FROMMER'S

MW00912371

BUDGET TRAVEL GUIDE

MEXICO '92 ON $45 A DAY

by Marita Adair

Assisted by Reed Glenn,
Maribeth Mellin, Elena Hannan de Renero,
Michelle da Silva Richmond, and Melanie Young

PRENTICE HALL TRAVEL

NEW YORK • LONDON • TORONTO • SYDNEY • TOKYO • SINGAPORE

FROMMER BOOKS

Published by Prentice Hall Travel
A division of Simon & Schuster Inc.
15 Columbus Circle
New York, NY 10023

ISBN 0-13-334988-8
ISSN 0899-2835

Design by Robert Bull Design
Maps by Geografix Inc.

Manufactured in the United States of America

FROMMER'S MEXICO '92 ON $45 A DAY

Editor-in-Chief: Marilyn Wood
Senior Editors: Judith de Rubini, Amit Shah
Editors: Alice Fellows, Paige Hughes, Theodore Stavrou
Assistant Editors: Suzanne Arkin, Peter Katucki, Lisa Renaud
Contributing Editors: Alan LaDuca, Lisa Legarde
Managing Editor: Leanne Coupe

CONTENTS

LIST OF MAPS

INVITATION TO THE READERS

In researching this book, our author has come across many wonderful establishments, the best of which we have included here. We are sure that many of you will also come across wonderful hotels, inns, restaurants, guest houses, shops, and attractions. Please don't keep them to yourself. Share your experiences, especially if you want to comment on places that have been included in this edition that have changed for the worse. You can address your letters to:

Marita Adair
Mexico '92 on $45 A Day
Prentice Hall Travel
15 Columbus Circle
New York, NY 10023

A DISCLAIMER

Readers are advised that prices fluctuate in the course of time and travel information changes under the impact of the varied and volatile factors that affect the travel industry. Neither the author nor the publisher can be held responsible for the experiences of readers while traveling. Readers are invited to write to the publisher with ideas, comments, and suggestions for future editions.

A WORD ABOUT PRICES

The $45 daily budget, which provides the title for this book, is intended to cover only the cost of your hotel room and three meals, and not your entertainment and transportation expenses. As a result, the accommodations listed in this book are, in my opinion, generally moderately priced, and not rock-bottom. The book can be used with safety by persons of both sexes and of all ages.

Mexico has a Value Added Tax of 15% (*Impuesto de Valor Agregado,* or "IVA," pronounced "ee-bah") on almost everything, including hotel rooms, restaurant meals, bus tickets, and souvenirs. In 1985 the Mexican government passed a law requiring that this tax be included, or "hidden" in the price of goods and service, not added at the time of sale. Thus, prices quoted to you should be *IVA incluido,* "tax included." All prices given in this book already include the tax.

In this book, I've listed only dollar prices, which are a more reliable guide than peso prices. In this age of inflation, prices may change by the time you reach Mexico. Mexico's inflation has been running nearly 20% to 30% a year.

Important note: In Mexico, the dollar sign is used to denote pesos, and a Mexican sign reading $5,000 means 5,000 pesos, not 5,000 dollars. To eliminate confusion, the dollar sign in this book is used only to indicate U.S. dollars.

As of this writing, the rate of exchange in Mexico is about 3,000 pesos for U.S. $1. This will certainly change by the time you visit Mexico, but any commercial bank will be glad to provide you with the current rate.

CHAPTER 1

GETTING TO KNOW MEXICO

Everyone north of the Rio Grande has at least some idea (usually an old-fashioned one) about what Mexico is like, but only those who go there can know the real Mexico, for the country is undergoing fast-paced and far-reaching change, as are most countries touched by modern technology. Being so close to the United States and Canada, Mexico is so forcefully affected by what goes on in its neighboring countries to the north that the Old Mexico of cowboy songs and the movies has long ago been replaced by a land full of the familiar signs of 20th-century life.

But this does not mean that a trip to Mexico will reveal people, sights, and sounds just like home. Mexico is very much its own country, the result of a particular blending of the land and the people and of ancient Indian, colonial European, and modern industrial influences. These elements are the basis of a unique culture and tradition.

1. GEOGRAPHY, HISTORY & POLITICS

GEOGRAPHY

Mexico includes seemingly trackless desert in the north, thousands of miles of lush seacoast, tropical lowland jungle, volcanic peaks, and the snow-capped mountains of the Sierra Madre. From the breathtaking gorges of Chihuahua to the jungle coastal plain of Yucatán, from the Pacific at Baja California to the Caribbean at Quintana Roo, Mexico stretches 2,000 miles from sea to sea. Four times the size of Texas, it's bordered on the north by the United States and to the southeast by Belize, Guatemala, and the Caribbean; to the east by the Gulf of Mexico; and to the west by the Sea of Cortez and the Pacific Ocean.

Mexico lacks an extensive river system, but the longest is the Río Balsas, which empties into the Pacific near Lázaro Cárdenas. The Río Grande/Río Bravo separates Texas from Mexico and the Río Usumacinta separates Mexico from Guatemala. The highest volcanic peak is the Pico de Orizaba at 18,201 feet, and the largest lake is Chapala at 666 square miles.

HISTORY

The earliest "Mexicans" were Stone Age men and women, descendants of the race that had crossed the Bering Strait and reached North America before 10,000 B.C. These were *Homo sapiens* who hunted mastodons and bison, and gathered other food as they could. Later (Archaic Period, 5200–1500 B.C.), signs of agriculture and domestication appeared: baskets were woven; corn, beans, squash, and tomatoes were grown; turkeys and dogs were kept for food. By 2400 B.C. the art of pot making had been discovered (the use of pottery was a significant advance). Life in these times was still very primitive, of course, but there were "artists" who made clay figurines for use as votive offerings or household "gods." Actually, "goddesses" is a better term, for all the figurines found so far have been female, and are supposed to symbolize Mother Earth or Fertility. (Use of these figurines predates any belief in well-defined gods.)

THE PRECLASSIC PERIOD It was in the Preclassic Period (1500 B.C.–A.D. 300) that the area known by archeologists as Mesoamerica (from the northern Mexico Valley to Costa Rica) began to show signs of a farming culture. They farmed either by the "slash-and-burn" method of cutting grass and trees, then setting fire to the area to clear it for planting; or by constructing terraces and irrigation ducts, a method used principally in the highlands around Mexico City, where the first large towns developed. At some time during this period, religion became an institution as certain men took the role of shaman, or guardian of magical and religious secrets. These were the predecessors of the folk healers and nature priests still found in modern Mexico.

The most highly developed culture of this Preclassic Period was that of the Olmecs, which flourished from 1500 to 100 B.C. They lived in what are today the states of Veracruz and Tabasco, where they used river rafts to transport the colossal multiton blocks of basalt used to carve roundish heads. These sculptures still present problems to archeologists: What do they signify? The heads seem infantile in their roundness, but all have the peculiar "jaguar mouth" with a high-arched upper lip that is the identifying mark of the Olmecs, and that was borrowed and adapted by many later cultures. The artists seemed obsessed with deformity, and many smaller carved or clay figures are of monstrosities or misshapen forms. Those with open eyes are slightly cross-eyed. Besides their achievements in sculpture, the Olmecs were the first in Mexico to use a calendar and to develop writing, both of which were later perfected by the Maya.

The link between the Olmecs and the Maya has not been clearly made, but Izapa (400 B.C.–A.D. 400), a ceremonial site in the Chiapan cacao-growing region near the Pacific coast, appears to be one of several transitional sites between the two cultures. When it was discovered, the monuments and stelae were in place, not having undergone destruction as have so many sites.

THE CLASSIC PERIOD Most artistic and cultural achievement came during the Classic Period (A.D. 300–900), when life centered in cities. Class distinctions arose as the military and religious aristocracy took control; a class of merchants and artisans grew, with the independent farmer falling under a landlord's control. The cultural centers of the Classic Period were Yucatán and Guatemala (also home of the Maya), the Mexican Highlands at Teotihuacán, the Zapotec cities of Monte Alban and Mitla (near Oaxaca), and the cities of El Tajín and Zempoala on the Gulf Coast.

The Maya are at the apex of pre-Columbian cultures. Besides their superior artistic achievements, the Maya made significant discoveries in science, including the use of the zero in mathematics and a complex calendar with which the priests could predict eclipses and the movements of the stars for centuries to come. The Maya were warlike, raiding their neighbors to gain land and subjects as well as to take captives for their many blood-centered rituals. Recent studies, notably *Blood of Kings* (Braziller, 1986) by Linda Schele and Mary Ellen Miller, debunked the long-held theory that the Maya were a peaceful people. Scholars continue to decipher the Maya hieroglyphs, murals, and relief carvings to reveal a Maya world tied to a belief that blood sacrifice was necessary to communicate with celestial gods and ancestors and to revere the dynasties of earthly blood kin. Thus, through bloodletting and sacrifice they nourished their gods and ancestors, and honored royal births, deaths, marriages, and accessions during a calendar full of special occasions. Numerous carvings and murals show that members of the ruling class, too, ritualistically mutilated themselves to draw sacrificial blood.

Who exactly inhabited Teotihuacán (100 B.C.–700 A.D.—near present-day Mexico City) isn't known, but it is thought to have been a city of 200,000 or more inhabitants covering 9 square miles. At its height, Teotihuacán was the greatest cultural center in Mexico, with influence as far southeast as Guatemala. Its layout has religious significance; on the tops of its pyramids consecrated to the sun and moon, high priest's rituals were attended, but not observed, by the masses of the people at the foot of the pyramid. Some of the magnificent reliefs and frescoes that decorated the religious monuments can be seen in Mexico City's museums.

The Zapotecs, influenced by the Olmecs, raised an impressive culture in the region of Oaxaca. Their two principal cities were Monte Alban (500 B.C.–A.D. 800), inhabited by an elite of merchants and artisans, and Mitla, reserved for the high priests. Both cities exhibit the artistic and mathematical genius of the people: characteristic geometric designs, long-nosed gods with feathered masks,

DATELINE

Chichén-Itzá.

• **1156–1230**
Toltecs abandon Tula and El Tajín.

• **1290** Zapotecs decline and Mixtecs emerge at Monte Alban; Mitla becomes refuge of Zapotecs.

• **1325–45** Aztec capital Tenochtitlán founded; Aztecs dominate Mexico.

• **1519–21**
Conquest of Mexico: Hernán Cortés and troops arrive near present-day Veracruz.

• **1521** Cortés defeats Aztecs at Tlaltelolco near Tenochtitlán.

• **1521–24**
Cortés organizes Spanish empire in Mexico and begins building Mexico City on the ruins of Tenochtitlán.

• **1524** First Franciscan friars arrive from Spain.

• **1524–35**
Cortés removed from leadership; Spanish king sends officials, judges, and finally an audiencia to govern.

• **1535–1821**
Viceregal Period: Mexico governed by 61 viceroys appointed by the King of Spain; a landed aristocracy emerges with ownership of huge portions of land (haciendas).

(continues)

N
0 ▢▰▰▰▰▰ 150 mi
240 km

Tijuana
Mexicali
Ensenada

Puerto Penasco
Nogales
Ciudad Juárez

UNITED STATES

San Quintin

Baja California

2

23

10

15

Ojinaga

Hermosillo

16

18

Chihuahua

Isla Cedros

Guaymas

16

Cuauhtémoc

Delicias

Santa Rosalia

Ciudad Obregon

Baja California Sur

Loreto

Los Mochis

Hidalgo del Parral

45

49

30

Monclova

CONTINENTAL DIVIDE

Torreon

Saltillo

Culiacán

15

Durango

54

40

Fresnillo

Gulf of California

La Paz

San Lucas

Pacific Ocean

Zacatecas

San Luis Potosi

15

SIERRA MADRE OCCIDENTAL

1

Tuxpan
San Blas

Aguascalientes

Islas Marias

Tepic

Guanajuato

Leon

Puerto Vallarta

Guadalajara

2

Barra de Navidad

Morelia

Uruapan

Manzanillo

Colima

37

Lazaro Cardenas

200

Key to states in central Mexico

1 Aguascalientes
2 Guanajuato
3 Queretaro
4 Hidalgo
5 Mexico
6 Distrito Federal
7 Morelos
8 Tlaxcala

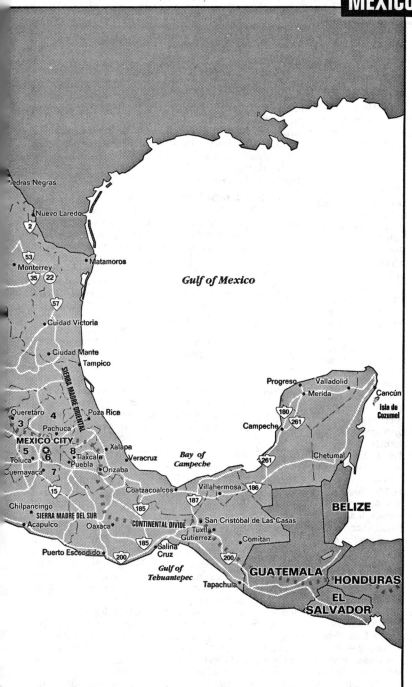

MEXICO

Piedras Negras

Nuevo Laredo

②

㊿

Monterrey

㉟ ㉒

㊳

Ciudad Victoria

Ciudad Mante

Tampico

Gulf of Mexico

Progreso   Valladolid

Merida

Cancún

Isla de
Cozumel

Campeche

⑱⓪

②⑥①

Querétaro   ④   Poza Rica

③

Pachuca

MEXICO CITY

⑤   ⑧   Xalapa

Toluca   ⑥   Tlaxcala   Veracruz

Cuernavaca   Puebla

⑦   Orizaba

②⑥①

Chetumal

Bay of
Campeche

SIERRA MADRE ORIENTAL

⑮

Coatzacoalcos

Villahermosa

①⑧⑥

⑱⑦

Chilpancingo

①⑧⑤

SIERRA MADRE DEL SUR

BELIZE

Acapulco   Oaxaca

CONTINENTAL DIVIDE

San Cristóbal de Las Casas

Tuxtla
Gutierrez

Comitan

Puerto Escondido   ①⑧⑤   Salina
Cruz

②⓪⓪

②⓪⓪

Gulf of
Tehuantepec

GUATEMALA

HONDURAS

Tapachula

EL
SALVADOR

DATELINE

- **1537** Mexico's first printing press is installed in Mexico City.
- **1562** Friar Diego de Landa destroys 5,000 Mayan religious stone figures and burns 27 hieroglyphic painted manuscripts at Maní, Yucatán.
- **1571** The Inquisition is established in Mexico.
- **1767** Jesuits expelled from New Spain.
- **1810–21** War of Independence Fr. Miguel Hidalgo starts movement for independence from Spain, but is executed within a year; leadership and goals change during the war years, but a compromise between monarchy and a republic is outlined by Augustín de Iturbide.
- **1821** Independence from Spain achieved.
- **1822** First Empire: Augustín de Iturbide, independence leader, ascends the throne as Emperor of Mexico.
- **1824** Iturbide is expelled, returns, and is executed.
- **1824–55** Federal Republic Period: Guadalupe Victoria is elected first president of Mexico in 1824, is

(continues)

hieroglyph stelae, a bar-and-dot numerical system, and a 52-cycle calendar. Like the Olmecs, the Zapotecs favored grotesque art, of which the frieze of the "Danzantes" at Monte Alban—naked figures of distorted form and contorted position—is an outstanding example.

El Tajín (A.D. 300–1100), covering at least 2,600 acres on the upper Gulf Coast of Veracruz, continues to stump scholars. The Pyramid of the Niches there is unique and recent excavations have uncovered a total of 17 ballcourts and Teotihuacán-influenced murals. Although Huastec Indians inhabited the region, who built the site and occupied it remains a mystery. Death and sacrifice are recuring themes depicted in relief carvings. Pulque (pre-Hispanic fermented drink), cacao (chocolate) growing, and the ball game figured heavily into Tajín society.

THE POSTCLASSIC PERIOD In the Postclassic Period (A.D. 900–1500), warlike cultures developed impressive societies of their own, although they never surpassed the Classic peoples. All paintings and hieroglyphs of this period show war, migration, and disruption. Somehow the glue of society became unstuck, people wandered from their homes, and the religious hierarchy lost influence. Finally, in the 1300s, the warlike Aztecs settled in the Mexico Valley on Lake Texcoco (site of Mexico City), with the island city of Tenochtitlán as their capital. Legend has it that as the wandering Aztecs were passing the lake they saw a sign predicted by their prophets: an eagle perched on a cactus plant with a snake in its mouth. They built their city there and it became a huge (pop. 300,000) and impressive capital. The Aztec empire was a more or less loosely united territory of great size. The high lords of the capital became fabulously rich in gold, stores of food, cotton, and perfumes; skilled artisans were prosperous; events of state were elaborately ceremonial. Victorious Aztecs returning from battle sacrificed thousands of captives on the altars atop the pyramids, cutting their chests open with stone knives and ripping out their still-beating hearts to offer to the gods.

QUETZALCOATL The legend of Quetzalcoatl, a holy man who appeared during the time of troubles at the end of the Classic Period, is one of the most important tales in Mexican history and folklore, and contributed to the overthrow of the Aztec empire by the Spaniards. Quetzalcoatl means "feathered serpent." Learned beyond his years, he became the high priest and leader of the Toltecs at Tula, and put an end to human sacrifice. His influence completely changed the Toltecs from a group of warriors to peaceful and productive farmers, artisans, and craftsmen. But his successes upset the old priests, and they called upon their ancient god of darkness, Texcatlipoca, to degrade Quetzalcoatl in the eyes of the people. One night the priests conspired to dress Quetzalcoatl in ridiculous garb, get him drunk, and tempt him to break his vow of chastity. The next morning the shame of this night of debauchery drove him out of his own land and into the wilderness, where he lived for 20 years. He emerged in Coatzacoalcos, in the

Isthmus of Tehuantepec, bade his few followers farewell, and sailed away, having promised to return in a future age. But artistic influences noted at Chichén-Itzá in the Yucatán suggest that in fact he landed there and, among the Maya, began his "ministry" again, this time called Kukulkán. He died there, but the legend of his return in a future age remained.

SPANISH CONQUISTADORES When Hernán Cortés and his men landed in 1519, in what would become Veracruz, the Aztec empire was ruled by Moctezuma (often misspelled Montezuma) in great splendor. The emperor was not certain what course to pursue: If the strangers were Quetzalcoatl and his followers returning at last, no resistance must be offered; on the other hand, if the strangers were not Quetzalcoatl, they might be a threat to his empire. Moctezuma tried to bribe them with gold to go away, but this only whetted their appetites. Despite the fact that Moctezuma and his ministers received the conquistadores with full pomp and glory when they reached Mexico City, Cortés eventually took Moctezuma captive.

Though the Spaniards were no match for the hundreds of thousands of Aztecs, they skillfully kept things under their control until a revolt threatened Cortés's entire enterprise. He retreated to the countryside, made alliances with non-Aztec tribes, and finally marched on the empire when it was governed by the last Aztec emperor, Cuauhtémoc. Cuauhtémoc defended himself and his people valiantly for almost 3 months, but was finally captured, tortured, and ultimately executed.

The Spanish conquest had started out as an adventure by Cortés and his men, unauthorized by the Spanish Crown or its governor in Cuba. Soon Christianity was being spread through "New Spain." Guatemala and Honduras were explored and conquered, and by 1540 the territory of New Spain included Spanish possessions from Vancouver to Panama. In the 2 centuries that followed, Franciscan and Augustinian friars converted great numbers of Indians to Christianity, and the Spanish lords built up huge feudal estates on which the Indian farmers were little more than serfs. The silver and gold that Cortés had sought made Spain the richest country in Europe.

INDEPENDENCE Spain ruled Mexico until 1821, when Mexico finally gained its independence after a decade of upheaval. The independence movement had begun in 1810 when a priest, Fr. Miguel Hidalgo, gave the cry for independence from his pulpit in the town of Dolores, Guanajuato. The revolt soon became a revolution, and Hidalgo, Igancio Allende, and another priest, José María Morelos, gathered an "army" of citizens and threatened Mexico City. Ultimately Hidalgo was executed, but he is honored as "the Father of Mexican Independence." Morelos kept the revolt alive until 1815, when he, too, was executed.

When independence finally came, Augustín Iturbide was ready to take over. In 1822 Iturbide founded a short-lived "empire" with himself as emperor. The next

DATELINE

followed by 26 presidents and interim presidents, among them José Lopez de Santa Anna.
- **1828** Slavery abolished.
- **1835** Texas declares independence from Mexico.
- **1836** Santa Anna defeats Texans at Battle of the Alamo, but is later defeated and captured at the Battle of San Jacinto, outside Houston, Texas.
- **1838** France invades Mexico at Veracruz.
- **1845** United States annexes Texas.
- **1846–48** War with the United States; for $15 million Mexico relinquishes half its national territory to the United States in the Treaty of Guadalupe Hidalgo.
- **1855–67** Reform Years: Include a 3-year war pitting cities against villages and rich against poor, in a search for ideology, stability, and political leadership.
- **1855–72** Benito Juárez is president; he nationalizes church property and declares separation of church and state.
- **1864–67** Second Empire in-

(continues)

terim period: Napoléon III sends Maximilian of Hapsburg to be Emperor of Mexico.

• **1867** Juárez orders execution of Maximilian and resumes presidency until his death in 1872.

• **1872–84** Post-Reform Period: Only four presidents hold office, but the country is nearly bankrupt.

• **1876–1911** Porfiriato: Porfirio Díaz, president/dictator of Mexico for 35 years, leads the country to modernization.

• **1911–17** Mexican Revolution: Franciso Madero drafts revolutionary plan; Díaz resigns; leaders jockey for power during a period of great violence, national upheaval, and tremendous loss of life.

• **1913** President Madero assassinated.

• **1914–1916** Two U.S. invasions of Mexico.

• **1917–40** Reconstruction: New constitution; land and education reforms are initiated and labor unions strengthened; Mexico expells U.S. oil companies and nationalizes all
(continues)

year it fell and was followed by the proclamation of a republic with Gen. Guadalupe Victoria as first president. A succession of presidents and military dictators followed Guadalupe Victoria until the French intervention, one of the most bizarre and extraordinary episodes in modern times. In the 1860s, Mexican factions offered Archduke Ferdinand Maximilian Joseph of Hapsburg the crown of Mexico, and with the support of the ambitious French emperor, Napoléon III, the young Austrian actually came to Mexico and "ruled" for 3 years (1864–67), while the country was in a state of civil war. This European interference in New World affairs was not welcomed by the United States, and the French emperor finally withdrew his troops, leaving the misguided Maximilian to be captured and executed by a firing squad in Querétaro. His adversary and successor (as president of Mexico) was Benito Juárez, a Zapotec Indian lawyer and one of the most heroic figures in Mexican history. After victory over Maximilian, Juárez did his best to unify and strengthen his country before dying of a heart attack in 1872. His effect on Mexico's future was profound, however, and his plans and visions bore fruit for decades. From 1877 to 1911, a period now called the "Porfiriato," the prime role in Mexico was played by Porfirio Díaz, a general under Juárez. Recognized as a modernizer, he was a terror to his enemies and to challengers of his absolute power. He was forced to abdicate in 1911 by Francisco Madero and public opinion.

After the fall of the Porfirist dictatorship, several factions split the country, including those led by "Pancho Villa" (whose real name was Doroteo Arango), Alvaro Obregón, Venustiano Carranza, and Emiliano Zapata. The decade that followed is referred to as the Mexican Revolution. Drastic reforms occurred in this period, and the surge of vitality and progress from this exciting if turbulent time has inspired Mexicans to the present. Succeeding presidents have invoked the spirit of the Revolution, which is still studied and discussed.

THE 20TH CENTURY After the turmoil of the Revolution, Mexico sought stability in the form of the Partido Revolucionario Institucional (el PRI), the country's dominant political party. With the aim of "institutionalizing the revolution," el PRI (pronounced "ell-pree") literally engulfed Mexican society, leaving little room for vigorous, independent opposition. For over half a century the monolithic party has had control of the government, labor unions, trade organizations, and other centers of power in Mexican society.

The most outstanding Mexican president of the century was Gen. Lázaro Cárdenas (1934–40). An effective leader, Cárdenas broke up vast tracts of agricultural land and distributed parcels to small cooperative farms called *ejidos*, reorganized the labor unions along democratic lines, and provided funding for village schools. His most famous action was the expropriation of Mexico's oil industry from U.S. and European interests, which became Petroleros Mexicanos (Pemex), the government petroleum monopoly.

The PRI has selected Mexico's president (and, in fact,

virtually everyone else on the government payroll) from its own ranks after Cárdenas, the national election being only a confirmation of the choice. Among these men have been Ávila Camacho, who continued many of Cárdenas's policies; Miguel Aleman, who expanded national industrial and infrastructural development; Adolfo Lopez Mateos, who expanded the highway system and increased hydroelectric power sources; and Gustavo Díaz Ordaz, who provided credit and technical help to the agricultural sector.

In 1970 Luis Echeverria came to power, followed in 1976 by José Lopez Portillo. During their presidencies there emerged a studied coolness in relations with the United States and an activist role in international affairs. This period also saw an increase in charges of large-scale corruption in the upper echelons of Mexican society. The corruption, though endemic to the system, was encouraged by the river of money from the rise in oil prices. When oil income skyrocketed, Mexican borrowing and spending did likewise. The reduction of oil prices in the 1980s left Mexico with an enormous foreign bank debt and serious infrastructure deficiencies.

MEXICO TODAY Without King Oil, Mexico must rebuild agriculture and industry, cut expenditures, tame corruption, and keep its creditors at bay. President Miguel de la Madrid Hurtado, who assumed the presidency in 1982, struggled with these problems and made important progress. The present president, Carlos Salinas de Gortari, has managed to slow inflation from 200% annually to between 20% and 30%. But the economy, and society, are still under tremendous economic pressure, and charges of government corruption, although less than in the past, still abound.

Economically, Mexico is not by any means a poor country. Only about a sixth of the economy is in agriculture. Mining is still fairly important. Gold, silver, and many other important minerals are still mined, but the big industry today is oil. Mexico is also well industrialized, manufacturing textiles, food products, and everything from tape cassettes to automobiles.

DATELINE

natural resources and railroads; assassinations of Presidents Obregón and Carranza and of Pancho Villa and Zapata.

• **1940** Mexico enters period of political stability and begins economic progress and improvement in the quality of life, though not without corruption, inflation, and unresolved national health, land, and agricultural issues.

• **1955** Women given full voting rights.

• **1982** Nationalization of banks.

• **1988** Mexico enters the General Agreement on Tariffs and Trade (GATT).

• **1991** Mexico, Canada, and the United States begin Free Trade Agreement negotiations.

POLITICS

The Republic of Mexico today is headed by an elected president and a bicameral legislature. It is divided into 31 states, plus the Federal District (Mexico City).

Mexico's current economic difficulties have led to a newly vigorous and open political life with opposition parties gaining strength. The traditionally victorious PRI party won the hotly contested presidential election in 1988, but its candidate, Carlos Salinas de Gortari, only managed to claim a historically low 50.36% of the vote amid claims of fraud by his chief rival, Cuauhtémoc Cárdenas of the newly formed National Democratic Front (FDN). Ironically, Cárdenas is the son of Mexico's beloved president who founded the PRI. However, opposition parties managed to win a few Senate seats for the first time since the PRI came to power, and recent local elections produced strong opposition candidates. Whether Sr. Salinas de Gortari's promised reforms for greater democracy will be lasting is debatable, but Mexico remains the most stable country in Latin America.

DID YOU KNOW . . . ?

- During the 300 years that Mexico belonged to Spain, no Spanish king ever visited the country.
- Nearly 300 Union veterans of the U.S. Civil War joined the side of Benito Juárez and fought against French intervention in Mexico in 1866.
- The Mexican territory ceded to the United States by the Treaty of Guadalupe in 1848 after the Mexican-American War makes up almost one third of United States territory, encompassing Texas, New Mexico, Arizona, Nevada, California, Utah, and part of Colorado.
- In 1841 Yucatán hired the Texas Navy to protect the peninsula from invasion by Mexico.
- With 120,000 square miles, Chihuahua is the largest Mexican State.
- In 1519 Mexico's Indian population was approximately 30 million; by 1550 it was reduced to 3 million due to smallpox, measles, and other diseases to which the Indians had no immunity, brought to the New World by the Spaniards.

In short, Mexico is well into the 20th century, with all the benefits and problems of contemporary life, and although vast sums are spent on education and public welfare, a high birth rate, high unemployment, and unequal distribution of wealth show that much remains to be done.

2. ART, ARCHITECTURE & LITERATURE

ART & ARCHITECTURE Mexico's artistic and architectural legacy began more than 3,000 years ago. Until the fall of the Aztec Empire in A.D. 1521, art, architecture, politics, and religion in Mexico were inextricably intertwined and remained so in different ways through the colonial period.

World-famous archeological sites in Mexico—more than 1,500 of them—are individually unique even when built by the same groups of people. Each year scholars decipher more information about the ancient groups who built these cities, using information they left in bas-relief carvings, sculptures, murals, and hieroglyphics.

Mexico's pyramids are truncated platforms, not true pyramids, and come in many different shapes. At Tzintzuntzán, near Lake Pátzcuaro, the buildings, called *yacatas,* are distinguished by semicircular buildings attached to rectangular ones. Many sites have circular buildings, usually called the observatory and dedicated to Ehécatl, god of the wind. At El Tajín, the Temple of the Niches has 365 niches, one for every day of the year, while El Castillo at Chichén-Itzá has 365 steps. The Temple of the Magicians at Uxmal has beautifully rounded and sloping sides. The Huastecas of northern Veracruz and Tamaulipas states were known for their many circular ceremonial platforms. Evidence of building one pyramidal structure on top of another, a widely accepted practice, has been found throughout Mesoamerica.

The largest pyramid by volume is the Tepanapa pyramid at Cholula. The Temple of the Inscriptions at Palenque is the only pyramid built specifically as a tomb, although tombs have been found in many other pyramids. Cobá has the longest road (*sacbe*), stretching 62 miles. Numerous sites in Mesoamerica had ballcourts. In Mexico the longest is at Chichén-Itzá—nearly the length of a football field. El Tajín, with 17 ballcourts, has the most.

Architects of many of these edifices used a sloping panel (*tablud*) alternating with a verticle panel (*tablero*). Good examples are at Teotihuacán and Cholula.

The true arch was unknown in Mesoamerica, so the Maya made multiple use of the corbelled arch in which a keystone juts out over the others and is used to build a modified inverted V-shaped arch.

The Olmecs, considered the mother culture in Mexico, built pyramids of earth, so little remains to tell us what their buildings looked like. The Olmecs, however, left an enormous sculptural legacy from small, intricately carved pieces of jade to 40-ton carved basalt rock heads that were, amazingly, shipped to their homesites by river raft.

Throughout Mexico, the pyramids were embellished with carved stone or mural art, not for the purpose of pure adornment, but for religious and historic reasons. Hieroglyphs, picture symbols etched on stone or painted on walls or pottery, function as the written language of the ancient peoples, particularly the Maya. By deciphering the glyphs, scholars allow the ancients to speak again, giving us specific names to attach to rulers and their families, demystifying the great dynastic histories of the Maya. For more on this, be sure to read *A Forest of Kings* (1990) by Linda Schele and David Freidel. Good hieroglyphic examples can be seen in the site museum at Palenque.

Carving important historic figures on free-standing stone slabs, or *stelae*, was a common Maya commemorative device. Several are in place at Cobá, and good examples are in the Museum of Anthropology in Mexico City and the Carlos Pellicer Museum in Villahermosa.

Pottery played an important role, and different indigenous groups are distinguished by their use of color and style in pottery. The Cholulans had distinctive red-clay pottery decorated in cream, red, and black; Teotihuacán was noted for its three-legged painted orangeware; Tenochtitlán for its use of brilliant blue and red; Casas Grandes for anthropomorphic and zoomorphic images on clay vessels; and the Maya for pottery painted with scenes from daily and historic life. Besides regional museums, the best collection of all this work is in the Museum of Anthropology in Mexico City.

Pre-Hispanic cultures left a number of fantastic painted murals, some of which are remarkably preserved, such as those at Bonampak and Cacaxtla, and others of which are fragmentary, such as those at Teotihuacán, Cholula, and El Tajín. Amazing stone murals or mosaics using thousands of pieces of fitted stone to form figures of warriors, snakes, or geometric designs decorate the pyramid facades at Xochicalco, Mitla, Uxmal, and Chichén-Itzá.

With the arrival of the Spaniards a new form of architecture came to Mexico (the next 300 years is known as the Viceregal Period, when Spain's appointed viceroys ruled Mexico). Many sites that were occupied by indigenous groups at the time of the Conquest were razed, and in their place appeared Catholic churches, public buildings, and palaces for conquerors and the king's bureaucrats. Indian artisans, who formerly worked on pyramidal structures, were recruited to give life to these structures, often guided by drawings of European buildings the Spanish architects tried to emulate. Frequently left on their own, the indigenous artisans sometimes implanted traditional symbolism in the new buildings: a plaster angel swaddled in feathers, reminiscent of the god Quetzalcoatl; or the face of an ancient god surrounded by corn leaves. They used pre-Hispanic calendar counts, the 13 steps to heaven, or the nine levels of the underworld to determine how many flowerettes to carve around the church doorway. Good examples of native symbolism can be seen at the church in Xochimilco near Mexico City and in Santa María Tonanzintla near Puebla. Native muralists had a hand in painting a knight in tiger skin on the Augustinian monastery in Ixmiquilpan, Hidalgo.

To convert the native populations, New World Spanish priests and architects altered their normal ways of building and teaching. Often before the church was built, an open-air atrium was first constructed so that large numbers of parishioners could be accommodated for service. *Posas* (shelters) at the four corners of churchyards were another architectural technique unique to Mexico, again for the purpose of accommodating crowds during holy sacraments. Because of the language barrier between the Spanish and the natives, church adornment became more graphic. Biblical tales came to life in frescoes splashed across church walls; Christian symbolism in stone supplanted that of pre-Hispanic times. Out went the eagle (sun symbol), feathered serpent (symbol of fertility, rain, earth, and sky), and jaguar (power symbol), and in came Christ on a cross, saintly statues, and Franciscan, Dominican, and Augustinian symbolism. It must have been a confusing time for the indigenous peoples, which accounts for the continued intermingling of Christian and pre-Hispanic ideas as they tried to make sense of it all. The convenient apparition of the Virgin Mary on former pre-Hispanic religious turf made it "legal" to return there to worship and build a "Christian" shrine. Baroque became even more baroque in Mexico and was dubbed *Churrigueresque.* Excellent Mexican baroque examples are the Santa Prisca Church in Taxco and the San Cayetano de la Valencia Church near Guanajuato. The term *Plateresque* was given to facade designs resembling silver design, but more planted on a structure than a part of it. The Acolman Convent near the ruins of Teotihuacán has one of the best Plateresque facades in Mexico. The Viceregal Museum in Tepozotlán, north of Mexico City, holds a wealth of artwork from Mexican churches during this period.

Concurrently with the building of religious structures, public buildings took shape, modeled after those in European capitals. Especially around Puebla, the use of colorful locally made tile, a fusion of local art and Talavera style from Spain, decorated public walls and church domes. The hacienda architecture sprang up in the countryside, resulting in massive, thick-walled, fortresslike structures built around a central patio. Remains of haciendas, some of them still operating, can be seen in almost all parts of Mexico. The San Carlos Academy of Art was founded in Mexico City in 1785, taking after the renowned academies of Europe. Though the emphasis was on a Europeanized Mexico, by the end of the 19th century the subject matter of easel artists was becoming Mexican: Still-lifes with Mexican fruit and pottery and Mexican landscapes, with cactus and volcanoes, appeared, as did portraits whose subjects wore Mexican regional clothing. José María Velasco (1840–1912), the father of Mexican landscape painting, emerged during this time. His work and that of others of this period are at the National Museum of Art in Mexico City.

With the late 19th century entry of Porfirio Díaz into the presidency came another infusion of Europe. Díaz idolized Europe, and during this time he lavished on the country a number of striking European-style public buildings, among them opera houses still used today. He provided European scholarships to promising young artists who later returned to Mexico to produce clearly Mexican subject paintings using techniques learned abroad. While the Mexican Revolution, following the resignation and exile of Díaz, ripped the country apart between 1911 and 1917, the result was the birth of Mexico, a claiming and appreciation of it by Mexicans. In 1923 Minister of Education José Vasconcelos was charged with educating the illiterate masses. As one means of reaching many people, he started the muralist movement when he invited Diego Rivera and several other budding artists to paint Mexican history on the walls of the Ministry of Education building and the National Preparatory School in Mexico City. From then on, the "big three" muralists—David Siquieros, José Clemente Orozco, and Rivera—were joined by others in bringing Mexico's history in art to the walls of public buildings throughout the country for all to see and interpret. The years that followed eventually brought about a return to easel art, an exploration of Mexico's culture, and a new generation of artists and architects who were free to invent and draw upon subjects and styles from around the world. Among the 20th-century greats are the "big three" muralists, as well as Rufino Tamayo, Gerardo Murillo, José Guadalupe Posada, Saturnino Herrán, Franciso Goitia, Frida Kahlo, José María Velasco, Pedro and Rafael Coronel, Miguel Covarrubias, Olga Costa, and José Chávez Morado. Among important architects during this period, Luis Barragán incorporated design elements from haciendas, and from Mexican textiles, pottery, and furniture, into sleek, marble-floored structures splashed with the vivid colors of Mexico. His ideas are used by Mexican architects all over Mexico today.

LITERATURE By the time Cortés arrived in Mexico, the people were already masters of literature, recording their poems and histories by painting in fanfold books (codices) made of deerskin and bark paper or carving on stone. To record history, gifted students were taught the art of book making, drawing, painting, reading, and writing, abilities the general public didn't have. The ancient Maya produced two important epic works, the *Book of Popol Vuh* and the *Chilam Balam.* Unfortunately, very little survives, for after the Conquest the Spaniards deliberately destroyed native books. However, several Catholic priests, among them Bernardo de Sahugun and Diego de Landa (who was one of the book destroyers), encouraged the Indians to record their customs and history. These records are among the best we have to document life before the Conquest.

IMPRESSIONS

Considering the variety of nations, tongues, cultures, and artistic styles, the unity of these peoples comes as a surprise. They all share certain ideas and beliefs. Thus it is not inaccurate to call this group of nations and cultures a Mexoamerican civilization. Unity in space and continuity in time; from the first millennium before Christ to the sixteenth century, these distinct Mexoamerican peoples evolve, reelaborate, and re-create a nucleus of basic concepts as well as social and political techniques and institutions. There were changes and variations . . . but never was the continuity broken.
—OCTAVIO PAZ, 1990

During the Conquest, Cortés wrote his now-famous five letters to Charles V, which give us the first printed Conquest literature, but the most important record is that of Díaz de Castillo. Enraged by an inaccurate account of the Conquest written by a flattering friend of Cortés, 40 years after the Conquest Bernal Díaz de Castillo, one of the conquerors, wrote his lively and very readable version of the event, *True History of the Conquest of Mexico;* it's regarded as the most accurate.

The first printing press appeared in Mexico in 1537 and was followed by a proliferation of printing, mostly on subjects about science, nature, and getting along in Mexico. The most important literary figure during the 16th century was Sor Juana Inez de la Cruz, child prodigy and later poet-nun whose works are still treasured. The first Spanish novel written in Mexico was *The Itching Parrot* by José Joaquín Fernández de Lizardi, about 19th-century Mexican life. The first daily newspaper appeared in 1805. Nineteenth-century writers produced a plethora of political fiction and nonfiction. Among the more explosive was *The Presidential Sucession of 1910* by Francisco Madero (who later became president), which contributed to the downfall of Porfirio Díaz, and *Regeneración,* a weekly anti-Díaz magazine published by the Flores Mignon brothers.

Among 20th-century writers of note are Octavio Paz, author of *The Labyrinth of Solitude* and winner of the 1991 Nobel prize for literature, and Carlos Fuentes, who wrote *Where the Air Is Clear.*

Books in Mexico are relatively inexpensive, but editions are not produced in great quantity. Newspapers and magazines proliferate, but the majority of those who read devour comic-book novels, the most visible form of literature.

3. RELIGION, MYTH & FOLKLORE

Mexico is a predominantly Roman Catholic country, a religion introduced by the Spaniards during the Conquest of Mexico. Despite its preponderance, the Catholic faith, in many places (Chiapas and Oaxaca, for example), has pre-Hispanic overtones. One need only visit the *curandero* section of a Mexican market, or attend a village festivity featuring pre-Hispanic dancers to understand that supernatural beliefs often run parallel to Christian ones.

Mexico's complicated mythological heritage from pre-Hispanic literature is jammed with images derived from nature—the wind, jaguars, eagles, snakes, flowers, and more—all intertwined with elaborate mythological stories to explain the universe, climate, seasons, and geography. So strong were the ancient beliefs that Mexico's indigenous peoples built their cities according to the four cardinal points of the compass, with each compass point assigned a particular color (the colors might vary from group to group). The sun, moon, and stars took on godlike meaning and the religious, ceremonial, and secular calendars were arranged to show tribute to these omnipotent gods.

Most groups believed in an underworld (not a hell), usually of 9 levels, and a heaven of 13 levels, so the numbers 9 and 13 become mythologially significant. The solar calendar count of 365 days and the ceremonial calendar of 260 days are numerically significant. How one died determined where one wound up after death: in the underworld, in heaven, or at one of the four cardinal points. Everyone had first to make the journey through the underworld.

One of the richest sources of mythological tales is the *Book of Popul Vuh*, a Maya bible of sorts, that was recorded after the Conquest. The *Chilam Balam,* another such book, existed in hieroglyphic form at the Conquest and was recorded, using the Spanish alphabet to transliterate Mayan words that could be understood by the Spaniards. The *Chilam Balam* differed from the *Popul Vuh* in that it is the collected histories of many Maya communities.

Each of the ancient cultures had its set of gods and goddesses, and while the names might not cross cultures, their characteristics or purpose often did. Chac, the hook-nosed rain god of the Maya, was Tlaloc, the mighty-figured rain god of the Aztecs; Queztalcoatl, the plumed-serpent god/man of the Toltecs, became Kukulkán of the Maya. The tales of the powers and creation of these deities make up Mexico's rich mythology. Sorting out the pre-Hispanic pantheon and mythological beliefs in ancient Mexico can become an all-consuming study (the Maya alone had 166 deities), so below is a list of some of the most important gods:

Chac	Maya rain god
Cinteotl	Huastec corn god
Coatlíque	Huitzilopochtli's mother, whose name means "she of serpent skirt," goddess of death and earth
Cocijo	Zapotec rain god
Ehécatl	Wind god, whose temple is usually round; another aspect of Quetzalcoatl
Huitzilopochtli	War god and primary Aztec god, son of Coatlique
Itzamná	Maya god above all, who invented corn, cacao, and writing and reading
Ixchel	Maya goddess of water, weaving, and childbirth
Kinich Ahau	Maya sun god
Kukulkán	Quetzalcoatl's name in the Yucatán
Mayahuel	Goddess of pulque
Ometeotl	God/goddess all-powerful creator of the universe, ruler of heaven, earth, and the underworld
Quetzalcoatl	A mortal who took on legendary characteristics as a god (or visa versa)—when he left Tula in shame after a a night of succumbing to temptations, he promised to return; he reappeared in the Yucatán—he is also symbolized as Venus, the morning star, and Ehécatl, the wind god.
Tezcaltipoca	Aztec sun god known as "Smoking Mirror"
Tláloc	Aztec rain god
Tonantzin	Aztec motherhood goddess
Xochipilli	Aztec god of dance, flowers, and music
Xochiquetzal	Flower and love goddess

4. CULTURAL & SOCIAL LIFE

The population of Mexico is 85 million, 15% of them white (most of Spanish descent), 60% mestizo (mixed Spanish and Indian), and 25% pure Indian (descendants of the Maya, Aztecs, Huastecs, Otomies, Totonacs, and other peoples). Added to this ethnic mix are Africans brought as slaves, European merchants and soldiers of fortune, and the lingering French influence from the time of Maximilian's abortive empire in the New World.

Although Spanish is the official language, about 50 Indian languages are still spoken, mostly in the Yucatán peninsula, Oaxaca, Chiapas, Chihuahua, Nayarit, Puebla, Sonora and Veracruz, Michoacan, and Guerrero.

Modern Mexico clings to its identity while embracing outside cultures, so Mexicans enjoy the Bolshoi Ballet as easily as a family picnic or village festival. Mexicans have a knack for knowing how to enjoy life, and families, weekends, holidays, and festivities are given priority. They also enjoy stretching a weekend holiday into 4 days called a *puente* (bridge) and, with the whole family in tow, flee the cities en masse to visit relatives in the country, picnic, or relax at resorts.

The Mexican work day is a long one: laborers begin around 7am and get off at dusk; office workers go in around 9am and, not counting the 2- to 3-hour lunch, get off at 7 or 8pm. Once a working career is started, there is little time for additional study. School is supposedly manditory and free through the sixth grade, but many youngsters quit long before that, or never go at all.

Sociologists and others have written volumes trying to explain the Mexican's special relationship with death. It is at once mocked and mourned. The Days of the Dead, November 1 and 2, a cross between Halloween and All Saints' Day, is a good opportunity to observe Mexico's relationship with the concept of death.

MUSIC & DANCE   One has only to walk down almost any street or attend any festival to understand that Mexico's vast musical tradition is inborn; it predates the Conquest. Musical instruments were made from almost anything that could be made to rattle or produce a rhythm or a sound—conch-shell trumpets, high-pitched antler horns, rattlers from sea shells and rattlesnake rattlers, drums of turtle shell as well as upright leather-covered wood (*tlalpanhuéhuetl*), and horizontal hollowed logs (*teponaztli*), bells of gold and copper, wind instruments of hollow reeds or fired clay, and soundmakers from leather-topped armadillo shells and gourds. Many were elaborately carved or decorated, befitting the important ceremonies they accompanied. So important was music that one of Moctezuma's palaces, the Mixcoacalli, was devoted to the care and housing of musical instruments, which were guarded around the clock. In Aztec times, music, dance, and religion were tied together with literature. Music was usually intended to accompany the poems that were written for religious ceremonies. Children with talent were separated and trained to adulthood especially as musicians and poets, two exacting professions in which mistakes carried extreme consequences. The dead were buried with musical instruments for their journey into the afterlife.

Music and dance in Mexico today are divided into three kinds: pre- and post-Hispanic and secular. Besides very regional village fiestas, two of the best places to see pre-Hispanic dancing are the Ballet Folklorico de México in Mexico City and the summer Guelaguetza in Oaxaca. Among pre-Hispanic dances still performed there or elsewhere in Mexico are "The Flying Pole Dance," "Dance of the Quetzales" (the sacred quetzal bird), "Deer Dance," and dances of the Huicholes and Coras of Jalisco and Nayarit. Post-Hispanic music and dance evolved first in order to teach the native inhabitants about Christianity with such dances as "Los Santiagos," with St. James battling heathens, and "Los Moros," with Moors battling Christians. Others, like "Los Jardineros," were spoofs on pretentious Spanish life. Secular dances are variations of Spanish dances performed by both men and women characterized by lots of foot-tapping, skirt-swishing, and innocent flirtation. No "Mexican fiesta night" would be complete without the "Jarabe Tapatío," the national folk dance of Mexico. The "Huapango," accompanied by violins and guitars, is a native dance of Veracruz, Tamaulipas, and San Luis Potosí. "Jaranas" are folk dances of the Yucatán, danced to the lively beat of a ukelele-like instrument and drums.

Besides the native music and dances, there are regional, state, and national orchestras. On weekends state bands often perform free in central plazas. Mexicans have a sophisticated enjoyment of performing arts from around the world and the world-class auditoriums in which they perform. Any such performance will be a sell-out, so it's possible to find national as well as international groups touring most of the year, but especially in conjunction with the Cervantino Festival, which takes place in Guanajuato in October and November. Invited groups perform throughout the country before and after the festival.

5. SPORTS & RECREATION

The precise rules of the ball game played by pre-Hispanic Mexicans isn't known, but it is fairly well established that some of the players were put to death when the game was over—whether the victors or the losers is unknown. Stone carvings of the game left on the walls of ballcourts throughout Mesoamerica depict heavily padded players elaborately decked out. With that interesting beginning, team sports are popular in Mexico. Probably the most popular team sport today is soccer; turn on the TV almost anytime to catch a game.

Bullfighting, introduced by the Spaniards, is performed countrywide today; the best venues are in Aguascalientes, Guadalajara, and Mexico City. Jai alai, another Spanish game, is played in arenas in Mexico City and Tijuana. By the 18th century the Mexican gentleman-cowboy, the *charro*, displayed skillful horsemanship during the *charreada*, a Mexican-style rodeo; today charro associations countrywide compete all year, usually on Sunday mornings. Although supposedly illegal, in many places cockfights are held in specially built arenas.

Mexico has numerous golf courses, especially in the resort areas, but also excellent ones in Mexico City and Guadalajara. It is sometimes easier to rent a horse in Mexico than a car, since it is a pastime enjoyed by many people at beach resorts as well as in the country. Sport bicycling has grown in popularity, so it isn't unusual to see young men making the grind of steep mountain passes during cycling club marathons.

Tennis, racquetball, squash, waterskiing, surfing, and scuba diving are all sports visitors can enjoy in Mexico. While it's possible to scuba dive in the Pacific, the best place for that sport is Mexico's Yucatán Caribbean coast. Mountain climbing and hiking volcanoes is a rugged sport where you'll meet like-minded folks from around the world.

6. FOOD & DRINK

Mexican food served in the United States isn't really Mexican food, it's a transported variation that gets less Mexican the farther you get from the border. True Mexican food usually isn't fiery hot; hot spices are added from sauces and garnishes at the table. While there are certain staples like tortillas and beans that appear almost universally, Mexican food and drink varies considerably from region to region; even the beans and tortillas sidestep the usual in some areas just to keep you on your toes.

DINING CUSTOMS   Who you are and what you do makes a difference on when you eat. If you're a businessperson, you may grab a cup of coffee or *atole* and a piece of sweet bread just before heading for work around 8am. Around 10 or 11am it's time for a real breakfast, and that's when restaurants fill with men (usually) eating hearty breakfasts that may look more like lunch with steak, eggs, beans, and tortillas. Between 1 and 5pm patrons again converge for lunch, the main meal of the day, that begins with soup, then rice, then the main course with beans and tortillas and maybe a meager helping of a vegetable, followed by dessert and coffee. Workers return to their jobs until 7 or 8pm. Dinner is late, usually around 9 or 10pm. Although you may see many Mexicans eating in restaurants at night, big evening meals aren't traditional; a typical meal at home would be a light one with leftovers from breakfast or lunch, perhaps soup, or tortillas and jam, or a little meat and rice.

Foreigners searching for an early breakfast will often find that nothing gets going in restaurants until around 9am; that's a hint to bring your own portable coffee pot and coffee, buy bakery goodies the night before, and make breakfast yourself. Markets, however, are bustling by 7am and that's the best place to get an early breakfast. Though Mexico grows flavorful coffee in Chiapas, Veracruz, and Oaxaca, a jar of instant coffee is often all that's offered, especially in budget restaurants.

Some of the foreigner's greatest frustrations in Mexico have to do with getting and retaining the waiter and receiving the final bill. If the waiter arrives to take your order before you are ready, you may have trouble getting him again when you are ready. Once an order is in, ordinarily the food arrives in steady sequence. Getting the check is another matter. It's considered rude for the waiter to bring it before it's requested, so you have to ask for it (sometimes more than once, when at last you've found the waiter). To summon the waiter, wave or raise your hand, but don't motion with your index finger, a demeaning gesture that may even cause the waiter to ignore you. Or if it's the check you want, a smile and a scribbling motion into the palm of your hand can send the message across the room. In many budget restaurants, waiters don't clear the table of finished plates or soft-drink bottles because they use them to figure the tab. Always double-check the addition.

REGIONAL CUISINE Mexico's regional foods are a mixture of pre-Hispanic, Spanish, and French cuisines, and at their best are among the most delicious in the world. Recipes developed by nuns during colonial times to please priests and visiting dignitaries have become part of the national patrimony, but much of Mexico's cuisine is derived from pre-Hispanic times. For the visitor, finding hearty, filling meals is fairly easy on a budget, but finding truly delicious food is not as easy. However, some of the best food is found in small, inexpensive restaurants where regional specialties are made to please discerning locals.

Tamales are one of Mexico's traditional foods, but regional differences make trying them a treat as you travel. In northern Mexico they are small and thin with only a tiny sliver of meat inside. Chiapas has many tamal types, but all are plump and usually come with a sizable hunk of meat and sauce inside. A *corunda* in Michoacan is a triangular tamal wrapped in a corn leaf rather than the traditional corn husk. In Oaxaca traditional tamales come steaming in a banana leaf. The *zacahuil* of coastal Veracruz is the size of a pig's leg (which is in the center) and is pit-baked in a banana leaf. *Molote,* a tiny football-shaped tamal, is a specialty around Papantla, Veracruz.

Tortillas, another Mexican basic, are not made or used universally. In northern Mexico flour tortillas are served more often than corn tortillas. Blue-corn tortillas, once a market food, have found their way to gourmet tables throughout the country. Oaxaca state boasts a large assortment of tortillas, including a hard, thick one with tiny holes used like a cracker, and the huge *tlayuda* that holds an entire meal. Tortillas are fried and used as garnish in tortilla and Tarascan soup. Filled with meat they become *tacos.* A tortilla stuffed, rolled, or covered in a sauce and garnished results in an *enchilada.* A tortilla filled with cheese and lightly fried is a *quesadilla.* Rolled into a narrow tube, stuffed with chicken, then deep-fried, it's known as a *flauta.* Leftover tortillas cut in wedges and crispy fried are called *totopos* and used to scoop beans and guacamole salad. Yesterday's tortillas mixed with eggs, chicken, peppers, and other spices are called *chilaquiles.* Small fried-corn tortillas are delicious with ceviche, or when topped with fresh lettuce, tomatoes and sauce, and chicken they become *tostadas.* Each region has a variation of these tortilla-based dishes.

Northern Mexico is known for charro beans, made with beer, *cabrito* (roast kid), *machacada* (shredded beef), Mennonite cheese, and a round Saltillo pulque bread, made with the alcoholic drink distilled from the maguey cactus.

Gulf Coast **Veracruz** specialties include combo plates of black beans and fried bananas and *pelliscadas,* tortillas refried in lard and salted. Around Lake Catemaco smoked meats are specialties.

The **Yucatán** Peninsula has some of the most varied regional food, including papadzul, huevos motuleños, poc-chuc, cochinita and pollo pibil, escabeche, and lime soup.

Besides being known for tamales, **Oaxaca** has delicious regional cheeses, and green, yellow, red, and black *mole.*

Puebla is known for the many dishes created by colonial-era nuns, among them traditional *mole poblano,* Mexican-style barbecue, lamb *mixiotes, tinga,* and the eggnoglike *rompope.*

Regional drinks are almost as varied as the food in Mexico. *Tequila* comes only from the blue agave grown near Guadalajara. Hot *ponche* (punch) is often found at festivals and is usually made with fresh fruit and spiked with tequila or rum. Baja California and the region around Querétaro are prime grape-growing land for Mexico's wine production. The best *pulque* supposedly comes from Hidalgo state. Beer is produced in Monterrey, the Yucatán, and Veracruz. Delicious fruit-flavored waters appear on tables countrywide made from hibiscus flowers, ground rice and melon seeds, watermelon, and other fresh fruits. Sangría is a spicy tomato/orange-juice and pepper-based chaser for tequila shots.

---

7. RECOMMENDED BOOKS, FILMS & RECORDINGS

BOOKS

There is an endless supply of books written on the history, culture, and archeology of Mexico and Central America. I have listed those that I especially enjoyed.

HISTORY *A Short History of Mexico* (Doubleday, 1962), by J. Patrick McHenry, is a concise historical account. A remarkably readable and thorough college textbook is *The Course of Mexican History* (Oxford University Press, 1987), by Michael C. Meyer and William L. Sherman. *The Conquest of New Spain* (Shoe String, 1988), by Bernal Díaz, is the famous story of the Mexican Conquest written by Cortés's lieutenant. *The Crown of Mexico* (Holt Rinehart & Winston, 1971), by Joan Haslip, a biography of Maximilian and Carlotta, reads like a novel. *Sons of the Shaking Earth* (University of Chicago Press), by Eric Wolf, is the best single-volume introduction to Mexican history and culture that I know of. *Ancient Mexico: An Overview* (University of New Mexico Press, 1985), by Jaime Litvak, is a short, very readable history of pre-Hispanic Mexico.

The Wind That Swept Mexico (University of Texas Press, 1971), by Anita Brenner, is a classic illustrated account of the Mexican Revolution. Charles Flandrau wrote the classic *Viva Mexico: A Traveller's Account of Life in Mexico* (Eland Books, 1985) early this century, a blunt and humorous description of Mexico. Most people can't put down Gary Jennings's *Aztec* (Avon, 1981), a superbly researched and colorfully written fictionalized account of Aztec life before and after the Conquest.

CULTURE *Five Families* (Basic Books, 1979) and *Children of Sanchez* (Random House, 1979), both by Oscar Lewis, are sociological studies written in the late 1950s about typical Mexican families. *Mexican and Central American Mythology* (Peter Bedrick Books, 1983), by Irene Nicholson, is a concise illustrated book that simplifies the subject.

A good, but controversial, all-around introduction to contemporary Mexico and its people is *Distant Neighbors: A Portrait of the Mexicans,* (Random House, 1984), by Alan Riding. In a more personal vein is Patrick Oster's *The Mexicans: A Personal Portrait of the Mexican People* (Harper & Row, 1989), a reporter's insightful account of ordinary Mexican people. A book with valuable insights into the Mexican character is *The Labyrinth of Solitude* (Grove Press, 1985), by Octavio Paz.

Anyone going to San Cristóbal de las Casas, Chiapas, should first read *Living Maya* (Harry N. Abrams, 1987), by Walter F. Morris, with excellent photographs by Jeffrey J. Foxx, all about the Maya living today in the state of Chiapas. For some fascinating background on northern Mexico and the Copper Canyon, read *Unknown*

Mexico (Dover Press, 1987), by Carl Lumholtz, an intrepid writer and photographer around the turn of the century.

The best single source of information on Mexican music, dance, and mythology is Frances Toor's *A Treasury of Mexican Folkways* (Crown, 1967). *Life in Mexico: Letters of Fanny Calderón de la Barca* (Doubleday, 1966), edited and annotated by Howard T. Fisher and Marion Hall Fisher, is as lively and entertaining today as when it first appeared in 1843, but the editor's illustrated and annotated update makes it even more contemporary. Scottish-born Fanny was married to the Spanish ambassador to Mexico and the letters are the accounts of her experiences.

ART, ARCHEOLOGY & ARCHITECTURE   Anyone heading for Yucatán should first read the wonderfully entertaining accounts of travel in that region by the 19th-century traveler, New York lawyer, and amateur archeologist John L. Stephens. His books, *Incidents of Travel in Central America, Chiapas and Yucatán*, and also the account of his second trip, *Incidents of Travel in Yucatán*, have been reprinted by Dover Publications. The series also includes Friar Diego de Landa's *Yucatán Before and After the Conquest* (Dover, 1978) written in the 1560s. Friar Diego's account is a detailed description of Maya daily life, much of which has remained the same from his time until today. Another must is *The Maya* (Thames and Hudson, 1987), by Michael Coe, which is helpful in relating to the different Maya periods. *A Forest of Kings: The Untold Story of the Ancient Maya* (William Morrow, 1990), by Linda Schele and David Freidel, uses the written history of Maya hieroglyphs to tell the dynastic history of selected Maya sites. *The Blood of Kings: Dynasty and Ritual in Maya Art* (George Braziller, Inc., 1986), by Linda Schele and Mary Ellen Miller, a pioneer work, unlocks the bloody history of the Maya.

A book that tells the story of the Indians' "painted books" is *The Mexican Codices and Their Extraordinary History* (Ediciones Lara, 1985), by María Sten. *Mexico Splendors of Thirty Centuries* (Metropolitan Museum of Art, 1990), the catalog of the 1991 traveling exhibition, is a wonderful resource on Mexico's art from 1500 B.C. through the 1950s. Another superb catalog, *Images of Mexico: The Contribution of Mexico to 20th Century Art* (Dallas Museum of Art, 1987) is a fabulously illustrated and detailed account of Mexican art gathered from collections around the world. *Art and Time in Mexico: From the Conquest to the Revolution* (Harper & Row, 1985), by Elizabeth Wilder Weismann, illustrated with 351 photographs, covers Mexican religious, public, and private architecture with excellent photos and text. *Casa Mexicana* (Stewart, Tabori & Chang, 1989), by Tim Street-Porter, takes readers through the interiors of some of Mexico's finest homes-turned-museums or public buildings and private homes using color photographs. *Mexican Interiors* (Architectural Book Publishing Co., 1962), by Verna Cook Shipway and Warren Shipway, uses black-and-white photographs to highlight architectural details from homes all over Mexico.

FOLK ART   Chloë Sayer's *Costumes of Mexico* (University of Texas Press, 1985) is a beautifully illustrated and written work. *Mexican Masks* (University of Texas Press, 1980), by Donald Cordry, based on the author's collection and travels, remains the definitive work on Mexican masks. Cordry's *Mexican Indian Costumes* (University of Texas Press, 1968) is another classic on the subject. Carlos Espejel wrote both *Mexican Folk Ceramics* and *Mexican Folk Crafts* (Editorial Blume, 1975 and 1978), two comprehensive books that explore crafts state by state. *Folk Treasures of Mexico* (Harry N. Abrams, 1990), by Marion Oettinger, curator of folk art and Latin American art at the San Antonio Museum of Art, is the fascinating illustrated story behind the 3,000-piece Mexican folk art collection amassed by Nelson Rockefeller over a 50-year period, as well as much information about individual folk artists.

NATURE   *Peterson Field Guides Mexican Birds* (Houghton Mifflin), by Roger Tory Peterson and Edward L Chalif, is an excellent guide to the country's birds. *Birds of the Yucatán* (Amigos de Sian Ka'an) has color illustrations and descriptions of 100 birds found primarily in the Yucatán Peninsula. *A Guide to Mexican Mammals &*

Reptiles (Minutiae Mexicana), by Norman Pelham Wright and Dr. Bernardo Villa Ramírez, is a small but useful guide to some of the country's wildlife.

FILMS

Mexico's first movie theater opened in 1897 in Mexico City. Almost immediately men with movie cameras began capturing everyday life in Mexico as well as both sides of the Mexican Revolution. All these early films are safe in Mexican archives. As an industry, it had its Mexican start with the 1918 film *La Banda del Automóvil Gris* (The Gray Automobile Gang) by Enrique Rosas Priego, based on an actual cops-and-robbers event in Mexico, but the industry's heyday really began in the 1930s and lasted only until the 1950s. Themes revolved around the Mexican Revolution, handsome but luckless singing cowboys, and helpless, poor-but-beautiful maidens all against a classic Mexican backdrop, at first rural or village (*rancho*) and later city neighborhood.

Classic films and directors from that era are *Alla en el Rancho Grande* and *Vamonos Con Pancho Villa*, both by Fernándo de Fuentes; *Campeón sin Corona* (Champion Without a Crown), a true-life boxing drama, by Alejandro Galindo; *La Perla* (The Pearl), by Emilio Fernández, based on John Steinbeck's novel; *Yanco*, by Servando González, about a poor, young boy of Xochimilco who learned to play a violin; and the sad tale of *María Candelaria*, also set in Xochimilco, another Fernández film starring Dolores del Río. Comedian Cantinflas starred in many Mexican films, and became known in the U.S. for his role in *Around the World in Eighty Days*.

If Mexico's golden age of cinema didn't last long, Mexico as subject matter and location has had a long life. The Durango mountains have become the film backdrop capital of Mexico. *The Night of the Iguana* was filmed in Puerto Vallarta, putting that seaside village on the map. *The Old Gringo* was filmed in Zacatecas and *Viva Zapata* and *Under the Volcano* were both set in Cuernavaca.

RECORDINGS

Mexicans take their music very seriously—notice the tapes for sale almost everywhere, ceaseless music in the streets, and the bus drivers with collections of tapes to entertain passengers by. For the collector there are choices from contemporary rock to revolutionary ballads, ranchero, salsa, and sones, and romantic trios.

For trio music, some of the best is by Los Tres Diamantes, Los Tres Reyes, and Trio Los Soberanos. If you're requesting songs of a trio, good ones to ask for are "Sin Ti," "Usted," "Adios Mi Chaparita," "Amor de la Calle," and "Cielito Lindo." Traditional ranchero music to request, which can be sung by soloists or trios, are "Tu Solo Tu," "No Volveré," and "Adios Mi Chaparita."

Music from the Yucatán would include the recordings by the Trio Los Soberanos and Dueto Yucalpeten. Typical Yucatecan songs are "Las Golondrinas Yucatecas," "Peregrina," "Ella," "El Pajaro Azul," and "Ojos Tristes." Hearthrob soloists from years past include Pedro Vargas, Hector Cabrera, Lucho Gatica, Pepe Jara, and Alberto Vazquez.

Peña Ríos makes excellent marimba recordings. Though marimba musicians seldom ask for requests, some typical renditions would include "Huapango de Moncayo" and "El Bolero de Ravel."

Mariachi music is played and sold all over Mexico. Among the top recording artists is Mariachi Vargas. No mariachi performance is complete without "Guadalajara," "Las Mañanitas," and "Jarabe Tapatío." Broncos' "Cuentame, Cuentame" is played so often you'd think it was the national song.

One of the best recordings of recent times is the Royal Philharmonic Orchestra's rendition of classic Mexican music titled *Mexicano;* it's one purchase you must make.

CHAPTER 2

PLANNING A TRIP TO MEXICO

In this chapter, the where, when, and how of your trip is discussed—the advance planning that gets your trip together and takes it on the road.

After they decide where to go, most people have two fundamental questions: What will it cost? and How do I get there? This chapter not only answers those questions, but addresses such important issues as when to go, whether or not to take a tour, what pretrip health precautions should be taken, what insurance coverage to investigate, where to obtain additional information, and more.

1. INFORMATION, ENTRY REQUIREMENTS & MONEY

SOURCES OF INFORMATION

TOURIST OFFICES   Mexico has tourist offices throughout the world, including the following:

United States: 70 East Lake Street, Suite 1413, Chicago, IL 60601 (tel. 312/565-2786); 2707 North Loop West, Suite 450, Houston, TX 77008 (tel. 713/880-5153); 10100 Santa Monica Boulevard, Suite 224, Los Angeles, CA 90067 (tel. 213/203-8191); 128 Aragon Avenue, Coral Gables, FL 33134 (tel. 305/443-9167); 405 Park Avenue, 14th Floor, New York, NY 10022 (tel. 212/755-7261); and 1911 Pennsylvania Avenue NW, Washington, DC 20006 (tel. 202/728-1750).

Canada: One Place Ville-Marie, Suite 2409, Montréal, PQ H3B 3M9 (tel. 514/871-1052); and 2 Bloor Street West, Suite 1801, Toronto, ON M4W 3E2 (tel. 416/925-0704).

Europe: Weisenhuttenplatz 26, 06000 Frankfurt-am-Main 1, Germany (tel. 4969/25-3541); 60 Trafalgar Square, 3rd Floor, London WC2 N5DS, U.K. (tel. 441/839-3177); Calle de Velázquez 126, Madrid 28006, Spain (tel. 34/261-1827); 4 rue Notre-Dame-des-Victoires, 4, 75002 Paris, France (tel. 331/40-210-0734); and Via Barberini 3, 00187 Roma, Italy (tel. 396/474-2986).

Asia: 2.15.1 Nagata-Cho, Chiyoda-Ku, Tokyo 100, Japan (tel. 813/580-2961 or 580-5539).

OTHER SOURCES   The following newsletters may be of interest to readers.

Sanborn's News Bulletin, Dept. FR, P.O. Box 310, McAllen, TX 78502, is a free newsletter produced by Sanborn's Insurance and it's full of tips on driving conditions, highways, hotels, economy and business, RV information, fishing, hunting, and so forth.

Travel Mexico, Apdo. Postal 6-1007, México, DF 06600, is issued six times a year by the publishers of *Traveler's Guide to Mexico,* the book frequently found in hotel rooms in Mexico. The newsletter covers a variety of topics from news about archeology, to hotel packages, new resorts and hotels, and the economy. A subscription costs $15.

ENTRY REQUIREMENTS

DOCUMENTS   You'll need valid proof of citizenship to qualify for the **Mexican Tourist Card** which is issued free at border crossings, by travel agencies, and airlines. Proof of citizenship is also required for re-entry into the United States. You must show proof such as a valid passport, naturalization papers, or a birth certificate with a raised seal (not a photocopy) or a current voter's registration.

A Tourist Card may be issued for up to 180 days, and you should get the card for the maximum time, just in case. Sometimes the officials don't ask, they just stamp a time limit, so be sure to say "six months," or at least twice as long as you think. You may decide to stay, and you'll eliminate hassle by not needing to renew your papers. This is especially important for people who take cars into Mexico.

Guard your tourist card carefully—if you lose it, you may not be permitted to leave the country until you replace it, a bureaucratic hassle that takes from several days to a week.

Lost Documents   To replace a lost passport, contact your embassy or nearest consular agent, listed in "Fast Facts: Mexico," below. You must establish a record of your citizenship, and also fill out a form requesting another Mexican Tourist Card. Without the tourist permit you can't leave the country, and without an affidavit affirming your passport request and citizenship, you may have hassles at Customs when you get home. So it's important to clear everything up *before* trying to leave.

CUSTOMS   When you enter Mexico, Customs officials will be tolerant as long as you have no illegal drugs or firearms. You're allowed to bring in two cartons of cigarettes, or 50 cigars, plus a kilogram (2.2 lb.) of smoking tobacco; the liquor allowance is two bottles of anything, wine or hard liquor.

When you're reentering the United States, federal law allows, duty free, up to $400 in purchases every 30 days. The first $1,000 over the $400 allowance is taxed at 10%. You may bring in a carton (200) of cigarettes, or 50 cigars, or 2 kg (total, 4.4 lb.) of smoking tobacco, plus 1 liter of alcoholic beverage (wine, beer, or spirits).

Canadian citizens are allowed $20 in purchases after a 24-hour absence from the country or $100 after a stay of 48 hours or more.

MONEY

CASH/CURRENCY   The Mexican unit of currency is the **peso.** Peso coins come in denominations of 20, 50, 100, 500, and 1,000. Bills come in denominations of 2,000, 5,000, 10,000, and above. Small bills and change are hard to come by, so try to keep the 500 and 1,000 peso coins and the 2,000, 10,000, and 20,000 bills on hand.

The dollar sign ($) is used to indicate pesos in Mexico. When a Mexican menu lists a glass of orange juice for $1,500, this means 1,500 pesos. To avoid confusion, I will use the dollar sign in this book *only* to denote U.S. currency.

Many establishments dealing with tourists quote prices in dollars, and to avoid confusion, they use the abbreviations "Dlls." for dollars and "m.n." (*moneda nacional,* national currency) for pesos: "$1,000.00 m.n." means 1,000 pesos.

Only dollar prices are listed in this book; they are a more reliable guide than peso prices. Inflation in Mexico is increasing 20% to 30% per year. Every effort is made to provide the most accurate and up-to-date information in this book, but price changes are inevitable.

WHAT THINGS COST IN MEXICO CITY — U.S. $

	U.S. $
Taxi from airport to Zona Rosa	$7
Bus from Zócalo to Chapultepec Park	50¢
Local telephone call from public street booth	Free
Local telephone call from airport or bus station booth	3¢
Double room at Hotel Emporio (expensive)	$55
Double room at Hotel Capitol (moderate)	$33
Double room at Hotel Montecarlo (budget)	$16
Lunch for one at Focalare (expensive)	$12
Lunch for one at Fonda Santa Anita (moderate)	$7
Lunch for one at Restaurant Mariane (budget)	$5
Dinner for one at Passy (expensive)	$25
Dinner for one at Lincoln Restaurant (moderate)	$15
Dinner for one at Cafe El Popular (budget)	$5
Margarita	$3
Coca-Cola	75¢
Cup of Coffee	75¢
Admission to Museo de Antropologia	$3.50
Ticket to Bellas Artes Ballet Folklorico	$15–$21

EXCHANGING MONEY Cash can sometimes be difficult to exchange because counterfeit U.S. dollars have been circulating recently in Mexico; merchants and banks are wary, and many, especially in small towns, refuse to accept dollars in cash.

Banks in Mexico often give a rate of exchange below the official daily rate, and hotels usually exchange below the bank's daily rate. Personal checks may be cashed, but will delay you for weeks since a bank will wait for your check to clear before giving you your money. Canadian dollars seem to be most easily exchanged for pesos at branches of Banamex and Bancomer.

Banks are open Monday through Friday from 9am to 1:30pm; a few banks in large cities offer extended afternoon hours. You'll save time at the bank or currency-exchange booths by arriving no earlier than 10am, about the time the official daily rate is received. Usually they won't exchange money until they have the official rate. Large airports have currency-exchange counters that sometimes stay open as long as flights are arriving or departing.

TRAVELER'S CHECKS For the fastest and least complicated service, you should carry traveler's checks, which are readily accepted nearly everywhere. Mexican banks pay more for traveler's checks than for dollars in cash—but Casas de Cambio (exchange houses) pay more for cash than for traveler's checks. Some banks, but not all, charge a service fee, as high as 5%, to exchange either traveler's checks or dollars. Sometimes banks post the service charge amount so you can see it, but they might not, so it pays to ask first and shop around for a bank without a fee.

CREDIT CARDS You'll be able to charge some hotel and restaurant bills, almost all airline tickets, and many store purchases on your credit cards. You can get cash advances of several hundred dollars on your card, but there may be a wait of 20 minutes to 2 hours. However, you can't charge gasoline purchases in Mexico.

VISA ("Bancomer" in Mexico), MasterCard ("Carnet" in Mexico), and, less widely, American Express are the most accepted cards. The Bancomer bank, with branches throughout the country, has inaugurated a system of Automatic Teller Machines linked to VISA International's network. If you are a VISA customer, you may be able to get peso cash from one of the Bancomer ATMs.

BRIBES & SCAMS

BRIBES   Called *propina* (tip), *mordida* (bite), or worse, the custom is probably almost as old as mankind. Bribes exist in every country, but in Third World countries the amounts tend to be smaller and collected more often. You will meet with bribery, so you should know how to deal with it.

With the administration of President Salinas de Gortari, border officials have become more courteous, less bureaucratic, and less inclined to ask/hint for a bribe. I'm still wary, however; just so you're prepared, here are a few hints based on the past.

Some border officials will do what they're supposed to do (stamp your passport or birth certificate and inspect your luggage) and then wave you on through. If you don't offer a tip of a few dollars to the man who inspects your car (if you're driving), he may ask for it, as in "Give me a tip (*propina*)." If you're charged for the stamping or inspection, ask for a receipt. If you get no receipt, you've paid a bribe.

Officials don't ask for bribes from everybody. Travelers dressed in a formal suit and tie, with pitch-black sunglasses and a scowl on the face, are rarely asked to pay a bribe. Those who are dressed for vacation fun or seem good-natured and accommodating are charged every time. You should at least act formal, rather cold, dignified, and businesslike, perhaps preoccupied with "important affairs" on your mind. Wear those dark sunglasses. Scowl. Ignore the request. Pretend not to understand. Don't speak Spanish. But whatever you do, avoid impoliteness, and absolutely *never* insult a Latin American official! When an official's sense of machismo is roused, he can and will throw the book at you, and you may be in trouble. Stand your ground—politely.

SCAMS   As you travel in Mexico, you may encounter several types of scams. The **shoeshine scam** is an old trick, used most often in Mexico City. Here's how it works. A tourist agrees to a shine for, say, 3,000 pesos. When the work is complete the vendor says "that'll be 30,000" and insists that the shocked tourist misunderstood. A big brouhaha ensues involving bystanders who side with the shoeshine vendor. The object is to get the bewildered tourist to succumb to the howling crowd and embarrassing scene and fork over the money. A variation of the scam has the vendor saying the price quoted is per shoe. To avoid this scam, ask around about the price of a shine, and when the vendor quotes his price, write it down and show it to him *before* the shine.

Tourists are suckered daily into the **iguana scam,** especially in Puerto Vallarta and nearby Yelapa beach. Someone, often a child, strolls by carrying a huge iguana and says "Wanna take my peekchur." Photo-happy tourists seize the opportunity. Just as the camera is angled properly, the holder of the iguana says (more like mumbles) "One dollar." That means a dollar per shot. Sometimes they wait until the shutter clicks to mention money.

Because hotel desk clerks are usually so helpful, I hesitate to mention the **lost objects scam** for fear of tainting them all. But here's how it works. You "lose" your wallet after cashing money at the desk, or you leave something valuable such as a purse or camera in the lobby. You report it. The clerk has it, but instead of telling you that he does, he says he will see what he can do; meanwhile, he suggests that you offer a high reward. This one has all kinds of variations. In one story a reader wrote about, a desk clerk in Los Mochis was in cahoots with a bystander in the lobby who lifted her wallet in the elevator.

Another scam readers have mentioned might be called the **infraction scam.** Officials, or men presenting themselves as officials, demand money for some supposed infraction. Never get into a car with them. I avoided one begun by a bona fide policeman-on-the-take in Chetumal when my traveling companion feigned illness and began writhing, moaning, and pretending to have the dry heaves. It was more than the policeman could handle.

Legal and necessary car searches by military personnel looking for drugs are mentioned elsewhere. But every now and then there are police-controlled illegal roadblocks where motorists are forced to pay before continuing. There has been a long-standing police roadblock outside Saltillo at the turnoff to Guadalajara. Here they only stop cars with the official tourist window decal and demand a "road use" fee of $20.

Along these lines, if you are stopped by the police, I also suggest that you avoid handing your driver's license to a policeman. Hold it so that it can be read, but don't give it up.

Although you should be aware of such hazards and how to deal with them, I log thousands of miles and many months in Mexico each year without serious incident, and I feel safer there than at home (see also "Emergencies" and "Safety" in "Fast Facts: Mexico," below).

2. WHEN TO GO — CLIMATE, HOLIDAYS & EVENTS

CLIMATE

From Puerto Vallarta south to Huatulco, Mexico offers one of the world's most perfect winter climates—dry, balmy, with temperatures ranging from the 80s by day to the 60s at night. (Although geographically within the tropic zone, Mazatlán is excluded from this perfect weather belt.) From Puerto Vallarta south you can swim year round.

The winter climate on the Gulf Coast is very different. While high mountains shield Pacific beaches from *nortes* (northers—freezing blasts out of Canada via the Texas Panhandle), the gulf enjoys no such immunity. The most disconcerting thing about nortes is that they strike so suddenly. You can be luxuriating on a Cancún beach, enjoying flawless weather, when all of a sudden you'll notice a slight haze obscuring the sun. Within an hour it's like March in New York—gray skies, a boisterous wind, and chilly rain whipping your cheeks. In that brief hour the temperature will have dropped as much as 40°. But here's an interesting twist. While nortes hit Veracruz (latitude 19) with vicious intensity, their sting is far less severe in the most northerly Yucatán Peninsula. Gales hit Veracruz over land and Mérida over water; the gulf has a warming effect.

In summer the difference between West Coast and Gulf Coast temperatures is much less. Both areas become warm and rainy. Of the two regions, the gulf is far rainier, particularly in the states of Tabasco and Campeche.

HOLIDAYS

On national holidays, banks, stores, and businesses are closed, hotels fill up quickly, and transportation is crowded. Mexico celebrates the following national holidays:

January 1	New Year's Day
February 5	Constitution Day
March 21	Birthday of Benito Juárez
March–April (moveable)	Holy Week (Good Friday through Easter Sunday)
May 1	Labor Day
May 5	Battle of Puebla, 1862 (Cinco de Mayo)
September 1	President's Message to Congress
September 16	Independence Day
October 12	Day of the Race (Columbus Day in the U.S.)
November 1–2	All Saints' and All Souls' days (Day of the Dead)
November 20	Anniversary of the Mexican Revolution
December 11–12	Feast Day of the Virgin of Guadalupe (Mexico's patron saint)
December 24–25	Christmas Eve and Christmas Day

MEXICO
CALENDAR OF EVENTS

JANUARY

☐ **Three Kings Day** Commemorates the Three Kings bringing of gifts to the Christ Child. On this day the Three Kings "bring" gifts to children. January 6.

FEBRUARY

☐ **Candlemas** On January 6, Rosca de Reyes, a round cake with a hole in the middle, is baked with a tiny doll inside representing the Christ child. Whoever gets the slice with the doll must give a party on February 2.

❂ *CARNAVAL Resembles New Orleans's Mardi Gras, a festival atmosphere with parades. In Chamula, however, the event hearkens back to pre-Hispanic times with ritualistic running on flaming branches. On the Tuesday before Ash Wednesday, in Tepoztlán and Huejotzingo masked and brilliantly clad dancers fill the streets. In some towns there will be no special celebration, in others a few parades.*
  Where: Especially celebrated in Tepoztlán, Mor.; Huejotzingo, Pue.; Chamula, Chi.; Veracruz, Ver.; Cozumel, Q. Roo; and Mazatlán, Sin. When: Date variable, but always the 3 days preceding Ash Wednesday and the beginning of Lent. How: Transportation and hotels will be clogged, so it's best to make reservations 6 months in advance and arrive a couple of days ahead of the beginning of celebrations.

☐ **Ash Wednesday** The start of Lent and time of abstenance. It's a day of reverence nationwide, but some towns honor it with folk dancing and fairs. Moveable date.

MARCH

☐ **Benito Juárez's Birthday** Small hometown celebrations countrywide, but especially in Juaréz's birthplace, Gelatao, Oaxaca.

❂ *HOLY WEEK Celebrates the last week in the life of Christ from Good Friday through Easter Sunday with almost nightly somber religious processions, spoofing of Judas, and reenactments of specific biblical events, plus food and craft fairs. Among the Tarahumara in the Copper Canyon, celebrations have pre-Hispanic overtones. Businesses close and Mexicans travel far and wide during this week.*
  Where: Special in Pátzcuaro, Taxco, Malinalco, and among the Tarahumara villages in the Copper Canyon. When: March or April. How: Reserve early with a deposit. Airlines into and out of the country will be reserved months in advance. Buses to these towns, or almost anywhere in Mexico, will be full, so try arriving on the Wednesday or Thursday before Good Friday. Easter Sunday is quiet.

MAY

☐ **Labor Day** Workers' parades countrywide and everything closes. May 1.
☐ **Holy Cross Day** Día de la Santa Cruz. Workers place a cross on top of unfinished buildings and celebrate with food, bands, folk dancing, and fireworks around the worksite. Celebrations are particularly colorful in Valle de Bravo, state of Mexico, and Paracho, Michoacan. May 3.

☐ **Cinco de Mayo** A national holiday that celebrates the defeat of the French at the Battle of Puebla. May 5.

☐ **Feast of San Isidro** The patron saint of farmers is honored with a blessing of seeds and work animals. May 15.

JUNE

☐ **Navy Day** Celebrated by all port cities. June 1.

✪ *CORPUS CHRISTI Honors the Body of Christ—the Eurcharist—with religious processions, mass, food. Celebrated nationwide. Festivities include numerous demonstrations of the voladores (flying pole dancers) beside the church and at the ruins of El Tajín.*
Where: Particularly special in Papantla, Ver. When: Variable date 66 days after Easter. How: By bus from Tampico, Tuxpan, or Poza Rica. Make reservations well in advance.

☐ **Saint Peter's Day** Día de San Pedro. Celebrated wherever St. Peter is the patron saint and honors anyone named Pedro or Peter. It's especially festive at San Pedro Tlaquepaque, near Guadalajara, with numerous mariachi bands, folk dancers, and parades with floats. June 29.

JULY

☐ **Virgin of Carmen** A nationally celebrated religious festival centered at churches nationwide. July 16.

☐ **Saint James Day** Día de San Juan. Observed countrywide wherever St. James is the patron saint, and for anyone named Juan or John, or any village with Santiago in the name. Often celebrated with rodeos, fireworks, dancing, and food. July 25.

AUGUST

✪ *ASSUMPTION OF THE VIRGIN MARY Venerated throughout the country with special masses and in some places processions. Streets are carpeted in flower petals and colored sawdust. At midnight on the 15th a statue of the Virgin is carried through the streets; the 16th is a running of the bulls. On August 15 in Santa Clara del Cobre, near Pátzcuaro, Our Lady of the Cibary is honored with a parade of floats, dancers on the main square, and an exposition of area crafts, especially copper.*
Where: Special in Huamantla, Tlaxcala, and Santa Clara del Cobre, Michoacan. When: August 15–16. How: Buses to Huamantla from Puebla or Mexico City will be full and there are few hotels in Huamantla. Plan to stay in Puebla and commute for the festivities.

SEPTEMBER

☐ **Independence Day** Celebrates Mexico's independence from Spain. A day of parades, picnics, and family reunions throughout the country. At 11pm on September 15 the president of Mexico gives the famous independence *grito* (shout) from the National Palace in Mexico City. It's also elaborately celebrated in Querétaro and San Miguel de Allende where Independence conspirators lived and met. September 16 (parade day).

OCTOBER

☐ **Cervantino Festival** Begun in the 1970s as a cultural event bringing performing artists from all over the world to the Guanajuato, a picturesque village northeast of Mexico City, now the artists travel all over the republic after appearing in

Guanajuato. Check local calendars for appearances. Mid-October through November.

☐ **Feast of San Francisco de Asis** Anyone named Frances or Francis or Francisco, and towns whose patron saint is San Francisco, will be celebrating with barbecue parties, regional dancing, and religious observances. October 4.

☐ **Día de la Raza** Day of the Race, or Columbus Day (the day Columbus discovered America), commemorates the fusion of two races—Spanish and Mexican. October 12.

NOVEMBER

❂ *DAY OF THE DEAD   What's commonly called the Day of the Dead is actually 2 days, All Saints' Day, honoring saints and deceased children, and All Souls' Day, honoring deceased adults. Relatives gather at cemeteries countrywide, carrying candles and food often spending the night beside graves of loved ones. Weeks before, bakers begin producing bread formed in the shape of mummies or round loafs decorated with bread bones. Decorated sugar skulls emblazoned with glittery names are sold everywhere. Many days ahead, homes and churches erect special altars laden with Day of the Dead bread, fruit, flowers, candles, and favorite foods and photographs of saints and of the deceased. On the 2 nights of the Day of the Dead children dress in costumes and masks, often carrying mock coffins through the streets and pumpkin lanterns into which they expect money will be dropped.*

*   **Where:** *The most famous celebration is on Janitzio, an island on Lake Pátzcuaro, Michoacan, west of Mexico City, but it has become almost too well known. Mixquic, a mountain village south of Mexico City, hosts an elaborate street fair, and around 11pm on both nights, solemn processions lead to the cemetery in the center of town where villagers are already settled in with candles, flowers, and food.* **When:** *November 1–2.*

☐ **Revolution Day** Commemorates the start of the Mexican Revolution in 1910, with parades, speeches, rodeos, and patriotic events. November 20.

DECEMBER

☐ **Feast of the Virgin of Guadalupe** Throughout the country the Patroness of Mexico is honored with religious processions, street fairs, dancing, fireworks, and masses. The Virgin of Guadalupe appeared to a small boy, Juan Diego, in December 1531 on a hill near Mexico City. He convinced the bishop that the apparition had appeared by revealing his cloak, upon which the Virgin was emblazoned. It's customary for children to dress up as Juan Diego, wearing mustaches and red bandanas. The most famous and elaborate celebration takes place at the Basilica of Guadalupe, north of Mexico City, where the Virgin appeared. But every village celebrates this day, often with processions of children carrying banners of the Virgin, and with *charreadas,* bicycle races, dancing, and fireworks. December 12.

☐ **Christmas Posadas** Each of the 12 nights before Christmas it's customary to reenact the Holy Family's search for an inn, with door-to-door candlelit processions in cities and villages nationwide. You may see them especially in Querétaro and Taxco.

☐ **Christmas** Mexicans extend this celebration and leave their jobs, often beginning 2 weeks before Christmas, all the way through New Year's. Many businesses close and resorts and hotels fill up. December 23 there are significant celebrations. Querétaro has a huge parade. In Oaxaca, it's the "Night of the Radishes," with displays of huge carved radishes. On December 24 in Oaxaca processions culminate on the central plaza. On the same night Santiago Tuxtla, Veracruz, celebrates with dancing the huapango and with jarocho bands in the beautiful town square. In Quiroga, Michoacan, villagers present Nativity plays (*Pastorelas*) at churches around the city on the evenings of December 24 and 25.

☐ **New Year's Eve** Like the U.S., New Year's Eve is the time to gather for private parties of celebration and to explode fireworks and sound noisemakers. Places with special festivities include Santa Clara del Cobre, with its candlelit procession of Christs, and Tlacolula near Oaxaca, with commemorative mock battles for good luck in the new year.

MEXICO CITY
CALENDAR OF EVENTS

JANUARY

☐ **Feast of San Antonio Abad** Blessing of the Animals at the Santiago Tlatelolco Church on the Plaza of Three Cultures, at San Juan Bautista Church in Coyoacán, and at the Church of San Fernando, two blocks north of the Juárez/Reforma intersection.

MAY

☐ **Corpus Christi** Children dressed as Indians and their parents gather before the National Cathedral on the Zócalo, carrying decorated baskets of fruit for the priest's blessing. *Mulitas* (mules), handmade from dried corn husks and painted, often with a corn-husk rider, and sometimes accompanied by pairs of corn-husk dolls, are traditionally sold there on that day. Moveable date 66 days after Easter.

AUGUST

☐ **Fall of Tenochtitlán** The last battle of the Conquest took place at Tlatelolco, the ruins that are now a part of Plaza of Three Cultures. Wreath-laying ceremonies there and at the Cuauhtémoc monument on Reforma commemorate the event when thousands lost their lives and the last Aztec king, Cuauhtémoc, surrendered to Hernán Cortés. August 13.

SEPTEMBER

☐ **Independence Day** At 11pm on September 15, the president of Mexico gives the famous independence *grito* (shout) from the central balcony of the National Palace in Mexico City before at least half a million people crowded into the Zócalo, and to the rest of the country via television. The enormous military parade on September 16 starts at the Zócalo and ends at the Independence Monument on Reforma. Tall buildings downtown are draped in the national colors of red, green, and white, and the Zócalo is ablaze with lights; it's popular to drive downtown at night to see the lights—truly spectacular. September 15–16.

DECEMBER

✪ *DÍA DE GUADALUPE* *The Virgin of Guadalupe, Patroness of Mexico, is venerated where she appeared to young Juan Diego in 1531, at what is now the Basilica of Guadalupe, north of the historic center of Mexico City. Penitents come on their knees, or walking for days, and Indian dancers perform outside the church. The solemn celebration is almost ruined by vendors of food and religious objects who line the roadways around the basilica, and pickpockets come in droves.*

Where: Basilica of Guadalupe. *When:* December 12 and the week before. **How:** *Public transportation will be packed, so your best bet is a taxi, which will let you off several blocks from the basilica.*

3. HEALTH & INSURANCE

HEALTH PREPARATIONS

Of course, the very best way to avoid illness or to mitigate its effects are to make sure that you're in top health when you travel and that you don't overdo it. Travel tends to take more of your energy than a normal working day, and missed meals mean that you get less nutrition than you need. Make sure that you have three good, wholesome meals a day, get more rest than you normally do, and don't push yourself if you're not feeling in top form.

COMMON AILMENTS

TURISTA *Turista* is the name given to the pervasive diarrhea, often accompanied by fever, nausea, and vomiting, that attacks so many travelers to Mexico on their first trip. Doctors, who call it travelers' diarrhea, say it's not just caused by one "bug," or factor, but by a combination of different food and water, upset schedules, overtiring, and the stresses that accompany travel. Being tired and careless about food and drink is a sure ticket to turista. A good high-potency (or "therapeutic") vitamin supplement, and even extra vitamin C, is a help; yogurt is good for healthy digestion, but is not available everywhere in Mexico.

Preventing Turista: The U.S. Public Health Service recommends the following measures for prevention of travelers' diarrhea:

- Drink only purified water. This means tea, coffee, and other beverages made with boiled water; canned or bottled carbonated beverages and water; beer and wine; or water that you yourself have brought to a rolling boil or otherwise purified. Avoid ice, which is usually made with untreated water.
- Choose food carefully. In general, avoid salads, uncooked vegetables, and unpasteurized milk or milk products (including cheese). Choose food that is freshly cooked and still hot. Peel fruit yourself. Don't eat undercooked meat, fish, or shellfish.

The Public Health Service does not recommend that you take any medicines as preventatives. All the applicable medicines can have nasty side effects if taken for several weeks.

How to Get Well: If you get sick, there are lots of medicines available in Mexico which can harm more than help. You should ask your doctor before you leave home what medicine he or she recommends for travelers' diarrhea, and follow that advice.

Public Health Service guidelines are these: If there are three or more loose stools in an 8-hour period, especially with other symptoms such as nausea, vomiting, abdominal cramps, and fever, it's time to go to a doctor.

The first thing to do is go to bed and don't move until the condition runs its course. Traveling makes it last longer. Drink lots of liquids: Tea without milk or sugar, or the Mexican *te de manzanilla* (chamomile tea), is best. Eat only *pan tostada* (dry toast). Keep to this diet for at least 24 hours and you'll be well over the worst of it. If you fool yourself into thinking that a plate of enchiladas can't hurt, or that beer or liquor will kill the germs, you'll have a total relapse.

The Public Health Service advises that you be especially careful to replace fluids and electrolytes (potassium, sodium, etc.) during a bout of diarrhea. Do this by drinking glasses of fruit juice (high in potassium) with honey and a pinch of salt added; and also a glass of boiled pure water with a quarter teaspoon of sodium bicarbonate (baking soda) added.

ALTITUDE SICKNESS   At high altitudes it takes about 10 days to acquire the extra red blood corpuscles you need to adjust to the scarcity of oxygen. At very high-altitude places such as Ixta-Popo Park outside Mexico City (13,000 ft.), your car won't run very well, you may have trouble starting it, and you may not even sleep well at night.

This ailment results from the relative lack of oxygen and decrease in barometric pressure that come from being at high altitudes (5,000 ft./1,500 m, or more). Mexico City is at an altitude of more than 7,000 feet, as are a number of other central Mexican cities, so discomfort is possible. Symptoms include shortness of breath, fatigue, headache, and even nausea.

Avoid altitude sickness by taking it easy for the first few days after you arrive at high altitude. Drink extra fluids, but avoid alcoholic beverages, which not only tend to dehydrate you, but also are more potent in a low-oxygen environment. If you have heart or lung problems, talk to your doctor before going above 8,000 feet.

BUGS & BITES   Mosquitoes and gnats are prevalent along the coast and in the Yucatán lowlands. Insect repellent (*rapellante contra insectos*) is a must, and it's not always available in Mexico. If you're sensitive to bites, pick up some antihistamine cream from a drugstore at home (Di-Delamine is available without a prescription). Rubbed on a fresh mosquito bite, the cream keeps down the swelling and reduces the itch. In Mexico, ask for Camfo-Fenicol (Camphophenique), the second-best remedy.

Most readers won't ever see a scorpion, but if you're stung go to a doctor.

MORE SERIOUS DISEASES

You don't have to worry about tropical diseases if you stay on the normal tourist routes. You can protect yourself by taking some simple precautions. Besides being careful about what you eat and drink, don't go swimming in polluted waters. This includes any stagnant water such as ponds, slow-moving rivers, and Yucatecan cenotes. Mosquitoes can carry malaria, dengue fever, and other serious illnesses. Cover up, avoid going out when mosquitoes are active, use repellent, sleep under mosquito netting, and stay away from places that seem to have a lot of mosquitoes. The most dangerous areas seem to be on Mexico's west coast away from the big resorts (which are relatively safe).

To prevent malaria if you go to a malarial area, you must get a prescription for antimalarial drugs and begin taking them before you enter the area. You must also continue to take them for a certain amount of time after you leave the malarial area. Talk to your doctor about this. It's a good idea to be inoculated against tetanus, typhoid, and diphtheria, but this isn't a guarantee against contracting the disease.

The following list of diseases should not alarm you, as their incidence is rare among tourists. But if you become ill with something more virulent than travelers' diarrhea, I want you to have this information ready at hand:

DENGUE FEVER   Transmitted by mosquitoes, it comes on fast with high fever, severe headache, and joint and muscle pain. About 3 or 4 days after the onset of the disease, there's a skin rash. Highest risk is during July, August, and September. Risk for normal tourists is low.

DYSENTERY   Caused by contaminated food or water, either amoebic or bacillary in form, it is somewhat like travelers' diarrhea, but more severe. Risk for tourists is low.

HEPATITIS, VIRAL   This virus is spread through contaminated food and water (often in rural areas), and through intimate contact with infected persons. Risk for tourists is normally low.

MALARIA   Spread by mosquito bites, malaria can be effectively treated if caught soon after the disease is contracted. Malaria symptoms are headache, malaise, fever, chills, sweats, anemia, and jaundice.

RABIES   This virus is almost always passed by bites from infected animals or bats, rarely through broken skin or the mucous membranes (as from breathing rabid-bat-contaminated air in a cave). If you are bitten, wash the wound at once with large amounts of soap and water—this is important! Retain the animal, alive if possible, for rabies quarantine. Contact local health authorities to get rabies immunization. This is essential, as rabies is a fatal disease which may be prevented by prompt treatment.

SCHISTOSOMIASIS   This is a parasitic worm, passed by a freshwater snail larva that can penetrate unbroken human skin. You get it by wading or swimming in fresh water where the snails are, such as in stagnant pools, streams, or cenotes. About 2 or 3 weeks after exposure, there's fever, lack of appetite, weight loss, abdominal pain, weakness, headaches, joint and muscle pain, diarrhea, nausea, and coughing. Some 6 to 8 weeks after infection, the microscopic snail eggs can be found in the stools. Once diagnosed (after a very unpleasant month or two), treatment is fast, safe, effective, and cheap. If you think you've accidentally been exposed to schistosomiasis-infected water, rub yourself vigorously with a towel and/or spread rubbing alcohol on the exposed skin.

TYPHOID FEVER   Protect yourself by having a typhoid vaccination (or booster, as needed). Protection is not total—you can still get this very serious disease from contaminated food and water. Symptoms are similar to those for travelers' diarrhea, but much worse. If you get typhoid fever, you'll need close attention by a doctor, perhaps hospitalization for a short period.

TYPHUS FEVER   You should see a doctor for treatment of this disease, which is spread by lice. Risk is very low.

EMERGENCY EVACUATION   For extreme medical emergencies there's a service from the United States that will fly people to American hospitals: **Air-Evac,** 24-hour air ambulance (tel. collect, 713/880-9767 in Houston, 619/278-3822 in San Diego, or 305/772-0003 in Miami, 24 hours daily).

INSURANCE

HEALTH/ACCIDENT/LOSS   It can happen anywhere in the world—you discover you've lost your wallet, your passport, your airline ticket, and your tourist permit. Always keep a photocopy of these documents in your luggage—it makes replacing them easier. To be reimbursed for insured items once you return, you'll need to report the loss to the Mexican police and get a written report. If you don't speak Spanish, take along someone who does. If you lose official documents, you'll need to contact both Mexican and U.S. officials in Mexico before you leave the country.
  Health Care Abroad, 243 Church Street N.W., Vienna, VA 22180 (tel. 703/255-9800 or toll free 800/237-6616), and **Access America, Inc.,** 600 Third Avenue, New York, N.Y. 10016 (tel. toll free 800/955-4002) offer medical and accident insurance as well as coverage for luggage loss and trip cancellation.

4. WHAT TO PACK

CLOTHING   Mexico City and other high-elevation cities such as San Cristóbal de las Casas require a coat in winter and preferably a couple of sweaters. In summer it gets warm during the day and cool, but not cold, at night. Generally speaking, throughout Mexico it rains almost every afternoon or evening between May and October—so take rain gear. Mexico tends to be a bit conservative in dress, so shorts and halter tops are generally frowned upon except at seaside resorts. Lightweight cotton clothes are preferrable for the lowlands (the Yucatán, and coastal areas). For dining out in a nice restaurant in conservative and sophisticated cities like Monterrey, Guadalajara, and Mexico City, a jacket and tie for men and dress or suit for women are appropriate.

GADGETS Bring your own washcloth, or better yet a sponge (which dries quickly)—you'll rarely find washcloths in a budget-category hotel room. A bathtub plug (one of those big round ones for all sizes) is a help since fitted plugs are frequently missing, or don't work. Blow-up (collapsable) hangers and a stretch clothesline are handy. I never leave home without a luggage cart, which saves much effort and money, and is especially useful in small towns where there are no porters at bus stations. Buy a sturdy one with at least 4-inch wheels that can take the beating of cobblestone streets, stairs, and curbs. A heat immersion coil, plastic cup, and spoon are handy for preparing coffee, tea, and instant soup. For power failures, and if you plan to visit archeological sites with dark interiors, a small flashlight is a help. A combo pocketknife (for peeling fruit) with a screwdriver (for fixing cameras and eyeglasses), bottle opener, and corkscrew is a must.

5. TIPS FOR THE DISABLED, SENIORS, SINGLES, FAMILIES & STUDENTS

FOR THE DISABLED Travelers unable to walk, or who are in wheelchairs or on crutches, discover quickly that Mexico is one giant obstacle course. Beginning at the airport on arrival you may encounter steep stairs before finding a well-hidden elevator or escalator—if one exists. Airlines will often arrange wheelchair assistance for passengers to the baggage area. Porters are generally available to help with luggage at airports and large bus stations, once you've cleared baggage claim. Escalators (and there aren't many in the country) are often not operating. Few handicapped-equipped rest rooms exist, or when one is available, access to it may be via a narrow passage that won't accommodate a wheelchair or someone on crutches. Many five-star and Gran Turismo hotels (the most expensive) now have rooms with bathrooms for the handicapped and handicapped access to the hotel. For those traveling on a budget, stick with one-story hotels or those with elevators. Even so there will probably still be obstacles somewhere. Stairs without handrails abound in Mexico. Intracity bus drivers generally don't bother with the courtesy step upon boarding or disembarking. On city buses the height between the street and the bus step can require considerable force to board. Generally speaking, no matter where you are, someone will lend a hand, although you may have to ask for it.

FOR SENIORS Handrails are often missing. Unmarked or unguarded holes in sidewalks countrywide present problems for all visitors.

Retiring Mexico is a popular country for retirees, although income doesn't go nearly as far as it once did. Do several things before venturing south permanently: Stay for several weeks in any place under consideration; rent before buying; and check on the availability and quality of health care, banking, transportation, and rental costs. How much it costs to live depends on your life-style and where you choose to live. Car upkeep and insurance, and clothing and health costs are important variables to consider.

The Mexican government requires foreign residents to prove a specific amount of income before permanent residence is granted, but you can visit for 6 months on a tourist visa and renew it every 6 months without commiting to a "legal" status. Mexican health care is surprisingly inexpensive. You can save money by living on the local economy: Buy food at the local market, not imported items from specialty stores; use local transportation and save the car for long-distance trips. Some of the most popular places for long-term stays include Guadalajara, Lake Chapala, Ajijic, and Puerto Vallarta all in the state of Jalisco; San Miguel de Allende and Guanajuato in the state of Guanajauto; Cuernavaca, Morelos; Alamos, Sinaloa; and to a lesser extent Manzanillo, Colima, and Morelia, Michoacan. Crowds don't necessarily mean that there are no other good places: Oaxaca, Querétaro, Puebla, Guanajuato, Tepoztlán, and Valle de Bravo have much to offer, but Americans have yet to collect there in large numbers.

The following newsletters are written for prospective retirees: **AIM,** Apdo. Postal 31-70, Guadalajara 45050, Jal., México, is a well-written, plain-talk and very informative newsletter on retirement in Mexico. Recent issues reported on retirement background and considerations for Lake Chapala, Aguascalientes, Alamos, Zacatecas, West Coast beaches, Acapulco, and San Miguel de Allende. It costs $16 to the U.S. and $19 to Canada. Back issues are three for $5.

The annual *Retiring in Mexico,* Apdo. Postal 50409, Guadalajara, Jal., (tel. 36/21-2348 or 47-9924), comes in three editions—a large January issue and smaller spring and fall supplements—all for $12. Each newsletter is packed with information about retiring in Guadalajara. It's written by Fran and Judy Furton, who also sell other packets of information as well as host an open house in their home every Tuesday for $12.

Finally **Sanborn Tours,** 1007 Main Street, Bastrop, TX 78602 (tel. toll free 800/531-5440), offers a "Retire in Mexico" Guadalajara orientation tour.

FOR SINGLE TRAVELERS Mexico may be the land for romantic honeymoons, but it's also a great place to travel on your own without really being or feeling alone. Although combined single and double rates is a slow-growing trend in Mexico, most of the hotels mentioned in this book still offer singles at lower rates. There's so much to see and do that being bored needn't be a problem. Mexicans are very friendly and it's easy to meet other foreigners. Certain cities like Acapulco, Manzanillo, and Huatulco have such a preponderance of twosomes that single travelers there may feel as though an appendage is missing. On the other hand, singles can feel quite comfortable in Isla Mujeres, Puerto Vallarta, San Blas, Cancún, Zihuatanejo, Ixtapa, Puerto Angel, Celestún, La Paz, and Cabo San Lucas. In those places you'll find a good combination of beachlife, nightlife, and tranquility, whichever is your pleasure.

If you don't like the idea of traveling alone then you might try **Sanborn's Tripshare Service** (see "Saving Money on Transportation," in Section 9, below) **Travel Companion Exchange,** P.O. Box 833, Amityville, NY 11701 (tel. 516/454-0880; fax 516/454-0170), brings prospective travelers together. Members complete a profile, then place an anonymous listing of their travel interests in the newsletter. Prospective traveling companions then make contact through the Exchange. Membership costs $36 to $66 for 6 months.

For Women As a frequent female traveler to Mexico, most of it alone, I can tell you firsthand that I feel safer traveling in Mexico than in the U.S. Mexicans are a very warm and welcoming people, and I'm not afraid to be friendly wherever I go. But I use the same common-sense precautions I use traveling anywhere else in the world: I'm alert to what's going on around me.

Mexicans in general, and men in particular, are nosey about single travelers, especially women. They want to know with whom you're traveling, whether you're married or have a boyfriend, and how many children you have. My advice to anyone asked these details by taxi drivers, or other people with whom you don't want to become friendly, is to make up a set of answers (regardless of the truth): I'm married, traveling with friends, and I have three children. Divorce may send out a wrong message about availability.

Drunks are a particular nuisance to the lone female traveler. Don't try to be polite—just leave or duck into a public place.

Generally women alone will feel comfortable going to a hotel lobby bar, but are asking for trouble by going into a pulquería or cantina. In restaurants, as a general rule, single women are offered the worst table and service. You'll have to be vocal about your preference and insist on service. Tip well if you plan to return. Don't tip at all if service is bad.

And finally, remember that Mexican men learn charm early. The chase is as important as the conquest (maybe more so). Despite whatever charms *you* may possess, think twice before taking personally or seriously all the adoring, admiring words you'll hear.

For Men   I'm not sure why, but non-Spanish-speaking foreign men seem to be special targets for scams and pickpockets. So if you fit this description, whether traveling alone or in a pair, exercise special vigilance.

FOR FAMILIES   Mexico has a high birth rate, so small children make up a large part of the population. Mexicans travel extensively with their families, so your child will feel very welcome. Hotels will often arrange for a baby-sitter. Several hotels in the mid to upper range have small playgrounds and pools for children and hire caretakers on weekends to oversee them. Few budget hotels offer these amenities.

Before leaving, you should check with your doctor to get advice on medications to take along. Bring a supply, just to be sure. Disposable diapers are made and sold in Mexico (one popular brand is Kleen Bebe). The price is about the same as at home, but the quality is poorer. Gerber's baby foods are sold in many stores. Dry cereals, powdered formulas, baby bottles, and purified water are all easily available in mid-size to large cities.

Cribs, however, may present a problem. Except for the largest and most luxurious hotels, few Mexican hotels provide cribs.

Many of the hotels I mention, even in noncoastal regions, have swimming pools, which can be dessert at the end of a day of traveling with a child who has had it with sightseeing.

FOR STUDENTS   Students traveling on a budget may want to contact the student headquarters in the various cities that can supply information on student hostels. Maps and local tourist information are also available. The office in Mexico City is at Hamburgo 273 (tel. 5/514-4213); in Guadalajara, it's at Terranova 1220 (tel. 36/42-0025); and in Monterrey, at Padre Mier Poniente 665 (tel. 83/44-9588).

6. EDUCATIONAL/ADVENTURE TRAVEL

EDUCATIONAL/STUDY TRAVEL

SPANISH LESSONS   A dozen towns south of the border are famous for their Spanish-language programs. Mexican National Tourist Council offices may have information about schools in Cholula, Cuernavaca, Guadalajara, Mérida, Morelia, Oaxaca, and San Miguel de Allende. Go any time of year—you needn't really wait for a "semester" or course year to start. It's best to begin on a Monday, however.

Don't expect the best and latest in terms of language texts and materials—many are well out-of-date. Teachers tend to be underpaid and perhaps undertrained, but very friendly and extremely patient.

The **National Registration Center for Studies Abroad (NRCSA)**, 823 North 2nd Street, Milwaukee, WI 53203 (tel. 414/278-0631), has a catalog ($5) of schools in Mexico. They will register you at the school of your choice, arrange for room and board with a Mexican family, and make your airline reservations, all for no extra fee. Contact them and ask for a (free) copy of their newsletter.

Folk-art collectors may be interested in trips organized by two Texas museums.

The **McAllen International Museum**, 1900 Nolana, McAllen, TX 78504 (tel. 512/682-1564), through the museum's Friends of Folk Art, arranges once- or twice-a-year trips around folk themes.

The **Friends of Folk Art** of the San Antonio Museum Association, P.O. Box 2601, San Antonio, TX 78299-2601 (tel. 512/226-5544), organizes small groups for once-a-year trips led by the museum's folk-art curator, usually concentrating on a single region in Mexico.

HOMESTAYS   Living with a Mexican family is another way to learn Spanish.

Family stays are not particularly cheap, so you should get your money's worth in terms of interaction and language practice.

Spanish-language schools frequently provide lists of families who offer rooms to students. Often the experience is just like being one of the family.

ADVENTURE/WILDERNESS

Mexico is behind the times in awareness of tourist interest in ecology-oriented adventure and wilderness travel. As a result, most of the national parks and nature reserves are understaffed and/or not staffed by knowledgeable people. Most companies offering this kind of travel are U.S. operated and trips are led by specialists. The following companies offer a variety of off-the-beaten-path travel experiences:

The American Wilderness Experience, P.O. Box 1486, Boulder, CO 80306 (tel. 303/494-2992, or toll free 800/444-0099), leads catered camping, kayaking, biking, and hiking trips in Baja California and Copper Canyon.

Biological Journeys, 1696F Ocean Drive, McKinleyville, CA 95521 (tel. 707/839-0178, or toll free 800/548-7555), offers naturalist-led natural-history and whale-watching cruises off Baja California.

Columbus Travel, 6017 Callaghan Road, San Antonio, TX 78228 (tel. 512/523-1400, or toll free 800/843-1060 in the U.S. and Canada), has a variety of soft and hard adventures, primarily in the Copper Canyon, and can design trips for special-interest groups. The company also arranges trips to the monarch butterflies in Michoacan.

Victor Emanuel Tours, P.O. Box 33008, Austin, TX 78764 (tel. toll free 800/328-8368), is an established leader in birding and natural-history tours.

Far Flung Adventures, P.O. Box 377, Terlingua, TX 79852 (tel. 915/371-2489, or toll free 800/359-4138), takes clients on specialist-led Mexico river trips such as in Veracruz and Río Usumacinta that combine rafting and camping at archeological sites.

The **Foundation for Field Research,** P.O. Box 2010, Alpine, CA 91903 (tel. 619/445-9264), accepts volunteers who contribute a tax-deductible share to project costs during scientific work at Bajia de Los Angeles and Isla de Cedros in Baja California, Mexiquillo Beach in Michoacan state, Alamos in the state of Sonora, and in the state of Chiapas.

Mountain Travel, 6420 Fairmount Avenue, El Cerrito, CA 94530 (tel. 415/527-8100, or toll free 800/227-2384), leads mountain climbers up Mexico's two tallest peaks, Orizaba (18,851 ft.) and Popocatépetl (17,761 ft.).

Rancho del Cielo Tours, c/o. Fred S. Webster, Jr., 4926 Strass Drive, Austin, TX 78731 (tel. 512/451-1669), cooperates with the Gorgas Science Foundation of Texas Southmost College in once- or twice-a-year, week-long trips to the remote mountain El Cielo Biosphere Reserve, 50 miles south of Ciudad Victoria, Tamaulipas. The area is rich in birds, orchids, and bromiliads, and is home to endangered black bear, jaguar, and ocelot.

Toucan Adventure Tours, 3135 East 4th Street, Long Beach, CA 90814 (tel. 213/438-6293; fax 213/438-6228), organizes short Mexico hotel tours and 2-week overland camping tours of Mexico and Guatemala by 15-passenger van.

Wings, Inc., P.O. Box 31930, Tucson, AZ 85751 (tel. 602/749-1967), has a wide assortment of trips, including birding in Oaxaca, Chiapas, Colima, and Jalisco.

7. GETTING THERE

BY PLANE

The airline situation is changing rapidly, with many new regional carriers offering scheduled service to areas previously not served. Besides regularly scheduled service, charter service direct from U.S. cities to resorts is making Mexico more accessible.

THE MAJOR INTERNATIONAL AIRLINES   The main airlines operating direct or nonstop flights from the U.S. to points in Mexico include Aero California (tel. toll free 800/237-6225), Aeroméxico (tel. toll free 800/237-6639), Air France (tel. toll free 800/237-2747), Alaska Airlines (tel. toll free 800/426-0333), American (tel. toll free 800/433-7300), Continental (tel. toll free 800/231-0856), Delta (tel. toll free 800/221-1212), Lacsa (tel. toll free 800/225-2272), Lufthansa (tel. toll free 800/645-3880), Mexicana (tel. toll free 800/531-7921), Northwest (tel. toll free 800/225-2525), Pan Am (tel. toll free 800/221-1111), and United (tel. toll free 800/241-6522). Southwest Airlines (tel. toll free 800/531-5601) serves the U.S. border. The main departure points are Chicago, Dallas/Fort Worth, Denver, Houston, Los Angeles, Miami, New Orleans, New York, Orlando, Philadelphia, Raleigh/Durham, San Antonio, San Francisco, Seattle, Toronto, Tucson, and Washington D.C.

   Bargain hunters rejoice! Excursion and package plans proliferate, especially in the off-season. A good travel agent will be able to give you all the latest schedules, details, and prices, but you may have to sleuth regional airlines for yourself (see "By Plane" in Section 8, "Getting Around," below). The lowest airline prices are midweek all year, and in the off-season (after Easter to December 15). Sample round-trip fares are as follows: An excursion fare from New York to Mexico City, $372; to Guadalajara, $370. From Los Angeles to Guadalajara, a typical fare runs $283; to Cancún, $425; to Mexico City, $302. From Dallas/Fort Worth to Mexico City the cost is $200; to Cancún, $286. From Denver, a round-trip fare to Mexico City runs $332; to Guadalajara, $361.

CHARTERS   Charter service is growing and usually is sold as a package combination of air and hotel. Charter airlines, however, may sell air only, without hotel. Charter airlines include **Taesa Airline,** with direct service from New York to Cancún, Miami and Houston to Veracruz, and possible inauguration of charters from Minneapolis, New York, and San Antonio to Puerto Vallarta; plus Laredo to Mexico City. **Latur** offers charters from New York to Cancún, Puerto Vallarta, and Acapulco; Chicago to Cancún; and Boston to Cancún.

   Tour companies operating charters include: Club America Vacations, Asti Tours, Apple Vacations, Friendly Holidays, Gogo Tours, and Mexico Tourism Consultants (MTC).

BY TRAIN

For getting to the border by train, call **Amtrak** (tel. toll free 800/872-7245) for fares, information, and reservations.

BY BUS

Greyhound-Trailways, or its affiliates, offers service from around the U.S. to the border, where passengers disembark, cross the border, and buy a ticket for travel into the interior of Mexico. At many border crossings there are scheduled buses from the U.S. bus station to the Mexican bus station.

BY CAR

Driving is certainly not the cheapest way to get to Mexico, but it's the best way to see the country.

   Using your own car in Mexico, you will find that Mexican fuel prices, though lower than those in the U.S. and Canada, are in reality not that much of a bargain because the fuel tends to be of much lower octane. Remember, it's not just how much a gallon of gas costs, it's how far you can go that's important—and 82-octane Mexican Nova doesn't get you as far as 91-octane American regular.

   Insurance costs are high (see below). Parking is a problem in the cities. Unless you have a full carload, the bus and train come out cheaper per person, and with public transport you don't have to undertake the tedious amount of driving needed to see a country this big.

   If you want to drive to the Mexican border but not into Mexico, border area chambers of commerce or convention and visitor's bureaus can supply names of secured parking lots. You can leave your car there while you see the country by rail, bus, or plane.

CAR DOCUMENTS   At the border you will have to provide proof that you own the car, registration papers are sufficient for this. (If the car ownership is in two names, then bring a notarized letter from the other owner giving permission to drive the car into Mexico.) Your tourist permit will be stamped, and car papers will be issued for the same length of time as your tourist permit. It's a very good idea to greatly overestimate the time you'll spend in Mexico when applying for your permit, so that if something unforeseen happens and you have to (or want to) stay longer, you don't have to go through the long hassle of getting your papers renewed. The maximum term for tourist permit and temporary vehicle importation permit is 6 months.

You must carry your vehicle permit and tourist permit in the car at all times. Remember that the driver of the car will not be allowed to leave the country without the car (even if it's wrecked or stolen) unless he or she satisfies Customs that the import duty will be paid. In an emergency, if the car must be left behind, it must be put under Customs seal at the airport and have the driver's tourist permit stamped to that effect. There may be storage fees.

MEXICAN AUTO INSURANCE   You must purchase Mexican insurance, as U.S. or Canadian insurance is not valid in Mexico, and any party involved in an accident who has no insurance (or ready proof of it) is automatically sent to jail and the car is impounded until all claims are settled. This is true even if you just drive across the border to spend the day—and it may be true even if you are injured.

The insurance agency will show you a full table of current rates and will recommend the coverage it thinks adequate. The policies are written along lines similar to those north of the border. Again, it's best to overestimate the time, because it's a real runaround to get your policy term lengthened in Mexico. Any part of the term unused will be prorated and that part of your premium refunded to you in cash at the office on the American side on your return, or by mail to your home. Be sure the policy you buy will pay for repairs in either the U.S. or Mexico, and that it will pay out in dollars, not pesos.

One of the best insurance companies for south-of-the-border travel is **Sanborn's Mexico Insurance,** with offices at all border crossings. I never drive across the border without Sanborn's insurance. It costs the same as the competition, and you get a Travelog that's a mile-by-mile guide along your proposed route. Information occasionally gets a bit dated, but for the most part it's like having a knowledgeable friend in the car telling you how to get in and out of town, where to buy gas (and which stations to avoid), highway conditions, and scams. It's especially helpful in remote places. Most of Sanborn's border offices are open Monday through Friday, and a few are staffed on Saturday and Sunday as well. You can purchase your auto liability and collision coverage by phone in advance and have it waiting at a 24-hour location if you are crossing when their office is closed. As for costs, a car with a value of $10,000 costs $119 to insure for 2 weeks, or $61 for 1 week. For information, contact Sanborn's Mexico Insurance, P.O. Box 310, Dept. FR, 2009 South 10th, McAllen, TX 78502 (tel. 512/686-0711; fax 512/686-0732).

AAA auto club also sells insurance.

PREPARING YOUR CAR   Know the condition of your car before you cross the border. Parts made in Mexico may be inferior, but service generally is quite good and relatively inexpensive. Your cooling system should be in good condition, with the proper mixture of coolant and water. Don't risk disaster with an old radiator hose, and carry a spare fan belt. For long drives in summer, an air conditioner is not a luxury but a necessity. You might want a spare belt for this too, just in case. Be sure your car is in tune to handle Mexican gasoline.

Remember that Mexico is a big country, and that you may put several thousand miles on your tires before you return home—can your tires last a few thousand miles on Mexican roads?

Take simple tools along if you're handy with them, also a flashlight or spotlight, a cloth to wipe the windshield, toilet paper, and a tire gauge—Mexican filling stations generally have air to fill tires, but no gauge to check the pressure. When driving, I always bring along a combination gauge/air compressor sold at U.S. automotive stores; it plugs into the car cigarette lighter, making it a simple procedure to check the tires every morning and pump them up at the same time.

Not that many Mexican cars comply, but Mexican law requires that every car have **seat belts** and **a fire extinguisher.** Be prepared!

CROSSING THE BORDER WITH YOUR CAR   After you cross the border into Mexico from the U.S., you'll stop to get your tourist/car permit (now all in one), and a tourist decal will be affixed to a rear window. Somewhere between 12 and 16 miles down the road you'll come to a Mexican Customs post. In the past every motorist had to stop and present travel documents. Now, there is a new system that stops some motorists (chosen at random) for inspection. If the light is green, go on through; if it's red, stop for inspection. In the Baja Peninsula the procedures may differ slightly—first you get your tourist permit, then on down the road you stop for the car permit. Theoretically, you should not be charged for your tourist permit, auto permit, and inspection, but the uniformed officer may try to extract a bribe (see "Bribes & Scams" in Section 1, above).

Incidentally, when you cross back into the U.S. after an extended trip in Mexico, the American Customs officials may inspect every nook and cranny of your car, your bags, even your person. They're looking for drugs, which includes illegal diet pills.

BY SHIP

Numerous cruise lines serve Mexico. Possible trips might cruise from California down to the Baja Peninsula (including specialized whale-watching trips) and ports of call on the Pacific Coast, or from Miami to the Caribbean (which often includes stops in Cancún, Playa del Carmen, and Cozumel).

From a budget point of view, these are expensive if you pay full price. However, if you don't mind taking off at the last minute, several cruise tour specialists arrange substantial discounts on unsold cabins. One such company is **The Cruise Line, Inc.,** 260 Northeast 17th Terrace, Suite 201, Miami, FL 33132 (tel. toll free 800/777-0707 or 800/327-3021).

PACKAGE TOURS

Package tours offer some of the best values to the coastal resorts, especially during high season from December until after Easter. Off-season packages can be real bargains. But to know for sure if the package is a cost saver, you must price the package yourself by calling the airline for round-trip flight costs and the hotel for rates. Add in the cost of transfers to and from the airport (which packages usually include) and see if it's a deal. Packages are usually per person, and single travelers pay a supplement. In the high season a package may be the only way of getting there because wholesalers have all the airline seats. The cheapest package rates will be those in hotels in the lower range, always without as many amenities. But you can use the public areas and beaches of more costly hotels without being a guest.

Travel agents have information on specific packages.

8. GETTING AROUND

BY PLANE

To fly from point to point within the country you'll rely on Mexican airlines. Mexico has two privately owned, large national carriers, **Mexicana** (tel. toll free 800/531-7921 in the U.S.) and **Aeroméxico** (tel. toll free 800/237-6639 in the U.S.), and several up-and-coming regional carriers. Mexicana is Latin America's largest air carrier, and offers extensive connections to the U.S. as well as within Mexico. Aeroméxico also has U.S. connections.

Several of the new regional carriers are operated by, or can be booked through Mexicana or Aeroméxico. Regional carriers are: **Aero Cancún** (see Mexicana), **Aero Caribe** (see Mexicana), **Aero Leo Lopez** (tel. 915/778-1022 in El Paso; fax 915/779-3534), **Aerolitoral** (see Aeroméxico), **AeroMar** (tel. toll free 800/950-0747 in the U.S. or see Mexicana), **Aero Monterrey** (see Mexicana), **Aero Morelos** (tel. 73/17-5588 in Cuernavaca; fax 73/17-2320), **Aerovias Oaxaqueñas** (tel. 951/6-3824 in Oaxaca), and **Noroeste** (tel. 602/275-7950 in Phoenix or 621/7-5007 in Hermosillo). The regional carriers are expensive, but they go to places that are difficult to reach. In each section of this book, I've mentioned regional carriers with all pertinent telephone numbers.

Because major airlines can book some regional carriers, read your ticket carefully to see if your connecting flight is on one of these smaller carriers—they may leave from a different airport or check in at a different counter.

AIRPORT TAXES Mexico charges an airport tax on all departures. Passengers leaving the country on an international departure pay $12 in cash—dollars or the peso equivalent—to get out of the country. Each domestic departure you make within Mexico costs around $5 unless you're on a connecting flight and have already paid at the start of the flight—you won't be charged again if you have to change planes for a connecting flight.

RECONFIRMING FLIGHTS Although airlines in Mexico say that it's not necessary to reconfirm a flight, I always do. On several occasions I have arrived to check in with a valid ticket only to discover that my reservation had been canceled. Now I leave nothing to chance. Also, be aware that airlines routinely overbook. To avoid getting bumped, check in for an international flight the required hour and a half in advance of travel. That will put you near the head of the line.

BY TRAIN

Train travel is safer and more comfortable than going by bus. However, it is slower and costs more, and schedules are likely to be less convenient. I don't recommend train travel east of the Isthmus of Tehuantepec (that is, into Yucatán or Chiapas).

SERVICE CLASSES Traveling **segunda** (second class) is usually hot, overcrowded, dingy, and unpleasant; **primera** (first class) can be the same unless you ask for **primera especial** (first-class reserved seat), a day or so in advance, if possible. The top-of-the-line accommodations on trains, cheaper than flying but more expensive than the bus, are Pullman compartments (*alcoba* or *camarin*) for overnight travel.

Mexico has added first-class service to a number of trains under a general title of **Servicio Estrella** (Star Service). Estrella trains are more expensive but they are superior to regular trains in comfort, and the price difference between Estrella and regular trains is small compared to what you get. At least one light snack is usually served at your seat, airline style, and is included in the price of the ticket. There may also be a dining car. (*Important Note:* Although this Service Estrella is described here, and I've given specific information by town throughout the book, there is a possibility that Estrella Service will undergo drastic changes this year, and the timetables could be altered considerably and service interrupted for a time. Please double-check before planning an itinerary around train travel.)

To reserve a place in an Estrella chair car, be sure to specify *primera especial* and not simply *primera*, which may also be offered. Service and cleanliness may vary dramatically on the Estrella trains, but generally I've found them to be a delightful experience. This qualified statement means that the cars will be clean at the start of the journey, but little may be done en route to keep them that way. Trash may accumulate, toilet paper vanishes, the water cooler runs dry or has no paper cups, and the temperature may vary between freezing and sweltering. Conductors range from solicitous to totally indifferent. Considering the overall comfort, though, they are a good value.

Sleeping compartments—called a *camarin* for one person, an *alcoba* for two (with two beds)—are available on overnight journeys on many trains. These convert to private sitting rooms during the day. Tickets may be sold for more than one or two people in either size compartment, but considering the space available, is not recommended.

MAJOR TRAINS There are two major train hubs—Mexico City and Guadalajara. If you plan to get on and off before your final destination, you must tell the agent your exact on-off schedule at the time of your ticket purchase. Estrella trains are often fully booked with tour groups or during holiday periods.

Here is a summary of the major rail connections:

Mexico City Hub

El Regiomontaño: Runs between Nuevo Laredo (at the Texas border) and Mexico City, through Monterrey and Saltillo.

El Constitucionalista: Between Mexico City and Guanajuato, through Querétaro and Irapuato.

El Tapatío: Between Mexico City and Guadalajara (overnight).

El Oaxaqueño: Between Mexico City and Oaxaca (overnight).

El Jarocho: Between Mexico City and Veracruz, passing Fortín de las Flores, Orizaba, and Córdoba en route (overnight).

El Purépecha: Between Mexico City and Uruapan, through Morelia and Pátzcuaro (overnight).

El San Marqueño–Zacatecano: Between Mexico City and Juárez, through Irapuato, León, Lagos de Moreno, Aguascalientes, and Zacatecas.

Guadalajara Hub

El Tren del Pacífico: Between Guadalajara and Mexicali at the California border, running along the Pacific coast through a dozen cities including Tepic, Mazatlán, Culiacán, Obregón, Hermosillo, Nogales, and Puerto Penasco.

El Sinaloense: Between Guadalajara and Los Mochis, through Tepic, Mazatlan, and Culiacán.

Other Trains

El Nuevo Chihuahua–Pacífico: Begins at both Los Mochis and Chihuahua City, and passes through Mexico's beautiful Copper Canyon.

El Rapido de la Frontera: Between Chihuahua and Ciudad Juárez at the Texas border.

El Tamaulipeco: Between Monterrey and the Texas border towns of Reynosa and Matamoros.

El Coahuilense: Between Saltillo and Piedras Negras on the Texas border, via Ciudad Frontera and Barroteran.

TICKETS & RESERVATIONS If you purchase your ticket at the train station, do it as soon as your plans are firm. In cities served by Estrella trains, you may find travel agents who will arrange your tickets, but they usually charge a service fee of up to 25% of the price of the ticket.

For advance planning using Estrella trains, your best bet is **Mexico by Rail,** P.O. Box 3508, Laredo, TX 78044 (tel. toll free 800/228-3225). Given 15 days' notice they will prepurchase your Estrella train ticket and mail it to you. For holiday travel, make plans 45 days ahead. If you leave from Nuevo Laredo, the company will arrange secured parking, a prestamped tourist card, and transfers across the border. They charge a percentage on top of the regular price of the train ticket. For example, the *Constitucionalista* costs $9.50 round-trip between Mexico City and Querétaro; *Mexico by Rail* charges $17.50.

To contact the trains directly for fares and schedule information in Mexico City, phone 5/547-6593, 547-1097, or 547-1084.

When deciding whether to use Mexico by Rail or another agent, consider the cost of going to the train station yourself and the uncertainty about space if you wait until you get there to reserve a seat. Although they seldom reply to mail, you can try writing well in advance to Commercial Passenger Department, **National Railways of Mexico,** Buenavista Grand Central Station, México, D.F. 06358 (tel. 5/547-8972).

For the **Pacific Railroad Company,** write Tolsa 336, Guadalajara, Jal. 44190. Both companies have special personnel and divisions to handle group train travel. With enough lead time, they'll even put on extra cars.

TRAVEL TIME   From Nuevo Laredo, it's a 25-hour, 735-mile ride to Mexico City. Other border towns are farther from the capital. The trip from Ciudad Juárez, across from El Paso, takes over 35 hours to Mexico City. There is a daily train from Matamoros, across from Brownsville, Texas, to Monterrey. This trip takes 8 hours and then a change of trains is made to an overnight sleeper train daily between Monterrey and Mexico City. From Nogales, the trip takes 26 or 36 hours, depending on which train you take. From Mexicali, the fast train takes 30 hours to Guadalajara, 45 to Mexico City. Pacific Coast trains and those from Mexico City to the Yucatán are notorious for running as much as 24 hours behind time.

BY BUS

Except for the Baja and Yucatán peninsulas, where bus service is not well developed, buses are frequent and readily accessible, and can get you to almost anywhere you want to go. More than a dozen Mexican companies operate large air-conditioned Greyhound-type buses between most cities. The cost is very reasonable, working out to around $1 an hour. Modern buses have replaced most of the legendary overloaded "village buses" that growled and wheezed along. Today it's best to buy your reserved-seat ticket, often via a computerized system, a day in advance on many long-distance routes. Schedules are fairly dependable, so be at the terminal on time for departure.

New buses are being added all over the country featuring large windows with an unobstructed view from every seat. Omnibus de México has added Executive Service from several cities. These cost much more than regular buses, carry half the number of passengers, have stewards, and include a club and movie section.

Many Mexican cities have replaced the bewildering array of tiny private company offices scattered all over town with new central bus stations, much like sophisticated airport terminals.

I've included information on bus routes in my suggested itineraries. Keep in mind that routes, times, and prices may change, and as there is no central directory of schedules for the whole country, current information must be obtained from local bus stations or travel offices.

For long trips, carry some food, water, toilet paper, and a sweater (in case the air conditioning is too strong).

See the Appendix for a list of helpful bus terms in Spanish.

BY CAR

Most Mexican roads are not up to northern standards of smoothness, hardness, width of curve, grade of hill, or safety marking. *Cardinal Rule:* Never drive at night if you can avoid it—the roads aren't good enough; the trucks, carts, pedestrians, and bicycles usually have no lights; you can hit potholes, animals, rocks, dead ends, or bridges out with no warning. Enough said!

You will also have to get used to the spirited Latin driving styles, which tend to depend more on flair and good reflexes than on system and prudence. Be prepared for new procedures, as when a truck driver flips on his left-turn signal when there's not a crossroad for miles. He's probably telling you that the road's clear ahead for you to pass—after all, he's in a better position to see than you are. It's difficult to know, however, whether he really means that he intends to pull over on the left-hand shoulder. You may have to follow trucks without mufflers and pollution-control devices for miles. Under these conditions, drop back and be patient, take a side road, or stop for a break when you feel tense or tired.

Take extra care not to endanger pedestrians. People in the countryside are not good at judging the speed of an approaching car, and often panic in the middle of the road even though they could easily have reached the shoulder.

Be prepared to pay tolls on some of Mexico's expressways and bridges. Tolls are high in this country, at least as high as in the U.S. The word for "toll" in Spanish is *cuota*.

CAR RENTALS With some trepidation I wander into the subject of car-rental rules, which change often in Mexico. The best prices are obtained by reserving your car a week in advance in the U.S. Mexico City and most other large Mexican cities have rental offices representing the various big firms and some smaller ones. You'll find rental desks at airports, at all major hotels, and at many travel agencies. The large firms like Avis, Hertz, National, and Budget have rental offices on main streets as well.

I don't recommend renting a car in Mexico City or for 1-day excursions from the city. It can be a real hassle, and parking is also a problem. Cars are a good option only if you have enough people to fill one and can share the cost.

Cars are easy to rent if you have a credit card (American Express, VISA, MasterCard, etc.), are 25 or over, and have a valid driver's license and passport with you. (One exception: Budget will hold a car reservation only with an American Express or Diner's Club credit card, but you can pay the rental with another card.) Without a credit card you must leave a cash deposit, usually a big one. Rent-here/leave-there arrangements are usually simple to make, but are very costly.

For a short 1-day trip to Cuernavaca (50 miles from Mexico City), through Budget Rental Cars you'll pay $66 with unlimited mileage, including 15% tax and $12 daily insurance; through Avis the cost would be $36.

If you choose to take mileage added, our completed estimate for Mexico City should look something like this, based on traveling 170km (105 miles) in a VW Beetle rented from Budget:

Basic daily rental	$47.00
170km (105 miles) at 25¢ each	42.50
Collison/Damage and personal accident insurance	12.00
IVA tax (15%)	15.23
Subtotal	116.73
Gas ($1 per gallon)	5.00
Tolls and parking	7.00
Grand Total	$128.73

If you purchase Budget's collision/damage insurance, the deductible is $250 if the car is repairable, $400 if it's unrepairable.

A car rented for 1 day through Avis, which from the U.S. only rents with unlimited mileage, would be:

Basic daily rental	$38.00
Insurance	12.00
IVA tax (15%)	7.50
Subtotal	56.50
Gas $1 gallon	5.00
Tolls and parking	7.00
Grand Total	$69.60

The Avis deductible is 5 days of the basic car rental, which in this case would be 5 × $38 = $190, if you buy their insurance.

Costs in the resorts vary: sometimes more, sometimes less than in Mexico City. Deductibles vary greatly so don't fail to get that information.

If you have an accident in Mexico, all parties can be carted off to jail until it's determined who is at fault or until you can show proof of insurance. Insurance bought with the car rental is usually sufficient proof. If you pay for your car rental on a credit card, you may be entitled to waive the insurance, which may be covered by the credit-card company. Before assuming that it is, check with the credit-card company, and get a letter stating the terms. (A letter in Spanish may help in case of an accident.) Without proof of insurance, you may have to pay for repairs, get a police report of the accident, and settle up with the credit-card insurer later.

Read the fine print on the back of your rental agreement and note that insurance is invalid if you have an accident while driving on an unpaved road.

One last recommendation: Before starting out with a rental car, be sure you know the **trouble number.** The large firms have toll-free numbers, which may not be well staffed on weekends.

GASOLINE   There's one government-owned brand of gas and one gasoline station name throughout the country—Pemex (Petroleras Mexicanas). Each station has a franchise owner who buys everything from Pemex. There are two types of gas in Mexico: Nova, an 82-octane leaded gas, and Magna Sin, 87-octane unleaded gas. Magna Sin is sold from brilliantly colored pumps and costs around $1.20 a gallon; Nova costs around $1 per gallon. In Mexico, fuel and oil are sold by the liter, which is slightly more than a quart (40 liters equals about 10½ gallons). Nova is readily available. Magna Sin is now available in most areas of Mexico, along major highways, and in the larger cities. Even in areas where it should be available, you may have to hunt around. The usual station may be out of Magna Sin for a couple of days—on weekends especially. Or you may be told that none is available in the area, just to get your business. Plan ahead: Fill up every chance you get; keep your tank topped off. Pemex publishes a helpful *Atlas de Carreteras* (road atlas), which includes a list of filling stations with Magna Sin gas, although there are some inaccuracies in the list. *No credit cards are accepted for gas purchases.*

Here's what to do when you have to fuel up: Drive up to the pump, close enough so that you will be able to watch the pump run as your tank is being filled. Check that the pump is turned back to zero, go to your fuel filler cap and unlock it yourself, and watch the pump and the attendant as the gas goes in. Though many service-station attendants are honest, most are not. It's good to ask for a specific peso amount rather than saying "full." This is because the attendants tend to overfill, splashing gas on the car and anything within range.

As there are always lines at the gas pumps, attendants often finish fueling one vehicle, turn the pump back quickly (or don't turn it back at all), and start on another vehicle. You've got to be looking at the pump when the fueling is finished, because it may show the amount you owe for only a few seconds. This "quick draw" from car to car is another good reason to ask for a certain peso amount of gas. If you've asked for 20,000 pesos' worth, the attendant can't charge you 22,000 for it.

Once the fueling is complete, let the attendant check the oil, or radiator, or put air in the tires. Do only one thing at a time, be with him as he does it, and don't let him rush you. Get into these habits or it'll cost you.

If you get oil, make sure that the can that is tipped into your engine is a full one. If in doubt, have the attendant check the dipstick again after the oil has supposedly been put in. Check your change, and again, don't let them rush you. Check that your locking gas cap is back in place.

DRIVING RULES   If you park illegally, or commit some other infraction, and you are not around to discuss it, police are authorized to remove your license plates (*placas*). You must then trundle over to the police station and pay a fine to get them back. Mexican car-rental agencies have begun to weld the license tag to the tag frame; you may want to devise a method of your own to make the tags difficult to remove. Theoretically, this will make the policeman move on to another set of tags easier to confiscate. On the other hand, he could get his hackles up and decide to have your car towed. To weld or not to weld is up to you.

Be attentive to road signs. A drawing of a row of little bumps means that there are speed bumps (*topes*) across the road to warn you to reduce speed while driving through towns or villages. Slow down when coming to a village whether you see the sign or not—sometimes they install the bumps but not the sign!

Kilometer stones on main highways register the distance from local population centers. There is always a shortage of directional signs, so check quite frequently that you are on the right road. Other common road signs include:

Camino en Reparación	Road Repairs
Conserva Su Derecha	Keep Right
Cuidado con el Ganado, el Tren	Watch Out for Cattle, Trains
Curva Peligrosa	Dangerous Curve
Derrumbes	Earthquake Zone
Deslave	Caved-in Roadbed
Despacio	Slow
Desviación	Detour
Disminuya Su Velocidad	Slow Down
Entronque	Highway Junction
Escuela	School (Zone)
Grava Suelta	Loose Gravel
Hombres Trabajando	Men Working
No Hay Paso	Road Closed
Peligro	Danger
Puente Angosto	Narrow Bridge
Raya Continua	Continuous (Solid) White Line
Tramo en Reparación	Road Under Construction
Un Solo Carril a 100 m.	One-Lane Road 100 Meters Ahead
Zona Escolar	School Zone

To reduce air pollution, Mexico City prohibits the use of vehicles on certain days (see Chapter 9 for details). The ban on cars includes rental cars and tourist cars, but it is not in effect on Saturday and Sunday. There's a large fine for violating this regulation.

MAPS Guía Roji and AAA have good maps to Mexico. In Mexico, maps are sold at large drugstores like Sanborn's, at bookstores, and in hotel gift shops.

BREAKDOWNS Your best guide to repair shops is the *Yellow Pages*. For specific makes and shops that repair them, look under "Automoviles y Camiones: Talleres de Reparación y Servicio"; auto-parts stores are listed under "Refacciones y Accesorios para Automoviles." On the road, often the sign of a mechanic simply says TALLER MECHANICO.

I've found that the Ford and Volkswagen dealerships in Mexico give prompt, courteous attention to my car problems, and prices for repairs are, in general, much lower than in the U.S. or Canada. I suspect that other big-name dealerships give similar satisfactory service. Often they will take your car right away and make repairs in just a few hours, sometimes minutes.

If your car breaks down on the road, help might already be on the way. Green, radio-equipped repair trucks manned by uniformed, English-speaking officers patrol the major highways during daylight hours to aid motorists in trouble. The "Green Angels" will perform minor repairs and adjustments free, but you pay for parts and materials.

MINOR ACCIDENTS Most motorists think it best to drive away from minor accidents if possible. Without fluent Spanish, you are at a distinct disadvantage when it comes to describing your version of what happened. Sometimes the other person's version is exaggerated, and you may end up in jail or spending days straightening out things that were not even your fault.

Also, see "Mexican Auto Insurance" in Section 7, "Getting There," "By Car," above.

PARKING When you park your car on the street, lock up and leave nothing within view inside (day or night). I use guarded parking lots, especially at night, to avoid vandalism and break-ins. This way you also avoid parking violations. When pay lots are not available, dozens of small boys will surround you as you stop, wanting to "watch your car for you." Pick the leader of the group, let him know you want him to guard it, and give him a peso or two when you leave. Kids may be very curious about the car and may look in, crawl underneath, or even climb on top, but they rarely do any damage.

BY RV

Touring Mexico by recreational vehicle is a popular way of seeing the country. Many hotels have hookups. RV parks, while not as plentiful as in the U.S., are available throughout the country.

BY FERRY

Ferries connect Baja California at La Paz and Santa Rosalia with the mainland at Topolobampo and Mazatlán. In the Yucatán ferries also take passengers between Puerto Juárez and Isla Mujeres and Playa del Carmen and Cozumel.

HITCHHIKING

You see Mexicans hitching rides for example, at crossroads after getting off a bus, but as a general rule hitchhiking isn't done. It's especially unwise for foreigners, who may be suspected of carrying large amounts of cash.

SUGGESTED ITINERARIES

IF YOU HAVE 1 WEEK

Day 1: Explore the museums and sites of Mexico City.
Day 2: Spend the day at the archeological site of Teotihuacán.
Day 3: Hop a train or a bus to one of the colonial regions around the capital: north to Querétaro, San Miguel de Allende, and Guanajuato; southwest to Taxco; northwest to Morelia, Pátzcuaro, and Uruapan; or east to Puebla.
Days 4 and 5: Center yourself in one of these towns and spend the other days seeing it and the surrounding areas.
Day 6: Return to Mexico City for an overnight and any last-minute sightseeing or shopping.
Day 7: Flight home.

IF YOU HAVE 2 WEEKS

Day 1: See the museums of Mexico City, especially those pertaining to areas covering the remainder of your trip.
Day 2: See the ruins of Teotihuacán, 30 miles east of Mexico City.
Day 3: Hop a train or a bus to one of the colonial regions around the capital: north to Querétaro, San Miguel de Allende, and Guanajuato; southwest to Taxco; northwest to Morelia, Pátzcuaro, and Uruapan; or east to Puebla.
Days 4 and 5: Explore your selected village or area.
Day 6: Return to Mexico City and take a flight, bus, or train to one of Mexico's larger colonial-era cities such as Mérida in Yucatán, or Guadalajara near the Pacific Coast.
Days 7 and 8: Explore the museums, restaurants, and nightlife of your chosen city. In Guadalajara don't miss market days in Tonala and shopping in Tlaquepaque. In Mérida you have the option of making day trips to the archeological sites of Uxmal and Chichén-Itzá, but I suggest that you cut your beach stay short (suggested below) and spend at least 2 nights at Chichén-Itzá.
Days 9–14: Spend the remainder of your stay in one coastal resort or exploring a coastline. If your choice is the Yucatán, head for one of the less costly resort areas such as Isla Mujeres north of Cancún, or go south of Cancún to Pamul, Playa del Carmen, or Punta Allen. Another option would be to continue exploring the archeological sites of the Yucatán's interior, leaving a couple of days at the end for beach relaxing. If your choice is the Pacific Coast area, spend a night or two in

Puerto Vallarta. From there it's easy to continue up the coast to more economical San Blas, or south to Barra de Navidad, Melaque, or Manzanillo, all of which are smaller, slower paced, and easier on the wallet.

IF YOU HAVE 3 WEEKS

Day 1: See the museums of Mexico City, especially those pertaining to areas covering the remainder of your trip.
Day 2: See the ruins of Teotihuacán, 30 miles east of Mexico City.
Day 3: Hop a train or a bus to one of the colonial regions around the capital: north to Querétaro, San Miguel de Allende, and Guanajuato; southwest to Taxco; northwest to Morelia, Pátzcuaro, and Uruapan; or east to Puebla.
Days 4–6: Explore your selected village or area.
Days 7–21: From any of the above your choices are many. From San Miguel you could continue north to the colonial silver cities of San Luis Potosí, Aguascalientes, and Zacatecas, and farther on to a week in the Copper Canyon, going from Chihuahua to Los Mochis and winding up for a few days on the beach at Mazatlán. Or spend less time in the canyon and end up the trip on the Baja Peninsula. If you are in Puebla the choice might be to continue on over the mountains to the city of Oaxaca (spend at least 5 days there) and wind up on a Oaxaca beach such as Huatulco, Puerto Angel, or Puerto Escondido. Or the coast of Veracruz offers a number of delightful off-the-beaten-path villages at very reasonable prices. If you're in the Lake Pátzcuaro region, the continued travel choices abound. From there head back to Toluca and south to Cuernavaca, Taxco, and Acapulco for a few days or on to more slow-paced Ixtapa/Zihuatanejo.

THEMED CHOICES

Travelers interested in **archeology** can spend weeks in the Yucatán, around Oaxaca and the Veracruz coast. **Folk art** lovers will find the states of Oaxaca, Chiapas, Puebla, and Guerrero to be especially rich in indigenous crafts, with especially good shopping in Mexico City, Oaxaca, and San Miguel de Allende. Planning your time around Mexico's **festival calendar** makes a unique, pleasurable, and colorful trip. Searching out Mexico's **cuisines** makes a wonderfully purposeful trip which would especially include Puebla, Michoacan, Oaxaca, the Yucatán Peninsula, and Veracruz. **Geologists and mountain climbers** could organize a trip around Mexico's mountain and volcanic peaks of Orizaba, Paricutín, Perote, Popocatépetl, Iztaccíhuatl, and Nevado de Toluca, and the Copper Canyon. **Naturalists** will find good birding or turtle-nesting opportunities on the Veracruz coast, Tamaulipas, Yucatán Peninsula, or Pacific Coast.

9. ENJOYING MEXICO ON A BUDGET

A trip to Mexico can be the most inexpensive foreign vacation you'll ever experience if you follow the suggestions in this guide. Guests at the posh hotels are tempted to stay there and not risk discomfort or inconvenience. As a result, they miss out on the Mexico of the Mexicans. Readers of *Frommer's Mexico on $45 a Day* have at their fingertips information that gets the basics of travel—hotels, meals, and transportation—out of the way as quickly and as cheaply as possible so they can turn their attention to the real Mexico: rubbing shoulders with Mexicans in the street, in the subway, on buses, or in colectivos (shared taxis or vans); staying in small hotels; and eating in local restaurants which present the outsider with new delights (and some perils!).

THE $45-A-DAY BUDGET

Our $45-a-day budget is intended to cover only the expenses of room and three meals each day. I will recommend hotels where you will be able to stay for about $18 to $25 per person per night, and restaurants in which it will be possible to have breakfast for about $3.50, lunch (the largest meal in the Mexican's day) for about $4 to $8, and supper for about $6 to $10. If you spend a few dollars more, you can live more comfortably—even luxuriously—for $50 or $60 a day.

If you like air travel, expect to pay well for the ease and speed; if you don't mind buses (the easiest and cheapest way to go), extra costs for transportation will be minimal. Add a few dollars a day for entertainment if you're a nightclub fan, but add only 50¢ to $4 for museums and exhibitions.

The hotels recommended in this book will be clean, respectable places, sometimes with comforts and conveniences such as a multilingual staff, swimming pools, and usually bathrooms in the rooms. These hotels are not standardized; each will have its own personality. If you want a room with a view over the lovely plaza in the center of Mexico City, then you must consider if you will be bothered by cars buzzing under your window and revelry during flag raising at 6am. If you hate noise, look for a hotel on a side street, perhaps with rooms around an inner court; or even a motel on the outskirts of town, which may be slightly more expensive but much more peaceful.

There will be times when you'd like to treat yourself to something special, so for those times I have included hotel and restaurant choices that are "Worth the Extra Bucks."

American-style restaurants are also noted now and then so you may, if you wish, give your stomach a respite from unfamiliar food. But don't forget that the reason you bought this book was so you could experience Mexican culture and save money at the same time.

SAVING MONEY ON ACCOMMODATIONS

Mexican hotels, like hotels throughout the world, have an assortment of rooms in a range of prices. Rooms with bath or air conditioning are always more expensive. In addition, rooms with a view of the street may be more expensive (and noisier) than those with windows opening onto an airshaft. Rooms may be furnished with a single bed, a double bed, or two twin beds; the best buy is for two people to take the double bed—twins are almost always more expensive. Ask for *una cama matrimonial.* When the desk clerk asks "How many beds?" don't necessarily answer "Two." Or if the clerk shows you a room with two beds, ask if he has one with a double bed. The price the desk clerk quotes you for a room often won't be the cheapest room he has available. Ask to see a cheaper room (*Quiero ver un cuarto más barato, por favor*)—it can't hurt.

The maximum price a hotel can charge for its rooms is controlled by the Mexican government. Often desk clerks will quote a lower price if business is slack or if you suggest a slight reduction. Room rates are required to be posted in plain view near the reception desk, and as a rule they are (places like Acapulco are the exception). Ask the clerk to show you the *Tarifa,* and learn to recognize its official form so you can locate it in other hotels.

Finally, test the beds if you intend to stay any length of time. Price often has nothing to do with the comfort of the beds. Often the cheaper hotels will have beds bought at different times, so one room may have a bad bed while another one has a good bed.

Remember also that the 15% IVA tax will be included in your bill except in a few low-budget places. When you register, ask if the tax has been included in the rate quoted to you.

HOLIDAY RESORTS Those planning to be in resorts like Mazatlán, Acapulco, Puerto Vallarta, Manzanillo, Cozumel, and Isla Mujeres should write ahead for hotel reservations on major holidays (Mexican as well as international). Christmas through New Year's and Easter week are the worst for crowding. If you discover it's a holiday when you're en route to the resort, plan to arrive early in the day.

Several readers have written to me about difficulties they encountered in making reservations by mail, and even by toll-free reservation numbers. Some report no answer or no record of their request (or deposit check) when they've arrived. Or they are quoted a higher price than one they might have paid by just arriving without a reservation. I've experienced the same frustrations. Here's a suggestion: Only make reservations during high season if you are going to a beach area. Off-season, just arrive and find out what's available by calling when you arrive. If you truly want a reservation, write or fax well in advance, saying in your letter that you'll forward a deposit upon receipt of a confirmation. Or, instead, call the hotel, make the reservation, get the name of the person who takes the reservation, and then send your deposit by registered mail, return receipt requested—all of which can take a good deal of time. If the clerk asks where you're calling from, pick someplace nearby in Mexico; if you say the U.S. or some distant Mexican City, the quoted rate could be two to three times the current local price (this is especially true in Acapulco); if they think you're nearby, they know you can easily find out the true rate. If in doubt about the price on arrival, ask the price as though you're just another tourist looking for a room. Don't tell them you've made a reservation and see what price they quote you. If it's a lot lower than the price quoted in the reservation, accept the lower price and register. If you've paid a deposit, make sure it's applied to your bill. You may have to debate the point with them a bit, but it's worth it.

VILLAS & CONDOS   Renting a private villa or condominium home for a vacation is a popular vacation alternative. The difference between the two, of course, is that villas are usually free-standing and condos may be part of a large or small complex and may seem more like a hotel. Often the villas are true private homes, in exclusive neighborhoods and rented out seasonally by their owners. Either accommodation comes with private kitchen and dining area, maid service, and pool. Often a full-time cook, maid, or gardener/chauffeur is on duty. Prices may be as low as $80 a night, or may be as high as $500. Rates are seasonal, with the best deals between May and October.

Four companies specializing in this type of vacation rental are: **Creative Leisure,** 951 Transport Way, Petaluma, CA 94954-1484 (tel. 707/778-1800, or toll free 800/426-6367); **Travel Resources,** P.O. Box 1042, Coconut Grove, FL 33133 (tel. 305/444-8583; fax 445-5729); **Mexico Condo Reservations,** 5801 Soledad Mountain Road, La Jolla, CA 92037 (tel. toll free 800/262-4500, 800/654-5543 in Canada); and **Casa Cozumel,** V.I.P. Services, Apdo. Postal 312, Cozumel, Q. Roo 77600 (tel. 987/2-2259; fax 987/2-2348), which only has listings on the island of Cozumel. All four have brochures with photographs of potential properties.

YOUTH HOSTELS   Mexico has some beautiful hostels built and maintained by the government. Prices are very low. For a list, stop by **SETEJ,** Hamburgo 273 in Mexico City (tel. 5/211-0743), or write to **Red Nacional de Albergues Tursticos (CREA),** Oxtopulco 40, Colonia Oxtopulco, Universidad, México, D.F. 04310.

A source of information on inexpensive youth hostel tours is the **Agencia Nacional de Turismo Juvenil,** Glorieta del Metro Insurgentes, Local C-11, Mexico 6, D.F. (tel. 5/525-2699 or 525-2974), at the Insurgentes Metro plaza.

CAMPING   It's easy and relatively cheap to camp south of the border if you have a recreational vehicle or trailer. It's more difficult if you have only a tent. Some agencies selling Mexican car insurance in the U.S. (including Sanborn's) will give you a free list of campsites if you ask. The AAA also has a list of sites. The *RV Park & Campground Directory* (previously published by Rand McNally, now published by Prentice Hall, New York) covers Mexico.

Campgrounds tend to be slightly below U.S. standards. Remember that campgrounds fill up just like hotels during the winter rush-to-the-sun and at holiday times, so get there early.

SAVING MONEY ON MEALS

You can save more money on meals than on any other expense of your trip, but I rush to add that eating well is one of the most important things you can do to make your trip enjoyable. Avoid "junk" foods, a luxury item in Mexico. Good nutrition is one of the keys to avoiding or mitigating the dread "turista" diarrhea (see Section 3, "Health and Insurance," above).

BREAKFAST Breakfast is the most overpriced meal in the world, and Mexico is no exception. Drop by a pañadería or pastelería (bakery or pastry shop) and get a few delicious sweet rolls or some pastry for incredibly low prices. This, plus perhaps a glass of milk or a piece of cheese (available in the markets), can keep you going until you have your big meal at noon.

If you pack an immersion coil and have a heat-resistant plastic cup, instant coffee or a tea bag, and powdered milk, you'll be able to make your own coffee or tea in the morning at a fraction of the restaurant price. Coffee in Mexico normally costs 75¢ a cup. Having a coil or a hot pot is also very handy if you are ill and can only stomach chamomile tea or bouillon. Coffee (ground and instant), tea bags, powdered milk (*leche en polvo*), and bouillon cubes are all readily available in Mexico, and I've indicated the location of pastry shops in most cities.

LUNCH Your best value by far will be to eat a big meal at noon. Most of Mexico is warm or hot during most of the day, so plan to be up and out to see the local sights early in the morning after a light breakfast. Then relax and collect your thoughts over a large lunch at about 1 o'clock and take it easy during the hottest part of the day. Set out again in the late afternoon and evening for more exploration, and have a light supper before returning to your hotel. This is what Mexicans do, and so most restaurants offer a *comida corrida*, or lunch special, of several courses at a fixed price between 1 and 4pm. Usually the meal will include soup, pasta, main course, dessert, and coffee, and will cost $2 to $8. The comida corrida, however, isn't always the cost-saving tanker-upper it once was. Portions are smaller these days, and often the price doesn't include dessert or a drink. One sign of a good comida is the number of Mexicans the place attracts; look to see what others are having. Sometimes a main course alone is the best bargain.

DINNER For dinner you'll want to eat lightly, having eaten heavily at 1 or 2 o'clock, and if you can make do with a good bowl of soup and a plate of enchiladas you'll need to spend very little. Avoid the long, luxurious dinners so popular in Europe and the U.S., unless you've decided to splurge. Such evening meals are not truly Mexican, and are therefore more expensive.

MARKETS Every town in Mexico has a market, and those found in the cities are often fabulous modern affairs. A full range of local produce, cheese, eggs, bread, and inexpensive fresh fruit is sold. The location of the market is given for most towns; if in doubt, ask for the *mercado*. Avoid milk and cream in open containers. In most places you should be able to find modern factory-packaged milk; if not, the powdered whole milk sold everywhere is almost as good (much better than powdered skim milk sold in the U.S.).

SAVING MONEY ON SIGHTSEEING & ENTERTAINMENT

Museums and archeological sights are free on Sunday and holidays. Local buses in villages and cities generally cost 20¢ to 35¢, and while they're often worn and noisy, using them will save a great deal of money in getting around. In resort areas, with a high number of discos, check hotel lobbies for free or discounted coupons to the nightspots. Free Sunday or weekend concerts are often presented in central parks and plazas all over Mexico.

SAVING MONEY ON SHOPPING

The charm of Mexico is no better expressed than in the arts and crafts. Hardly a tourist will leave this country without having bought at least one handcrafted item. Mexico is famous for textiles, ceramics, baskets, and onyx and silver jewelry, to mention only a few.

Prices for the crafts are really dependent on your bargaining ability. It's very helpful to visit a government fixed-price shop (usually called the Artes Populares or

FONART) before attempting to bargain. This will give you an idea of the cost versus quality of the various crafts.

Following, now, are the various crafts, in alphabetical order. The first city or village listed is the best place to buy.

Baskets: Woven of reed or straw—Oaxaca, Copper Canyon, Toluca, Yucatán, Puebla, Mexico City.

Blankets: Saltillo, Toluca, Santa Ana Chiautempan, north of Puebla, Oaxaca, and Mitla (made of soft wool with some synthetic dyes; they use a lot of bird and geometric motifs). Make sure that the blanket you pick out is in fact the one you take since often the "same" blanket in the wrapper is not the same.

Glass: Hand-blown and molded—Monterrey and Tlaquepaque; Mexico City at the Avalos Brothers glass factory, Carretones 5 (Metro: Pino Suárez).

Guitars: Made in Paracho, 25 miles north of Uruapan on Highway 37.

Hammocks and Mosquito Netting: Mérida, Campeche, Mazatlán. See market section in Mérida (Chapter 00) for details on buying.

Hats: Mérida (Panama), made of sisal from the maguey cactus; finest quality weaving; easy to pack and wash. San Cristóbal de las Casas, Chiapas, is a good place for varied regional hats.

Huaraches: Leather sandals, often with rubber-tire soles—San Blas, Mérida, Mexico City, Guadalajara, Hermosillo, San Cristóbal de las Casas, and in fact most states.

Huipils: Hand-woven, embroidered or brocaded overblouses indigenous to almost all Mexican states but especially to Yucatán, Chiapas, Oaxaca, Puebla, Guerrero, and Veracruz. Most of the better huipils are used ones bought from the village women. Huipils can be distinguished by villages; look around before buying— you'll be amazed at the variety.

Lacquer Goods: Olinala, Guerrero, northeast of Acapulco, is known for ornate lacquered chests and other lacquered decorative and furniture items. Pátzcuaro and Uruapan, west of Mexico City, are also known for gold-leafed lacquered trays.

Leather Goods: Monterrey, Saltillo, León, Mexico City, San Cristóbal de Las Casas, and Oaxaca.

Masks: Wherever there is locally observed regional dancing you'll find mask makers. The tradition is especially strong in the states of Guerrero, Chiapas, Puebla, Oaxaca, and Michoacan.

Onyx: Puebla (where onyx is carved), Querétaro, Matehuala, Mexico City.

Pottery: Tlaquepaque, Tonala, Oaxaca, Puebla, Michoacan, Coyotepec Izucar de Matamoros, Veracruz, Copper Canyon, Dolores Hidalgo, and Guanajuato.

Rebozos: Woman's or man's rectangular woven cloth to be worn around the shoulders, similar to a shawl—Oaxaca, Mitla, San Cristóbal de las Casas, Mexico City, and Pátzcuaro. Rebozos are generally made of wool or a blend of wool and cotton, but synthetic fibers are creeping in, so check the material carefully before buying. Also, compare the weave from different cloths since the fineness of the weave is proportional to the cost.

Serapes: Heavy woolen or cotton blankets with a slit for the head, to be worn as a poncho—Santa Ana Chiautempan (30 miles north of Pueblo near Tlaxcala), San Luis Potosí, Santa María del Río (25 miles south of San Luis Potosí), Chiconcoac (1 hour's drive northeast from Mexico City, near Texcoco), Saltillo, Toluca, Mexico City.

Silver: Taxco, Mexico City, Zacatecas, Guadalajara. Sterling silver is indicated by "925" on the silver, which certifies that there are 925 grams of pure silver per kilogram, or that the silver is 92.5% pure. A spread-eagle hallmark is also used to indicate sterling. Look for these marks or you may pay a high price for an inferior quality that is mostly nickel, or even silverplate called alpaca.

Stones: Chalcedony, turquoise, lapis lazuli, amethyst—Querétaro, San Miguel del Allende, Durango, Saltillo, San Luis Potosí. The cost of turquoise is computed by weight, so many pesos per carat.

Textiles: Oaxaca, Chiapas, Santa Ana near Puebla, Guerrero, and Nayarit are known for their excellent weaving, each culturally distinct and different.

Tortoise Shell: It's illegal to bring it into the U.S.

SAVING MONEY ON TRANSPORTATION

If you plan to rent a car, you can save money by reserving it 7 days before you leave the States and for only as long as you need. Make sure that the company you select offers the VW Beetle or Nissan—usually the cheapest car—and that they will have one on hand to rent you. Sometimes when you arrive at the office the cheapest cars will be "all booked up," so a more expensive car (that's also more expensive to operate) is substituted at the same price. Ask if you are guaranteed the quoted rate even if that size isn't available when you arrive. Take the name of the person you spoke with and ask for your confirmation number and keep it handy.

Shop for a good price before renting, as there is a great variation between the quoted prices. Pay attention to insurance deductibles. Lets hope you don't have an accident, but if you do, one company may charge you the first $250 in damages while another may charge the first $1,000. Weekly rentals often don't charge for the mileage, which can be a considerable savings. Be sure to double-check all math on the rental form; if you were quoted rates in the States, be sure they are the same after the peso conversion appearing on the form. Return the car with the same level of gas; rental companies sock it to you on gas charges.

If you plan to drive to Mexico, consider **Sanborn's Tripshare Service,** a new offering by Sanborn's Mexico Insurance Services, Dept. FR, P.O. Box 310, McAllen, TX 78502. For $2 you can get on a computerized tripsharers' list. To receive a list of prospective tripsharers will cost $3 to $6, depending on whether you are a student, a member of one of their clubs, or neither of the two.

SAVING MONEY ON SERVICES

Throw out the iron-clad 15% **tipping** rule in budget restaurants no matter what other travel literature may say. Do as the locals do: For meals costing under $3, leave the loose change; for meals costing $4 to $5, leave 6% to 10%, depending on service. Above $5, you're into the 10% to 15% bracket. Some of the more crass high-priced restaurants will actually add a 15% "tip" to your bill—leave nothing extra if they do.

Bellboys and porters will expect about 25¢ per bag. You needn't tip taxi drivers unless they've rendered some special service—carrying bags or trunks.

 MEXICO

Abbreviations Dept.=apartments; Apdo.=post office box; Av.=Avenida; Calz.=Calzada (boulevard). C on faucets stands for *caliente* (hot), and F stands for *fría* (cold). In elevators, PB (*planta baja*) means ground floor.

American Express Wherever there is an office, I've mentioned it.

Business Hours In general, Mexican businesses in larger cities are open between 9am and 7pm; in smaller towns many close between 2 and 4pm. Most are closed on Sunday. Bank hours are 9 or 9:30am to 1pm Monday through Friday. A few banks in large cities have extended hours.

Camera/Film Both are more expensive in Mexico than in the U.S.; take full advantage of your 12-roll film allowance by bringing 36-exposure rolls. Also bring extra batteries: AA batteries are generally available, but AAA and small disk batteries for cameras and watches are rarely found. A few places in resort areas advertise color film developing, but it might be cheaper to wait until you get home. If you're a serious photographer, bring an assortment of films of various speeds as you will be photographing against glaring sand, in gloomy Maya temples, and in dusky jungles. Proper filters are a help.

Cigarettes Cigarettes are much cheaper in Mexico, even U.S. brands, if you buy them at a grocery or drugstore and not a hotel tobacco shop.

Climate   See Section 2, "When to Go," above.

Crime   See and "Legal Aid" and "Safety," below, and "Bribes and Scams" in Section 1, "Information, Entry Requirements, and Money," above.

Currency   See Section 1, "Information, Entry Requirements, and Money," above.

Customs   Mexican Customs inspection has been streamlined. At most border crossings entering tourists are requested to punch a button: If the resulting light is green, you go through without inspection; if it's red, your luggage or car may be inspected thoroughly or briefly.

Doctors and Dentists   Every embassy and consulate is prepared to recommend local doctors and dentists with good training and modern equipment; some of the doctors and dentists even speak English. See the list of embassies and consulates under "Embassies and Consulates" (below), and remember that at the larger ones a duty officer is on call at all times. Hotels with a high clientele of foreigners are often prepared to recommend English-speaking doctors. Almost all first-class hotels in Mexico have a doctor on call.

Documents Required   See Section 1, "Information, Entry Requirements, and Money," above.

Driving Rules   See Section 8, "Getting Around," above.

Drug Laws   Briefly, don't use or possess illegal drugs in Mexico. Mexicans have no tolerance of drug users and jail is the solution, with very little hope of getting out until the sentence (usually a long one) is completed or heavy fines or bribes are paid. (*Important Note*: It isn't uncommon to be befriended by a fellow user only to be turned in by that "friend," who then collects a bounty for turning you in. It's no win!) Bring prescription drugs in their original containers. If possible, pack a copy of the original prescription with the generic name of the drug.

I don't need to go into detail about the penalties for illegal drug possession upon return to the U.S. Customs officials are also on the lookout for diet drugs sold in Mexico, possession of which could also land you in jail in the U.S. because they are illegal there. If you buy antibiotics over the counter (which you can do in Mexico), say, for a sinus infection and still have some left, you probably won't be hassled by U.S. customs.

Drugstores   Drugstores (*farmacia*) will sell you just about anything you want, with prescription or without. Most are open Monday through Saturday from 8am to 8pm. If you need to buy medicines after normal hours, ask for the *farmacia de turno*—pharmacies take turns staying open during the off-hours. Find any drugstore and in its window may be a card showing the schedule of which farmacia will be open at what time.

Electricity   The electrical system in Mexico is 110 volts, 60 cycles, as in the U.S. and Canada, with the same flat-prong plugs and sockets. Some light bulbs have bayonet bases.

Embassies and Consulates   They provide valuable lists of doctors, and lawyers, as well as regulations concerning marriages in Mexico. Contrary to popular belief, your embassy cannot get you out of a Mexican jail, provide postal or banking services, or fly you home when you run out of money. Consular officers can provide you with advice on most matters and problems, however. Most countries have a representative embassy in Mexico City and many have consular offices or representatives in the provinces.

The Embassy of **Australia** in Mexico City is at Jaime Balmes 11, Plaza Polanco (tel. 5/395-9988); it's open Monday through Friday from 8am to 1pm.

The Embassy of **Canada** in Mexico City is at Schiller 529, in Polanco (tel. 5/254-3288); it's open Monday through Friday from 9am to 1pm and 2 to 5pm (at other times the name of a duty officer is posted on the embassy door). In Acapulco, the Canadian consulate is in the Hotel Club del Sol, Costera Miguel Aleman, at the corner of Reyes Católicos (tel. 748/5-6621); open from 8am to 3pm.

The Embassy of **New Zealand** in Mexico City is at Homero 229, 8th Floor (tel. 5/250-5999); it's open Monday through Thursday from 9am to 2pm and 3 to 5pm, and on Friday from 9am to 2pm.

The Embassy of the **United Kingdom** in Mexico City is at Lerma 71, at Rio Sena (tel. 5/207-2089 or 207-2186), Monday through Friday from 8:30am to 3:30pm. There are honorary consuls in the following cities: Acapulco, Hotel Las Brisas, Carretera Escenica (tel. 748/4-6605 or 4-1580); Ciudad Juárez, Calle Fresno 185 (tel. 161/7-5791); Mérida, Calle 58 no. 450 (tel. 99/21-6799); Monterrey, Privada de Tamazunchale 104 (tel. 83/78-2565); Veracruz, Avenida Morelos 145 (tel. 29/31-0955); Guadalajara (tel. 36/35-8295); and Tampico (tel. 12/12-9784).

The Embassy of the **United States** in Mexico City is right next to the Hotel María Isabel Sheraton at Paseo de la Reforma 305, at the corner of Río Danubio (tel. 5/211-0042, or 5/211-4536 for emergencies). There are U.S. consulates in Ciudad Juárez (tel. 1/613-4048), Guadalajara (tel. 3/625-2998), Hermosillo (tel. 6/217-2382), Matamoros (tel. 8/912-5251), Mazatlán (tel. 6/781-2685), Mérida (tel. 9/925-5011), Monterrey (tel. 8/345-2120), Nuevo Laredo (tel. 8/714-0696), and Tijuana (tel. 6/681-7400). In addition, consular agents reside in Acapulco (tel. 748/3-1969 or 485-7207); Cancún (tel. 988/4-1437), open from 10am to 2pm and 4 to 7pm; Durango (tel. 181/1-4445), open from 8am to 3pm; Mulege (tel. 685/3-0111); Oaxaca (tel. 951/6-0654); Puerto Vallarta (tel. 322/2-5769); San Luis Potosí (tel. 481/7-2510), open from 9am to 1pm and 4 to 7pm; San Miguel de Allende (tel. 465/2-2357), open Monday and Wednesday from 9am to 2pm and 4 to 7pm, on Tuesday and Thursday from 4 to 7pm, and by appointment on Friday, Saturday, and Sunday; Tampico (tel. 121/3-2217); and Veracruz (tel. 29/31-0142).

Emergencies The 24-hour **Tourist Help Line** in Mexico City is 5/250-0151; for legal assistance call 5/525-9380 or 525-9384.

Etiquette As a general rule, Mexicans are very polite. Foreigners who ask questions politely, and say "Please" and "Thank you" will be rewarded. Mexicans are also very formal; an invitation to a private home, no matter how humble, is an honor. And although many strangers will immediately begin using the familiar form of the pronoun *tu* and its verb form, if you want to be correct, the formal *usted* is still preferred until a friendship is established. When in doubt use the formal form and wait for the Mexican to change to the familiar. Mexicans are normally uncomfortable with our "dutch treat" custom of dining, and will usually insist on paying. It can be touchy and you don't want to be insulting. But you might offer to get the drinks or insist on paying the tip. If you're invited to a home, it's polite to bring a gift, perhaps a bottle of good wine or flowers.

Guides Most guides in Mexico are men. Many speak English (and occasionally other languages) and are formally trained in history and culture to qualify for a federally approved tourism license. Hiring a guide for a day at the ruins, or to squire you around Mexico City, may be a worthwhile luxury *if* you establish boundaries in the beginning. Be specific about what you want to do and how long you want the service. The guide will quote a price. Discussion may reduce the initial quote. If your guide is using his own car, is licensed (something he can prove with a credential), and speaks English, the price will be higher and is generally worth it. If you are together at lunch, it's customary to buy the guide's meal. When bus tours from the U.S. diminished a few years ago, many licensed English-speaking guides became taxi drivers, so it isn't unusual to find incredibly knowledgeable taxi drivers who are experienced guides. In Mexico City these licensed guides/taxi drivers often have a permanent spot outside the better hotels and are available for private duty. If the service has been out of the ordinary, a tip is in order—perhaps 10% of the daily rate. On tours, the recommended tip is $1.50 to $2 per day per person.

Hitchhiking Generally speaking hitchhiking is not a good idea in Mexico. Take a bus instead—they're cheap and go everywhere.

Holidays See Section 2, "When to Go," above.

Information See Section 1, "Information, Entry Requirements, and Money," above, and specific city for local information offices.

Language The official language is Spanish, but there are at least 50 Indian languages spoken and more than four times that many Indian dialects. English is most widely spoken in resort cities and in better hotels. It's best to learn some basic phrases.

Legal Aid Procuraduria Federal de Consumedor (**Proseco**), Calle Doctor Navarro 210, 4th Piso, Col. de los Doctores, México D.F. 06720 (tel. 525/761-4546; fax 525/761-3885), is a contact for tourists with legal problems. **International**

Legal Defense Counsel, 111 South 15th Street, Packard Building, 24th Floor, Philadelphia, PA 19102 (tel. 215/977-9982), is a law firm specializing in legal difficulties of Americans abroad. See also "Embassies and Consulates" and "Emergencies," above.

Mail Mail service south of the border tends to be slow (sometimes glacial in its movements) and erratic. If you're on a 2-week vacation, it's not a bad idea to buy and mail your postcards in the Arrivals lounge at the airport to give them maximum time to get home before you do.

For the most reliable and convenient mail service, have your letters sent to you c/o the American Express offices in major cities, which will receive and forward mail for you *if* you are one of their clients (a travel-club card or an American Express traveler's check is proof). They charge a fee if you wish them to forward your mail.

If you don't use American Express, have your mail sent to you care of *Lista de Correos* (General Delivery), followed by the Mexican city, state, and country. In Mexican post offices there may actually be a "lista" posted near the Lista de Correos window bearing the names of all those for whom mail has been received. If there's no list, ask and show them your passport so they can riffle through and look for your letters. If the city has more than one office, you'll have to go to the central post office—not a branch—to get your mail. By the way, in many post offices they return mail to the sender if it has been there for more than 10 days. Make sure people don't send you letters too early.

Maps AAA maps to Mexico are quite good and available free to members at any AAA office in the U.S.

Newspapers and Magazines The English-language newspaper *The News,* published in Mexico City, carries world news and commentaries, and a calendar of the day's events including concerts, art shows, and plays. Newspaper kiosks in larger Mexican cities will carry a selection of English-language magazines.

Passports See Section 1, "Information, Entry Requirements, and Money," above.

Pets Taking a pet into Mexico entails a lot of red tape. Consult the Mexican Government Tourist Office nearest you (see Section 1, "Information, Entry Requirements, and Money," above).

Police Police in general in Mexico are to be suspected rather than trusted; however, you'll find many who are quite helpful with directions, even going so far as to lead you where you want to go.

Radio/TV Many hotels now have antennas capable of bringing in U.S. TV channels. Large cities will have English-language stations and music.

Rest Rooms The best bet in Mexico is to use rest rooms in restaurants and hotel public areas. Always carry your own toilet paper and hand soap, neither of which is in great supply in Mexican rest rooms. Public facilities, usually near the central market, vary in cleanliness and usually have an attendant who charges a few pesos for toilet use and a few squares of toilet paper. Pemex gas stations have improved the maintenance of their rest rooms along major highways. No matter where you are, even if the toilet flushes with paper, there'll be a waste basket for paper disposal. Many people come from homes without plumbing and are not accustomed to toilets that will take paper, and will throw paper on the floor rather than put it in the toilet—thus you'll see the basket no matter what quality of place you are in. On the other hand, the water pressure in many establishments is so low that paper won't go down. There's often a sign saying "do," or "don't" flush paper.

Safety Whenever you're traveling in an unfamiliar city or country, stay alert. Be aware of your immediate surroundings. Wear a moneybelt and don't sling your camera or purse over your shoulder. This will minimize the possibility of your becoming a victim of crime.

Crime is more of a problem in Mexico than it used to be. Although you will feel physically safer in most Mexican cities than in comparable big cities at home, you must take some basic, sensible precautions.

First, remember that you're a tourist, and an obvious target for crime. Beware of pickpockets on crowded buses, the Metro, in markets. Guard your possessions very carefully at all times; don't let packs or bags out of your sight even for a second (the big first-class bus lines will store your bag in the luggage compartment under the bus, and that's generally all right, but keep your things with you on the less responsible village and some second-class buses on country routes).

Next, if you have a car, park it in an enclosed or guarded lot at night. Vans are a special mark. Don't depend on "major downtown streets" to protect your car—park it in a private lot with a guard, or at least a fence.

Women must be careful in cities when walking alone, night or day. Busy streets are no problem, but empty streets (even if empty just for afternoon siesta) are lonely places.

Important Warning: Agreeing to carry a package back to the States for an acquaintance or a stranger could land you in jail for years if it contains drugs or some other contraband. Never do it no matter how friendly, honest, or sincere the request. Perpetrators of this illegal activity prey on innocent-looking single travelers and especially senior citizens.

Taxes There's a 15% tax on goods and services in Mexico and it's supposed to be included in the posted price.

Telephone/Telex/Fax Telephone area codes were gradually being changed as this book went to press. Usually the change affects area code and first digit, or area code only. But some cities, such as Veracruz, are adding exchanges and changing numbers. If you have difficulty calling long distance, ask the operator for assistance. Also see the Appendix for detailed information about making long distance calls.

Time Central standard time prevails throughout most of Mexico. The west-coast states of Sonora, Sinaloa, and parts of Nayarit are on mountain standard time. The state of Baja California Norte is on Pacific standard time, but Baja California Sur is on mountain time.

Note that daylight saving time is not used in Mexico, except in Baja California Norte (late April to late October).

Tipping See "Saving Money on Services" in Section 9, "Enjoying Mexico on a Budget," above.

Tourist Offices See Section 1, "Information, Entry Requirements, and Money," above, and also each specific city.

Visas See Section 1, "Information, Entry Requirements, and Money," above.

Water Most hotels have decanters or bottles of purified water in the rooms, and the better hotels have either purified water from regular taps or special taps marked AGUA PURIFICADA. In the resort areas, especially the Yucatán, hoteliers are beginning to charge for in-room bottled water. Virtually any hotel, restaurant, or bar will bring you purified water if you specifically request it, but you'll usually be charged for it.

CHAPTER 3

THE PACIFIC COAST FROM HERMOSILLO TO MAZATLÁN

The route along the western coast of Mexico, with its hazy pinnacled desert mountains, is an attractive one. It takes you straight down to Mexico's well-known Pacific beach resorts. This chapter covers two states, Sonora and Sinaloa. Well traveled by Mexican and American tourists, truckers, and locals, the area poses few problems. However, since Sinaloa has long been known as a drug-trafficking center, it would be wise not to make any adventurous side trips into out-of-the-way villages.

SEEING THE NORTHERN PACIFIC COAST

Your first main destination will be the coastal resort city of Mazatlán, 735 miles to the south. Much of this long stretch is desert country, broiling hot in the summer. You'll pass through Hermosillo, capital of the state of Sonora, a good place for an overnight stop. Guaymas, farther south, is the first coastal town you'll reach, noted for its enormous shrimp, a good stopoff for a day or two of fishing. Here you'll have your first glimpse of the Sea of Cortez (called the Gulf of California on U.S. maps), dubbed "the world's greatest fish trap." Continuing on past Ciudad Obregón to Navajoa, turn left and follow the signs to Alamos, Mexico's jumping-bean capital, a restored colonial-era silver-mining ghost town. Los Mochis is the next coastal port. An unimpressive tourist destination, it has wonderful seafood and is the Pacific Coast starting point for the famed Copper Canyon Train (see Chapter 4). And finally there's Mazatlán—seaport, super fishing hub, and noted as one of the Pacific Coast's most reasonably priced resort cities.

CROSSING THE BORDER

BY TRAIN   You can catch the southbound *El Tren del Pacífico* at the beginning of the line, either in Mexicali or in Nogales. (If you want to switch over from bus to train in Mexicali, you can walk the few blocks from the Central Camionera to the train station, or take a taxi.) The train departs daily from Mexicali around 9am and from Nogales at 2:20pm. (Be sure to check these schedules; they may change.)

BY BUS   To cross over by bus from San Diego, go to the Greyhound Bus Station at 120 West Broadway at 1st Street (tel. 619/239-9171). Buy your **Greyhound** ticket through to either the Tres Estrellas de Oro station (tel. 66/5-1722; 18 Greyhound buses daily) or to the Central Camionera (4 buses daily, 5:15, 7:15, 8:40, and

WHAT'S SPECIAL ABOUT THE NORTHERN PACIFIC COAST

Water Sports
- ☐ Deep-sea fishing in the Sea of Cortez at Guaymas, Kino Bay, and Puerto Penasco, and in the Pacific at Mazatlán.
- ☐ Bass fishing near Alamos.

Nature/Museums
- ☐ Ecologial Center of Sonora, a 2,471-acre open-air reserve south of Hermosillo, featuring animals and 1,000 species of plants native to the region and from world deserts.

A Ghost Town
- ☐ Alamos, a 17th-century silver-mining village, returned to life with restored mansions.

Unusual Natural Phenomena
- ☐ Mexican jumping beans, which start rattling the forest floor in June near Alamos.

☐ Aquarium in Mazatlán, an informative living display of fish native to the Pacific.

10:40am), both on the Mexican side. The Greyhound bus stops at the border station for you to obtain your Tourist Card. The Greyhound bus continues to the two bus stations in downtown Tijuana and from there you can buy your ticket to your Mexican destination. Call the Greyhound information number above to verify these times. (See Appendix for a list of bus terminology.)

BY CAR   Coming from California by car, the best route is **I-10 or I-8 to Tucson and then I-19 to Nogales.** Be sure you have Mexican auto insurance and proper car ownership papers. (See "Getting There" in Chapter 2). Stop at the border station and pick up your Tourist Card, if you don't already have one. The cars that are zipping right through the border station without stopping are not heading south, but are just crossing over for the day. A few miles farther along the road south there will be a Customs checkpoint. You stop to punch a button: if the light turns green, there's no Customs check; if it turns red, stop and officials will check your tourist permit and/or car-entry permit, and may inspect your luggage.

ON FOOT   From downtown San Diego, take the **Tijuana Trolley** to San Ysidro, walk through the border station, and pick up a "Centro" or "Central Camionera" local city bus—tell the driver you want to get to the Central Camionera. You can also take a taxi from the fleet of taxis you see waiting just across the border.

---

1. HERMOSILLO

250 miles S of Nogales, 86 miles N of Guaymas, 385 miles NW of Chihuahua

GETTING THERE   By Plane   Aeroméxico flies to Tucson, Chihuahua, Los Mochis, Mazatlán, Cd. Obregón, and Tijuana. **Noroeste** flies to Mexicali, Cd. Juárez, Chihuahua, Mazatlán, Culiacán, and Cd. Obregón.

By Bus   Hermosillo is well served by buses from the border and along the Pacific Coast.

By Car   Mexico Highway 15 leads from Nogales and connects with Highway 2 from Mexicali and Tijuana.

DEPARTING   By Plane   Aeroméxico is at Boulevard Navarette 165 (tel.

16-8259 or 16-8206, or 16-0772 at the airport). **Noroeste,** Boulevard Reed 99, opposite Nissan (tel. 17-3606 or 17-4988 for reservations, or 17-5007 or 173446 for ticket sales).

By Train   The train station is at Transversal and M. González (tel. 17-1711 or 14-3200). You can buy tickets Sunday through Friday from 7am to 3pm and on Saturday between 10 and 11am. If you are going south, they go on sale only 30 minutes before the train's departure. If you're going north to the border, you can buy them a day ahead. The *Tren del Pacífico* from Hermosillo to Nogales (a 4-hour trip) leaves at 7:45am; going south to Guadalajara (a 24-hour trip) it leaves at 7:55pm. *Note:* Pacific Coast trains often run hours behind schedule.

By Bus   The bus station is north of the town center at Boulevard Transversal 400 at Los Piños. It's small, hot, and dirty, and full of expensive fast-food restaurants. To get there, take the Ranchito Mendoza bus from Juárez Plaza downtown. **Transportes del Pacífico** (tel. 17-0580) has four daily expresses to Guadalajara, and local buses every half hour. Hourly *de paso* buses go to Guaymas (1½ hrs.), Empalme, Cd. Obregón, Navajoa, Los Mochis (8 hrs.), Mazatlán, and Tepic. **Tranportes Norte de Sonora** goes to Mexicali and Tijuana several times daily and to Guaymas hourly. **Tres Estrellas de Oro** (tel. 13-2416) goes to Mexico City and Cd. Juárez hourly (very full on weekends). Buses to Mazatlán are *de paso:* they originate elsewhere and stop if they have room; first-class buses with assigned seats go to Cd. Obregón, Juárez, Guaymas, Nogales, and Tijuana.

By Car   Highway 2 from Tijuana and Mexicali connects with Highway 15 south of Magdelena and continues down the Pacific Coast/Sea of Cortez. From Nogales, it's Highway 15 all the way south.

This city (alt. 720 ft.; pop. 500,000), capital of the state of Sonora, is the center of a fruit- and vegetable-farming area—much of which is shipped to the U.S., by the way. You enter on a lovely tree-lined boulevard, which in summer is vibrant with the orange flowers of the yucatecos.

ORIENTATION

ARRIVING   The **airport** is 6 miles from the city center on Boulevard Garcia Morales. Colectivo taxis cost $5 to city center.

The **Central Camionera** (bus station) is 5 miles north of the town center. Take the "Rancho Mendoza" city bus to downtown. You can get on with luggage providing it doesn't crowd the aisle too much; taxis cost $3.50.

The **Estación Ferocarrile** (train station) is even farther from town. To get a bus from the train station, walk out the front of the station one block straight ahead to four-lane Boulevard Kino; cross it and turn left, and walk half a block to the street just before the Motel Costa Rica. The bus to town ("Estación") stops on the corner—the school bus type with cassette entertainment. Taxis from the train station cost around $7.

INFORMATION   The **State Tourism Office** is at Boulevard Rodríguez 138 (tel. 14-7399 or 14-8407). It's open Monday through Friday from 9am to 3pm.

FAST FACTS

American Express   The local representative is Termex Travel, Rosales and Monterrey, Edifición Lupita (tel. 13-4415 or 17-1718).

   Area Code   The telephone area code is 621.

   Market   The market is at the corner of Monterrey and Matamoros. Orient yourself at Juárez Park, walk toward the mountain and you'll find the market.

WHAT TO SEE & DO

Located in the foothills of near-town mountains, the **Museo de Sonora**, at Jesús García and California, opened in 1985, is housed in a fortresslike building that was a penitentiary from 1907 to 1979. Now it's a fine museum with 18 rooms of subjects ranging from astonomy, geology, and ecology to pre-Hispanic artifacts, and history of the area from the Conquest to the present day. Admission is $2. The museum is open Wednesday through Saturday from 9am to 3:30pm; the library, Monday through Friday from 9am to 2pm (closed most holidays). From Plaza Juárez, walk toward the mountain nearest town (just a few blocks) past the market; the museum is at the bottom of the mountain.

WHERE TO STAY & EAT

You will note that there are many expensive hotels in Hermosillo. You'll also see *casas de huespedes* (guesthouses), especially in the area near Plaza Juárez; these are cheaper, but also inferior, accommodations.

HOTEL MONTE CARLO, on the corner of Juárez and Sonora, Hermosillo, Son. 83000. Tel. 621/2-0853. 36 rms (all with bath). A/C
$ Rates: $20 single; $22 double.
The name is grander than the place, which from the outside appears seedy, as does the surrounding area opposite Plaza Juárez. But don't pass it by. Inside it has been nicely remodeled including all new fawn-colored tile floors, new bathroom fixtures, and fresh paint. While the rooms are still basic, beds are firm and covered with cheap bedspreads. It's not the Ritz, but the price is right and the management is helpful.

HOTEL SAN ALBERTO, corner of Serdan and Rosales, Hermosillo, Son. 83000. Tel. 621/13-2840. 174 rms (with bath). A/C TV TEL
$ Rates: $40 single; $45 double. **Parking:** Free.
It's an older, five-story structure on the outside, but a warm and well-run hotel on the inside. There's a swimming pool, off-street parking, cafeteria, bar, travel agency, beauty parlor, and tobacco shop. It's in the central city at Highway 15 and Serdan, opposite the Telegraph Office.

EASY EXCURSIONS FROM HERMOSILLO

About 2½ miles (km 4) south of Hermosillo on Highway 15 to Guaymas is the ✪ **Ecological Center of Sonora,** a 2,471-acre mostly open-air museum set aside to protect plants and animals native to the desert, with a modern visitor's center. By strolling the meandering walkways through the open desert you see plants and animals in their native habitat, including wild sheep. One section compares the Sonora Desert with other deserts in the world. Open in summer, daily from 8am to noon and 4:30 to 8pm; in winter, Wednesday through Sunday from 9am to 5pm.

Almost 70 miles west of Hermosillo on a fairly good road lies **Kino Bay.** Actually there are two Kinos: Kino Viejo, a small, somnolent fishing village, and Kino Nuevo, an area that has become popular with wealthy Americans and condominium owners. Part of the attraction is the good fishing, and in June the **International Sport Fishing Tournament** draws crowds. The beach is beautiful, with miles of white sand and gorgeous houses lining it. Many public *palapas* (open palm-roofed shelters) dot the shore offering shade from the glittering sun. If you feel like spending some time in total relaxation, enjoying pure tranquility, sparkling water, fishing, and sun before you continue on into Mexico, Kino is a good place to do it.

At the harbor, the fishermen come to beach their boats. Many open-air shacks offer wares, and the carvings of the Seris. Occasionally a group of Seri will be camped beyond the end of the road in Kino Nuevo on their way to or from Desemboque. The Seri are known for their ironwood carvings; you can find them at work in Kino Viejo as well.

Second-class buses leave daily from Hermosillo to Kino Bay, from the station of Autobuses de Municipio de Hermosillo, 1½ blocks up Calle Sonora from the Hotel

Monte Carlo, at Manuel González 44 (tel. 621/2-2556). Travel time is roughly 2 hours. If you don't want to stay over in Kino, there's nothing to prevent you from getting an early start, making a day of it at the beach, and returning to Hermosillo in the late afternoon. From Hermosillo there are seven buses a day to Kino, the first at 5:45am and the last at 6:30pm. Return buses from Kino are at 6, 8, and 10am, noon, and 2, 4, and 6pm.

2. GUAYMAS

86 miles S of Hermosillo, 112 miles N of Cd. Obregón,
140 miles N of Navajoa, 130 miles NW of Alamos

GETTING THERE   By Air   Guaymas has Aeroméxico from Mexico City, La Paz, León, and Tucson. In Guaymas, the Aeroméxico office is at Aquiles Serdan 236, at Avenida 15 (tel. 622/2-0123 or 2-0266, or 2-7111 or 2-3266 at the airport).

By Train   El Tren del Pacífico stops at Empalme, about 10 miles to the south of Guaymas.

By Bus   Guaymas is served by most buses coming down the coastal route.

By Car   Guaymas is on the Pacific Coastal Highway (Hwy. 15).

By Ferry   A ferry runs from Guaymas to Santa Rosalía, in Baja California, every Tuesday, Friday, and Sunday at 10am. The return ferry, from Santa Rosalía to Guaymas, leaves at 11pm and arrives in Guaymas at 7am. There are two classes of tickets: *Turista,* which is a private room, and *Salón* class with chairs. You can buy tickets a day ahead or on the day of departure, but if you wait until the day of departure, get there at least an hour early. The ferry terminal in Guaymas (tel. 622/2-2324) is located at the east end of town; you can buy your tickets there during morning hours.

ESSENTIALS   The **telephone area code** for Guaymas is 622.

DEPARTING   By Train   You must buy your tickets at the train station in Empalme (tel. 622/3-0616), which opens about an hour before each train arrives. Coastal trains are often late, so prepare for a long wait.

By Bus   The first-class **Tres Estrellas de Oro** (tel. 2-1271) and **Transportes Norte de Sonora** bus station is on the corner of Calle 14 Sur and Avenida 12 Poniente, about two blocks from the main street (Avenida Aquiles Serdan). The second-class **Transportes del Pacífico** bus station is around the corner, at Calle 13 and Avenida 10 Poniente. Both stations are located nine short blocks west of the central plaza. Buses on Serdan go east to the town center. There's frequent service south along the coast and inland to Guadalajara. Buses go hourly to Tijuana and six daily go to Nogales.

Guaymas (pop. 130,000), on the coast, owes its reputation to fishing, both commercial and sport. Runs of marlin and sailfish generally occur between February 15 and August 15. Lobster, sea turtles, and clams abound in nearby waters as well.
     The town (pronounced "*Ee*-mahs") is divided by a hilly range, the port on one side and the resort plus Miramar Beach on the other. Unfortunately, it's not much of a resort. The beach is unexceptional and the majority of the hotels and motels in the area customarily charge more in the scorching off-season summer months than they do in winter to defray the cost of the electrical current used by the air conditioner (which you must take advantage of).

ORIENTATION

ARRIVING   Colectivo vans take passengers from the airport, quite a distance west of town, for around $5. Don't tarry after arrival, since the vans leave as soon as they fill up. From the train in Empalme a taxi costs between $7 and $9. The bus station is within walking distance of downtown hotels.

INFORMATION   The **State Tourism Office** (tel. 622/2-2932) is on the second floor of the Palacio Municipal, on Calle 23 at Aquiles Serdan (the town's only main street), across from a wide plaza. The helpful staff has information in English and Spanish, covering Guaymas, San Carlos, and Sonora state. It's open Monday through Friday from 9am to 1pm and 3 to 6pm, and on Saturday from 9am to 1pm.

CITY LAYOUT   Guaymas is anchored by a grand open plaza, bounded by Serdan and Rodríguez, dedicated to three of the state's favorite sons. Next to it is another small shady plaza and a children's park. All are framed on one side by the pier and harbor. The Palacio Municipal (housing the tourist office) is a grand old building facing one side of the open plaza. From the plaza you can see the twin white spires of the San Fernando Church. Serdan, the main street, passes in front of the main plaza. The city is divided into *calles* running east-west and *avenidas* running north-south, with a few named streets thrown in. Calle numbers ascend going toward the plaza; avenidas change directions going north and south on Serdan.

GETTING AROUND   City buses go up and down Calle Serdan, the main east-west artery through town. They are convenient for reaching all the restaurants, hotels, and sights mentioned in this section. Streets crossing Serdan are well marked, making it easy to know when to get on and off the bus. Going toward the central plaza, Calle 20 is the last stop the bus makes before reaching the plaza three blocks farther.

WHERE TO STAY

CASA DE HUESPEDES LUPITA, Calle 15 no. 125 Sur, Guaymas, Son. 85400. Tel. 622/2-8409. 31 rms (7 with bath).
$ Rates: $11 single with bath; $15 double with bath, for two to four people; $4 less for rooms with shared bath.
For travelers on a tight budget, try these basic but clean rooms that open onto a shady but grassless inner patio. The rooms are cheerful enough with fans and bright-blue walls, but otherwise very plain. They fill up by nightfall, so get here early.
  To find the place, walk two blocks east of the bus station opposite the jail (which looks like a castle); it's at the corner of Calle 10—ask directions.

HOTEL ANA, Calle 25 no. 135, Guaymas, Son. 85400. Tel. 622/2-3048. 35 rms (all with bath). A/C
$ Rates: $18 single; $22 double; $22 triple.
The Hotel Ana is in a quieter part of town a couple of blocks north of the church, on Calle 25 at the corner of Serdan. The clean rooms are pleasant but humble, all with two double beds, red-and-white-checked floors, and barred windows that open onto the fresh air of the small central walkway.

DEL PUERTO MOTEL, Yañez 92, Guaymas, Son. 85400. Tel. 622/2-3408 or 2-2491. 72 rms (all with bath). A/C
$ Rates: $20 single; $24 double; $29 triple.
Rooms here are modern and clean with red-tile floors. Rooms for two people have both a double and a twin-size bed. To get here, walk three blocks west of the main plaza; the hotel is near the corner of Calle 19, one block from the big mercado (market) at Rodríguez; turn left at the tortilla factory.
  The owners of the Del Puerto also operate the 40-room Malibu Motel, located north of town on the International Highway, km 1,983, with similar services and rates.

HOTEL IMPALA, Calle 21 no. 40, Guaymas, Son. 85400. Tel. 622/2-1335 or 2-0922. 46 rms (all with bath). A/C TV TEL
$ Rates: $23 single; $27 double; $33 triple.
The lobby is furnished with plastic waiting-room seats and a TV. The hotel is old but

freshly painted and clean. The hotel's air-conditioned Restaurant Mandarin specializes in Chinese food; it's open daily from 7am to 11pm.

To get here, walk two blocks west of the central plaza; it's between Serdan and Rodríguez.

HOTEL SANTA RITA, Calle 9 at the corner of Aquiles Serdan, Guaymas,
Son. 85400. Tel. 622/2-8100 or 2-6463. 36 rms (all with bath). A/C
$ Rates: $23 single; $27 double; $33 triple. **Parking:** Free.
Right on the main boulevard, 12 blocks west of the central plaza, is the Hotel Santa Rita. The decor is pleasant, with dark Spanish-style heavy wooden furniture, and red curtains and red-and-black bedspreads set against tile walls and white-tile floors. Rooms are very clean and comfortable; some have windows facing the interior and others have windows on the street.

WORTH THE EXTRA BUCKS

MOTEL ARMIDA, on the International Hwy. (Hwy. 15), Guaymas, Son.
85400. Tel. 622/2-3050. 125 rms (all with bath). A/C TV TEL
$ Rates: $40–$64 single or double. **Parking:** Free.
This thoroughly modern hotel is a town social center of sorts—very popular and bustling. The more expensive rooms were built in 1989 and are especially large, with modern bathrooms and TVs with U.S. channels. The large motel has a swimming pool, bar, discothèque, and several restaurants.

WHERE TO EAT

JAX SNAX, at the corner of Aquiles Serdan and Calle 14 Sur. Tel.
2-3865.
Specialty: FAST FOOD.
$ Prices: Pizza $4–$6.50; hamburgers $2.50–$5.
Open: Tues–Sun 7am–11pm.
Small and pleasant, with a pizza-parlor decor and ceiling fan, Jax Snax has 13 kinds of pizza in four sizes; chicken, fish filets, and carne asada, all served with green salad, french fries, beans, guacamole, and tortillas or bread; and nine kinds of hamburgers, all served with french fries. For naturalists, there's a big bowl of yogurt with honey, fruit, and granola. The place is eight blocks west of the central plaza.

JUGOS CHAPALITA, Rodríguez 22.
Specialty: FRUIT/FRUIT DRINKS.
$ Prices: Fruit drinks $1.50.
Open: Daily 7:30am–9pm.
Jugos Chapalita, two blocks west of the plaza, on the same block as the Restaurant El Paradise and the Hotel Impala, is decorated with pyramids of fruit. *Licuados* of fresh fruit blended with milk come in 11 tropical flavors and cost more if they're made with eggs. The Especial Chapalita comes with seven to nine fruits, two eggs, and chocolate milk.

RESTAURANT EL PARADISE, at Rodríguez 20. Tel. 2-1181.
Specialty: SEAFOOD.
$ Prices: Appetizers $4–$7.50; seafood combo $12; seafood cocktails, salads, basic enchiladas $4–$6.
Open: Daily noon–10pm.
Restaurant El Paradise is two blocks west of the plaza, across from the Hotel Impala and one block from the market. There's an English menu, waiters who speak your lingo, air conditioning, and big portions. The seafood is fresh from Guaymas harbor. The seafood combo comes with deviled crab, fish filets, broiled shrimp, clams ranchero style, french fries, vegetables, and rolls with butter. On this menu you can choose from shrimp prepared 13 different ways, or enchiladas, tacos, and steak.

TODOS COMEN, Serdan 283, near Calle 15. Tel. 2-1100.
Specialty: MEXICAN.
$ Prices: Breakfast $1.75–$2.50; main courses $1.25–$8.

Open: Daily 24 hours.

At Todos Comen, seven blocks west of the plaza, a basic low-priced menu of seafood, chicken, and Mexican specialties is served for all meals. It's a tiny place, with air conditioning and ceiling fans, and plastic-covered tables. It's good to know about for those after-hours times when you're looking for a bite.

SHOPPING

At the **mercado** (market), located on Avenida Rodríguez on the entire block between Calle 19 and Calle 20, you can find economical breakfasts and lunches, licuados, vegetables and fruits, meats and groceries, clothes, sombreros (hats), shoes and huaraches (sandals), rugs and blankets. You may get a good deal or two, and if you're not going much farther south, you can buy beautiful Mexican embroidered dresses and blouses here at the Guaymas market. Otherwise, wait to make your purchases later in your trip.

EASY EXCURSIONS FROM GUAYMAS
SAN CARLOS

About 12 miles west of Guaymas off Highway 15 is the resort area of San Carlos. The beaches are nice, but the hotels and restaurants are fairly expensive. Once off the highway, drive east for 7 miles through a riot of billboards advertising house lots for sale, condos, time-sharing, trailer parks, and all types of *bienes raices* (real estate).

Set in the midst of striking scenery—pinnacled mountains on a beautiful bay—San Carlos is not at all like Puerto Vallarta or Acapulco. Rather, it's new, growing, and aimed not at the casual tourist but at the condo crowd. Restaurants tend to be expensive. If you want to see San Carlos, I'd recommend taking only a day trip. You can take the Guaymas city bus ("San Carlos") for 35¢.

PLAYA MIRAMAR

Guaymas's beach area, west of town across the hills, is called Playa Miramar, on Bocochibampo Bay. The city bus ("Miramar") will take you on the 25-minute ride from Guaymas for 25¢, driving north along the beach past beachfront homes and finally terminating at a small beachfront complex of shops, little restaurants, a trailer park, and a hotel.

Where to Stay at Playa Miramar

LEO'S INN, Calle 28 no. 133 (Apdo. Postal 430), Guaymas, Son. 85400. Tel. 622/2-9490 or 622/2-1337. 43 rms (all with bath). A/C **Bus:** "Miramar" to the north end of Miramar Beach; the bus stops at the beach restaurants next door.
$ Rates: $30 single; $35 double. **Parking:** Free.

Leo's is a nice, modern little place with a verdant garden on one side and two floors of tidy rooms with bug screens and screen doors. Ask for a discount in September and October. Rooms 1 and 2 have balconies overlooking the beach; they're large rooms with comfortable furniture, tile floors, and area rugs. Other rooms are smaller, with a narrow terrace walkway overlooking the front lawn/garden. There's an outdoor grill for guest use.

Where to Eat at Playa Miramar

RESTAURANT LA BOCANA. Tel. 2-4822.
Specialty: SEAFOOD. **Bus:** "Miramar" to the north end of Miramar Beach; the bus stops in front.
$ Prices: Breakfast $1.50–$3; lunch/dinner $5.50–$15.
Open: Daily 9am–9pm (off-season, hours are erratic—don't come early).

The Restaurant La Bocana, next to Leo's Inn, is an airy glassed-in room on the beach with an informal ambience, and seafood. You can get filete de pescado al mojo de ajo (fish filet in garlic sauce), meat dishes, shrimp, and lobster. The house specialty is a seafood platter of breaded and grilled shrimp, fried fish filet, fried perch, clams, rice, and salad.

VENENO'S RESTAURANT.
   Specialty: SEAFOOD. **Bus:** "Miramar" to the north end of Miramar Beach; the bus stops in front.
$ Prices: Slightly cheaper than La Bocana, above.
   Open: Daily 9:30am–9pm (off-season, hours are erratic—don't come early).
Veneno's, also next to Leo's Inn, is similarly styled to Restaurant La Bocana with windows open to the sea, but it's much more informal. The menu features a basic selection of very fresh seafood at slightly lower prices than the place next door.

EN ROUTE TO ALAMOS

From Guaymas, the route leads south to **Cd. Obregón.** A model city founded in 1928 (pop. 270,000), it has probably the flattest location, widest streets, and least colonial atmosphere of any community in Mexico. With the modernity of 20th-century buildings, it differs from such settlements as San Cristóbal de las Casas and Guanajuato as the Yukon does from the Congo. The regional economy is based on cotton cultivation, but rice, sesame, and cotton are all grown because of the irrigation of this desert land over the last 30 years.

About 42 miles south of Cd. Obregón is **Navojoa,** Sonora (alt. 125 ft.; pop. 125,000). It's an agricultural town famous for its wheat production and flour mills. Navojoa's touristic importance is its proximity to other, more attractive places, such as **Alamos** (35 miles east) and the beach at **Huatabampo** (25 miles west). Tourists can take buses leaving Navojoa for one of these destinations. Buses to Huatabampo leave Navojoa from the bus station at the corner of Calle Guerrero and Rincón, six blocks west of the Central Camionera (the Tres Estrellas de Oro station) about every 15 minutes from 5:45am to 8pm. It's a 30- to 40-minute trip by bus. By car to Huatabampo, drive 25 miles south on Calle Talamante, running parallel to Calle Pesquiera, six blocks to the west.

---

3. ALAMOS

130 miles SE of Guaymas, 35 miles E of Navojoa

GETTING THERE By Plane The nearest commercial airport is in Obregón, served both by **Aeroméxico** with direct flights from Hermosillo, Culiacán, and Guadalajara; and **Noroeste** with direct flights from Hermosillo. Alamos has a 3,900-foot paved airstrip (elev. 1,347 ft.) for private planes; circle the town before landing and a taxi will meet the plane.

By Bus In Navojoa you'll probably arrive at the Tres Estrellas de Oro station on Calle Guerrero. The small bus station for Alamos is on Calle Guerrero at Rincón, six blocks west of the Tres Estrellas station. From there it's a 40-minute ride or more (lots of stops) to Alamos, with buses leaving every 30 to 45 minutes between 6:30am and 7pm.

By Car To drive to Alamos, turn east off Highway 15 in Navojoa onto Avenida Abasolo and follow the road for 35 miles.

ESSENTIALS Information The **State Tourism Office** faces the main square below the Hotel Los Portales. It's open Monday through Friday from 9am to 1pm and 3 to 6pm; and on Saturday from 9am to 1pm. Local tour guides can be arranged at the tourist office, and while the price quoted is very low, it's for the guide only; in addition you'll need to hire a taxi, so that the total price for a half-day comes to about $40. The tourist office can also help arrange local guides for bass fishing and dove hunting.

Fast Facts The **telephone area code** is 642. Because of the valley's sheltered location and altitude (1,440 ft. above sea level), it has an excellent **climate** and flowers are abundant. This part of northern Mexico is cold in winter.

A dead-end road will take you to the colonial-era silver-mining village of Alamos, Sonora (pop. 25,000). This city was already more than a century old when the king of Spain sent out a surveyor-general to plan out the main streets in 1750. Early Catholic missions were maintained in this isolated valley as early as 1613, and by 1685 some of the richest silver mines in the world were operating nearby.

The silver finally gave out (around 1900), and people began to drift away. In the 1940s a few Americans discovered the town and began restoring the mansions as second homes. Since then many Americans have come and gone, or remained permanently, preserving many homes in the process, and making Alamos a beautiful village. Today Alamos is a State Monument Town and new construction must conform to colonial structures. Cobbled streets wind around arcaded porticos. Despite the town's rebirth, the visitor quickly notices its isolation.

WHAT TO SEE & DO

Alamos is a small town, centered by a lovely **plaza** complete with white iron bandstand, a beautiful place for relaxing and strolling around. Ask your hotel for a map of Alamos; it will alert you to the many interesting sights tucked away all over town. For a more intimate view of the mansions, be at the bank side of the church plaza any Saturday at 10am for the **Home-and-Garden Tour** sponsored by Alamos's Friends of the Library. The cost is $5 and includes coffee and cookies at the library, which is in the government Palacio just behind the cathedral.

The **Palacio,** built in 1899, is a lovely building as is the cathedral, one block away. Also facing the plaza is the museum of customs and traditions, **Museo Costumbrista de Sonora** (tel. 8-0053), open Wednesday through Sunday from 9am to 1pm and 3 to 6pm. Admission is free, but donations are appreciated. Nicely laid out, with excellent displays, it exhibits artifacts from the city's history, including a replica of a mine shaft, agricultural implements, home furnishings, photographs, and a large collection of coins minted in Alamos when it was part of the state called Estado do Occidente.

Attached to the back section of the museum is the **Centro Cultural,** which offers laser-disk cultural shows, such as Placido Domingo at the Metropolitan Opera. Check for local schedules. Aside from these shows and the Hotel Tesoro's low-key entertainment (see below), there is no nightlife to speak of. This is the place for a good, thick book, perhaps on regional lore.

A SPECIAL EVENT Exactly 21 days after the first rain of the season, usually in June, the Sierra des Alamos start to crackle with the sound of **Mexican jumping beans,** and people take to the hills to hunt *los brincadores.* Early in the morning when the sun begins to warm them up, they start jumping—actually a worm inside causes the beans to move. Storeowners bring them back to sell, until they stop jumping, around December.

WHERE TO STAY

HOTEL ENRIQUE, Juárez 5, Alamos, Son. 85760. Tel. 642/8-0280. 10 rms (1 with bath).
$ Rates: $6 without bath; $8 with bath.
This hotel has no redeeming qualities, but I mention it in case you arrive and there are no rooms anywhere else. It's below the Hotel Los Portales and faces the main plaza (there's no sign). This will do for a night until you can find something better. It's a group of dark, marginally kept rooms with fans, laid out around a sunny courtyard. The dirty bath/shower is shared by men and women.

HOTEL LOS PORTALES, Juárez 6, Alamos, Son. 85760. Tel. 642/8-0211. 10 rms (all with bath).
$ Rates: $33 single; $38 double.
Once a city mansion belonging to silver-mine owners, the Hotel Los Portales exudes

the charm of bygone days. Like many elegant town homes when silver reigned, interior entry walls are elaborately stenciled to resemble elegant wallpaper; this is one of the few remaining examples of this art in town. Though aged, the walls are part of the hotel's charm. The comfortable, high-ceilinged rooms flanking the inner courtyard have tile floors, fireplaces, fans, and one or two double beds. At night it's nice to sit in one of the *equipale* chairs under the portal in front and watch what little goes on in the plaza and prompt a local to tell ghost stories. The hotel office sells soft drinks and beer.

To get here from the bus stop, face the plaza, then walk left for two blocks up the same side of the street as the bus stop and turn right up a narrow cobbled street to the central plaza; the hotel is ahead on the right facing the plaza.

HOTEL MANSION DE LA CONDESA MAGDELENA, Obregón 2, Alamos, Son. 85760. Tel. 642/8-0221. 13 rms (all with bath).
$ Rates: Low season, $30 single; $40 double; $50 triple. High season, 50% more.
The mansion was built in 1865 by the Salido family of miners, ranchers, and merchants, and Rafaela Adriana Marcor Glaxiola, a descendant of the original family owners, who lived here until 1979 teaching English, French, and music to local students. She hosted Francisco Madero in 1910 (he later became president of Mexico). The mansion (often called by its former name, the Glaxiola House) opened as a hotel in 1986 with 13 large and nicely furnished rooms, all with tile floors and Mexican tile accents, flanking the pleasant inner courtyard. The then president of Mexico, Miguel de la Madrid, stayed here for the hotel's inauguration. Each room is slightly different in size and antique decor, and each has a fireplace. There's a crafts shop in the lobby. The restaurant is open during high season November through Easter.

To get here, with the main plaza on your left, walk on Juárez past the church two blocks and turn left onto Obregón and walk three more blocks; the hotel is on the right.

CASA DE LOS TESOROS, Av. Obregón 10 (Apdo. Postal 12), Alamos, Son. 85760. Tel. 642/8-0010. 14 rms (all with bath). A/C.
$ Rates: June–Sept, $40 single; $45 double. Oct–May (including meals), $70 single; $100 double.
Built in the 18th century by the first priest who came to Alamos, it was later converted to a convent and finally a hotel. Rooms line up along one side of the central patio and restaurant. In back, behind the restaurant, is a lovely pool. Each room is slightly different in furnishings and each has a fireplace—essential in winter. It's very popular with tour groups, which accounts for the high prices. You'll find it two blocks behind the church and central plaza.

WHERE TO EAT

RESTAURANT LAS PALMERAS, Cárdenas 9. Tel. 8-0065.
Specialty: MEXICAN.
$ Prices: Breakfast $3.50–$4; main courses $2.50–$7.
Open: Daily 7am–10pm.
This simple, family-run restaurant opposite the church and museum on the main plaza can fill most of your dining needs. Tables are set out under the portals or inside. The food is better than at Los Tesoros at a fraction of the price. House specialties are milanesa (breaded beef), fried fish from the nearby reservoir Presa Macusare, and a Sunday special of oven-roasted leg of pork.

CASA DE LOS TESOROS, Av. Obregón 10. Tel. 8-0010.
Specialty: MEXICAN/INTERNATIONAL.
$ Prices: Breakfast $3.50–$5; main courses $4–$10; fixed-price meals $10 at lunch, $15 at dinner.
Open: Daily 7am–9pm (lunch by reservation at 1:30pm and dinner by reservation at 7:30pm; off-hours, order à la carte).
If there is any ongoing action in Alamos it will be here at this hotel-restaurant. Prices reflect its focal point as practically the only game in town. Groups on tour almost

always stay and eat here and management caters to their needs. A guitar trio plays some evenings.

On Saturday nights the Hotel de Los Tesoros organizes a Mexican Night, which for a fixed price includes dinner and entertainment by local Mayo Indian dancers. The restaurant's food and service are good, but too expensive. Eat here before or after formal dining hours and order from the less expensive à la carte menu.

EASY EXCURSIONS FROM ALAMOS

Outside of town, 8 miles to the south on Carretera Guirocoba, the natural springs/swimming hole at **Cuchujaki** draws visitors year round, but especially in summer, when in addition to swimmers there are American students who come to camp out. If you don't have a car, a taxi will take you from Alamos for $20, returning for you at the time you specify if you ask the driver.

To the west of Alamos, the park **El Chaloton** is about 1¼ miles from downtown, especially popular during the months of June through October. Half a mile farther on is **Solipasos,** another popular swimming hole. The *presa* (reservoir) **Macusare** on the highway between Navojoa and Alamos, about equidistant between the two, is another fine place for swimming—and for fishing too.

EN ROUTE TO MAZATLÁN

About halfway between Alamos and Culiacán is **Los Mochis,** the best boarding point for the **Copper Canyon Train,** *El Chihuahua al Pacífico.* Los Mochis, the Copper Canyon, and Chihuahua are covered in Chapter 4.

Almost equidistant between Los Mochis and Mazatlán (130 miles from the former, 140 miles from the latter) is **Culiacán,** capital of Sinaloa. The surrounding region, located between the foothills of the Sierra Madre and the Pacific, is a rich agricultural area abounding in cotton, peanuts, and some of the world's finest tomatoes, as well as abundant poppy fields. Along with Southeast Asia, the Culiacán area is one of the world's greatest producers of crude opium, and it has the crime problems of any drug-region city.

Culiacán itself is a humming, progressive city of 560,000, where modern buildings stand cheek-by-jowl with structures dating back to colonial times. Examples of both can be seen on **Plaza Obregón,** where a lovely old cathedral looks across the park at some of the most futuristic architecture in Mexico.

From Culiacán it's an easy 3-hour drive to Mazatlán, the most northerly of Mexico's fabulous Pacific resorts. Pretty country separates the two cities, with rolling uplands gradually yielding to fertile tropic savannahs.

---

4. MAZATLÁN

674 miles NW of Mexico City, 314 miles NW of Guadalajara,
976 miles S of Mexicali

GETTING THERE   By Plane   There are some direct or nonstop flights to Mazatlán, most of them from the West Coast: **Aero California** has nonstop flights from Phoenix and San Diego; **Aeroméxico** flies from Los Angeles, Tucson, Mexico City, Aguascalientes, Los Mochis, Durango, Tijuana, and León; **Alaska Airlines** flies from Los Angeles, San Francisco, and Anchorage; **Delta** flies from Los Angeles; **Mexicana** offers service from Los Angeles, Denver, San Francisco, Mexico City, Guadalajara, and Los Cabos. The regional carrier **Noroeste** flies from Chihuahua, Cd. Obregón, Culiacán, Hermosillo, and Mexicali. Check with a travel agent for the latest **charter flights;** charters from Boston, Los Angeles, Salt Lake City, and San Antonio are anticipated for 1992.

By Train   The northbound *El Tren del Pacífico* begins in Guadalajara, stops in Tepic around 2pm, and arrives in Mazatlán around 6pm; from Mexicali at the U.S. border it leaves at 9am and pulls into Mazatlán around 6am the next morning. Another train, *El Sinaloense,* arrives from Guadalajara around 5am; from Mexicali it reaches Mazatlán around 11pm. The *Pacífico* is a newer, nicer train than the *Sinaloense,* but has no sleeping compartments.

By Bus Mazatlán is a popular stop on the way to and from the U.S.–Mexico border at Nogales or Mexicali. More than half a dozen bus lines offer service from points north and south as well as from Mexico City and Guadalajara.

By Car From Culiacán to the north or Tepic and Guadalajara to the south/ southeast, take Highway 15. From Durango to the northeast, the only choice is Highway 40 through the mountains, a winding but scenic trip.

By Ferry The ferries that were operated by SEMATUR and Baja Express between La Paz and Mazatlán are not running at the moment, but there's talk that the service may be reinstated. For more information, see Section 2, "La Paz," in Chapter 7 on Baja California.

DEPARTING By Plane Airline offices are located downtown: **Aero California,** in the Hotel Posada de Don Pelayo, Avenida del Mar 1100 (tel. 83-2024, 83-2042, or 83-0242); **Aeroméxico,** Camaron Sabalo 310 (tel. 84-1609, 84-1111, or 84-1621); **Alaska Airlines,** in the El Cid Resort, Camaron Sabalo (tel. 84-4767 or 84-4745, or 85-2731 or 85-2730 at the airport, or toll free in Mexico 95-800/426-0333); **Delta,** Camaron Sabalo 5N, near the El Cid Resort (tel. 83-2709, or 82-3354 at airport); **Mexicana,** Paseo Claussen 101B (tel. 82-7722); and **Noroeste,** in the El Cid Resort, Camaron Sabalo (tel. 84-3944, 84-3855 or 84-3833).

By Train The northbound *El Tren del Pacífico* (tel. 81-5892 or 84-6710) departs Mazatlán at 6:50pm, making stops in Culiacán, Cd. Obregón, Hermosillo, Nogales (11:05am), and Puerto Penasco before arriving in Mexicali at 4:30pm the next day. The southbound *Pacífico* leaves at 6:55am and stops in Tepic (12:25pm) before arriving in Guadalajara at 6:05pm, an especially scenic trip through the Sierras. The northbound *El Sinaloense* departs Mazatlán at 5:35am; its southbound train leaves at 11:40pm and arrives in Guadalajara around 10am the next morning. *Note:* Trains are not always on time; you may have a long wait at the station.

Tickets are sold Monday through Saturday from 9am to 12:30pm and 3 to 5pm; and on Sunday and holidays from 9am to noon. For a small fee a travel agency may be willing to purchase the tickets for you.

By Bus Major bus lines include **Transportes del Norte** (tel. 81-2335), **Tres Estrellas de Oro** (tel. 81-3680); **Autobuses Estrella Blanca** (tel. 81-5381); **Transportes Norte de Sonora** (tel. 81-3684 or 81-3846); **Transportes del Pacífico** (tel. 82-0577), and **Trans Monterrey Saltillo** (tel. 81-5381). Buses heading north and south along the coast as well as inland to Guadalajara and Mexico City are available. In some cases you can buy a reserved seat the day before departure. Check more than one bus line.

Mazatlán, Sinaloa (pop. 500,000), was once best known as a resort for sportsmen who came to catch sailfish and marlin. You can still hire a boat for big-game fishing, or guns and a guide for a hunting expedition to the countryside. However, Mazatlán has been promoted by the Mexican government as an international attraction, and has many resort hotels.

Travel writers have been kind to Mazatlán, dreaming up such sugary phrases as "jewel of the West," "pearl of the Pacific," and "place of the deer" (this last being a literal translation of the Nahuatl word). The beaches are nice enough, especially Sabalo Beach, to the north of the town and accessible by bus from the zócalo. The beach right downtown, Olas Altas (High Waves), is best for watching sunsets from sidewalk cafés where the resort got its start.

ORIENTATION

ARRIVING The **airport** is about 10 miles south of town. Minivans from the airport to hotels charge $5 per person; a taxi from the airport will cost $15. There's

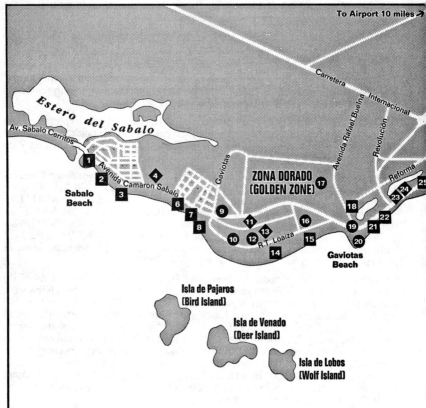

Estero del Sabalo

Av. Sabalo Cerritos

Carretera Internacional

Avenida Rafael Buelna

Revolución

Reforma

Avenida Camaron Sabalo

Sabalo Beach

Gaviotas

ZONA DORADO (GOLDEN ZONE)

R.T. Loaiza

Gaviotas Beach

1
2
3
4
6
7
8
9
10
11
12
13
14
15
16
17
18
19
20
21
22
23
24
25

Isla de Pajaros (Bird Island)

Isla de Venado (Deer Island)

Isla de Lobos (Wolf Island)

B a h í a   d e l

Mazatlán

MEXICO CITY

ACCOMMODATIONS:
Aqua Marina Hotel 30
El Cid Resort 6
Cabinas al Mar Hotel 22
Camino Real Hotel 1
Costa de Oro Hotel 8
Motel del Sol 29
Hacienda Hotel 31
Holiday Inn Hotel 3
Hotel Inn at Mazatlán 7

Los Sabalos Hotel 15
Playa Mazatlán Hotel 14
Posada de Don Pelayo 21
Pueblo Bonito Hotel 2
Motel San Diego 18
Sands Hotel 25

DINING:
El Faro Restaurant 36
Restaurant Jungle Juice 11
Restaurant Los Arcos 4

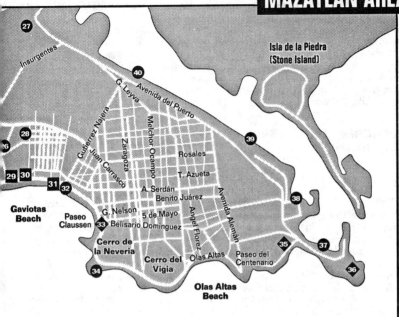

MAZATLÁN AREA

Isla de la Piedra
(Stone Island)

Insurgentes

G. Leyva
Avenida del Puerto

Gutierrez Najera

Juan Carrasco

Zaragoza

Melchor Ocampo

Rosales

T. Azueta

A. Serdán
Benito Juárez

Avenida Alemán

Angel Florez

Gaviotas
Beach

Paseo
Claussen

G. Nelson
Belisario Dominguez

5 de Mayo

Cerro de
la Neveria

Cerro del
Vigia

Olas Altas

Paseo del
Centenario

Olas Altas
Beach

Puerto Viejo

El Marinero Restaurant 33
El Mirador Restaurant 35
Parrillada No. 1 Restaurant 23
Pepe Toro Restaurant 13
Señor Frog's Restaurant 24

ATTRACTIONS:
American Express Office 9
Aquarium 26
Bullring/Plaza de Toros 17
Bus Station 28

Cruise Ship and
  Freight Docks 39
Ferry Dock 38
Fisherman's Monument 32
Mazatlan Arts and
  Crafts Center 10
El Mirador Lookout Point 35
Sabalo Traffic Circle 19
Sea Shell City 12
Spanish Fort 34

Sport Fishing
  Fleets/Docks 37
Stone Island,
  launches to 40
Tourism Office 16
Train Station 27
Valentino's Disco/
  Cameron Point 20

also a bus that charges the same as the minivans and makes the rounds of hotels, but it's quite slow and sometimes careless with the luggage.

The **train station** (tel. 81-2802, 81-5892, or 81-2034) is about 3 miles northeast of downtown in Colonia Esperanza behind the Cafe El Marino coffee-processing plant. A taxi from the train station to most hotels will cost between $6 and $10.

The **Central de Autobuses** (main bus terminal), at Carretera Internacional Norte (International Highway) and Chachalacas, is three blocks inland from the Malecón on Río Tamazula. A taxi from the bus station to most hotels will cost around $5. You can catch a local bus for 15¢, but you may have to change buses en route.

INFORMATION   The **City Tourism Office** is in the Golden Zone, across the street from the large Hotel Los Sabalos, at Rodolfo T. Loaiza 100, downstairs (tel. 69/83-2545 or 84-0222; fax 69/86-0120). The staff members are friendly and speak English. It's open Monday through Friday from 9am to 4pm and on Saturday from 9am to 1pm.

CITY LAYOUT   Mazatlán extends from the historic downtown and port area on the peninsula, with its harbor and Olas Atlas Beach where the first glamorous hotels were built, to the "Golden Zone" and Los Cerritos area to the north, where the fashionable and luxurious hotels rise today. More hotels, shops, and restaurants edge the curving seaside boulevard, or **Malecón,** that connects these areas. This waterfront drive changes names several times, starting out as Avenida Olas Atlas downtown, then becoming Paseo Claussen, Avenida del Mar, Avenida Camaron Sabalo (in the Golden Zone), and finally Avenida Sabalo Cerritos.

About 4 miles north of downtown lies the Sabalo traffic circle of the **Golden Zone** near Punta Camaron, a rocky outcropping over the water. From here the resort hotels, including the huge El Cid Resort complex, continue to spread northward along and beyond **Sabalo Beach,** one of Mazatlán's best. It's another 5 miles to **Los Cerritos** (The Little Hills), the northern limit of the resort.

Keep in mind that Mazatlán is fully 10 miles long, and use the landmarks of downtown, the Sabalo traffic circle, El Cid Resort, and Los Cerritos to find your way. Street numbers are of little practical use.

GETTING AROUND

The downtown transportation center for buses, taxis, and *pulmonías* is on the central plaza, or zócalo, that faces the cathedral.

By Bus   Buses painted blue or green make getting around this long resort relatively easy. The "Sabalo Basilica" buses run from the Golden Zone along the waterfront to downtown and back, and one of their stops is the downtown market. The "Cerritos-Juárez" line starts near the train station, cuts across town to the Malecón beside the Golden Zone, and heads north to Cerritos and back. The "Sabalo Cocos" line runs through the Golden Zone, heads inland to the bus station, and on to downtown by a back route (instead of the waterfront), also stopping at the market. Buses run daily from 5am to 10pm and charge under 50¢.

At the bus station you can also catch buses to nearby picturesque towns such as Copala and Concordia, and save money over the tour price. Just be sure to go early and verify the time of the last afternoon bus back.

By Pulmonía   These Jeep-type open-air vehicles carry up to three passengers anywhere for the same or a bit less than taxi fare. Called *pulmonías* (literally, "pneumonias"), they have surreylike tops and open sides to let in the breezes. As with taxis, haggle for a good price before boarding.

FAST FACTS

American Express   The AMEX office is on Camaron Sabalo in the Centro Comercial Balboa shopping center, Loc. 4 and 16 (tel. 83-0600), between the traffic circle and El Cid Resort; it's open Monday through Friday from 9am to 5pm and on Saturday from 9am to noon.

Area Code   The telephone area code is 69.

Banks   Foreign currency is exchanged Monday through Friday from 9 to 11:30am.

Climate   As the northernmost major beach resort on the mainland, Mazatlán can be cooler in the summer than the resorts farther south. The wettest month is September.

Legal Aid   The Attorney Agency (tel. 84-3222) next door to the City Tourism Office helps tourists with legal problems and complaints.

Market   The mercado covers the downtown block bordered by Serdan, Juárez, Ocampo, and Valle.

Post Office   The Correo is downtown on the east side of the main plaza, on Juárez just off Angel Flores.

U.S. Consulate   It's downtown at Circunvalación 6 and Venustiano Carranza (tel. 85-2205), one block from the Olas Atlas beach. Open Monday through Friday from 8 to 11am for visas and other services, and 2 to 4pm for passports.

WHAT TO SEE & DO

To orient yourself, hike up and enjoy the panoramic view from the famous **Faro (lighthouse),** on the point at the south end of town. It's the second-highest lighthouse in the world (only Gibraltar is higher), towering 447 feet over the harbor.

MUSEUMS

MUSEO ARQUEOLÓGICO DE MAZATLÁN, Sixto Osuna 76, a block in from Paseo Olas Altas. Tel. 85-3502.
This small but attractive museum exhibits both pre-Columbian artifacts and occasional contemporary artists.
Admission: $2.
Open: Tues–Sun 10am–1pm and 4–6:30pm.

ACUARIO MAZATLÁN AQUARIUM, one block off Av. del Mar. Tel. 81-7815, 81-7816, or 81-7817.
Besides the beaches, children and adults interested in the sea will love what is one of the largest and best aquariums in Mexico. To find it, look for the turn near the Motel del Sol and the Pizza Hut.
Admission: $2 adults, $1 kids 3–14.
Open: Daily 10am–6pm; sea lion shows daily at 11am and 1, 3, and 5pm.

MUSEO DE CONCHAS (Sea Shell City), Rodolfo Loaiza 407, in the Golden Zone. Tel. 83-1301.
Shell collectors and kids will enjoy this vast and fascinating collection of shells and shell art, much of which is for sale.
Admission: Free.
Open: Daily 9am–7pm.

ARCHITECTURE

Two blocks south of the zócalo stands the lovely and historic **Angela Peralta Theater,** which in 1989 celebrated its first full season since renovation began 4 years ago. The theater was named for one of the world's great divas, who, along with the director and 30 members of the opera, died in Mazatlán of cholera in the epidemic of 1863.

The 20-block historic area near the theater, including the small square **Plazuela Machado** (bordered by Frías, Constitución, Carnaval, and Sixto Osuna) is packed with beautiful old buildings and rows of colorful town houses trimmed with wrought iron and carved stone; many have recently been restored as part of a city project. Check out the **town houses** on Libertad between Domínguez and Carnaval, and the two lavish **mansions** on Ocampo at Domínguez and at Carnaval. For a rest stop, try the restaurant Hostería de Pepe (decorated with historic pictures of Mazatlán) or the bar Cafe Pacífico on Plazuela Machado.

Back at the zócalo, be sure to take a look at the unusual yellow-tiled **cathedral.** The zócalo itself is the heart of the city, filled with vendors, shoe-shine stands, and people of all ages out for a stroll. At its center is a Victorian-style wrought-iron bandstand.

THE BEACHES

At the western edge of downtown is the rocky, pebbly **Playa Olas Altas,** a lovely little cove, but not the best for swimming. Around a rocky promontory to the north of Olas Altas is **Playa Norte,** several miles of good sand beach.

At the Sabalo traffic circle, Punta Camaron juts into the water, and on either side of the point is **Playa Las Gaviotas.** Farther north, **Playa Sabalo** is perhaps the very best of all. The next point jutting into the water is Punta Sabalo, past which is a bridge over the channel that flows in and out of a lagoon. North of the bridge lie even more beaches, all the way to Los Cerritos. Remember that all beaches in Mexico are public property, so feel free to wander where you like.

Another nice beach that makes a pleasant outing is on the ocean side of **Isla de la Piedra (Stone Island),** on the southeast side of town. From the center of town, board a "Circunvalación" bus from the north side of the zócalo for the ride to the boat landing, called "Embarcadero Isla de la Piedra." Small motorboats make the 5-minute trip to the island every 15 minutes or so, from 7am to 11pm, and charge $1 round-trip, $2 after 5pm. When you alight on the island, walk through the sleepy little village to the ocean side, where the pale sandy beaches, bordered by coconut groves, stretch for miles. On Sunday afternoons the *palapa* restaurants on the shore have music and dancing, attracting families and young people; on other days the beach is almost empty. Carmelita's palapa has delicious fish called "lisamacho," served grilled and slightly blackened (over an open fire) with fresh, hot corn tortillas and salsa for about $3.50.

Camping here is possible but not recommended.

CRUISES & BOAT RENTALS

The **Fiesta Yacht Cruise** (tel. 81-3041) runs a large double-deck boat every morning at 11am, leaving from the south beach near the lighthouse. The 3-hour cruise takes in the harbor and bay, with bilingual guides to explain the marine life, plus a marimba band to entertain. Bring a swimsuit in case the boat stops at one of the small islands. Tickets run $6 per person (youngsters ages 5 to 8 pay half price). In December and January there's also a Friday moonlight cruise from 7 to 10pm for $9 per person. Purchase tickets through a major hotel or travel agency.

Amphibious boats heading for Isla de Venados (Deer Island), one of the three big islands off the coast, leave from the beaches of the El Cid Resort (tel. 83-3333) and the Inn at Mazatlán (tel. 83-5500) continuously throughout the day.

SPORTS & RECREATION

Fishing can be arranged on the south side of town, at the base of the 515-foot hill that supports the lighthouse. Rates range from $140 a day and up for deep-sea cruises

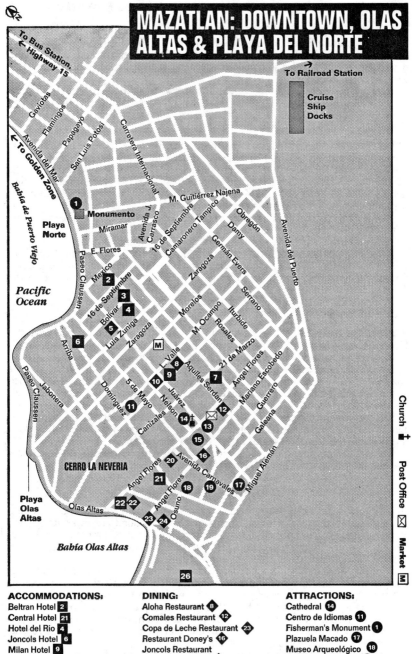

MAZATLAN: DOWNTOWN, OLAS ALTAS & PLAYA DEL NORTE

To Bus Station,
Highway 15

To Railroad Station

Cruise
Ship
Docks

To Golden Zone

Bahía de Puerto Viejo

Gaviotas

Flamingos

Papagayo

San Luis Potosí

Avenida del Mar

Carretera Internacional

Monumento

1

M. Guitiérrez Najena

Obregón

Damy

Avenida J. Carrasco

Miramar

Playa Norte

E. Flores

Paseo Clausen

México

16 de Septiembre

Camaronero Tampico

Germán Eyers

Serrano

Avenida del Puerto

Pacific Ocean

2

16 de Septiembre

Bolívar

3

4

Zaragoza

Morelos

M. Ocampo

Iturbide

Luis Zuniga

5

Rosales

Arriba

6

Zaragoza

M

Valle

Aquiles Serdan

21 de Marzo

Angel Flores

Mariano Escobedo

Jabonera

5 de Mayo

Domínguez

8

9

10

Juárez

7

Guerrero

Paseo Clausen

11

Nelson

Canizales

14 †

12

13

Galeana

15

CERRO LA NEVERIA

20

Avenida Carnavales

16

21

Angel Flores

18

19

17

Miguel Alemán

Playa Olas Altas

Olas Altas

22 **22**

Angel Flores

23 **24**

Osuno

Bahía Olas Altas

26

Church †

Post Office ⊠

Market M

ACCOMMODATIONS:
Beltran Hotel **2**
Central Hotel **21**
Hotel del Rio **4**
Joncols Hotel **6**
Milan Hotel **9**
Olas Altas Hotel **26**
Hotel Santa Barbara **3**
Siesta Hotel **22**
Villa del Mar Hotel **7**

DINING:
Aloha Restaurant **8**
Comales Restaurant **12**
Copa de Leche Restaurant **23**
Restaurant Doney's **16**
Joncols Restaurant
Madrid Restaurant **24**
Mamucas Restaurant **5**
Menudo Restaurant **19**
Restaurant El Shrimp Bucket **22**
Tortas Hawaii **10**

ATTRACTIONS:
Cathedral **14**
Centro de Idiomas **11**
Fisherman's Monument **1**
Plazuela Macado **17**
Museo Arqueológico **18**
Post Office/Correos **13**
Teatro Angela Peralta **19**
Zócalo (Main Square) **15**

including all equipment (or $45 per person if there's a group you can join). Try **Mike Maxemin's Faro Fleet** (tel. 81-2824 or 82-4977) or **Bill Heimpel's Star Fleet** (tel. 82-2665 or 82-3828). A fishing license is necessary; you can buy one for $4 on the day of your trip. You can also rent scuba-diving or waterskiing equipment, but prices vary, so shop around and bargain.

If you want to rent **bicycles, motor scooters, or sailboats,** or soar above the Pacific with a **parachute,** go to the Hotels Playa Mazatlán (tel. 83-4444), El Cid Resort (tel. 83-3333), Costa de Oro (tel. 83-5344), or Oceano Palace (tel. 83-0666), 4 miles north of downtown, past the traffic circle.

Land Sports   Mazatlán has 127 **tennis** courts. Try the ones at the El Cid Resort, Camaron Sabalo (tel. 83-5611, ext. 1366), though these are reserved primarily for hotel guests; the Racquet Club Gaviotas, Ibis and Río Bravo in the Golden Zone (tel. 83-5939 or 83-5930); Club Deportivo Reforma, on Rafael Buelna near the bullring (tel. 83-1200, 83-1210, or 83-3576); or Nuevo Club de Tenis (tel. 83-3576). Many of the larger hotels in Mazatlán also have courts.

As for **golf,** try the 18-hole course at the El Cid Resort (tel. 83-3333), mainly for hotel guests; or the 9-hole course at the Club Campestre Mazatlán (open to the public), on Highway 15 on the outskirts of downtown (tel. 82-5702).

In addition to its worldwide reputation for year-round sportfishing (especially sailfish and marlin), Mazatlán is known for good **hunting,** principally duck and dove. For information about transportation, guides, equipment, and licenses, call Roberto Aviles (tel. 81-6060), or the Tourism Office (tel. 83-2545 or 84-0222).

You can rent horses for **horseback riding** at the Guadalupe Ranch near the El Cid Resort for $6 an hour.

Spectator Sports   There's a bullring on Rafael Buelna, about a mile from the Golden Zone (take the "Sabalo-Cocos" bus). From December through April, **bullfights** are held every Sunday and on holidays at 4pm; locals recommend arriving at 2pm. Tickets range from $10 for general admission (ask for the shady side, *la sombra*) to $25 for the front of the shaded section, and can be purchased in advance at the El Camaron Motel next to Valentino's Disco near the Sabalo traffic circle (tel. 84-1666).

On Saturday in the summer, Mexican rodeos, or ***charreadas,*** are held at the Lienzo Charro (ring) of the Association of Charros of Mazatlán (tel. 83-3154). Tickets are available through most major hotels and travel agencies.

During the Cultural Festival of Sinaloa in November, **pelota and hulama games** are played (see "Special Events," below).

ORGANIZED TOURS

In addition to a daily **city tour,** there are excursions to many colorful and interesting villages nearby, such as Concordia, Copala, and San Blas. Some are towns dating back to the Spanish conquest during the 16th century; others are quaint farming or fishing villages. Information and reservations are available at any travel agency or major hotel. Among the options:

Copala-Concordia: This popular countryside tour stops at several mountain villages where furniture and other items are crafted. Copala has a pretty Spanish colonial church. Lunch is usually included in the $35 to $40 tour.

San Blas Jungle Tour: This all-day excursion includes a boat trip up a mangrove-shrouded jungle river to a lovely pool created by natural springs, where you can swim. Sometimes there's a stop in Rosario, famous for it's colonial church's gold altar screen. Cost is $45 to $50, including lunch.

Stone Island: The boat trip and tour (10am to 4pm) costs $25, including lunch. Tickets purchased at Viajes el Sabalo (tel. 83-3560 or 84-3009) at the Hotel Los Sabalos are discounted. Optional horseback riding on the island costs $10 an hour.

Teacapan: This is a picturesque fishing village south of Mazatlán, with jungle river cruise. Stops along the way may include Esquinapa, known for its shrimp-stuffed tamales, and the hot springs at Agua Caliente.

Note: It's possible to get to Copala, Rosario, Teacapan, and other nearby towns by bus from the main terminal. But leave early and find out beforehand when to catch the last bus back.

A LANGUAGE SCHOOL

Classes in Spanish, with a maximum of six students, begin every Monday at the **Centro de Idiomas,** three blocks west of the cathedral, at Belisario Domínguez 1908, between 21 de Marzo and Canizales. In addition to small-group and individual instruction, the Language Center offers a Homestay Program, in which one lives with a Mexican family; and a Person-to-Person program that matches students with local people of similar interests and vocation. And on Friday evenings at 7pm the center holds free Spanish and English conversation groups open to both visitors and locals. For more information, call Dixie Davis, the American founder of the school (tel. 69/82-2053 or 81-3784; fax 69/85-5606).

SPECIAL EVENTS

The week before Lent (usually in February) is Mazatlán's famous **Carnaval,** or Mardi Gras. People come from all over the country and abroad for this flamboyant celebration.

Parades, special shows, the coronation of the Carnaval Queen, and many other extravaganzas take place all over town (for event information, check at major hotels or the Tourism Office, and look for posters). Every night during Carnaval week, all along the Olas Altas oceanfront drive in the southern part of town, music fills the street with roving mariachi groups, the local traditional *bandas Sinaloenses* (lots of brass instruments), and electrified bands set up under tarpaulin shades. Everyone is dancing, laughing, and milling about. The crowd increases each day, until on the last night (Tuesday), the Malecón is packed with musicians, dancers, and people out for a good time.

Even children have their own events during Carnaval, including the **Carnaval Infantil,** in which the Junior King and Queen of Carnaval are crowned; a musical show and *ballet folklorico* presented by an all-child cast; and the **Desfile Infantil,** a children's parade. Parents can also take their kids for a spin on the ferris wheel and other rides at the amusement area "Los Juegos La Verbena," set up near the bus station. Admission is free but the rides are not.

The following day, Ash Wednesday, the party is over. People receive crosses of ashes on their foreheads at church, and that's the beginning of Lent.

If you plan to be in Mazatlán for Carnaval or Semana Santa (Holy Week), be sure to make reservations well in advance. Hotels fill up and their prices usually rise, too.

Starting in mid-November, the 2-week **Cultural Festival of Sinaloa** takes place in Mazatlán and all over the state, with outstanding dance groups (from folkloric to classical ballet), operas, symphony concerts, art exhibits, literary competitions, music of all kinds, and even a children's *ballet folklorico.* Sports events include pelota (jai alai) and the pre-Hispanic ball game known as "hulama." For more information, call the Tourist Office (tel. 69/83-2545 or 84-0222).

Mazatlán's largest religious celebration, outside of Christmas and Holy Week/ Easter, is the **Feast of the Immaculate Conception** on December 8.

IN NEARBY VILLAGES On the weekend of the first Sunday in October **Rosario,** a small town known for the gold altar screen of its colonial church, holds a **festival honoring Our Lady of the Rosary.** Games, music, dances, processions, and festive foods mark the event. From May 1 to 10 Rosario holds its **Spring Festival.**

From October 12 to 19, the village of **Escuinapa** holds a **Mango Festival.**

WHERE TO STAY

The hotels in downtown Mazatlán are generally older and cheaper than those along the beachfront heading north. Most beachfront hotels are relatively new, flashy, and expensive, although some fit our budget. The three major areas are the downtown seafront, midtown, and the Golden Zone (Zona Dorada).

DOWNTOWN SEAFRONT/PLAYA OLAS ALTAS

The old section of Mazatlán is spread around a tiny, picturesque cove a short walk from downtown. It was here that the movie stars of the past came to play in the sun and surf; the hotels where they stayed are still here, seeming to whisper of their former glory. All are right on the waterfront, and their seaside rooms all have large private balconies, with beautiful views of the cove and the sunset. There are several nice seafront restaurants along here too, open from early until late, making it easy to dine near your hotel.

Doubles For Less Than $40

HOTEL LA SIESTA, Av. Olas Altas 11, Mazatlán, Sin. 82000. Tel. 69/81-2640. 56 rms (all with bath). A/C TEL

$ Rates: $20 single; $24 double.

One of the most attractive hotels in this area (on the Malecón at Angel Flores) offers comfortable, simple rooms that open onto a lush central palm court lined with green balconies; 30 rooms come with TVs. The restaurant El Shrimp Bucket (see "Where to Eat," below) offers tables with colorful umbrellas set up on the court. On the street side, the piano bar La Cantina has indoor as well as sidewalk tables.

HOTEL OLAS ALTAS, Calle Centenario 14, Mazatlán, Sin. 82000. Tel. 69/81-3192. Fax 69/85-3720. 50 rms (all with bath). A/C TV TEL

$ Rates: Summer, $35–$40 single or double; the rest of the year, $45 single or double. **Parking:** Free.

The upstairs lobby of this simple, three-story hotel is a cool delight, with white wicker chairs and a balcony overlooking the ocean; it's up the hill on the south side of the Olas Altas cove. Ask for one of the seaside rooms, which have large balconies. All rooms have ceiling fans, and 10 have king-size beds (the rest have two full beds). The restaurant and bar are open daily from 7am to 10:30pm. Parking is enclosed.

DOWNTOWN/MIDTOWN

This downtown area, spreading from the zócalo to Playa Norte and nearly to Playa Olas Altas, includes the commercial hub of the town with bustling streets, countless shops, chronic parking problems, and a hundred little Mexican restaurants. Beware of traffic noise; at some hotels an interior room may be preferable.

Doubles For Less Than $15

HOTEL BELTRAN, Aquiles Serdan 2509 Nte., Mazatlán, Sin. 82000. Tel. 69/82-2776. 28 rms (all with bath).

$ Rates: $9 single; $11 double.

The rather dim, cubiclelike rooms of this two-story hotel two blocks in from the waterfront of Playa Norte overlook a narrow courtyard with a few benches. All come with two double beds, fans, and a small desk with wall mirror against the burgundy walls. There's a TV in the lobby.

HOTEL SANTA BARBARA, Juárez and 16 de Septiembre, Mazatlán, Sin. 82000. Tel. 69/82-2120. 31 rms (all with bath).

$ Rates: $10 single; $13 double.

Two blocks in from the waterfront of Playa Norte, the comfortable lobby has a group of rocking chairs, and the rooms are simple and clean cubicles. Some are a bit musty and dim, but all have fans and are pleasantly decorated with chenille bedspreads, wood furniture, and peach walls; six rooms are air-conditioned.

Doubles For Less Than $25

JONCOL'S HOTEL, Domínguez 2701 Nte., Mazatlán, Sin. 82000. Tel. 69/81-2131 or 81-3151. 37 rms (all with bath). TEL

$ Rates: $14 single; $16 double.

This large hotel on the first block in from the waterfront of Playa Norte offers large, clean rooms. Some have ceiling fans (15 are air-conditioned), balconies, and sea views. There's a TV in the lobby.

HOTEL MILAN, Canizales Pte. 717, Mazatlán, Sin. 82000. Tel. 69/81-3588. 24 rms (all with bath). TV TEL
$ Rates: High season, $15 single; $17 double. Low season, $11–$13 single or double.
The Milan is one block east of the cathedral between Aquiles Serdan and Benito Juárez. Rooms tend to be dark, but 17 are air-conditioned and all have fans. The staff is amiable and there's a cafeteria downstairs off the lobby, open Monday through Saturday from 8am to 9pm.

HOTEL VILLA DEL MAR, Aquiles Serdan Nte. 1506, Mazatlán, Sin. 82000. Tel. 69/81-3426. Fax 69/81-5221. 26 rms (all with bath). **Parking:** Free; space for eight cars.
$ Rates: $17 single or double.
Located in the center of town two blocks east of the cathedral near 21 de Marzo, this hotel offers at least six rocking chairs in the lobby. Rooms are simple and aging, but clean; all have fans, eight have air conditioners, and eight have TVs.

HOTEL DEL RÍO, Benito Juárez and Quijano, Mazatlán, Sin. 82000. Tel. 69/82-4654. 17 rms (all with bath).
$ Rates: $10 single; $18 double.
The rooms are small and austere but clean, with carved-wood headboards for a softening touch. Ask for one of the rooms with windows overlooking the street, as those facing the interior courtyard tend to be dark. A small flourescent bulb on the wall lights them at night. All have fans, most come with one full bed, and four have two double beds. The hotel is several blocks in from the waterfront of Playa Norte.

HOTEL CENTRAL, Domínguez Sur 2, Mazatlán, Sin. 82000. Tel. 69/82-1888. 67 rms (all with bath). A/C TEL
$ Rates: $20 single; $22 double.
Although a bit expensive, this hotel three blocks from the waterfront of Playa Olas Altas (near Angel Flores) offers pleasant, clean rooms with good beds; most have one single and one double bed, and 40 have TVs. The small café upstairs is open Monday through Saturday from 7am to 8pm.

THE GOLDEN ZONE [ZONA DORADA]

The Golden Zone is an elegant arc of golden sand serviced by a palm-lined boulevard and bordered by flashy hotels and a sprinkling of elaborate beach houses complete with high walls and watchdogs. A special bonus here is the sunset view, unique because of the three islands just offshore, which seem to melt gradually into the fading colors of evening. In summer as well as May and September, many hotels along this beach cut their prices.

Doubles For Less Than $20

HOTEL CABINAS AL MAR, Av. del Mar 123 (Apdo. Postal 444), Mazatlán, Sin. 82000. Tel. 69/81-5752. 24 rms (all with bath), 11 apartments. **Parking:** Free and protected.
$ Rates: $11 single; $14 double; $18 apartment for four.
Several rooms have one double bed and two singles—perfect for a family. All rooms have ceiling fans and the ones facing the sea have private balconies.

MOTEL SAN DIEGO, Camaron Sabalo and Rafael Buelna (Apdo. Postal 295), Mazatlán, Sin. 82000. Tel. 69/83-5703. 40 rms (all with bath). **Parking:** Free in front, but unprotected.
$ Rates: $12 single; $17 double.

Clean and comfortable, this budget establishment is actually two motels next door to each other and under the same management. There's no sea view here (it's on the traffic circle of the waterfront drive near Sabalo Beach, at the beginning of the Golden Zone), but it's only a few minutes' walk to one of Mazatlán's best beaches. Nine rooms are air-conditioned and 21 rooms have fans.

Doubles For Less Than $40

MOTEL DEL SOL, Av. del Mar (Apdo. Postal 400), Mazatlán, Sin. 82000. Tel. 69/85-1103. Fax 69/85-2603. 21 rms (all with bath). A/C TV TEL
$ Rates: $27 single or double; $35 with kitchenette. **Parking:** Free.
This modern brown hotel with shuttered windows is on the waterfront near the Pizza Hut, near the street leading to the Aquarium. It looks small from the street, but extends far back. Most rooms are modern and small; some have kitchenettes. Facilities include a swimming pool, travel agency, and parking spaces.

HOTEL SANDS, Av. del Mar 1910 (Apdo. Postal 309), Mazatlán, Sin. 82000. Tel. 69/82-0000 or 82-0600. 73 rms, 12 suites (all with bath). A/C TV TEL
$ Rates: $35 single or double; $44 suite for two. **Parking:** Free.
This three-story hotel on the waterfront drive a block from the bus station offers air-conditioned rooms with ceiling fans and refrigerators; some have balconies with a sea view. It also has a swimming pool and a restaurant nearby, La Rana Sonriente. Parking is enclosed.

POSADA DE DON PELAYO, Av. del Mar 1111 (Apdo. Postal 1088), Mazatlán, Sin. 82000. Tel. 69/83-1888. Fax 69/84-0799. 80 rms, 76 suites (all with bath). A/C MINIBAR TEL
$ Rates: $35 single or double; $48 suite for two. **Parking:** Free.
⭐ If you can afford to pay a little more, you can stay in this attractive and imposing hotel on the waterfront a few blocks south of the traffic circle. Every room has a king-size bed or two double beds, and those in front have beautiful sea views. Facilities include a restaurant, bar, two swimming pools, and tennis courts. Parking is enclosed.

WORTH THE EXTRA BUCKS

HOTEL AQUA MARINA, Av. del Mar 110 (Apdo. Postal 301), Mazatlán, Sin. 82000. Tel. 69/81-7080 or 81-7085, or toll free 800/528-1234 in the U.S. 100 rms (all with bath). A/C MINIBAR TV TEL
$ Rates: $46 single or double.
This two-story motel has palm trees, a parking lot, and a little pool in front. The beach is across the street, and if you get a room on the second floor, you'll be able to sit out on a small private terrace and enjoy the view. On the premises are a restaurant, bar, travel agency, and tobacco shop. The Aqua Marina is part of the Best Western chain, so you can call the toll-free number above to reserve a room; however, the rates will be several dollars higher than if you contact the hotel directly.

EL CID RESORT, Av. Camaron Sabalo, Mazatlán 82000, Sin. Tel. 69/83-3333, or toll free 800/525-1925 in the U.S. Fax 69/84-1311. 1,000 rms and suites (all with bath). A/C MINIBAR TV TEL
$ Rates: $75–$110 single or double; more for suites; 15% less in summer.
⭐ This huge resort at the northern end of the Golden Zone is the city's largest employer, with a staff of more than 2,000. The 1,000-acre complex includes 17 restaurants and lounges, a disco, a health spa and fitness center, six heated swimming pools, 17 lighted tennis courts, and an 18-hole golf course. The Hotel Granada Country Club section, across the street near the golf course (not on the beach), generally charges lower rates than the two waterfront towers. Rooms in the newer tower, El Moro, are spacious and contemporary (many are suites), with private balconies and marble-trimmed baths; suites have kitchenettes. Rooms in the four-story older section overlooking the sea (my preference) come with two double beds that slide partially under counters during the day to appear like couches, and chunky

contemporary wood furniture. But ask to see the room first and make sure the air conditioning and elevator work before splurging here.

WHERE TO EAT

Mazatlán is a great town for tasty seafood prepared in a variety of ways, and boasts the largest shrimp fleet in the world. Yet seafood here is not cheap, and often Mexican plates are the best bargain.

An alternative to eating in a restaurant is to stop at one of the many *loncherías* scattered throughout the downtown area. A torta (a sandwich on a small French roll), stuffed with a variety of meats, cheeses, tomatoes, onions, and chiles, generally costs $1 or less.

DOWNTOWN & PLAYA OLAS ALTAS
Meals For Less Than $5

MENUDO, B. Domínguez and Escobedo.
  Specialty: MEXICAN.
$ **Prices:** Breakfast with eggs $2; menudo $3.50; comida corrida $3.50.
  Open: Mon–Sat 8am–4pm (comida corrida served noon–4pm).

Named after the hearty tripe stew that is the Mexican cure for a hangover, this plain lunchroom with wooden tables dishes up inexpensive breakfasts, menudo, and plate-lunch specials. It's on a corner two blocks west of the zócalo.

TORTAS HAWAII, Valle and Nelson.
  Specialty: SANDWICHES.
$ **Prices:** Sandwiches $2.50–$4.50.
  Open: Mon–Sat 9am–10pm.

This Mexican franchise one block north of the cathedral serves large, round tortas (Mexican sandwiches) stuffed with a variety of meats and melted cheeses. They're quick, inexpensive, and tasty—some locals swear they're the best sandwiches in the city. There's another branch on the Malecón near the Golden Zone.

Meals For Less Than $10

LOS COMALES, Angel Flores 908.
  Specialty: MEXICAN.
$ **Prices:** Appetizers $1–$6; main courses $3.50–$8; sandwiches $2; enchiladas, tacos, chilaquiles, or quesadillas $2.50–$3.50; beef, chicken, or fish $5–$7; chicken mole $6.
  Open: Daily 8am–10:30pm.

High ceilings with fans keep this neighborhood restaurant cool, while bright plaid tablecloths and murals portraying birds, butterflies, and fish provide the funky decor. Mexican home-cooking stars here, including some of the best chicken mole—rich, dark, and velvety—in town. Other dishes from the bilingual menu worth sampling are pork in green sauce, beef stew, pozole (a hearty pork-and-hominy stew), and beef liver with onion sauce. Los Comales is a block east of the cathedral and zócalo.

RESTAURANT MADRID, Olas Altas 166. Tel. 81-7480.
  Specialty: MEXICAN.
$ **Prices:** Appetizers $1.25–$7; main courses $3.50–$9; comida corrida $5.50; cheese fondue or guacamole for two $5.25–$6.25; red snapper or steak for two (including glass of wine) $13; full breakfast $2.50.
  Open: Daily 7am–midnight

It's easy to linger over a meal or drinks at the sidewalk tables of this leisurely establishment, with its lovely view of tiny Olas Altas Beach. The service here is slow but friendly. The bilingual menu includes a different special every day.

RESTAURANT ALOHA, Canizales 725. Tel. 81-6710.
  Specialty: MEXICAN.

$ Prices: Soup $1–$6; main courses $3.50–$11; fish $3–$5; shrimp dishes $11; beefsteak $5; comida corrida $4.
Open: Daily 7am–10pm (comida corrida served noon–5pm).

This plain Formica-dinette café is short on ambience, but the shrimp dishes are about half the Golden Zone price. The menu also includes Mexican antojitos (appetizers). The front is open to the sidewalk. It's a block east of the cathedral, near the Hotel Milanut (Canizales becomes 21 de Marzo).

JONCOL'S, Flores 608 Pte. Tel. 81-2187.
Specialty: MEXICAN.
$ Prices: Appetizers $1.50–$6; main courses $3.50–$11; ham and eggs $2.50; shrimp soup $6; comida corrida $5; meat, fish, or chicken $5–$8.50; enchiladas $3.50.
Open: Daily 7am–11pm (comida corrida served noon–4pm).

This well-established, air-conditioned restaurant two blocks west of the zócalo has the feeling of a diner with a dining room. Wood paneling covers the walls and red tablecloths brighten up the room. Patrons can choose from 13 different kinds of soup.

Meals For Less Than $15

COPA DE LECHE, Olas Altas 33 Sur. Tel. 82-5753.
Specialty: MEXICAN.
$ Prices: Appetizers $2.50–$6; main courses $4–$13; banana split $2; fish soup $2.50; shrimp stuffed with cheese and bacon $13; Alambre barbecue for two $11.
Open: Daily 7am–11pm.

This shaded sidewalk café on the waterfront at Playa Olas Altas has the feeling of Mazatlán in the 1930s, and it's still the most popular in town. The food is consistently as good as the ocean view. Its menu includes Alambre barbecue (beef cooked with onion, peppers, mushrooms, ham, and bacon) and fresh seafood. The bar is an old wooden boat.

DONEY'S, Mariano Escobedo 610. Tel. 81-2651.
Specialty: MEXICAN.
$ Prices: Appetizers $1.50–$8; main courses $4–$13; comida corrida $8; Mexican plate $7.
Open: Daily 8am–10pm (comida corrida served 1–4pm).

This tried-and-true favorite, in a converted colonial home immediately south of the zócalo on the corner of 5 de Mayo, is regarded by many locals as the best moderately priced restaurant downtown. The mood under the brick domes covering the interior courtyard is serene, while stained glass, handsome woodwork, and old sepia photographs add a turn-of-the-century flavor, especially when piano music fills the air. The large menu includes what some claim is the best apple pie in town.

RESTAURANT MAMUCAS, Bolívar Pte. 404. Tel. 81-3490.
Specialty: MEXICAN.
$ Prices: Appetizers $6; main courses $8–$20; seafood soup $6; fish $8; seafood grill for two $28.
Open: Daily 10:30am–9:30pm.

Fresh, moderately priced seafood is the specialty here. Have a feast beginning with shrimp cocktail or oysters, then grilled fish, coffee, and dessert. The bilingual menu includes smoked marlin, a mixed platter, stuffed squid, octopus, oysters, and seafood soup. For a big meal, the best deal is the seafood grill for two. The Mamucas is 1½ blocks east of Joncol's Hotel.

NORTH BEACH & THE GOLDEN ZONE
Meals For Less Than $10

LA CARRETA, in the Costa de Oro Hotel, Camaron-Sabalo. Tel. 83-5344.
Specialty: MEXICAN/BREAKFAST.
$ Prices: Breakfast $2–$6.
Open: Breakfast 7–11:30am.

A delightful place to eat breakfast by the sea is this outdoor restaurant, on a platform overlooking the waves in the Golden Zone, a bit south of the El Cid Resort. Tables are shaded by thatched palapas. Service is friendly and attentive, and the waiter leaves a thermal pot of coffee on your table.

LA PARRILLADA No. 1, Av. del Mar 1004.
 Specialty: MEXICAN.
$ Prices: Appetizers $1.50–$4; main courses $4–$7.50; T-bone steak or chuleta (pork chop) $7.50.
 Open: Dinner only, daily 5pm–midnight.
Grilled meat is the specialty at this small, open-air restaurant on the waterfront drive north of Señor Frog's. Here you can watch the food sizzling in the open kitchen under a tile roof. Diners sit at a dozen umbrella-shaded tables. There's another Parrillada No. 1 in front of the Aquarium, just a block off the Malecón.

Meals For Less Than $15

PEPE TORO, Las Garzas 18. Tel. 84-4176.
 Specialty: MEXICAN.
$ Prices: Appetizers $2.50–$5; main courses $5–$14; beef burrito, chimichanga, cheese-stuffed chili, bean enchilada, or red enchilada combo $8.
 Open: Daily 8am–11pm.
Open in the front, with tables looking out on the sidewalk, this restaurant serves Mexico City–style food in a rustic setting reminiscent of Mexican ranches. Patrons at leather *equipales* tables and chairs dine under brick arches and wrought-iron fixtures. Some dishes are grilled outside. Pepe Toro is in the Golden Zone one block from Jungle Juice and close to the waterfront drive.

JUNGLE JUICE, Las Garzas and Laguna. Tel. 83-3315.
 Specialty: MEXICAN.
$ Prices: Appetizers $1.25–$5; main courses $7–$17; lobster, shrimp, or steak-and-lobster dinner $15; bananas flambé $5.
 Open: Restaurant, daily 7:30am–10:30pm; bar, daily 4pm–midnight (happy hour at 6–7pm and 9–10pm with two drinks for the price of one).
A front patio surrounded by lattice and an upstairs bar hung with piñatas give this restaurant a festive air. Smoothies and many kinds of juices are specialties, plus dishes grilled over mesquite on the patio. This casual spot also serves good breakfasts and makes a nice stop after shopping in the Golden Zone (it's about a block in from the waterfront drive and a block east of the Hotel Playa Mazatlán). Look for daily specials on the blackboard.

WORTH THE EXTRA BUCKS

SEÑOR FROG'S, North Beach Malecón, Av. del Mar. Tel. 85-1110 or 82-1925.
 Specialty: MEXICAN.
$ Prices: Appetizers $2.50–$5; main courses $3.50–$20; seafood or meat dishes $8–$20.
 Open: Daily noon–midnight.
A sign over the door says JUST ANOTHER BAR & GRILL, but the line waiting to get in says just the opposite. The decor is delightfully silly, the food and loud music are great, and the atmosphere is friendly and lively. Revelers have been known to dance on the tables late at night. And the food is among the best in town. Try the great ribs, Caesar salad, or mango crêpes. It's on the waterfront drive at Playa Norte, next to the Frankie Oh! disco.

EL MARINERO, Paseo Claussen and 5 de Mayo. Tel. 81-7682.
 Specialty: MEXICAN/SEAFOOD.
$ Prices: Appetizers $2–$7; main courses $7–$20; shrimp $10; chicken mole $7.
 Open: Daily noon–11pm (mariachis play 7:30–10pm).
Festooned with shell curtains made by local fishermen, seashell chandeliers, columns wrapped with rope, and other nautical bric-a-brac, this casual, friendly restaurant is a

fine place for a leisurely dinner while mariachis play. Shrimp is prepared at least half a dozen ways, all of them delicious, especially the "Adobo"—made with roasted red peppers and almonds. Some dishes are brought sizzling to the table on a ceramic grill. El Marinero is on the waterfront drive at Playa Norte, near the Fisherman's Monument.

LOS ARCOS, Camaron Sabalo. Tel. 83-9577.
   Specialty: MEXICAN/SEAFOOD.
$ Prices: Appetizers $2–$6; main courses $8–$15.
   Open: Daily noon–10pm.
Piñatas, shell mobiles, plants, and twinkle lights are suspended beneath the big, round thatched roof of this lively restaurant that's popular with locals. Delicious sauces with seafood are the house specialty, among them a mole, a green sauce, a mushroom sauce with chiles, and a tequila and red wine sauce. The fish "chilico"—baked in a zesty green sauce topped with bubbling white cheese—is highly recommended. You'll find Los Arcos between the El Cid Resort and the Holiday Inn, but on the opposite (east) side of the street.

EL SHRIMP BUCKET, in the Hotel La Siesta, Av. Olas Altas 11. Tel. 81-6350 or 82-8019.
   Specialty: MEXICAN/SEAFOOD. **Reservations:** During major holidays.
$ Prices: Appetizers $3–$10; main courses $8–$20; fish or steak $9–$11; shrimp or seafood $16–$20.
   Open: Daily 6am–11pm; separate piano bar, La Cantina, daily 3–11pm.
★ Sample some of the best shrimp in town in the air-conditioned dining room or under umbrellas on the patio. The marimbas start tinkling around 7pm, and for wining, dining, and dancing, this is a great place for a splurge. Opened in 1962, this restaurant on the waterfront at Playa Olas Altas launched the Carlos Anderson chain, which now includes more than 50 restaurants in four countries.

READERS RECOMMEND

Pastelería Panama, Domínguez and Sixto Osuna (tel. 81-7517).—*"After we discovered the Pastelería Panama we ate the rest of our meals there. We like to get up and eat breakfast early and they open at 7am."*—Helen Prouix, Lakeside, Ore. [*Author's Note:* Ms. Prouix thoughtfully sent along a menu, which shows a full range of Mexican breakfast favorites for $3.50 to $4, a good selection of sandwiches for $2 to $3, Mexican plates for $2.50 to $4, and soups for $1.50. There are three other locations.]

SHOPPING

The **Golden Zone** is the place to shop. For a huge selection of handcrafts from all over Mexico, visit the **Mazatlán Arts and Crafts Center** Calle Gaviotas and Loaiza (tel. 83-5022); the shop sometimes organizes crafts-oriented tours of mountain villages. For interesting fabrics and clothing, check out the **Tequila Tree,** Rodolfo Loaiza 401 (tel. 83-5323), north of the Hotel Playa Mazatlán. **O'Houlihan's,** Camaron Sabalo 777 (tel. 84-0478), south of the El Cid Resort, has a good selection of silver jewelry. Most stores in the Golden Zone open Monday through Saturday at 9 or 10am and close between 6 and 8pm; some close for lunch between 1 and 4pm. Some stores are also open on Sunday afternoon.

EVENING ENTERTAINMENT

There's a **fireworks** show every Sunday, beginning at 8pm, on the beach fronting the Hotel Playa Mazatlán in the Golden Zone on Camaron Sabalo (tel. 83-4444). The display is visible from the beach or from the hotel's terrace restaurant. The restaurant offers a great view of the sunset and live music for dancing nightly from 7pm to midnight.

    This hotel also presents an excellent **Fiesta Mexicana,** complete with buffet, open bar, folkloric dancing, and live music for some high-stepping of your own.

Fiestas are presented nightly, beginning at 7pm; try to arrive at 6pm to get a good table. Tickets are $25.

Several other hotels in this area also have similar shows. The **Maya Show** in the Maya Pyramid building across from the Hotel Flores in the Golden Zone is held on Tuesday, Thursday, and Saturday at 7pm (tel. 84-5380). Admission is $25.

Check with the Tourism Office (tel. 83-2545 or 84-0222) or a local travel agency for details; most travel agencies can arrange tickets.

DISCOS & BARS

VALENTINO'S, Punta Camaron, near the Camaron Sabalo traffic circle. Tel. 83-6212 or 83-5111.

Dramatically perched on a rocky outcropping overlooking the sea, this disco offers a magnificent view from one of its dance floors (there are two). It also puts on a good hi-tech light show complete with green laser beams, and for a break from the pulsating dance floor there are pool tables in another room and some quiet (relatively) areas for talking. Open daily from 9pm until 4am. Drinks run $2 to $4.
Admission: $8.

EL CARACOL, at the El Cid Resort, Camaron Sabalo. Tel. 83-3333.

This large, multilevel disco has modern lights, video screens, and a booming sound system. Spiral slides connect several levels, making possible a quick arrival at the dance floor. Open daily from 9pm to 4am (closed on Monday during low season). Drinks cost $2 to $4.
Admission: Sun–Thurs $5, Fri–Sat $6.50.

JOE'S OYSTER BAR, off Loaiza on the beachfront at Los Sabalos Hotel. Tel. 83-5333.

Beer, burgers, fresh oysters, and loud music are the house specialties at this casual, open-air gathering place, where patrons watch over the beach activities below from rustic picnic tables. Open daily from 11am to 2am. Beer runs $2; margaritas, $3.
Admission: Free.

CAFE PACÍFICO, Frías and Constitución. Tel. 85-2583.

If you're staying downtown, this bodegalike bar in a restored historic building on Plazuela Machado is a pleasant place to spend some time. The doors are inset with stained glass, while the thick roof beams and walls are hung with braided garlic, dried peppers, and old photographs. Another room contains a pool table. Open Monday through Saturday from 11am to midnight and on Sunday from 3pm to midnight. Beer costs $1.50, and margaritas are $2.50 to $5.
Admission: Free.

CHAPTER 4

THE COPPER CANYON

The Copper Canyon (Canyon del Cobre) is said to be four times larger than the Grand Canyon, made up of 20 canyons. Through the Copper Canyon runs the famed *Chihuahua al Pacífico* Railway. Acclaimed as an engineering miracle, it covers 390 miles, has 39 bridges and 86 tunnels, and loops down to sea level and up to 9,000 feet and back again through some of Mexico's most majestic pastel-colored, rugged mountain and pine-forest country.

The name of the train line conceptualizes the idea of linking arid, desertlike Chihuahua with the natural port of Topolobampo, a few miles west of Los Mochis. American Albert Kinsey Owen, who invested in the project of building the railroad, envisioned it as the shortest route for goods from Kansas City to the Pacific.

Within the Copper Canyon region live the reclusive Tarahumara Indians, in tiny settlements of small log huts in summer and in caves in winter. They have remained aloof from modern civilization, retreating to the rugged canyons and subsisting on corn, tortillas, beans, and herding a few goats and cattle. The men wear sandals, white loincloths, and colorful headbands. Women, who often go barefoot, wear colorful cotton skirts and ruffled blouses. Although they weave fine thick wool blankets, they don't wear wool, even in harsh canyon winters. Social and ritual gatherings are centered around *tesguino,* a fermented corn drink, and because of the frequency of these gatherings, many Tarahumara are alcoholics. They suffer from tuberculosis and other respiratory diseases, but their plight has been addressed by Father Verplunken, a Jesuit missionary based in Creel, and by the Flying Doctors, a group of volunteer U.S. medical professionals, who provide health care. Many Tarahumara children attend boarding school in Creel or Cerocahui, returning home on weekends.

SEEING THE COPPER CANYON

Los Mochis is one of the entrances to the fabulous Canyon del Cobre (Copper Canyon) aboard the Chihuahua–Pacifico train. Chihuahua, on the other side of the canyons, is the other boarding point. Generally speaking Los Mochis is recommended as the preferable starting place for this trip because the most scenic part of the 12- to 15-hour journey is between El Fuerte and Creel, and the chances of seeing it in good daylight are best if the trip begins in Los Mochis. If the train from Chihuahua to Los Mochis runs on schedule (and it has all the times I've taken it) you can also be assured of daylight during the best part of the trip; but if you don't want to take a chance, then it's best to start in Los Mochis or El Fuerte. Chihuahua, however, is the more interesting starting point.

A trip on the train with stops to stay at lodges en route is an adventure, fraught with the possibility of uncertainty even when you've planned every last detail. Accommodations are comfortable but rustic; most don't have electricity (lanterns provide light), and only in Creel and El Fuerte are there telephones. Rooms have wood-burning stoves for heat in winter.

Peak travel times in the canyon are at the end of February, in March, April, and October, and at the beginning of November. Off-season months are July, August,

WHAT'S SPECIAL ABOUT THE COPPER CANYON

The Canyons
- ☐ Four times larger than the Grand Canyon, comprised of approximately 20 canyons.

The Railroad
- ☐ The Copper Canyon Railroad, covering 390 miles, took 112 years to build and has 86 tunnels and 39 bridges.

Tarahumara Indians
- ☐ Nomadic, shy Tarahumara Indians numbering around 50,000, famous as long-distance runners, for pre-Hispanic customs and Easter celebrations, and as rug and basket weavers.

Excursions
- ☐ Hiking deep into the canyon or going by four-wheel-drive vehicle, and staying in rustic lodges, some with canyon vistas.

Museums
- ☐ Pancho Villa Museum, where Villa lived in Chihuahua, now the Museum of the Revolution.
- ☐ Architecturally exquisite, the Regional Museum of Chihuahua, an exact replica of a French Second Empire neoclassical mansion built in 1910.

Special Cities and Villages
- ☐ Batopilas, an 18th-century silver-mining village hidden at the bottom of the canyon.
- ☐ Modern Chihuahua, capital of Chihuahua state, noted for its colonial architecture, beefsteaks, and museum/home of Pancho Villa.
- ☐ Mennonite farming community at Cuauhtémoc near Chihuahua.

January, mid-November, and December. You can pass through the Copper Canyon in one 15-hour day, spending a night in Chihuahua and another in Los Mochis, but you miss the essence of the canyon. I'd recommend at least 1 or 2 nights with stops along the way.

If you spend a night en route, you'll have roughly 24 hours at each destination—usually enough time for one or two excursions. Creel, a rustic lumber town, offers the only economical lodgings in the canyon and some of the best side trips, especially hiking and overnight camping—but there are van tours too. Every stop is interesting, but Creel and Cerocahui offer the most possibilities.

Drivers from all canyon hotels await trains, and if you don't have a reservation you can ask the driver about room availability. However, the hotels are quite small and groups often fill them up, so it's almost imperative to make reservations in advance, especially in peak season.

1. LOS MOCHIS

126 miles S of Alamos, 50 miles W of El Fuerte,
193 miles S of Guaymas, 260 miles N of Mazatlán

GETTING THERE By Plane Aeroméxico, Gabriel Leyva 168 (tel. 5-2580 or 2-0062, or 5-2575 at the airport), has direct service with Hermosillo. **Servicio Aereo Leo Lopez,** Guillermo Prieto 864 (tel. 2-9482 or 2-9483), flies between El Paso and Chihuahua daily and between Chihuahua and Los Mochis on Monday, Wednesday, and Friday. **Aero California,** Hidalgo 440 Poniente (tel. 2-8466 or 2-6790), flies from La Paz.

By Train *El Sinaloense* leaves Guadalajara at midnight and passes through

Mazatlán before arriving in Los Mochis at 11:30am. The Copper Canyon train, known as *El Nuevo Chihuahua–Pacífico* (mentioned above), runs daily between Chihuahua (leaving at 7am) and Los Mochis (arriving at 7pm). You'll find complete Copper Canyon train information in Section 2.

By Bus   Los Mochis is marginally served by buses. Most passing through are *de paso*. Tres Estrellas de Oro is the first-class line, with buses hourly from Mazatlán, Guadalajara, and Mexico City. All buses from Navojoa (the connecting point from Alamos) are *de paso*.

By Car   Coastal Highway 15 is well maintained in both directions leading into Los Mochis.

By Ferry   From La Paz to Topolobampo, the daily SEMATUR ferry leaves La Paz at 8pm and arrives in Los Mochis at 4am. Dangerous cargo is carried on Monday and Tuesday. Only chair seats are available.

DEPARTING   By Plane   The **Aeroméxico** office is at Gabriel Leyva 168 (tel. 5-2580 or 2-0062, or 5-2575 at the airport). The office of **Servicio Aereo Leo Lopez** is at Guillermo Prieto 864 (tel. 2-9482 or 2-9483). The **Aero California** office is at Hidalgo 440 Poniente (tel. 2-8466 or 2-6790).

By Train   *El Sinoalense* leaves Los Mochis at 4:40pm and arrives in Guadalajara the next day at 10am. The *Chihuahua al Pacífico/Copper Canyon* train leaves at 6am (mountain/Los Mochis time); taxis charge $6 from downtown to the station.

By Bus   Each bus line has its own terminal in this city. **Tres Estrellas de Oro,** Calle Obregón 61 Pte., at Allende (tel. 2-1757), is in the center of town, but the others are only six blocks away; it serves Mexico City (24-hour trip), Guadalajara (16-hour trip), and Mazatlán hourly. The *Expreso de Lujo* (luxury express) between Mazatlán and Los Mochis has half the seats of a regular bus, a club section, and video movies, and costs $15 one way. From Navojoa (the crossroads connection to Alamos, 2½ hours north) all buses are *de paso*. **Transportes Norte de Sonora,** Avenida Morelos 33 Pte., at Zaragoza (tel. 2-0411), and **Transportes del Pacífico,** Avenida Morelos 337 Pte. (tel. 2-0347 or 2-0341), next door, make the same runs but almost all are *de paso*. For buses that originate here and pass through Navojoa (crossroads to Alamos) go to the ticket booth in the back of the station. Eleven buses go to Navojoa, the first at 5am and the last at 5pm. The awful bus station for **El Fuerte** (1½ hours) is around the corner and through the alley from the Santa Anita Hotel. Buses, which run frequently throughout the day, are the school-bus variety and the purser stows luggage in the back of the bus. Were it not for the numerous stops en route, the trip would take an hour.

By Ferry   The **SEMATUR ferry** to La Paz, Baja California, leaves the nearby port of Topolobampo daily at 10pm, an 8-hour trip. For tickets and information, the SEMATUR ferry office in Los Mochis is at R. G. Castro 132 Oeste, Los Mochis, Sin., 81200 (tel. 681/5-8262). Bring your own food and drink. The newer and faster *Baja Express* leaves Topolobampo daily at 3pm for a 5-hour trip to La Paz. Travel agents sell *Baja Express* tickets or you can go to the office in Los Mochis at Hidalgo 546 (tel. 681/2-0302).

Los Mochis, Sinaloa (alt. 243 ft.; pop. 350,000), founded in 1703 by an American, Benjamin Johnson of Pennsylvania, is a wealthy city in a fertile agricultural area and, aside from the enormous sugar mill at the northwestern end of town, there's not much of note. The city's architecture is distinctly American. The town's importance to the tourist is as a boarding point for the Ferrocarril Chihuahua al Pacífico train. From the port at Topolobampo Bay nearby, you can take a ferry to get to La Paz, in Baja California.

ORIENTATION

ARRIVING The **airport** is several miles north of town. Take a *combi* (van) from the airport into town for $6.25; taxis are twice that. All **bus stations** are downtown within walking distance of the hotels. By **ferry** in Topolobampo, you'll have to bargain with waiting taxis for the fare to Los Mochis. The **train station** is about 3 miles from town and taxis charge around $6 to the central city.

INFORMATION The **City Tourist Office,** at Cuauhtémoc and Allende (tel. 681/5-0405), has a helpful staff and usually someone who speaks English is around. The office is open Monday through Friday from 8am to 3pm.

CITY LAYOUT Los Mochis contains no central plaza. To acquaint yourself with this city, use the Tres Estrellas de Oro bus station, Calle Obregón 61 Pte., at Allende, as an orientation point. The other bus stations, hotels, and restaurants are within two to six blocks of the station.

Plaza Fiesta Las Palmas, at the corner of Obregón and Rosales, is the shopping mall and the main spot where people of all ages gather, an interesting slice of Mexican life. Ley, a large store, sells everything from groceries to clothes to televisions.

GETTING AROUND Hotels, restaurants, and the Plaza Fiesta Las Palmas are all within walking distance of downtown.

FAST FACTS

American Express The local representative is Viajes Kristal, Avenida Alvaro Obregón 471-A Pte. (tel. 681/2-2084; fax 681/5-6827).

Area Code The telephone area code is 681

Time The entire railroad operates on central time, despite the fact that Los Mochis is in the mountain time zone.

WHAT TO SEE & DO

For most travelers, Los Mochis is a stopover en route to somewhere else. There isn't much of importance here, but the town is pleasant, and you can enjoy some of the best seafood in Mexico.

A city tour, hunting and fishing trips, and boat rides around Topolobampo Bay can be arranged through the **Viajes Flamingo** travel agency, on the ground floor of the Hotel Santa Anita; it's open from 8:30am to 1pm and 3 to 6pm. The boat ride is really just a spin in the bay, and not particularly noteworthy although the bay is pretty.

Topolobampo also has a nice beach, but the town isn't much. To get to Topolobampo, catch the bus at the corner of Obregón and Degollado, across from the Hotel Catalina.

WHERE TO STAY

HOTEL FENIX, Angel Flores 365, Los Mochis, Sin. 81200. Tel. 681/2-2623. 40 rms (all with bath). A/C TV TEL

$ Rates: $17 single; $21 double; $24 triple.

The Hotel Fenix is a good downtown choice. Make reservations or arrive before noon, as it fills up early. It's clean, carpeted, and offers laundry and dry-cleaning service. A small cafeteria, serving Monday through Saturday from 7am to noon and 5 to 10pm, opens onto the hotel lobby.

From the Tres Estrellas bus station, walk left four blocks, then turn right onto Flores; the hotel is behind the Hotel Santa Anita.

HOTEL AMERICA, Allende 655 Sur, Los Mochis, Sin. 81200. Tel. 681/2-1355, 2-1905, or 2-1356. 46 rms (all with bath). A/C TEL

$ Rates: $17 single; $21 double. **Parking:** Free.

The clean marble-floored lobby is an indication of the maintenance of this hotel 2½ short blocks from the Tres Estrellas bus station. The freshly painted rooms have tile floors and large windows facing the street. Rooms away from the Allende side will avoid the noise of the early-morning mufferless local buses. On the second floor there's a sitting area, purified water, and ice-making machine. Parking is off-street and enclosed.

HOTEL CATALINA, Obregón 48 Pte., Los Mochis, Sin. 81200. Tel. 681/2-1246 or 2-1137. 50 rms (all with bath). A/C TV TEL
$ Rates: $17 single; $23 double.

The Hotel Catalina, opposite the Tres Estrellas bus station, at the corner of Allende, is grossly overpriced for the quality of maintenance. Walls are dirty and the air conditioning may not function, so check first. This is a last-ditch suggestion if you can't find anything else. The lobby is spartan but functional, with a color TV.

HOTEL BELTRAN, Hidalgo 281 Pte., Los Mochis, Sin. 81200. Tel. 681/2-0710. 53 rms (all with bath). A/C TEL
$ Rates: $17 single; $21 double (one bed).

The Hotel Beltran continues to have its ups and downs. Rooms are clean, with old-fashioned furniture and air conditioning that may or may not work. Some of the rooms have a view of the city and 15 have TVs. Bottles of purified water are on each floor and there's an ice-making machine in the lobby. On the second floor are sitting areas with rocking chairs.

From the Tres Estrellas bus station, turn left onto Obregón for one block, turn right onto Prieto for one block, and then left onto Hidalgo; the hotel is at the corner of Zaragoza, on left around the corner from the Hotel Santa Anita.

HOTEL LORENA, Obregón 186 Pte., Los Mochis, Sin. 81200. Tel. 681/2-0239 or 2-0958. 40 rms (all with bath). A/C TV TEL
$ Rates: $19 single; $23 double; $31 triple.

All the rooms in the Hotel Lorena, at the corner of Obregón and Guillermo Prieto, a block from the Tres Estrellas bus station, open on to wide hallways lined with big, comfortable rocking chairs, with groups of tables and chairs at either end of the hall. All rooms have windows but only a few have views. Owner Yoni Felix speaks English. A third-floor cafeteria is open Monday through Saturday from 7 to 11am and 7 to 11pm.

WORTH THE EXTRA BUCKS

HOTEL SANTA ANITA, Leyva at the corner of Hidalgo (Apdo. Postal 159), Los Mochis, Sin. 81200. Tel. 681/5-7046. Fax 681/2-0046. 133 rms (all with bath). A/C TV TEL
$ Rates: $65 single; $75 double. **Parking:** $1.75 daily.

The nicest hotel in Los Mochis is the Hotel Santa Anita, 4½ blocks down Obregón from the Tres Estrellas bus station. Recently completely remodeled, the rooms are nicely furnished although most are small. All are carpeted and have comfortable beds, color TV with U.S. channels, and tap water purified for drinking. The hotel's excellent and popular restaurant is off the lobby. There are two bars, one of them with live music at least 1 day a week.

Another special feature: Every morning at 5:15am a private hotel bus takes guests to the *Chihuahua al Pacifico* train, which departs daily at 6am. That saves the $6 taxi ride. The lobby travel agency, Viajes Flamingo (tel. 681/2-1613 or 2-1929), is about the best in town; you can buy your train tickets here, and find out about all the other touristic activities in the area.

WHERE TO EAT

RESTAURANT EL GORDO, Zaragoza and Morelos. Tel. 2-0099.
Specialty: MEXICAN.
$ Prices: Comida corrida $3.25.

Open: Daily 7am–5pm (comida corrida served 1–5pm).

This delightful and spotless little restaurant was created for locals on a budget and suits me just fine. Presided over by three stalwart dueñas, it's decorated in green-and-white checks and has windows on two sides. The food is excellent and you have a choice of three filling comidas which might include meatballs in chipotle sauce, chiles relleños, fish, or a pork stew. All come with rice, soup, tortillas, and a soft drink. Highly recommended.

To get here, facing the Santa Anita Hotel, walk right for four blocks and then turn right onto Morelos for one block; it's half a block from the Norte de Sonora bus station.

EL TAQUITO, Leyva at Barrera.
Specialty: MEXICAN.
$ Prices: Breakfast $1.75–$7; main courses $2–$10.
Open: Daily 24 hours.

Any time of the day or night, El Taquito has its share of locals enjoying some of the best food in town or lingering over a third cup of coffee. The café, 1½ blocks left of the Hotel Santa Anita, looks like an American fast-food place with orange Formica tables and booths. The tortilla soup comes in a large bowl, and main-course portions are large.

RESTAURANT HENRY, Hidalgo 147 Pte. Tel. 2-3959.
Specialty: SEAFOOD.
$ Prices: Soup $3.50; main courses $4–$6.
Open: Daily 9am–8pm.

Restaurant Henry is a large restaurant specializing in seafood; you'll see fresh oysters being opened in the window, and aquariums inside. The restaurant is popular for its fresh seafood and low prices: shrimp (prepared nine ways), fish filets (prepared in 13 ways), and machacas (six different kinds), Chinese platters (16 different dishes), and several kinds of seafood cocktails and soups. The restaurant is 1½ blocks south of the Hotel Beltran, between Prieto and Allende.

WORTH THE EXTRA BUCKS

RESTAURANT ESPAÑA, Obregón 525. Tel. 2-2221 or 2-2335.
Specialty: SEAFOOD/INTERNATIONAL.
$ Prices: Breakfast $4–$7; comida corrida $7–$16; main courses $6–$18; paella $6.
Open: Daily 7am–midnight (comida corrida served Mon–Fri 1–4:30pm).

Bullfighting prints decorate the walls of this modern restaurant (opened in 1988); many plants, and both air conditioning and ceiling fans, complement the pleasant decor. The food is good, the portions are large, and the prices are moderate to high. There's a full page of seafood followed by other choices such as filet mignon with mushrooms or chateaubriand, liver and onions, or chicken enchiladas. Thursday or Sunday you can order the special paella valenciana. There's full bar service as well.

To get here from the Hotel Santa Anita, walk south on Obregón one block to the corner of Flores; the restaurant is on the right.

EL FARALLON, Obregón 495. Tel. 2-1428 or 2-1273.
Specialty: SEAFOOD.
$ Prices: Appetizers $3.50–$6; main courses $7.50–$12.
Open: Daily 8am–11pm.

If your budget can stand a splurge, try the finest restaurant in Los Mochis; it's 1½ blocks from the Hotel Santa Anita, on the left at the corner of Flores. The walls are painted with murals depicting the wealth of the Sea of Cortez and also the new agricultural pride of the area: the dam on the Fuerte River. Fish nets strung about, seashells, sharks' jaws, and glass fishing floats complete the nautical decor. The food here is excellent. You can get a dinner of fish or shrimp, frog's legs, and crab, and for dessert you might want to try a fresh melon with ice cream. There's full bar service too, and the margaritas are excellent.

2. THE COPPER CANYON TRAIN

TRAIN DEPARTURE TIMES

From Los Mochis		From Chihuahua	
Los Mochis	6am (Mountain Time)	Chihuahua	7am
El Fuerte	7:30am	Creel	noon
Bahuichivo/Cerocahui	9:30am	El Divisadero	1pm
El Divisadero	noon	Bahuichivo/Cerocahui	3:30pm
Creel	1pm	El Fuerte	5:30pm
Chihuahua (arrives)	6pm	Los Mochis (arrives)	7pm

Note: The railroad runs on central time, although Los Mochis is on mountain time. This means that if the train is scheduled to depart Los Mochis at 7am railway time, it pulls out at 6am local time. Be aware of that when reading a printed schedule.

The longest train stop where passengers can see the canyons is the 10-minute stop at El Divisadero—barely enough time to dash to the canyon's edge for a look.

BUYING A TICKET In Los Mochis, the Ferrocarril Chihuahua al Pacífico station is about 3 miles from the center of town on a Netzahualcoyotl Street. This is the station for *El Nuevo Chihuahua–Pacífico,* which runs between Los Mochis and Chihuahua from both directions simultaneously daily. Tickets are on sale Monday through Friday from 5:30am to 9am and 11am to 2pm, on Saturday from 5:30 to 8:30am, and on Sunday between 6 and 9am; and every afternoon from 4 to 6pm. A one-way ticket in either direction in Primera Especial costs $25, or double that if you want a round-trip. There's a $3 to $5 extra charge for any stops you make en route.

There are four ways to obtain tickets. The first is from a local travel agency in Los Mochis or Creel. The second is at the train station a day ahead, or the same day of your travel (same-day ticket purchase isn't advised, since there may be no seats). A third way is through Mexico by Rail (see "Getting Around" in Chapter 2). A fourth, and the most reliable, is through a U.S. travel agency specializing in the Copper Canyon and selling air/train/hotel packages (not tickets alone). The least preferable option is to use a travel agent in Chihuahua, because several agencies may sell the same seat more than once, requiring travelers to decide how to share a seat. In Los Mochis I've had good luck using Viajes Flamingo at the Hotel Santa Anita.

If you plan to stop off en route, you must tell the ticket agent at the time you purchase your ticket, and know in advance how long you will be staying at the various stopoffs. Once purchased, the ticket is good for those dates only, and cannot be changed. A reserved seat is a necessity, but your reserved seat number is good only until your first stopoff; thereafter, when you reboard you'll have to take what's available. On my last trip, conductors had my name on a list at each stop and had an assigned seat for me. You can buy a ticket for shorter distances along the way, enabling you to spend as much time as you like in any location, but if you're traveling during a peak season, it may mean that you'll have to take your chances finding a seat when you reboard the train—or stand in any available space between cars as many locals do.

Planning a trip, balancing train stops with hotels, obtaining train tickets, and making reservations can be done in the Copper Canyon with perseverance—especially using Creel as a base. You can arrange your own trip by contacting the hotels directly and buying your ticket when you arrive in Los Mochis or Chihuahua. Or you can travel in the off-season without hotel reservations and take pot luck.

Travel Agents However, a tour company specializing in the Copper Canyon area can save headaches. I highly recommend the services of **Columbus Travel,** 6017 Callaghan, San Antonio, TX 78228-1115 (tel. 512/523-1400, or toll free 800/843-1060), which arranges group tours as well as individualized and special-interest trips in the Copper Canyon. You can also join groups organized by **Sanborn's Tours,** 1007 Main Street, Bastrop, TX 78602 (tel. toll free 800/531-5440), or **Armadillo Tours International,** 901 Mopac Expressway South, Building

2, Suite 120, Austin, TX 78746 (tel. toll free 800/284-5678). **Mexico By Rail** (tel. toll free 800/228-3225), can also book and send your tickets before you leave home. You don't have to travel with a group to use these agencies.

WHAT TO PACK   While Los Mochis is warm all year round, Chihuahua can be blistering in summer, windy just about any time, and freezing, even snowy, in the winter. Both cities are wealthy, and Chihuahua in particular can be somewhat on the dressy side.

The canyon is blue-jeans and hiking-boot country, but pay special attention to the climate. From November through March it may snow; even in the tropical bottom of the canyon you may need a sweater. In the upper elevations, be prepared for freezing temperatures at night, even in spring and fall. Long johns and gloves are a must in winter. Sturdy shoes or hiking boots are essential anytime if you plan even a little walking and hiking.

CONDITIONS OF TRAVEL   The first-class *Chihuahua al Pacífico* has adjustable cloth-covered seats, air conditioning in summer (usually), and heating (maybe) in winter. There's a dining car, but food vendors come to the train doors, selling an assortment of pies, tacos, empanadas, fruit, and soft drinks. Toilet paper and water may not be replenished; bring your own.

The train stops many times, but the following are stops with hotels:

STOP 1: EL FUERTE

Though not yet in the Copper Canyon proper, the train stops here first. El Fuerte, with its cobblestone streets and handsome old colonial mansions, is a former silver-mining town about an hour out of Los Mochis. Were it not for its proximity to the railroad, El Fuerte might have become a ghost town as did Alamos (see Chapter 3). A few years ago El Fuerte got a facelift, with a refurbished plaza and bandstand, cultural center, museum, and freshly painted buildings around the square. I prefer to skip Los Mochis and start my train journey here.

ESSENTIALS   The **bus stop** (not really a station) is about a block and a half from where the bus from Los Mochis lets you off on the cobblestoned street. Ask directions to the plaza and hotel. The **train station** is several miles from town. Taxis meet each train and cost $6 per taxi into town; get others to share the price in advance so you look like a group together, otherwise the taxi charges per person.

WHAT TO SEE & DO

Canyon country hasn't begun yet and the main reason for stopping here would be to explore the town, **fish** for black bass and trout, or **hunt** for duck and dove. The Posada Hidalgo can arrange guides and all equipment for both if notified in advance.

The **museum,** in the cultural center on the square, is small but has some good examples of area crafts. A branch of the government-operated **Artes Populares e Industrias Populares** next door has a great selection of folk art.

WHERE TO STAY & EAT

HOTEL POSADA HIDALGO, Hidalgo 101. El Fuerte, Sin. 81820. Tel. 681/3-0242 or 5-7046. 30 rms (all with bath). A/C
$ Rates: $55 single; $65 double.
This delightful hotel, four blocks from the bus stop and 3 miles from the train station, has two parts. The mansion section, with open portals around a central patio, belonged to silver grandees in the 18th century; there's even a steep carriage ramp from when it was a stagecoach stop. The new section is adjacent. President Salinas de Gortari slept here in 1990, as did Venustiano Carranza early this century. Rooms in the old section are high-ceilinged ones with hardwood floors. New rooms are

similarly decorated with two double beds, and all open onto a shady courtyard with covered walkway.

Meals are expensive, but there are inexpensive eateries near the hotel.

You can also make room reservations through the Hotel Santa Anita, Apdo. Postal 159, Los Mochis, Sin. 81200 (tel. 681/5-7046; fax 681/2-0046).

STOP 2: BAHUICHIVO

This is the first stop in canyon country. Bahuichivo consists mainly of the station and a few humble abodes. Your destination is the village of **Cerocahui** (alt. 5,550 ft.), in a valley about 6 miles from the train stop. Because of the rough, teeth-jarring road, the ride lasts an hour before you see the village, which is home to 600 inhabitants.

WHAT TO SEE & DO

The Paraíso del Oso is about a mile from the village. The Hotel Mision is in **Cerocahui.** Built around a mission church, Cerocahui consists of little more than rambling unpaved streets and a hundred or so homes. Mountains surround the town, but you have to take the Gallego excursion for real canyon vistas. In Cerocahui children beseige tourists to be escorts to the waterfalls. Both hotels can arrange **horseback riding** to the falls and other lookout points ($4 an hour), and by truck to **Cerro Gallego** ($15 per person), a lookout high in the mountains around the town and worth the trip.

Only the Paraíso del Oso offers a trip to the mining town of **Urique** at the bottom of the Urique Canyon (one of several canyons that make up the Copper Canyon). You can go down and back in a day, or schedule an overnight. The Urique trip costs $100 and can be split among four to six people. It's possible to see the waterfall on arrival and schedule the Gallegos trip for the next morning, have lunch, and make the train. The Urique trip would require another day.

WHERE TO STAY & EAT

HOTEL MISION. 30 rms (all with bath).
$ Rates (including meals): $85 single; $132 double. No checks or credit cards accepted.

Established years ago in the village of Cerocahui, the Hotel Mision, is the lodging of choice. Guest rooms have hot water, and wood-burning stoves and electricity until 10pm. The lobby-restaurant area surrounds a large rock fireplace where a local guitarist and singer entertain informally in the evenings. The food is excellent and the ranch-style rooms, with tile floors, are comfortable.

Reservations: Hotel Santa Anita, Apdo. Postal 159, Los Mochis, Sin. 81200 (tel. 681/5-7046; fax 681/2-0046).

PARAÍSO DEL OSO. 12 rms (all with bath).
$ Rates (including all meals): $75 single; $100 double; $120 triple.
Opened in 1990, it's the newest of canyon lodges, and was finishing construction but accepting guests when I was there. More rustic than the Hotel Mision, but with hot water in the rooms, it's a second choice until construction is completed. Its setting by a stream is what you come to the canyon for, and it's at the foot of a toothy mountain with a natural rock profile of an *oso* (bear)—thus its name. Eventually there will be more rooms and a larger restaurant. Food here doesn't compare to the Mision. Rooms have two double beds, nice tile floors, and log furniture. Rates include a trip to town, but it's also a nice walk.

Reservations: Adobe Tours, P.O. Box 12334, Albuquerque, NM 87195-0334 (tel. 505/873-1155, or toll free 800/852-2054; fax 505/877-1159).

STOPS 3 & 4: EL DIVISADERO

Stops 3 and 4 are only 2 miles apart. Stop 3 (coming from Los Mochis) is in front of the Posada Barrancas and opposite the Mansion Tarahumara. Stop 4 is El Divisadero proper (alt. 9,000 ft.), consisting of the Hotel Cabañas Divisadero, Barrancas, taco stands at train time (delicious), and the most spectacular overlook of the canyon that you'll see if you make no overnight stops en route. The train stops for only 10 minutes, long enough for a mad dash to the lookout to see the view and to make some hurried purchases from the Tarahumara Indians who appear at train time to display their beautiful baskets, homemade violins, and wood and cloth dolls.

Hotels can arrange various excursions, including visits to cave-dwelling Tarahumara, hiking, and horseback riding.

WHERE TO STAY & EAT

MANSION TARAHUMARA. 15 cabañas (all with bath and fireplace).
$ Rates (including meals): $75 single; $110 double; $130 triple.

Built like an enormous stone castle, it's perched on a hillside opposite the train stop at Posada Barrancas. A van meets the train and carries guests and luggage across the tracks to the hotel. This is among my favorite of the canyon lodges, because of the setting, the rooms, and the management's interest in guest comfort. Rock-walled bungalows are behind the castle and each has a big fireplace and is nicely furnished with two double beds and windows facing the view.

The castle contains the restaurant with a big window view, and a large area ideal for dancing or live entertainment which the hotel sometimes sponsors. Most nights a guitarist stops in for a sing-along after dinner. Besides the usual cave tours or horseback riding, the hotel can also arrange guided hiking to the bottom of the canyon or to Batopilas (see Batopilas description in "Stop 5: Creel," below).

Reservations: Sierra Madre Tours, Libertad 1204-C (Apdo. Postal 1666 D), Chihuahua, Chih. 31000 (tel. 14/12-7943; fax 14/16-5444).

HOTEL POSADA BARRANCAS. 36 rms (all with bath).
$ Rates (including meals): $85 single; $132 double.
The train stops right in front of this inn and hotel employees arrive to help with luggage. Rooms are comfortable, with two double beds and a very warming iron wood-burning stove. Like other lodges, meals are a communal affair in the cozy living-restaurant area and the meals are quite good. You can hike to the Tarahumara caves and to the rim of the canyon where the hotel has a beautiful log-walled enclosed bar with a magnificent view.

Reservations: Hotel Santa Anita, Apdo. Postal 159, Los Mochis, Sin. 81200 (tel. 681/5-7046; fax 681/2-0046).

HOTEL CABAÑAS DIVISADERO-BARRANCAS. 32 rms (all with bath).
$ Rates (including three meals): $85 single; $120 double; $160 triple; $200 quad.
The first hotel in the canyon, at the first train stop in the canyon, it caters to groups and remains popular because of its location on the edge of the canyon overlook—the most spectacular view of any hotel in the canyon. The restaurant has a large picture window, perfect for sitting and gazing for hours. Rooms are beautifully rustic with foot-loomed hot-pink and lime-green bedspreads and matching curtains, two double beds, fireplace, and 24-hour electricity.

Reservations: Calle 7a no. 1216 at Paseo Bolívar (Apdo. Postal 661), Chihuahua, Chih. 31300 (tel. 14/2-3362 or 15-1199; fax 14/15-6575).

STOP 5: CREEL

This rustic logging town (alt. 8,400 ft.; pop. 6,000), with newly paved streets, offers the only economical lodgings in the canyon, as well as some of the best side trips, especially hiking and overnight camping.

When you are ready to get off the train, keep a lookout for the station because the trains stop here for only a few minutes. When you're ready to reboard, be sure to be at the station before the arrival time of the train. You'll need to be ready to jump on when you see it coming.

GETTING THERE & DEPARTING Besides the *Chihuahua al Pacífico* train, you can also get to Creel by bus and car.

By Bus The **Chihuahua Madera Line,** next to the Hotel Korachi, serves Creel and Chihuahua eight times daily. The first bus leaves Creel at 7am and the last at 3pm; six of these buses make the trip in 5 hours, stopping 13 times en route. Buses at 11am and 2pm are direct and make the trip in 4 hours. (See also buses to Batopilas "What to See and Do," below). In Chihuahua bus tickets to Creel are sold at the far-right section of the main bus terminal.

By Car   From Chihuahua, follow the signs to Cuauhtémoc and then to Creel; the trip takes about 4 hours on a paved road.

ORIENTATION

The station, opposite the main plaza, is in the heart of the village and within walking distance of all lodgings except the Copper Canyon Hiking Lodge. Except for the Casa de Huespedes Margarita, which is close by, look for your hotel's van, which will be waiting at the station. There's one main street, Lopez Mateos, and almost everything is on it and within walking distance.

FAST FACTS

Area Code   The telephone area code is 145.
Electricity   There's electricity 24 hours daily in all Creel hotels.
Information   The best sources of information are the Mission Store and the hotels.
Telephone   The long-distance office is at Mateos 30, one block east of the plaza. It's open Monday through Saturday from 9am to 1:30pm and 3 to 8pm, and on Sunday from 9am to 2pm.

WHAT TO SEE & DO

You'll occasionally see the Tarahumara as you walk around town, but mostly you'll see rugged logging types and tourists from around the world.

There are several stores around Creel that sell Tarahumara arts and crafts. The best is **Artesanías Mission** (Mission Crafts), which has quality merchandise and reasonable prices, with all profits going to the Mission Hospital, run by Father Verplunken, a Jesuit priest, and benefiting the Tarahumara. Here you'll find Tarahumara crafts: dolls, pottery, woven purses and belts, drums, violins (a craft inherited from the Spanish), bamboo flutes, bead necklaces, bows and arrows, cassettes of Tarahumara music, wood carvings, baskets, and heavy wool rugs, as well as an excellent supply of books and maps relating to the Tarahumara and the region. It's open Monday through Saturday from 9am to 7pm and on Sunday from 9am to 2pm. It's beside the railroad tracks, on the main plaza.

Nearby Excursions

Close by there are several canyons, waterfalls, a lake, hot springs, Tarahumara villages and cave dwellings, and an old Jesuit mission. Batopilas, a fascinating 18th-century silver-mining village is at the bottom of the canyon, an overnight jaunt. You can ask for information about these and other things to do from your hotel.

Whether you go by foot, horseback, bus, or guided tour, if you're planning to do any strenuous hiking, rock climbing, or adventuring, it's strongly recommended that you take someone with you who knows the area—you're in the wilderness out here, and you can't count on anyone coming along to rescue you should an accident occur.

A nice walk you can do on your own is to head out of town on Avenida Lopez Mateos, past the Motel Parador de la Montaña; go past the lumber mill, and keep going, taking the left fork in the road when you pass the cemetery. Continuing along this road, you come to a valley where the Tarahumara live; you'll see their footpaths, domestic animals, and cave dwellings. If you continue on this same road, you pass the **Valley of the Mushroom Rocks**, about 2½ miles from town, and finally reach the tiny village of **San Ignacio**, where there is a 400-year-old mission. From here, you can continue on to **Lake Arareco**, about 4½ miles from Creel.

ORGANIZED TOURS   Hotels offer organized tours. The **Motel Parador de la**

Montaña has 10 different tours, ranging from 2 to 10 hours, and priced from $10 to $30 per person (four people minimum); $100 for the Batopilas trip. The **Hotel Nuevo** and **Casa de Huespedes Margarita** offer the most economical tours in town, priced around $10 for a day-long canyon and hot-springs tour. All tour availability depends on if a group can be gathered, and your best chance of that is at the Parador de la Montaña, which caters to groups. The **Copper Canyon Hiking Lodge** arranges overnight and longer hikes into the mountains.

BATOPILAS You can make an overnight side trip on your own from Creel to the silver-mining village of Batopilas, founded in 1708. It's 7 to 9 hours from Creel by bus (the school-bus type) along a narrow dirt road winding down through some of the most beautiful scenery in the Copper Canyon. Beside a river at the bottom of a deep canyon, the weather is tropical. There's a beautiful little church, and several walks and a hike to Mision Sotevo that you can do from there. The town itself is like something from a 17th-century time-warp: The drygoods store has the original shelving and cash register, cobblestone streets twist past whitewashed town homes, miners and ranchers come on horseback, and Tarahumara are frequent visitors. A considerable number of pigs, dogs, and flocks of goats wander at will—this is Chihuahua's goat-raising capital.

Where to Stay and Eat Batopilas has several little restaurants and three hotels, ranging in price from about $10 to $75 per person per night. There are no telephones so you can't make firm reservations. However, the Parador de la Montaña in Creel operates the 10-room Parador Batopilas and can tell you the likelihood of vacancies. All rooms share two baths, separate for men and women, and cost around $25 a night. The Copper Canyon Hiking Lodge recently opened a mansion-turned-hotel and rents rooms for $70 a night. Check with them in Creel regarding vacancies. There's another nameless hotel with five or six rooms, and if all else fails, you can probably find a family willing to let you stay in an extra room. One night isn't enough since you arrive in late afternoon and must leave at 4am the next morning.

Getting to Batopilas To get to Batopilas, take a bus from the unmarked storefront at Mateos 39 next to D'Flor variety store and opposite the Restaurant Lupita. Buses go to Batopilas on Tuesday, Thursday, and Saturday, leaving Creel at 7am and arriving in Batopilas around 3:30pm. From Batopilas, the return bus leaves for Creel on Monday, Wednesday, and Friday at 4am in summer, 6am in winter, supposedly to arrive in Creel around noon, in time to meet the connecting *Chihuahua al Pacífico* trains leaving for Los Mochis and Chihuahua. In the rainy months of June through August it arrives later. Tickets are supposedly sold between 11am and 8pm the day before; the cost is $6.50.

WHERE TO STAY

For a small town, Creel has quite a number of places to stay because of its popularity with international tourists and loggers on business. Be sure to have a reservation during high season.

HOTEL KORACHI, Calle Francisco Villa 116, Creel, Chih. 33200. Tel. 145/6-0207. 22 rms (14 with bath).
$ Rates: $6–$14 single; $14–$20 double cabaña.
The eight regular rooms in the main building, across the railroad tracks from the station, share common bathrooms, are dark, and have only the heat from the central hallway (which has a hard time making it into your room whenever your door is closed). There are also 14 cabañas in the back, with wood stoves and large private baths, two double beds, plus a terrace to sit on out front. Be sure to inspect the facilities first since housekeeping standards vary. Higher rates are for rooms with a private bathroom.

CASA DE HUESPEDES MARGARITA, Lopez Mateos 11, Creel, Chih. 33200. Tel. and fax 145/6-0045. 23 rms (all with bath).
$ Rates (including breakfast and dinner): $10 sleeping bag space (10 spaces); $15 share in a four-bed dormitory; $17–$21 single or double private room; $17 double private cabaña.

⭐ With its youth hostel–type atmosphere, this signless white house between the two churches on the main plaza is the most popular spot in town with international backpacking, student, and minimal-budget travelers. It's also one of the cleanest hotels in the country. Rooms have pine details and tile floors and are decorated with frilly curtains and spreads. There's plenty of hot water and gas heat in each room. Meals are taken family style around a big dining table. Nonguests can eat here too—just let them know in advance; breakfast and lunch are $2.75 each.

HOTEL NUEVO, Calle Francisco Villa 121, Creel, Chih. 33200. Tel. 145/6-0022, or 14/17-5539 in Chihuahua for reservations. 27 rms (all with bath).
$ Rates: $17 single; $33–$51 double.

Ⓢ There are two hotel sections, the older one across the tracks from the train station next to the restaurant and variety store, and new log cabañas in back, which are carpeted and have TV and are the highest price. All except six rooms have a heater or fireplace. There is a nice hotel restaurant open for breakfast (8:30 to 10am) and dinner (6:30 to 8pm), and a small general store that sells local crafts as well as basic supplies. Ask at the store about rooms.

MOTEL PARADOR DE LA MONTAÑA, Av. Mateos, Creel, Chih. 33200. Tel. 145/6-0075. Fax 145/6-0085. 49 rms (all with bath).
$ Rates: $35–$55 single; $52 double; $60 triple; $70 quad.
The nicest accommodation in town is the Motel Parador de la Montaña, located two blocks west of the plaza. The rooms are large, with two big double beds, high wood-beamed ceilings, central heating, and tiled bathrooms. Guests congregate in the restaurant, the bar, and the lobby with its roaring fireplace. The bar is the town's evening action spot. Since the motel caters to groups, the best chance of joining one of the 10 area tours is here. The hotel also owns the Parador Batopilas in Batopilas.

For reservations in Chihuahua, contact Calle Allende 114, Chihuahua, Chih. 31300 (tel. 14/12-2062 or 15-5448).

COPPER CANYON HIKING LODGE. 18 rms (all with bath).
$ Rates (including meals): $72 single; $107 double; $142 triple; $185 quad. Ask about packages and specials.

⭐ About 20 minutes (12 miles) southwest of Creel proper is everything you imagine a mountain lodge should be—rock-walled, beamed ceilings, lantern lights, and wood-burning stoves—in short, rustic/comfortable and no electricity. It's out-of-town location offers a great starting point for guided or self-guided hikes and walks in the mountains to the Cusarare Waterfalls, cave paintings, and to the present-day Tarahumara cave dwellings. Owner Skip McWilliams holds special reverence for the Tarahumara and has made an effort to become friends with those who live near the lodge. On nights that he lights a bonfire, they come for whatever gathering is planned. Admittedly there is usually a language barrier with the guests, and the Tarahumara are shy, but hand gestures and friendliness go a long way. McWilliams specializes in overnight or longer hikes in the canyons and often leads these expeditions himself. The Tarahumara come along as well, and everyone is expected to pitch in with whatever needs doing.

The hotel bus meets the train. If you show up without reservations, try bargaining for a discount, especially if the hotel has vacancies. The hotel also owns the newly opened 15-room Hacienda Batopilas in Batopilas.

Reservations: Copper Canyon American Eagle Company, 1100 Owendale, Suite G, Troy, MI 48083 (tel. toll free 800/543-4180).

WHERE TO EAT

LA CABAÑA, Lopez Mateos. Tel. 6-0068.
   Specialty: MEXICAN.
$ Prices: Breakfast $2–$3; Mexican plates $2.50–$5; main courses 60¢–$2.
   Open: Daily 9am–9pm.
There's a good variety on the menu at the log cabin, La Cabaña, on the right, one block west of the plaza. The chicken mole is tasty, as are the antojito plates

(enchiladas, tacos, quesadillas). Several breakfasts are available. Service is slow and informal, but the wide variety of colorful regional decorations will keep you busy as you wait for your order.

RESTAURANT VERONICA, Mateos 34.
Specialty: MEXICAN.
$ Prices: Soup $1.50; antojitos $1.50–$3.
Open: Daily 8am–10pm.

The pink-painted ceiling and walls provide a perfect backdrop for the five tables and chairs. The menu includes a delicious large bowl of vegetable soup, assorted antojitos, seafood, and sandwiches. The burritos de pollo are large, fresh, and filling. The restaurant is two blocks west of the plaza.

MOTEL PARADOR DE LA MONTAÑA, Lopez Mateos. Tel. 6-0075.
Specialty: INTERNATIONAL.
$ Prices: Breakfast, sandwiches, and hamburgers $4–$5; main courses $6–$12.
Open: Daily 7:30am–10pm.

Easily the most popular restaurant in town for an all-out dinner of soup, salad, steak, dessert, and coffee, or just a simple grilled half-chicken dinner. There's full bar service from the cozy little bar attached, which is open all day and evening until around midnight. With its hanging lanterns, high wood-beamed ceiling, huge fireplace, and friendly atmosphere, this is well worth a stop in. It's two blocks west of the plaza.

3. CHIHUAHUA
213 miles S of El Paso, 275 miles N of Torreón

GETTING THERE   By Air   Southwest Airlines (tel. toll free 800/531-5601) serves El Paso from various U.S. cities. **Aeroméxico** flies from Guadalajara, Hermosillo, Cd. Juárez, Mexico City, Monterrey, and Torreón. **Servicio Aereo Leo Lopez** has daily flights to El Paso and Monday, Wednesday, and Friday service to Los Mochis. **AeroLitoral** (Aeroméxico affiliate) flies from Tampico twice each day five times a week. **Noroeste** serves Mazatlán, Hermosillo, and Tijuana.

By Train   *El Rapido de la Frontera* runs the 4-hour trip between Cd. Juárez, across from El Paso on the Texas border, to Chihuahua daily; it leaves Juárez at 6pm and arrives in Chihuahua at 10pm.

By Bus   Transportes Chihuahuenses (tel. 12-1054 or 12-1910) is the big local line, but **Omnibus de México** (tel. 15-0665), **Tres Estrellas de Oro** (tel. 12-0257), **Transportes del Norte** (tel. 12-4773), and **Autobuses Estrella Blanca** (tel. 12-4721) also runs buses hourly from the border through Chihuahua to points south. Check with them at the Central Camionera.

By Car   Highway 45 leads south from Cd. Juárez and Highway 49 leads north from Torreón.

DEPARTING   By Plane   Transportes Aeropuerto (tel. 20-1124) runs colectivo service to and from the airport for $1.75 per person. Taxis charge $8 to $10 and up. **Aeroméxico/AeroLitoral** is at Calle Victoria 106 (tel. 15-6303); **Servicio Aereo Leo Lopez,** at Coronado 421 (tel. 16-2828, or 20-0259 at the airport); and **Noroeste** is at Jimenez 1204 (tel. 16-5146).

By Train   For the ***Chihuahua al Pacífico*** (tel. 14/12-2284 or 15-7756) through the Copper Canyon to Los Mochis, the station is two blocks behind the prison on 20 de Noviembre, near the intersection with Ocampo. The train leaves promptly at 7am daily. (The complete train schedule and the train route are in Section 2 of this chapter, above). To get there from the Plaza Principal and Avenida Juárez take a bus named "Cerro de la Cruz" or "Ramiro Valles/Penitenaria." It lets you off two blocks from the station. Tickets are on sale 6am to 6pm daily.

At a different station you take *El Rapido de la Frontera* (tel. 14/13-0093) which runs the 4-hour trip to El Paso on the Texas border daily. It leaves at 7am and arrives in Cd. Juárez at 11am. Buy your tickets a day in advance between 8:30am and 12:30pm. To get to the *Rapido de la Frontera* station from Plaza Principal, take any "Colón" bus on Niños Héroes or Aldama (Colón becomes Tecnológico). Get off at Division del Norte or when you see the El Capitan Motel on the right. Walk right on Division and the station is a half a block ahead.

If you arrive in Cd. Juárez and you intend to cross the border immediately, you have two choices: Negotiate with a taxi to take you across (to the airport it's about $35); a cheaper way is to take a taxi only to the border, then walk across and get another taxi on the other side.

By Bus   Buses leave every hour from the Central Camionera heading for major points. **Omnibus de México** has a new first-class bus between Juárez and Chihuahua, Real Executivo, with only 20 seats, VCRs, and earphones, and makes no stops during the 4½-hour ride. It leaves twice daily, at 8am and 5pm. Tickets are $15 and reservations can be made up to 1 week in advance. To Creel look for the Chihuahua Madera line (tel. 12-9833 or 15-6282) at the far right end of the station. Buses leave at 6, 8, and 10am and 1, 3, 4, and 5pm. The trip takes 5 hours.

Chihuahua (alt. 4,700 ft.; pop. 531,000), a city of wide boulevards and handsome buildings, is the capital of the state of Chihuahua, the largest and richest state in Mexico. The money comes from mining, timber, cattle raising, many *maquiladoras* (U.S. assembly plants), and tourism—it's one of two major departure points for the Copper Canyon train.

Aside from its industry, Chihuahua boasts a modern university and a museum in the house where Pancho Villa lived, but very few of the tiny, hairless Chihuahua dogs.

ORIENTATION

ARRIVING   From the **airport**, it's a half-hour trip downtown on the express van for $1.60 per person, and Transportes Aeropuerto (tel. 20-1124) runs colectivo service to and from downtown for $1.75 per person.

The *El Rapido de la Frontera* train arrives at the **Nacionales de México train station** in Chihuahua. It's at the northeastern end of Avenida Division del Norte about 3 miles from city center.

From the **Central Camionera,** orient yourself to the town center by walking toward the tall buildings six blocks or so away.

INFORMATION   The **State Tourism Office** is at Calle Libertad and Calle 13, on the second floor of the Augustín Melgar building, six blocks north of the cathedral. It's open Monday through Friday from 9am to 3pm with extended hours in December, during Holy Week, and in July and August.

CITY LAYOUT   The town center is Plaza Principal and the cathedral, flanked by Avenidas Libertad and Victoria, which run north and south, and Avenida Independencia and Calle 4, running east and west.

GETTING AROUND

Local buses run along main arteries beginning at the central plaza. Taxis can be taken from the center of town to most major sights. For early morning transportation to the train station, it's best to make pick-up arrangements with one of the travel agencies, since taxis are scarce at that hour.

FAST FACTS

American Express   The local representative is Viajes Rojo y Casavantes, in the Hotel San Francisco, Guerrero 1207 (tel. 14/12-5888; fax 14/15-5384).

Area Code   The telephone area code is 14.

Canyon Arrangements   If you wait to make overnight hotel reservations in the canyon until you are in Chihuahua, consider using a local travel agent. I recommend **Turismo Al Mar,** Reforma 1600-2, Chihuahua, Chih. 31207 (tel. 14/16-5950); **Cañon de Urique,** Avenida Revolución 100, Chihuahua, Chih. 31310 (tel. 14/16-2672); or **Sierra Madre Tours,** Calle Libertad 1204 C (Apdo. Postal 1666-D), Chihuahua, Chih. 31000 (tel. 14/12-7943; fax 14/16-5444). For buying train tickets, however, do it yourself at the station.

WHAT TO SEE & DO

To see all the sights of Chihuahua in one day, there are 3-hour **city tours,** with English-speaking guides available. Two recommended agencies are **Turismo Al Mar,** Reforma 400 (tel. 16-9232 or 16-5950; fax 16-6589), and **Rojo y Casavantes,** in the lobby of the Hotel San Francisco, Vicente Guerrero 1207 (tel. 15-4636 or 12-6030). Either agency will pick you up at your hotel for tours at 10am or 4pm. They'll take you to see the museums, the churches, the colonial aqueduct, the state capitol building, the state penitentiary, and more. Cost is $12 per person. A trip to the Mennonite village near Cuauhtémoc costs $22 per person, with a minimum of four people.

MUSEUM OF THE REVOLUTION, Calle 10 no. 3014, at the corner of Mendez. Tel. 16-2958.

This museum is located in Pancho Villa's former house on what was once the outskirts of the city. Luz Corral de Villa, Villa's legitimate wife (he had others, they say), lived in the house until her death in 1981. Exhibits include Villa's weapons, some personal effects, lots of period photos, and the 1922 Dodge in which he was shot in 1923, complete with bullet holes. It's one of the most interesting museums in the country.

Admission: 25¢.

Open: Daily 9am–1pm and 3–7pm. **Bus:** "Colonia Dale" heads west down Juárez, turning south onto Ocampo, and will let you off on the corner of Ocampo and Mendez.

MUSEO REGIONAL DE CHIHUAHUA [Quinta Gameros], Paseo Bolívar 401. Tel. 12-3834.

If you've ever been to France and visited some of the kingly palaces there, you'll think you are experiencing déjà vu when you see Quinta Gameros, an exact replica of a French Second Empire neoclassical mansion. The mansion was built in 1910 for Manuel Gameros and was converted to a museum in 1961. Pancho Villa used it as a headquarters for a while. Notice the wealth of decorative detail from floor to ceiling, inside and out. There are permanent exhibits of turn-of-the-century art nouveau furnishings, and other salons containing exhibits of historical Chihuahuense photographs; an exhibit on the Mennonites of Cuauhtémoc, near Chihuahua; and an exhibit of artifacts from the ancient pre-Hispanic ruins of Paquime, about 5 hours to the north.

Admission: 50¢.

Open: Tues–Sun 10am–1pm and 4–7pm. **Directions:** Heading away from Plaza Principal with the cathedral on your right, walk eight blocks on Independencia to Bolívar, turn right, and then walk one more block; it's on the right.

MUSEO DE ARTE DE INDUSTRIAS POPULARES, Av. Reforma 5. Tel. 13-3119.

This small museum has excellent life-size displays of Tarahumara Indians at work in their village settings and surrounded by the pottery, rugs, and other crafts for which they are famous. The showroom next to the museum has crafts from around the country for sale.

Admission: Free.

Open: Tues–Sat 10am–1pm and 4–7pm. **Directions:** From Plaza Principal, walk seven blocks east on Independencia and cross Revolución and Reforma; it's in an obscure house, with a sign, to the right of Hobbit.

MUSEO CASA DE JUÁREZ, at the corner of Juárez and Calle 5a.

This was the Mexican National Palace in 1864 when Benito Juárez was leading the fight for independence from the French occupation. Detailed exhibits tell the history of that stormy epoch, how the armed struggle proceeded from place to place; and you'll see the various plans and constitutions that were drawn up, with photographs, documents in Spanish, and exhibits of period furnishings.

Admission: Free.

Open: Mon–Fri 9am–3pm and 4–6pm. **Directions:** From Plaza Principal, walk north on Independencia for two blocks, then turn right on Juárez for one long block; it's on the left almost at Calle 5.

PALACIO DEL GOBIERNO, Calle Aldama between Guerrero and Carranza.

The Palacio del Gobierno is a magnificently ornate structure dating from 1892. A colorful, expressive mural encompasses the entire first floor of the large central courtyard, telling the history of the area around Chihuahua from the time of the first European visitation up through the time of the Revolution. In the far-right corner, note the scene depicting Benito Juárez flanked by Abraham Lincoln and Simon Bolívar, Liberator of South America. Also in the far-left back courtyard is a plaque and altar commemorating the execution of Miguel Hidalgo, the father of Mexican independence, at 7am on July 30, 1811; the plaque marks the very spot where the hero was killed (it was then a Jesuit convent), and a mural portrays the scene.

Admission: Free.

Open: Daily 8am–9pm. **Directions:** From Plaza Principal, walk east on Independencia one block, then turn left on Aldama for two long blocks; cross Guerrero and the entrance is on the left.

HIDALGO'S DUNGEON, in the Palacio Federal, Calle Juárez at Guerrero.

Father Miguel Hidalgo y Costillo was a priest in Dolores, Guanajuato, when he started the War of Independence on September 15, 1810. A few months later he was captured by the Spanish, brought to Chihuahua, and kept in a dungeon for 98 days, before being shot with his lieutenants, Allende, Aldama, and Jimenez. The four were beheaded, and their heads hung in iron cages for 9½ years on the four corners of the Alhondiga granary in Guanajuato, as examples of what happens to revolutionaries. It was here in this cell that Hidalgo was kept on bread and water before his execution. The night before his death, he wrote a few words on the wall with a piece of charcoal to thank his guard and the warden for the good treatment they gave him. A bronze plaque commemorates his final message.

Admission: 50¢.

Open: Daily 9am–7pm. **Directions:** From Plaza Principal, walk north on Libertad for three long blocks, cross Guerrero, and turn left on it to the corner of Juárez; the entrance to the museum is on the right, below the post office.

NEARBY EXCURSIONS

The **Mennonite village of Cuauhtémoc,** 2 hours west of Chihuahua, makes an unusual side trip. Originally from northern Germany, they became an official reformist religious sect under Mennon Simmons in the early 16th century. With a strict Bible-based philosophy governing their daily lives, prohibiting them from engaging in war and many other aspects of popular culture, they immigrated to other lands rather than violate their beliefs.

The group of 5,000 that in 1920 migrated to Cuauhtémoc from Canada petitioned the Mexican government for permission to settle here and maintain their own community traditions; Cuauhtémoc was little more than desert then, and Mexico was trying to develop its lands. The Mennonites have transformed this desert into a productive and prosperous farming community. They still maintain their 16th-century customs, religion, dress, and language (a dialect of Old German); you'll see them riding around in horse and buggies, since they eschew the use of cars and other modern technology, although one sect here does allow use of mechanized farm implements. They are especially famous for their delicious cheese, fine woodwork, and embroidery, as well as their agricultural products.

An all-day Mennonite tour to Cuauhtémoc, includes a visit to the Mennonite village and agricultural lands, and a cheese factory, and lunch in a Mennonite home, meeting the people and learning about their culture and history. The tour companies mentioned above can arrange the tour.

Another interesting side trip is to the **Ruins of Paquime** (A.D. 900–1340), near the town of Casas Grandes, about 5 hours to the north of Chihuahua on Highway 10. Here you'll find the pueblo-like mud-walled remains of northern Mexico's most important pre-Hispanic city. Few tour agencies arrange a trip from Chihuahua unless there is a group of six or more. You can stay over in the nearby town of Nuevo Casas Grandes, about 5 miles to the northeast of the ruins.

EVENING ENTERTAINMENT

Most downtown action takes place in hotel lobby bars. At the **Hotel San Francisco,** Victoria 1207, behind the cathedral, there's live music (piano in the lobby bar, a band in the Los Primos bar) Monday through Saturday, with happy hour from 5 to 8pm. The **Posada del Sol** (formerly the Hyatt Hotel), at Independencia 500, has different live entertainment nightly in the lobby bar. The **Hostería 1900,** at Independencia 903 (see "Where to Eat," below), has live entertainment weekends from 9:30pm to 2am.

WHERE TO STAY

HOTEL SAN JUAN, Victoria 823, Chihuahua, Chih. 31300. Tel. 14/14-2849. 61 rms (all with bath).
$ Rates: $10 single; $16 double with one bed, $18 double with two beds.
Once a beautiful town house with ornate carving and beautiful tile, now it has fallen on humble times. Rather dreary, the rooms face onto long hallways, but most rooms have a window facing outside. The hotel restaurant is open from 8am to 10pm, and there's a bar too, open from 11am to 11pm. The hotel is two blocks behind the cathedral.

HOTEL DEL COBRE, Calle 10 no. 905, Chihuahua, Chih. 31300. Tel. 14/15-1660. 93 rms (all with bath). A/C TEL
$ Rates: $10–$24 single; $13–$28 double. **Parking:** Free.
To the left of the bus station, at the corner of Calle 10 and Progreso, the Hotel del Cobre is clean and modern, and popular with businessmen. There are two price categories here: Simple rooms have the general heat and air conditioning operating throughout the building; the 42 somewhat nicer rooms have individually controlled heat and air conditioning and TV. The restaurant is open daily from 7am to 10pm.

HOTEL REFORMA, Calle Victoria 809, Chihuahua, Chih. 31300. Tel. 14/12-5808. 49 rms (all with bath).
$ Rates: $11 single or double with one bed, $13 single or double with two twin-size beds; $15 with two double-size beds, for up to four people.
An old mansion two blocks behind the cathedral near Ocampo, this was evidently a fancy place when it was built in 1913. Today it's a humble shadow of its former self, but enjoyable if you can get one of the brighter rooms facing the street, with French doors opening onto little balconies. Rooms facing the back have small windows facing outside. Many rooms face the large covered inner courtyard, which serves as the lobby, and these rooms are dark. There's a simple but good restaurant, Mi Cafe, which is open daily from 8am to 11pm.

HOTEL BAL-FLO, Calle 5a no. 702, Chihuahua, Chih. 31300. Tel. 14/16-0300. 91 rms (all with bath). A/C TEL
$ Rates: $26 single; $30 double. **Parking:** Free.
All rooms at the Bal-Flo are heated and carpeted. Some rooms have windows on the street; others open onto an air shaft. Rental TVs are extra. The proprietor, Sr. Baltazar Flores, speaks English and is quite helpful. The cafeteria, open daily from 7am to 11pm, serves good, inexpensive food.

To get here from Plaza Principal, walk four long blocks east on Independencia and turn right for two blocks on Niños Héroes; it's on the left at Calle 5.

HOTEL SANTA REGINA, Calle 3a no. 107, Chihuahua, Chih. 31300. Tel. 14/15-3889. 102 rms (all with bath) A/C TV TEL
$ Rates: $28 single; $30 double.
The three-story Santa Regina has carpeted rooms that are heated in winter and TVs that receive U.S. channels. More than half the rooms have windows facing outside; others have windows on the hall.
To get here from Plaza Principal, walk two blocks to Doblado and turn right for 2 more blocks; the hotel is between Juárez and Doblado.

HOTEL EL DORADO, at the corner of Calle 14 and Julian Carrillo, Chihuahua, Chih. 31300. Tel. 14/12-5770. 70 rms (all with bath). A/C TV TEL
$ Rates: $28 single; $32 double. **Parking:** Free.
The Hotel El Dorado has modern, carpeted, and clean rooms. A few rooms don't have TV and rent for $4 less. There's 1-day laundry service, a restaurant open from 7:30am to 10pm, a color TV and nice sitting area in the bright lobby, and a ladies' bar open nightly with a variety show from 9pm to 3am ($4 cover charge).
To get here, turn right out the door of the bus station, then right again when you get to the street; go to the first corner, turn left, and the El Dorado is half a block up on the right.

WHERE TO EAT

For some very inexpensive meals, head for Avenida Victoria behind the cathedral, to the restaurants of the **Hotel Reforma** and the **Hotel San Juan,** mentioned above. Both restaurants are clean, small, and friendly, and serve basic Mexican food at low prices. Mi Cafe, in the Hotel Reforma, serves a comida corrida from 1pm until it runs out for $4.50 to $9.50, and is open daily from 8am to 11pm. The Restaurant San Juan offers one of the least expensive comida corridas in town from 1 to 3pm for $2.75; it's open from 8am to 10pm.

LIVEER RESTAURANTE DE AUTO SERVICIO, Libertad 318. Tel. 15-4902.
Specialty: MEXICAN.
$ Prices: Main courses $1.25–$3; plate lunch $2.15–$3.50.
Open: Daily 11am–9pm.
This is a walk-down-the-line–style cafeteria. Bright and clean, it serves a variety of main dishes, side dishes, salads, desserts, and drinks at reasonable prices. You can also get hot snacks "to go" from the window out front.
To get here from Plaza Principal, walk 1½ blocks north on Libertad; it's on the right opposite the Salinas y Rocha store.

LA PARILLA, Victoria 420. Tel. 15-5856.
Specialty: STEAKS.
$ Prices: Steaks $6–$10; fajitas $6; tacos $1.50; soft drinks 50¢.
Open: Daily noon–midnight.
With its ranch-style café decor of dark-wood tables and plastic-covered chairs, La Parilla features Chihuahua-bred beef cuts—sirloin, filet mignon, and club. All meat platters come with consommé, salad, and potato. There are 21 kinds of tacos and lots of side orders like northern-style pinto beans cooked in beer, hot cheese, tortilla soup, and grilled onions. The restaurant is 1½ blocks south of the cathedral past the Hotel San Francisco, on the left.

HOSTERÍA 1900, Independencia 903. Tel. 16-1990.
Specialty: INTERNATIONAL.
$ Prices: Appetizers $2.75–$6.50; crêpes $6.50–$8.50; fondue $10.50–$20.
Open: Mon–Thurs 1pm–midnight, Fri–Sun 1pm–2am.
Cozy and charming in a Greenwich Village way, it's decorated with black tables and chairs with accents of turquoise, hot pink, and black. Besides fondue and crêpes with

six different sauces and fillings, there are meat dishes and soups. There's live trio music weekends from 9:30pm to 2am and happy hour most afternoons when two drinks for the price of one are served with free snacks. The Hostería 1900 is three blocks east of Plaza Principal, half a block past the Posada del Sol.

EL TRASTEVERE, Victoria 410. Tel. 15-8719.
   Specialty: ITALIAN.
$ **Prices:** Appetizers $2.50–$7.50; main courses $6.50–$10; Mexican specials $3.25–$8.25; pizza $2.90–$9.50.
   Open: Daily 8am–11pm.
   Decorated like an Italian country kitchen, with brick columns and a dozen tables and chairs, El Trastevere is a block behind the cathedral, opposite the Hotel San Francisco. Here you can get flavorful Italian food. Besides 14 varieties of pizza, there are crêpes six ways, different Mexican specialties daily, and fondue appetizers with beer or white wine and cheese. The spaghetti bolognese, enough for two, has a thick, flavorful meat sauce.

DEGA, Calle Victoria 409. Tel. 16-7550.
   Specialty: MEXICAN/INTERNATIONAL.
$ **Prices:** Breakfast $2–$6; Sun buffet $8; lunch buffet $10; menu ejecutivo $8; plato Mexicano $5.50.
   Open: Daily 7am–10:45pm; lunch buffet Mon–Sat 1–5pm; brunch buffet Sun 10am–1pm; menu ejecutivo Mon–Sat 1–4pm.
The hotel is beyond our budget, but the restaurant/cafeteria/bar is very popular for its good food. The four-course "menu ejecutivo" is served with several choices. The "plato Mexicano" comes with a tamale, a chile relleño, beans, chips, and guacamole. Fish, charcoal-grilled chicken, barbecue, and salads are all reasonably priced. It's next to the Hotel San Francisco, half a block behind the cathedral on Victoria.

CHAPTER 5

THE PACIFIC COAST FROM SAN BLAS TO IXTAPA

- **WHAT'S SPECIAL ABOUT THE CENTRAL PACIFIC COAST**
1. **SAN BLAS**
2. **PUERTO VALLARTA**
3. **BARRA DE NAVIDAD & MELAQUE**
4. **MANZANILLO**
5. **ZIHUATANEJO & IXTAPA**

Mexico's Pacific Coast is over 2,000 miles long. Although the northern reaches of the coast are the western edges of the Sonoran Desert, once you get south of Culiacán the lush tropical climate is perfect for beach resorts. Several have come of age as glittering resorts served by jet aircraft and guarded from the sea by towering walls of high-rise luxury hotels. Nevertheless, there are inexpensive hotels and restaurants in the older downtown sections of most cities. Best of all, some villages are still laid-back, undiscovered, and inexpensive, especially San Blas and Barra de Navidad.

Each of Mexico's fabled Pacific resorts has its own special *ambiente,* which you will discover more readily by traveling on $45 a day than if you zip in by Lear Jet and stay at the Westin. This chapter describes the most northerly of this section's resort cities.

SEEING THE PACIFIC COAST FROM SAN BLAS TO IXTAPA

It's difficult to make suggestions on how to parcel your time since Mexico's mid Pacific Coast caters to so many kinds of vacationers. For a combination of glitz and laid-back village Mexico, but at reduced prices, it's hard to beat Ixtapa-Zihuatanejo. A few of the cities and villages are close together, so you could easily try out several before heading home. The best time to go is off-season, especially October to mid-December, when prices are their lowest and the hotels less crowded; some are almost empty.

1. SAN BLAS

550 miles NW of Mexico City, 190 miles NW of Guadalajara, 150 miles N of Puerto Vallarta, 1,173 miles S of Mexicali, 220 miles S of Mazatlán

GETTING THERE By Bus From Puerto Vallarta, **Transportes del Pacífico,** Insurgentes 160 (tel. 2-1015), has hourly service to Tepic. From Tepic to San Blas buses leave frequently. The bus station is conveniently located on the main square, Calle Sinaloa (tel. 5-0043).

WHAT'S SPECIAL ABOUT THE CENTRAL PACIFIC COAST

Birding
☐ San Blas, famous for its mangrove trips and 300 bird species.

☐ Colima, with rich bird life that can be seen from the highway, but especially around Laguna Cuyutlan, Manzanillo lagoon, and near the volcanoes east of Colima City.

Fishing
☐ Mexico's Pacific Coast is known for its abundance of marlin and sailfish.

Museums
☐ Museum of Western Cultures, in Colima, full of pre-Hispanic artifacts including clay dancing dogs.

☐ Museum of Popular Culture Pomar, in Colima, displaying regional clothing from throughout Mexico.

Phenomena
☐ Magnetic field near Comala causes vehicles to move without motors turned on.

By Car From Tepic take the four-lane toll road ("Cuota") north to the exit for San Blas; the toll is about $3. From here to the coast, the two-lane highway takes about an hour to wind through ever-lusher tropical country, finally emerging into the sleepy town on the Pacific.

ESSENTIALS The **telephone area code** is 321.

Climate The rainy season is May through October, though this usually means brief showers, with September and October the wettest months. The no-see-ums are worst during the rainy season, so bring plenty of repellent. Summer can be hot and steamy.

DEPARTING By Bus The bus station is conveniently located on the main square, Calle Sinaloa (tel. 5-0043). **Transportes del Noroeste, Norte de Sonora,** and **Tres Estrellas de Oro** each has several runs a day to Tepic and two a day each to Guadalajara. From Tepic there are buses north to Mazatlán and south to Puerto Vallarta, and beyond.

San Blas, Nayarit (pop. 10,000) is an easy-going fishing village and tourist town on a lush section of the Pacific Coast. It has beaches edged with coconut palms and palapa beach-shack restaurants selling fresh grilled fish, and its slow, dreamy pace makes visitors want to linger. It is known for its excellent surfing (one beach is said to have the longest waves in the world), its great variety of birds (more than 300 species), and the idyllic jungle cruise up a river to the Tovara springs. Along the road into town, watch for stands selling smoked fish and tiny houses woven of mangrove branches.

ORIENTATION

INFORMATION The **Tourist Office** is next door to McDonald's Restaurant on Calle Juárez, open daily (usually) from 4 to 6pm.

CITY LAYOUT As you enter the village of San Blas on the principal street, **Juárez,** the main square is on the right. At its far end sits the old church, with a new one next to it. Next door is the bus station, and on the other side of the churches, the mercado (market). After passing the square, the first one-way street to the left is **Batallon,** an important thoroughfare that passes a bakery, a medical clinic, several hotels, and Los

Cocos Trailer Park, and ends at **Borrego Beach,** with its many outdoor fish restaurants.

GETTING AROUND

Nearly everything is within walking distance, and there are public buses that go to the farther beaches, Matanchen and Los Cocos, on their way to the next village to the south, Santa Cruz.

WHAT TO SEE & DO

After you've walked around the town and taken the river cruise, there's not a lot to do besides relax, swim, read, walk the beach, and eat fish—unless you're a serious birdwatcher or surfer. During the winter months, however, you can also look for **whales** off the coast of San Blas.

PORT OF SAN BLAS   Like Acapulco, San Blas was once a very important port for New Spain's trade with the Philippines. Pirates would attempt to intercept the rich Spanish galleons headed for San Blas, and so the town was fortified. Ruins of the fortifications complete with cannons, the old church, and houses all overgrown with jungle are still visible atop the hill, **La Contadura.** The fortress settlement was destroyed during the struggle for independence in 1811, and has been in ruins ever since. Also, it was from San Blas that Fr. Junípero Serra also set out to establish missions in California during the 18th century.

The view from La Contadura is definitely worth the trouble to get there: The entire surrounding area stretches out before you, a panorama of coconut plantations, coastline, town, and lighthouse at Playa del Rey.

To reach the ruins from San Blas, head east on Avenida Juárez about half a mile, as if going out of town. Just before the bridge, take the stone path that winds up the hill to your right.

BEACHES & WATER SPORTS   One of the closest beaches is **Borrego Beach,** south from the town plaza on Batallon until it ends. This is a gray sand beach edged with palapa restaurants selling fish. For a more secluded place to swim, pay a fisherman to take you across Estuary El Pozo at the southwest edge of town to the "island," actually **El Rey Beach.** Walk to the other side of the island and you might have it all to yourself. Or try the beach on the other side of the lighthouse on this island. Bring your own shade, for there are no trees. The fisherman "ferry" charges about $1 one way and operates from 6am to 6pm. Canoes and small boats can also be rented at the harbor on the west side of town, following Avenida Juárez.

About 3 miles south of San Blas is **Matanchen Bay.** If driving, head out Avenida Juárez toward Tepic, cross the bridge, and turn right at the sign to Matanchen. A bus also stops there on its way south to the village of Santa Cruz, departing from the bus station on the main square at 9am, 11am, 1pm, 3pm, and 5pm; check on the return stops at Matanchen Bay, which are generally an hour later. There's a little settlement here where you can have a snack or a meal, or rent a boat and guide for the jungle river cruise.

Half a mile past the settlement is a dirt road to **Las Islitas Beach,** a magnificent swath of sand stretching for miles, with a few beach-shack eateries. This is the famous surfing beach of the mile-long waves, and real and would-be surfing champions come from Mexico and the U.S. to test their mettle here, especially during September and October, when storms create the biggest waves. If you don't have a surfboard, you can usually rent one from one of the local surfers for around $2 an hour. The body-surfing at Islitas and Matanchen is good, too. A taxi to Islitas will cost about $4 from downtown San Blas.

Farther south from Matanchen is beautiful **Playa Los Cocos,** lined with coconut palms. It's also on the bus route to Santa Cruz, but double-check on stops and schedules before boarding in San Blas.

JUNGLE CRUISE TO TOVARA SPRINGS   Almost the moment you hit San Blas, you'll be approached by a "guide" who offers "a boat ride into the jungle." This can be exciting, but expensive as well, depending on how many people share the cost: about $40 for a boatload of one to four people for the 3- to 4-hour trip from the bridge at the edge of town on Juárez. It's less (about $30) for the shorter, 2-hour trip from the Embarcadero near Matanchen Bay, out of town. Either way it's worth it if you take the early-morning cruise—through shady mangrove mazes and tunnels, past tropical birds and cane fields, to the beautiful natural springs, La Tovara, where you can swim. There's a restaurant here too, but stick to soft drinks or beer. This is one of the unique tropical experiences in Mexico, and to make the most of it, find a guide who will leave at 6:30 or 7am: The first boat on the river encounters the most birds, and the Tovara River is like glass then, unruffled by breezes. Around 9am the boatloads of tour groups start arriving and the serenity evaporates like the morning mist.

Note: The guide may also offer to take you to "The Plantation"—pineapple and banana plantations on a hill outside of town. The additional cost of this trip, for most people, is not worth it.

BIRDWATCHING   As many as 300 species of birds have been sighted here, one of the highest counts in the western hemisphere. Birders and hikers should pick up a copy of the booklet "Where to Find Birds in San Blas, Nayarit," on sale at the Hotel Las Brisas Resort. With maps and directions, it details all the best birding spots and walks—including hikes to some lovely waterfalls where nonbirdwatchers can swim, too. Probably the best bilingual guide to birds and the area is **Manuel Lomelli**, who can be reached through the Las Brisas Motel (tel. 321/5-0307 or 5-0558). A day's tour will cost around $100, which can be divided among the participants. Birding is best from mid-October to April.

WHERE TO STAY
DOUBLES FOR LESS THAN $20

FLAMINGO HOTEL, Av. Juárez 105 Pte., San Blas, Nayarit 63740. Tel. 321/5-0448. 25 rms (all with bath).
$ Rates: $15 single; $17 double.
Built in 1863, this two-story hotel two blocks west of the main square housed the German Consulate in its grander years. And it retains some of its colonial charm in spite of its run-down condition. Some of the rooms are shabby (especially those upstairs), but those on either side of the courtyard are quite nice, with ceiling fans, 20-foot-high beamed ceilings, and barred windows. The quiet inner courtyard has high arches, a red-tile floor, massive Spanish furniture, and lush tropical plants. Manager Jimmy Mendosa speaks perfect English.

MISSION SAN BLAS HOTEL, Av. Cuauhtémoc 197, San Blas, Nayarit 63740. Tel. 321/5-0023. 20 rms (all with bath).
$ Rates: $15 single; $17 double. Extra person $4.
Formerly the Posada Casa Morales, this group of bungalows, on the waterfront at El Pozo Estuary, is within walking distance of town. Some of the bungalows have a view of the ocean; others overlook the pool and garden. The large rooms have cinderblock walls and fans, with two double beds or three singles.

HOTEL LOS BUCANEROS, Av. Juárez 75 Pte., San Blas, Nayarit 63740. Tel. 321/5-0101. 33 rms (all with bath).
$ Rates: $15 single; $19 double.
A 6-foot-long stuffed crocodile smiles at visitors with open jaws in the lobby. An equally large cayman lives in a pen out back; although it looks fierce, it flees from humans. Rooms are arranged around a courtyard and all have fans. Guests enjoy the swimming pool with lots of deck space. The hotel is on the main street near the town plaza.

DOUBLES FOR LESS THAN $35

MOTEL POSADA DEL REY, Calle Campeche 10, San Blas, Nayarit 63740. Tel. 321/5-0123. 12 rms (all with bath).

$ Rates: $26 single; $28 double.
Rooms, all with fans, are arranged around a tiny courtyard taken up entirely by a little swimming pool that could be cleaned more frequently. An open-air bar and restaurant on the third floor provides a lovely view of ocean and palms. The motel is one block in from the waterfront at El Pozo Estuary, five blocks south of the town plaza.

SUITES SAN BLAS, Matanchen and Las Palmas (Apdo. Postal 12), San Blas, Nayarit 63740. Tel. 321/5-0047 or 5-0505. 23 suites (all with bath).
$ Rates: $30 suite for two; $35–$45 suite for four to six. Extra person $6.
This three-story apartment house has one- and two-bedroom suites with dark, Spanish-style furniture, fans, multiple beds, kitchen, and balcony. There's a restaurant, swimming pool, children's pool, and a grassy children's playground with tall coconut palms. It's about seven blocks south on Batallon and then left on Las Palmas one block to Matanchen.

DOUBLES FOR LESS THAN $45

MARINO INN, Av. Batallon and Av. Las Islitas, San Blas, Nayarit 63740. Tel. 321/5-0303. 54 rms (all with bath). A/C
$ Rates: $35 single; $42 double; extra person $8.
This four-star hotel about six blocks south of the main square looks like a typical American hotel and lacks all Mexican charm. But it's the only totally air-conditioned hotel in town and has the largest swimming pool, plus a separate pool for kids. Ask to see a room first—some can be dark and musty.

WORTH THE EXTRA BUCKS

HOTEL LAS BRISAS RESORT, Calle Paredes Sur, San Blas, Nayarit 63740. Tel. 321/5-0480, 5-0307, or 5-0308. Fax 321/5-0112. 42 units (all with bath), 5 minisuites (3 with kitchenette).
$ Rates (including breakfast): $40 single ($50 with A/C); $47 double ($54 with A/C); more for suites. **Parking:** Free.
A block inland from the waterfront, nestled among pretty gardens of palms, hibiscus, and other tropical plants are the cottagelike quadruplexes and other buildings (one with three stories) of this oasislike resort. The tranquil ambience, two pools (one for toddlers), and one of the best restaurant/bars in town all add to the appeal of the nicest place to stay in San Blas. The rooms (all with fans, 18 with air conditioning) are modern, bright, and airy. Another bonus is the manager, María Josefina Vazquez, one of the most knowledgeable and helpful people I've met on the Pacific Coast!
To get here, walk south from the square on Batallon for about six blocks, turn right on Campeche across from the Marino Inn, and then left on the next street, Paredes Sur.

CAMPING

For camping, try the **Los Cocos Trailer Park,** at Avenida Batallon and Calle Jose Azueta (tel. 321/5-0055), near the beach. It has 100 spaces and charges $6 single, $8 double, per day for a basic hookup in its grassy park with palm trees. It also has a self-service laundry and a bar.

WHERE TO EAT

Sad to report, the long-established, popular restaurant Diligencias, at Juárez 93 Pte., is now a gift shop. The owners remember their long-time Frommer friends and want them to know they're still there to offer advice. They also said that you are welcome to use their address to receive mail from home.

For an inexpensive meal, try fresh grilled fish from one of the little shacks on the beach. A fairly large fish (filet or whole) with hot tortillas and fresh coconut milk to drink will cost about $5. The prices are the same at all of these places. From town, take Avenida Batallon south from the plaza—follow your nose when you smell the fish grilling.

MEALS FOR LESS THAN $15

TONY'S LA ISLA, Mercado and Paredes. Tel. 5-0407.
   Specialty: MEXICAN.
$ Prices: Appetizers $2–$4; main courses $4–$10.
   Open: Tues–Sun 2–10pm.

Some swear that the best seafood in San Blas is served at "Chef Tony's." Hanging shark jawbones, fish nets, and shells set the mood for the excellent shrimp, oysters, lobster, and fish. Or try the filet mignon with mushrooms. It's about two blocks south of the plaza, near the post office.

McDONALD'S, Juárez 36 Pte.
   Specialty: MEXICAN.
$ Prices: Appetizers $2–$5; main courses $5–$10; beef and seafood shish kebab $7.
   Open: Nov–June, daily 7am–10pm; July–Oct, Wed–Mon 7am–10pm.

This isn't what you're thinking—in fact, this family-run restaurant, founded by Glenn McDonald of Iowa, has been operating in San Blas for 35 years. Specialties of the house include a seafood platter of fish, oysters, and shrimp, and a shish kebab of seafood and beef tenderloin. It's ½ block west of the town square.

WORTH THE EXTRA BUCKS

RESTAURANT EL DELFIN, in the Hotel Las Brisas Resort, Calle Paredes Sur. Tel. 5-0112 or 5-0480.
   Specialty: MEXICAN.
$ Prices: Appetizers $3–$6; main courses $7–$20.
   Open: Daily 8am–9:30pm.

This hotel restaurant serves the best food in San Blas, in an open-air dining room protected by screens and cooled by ceiling fans. Soft light, soft music, and comfortable captain's chairs add to the serene ambience. The chef masterfully plays from a wide repertoire of sauces: try the steak with mustard sauce, the chicken "orange," or the exquisite shrimp or fish with a creamy *chipotle* pepper sauce. Homemade soups and desserts deserve encores, too.

EVENING ENTERTAINMENT

At the moment, San Blas has two discothèques: **Disco Laffite** at the Hotel Los Bucaneros (tel. 5-0101) opens on weekends, while the **Marino Inn's disco** (tel. 5-0303) is open only during the Christmas and Easter (Holy Week) holidays. Both start around 10pm and close during the wee hours. But discos and their schedules come and go, so check locally upon arrival.

On most evenings (especially Sunday night), the plaza fills up with young people, talking and laughing while eating ice cream.

MIKE'S PLACE, Av. Juárez. Tel. 5-0432.
   Live music is featured at this nightclub above McDonald's Restaurant, just west of

the square. Here patrons can enjoy the view of the square and street from a balcony with tables. Manager Mike McDonald plays the organ and sings most nights from 9pm until 1 or 2am. When flamenco or folk groups perform, however, there's a cover charge. Open Monday through Saturday from 6pm to 2am and on Sunday from noon to 9pm; there's live music Wednesday through Saturday. Drinks run $2 to $5.

Admission: Usually free.

VIEJANOS, Av. Batallon 25.
This bar a few doors south of the plaza offers recorded music, TV, and videos. The sign says LADIES' BAR, but it's really more of a cantina and sports bar for men, though couples are fine. Open Monday through Saturday from 9am to 1am. Drinks cost $2.50.

LA FAMILIA, Av. Batallon 18. Tel. 5-0258.
This relatively new restaurant and video bar creates a festive mood with colorful tablecloths, bright *papel picado* hung here and there, and Mexican folk art and doodads on the walls. Open daily from 7:30am to 10pm. Drinks are $2 to $4.

EN ROUTE

Capital of the state of Nayarit, **Tepic** is a busy, dusty city with little in the way of tourist attractions. But it can be a convenient overnight or meal stop on the way to other places, and serves as the principal bus and train terminus for those going to or from San Blas, 40 miles away on the coast.

---

2. PUERTO VALLARTA

620 miles W of Mexico City, 260 miles W of Guadalajara,
175 miles N of Manzanillo, 300 miles S of Mazatlán,
112 miles S of Tepic.

GETTING THERE By Plane Aero California has nonstop or direct flights from Phoenix and San Diego. **Aeroméxico** flies from Los Angeles as well as from Guadalajara, La Paz, León, Mexico City, and Tijuana. **Alaska Airlines** flies from Los Angeles and San Francisco. **American Airlines** has direct flights from Dallas/Fort Worth. **Continental** flies nonstop from Houston. **Delta** flies nonstop from Los Angeles. **Mexicana** has direct or nonstop flights from Chicago, Dallas/Fort Worth, Denver, Los Angeles, and San Francisco, plus Guadalajara, Mazatlán, and Mexico City. **TAESA** has direct charter flights from San Antonio. The regional airline **Aero Vallarta** flies to and from Manzanillo November through Easter.

Check with a travel agent regarding charter service; **charters** from New York, Los Angeles, Minneapolis, and other cities are anticipated during 1992.

By Bus From Mexico City, Guadalajara, or points north and south along the coast, Puerto Vallarta is served by a whole slew of bus lines: **Tres Estrellas de Oro** (first class), **Estrella Blanca** (first class), **Tranportes del Pacífico** (first and second class), **Transportes Norte de Sonora** (first and second class), and **Autotransportes del Pacífico** (second class).

By Car From Mazatlán to the north (6 hrs.) or Manzanillo to the south (3.5 hrs.), the only choice is the coastal highway. From Guadalajara (8 hrs.), take Highway 15 to Tepic, then Highway 200 south.

By Ferry Ferry service between Puerto Vallarta and Cabo San Lucas in Baja California has been suspended. Inquire at the tourist office for the latest information or call the SEMATUR ferry office in Mexico City (tel. 5/53-7957).

DEPARTING By Plane Most airline offices are downtown: **Aero California,**

Plaza Caracol, Marina 23G (tel. 1-1571, or 1-1444 at the airport); **Aeroméxico,** Juárez 255 (tel. 1-1897, 2-5898, or 2-0031, or 2-1055 or 2-1204 at the airport); **Alaska Airlines,** at the airport (tel. 3-0350 or 3-0351, or toll free 95-800/426-0333 in Mexico); **American Airlines,** at the airport (tel. 1-1927, 2-3788, 2-3878 or 2-3787); **Continental,** at the airport (tel. 2-3095 or 2-3096); **Delta,** at the airport (tel. 2-4032 or 2-3919, or toll free 91-800/9-0221 in Mexico); **Mexicana,** Juárez 202 (tel. 2-5000); and **Aero Vallarta,** Zaragoza and Juárez (tel. 2-2210, or 2-0999 or 2-5354 at the airport).

By Bus   The second-class **Autotransportes del Pacifico,** at the corner of Constitución and Madero (tel. 2-3436), has hourly buses to Manzanillo from 5am to 6pm (a 6-hour trip), and service almost as frequent to Melaque (a 4½-hour trip). It also has four buses a day to Guadalajara between 8am and 10pm. Buy your ticket an hour before departure or even a day ahead. This is the best line for Manzanillo and Melaque.

The first-class **Tres Estrellas de Oro,** Insurgentes 210 (tel. 2-1019), offers 12 buses daily for the 12-hour trip to Guadalajara; you can buy a reserved-seat ticket the day before. It also has *de paso* buses to Culiacán, Mazatlán, and Manzanillo. The station is small and understaffed, and what staff there is tends to be surly and gleefully unhelpful.

Transportes Norte de Sonora, at Madero 343, near Insurgentes (tel. 3-1322), has one bus to Tepic at 6am (a 3-hour trip). In addition, it offers a 3pm bus to Mexico City and two to Guadalajara, including one first-class bus at 11pm.

Transportes del Pacifico, Insurgentes 160 (tel. 2-1015), has both first- and second-class service to Guadalajara and Mexico City, and second-class buses to Tepic. The Tepic buses depart almost hourly from 5am to 9pm (a 3½-hour trip). **Estrella Blanca** (first class), Insurgentes 180 (tel. 2-0613), goes to Tepic (at 10am and 5pm), Irapuato, Mexico City (three buses daily), and Guadalajara (four buses daily).

Puerto Vallarta (pop. 250,000) is gorgeous, with its tropical mountains right beside the sea, its coves and beaches, and its Mexican town of white buildings with red-tile roofs. Puerto Vallarta's development—mostly on the outskirts of the original town—has lent prosperity without destroying the charm.

Once an agricultural village on the Bay of Banderas, far from roads, airports, electricity, and tourism, Puerto Vallarta ceased to be a secret with the filming of *Night of the Iguana.* Elizabeth Taylor bought a house in the village and the growth of a booming resort started with a good highway and a jetport.

Growth has been to the north and south along the beach. Marina Vallarta, a resort-city-within-a-city, is at the northern edge of the hotel zone not far from the airport. It boasts half a dozen luxury hotels and condominium projects, a huge marina with 300 yacht slips, a golf course, restaurants and bars, an office park, and a shopping plaza. Between it and downtown are many more luxury hotels such as the Krystal and Fiesta Americana. Nuevo Vallarta, another masterplanned resort, is just north of Marina Vallarta and across the Ameca River in the state of Nayarit (about 8 miles north of downtown). It also has hotels, condominiums, and a yacht marina, plus a convention center under construction. Another complete new resort complex is on the drawing board for Nueva Vallarta and we'll be hearing more about it. For now, though, Nueva Vallarta is too difficult to reach by public transportation and all hotels are out of our budget range.

South of town about 6 miles on Mismaloya Beach, where *Night of the Iguana* was filmed, lies the Jolla de Mismaloya Resort & Spa, which marks the farthest development to the south. Between it and downtown are more five-star hotels on the beach and mountainside.

ORIENTATION

ARRIVING   By Plane   The airport is close to the north end of town on the main highway, only about 6 miles from downtown, where most of the budget hotels are located. Upon arriving, take the airport minivan (*colectivo*) for about $5 (the exact

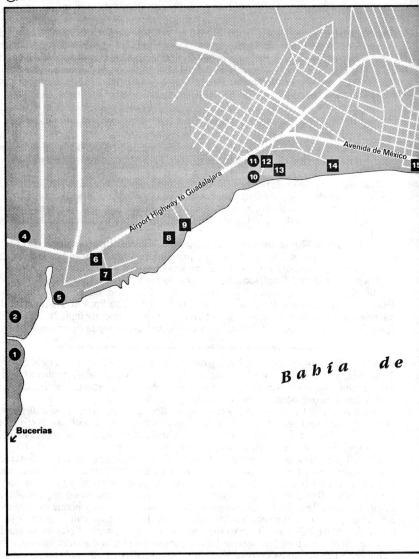

Avenida de México

Airport Highway to Guadalajara

Bucerias

Bahía de

Puerto Vallarta

MEXICO CITY

ACCOMMODATIONS:

Hotel Buenaventura 15	Krystal Hotel 7
Hotel Camino Real 22	Nueva Rosita Hotel 16
Fiesta Americana Hotel 9	Playa de Oro Hotel 6
Garza Blanca Hotel 23	Plaza Las Glorias Hotel 12
Holiday Inn Hotel 8	Plaza Vallarta Fiesta
Hyatt Coral Grand Hotel 24	Americana Hotel 13
Jolla de Mismaloya Hotel 25	Sheraton Hotel 14

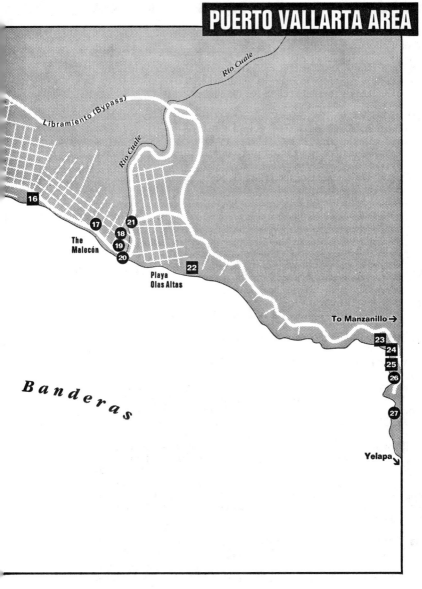

PUERTO VALLARTA AREA

Río Cuale

Libramiento (Bypass)

Río Cuale

Río Cuale

16

17

The Malecón

21

18

19

20

Playa Olas Altas

22

To Manzanillo →

23

24

25

26

27

B a n d e r a s

Yelapa ↘

ATTRACTIONS:

Airport **2**

American Express Office **11**

Boca de Tomatlán (village) **26**

Bullring/Plaza de Toros **4**

Cathedral **18**

Restaurant Chico's Paradise **27**

Marina Vallarta **1**

Nueva Vallarta **1**

Pier/Muelle **5**

Post Office/Correos **17**

Tourist Office **19**

Villa Vallarta Center **10**

Zócalo/Main Square **20**

Market **21**

fare depends on where you're going); or walk a block to the highway and catch a city bus for about 35¢.

By Bus   If you arrive by bus, you'll be south of the river on Madero, Insurgentes, or Constitución, and close to many of our hotel selections. Most of the bus "stations" are small offices or waiting rooms for the various lines.

INFORMATION   The **State Tourism Office,** at Juárez and Independencia (tel. 322/2-0242, 2-0243, or 3-0744), is in a corner of the white Presidencia Municipal building near the main square. This is also the office of the tourist police. Open Monday through Friday, 9am to 9pm; Saturday from 9am to 1pm.

CITY LAYOUT   Once in the center of town, nearly everything is within walking distance. The seaside promenade, or **Malecón,** follows the rim of the bay from north to south, and the town stretches back into the hills half a dozen blocks. Coming in from the airport, north of town, you'll pass the town pier, the Marina Vallarta development, and many luxury hotels; downtown the Malecón is lined with more hotels.

The area north of the **Río Cuale** is the oldest part of town—the original Puerto Vallarta. The area south of the river used to be only beach, but in the last decade it has become as built-up as the old town. Today the best budget lodgings, as well as the bus "stations," are here.

GETTING AROUND

BY BUS & COLECTIVO   City buses run from the airport through the expensive hotel zone along 31 de Mayo (the waterfront street), across the Río Cuale and inland on Vallarta, looping back through the downtown hotel and restaurant districts, on Insurgentes and several other downtown streets. These will serve just about all your transportation needs frequently and cheaply—about 35¢ a ride.

All local buses leave from the same plaza, **Plaza Lázaro Cárdenas,** a few blocks south of the river at Cárdenas and Suarez. Hours are generally from 6am to 8 or 9pm. The buses heading north leave from the beach side of the plaza, on Olas Altas. If you want to go north to the airport, take a bus marked "Ixtapa" or "Junta."

If you want to go south, take the no. 02 minivan (*colectivo*), which leaves from the east side of the plaza, away from the beach, every 10 to 15 minutes all day until 5pm, then every half hour until 8 or 9pm. Be sure to ask if you want to go to Mismaloya Beach; another no. 02 goes farther to Boca de Tomatlan (a fishing village) and may not stop at Mismaloya. Otherwise there are few regular stops—you just tell the driver where you want to get out. The fare is about 50¢. As a rule, locals riding the buses and minivans are very helpful to tourists.

BY BOAT   The town pier (*muelle*), where you'll catch pleasure boats to Yelapa and for fishing excursions, is north of town near the airport and a convenient, inexpensive bus ride from town. Just take any bus marked "Pittalal" and tell the driver to let you off at the *muelle*. Do not confuse the town pier with the new pier south of the river at Playa Olas Altas.

BY TAXI   Most trips downtown cost $2 to $3; to or from Mismaloya Beach to the south costs $8 to $10. But with such good bus service there's little reason to use them.

FAST FACTS

American Express   The local office is located in the Villa Vallarta shopping center on the main highway to the airport (Carretera Aeropuerto km 2.5), north of downtown (tel. 2-6876, or toll free 91-800/0-0333 in Mexico).

Area Code   The telephone area code is 322.

Climate   It's hot and humid in the summer.

Laundry   The **Lavandería Nelly,** on Guerrero near Matamoros, will wash and dry a load of clothes for about $3. Open Monday through Friday from 9am to 1:30pm and 4 to 8pm, and on Saturday from 9am to 1:30pm.

U.S. Consular Agency   The office is at Miramar and Libertad, on the second floor of Parian del Puente 12B, just north of the river bridge near the market (tel. 322/2-0069, 24 hours a day for emergencies). Open Monday, Wednesday, and Friday from 9am to 1pm; on Tuesday and Thursday from 10am to 1pm.

WHAT TO SEE & DO

The Tourism Office and travel agencies can provide information on what to see and do, and travel agencies can arrange tours, car rentals, and other activities. I highly recommend the agencies **Viajes Toucan Tours** (tel. 2-4600 or 2-4646) and **Viajes Marely** (tel. 2-5973).

Note: Beware of "tourist information" booths along the street—they are usually time-share hawkers offering "free" or cheap Jeep rentals, cruises, breakfasts, etc., as bait. If you're suckered in, you may or may not get what is offered and the experience will cost at least half a day of your vacation.

THE BEACHES   Its beaches are Puerto Vallarta's main attraction. They start well north of town, out by the airport, with **Playa de Oro,** and extend all around the broad Bay of Banderas. The most popular are **Playa Olas Altas,** also known as Playa Muertos or Playa del Sol, just off Calle Olas Altas, south of the Río Cuale; and **Playa Mismaloya,** in a beautiful sheltered cove about 6 miles south of town along Highway 200. It was at Mismaloya that *Night of the Iguana* was filmed. You can still see and hike up to the stone buildings that were constructed for the movie, on the point framing the south side of the cove. The Jolla de Mismaloya Resort is on this beach, as well as several rustic seafood restaurants; this and all beaches in Mexico are public.

Along the route to Mismaloya (see "Getting Around," above) are many other fine beaches, including **Punta Negra,** with soft white sand, an enjoyable view, and a little palapa restaurant. You can ask the driver to let you off at any point and explore the area for yourself.

Around the rocky point **south of Playa Olas Altas** are quite a number of small, sheltered coves that get very little use and are much nicer than the Coney Island atmosphere of the main beach.

BOAT TRIPS   Puerto Vallarta offers a number of different boat trips, including **sunset cruises** and **excursions to Yelapa** (a tiny town on a lovely cove), **Las Animas Beach, La Manzanilla Beach,** and **Quimixto Falls.** Some make a stop at the **Los Arcos** rock formations for **snorkeling,** some include lunch, and most provide music and an open bar on board. Prices range from $20 for a sunset cruise to $50 for an all-day outing. Viajes Toucan Tours (tel. 2-4600 or 2-4646) and other travel agencies have tickets and information. **Scuba diving** and **fishing** excursions can also be arranged through travel agencies; or you can try your luck by negotiating directly at the town pier or the marina Las Peinas farther north, where many dive and charter boats are docked. Fishing charters run $60 to $300 a day. Dive trips start around $50 per person.

Note: The town pier/marina used by most pleasure boats is north of downtown near the airport. Don't confuse it with the new pier at Playa Olas Altas south of the river.

SPORTS & RECREATION   Puerto Vallarta has two **golf** courses: an 18-hole private course at Marina Vallarta for members only; and the 18-hole Los Flamingos Club de Golf, 5 minutes north of Nuevo Vallarta (tel. 2-5025, ext. 1203). Golf packages are available at the Villas Quinta Real and Marriott Casa Magna in Marina Vallarta.

Waterskiing, parasailing, and other water sports are available at many beaches along the Bay of Banderas.

Bullfights are held from November through April on Wednesday afternoon at the Bullring "La Paloma," across the highway from the town pier. Tickets can be arranged through a travel agency or through Foto Taurina (tel. 2-1158).

TOURS   You can join **city tours, jungle tours,** and **horseback-riding tours** at several different ranches in the country, arranged through Viajes Marely (tel. 2-5973) and other travel agencies. They cost $15 to $35 per person.

A **house-and-garden tour** of four private homes in town is offered every Saturday by the International Friendship Club for a donation of $12 per person. The tour bus departs from the main plaza by the Tourism Office (which has information about this event) at 11am. Proceeds are donated to local charities.

A STROLL THROUGH TOWN   Puerto Vallarta's tightly knit cobblestone streets are a delight to explore (with good walking shoes!), full of tiny shops, rows of windows edged with curling wrought iron, and vistas of red-tile roofs and sea. Start with a walk up and down the Malecón, the seafront boulevard. Among the sights not to miss is the **municipal building,** on the main square (next to the Tourism Office), which has a large mural by Manuel Lepe inside in its stairwell. Nearby, up Independencia, sits the **cathedral,** topped with its curious crown; on its steps women sell colorful herbs and spices to cure common ailments. Here Richard Burton and Elizabeth Taylor were married the first time—she in a Mexican wedding dress, he in a Mexican *charro* outfit.

Three blocks south of the church, head uphill on **Libertad,** lined with small shops and pretty upper windows; it brings you to the **public market,** on the river. After exploring the market, cross the bridge to the **island in the river;** sometimes a painter is at work on its banks. Walk down the center of the island toward the sea, and you come to the tiny **Museo del Cuale,** which exhibits pre-Columbian ceramics and local artists; it's open daily from 9am to 2pm and 3 to 8pm.

Retrace your steps back to the market and Libertad, and climb up steep Miramar to **Zaragoza:** At the top is a magnificent view over rooftops to the sea. Up Zaragoza to the right two blocks is the famous pink arched bridge that once connected Richard Burton's and Elizabeth Taylor's houses. This area is known as **Gringo Gulch,** where many Americans have houses.

SPECIAL EVENTS   The week leading up to **December 12**—the "birthday" of Mexico's patron saint, the Virgin of Guadalupe—is celebrated with processions of Las Peregrinas (religious pilgrims) and much merry-making.

WHERE TO STAY

Most of the bargain hotels are south of the Río Cuale. You may find even better prices than those below if you travel during May, August, and September—the slowest months of the off-season. Prices go up anywhere from 25% to 50% from mid-December through Easter Week, when all the best rooms are generally booked. It's best to have reservations in high season, but if you want to chance it, arrive early in the day and start your search. If you are told that the rooms are full, ask if you can leave your name and return at checkout time to see if anyone has vacated.

SOUTH OF THE RÍO CUALE
Doubles For Less Than $15

Along Madero and not far from the city's bus stations lie several hotels, the **Analiz, Azteca** and **Villa del Mar,** with the lowest rates in town. All are clean and have ceiling fans, private baths, and hot water. One drawback, however, is that many of the rooms have windows facing an indoor hallway. When the windows are open your neighbors can look in; when they're closed, you may feel as if you're in a closet. Another drawback is that some appear to rent rooms by the hour at night. They're also a five- to six-block walk from the beach. Ask to see the room before deciding.

HOTEL BERNAL, Madero 423, Puerto Vallarta, Jal. 48380. Tel. 322/2-3605. 34 rms (all with bath).

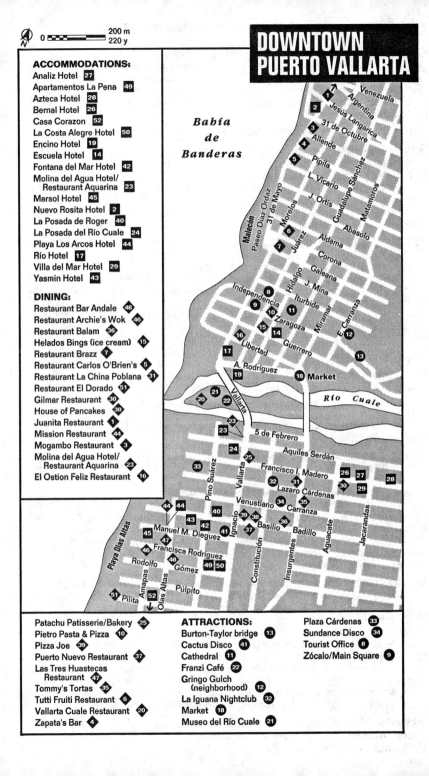

$ Rates: $11 single; $13 double; $15 triple; $17 quad.

The pink or yellow walls enclose small, clean rooms with two or three beds plus a fan and a chair and table. Generally this hotel is quiet and sheltered from bus noise, but a room away from the street may be preferable.

To get here, walk two blocks south of the river on Vallarta, then left onto Madero for four blocks.

Doubles For Less Than $25

HOTEL YASMIN, Badillo 168, Puerto Vallarta, Jal. 48380. Tel. 322/2-0087. 27 rms (all with bath).
$ Rates: $20 single; $23 double.
Located about a block from the beach (walk five blocks south of the river on Vallarta, then turn right onto Badillo about a block), this three-story hotel has a garden courtyard with sturdy metal tables and chairs. The rooms are clean but a bit shabby, with white-brick walls, fans, a chair, and a single light between the two beds.

HOTEL POSADA DE ROGER, Badillo 237, Puerto Vallarta, Jal. 48380. Tel. 322/2-0836 or 2-0639. 52 rms (all with bath).
$ Rates: $20 single; $23 double. Extra person $4.

This former pension is now a hotel with simple but homey, comfortable, and spotless rooms (all with fans, 24 with air conditioning) at a good price. Guests enjoy the small second-floor swimming pool and choose from several levels of terraces with tropical plants and bougainvillea. The hotel, five blocks south of the river (head down Vallarta, then turn right onto Badillo), has retained its friendly ambience, and guests still gather in the attractive courtyard for conversation and entertainment. The hotel's restaurant/bar, El Tucan, is downstairs.

The Hotel Posada de Roger also rents six apartments with bath and fans at two nice locations about two blocks away, but by the month only: $350 a month for two to four people. Some have kitchenettes. Reserve as early as possible.

Doubles For Less Than $40

Though some are beyond our range in high season, the hotels below offer excellent values in the off-season.

HOTEL COSTA ALEGRE, Rodríguez 168, Puerto Vallarta, Jal. 48380. Tel. 322/2-4793, or toll free 800/458-6888 in the U.S. 28 rms (all with bath). A/C TV TEL
$ Rates: $32 single; $36 double. 45% less in summer.
Next door to the Apartments La Pena seven blocks south of the river (walk down on Vallarta, then turn right on Rodríguez for half a block), this "sister" hotel of the Hotel Playa Los Arcos (see below) offers clean rooms with flowered bedspreads, wooden trunks, tile floors, and small refrigerators. A small swimming pool borders a well-tended garden. Guests can use the beach-club facilities of the Hotel Playa Los Arcos, a few blocks away.

APARTMENTS LA PENA, Rodríguez 174 (Apdo. Postal 177), Puerto Vallarta, Jal. 48380. Tel. 322/2-1213, or 313/661-1554 in the U.S. Fax 313/354-1089. 9 apartments (all with bath).
$ Rates: High season, $35 for a one-bedroom, $50 for a two-bedroom; off-season, $25 for a one-bedroom, $40 for a two-bedroom.
These recently painted apartments (eight one-bedroom and one two-bedroom) have fully equipped open-air kitchenettes on the balconies, fans, and filters to purify water; three have patios. The apartments are up on the rocks (that's what *pena* means) facing a garden, and all enjoy the ocean breeze. Maid service and clean towels are provided daily. Make reservations well in advance. The Rocks are seven blocks south of the river; walk down Vallarta, then turn right on Rodríguez for half a block.

POSADA RÍO CUALE, Serdan 242 (Apdo. Postal 146), Puerto Vallarta, Jal. 48380. Tel. 322/2-0450 or 2-0914. 21 rms (all with bath). A/C
$ Rates: $31 single; $36 double.

This delightful two-story hotel occupies one of the town's busiest intersections, a block south of the river at Serdan and Vallarta. Its large rooms have arched brick windows and wooden shutters; the quietest are away from Calle Vallarta. At night the swimming pool becomes a lighted fountain, and the courtyard around it is part of the popular Restaurant Gourmet, which has mariachi music on Friday, Saturday, and Sunday nights from 8 to 10:30pm. Park in front on the street.

HOTEL FONTANA DEL MAR, Dieguez 171, Puerto Vallarta, Jal. 48380. Tel. 322/2-0583 or 2-0712, or toll free 800/458-6888 in the U.S. 27 rms, 15 suites (all with bath). A/C TV TEL

$ Rates: High season, $35 single; $40 double. Off-season, $25 single; $30 double. $5–$7 more for suites.

One of the best budget hotels in the area is on a quiet side street in downtown Vallarta, six blocks south of the river on Vallarta and only two blocks from the Playa del Sol. The inviting decor includes curly white iron trim and royal blue. The clean, comfortable rooms overlook the plant-filled courtyard with more frilly iron trim. All rooms have showers, and the suites come with balconies or kitchenettes. Guests can use the small rooftop swimming pool or the pool and beach-club facilities at the Hotel Playa Los Arcos, a block away.

Worth the Extra Bucks

HOTEL MARSOL, Rodríguez 103 (Apdo. Postal 4), Puerto Vallarta, Jal. 48380. Tel. 332/2-1365 or 2-0865. 138 rms, 22 apartments (all with bath).
$ Rates: $28 single; $36 double; $46 apartment for one or two.
Right on Playa del Sol, this large, airy hotel has nothing but a row of coconut palms and a retaining wall between its veranda and the beach, while oceanside restaurants are a mere 50 yards away. The apartments have air conditioners, balconies facing the sea, and aging kitchenettes. The other rooms have fans and face the mountains and town. There's also a pool.

To get here, walk seven blocks south of the river on Vallarta, then turn right onto Rodríguez to the beach.

HOTEL MOLINO DE AGUA, Vallarta 130 (Apdo. Postal 54), Puerto Vallarta, Jal. 48380. Tel. 322/2-1907 or 2-1957, or toll free 800/826-9408 in the U.S., 800/423-5512 in California. Fax 322/2-6056. 20 rms, 16 suites, 29 cabins (all with bath). A/C

$ Rates: High season, $55–$85; low season, $35–$70. **Parking:** Free.
This complex of luxury cabins and small buildings, reached by winding walkways, is nestled into lush tropical gardens beside the river and sea; it's half a block south of the river on Vallarta. Although it's on a main street and centrally located, with all its big trees and open space it's a completely tranquil oasis. Some units are individual bungalows with private patios, and there's a small two-story building near the beach. Its amenities include a Jacuzzi beside the pool and an excellent restaurant/bar, the Aquarena. Parking is protected.

CASA CORAZON, 326 Amapas (Apdo. Postal 66), Puerto Vallarta, Jal. 48380. Tel. 322/2-1371 at the restaurant. 12 rms (all with bath).
$ Rates (including breakfast): High season, $55–$60 single or double; off-season, $20–$25 single or double.
Perched on a hill beside the Playa del Sol, this four-story villa has been converted by its American owners into a delightful bed-and-breakfast inn with fans in every room. It prides itself on its friendly, casual atmosphere, where guests get together over the complete breakfast served on the expansive terrace. The front gate opens onto the beach, where the inn has a bar and restaurant. No children under 12.

To get there, walk 10 blocks south of the river on Vallarta, turn right onto Pilita for 3 blocks, then left for half a block on Amapas.

Reservations: P.O. Box 937, Las Cruces, NM 88004 (tel. 505/523-4666 or 522-4684).

HOTEL PLAYA LOS ARCOS, Olas Altas 390, Puerto Vallarta, Jal. 48380.

Tel. 322/2-1583, or toll free 800/458-6888 in the U.S. Fax 322/2-0583. 135 rms, 10 suites (all with bath). A/C TEL

$ Rates: Dec 18–Easter, $40–$50 single; $50–$60 double; $70–$90 suites. Off-season, $46 double. Ask about further discounts in June, Sept, and Oct.

Conveniently located downtown, this popular four-story hotel is shaped like a U facing the beach, with a swimming pool in the courtyard. Rooms with private balconies overlook the pool, while the 10 suites have ocean views and kitchenettes. The standard rooms are small but pleasantly decorated with pink floral spreads and carved wooden furniture painted pale pink—two double beds, a dresser, a table, and two chairs. On the premises are tennis courts, a restaurant, a coffee shop, and a thatch-roofed beachside bar with occasional live music.

To get here, walk five blocks south of the river on Vallarta, then right onto Badillo for two blocks, and then left onto Olas Altas.

NORTH OF THE RÍO CUALE

This is the real center of town, where the market, principal plazas, church, and town hall all lie. Budget lodgings are scarce here, although most of the hotels are moderately priced.

Doubles For Less Than $30

HOTEL ESCUELA CECATTUR, Guerrero and Hidalgo, Puerto Vallarta, Jal. 48380. Tel. 322/2-4910. 14 rms (all with bath).
$ Rates: $17 single; $21 double.
Centrally located and next door to a public school, this clean, three-story hotel has the feeling of a pleasant dormitory or youth hostel. Each plain, spacious room comes with a fan (two have air conditioning), several beds, Formica furniture, and usually a large window. And because the hotel's in the heart of town—two blocks north of the river and three blocks in from the beach—restaurants and shops are just steps away.

HOTEL ENCINO, Juárez 122, Puerto Vallarta, Jal. 48380. Tel. 322/2-0051. Fax 322/2-2573. 75 rms (all with bath). A/C TEL
$ Rates: $22 single; $26 double.
The hotel's spotless rooms are cheerfully decorated with turquoise-blue furniture and other bright touches against the white walls and tile floors. Most have their own private balconies with sliding glass doors and views of the ocean, river, or mountains and town. Rooms also come with radios. Especially nice are the rooftop swimming pool and the restaurant/bar, Vista Cuale, which enjoy lovely vistas of mountains and sea.

To get here, head south on Juárez to the place where Vallarta crosses the river; the hotel is next to the bridge.

HOTEL RÍO, Morelos 170 (Apdo. Postal 23), Puerto Vallarta, Jal. 48300. Tel. 322/2-0366. 46 rms (all with bath).
$ Rates: $23 single; $26 double; $48 large room for six.
This three-story hotel a block north of the Río Cuale and about a block in from the beach has the same white concrete architecture as the Hotel Rosita. Its shady, lush courtyard surrounds a tiny kidney-shaped pool. The very clean rooms come with balconies and ceiling fans. Ask for one of the big corner rooms with extra-spacious balconies.

Worth the Extra Bucks

HOTEL BUENAVENTURA, Av. México 1301, Puerto Vallarta, Jal. 48350. Tel. 322/2-3737, or toll free 800/458-6888 in the U.S., 800/227-0212 in California. 210 rms (all with bath). A/C TEL
$ Rates: High season, $60 single; $70 double; $80 triple. Off-season, $40 single; $45 double; $50 triple.

⭐ The giant palapa roof of the hotel lobby and restaurant set the tone for the breezy, jungle-lush interior filled with *equipales* leather furniture. Somewhat off the beaten tourist track, the Buenaventura holds its place in the market with appealing prices, comfort, and a beautiful beachfront, on the beach about six blocks north of the Malecón at Nicaragua. The attractive rooms have balconies, beam-and-brick ceilings, and tile floors. There's also a swimming pool next to the beach. Only the fourth floor has color TV with U.S. channels.

READERS RECOMMEND

Bucerias Trailer Court, Bucerias, Nayarit, 12 miles north of Puerto Vallarta. "The Bucerias Trailer Court is a very clean AAA-recommended RV park and camping area on the beach. Camping spots with electric hookups go for $11.50 for two people, and they allow pets."—Jo Ann Farver, Stillwater, Okla. [*Author's Note*: Bucerias is a fishing village that has grown into a tourist area. Currently the town is still a little "sleepy" compared to Puerto Vallarta and other Pacific Coast spots (the coast of Nayarit is slated for intensive tourism development over the next decade).]

WHERE TO EAT

Although eating out in Puerto Vallarta has become more expensive, some bargains and good values remain. South of the river is the best area for finding inexpensive-to-moderate restaurants.

North of the river, a nice snack as you stroll along the Malecón is an *elote*—corn-on-the-cob served on a stick and either roasted or broiled, sold at little stands in the evening.

You can pick up inexpensive fruit, vegetables, and picnic fixings at the municipal market beside the Río Cuale where Libertad and Rodríguez meet. You can also eat upstairs at one of the many little *loncherías*—just choose something freshly cooked and hot.

SOUTH OF THE RÍO CUALE

Meals For Less Than $5

PATACHU PASTELERÍA, Vallarta 179.
  Specialty: FRENCH BAKERY.
$ **Prices:** Bread, pastries, and quiche by the piece 25¢–$2.
  Open: Daily 9am–9pm.
⭐ The young Parisian Frédéric Leborgne came all the way to Puerto Vallarta to open his French bakery. It's the real thing—selling authentic baguettes (both white and whole wheat), flaky croissants, individual fruit tarts, pies, and quiche (whole or by the slice). Drop in for a pastry with coffee or to get picnic supplies. It's two blocks south of the river on Vallarta.

TOMMY'S TORTAS, Insurgentes 323. Tel. 2-0175.
  Specialty: SANDWICHES.
$ **Prices:** Sandwiches $2.50–$4; fries $1.25; beer $1.25.
  Open: Daily 8am–midnight.
⭐ On the southern edge of the bus district, four blocks south of the river on Insurgentes between Cárdenas and Carranza, this neat new restaurant turns out delicious Mexican tortas (sandwiches made with various combinations of meat and cheese) and french fries, which diners wash down with beer or soft drinks. It's painted in dusky Santa Fe pastels and has three open arches across the front, with indoor and sidewalk tables.

Meals For Less Than $10

FONDA LA CHINA POBLANA, Insurgentes 222. Tel. 2-4049.
  Specialty: MEXICAN.

$ Prices: Breakfast $2–$2.50; appetizers $2–$6; main courses $3–$8; tacos $3.
Open: Daily 24 hours.

In the heart of the bustling bus station area, three blocks south of the river on Insurgentes between Madero and Cárdenas, this orderly café with checked tablecloths and brick arches is a real find—and it's open around the clock. You can watch food sizzling on the grill while downing tacos, steak, black-bean soup, or shrimp or oysters prepared five ways.

CASA DE HOTCAKES (The Pancake House), Badillo 289.
Specialty: AMERICAN/MEXICAN BREAKFAST.
$ Prices: Breakfast $3.50–$6.
Open: Breakfast/brunch only, Tues–Sun 8am–2pm.

For a hearty, American-style breakfast or brunch, stop at "the only pancake house on the west coast of Mexico." Mouth-watering pancakes and waffles are imaginatively mixed with fruit, chocolate, nuts, and even peanut butter. You can also pig out on eggs Benedict, cheese blintzes, breakfast burritos, or Belgian waffles. Owner and travel writer Memo Barroso and his Canadian wife recently remodeled the place with lots of tile and white stucco in a style suggesting an airy, contemporary hacienda. It's five blocks south of the river on Vallarta, then left on Badillo a block.

LAS TRES HUASTECAS, Olas Altas 444, at Rodríguez.
Specialty: MEXICAN.
$ Prices: Appetizers $2–$3.50; main courses $4.50–$8; eggs $1.50–$2; enchiladas Huastecas (meat, cheese, beans, and salsa) $4.
Open: Daily 8am–8:30pm.

Locals and tourists gather at this tried-and-true place near the Hotel Marsol (it's seven blocks south of the river on Vallarta, then right on Rodríguez two blocks to Olas Altas). The decor is cheery and bright, with colorful murals and ceilings painted with tropical Mexican scenes. Humorous Spanish poems by the owner, "El Querreque," are posted around the dining room; if you don't understand Spanish, ask someone to explain them to you. The menu is bilingual.

EL DORADO, Pulpito. Tel. 2-1511.
Specialty: MEXICAN.
$ Prices: Breakfast $1.50–$5; appetizers $2.50–$7; main courses $4.50–$12; green salad or sandwiches $3.50–$7.
Open: Daily 8am–9pm.

This open-air, palapa-roofed restaurant on the beach is a local favorite, especially for a hearty breakfast by the sea. Try the huevos Motulenos—Yucatecan-style eggs on tortillas with black beans, cheese, and a tangy salsa. In the late afternoon watch the surfers and parasailors while sipping a cool drink. Seafood is another specialty, and iced tea is always available.

To get here, walk nine blocks south of the river on Vallarta, then turn right onto Pulpito to its end at the beach.

RESTAURANT GILMAR, Madero 418. Tel. 2-3923.
Specialty: MEXICAN.
$ Prices: Appetizers $3–$4; main courses $4.50–$13; comida corrida $2–$4.50; pozole $3; carne asada $7.
Open: Daily 7am–11pm (comida corrida served 1–5pm).

The personal attention of owner Gilbert Martinez makes this modest Mexican diner a pleasant stop with good food. The house specialty is carne asada a la Tampiqueña, which comes with beef, salad, beans, rice, a quesadilla, an enchilada, and guacamole. Or try the spicy shrimp "diabla."

You can get here by walking two blocks south of the river on Vallarta and then turning left onto Madero for 3½ blocks.

Meals For Less Than $15

ARCHIE'S WOK, Rodríguez 130. Tel. 2-0411.
Specialty: ORIENTAL/ECLECTIC.

$ Prices: Appetizers $2–$4; main courses $4.50–$12.
Open: Daily 1–10pm.

After training as a chef in California, Archie Alpenia brought his family to Puerto Vallarta and ended up as chef to the late John Huston, the director who filmed *Night of the Iguana*. Today Archie's Wok stirs up delightfully eclectic Oriental fare: Filipino egg rolls, Thai coconut fish, chicken Singapore, and spicy red curry, to name but a few dishes. Desserts surprise with homemade fudge brownies, lime pie, and carrot cake. Archie's Wok is seven blocks south of the river on Vallarta, then left on Rodríguez for 2½ blocks.

PIZZA JOE, Badillo 269. Tel. 2-2477.
Specialty: ITALIAN.
$ Prices: Salad $4; main courses $5–$17; large pizza (14 in.) with everything $17; lasagne $8; pasta $5–$7; slice of cheesecake $2.50.
Open: Mon–Sat 2–11pm.

Behind a high brick wall lies a garden patio with twinkle lights in the trees, soft music, and red-checked tablecloths, where you can *mangi* under the stars on some of the best Italian *cuccina* in town. Besides pizza there's a good range of pastas, as well as vegetarian and meat lasagne. The decadent homemade cheesecake comes in several flavors: lemon-lime, orange, Kahlúa, and chocolate-almond. The young American-Canadian couple who own it, Joe and Clara, make everyone feel welcome. You'll find them five blocks south of the river on Vallarta, then left on Badillo half a block.

PUERTO NUEVO, Badillo 284.
Specialty: MEXICAN/SEAFOOD.
$ Prices: Appetizers $3–$6; main courses $6–$13; daily special $11.
Open: Daily 12:30–11pm.

Owner and chef Roberto Castellon presents seafood with inventive flair: Try the crab enchiladas, shrimp "filet mignon," or smoked marlin—or the unusual manta ray tacos. Dine inside or in the roofed, open-air sidewalk area hung with plants for a jungley effect. The restaurant is five blocks south of the river on Vallarta, then half a block left on Badillo.

RESTAURANT/BAR AQUARENA, in the Hotel Molino de Agua, Vallarta 130. Tel. 2-1907 or 2-1957.
Specialty: MEXICAN/SEAFOOD.
$ Prices: Breakfast $3–$6; appetizers $3.50–$6; main courses $3.50–$6 at lunch, $7–$15 at dinner; grilled seafood platter for two $30; Sat-night cook-out $10–$18.
Open: Breakfast daily 7:30–11:30am; lunch/dinner 11:30am–11pm (happy hour 6–9pm).

Have a relaxing meal immediately south of the river in the beautiful dining room decorated with bamboo, or on the shady terrace looking out on the pool and tropical gardens. While the pianist plays every night from 6 to 9:30pm (during high season), savor well-executed margaritas followed by the grilled seafood platter—a large tray of succulent lobster, shrimp, fish, and tender squid, the latter in a velvety, exquisitely spiced adobo sauce. For lunch, the tortilla soup is a filling and budget-wise winner. Afterward, take a stroll around the romantic gardens.

Worth the Extra Bucks

One of the unique attractions of Puerto Vallarta is its half-dozen **"jungle restaurants"** that offer open-air dining in a magnificent tropical setting by the sea or beside a mountain river.

CHICO'S PARADISE, Km 20 on Hwy. 200 south of town. Tel. 2-0747.
Specialty: MEXICAN/SEAFOOD. **Directions:** See below.
$ Prices: Appetizers $3–$11; main courses $8–$25; soups $3–$6; barbecued ribs $10; grilled seafood platter for two $50.
Open: Daily 11am–7pm.

Lunch at this lively tropical place, perched on the edge of a river gorge under a big thatched roof, can easily be a day's outing. Arrive early (noon) to get a good table, then enjoy the river view and the mariachis. Among the tasty dishes are barbecued ribs, fish sarandeado (grilled in a special way), seafood cazuelas (casseroles), black-bean soup, and the seafood platter for two. After dining, hike down to the river to swim and sunbathe, or explore the crafts and souvenir shops on the premises. Don't forget to bring your swimsuit, tennis shoes, and beach towels!

The restaurant is about 13 miles south of town on the main highway. Round-trip cab fare is about $30 (get a group of four to share). Or take the no. 02 minivan (50¢) to Boca de Tomatlán, a fishing village, and then get a taxi from there—a relatively short distance.

NORTH OF THE RÍO CUALE
Meals For Less Than $5

HELADOS BING, Juárez 280. Tel. 2-1627.
  Specialty: ICE CREAM.
  $ Prices: Single cone 90¢; special sundae $3.
  Open: Daily 8:30am–10:30pm.
The most popular ice-cream shop in town has a long list of flavors to choose from. It also has branches at Cárdenas and Constitución south of the river; at the airport; and at Villa Vallarta, the shopping center near the big hotels north of town. Just look for its pink-and-white decor. This one is on Juárez near Guerrero, about two blocks in from the Malecón and half a block from the main plaza.

TUTTI FRUTTI, Morelos and Corona. Tel. 2-1068.
  Specialty: HEALTH/VEGETARIAN/AMERICAN.
  $ Prices: Appetizers $1.50; main courses $1.50–$5; cinnamon coffee 50¢; fresh juices or licuados made with fresh fruit and milk or purified water $1.50; sandwich $1.50–$2; three quesadillas and beans $3; hamburger and fries $4.
  Open: Mon–Sat 8am–10pm.
This is a good spot for a quick snack near the Malecón. The menu includes grilled or cold sandwiches with all the trimmings. Eat at the counter or take your meal out.

Meals For Less Than $10

RESTAURANT JUANITA, Av. México 1067. Tel. 2-1458.
  Specialty: MEXICAN.
  $ Prices: Appetizers $1.50–$2.50; main courses $3–$10; comida corrida $3–$4; pozole $2; giant shrimp $10.
  Open: Daily 8am–10:30pm (comida corrida served noon–5pm).
Decorated with bright piñatas, paintings, and plaid tablecloths, this simple and cheerful restaurant is open to the sidewalk. Try the pozole (a hearty stew with meat and hominy) or splurge on the giant shrimp with garlic. It's on México near Venezuela, several blocks north of the Malecón.

PIETRO PASTAS & PIZZAS, Zaragoza 245, at Hidalgo. Tel. 2-3233.
  Specialty: ITALIAN.
  $ Prices: Appetizers $3.50–$7; main courses $6–$8; 12-in. pizzas $6–$8; pasta $6.50.
  Open: Daily noon–midnight.
Italian music and swags of braided garlic on the wall above a big brick oven wall set the mood for the menu offerings: ravioli, canneloni, lasagne, calzone, and of course, pizza. And the pasta is homemade. Pietro's is across the street and just south of the cathedral.

Meals For Less Than $15

BRAZZ, Morelos and Galeana. Tel. 2-0324.
  Specialty: MEXICAN.
  $ Prices: Breakfast $5–$6; appetizers $2.50–$6; main courses $7–$17; seafood casseroles $10.
  Open: Daily 8am–1am.
Lunch bargains are served in the air-conditioned dining room, surrounded by a large

open-air bar with leather *equipales* furniture. Festive *papel picado* (cut-out paper) and bits of painted fabric hang from the bar's high ceiling and flutter in the breeze. In the evening mariachis and marimbas play from 7pm to 1am. Brazz is just off the south end of the Malecón.

EL OSTION FELIZ, Libertad 177. Tel. 2-2508.
   Specialty: MEXICAN/SEAFOOD.
$ **Prices:** Appetizers $4.50–$7; main courses $8–$17; seafood salad $6; crab tacos $4; seafood casseroles $10; oyster cocktail or stew $6.
   Open: Daily 10am–midnight or 1am.
One block north of the river on Libertad just off Morelos, across from the Hotel Río, "The Happy Oyster" serves a cornucopia of seafood, including a salad of squid, octopus, frogs' legs, conch, and shark. Choose from seven different seafood casseroles or be macho and go for the shark ceviche! Crayfish from local rivers is available in season.

Worth the Extra Bucks

BOGART'S, in the Krystal Vallarta Hotel, Av. de las Garzas. Tel. 2-1459.
   Specialty: CONTINENTAL/ECLECTIC.
$ **Prices:** Appetizers $6–$20; main courses $12–$30.
   Open: Daily 6pm–midnight.
Pointed Moorish arches, murmuring fountains, a silky tent ceiling, and high-backed peacock chairs create the mysterious mood of Casablanca in this softly lighted, sumptuous restaurant. A pianist plays in the background while waiters out of *Arabian Nights* serve such delicacies as Persian crêpes (sour cream, cheese, and caviar), escargots, sorbet between courses, and flambéed shrimp Krystal. For a big splurge or a special occasion, a dinner in this fantasy place is unforgettable. It's north of downtown near the town pier; take the "Muelle" bus.

READERS RECOMMEND

Balam, Badillo 425, between Aguacate and Jacarandas (tel. 2-3451). *"Fresh seafood restaurant 1½ blocks east of Insurgentes. Only about 10 tables, and the food is fabulous. Try the lobster and pasta, or shrimp and pasta, or the seafood salad, or the fresh lobster, etc. I had them all. The main dishes run around $9 a plate. Tony (the owner) creates all recipes and visits every table."*—Kathleen R. Schweizer, Seattle, Wash.

SHOPPING

Excellent-quality merchandise is brought to Puerto Vallarta from all over Mexico. Prices are higher than in the places where the things originated, and if you're planning to visit other parts of Mexico, you might want to wait and make your purchases at the source. In Guadalajara, 6 hours away by bus, prices are considerably lower.

Puerto Vallarta's **municipal market** is just north of the Río Cuale where Libertad and Rodríguez meet. The mercado sells clothes, jewelry, serapes, shawls, leather accessories and suitcases, papier-mâché parrots, stuffed frogs and armadillos, and of course T-shirts. Be sure to do some comparative shopping before buying. It's open daily from 8am to 8pm.

Calle Libertad next to the market is the place to buy huaraches—comfortable, practical sandals made of leather strips and rubber-tire soles. Buy a pair that fits very tightly—they stretch out quickly and can become too floppy.

CRAFTS & FOLK ART

The **Olinala Gallery,** Cárdenas 274, tel. 2-4995, has fine indigenous Mexican crafts and folk art, including an impressive collection of authentic masks and Huichol beaded art. Priced at $45 to $2,000 for museum-quality pieces, most of the masks have been worn in ceremonies rather than created for tourists. Reference books and other literature are available in English, and the knowledgeable staff will gladly answer questions. Open Monday through Saturday from 10am to 2pm and 5 to 9pm.

Gallery Indigena, Cárdenas 288, with more Mexican folk art and handmade wares is down the street from Olinala Gallery; open Monday through Saturday from 10am to 2pm and 5 to 8pm. **La Reja,** Juárez 501, tel. 2-2272, has a great selection of Mexican ceramics and some lovely Guatemalan fabrics are among the crafts here; open Monday through Saturday 9am to 2pm and 4 to 8pm. **Querubines,** Juárez 501-A, tel. 2-3475, offers Guatemalan and Mexican wares, including embroidered and hand-woven clothing, wool rugs, jewelry, straw bags, and Panama hats. Open Monday through Saturday from 9am to 9pm.

Arte Magico Huichol, Corona 164, may be the best gallery of Huichol Indian art in all of Mexico. It carries very fine large and small yarn paintings by recognized Huichol artists, as well as intricately beaded masks, bowls, and ceremonial objects; open Monday through Saturday from 10am to 9pm. At **Nacho's,** Libertad 160A, beautifully made silver jewelry from Taxco and lacquerware from Olinala are sold. When buying sterling, always look for the .925 stamp on the back. Open Monday through Saturday from 10am to 2pm and 5 to 8pm.

CONTEMPORARY ART

The following galleries carry contemporary Mexican and/or foreign artists: **Galería Pacífico,** Juárez 519 (tel. 2-6768), open Monday through Saturday from 10am to 9pm; **Fitzpatrick/De Gooyer,** Morelos 589 (tel. 2-1982), open Monday through Saturday from 10am to 2pm and 4 to 8pm; **Galería Uno,** Morelos 561 (tel. 2-0908), open Monday through Saturday from 10am to 9pm; and the **Sergio Bustamante Gallery,** Juárez 275 (tel. 2-1129), open Monday through Saturday from 9am to 9pm, where fantastic creatures emerging from eggs and other colorful, surreal images in three-dimensional ceramics are the trademark.

EVENING ENTERTAINMENT

Wander down the Malecón after dark and you'll hear music pouring out from half a dozen inviting restaurant/bars with their windows open to the sea. The beach doesn't go to sleep at night, either. Bands play under the palapas and there's dancing on the beach.

RESTAURANT/BARS

CARLOS O'BRIAN'S, Paseo Díaz Ordaz 786 (the Malecón), at Pipila. Tel. 2-1444.

The young-at-heart form a long line out front in the evening as they wait to get inside and join the party. Late at night the scene resembles a rowdy college party. Revelers have been known to dance on the tables and chairs. Open daily from 11am to 2am. Drinks run $2.50 to $6.

RESTAURANT/BAR ZAPATA, Paseo Diaz Ordaz 522 (the Malecón). Tel. 2-4748.

Photographs and memorabilia from the Mexican Revolution surround you as you listen to live South American music. You can sit at the bar on one of the revolving horse-saddle stools. Open nightly from 7pm to 1:30am, with live music until midnight. National drinks cost $3.

Admission: Free.

MOGAMBO, Paseo Diaz Ordaz 644 (the Malecón). Tel. 2-3476.

Live jazz lures in passersby to sit beneath the crocodiles and other stuffed creatures on the walls of this African-theme bar and restaurant. Open daily from 8am to 2pm, with live jazz nightly from 8pm to 2am. Drinks are $2 to $4; fancy coffee, $5.50.

Admission: Usually free.

FRANZI CAFE, Río Cuale.

At this pleasant spot under shady trees on the island in the middle of the river, talented groups play live jazz in the evening. Dinner is expensive, but you can always stop by for drinks. The Sunday champagne brunch from 8am to noon also features live music (sometimes a harpist). Open daily from 8am to midnight, with live jazz nightly from 8 to 11pm. Drinks are $2.50; fancy coffee, $6. Sunday brunch will run about $12.

RESTAURANT/BAR VALLARTA CUALE, Río Cuale.

At the tip of the island where the river flows into the sea, this restaurant has a beautifully decorated terrace with leather furniture and scarlet tablecloths. Hit the bar for happy hour and sunset-watching, or in the evening when a romantic trio serenades diners. Food prices are a bit steep. Open daily from 8am to 11pm; happy hour (with two drinks for the price of one) is on from 6 to 8pm, and there's live music from 7:30 to 10:30pm. Beer is $1.50; margaritas, $2 to $4.

ANDALE, Olas Altas 425. Tel. 2-1054.

South of the river, Andale can be one of the wildest watering holes in town for youthful vacationers. Drinks are reasonably priced and sometimes the tequila Slammers are on the house. The restaurant upstairs is a bit quieter, with tables overlooking the street. Open daily from 4pm to midnight. Margaritas cost $2.50 and beer is $1.50.

DISCOS

The discos are loud and expensive, but a lot of fun. Admission is $5 to $10, and you'll generally pay $3 for a margarita, $2 for a beer, more for a whisky and mix. Keep an eye out for the free disco passes that are frequently available in hotels, restaurants, and other tourist spots. Most discos are open from 10pm to 4am.

CACTUS, Dieguez and Vallarta. Tel. 2-6037 or 2-6077.

A current favorite, this large disco offers pounding music, sculpted cavelike walls sprouting trees and cactus, and several tiers of seating that frames the large, hi-tech dance floor on three sides. Open nightly from 10pm to 5am. Drinks run $2 to $5.
   Admission: $10.

SUNDANCE, Cárdenas 329. Tel. 2-2296.

Columns, arches, and comfortable furniture surround the black-lighted dance floor in the middle of the large room. This nightspot is popular with well-heeled locals, but draws its share of tourists, too. Open nightly from 10pm to 4am. Drinks cost $2.50 to $5.
   Admission: Sun–Thurs free, Fri–Sat $8.

FRIDAY LOPEZ, in the Hotel Fiesta Americana Puerto Vallarta, north of downtown off the airport road. Tel. 2-2010.

Live bands and the upstairs-downstairs Spanish-colonial-style setting keep everyone hopping in this festive nightspot. Classic rock-and-roll "gold" is the music of choice. Open nightly from 10:30pm to 3am. Drinks run $2.50 to $5.
   Admission: $8; women free on Wed.

CHRISTINE, in the Krystal Vallarta Hotel, Av. de las Garzas, north of downtown off the airport road. Tel. 2-1459.

With its Victorian "streetlamps" and ceiling spangled with tiny lights, the interior resembles a cross between an octagonal jewelbox and a turn-of-the-century gazebo in a park—until the opening light show. Then the stage fogs up, lights swing down and start flashing, and suddenly you're enveloped in booming classical music like you've *never* heard it before. After the show, video screens and disco sounds take over. Open nightly from 10:30pm to 4am; the opening light show begins at 11pm. Drinks go for $2 to $5. *Note:* No shorts for men, tennis shoes, or thongs.
   Admission: $11.

IGGY'S, in the La Jolla de Mismaloya Resort, km 11 on the main highway south of town. Tel. 2-1374.

Every night at 7pm this disco shows the movie that put Puerto Vallarta on the map: *Night of the Iguana.* Afterward you can dance or enjoy the wonderful view of Mismaloya Beach below, where the movie was filmed. The remains of the movie set can be seen on the southern point above the beach. Open nightly from 7pm to 1am. Drinks cost $2 to $3. No dress code.

Admission: Free. **Directions:** The minivan no. 02 (50¢) runs up to Mismaloya until 9pm or so (see "Getting Around," above). A taxi back will cost around $8 (gather a group of four to share).

MEXICAN FIESTAS & HOTEL EVENTS

LA IGUANA, Cárdenas 311, between Constitución and Insurgentes. Tel. 2-0105.

For a real extravaganza, go to La Iguana for an evening of entertainment that includes an open bar and an all-you-can-eat buffet. The owner-chef-showman-host, Gustavo Fong Salazar, was born in Mexico to a Chinese father and a Mexican mother, went to school in Hong Kong, managed the American Club there, and served in the American armed services in China during World War II. Returning to Mexico 28 years ago, after seeing great shows in many parts of the world, he originated the concept of Mexican folk shows for tourists, which have since become popular all over the country. The show is as eclectic as its owner's experience, with Mexican folkloric dancing, mariachis, rope-twirling, piñatas, fireworks, and an orchestra for dancing. Open on Thursday and Sunday from 7 to 11pm.

Admission: $30.

KRYSTAL VALLARTA HOTEL, Av. de las Garzas, north of downtown off the airport road. Tel. 2-1459.

Mexican Fiestas are held just about every night at major hotels around town and generally include a Mexican buffet, open bar, and live music and entertainment. One of the best is hosted by the Krystal Vallarta on Tuesday and Saturday at 7pm. The hotel also puts on a comic **Charreada**—a Mexican rodeo—with lots of audience participation (it also includes dinner and drinks) on Thursday at 7pm. The Tourism Office and local travel agencies can provide information on these and other hotel events; agencies can arrange tickets.

Admission: $25–$35.

AN EXCURSION TO PLAYA YELAPA

A cove as inviting as a tropical fantasy is a 2-hour trip by boat down the coast. Go to the town marina and catch the 9am boat, the *Serape,* to Yelapa for $17 round-trip, returning around 4pm. The fare includes two drinks on board, but you need to bring your own lunch or buy it in Yelapa. Several other boats and cruises go to Yelapa and include lunch and open bar for $30 to $35. Travel agencies can provide tickets and information.

At Yelapa you can lie in the sun, swim, eat fresh grilled crayfish or seafood at a restaurant right on the beach (try Vagabundo's), have your picture taken with an iguana (for $1 a shot!), let local "guides" take you on a tour of the town or up the river to see the waterfall, and hike up to visit Rita Tillet's crafts shop on the edge of the mountain. If it's still open, have your guide take you to see Rancho Sueno (Dream Ranch), unusual lodgings with waterbeds, hanging beds, and "outdoor rooms" carved right out of the cliff. *Note:* If you use a local guide, agree on a price *before* you start out!

WHERE TO STAY

For cheap accommodations ask around to see if residents are renting rooms, or rent a palapa hut with a dirt floor.

HOTEL LAGUNITAS. 20 cottages (all with bath).

$ Rates: $18 single; $30 double (rate varies according to season and demand). The rock-and-stucco cottages with thatched roofs and screened windows are rustically agreeable. They're on the far-left end of the beach in Yelapa. Services are unpredictable, but you might spend a blissful few days in these cottages. Beach palapa restaurants are steps away, but it wouldn't hurt to bring a supply of snacks and drinking water. There's electricity from 7 to 11pm, but there are no telephones in Yelapa.

Reservations: Contact Sergio Garcia in Puerto Vallarta (tel. 322/2-1932).

3. BARRA DE NAVIDAD & MELAQUE

133 miles S of Puerto Vallarta, 65 miles N of Manzanillo, 162 miles E of Guadalajara

GETTING THERE   By Bus   There are many bus routes between Puerto Vallarta and Manzanillo, and between Guadalajara and Manzanillo. Most of these buses stop in Barra de Navidad (and Melaque/San Patricio, the next village, 3 miles away). Buses run frequently between Barra de Navidad and Manzanillo for 35¢.

By Car   Coastal Highway 200 leads from both Puerto Vallarta and Manzanillo. Highway 54 to Guadalajara intersects at Melaque and Barra de Navidad.

ESSENTIALS   The telephone area code is 333.

In the 17th century, Barra de Navidad was a harbor for the Spanish fleet, and it was from here, in 1654, that galleons set off to conquer the Philippines. Located on a crescent-shaped bay with curious rock outcroppings, Barra de Navidad and neighboring Melaque (both on the same bay) boast a perfect beach, with a peaceful ambience unfettered by the trappings of jet-set Mexico. Barra has been "discovered," but only by a small number of people from December through Easter. Most of the year it's a real getaway, with a pick of rooms and an easy pace.

ORIENTATION

ARRIVING   The bus will let you off in the town center in front of the bus station office, painted hot pink and lime green, near the central plaza. The main beach street is **Legazpi,** and the hotels are in the first two blocks back from the beach. Two blocks behind and to the right is the lagoon side, with its main street **Morelos/Veracruz** and more hotels and restaurants. Few streets are marked, but 10 minutes of wandering will give you the village's entire layout.

INFORMATION   The **Tourism Office** for both Barra de Navidad and Melaque is at Sonora 15 (tel. 333/7-0100), half a block and around the corner from the Hotel Tropical. The office is open Monday through Friday from 9am to 7pm and on Saturday from 9am to noon or 1pm. They have good maps of Barra.

WHAT TO SEE & DO

Swimming and enjoying the lovely beach and bay view take up most people's time.

If you want to rent a small boat, you can go to your right, just about half a block south of the Restaurant Eloy on Calle Veracruz, until you come to the tiny boatmen's cooperative, with fixed prices posted on the wall. Someone will take you wherever you want to go. A round-trip to the village of **Colimilla,** just across the lagoon, popular for its many pleasant restaurants, costs $8.50 for up to eight people and you stay as long as you like; for a 30-minute **tour around the lagoon,** it's $10; or out on the sea, $12.50. **Sportfishing** is $17 per hour and up to six people can share the cost. **Waterskiing** costs $50 an hour. Ask for boatman Sergio Barcena Monzalez, who speaks excellent English.

WHERE TO STAY

HOTEL JALISCO, Jalisco 81, Barra de Navidad, Jal. 48987. 13 rms (12 with bath).

$ Rates: $12 single; $15 double.

For those on a strict budget, this may be a choice, but it's no place to write home about. It's strictly no frills, just basic dark rooms, (10 with fans), unreliable hot water, close to the beach and restaurants, and overpriced for what you get. Ask for a discount. It's around the corner from the Hotel Delphín at Jalisco and Morelos.

HOTEL DELPHÍN, Calle Morelos 23, Barra de Navidad, Jal. 48987. Tel. 333/7-0068. 25 rms (all with bath), 3 apartments.
$ Rates: $25 single; $35 double. **Parking:** Free across the street.

Among Barra's better-maintained hotels, the three-story Delphín, on the landward side of the lagoon, offers nice, well-cared for rooms, each with red-tile floors, fans, and either a double or two single beds. Outside each room are tables and chairs on the covered walkways. The courtyard with small pool and lounge chairs is shaded by an enormous tree. A breakfast buffet is served during high season on the lovely second-level breakfast terrace and costs $6. The menu includes banana hotcakes, a tradition at the Delphín.

HOTEL SANDS, Morelos 24, Barra de Navidad, Jal. 48987. Tel. 333/7-0018 or 7-0148. 43 rms (all with bath).
$ Rates: $30 single; $38 double; $78 bungalow for four, $104 bungalow for six.
The colonial-style Sands, cater-corner from the Hotel Delphín, on the lagoon side at Jalisco, offers small but homey rooms, with red-tile floors, fans, and windows with both screens and glass. Lower rooms look onto a public walkway and wide courtyard; upstairs rooms are brighter. In back is a beautiful pool by the lagoon. The hotel is known for its high-season "happy hour" from 2 to 6pm at the pool terrace bar. After 6pm, the hotel is quiet again.

HOTEL TROPICAL, Legazpi 96, Barra de Navidad, Jal. 48987. Tel. 333/7-0020. Fax 333/7-0149. 57 rms (all with bath).
$ Rates: $30 single; $38 double.
Located on the beach at the far end of Legazpi, facing the bay, this hotel offers nice rooms with a view of either the sea or the lagoon. Rooms all have fans and two double beds. Ocean-view rooms have a narrow terrace and a wall of windows, making the rooms bright and cheery. The breezy sea-view terrace restaurant has a separate bar, and there's a tiny children's pool.

WHERE TO EAT

PANCHOS, Legazpi 53. Tel. 7-0176.
Specialty: SEAFOOD.
$ Prices: Breakfast $1.50–$3; main courses $4–$12; deviled shrimp $8.
Open: Daily 9am–11pm.

Toward the far end of Legazpi, next to the Restaurant Pacífico, is the most popular place in town, where locals hang out for the food and conversation. Pull up a chair on the sand floor and join them. You must try the spicy deviled shrimp, which was invented here. The ground marlin ceviche is fabulous in a sauce of tomatoes and hot peppers; an order is plenty for two people.

VELEROS, Veracruz 64.
Specialty: SEAFOOD/BEEF.
$ Prices: Appetizers $1.75–$4; main courses $5–$10.
Open: Low season, daily noon–11pm; high season, daily 8am–11pm.

At this restaurant near the lagoon boat rental and the Restaurant Eloy (see below), it's tranquilizing to watch fishermen float by. The ambience is clean, classy, and casual, with cloth-covered tables, an ivy-covered brick wall, impeccable service, and dependably good food. Seafood specialties include shrimp brochette and fish filet, but there's also pepper steak, filet mignon, and grilled chicken.

RESTAURANT ELOY, Calle Yucatán 47. Tel. 7-0365.
Specialty: SEAFOOD.
$ Prices: Breakfast $2–$4.50; main courses $3.50–$7.
Open: Daily 9am–9pm.
Go down the street crossing Lopez de Legazpi between the Restaurant Pacífico and the Hotel Tropical, walk one short block, and you'll see the sign for the Eloy, at the

corner of Veracruz. A dozen white-clad tables and chairs topped with little vases of flowers greet you as you enter this simple family-run restaurant facing the lagoon. The specialty is fish filet, fried and covered in a special tomato sauce. The combination plate comes with shrimp, octopus, and scallops. All orders come with salad, french fries, and rice.

EVENING ENTERTAINMENT

During high season there is always happy hour (2 to 6pm) at the **Hotel Sands** poolside/lagoonside bar.

At the **Disco El Galleon,** in the Hotel Sands on Calle Morelos, cushioned benches and cement tables encircle the round dance floor. It's all open air, but garden walls restrict air flow and there are few fans so you can really work up a sweat dancing the night away. They serve drinks only, no snacks. Admission is $1.75 to $2.50 Sunday through Thursday, $3.50 on Friday and Saturday. It's open daily from 8pm to 2am.

AN EXCURSION TO MELAQUE/SAN PATRICIO

For a change of scenery, you may want to wander over to Melaque (also known as San Patricio), 3 miles from Barra and on the same bay. You can walk to it on the beach from Barra or take one of the frequent local buses from the bus station near the main square in Barra.

Melaque's pace is even more laid back than Barra's, and though it's a larger village, it seems smaller: It has fewer restaurants and less to do. The paved road ends where the town begins. A few yachts bob in the harbor and the palm-lined beach is gorgeous.

If you come by bus from Barra, you'll be dropped off near the highway several blocks from the town center and the beach. (If you're coming from Manzanillo, Guadalajara, or Puerto Vallarta, the thatch-roofed bus stop is near the center of the village, a block from the beach.) Restaurants and hotels line the beach and it's impossible to get lost, but a word of orientation will help. Coming into town from the main road, you'll be on the town's main street, **Avenida Lopez Mateos.** You'll pass the main square and come down to the waterfront, where there's a trailer park. The street going left (southeast) along the bay is **Avenida Gomez Farías;** the one going right (northwest) is **Avenida Miguel Ochoa Lopez.**

WHERE TO STAY

The prices mentioned below are for low season (May to October). From November to the end of Easter week prices may go up 25% to 30% in some hotels.

All along the seaside avenue you'll see signs for hotels as well as bungalows. In Melaque, bungalows are rooms with a kitchen and sometimes a sitting room as well.

Doubles For Less Than $35

POSADA LAS GAVIOTAS, Hidalgo 1, Melaque, Jal. 48980. Tel. 333/7-0129; or 36/15-9903 in Guadalajara. 24 rms (all with bath).
$ Rates: $22 double.
Walk west from the bus station on Farías to Hidalgo, turn right, and you'll come on the simple, well-used, but breezy rooms built under the long arches that stretch from Gomez Farías all the way down to the beach. All rooms have fans and 15 have a kitchenette. Two tiled pools (one for kids), garden, palms, and patio make the elevated beachfront terrace a pleasant place to relax.

BUNGALOWS VILLAMAR, Hidalgo 1, Melaque, Jal. 48980. Tel. 333/7-0005. 5 bungalows.
$ Rates: $17 small bungalow; $25 larger bungalow single or double. Discounts for longer stays.
It's a quiet place where you can hear waves breaking and the palm trees swishing in the garden. Clean, but well used, the bungalows enjoyed a fresh coat of paint in 1990. Most have two bedrooms, a living room and kitchen, bath, a private patio out back,

and a private sitting terrace with chairs out front by the garden; all have fans. There is also an elevated terrace overlooking the beach and bay. Manager Roberto Ramírez speaks perfect English and is friendly and helpful. It's almost always full during winter months, so make reservations well ahead. You'll find it on the corner, next to the Hotel Gaviotas.

POSADA PABLO DE TARSO, Gomez Farías 49, Melaque, Jal. 48980. Tel. 333/7-0117 or 7-0268, or 36/16-4850 in Guadalajara. Fax 36/16-4850 in Guadalajara. 27 rms (all with bath).
$ Rates: $30 single or double. **Parking:** Free.
This two-level hotel offers exceptionally tidy rooms, 14 with air conditioning and 13 with fans. Two have kitchens and sitting rooms. There's a grassy courtyard, and a seaside terrace and large swimming pool. It's left of the bus station, past the Motel Vista Hermosa.

HOTEL DE LEGAZPI, Av. de Las Palmas, Melaque, Jal. 48980. Tel. 333/7-0397, or Apr–Nov 317/846-2566 in the U.S. (ask for owner Martin Curley). 14 rms (all with bath).
$ Rates: $25 single; $30 double. Prices 50% higher in the winter season.
American owned, this two-story hotel at the north end of the bay has a nice secluded location on a beautiful portion of beach. The large rooms are simply furnished and have tile floors and fans. It's a 10-minute walk to town and there are several palapa-style restaurants nearby. There's lobby TV with U.S. channels, a community kitchen, and a swimming pool in front of the hotel.

Worth the Extra Bucks

CLUB NAUTICO MELAQUE, Madero 1, Melaque, Jal. 48980. Tel. 333/7-0239. 35 rms (all with bath).
$ Rates: $30 single; $40 double.
East of the bus station, on the left facing the beach, is one of Melaque's better inns. Rooms are nicely furnished and immaculate; all have fans and some have private balconies. There's a swimming pool in front (street side) of the hotel. The hotel's huge breezy beachside palapa restaurant and bar with a total bay view is one of the nicest on the beach. Breakfast costs $1.50 to $3, seafood runs $6 to $9, and other main courses of chicken or beef are between $6 and $15. Try the amandine fish in an almond-butter sauce, which, like all the main courses, comes with rice and vegetables. It's open daily from 7:30am to 10:30pm.

WHERE TO EAT

FONDA LOS PORTALES, Gomez Farías 358. Tel. 7-0268.
Specialty: SEAFOOD.
$ Prices: Breakfast $1.75–$2.25; seafood platter $5–$7.50.
Open: Daily 8am–6pm.
With its new brick floor and freshly painted chairs, Los Portales has lost its rough edges and looks more inviting. This simple family-run restaurant is popular for its seafood platters at good prices, but there's fried chicken too, and side orders of rice and vegetables. It's near the Posada Gaviotas.

EL BUEN GUSTO, Lopez Mateos 18, at Gomez Farías.
Specialty: MEXICAN.
$ Prices: Soft drinks 40¢; beer 75¢; tamales 50¢; tacos 35¢; pozole $1.75; roast chicken $2.
Open: Daily 9am–11pm.
Run by the Benjamin Macías Solis family, this eatery, currently half a block from the square going toward the beach, keeps moving and I keep finding it because the food is both good and cheap. Wherever they are, the decor always features metal tables and chairs. The food is home-style, which is why there's always a loyal following of Mexicans around. The bowl of pozole is large, tasty, and filling. They were planning to add seafood and hamburgers. If they've moved again ask around, or look for the Buen Gusto sign.

READERS RECOMMEND

Los Pelicanos, at the north end of the beach, Melaque. "*Owners Phil and Trine, formerly from the U.S., have settled in Melaque. It's a friendly place, you can use the restaurant for international mail. Phil has written a local guidebook and created numerous fabulous sauces which he serves in the restaurant and also sells. The food is inexpensive and tasty, and Trine plays a mean game of dominoes.*"—Kathleen R. Schweizer, Seattle, Wash.

EN ROUTE TO MANZANILLO

At Barra, Highway 80 goes up into the hills of Guadalajara, but if you're heading south down the coast, you'll pass Playa de Oro and Manzanillo's airport, Santiago, Las Hadas, Las Brisas, and finally Manzanillo. The last is 40 miles from Barra over a beautiful curving mountain road.

4. MANZANILLO

160 miles S of Puerto Vallarta, 167 miles SW of Guadalajara, 40 miles S of Barra de Navidad

GETTING THERE   By Air   Aeroméxico and **Mexicana** offer flights between Manzanillo and Mexico City, Guadalajara, and Los Angeles. There are connecting flights several times a week for Chicago, Dallas/Fort Worth, Monterrey, Reno, Sacramento, San Diego, San Francisco, and a few other cities.

By Train   *El Colimense* leaves Guadalajara at 9am, stops in Colima at 2:25pm, and arrives in Manzanillo at 4pm. It's a comfortable and beautiful ride, passing over some scenic mountain gorges. A snack is included.

By Bus   The service is very good to and from Manzanillo, up and down the coast, and inland to Colima and Guadalajara.

By Car   Coastal Highway 200 leads from Acapulco and Puerto Vallarta. From Guadalajara, take Highway 54 through Colima (outside Colima you can switch to a toll road, which is faster but less scenic, into Manzanillo).

DEPARTING   By Plane   The airport is 45 minutes northwest of town at Playa de Oro. The colectivo airport service, **Transportes Terrestres** (tel. 3-2470) picks up passengers at hotels. Call a day ahead for reservations. One way, the cost is $4. The Manzanillo office of **Aeroméxico** is in the Centro Comercial "Carrillo Puerto," between Quintero and Galindo (tel. 333/2-1267 or 2-1711). **Mexicana** is at Avenida Mexico 380 (tel. 333/2-1972 or 2-1009, or 3-2323 at the airport).

By Train   Make train reservations and get seat assignments between 10:30am and 5:30pm, but ticket sales are in a separate line from 10:30am to 3pm (on Saturday, Sunday, and festival days ticket sales are 10:30am to 1pm). Don't wait until the last minute. *El Colimense* leaves Manzanillo at 1pm, arrives in Colima at 2:45pm, Cd. Guzman at 5pm, and Guadalajara at 8pm.

By Bus   Manzanillo's **Central Camionera** (bus station) is a few blocks east of town, at Vicente Suárez and Galeana, just off the road to Colima. Follow Hidalgo east until you come to Galeana and the camionera will be off to the right. **Auto Transportes Colima** goes to Colima every 15 minutes and the trip takes 2 hours on a *de paso/ordinario* and 1½ hours on a *directo*. **Tres Estrellas de Oro** has six buses daily to Guadalajara and one of them is an express (no stops). They also can get you to Mexico City, and back up the coast to Culiacán, Guaymas, Mazatlán, Puerto Vallarta, Mexicali, and Tijuana. **Norte de Sonora** (tel. 2-0432) has twice-weekly service to Tepic, Los Mochis, and Mazatlán. The most frequent service to Guadalajara (6 to 7 hrs.), Puerto Vallarta (6 hrs.) via Melaque (San Patricio) and Barra de Navidad (1½ hrs.) is on **Auto Camiones de Pacífico** (tel. 2-0515), with first-class service 25 times a day and second-class service almost as frequently. **Autobuses de Occidente** has frequent service to Colima and express service to Mexico City via Morelia and Toluca, and direct and express service to Guadalajara. **Flecha Amarilla** (tel. 2-0210) also has assigned-seat service to Guadalajara, and other buses inland to León and San Luis Potosí.

Today, Manzanillo, Colima (pop. 70,000), is Mexico's main seaport on the Pacific. The chief local industries are fishing, mining, and tourism, which is booming. Unfortunately, none of the new construction benefits the budget traveler.

ORIENTATION

ARRIVING The **airport** is a 45-minute ride north of the town center. Colectivo vans meet each flight and you buy tickets ($4) inside the terminal. The **train station** is conveniently located downtown on the waterfront, within walking distance of several hotels. City buses stop in front. The **bus station** is several blocks inland.

INFORMATION The **Tourism Office,** is in Salahua on the main highway between Centro and Santiago, next to Avis and Budget car rental (no phone). It's open Monday through Friday from 9am to 3:30pm.

CITY LAYOUT The town, which is less attractive than you might expect, is at one end of a 7-mile-long curving beach, **Playa Azul,** whose northern terminus is the **Santiago Peninsula.** Santiago is 7 miles from downtown; it's the site of many beautiful homes and the best hotel in the area, Las Hadas.

There are two lagoons, one, **Laguna de Cuyutlan,** almost behind the city and the other, **Laguna de San Pedrito,** behind the beach. Both of these are good for birdwatching. There are also two bays. **Manzanillo Bay** has the harbor, town, and beaches, and it's separated by the Santiago Peninsula from the second bay— **Santiago.**

Downtown activity centers around the plaza, which is separated from the waterfront by railroad and shipyards. The plaza has a brilliant poinciana tree with red blossoms, a fountain, kiosk, and a view of the bay. Large ships dock at the pier nearby. **Avenida México,** the street leading out from the plaza's central gazebo, is the town's principal commercial thoroughfare. Walking along here you will find a few shops, small eateries, and juice stands.

GETTING AROUND

BY BUS The local buses (called *camionetas*) make a circuit along the lagoon behind the downtown area, and out along the Manzanillo Bay to the Santiago Peninsula and the Bay of Santiago to the north. This is a cheap way to see the coast. Departures are every 20 minutes from in front of the train station.

BY TAXI Taxis in Manzanillo supposedly have fixed rates for trips within town, as well as to points more distant, but they aren't posted; ask your hotel what a ride should cost to get a feel for what's right—then bargain with the driver.

FAST FACTS

American Express The local representative is Bahías Gemelas Travel Agency, Blvd. Costeera M. Madrid, km 10 (tel. 333/3-2100; fax 333/3-0649).

Area Code The telephone area code is 333.

Laundry There's a self-service laundry at the junction of the Manzanillo, Las Brisas, and Santiago roads called Lavandería Automatica Gissy (that's "*Hee*-see"), in a little complex of shops.

WHAT TO SEE & DO

Activities depend on where you stay. Most resort hotels here are completely self-contained, with restaurants and sports all on the premises. This isn't necessarily

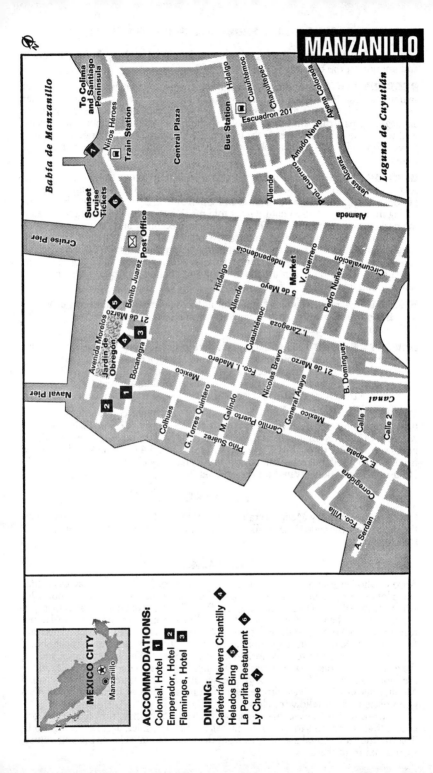

true of my hotel recommendations, however, since several of them do not have pools and are not on the beach.

BEACHES **La Audiencia Beach,** on the way to Santiago, offers the best swimming, but **San Pedrito,** shallow for a long way out, is the most popular because it's much closer to the downtown area. **Playa Miramar,** on the Bahía de Santiago, up past the Santiago Peninsula, is another of the town's popular beaches, well worth the ride out there on the local bus from town. The major part of **Playa Azul** drops off a little too steeply for safe swimming, and is not recommended for waders.

BIRDING There are many lagoons along the coast. As you go from Manzanillo up past Las Brisas to Santiago, you'll pass **Laguna de Las Garzas** (Lagoon of the Herons), also known as **Laguna de San Pedrito,** where you'll see many big herons fishing in the water. A local nature-lover told me that the white ones are the females; the darker ones are the males. They nest here in December and January.

Back of town, on the road leading to Colima (the capital) is the **Laguna de Cuyutlan** (follow the signs to Cuyutlan). Just before the town of Cuyutlan (which faces the ocean) you'll come to a bridge. Park on either side of it and follow a path to the lagoon, where birds can usually be found in abundance; species vary between summer and winter.

FISHING Manzanillo is also famous for its fishing—**marlin, sailfish, dolphin, sea bass, and manta ray.** Competitions are held around the November 20 holiday, and in February.

SUNSET CRUISES Many charter boats are available along the waterfront. For a sunset cruise, buy tickets downtown at La Perlita Dock (across from the train station) fronting the harbor. Tickets go on sale daily from 10am to 2pm and 4 to 7pm, and cost around $15, which includes two drinks. It's a good idea to buy the ticket a day ahead, since the cruise can be booked up by hotels and travel agencies.

TOURS Because Manzanillo is so spread out, you might consider a city tour. I highly recommend the services of Luis Jorje Alvarez at **Viajes Lujo,** Avenida México 143-2, Manzanillo, Col. 28200 (tel. 333/2-2919; fax 333/2-4075). Office hours are Monday through Friday from 9am to 2pm and 4 to 7pm, and on Saturday from 9am to noon, but tours can be any time. A half-day city tour costs around $12. He uses air-conditioned vans and speaks English.

SHOPPING

Only a few shops carry Mexican crafts and clothing, and almost all are downtown on the streets near the central plaza. You can also try exploring the new malls on the road to Santiago.

LAS HADAS

Anyone who has ever heard of Manzanillo has heard of Las Hadas; or say Las Hadas and a lot of people think that *is* Manzanillo. You may remember it from the movie *10,* which featured Bo Derek and Las Hadas. The self-contained Eden that put Manzanillo on the map, the brainchild of the Bolivian entrepreneur Antenor Patino, features lavish Moorish-style architecture that started a trend in Mexico. There are four restaurants, four bars, two pools, a marina, a golf course, and lots of posh shops. Visitors who come just to look around are discouraged, so go before sunset and tell the guard you're going to the marina restaurants. Adjacent to the hotel complex, these are not owned by the hotel and are set up on the waterfront like a small Mediterranean village: Neat little eateries feature all kinds of food and drink. It's a good place to meet fellow travelers.

To drive to Las Hadas, take Highway 80 to Santiago Bay, turn left at the golf course (follow the signs to Club Las Hadas), and then turn left again at the sign to El Tesoro. You can also take a city bus from the train station as far as the golf course, then a taxi from there.

WHERE TO STAY

The strip of coastline on which Manzanillo is located can be divided into three areas: **downtown,** with its shops, markets, and continual activity; **Las Brisas,** the motel-lined beach area immediately to the north of the city; and **Santiago,** which is virtually a suburb situated even farther north at the end of Playa Azul. All areas are reasonably convenient to one another by either bus or taxi. Reservations are recommended for the Christmas and New Year's holidays.

DOWNTOWN

HOTEL FLAMINGOS, Madero 72, Manzanillo, Col. 28200. Tel. 333/2-1037. 34 rms (all with bath).
$ Rates: $10 single; $13 double.
Although the reception is not very friendly, this worn-out hotel offers basic, clean rooms and table fans. Windows look out onto ugly buildings across the street. It's half a block east of the plaza, near the Restaurant Chantilly.

HOTEL EMPERADOR, Balvino Davalos 69, Manzanillo, Col. 28200. Tel. 333/2-2374. 28 rms (all with bath).
$ Rates: $8.50–$13 single or double with one bed, $15–$19 single or double with two beds.
This very basic low-budget hotel offers clean, bare rooms with hot water and a fan. Most look out onto the tiny inner courtyard, which is more like an airshaft. The hotel is a block west (left of) the plaza almost at the corner of Carrillo Puerto.

HOTEL COLONIAL, Av. México 100 at Gonzales Bocanegra, Manzanillo, Col. 28200. Tel. 333/2-1080 or 2-1134. 40 rms (all with bath).
$ Rates: $27–$30 single or double.
An old favorite, this three-story colonial-style hotel changes little from year to year—same minimal furniture, red-tile floors, and comfort at ever-increasing prices. Higher prices are for the 25 rooms with air conditioning (the rest have fans). In the central courtyard is a restaurant/bar. The Colonial is a block inland from the plaza on Galindo, on the right corner.

LAS BRISAS

Buses run out to Las Brisas from downtown. Look for "Brisas Direc" on the signboard. It's a 6-mile trundle around Manzanillo Bay, ultimately curving southward. Most hotels, bungalows, and condominiums are on the single main road.

CLUB VACACIONAL LAS BRISAS, Av. Lázaro Cárdenas 207, Las Brisas, Manzanillo, Col. 28200. Tel. 333/3-2075 or 3-1717. 56 bungalows.
$ Rates: $27 bungalow for one; $40 bungalow for two. **Parking:** Free in front.
This beachfront hostelry about halfway down the Las Brisas peninsula has plain but comfortable bungalows with kitchenettes (24 with air conditioning, 32 with fans) surrounding a large pool and grassy interior lawn shaded by palms. Besides the pool, there's one tennis court and a restaurant open for all three meals. It's extremely popular with Mexican families on weekends.

HOTEL LA POSADA, Av. Lázaro Cárdenas 201, Las Brisas (Apdo. Postal 135), Manzanillo, Col. 28200. Tel. and fax 333/3-1899. 24 rms (all with bath).
$ Rates (including breakfast): Off-season, $42 single; $48 double. High season, 10%–15% higher.
Another long-time favorite of traveling cognoscenti, this small inn at the far end of the Las Brisas peninsula has a shocking-pink stucco facade with a large arch that leads to a broad tile patio smack on the beautiful beach. The rooms have natural brick walls and simple but very tasteful furnishings; all have fans. The atmosphere here is casual and informal—you can help yourself to beer and soft drinks all day long, and at the end of

your stay owner Bart Varelmann (a native of Ohio) will ask you how much you owe for refreshments. All three meals are served in the dining room or out by the pool. If you want to come for a meal, breakfast (served between 8 and 11am), lunch, or dinner (between 1:30 and 9pm) costs around $4.

SANTIAGO

Three miles north of Las Brisas is the peninsula and village of Santiago. The hotels below are on the beach next to each other, out on a bluff at one end of the lovely Santiago Bay—not in Santiago itself. Get off the bus at the main Santiago bus stop and transfer to a taxi (they're available 24 hours a day). The ride out to the hotels takes 5 minutes and costs $2.

HOTEL ANITA, Dom. Playa Santiago (Apdo. Postal 15), Manzanillo, Col. 28200. Tel. 333/3-0161. 57 rms (all with bath).
$ Rates: $13 single; $17 double; $25 triple.
If you don't mind a fading beauty that has seen many better days, but has a great view, then the Anita is for you. Furnishings are from the '40s (maybe earlier), beds may sag, and hot water may never appear. But all rooms have fans and the large covered patio/walkway lining the rooms has comfortable chairs, good breezes, and great views of the cliffs and bay below. It's on the Playa Audiencia side of the Santiago Peninsula.

HOTEL MARLYN, Peninsula de Santiago (Apdo. Postal 288), Manzanillo, Col. 28200. Tel. 333/3-0107. 38 rms (all with bath), 4 suites.
$ Rates: $30 single or double; $44 suite for four; $90–$95 bungalows for four.
White and airy, this hotel facing Audiencia Bay on the Santiago Peninsula has a little swimming pool and a beachfront café. Some rooms have a sea view, but rates are much lower on the inland side. The suites are air-conditioned; the rooms have fans.

HOTEL PLAYA DE SANTIAGO, Santiago Peninsula (Apdo. Postal 90), Manzanillo, Col. 28200. Tel. 333/3-0055 or 3-0270. Fax 333/3-0344. 107 rms (all with bath), 24 bungalows. A/C TEL
$ Rates: $30 single or double. **Parking:** Free.
This is one of those 1960s-era hotels aimed at the jet set who've since migrated around the peninsula to Plaza Las Glorias and Las Hadas. You get the essence of glamour at a fraction of the price, but no beach—it's on a cliff overlooking Audiencia Bay. Bungalows have kitchenettes. The restaurant and bar are positioned for views, and there's a swimming pool and tennis court. The hotel is at the south end of the road around Santiago Bay.

WHERE TO EAT

For picnic fixings there's a big supermarket, the **Centro Comercial Conasuper,** on the road leading into town, half a block from the plaza at Morelos. The huge store sells food, produce, household goods, clothes, hardware, and more. Open daily from 8am until 8pm.

CAFETERÍA/NEVARÍA CHANTILLY, Juárez and Madero (across from the plaza). Tel. 2-0194.
Specialty: MEXICAN. **Directions:** Faces main plaza.
$ Prices: Breakfast $1.25–$3; main courses $1.50–$7; comida corrida $4.
Open: Sun–Fri 7am–10pm.
Join the locals at this informal corner café. The large menu includes club sandwiches, hamburgers, carne asada a la Tampiqueña, enchiladas and vegetable salads, and a daily lunch special—all moderately priced.

HELADOS BING, Av. Morelos and 21 de Marzo.
Specialty: ICE CREAM.
$ Prices: Ice-cream cone 60¢ single scoop, $1.25 double scoop; Bing Special $2.50; Bing Roll $9.
Open: Daily 8am–10pm.

Look for Bing's pink-and-white awning on the northeast corner of the main plaza, opposite the harbor, and trundle over for the best ice cream in Mexico. Have it by the cone, in a cup, or piled with calories like the Bing Special—in a glass with fruit, hot chocolate cream, and nuts—or a Bing roll, a 10-inch roll of cake and ice cream.

LY CHEE, Niños Héroes 397. Tel. 2-1103.
Specialty: CHINESE.
$ **Prices:** Appetizers $7.50; main courses $3.50–$10.
Open: Tues–Sun 2–10pm.
This most pleasurable waterfront restaurant faces the harbor cater-corner from the train station and plaza under a huge palapa. The fare is mainly Chinese with dishes similar to any Chinese restaurant, though several Mexican dishes are also offered.

LA PERLITA RESTAURANT, Perlita Plaza. Tel. 2-2770.
Specialty: MEXICAN.
$ **Prices:** Main courses $2–$9; tacos, quesadillas, tortas (sandwiches), or french fries $1.75–$3; seafood $3.75–$15.
Open: Daily 9am–midnight.
Look for the orange awnings at this economical fast-food stop on the waterfront where metal tables are set out on the shady plaza opposite the train station and next to the cruise ticket office. Besides a good fast-food menu, they offer a full range of fruit and mixed drinks, with purified bottled water in the fruit drinks.

WORTH THE EXTRA BUCKS

OSTERÍA BUGATTI, a few doors north of the Las Brisas crossroads. Tel. 3-2999.
Specialty: INTERNATIONAL. **Reservations:** Recommended after 8pm. **Bus:** Take a *caminota* from the train station as far as Las Brisas crossroads.
$ **Prices:** Appetizers $4–$5.50; Sonora steaks $12–$14; seafood $12–$15; pasta $6–$7.50.
Open: Daily 1pm–1am. **Closed:** Sept 15–27.
One of the best restaurants in town is in a dark, vaulted cellar with a brick ceiling and soft lighting. Your English-speaking waiter arrives bearing a platter laden with quality beef, pork, and seafood. Your selection will be cooked to your specifications. Seafood selections include lobster, red snapper, and shrimp. Air conditioning, plus a complete international bar, help make this a popular place.

LA PLAZUELA RESTAURANT, in the Hotel Plaza Las Glorias, Av. de Tesoro, Santiago Peninsula. Tel. 3-0440 or 3-0550.
Specialty: INTERNATIONAL.
$ **Prices:** Appetizers $7.50–$10; main courses $6–$10; chilaquiles $4; lobster $18–$25; seafood grill $50.
Open: Breakfast daily 8:30–11am; lunch daily 1–5pm; dinner daily 7–11:30pm.
For a meal on an outdoor terrace with a fabulous bay view, try the restaurant in this expensive hotel on the mountainside on the Manzanillo Bay side of the Santiago Peninsula near Las Hadas. It's great for a splurge night out with the city lights twinkling around the bay, but lunch is much less expensive, with less exotic dishes such as fajitas and black-bean soup, quesadillas, burritos and chicken tacos, and seafood salad. The striking Santa Fe–style hotel is out of our range, charging $110 to $140 for a single room in the off-season.

AN EXCURSION TO COLIMA

The attractive capital of the state of Colima, also called Colima, is 60 miles southeast of Manzanillo and has a number of interesting museums. A balmy metropolis that dates back to 1523, its founder was the conquistador Gonzalo de Sandoval, youngest member of Cortes's staff. It can be reached by a picturesque road that skirts the 12,870 foot Volcano de Colima, which last erupted in 1991. Also visible on this trip is the 14,000-foot Nevado de Colima, which actually lies in the state of Jalisco. Colima can be reached by frequent bus service from Manzanillo.

WHAT TO SEE & DO

MUSEO DE OCCIDENTE DE GOBIERNO DE ESTADO (Museum of Western Cultures), Galvan at Ejercito Nacional.

Also known as the Museum of Anthropology, this is one of my favorite museums in the country. It has many pre-Hispanic pieces, including the famous clay dancing dogs of Colima. There are fine examples of clay, shell, and bone jewelry, exquisite human and animal figures, and diagrams of tombs showing unusual funeral customs.

Admission: Free.

Open: Daily 9am–7:30pm.

MUSEUM OF POPULAR CULTURE MARÍA TERESA POMAR, University of Colima, 27 de Septiembre and Gabino Barrera. Tel. 2-5140.

One of the city's most interesting museums contains regional costumes and musical instruments from all over Mexico, photographs showing the day-to-day use of costumes and masks, and folk art from Oaxaca, Guerrero, and elsewhere. The section devoted to Mexico's sweet bread (*pan dulce*) is set up like an authentic bakery, with each bread labeled. At the entrance is a shop selling Mexican folk art.

Admission: 35¢.

Open: Tues–Sat 9am–2pm and 4–7pm, Sun 9am–2pm. **Directions:** From the Museum of Western Cultures, go left out the front door and walk five blocks to the wide Avenida Galvan, at Ejercito; cross it and the museum is on your right.

MUSEO DE HISTORIA DE COLIMA, Portal Morelos 1.

Opened in 1988, the city's newest showcase is dedicated to state history. The beautiful colonial building, on the plaza opposite the Hotel Ceballos, is the former Hotel Casino, the birthplace of former Mexican president Miguel de la Madrid Hurtado. The collection includes pre-Hispanic pottery, baskets, furniture, and dance masks. More than 5,000 pre-Hispanic pieces are packed away awaiting the renovation of the upper floor. After seeing the pottery here and at the Museo Occidente, you'll begin to understand why the Aztec name for Colima meant "place where pottery is made." Colima is also known for the variety of pre-Hispanic tombs, and one of the best displays here shows drawings of many kinds of tombs. You may be asked to leave your purse or bag with the guard as you enter.

Admission: Free.

Open: Mon–Sat 10am–2pm and 4–8pm; Sun, bookstore only, same hours.

COMALA

From the old Colima bus station, three blocks south of the central plaza at Nicolas Bravo and Medellin, buses run to Comala every 15 minutes. The trip takes 20 minutes and costs 15¢ ($6 by taxi).

This picturesque little village is near a mysterious **magnetic zone** out on the highway. Get one of the taxi drivers on Comala's square to run you out to this area, a few miles from town. When he gets there, he'll kill the engine. Then the magnetic pull takes control and the car gathers speed uphill without engine power. The phenomenon was discovered by accident a few years ago when a motorist had car trouble but couldn't get the vehicle to stop.

Comala is liveliest on Sunday when roving bands of **mariachis** gather to serenade diners under the arcades around the central plaza. As many as five different groups sing at once. The food, drink, and atmosphere of this village makes a perfect outing. Arrive before 3pm for a good seat for all the wholesome revelry that gets going around 3:30pm.

On the outskirts of town is an **artisans' school** that's open Monday through Saturday. Visitors are welcome to come in and browse.

WHERE TO EAT

LOS NARANJOS (The Orange Trees), Gabino Barrera 43. Tel. 2-0029.

Specialty: MEXICAN.

$ Prices: Main courses $2–$6; tacos 75¢–$3.

Open: Daily 8am–11:30pm.

The leading restaurant downtown is handsomely decorated with orange and white linens, light-blue walls, and orange fruit designs hand-painted on the chairs. For the quality of decor you'd expect higher prices. I recommend the pollo caserola, a vegetable-and-meat stew of carrots, potatoes, and peas in a delicious tomato broth, all served in a clay casserole with a side order of fresh corn tortillas. It's enough for two.

To get here from the plaza, walk down Madero (to the left of the cathedral) and take the first street on the left.

LAS PALMAS, Callejon del Caco. Tel. 2-4444 or 4-0388.
  Specialty: MEXICAN.
  $ Prices: Breakfast $1.75–$3.50; main courses $1.75–$5.
  Open: Mon–Sat 8am–10pm.
Behind the Hotel Ceballos (on the plaza), off a pedestrians-only street, there's a sign on the sidewalk directing you through a small interior mall to the back and this tranquil little restaurant with covered dining space as well as umbrella-shaded patio tables. The food is Mexican fast food, such as tacos, quesadillas, and soup, plus hamburgers and french fries.

---

5. ZIHUATANEJO & IXTAPA

360 miles SW of Mexico City, 353 miles SE of Manzanillo.
158 miles NW of Acapulco

GETTING THERE By Plane Aeroméxico has nonstop flights from Mexico City and Houston. **Delta** flies nonstop from Los Angeles. **Mexicana** has nonstop or direct flights from Dallas, Los Angeles, San Francisco, Guadalajara, Mexico City, and Puerto Vallarta. The regional carrier **AeroMorelos** flies to and from Acapulco, Cuernavaca, Mexico City, and Puebla. Check with a travel agent on **charter flights.**

By Bus The bus lines **Estrella Blanca** and **Tres Estrellas de Oro** (first class) and **Blanco Frontera** and **Flecha Roja** (second class) serve Zihuatanejo/Ixtapa daily with numerous buses from Acapulco, Mexico City, and nearby cities and towns. The trip from Mexico City takes 10 to 12 hours; from Acapulco, 4 to 5 hours. From Mexico City, Tres Estrellas de Oro buses to Zihuatanejo depart from the Terminal Central de Autobuses del Sur (South Bus Station) near the Tasqueño Metro line.

By Car From Mexico City the shortest route is Highway 15 to Toluca, then Highway 130/134 the rest of the way, though on the latter highway gas stations are few and far between. The other route is Highway 95D (four lanes) to Iguala, then Highway 51 west to Highway 134.

From Acapulco or Manzanillo, the only choice is the Coastal Highway, Highway 200. The ocean views along the winding, mountain-edged drive from Manzanillo can be spectacular.

DEPARTING By Plane Airline offices are either downtown or at the airport: **Aeroméxico,** Juan Alvarez 34 and 5 de Mayo, near the Banco Banamex (tel. 4-2018 or 4-2019), open daily from 8am to 6:30pm; **Delta,** at airport (tel. 4-3386 or 4-3387, or toll free in Mexico 91-800/9-0221); **Mexicana,** Vicente Guerrero and Nicolas Bravo (tel. 3-2208 or 3-2209, or 4-2227 at the airport), open daily from 9am to 5:30pm; and **AeroMorelos,** at the airport (tel. 4-4960; fax 753/4-4961).

Taxis are the only option for returning to the airport, and charge around $16 for up to three people.

By Bus Tres Estrellas de Oro (tel. 4-3802 or 4-2175) runs five buses to Acapulco daily between 8am and 8:30pm; the trip takes 4 to 5 hours (and the Tres Estrellas de Oro station in Acapulco is near many budget hotels). To Mexico City, one direct bus makes the trip in 10 hours; five make a 12-hour trip via Acapulco. This first-class line also goes to León and Querétaro.

At the Central de Autobuses, several companies offer service to Acapulco and other cities: first-class **Estrella Blanca** (tel. 4-3478), and the second-class lines

Flecha Roja (tel. 4-3477 and 4-3483) and **Blanco Frontera.** If possible, buy your ticket the day before and get a reserved seat on one of Estrella Blanca's six nonstop buses that originate in Zihuatanejo and depart daily between 8am and 5:30pm. Estrella Blanca's buses are air-conditioned—when it works (but keep in mind that the Estrella Blanca station in Acapulco is far from suggested hotels and means at least a $3 taxi ride upon arrival). Flecha Roja and Blanco Frontera run buses to Acapulco every hour or so; these stop in Zihuatanejo and take on passengers as space permits. The cost is the same as first class, but there are at least 10 stops en route and the trip takes 6 hours instead of the promised 4.

As Mexico develops, the secluded hideaways that made the Pacific Coast an intrepid tourist's dream-come-true are being discovered en masse. Such is the fate of Zihuatanejo, in the state of Guerrero, a town that shut off its electricity at 11pm only 10 years ago. Now the lights are on 24 hours a day, and the primitive airstrip has been turned into a jetport welcoming daily flights from Mexico City and the U.S. In 1972 Zihuatanejo had a population of about 4,000; now it's 50,000 (both towns together).

Despite all this, Zihuatanejo has kept its rustic, unpretentious charm. The beach curves around a small, natural bay in which fishing boats and sailboats bob at anchor, and the town retains its feeling of village life. Costs are lower here than in Ixtapa, a modern planned resort 7 miles northwest. This resort pair, which combines Ixtapa's sleek sophistication with "Zihuat" 's rustic charm, is also developing some of the vibrancy of Puerto Vallarta—good restaurants, shopping, and a growing nightlife. And more than either Puerto Vallarta or Acapulco, food and lodging are still reasonably priced—if you know where to look.

Ixtapa has a wide beach lined with high-rise hotels against a backdrop of lush palm groves and mountains. On the opposite side of its main boulevard lies a huge area of shopping malls (most of them air-conditioned), restaurants, and discos. This resort also has a fine golf course, and by 1992 the new Marina Ixtapa should be operating. Of course, the most economical way of enjoying Ixtapa's beach and other attractions is through quick trips over on the shuttle bus (remember that all beaches in Mexico are public, including those in front of hotels). Ixtapa was originally planned for charter- and package-tour visitors, and the most budget-wise way of staying here is with an all-inclusive package purchased through a travel agency.

ORIENTATION

ARRIVING   By Plane   The Ixtapa/Zihuatanejo airport is 20 minutes (about 10 miles) south of Zihuatanejo. Minivans, or *colectivos,* transport travelers to hotels in Zihuatanejo and Ixtapa for $6 per person; colectivo tickets are sold just outside the baggage-claim area. A taxi for up to three people will cost $16 to either town.

By Bus   In Zihuatanejo, the **Tres Estrellas de Oro bus station,** Paseo del Palmar 54, at Paseo Zihuatanejo (also called Morelos), is a few blocks beyond the market and within walking distance of some suggested downtown hotels. The clean, new **Central de Autobuses,** the main terminal where all other buses converge, is a mile or so farther on Paseo Zihuatanejo at Paseo la Boquita. A taxi from either bus station to most Zihuatanejo hotels costs $1 or $2; to go on to Ixtapa would add another $5 or so to the fare.

INFORMATION   The **Zihuatanejo Tourism Office** is on the main square on Alvarez (tel. 4-2000), open Monday through Friday from 9am to 2pm and 4 to 7pm. The local tourism representative, Adrian Abarca, is another source of information (tel. 4-2001).

Ixtapa has a **tourist information kiosk** in the mall area across from the hotel zone, as well as a **Federal Tourism Office** in La Puerta shopping center, across from the Stouffer Presidente Hotel, (tel. 3-1967 or 3-1968), open Monday through Friday from 9am to 3pm.

CITY LAYOUT   The fishing village and resort of Zihuatanejo spreads out around the **Bay of Zihuatanejo,** the bay framed by the downtown to the north and a

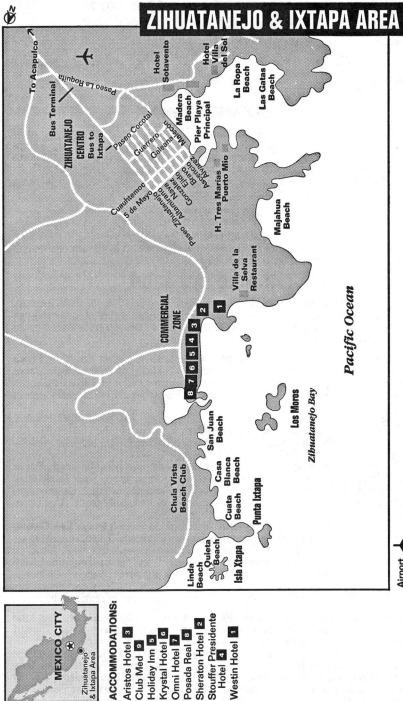

ZIHUATANEJO & IXTAPA AREA

To Acapulco

Paseo La Ropita

Bus Terminal

ZIHUATANEJO
CENTRO

Bus to
Ixtapa

Paseo Cocotal

Hotel
Sotavento

Hotel
Villa
del Sol

La Ropa
Beach

Las Gatas
Beach

Madera
Beach

Malecón

Guerrero

Galeana

Pier Playa
Principal

Cuauhtemoc

5 de Mayo

Nava

Altamirano

Gonzalez

Ejido

Bravo

Ascencio

Alvarez

Paseo Zihuatanejo

H. Tres Marias
Puerto Mío

Majahua
Beach

Villa de la
Selva
Restaurant

2

1

COMMERCIAL
ZONE

3

4

5

6

7

8

San Juan
Beach

Los Moros

Zihuatanejo Bay

Pacific Ocean

Chula Vista
Beach Club

Casa
Blanca
Beach

Cuata
Beach

Punta Ixtapa

Linda
Beach

Quieta
Beach

Isla Xtapa

Airport

MEXICO CITY

Zihuatanejo
& Ixtapa Area

ACCOMMODATIONS:

Aristos Hotel **3**
Club Med **9**
Holiday Inn **5**
Krystal Hotel **6**
Omni Hotel **7**
Posada Real **8**
Sheraton Hotel **2**
Stouffer Presidente
Hotel **4**
Westin Hotel **1**

beautiful long beach and Sierras foothills to the east. The heart of Zihuatanejo is the waterfront walkway **Paseo del Pescador** (also called the Malecón), bordering the Municipal Beach. The main thoroughfare for cars, however, is **Juan Alvarez**, a block behind the Malecón. A good highway connects "Zihuat" to **Ixtapa**, 7 miles to the northwest. Eight tall hotels line Ixtapa's beach, Playa Palmar, accessed by the main street, **Boulevard Ixtapa.**

GETTING AROUND

A **shuttle bus** goes back and forth between Zihuatanejo and Ixtapa every 15 to 20 minutes from 6am to 10pm daily, charging about 25¢ one way. In Zihuatanejo it stops near the corner of Morelos/Paseo Zihuatanejo and Juárez, about three blocks north of the market. In Ixtapa it makes numerous stops along Boulevard Ixtapa. A **taxi** from one town to the other costs about $5 to $6 one way; after 10pm rates increase, sometimes as much as 50% (agree on a price before getting in).

FAST FACTS

Area Code   The telephone area code is 753.
Climate   Summer is hot and humid, though tempered by the sea breezes and occasional brief showers; September is the wettest month.

WHAT TO SEE & DO

The **Museo de Arqueología,** at the east end of Paseo del Pescador, near Guerrero, was being remodeled recently, with tentative new hours set as Monday through Saturday from 10am to 8pm. Artifacts discovered a few years ago at the archeological site near the airport will be displayed.

THE BEACHES   In Zihuatanejo   At Zihuatanejo's town beach, or **Playa Municipal,** the local fishermen pull up their colorful boats on the sand. Small shops and restaurants line its waterfront, making this a great spot for people-watching and absorbing the flavor of daily village life. This beach is protected from the main surge of the Pacific.

Besides the peaceful Playa Municipal, Zihuatanejo has three other beaches: Madera, La Ropa, and Las Gatas. **Madera Beach,** just east of the Municipal Beach, is open to the surf but generally tranquil. Many attractive budget lodgings overlook this area from the hillside.

South of Playa Madera is Zihuatanejo's largest and most beautiful beach, **Playa La Ropa,** a long sweep of sand with a great view of the sunset. Some lovely small hotels and restaurants nestle into the hills and palm groves edge this shoreline. Although it's also open to the Pacific surge, the waves are usually gentle. A taxi from town costs $1.75.

Along a rocky seaside path that leads south from La Ropa is **Playa Las Gatas,** which is protected by a coral reef and popular with snorkelers. The open-air seafood restaurants on this beach also make it an appealing lunch spot for a splurge. Although you can hike here, it's much easier to take the hourly "ferry" (a small motorboat with a sunshade) at the Zihuatanejo town pier, which runs from 9am to 4:30pm (a 10-minute trip; round-trip fare is about $2). Usually the last ferry back leaves Las Gatas at 4:30pm; be sure to double-check! Snorkeling gear can be rented at the beach.

In Ixtapa   Ixtapa's main beach, **Playa Palmar** is a lovely arc of white sand edging the hotel zone, with dramatic rock formations silhouetted in the sea. The surf here can be rough; use caution and never swim when a red flag is posted.

Other beaches in the area include **Playa Quieta,** a tranquil beach on the mainland across from Isla Ixtapa, about 7 miles north of Ixtapa. Water-taxis here ferry passengers to Isla Ixtapa for about $2.50 round-trip. **Playa Las Cuatas,** a pretty beach and cove, is a few miles north of Ixtapa, where the Chula Vista Beach Club (restaurant/bar) is located. **Playa Vista Hermosa** is another pretty beach framed by striking rock formations and bordered by the Camino Real Ixtapa Hotel high on

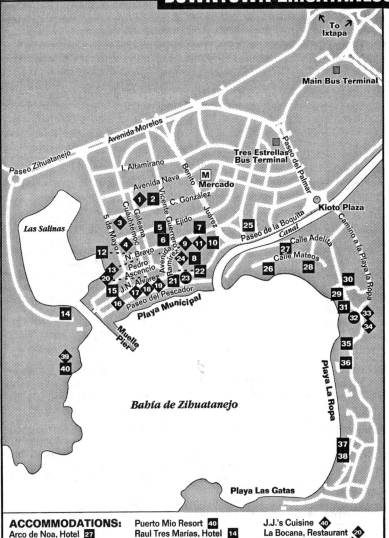

DOWNTOWN ZIHUATANEJO

To Ixtapa

Main Bus Terminal

Avenida Morelos

Paseo Zihuatanejo

I. Altamirano

Tres Estrellas
Bus Terminal

Paseo del Palmar

Avenida Nava

Benito Juárez

M Mercado

Kioto Plaza

C. González

Vicente Guerrero

Ejido

Galeana

Cuáuhtémoc

5 de Mayo

Las Salinas

Paseo de la Boquita

Canal

Calle Adelita

Calle Mateos

N. Bravo

Pedro
Ascencio

J.N. Álvarez

Avenida Ramírez

Paseo del Pescador

Playa Municipal

Muelle
Pier

Bahía de Zihuatanejo

Playa La Ropa

Playa Las Gatas

ACCOMMODATIONS:

Arco de Noa, Hotel **27**
Apartamentos
  Amueblados Valle **5**
Avila, Hotel **21**
Bungalows Allec **28**
Bungalows Pacificos **26**
Casa Aurora **6**
Catalina, Hotel **36**
Casa Bravo **7**
Hotel Flores **25**
Imelda, Hotel **2**
Irma, Hotel **31**
Palacios, Hotel **29**
Posada Citlali, Hotel **8**
Posada Celeste **12**

Puerto Mio Resort **40**
Raul Tres Marías, Hotel **14**
Raul Tres Marías
  Centro,Hotel **15**
Sotavento, Hotel **35**
Susy, Hotel **22**
Villa del Sol, Hotel **37**
Villas Miramar **30**
Zihuatanejo Centro, Hotel **10**

DINING:

Bay Club Restaurant, The ◆**33**
Cafe La Marina ◆**19**
Casa Elvira, Restaurant ◆**13**
Canaima, Restaurant ◆**17**
Coconuts, Restaurant ◆**24**

J.J.'s Cuisine ◆**40**
La Bocana, Restaurant ◆**20**
Kapi Kofi, Restaurant ◆**11**
Kon-Tiki, Restaurant ◆**34**
La Mesa del Capitan,
  Restaurant ◆**9**
La Perla, Restaurant ◆**39**
La Serena Gorda,
  Restaurant ◆**18**
Nueva Zelana, Restaurant ◆**4**
100% Natural ◆**3**
Panadería Frances/Bakery ◆**1**

SIGHTS:

Ibiza Disco **32**
Museo de Archeología ◆**23**

the hill. **Playa Majahua,** an isolated beach just west of Zihuatanejo, can be reached by a dirt road. Majahua is for picnicking only—its big surf makes swimming dangerous (people have drowned here).

WATER SPORTS & BOAT TRIPS   Probably the most popular boat trip is to **Isla Ixtapa** for snorkeling and lunch at El Marlin restaurant. Though available as a tour through local travel agencies, you can go on your own from Zihuatanejo by catching the boat that leaves the boat cooperative at the town pier around 11am for Isla Ixtapa and returns by 5pm, charging about $6 for the round-trip (lunch not included). Along the way you'll pass dramatic rock formations and the Los Moros de Los Pericos islands, known for the great variety of birds that nest on its rocky points jutting out into the blue Pacific. To go on your own from Ixtapa, take a taxi to Playa Quieta (20 minutes, about $5, one way), then catch a water-taxi ($2.50 round-trip) to the island. On the island you'll find good snorkeling and a nature trail through an unfenced wildlife area with a few exotic birds and animals. Oliverio rents snorkeling gear on the island. Be sure to catch the last water-taxi back at 4:30pm; there should be plenty of taxis for the return to Ixtapa.

Separate excursions to **Los Moros de Los Pericos islands** for birdwatching can usually be arranged through local travel agencies, though it would probably be less expensive to rent a boat with a guide at the town pier in Zihuatanejo. The islands are offshore from Ixtapa's main beach.

Sunset cruises on the yacht *Fandango-Zihua* depart from the Zihuatanejo town pier daily from 5 to 8pm. They include live music and an open bar. Tickets purchased at the town pier cost about $20. Sometimes night and moonlight cruises are available.

Fishing trips can be arranged with the boat cooperative at the Zihuatanejo town pier and cost $80 to $180, depending on the size of boat, length of time (though most trips are 6 hours), etc. The cost is higher through a local travel agency ($180 to $250). Both small-game and deep-sea fishing are offered. Trips that combine fishing with a visit to near-deserted ocean beaches that extend for miles along the coast from Zihuatanejo can also be arranged.

Sailboats, windsurfers, and other water-sports equipment rentals are usually available at Club de Playa Omar, La Ropa Beach in Zihuatanejo (tel. 4-3873), and at the main beach, Playa Palmar, in Ixtapa. **Parasailing** is also available at both beaches. Arrange **waterskiing** for $25 an hour at the town pier in Zihuatanejo and on the main beach in Ixtapa.

Scuba-diving trips are arranged through the Zihuatanejo Scuba Center, at Paseo del Pescador 4 (tel. 4-2147; fax 753/4-2048). Fees start around $60 for two dives, including equipment and lunch. Marine biologist and dive instructor Juan Barnard is extremely helpful and knowledgeable about the area, which has nearly 30 different dive sites. Diving is done year round, though the water is clearest in the summer, with 100-foot visibility or better.

Surfing is good at Petacalco Beach, north of Ixtapa.

The new **Marina Ixtapa,** a bit north of the Ixtapa hotel zone, should be finished and operating by late 1991.

LAND SPORTS & ACTIVITIES   In Ixtapa, the **Club de Golf Ixtapa** has an 18-hole course designed by Robert Trent Jones, Jr. Bring your own clubs or rent them here. The greens fee is $33. Call for reservations (tel. 4-2280 or 4-3245).

To polish your **tennis** serve in Zihuatanejo, try the La Ceiba Tennis Club near Playa Madera, or the Hotel Villa del Sol at Playa la Ropa (tel. 4-2239 or 4-3239). In Ixtapa, the Club de Golf Ixtapa has five tennis courts, lighted at night; it also rents equipment. Fees are $8 an hour, $10 an hour at night. Call for reservations (tel. 4-2280 or 4-3245). In addition, the Sheraton and many hotels on the main beach of Ixtapa have courts.

For **horseback riding,** guided trail rides from the Playa Linda Ranch (about 7 miles north of Ixtapa) to Posquelite in the countryside can be arranged through the travel agency Turismo Caleta (tel. 4-2491 or 4-2493) for $30.

The Chula Vista Beach Club on Playa Las Cuatas, north of Ixtapa, offers free **miniature golf, volleyball, and Ping-Pong,** but bring your own water-sports equipment. The attractive restaurant/bar on the beach is open daily from 11am to 6pm; no admission fee. Taxi fare is about $8 to $10 round-trip from Ixtapa, $15 from Zihuatanejo.

Bullfights are held on Sunday or Wednesday afternoon during the winter season at the Plaza de Toros (bullring) in Zihuatanejo. Most hotel travel agencies can arrange tickets.

A **countryside tour** of fishing villages, coconut and mango plantations, and the Barra de Potosí Lagoon (known for its tropical birds), 14 miles south of Zihuatanejo, is available through Turismo Caleta (tel. 4-2491 or 4-2493) and other local travel agencies for $30.

WHERE TO STAY

Because the most economical hotels are in Zihuatanejo rather than Ixtapa, all the lodging selections—with two exceptions—are in this village or near its beaches, Madera and La Ropa. Some of the best low-budget accommodations on the Pacific Coast are here.

Playa Madera and Playa La Ropa, separated from each other only by a craggy shoreline, are both accessible by road. Prices here tend to be higher than those in town, but some people find that the beautiful and tranquil setting is worth the little extra. Town is just 5 to 20 minutes away, depending on whether you walk or take a taxi.

Note: If you arrive without reservations during the busiest times of the year—the Christmas holidays and Easter week (when hotel prices are higher and vacancies rare)—take the first room available. Then, with more time, search for what suits you best. If there are no vacancies, look in higher-priced Ixtapa or in Petatlan, 22 miles down the coast (southeast).

IN TOWN
Doubles For Less Than $25

CASA AURORA, Nicolas Bravo 27, Zihuatanejo, Gro. 40880. Tel. 753/4-3046. 12 rms (all with bath).
$ Rates: $11 per person.
Located a few minutes from the beach (walk inland on Guerrero to Nicolas Bravo), this hotel offers small rooms and a comfortable second-story porch. All rooms have hot water. The best rooms are no. 12 (a double) and no. 13 (a triple), with windows facing the street.

POSADA CELESTE, Galeana 5, Zihuatanejo, Gro. 40880. Tel. 753/4-2047. 2 rms (all with bath).
$ Rates: $15 single or double.
This friendly, family-run hotel has bright, clean rooms with ceiling fans and large bathrooms. It's especially good for families and has a place for washing clothes by hand.

To get here, walk two blocks inland from the main street (Alvarez) and turn south on Nicolas Bravo.

CASA BRAVO, Nicolas Bravo 11, Zihuatanejo, Gro. 40880. Tel. 753/4-2548. 6 rms (all with bath).
$ Rates: High season, $15 single; $19 double. Off-season, $12 single; $15 double.
A good value for its budget price, this two-story hotel offers clean, plain rooms with mismatched furniture, fans, and bare bulbs above the beds. Three second-story rooms at the front of the building have balconies, though this means a bit of street noise. Guests can lounge in the two hammocks in the open-ceilinged lobby.

You'll find it by walking inland on Guerrero to Bravo and turning right.

HOTEL RAUL TRES MARÍAS, Calle Noria 4, Colonia Lázaro Cárdenas, Zihuatanejo, Gro. 40880. Tel. 753/4-2191 or 4-2591. 25 rms (all with bath).
$ Rates: $14 single; $20 double. Discounts for long stays off-season.

Don't let the well-worn exterior discourage you. This aging budget standard was here a decade ago when Zihuatanejo was at the end of a dirt road; like the village, the hotel has grown, and retains the same friendly atmosphere of previous years. Several levels of terraces offer a marvelous view of the whole town. Rooms are plain and simple, but bright and clean; all have fans and screens.

The hotel is across the wooden footbridge on the west side of town. From the bus station, walk south on Juárez toward the beach, turn right on the last street before the beach (Alvarez), follow it to the end, and cross the footbridge.

HOTEL SUSY, Juan Alvarez 3, Zihuatanejo, Gro. 40880. Tel. 753/4-2339. 17 rms (all with bath).
$ Rates: High season, $19 single; $27 double. Off-season, $15 single; $19 double.
Shiny and clean, with lots of plants along a shaded walkway set back from the street, this two-story hotel offers small rooms with ceiling fans (two with air conditioning) and louvered glass windows. Rooms on the upper floor have balconies overlooking the street. Late sleepers and nap-takers should keep in mind that the schoolyard across the way can be noisy. It's on the east end of the main street, half a block in from the town beach.

POSADA CITLALI, Vicente Guerrero 3, Zihuatanejo, Gro. 40880. Tel. 753/4-2043. 17 rms (all with bath).
$ Rates: High season, $19 single; $27 double. Off-season, $15 single; $23 double.
The small rooms in this three-story hotel are arranged around a little courtyard with trees, flowering plants, a hammock, and rocking chairs. Furnishings include ceiling fans, chenille bedspreads, and a large wall mirror with a shelf beneath it. The posada is inland from the main street (Alvarez), a short walk from the town beach.

Doubles For Less Than $30

APARTAMENTOS AMUEBLADOS VALLE, Vicente Guerrero 14, Zihuatanejo, Gro. 40880. Tel. 753/4-3220 or 4-2084. 8 apartments.
$ Rates: $25–$30 one-bedroom apartment; $40 two-bedroom apartment. Off-season 15%–20% less.
You can rent a well-furnished apartment for a little more than the price of a hotel room. The five one-bedroom apartments accommodate up to three people; the three two-bedroom apartments can fit four comfortably. Each apartment is different, but all are clean and airy, with ceiling fans, private balconies, and kitchenettes. Maid service is provided daily. Reserve well in advance during high season. It's on Guerrero about two blocks in from the waterfront.

Worth the Extra Bucks

HOTEL ÁVILA, Juan Alvarez 8, Zihuatanejo, Gro. 40880. Tel. 753/4-2010. 27 rms (all with bath).
$ Rates: $48 single or double; $55 with ocean view. **Parking:** Free.
This hotel offers pricey rooms conveniently located on the beach. Eighteen rooms have private balconies facing town, but no ocean view. The rest share a terrace facing the sea. Rooms with ceiling fan or air conditioning cost the same.

HOTEL ZIHUATANEJO CENTRO, Ramírez 2, Zihuatanejo, Gro. 40880. Tel. 753/4-3661. Fax 753/4-2669. 70 rms (all with bath). A/C TV TEL
$ Rates: $48 single or double.
Arranged around a small courtyard with a swimming pool and a colorful mural on one side of the building, this modern four-story hotel offers clean, comfortable, motel-size rooms with bright bedspreads and wooden headboards. Some have tiny balconies and a view of the pool or street. Guests can enjoy the poolside bar and restaurant. TVs bring in U.S. channels. The hotel is about a block inland on a curving street that runs from Alvarez to Guerrero.

PLAYA MADERA

Madera Beach is a 15-minute walk or a $1.75 taxi ride from town. Most of the accommodations are on Calle Eva S. de Lopez Mateos, the road that overlooks

Madera Beach. If you walk 15 minutes east of town beside the canal, crossing a footbridge, and following the road running uphill, you will intersect Mateos.

Doubles For Less Than $25

ARCO DE NOA, Calle Eva S. de Lopez Mateos, Playa Madera, Zihuatanejo, Gro. 40880. Tel. 753/4-2272. 10 rms (all with bath).
$ Rates: High season, $23 single or double; off-season, $12–$15 single or double.
An excellent value, Arco de Noa is a two-story house on the inland side of Mateos set back from a front patio landscaped with flowers and a shaded sitting area. The neat, pleasant rooms have large windows with glass louvers, white walls, bright-colored bedspreads, and ceiling fans. Guests are free to use the kitchen and dining room on the premises. Four rooms have sea views.

Doubles For Less Than $45

HOTEL PALACIOS, Playa Madera (Apdo. Postal 57), Zihuatanejo, Gro. 40880. Tel. 753/4-2055. 28 rms (all with bath).
$ Rates (including breakfast): High season, $38 single; $44 double. Off-season, about 20% less.
This is one of the older hotels on the beach, and it shows. Its good points include separate children's and adults' pools on a beachside terrace, and the ceiling fans and sea breezes. Few rooms have ocean views, although no. 10 and nos. 17 through 21 all have windows on two sides, good vistas, and shared balconies. Five rooms are air-conditioned.

BUNGALOWS ALLEC, Calle Eva S. de Lopez Mateos, Playa Madera (Apdo. Postal 220), Zihuatanejo, Gro. 40880. Tel. 753/4-2002 or 4-3679. 12 apartments.
$ Rates: High season, $45 apartment for one or two, $65 apartment for four; off-season, $35 apartment for one or two, $50 apartment for four.
These popular bungalows are managed by a delightful English-speaking couple, Klaus and Carola Ellrodt. The six two-bedroom apartments include kitchens, and the six one-bedroom apartments have kitchenettes, narrow balconies, and loft bedrooms; all come with fans. A formidable flight of stairs leads down the hillside to the beach. Reserve at least 2 months in advance for high season.

BUNGALOWS PACÍFICOS, Playa Madera (Apdo. Postal 12), Zihuatanejo, Gro. 40880. Tel. 753/4-2112. 6 bungalows.
$ Rates: High season, $45 bungalows for one or two; $10 extra person. Off-season, $40 bungalows for one or two; $5 extra person.
Providing ample comfort, beauty, and tranquility, these bungalows come with two bedrooms, fans, fully equipped kitchens, and lovely terraces serving as living areas with table and chairs, hammock, flowering plants, and magnificent views. The hostess, Anita Hahner, will gladly answer all your questions in four languages, including English. The three-story building is arranged in tiers down the steep hillside, and the beach is just a 5-minute walk away.
To get here, facing Bungalows Allec (see above) on Mateos, take the road to the right until you reach its terminus overlooking the town.

Worth the Extra Bucks

VILLAS MIRAMAR, Calle Adelita, Playa Madera (Apdo. Postal 211), Zihuatanejo, Gro. 40880. Tel. 753/4-2106 or 4-2616. Fax 753/4-2149. 18 suites. A/C TEL
$ Rates: High season, $60 one-bedroom suite for one or two, $75 with ocean view; $115 two-bedroom suite. Off-season, $45 one-bedroom suite for one or two, $50 with ocean view. **Parking:** Free.
Some of these elegant suites are built around a beautiful shady patio that doubles as a restaurant. Those across the street center around a lovely pool and have private balconies and sea views. Parking is enclosed.
To find Villas Miramar, on the road leading south out of town toward Playa La Ropa, take the first right after the traffic circle; then turn left onto Adelita.

PLAYA LA ROPA

Some travelers consider Playa La Ropa the most beautiful of Zihuatanejo's beaches. It's a 20- to 25-minute walk south of town on the east side of the bay, or a $1.75 taxi ride. The hotels here are beyond our budget, but may be worth the extra expense for the peaceful and gorgeous setting.

Worth the Extra Bucks

BUNGALO PALACIOS VEPAO, Playa La Ropa, Zihuatanejo, Gro. 40880. Tel. 753/4-2631. 15 rms (all with bath).

$ Rates: High season, $60 single or double; less in off-season.

This two-story beachside hotel breaks our budget, but offers comfortable rooms at a reasonable price. Twelve of the sunny rooms have kitchens; the other three share one. Most are spacious and all have fans and balconies with ocean vistas. Management is indifferent, but the rooms' location is ideal. Make reservations well in advance.

HOTEL CATALINA and HOTEL SOTAVENTO, Playa La Ropa, Zihuatanejo, Gro. 40880. Tel. 753/4-2032 or 4-2088. 124 rms (all with bath).

$ Rates: High season (including two meals), $60–$80 single; $85–$105 double. Off-season (without meals), $40–$60 single or double.

Perched high on the hill close to each other and managed together by the same owners, these two attractive hotels were among the first in the area and retain the slow-paced, gracious mood of Zihuatanejo in its early days as a little-known hideaway. The spectacular panoramic views of Playa La Ropa below alone are worth the price of staying here.

The 85 terrace rooms of the Sotavento are quite large, with telephones, and decorated with wood furniture that evokes the 1950s and 1960s, including one double and one single bed. Best of all is the large, shared ocean-view terrace, equipped with a hammock and two chaise longues for each room—great for sunning and sunset-watching. The Catalina has recently remodeled many of its 39 rooms with Mexican tile, wrought iron, and other handcrafted touches; these also have lovely terraces with ocean views and come with two queen-size beds.

Between them the two hotels cover eight stories climbing the slope and have several restaurants and bars. Do ask to see at least a couple of rooms first as they can vary quite a bit in furnishings and price. Also keep in mind the hike down many steps to the beach (depending on the room level) and the lack of air conditioning, compensated for by the ceiling fans and sea breezes. Nor is there a swimming pool.

To get here, take the highway south of Zihuatanejo about a mile, turn right at the hotel sign, and follow the road downhill to the hotels. Or you can hike up the hill from La Ropa Beach.

IXTAPA

Although the two hotels below are beyond our budget, they remain the best bargains in Ixtapa, which caters primarily to the charter- and package-tour business. If you want to stay at a hotel on Ixtapa's beautiful beach, your best bet is to buy a hotel-and-airfare package in advance.

Worth the Extra Bucks

BEST WESTERN POSADA REAL, Blvd. Ixtapa, Ixtapa, Gro. 40380. Tel. 753/3-1625 or 3-1745, or toll free 800/528-1234 in the U.S. (Best Western). Fax 753/3-1805.

$ Rates: High season, $80 single or double; Off-season $70 single or double. **Parking:** Free.

The plain, motel-type rooms have two comfortable double beds, a wall-desk/counter and minicouch, and a small window (some with sea view but no balcony) with an air conditioner beneath it. The TV brings in U.S. channels. Request a room on the lower floors; there are no elevators in this four-story hotel. Among the facilities are two pools, two outdoor restaurants, a gift shop, and a travel desk. Coco's, its pirate-theme restaurant/bar on the beach with hanging basket chairs and music, can be fun. The Lighthouse Restaurant and Euphoria Disco are set apart on the front part of the property, just off Boulevard Ixtapa. Booking directly with the hotel or buying a package may be cheaper than reserving through Best Western. Parking is in an open lot off Boulevard Ixtapa. The posada is on Ixtapa's main beach next to Carlos 'n' Charlie's restaurant at the northern end of the hotel zone.

HOTEL ARISTOS, Blvd. Ixtapa, Ixtapa, Gro. 40380. Tel. 753/3-0011, or toll free 800/527-4786 in the U.S. Fax 753/3-2031. 225 rms (all with bath). A/C TV TEL

$ Rates: High season, $85 single or double; less in off-season. **Parking:** Free.

Since the earthquake of 1985, this hotel on the main beach of Ixtapa has been completely rebuilt. Standard rooms are medium-sized with a sea view (some have balconies) and come with two double beds, marble-trimmed bath, slick contemporary furniture, and TV with U.S. channels. The decor might be called "Moorish modern," mixing pointed arches with contemporary lines. Facilities include three restaurants, piano bar, nightclub, swimming pool, travel agency, shops, two tennis courts, and exercise and water-sports equipment. Laundry, baby-sitting, secretarial, and business services are also available. Parking is in an open lot off Boulevard Ixtapa.

CHAPTER 6

THE PACIFIC COAST FROM ACAPULCO TO BAHÍAS DE HUATULCO

Visitors from North America enjoyed sunning and swimming in Acapulco long before their Mexican neighbors caught on. A half century ago Acapulco was a sleepy fishing port with only a few renegade "Norteamericanos" living on low budgets. Since then, things have changed. Although the small fishing ports still exist, you have to forge ever southward to find them.

SEEING THE SOUTHERN PACIFIC COAST

The southern reaches of the Pacific Coast cater to varying tastes. If you are interested in nightlife, glitz, and luxury hotels, Acapulco wins hands down. For a touch of colonial Mexico, take a side trip from Acapulco to Taxco (see Chapter 13). If you want to get away from everything in a quiet atmosphere with beautiful scenery and unspoiled nature, you should choose one of the other destinations. Puerto Angel is the perfect spot for kicking back and spending little money, and while Huatulco is overpriced and hard to get to, it still offers the untouched beauty of the Oaxaca coastline with its beaches and hidden coves.

1. ACAPULCO

262 miles S of Mexico City, 170 miles S of Taxco,
612 miles SE of Guadalajara, 158 miles SE of Ixtapa/Zihuatanejo,
470 miles NW of Huatulco

GETTING THERE By Plane The following major airlines have nonstop or direct service to Acapulco: **Aeroméxico,** from Houston, New York, Guadalajara, Mexico City, and Tijuana; **American,** from Dallas/Fort Worth; **Continental,** from Houston and Newark; **Delta,** from Dallas/Fort Worth and Los Angeles; and **Mexicana,** from Chicago, Los Angeles, and Mexico City. Regional carriers include **AeroLibertad,** from Ixtapa/Zihuatanejo and Oaxaca; and **AeroMorelos,** from Cuernavaca and Puebla.

WHAT'S SPECIAL ABOUT THE SOUTHERN PACIFIC COAST

Beaches
- ☐ One of the most beautiful beaches in the country is in Puerto Escondido.
- ☐ The unspoiled beaches and beautiful coastline of Huatulco, with pristine bays and crystal-clear water.

Nightlife
- ☐ Acapulco's varied and vibrant nightlife, unrivaled in all of Mexico.

- ☐ The breathtaking glittering night view of Acapulco's bay.

Towns
- ☐ Puerto Escondido, an example of a coastal predevelopment town with palm-lined beaches and green hills.

Check with a travel agent about **charter flights.** Charters from Atlanta, Cinncinnati, Oakland, and other U.S. cities are anticipated during 1992.

By Bus   Buses from Mexico City to Acapulco leave from the Terminal Central de Autobuses del Sur (Taxqueño Metro line) for the 7-hour trip. **Estrella de Oro** has hourly service from Mexico City to Acapulco, but try to reserve your seat a few days in advance. There's little difference between express and deluxe service. **Lineas Unidas del Sur/Flecha Roja** also runs 24 daily buses to Acapulco from Mexico City's south bus station, but the equipment is inferior to that of Estrella de Oro. The road between Mexico City and Acapulco is curvy.

From Ixtapa/Zihuatanejo, **Estrella Blanca** has six direct buses daily and nine *de paso* buses to Acapulco.

By Car   From Mexico City, take Highway 95 south, a curvy highway. A much straighter four-lane toll highway is under construction. From points north or south along the coast, the only choice is Highway 200.

DEPARTING By Plane   Airline offices are at the airport and/or downtown: **AeroLibertad,** at airport (tel. 84-2443 or 84-2521; fax 74/84-2521), or use the Mexicana office below (Mexicana owns AeroLibertad); **Aeroméxico,** Costera Aleman 251 (tel. 85-1625, 85-1600, or 85-1543, or 84-0035 at the airport); **AeroMorelos,** at the airport (tel. 84-7965 or 81-0852; fax 74/84-3141); **American,** Costera Aleman 239 (tel. 84-1734 or 84-1814); **Continental,** at the airport (tel. 84-7003 or 84-6900); **Delta,** in the Hotel Continental Plaza, Costera Aleman (tel. 84-0716 or 84-0717, or toll free 91-800/9-0221 in Mexico); **Mexicana,** Costera Aleman 1252 (tel. 4-6943 or 84-6890, or 84-1815 at the airport).

Transportación Aeropuerto (tel. 85-2332, 85-2591, or 85-2226) has colectivo service to and from the airport. Call the day before your departure for a reservation. One-way trip costs $5.50 per person; children pay half price. The service picks you up 90 minutes (flights within Mexico) to 2 hours (international flights) before your departure time. **Taxis** cost $13 to $18.

By Bus   From Acapulco, **Estrella de Oro** (tel. 85-8705 or 85-9360) has more than a dozen direct buses daily to Mexico City, three to Taxco (at 7am, 9am, and 4:30pm), and several to Ixtapa/Zihuatanejo daily. **Lineas Unidas del Sur/Flecha Roja** (tel. 82-0351) also has frequent buses to Mexico City, but they're not as nice as those of Estrella de Oro. **Estrella Blanca** (tel. 83-0802) has service to Ixtapa/Zihuatanejo, Monterrey, Zacatecas, Guadalajara, and the region around San Luis Potosí.

The astounding thing about Acapulco (pop. 600,000) is its perennially romantic reputation and its jet-set image. This city spreading across foothills around a vast blue bay is an exciting playground and bustling commercial center. A real city rather

ACCOMMODATIONS:

Acapulco Plaza Hotel	20
Acapulco Princess Hotel	39
Acapulco Ritz Hotel	19
La Angosta Hotel	12
Belmar Hotel	8
Boca Chica Hotel	6
Bonanza Hotel	3
Hotel Caleta	1
Calinda Hotel	25
Continental Plaza Hotel	21
Hotel El Faro	14
Fiesta Americana Condesa Hotel	23
Hyatt Regency Hotel	31
Motel la Jolla	4
Las Brisas Hotel	36
Lindavista Hotel	2
Paraiso Radisson Hotel	18
Pierre Marqués Hotel	38
Plaza Las Glorias Hotel/El Mirador	13
Punta Diamante (resort development)	24
Suites Imperial Jazmin	9

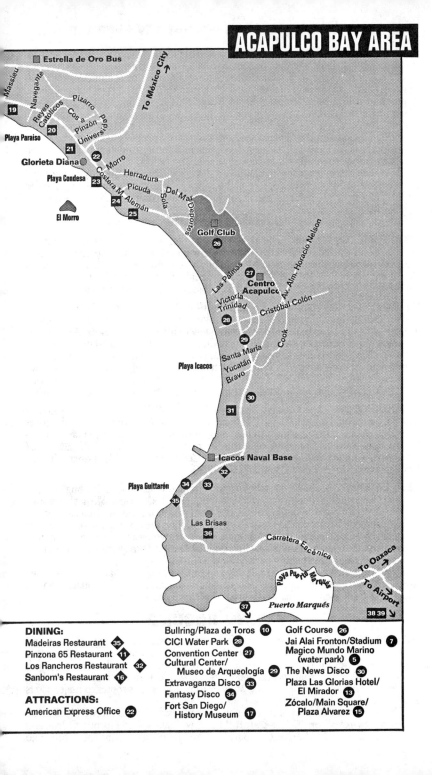

ACAPULCO BAY AREA

Estrella de Oro Bus

To México City →

Massieu

Navegante

Reyes Católicos

Pizarro

Cos a Pinzón

Popo

Universi

19

20

Playa Paraiso

21

22

Glorieta Diana

Playa Condesa

23

Morro

Herradura

Picuda

Del Mar

Sola

Deportes

24

25

El Morro

Golf Club

26

Las Palmas

27

Centro
Acapulco

Victoria
Trinidad

Cristóbal Colón

Av. Alm. Horacio Nelson

28

29

Cook

Santa María

Yucatán

Bravo

Playa Icacos

30

31

Icacos Naval Base

32

Playa Guittarón

34

33

35

Las Brisas

36

Carretera Escénica

To Oaxaca →

To Airport →

Playa Pue. rto Marqués

37

Puerto Marqués

38 39 ↘

DINING:
Madeiras Restaurant **35**
Pinzona 65 Restaurant **11**
Los Rancheros Restaurant **32**
Sanborn's Restaurant **16**

ATTRACTIONS:
American Express Office **22**

Bullring/Plaza de Toros **10**
CICI Water Park **28**
Convention Center **27**
Cultural Center/
  Museo de Arqueología **29**
Extravaganza Disco **33**
Fantasy Disco **34**
Fort San Diego/
  History Museum **17**

Golf Course **26**
Jai Alai Fronton/Stadium **7**
Magico Mundo Marino
  (water park) **5**
The News Disco **30**
Plaza Las Glorias Hotel/
  El Mirador **13**
Zócalo/Main Square/
  Plaza Alvarez **15**

than simply a resort, Acapulco also has its share of grit along with the glitz. There are slums as well as villas. Some of the hotels could use a facelift.

Acapulco has been working hard lately to regain some of the old glamour that originally put it on the map in the 1960s, when many Hollywood stars hung out here. A program called ACA-Limpia ("Clean Acapulco") is cleaning up the bay (where whales have been sighted recently for the first time in years) and sprucing up the Costera. Itinerant vendors have been moved to newly created market areas such as the Diana traffic circle on the Costera so they don't annoy people on the beach.

Acapulco is still growing: Its latest development is the upscale Punta Diamante, on the coast east of town. It will include several luxury hotels.

Of course, when it comes to nightlife, the vibrant variety of this city's discos and clubs is hard to top in Mexico, just as the view of Acapulco Bay at night, spangled with twinkling lights, remains one of the most breathtaking views in the world.

ORIENTATION

ARRIVING   By Plane   The **airport** is 14 miles southeast of town near Puerto Marqués, over the hills lying east of the bay. **Transportación Aeropuerto** desks at the front of the airport sell tickets for minivan colectivo transportation into town ($5.50 per person), or by taxi ($12 for two people, slightly more for three or four); children pay half price. A round-trip ticket costs twice the one-way fare.

By Bus   The bus station for **Lineas Unidas del Sur/Flecha Roja** is in the market area at Cuauhtémoc 97, about six blocks from the zócalo, or main square (downtown), and close to many downtown budget hotels. The **Estrella de Oro** bus station is much farther from downtown at Cuauhtémoc 1490 and Massieu, but still within walking distance of some economical accommodations. Local buses pass the terminal going both directions on Cuauhtémoc. The relatively new (1990) **Estrella Blanca** terminal at Ejido 47 is north of downtown and farthest from our hotel selections. The station has a hotel-reservation service, "Sendetur," open 24 hours.

INFORMATION   The **Federal Tourism Office (SECTUR)** is on the Costera at Río de Camaron 187 (tel. 785-1041), near Hornos Beach. Attendants will answer questions about buses, airlines, hotels, and other topics. Open Monday through Friday from 8am to 8pm and on Saturday from 10am to 2pm. The **State of Guerrero Tourist Office,** in the Convention Center (tel. 84-1014), is open Monday through Friday from 9am to 3pm and 6 to 8:30pm.

CITY LAYOUT   Acapulco stretches for more than 4 miles around the huge bay, so walking to see it all is impractical. The main boulevard, **Costera Miguel Aleman** (the Costera), follows the outline of the bay from downtown on the west side, where "Old Acapulco" began, to the Hyatt Regency Hotel on the east side. Most hotels are either on the Costera and the beach, or a block or two away; as you go east from downtown they become increasingly luxurious. **Avenida Cuauhtémoc** is the major artery inland and runs roughly parallel to the Costera.

Street names and numbers in this city can be confusing and hard to find—many streets are not well marked, or change names unexpectedly. Fortunately you're seldom far from the Costera, so it's hard to get really lost.

GETTING AROUND

BY BUS   For a city with such a confusing street system, it's amazingly easy and inexpensive to use city buses. Two kinds of buses run along the Costera: pastel color-coded buses for tourists and regular "school buses" for locals. As a rule, both types seem to pick up tourists and nontourists alike. Covered bus stops are all along the Costera with handy maps on the walls showing tourist bus routes to major sights and hotels.

The best place near the zócalo to catch a bus is beside Sanborn's, two blocks east. **"Caleta Directo"** or **"Base-Caleta"** buses will take you to Hornos, Caleta, and Caletilla beaches along the Costera; some buses return along the same route; others go

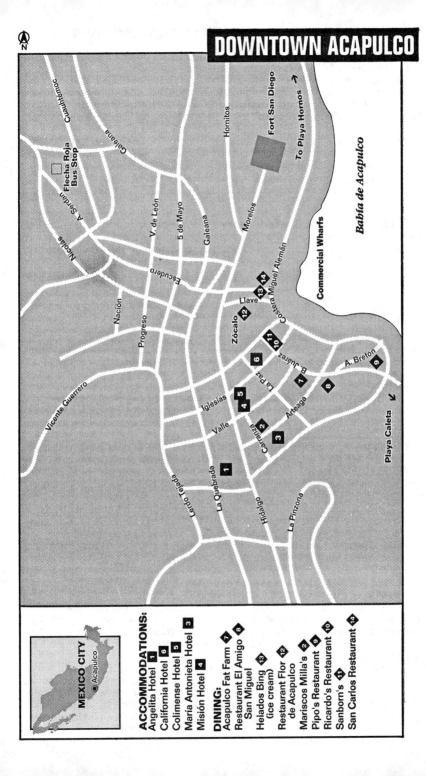

DOWNTOWN ACAPULCO

MEXICO CITY

Acapulco

ACCOMMODATIONS:

Angelita Hotel **1**
California Hotel **6**
Colimense Hotel **5**
María Antonieta Hotel **3**
Misión Hotel **4**

DINING:

Acapulco Fat Farm **7**
Restaurant El Amigo
 San Miguel **8**
Helados Bing
 (ice cream) **13**
Restaurant Flor
 de Acapulco **12**
Mariscos Milla's **2**
Pipo's Restaurant **9**
Ricardo's Restaurant **10**
Sanborn's **11**
San Carlos Restaurant **14**

around the peninsula and return to the Costera. As for the restaurants and nightspots in the upscale hotel district on the north and east sides of the bay, catch a **"Base–Cine Río–Caleta"** bus beside Sanborn's. It runs inland along Cuauhtémoc to the Estrella de Oro bus terminal, then heads back to the Costera and beach at the Ritz Hotel and continues east along the Costera to Icacos Beach near the Hyatt Regency Hotel. **"Zócalo Directo"** and **"Caleta Directo"** buses follow the same route in the opposite direction.

For longer expeditions there are buses to Puerto Marqués to the east ("Puerto Marqués–Base") and Pie de la Cuesta to the west ("Zócalo–Pie de la Cuesta"). Be sure to verify the time and place of the last bus back if you hop one of these!

For a cheap way to get to the discos and restaurants east of town near the Las Brisas Hotel, take a "Base" bus as far as the Hyatt Regency. Then take a taxi the rest of the way for $4. City buses stop at 10pm.

BY TAXI   Taxis charge $3 to $4 for a ride within the city and more if you go farther out. For approximate prices, ask at your hotel or scan one of the taxi tariff lists found in most major hotel lobbies. Always establish the price with the driver before starting out. Report any trouble or overcharges to the Procuradura del Turista—the Tourist Assistance Office on the Costera next to the Convention Center (tel. 74/84-4416 or 84-6136).

FAST FACTS

American Express   The main office is at Costera Aleman 709, east of the Diana traffic circle (tel. 84-1095 for travel services, 84-5200 for financial services, 84-5550 for customer service, 84-6060 for tours); another branch is at the Hyatt Regency (tel. 84-2888).

Area Code   The telephone area code is 74.

Changing Money   Banks along the Costera are open Monday through Friday from 9am to 1 or 1:30pm (though hours for exchanging money may be shorter) and generally have the best rates. *Casas de cambio* (currency booths) along the street may have better exchange rates than hotels.

Climate   Although June through October is the rainy season, June, September, and October are the wettest months, while July and August are relatively dry.

Consular Agents   The **United States** has an agent at the Hotel Club del Sol (tel. 85-6600 ext. 7348, or 85-7207), across from the Hotel Acapulco Plaza, open Monday through Friday from 10am to 2pm. The agent of **Canada** is also at the Hotel Club del Sol (tel. 85-6621), open Monday through Friday from 9am to 1pm. The agent of the **United Kingdom** is at the Las Brisas Hotel (tel. 84-6605), open Monday through Friday from 9am to 6pm.

Post Office   The central post office (Correo) is on the Costera near the zócalo and Sanborn's. Other branches are located in the Estrella de Oro bus station on Cuauhtémoc, inland from the Acapulco Ritz Hotel; and on the Costera near Caleta Beach.

Safety   Pay careful attention to **warning flags** posted on Acapulco beaches! These alert you to the presence of rip tides, which claim a few lives every year. Red or black flags mean stay out of the water, yellow signifies caution, and white or green flags mean it's safe to swim. Don't swim on any beach that fronts an open sea. But don't let down your guard on the bays either. It's difficult to imagine how powerful an undertow can be.

As always, tourists are vulnerable to **thieves.** This is especially true when you're shopping in a market, lying on the beach, wearing jewelry, or carrying a camera, purse, or bulging wallet. Tourists out for a morning walk on the beach should be especially alert. Pay attention to joggers coming from both directions—one knocks you down, then they rob you. To remove temptation from would-be thieves, purchase one of those waterproof plastic tubes on a string to wear around your neck at the beach—it's big enough for a few bills and your room key. Street vendors and hotel variety shops sell them.

Tourist Police If you see policemen in uniforms of white and light blue, they're from a special corps of English-speaking police who assist tourists.

WHAT TO SEE & DO

Acapulco abounds with great beaches and opportunities for water sports. But it's also pleasant to take a walk early in the day (before it gets too hot) around the **zócalo,** called Plaza Alvarez. Visit the cathedral—the bulbous blue onion domes make it look more like a Russian Orthodox church, and it was actually designed as a movie theater! From the church, turn east along the side street going off at a right angle (Calle Carranza, without a marker), where an arcade offers newsstands and shops.

A fabulous view of Acapulco awaits from the top of the hill behind the cathedral. Take a taxi up the hill from the main plaza, following the signs leading to **La Mira.**

City tours, day trips to Taxco, cruises, and other excursions and activities are offered through local travel agencies.

THE BEACHES

Here's the rundown, from west to east around the bay: **Playa la Angosta** is a small, sheltered, and often-deserted cove just around the bend from La Quebrada (where the cliff divers perform).

South of downtown on the Peninsula de las Playas lie **Caleta and Caletilla beaches,** separated by a small outcropping of land where the new aquarium and water park, Magico Mundo Marino, stands. You'll find thatch-roofed restaurants, water-sports equipment to rent, and the brightly painted boats that ferry passengers to Roqueta Island. Mexican families favor these beaches because they're close to several inexpensive hotels. And in the late afternoon fishermen pull their colorful boats up on the sand and sell their catch, and sometimes oysters on the half shell.

The pleasure boats dock at **Playa Larga,** also south of the zócalo. Charter fishing trips sail from here. In the old days these downtown beaches—Larga, Caleta, Caletilla—were what Acapulco was all about and where it began. Nowadays the beaches and the resort development stretch the entire 4-mile length of the bay's shore.

Going east from the zócalo, the major beaches are **Hornos** (near Papagayo Park), **Hornitos, Condesa,** and **Icacos,** followed by the naval base (La Base) and **Punta del Guitarron.** After Guitarron Point the road climbs to the legendary hotel Las Brisas, where many of the 300 casitas (bungalow-type rooms) have their own swimming pools (there are 250 pools in all) and start at $200 per day in winter, $125 in the off-season. Past Las Brisas, the road continues on to **Puerto Marqués** and **Punta Diamante,** about 12 miles from the zócalo. The fabulous Acapulco Princess and Pierre Marqués hotels dominate the landscape.

The bay of Puerto Marqués is an attractive area for swimming. The water is calm, the bay sheltered, and waterskiing available. Past the bay lie **Revolcadero Beach** and a fascinating jungle lagoon.

Warning: Each year in Acapulco at least one or two unwary swimmers drown because of deadly rip tides and undertow (see "Safety" in "Fast Facts," above). *Swim only in Acapulco Bay or Puerto Marqués Bay*—but even there be careful of undertows!

Other beaches are difficult to reach without a car. **La Pie de la Cuesta** is 8 miles west of town (buses leave town every 5 or 10 minutes). You can't swim here, but it's a great spot for watching big waves and the sunset, especially over *coco locos* (made with a fresh coconut with the top whacked off) at one of the rustic beachfront restaurants hung with hammocks. If boys try to collect money from you for sitting under the thatched palapas on the public beach, you don't have to pay them.

If you drive, continue west along the peninsula, passing Coyuca Lagoon on your right, until you have almost reached the small air base at the tip. Along the way, you'll be invited to drive into different sections of beach by various private entrepreneurs, mostly small boys.

BAY CRUISES & ROQUETA ISLAND

A wonderful way to see the whole bay is from the deck of a yacht, and Acapulco has a variety of cruises to choose from. The *Fiesta* (tel. 83-2531) offers an afternoon cruise leaving at 4:30pm for $10 (drinks not included), and evening trips at 7:30 and 8pm with dinner, drinks, live music, and a show for $35 to $48. Two other motor yachts, the *Hawaiian* (tel. 82-0785) and the *Bonanza* (tel. 83-1803), make similar trips during the day and evening.

The trimaran *Aca Tiki* (tel. 84-6140 or 84-6786) and the large yacht *Fiesta Cabaret* (tel. 83-2531) offer nightly dinner/dance cruises with an open bar for around $48. The *Aca Tiki* is quieter and more sophisticated, serving dinner at the table. The *Fiesta Cabaret* features a buffet, loud music, and enthusiastic leadership. The **Fishing Factory** (tel. 82-1398) offers a $30 sunset cruise departing at 5:30pm to watch the cliff divers and includes an open bar. The *Aca Tiki* also offers daytime snorkeling and lunch cruises to Roqueta Island.

Schedules change, so call the cruise operators above or consult a local travel agency for additional information and reservations. Be sure you understand what the price covers—tips and drinks may be extra, for example.

A TRIP TO ROQUETA ISLAND Boats from Caletilla Beach to Roqueta Island—a delightful place to snorkel, sunbathe, hike to a lighthouse, visit a small zoo, or eat lunch—leave every half hour from 9:30am until the last one returns at 5pm. The cost is $3 round-trip, or $6 on a glass-bottom boat (use the same ticket to return on any launch). You may disagree, but I don't think the glass-bottom-boat ride is worth the bucks. Purchase tickets directly from any boat that is loading or from the information booth on Caletilla Beach (tel. 82-2389). The booth also rents inner tubes, small boats, canoes, peddle boats, and beach chairs; it can also arrange waterskiing and scuba diving.

SPORTS

WATER SPORTS An hour of **waterskiing** can cost as little as $20 or as much as $50. Caletilla Beach, Puerto Marqués Bay, and Coyuca Lagoon have waterskiing facilities.

Scuba diving costs $25 for an hour and a half of instruction if booked directly with the instructor on Caleta Beach, or $30 to $50 if arranged through a hotel or travel agency. Dive trips start around $35 per person for one dive.

Boat rentals are the least expensive on Caletilla Beach, where an information booth (tel. 82-2389) rents inner tubes, small boats, canoes, peddle boats, and beach chairs; it can also arrange waterskiing and scuba diving.

For **deep-sea fishing** excursions, go to the docks at Playa Larga (south of the zócalo). Charter fishing trips from here run $100 to $150 for 7 hours, arranged through the Boat Cooperative (tel. 82-1099). Another charter-boat dock (tel. 83-9107) is next to the Colonial Restaurant and Beach Club across from Fort San Diego. Booked through a travel agent or hotel, fishing trips start around $200 for four people.

Parasailing, though not without risks, can be a fantastic thrill. The pleasure of floating high over the bay hanging from a parachute towed by a motorboat is yours for $25. Most of the parachute rides operate on Condesa Beach.

LAND SPORTS A round of 18 holes of **golf** at the Acapulco Princess Hotel (tel. 84-3100) costs $64. At the Club de Golf Acapulco, off the Costera next to the Convention Center (tel. 84-0781 or 84-0731), play nine holes for $25 or 18 for $35. The Pierre Marqués Hotel (tel. 84-2000) also has a course.

Tennis at one of the tennis clubs open to the public costs around $8 per hour. Try the Club de Golf Acapulco (tel. 84-4824), open daily from 7am to 6:30pm. Singles cost $8 an hour; doubles, $12.

Horseback-riding tours on the beach are available through the Lienzo Charro "México Real" (tel. 85-0331) near the Acapulco Princess Hotel. The 2-hour rides depart at 9:30am, 11:30am, and 3:30pm daily, and cost $30, including two beers or soft drinks.

Traditionally termed the Fiesta Brava, the **bullfights** are held during Acapulco's winter season at a ring up the hill from Caletilla Beach. Tickets purchased through travel agencies cost around $35 and usually include transportation to and from your hotel. The festivities begin each Sunday in winter at 5:30pm.

MUSEUMS & SPECIAL ATTRACTIONS

CENTRO CULTURAL DE ACAPULCO, Costera Aleman.

The State of Guerrero's Instituto Guerrerense de la Cultura sponsors this cultural center, located one block east of CICI in a complex of small buildings in a shady grove across from the Acapulco Dolphins Hotel and Fersato's Restaurant, near the eastern end of the Costera. It includes an archeological museum with an interesting collection of pre-Columbian artifacts. Other buildings contain crafts exhibits (many for sale), or host classes in painting or guitar, poetry readings, and performances of music and dance.

Admission: Free.
Open: Daily 9am–2pm and 5–8pm.

FORT SAN DIEGO, Costera Aleman, east of the Zócalo.

The original Fuerte de San Diego was built in 1616 to protect the town from pirate attacks. At that time, the port was wealthy from its trade with the Philippine Islands, which like Mexico were part of Spain's enormous empire. The fort you see was rebuilt after extensive damage by an earthquake in 1776.

Today it houses the **Museo Histórico de Acapulco** (Acapulco Historical Museum). The vaulted chambers of the old fort have been repaired, lighted, air-conditioned; and filled with exhibits that tell the fascinating story of Acapulco as a port for conquest of the Americas, conversion of the natives to Catholicism, and trade with the Orient. Though all is in Spanish, most of the exhibits are self-explanatory.

The first room has changing shows. Recently it displayed artifacts from the Aztec Templo Mayor excavation in Mexico City. Other rooms chronicle Acapulco's pre-Hispanic past and the coming of the conquistadors, complete with Spanish armor, the Spanish imperial conquest of the South Seas, for which Acapulco was a base, and a 6-foot-tall model of the *Manila Galeon,* one of the famous ships that sailed back laden with treasures from the Orient as well as artifacts from the China trade, including fine chests, vases, textiles, and furniture. The fort's kitchen has been restored, as has the chapel.

Admission: $4, free Sun.
Open: Tues–Sun 10:30am–4:40pm. Best time is in the morning, for the "air conditioning" is minimal. **Directions:** Follow Costera Aleman past old Acapulco and the zócalo; the fort is on a hill on the right. *Note:* You can reach the fort by a road through a military zone; coming from the main plaza, look for the road on the left, landward side of the Costera. If you're in good shape, you can climb a cascade of stairs opposite the cargo docks.

MAGICO MUNDO MARINO, Caleta and Caletilla beaches. Tel. 83-1215.

It's easy to spend at least half a day at this new water park and aquarium, which offers tanks of sea lions, turtles, and dolphins, as well as aquariums of tropical fish, exhibits of shells, popular movies (many from the U.S.), a swimming pool with a water slide, an ocean swimming area, jet-ski rentals, two bars, and an attractive terrace restaurant overlooking the water. At the umbrella-shaded restaurant you can order breakfast, lunch, snacks, and drinks, including fresh oysters and clams right out of a tank.

Admission: $6 adults, $4 children.
Open: Daily 9am–7pm (restaurant, daily 10am–7pm).

CENTRO INTERNACIONAL DE CONVIVENCIA INFANTIL (CICI), Costera Aleman, at Colón. Tel. 84-1970.

This sea life and water park east of the Convention Center offers a variety of swimming pools with waves, water slides, and water toboggans. Dolphin shows at 12:30, 3:30, and 5:30pm are in English and Spanish. Amenities include a cafeteria and changing rooms.

Admission: $8 adults, $6 children (under 2 years old, free).

Open: Daily 10am–6pm.

WHERE TO STAY

Acapulco's downtown section has seen a slight increase in petty crime. Therefore, you might want to spend a little more money and stay near one of the beaches. If you do decide to stay downtown, choose your hotel carefully and stick to the ones recommended below. The good downtown hotels are indeed lodging bargains. Crime is a reality in any city, so just take normal precautions and use common sense.

If you need a room on arrival, both the Estrella de Oro and Estrella Blanca bus stations have **hotel-reservation services,** operated by the Hotel and Motel Association. They will either call a hotel of your choosing or try to find one to suit your requirements. If they make the reservation, you pay them for 1 night in advance (they'll give you a voucher for the hotel). The drawback is that they can only make reservations at hotels that belong to the association. But they may allow you to use the telephone to call a nonmember hotel yourself.

If you plan to make reservations before leaving home, be aware that the hotel may quote you a higher price than if you walked in off the street and asked for a room: The quote might be as much as $60 as opposed to $25! Why? Because they know that if you're reserving in advance, they already have your business, so they might as well raise the price. They also assume that North Americans can afford a higher price.

EAST OF DOWNTOWN NEAR HORNOS BEACH

East of the zócalo along the Costera, most lodgings are beyond our stated range, but several hotels in this area offer budget rates in the off-season (from May through November).

Doubles For Less Than $40

HOTEL VILLA RICA, Universidad, Acapulco, Gro. 39300. Tel. 74/87-4646. Fax 74/87-4624. 55 rms (all with bath). A/C TEL
$ Rates: Off-season, $36 single or double; high season, $44 single or double. Discounts available for longer stays. **Parking:** Free.

Located on a quiet hillside two blocks inland from the Costera on Reyes Católicos this modern hotel offers spacious rooms with firm beds. The front rooms have balconies with grand bay views. Amenities include a beautiful swimming pool and a restaurant/bar on the premises. Parking is enclosed.

HOTEL DEL VALLE, Espinoza 150, Acapulco, Gro. 39300. Tel. 74/85-8336 or 85-8388. 19 rms (all with bath).
$ Rates: $25 single or double, $30 single or double with A/C.

As you drive along the Costera, look for the tiny Hotel Jacqueline and you'll find the Hotel del Valle just behind it, off the Costera on Espinoza, near Paraíso Beach. The rooms are simple and well kept with fan (13 rooms) or air conditioner (6 rooms). There is also a little swimming pool. Paraíso Beach is half a block away.

NEAR THE ESTRELLA DE ORO BUS STATION

If you're taking the Estrella de Oro bus to Acapulco from Mexico City or Taxco, you'll be glad to know that there are two budget-to-moderate hotels within easy walking distance of the terminal.

AUTOTEL RITZ, Magallanes (Apdo. Postal 257), Acapulco, Gro. 39300. Tel. 74/85-8023 or 85-8075, or toll free 800/527-5919 in the U.S. 102 rms (all with bath). A/C TEL
$ Rates: Off-season, $35 single or double; high season, $55 single or double.

This L-shaped hotel has a swimming pool and a garden restaurant called El Jardín. Elevators take you up to the comfortable rooms that have small balconies with flower boxes. If you want a view of the sea, request a room on the seventh floor. Don't confuse the Autotel Ritz with the more expensive Ritz Acapulco Hotel, which is under the same management. Rental TVs are available.

To get here from the bus station, walk 2½ blocks on Magallanes toward the beach; it's half a block from the beach.

NEAR ICACOS BEACH

These hotels are all on the far eastern side of the bay, near the Convention Center (Centro Acapulco) and CICI (Centro Internacional de Convivencia Infantil), Acapulco's fabulous children's water amusement park.

Doubles For Less Than $50

HOTEL SOL-I-MAR, Bravo 5, Acapulco, Gro. 39850. Tel. 74/84-1534 or 84-1536. Fax 74/84-2082. 39 rms (all with bath). A/C
$ Rates: $27 single; $42 double; $90 bungalows for four to six people.

Several two-story neocolonial buildings with lots of brick, tile, and wrought ironwork comprise this hotel complex just a block from the beach and half a block from the Romano Days Inn. Most of the rooms have kitchens and large private patios, and there are two small swimming pools.

Doubles For Less Than $65

POSADA DEL SOL, Costera Aleman 1390, Acapulco, Gro. 39300. Tel. 74/84-1010. 240 rms (all with bath). A/C TEL
$ Rates: $55 single or double.
This three-story motel is built around a spacious, palm-shaded courtyard with a large swimming pool. Lounge chairs are scattered around the pool, and barmen wait attentively at a little poolside stand. The rooms are fairly small, with small showers. The attractive streetside restaurant is popular for its reasonable prices and arctic air conditioning. The posada is on the ocean side of the Costera just east of the Convention Center, one block from the beach.

ACAPULCO DOLPHINS HOTEL, Costera Aleman 50, Acapulco, Gro. 39300. Tel. 74/84-6630 or 84-6678. Fax 74/84-3072. 185 rms (all with bath). A/C MINIBAR TV TEL
$ Rates: Off-season, $55 double; winter, $85 double.
This new hotel on the Costera east of CICI attracts a young and lively clientele that includes many French-speaking Canadians. The rooms are tidy, modern, and nicely furnished. There's a swimming pool in an interior courtyard.

MOTEL QUINTA MICA, Colón 115, Acapulco, Gro. 39850. Tel. 74/84-0121 or 84-0122. 31 rms (all with bath). A/C
$ Rates: $60 single, double, or triple; $120 large rooms for up to six people; $160 suite for 10.
Prices are higher here, but almost all rooms have a kitchenette and fridge so you can prepare inexpensive meals. The premises include a swimming pool for adults and a wading pool for children. The motel is next to CICI on Colón, half a block from the beach.

Worth the Extra Bucks

HOTEL ROMANO DAYS INN, Costera Aleman 2310, Acapulco, Gro. 39850. Tel. 74/84-5332, or toll free 800/325-2525 in the U.S. 328 rms (all with bath). A/C TEL
$ Rates: Off-season, $70 double.
Nicely redecorated in a contemporary style with pastels and rattan furniture, this 16-story hotel has a pleasant open-air restaurant and an attractive swimming pool.

Standard rooms come with two double beds, a dresser, and a table with two chairs; balconies offer a sea or city view. Superior rooms are more elegantly furnished with floral spreads and marble accents, and include a TV and minibar. The hotel is on the ocean side of the Costera a few blocks east of CICI and close to the Hyatt Regency.

DOWNTOWN–ON LA QUEBRADA

Up the hillside west of the zócalo, near the cliff divers' area known as La Quebrada, lie several busy streets dotted with some of the best budget hotels in town. The disadvantage of this area is that every evening until around 11pm, tour buses roar up and down the hill for the high divers' act.

Doubles For Less Than $25

HOTEL ANGELITA, Quebrada 37, Acapulco, Gro. 39300. Tel. 74/83-5734. 10 rms (all with bath).
$ Rates: $8 per person single or double, $10 per person triple or quad. 10% discount for longer stays; 5% discount off-season.
This three-story, white stucco hotel on Quebrada a few blocks west of the zócalo advertises *limpieza absoluta* (absolute cleanliness), and that's what you'll find in this bright place. White, simply furnished rooms have blue-tile baths and ceiling fans, and the airy central hallway is lined with plants. The two largest rooms have balconies.

HOTEL EL FARO, Quebrada 83, Acapulco, Gro. 39300. Tel. 74/82-1365 or 82-1366. 33 rms (all with bath). TEL
$ Rates: $10 single; $20 double; slightly less off-season. Discounts for long stays. **Parking:** Free.
A long time ago this was one of Acapulco's top hotels. The big old rooms have well-used old-fashioned furniture, fans, and louvered shutters, and some have big terrace-balconies overlooking the square. But this hotel's good old days are long gone; be sure to inspect your room before you sign in, and if you're not satisfied, ask to see another. A friendly family manages the hotel. Parking is on the street and plaza in front of the hotel, which they say is patrolled by the police 24 hours. It's at the top of the hill, cater-corner from the Plaza Las Glorias Hotel (the Mirador).

Worth the Extra Bucks

PLAZA LAS GLORIAS/EL MIRADOR, Quebrada 74. Tel. 74/83-1155, or toll free 91-800/9-0027 in Mexico. Fax 74/82-0638. 100 rms (all with bath). A/C TV TEL
$ Rates: Off-season, $52 single; $64 double. Winter, $64 single; $75 double.
One of the landmarks of "Old Acapulco," the former El Mirador Hotel, on the plaza at the top of Quebrada, overlooks the famous cove where the cliff divers perform. Renovated with lush tropical landscaping and lots of handsome Mexican tile, this romantic hotel offers attractively furnished rooms with double or queen-size beds, mini-refrigerator and wet bar, and large bathrooms with marble counters. Ask for a room with a balcony (there are 42) and ocean view (95 rooms). There are three pools and a protected area beside a cove with good snorkeling. The hotel's La Perla Restaurant has an evening buffet ($30) and tables with great views of the cliff-diving show. The Don Carlos coffee shop offers mediocre food and outrageously slow service.

DOWNTOWN — THE ZÓCALO/LA PAZ AREA

There are several budget hotels on La Paz, which runs southwest from the zócalo several blocks.

Doubles For Less Than $25

HOTEL COLIMENSE, Iglesias 11, Acapulco, Gro. 39300. Tel. 74/82-2890. 10 rms (all with bath).
$ Rates: $11 single; $15 double.
The shabby but clean rooms with fans are on the second floor and overlook an

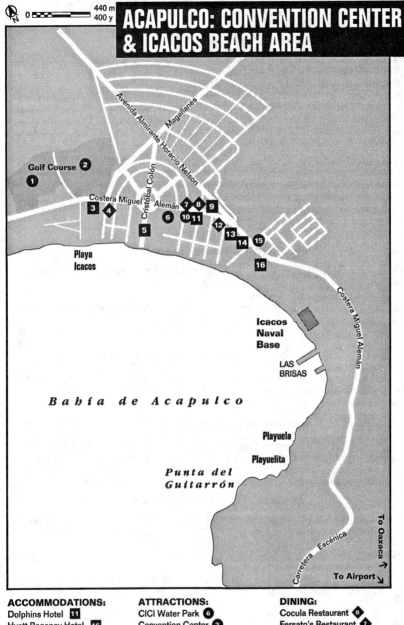

ACAPULCO: CONVENTION CENTER & ICACOS BEACH AREA

0 — 440 m
— 400 y

Avenida Almirante Horacio Nelson

Magallanes

Golf Course ②

①

Cristóbal Colón

Costera Miguel Alemán

③ ④

⑦ ⑧ ⑨

⑥ ⑩ ⑪

⑤

⑫

⑬

⑭ ⑮

⑯

Playa Icacos

Icacos Naval Base

LAS BRISAS

Costera Miguel Alemán

Bahía de Acapulco

Playuela

Playuelita

Punta del Guitarrón

Carretera Escénica

To Oaxaca ↗

To Airport ↘

ACCOMMODATIONS:
Dolphins Hotel ⑪
Hyatt Regency Hotel ⑯
Posada del Sol ③
Quinta Mica Hotel ⑤
Romano Days Inn ⑭
Sol-I-Mar Hotel ⑬
El Tropicano Hotel ⑨

ATTRACTIONS:
CICI Water Park ⑥
Convention Center ②
Cultural Center/ Museo Antrolopolgía ⑩
Golf Course ①
The News Disco ⑮

DINING:
Cocula Restaurant ⑧
Fersato's Restaurant ⑦
100% Natural ⑫
Pipo's Restaurant ④

unkempt but shaded courtyard with swings and rocking chairs. Windows are well screened. It's two blocks west of the zócalo.

HOTEL MARÍA ANTONIETA, Azueta 17, Acapulco, Gro. 39300. Tel. 74/82-5024. 30 rms (all with bath).
$ Rates: $10 single; $20 double; $40 triple.
This well-kept, two-story hotel offers rooms off an airy central corridor festooned with plants. The clean, white rooms come with two double beds, white spreads and curtains, fans, and louvered glass windows. Upstairs rooms have larger windows and are brighter. A communal kitchen and dining area is available for the use of the guests. The hotel is three blocks southwest of the zócalo.

HOTEL CALIFORNIA, La Paz 12, Acapulco, Gro. 39300. Tel. 74/82-2893. 24 rms (all with bath).
$ Rates: $13 single; $22 double; 15% less off-season.
The rooms at the Hotel California are arranged around a paved open patio. All have fans (two are air-conditioned) and are decorated with nice white drapes and Formica furniture. It's a block southwest of the zócalo; two blocks east on the Costera are convenient bus stops.

Doubles For Less Than $40

HOTEL MISION, Felipe Valle 12, Acapulco, Gro. 39300. Tel. 74/82-3643. 27 rms (all with bath).
$ Rates: $18 single; $35 double.
Enter the brick, plant-filled courtyard shaded by an enormous mango tree and step back in time to an earlier Acapulco at this tranquil, 19th-century hotel two blocks inland from the Costera and the zócalo. Old photos of Acapulco show similar hacienda-style architecture, with white stucco walls, red-tile roofs, and a courtyard. And in fact the original L-shaped building is at least 100 years old. The rooms have colonial touches such as colorful tile and wrought iron, and come simply furnished with one or two beds and ceiling fans. Breakfast is served on the patio (be patient with the slow, inexperienced staff). Soft drinks and beer are usually available all day.

NEAR PLAYA LA ANGOSTA

If you stand in the zócalo and face the water, to your right the Costera leads to hotels on the hilly peninsula that curves back into the bay. Their location gives these hotels great views of the city and bay. Take any bus along the Costera which runs along the base of the peninsula; then hike up the slopes to your hotel or take a cab.

Doubles For Less Than $30

HOTEL LA ANGOSTA, Lopez Mateos (Apdo. Postal 88), Acapulco, Gro. 39300. Tel. 74/83-7670. Fax 74/82-1629. 25 rms, 5 suites (all with bath). A/C MINIBAR
$ Rates: $27 double with fan, $48 with A/C; $100 suite for two to four people. Discount off-season.
This elegant little hotel is a real find. Once the summer home of former Mexican President Portes Gil, and formerly the Hotel Mocambo, this hotel resembles a Mediterranean villa with white exterior, front patio behind a stucco wall, French windows, wrought iron, and arches. Completely renovated in 1990, there are five spacious, one- and two-bedroom suites and 25 smallish rooms with sienna-colored Saltillo tile floors, whitewashed leather *equipale* furniture, and king-size beds. There's a tiny pool on the front patio and the small beach, Playa la Angosta, is just across the street. A bar and restaurant in the open lobby offer views of Acapulco's famous sunsets.
To get here, head south on the Costera from the zócalo, pass the Club de Esquies, and turn right onto the road across the isthmus of the peninsula (a distance of 100 yards) to Playa la Angosta, at the head of a pretty cove; this road intersects Lopez Mateos.

NEAR PLAYAS CALETA & CALETILLA

The layout of streets in the peninsula that separates the two beaches is confusing, and the disorganization in street names and numbers is enough to drive one to tears. A street will be named Avenida Lopez Mateos, but so will the street meeting it at a 90° angle; some streets have two names, while others have none; many buildings have two street numbers.

Here are explicit directions to my hotel choices in this area: Facing Caletilla Beach is a semicircular array of little restaurants, and behind this semicircle and across the street is a large, tree-lined parking lot for the Jai Alai Fronton, a peeling yellowish building at the far end of the parking lot. As you face the parking lot (your back to the water), a street runs along the left side of the lot up the hill. This is supposedly Avenida Lopez Mateos (also marked as Avenida Flamingos) and along it, on the left-hand side of the street, are several good hotels only a few minutes' walk from the beach.

Doubles For Less Than $35

HOTEL BONANZA, Lopez Mateos 14, Acapulco, Gro. 39360. Tel. 74/83-7765. 26 rms (all with bath).
$ Rates: $15 single; $23 double; $40 quad.

There is a little fountain in the entry court of this hotel at the base of the hill. The rooms have ceiling fans and louvered windows for good cross ventilation. There's also a tiny swimming pool. This is as close to the beach as you can get.

HOTEL LINDAVISTA, Playa Caleta (Apdo. Postal 3), Acapulco, Gro. 39360. Tel. 74/82-2783 or 82-5414. 43 rms (all with bath).
$ Rates: $27 single or double with fan, $40 single or double with A/C. **Parking:** Free.

The old-fashioned Lindavista snuggles into the hillside above Caleta Beach to the left of the Hotel Caleta. Older American and Mexican couples are drawn to the well-kept rooms (20 with air conditioning, 23 with fans), beautiful views, and slow pace of the area here. There's a small swimming pool and a terrace restaurant/bar.

SUITES IMPERIAL JAZMIN, Lopez Mateos 433, Acapulco, Gro. 39360. Tel. 74/82-3420 or 82-5364. 27 rms (all with bath).
$ Rates: $20 single; $32 double; $60 two-bedroom suite for up to eight people. **Parking:** Free.

Families love this modern hotel across the street from the more visible Motel Caribe. Rooms are cheery if tiny, and grouped around a postage-stamp-size swimming pool. Eight rooms come with kitchens, three are air-conditioned, and all have fans.

Doubles For Less Than $50

HOTEL BELMAR, Gran Via Tropical and Av. de la Cumbre, Acapulco, Gro. 39360. Tel. 74/82-1525 or 82-1526. 80 rms (all with bath).
$ Rates: $33 single; $48 double.

Two small pools and shady patios fill the grassy lawn in front of the hotel. Built in the 1950s, it's among those immaculately kept hotels from that era, with large, well-kept, and breezy rooms, all with fans, enormous balconies, and relaxing views; 70 rooms are air-conditioned. It's an ideal place to spread out and unwind. There's a comfortable restaurant/bar.

To get here, facing the Hotel de la Playa between Caleta and Caletilla beaches, take the street to your left up the hill about 1½ blocks.

Doubles For Less Than $60

MOTEL LA JOLLA, Costera Aleman and Lopez Mateos, Acapulco, Gro. 39360. Tel. 74/82-5862, or 5/566-2377 in Mexico City. 73 rms (all with bath). A/C TEL
$ Rates: $48 single; $55 double. **Parking:** Free.

Bright and modern, this two-story, L-shaped motel surrounds a beautiful swimming pool bordered with coconut palms. Although you're quite near the beach here (half a block away), you can't see it. You'll spot the hotel first by its restaurant, shaped like a flying saucer.

Worth the Extra Bucks

HOTEL BOCA CHICA, Privada de Caletilla (Apdo. Postal 1211), Acapulco, Gro. 39360. Tel. 74/83-6741. Fax 74/83-9513. 45 rms (all with bath). A/C TEL

$ Rates: Winter (including breakfast and dinner), $107 single; $136 double. Off-season, $65 single; $80 double. **Parking:** Free.

This five-story hotel on the headland of the beach at the end of the Costera, overlooking Caletilla Beach and Roqueta Island, offers 180° panoramic views. Lawns, terraces, the pool, and the bar and restaurant are arrayed on different levels. All rooms have a little veranda, many windows, marble and tile baths, and plenty of space to unwind. The hotel can also arrange for waterskiing, sailing, scuba diving, deep-sea fishing, surfing, golf, and tennis. Its Japanese restaurant has a sushi bar.

WHERE TO EAT

THE COSTERA FROM PAPAGAYO PARK TO ICACOS BEACH

Meals For Less Than $15

PASTELERÍA VIENA, Costera Aleman 715A. Tel. 84-2551.
  Specialty: BAKERY.
$ Prices: Breakfast $2–$3; sandwiches $3–$4; pastries $1.50.
  Open: Daily 8:30am–11pm.

Air-conditioned to alpine freshness, this tiny Central European–like haven is decorated with lace tablecloths and posters of the Tirol. Tempting baked goods are displayed in the window and pastry cases. It's half a block east of the Diana traffic circle on the inland side of the Costera.

MARÍA BONITA, Sandoval 26. Tel. 86-2930.
  Specialty: MEXICAN.
$ Prices: Breakfast $2.50–$4; lunch special $5–$6; appetizers $2–$4; main courses $4–$12.
  Open: Daily 8am–11pm.

This lively restaurant, on the beach side of the Costera behind the Vaca Negra restaurant and west of the Acapulco Plaza Hotel, is like a fiesta inside, its thatched roof hung with piñatas and *papel picado*. Tablecloths are green, the chairs red—Mexico's colors. The name comes from the nickname of María Felix, the Mexican movie star.

LA TORTUGA, Costera Aleman 5-A. Tel. 84-6985.
  Specialty: MEXICAN.
$ Prices: Appetizers $2–$4; main courses $4–$13.
  Open: Daily 10am–1am.

This small, congenial outdoor restaurant is quiet and shady, with tables set out on numerous terraces filled with greenery. Try the tasty fish filet stuffed with shrimp from the full restaurant menu, or have just a sandwich or a plate of tacos and a beer. The "Turtle" is half a block inland from the Costera at the corner of Lomas del Mar and across from La Torre de Acapulco Hotel.

MIMI'S CHILI BAR, at Blackbeard's, Costera Aleman. Tel. 84-2549.
  Specialty: MEXICAN.
$ Prices: Appetizers $2–$4; main courses $5.50–$15; chili, burger, or burrito $5–$7.
  Open: Daily noon–3am (sometimes to 5am).

Blackbeard's is too expensive, but its annex, Mimi's, serves burgers, salads, and bowls of chili in a funky Old West–meets–beach shack setting with sawdust on the floor.

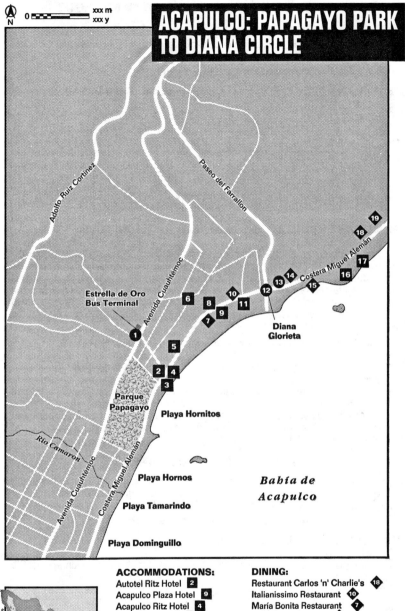

ACAPULCO: PAPAGAYO PARK TO DIANA CIRCLE

Adolfo Ruiz Cortínez

Paseo del Farallon

Costera Miguel Alemán

Avenida Cuauhtémoc

Estrella de Oro Bus Terminal

Diana Glorieta

Avenida Cuauhtémoc

Río Camarón

Costera Miguel Alemán

Parque Papagayo

Playa Hornitos

Playa Hornos

Bahía de Acapulco

Playa Tamarindo

Playa Dominguillo

0   xxx m
     xxx y

MEXICO CITY

Acapulco

ACCOMMODATIONS:
Autotel Ritz Hotel **2**
Acapulco Plaza Hotel **9**
Acapulco Ritz Hotel **4**
Club de Sol Hotel **8**
Continental Plaza Hotel **11**
Del Valle Hotel **5**
Fiesta Americana
  Condesa Hotel **16**
Paraiso Radisson Hotel **3**
Presídente Hotel **17**
Villa Rica Hotel **6**

DINING:
Restaurant Carlos 'n' Charlie's **18**
Italianissimo Restaurant **10**
María Bonita Restaurant **7**
Mimi's Chile Saloon **15**
Pastelería Viena **14**
La Tortuga Restaurant **19**

ATTRACTIONS:
American Express Office **13**
Diana Glorieta (traffic circle) **12**
Estrella de Oro Bus Terminal **1**

Drinks are two for the price of one all day. It's on the ocean side of the Costera a few blocks east of the Diana traffic circle and just before the Fiesta Americana Condesa Hotel.

Meals For Less Than $20

RESTAURANT FERSATO'S, Costera Aleman 44. Tel. 84-3949.
Specialty: MEXICAN.
$ Prices: Appetizers $2–$5; main courses $3–$13; jumbo shrimp $13.
Open: Daily 7am–midnight.

A charming young hostess in traditional dress welcomes you to the big dining room beneath the tile roof and stone arches. You take a seat at one of the wrought-iron or bamboo tables, and are soothed by soft music as you order from the extensive menu of authentic Mexican food. Try the mole, the black beans, or the mixiotes wrapped in maguey leaves. The restaurant is on the inland side of the Costera across from the State of Guerrero Cultural Center and the Archeological Museum.

RESTAURANT COCULA, Costera Aleman 10. Tel. 84-5079.
Specialty: MEXICAN.
$ Prices: Appetizers $3–$5; main courses $6–$13.
Open: Mon–Wed and Fri 6pm–1am, Thurs and Sun 2pm–1am.
You can dine on the patio out front, or on one of the two levels of terraces. Appetizers include guacamole, black-bean soup, and cheese fondue. Grilled meats are the specialty, and you can choose broiled chicken, quail, spiced pork sausage, ribs, shish kebab, or a mixed grill. The restaurant is on the inland side of the east end of the Costera, across from the Magic Disco.

MARISCOS PIPO, Costera Aleman and Victoria. Tel. 84-0165.
Specialty: MEXICAN/SEAFOOD.
$ Prices: Appetizers $3.50–$5; main courses $10–$30; lobster $30.
Open: Daily 1–9:30pm.
This famous zócalo-area seafood restaurant has a reputation spanning decades, and now it has this second branch that's a bit fancier with slightly higher prices. A typical meal might include soup, grilled red snapper (huachinango a la parrilla), dessert, and wine or beer. It's on the ocean side of the Costera east of the Convention Center and close to CICI and the Posada del Sol Hotel.

DOWNTOWN/ZÓCALO AREA

To explore this area, start right at the zócalo and stroll west along Juárez. After about three blocks you'll come to Azueta, lined with small seafood cafés and streetside stands selling fresh oysters and clams on the half shell.

Meals For Less Than $10

RESTAURANT RICARDO'S, Juárez 9. Tel. 82-1140.
Specialty: MEXICAN.
$ Prices: Appetizers $2–$3; main courses $2–$4; breakfast or lunch special $3; sandwich $1.50.
Open: Daily 8am–1am.

This small, narrow café half a block west of the zócalo is usually jammed with happy, hungry customers. The lunch special is very popular; it might include soup, rice or noodles, main dish, and ice cream or coffee. Try the cheese-filled chiles relleños or the delicious cabrito en chile ajo—goat baked in a garlicky, brick-red pepper sauce (moderately spicy).

SAN CARLOS, Juárez 5. Tel. 82-6459.
Specialty: MEXICAN.
$ Prices: Appetizers $1–$4; main courses $2.50–$7; meat or fish $3–$4; comida corrida $3; soup $1–$2.
Open: Daily 7:30am–11:30pm (comida corrida served 1–6pm).

Western-style food such as charcoal-broiled chicken or fish is served at chuck-wagon prices on the front patio or in the dining room. Yellow tablecloths brighten this otherwise plain café a few steps west of the zócalo. On Sunday the specialty is chicken mole.

THE ORIGINAL ACAPULCO FAT FARM/LA GRANJA DEL PINGUE, Juárez 10. Tel. 83-5339.

Specialty: ECLECTIC/PASTRIES/ICE CREAM.

$ **Prices:** Appetizers $2–$3.50; main courses $3–$8; dessert $2–$3; soup, sandwiches, or spaghetti $2–$5; dinner special $6–$8.

Open: Winter, daily 9am–10pm; off-season, daily 10am–10pm.

Specializing in ice cream and French/Viennese pastries, this unusual restaurant is the cooperative effort of alumni and prep-school students of the Acapulco Children's Home. Its eclectic menu includes a dinner special after 5pm, usually in the American–home-cooking genre. It also claims to have the best coffee in town. The dining area is a pretty shaded patio hung with folk-art masks and piñatas. Bring your paperback novels to exchange here. It's two blocks west of the zócalo.

MARISCOS MILLA'S, Azueta and Carranza. Tel. 83-8445.

Specialty: MEXICAN.

$ **Prices:** Appetizers $1.50–$3.50; main courses $3.50–$6.50; fish dinner $4; fish almendrado $4.

Open: Daily 8am–8pm.

The open-air dining room of this corner restaurant is decorated with photographs of Old Acapulco. You can watch the cooks at work in the open kitchen behind the neat tile counter. The house specialty is pescado almendrado—fish prepared with almonds.

To get here, walk three blocks inland from the Costera on Azueta to Carranza; it's across the street from the Hotel Sacramento.

RESTAURANT LA FLOR DE ACAPULCO, Zócalo. Tel. 82-1073 or 82-5018.

Specialty: MEXICAN.

$ **Prices:** Appetizers $1–$4; main courses $3–$10; comida corrida $4–$5; soups $1–$4; grilled chicken $10.

Open: Daily 8am–11pm (comida corrida served from 1:30pm until it runs out).

The best place to people-watch in Acapulco is on the east side of the zócalo at the downtown branch of this restaurant, which has another farther east on the Costera. Tables with bright-orange cloths are set out on the sunny plaza and in an airy dining room with ceiling fans. The extensive menu includes chicken mole, enchiladas, and carne asada a la Tampiqueña, as well as breakfasts and late-night snacks. Grilled chicken is the house specialty.

Meals For Less Than $20

EL AMIGO MIGUEL, Juárez 31 at Azueta. Tel. 83-6981.

Specialty: MEXICAN/SEAFOOD.

$ **Prices:** Appetizers $2–$4; main courses $2.50–$13; fish $4–$10; lobster $15.

Open: Daily 10:30am–9:30pm. **Closed:** New Year's Day.

Red tablecloths and fish on the wall decorate this simple restaurant three blocks west of the zócalo where fresh seafood is king. The large open-air dining room is usually brimming with seafood lovers. Try the stuffed crab, the snapper, or the baby shark.

MARISCOS PIPO, Almirante Breton 3. Tel. 83-8801 or 82-2237.

Specialty: MEXICAN/SEAFOOD.

$ **Prices:** Appetizers $2–$13; main courses $3–$25; almendrado (fish baked with cheese and almonds) $4; red snapper $8; lobster $25.

Open: Daily 11am–8pm.

Diners can look at photographs of Old Acapulco on the walls while sitting in the airy dining room, decorated with hanging nets, fish, glass buoys, and shell lanterns. The English-language menu lists a wide array of seafood, including ceviche, lobster, octopus, crayfish, and baby-shark quesadillas. This classic place is a local favorite.

To get here, walk five blocks west from the zócalo on Juárez, past Azueta, and bear left at the fork in the road.

CERRO LA PINZONA/PLAYA LARGA AREA

Meals For Less Than $20

PINZONA 65, Pinzona 65. Tel. 83-0388 or 82-3832.
  Specialty: MEXICAN.
$ Prices: Appetizers $3–$4; main courses $8–$12; dessert $2–$3.
  Open: High season, daily 4pm–midnight. **Closed:** Easter Mon–Nov 1.

This elegant restaurant is upstairs on the open rooftop terrace. Guests dine under the stars at tables topped by royal-blue and white cloths, matching ceramic plates, crystal, and flickering candles. Owner Bennie Hudson formerly worked as a food and beverage manager for the Hyatt hotel chain. Try to arrive in time to watch daylight fade on the bay and lights twinkle on across the mountains. Delicious choices might include watercress salad, sea bass in garlic butter, and cafe Pinzona, a flaming brew of Kahlúa, coffee, and ice cream. Though prices are a bit higher here, you're paying for one of the most panoramic hilltop views in Acapulco.

To get here, take the "Caleta" bus south past the zócalo to the Pemex gas station in the Playa Larga area; then take a cab ($2) up the steep hill to Pinzona 65, across the street from the Casa Blanca Hotel.

CALETA/CALETILLA BEACH AREA

The area around Caleta and Caletilla beaches used to be rather down-at-the-heels, but not long ago the municipal authorities pumped lots of money into public facilities here. Now the beaches have nice shady palapas and beach chairs, clean sand, and fine palm trees. Three buildings have been built to house "vestidores, regarderas" (changing rooms, showers, and lockers) and restaurants. Little dining places line the outer periphery of the buildings, and the kitchen work is done at the center (peek around to the kitchen to see boys cutting up fish for the pot).

To find a good meal, wander along the rows of restaurants, looking for busy spots where people are eating (and not just sipping drinks). Study menus, which will either be displayed or handed to you on request. Although the restaurants may tend to look all the same, you'll be surprised at the difference in prices. Filete de pescado (fish filet) might be $2.50 at one place and twice as much at another; beer can cost anywhere from 65¢ to $2. Some offer inexpensive fixed-price meals for little over a dollar or two.

Meals For Less Than $10

HELADOS BING'S, Costera Aleman at Ignacio de la Llave. Tel. 83-7574.
  Specialty: ICE CREAM.
$ Prices: Ice-cream cone $1; special sundae $3.50.
  Open: Daily 10am–10:30pm.
The ice cream is smooth and delicious—you'll be hooked in no time. Look for Bing's hot-pink motif along the Costera a block east of the zócalo. You'll find other branches at the Diana traffic circle and near the Torre de Acapulco Hotel.

100% NATURAL, Costera Aleman 2280. Tel. 84-4562.
  Specialty: MEXICAN/VEGETARIAN.
$ Prices: Breakfast $2–$4; appetizers $3–$6; main courses $3–$6; fruit and vegetable drinks $2; sandwiches $2.50–$4; soups $2.50–$4.
  Open: Daily 24 hours.

You'll see branches of 100% Natural in just about every area of Acapulco, some with green awnings and others with yellow. Actually the green and yellow signs are rival chains, but their menus are quite similar—soups, salads, sandwiches, fruit, yogurt, shakes, and pasta dishes that please vegetarians and carnivores alike. Although each is part of a franchise, they're individually owned, so the hours vary—not all stay open 24 hours. This one is on the east end of the Costera near the Romano Days Inn.

SANBORN'S, Costera Aleman and Escudero. Tel. 82-6167.
Specialty: AMERICAN/MEXICAN.
$ Prices: Breakfast $3–$5; appetizers $2–$7; main courses $3.50–$12; shrimp $12.
Open: Daily 7:30am–11pm.

The best of the American-style restaurants, Sanborn's cool dining area is reminiscent of upscale dining rooms of the 1950s with its American colonial decor, brass light fixtures, and well-padded booths around the walls. It's especially good for breakfast, though it also has good enchiladas, club sandwiches, burgers, sincronizadas (ham and cheese melted between corn tortillas), pastas, and fancier fare such as fish and steaks. Beer, wine, and cocktails are served, too. For an inexpensive snack, buy pastries to go at the store's bakery. Upstairs are clean bathrooms. You'll find it two blocks east of the zócalo on the Costera.

The other Sanborn's is in a high-rise building on the Costera at Condesa Beach near the Stouffer Presidente Hotel (tel. 84-4465).

Worth the Extra Bucks

ITALIANISSIMO, in El Patio Center, Costera Aleman. Tel. 84-2470.
Specialty: ITALIAN.
$ Prices: Appetizers $3–$9; main courses $6–$15; pasta dishes, pizza, or lasagne $7–$8; jumbo shrimp $15.
Open: Oct–May, daily noon–midnight; June–Sept, Mon–Sat noon–midnight.

On a patio shaded by large trees this small Italian restaurant does delicious tableside preparations with pizzazz—such as the "scampi Stroganoff" with vodka sauce. And the pastas are homemade. For appetizers, try the Caesar salad or the heavenly mussels in white wine sauce. Dessert could be Irish coffee and chocolate cake. The restaurant is two blocks west of the Diana traffic circle, on the inland side of the Costera across the street from the Continental Plaza Hotel.

CARLOS 'N' CHARLIE'S, Costera Aleman 999. Tel. 84-1285 or 84-0039.
Specialty: MEXICAN
$ Prices: Appetizers $4–$8; main courses $8–$15; fajitas $8; fish or meat $11; shrimp $15.
Open: Dinner only, nightly 6:30pm–midnight.

At this Carlos Anderson restaurant you'll find the usual posters, silly sayings, bric-a-brac, sassy waiters, and menu humor ("splash" for seafood, "moo" for beef). The food is good and the place is always packed, an indication that people like what they get for the price they pay. Come early and get a seat on the terrace overlooking the Costera. The place is on the Costera east of the Diana traffic circle and across the street from the Stouffer Presidente Hotel.

RESTAURANT LOS RANCHEROS, Carretera Escenica. Tel. 84-1908 or 84-5394.
Specialty: MEXICAN.
$ Prices: Appetizers $3–$6; main courses $11–$16.
Open: Daily noon–1am.

Hearty Mexican food is served in this old-time northern Mexican ranch house with red-tile roof and rough wood construction. The little bar is decorated with old U.S. auto license plates, and old farm implements and spoof "Wanted" posters hang on the walls. The wide, roofed terrace with ceiling fans provides a good place to dine and enjoy the view, but the traffic is a bit annoying. The menu includes beef or chicken fajitas, T-bone steak Jalisco style, carne asada a la Tampiqueña, and red snapper. Mexican wines cost about $12 per bottle. Los Rancheros is east of town on the scenic highway between the naval base and the Las Brisas Hotel.

MADEIRAS, Carretera Escenica. Tel. 84-4378.
Specialty: MEXICAN/CONTINENTAL. **Reservations:** Required.
$ Prices: Fixed-price dinner $30.
Open: Dinner only, nightly 6:30–10:30pm (two seatings: at 6:30–8pm and 9–10:30pm).

Enjoy an elegant meal and a fabulous view of glittering Acapulco Bay at night at Madeiras, east of town on the scenic highway, before the Las Brisas Hotel. The several small dining areas have ceiling fans and are open to the evening breezes. If you arrive before your table is ready, have a drink in the comfortable lounge. There's also an outlet of Los Castillo Silver from Taxco off the lobby.

Selections might include tamal al chipotle (a corn tamale made with tangy chipotle sauce), roasted quail stuffed with tropical fruits, fish cooked in an orange sauce, or old favorites such as filet mignon, beef Stroganoff, and frogs' legs in garlic and white wine. Wines are reasonably priced if you stick to the Mexican labels.

SHOPPING

Acapulco is not the best place to buy Mexican crafts, but there are a few interesting shops. The best places are at the **Mercado Parazal** (often called the **Mercado de Artesanías**) on Calle Velasquez de León near 5 de Mayo in the downtown zócalo area (when you see Sanborn's, turn right and go behind it several blocks). Stall after covered stall of curios from all over the country are here, including silver, embroidered cotton clothing, rugs, pottery, and papier-mâché. Artists paint ceramics with village folk scenes while waiting for patrons. It's a pleasant place to spend a morning or afternoon. Shopkeepers are vigilant and not too pushy—but they'll test your bargaining mettle. The starting price will be astronomical, and getting the price down may take more time than you have. But as always, acting disinterested enough to walk away often brings it down in a hurry. Before buying silver here, examine it carefully and be sure it has the .925 stamp on the back. The market is open daily from 9am to 8pm.

For a familiar, brightly lit department store with fixed prices, try **Artesanías Finas de Acapulco** (tel. 84-8039), called AFA-ACA for short. To find it, go east on the Costera until you see the Hotel Romano Days Inn on the seaward side and Baby-O disco on the landward side. Take the street between Baby-O and the Hotel El Tropicano—that's Avenida Horacio Nelson. On the right, half a block up, is AFA-ACA, a huge air-conditioned store, popular with tour groups. The merchandise includes clothes, marble-top furniture, saddles, luggage, jewelry, pottery, papier-mâché, and more. The store is open Monday through Saturday from 9am to 7:30pm and on Sunday from 9am to 2pm. **Sanborn's** is another good department store.

The **Costera Aleman** is crowded with boutiques selling resort wear. Look for a sale. These stores have an abundance of attractive summer clothing at prices that are lower than you might pay in the U.S. When they have a sale, that's the time to stock up on some incredible bargains. Pay close attention to the quality of zippers; sometimes Mexican zippers are not up to the task. One of the nicest air-conditioned shopping centers on the Costera is **Plaza Bahía**, Costera Aleman 125 (tel. 86-2452), which has two stories of shops and small fast-food restaurants, including a tempting pastry shop, Café Paris. It's located just west of the Acapulco Plaza Hotel. The shops in front of the Acapulco Plaza Hotel include a fine silver shop, Tane.

EVENING ENTERTAINMENT

SPECIAL ATTRACTIONS

High divers perform at La Quebrada each day at 1pm, 7:30pm, 9:30pm, and 10:30pm for $2 admission. From a spotlit ledge on the cliffs in view of the lobby bar and restaurant terraces of the Hotel Plaza Las Glorias/El Mirador, each solitary diver plunges into the roaring surf 130 feet below after praying at a small shrine nearby. To the applause of the crowd that has gathered, he then climbs up the rocks and accepts congratulations and gifts of money from onlookers. The best show is at 10:30pm, when they dive with torches.

If you want to watch from the hotel terraces, there's a cover charge of $6 to $8 in the evening if you're not having dinner (the buffet at La Perla restaurant is $30 per person). However, you might try arriving at the lobby bar 30 minutes before a performance and ordering drinks; they don't always collect the cover charge from people who are already there. The hotel coffee shop Don Carlos, which also has a terrace with good views, serves snacks and drinks but has unbelievably slow service.

The **"Gran Noche Mexicana"** with the **Acapulco Ballet Folklórico** is held in the plaza of the Convention Center every Tuesday, Thursday, and Saturday night at 8pm. With dinner and open bar the show costs $35; general admission (including three drinks) is $20. Call for reservations (tel. 84-7050) or consult a local travel agency.

Another excellent **Mexican Fiesta and folkloric dance show,** which includes *voladores* from Papantla (flying pole dancers) is held at Marbella Plaza near the Continental Plaza Hotel on the Costera on Monday, Wednesday, and Friday at 7pm. The $42 fee covers the show, buffet, open bar, taxes, and gratuities. Make reservations through a travel agency.

Many major hotels also host Mexican fiestas and other theme nights that include dinner and entertainment. Consult a travel agency for information.

NIGHTCLUBS & DISCOS

Acapulco is more famous for its nightclubs than it is for its beaches. The problem is that the clubs open and close with shocking regularity, making it very difficult to make specific recommendations that will remain accurate. Some general tips will help: Every club seems to have a cover charge ranging from $8 to $20; drinks can cost anywhere from $4 to $9.

The high-rise hotels have their own bars, supper clubs, and nightclubs with floor shows, and the informal lobby or poolside cocktail bars often offer live entertainment.

Now that Acapulco has so many discos, many of them periodically waive the cover charge or offer some other promotion to attract customers. Another trend is a big cover charge with an open bar. Call the disco, or look for promotional material around hotel reception areas, at travel desks or concierge booths, and in local publications.

Acapulco also has its own spectacular culture and convention center, called the **Centro Acapulco,** on the eastern reaches of the bay between Condesa and Icacos beaches. Designed with extravagant Mexican taste, the Centro has rolling lawns and you enter via a grand promenade framing a central row of pools and high-spouting fountains. Within the modern center are several forms of entertainment: a mariachi bar, a piano bar, a disco, a movie theater, a legitimate theater, a café, a nightclub, several restaurants, and outdoor performance areas.

EXTRAVAGANZZA, Carretera Escenica. Tel. 84-7154 or 84-7164.

If you have something trendy and dressy to wear, you might venture up to this snazzy neo-deco, chrome-and-neon extravaganza, perched on the side of the mountain between Los Rancheros Restaurant and La Vista Shopping Center. You can't miss the neon lights. The plush, dimly lit interior dazzles with a sunken dance floor and panoramic view of Acapulco Bay. The door attendants wear tuxedos, so don't expect to get in wearing shorts, jeans, T-shirts, tennis shoes, or sandals. It opens nightly at 10:30pm; fireworks blast off at 3am. Call to find out if reservations are needed. National drinks run $5 to $6.

Admission: $11–$16.

FANTASY, Carretera Escenica. Tel. 84-6727 or 84-6764.

Recently redecorated, this club has a fantastic bay view and sometimes waives the cover charge as a promotion. Periodically during the evening it puts on a good show with green lasers, which it also shoots out across the bay. The dress code does not permit shorts, jeans, T-shirts, or sandals. Reservations are recommended. Located in the La Vista Shopping Center, it's open nightly from 10:30pm to 4am. Drinks go for $6.

Admission: $12.

BABY-O, Costera Aleman. Tel. 84-7474.

Across from the Romano Days Inn, this intimate disco has a small dance floor surrounded by several tiers of tables and sculpted, cavelike walls. It even has a hot tub and a breakfast area—well-heeled locals like to come here to wind down and end the evening—or morning, as it were. Drinks run $5 to $6.

Admission: Men $12, women free.

EVE, Costera Aleman 115. Tel. 84-4778.

This club once required glitzy dress and buckets of money to get in and stay there. On a recent visit, couples danced the night away in cool, casual clothes. But though there's no strict dress code, jeans and T-shirts are best left in your room. Open nightly at 10pm; the open bar closes at 3am. Drinks cost $4.

Admission: $8, $16 with open bar.

YESTERDAY'S, in El Patio Center, Costera Aleman. Tel. 84-8295.

Across from the Continental Plaza Hotel, this disco specializes in music of the '50s, '60s, and '70s. No shorts are allowed. Sometimes the cover charge includes an open bar with national drinks. Open nightly at 9pm. Drinks are $4 to $5.

Admission: $10–$12.

AFRO ANTILLANOS, Costera Aleman at Cuando la Cosa 32. Tel. 84-7235.

Live tropical music is the specialty of the house at this relatively new disco not far from the Continental Plaza Hotel. Shorts are a no-no. Open nightly from 10pm to 4am; open bar closes at 3am.

Admission: $19 with open bar.

LE DOME, Costera Aleman 402. Tel. 84-1190.

The flashy lighting and unusual chandelier at this long-running favorite attract a young yuppie crowd from Mexico City. Tuesday night is Tequila Night, with games and prizes. It's across from the Calinda Quality Inn. Don't show up in shorts. Open nightly from 10:30pm to 5 or 6am. Drinks run $5.

Admission: $12.

THE PLANET, Costera Aleman. Tel. 84-3252.

Taking its name from the *Daily Planet* newspaper in *Superman*, this vast disco has John Lennon's psychedelic-painted Rolls-Royce permanently on display. Shorts, jeans, tennis shoes, and sandals are not permitted. It's on the east end of the Costera near the Hotel Palapa. Open nightly from 10pm to 4am.

Admission: $19 with open bar.

MAGIC, Costera Aleman at Yucatán. Tel. 84-8816.

One of the newer discos, Magic draws a youthful crowd to its pyramid-shaped building with a waterfall in front. It lies on the east end of the Costera near the Romano Days Inn. The dress code frowns on shorts, tennis shoes, and sandals. Open nightly at 10:30pm. Drinks are $5.

Admission: $12.

THE NEWS, Costera Aleman. Tel. 84-5904.

The booths and love seats ringing the vast dance floor can seat 1,200, so this disco can double as a concert hall. But while high-tech in style, it's laid-back and user-friendly. It doesn't even have a dress code! Across the street from the Hyatt Regency, it opens at 10:30pm nightly.

Admission: $19 with open bar.

EL FUERTE, Costera Aleman 239. Tel. 82-6161.

For something completely different, see dancing and music so carefully patterned it seems the antithesis of disco—the flamenco show at El Fuerte nightclub. Old Spain's traditions come to life with both color and austerity here. Shows are Monday through Saturday at 10 and 11:30pm.

---

2. PUERTO ESCONDIDO

230 miles SE of Acapulco, 150 miles N of Salina Cruz,
50 miles N of Puerto Angel

GETTING THERE   By Plane   AeroLibertad flies from Oaxaca on Monday, Wednesday, and Friday, and to and from Acapulco on Friday. There's one flight daily from Oaxaca on a 28-passenger plane on **Aerovias Oaxaqueñas.** Buy tickets as far in advance as possible, directly from the offices; because reservations are not computerized, there can be mix-ups. Reconfirm the flight a day in advance. **Aero Vega Jr.** has two flights a day between Oaxaca and Puerto Escondido on three-, six-, and nine-passenger planes. **AeroMorelos** flies between Puerto Escondido and Oaxaca with one flight daily.

Warning: Your flight from Oaxaca to Puerto Escondido may touch down in the little coastal town of Pinotepa Nacional. There will be no sign and no announcement of where you have landed. Ask the flight attendant "Puerto Escondido?" before you get off, just to be sure.

Mexicana (tel. 2-0300 or 2-0098) flies from Mexico City to Puerto Escondido daily, arriving at 10:30am.

If space on flights to Puerto Escondido is booked solid, you have the option of flying Aeroméxico into the Huatulco airport. This is an especially viable option if your destination is Puerto Angel, which lies between Puerto Escondido and Huatulco but is closer to the Huatulco airport. There is frequent bus service between the three destinations.

By Bus Buses are frequent between Acapulco, Oaxaca, and south along the coast to and from Huatulco and Puerto Angel.

Warning: Along the coastal highway from Acapulco and from the mountains inland from Oaxaca, the bus may be stopped for army inspections for drugs and firearms. Watch the soldiers closely as they inspect your baggage; they have been known to steal from unwary travelers. They may ask passengers to get off, so take your purse, cameras, and money with you and wait outside.

By Car From Oaxaca, Highway 175 via Pochutla is the least bumpy road. The 150-mile trip takes 10 or 12 hours. Highway 200 from Acapulco is also a good road. There are frequent army inspections (they're looking for drugs and firearms); see the warning above. Keep your eyes open; most soldiers are intent on doing their duty, but a few have sticky fingers.

From Salina Cruz to Puerto Escondido is a 4- or 5-hour drive, past the Bahías de Huatulco and the turnoff for Puerto Angel. A few stretches are paved, but a good two-thirds of it is dusty and rutty in the dry season, muddy and rutty—and even washed out—in the rainy season.

DEPARTING By Plane **Aerotransportes Terrestes** sells colectivo transportation tickets to the airport from their office at the north end of Gasga, halfway up the hill. The price is $2.25 one way and includes pickup at your hotel. The office is open daily from 8am to 2pm and 5 to 7pm. The office of **AeroLibertad** is in the Hotel Rincón del Pacífico (tel. 2-0056, or 2-0483 at the airport). **Aerovias Oaxaqueñas** is located next to the Hotel Rincón del Pacífico, near the end of Avenida Gasga (tel. 2-0132). The office of **Aero Vega Jr.** is opposite the Rocamar Hotel (tel. 6-8466 or 6-2777; fax 958/6-3265) and there's a desk at the airport (tel. 2-0443).

Tickets for **AeroMorelos** are handled by Turismo Rodimar, Avenida Gazca 905-B (tel. 2-0734; fax 958/2-0789).

Mexicana flies a Boeing 727-200 between Mexico City and Puerto Escondido daily. The jet departs Puerto Escondido for Mexico City at 11am.

By Bus The three bus stations are all within a three-block area. For **Graciela Amarillas** (Yellow Fox), **Graciela Verde** (Green Fox), and **Estrella Blanca Cuauhtémoc** (White Star) the station (tel. 2-0427 and 2-0181) is across the highway at the south end of the tourist zone. Cuauhtémoc goes to Puerto Angel, Pochutla, and Huatulco; the Graciela lines go almost hourly to Acapulco and Zihuatanejo, and several a day go to Puchutla and Huatulco. There are only three direct buses to Acapulco with assigned seats, and two to Mexico City.

A block north on Hidalgo is **Transportes Oaxaca Istmo** (tel. 2-0392), in a thatched hut with bamboo walls. There are three buses daily to Pochutla (1 hr.) Salina Cruz (5 hrs.), or Oaxaca (10 hrs.). The terminal for **Lineas Unidas Estrella del Valle** and **Oaxaca Pacífico** is a block or so farther down on Hidalgo. Four buses go to Salina Cruz and Santa Cruz de Huatulco; two are direct buses, at 8am and 10:40am.

Lineas Solteca, far out on the road to Oaxaca, has school-bus-type, very second-class service to and from Oaxaca two or three times a day and is a choice if you are desperate.

Puerto Escondido (pop. 50,000) means "Hidden Port," and although it has been "discovered," development has stalled. Anyone who wandered into Acapulco a half century ago might have found a similar scene and a similar ambience. The thing to do while you're in Puerto Escondido is to catch it before it's gone forever. The lush palm-lined beach off the town center is one of the most beautiful in the country, with colorful boats pulled up on the sand—a long-gone scene in more developed resorts.

Looking out on the main beach, ahead of you is a range of low hills overlooking the bay. Beyond that are palm groves and a stretch of the most glorious beach you've ever seen. This is particularly true if you're facing east. The bay is irregular in shape; its western promontory consists of a tiny beach followed by rocks jutting into the sea. By way of contrast, the eastern peninsula is about a mile long with low green hills descending to meet a long stretch of fine sand. The coastline is slowly being developed. Where there was once nothing, there are now several restaurants, bungalows, and hotels. However, the construction is well back from the shoreline.

Laziness is a state of mind here, sipping a cool bottle of something refreshing, feeling the sea breeze, watching the pelicans soar and wheel and then come down to race across the surface of the water. Duck into a fan-cooled restaurant by day, or return in the cool evening and find informal groups discussing the day's events.

ORIENTATION

ARRIVING The **airport** is about 2½ miles from the center of town near Playa Bachoco. Prices for the minibus to hotels are posted: $1.15 to $2.25 per person. There's no central **bus station** in Puerto Escondido so you could arrive at one of several places; all except Lineas Solteca are within a short walk or taxi ride to hotels. Minibuses from Huatulco may let you off on a street corner (not a station) in the old section of Puerto Escondido.

INFORMATION Plans were underway to move the tourism office, so I'll give you the old location first, then the proposed new one. The **State Tourist Office** is in the old town across the highway from Gasga and up the hill near the market, on top of the Super Estrella store at the corner of Oaxaca and Hidalgo (tel. 958/2-0175). The office is open Monday through Friday from 9am to 2pm and 5 to 8pm, and on Saturday from 10am to 1pm. The new office was to open on Highway 200 between town and the Bacocho development, at the corner of 3 Norte and the highway, near the Hotel Gaviota.

CITY LAYOUT There's a **paved tourist zone** east of coastal Highway 200 (which runs north and south) and an **unpaved town zone** west of the highway. The towns streets were recently numbered, with Avenida Oaxaca the dividing line between east (*oriente*) and west (*poniente*) and north (*norte*) and south (*sur*). Formerly they were named by historic dates and famous people. But the streets are not marked, so finding your way is a bit of guesswork and asking directions. Most of the hotels and restaurants mentioned here are in the tourist zone along the long hill of **Avenida Gasga** that makes a loop from the coastal highway through the tourist zone. At the foot of the hill, Gasga becomes closed to traffic for about three blocks, and becomes a pleasant pedestrians-only zone (or PZ) chock-a-block with small restaurants, shops, and hotels. The PZ is flat and parallels the beach, which is just steps away. The airline offices, travel agencies, and other services are all located along the PZ. The Hotel Las Palmas is more or less at the center of the PZ. At the northern end of the PZ, Gasga is open to traffic and climbs a hill where some of my recommended hotels are located.

The **beaches,** Playa Principal in the center of town and Marinera and Zicatela, south of the town center, are interconnected and it's easy to walk from one to the other. Bacocho, Puerto Angelito, and Carrizalillo beaches are north of town and can be reached by road or boat. Because Gasga is closed off for three blocks, it's impossible to drive along the beach from one beach to another, which means that if you're staying south of town, you'll have to walk along the beach or up on the highway to get from your hotel to the PZ. Surfers find Zicatela Beach's big curling waves are the best for board surfing. New development has taken place on **Playa Bacocho,** north of town, and the two large hotels there cater mainly to charter groups.

GETTING AROUND

Almost everything is within walking distance of the pedestrian zone. Taxis cost no more than $2 to $3 to beaches or anywhere in town.

FAST FACTS

Area Code   The telephone area code is 958.

Money Exchange   There is a money exchange office near the middle of the mall, open Monday through Saturday from 9am to 2pm and 5 to 8pm.

Safety   Puerto Escondido's petty crime has risen. Don't leave your belongings unattended on the beach, and deposit other valuables in the hotel safe. For sure, don't take a midnight stroll down the deserted beach.

Seasons   High season is mid-December through Easter, with another influx of visitors in July and August.

Telephone   The long-distance telephone office is open daily from 9am to 10pm.

WHAT TO SEE & DO

BEACHES   **Playa Principal** and **Playa Marinera,** both adjacent to the town center, are the best swimming beaches and both are on a deep bay. **Zicatela** beach adjoins Playa Marinera and spreads out for several miles. The surfing part of Zicatela, with large curling waves, is a mile and a half or more from the town center.

Barter with one of the fishermen on the main beach for a ride to **Puerto Angelito,** a small cove just north of town, where the swimming is safe and the pace decidedly calmer than in town. **Playa Carrizalillo,** near Angelito, is another calm cove (topless sunbathing is not tolerated). **Playa Bacocho** is on a shallow cove north of Playa Carrizalillo, and is best reached by taxi or boat rather than walking from Carrizalillo. The townspeople are becoming less tolerant of nude sunbathing, and the police sometimes walk the beach requesting that bathers put their clothes on. Better that than a visit to jail.

Warning: Swimming at a beach that fronts on open sea is a risk to your life. The tide is unpredictable—you're floating peacefully in shoulder-deep water when suddenly the water sinks to knee level, and before you can blink it's crashing over your head. Don't follow the surfers' example; they have surfboards to cling to, and they know waves and tides. Despite big warning signs, someone drowns every year. Swim at the beach in town, or at other sheltered beaches in bays and coves.

NATURE TOURS   The **Garcia Rendon Travel Agency,** on Avenida Gasga near the Las Palmas Hotel (tel. 958/2-0114; fax 958/2-0114), offers full-day land and sea trips to explore the nature in the area. This office has a helpful English-speaking staff and is a good source of information. It's open daily from 7am to 10pm.

A dawn or sunset trip to **Manialtepec Lagoon,** a bird-filled mangrove lagoon, costs $25 to $35 and includes a stop on a secluded beach for a swim and snack. Trips can also be arranged at your hotel.

Fishermen keep their colorful *pangas* (small boats) on the beach beside the PZ. A **fisherman's tour** around the coastline in his boat will cost about $30, but a ride to Zicatela or Puerto Angelito costs around $5.

SHOPPING   The PZ has sprouted a row of tourist shops selling straw hats and Puerto Escondido T-shirts and a few stores featuring Guatemalan and Oaxacan clothing.

EVENING ENTERTAINMENT **Sunset-watching** is a ritual you won't tire of, since there are many good lookout points. Watch the surfers at Zicatela from the Los Tres Osos restaurant, a second-story affair at the far south end of the beach, or from the Hotel Santa Fe on Marinero Beach. Dedicated sunworshippers might want to spring for a cab (about $3) or walk half an hour or so north to the Hotel Posada Real on Playa Bacocho. The hotel's clifftop lawn is a perfect sunset-watching perch. Or you might climb down the cliff side (or take the hotel's shuttle bus) to the pool and restaurant complex on the beach below. The food isn't great, but the restaurant is an amazing sight, with a man-made tropical lagoon in the middle and leopard-skin swings at the bar.

There's not much evening entertainment in Puerto Escondido after the restaurants on the pedestrian mall close near midnight. **El Tubo** is an open-air beachside disco behind the telephone office on Gasga, which was not charging a cover when I was there.

WHERE TO STAY

Note that the rates quoted for most hotels are off-season prices; winter rates are higher.

DOUBLES FOR LESS THAN $25

HOTEL SAN JUAN, Felipe Merklin 503, Puerto Escondido, Oax. 71980. Tel. 958/2-0336. 26 rms (all with bath).
$ Rates: $9–$15 single; $15–$19 double. **Parking:** Free.
The best budget choice in the area is at the top of the Avenida Gasga hill, on the west side of the highway opposite the Hotel Crucero (look for a dirt road behind/below the curve in the highway). It's easy to get to as you come into town on the bus or by car, but the return trip on foot up the hill after a hot day at the beach is rough. Dozens of blue and green canaries greet you by the desk. A new restaurant has been added to the pretty patio on the right as you enter. The spare but bright, sparkling clean rooms have painted concrete floors, either two double or two twin beds, small closets, fans, and windows with screens. Second- and third-floor rooms have fantastic views from the balcony walkway.

LA CASA DE LOS HUESPEDES NAXHIELY, Av. Gasga 301, Puerto Escondido, Oax. 71980. 8 rms (all with bath).
$ Rates: $9 single; $14 double.
This good budget-conscious choice is managed by a young, cheerful couple. Each of the clean small rooms has a double bed, a fan, and sliding glass windows, but no screens and no bathroom doors. It's up the hill beyond the northern end of the pedestrian zone, on the right.

HOTEL LUZ DEL ANGEL, Calle Primero Norte 102, Puerto Escondido, Oax. 71980. Tel. 958/2-0122. 28 rms (all with bath).
$ Rates: $15 single; $18 double. Discounts available if business is slow.
Though not near the beach, this clean, quiet hotel is a popular choice. It's across from the market and near the bus stations, across Highway 200 on the landward side, off Avenida Oaxaca. The sparsely furnished but clean rooms have fans and either two double or two twin beds; 10 rooms have TV. If you get a room on the street you'll be able to watch the market come alive in the morning. There's a cheery, inexpensive restaurant just off the lobby, but you can wander over to the juice stand diagonally across from the hotel in the morning.

HOTEL LAS PALMAS, Av. Gasga, Puerto Escondido, Oax. 71980. Tel. 958/2-0230. 38 rms (all with bath).
$ Rates: $23 single or double; $28 triple.
This traditional favorite has an overgrown courtyard surrounded by a three-story U-shaped building in the center of the tourist zone facing the ocean and the beach. Each nicely furnished room has a fan and a double and a twin bed covered in tasteful foot-loomed bedspreads and matching drapes. The glass doors offer little privacy to

guests staying on the first floor, especially by the pool. The best rooms are on the second and third floors, facing the sea. While the food isn't particularly outstanding, the hotel's beachfront restaurant location is a comfortable place to dawdle away the hours watching the passing beach scene. Beside the restaurant is a comfy shaded bar with lounge chairs where guests become engrossed in thick novels.

HOTEL RINCÓN DEL PACÍFICO, Av. Gasga, Puerto Escondido, Oax. 71980. Tel. 958/2-0056. 28 rms (all with bath).
$ Rates: $20 single; $24 double.
This two-story U-shaped hotel surrounds a patch of sand shaded by a few tremendous palms. It's opposite Bancomer, close to the center of the PZ, and to the Hotel Las Palmas, facing the Pacific. In fact the rooms are similar to those at Las Palmas, with a glass wall and doors, although the decor is 1960s. All except two rooms have a double and one twin bed, and fans. Two suites facing the beach have a living room, minibar, air conditioning, TV, and a small patio on the beach. The beachside restaurant is open daily from 7:30am to 11pm. The restaurant on the beach level is open daily from 7am to 11pm.

MARGEOS, Av. Gasga, at Carretera Costera, Puerto Escondido, Oax. 71980. Tel. and fax 958/2-0525. 10 rms (all with bath).
$ Rates: Low season, $18 single; $24 double. High season, $24 single; $32 double. Add 20% for children under 12 in their parent's room. **Parking:** Free.
This small, two-story family-operated hotel has its back to Highway 200. The beach and the south end of the PZ are half a block away. The large rooms with fans are clean, colorful, and well kept, but are expensive for the off-beach location and room quality. An open-air lobby restaurant serves all meals, and you'll find the owners, a big clan of Morgans, to be friendly and helpful. Parking is on the street in front.

HOTEL NAYAR, Av. Gasga 407, Puerto Escondido, Oax. 71980. Tel. 958/2-0113 or 2-0319. 36 rms (all with bath).
$ Rates: $19 single; $24 double; $28 triple. **Parking:** Free.
Enter the Nayar via a cobbled drive shaded by enormous palms. There's parking for several cars along the entryway. On the left is a nice-size pool. This is an old-fashioned, rambling, two-story hotel with clean but dated rooms with fans. Rooms have either two double beds or a double and a twin. All have balconies, but only upper-story rooms have views. And only certain parts of the hotel have hot water. It's past the PZ, up the hill at the north end of Avenida Gasga.

HOTEL LOREN, Av. Gasga 507, Puerto Escondido, Oax. 71980. Tel. 958/2-0591. Fax 958/2-0057. 23 rms (all with bath).
$ Rates: $19 single; $24 double; $28 triple. **Parking:** Free.
The three-story hotel is tucked in a shady bend of Avenida Gasga past the north end of the pedestrian zone (it can also be reached off Highway 200) around the corner from both the Hotel Nayar and the Hotel Paraíso Escondido. It faces an open interior patio with an inviting pool. A restaurant should be in service when you travel. The best views are on the upper two levels, but there are no elevators. Rooms are immaculate, but sparsely furnished, with fans, two double beds, a chair, and a table. Parking is enclosed.

CASTILLO DE LOS REYES, Av. Gasga, Puerto Escondido, Oax. 71980. Tel. 958/2-0442. 16 rms (all with bath).
$ Rates: $19 single; $24 double; $28 triple. 20% discount May–July.
Don Fernando, the proprietor, has a gift for making his guests feel at home. Guests converse around tables on a shady patio near the office. Your white-walled room will have a fan as well as some special touch—a deer skin stretched across one wall, a gourd mask hanging over the bed. There's hot water, and the rooms are shaded from the sun by aging palms. A small new restaurant should be ready when you travel. It's up the hill on Gasga past the pedestrian zone on the left side (you can also enter Gasga off Highway 200).

HOTEL ROCAMAR, Av. Gasga 601, Puerto Escondido, Oax. 71980. Tel. 958/2-0339. 16 rms (all with bath).

$ Rates: $18 single; $36 double.

Although the hotel is not facing the beach, you're at the north end of the pedestrian zone and Andador la Soledad, only 90 seconds away from the surf on the city's main swimming beach and surrounded by restaurants. The tidy rooms have screens on the windows, a shower, and a fan (15 rooms) or air conditioning (6 rooms).

WORTH THE EXTRA BUCKS

HOTEL PARAÍSO ESCONDIDO, Calle Union 10, Puerto Escondido, Oax. 71980. Tel. 958/2-0444. 20 rms (all with bath). A/C
$ Rates: $30 single; $40 double.

This quaint little hacienda has numerous artistic touches, beautiful stonework, stained-glass windows, and tiles. The tastefully decorated rooms, reached by a series of stairs, all have two double beds and either a patio or private balcony. Second- and third-floor rooms have beautiful bay views. The second-level patio has a lovely lawn shaded by almond, flame, and palm trees; an open-air restaurant/bar (open in high season only) by a swimming pool has bay views. Though it's not on the beach, the comforts more than make up for the short walk to the beach. Highly recommended. It's up the hill on Avenida Gasga, past the north end of the pedestrian zone and behind the more visible Hotel Nayar.

HOTEL SANTA FE, Calle del Morro (Apdo. Postal 96), Puerto Escondido, Oax. 71980. Tel. 958/2-0170. Fax 958/2-0260. 39 rms, 4 bungalows (all with bath). A/C TEL
$ Rates: Low season, $35 single; $40 double; bungalow $45–$55. High season, $45 single; $50 double; $75 bungalow. **Parking:** Free.

The best hotel in town is about half a mile south of the town center off Highway 200, between the town beach and Zicatela Beach beside a rock outcropping that's a prime sunset-watching spot. The hacienda-style buildings have tiled stairs and archways laden with blooming bougainvillea. The large rooms have huge tile baths, colonial furnishings, foot-loomed bedspreads, Guerrero pottery lamps, and both air conditioning and ceiling fans. There is a small pool in the shade, and the restaurant is by far the finest in town. Though the prices are a bit steep for Puerto Escondido, they would be twice as high anywhere else. Bungalows are next to the hotel and come equipped with living room, kitchen, and one bedroom with two double beds. The road from the highway to the hotel is rutted and ends on the beach. Park in front of the hotel entrance.

LOS DELFINES, Hwy. 200, km 2, Cerro de la Iguana (Apdo. Postal 150), Puerto Escondido, Oax. 71980. Tel. and fax 958/2-0467, or 951/5-0546 in Oaxaca. 8 rms (all with bath). TV
$ Rates: Low season, $45; high season, $75.

Secluded and away from town, the eight earth-toned bungalows are on the edge of the cliff overlooking Zicatela Beach. Touches of Mexico are scattered throughout the property, from the hammocks stretched out in the open-air living room of the main house to the llamarada vines twisting over the front gate. There's a path to the beach, a lap pool, and a palapa restaurant/bar where the owner's gourmet meals are served. Rooms all come with fans, fully equipped kitchens, one or two bedrooms, hammocks on the individual terraces, and eating and living areas. There's good cross ventilation and screened windows and doors. All rooms face the ocean. Los Delfines is about a mile south of the town center: If you're arriving from Huatulco, it's on the left before the town center; from Acapulco or Oaxaca, pass through town and it's on the right.

WHERE TO EAT

For the lowest prices, wander across the landward side of the highway until you find the **market** and little cookshops on Hidalgo, a block off the highway. Before you order, ask the price—you'll be sorry if you ignore this advice.

MEALS FOR LESS THAN $5

RESTAURANT ALICIA, Av. Gasga. Tel. 2-0690.
Specialty: MEXICAN.
$ Prices: Breakfast $1.75–$3; main courses $1.50–$3.50.
Open: Daily 7am–11pm.
Here in the middle of the pedestrian zone, between the Hotel Palmas and the long-distance office, is Puerto Escondido's honorary United Nations. Foreigners from all over enjoy the inexpensive meals and good service here. Decor is simple; a half dozen cloth-covered tables look onto Gasga's passing scene. The menu isn't lengthy, but features fish, chicken, and beef dishes as well as tacos and enchiladas served with a small salad. Drink specialties are fruit milkshakes.

BANANAS, Av. Gasga. Tel. 2-0005.
Specialty: INTERNATIONAL.
$ Prices: Breakfast $1.75–$3.50; appetizers $3–$4.
Open: Daily 7:30am–1am.
You'll see this bamboo and thatch-roofed, two-story restaurant at the southern entrance to the PZ. Breakfast includes fresh yogurt, crêpes, and fresh fruit drinks. A range of light appetizers includes quesadillas with potato or squash flowers, tacos, and stuffed tortillas.

MEALS FOR LESS THAN $10

PERLA FLAMEANTE, Av. Gasga.
Specialty: SEAFOOD.
$ Prices: Appetizers $2–$3; main courses $2–$5.
Open: Breakfast/lunch daily 7am–2pm; dinner daily 4–11pm.
The best deal on savory fish filets is at this bamboo-walled restaurant on the sea side of Gasga at the south end of the pedestrian zone next to Bananas. The menu includes grilled shark, tuna, and mackerel in teriyaki, Cajun, garlic butter, or wine-and-herb sauce, all served with rice and salad. Upstairs a dozen tables overlook a shady palm grove.

LA POSADA D'LOREN, Av. Gasga. Tel. 2-0448.
Specialty: SEAFOOD/STEAK.
$ Prices: Appetizers $3–$5; main courses $3–$13; filet mignon $7; lobster $15.
Open: Daily 3–11pm.
A tempting aroma of charred steaks and lobster wafts from this seaside restaurant near the north end of the pedestrian zone at Andador Libertad. The open-air dining room and outdoor patio are a few steps lower than the street. The sounds of '50s hits and show tunes are a pleasant reprieve from rock and mariachis. The best deal is grilled fresh fish (snapper, bass, shark, and the catch of the day), served with a tangy peanut sauce on the side, and both baked potato and rice. Try the house drink, a soothing blend of banana, coconut, pineapple, and tequila.

NAUTILUS, Av. Gasga.
Specialty: INTERNATIONAL.
$ Prices: Appetizers $3–$4; main courses $2.75–$14.50; comida corrida $5–$10.
Open: Daily 8am–midnight, comida corrida served 1-5pm.
Here, at the north end of pedestrian zone, you may hear exhilarating mariachi music, Billy Holiday, or Patsy Klein coming from the tape player. From the second-story dining room there's a fabulous bay view where you can watch fishermen and brown pelicans. Breakfast specialties feature German-style dishes as well as traditional Mexican eggs. Usually there are three comida corridas featuring soup through dessert in various price ranges. For spurge specialties, try huachinango Hindu style with fruit, wine, and curry. Hungarian and Italian pasta and sushi with vegetables are more moderately priced, as well as chicken and a small selection of vegetarian dishes.

SPAGHETTI HOUSE, on the beach. Tel. 2-0005.
    Specialty: ITALIAN.
$ **Prices:** Appetizers $3.25–$7; main courses $3.50–$11; pasta $3–$6.50; pizza $4–$5.
    Open: Daily noon–11pm; happy hour, with drinks at two for the price of one, 6–7pm.

Facing the beach off the south end of the pedestrian zone, take a seat at one of the clean cloth-covered tables with matching cushions under a tile roof open to great sea breezes and the sound of pounding rolling surf. Pasta runs the gamut from basic spaghetti Napoletana to canellone and seafood fettuccine. Seven salads and pizza seven ways, plus an extensive bar list, ought to please most anyone.

WORTH THE EXTRA BUCKS

RESTAURANT SANTA FE, in the Hotel Santa Fe, Playa Marinero. Tel. 2-0170.
    Specialty: INTERNATIONAL.
$ **Prices:** Appetizers $3–$8; main courses $3.75–$12; tostadas especiales $3.65.
    Open: Daily 7:30am–11pm.

The atmosphere is cool and breezy, with fantastic views of the sunset and the waves on Zicatela Beach. The seafood dishes are a little expensive, but the vegetarian dishes are reasonably priced and creative, adapting traditional Mexican and Italian dishes. One of my favorites is the house specialty, chiles relleños: mild green peppers stuffed with cheese, raisins, and nuts, then baked in a mild red-chile sauce, served with brown rice, beans, and salad. The other favorite is the tostada special—big crispy tortillas heaped high with beans, lettuce, cheese, avocado, and salsa. The restaurant is on the beach about half a mile south of the town center.

EXCURSION TO PUERTO ANGEL

Fifty miles southwest of Puerto Excondido, and 30 miles north of Huatulco Bays, is the tiny fishing port of Puerto Angel (pop. 15,000), known to a handful of vacationers who come here regularly, mostly from Mexico City and Oaxaca. A small, beautiful bay and several inlets provide peaceful swimming and good snorkeling, and the village's position assures a sleepy, tranquil atmosphere.

    There are no direct buses from Puerto Escondido to Puerto Angel; however, numerous buses leave Puerto Escondido for Pochutla, 7 miles east of Puerto Angel, where you can transfer for the short ride to the village. The Pochutla bus yard is a confusing cacophony of drivers shouting their destinations, so listen carefully and double-check as you board. Buses depart from Pochutla for Puerto Angel every 20 minutes or so and cost 25¢. By car, travel on coastal Highway 200, and in Pochutla look for the well-marked turnoff off Highway 175 to Puerto Angel.

    The bus will let you off in the central village. The paved road from Pochutla ends at the edge of Puerto Angel and narrows to a dirt-and-sand track that goes through the village and winds up into the hills. The town center is only about four blocks long. There are few signs in the village giving directions, so I use the term "block" more as an idea of distance than as an identifier—so much of Puerto Angel is a path. The navy base is toward the far end of town, just before heading out to Playa Panteón; the rough road gets narrow and rutted at this point as it travels around the bay. The tourist office in Puerto Escondido has maps of Puerto Angel.

    Puerto Angel has only one telephone (tel. 958/4-0398, 4-0397, or 4-0399), in the long-distance office on the main street opposite the pier, open daily from 9am to 2pm and 4 to 8pm. You can try leaving a message for a hotel, but there's no guarantee that it will be passed on.

WHAT TO SEE & DO

The golden sands of Puerto Angel and the peaceful village life are the attractions here, so in the "where to soak" category let's begin with **Playa Principal,** directly in the central village. You can't miss it as the beach lies between the pier from which the bulk of the local fishing fleet works and the Mexican navy base. On one end near the pier, fishermen pull their colorful boats on the beach and unload their catch in the mornings while trucks from as far away as Mexico City, Acapulco, Oaxaca, and Huatulco wait to haul it off. The rest of the beach is for enjoyment, and except on Mexican holidays, it's usually deserted. It's important to note that Pacific Coast currents deposit trash on Puerto Angel beaches. The townsfolk do a fairly good job of keeping it picked up, but those currents are constant.

Playa Panteón is the main swimming and snorkeling beach. It's about a 15-minute walk from the town center, straight through town on the main street that skirts the beach. Just before you reach Playa Panteón you pass the *panteón* (cemetery) for which the beach is named.

The 3.7 miles of rough road to **Playa Zipolite** (that's "See-poh-*lee*-teh") can be negotiated on foot in 45 minutes or by taxi for $6. You'll have to ask someone to point you to the right path if you walk. The partially shaded road can sap the last bit of your energy if you attempt to walk back to town in the midday heat, so wear a hat. Zipolite is a beach without protection from the open surf. Consequently, swimming can be very dangerous. The beach's main claim to fame is surfing, with many surfers ensconced in hammocks under numerous palapas along the beach. Beyond a large rock outcropping at the far end of the beach is an area where nude bathing has been tolerated for several years. One caveat: Police could roust *au naturel* bathers at any time as they are technically breaking the law.

WHERE TO STAY

There are two areas in Puerto Angel to look for accommodations: Playa Principal in the tiny town, and Playa Panteón, the pretty beach area beyond the village center. Because the bus route ends by the navy base in town and it can be scaldingly hot on the sandy road to Playa Panteón, you might consider taking a taxi for about $2.

Between Playa Panteón and town there are numerous bungalow and guesthouse set-ups with budget accommodations.

Most hotels receive mail in Pochutla. During the high seasons, December through Easter and July and August, rates can go up and you should reserve well in advance.

CAPY'S, Apdo. Postal 135, Pochutla, Oax. 70900. 8 rms (all with bath).
$ Rates: $7 single; $9 double.
You'll see Capy's sign hanging over the street; it's on the right, before the cemetery and Playa Panteón. Go up a flight of stairs to the second-story restaurant and someone can show you one of the very plain rooms. It's a decent enough budget choice, with simple furnishings, fans, and well-screened windows. Room 6 has a great patio out front with a splendid bay view.

The pleasant, covered, but open-air restaurant is open daily from 8am to 9pm. Breakfast is served between 8am and noon and costs $2 to $3; lunch and dinner are served from 1 to 9pm and main courses cost between $2 and $6.

CASA HUESPEDES GANDI Y TOMAS, Playa Principal, Puerto Angel, Oax 70900. 8 rms (3 with bath).
$ Rates: $9 single; $11 double.
You may have to shoo a few chickens from underfoot while trudging up the brick stairs, but it's an acceptable budget choice that's almost always full. Come early to get a room with a private bath. Rooms are nice but sparsely furnished, with several pleasant balconies with tables and chairs and paperback books to borrow. There are no fans. It's on the hill in back of the town center, above and to right of the Naval Fisheries building.

POSADA RINCÓN SABROSO, Playa Principal, Puerto Angel, Oax 70900. 8 rms (all with bath).
$ Rates: $12 single; $14 double.
A sign on the street marks the entrance up a flight of stairs. Rooms have nice tile floors, plaster walls, fans, and screened windows. Hammocks hang between posts on the tile patio walkway, which is also furnished with tables and chairs outside each room. A jungle of plants blocks the view and breezes. It's on the right as

you enter town, near the base of the bridge and opposite the main pier, by the Hotel Soraya.

HOTEL LA CABAÑA DE PUERTO ANGEL, Apdo. Postal 22, Pochutla, Oax. 70900. Tel. 951/4-0026. 23 rms (all with bath).

$ Rates: $15 single; $19 double; triple $24.

Covered in vines and plants, with lots of shade, this hacienda-style hotel is efficient and accommodating, with friendly, helpful desk clerks. The clean, sunny rooms have louvered windows and screens, ceiling fans, and firm double beds. The rooftop patio is a nice place to sunbathe peacefully, but the hotel is on Playa Panteón on the landward side of the road, just steps from the beach and several restaurants. Highly recommended.

LA BUENAVISTA, Apdo. Postal 48, Pochutla, Oax. 70900. 13 rms (11 with bath).

$ Rates: Low season, $18–$22 single or double; high season, $25–$30 single or double.

To find La Buenavista, follow the dirt road through town, and shortly you'll see a sign pointing right to the hotel. It's on a hillside, so to get to the lobby/patio you have to climb a formidable flight of stairs, after which you'll discover why this hotel's name means "good view," with the bay and village in the distance. The rooms, all with natural tile floors, one or two double beds, fans, and well-screened windows, are tastefully furnished with Mexican accents. On the roof is a wonderful little reasonably priced restaurant also open to breezes and with bay views. It's open for breakfast at 7:30am and for dinner around 6pm. Breakfast costs $2 to $3; dinner, $4 to $8.

Worth the Extra Bucks

POSADA CAÑON DE VATA, Calle Canyon del Vata (Apdo. Postal 74) Pochutla, Oax. 70900. 10 rms, 4 bungalows (all with bath).

$ Rates: $25–$30 single; $35–$40 double; $50 bungalow for two. **Closed:** May–June.

The most inviting place in Puerto Angel is a 3-minute walk from Playa Panteón; Suzanne and Mateo Lopez call their posada "A Place to Rest from the World." It's a homey, cool, wooded oasis in a narrow canyon with shelves of paperback books to trade and coffee always ready in the dining room. Rooms are agreeably rustic-chic, with fans, beds covered in Guatemalan tie-died cloth, and Mexican artistic touches throughout. Room 4 is larger than most and has a private balcony. The four bungalows are a long walk up the hill from the restaurant and up a flight of stairs, but the seclusion is nice. The patio restaurant serves delicious food featuring home-baked bread and a fixed-price menu with breakfast, beginning at 7am, costing $2 to $3; lunch is $3 and dinner, at around 7pm, runs about $8. Highly recommended. It's near Playa Panteón. Walk one block past the Hotel Cabaña del Puerto Angel and look right; it's in a lush ravine without a street sign.

HOTEL SORAYA, Playa Principal, Puerto Angel, Oax 70900. 32 rms (all with bath). A/C

$ Rates: Low season, $20 single; $24 double; $28 triple. High season, 20% more. Ask for a discount May–Sept.

Within the town itself, the top choice for lodging sits atop a small cliff. (It's on the right by the bridge entering town where the pavement ends, opposite the main pier.) The clean rooms, all with tile floors, are sparsely furnished. Some have ocean views. Rooms 22, 23, and 24 have large terraces with hammocks and sea views. The restaurant has a magnificent view of the bay and village.

WHERE TO EAT

Besides the hotel restaurants mentioned above, several beach palapa restaurants are worth noting.

On Playa Panteón, one of the best is the family-owned **Restaurante Bricio y Cordelia,** with good, friendly service. It's a spotless, covered restaurant with 15 or so tables and chairs, ideally situated for watching the beach and bay while enjoying some well prepared seafood. There's beef, chicken, and pasta, too—but seafood is the specialty. If you want to use this restaurant as a base on the beach, there's no charge for using their lounge chairs and thatched palapas, providing you buy your refreshments here. It's open daily from 7:30am to 9pm in the off-season and until 10 or 11pm in high season.

3. BAHÍAS DE HUATULCO

40 miles S of Puerto Angel, 425 miles S of Acapulco

GETTING THERE By Plane Mexicana connects Huatulco with Cancún, Guadalajara, Los Angeles, and Mexico City. **Aeroméxico** offers service from Mexico City. **Aviacsa** arrives from Tuxtla Gutiérrez and Mexico City. **AeroMorelos** has daily flights from Oaxaca. **Club Med charter flights** originate at the Dallas/Fort Worth Airport.

Shuttle buses from Huatulco's international airport, about 11 miles north of the Bahías de Huatulco, to the hotels cost $13 per person.

By Bus To reach Huatulco by bus from Puerto Escondido or Puerto Angel you must change buses in Pochutla at a huge dirt lot where the drivers shout out their destinations and wait to leave until the bus is at least semi-full, regardless of schedule. The situation here is absurdly confusing, since the buses marked "Huatulco" actually go to Santa María Huatulco, nowhere near the bays. The buses to Salina Cruz stop in Crucecita, as do those marked "Santa Cruz." Be specific when you ask the driver where he's going, and ask for Bahías de Huatulco or Crucecita. The fare is 75¢ and the ride takes about an hour.

By Car The coastal Highway 200 leads to Huatulco from the north and is generally in good condition. Allow at least 8 hours for the trip from Oaxaca City on mountainous Highway 175.

DEPARTING By Plane Phone calls from Huatulco to the **international airport,** about 11 miles north of the Bahías de Huatulco, are long distance, so use a travel agent in town to check or change flights. The **Mexicana** office is in the Hotel Castillo Huatulco in Santa Cruz (tel. 958/4-0077). **Aeroméxico** is reached at the airport (tel. 958/4-0328). **Aviacsa** (tel. 958/4-0125) goes to Tuxtla Gutiérrez and Mexico City. **AeroMorelos** is in the Sheraton Hotel at the travel agency Servicios Turisticos del Sur (tel. 958/1-0055).

By Bus There are four bus stations in Crucecita and one in Santa Cruz.

From **Santa Cruz,** the most convenient and frequent buses to Pochutla are the minibuses that gather in the bus yard by the yacht basin in Santa Cruz. They leave every 15 minutes between 6:30am and 7:30pm. There are no signs, so tell one of the drivers where you want to go and he'll tell you which bus (put your luggage by the driver). At the Pochutla bus yard you switch to buses to Puerto Esondido or Puerto Angel.

Bus stations in **Crucecita** are all within three blocks of each other. **Cristobal Colón** buses (tel. 7-0261) are at Cardenias at Ocotillo. Most of these buses go south toward Tehuantepec and across the isthmus of Tehuantepec to Acayucán, San Cristóbal de las Casas, and Tuxtla Gutiérrez. One block farther, opposite the telephone office, is another storefront station, which doubles as a record shop and video-rental outlet. Buses here go to Salina Cruz, Pochutla, and Puerto Escondido. The **Lineas Unidas del Sur** station is at the corner of Gardenia and Palo Verde (tel. 7-0103), open daily from 7am to 9pm. From here buses go to Acapulco, Puerto Angel via an Acapulco bus, and Puerto Escondido and Mexico City.

❝The next Cancún!" trumpets the tourist literature—but it's going to be a while. Oaxaca's coastline is one of the last undeveloped stretches of pure white sands and isolated coves in Mexico, and it's a joy to see. Birds and tropical blossoms abound. The sea is crystalline clear and bathwater warm, and the air blessedly free of gasoline fumes. It takes some creative resourcefulness to explore this region on a budget, but the natural beauty is worth the effort.

The FONATUR development of the Bahías de Huatulco, a government megaresort on the nine pristine bays of Huatulco, is an ambitious project that includes 124,000 acres of land, mostly undeveloped. The small communities of locals have been transplanted away from the coast into Crucecita and Santa Cruz, and corporate giants are vying for the rights to huge parcels of prime, pristine bayfront jungle.

After the turn of the century Huatulco is supposed to have over a million visitors each year. Right now, there are three luxury resorts, another under construction, several mid-range hotels, about a dozen restaurants, and a few tourist amenities. Phone service is gradually reaching hotels, restaurants, and businesses. The airport consists of three sky-high palapas, but to call there is a long-distance call. The bus stations are spread out. The area's two towns, Crucecita and Santa Cruz, have pretty new plazas and lots of colonial-style shops and restaurants, and the trees and flowers planted in 1985 are finally giving color and shade. There are still a few families complete with roosters and dogs living in makeshift residences under the trees beside unfinished hotels, but there's less of that. The restaurant shacks in Santa Cruz Bay are giving way to new buildings for these businesses, and the beautiful marina there is finished. Huatulco's rough edges are smoothing out, so plan to get there soon, before glitz, glamour, and high prices take over.

ORIENTATION

ARRIVING   The **airport** is 13 miles from town and the trip costs $6 in a colectivo bus. If you arrive by **bus** in Crucecita, you'll be dropped at one of the bus stations on Avenida Gardenias. If you come on one of the white **minibuses** from Pochutla, you'll arrive in Santa Cruz at the marina.

INFORMATION   The **Tourism Office** is in Tangolunda, cater-corner from the Sheraton on a road sometimes called Paseo Tangolunda (tel. 958/1-0032); it's open Monday through Friday from 9am to 2pm, with extended afternoon hours in high season. Another **quasi-tourism office** (tel. 7-0027) is located in Crucecita near the corner of Bugambilias, just a few steps from the Plaza Principal. It belongs to the tourist publication *Huatulco Espacio 2000* and has helpful if somewhat overglowing descriptions of what to see and do in Huatulco. You can get maps of Puerto Angel and Puerto Escondido here. It's open Monday through Friday from 9am to 2pm and 4 to 6pm.

CITY LAYOUT   Just naming where you want to go in Huatulco can be confusing. The FONATUR resort area is called **Bahías de Huatulco,** not to be confused with Santa María Huatulco, some 17 miles inland. Then there's **Santa Cruz Huatulco,** which is normally just called Santa Cruz and is the original coastal settlement on the bay. It has the dock where bay tours and glass-bottom-boat trips begin. Rows of bright blue, pink, and yellow shacks are part of a large artisans' market on the waterfront next to the marina. **Juárez** is Santa Cruz's main street, only about four long blocks in all, anchored at one end by the new Hotel Castillo Huatulco and at the other end by the Hotel Binneguenda. Opposite the Castillo is the **marina,** now taking on a handsome look with pale sienna-colored colonial-style buildings around it and beyond it a beach littered with small boats and makeshift restaurants. Buses to Pochutla are corraled in a dirt lot next to the marina. The area's banks and a small supermarket are on Juárez. It's impossible to get lost—you can see almost everything at a glance.

A mile and a half inland from Santa Cruz is **Crucecita,** a planned city which sprang up in 1985 centered on a lovely new, grassy plaza edged with flowering hedges. It's the residential area for the resorts, with neighborhoods of new stucco homes mixed with makeshift wooden ones and small apartment complexes, plus a few new hotels. Most of the restaurants are here.

For a sampling of the luxurious Huatulco of tomorrow, take a cab 3 miles from

Santa Cruz to **Tangolunda Bay,** the focal point of development for the nine bays. Gradually, half the bays will have resorts where guests arrive on a shuttle from the airport and stay put. For now, Tangolunda has the golf course, the tourist office, and the Club Med, Sheraton, Club Maeva, and a new Holiday Inn Crowne Plaza under construction, all far beyond our budget yet much less expensive than they will be someday. Chahue Bay, between Tangolunda and Santa Cruz is a beautiful bay set aside for trailers and campers, but is little used.

GETTING AROUND

It's a long walk between the three destinations of Crucecita, Santa Cruz, and Tangolunda. There is no public bus transportation to Tangolunda, but the minibuses near the marina all make stops in Crucecita gathering passengers on the way to Pochutla; even if you pay the full fare to Pochutla, it'll be cheaper than a taxi to Crucecita. Cab rides between these areas cost about $3, though I've seen locals get by for much less.

FAST FACTS

Area Code   The telephone area code is 958.

Banks   There are two banks in Santa Cruz, one on Juárez and the other in the same area but set back closer to the water.

Supermarket   The **Super Mas** market, on Juárez near the Hotel Binneguenda (tel. 7-0337), has a good supply of the basics.

Taxis   In **Crucecita,** there's a taxi stand opposite the Hotel Griffer. To or from Santa Cruz costs $1. Between either Crucecita and Tangolunda Bay the cost is $2 to $3, depending on if you hail a street taxi or a more expensive hotel taxi.

Telephone   The **long-distance telephone office** is on Avenida Gardenias at Maciul, in Crucecita. It's open Monday through Saturday from 7:30am to 9:30pm and on Sunday and holidays from 1:30 to 3:30pm.

WHAT TO SEE & DO

BEACHES   The beach at **Santa Cruz** has too many restaurants and small boats on it to be inviting as a sunning spot. **Tangolunda Bay** beaches are nice and access to them is through the hotels; the beaches are public, so feel free to enjoy any spot that suits you. For about $4 one way, *pangas* from the marina in Santa Cruz will ferry you to **La Entrega** beach, on the bay over from Santa Cruz; you can split the price with others. There you'll find a row of palapa restaurants all with beach chairs out front. Find an empty one and use that restaurant for your refreshment needs in return. A snorkel equipment-rental booth is about midway down the beach and there's some fairly good snorkeling on the end away from where the boats arrive; be careful of wave action pushing you against the rocks.

BAY CRUISES/TOURS   Huatulco's major attraction is the coastline, that magnificent stretch of pristine bays. The only way to really grasp the beauty of the place is by taking a **cruise of the bays,** stopping at Chahue or Maguey Bay for a dip in the crystal-clear water and a fish lunch from one of the palapas on the beach. You can catch a boat from Santa Cruz at $3 to $5 per hour, or take one of the cruise tours from the travel agencies at the hotels, for 6 hours for $25, which includes a bay tour, lunch, and snorkeling.

Servicios Turisticos del Sur in the Sheraton Hotel or at the Hotel Castillo in Santa Cruz (tel. 1-0055) has full-day tours of the bays, as well as tours to Oaxaca, Puerto Escondido, and Puerto Angel. **Turismo Tangolunda** in the Royal Maeva (tel. 1-0094) and **Viajes y Excursiones Santa Cruz Huatulco** in the Posada Binniguenda have similar tours and prices.

BIRDING   Although there are no formal birding walks or tours, if birds are your interest Huatulco will be rewarding. Before setting out, be sure to wear protective clothing and sturdy shoes.

FISHING   Deep-sea fishing costs $100 an hour with a 2-hour minimum if arranged directly with a boat owner at the pier; 4 to 6 hours is recommended, and the price can be split with up to six people. Don't hesitate to bargain the price down. It may be less of a hassle and end up costing less (between $35 and $50 per person) if arranged through a hotel travel agency. Fishing is good all year, but best in winter and spring for sail fish, mahi mahi, bonito, and tuna.

SHOPPING   There's a good folk-art store in the **Sheraton Hotel,** but for the most part shopping is confined to the **Santa Cruz market,** by the marina, and the **Crucecita market,** on Guamuchil half a block from the plaza.

WHERE TO STAY

Besides the hotels listed below, there's one **trailer park** near Santa Cruz, but tent camping is not allowed. Hotels in Santa Cruz and Crucecita are generally overpriced. Off-season there are lots of vacancies in Crucecita, so try bargaining for a discount.

GRIFFER, Av. Guamuchil (Apdo. Postal 159), Crucecita, Oax. 70900. Tel. 958/7-0048. 20 rms (all with bath). TV TEL
$ Rates: $24–$36 single or double.

There's nothing special about this hotel except its prices. The tidy rooms have tile floors, fans, one or two double beds, space for a table and chair, and small showers. Some of the rooms have small balconies overlooking the street.

To get here, walk away from Plaza Principal on Guamuchil; the hotel is on the right at the end of the block at the corner of Carriza.

SUITES BUGAMBILIAS, Bugambilias and Flamboyan, Crucecita, Bahías de Huatulco, Oax. 70900. Tel. 958/7-0018. 20 rms (all with bath).
$ Rates: Low season, $32 single; $35–$50 double. High season, slightly higher. The smallish rooms are open and airy, with orange-and-black bedspreads, fans, and festive talavera lamps. Two large rooms overlook Guamuchil and have table and chairs and a small balcony. Supposedly air conditioning and TVs are being added; if so, look for prices to go up. It's on the Crucecita Plaza Principal.

POSADA DEL PADRINO, Calle Guamuchil, Crucecita, Santa Cruz de Huatulco, Oax. 70900. Tel. 958/7-0060. 8 rms (all with bath). A/C
$ Rates: $40 single or double.
All the rooms are nice size, with tile floors, decorated in cool blue and rattan with lots of storage shelves. Baths are small, but overall the small inn is cheery and clean. It's across from the market half a block off Plaza Principal on Guamuchil, next to the Rancho del Padrino restaurant; the lobby is upstairs.

WORTH THE EXTRA BUCKS

POSADA BINNIGUENDA, Benito Juárez 5 (Apdo. Postal 44), Santa Cruz de Huatulco, Oax. 70900. Tel. 958/7-0077. Fax 5/660-1006 in Mexico City. 73 rms (all with bath). A/C TV TEL
$ Rates: $50 single; $62 double.

This was Huatulco's first hotel and it retains the Mexican charm and comfort that made it memorable. Rooms have Mexican tile floors, foot-loomed bedspreads, colonial-style furniture, and French doors opening onto tiny wrought-iron balconies overlooking Juárez. TVs bring in U.S. channels. There's a nice shady area around the hotel's beautiful pool in back of the lobby. The restaurant is only fair, but the fresh lemonade is superb. It's away from the marina at the far end of Juárez, only a few blocks from the water.

CASTILLO HUATULCO, Juárez, Manzana 1, Lote 2a, Santa Cruz de Huatulco, Oax. Tel. 958/7-0051. Fax 958/7-0131. 58 rms, 4 suites. A/C TV TEL
$ Rates: $75 single or double.

The hotel opened its first half in 1990. Because it's ideally situated opposite the market and marina, Santa Cruz beach, and buses to Crucecita, you'll save money on transportation by staying here. Rooms are nicely proportioned, with beige tile floors, two double beds, and small balconies, some with sea views. The four loft suites, which cost more, probably looked good on paper, but are ridiculous in reality: One bedroom, the living room, and the only bath are downstairs; the second bedroom is up a very tall spiral staircase (imagine hauling luggage up). There's a nice-size pool with a swim-up bar and the restaurant opens to the pool.

ROYAL MAEVA, Paseo Tangolunda (Apdo. Postal 227), Bahías de Huatulco, Oax. 70900. Tel. 958/1-0000, or toll free 800/431-2138 in the U.S. and Canada. Fax 958/1-0220. 350 rms (all with bath). A/C TV TEL

$ Rates (including all meals, taxes, and tips): Low season, $95 per person; high season, $125 per person.

It's sprawling and breezy, right at the end of Tangolunda beach and bay. Room design is similar to the Sheraton next door, but the decor is less lavish. A fun-loving crowd listens to loud music in the pool area. If you're sensitive to sound, choose a room far enough away. Lavish buffets with communal seating are served indoors and outdoors. The beach is spectacular, and most water sports—windsurfing, canoeing, snorkeling—are included in the daily rate. I should mention that they don't have an abundance of equipment, so although it's free, you may have to wait. Maeva is a poor copy of Club Med.

CLUB MED, Tangolunda Bay, Santa Cruz de Huatulco Oax. 70900. Tel. 958/1-0033, or toll free 800/258-2633 in the U.S. Fax 958/1-0101. 500 rms (all with bath). A/C

$ Rates (including all meals and activities): Low season, $1,380 per person per week, double occupancy, including airfare from New York; $1,180 per person per week, double occupancy, including airfare from Dallas/Fort Worth. Ask about other cities and low-season discounts.

⭐ In my opinion the best splurge value in Huatulco is Club Med. I think it's also the best Club Med in the country because it caters to all ages, is more like a country club for the sports- or relaxation-minded, and has the most beautiful setting and spectacular view on Tangolunda Bay. It's also the largest Club Med in Mexico, but because of its room configuration, spread out over a fabulous promontory, it still manages a feeling of personal seclusion. The best time to come is in low season, when prices are lower and there are fewer guests vying for dining room seats and turns on the equipment. Rooms and bathrooms are larger than other Club Meds, with sliding closets that separate the two bed areas. Each room has a private patio with hammock and all rooms have sea views. Rooms have both air conditioning and fans, and you need both—the air conditioning isn't very cool.

Four restaurants feature different cuisines with an emphasis on fresh seafood, French, and Moroccan specialties (but all may not be open in low season). There's a nightly disco by the beach. Water sports include windsurfing, kayaking, and snorkeling. There's also an air-conditioned workout room, with a daily schedule of aerobics, and workout equipment, three air-conditioned squash courts, and a practice golf course with professional instruction. The snorkeling is quite good on a coral reef on one of the club's beaches. Six of the 12 tennis courts are lighted for night play. Deep-sea fishing costs extra. A taxi to town for shopping is cheaper than the hotel's boat excursion.

WHERE TO EAT

Outside of the hotels, the best choices are in Crucecita and on the beach in Santa Cruz.

RESTAURANT AVALOS DOÑA CELIA, Santa Cruz Bay. Tel. 7-0128.
   Specialty: SEAFOOD/MEXICAN.
$ Prices: Breakfast $2–$4; Mexican specialties $4–$8; seafood $6–$15.
   Open: Daily 7:30am–9pm.

Doña Celia, an original Huatulco resident, chose to stay in business in the same area where she started her little thatch-roofed restaurant years ago. Now she's in a new building at the end of Santa Cruz's beach, serving the same good food. Her specialties are filete empapelado, a foil-wrapped fish baked with tomato, onion, and cilantro, and filete almendro, a fish hot cake with almonds.

FAST, Av. Guamuchil, Crucecita.
Specialty: SANDWICHES.
$ Prices: Breakfast $1.50–$3.50; tortas $1.50–$3.
Open: Wed–Mon 8am–2am.
This narrow eatery stays busy all day serving up an assortment of tortas (sandwiches) with a variety of fillings, plus baked potatoes, french fries, chicken, and treats such as ice cream, fresh juice, and malts. It's a few steps off Plaza Principal on Guamuchil, by Posada Padrino.

RESTAURANT LOS PORTALES, Bugambilias at Guamuchil, Crucecita.
Specialty: TACOS.
$ Prices: Breakfast $1.75–$3.50; tacos 40¢–$4.50.
Open: Daily 6:30pm–1am.
Pull up a stool and watch the cooks create tacos on an open grill, or sit at a table on the sidewalk right on Plaza Principal. Select from tacos 20 different ways: al pastor, beef, pork, sausage. The king of tacos is the alambre, with chiles, beef, bacon, and onions.

RESTAURANT RANCHO DEL PADRINO, Calle Guamuchil, Crucecita. Tel. 7-0060.
Specialty: OAXACAN.
$ Prices: Breakfast $5–$8; Mexican/Oaxacan specialties $1–$8.
Open: Tues–Sun 8am–11pm.
Basket lamps, sombreros, and sienna-colored walls set a background for casual dining and soft music. Half a block on Guamuchil off Plaza Principal, this is one of the village's more inviting restaurants. The Oaxaca *botana* (snack) platter is enough for two.

RESTAURANTE MARÍA SABINA, Flamboyanes 15, Crucecita. Tel. 7-0219.
Specialty: SEAFOOD/OAXACAN.
$ Prices: Appetizers $1.25–$5; main courses $5.75–$18.50.
Open: Mon–Sat 1pm–midnight.
This popular restaurant, which some say is the best in town, is on the far side of Plaza Principal. Carne asada, chicken, and fresh fish cook on the big open grill on the sidewalk beside the café tables. The lengthy menu also features Oaxacan dishes.

FOG CUTTER, Av. Colorines and Laurel, Crucecita.
Specialty: BEEF/SEAFOOD.
$ Prices: Appetizers $6–$8; main courses $9.50–$18.
Open: Tues–Sun 2–11pm.
Small and cozy, with fewer than 10 tables, and a bit isolated from mainstream Crucecita, this is a good place for a full-scale beef or fish dinner and a taste of what local life is like. Prices are a bit high, so you might try an appetizer to see if you want a full meal. Besides steak and seafood, paella makes a frequent appearance on the menu.

To get here, face the Plaza Principal on Bugambilias, cross it to Gardenia, turn left and walk two blocks, then turn right for two more blocks; it's next to Canada shoes.

EVENING ENTERTAINMENT

Bring a supply of books—Huatulco is short on entertainment. Besides the disco below, a lot of people finish off an evening at one of the eateries on Santa Cruz Bay.
Disco Magic Circus, Santa Cruz Bay (tel. 7-0017 or 7-0037), is one block opposite the Hotel Binneguenda going toward the bay. The music is a mix of salsa and rock. Admission is $10 (women free on Sunday). In low season it's open Tuesday through Saturday from 10pm to 3am; in high season, open daily.

BAJA CALIFORNIA

A peninsula longer than Italy, Baja California stretches 876 miles from Tijuana at its northern edge to Los Cabos at its southern tip. Its desert terrain rises up from both coasts—the Pacific Ocean on the west and the Sea of Cortez to the east—to form a spine of craggy mountains that can change from burnt sienna to vermillion, orange, purple, apricot, or rose, depending on the time of day. Whole forests of majestic cardon cactus, spiky joshua trees, and spindly ocotillo bushes populate this raw, untamed landscape where volcanoes once roared. Baja's wide-open spaces seem to echo with geological time: It's easy to imagine the toothy Sierras heaving up while seas rolled across the flat lands at their feet.

Georgia O'Keeffe probably would have loved Baja's painted-desert colors and sculpted terrain beside the sea; others might find it barren. For Baja is a place that, depending on your mood, can be boring or breathtakingly beautiful. Its austere but dramatic landscape resembles the American West—beside a brilliant blue sea. Or it brings to mind the moon—a moon with palm trees and turquoise bays. Scattered along its coastline and tucked among its mountains are tropical hamlets and little oasislike towns planted like rewards at the end of a long road.

Baja has always been a land of striking oppositions and paradox. It has some of the most beautiful beaches in Mexico, many of them isolated and blissfully unpopulated, while others are lined with semipermanent trailers and RVs that have settled in with their satellite dishes on the sand. Often Baja seems like one of the least crowded corners of Mexico. At other times it appears to be the southern playground of America's west coast. Baja's terrain and climate can be as inviting as a Caribbean isle or as unforgiving as a norther.

Baja is a land of secrets too, a place that takes patience to penetrate. Its mountains are riddled with caves painted with bold prehistoric pictures and petroglyphs, though reaching them is an adventure requiring horses, mules, or Jeeps. A wealth of untamed marine life plays beneath its waves: Besides the flying marlin and other game fish that have lured wealthy anglers to this peninsula since the 1950s, there are wave-leaping dolphins, colonies of sea lions, giant manta rays, and lagoons full of whales, the latter migrating to Baja's bays in the winter to breed. This land's wild beauty brings out the explorer in visitors.

SEEING BAJA CALIFORNIA

To drive on Mexico Highway 1 (the Transpeninsular Highway) from Tijuana at the U.S. border to Cabo San Lucas at the southern tip of the Baja (1,125 miles) count on 25 hours of driving time (excluding stops) and at least two overnight stops. The distances are vast and there are numerous side trips to lengthen the journey—isolated coves and beaches to explore, whales in the bays, and caves painted with ancient pictures. With the exception of such detours, you'll stay on Highway 1 until you're south of La Paz, where Highway 1 goes to San José del Cabo and Highway 19 branches off to Cabo San Lucas. The two-lane highway is reasonably well maintained (watch for occasional potholes and rocks in the road) but has no shoulders, so drive carefully and fill your tank at every opportunity—the stretches in between can be long. Livestock is not fenced, so you should never drive after dark.

There are express buses that start in Tijuana and go all the way to the capital, La

WHAT'S SPECIAL ABOUT BAJA CALIFORNIA

Ancient History
☐ Mysterious petroglyphs painted in more than 100 Baja caves.

Architecture
☐ The 19th-century French architecture of Santa Rosalía, including a prefabricated-iron church designed by Gustave Eiffel.

Beaches
☐ Beaches and coves of the 22-mile "Corridor" coast between San José del Cabo and Cabo San Lucas, especially Bahía Chileno and Playa Santa María for snorkeling.

☐ Beaches edging the peninsula north of La Paz, especially Puerto Balandra, where the rock formations around the sweeping crystalline coves rise up like humpbacked whales.

Events/Festivals
☐ Carnaval (Mardi Gras) week in La Paz.

Natural Spectacles
☐ Isla Espíritu Santo and the sea lion colony at Los Islotes north of La Paz.

☐ Isla Coronado where dolphins leap and sea lions play.

☐ Whales in Magdalena Bay, Laguna San Ignacio, or Scammon's Lagoon on the Pacific coast.

☐ El Arco at Land's End in Cabo San Lucas—towering rock pinnacles and an arch where the Pacific Ocean and the Sea of Cortez meet.

☐ The Sierra de la Giganta soaring up beside the coastline near Loreto.

☐ Palm-fringed oasis rivers in Mulege and San Ignacio.

Sports
☐ Fishing for marlin that weigh more than 100 pounds in Los Cabos, or yellowtail in Loreto.

☐ The Tennis Center in Loreto, the best in Mexico.

Paz, with minimal intermediate stops. In La Paz you change for one of the many buses south to Los Cabos (San José del Cabo and Cabo San Lucas) or points in between. Bus service is frequent enough that you can use it to see Baja's main towns. One caution, however: Busing in Baja is best in the cool winter months, for the buses are not air-conditioned and Mexicans often prefer to keep the windows shut, even in hot weather.

Ferryboats operate between La Paz (Pichilingue dock) and Los Mochis (Topolobampo dock), between La Paz and Mazatlán, and between Santa Rosalía and Los Mochis. One ferry system, owned by the private company SEMATUR, was purchased from the government in 1989. It uses several large, multideck ships that carry from 100 to nearly 700 passengers, as well as cars and freight. The other line, called Baja Express, is also privately owned and began service in 1990. Its compact, catamaran-type "waterjets" carry passengers only, and are faster than the SEMATUR ships. Baja Expeditions (tel. toll free 800/843-6967 and Pacific Sea Fari Tours (tel. 619/226-8224) offer cruises to Baja from San Diego and Los Angeles.

Baja brings out creativity in budget-minded travelers, for as a rule its price structure is rather upscale. Baja first became popular as a private fishing club for wealthy Americans, and some of this country-club ambience still exists, especially in Los Cabos, and has tended to push up prices. Budget hotels and restaurants exist too, but are fewer and farther between than in many other parts of Mexico.

WHAT TO SEE & DO Though the superb sport fishing is still one of the best reasons for coming to Baja, the list of other options continues to grow as Baja develops and becomes more popular. Scuba diving, snorkeling, sailing, outings to see whales or ancient cave paintings or villages hidden in the mountains, exploring dreamy and isolated beaches—these all draw visitors to Baja.

IMPRESSIONS

Below the Mexican border [of Baja California] the water changes color; it takes on a deep ultramarine blue—a washtub bluing blue, intense and seeming to penetrate deep into the water; the fishermen call it "tuna water."
—JOHN STEINBECK, *LOG FROM THE SEA OF CORTEZ*, 1941

It's important to remember, however, that many of these outings involve excursions that are difficult to organize independently. Most can be arranged through local travel agencies, but this adds to the price of playing in Baja. Also keep in mind that many organized trips require a minimum of four to six people, so traveling with a small group of friends can be helpful.

Shopping, especially in Cabo San Lucas and La Paz, has become much more varied and interesting over the past 5 years. And because Baja is a special duty-free zone (a government-conferred status to bolster commerce), imported products are cheaper here than they are on the mainland. This also means that you (and your car) may be subject to a Customs check as you pass from Baja to other parts of Mexico.

A NOTE ON THE WEATHER   Baja is a land of extremes: It can be skillet-hot in summer and sometimes cold and windy in winter—so windy that fishing and other nautical expeditions may be grounded for a few days. Though winter can be warm enough for water sports, bring a wetsuit along if you're a serious diver or snorkeler, as well as a change of warm clothes for unexpectedly chilly weather. Rather than set your heart on one activity—such as fishing or whale-watching—have some alternatives in mind, too.

1. LOS CABOS

Los Cabos means "the Capes" and refers to two resort towns that perch on the southern tip of Baja 22 miles apart: San José del Cabo and Cabo San Lucas. Because each has its own distinctive character and attractions, they are treated separately. It is possible to stay in one and make day trips to the other.

Note: The one airport that serves both towns is 7½ miles northwest of San José del Cabo and 22 miles northeast of Cabo San Lucas.

SAN JOSÉ DEL CABO

122 miles S of La Paz, 22 miles E of Cabo San Lucas,
1,100 miles S of Tijuana

GETTING THERE   **By Plane**   **Aero California** has nonstop or direct flights from Los Angeles, Phoenix, and San Diego, and anticipates adding service from Dallas/Fort Worth; **Alaska Airlines** flies from Los Angeles, San Diego, San Francisco and Seattle; and **Mexicana Airlines** flies from Denver, Guadalajara, Los Angeles, Mazatlán, Mexico City, Monterrey, Puerto Vallarta, and San Francisco.

By Bus   The companies **Tres Estrellas de Oro** (first class) and **Aguila** (second class) operate buses arriving from Cabo San Lucas and La Paz almost hourly throughout the day and early evening. The trip from Cabo San Lucas takes 40 minutes; from La Paz the *Via Corta* (shorter route) buses take 2½ hours and the other buses 3½ hours.

By Car   From La Paz take Hwy 1 south, a scenic and curvy route that winds through foothills and occasionally skirts the eastern coastline; the drive takes 3 to 4 hours. Or from La Paz take Hwy 1 south just past the village of San Pedro, then Hwy 19 south (a less winding road than Hwy 1) through Todos Santos to Cabo San Lucas, where you pick up Hwy 1 east to San José del Cabo; this route takes 2 to 3 hours. From Cabo San Lucas it's a half-hour drive.

DEPARTING By Plane Airline offices: **Aero California,** no office in town (airport tel. 2-0943), **Aeroméxico,** Zaragoza and Hidalgo (tel. 2-0398, 2-0598, or airport tel. 2-0399), **Alaska Airlines,** no office in town (airport tel. 2-1015, 2-1016, or 2-1017), **Mexicana Airlines,** Plaza Los Cabos on Paseo San José across from the hotel zone (tel. 2-0192 or 2-0230).

By Bus The companies **Tres Estrellas de Oro** (first class) and **Aguila** (second class) operate buses to Cabo San Lucas almost hourly from around 6am to 10pm, and to La Paz every hour or two between 6am and 7pm (for points farther north you usually change buses in La Paz). For La Paz, buy a ticket the day before for the *Via Corta* (the shorter route), and request a window seat on the shady side of the bus (depending on the time of day). At the moment, the *Via Corta* buses depart at 7am, 9:30am, 3pm, and 4pm. The new bus station (*Terminal de Autobuses*), on Valerio Gonzalez a block east of Hwy 1 (tel. 2-1100), is open daily from 5:30am to 9pm—though buses can arrive and depart later.

Despite the tap-tap-tap of new construction, San José del Cabo retains the air of a provincial Mexican village, with its one- and two-story pastel buildings crowding narrow streets and the shady plaza, church, and bandstand at its heart. This town of 24,000 people seems older and more typically Mexican than Cabo San Lucas, and though it does have a modest nightlife, San José is the more sedate of the two "Cabos."

ORIENTATION

ARRIVING By Plane Upon arriving at the airport, buy a ticket inside the building for a colectivo, vans that take groups of passengers to hotels. The fare to San José del Cabo is $4 per person. The taxi fare is $9, which could be shared by four people.

By Bus From the bus station to the budget hotels downtown or the beachside hotel zone is too far to walk with luggage. A taxi from the bus station to either area costs $1.50 to $2.50.

INFORMATION Tourist information booths at the Los Cabos airport and on San José's town square should be open soon, daily from 9am to 5pm. Until then, gather information at travel agencies in the hotels or in town.

CITY LAYOUT San José del Cabo consists of two zones: **downtown,** where the budget hotels are located, and the ritzier hotel zone along the beach, called **Playa Hotelera.**

Zaragoza is the downtown's main street; **Malecón San José** (also called Paseo San José) runs parallel to the beach and is the principal boulevard of the hotel zone. Mile-long **Boulevard Mijares** connects the two areas.

GETTING AROUND

There is no local bus service between downtown and beach; a **taxi** from one to the other costs $2.50 to $3.

For day trips to Cabo San Lucas, catch a bus for $1.50 (see "Departing," above) or a cab for $20 one way. **Bicycles** rent for $8 to $10 a day from the Stouffer Presidente Hotel (tel. 2-0211) or Las Misiones Hotel (tel. 2-0985), both on Malecón San José in the hotel zone. **Vagabundo's,** also on Malecón San José, near the Stouffer Presidente, rents motorcycles, scooters, and ATVs (all-terrain vehicles) for $22 a day and up; scooters can also be rented at the Fiesta Inn on Malecón San José (tel. 2-0701) for $7 an hour or $22 a day and up.

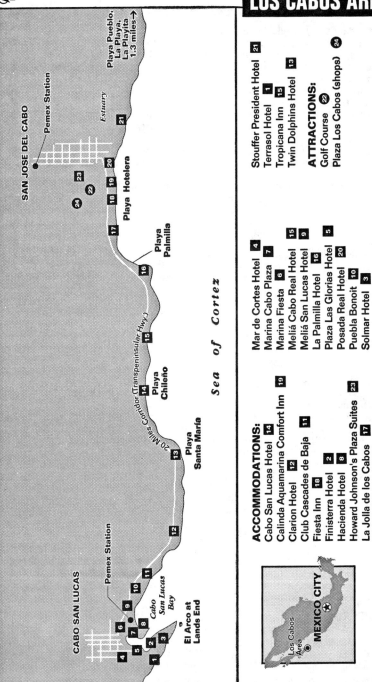

LOS CABOS AREA

ACCOMMODATIONS:

Cabo San Lucas Hotel [14]
Calinda Aquamarina Comfort Inn [19]
Clarion Hotel [12]
Club Cascades de Baja [11]
Fiesta Inn [18]
Finisterra Hotel [2]
Hacienda Hotel [8]
Howard Johnson's Plaza Suites [23]
La Jolla de los Cabos [17]

Mar de Cortes Hotel [4]
Marina Cabo Plaza [7]
Marina Fiesta [6]
Meliá Cabo Real Hotel [15]
Meliá San Lucas Hotel [9]
La Palmilla Hotel [16]
Plaza Las Glorias Hotel [5]
Posada Real Hotel [20]
Puebla Bonoit [10]
Solmar Hotel [3]

Stouffer President Hotel [21]
Terrasol Hotel [1]
Tropicana Inn [15]
Twin Dolphins Hotel [13]

ATTRACTIONS:

Golf Course [22]
Plaza Los Cabos (shops) [24]

MEXICO CITY

Los Cabos Area

FAST FACTS

Area code   The telephone area code is 684.

Banks   Banks exchange currency Monday through Friday from 9 to 11am. There are two banks on Zaragoza between Morelos and Degollado.

Books   Used paperbacks in English are for sale or exchange at **Andre Mar** restaurant, Boulevard Mijares 34 (tel. 2-0374), open daily from 8am to 10pm.

Business Hours   Shops are generally open Monday through Saturday from 9 or 10am to 7 or 8pm; some close for lunch between 1 and 4pm.

Municipal Market   It's on Mauricio Castro and Green, two long blocks south of the main street, Zaragoza. It's short on handcrafts but long on produce and local color.

Post Office   The Correos is on Zaragoza just west of the main square, open Monday through Friday from 8am to 1pm and 3 to 7pm, and on Saturday from 9am to 1pm.

Telephone   Long-distance calls can be made from the building on Zaragoza near Morelos, open Monday through Saturday from 9am to 9pm and on Sunday from 9am to 2pm.

WHAT TO SEE & DO

San José del Cabo is a fine place to unwind, ride horses across the sand, play golf, shop, and absorb its authentic Mexican flavor. Although many water sports can be arranged, the town beach, or Playa Hotelera, is not a true swimming beach because the currents and undertow make swimming risky. At the moment San José has no marina, though construction of one between the town beach and Pueblo La Playa to the east was scheduled to begin in 1991. Beach aficionados who would like to explore the beautiful coves and beaches along the 22-mile coast between the two Cabos should factor in the cost of a rental car ($50 a day and up) for a day or two. Frequent bus service between San José del Cabo and Cabo San Lucas make it possible to take in the pleasures of both towns.

BEACHES   The nearest safe swimming beach is **Playa Pueblo la Playa** (also called "La Playita"), located about 2 miles east of town: From Boulevard Mijares, turn east at the small sign PUEBLO LA PLAYA and follow the dirt road through cane fields and palms to a beach where a number of *pangas* (skiffs) belonging to local fishermen are pulled up. Not far from the beach is a good restaurant (see "Where to Eat," below). A taxi to Puebla la Playa beach costs about $5 one way. Or you can walk to this beach from the beach beside the Stouffer Presidente Hotel—it's a little over a mile east.

A fine swimming beach with beautiful rock formations is **Playa Palmilla,** 5 miles west of San José, near the Spanish colonial-style Hotel Palmilla—an elegant place to splurge on lunch or dinner. To reach Playa Palmilla, take a taxi to the road that leads to the Hotel Palmilla grounds for about $5, then take the fork to the left (without entering the hotel grounds) and follow signs to Pepe's restaurant on the beach. Cheaper still, buy a ticket on the bus to San Lucas and ask the driver to drop you at the Hotel Palmilla turnoff. To return, stand near the highway and flag down the next bus back to San José: Buses generally run until 9 or 10pm, but stick to daylight hours for such "bus-hiking." Another option is catching a cab from the Hotel Palmilla, though it's a long walk into the hotel's grounds where the cabs are stationed.

For other beaches worth exploring if you have a rental car, see "What to See and Do" in Cabo San Lucas, below.

SUNSET CRUISES   Boats depart from Cabo San Lucas and the cruise includes music, open bar, and dinner at a seafood restaurant for $40 per person. Arrange through a travel agency.

Surfing   Boardheads can test their skills from March to November at Punta Colorada, up the east coast from San José del Cabo.

WATER SPORTS Fishing   At **Playa Pueblo la Playa,** local fishermen take visitors deep-sea fishing for $130 for 6 hours, generally from 6am to noon. This cost

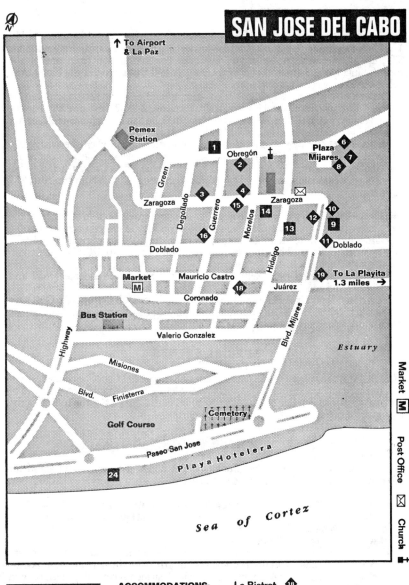

SAN JOSE DEL CABO

To Airport & La Paz

Pemex Station

Obregón

Plaza Mijares

Green

Zaragoza

Degollado

Guerrero

Morelos

Hidalgo

Zaragoza

Doblado

Doblado

Market

Mauricio Castro

To La Playita 1.3 miles →

Coronado

Juárez

Bus Station

Valerio Gonzalez

Blvd. Mijares

Estuary

Misiones

Blvd. Finisterra

Golf Course

Cemetery

Paseo San Jose

Playa Hotelera

Highway

Sea of Cortez

Market Ⓜ

Post Office ✉

Church ✝

San Jose del Cabo

MEXICO CITY

ACCOMMODATIONS:
Calinda Hotel 24
Ceci Hotel 14
Colli Hotel 13
San José Inn 1
Tropicana Inn 9

DINING:
Andre Mar Restaurant 19
Los Arcos Restaurant 3
La Baguette 6

Le Bistrot 18
Café Europa 8
Chino Bar Canton 4
Damiana Restaurant 7
Diana Restaurant 15
Kepy's Pizza 2
Posada Terranova 16
Sandricks 11
Tropicana del Cabo 10

can be divided among two or three people, depending on how many the *panga* holds. The **Hotel Palmilla** (tel. 2-0582), which has its own fleet, offers an afternoon trip for $75 (up to three anglers can share the cost). For information from one of the sport-fishing operators in Puebla la Playa, contact **Bill Sorenson** at the Hotel Colli (tel. 2-0052) between 2pm and 4pm.

Snorkeling and Diving   Trips start around $35 per person and can be arranged through travel agencies (try TourCabos, tel. 2-0982), the dive shop at the Hotel Palmilla (tel. 2-0582), or Amigos del Mar in Cabo San Lucas (tel. 3-0022, or toll free 800/447-8999 in the U.S., or in California 213/546-1447).

Whale Watching   From December through March, when the whales are offshore, the fishermen at **Playa Pueblo la Playa** will take small groups out to see the whales; a 4-hour trip runs about $40 per person. **TourCabos** (tel. 2-0982) arranges whale watching for groups of four or more people; the 2-hour trip costs $35 per person.

LAND SPORTS   Golf   Tee off from 7am to 4pm (to 4:30pm in summer) at the nine-hole **Club Campo de Golf Los Cabos,** on Paseo Finisterra across from the Howard Johnson Hotel (tel. 2-0905 for golf reservations). The greens fee is $18 for nine holes and $27 for 18 holes; clubs are $12; a golf cart, $14 to $20. Club guests can use the swimming pool.

Horseback Riding   Rent horses near the Stouffer Presidente Hotel and canter along the beach for $8 to $10 an hour.

Tennis   Tennis is available at the two courts of the **Club Campo de Golf Los Cabos** (tel. 2-0905) for $7 an hour during the day, $11 an hour at night. Club guests can use the swimming pool.

SPECIAL EVENTS

March 19 is the festival of the patron saint of San José del Cabo, celebrated with a fair, music, dancing, feasting, horse races, and cock fights. **June 19** is the festival of the patron saint of San Bartolo, a village 62 miles north. **July 25** is the festival of the patron saint of Santiago, a village 34 miles north.

WHERE TO STAY

Because San José has only a handful of budget hotels, it's best to call ahead for reservations. If this is not possible, try to arrive early, when others are checking out.

HOTEL CECI, Zaragoza 22, San José del Cabo, B.C.S. 23400. Tel. 684/2-0051 (at the store next door, open Mon–Sat 9am–1pm and 3–7pm). 12 rms (all with bath).
$ Rates: $13 single; $18 double.
Be prepared to wake up at 6am when the church bells sound, and toll every hour until 9pm. The white walls could use fresh paint, but otherwise the plain, cell-like rooms are clean and come with table fans and a chair. A shaded second-floor terrace with metal chairs provides a bit more space. The hotel is two blocks west of the town square on Zaragoza, across from the church.

SAN JOSÉ INN, Obregón 2 (Apdo. Postal 192), San José del Cabo, B.C.S. 23400. Tel. 684/2-1428. 23 rooms (all with bath).
$ Rates: $20 single; $25 double.
★ Recently remodeled with pastel colors, this clean, two-story hotel has ceiling fans, TV in the lobby, and a patio and snack bar in the backyard, where a pool is planned. At the moment only 15 rooms are open. It's about three blocks west on Obregón (one street north of Zaragoza) from the town plaza to Guerrero.

HOTEL COLLI, Hidalgo 10, San José del Cabo, B.C.S. 23400. 12 rms (all with bath).

$ Rates: May–Oct, $22.50 single; $31.50 double; $40.50 triple. Nov–Apr, $28.50 single; $38 double; $47.50 triple.

Minimally decorated with boxy contemporary furniture, these small, clean rooms occupy the second and third floors of an apartmentlike building. Those facing the street have private balconies and all have fans. Guests can picnic in the sun at the three tables on the third-story terrace. Laundry service can be arranged with the maids. The hotel is one block south of Zaragoza on Hidalgo.

POSADA TERRANOVA, Degollado, San José del Cabo, B.C.S. 23400. Tel. 684/2-0534. 5 rms (all with bath). A/C TV

$ Rates: $39 single; $45 double. Extra person $7.

The nicest budget hotel in town offers clean, spacious rooms with generous windows and simple furniture. The upstairs room is actually a suite with two double beds and a small kitchen. Guests can watch TV in the cheerful restaurant and bar on the ground floor, which has a dining patio and tables covered with green linens (open daily from 7:30am to 3pm and 6 to 10:30pm). In the next year the owner hopes to build 15 more rooms behind the existing property. The Posada is on Degollado, between Zaragoza and Doblado.

Worth the Extra Bucks

CALINDA AQUAMARINA COMFORT INN, Malecón San José, San José del Cabo, B.C.S. 23400. Tel. 684/2-0110 or 2-0077, or toll free 91-800/90-000 in Mexico, 800/228-5151 in the U.S. Fax 684/2-0287. 99 rms (all with bath). A/C TEL

$ Rates: $67–$90 single or double. **Parking:** Free parking lot in front.

Right on the beach, the pleasant motel-style rooms occupy several three-story buildings arranged around a large pool (heated in winter) and cactus gardens. Upper rooms have balconies and guests enjoy a restaurant and lobby bar on the premises.

TROPICANA INN, c/o Tropicana del Cabo Restaurant, Blvd. Mijares 30, San José del Cabo, B.C.S. 23400. Tel. 684/5-2684 or 2-0907. 40 rms (all with bath). A/C TV TEL

$ Rates: $86 single or double. **Parking:** Free.

Scheduled to open in March 1991, this neo-Spanish colonial-style hotel frames a courtyard with a graceful arcade bordering the rooms. Each medium-sized room in the L-shaped building (a two- and a three-story wing) comes with two double beds, a TV with U.S. channels, a window looking out on the courtyard, and bath with shower. Amenities include parking, a swimming pool, and room service until 11pm from the adjacent Tropicana del Cabo Restaurant and Bar (owned by the hotel). It's behind the restaurant a block south of the town square.

FIESTA INN, Malecón San José, San José del Cabo, B.C.S. 23400. Tel. 684/2-0701, or toll free 800/FIESTA-1 in the U.S. Fax 684/2-0480. 157 rms (all with bath). A/C TV TEL

$ Rates: $105–$127 single or double.

A jumble of stucco arches painted soft colors dominates this beachside three-story hotel, which always appears to be hopping with activity. Amenities include a restaurant and outdoor snack bar, laundry service, in-house travel agency, and two bars: an open-air lobby bar with live music nightly, and another beside the beach and large swimming pool, which is heated in winter. Each room is decorated in cool pastels, with pale rattan furniture, a TV with U.S. channels, a marble-trimmed bathroom, and a tile balcony with table and chairs to add a touch of luxury. Scooters can be rented at the hotel travel agency for $7 an hour or $22 a day.

WHERE TO EAT
Meals For Less Than $5

LA BAGUETTE, San José town plaza. Tel. 2-1125.
  Specialty: FRENCH/MEXICAN BAKERY.
$ Prices: Bread and rolls 15¢–$2.

Open: Mon–Sat 8am–8pm.

Stock up on the staff of life *à la française,* with Mexican *pan dulce,* or hearty doughnuts at this new bakery with its spanking-white walls and its squeaky-clean, white tile floors. Besides slender baguettes, you can find whole-wheat bread here. This is a good stop for breakfast pastries or for picnic supplies. It's on the east side of the town square and next to the Damiana restaurant.

SANDRICK'S, Blvd. Mijares 28.
Specialty: MEXICAN.
$ **Prices:** Main courses $2–$4; beer $1.
Open: Wed–Mon 2–9pm.

This open-air, upstairs restaurant, on the second story above some offices, just south of Bing's pink ice-cream store, is shaded by a palapa hung with plants and cooled by breezes and fans. In the center is a small open kitchen where you can watch the fajitas, tacos, chimichangas, and burgers being made.

LOS TORITOS, Plaza Los Cabos, Malecón San José.
Specialty: MEXICAN.
$ **Prices:** Breakfast $3–$5; soup or quesadillas $2–$3; main courses $2–$7; fish tacos or burgers $4.50–$6.
Open: Daily 7am–10pm.

This cheerful, ranch-rustic eatery in a shopping center on Malecón San José, near Highway 1 and opposite the Fiesta Inn, is popular with the locals, especially in the morning when coffee is free with a full breakfast. Guests sit outdoors at umbrella-shaded tables or inside at substantial wooden tables watched over by bulls' heads mounted on the walls. American radio news may be playing in the background. For lunch or a snack, try the quesadillas or fish tacos.

Meals For Less Than $10

RESTAURANT CHINO BAR CANTON, on Zaragoza between Morelos and Guerrero. Tel. 2-0403.
Specialty: CHINESE.
$ **Prices:** Appetizers $1.50–$8; main courses $6.75–$11.25; soups $2.75–$10; daily special with drink (beer or soda) $7.75.
Open: Daily 1–10pm.

Diners with a yen for Oriental flavors chow down on Chinese noodles, chicken "Zsechuan," shrimp "embroiled," and myriad other dishes at tables set with colorful plastic dishes and bright-orange linens. An open-air roof terrace provides a fine view of hills and palm trees. Half the fun here is reading the menu. The restaurant is two blocks west of the town square, above the Curios Mexico shop.

KEPY'S PIZZA, Obregón, west of Hidalgo. Tel. 2-1426.
Specialty: ITALIAN.
$ **Prices:** Salads $2.25–$3.75; buffalo chicken wings $5.50; subs $3.75–$4.50; spaghetti dinner $5.50; pizza $6.75–$11.25.
Open: Daily 4–11pm.

Roosters crowing in not-too-distant backyards serenade diners downing pizza and pasta at the three tables on the tiny red-and-white porch overlooking the quiet street. Two more tables crowd inside the restaurant, which also makes deliveries.

LOS ARCOS, Zaragoza 222. Tel. 2-0022.
Specialty: MEXICAN/AMERICAN.
$ **Prices:** Soup of the day $3.50; sandwiches $4.25–$5; main courses $9.50–$12; tacos or ceviche $5.50.
Open: Mon–Sat 7am–10pm, Sun noon–10pm.

Half a dozen cloth-covered tables crowd the high porch shaded by a vine-draped trellis, where diners look out over the passing street scene. Inside, the simple fare is served up from behind a wooden counter. Los Arcos is on Zaragoza west of Guerrero.

RESTAURANT/BAR DIANA, Zaragoza 30. Tel. 2-0490.

Specialty: MEXICAN.

$ **Prices:** Soup $4.50–$7; tacos, enchiladas, burgers, or egg dishes $4.50; seafood dishes $8–$16; beer $1.50; margarita $2.25.

Open: Daily 8am–10pm.

Both locals and visitors enjoy the hearty fare dished up at the dozen or so dinette tables on the second-story, open-air terrace overlooking the street. A bar with a color TV is through a door in the back of the restaurant. It's on Zaragoza between Morelos and Guerrero.

LA PLAYITA, Pueblo la Playa. Tel. 2-1163.

Specialty: MEXICAN/SEAFOOD.

$ **Prices:** Appetizers $5.50–$8; main courses $6.50–$15; Mexican plate $8; beer $1.50.

Open: Daily 10am–10pm.

Jungley gardens lead to the entrance of this breezy, casual restaurant under a large thatched roof, while painted plaster fish and tortoise shells enliven the wall behind the long wooden bar. Some of the freshest fish in Los Cabos is served here since fishing is the main occupation of the village. You'll find La Playita set back from the beach at Pueblo la Playa, a fishing village 2 miles east of San José.

CAFE EUROPA, San José town plaza. Tel. 2-1218.

Specialty: EUROPEAN/DELI.

$ **Prices:** Not available.

Open: Daily 8am–10pm.

Though the paint was just drying and prices weren't set on my last visit, this sleek deli and café on the east side of the town square looks promising, and adds yet another European culinary presence to San José. It's owned by two women—one from Poland, the other from Ireland—who plan to serve espresso, cappuccino, sandwiches, salads, pizzas, homemade desserts, and a deli-style assortment of imported cheeses, pâtés, smoked salmon, and other goodies. Word also has it that an English-style pub is planned next door.

Worth the Extra Bucks

LE BISTROT, Morelos 4. Tel. 2-1174.

Specialty: FRENCH/ITALIAN. **Reservations:** Recommended in December and for groups of six or more.

$ **Prices:** Soup of the day $3.25; main courses $9–$20; sandwiches $3–$4.25; pizza or lasagne $7; breakfast buffet $7.

Open: Mon 6–10pm, Tues–Sun 8:30am–10pm (closed 4–6pm daily Sept–Oct).

For a special treat, seek out Le Bistrot, a European restaurant in a cozy stucco house with a fireplace and a pretty garden patio about five blocks south of Zaragoza on Morelos. The Belgian couple who own and run it prepare delicious soups, lasagne, beef or cheese fondue, meat and seafood dishes, and homemade desserts. Ask about the daily special.

DAMIANA, San José town plaza. Tel. 2-0499.

Specialty: MEXICAN/SEAFOOD. **Reservations:** Recommended during the Christmas and Easter holidays.

$ **Prices:** Appetizers $4–$8; main courses $8.50–$30; breakfast or light lunch dishes $5.50–$9; soup $6. Lower-priced menu daily 10:30am–5pm.

Open: Daily 10:30am–11pm. **Closed:** When it rains, which is very rare.

This elegant restaurant on the east side of the town plaza is decorated like an 18th-century mansion. Mariachis add to the romantic ambience by playing nightly from 6:30 to 9pm (mid-December to mid-May) in the tropical courtyard, where candles flicker under the trees and bougainvillea. For an appetizer, try the cheese soup—laced with cilantro, poblano peppers, and thick chunks of cheese—or the mushrooms "Diablo," a moderately zesty temptation.

LA PALOMA, in the Hotel Palmilla, Punta Palmilla. Tel. 2-0582.
Specialty: MEXICAN/CONTINENTAL. **Reservations:** Recommended.
$ Prices: Sun brunch $27, plus drinks and tip.
Open: Breakfast daily 6:30–10:30am; lunch daily noon–3pm; dinner daily 6–9:30pm; brunch Sun 11:30am–2:30pm.

Sunday brunch here is a lavish buffet with both Mexican and continental dishes, including pâté, ceviche (marinated fish), baked ham, crêpes, eggs Benedict, roast beef, enchiladas, chiles relleños, mousse, and cheesecake. But the spectacular setting provides the best sauce: an airy, Spanish hacienda–style room overlooking the sea, edged with terraces and high open arches that let in the breeze. Mariachis and sometimes a Peruvian group serenade diners. Take a swimsuit along for a dip at the beach later. It's about 5 miles east of San José on Highway 1.

SHOPPING

The handful of tourist shops are clustered around **Boulevard Mijares** and the town's main street, **Zaragoza.** Also worth exploring is **Obregón,** a block north of and parallel to Zaragoza, which is beginning to sprout with new shops. A few open-air stalls selling handcrafts and souvenirs, where bargaining is essential, edge Boulevard Mijares. The municipal market on Mauricio Castro and Green sells mainly edible and utilitarian wares.

LA CASA VIEJA BOUTIQUE, Blvd. Mijares 27. Tel. 2-0599.
One of the oldest and most beautiful shops in San José, this boutique brims with carefully selected Mexican crafts, unusual jewelry, and pretty resortwear. Open daily 9am to 7pm December through April; closed Sunday May through June; closed 2:30 to 4:30pm and Sunday July through September.

LA BAMBA, Blvd. Mijares 33. Tel. 3-0385.
This shop specializes in original hand-painted clothing, canvas shoes, and accessories. Open Monday through Saturday from 9am to noon and 4 to 7pm.

LA MINA, Blvd. Mijares 33.
Silver jewelry from Taxco, leather bags and accessories, and cowboy boots are featured in this new shop decorated to resemble a silver mine. It's open Monday through Saturday from 9am to 1pm and 4 to 7pm.

ANTIGUA LOS CABOS, Zaragoza 20. Tel. 2-0233.
Fine arts, crafts, jewelry, and furniture from Tlaquepaque spread from the high-ceilinged rooms to the patio out back. Especially nice is the selection of ceramics. Open Monday through Saturday from 9am to 6pm.

GALERIA DE LOS CABOS, Obregón 21 near Morelos.
Heavy carved-wood furniture and rustic *equipales* are the staples of this new shop. Open Monday through Saturday from 9am to 1:30pm and 4 to 7pm.

EVENING ENTERTAINMENT

Nightlife in San José revolves mainly around the restaurants and large hotels. So far there's only one disco (see below), though a new one is scheduled to open soon on Boulevard Mijares. This boulevard is the town's "restaurant row," where you can amble along until you find the restaurant or watering hole with the most appealing music. Several of the hotels have **"Mexican Fiestas"** and other weekly theme nights that include a buffet (usually all you can eat), drinks, live music, and entertainment for $25 to $35 per person. These can be both fun and a good value for a splurge. For more information, call the Stouffer Presidente (tel. 2-0211), Howard Johnson (tel. 2-0999), Fiesta Inn (tel. 2-0701), or Hotel Palmilla (tel. 2-0582).

IGUANA BAR & GRILL, Blvd. Mijares 24. Tel. 2-0266.

This lively, open-air bar and restaurant is sheltered by a broad thatched roof and boasts a patio under the stars. Live music and dancing get cranking around 9:30pm and can last until 1am. At the moment this is the most "happening" nightspot in San José. Should hunger strike, the house specialty is barbecued ribs. It's open Wednesday through Monday from 11am to 1am; happy hour is 5 to 6pm. Drinks run $1.50 to $3.50.

VIDEO DISCO CACTUS, in the Stouffer Presidente Hotel, Blvd. Mijares and Malecón San José. Tel. 2-0211.

The town's only disco, equipped with video screens and laser lighting effects, is at its best on weekends. Open Tuesday through Sunday from 10pm to 3am. Drinks cost $4 and up.
Admission: $5; free to hotel guests.

TROPICANA DEL CABO BAR & GRILL, Blvd. Mijares 30. Tel. 2-0907.

Ensconced in leather barrel chairs in the large bar, guests tune in to American sports events on the big-screen TV during the day. Come evening, mariachis play Wednesday through Saturday from 5 to 9pm. And on Friday and Saturday night in the patio restaurant in the next room, a Mexican folkloric dance show entertains diners from 7 to 8pm. After 9pm on some nights a rock band plays for those inclined to dance. It's open daily from 7am to 1am. Drinks go for $3 and up.

LOBBY BAR, in the Fiesta Inn, Malecón San José. Tel. 2-0701.

Set well back from the beach but within earshot of the waves, this open-air lobby bar features a singer Tuesday through Sunday night from 6 to 10:30pm. Drinks cost $3 and up.

LA PALOMA CANTINA, in the Hotel Palmilla, 5 miles east of San José on Hwy. 1. Tel. 2-0582.

Perched on rocky Punta Palmilla overlooking the sea, this is one of the most romantic spots in Los Cabos to watch the waves and setting sun. And during the "Fiesta Hour" from 4 to 6:30pm there are complimentary hot and cold hors d'ouevres. In the evening, Sunday through Wednesday from 6:30 to 9pm a guitar player entertains guests, while Thursday through Saturday a Latin American group plays haunting Peruvian music from 6 to 9pm, followed by a band for dancing from 9:30 to 11:30pm. Call ahead to confirm who is playing and when before spending the $12 or more for round-trip taxi fare from San José. The bar is open from 11:30am to 11:30pm daily.

CABO SAN LUCAS

110 miles S of La Paz, 22 miles W of San José del Cabo,
1,120 miles S of Tijuana

GETTING THERE   By Plane   Aero California has nonstop or direct flights from Los Angeles, Phoenix, and San Diego; **Alaska Airlines** flies from Los Angeles, San Diego, San Francisco, and Seattle; and **Mexicana Airlines** flies from Denver, Guadalajara, Los Angeles, Mazatlán, Mexico City, Monterrey, Puerto Vallarta, and San Francisco.

By Bus   The companies **Tres Estrellas de Oro** (first class) and **Aguila** (second class) operate buses arriving from San José del Cabo and La Paz almost hourly throughout the day and early evening. The trip from San José del Cabo takes 40 minutes; from La Paz, the "Via Corta" (shorter route) buses take 2½ hours, and the other buses 4 hours.

By Car   From La Paz, take Highway 1 south past the village of San Pedro, then Highway 19 south through Todos Santos to Cabo San Lucas, a 2-hour drive.

Todos Santos has several restored historic buildings and makes a pleasant stop for a meal—try El Molino, an American-run restaurant in a converted sugar mill.

DEPARTING   By Plane   Airline offices are in town and/or at the airport: **Aero California,** Centro Comercial Plaza on Hidalgo (tel. 3-0827 or 3-0848, or 2-0943 at the airport); **Aeroméxico** (tel. 2-0399 at the airport); **Alaska Airlines** (tel. 2-1015, 2-1016, or 2-1017 at the airport); and **Mexicana,** Niños Héroes and Zaragoza (tel. 3-0411 or 3-0412).

By Bus   The companies **Tres Estrellas de Oro** (first class) and **Aguila** (second class) operate buses to San José del Cabo almost hourly from around 6:45am to 8pm, and to La Paz every hour or two between 6am and 6:30pm (for points farther north you usually change buses in La Paz). For La Paz, buy a ticket the day before for the "Via Corta" (the shorter route) buses, and request a window seat on the shady side of the bus (depending on the time of day). At the moment, the "Via Corta" buses to La Paz depart at 7am, 7:30am, 10:30am, 1pm, 3:30pm, and 5:30pm. The main bus station is two blocks from the waterfront, at Zaragoza and 16 de Septiembre (tel. 3-0400), open daily from 5am to 8pm.

Another bus station, on 16 de Septiembre a block east of Morelos, serves the **Transportes de La Paz** line (second class) with buses to La Paz between 6am and 7pm. It's not recommended, however—the buses look dirty and the one-room station is quite seedy.

Cabo San Lucas, with a population of 25,000 is the faster growing of the two resort towns. In the past few years, swanky new hotels and sleek condos have nearly doubled around the harbor and in the steep hills that frame the picturesque blue bay where private American yachts have been dropping anchor since the 1950s. That era marked the beginning of Cabo San Lucas's fame as a mecca for marlin hunters (and other big-game fish), and many of its popular watering holes still retain the air of a yacht club mixed with the good-natured silliness of a fraternity party. San Lucas is definitely the party capital of Los Cabos, and has a flashy glamour that's less pronounced in San José. It's also the priciest resort in Baja.

ORIENTATION

ARRIVING   By Plane   Upon arriving at the airport, buy a ticket inside the building for a colectivo: The fare to Cabo San Lucas is $7 per person. The taxi fare is $28, which could be shared by four people. A new four-lane highway between the airport and Cabo San Lucas was scheduled to begin construction in 1991.

By Bus   From the bus station to most of the budget hotels downtown is not too far to walk with light luggage. A taxi from the bus station to most hotels should be under $4.

CITY LAYOUT   The small town spreads out north and west of the harbor of **Cabo San Lucas Bay,** edged by foothills and desert mountains to the west and south. The main street leading into town from the airport and San José del Cabo is **Lázaro Cárdenas;** as it nears the harbor, **Marina Boulevard** branches off from it and becomes the main artery that curves around the waterfront.

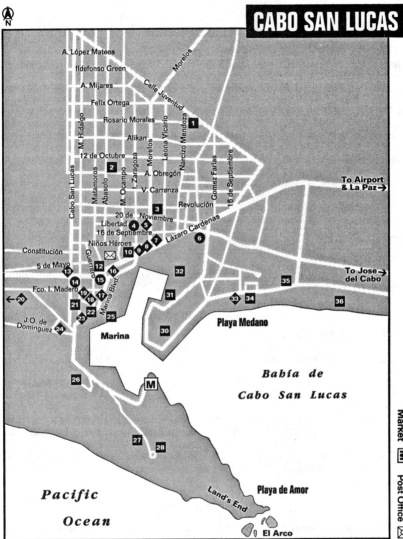

CABO SAN LUCAS

Market **M**

Post Office ⊠

ACCOMMODATIONS:
Club Cascades de Baja **36**
Crea Youth Hostel **21**
Finesterra Hotel **26**
Hacienda Hotel **30**
Las Margaritas Inn **10**
Mar de Cortez Hotel **12**
Marina Cabo Plaza **31**
Marina Fiesta **32**
Marina Hotel **22**
Melia San Lucas Hotel **34**
Plaza Las Glorias Hotel **25**
Pueblo Bonito **35**
Casa Blanca Hotel **3**

Scorpion Apartments **2**
Solmar Hotel **28**
Terrasol **1**

DINING:
Ali's Burger ◆**5**
El Faro Viejo II Deli ◆**20**
El Galeon Restaurant ◆**24**
Giggling Marlin ◆**16**
Kankun ◆**23**
Miguel's ◆**9**
Las Palmas ◆**33**
Papi's Deli ◆**19**
Pizza Oceano ◆**13**

Río Grill ◆**17**
Rosticería Pollo de Oro ◆**7**
Squid Row ◆**8**
Tacos Chidos ◆**18**

ATTRACTIONS:
Bus Station ●**4**
Cabo Wabo Cantina ●**15**
Lukas Disco ●**6**
Main Square ●**14**

GETTING AROUND

There is no local bus service in Cabo San Lucas; a **taxi** from downtown to the farthest hotels, such as the Solmar near Land's End or the Melia on Medano Beach, should run $4 to $6.

ATVs (all-terrain vehicles), **scooters,** and **motorcycles** rent for $8 to $15 an hour or $23 to $50 a day, and **bicycles** are $2.50 an hour or $10 a day from Chubasco's at Marina Boulevard 22 (tel. 3-0404), open daily from 8am to 6pm. *Note:* Be sure you are informed of the risks associated with ATVs, scooters, and motorcycles before riding one.

The quickest new way to get to Medano Beach from downtown is to catch the **water-taxi** at the marina by Plaza Las Glorias for $3. For day trips to San José del Cabo, catch a bus for $1.50 (see "Departing," above) or a cab for $20 one way.

Rental cars generally run $50 a day and up (try to negotiate one with free mileage). The Tourcabos Travel Agency, in the lobby of the Hotel Solmar (tel. 3-0449), had a special rate of $30 for a VW Beetle for 6 hours (including mileage, insurance, gas, and tax)—nice if you want to explore the beaches between the two towns.

INFORMATION Tourist information booths at the Los Cabos airport and on the town square (at Hidalgo and Madero) should be open soon, daily from 9am to 5pm. Until then, gather information at travel agencies in hotels or in town. For boating and other water sports, ask around at the town marina. *Note:* Beware of "Visitor Information" booths along the street—they're actually time-share hawkers.

FAST FACTS

Area Code   The telephone area code is 684.

Banks   Banks exchange currency Monday through Friday from 9 to 11am.

Business Hours   Shops are generally open Monday through Saturday from 9 or 10am to 7 or 8pm; some close for lunch between 1 and 4pm.

Groceries   The biggest and best supermarket is **Supermercado Plaza,** in Plaza Aramburo, on Cárdenas at Zaragoza (tel. 3-0939). It also has a good bakery. Open daily from 7am to 10pm.

Pharmacy   The largest drugstore in town, with a wide selection of toiletries as well as medicines, is **Farmacía Aramburo,** in Plaza Aramburo, on Cárdenas at Zaragoza, open daily from 7am to 9pm.

Post Office   The Correos is on Matamoros about a block north of Cárdenas, open Monday through Friday from 8am to 1pm and 3 to 7pm, and on Saturday from 9am to 1pm.

WHAT TO SEE & DO

Although superb sport fishing put Cabo San Lucas on the map, there's more to do here than dropping in your line and waiting for the Big One. But if that's your fancy, go for it. For most cruises and excursions, try to make reservations at least a day in advance; keep in mind that some trips require a minimum number of people. Fishing and most other sports and outings can be arranged through a travel agency.

SPORT FISHING   Begin at the town marina on the south side of the harbor, where you'll find about two dozen fleet operators with their stands beside the docks, waiting to sign up sports fishermen—and women. And you may save some money this way: At the north end of the marina, for instance, **Fernando Leyva** (tel. 3-0618) offers *pangas* with captain and equipment for $25 to $30 an hour (which could be divided among three people). The going rate for a day on a fully equipped Bertram with captain and guide (many of the larger hotels, like the Solmar, have their own fleets) starts around $200.

The fishing really is as spectacular as they say: Bringing in a marlin over 100 pounds is routine. Angling is good all year, though the catch varies with the season: Sailfish, swordfish, and wahoo are best from June through November; yellowfin tuna from

May through December; yellowtail from January through April; black and blue marlin July through December; and striped marlin all year.

BEACHES All along the curving sweep of sand known as **Medano Beach or Rafa's Beach,** on the east side of the bay, you can rent snorkeling gear, boats, kayaks, pedalboats, and windsurf boards (and get windsurfing lessons). This is the town's main beach—a great place for safe swimming as well as people-watching from one of the many outdoor restaurants along its shore.

Another good beach for swimming and snorkeling is **Playa de Amor (Lover's Beach),** south of town near the soaring rock formations that mark Land's End like exclamation points. It costs $25 an hour to rent your own *panga* to go to Playa de Amor from the marina. You can also negotiate with someone at the marina to take you and pick you up later for $15 to $20. Cheapest of all is to ride there on one of the glass-bottom boats ("Fondo de Cristal") from the marina for $5 round-trip: Because they come and go all day, you can catch a later one back (but make sure you check on the time of the last one).

Beach aficionados may want to rent a car (see "Getting Around," above) and explore the half dozen out-of-the-way beaches and coves between the two Cabos: **Playas Palmilla, Bledito, Chileno, Santa María, Barco Varado,** and **Vista del Arcos.** Palmilla, Bledito, and Santa María are generally safe for swimming; the others are for the view only or for experienced snorkelers. Always check at a hotel or travel agency for directions and swimming conditions. Although some travel agencies run snorkeling tours to some of these beaches, there's no public transportation: Your options are renting a car ($50 a day and up) or "bus-hiking"—catching the bus to San José and asking the driver to drop you off at one of the beach turnoffs (depending on the beach, it can be a long walk from the highway to the beach).

CRUISES   Glass-bottom boats leave from the town marina daily, every 20 minutes between 9am and 4pm. For $5 per person, the tour takes you past sea lions and pelicans to see the famous "El Arco" (rock arch) at Land's End, where the Pacific and the Sea of Cortez meet. Most make a brief stop at Lover's Beach or will drop you off there if you ask; you can use your ticket to catch a later boat back (but be sure to check on the time of the last boat). The Dos Mares glass-bottom boats (tel. 3-0402 or 3-0885) also depart from the Melia Hotel at Medano Beach; they also run **whale-watching cruises** when the leviathans come to call between December and March.

A **sunset cruise** on the 46-foot trimaran *Trinidad* (tel. 3-1477) also leaves from this dock at 5pm. The $25 cost of the cruise includes margaritas, beer, and other drinks. A 42-foot catamaran, the *Pez Gato,* offers a similar sunset cruise at 4:45pm for the same price. Look for a booth near the marina marked PEZ GATO or ENRIQUE'S PLACE (tel. 3-0408 or 3-1083). The *Pez Gato* has another 2-hour cruise daily at 10am. If the whales are in, you'll probably see some on any of the cruises—including the inexpensive glass-bottom-boat trips.

ATV TRIPS Expeditions on ATVs (all-terrain vehicles) to visit Cabo Falso, an 1890 lighthouse, and La Candelaría, an Indian pueblo in the mountains, are organized by Chubasco's, a shop that rents ATVs, scooters, motorcycles, and bicycles. The 3-hour tour to **Cabo Falso** includes time at the beach, a look at some sea-turtle nests (without disturbing them) and the remains of a 1912 shipwreck, a ride over 500-foot sand dunes, and a visit to the lighthouse. The three tours leave daily at 9am, 12:30pm, and 4pm (the last one is a sunset tour) and cost around $40 per person, or $55 for two riding on one ATV.

La Candelaría is an isolated Indian village in the mountains 25 miles north of Cabo San Lucas. Written about in *National Geographic,* the old pueblo is known for the white and black witchcraft still practiced here. Lush with palms, mango trees, and bamboo, the settlement is watered by an underground river that emerges at the pueblo. The return trip travels down a steep canyon, along a beach (with time to swim), and past giant sea-turtle nesting grounds. Departing at 9:30am, the La Candelaría tour costs around $70 per person or $90 for two on the same ATV (a 220-lb. limit per vehicle applies to both tours).

Both trips include bilingual guides, goggles, bandanas, backpacks, and soft drinks; bring your own lunch. **Chubasco's** is located at Marina Boulevard 22 and at the Melia Hotel on Medano Beach (tel. 684/3-0404, or 706/843-0404 in the U.S., for reservations). Chubasco's is open daily from 8am to 6pm.

DAY TRIPS   Day trips to **La Paz** through a travel agency cost around $60, including lunch and a tour of the countryside along the way. Usually there's a stop at the weaving shop of Fortunato Silva in La Paz, who spins his own cotton and weaves it into wonderfully textured rugs and textiles.

SPORTS   Golf   For playing in Los Cabos, see "What to See and Do" in San José del Cabo.

Horseback Riding   You can rent horses from **Marco's Horse Rentals** at the Hacienda Hotel (tel. 3-0123); **Rancho Collins,** north of the Hotel Melia; or the **Finisterra Hotel stables** (tel. 3-000) for around $15 per hour. All have guided beach rides and sunset tours to El Faro Viejo (the Old Lighthouse) for $20 to $30 per person. Marco's is open daily from 7am to 6pm; Rancho Collins, daily from 8am to 5:30pm. The Finisterra stables open for the ride to the lighthouse that leaves at 3:30pm and returns at 6pm.

Snorkeling and Diving   The *Trinidad, Pez Gato,* and *Dos Mares* boats (see "Cruises," above) also offer snorkeling cruises that range from $6 to $30 per person. Among the beaches visited on different trips are Lover's Beach, Santa María, Chileno, and Barco Varado. Snorkeling gear rents for $6 to $10. For scuba diving, contact **Amigos del Mar** (tel. 3-0022 or 3-0554, or toll free 800/447-8999 in the U.S. or 213/546-1447 in California), which has an office west of the town marina on Marina Boulevard. Dives are made along the wall of a canyon in Cabo San Lucas Bay, where you can see a "sandfalls" that even Jacques Cousteau couldn't figure out—no one knows its source or cause. There are also scuba trips to Santa María Beach and farther places, including the Gordo Banks and Cabo Pulmo. Dives start at $35; gear rental is $20 per day. April through November are the best diving months. Reservations can be made in advance.

Surfing   There's good surfing to be found from March to November all along the beaches west of town, and a famous right break at Chileno Beach, near the Cabo San Lucas Hotel east of town.

SPECIAL EVENTS

October 12 is the festival of the patron saint of Todos Santos, a town about 60 miles north. **October 18** is the festival of the patron saint of Cabo San Lucas, celebrated with a fair, feasting, music, dancing, and special events.

WHERE TO STAY

Budget lodging is scarce in Cabo San Lucas. The handful of inexpensive hostelries often have no vacancies, so it's wise to call ahead for reservations or arrive early when other travelers are checking out.

CREA YOUTH HOSTEL, Av. de la Juventud, (no number), **Cabo San Lucas, B.C.S. 23410. Tel. 684/3-0148.** 1 dorm (shared baths) and 11 rms (all with bath).
$ Rates: $8–$12 single; $13–$15 double, $5 dormitory bunk. **Parking:** On street, unprotected.
In spite of the institution's prisonlike appearance, its modern one-story, brick-and-concrete buildings inside the wall offer functional, minimally furnished (mostly single beds), and reasonably clean accommodations with fans. A shaded outdoor area with a sink and counters provides a place in the big courtyard to prepare picnic-type meals,

and you can watch TV in the lobby. There's no age limit, but be aware that no alcohol is permitted. Its biggest drawback is the long walk from the center of town: Walk eight long blocks north (of Cárdenas) on Morelos, then turn right on Juventud and walk two more blocks to the large walled compound with the letters ISJD on the front.

HOTEL DOS MARES, Emiliano Zapata, Cabo San Lucas, B.C.S. 23410. Tel. 684/3-0330. 19 rms (all with bath).
$ Rates: $23 single or double; $26 triple.
This somewhat run-down, three-story hotel offers simple shoeboxlike rooms arranged around a courtyard where a huge almond tree makes a pleasant, shady sitting area with a small pool and a few tables and chairs. These double as outdoor seating for the hotel's café and bar, and the place and its young patrons exude the laid-back, friendly outlook of the 1960s. Fourteen rooms have air conditioning and the rest have table fans; some bathrooms lack doors. Best ask to see the room first—some are dark and dismal. There's a TV in the bar. The hotel is on Zapata between Hidalgo and Guerrero, about a block inland from Marina Boulevard.

HOTEL CASA BLANCA, Revolución and Morelos (Apdo. Postal 79), Cabo San Lucas, B.C.S. 23410. Tel. 684/3-0260. 30 rms (all with bath).
$ Rates: $18 single; $25 double; $28 triple. **Parking:** Free; guarded.
Located three long blocks from the harbor (from Cárdenas, walk three blocks north on Morelos and turn right at Revolución), this L-shaped, two-story hotel frames a dusty courtyard with a few shade trees and a palapa over a couple of picnic tables on a cement patio. Neat and clean, all rooms have windows and either ceiling or table fans. Some are freshly painted—ask to see more than one room. Off-street parking is not behind a locked fence but is watched by the clerk in the 24-hour office. Expect to pay a towel deposit of $5. Laundry service is available.

HOTEL MARINA, Marina Blvd. at Guerrero, Cabo San Lucas, B.C.S. 23410. Tel. 684/3-0030. 23 rms, 7 suites (all with bath). A/C
$ Rates: Winter, $36 single; $46 double. Summer, about $10 less.
This two-story hotel on Marina Boulevard, facing the Plaza las Glorias Hotel on the harbor, has 23 very basic cubicles and seven generous suites, some overlooking the swimming pool and courtyard, others overlooking the street (the hotel's view of the harbor is blocked by the new Plaza las Glorias Hotel). The suites on the street side are quite large but can be a bit noisy; they come with minibars, two double beds, chairs, and other solid wood furniture, plus a balcony, large tile bath, and a small freezer. Regular rooms are minimally furnished with a double bed and a shelf with a small mirror. The hotel's cheerful outdoor café facing the street is open daily from 3 to 11pm; happy hour is 4 to 6pm.

SCORPION APARTMENTS, Abasolo and Obregón (Apdo. Postal 126), Cabo San Lucas, B.C.S. 23410. Fax 684/3-1279 (10am–noon). 6 apartments (all with bath). A/C
$ Rates: $500 a month; $38 daily if available.
Don't be scared off by the name. More daunting is the lengthy walk (six long blocks inland on Abasolo to the corner of Obregón) from the heart of town to get here. The one-bedroom apartments have white stucco walls and come equipped with a furnished minikitchen, queen-size bed, and nice bath finished with tiny blue mosaic tiles.

Worth the Extra Bucks

HOTEL MAR DE CORTEZ, Cárdenas at Guerrero, Cabo San Lucas, B.C.S. 23410. Tel. 684/3-0032. 66 rms, 16 suites (all with bath). A/C
$ Rates: Dec to mid-June, $39 single; $45 double in the old section; the larger rooms of the new section run about $10 more; suites $15 more. Mid-June to Nov, about 20% less. 10% service charge added to all bills. **Parking:** Free; protected.
In a great location, on Cárdenas one block in from the marina in the center of town, this attractive two-story hotel arranged its Spanish-style white stucco building around a rambling, landscaped courtyard with swimming pool. The

smaller rooms of the older section have charming, dark-wood furniture and one or two single beds, a desk, and a tiny front porch facing the courtyard. A semi-outdoor bar with a fireplace under its thatched roof (!) for the sometimes-cool winter nights provides a pleasant gathering place for guests who share the general feeling of camaraderie here. There's also a restaurant with a TV, and a freezer for storing your fish. The place books up quickly, apparently because many patrons are regulars who return every year.

You can make reservations in the U.S.: P.O. Box 1827, Monterey, CA 93942 (tel. 408/375-4755, or toll free 800/347-6847).

LAS MARGARITAS INN, Cárdenas at Zaragoza (Apdo. Postal 354), Cabo San Lucas, B.C.S. 23410. Tel. and fax 684/3-0450. 16 suites (all with bath).

$ Rates: Mid-Dec to mid-Apr, $60 one-bedroom suite for one or two people; $80 two-bedroom suite for three or four people. Mid-Apr to mid-Dec, about $10 less. **Parking:** Free; unprotected.

Located on Cárdenas at Zaragoza in Plaza Aramburo in the heart of town across from the marina, this new three-story property features 14 one-bedroom and two two-bedroom suites, attractively decorated in white and pastels with contemporary furniture and a furnished kitchen. Each bedroom has a double bed and the living-rooms have sleeper-sofas. All suites open off the balconies on the second and third stories overlooking the marina across the street. Four of the suites have fans rather than air-conditioning, so check first if that's important. For what you get, this is a good value.

WHERE TO EAT

Prices, as a rule, decrease the farther you walk inland from the waterfront. For the best dining bargains, walk north along Morelos, heading inland from the sea.

Meals For Less Than $10

TACOS CHIDOS, Zapata.
Specialty: MEXICAN.
$ Prices: Appetizers $1–$1.50; main courses $1.50–$3.50; tacos $1; tamales $1.50; soup $2.50.
Open: Wed–Mon 7am–10pm.

At this tiny family-run place with an open kitchen behind the wooden counter, you can sit on a stool and watch some of the most delicious cheap eats in Cabos being prepared. Everything's fresh and homemade here, including the corn tortillas and several different salsas—try the incendiary brick-red version in the big stone *molcajete* (grinding bowl) or the tangy green one (kept cold in the refrigerator) if you like things hot! Fish tacos made with fresh dorado are superb. The place is on Zapata between Hidalgo and Guerrero, about a block in from Marina Boulevard.

ROSTICERÍA POLLO DE ORO, Cárdenas. Tel. 3-0310.
Specialty: GRILLED/MEXICAN.
$ Prices: Main courses $3–$8.
Open: Daily 6am–11pm.

In this unprepossesing cinderblock building open to the sidewalk on Cárdenas at Morelos, patrons at dinette tables and chairs chow down on juicy roasted chicken and barbecued ribs. You can watch the chickens roasting on the grills in the walls, and on a hot day it can get pretty warm here in spite of the fans. The small menu features Mexican dishes, too.

PAPI'S DELI, Hidalgo at Zapata.
Specialty: MEXICAN/DELI.
$ Prices: Breakfast specials $1–$2; appetizers $1–$4; main courses $3–$10; sandwiches $2–$4.50; chile relleño plate $5.
Open: Daily 7am–6pm.
Sandwiches, Mexican food, and ice cream are served indoors or outside at tables

under the trees just off the sidewalk. The shop will also prepare a box lunch, but request it a day ahead. Papi's is on Hidalgo about a block inland from Marina Boulevard.

PIZZA OCEANO, Cárdenas. Tel. 3-0931.
   Specialty: ITALIAN.
   $ Prices: Main courses $3.50–$6; spaghetti $5; pizzas $5–$13.
   Open: Daily noon–10:30pm.
   The specialty here is 12- and 16-inch pizzas cooked in a wood-fired oven in this one-room cottage with red-brick walls inside, lots of plants, and bright murals twining up the interior columns. Eat inside or grab one of the two tables on the high front porch overlooking the quiet street at the west end of Cárdenas between Juárez and San Lucas—this end of Cárdenas is like a little eddy apart from the bustle of town. The hefty servings of spaghetti with meat sauce almost looked like enough for two.

ALI'S BURGER, Morelos and 16 de Septiembre.
   Specialty: MEXICAN/MIDDLE EASTERN.
   $ Prices: Breakfast $2.50–$3; appetizers $1–$2; main courses $4–$5; taco or burrito $1; burger or tortas $1.50–$2.50.
   Open: Daily 7am–10pm.
This small palapa-shaded patio a block inland from Cárdenas on Morelos is a casual crossroads for international travelers. Diners sit at picnic tables or pull up stools at the outdoor kitchen counter to watch owner and chef Ali Gagi (a native of Algeria) make Mexican food, burgers, and sometimes couscous. While he works he may chat with visitors in six languages, including English. By special arrangement, this lively former hotel chef will prepare couscous for a small group, and will also custom cook or smoke your freshly caught fish. Be sure to read and sign his multilingual guest book.

EL FARO VIEJO II DELI, Plaza El Pedregal 5.
   Specialty: AMERICAN/DELI/BAKERY.
   $ Prices: Breakfast $4–$6; sandwiches and burgers $4–$8; homemade pie and cheesecake $2.50–$3.
   Open: Daily 6am–4pm.
   When you're homesick for mom's apple pie, homemade bread, a thick juicy burger, or pastrami on rye, this is the place. Tasty coleslaw and potato salad come with the thick sandwiches, and the desserts still look tempting after eating one, so close your eyes. It's squeaky-clean and air-conditioned with contemporary art on the walls and English channels on the tube. Box lunches are available. You'll find it west of Marina Boulevard on the street that leads into El Pedregal (close to the traffic circle west of the town marina).

KANKUN RESTAURANT, Marina Blvd.
   Specialty: MEXICAN/SEAFOOD.
   $ Prices: Quesadillas $3.50; main courses $3.50–$15; breakfast specials $3; lunch special $3.50; dinner specials $12–$15.
   Open: Mon–Sat 8am–10pm, Sun 4–10pm.
   A streetside café with a few tables on the sidewalk and more inside, Kankun offers generous specials. For the breakfast special there are 13 choices; the lunch special (served from 11am to 4pm) might feature two well-stuffed burritos with rice and beans; and the dinner special could include breaded abalone with garlic sauce, lobster, and ribs. Kankun is on Marina Boulevard west of Guerrero.

Worth the Extra Bucks

EL GALEON, Marina Blvd. Tel. 3-0443.
   Specialty: ITALIAN. **Reservations:** Recommended during the Christmas and Easter holidays.
   $ Prices: Appetizers $2–$8; main courses $8–$20; soup $2–$3; dessert $2.50.
   Open: Daily 4–11pm.
On a hillside looking over the town and harbor, this Neapolitan-Italian restaurant

serves wonderful Caesar salad, homemade pasta, pizza, and seafood, all fussed over (in the kitchen) by the blond Italian chef Rafael. The night view of lights twinkling around the harbor is especially romantic while the pianist plays in the background. Have a cocktail first on the terrace of this somewhat old-fashioned, courtly place, and finish with cappuccino. It's on Marina Boulevard west of the town marina near the turnoff to the Solmar Hotel.

SHOPPING

The first stop should be the **open-air market** by the marina. Mixed in with the T-shirts and touristy junk are some nice crafts and jewelry—but be sure to bargain.

In town, most shops are on or within a block or two of the main streets, Cárdenas and Marina Boulevard, or along Hidalgo, which runs north beside the town plaza and the Centro Comercial Plaza, a white building with half a dozen shops selling jewelry, clothing, and Oaxacan weavings. Especially worth a look on Cárdenas are the shops **Temptations, Zen-Mar** (tel. 3-0661), **La Cucaracha de Oro** (tel. 3-0021), and **Rostros de México** (Faces of Mexico), the latter a gallery selling masks and folk art. For hand-painted clothing and "art to wear," stop by **La Bamba,** at Cárdenas and Guerrero (tel. 3-1140); and **Dos Lunas** at Guerrero and Madero (tel. 3-1270).

West of the town plaza on Calle Cabo San Lucas is **Mamma Eli's Curio Shop,** selling folk art, crafts, and clothing. Across the street at Hidalgo 10, a large selection of regional crafts and leisure clothing awaits at **Boutique La Paloma.** Check out **La Bugambilia,** on Hidalgo between Cárdenas and Madero, for quality leather goods. Across from the plaza on Hidalgo at Obregón, a small **Mexican market** sells typical embroidered dresses, weavings, silver, leather suitcases, and other handcrafts.

In the Medano Beach area, try **Galeries Gattamelata** (tel. 3-1166) for crafts, antiques, and colonial-style furniture. **Piñeda de Taxco** (tel. 3-1000) in the Hotel Melia has fine gold and silver jewelry.

EVENING ENTERTAINMENT

Cabo San Lucas is the nightlife capital of Baja, though after-dark fun is centered around the party ambience and camaraderie found in the casual bars and restaurants rather than a flashy disco scene. Finding a happy hour with live music and a place to dance, or a Mexican Fiesta with mariachis, is not difficult here. And discos there are, too.

Mexican Fiestas & Theme Nights

Some of the larger hotels have weekly "Fiesta Nights," "Italian Nights," and other buffet-plus-entertainment theme nights that can be fun as well as a good buy. Check at travel agencies and the following hotels: Solmar (tel. 3-0022), Finisterra (tel. 3-0000), Hacienda (tel. 3-0123), Plaza las Glorias (tel. 3-1220), and Melia San Lucas (tel. 3-0420). Prices range from $12 (drinks, tax, and tips extra) to $30 (for everything, including open bar with national drinks).

Sunset Watching

At twilight time, settle into one of these watering holes—on the slender point that leads to Land's End where the two seas meet—and watch the sun sink into the Pacific.

WHALE WATCHER'S BAR, in the Hotel Finisterra. Tel. 3-0000 or 3-0100.

S The high terrace offers a splendid view of sea and beach—and frolicking whales in season, from January to March. Mariachis play daily from 5 to 8pm. Open daily from noon to 11pm. "Whale" margaritas cost $2.50; beer, $1.50. There are two-for-one drinks during happy hour, 3:30 to 5:30pm.

EL TREBOL, in the Solmar Hotel. Tel. 3-0022.

On a broad beach under a big round palapa, listen to Pacific rollers thunder in the distance while mariachis play daily from 6:30 to 7:30pm. As the sun sets, it gilds the high outcropping of sienna rocks behind the hotel with golden light. Open daily from 7am to 11pm. Beer goes for $1.50; margaritas, $2.50.

Happy Hours

If you shop around, you can usually find an *hora alegre* somewhere in town between noon and 7pm.

GIGGLING MARLIN, Cárdenas across from the marina. Tel. 3-0606.

Live music alternates with tapes in blasting the merry patrons here, who occasionally jump up to dance in the small area in front of the makeshift stage for musicians. A contraption of winches, ropes, and pulleys above a mattress provides entertainment as couples literally string each other up by the heels, while a VCR shows slapstick tapes. Along with action there's decent food—especially if you bring your own catch of the day and let the chef cook it for you with all the trimmings (the grilled marlin was delicious!). Ribs are another specialty. The silliness and fun go on until midnight Sunday through Thursday, until 1am on Friday and Saturday. There is live music Wednesday through Sunday from 8pm to midnight. Open daily from 8am to midnight. Beer runs $1.50 to $2; schooner margaritas, $5. There are discounts during happy hour, 2 to 6pm.

EL SQUID ROE, Marina Blvd. Tel. 3-0655.

El Squid Roe is one of the late Carlos Anderson's inspirations that still attracts crowds with its eclectic-nostalgia decor and eclectic food that's far better than it deserves to be for a party place that's so much fun. A waiter dressed as a bug exterminator dispenses tequila from his backpack sprayer. As fashionable as blue jeans, this is a place to see and be seen in. There's a patio out back for dancing. Open daily from noon to 2am. Beer costs $1; margaritas, $3. There are two-for-one drinks during happy hour, 2 to 4pm daily.

MIGUEL'S BAR & GRILL, Cárdenas at Zaragoza.

Low-key but up high, this new open-air bar overlooks the main street and marina from tables on its outdoor, second-story terrace. Under the roof are booths and tables with pretty woven straw chairs on the clean tile floor. Miguel's is a nice place to chat without competing with loud music. The menu includes lots of munchies, such as buffalo wings, potato skins, and nachos. Open daily from noon to midnight. Beer goes for $2; margaritas, $2.50. Discounts are given during happy hour, 5 to 7pm.

RÍO GRILL RESTAURANT AND BAR, Marina Blvd. 31-A. Tel. 3-1335.

The curving bar in the middle of the room has a cozy neighborhood feeling, even though most of the patrons are tourists. Low-key bands play on the patio under the stars every evening from 7pm to midnight, and there's just enough room to dance. The restaurant specializes in shish kebabs. Open daily from noon to midnight. Margaritas run $3, but there are three-for-one margaritas and $1 beer during happy hour, 3 to 7pm.

LAS PALMAS, on Medano Beach. Tel. 3-0447.

People-watching is the prime pastime at this palapa-shaded restaurant with a ringside location on Medano Beach. Sports fans can pull up a leather *equipale* to the TV showing American sports events. Though the food is pricey, the drink prices are right during happy hour. Open daily from noon to 11pm. Drinks run $2 to $5. Beer and margaritas are $1 during happy hour, noon to 4pm.

Dancing

LUKAS, Marina Blvd. at Marina Plaza. Tel. 3-1744.

About as flashy as anything you'll find in Acapulco, this new disco has all the bells and whistles—neon and chrome, hi-tech lighting, tiered seating, booming sound system, and a snazzy opening light show around 11pm that starts with shrouding the stage in "fog." The owner says that tourists are seldom charged admission—even when there's an official cover charge. Check first, however, as policies can always change. Open nightly from 9pm to late (closed Sunday off-season). Drinks range from $2 to $7.

Admission: $10 on weekends during high season (Dec–Apr); otherwise free.

CABO WABO CANTINA, Guerrero at Cárdenas. Tel. 3-1188.

Owned by the Van Halen band and its Mexican and American partners, this "cantina" packs in youthful crowds, especially when rumors fly that a "surprise" appearance by one of the Van Halens is imminent (word has it that the Van Halens plan to show up spontaneously at least six times a year). Live rock bands from the U.S., Europe, and Australia perform frequently on the well-equipped stage. When live music is absent, a disco-type sound system blasts out mostly rock and roll; conversations must be shouted. Plush, overstuffed furniture frames the dance floor. For snacks, the "Taco-Wabo" just outside the club's entrance stays up late, too. Open nightly from 8pm to 4am. Drinks run $3 to $5, with $2 specials on Tuesday and Thursday.

Admission: $10 cover for live shows (includes two drinks); otherwise free.

---

2. LA PAZ

110 miles N of Cabo San Lucas, 122 miles N of San José del Cabo, 980 miles S of Tijuana

GETTING THERE   By Plane   Aero California has nonstop or direct flights from Los Angeles, Aguascalientes, Culiacán, Guadalajara, Loreto, Los Mochis, Mexico City, and Tijuana. **Aeroméxico** flies from Los Angeles, Tucson, Culiacán, Guaymas, Guadalajara, Mexico City, Puerto Vallarta, and Tijuana.

By Bus   The bus lines **Tres Estrellas de Oro** (first class), **Aguila** (second class), and **Transportes de La Paz** (second class) serve La Paz with buses from the south (Los Cabos) and north (as far as Tijuana). From Los Cabos it's 2½ hours (if you take the short route, the "Via Corta") to 3½ hours; from Loreto, 5 hours.

By Car   From San José del Cabo, Highway 1 north is the longer, more scenic route; flatter and faster is Highway 1 east to Cabo San Lucas, then Highway 19 north through Todos Santos. A little before San Pedro Highway 19 rejoins Highway 1 north into La Paz; allow 2 to 3 hours. From Loreto to the north, Highway 1 south is the only choice; allow 4 to 5 hours.

By Ferry   Two **SEMATUR car-ferries** serve La Paz: from Topolobampo (the port for Los Mochis), daily at 10pm (an 8-hour trip), and from Mazatlán, daily at 5pm (an 18-hour trip). On Monday and Tuesday the Topolobampo ferry carries dangerous cargo (chemicals, gas, etc.). Tickets can be purchased in Los Mochis at Boulevard R. G. Castro 132 Oeste (tel. 681/5-8262); and in Mazatlán at the Terminal Transbordadores (tel. 678/4-1198).

There's also a newer and much faster "waterjet" ferry, the **Baja Express,** which leaves Topolobampo daily at 3pm and arrives in La Paz at 7pm. Tickets can be purchased at the office in Los Mochis at Hidalgo 546 (tel. 681/2-0302) or through several U.S. tour operators (see "Departing," below). Another Baja Express ferry is planned for Mazatlán (tel. 678/5-3737 or fax 678/5-3730 for information).

DEPARTING   By Plane   You'll find the offices of **Aero California** at Paseo Obregón 550 (tel. 682/2-1112, 2-1113, or 2-8392), and **Aeroméxico** at Paseo Obregón between Hidalgo and Morelos (tel. 682/2-0091, 2-0093, or 2-1636).

By Bus   The Central Camionera (main bus station) is at Jalisco and Héroes de la Independencia, about 25 blocks southwest of the center of town, open from 6am to 10pm. Buses leave every 2 or 3 hours for Los Cabos (south) and points north (Loreto and beyond). To check on schedules, call the two main bus lines, **Tres Estrellas de Oro** (tel. 2-6476) and **Aguila** (tel. 2-4270). Buy your ticket in person the day before (though the clerk for Tres Estrellas says reservations can be made by phone).

To get to the station, catch the "Ruta S.E.P." city bus near the corner of Revolución and Degollado by the market. It's often crowded, so be prepared to stand. The fare is about 50¢; have some 500- and 100-peso coins on hand. Taxi fare from downtown to the station runs $2.50 to $3.

To Los Cabos, the **Aguila** line has a station, sometimes called the "beach bus station," on the Malecón at Independencia (tel. 2-3063, 2-4270, or 2-7094). Though little more than a parking lot with a tiny office (open from 8am to 6pm daily), it has "Via Corta" buses (the shorter route) departing for Cabo San Lucas at 8:30am, 10:30am, 1:30pm, 3:30pm, and 5:30pm daily.

By Ferry   The **SEMATUR car-ferry** departs for Topolobampo daily at 8pm (an 8-hour trip), and for Mazatlán daily at 5pm (an 18-hour crossing). The dock is at Pichilingue, 11 miles north of La Paz. The one-way fare to Topolobampo is $10 and only Salón class is available—about 440 bus-type seats in one or more large rooms on the lower deck. To Mazatlán, one-way fares are $16 for Salón class (which can become very crowded), $31 for Turista class (a bunk in a tiny room with four bunks, chair, sink, window, and individual baths/showers down the hall), and $47 for Cabina class (a small room with one bunk, chair, table, window, and private bath). Especial class for $62 (two rooms, comfortable though worn furniture, private bath, and air conditioning—when it works) is rarely available.

SEMATUR ferries are usually equipped with a cafeteria, restaurant-bar, and disco. Nevertheless, it's wise to bring some of your own food and bottled water. Also, except for Salón tickets (sold only the day of departure), reserve as early as possible and confirm your reservation 24 hours before departure; you can pick up tickets at the port terminal ticket office as late as the morning of the day you are leaving. If you are told that Cabina- and Turista-class are sold out, some extra money above the fare may result in a ticket being found. You can buy your SEMATUR tickets at the office at Guillermo Prieto 1465, between Independencia and Reforma, La Paz, B.C.S. 23000 (tel. 682/5-3833 or 2-9485), open daily from 8am to 8pm (it's best to call first to make sure). Tickets can also be purchased at the SEMATUR office at the Pichilingue ferry dock (tel. 682/2-9485 or 2-5117), open daily from 8am to 8pm; or in town at the following travel agencies: Turismo La Paz, at the Hotel Perla (tel. 682/2-7676 or 2-8300); Viajes Baja California Sur Internacional, at Paseo Obregón and Allende (tel. 682/2-3660 or 2-4130); and Viajes Transpeninsulares, at Zaragoza 1630 (tel. 682/2-0399). It's best to make your reservation in person.

Buses for the Pichilingue dock depart from the "beach bus terminal" on the Malecón at Independencia nearly every hour from 8am to 6pm. Bus fare is 75¢. A taxi from downtown La Paz to the dock will charge around $11.

The "waterjet" **Baja Express** ferry leaves for Topolobampo daily at 10am (a 4-hour trip). It departs from the town pier about midway on the Malecón at Muelle. The one-way fare is around $35 for Tourist class and $50 for Express class. Up to 280 passengers can go Tourist class, which includes seats on the air-conditioned lower deck, snacks, soft drinks, movies, and taped music. Express class is limited to 35 passengers, who receive the same amenities plus leather seats on the air-conditioned upper deck and an open bar. A "pier fee" of $2 is added to each ticket, which includes a free shuttle from the Topolobampo dock to Los Mochis. Passengers are advised to arrive an hour and a half before departure time.

In La Paz, purchase tickets from the Baja Express office on the Malecón at 16 de Septiembre (tel. 5-6311 or 5-6313), next to the State Tourist Office. Advance tickets can be arranged through several tour operators in the U.S.: Viajes de la Serna in Arizona (tel. toll free 800/828-3242), Sun Tours in California (tel. toll free 800/829-0510), and Pan American Tours in Texas (tel. toll free 800/876-3942).

L a Paz means "peace," and few things are more peaceful in Baja than relaxing in an open-air café along La Paz's palm-fringed seaside boulevard as the sun sets across the saucer-shaped bay. This laid-back yet thriving port city of 180,000 inhabitants is also the capital of the state of Baja California Sur. Though visitors are welcomed and can find plenty to do, La Paz doesn't have the feeling of a tourist town. And being a port as well as a duty-free zone, several of its streets bristle with small shops stuffed with foreign goods, including perfumes, high-tech gadgets, and silk pajamas from the Far East. La Paz is at the center of fine beach country, too; within a 50-mile radius lie some of the loveliest *playas* in Baja, many of them accessible by car or bus, or through organized tours. This casual capital is enjoyable anytime, though its carefree, raffish charm bursts into full bloom during Carnaval, when La Paz is *the* place to be in Baja for this Mexican version of Mardi Gras.

ORIENTATION

ARRIVING By Plane The **airport** (tel. 2-9386) is 11 miles southwest of town along the highway to Ciudad Constitución and Tijuana. Airport **colectivos** (minivans) to downtown cost around $4 (they run only from the airport to town, not vice-versa). The **taxi** fare to or from the airport is about $11.

By Bus Unless you take the Aguila bus from Los Cabos that arrives at the depot on the Malecón, you will arrive at the **Central Camionera** at Jalisco and Héroes de la Independencia, about 25 blocks southwest of downtown. A cab from here to hotels in the center of town will run $2.50 to $3.

By Ferry Buses line up in front of the ferry dock at Pichilingue to meet every arriving ferry and charge about 75¢ for the ride into town, stopping at the "beach bus station" on the Malecón at Independencia—within walking distance of many downtown hotels if you're not encumbered with luggage. A taxi from the ferry into downtown La Paz (11 miles) charges around $11.

INFORMATION The **State Tourist Office** (Secretaria Estatal y Delegación Federal de Turismo de B.C.S.) (tel. 682/2-1199, 2-7975, or 2-5939) is on the Malecón across from the intersection with Calle 16 de Septiembre. It's open Monday through Friday from 8am to 8pm and on Saturday from 9am to 1pm. The staff speaks English and can supply information on La Paz, Los Cabos, and the region.
    Another source of tourist information is the **booth in the lobby of the Hotel Los Arcos** (tel. 2-2744, ext. 608), open daily from 9am to 2pm and 4 to 7pm. The English-speaking staff can help you with everything from airline schedules to whale-watching trips, including water sports, tours, and cruises.

CITY LAYOUT Although La Paz sprawls well inland from the **Malecón** (the seaside boulevard, **Paseo Alvaro Obregón**), you'll probably spend most of your time in the older, more congenial downtown section along the waterfront.

GETTING AROUND

Because most of what you'll need in town is located on the Malecón between the State Tourist Office and the Hotel Los Arcos, or a few blocks inland from the waterfront, it's easy to get around La Paz on foot. There are public **buses** that go to some of the beaches north of town (see "What to See and Do," below), but to explore the many beaches within 50 miles of La Paz, the best bet is renting a car; several **auto-rental agencies** are on the Malecón.

FAST FACTS

Area Code The telephone area code is 682.
    Banks Banks generally exchange currency on business days between 9am and noon.

Business Hours Normal business hours are from 9 or 10am to 2pm and 4 to 7 or 8pm.

Marinas La Paz has two marinas: **Marina de La Paz,** at the west end of the Malecón at Legaspi (tel. 5-2112 or 5-1646); and **Marina Palmira,** north of town at km 2.5 on the Pichilingue Highway (tel. 5-3959). A third marina west of town in Fidepaz is being planned.

Municipal Market Three blocks inland at Degollado and Revolución de 1910, the public market sells mainly produce, meats, and utilitarian wares.

Post Office The Correos is three blocks inland at Constitución and Revolución de 1910.

WHAT TO SEE & DO

La Paz combines the un-self-conscious bustle of a small capital city and port with beautiful beaches not far from town. Everything from whale watching to beach tours and sunset cruises can usually be arranged through travel agencies in major hotels or along the Malecón.

BEACHES Near La Paz lie some of the loveliest beaches in Baja, many rivaling the Caribbean with their clear turquoise water. Don't be surprised if you have a beach or cove to yourself—some isolated shores are accessible only by dirt road or boat. Public buses from the "beach bus station" at Independencia on the Malecón depart almost every hour from 8am to 5 or 6pm for beaches to the north, stopping at **Playa Coromuel** (3.1 miles), **Playa Tesoro** (8.9 miles), and **Pichilingue** (10.5 miles; from the ferry stop you walk north to the beach). Both Pichilingue and Coromuel beaches have palapa-shaded bars and restaurants. The last bus back to town leaves the beaches around 6:30pm. The one-way fare is 75¢.

The beach at **La Concha Beach Resort,** km 5.5 on the Pichilingue Highway, about 6 miles north of town (tel. 2-6544), rents equipment for snorkeling, waterskiing, windsurfing, and sailing. Sunset cruises and other nautical adventures are also offered. The beach is open to the public (as are all Mexican beaches), and the hotel has a good poolside restaurant and bar. A taxi from town costs about $6 one way. For more information, call the resort.

Viajes Buendía Osorio (tel. 2-7800 or 5-1161) offers guided beach tours by car for $14 to $16 per person.

For more beach information and maps, check at the State Tourist Office on the Malecón.

MARINE EXCURSIONS The most fascinating cruise is to **Isla Espíritu Santo** and **Los Islotes** to visit the largest sea-lion colony in Baja, stunning rock formations, and remote beaches, with stops for snorkeling, swimming, and lunch (if conditions permit, you may be able to snorkel beside the sea lions!). *La Reina Calafia* (tel. 2-5837 or 5-1082), Viajes Coromuel at the Hotel Los Arcos (tel. 2-8006), and other travel agencies can arrange these all-day trips, weather permitting, for $32 to $40 per person. Sometimes a minimum of four to six people is required.

The glass-bottom boat *La Reina Calafia* (tel. 2-5837 or 5-1082) offers tours to **Puerto Balandra,** pristine coves within coves of crystal-blue water and ivory sand framed by bold rock formations rising up like humpbacked whales. The tour, from 9am to 4pm, includes snorkeling gear and 3 hours in this breathtaking, Crusoe-like spot with a cooler full of soft drinks and beer for about $25 per person; lunch at a beachside thatched restaurant at Pichilingue Beach is an optional extra.

Scuba-diving trips, best from mid-April through November, can be arranged with John Riffe at Marina de La Paz, just off the Malecón at Legaspi (tel. 5-2112 or 5-1646, or toll free 800/347-BAJA in the U.S.); or Fernando Aguilar at Independencia 107-B (tel. 2-1826 or 5-2575). Diving options include the sea-lion colony at Los Islotes, distant Cerralvo Island, the sunken ship *Salvatierra,* a 60-foot wall dive, several sea mounts (underwater mountains) and reefs, and a trip to see hammerhead sharks and giant manta rays. Rates start at $65 to $75 per person for an all-day excursion.

Whale watching on Magdalena Bay in the Pacific beside Puerto López

Mateos takes place December through March, depending on when the whales arrive and depart. The 12-hour excursion starts around $75 per person, including breakfast, lunch, transportation, and an English-speaking guide. Make reservations at the Hotel Los Arcos travel desk (tel. 2-2744, ext. 608) or Aventuras Turistica Calafia (tel. 5-1082 or 2-5837). Often a minimum of six people is required for the trip, so make friends quickly and sign up as a group.

SPORT FISHING   La Paz is justly famous for its sport fishing and attracts anglers from all over the world; it has more than 850 species of fish. Here's a list of the most sought-after fish, and when you can find them: black marlin (Aug–Nov), crevalle (Jan–Oct), dolphin (June–Dec), grouper (Apr–Oct), marlin (May–July), needlefish (May–Sept), roosterfish (Apr–Oct), sailfish (June–Nov), sierra (Oct–June), snapper (Apr–Oct), wahoo (Apr–Dec), yellowfin tuna (Apr–Dec), and yellowtail (Dec–May). Fishing expeditions start around $200 a day for a small boat for two people and a guide, $250 for a larger boat for four.

One of the best-known operations is Millo Velez's **Dorado Velez Fleet;** call him for reservations at the Hotel Los Arcos Fishing Desk (tel. 682/2-2744, ext. 637) or at his home (tel. 682/5-2816), or write to him at Apdo. Postal 402, La Paz, B.C.S. 23000. Other operations include the **Mosquito Fleet** (tel. 682/2-0815 or 2-1674) and **La Costa Fleet** (tel. 682/2-4030).

The most economical approach is to **rent a *panga* (skiff)** with guide and equipment for $25 an hour. They're available through Viajes Coromuel (tel. 2-8006) and the Hotel Los Arcos (tel. 2-2744).

CULTURE   At the **Anthropology Museum,** on Altamirano between Constitución and 5 de Mayo (tel. 2-0162), see large though faded color photos of Baja's prehistoric cave paintings and exhibits on the geological history of the peninsula, fossils, missions, colonial history, and daily life. All information is in Spanish. Free admission; open daily from 8am to 6pm.

A new **theater** (1986) near the museum stages all kinds of performing arts events in Spanish.

Our Lady of La Paz Mission (the La Paz cathedral), founded in 1720, is on the main square on Revolución between 5 de Mayo and Independencia. It was part of the chain of California Jesuit missions.

A DAY TRIP   A day trip by car or guided **tour to Los Cabos** at the southern tip of Baja California, where the Pacific Ocean meets the Sea of Cortez, will take you past dramatic scenery and many photogenic isolated beaches. A guided tour that includes lunch and a glass-bottom-boat tour to El Arco in Cabo San Lucas costs $35 to $40 per person and can be booked through most travel agencies. **Viajes Contreras** (tel. 2-5666 or 5-1998) does an especially interesting trip that stops at several small towns and sights on the way to Los Cabos. Most tours are from 7am to 6pm, and some include breakfast.

SPECIAL EVENTS

February features the biggest and best **Carnaval/Mardi Gras** in Baja. In March there's the **Festival of the Whale.** May features a **festival celebrating the city's founding** by Cortez in 1535. The annual **marlin-fishing tournament** is in August. And on **November 1–2,** the Day of the Dead altars are on display at the Anthropology Museum.

WHERE TO STAY
PENSIONS

PENSION CALIFORNIA, Degollado 209, La Paz, B.C.S. 23000. Tel. 682/2-2896. 25 rms (all with bath).

$ Rates: $7 single; $10 double.

In the middle of town, three blocks inland from the Malecón on Degollado at Madero, this pension in an old colonial home has cell-like rooms painted bright blue and white and furnished with ceiling fans, fluorescent lighting, and mattresses on concrete bases. They're arranged around a large unkempt courtyard spilling over with plants, trees, Mexican paintings, and bric-a-brac. The place has a friendly and casual personality all its own, and is a favorite with students and others on minimal budgets. Guests often gather in the courtyard to cook on the outdoor stoves, eat at the long tables, and watch the color TV.

HOSTERÍA EL CONVENTO, Madero 85, La Paz, B.C.S. 23000. Tel. 682/2-3508. 42 rms (all with bath).

$ Rates: $7 single; $10 double.

The owners of the Pension California around the corner manage this similar nearby establishment, also in a rambling old colonial home. It's a bit quieter and lacks the stoves in the courtyard, but otherwise it's much the same in facilities, friendly ambience, and youthful patrons traveling on a shoestring. The shoebox-size rooms have fans, brightly painted walls, and a shower curtain or corrugated tin for the bathroom door.

HOTELS & SUITES

Doubles For Less Than $25

HOTEL POSADA SAN MIGUEL, 16 de Septiembre and Domínguez, La Paz, B.C.S. 23000. Tel. 682/2-1802. 15 rms (all with bath).

$ Rates: $8 single; $11 double.

Tidy and spartan, this hotel three blocks inland from the waterfront (turn left on Domínguez) faces the Palacio Municipal on a busy street in the downtown commercial district. The rooms, which contain ceiling fans, are arranged around an attractive, small courtyard full of plants and flowers. Reserve in advance if possible—it's often booked.

HOTEL SAN BERNARDINO, Abasolo 436, La Paz, B.C.S. 23000. Tel. 682/2-9220 or 2-9210. 28 rms (all with bath). A/C TV

$ Rates: $14 single; $17 double.

On Abasolo near 5 de Febrero, a long (15- to 20-minute) walk west of the town center and three blocks in from the waterfront, this somewhat shabby, two-story motel around a courtyard/parking lot has clean rooms decorated with garish fabrics and colors. Most have two beds, a double and a single. On some days the washed sheets are draped over the balconies. There's a small restaurant on the premises.

HOTEL LORIMAR, Bravo 110 Pte., La Paz, B.C.S. 23000. Tel. 682/5-3822. 27 rms (all with bath). A/C

$ Rates: $17 single; $19 double.

Here you get a plain hotel room with the friendly, personal service of a *casa de huespedes*. The rooms are clean and simply furnished, with windows that open onto the hall. There's a TV in the lobby. The Lorimar is on Bravo between Madero and Mutualismo, about 1½ blocks inland from the waterfront.

Doubles For Less Than $35

HOTEL PURISIMA, 16 de Septiembre 408, La Paz, B.C.S. 23000. Tel. 682/2-3444. 110 rms (all with bath). TV

$ Rates: $21 single; $25 double.

About five blocks in from the Malecón on the busy 16 de Septiembre just before Serdan, this four-story hotel offers small rooms that are clean but rather worn-looking. They're furnished with a double bed, desk and chair, and ceiling fans. Those across the front of the building have a window overlooking the street—a mixed blessing. The elevator smells.

HOTEL GARDENIAS, Serdan 520 (Apdo. Postal 197), La Paz, B.C.S. 23000. Tel. 682/2-3088. Fax 682/5-0436. 56 rms (all with bath). A/C TV TEL
$ Rates: $25–$29 single; $33 double.

Ten blocks east of the town center on the Malecón and then about three blocks inland—a 15- to 20-minute walk—this pleasant, two-story hotel surrounds a large courtyard and pool. The decor is a blend of neo-Spanish colonial and 1950s modern motel. Ask for one of the recently remodeled rooms. A restaurant on the premises is open daily from 7:30am to 3pm.

HOTEL PLAZA REAL DE LA PAZ, Callejon La Paz and Esquerro, La Paz, B.C.S. 23000. Tel. 682/2-9333. Fax 682/2-4424. 18 rms, 3 suites (all with bath). A/C TV TEL
$ Rates: $27 single; $32 double; $36 triple; $42 suite.

This unfancy, homey hotel, a short block inland from the Malecón and not far from the Hotel Perla, has comfortable but worn vinyl couches and a TV in its tiny lobby, which opens onto the simple hotel restaurant with dinette tables and chairs. Ruffled bedspreads and wooden headboards on the two double beds soften the otherwise spartan, clean rooms in the three-story building. The hotel is popular with Mexican business travelers. The Mexican restaurant serves some interesting regional dishes daily from 7am to 11pm, and also offers room service the same hours.

HOTEL ACUARIO'S, Ramírez 1665, La Paz, B.C.S. 23000. Tel. 682/2-9266. 60 rms (all with bath). A/C TV TEL
$ Rates: $28 single; $32 double. **Parking:** Free, in an enclosed area with a gate.

This new-looking, well-maintained, three-story motel frames a protected parking lot and small pool. The comfortable, neat rooms come with small balconies, one or two double beds, a table and two chairs (wood-grain Formica), and a bath with a tub as well as a shower. A restaurant/bar on the premises is open daily from 7am to 11pm. Laundry service is available. You'll find the hotel six blocks inland from the Malecón on Degollado and to the left on Ramírez.

JARDÍN DE PAZ SUITES, Mutualismo 314 (Apdo. Postal 6, Jalisco Sucursal A), La Paz, B.C.S. 23000. Tel. 682/5-3630 or 2-3042. 8 suites (all with bath).
$ Rates: $30 one-bedroom suite for one or two people; $42 two-bedroom suite for three or four people.

Owned by a Canadian couple who also operate a leather-crafts shop next to the office, these suites—five one-bedroom and three two-bedroom—open onto a rambling hillside courtyard with a fountain and trees. The clean, simple suites have comfortable if somewhat worn furnishings, full kitchens and living rooms, and weekly maid service; six suites have air conditioning and two have fans. A self-service washer and dryer are available. A restaurant on the premises serves breakfast and lunch daily from 6am to 2pm. The suites are one block in from the west end of the Malecón, on Mutualismo between Ocampo and Bravo, near the Hotel Los Arcos.

Doubles For Less Than $45

HOTEL PERLA, Paseo Obregón 1570 (Apdo. Postal 207), La Paz, B.C.S. 23000. Tel. 682/2-0777. Fax 682/5-5363. 101 rms (all with bath). A/C TV TEL
$ Rates: $36–$37 single or double; $46 triple. Extra person $9.

Well situated in the center of the Malecón between Callejon La Paz and Arreola; near the State Tourist Office in the heart of town, this attractive three-story hotel overlooks the bay. Its recently remodeled rooms have white textured walls and chunky contemporary, blond-wood furniture, including queen-size beds in 10 rooms. Amenities include a pool and sundeck on the second floor, travel agency, nightclub, laundry service, and room service daily from 7am to

10:30pm. A local favorite is the hotel's airy streetside restaurant, La Terraza, a great spot for margaritas and sunsets over the water. Try to get one of the 28 rooms with a sea view.

SUITES MISION, Paseo Obregón 220, La Paz, B.C.S. 23000. Tel. 682/2-1888, 2-0014, or 2-0815. 8 suites (all with bath). A/C TV

$ Rates: $37 one-bedroom suite; $43 two-bedroom suite.

These attractive split-level suites open off the narrow interior courtyard of a two-story building set back from the Malecón near the Hotel Perla, and next door to the Curios Mary shop on Arreola. All come with kitchenette, living room (some with dining room, too), marble and tile floors, and pleasant Mexican furnishings. Most have a porch for sitting outside and three have balconies with ocean views. The owners can provide laundry, travel agency, and complete sport-fishing services, including cleaning and packing fish to go (they own the Mosquito Fishing Fleet). The four one-bedroom suites accommodate one or two people; the four two-bedroom suites, three or four. This place is an excellent value in a great location, so reserve as early as possible.

Worth The Extra Bucks

LA POSADA DE ENGELBERT, Av. Reforma and Playa Sur (Apdo. Postal 152), La Paz, B.C.S. 23000. Tel. 682/2-4011. Fax 682/2-0663. 26 suites, 4 casitas (all with bath). AC TV

$ Rates: $58 single; $65 double; $77 casita.

Singer Engelbert Humperdinck visited and liked this palmy little oasis by the sea so much that he decided to buy it (formerly called La Posada). It's tucked into palm-shaded gardens looking out on the bay, with suites and casitas in small one-story buildings scattered about the rambling grounds. A suite is actually a large room with a queen-size bed (or two doubles) and easy chairs beside the fireplace; there's a single bed in a tiny side room. Each casita is beautifully furnished in the Mexican style with crafts and hand-finished touches, plus a kitchen, living room with fireplace, and a high-walled private patio. The pretty pool area, palapa bar, and restaurant (open daily from 7:30am to 11pm), all looking out on the water, provide delightful places to spend time. For an escape with its own beach, this is a good value. It's a 10-minute taxi ride west of downtown, too far to walk. But the taxi fares to and from town ($2 to $3 each way) can add up.

HOTEL LOS ARCOS, Paseo Obregón 498 (Apdo. Postal 112), La Paz, B.C.S. 23000. Tel. 682/2-2744 or 2-2510; in the U.S., 213/583-3393, or toll free 800/347-2252. Fax 682/5-4313. 180 rms, 52 in bungalows, 8 suites (all with bath). A/C MINIBAR TV TEL

$ Rates: $61–$64 single; $64–$66 double (bungalows or hotel rms); $77–$80 suite (for one or two).

This three-story, neo-colonial-style hotel at the west end of the Malecón between Rosales and Allende is the best place to splurge downtown. While decidedly modern in its furnishings and amenities (room service, laundry, cafeteria, upscale restaurant, bar with live music, travel agency, fishing desk), its rambling nooks and crannies filled with fountains, plants, and even rocking chairs give it lots of old-fashioned charm. Most rooms come with two double beds and a balcony overlooking the inner courtyard's pool or the waterfront. Bungalows in the separate Cabañas de Los Arcos section are nestled into an appealing jungle garden shaded by large trees. This complex also offers two swimming pools (one heated), a sauna, Ping-Pong tables, and a tourist-information booth in the lobby. TVs are color with U.S. channels.

WHERE TO EAT

Although La Paz is no culinary mecca, it has a growing assortment of small pleasant restaurants that are good and reasonably priced. In addition to the usual seafood and Mexican dishes, Italian, French, Spanish, Chinese, and even "New Age" vegetarian health food can be found. Keep in mind that shrimp and lobster are usually the priciest dishes in Baja and that most restaurants offer an inexpensive meal of soup and tortillas that's satisfying and filling.

Calle Independencia, starting about a block in from the Malecón, is a "boutique street" with a block or two of little shops and restaurants. Restaurants along the seaside **Malecón** tend to be more expensive. Small streetside eateries with signs that say BIRRIERÍA specialize in roasted cabrito—baby goat—which can be delicious.

For quick snacks under a dollar, a couple of bakeries have appealing breads and sweets: the **panadería** at Independencia and Domínguez, and the **pastelería** at Altamirano and Bravo.

Sweeter still is the **Godiva chocolate shop** at Bravo 280. These are not the imported Godiva goodies, but the dark, white, and milk-chocolate morsels are tempting. The shop is open Monday through Saturday from 10am to 1pm and 3 to 8pm.

MEALS FOR LESS THAN $5

RESTAURANT TIP'S, Independencia 106.

Specialty: MEXICAN.

$ Prices: Main courses $2–$3; eggs $2; comida corrida $2.50–$3; burrito plate $1.75.

Open: Daily 9am–9pm (comida corrida served 1–5pm).

A neighborhood shoebox of a place with clean tile floors and red-checked tablecloths, this modest eatery serves good Mexican food and fresh-squeezed orange juice. The comida corrida comes with soup, salad, and main course; an order of machaca (a tasty dried meat) burritos is accompanied by salad and beans. Fans cool the air. It's two blocks inland from the Malecón on Independencia before Domínguez.

MENUDO'S & BEER, Esquerro and Callejon La Paz. Tel. 2-8099.

Specialty: MEXICAN.

$ Prices: Main courses $3–$5; omelets $2–$3; beer $1.50.

Open: Breakfast/lunch daily 8am–2pm; dinner daily 6pm–midnight.

Even without a raging *crudo* (hangover), a steaming bowl of menudo or pozole sometimes hits the spot (menudo is the traditional Mexican remedy for the day after). Menudo is made with tripe and spices; pozole, with hominy, pork, peppers, and spices. With the zesty, hearty soup, try an order of tamales, taquitos (mini-tacos), quesadillas, or sopes—thick corn pancakes with various toppings. Opened in 1990, this tiny Mexican diner has serapes on the wall, checked tablecloths, taped music, and air conditioning. Breakfast is served at night, too. You'll find the place up Callejon La Paz from the waterfront and across the street on Esquerro.

PARRILLADA NORTEÑA, 5 de Mayo 1007. Tel. 5-0570.

Specialty: MEXICAN TACOS AL CARBON/BURGERS.

$ Prices: Main courses (two to four tacos) $2.50–$7; Mexican beer $1.50.

Open: Daily 1–11pm.

Some of the best tacos in Baja are made at this *parrillada,* which means "grill." Taco meats and seafood are grilled quickly over a very hot fire, topped with melted white Chihuahua cheese ("Norteña" style), then served on thick handmade corn or flour tortillas with eight different sauces and condiments, which are brought to the table in little ceramic bowls. Half the fun here is mix-and-matching the 20 different taco combinations (including steak, pork, bacon, chorizo, chilorio, fish, clams, mushrooms, and slightly charred grilled onions) with the wonderful salsas. Chilorio is a delicious and spicy ground meat filling. Burgers are also available. It's an 11-block hike in from the Malecón on 5 de Mayo, on the corner at Josefa Ortiz.

MEALS FOR LESS THAN $10

CAFETERÍA, in the Hotel Los Arcos, Paseo Obregón 498 Sur. Tel. 2-2744.

Specialty: MEXICAN/AMERICAN.

$ Prices: Appetizers $1–$3; main courses $3–$11; breakfast $2–$7; soup and sandwich $5; box lunch $5; Mexican buffet (Sun 1–4pm) $7.50.
Open: Daily 6am–10pm.

The cheerful blue-and-green booths and tables of this American-style cafeteria look out on an interior courtyard with tropical plants and splashing fountain, where patrons can also dine. Mariachis play at the Sunday brunch. The hotel is at the west end of the Malecón between Allende and Rosales.

EL QUINTO SOL RESTAURANT AND NUTRITION CENTER, Independencia and Domínguez. Tel. 2-1692.

Specialty: NATURAL/VEGETARIAN.
$ Prices: Salads $2.50–$4; main courses $3.50–$7; rice-of-the-day plate $2; comida corrida $6.
Open: Mon–Sat 7:30am–9:30pm (comida corrida served 1–5pm).

This "New Age" natural foods and bookstore has a large menu featuring exotic juices, yogurt shakes, tamales, cheese and carrot tacos, and carrot croquettes at reasonably down-to-earth prices. It's two blocks inland from the Malecón on Independencia at Domínguez.

ROSTICERÍA CALIFORNIA, Serdan 1740. Tel. 2-5118.

Specialty: MEXICAN CHICKEN.
$ Prices: Main courses $3.50–$7.
Open: Daily 8am–8pm.

Tasty chicken is the main event here—roasted, fried, and sometimes cooked in a soup. Whole- and half-chicken orders are served with salad, french fries, tortillas, and salsa. The decor is cheerful, bright, and airy, with ceiling fans and colorfully embroidered tablecloths from Chiapas. There's also a small patio out back. The Rostic ería is five blocks inland from the Malecón on Degollado; then turn right on Serdan and it's not far from the public market.

TRATTORIA NAPOLI, Paseo Obregón and Hidalgo. Tel. 2-1183.

Specialty: ITALIAN.
$ Prices: Main courses $4–$10; spaghetti $3.50–$4; crêpes $3.50–$5; pizza $3–$9.
Open: Daily 10:30am–10:30pm.

In a historic stucco house under shady trees, at the east end of the Malecón at Hidalgo, this charming, cozy restaurant serves some of the town's best Italian food as well as crêpes filled with chicken, mushrooms, or mangos.

RESTAURANT/BAR LA TERRAZA, by the Hotel Perla, Paseo Obregón 1570. Tel. 2-0777.

Specialty: MEXICAN.
$ Prices: Appetizers $2.50–$10; main courses $5.50–$13.
Open: Daily 7am–11pm.

This comfortable, shaded, open-air restaurant in the middle of the Malecón beside the Hotel Perla has a great view of the bay and sunset. Plants, people, and a mural in the style of the famous ancient Baja cave paintings fill this La Paz institution where the local silver-haired *jefes* (bosses) and politicos hang out.

WORTH THE EXTRA BUCKS

RESTAURANT BERMEJO, in the Hotel Los Arcos, Paseo Obregón 498. Tel. 2-2744.

Specialty: MEXICAN/CONTINENTAL.
$ Prices: Appetizers $2–$8; main courses $4.50–$20; enchiladas $5.50; Mexican plate $10; desserts $2–$3.50.
Open: Dinner only, daily 7–11pm.

Ensconced in the deep padded booths lit by candles or beside a window with a view of the bay, patrons enjoy well-prepared steak and seafood as well as showy flambé dishes. Deep wine-red fabrics, dark woods, brick columns, and wrought iron add to the feeling of a Spanish bodega. On most nights a pianist plays from 8 to

11pm. The flambéed steak Mexican style is spicy and delicious. Sometimes there are lobster specials, so call ahead. The restaurant is on the west end of the Malecón at Hotel Los Arcos.

SHOPPING

Because Baja is a duty-free zone, La Paz has plenty of shops stuffed with electronic gear, perfumes, cosmetics, shoes, and trinkets from the Orient, especially along **16 de Septiembre.** The dense cluster of streets spreading out behind Hotel Perla **between 16 de Septiembre and Degollado** is chock full of small shops, some tacky but others quite upscale, such as **Importaciones Sara** at Esquerro 80-A (tel. 2-2111), and **La Perla de La Paz** at Mutualismo and Arreola—both department stores specializing in perfume, cosmetics, and other luxury imports. The municipal market at Revolución and Degollado, however, has little to interest visitors.

Stores selling crafts, folk art, clothing, and handmade furniture and accessories lie mostly along the **Malecón (Paseo Obregón)** or a block or two in from it. Among these, the **Cotton Club,** between Muelle and Lerdo, offers appealing resort wear and folk-artsy jewelry. For crafts and clothing, check out the following: **El Portal Bazar** (tel. 5-1172), near Muelle; **Antigua California** (tel. 5-5230), near Martínez; and **México Lindo** (tel. 2-1890), a half block from the Malecón on Lerdo. On the ocean side of the Malecón on the square by the Tourist Office, try **La Paloma,** which has nice crafts and local shellwork.

Freeport, a small shop next to the Hotel Perla, is the place to buy unmounted, irregular gray pearls and other jewelry (La Paz was once famous for its local pearls). And if you like beautiful hand-woven tablecloths, placemats, rugs, and other textiles, it's worth the long walk or taxi ride to Artesanías Cuauhtémoc, also called **The Weaver,** at Abasolo 3315, between Jalisco and Nayarit (tel. 2-4575), beyond the west end of the Malecón and across from the Conasupo building. In his 70s, Fortunato Silva weaves wonderfully textured cotton textiles from yarn he spins and dyes himself, and charges far less than what you'd pay for the equivalent in craftsmanship in the U.S. Open Monday through Saturday from 9am to 2pm and 4 to 6pm, and on Sunday from 10am to 1pm.

EVENING ENTERTAINMENT

La Paz nightlife begins in a café along the Malecón as the sun sinks into the sea—often painting a luminous, Maxfield Parrish sort of scene with gold-tinged, almost iridescent glowing colors streaking across the broad bay behind the palm trees silhouetted along the waterfront. Always have your camera ready at sunset.

A favorite ringside seat at dusk is a table at **La Terraza,** next to the Hotel Perla, which makes good schooner-size margaritas. Among the after-dark options are several discos, a few restaurants and nightclubs with live music, and hotel fiestas and theme nights with dinner and live music. Since most discos charge admission, it's best to peek in, if possible, before paying the cover charge: Too few or too many people may change your mind. An inexpensive alternative is to stroll along the Malecón and people-watch, stopping here and there for a drink or snack or to hear some wandering mariachis.

OLD WEST, Paseo Obregón and Lerdo. Tel. 5-4454.

On the Malecón, this rustic watering hole and restaurant is a comfortable drinking-and-dancing spot with sawdust on the floor, a long wooden bar, and leather *equipales* tables and barrel chairs. Open daily from noon to 2am. There are live bands Thursday through Sunday from 9:30pm to 2am; happy hour is daily from noon to 2pm and 6 to 7pm. Beer costs $1.50 to $2; margaritas, $1.25 to $2.25.

PELICANOS BAR, in the Hotel Los Arcos, Paseo Obregón 498. Tel. 2-2744.

Try to get a window table to enjoy the fine view of the bay in this quiet, sedate spot. Dark wood and old-fashioned chairs upholstered in red recall the "Spanish-Mediterranean" style popular in the 1960s. Open daily from 5pm to midnight;

mariachis play Thursday through Saturday from 7 to 10pm. Drinks run $1.50 to $3; snacks are $1.50 to $7.

OKEY LASER DISCO, Paseo Obregón. Tel. 2-3133.

Recently remodeled with lots of flashy mirrors and chrome against a black background, this compact disco sits in the middle of the Malecón, just half a block east of the Hotel Perla. Open Thursday through Saturday from 10pm to 3am. Drinks go for $2 to $5.
Admission: Varies.

LA CABAÑA DISCO, in the Hotel Perla, Paseo Obregón 1570. Tel. 2-0777.

For a lovely view of the bay from the dance floor, this is *the* place to be. The setting is contemporary, with a large rectangular dance floor framed by windows across the front and surrounded by many small tables. Occasionally live bands play here. It's open Tuesday through Thursday from 9:30pm to 3:30am and Friday through Sunday from 9:30pm to 4am. Beer costs $1 to $2; margaritas, $2.50.
Admission: $13 (includes three national drinks).

X-TASIS DISCO, Arreola and Domínguez.

Three blocks in from the waterfront on Arreola, this new disco was scheduled to open sometime in 1991. Check it out.

LA PAZ-LAPA, Paseo Obregón and Marqués de León. Tel. 2-6025.

This lively restaurant and bar, on the ocean side of the Malecón west of the Los Arcos Hotel, is a Carlos Anderson place (as in Carlos 'n' Charlie's) with circus-inspired decor and party atmosphere. But the fun can blast the budget unless you select food carefully (try the tortilla soup) and watch your drink tab. Open Wednesday through Monday from noon to 1am. Drinks are $2 to $5.

MEXICAN FIESTAS & THEME NIGHTS

This slightly out-of-town hotel presents Mexican Fiestas and other buffet-plus-entertainment events for $12 to $30 per person. When calling for information, be sure to check on what the price covers.

LA POSADA DE ENGELBERT, Av. Reforma and Playa Sur. Tel. 2-4011.

This charming hacienda-style hotel by the water puts on Mexican Fiestas and other theme nights on its garden patio. Call for current information. Round-trip taxi fare from downtown is $4 to $6.

3. LORETO

237 miles N of La Paz, 90 miles S of Mulege, 742 miles S of Tijuana

GETTING THERE   By Plane   Aero California has nonstop flights from Los Angeles and La Paz. **Charter flights** out of San Diego and Canada are anticipated.

By Bus   Frequent buses from towns both north and south of Loreto make stops here. From La Paz (south) the trip is 5 hours; from Santa Rosalía (north), 3 hours.

By Car   From major towns north or south take Highway 1. Coming from the north, the prettiest section is south of Mulege where the road skirts lovely coves along Concepción Bay. From the south the best views occur during the last 40 miles before Loreto, where the road edges the steep Sierra de la Giganta rising beside the sea. In view offshore are the islands Danzante (small) and Carmen (large).

DEPARTING   By Plane   The **Aero California** office is on Juárez between Misioneros and Zapata (tel. 683/3-0500 or 3-0566).

By Bus   The new **Terminal de Autobuses** shares a building with the Restaurant Don Luis, a modest taco-and-enchilada place on Juárez between Ayuntamiento and León. The schedules of buses going north and south are posted outside by the ticket window. For some destinations, such as La Paz, you can buy your ticket a day in advance. Otherwise (especially if you're heading north), when the bus arrives you buy your ticket from the driver and hope a seat is available. Buses heading north depart from 2 to 11pm; buses heading south leave from 7am to midnight. The bus station is open daily from 6am to 11pm.

Although Loreto has long been known among anglers as the Yellowtail Capital of Baja, it still has the feeling of a dusty little town that time forgot. Fences made of palm fronds rustle in the sea breeze along its mostly unpaved streets, where roosters crow and dogs bark. Set against the backdrop of the vermillion Sierra de la Giganta rising 5,000 feet above it, Loreto is small enough (pop. 12,000) that after a couple of days you feel like part of the family.

Yet Loreto is actually the oldest settlement in Baja; it was the place where the Jesuit padres first stepped ashore to found a mission in the Californias, in 1697. Their simple stone church stands at the heart of the town that served as the capital of Baja until 1830.

Moreover, this sleepy town is waking up: Over the past year it has paved and landscaped its Malecón (seaside boulevard) and officially constructed an aqueduct to bring fresh water from underground springs in the north. The last especially should boost tourism; before, the terrible-tasting tapwater was a constant complaint.

The "other" Loreto, much-touted in brochures, is the development south of town around Nopolo Bay, where the Stouffer Presidente Hotel, the Loreto Tennis Center, and a recently inaugurated (spring 1991) 18-hole golf course are located. Still more development is planned for Puerto Escondido, 20 miles south, where a marina and the first of several hotels are being built.

ORIENTATION

ARRIVING   By Plane   Airport colectivos (minivans) charge around $5 for the trip into town. Taxi fare to or from the airport (4 miles south of Loreto) is around $7.

By Bus   With the exception of the Motel Salvatierra, the hotels are too far to walk to from the bus station. A taxi to most hotels runs $2 to $3; to the Stouffer Presidente (5 miles south), $10.

INFORMATION   The **Ayuntamiento de Comondu (tourist office)** Loreto, B.C.S. 23880 (tel. 683/3-0689), faces the town plaza near Salvatierra and Madero. Here Estela Davis and Carlos Maraver provide information Monday through Saturday from 9am to 3pm and 5 to 8pm.

When the office is closed, the travel agency of **Alfredo's Sport Fishing,** on Juárez just west of the waterfront (tel. 683/3-0165), can also provide information in English.

CITY LAYOUT   Loreto's main street, **Salvatierra** (named after the priest who founded the Loreto mission), runs from the traffic circle at the town's entrance to the Malecón, **Boulevard López Mateos,** where there are several hotels. From the waterfront to the center of town (marked by the church and town plaza on Salvatierra) is a pleasant 10-minute walk. Most shops are on or close to Salvatierra.

GETTING AROUND

Although Loreto is small, its handful of hotels are quite spread out. **Bicycles** can be rented from the travel agency at the Stouffer Presidente Hotel, Turismo Los Candeleros (tel. 3-0700, ext. 453), for $5 an hour. **Rental cars,** starting around $50 a day, are available at Alfredo's Sport Fishing and Turismo Los Candeleros. A **public bus** (a minivan) runs along Salvatierra.

FAST FACTS

Area Code   The telephone area code is 683.

Books   Used English-language paperbacks are sometimes for sale at the history museum next to the church.

Business Hours   Shops are open Monday through Saturday, from around 10am to 2pm and 5 or 6 to 7pm.

Climate   During November through March, occasional days are too windy for fishing and other nautical expeditions.

WHAT TO SEE & DO

Fishing remains Loreto's number-one lure, though there are some beautiful white beaches on the offshore islands, Coronado, Carmen, and Danzante. The town also makes a good base for whale-watching trips and expeditions into the mountains, and boasts the best tennis facility in Mexico.

Fishing and most water sports, rentals, and excursions can be arranged through one or more of the following: **Alfredo's Sport Fishing,** on Juárez between the town and the waterfront (Apdo. Postal 39), Loreto, B.C.S. 23880 (tel. 683/3-0165); **Turismo Los Candeleros,** at the Stouffer Presidente Hotel, Boulevard Misión de Loreto, Loreto, B.C.S. 23880 (tel. 683/3-0700 ext. 453, or 3-0044); and the **Hotel Mision,** Boulevard López Mateos 1 on the waterfront (Apdo. Postal 49), Loreto, B.C.S. 23880 (tel. 683/3-0048). For activities based at the Stouffer Presidente Hotel, remember that a taxi there costs about $10 one way. Prices for outings do not include a tip for the guide or boat skipper, traditionally 10% to 15%.

BEACHES   Loreto's beaches are either rocky or made of brown sand. But there are beautiful white beaches on the islands off the coast. Closest to Loreto is **Coronado Island,** where you may spot dolphins or sea lions. A guided boat trip to Coronado takes 30 minutes to get there; Alfredo's Sport Fishing charges $30 per person for 4 hours, including lunch and drinks (minimum of four people). North of Loreto you'll also find gorgeous beaches along **Concepción Bay.** A 6-hour expedition there runs $35 to $40 per person with lunch and drinks (minimum of four people).

WHALE WATCHING   All-day excursions to see the whales (January through March) near Puerto López Mateos on the west coast run $65 per person and generally include car transportation, lunch, drinks, and 2 hours of whale watching in a boat with a guide (a minimum of four to six people is often required). For reservations, call Alfredo's, Los Candeleros, or Francisco Juárez at the Hotel Mision.

WATER SPORTS   **Scuba-diving trips** to Coronado, Carmen, and Danzante islands can be arranged through **Fantasía Divers de Loreto,** based at the Stouffer Presidente Hotel (tel. 3-0700, ext. 114; or toll free 800/336-DIVE in the U.S.). Diving is best from June through October, barring a rare tropical storm in August or September. Some days may be too windy, especially from December to March, and blooming plankton can cloud the water in February and March. The water doesn't warm up until June, so a quarter-inch wetsuit is essential from December to May. The best diving spots are around Coronado Island (1½ miles offshore, the closest to Loreto), Carmen Island (8½ miles offshore, the largest island), and Danzante Island (2½ miles offshore from Puerto Escondido, 20 miles south of Loreto). Diving classes are given by Fantasía Divers in the pool of the Stouffer Presidente Hotel between 9am and 5pm by reservation.

Fantasía Divers (tel. 3-0700, ext. 114) can also arrange **windsurfing, island trips, sailing trips,** and **sunset cruises.** The Hotel La Pinta also rents equipment.

DEEP-SEA FISHING   The season for yellowtail and amberjack is November through June; for roosterfish, October through April; bonita, March through December; dorado (dolphin fish), May through October; sailfish, June through September; yellowfin tuna, July through November; and cabrilla (sea bass), grouper, and red snapper, all year. Fishing trips start at around $90, including guide, and can be arranged through Alfredo's, Los Candeleros, the Hotel Mision, the Hotel Oasis, or Oscar Henaine at the Hotel La Pinta.

TENNIS   The excellent **Loreto Tennis Center,** across from the Stouffer Presidente Hotel on Nopolo Bay (tel. 3-0408), has nine courts (lighted at night), a stadium for tournaments, and a pool and locker room facilities for the use of paying guests. Make reservations by calling the center, which is privately managed (not part of the hotel). Rates are $7 an hour, $10 an hour after dark. Open daily from 7am to 7pm and at night from 7 to 10pm by advance reservation.

CULTURE   At the heart of town is **Our Lady of Loreto,** the oldest mission in the chain established by the Spanish Jesuits throughout the Californias. After its founding in 1697 by Padre Juan María de Salvatierra, Loreto grew and served as the capital of Baja California until 1830. The mission church, ornamented with baroque carved stone, has been well preserved and its altar screen restored—a group of paintings set in a baroque framework of red, blue, and gold trim. It's open during daylight hours.

Next to the church sits a small but fascinating **history museum,** displaying everything from Spanish colonial religious art to the tools of daily life when Loreto was an 18th-century outpost. Sometimes used paperbacks in English are on sale here for $1. Open Monday through Friday 9am to 12:30pm and 1 to 5pm. Admission is 25¢.

A DAY TRIP   The second-oldest mission in the Californias, **Misión San Francisco Javier** is perched high in the mountains about 25 miles southwest of Loreto. At the end of the 2-hour journey—over a scenic but rugged dirt road that requires a four-wheel-drive—is a baroque stone church completed in 1759. Inside sits a beautiful gold altar screen inset with paintings. You can climb up the winding stairs to the bell tower and roof, where you get a closer look at the intricately carved stone roof ornaments and a panoramic view of the valley. If the church is locked, ask around and a local "guide" is sure to let you in for a small fee (be sure to give him or her a "contribution" for the church).

For another small fee, ask your guide to show you the gigantic gnarled olive trees planted by the first Spanish friars. A tiny, dirt-floored snack bar near the church sells soft drinks, but it's best to bring lunch. On December 3 the town holds a big fiesta honoring its patron saint with music, dancing, food, and merrymaking, for which about 20,000 "pilgrims" show up!

This can be a difficult expedition to arrange because of the rough road (most taxi drivers don't want to take their cars on it). Tours (for a minimum of four people) can sometimes be arranged through Alfredo's or Los Candeleros for $37 to $40 per person, with lunch and drinks. Allow 6 hours for the outing and start early enough to return in daylight.

SPECIAL EVENTS

In March there's the **Festival of the Virgin of Loreto,** patron saint of pilots. The **"Loreto 400"** auto race is held annually in June, and July and August is the time for dorado **fishing tournaments.** On September 8 the 1697 founding of the **Loreto Mission** is celebrated. September 29 is the **Festival of San Miguel de Comondu,** patron saint of this village in the mountains about 60 miles northwest of Loreto. **October 25** is the festivities honoring the Virgin of Loreto and the city founding. And December 3 is the **Festival of San Francisco Javier,** patron saint of the village and historic mission church in the mountains 25 miles southwest of Loreto.

WHERE TO STAY

The only true budget lodgings in Loreto are either seedy or inconveniently far from town. Though more expensive, the three moderate hotels on Loreto's waterfront offer better value.

MOTEL SALVATIERRA, Salvatierra 123, Loreto, B.C.S. 23880. Tel. 683/3-0021. 30 rms (all with bath). A/C
$ Rates: $15 single; $23 double.

With little to recommend it besides its low prices, this run-down motel has rather dismal and minimally clean rooms with hot water. Make sure the air conditioner works before taking the room. Several restaurants are nearby, and a public minivan "bus" that runs along Salvatierra will take you closer to the beach. Otherwise it's a long walk to the water. The motel is on Salvatierra at León, about two blocks east of the traffic circle and on your left as you enter town.

HOTEL VILLA DEL MAR, Colonia Zaragoza, Loreto, B.C.S. 23880. Tel. 683/3-0299 or 3-0399. 84 rms (all with bath). A/C
$ Rates: $25 single or double.
Scattered about the arid grounds beside the sea are several trailerlike buildings. Inside, the neat and clean cubicles have light wood paneling, a bunk, and a double bed. Facilities include a tennis court and swimming pool, but no restaurant. A chain-link fence surrounds the "villa" and separates it from the rock-strewn beach. It's a mile south of town at the end of Calle Madero. If you don't have a car, try to rent a bicycle from the Stouffer Presidente Hotel. Otherwise the $2 taxi fare to or from town adds up—and it's too far to walk on a hot day or at night.

HOTEL LA PINTA, Calle Davis (Apdo. Postal 28), Loreto, B.C.S. 23880. Tel. 683/3-0025. Fax 683/3-0026. 49 rms (all with bath). A/C TV
$ Rates: $40–$52 "Hacienda" single, $53–$63 "Villa" single; $44–$56 "Hacienda" double, $56–$67 "Villa" double. Extra person $15.
★ Beyond the north end of the Malecón facing the smooth beach of brown sand, but entered from Calle Davis on the west side of the property, the La Pinta offers large, simply furnished rooms in several two-story, brick buildings that resemble apartment houses. All have sliding glass doors that open onto little balconies or patios with an ocean view. A "Hacienda" room, with a queen-size bed, appears to be the better value. Yet several people could share a "Villa" room, furnished with one single and two double beds, TV, and a fireplace. Hotel amenities include a restaurant, bar, and swimming pool. Fishing boats and kayaks are available for rent.

HOTEL MISION, Blvd. López Mateos 1 (Apdo. Postal 49), Loreto, B.C.S. 23880. Tel. 683/3-0048. Fax 683/3-0648. 36 rms (all with bath). A/C
$ Rates: High season $45–$55 single; $57–$67 double; $69–$79 triple (the higher rate includes breakfast or lunch). Off-season (Sept to mid-Dec), rates are 20% less.
A favorite for its Spanish colonial charm and central location on the town waterfront, on the Malecón at Juárez, this rambling hotel of white stucco arches and painted tile rises three stories behind a landscaped courtyard facing the sea. Some of the corner rooms are quite large with simple wood furniture and beds for four or five people; three rooms have TVs. Amenities include laundry service, a good restaurant, indoor and outdoor bars, gift shop, and swimming pool. The "beach" is rocky; for a sand beach walk north on the Malecón toward the Hotel La Pinta. The hotel can arrange fishing trips and other activities. Ask for a room with a sea view.

WORTH THE EXTRA BUCKS

HOTEL OASIS, Blvd. López Mateos (Apdo. Postal 17), Loreto, B.C.S. 23880. Tel. 683/3-0112 or 3-0211. Fax 683/3-0795. 35 rms (all with bath). A/C
$ Rates (including three meals a day): $70 single; $95 double.
Nestled into a pretty garden setting by the sea, beyond the southern end of the Malecón (Boulevard López Mateos), where it stops. The cottagelike stone buildings have generous rooms with substantial wood furniture, two double beds, and a big front porch. Guests can enjoy the tennis courts and swimming pool or arrange a fishing charter with the hotel's fleet. The attractive restaurant and bar look out on the waves. Laundry service is available.

STOUFFER PRESIDENTE HOTEL, Blvd. Misión de Loreto, Loreto, B.C.S. 23880. Tel. 683/3-0700, or toll free 800/HOTELS-1 in the U.S. Fax 683/3-

0377. 235 rms, including 8 suites (all with bath). A/C TV TEL **Taxi:** To or from town, $10; the airport, $6.
$ Rates: $75–$80 single or double. Extra person $25. **Parking:** Free.
This large resort hotel on Nopolo Bay, 7 miles south of Loreto and 1 mile south of the airport, is a world in itself, with beautifully landscaped grounds, its own beach and water-sports facilities (fishing, boat rentals, dive shop), two pools, four bars (the lobby bar has Ping-Pong and pool tables), a disco, three restaurants, a travel agency, and mini-shopping arcade. The contemporary-style rooms are scattered about the grounds in stone and stucco two-story buildings; each room comes with a balcony or patio and 42 have ocean views. Evening turndown, laundry, and room service (6am to midnight) are available. Just across the street is the Loreto Tennis Center. The in-house travel agency rents cars for $35 a day (including tax and insurance) plus 20¢ per kilometer to guests and others. For those who don't plan to spend much time in town, this resort can be a fine escape.

WHERE TO EAT

Local specialties include smoked fish (pescado ahumado), chocolate clams (a type of almeja, not the preparation), and fresh yellowtail tuna. Many restaurants are glad to custom-cook your catch: For fish grilled with garlic and butter, order *pescado al mojo de ajo* ("al *mo*-ho day *ah*-ho").

LA FUENTE, Salvatierra.
Specialty: MEXICAN.
$ Prices: Appetizers $1–$2; main courses $2–$8; comida corrida $3; breakfast dishes $2.50–$3; shrimp dinner $8.
Open: Daily 7am–9pm (comida corrida served noon–4pm).
This small family restaurant with a palapa roof and cactus-rib walls serves breakfast (try the huevos divorciados, with two sauces), a comida corrida, and dinners of fresh seafood caught by local fishermen. Typical dishes served with the daily special are chiles rellenos (stuffed with meat or cheese), garlic fish, and meat or chicken with pipian, a delicious sauce. On Saturday and Sunday try the hearty stews, menudo and pozole. La Fuente is on Salvatierra across from the long-distance telephone office and east of the Pemex gas station.

EL MESÓN, Salvatierra and Tamaral. Tel. 3-0767.
Specialty: MEXICAN.
$ Prices: Main courses $3.50–$4.
Open: Mon–Sat 7:30am–6pm, Sun 7:30am–4pm (comida corrida served 1–5pm).
Served on the front porch or inside this modest stucco building, the comida corrida comes with soup, beans, and rice. Typical main courses are ham and cheese enchiladas or chicken mole. El Mesón is on the north side of the main street just beyond the traffic circle at the entrance to town.

CAFE OLE, Madero. Tel. 3-0496.
Specialty: MEXICAN.
$ Prices: Breakfast $2–$5; main courses $3.50–$8; tortas or tacos $2–$4.
Open: Mon–Sat 7am–10pm, Sun 7am–2pm.
Popular with locals, this open-air eatery under a palapa roof dishes out decent budget eats. The kitchen is in view right behind the lunch counter, and patrons place their orders and wait on themselves. It's on Madero between Salvatierra and Hidalgo, just south of the town plaza and bandstand.

EL EMBARCADERO, Blvd. López Mateos. Tel. 3-0165.
Specialty: MEXICAN/SEAFOOD.
$ Prices: Appetizers $2–$5; main courses $5–$14; soup $2.50; daily specials $4.25–$7.

Open: Dinner only, Thurs–Tues 5–11pm.

⭐ At this simple brick building on the waterfront, on the Malecón north of Juárez and the Hotel Misión, seafood reigns supreme, some of it grilled to succulent perfection over a wood fire outdoors. Especially recommended are the clams steamed with a savory broth, and the grilled fish topped with scallops, almonds, and garlic-butter sauce. When available, a delicious dip made with fish smoked on the premises is served as a complimentary appetizer. The proprietors also own Alfred's Sport Fishing, so the fish here is usually fresh.

CESAR'S, Juárez at Zapata. Tel. 3-0203.
Specialty: MEXICAN.
$ Prices: Appetizers $3–$6; main courses $7–$14; soup $2.50–$6; crêpe suzettes for two $11.
Open: Daily 11am–11pm.

⭐ Loreto's oldest fine dining restaurant, on Juárez across from the supermarket and the Pemex gas station, still puts on a good show with tableside Caesar salad and flaming desserts served beneath the wood-beamed ceilings hung with fishnets and nautical doodads. For a splurge and the community camaraderie on Saturday night, it's *the* place to be. Locals and tourists often drift over to the bar after dinner to mingle and sing together if a musician strolls in with his guitar.

EL NIDO, Salvatierra 154. Tel. 3-0284.
Specialty: MEXICAN/STEAKHOUSE.
$ Prices: Appetizers $2–$5; main courses $8–$15; Mexican plate $8.
Open: Daily 1–11pm.

⭐ The rustic cactus-and-wagonwheel decor sets the tone for some of the best charcoal-grilled steaks and seafood in town. Some of the fresh seafood is local and the steaks are from the state of Sonora in northern Mexico, famous for its fine beef.

Ⓢ You'll find El Nido on the south side of the main street just beyond the traffic circle at the entrance to town.

SHOPPING

Loreto's crafts and clothing shops are clustered around Salvatierra near the mission church and along Madero near the town square. Among the best are **El Alacrán, El Sarape, Regalos Azteca,** and **Eclipse.** El Alacrán has especially nice crafts, while Eclipse specializes in hand-painted T-shirts.

EVENING ENTERTAINMENT

STOUFFER PRESIDENTE HOTEL, Blvd. Misión de Loreto. Tel. 3-0700.
The hotel holds a Mexican Fiesta on Saturday night from 8 to 10pm. It includes an open bar with national drinks, all-you-can-eat buffet, mariachis, folkloric dancers, and games.
Admission: $20.

DISCO DUNA, in the Stouffer Presidente Hotel, Blvd. Misión de Loreto. Tel. 3-0700.
This sleek disco is the lively late-night place in Loreto on the weekends, when it's popular with locals as well as tourists. Open Friday and Saturday from 10pm to 3am. Drinks cost $3–$5.
Admission: Men $5; women free.

CESAR'S RESTAURANT, Juárez at Zapata. Tel. 3-0203.
⭐ On Saturday night, a local guitarist or two often stroll in and sing Mexican songs in the bar with whomever wants to join in. Decorated with fish nets and rustic dark wood, this bar/restaurant has the comfortable feeling of a

neighborhood get-together. Open daily from 11am to 11pm, sometimes later on Saturday. Beer is $1.25; margaritas, $2.

PELICANOS BAR, in the Hotel Misión, Blvd. López Mateos 1. Tel. 3-0048.

American sports fishermen ready to party after a hard day battling yellowtail often fill the barstools of this cozy upstairs hangout overlooking the waterfront. Its walls testify to its steady patronage: Nearly every square inch is checkered with foreign business cards. Be ready with your jokes and fish tales here if you want to be one of the boys. Open daily from 1 to 9pm. Beer runs $1.50; margaritas, $2.50.

4. MULEGE

327 miles N of La Paz, 90 miles N of Loreto, 40 miles S of Santa Rosalía, 652 miles S of Tijuana

GETTING THERE By Bus North- and southbound buses pass through Mulege every few hours during the day and evening, letting off passengers at the bus stop on the edge of town beside the highway, where you can usually find a taxi in the daytime. There's no bus station.

By Car Coming from the north or south, the only choice is Mexico Highway 1. The 50-mile section just south of Mulege that edges Concepción Bay is especially scenic.

DEPARTING By Bus The bus stop is at the north end of town beside the highway (there's no bus station). For bus schedules, contact the local tourist representative, **Javier Aguiar,** at the Hotel Las Casitas at Madero 50 (tel. 3-0019). The first northbound bus arrives around 10am; the next at 1:30pm. The first southbound bus comes through around 11am. They pick up passengers if there's space on the bus.

A tropical hamlet on one of the few rivers in Baja, Mulege has the insouciant appeal of an oasis. Mangrove thickets edge its lazy, milky-green river, while dense groves of palm trees reach from the riverbanks to the pink and terra-cotta foothills of the Sierra. Over the years, this easy-going village of 5,000 inhabitants has attracted a community of around 1,000 Americans who live here semipermanently, many of them in the trailer parks along the river south of town. But whether it's the oasis ambience or the influence of the semi-expatriate milieu, Mulege has the air of a town on vacation. It's a good place simply to relax, do a little shopping or laundry, and meet other people in the area by going to the "fiesta nights" at local hotels. Mulege is not a beach town, however, for the nearest beach is about 3 miles south.

ORIENTATION

ARRIVING By Bus If your luggage is light, you can walk to the hotels in town, which is quite small. A taxi to any hotel in town shouldn't cost much more than $1; to the farthest hotel, the Serenidad, which is 2 miles south of town, the fare is $2.50.

INFORMATION There's no official tourist office here, but the local tourism representative, **Javier Aguiar,** owns the Hotel Las Casitas, at Madero 50 (tel. 3-0019), and can provide information.

CITY LAYOUT Mulege lies on the north side of the Mulege River and Highway 1, about 3 miles from the sea. It's organized around **Madero** and **Zaragoza** streets, which intersect by the main plaza next to the highway. Street signs are scarce, but the town is small: If you can't find a place, just ask—it can't be far. Mulege Divers and the Hotel Las Casitas on Madero sometimes have maps.

GETTING AROUND

You can walk all around the town proper in about 20 minutes. To get to the nearest beach or a hotel or restaurant out of town, you'll have to take a taxi or "bus-hike" (see "What to See and Do," below).

FAST FACTS

Area Code   The telephone area code is 685.

Business Hours   Shops are usually open Monday through Saturday from 9am to 1pm and 3 to 7pm, but posted hours are not always kept, however.

Currency Exchange   Hotels exchange currency for their guests.

Laundry   There's a good self-service **Laundromat Claudia** just up the hill on Zaragoza at Moctezuma (tel. 3-0057). Tokens for the machines cost $2 for a washer, $1 for a dryer. You can also buy detergent. Open Monday through Saturday from 8am to 6pm.

WHAT TO SEE & DO

ATTRACTIONS   On a bluff at the southern edge of Mulege rises the **Santa Rosalía de Mulege mission,** founded in 1705 by the Jesuits. Even better than the stark stone church, however, is the **mirador** behind it, an eyrie with a spectacular panoramic view of the town, its winding green river, and the thick palm groves spreading from the river to the desert mountains.

WATER SPORTS   In town, sign up for **scuba diving** or **snorkeling** trips with Mulege Divers at Madero 45, open Monday through Saturday from 9am to 1pm and 3 to 6pm. Snorkeling excursions start at $15, and scuba trips at $35, depending on what equipment you rent.

Fishing trips with Mario Yee's "Pelicano Fleet," located next to the Hotel Serenidad, start at $95 a day for a 22-foot skiff for three (including skipper and equipment). Reservations can be made in advance (tel. 685/3-0111 or 3-0179; 619/436-0212 in the U.S., fax 619/943-8665).

BEACHES   Mulege's nearest beach is about a mile hike south from the Hotel Serenidad, which is 2 miles south of town. Without a car, the options for reaching the beach are taxis and buses. The one-way taxi fare would range from $9 to $13. You might "bus-hike" from the bus stop (the first southbound bus comes through at 11am) if the driver will agree to drop you at the turnoff for one of the following beaches south of Mulege: **Punta Arena** or **"Raul's Beach"** (8 miles), **Playa Santispac** (10 miles), **Playa Los Cocos** (12 miles), and **Playa El Coyote,** the most scenic (15 miles). All are on magnificent, morning-glory-blue Concepcion Bay.

IMPRESSIONS

Probably nowhere in the world do two countries as different as Mexico and the United States live side by side. . . . Probably nowhere in the world do two neighbors understand each other so little. . . . More than by levels of development, the two countries are separated by language, religion, race, philosophy, and history.
—ALAN RIDING, *DISTANT NEIGHBORS,* 1986

But expect to share some of the beaches with campers and RV's, and wear sturdy shoes for hiking from the highway to the beach. The bus fare from Mulege to Loreto is around $3 one way, so negotiate for less than that. For the return trip, check locally on when the last northbound bus passes through during daylight hours.

CAVE PAINTINGS   Three-hour expeditions (round-trip) to see ancient petroglyphs and cave paintings near San Balthazar, San Patricio, or Trinidad can be arranged in advance through **Javier Aguiar** at the Hotel Las Casitas (tel. 685/3-0019) and start around $160 for the trip. He can also arrange longer trips to other caves by mule with local guides Narciso or Arturo Villavicencio. Rates for mules and guide start around $30 a day per person.

WHERE TO STAY

HOTEL VIEJA HACIENDA, Madero 3, Mulege, B.C.S. 23900. Tel. 685/3-0021. 14 rms (all with bath).
$ Rates: $14 single; $17 double.
This two-story hotel on Madero east of the town plaza lives up to its name ("Old Hacienda") with a certain shabby-genteel charm. The garden of the rambling patio it surrounds, partially shaded by trees, needs tending, and everything looks a bit run-down, including the pool and outdoor furniture by the open-air bar. Rooms are as plain as linoleum, with two double beds and sometimes a kitchenette; eight are air-conditioned and the rest have fans. The bar is open from noon to midnight daily.

HOTEL TERRAZAS, Zaragoza, Mulege, B.C.S. 23900. 20 rms (all with bath. A/C
$ Rates: $19 single; $25 double; $30 triple.
Stacked on the hillside on Zaragoza north of Moctezuma, in tiers softened by fuschia and orange bougainvillea, the four motellike buildings contain plain brick rooms with tile floors. From the roof patio you get a fine view of the town below; the rooftop bar is occasionally open.

HOTEL ROSITA, Madero 2, Mulege, B.C.S. 23900. Tel. 685/3-0270. 12 suites (all with bath). A/C
$ Rates: $24 suite for one or two, $27 suite for three or four.
This two-story mini-apartment building offers somewhat dusty and dim two-bedroom suites with kitchenettes and worn modern furniture. The central location, on Madero about a block east of the town plaza, is convenient.

HOTEL LAS CASITAS, Madero 50, Mulege, B.C.S. 23900. Tel. 685/3-0019. 8 rms (all with bath). A/C
$ Rates: $22 single; $29 double.
The most cheerful place to bunk right in town has clean, simple rooms arranged around a small patio spilling over with vines and flowering plants. Each room comes with two double beds and a shower. The hotel's reasonably priced restaurant and bar also have an attractive patio. It's located on Madero about a block east of the town plaza.

WORTH THE EXTRA BUCKS

HOTEL SERENIDAD, Apdo. Postal 9, Mulege, B.C.S. 23900. Tel. 685/3-0111203. Fax 685/3-0311. 55 rms (all with bath). A/C
$ Rates: $60–$65 single or double.
This hotel captures the casual grace of a Spanish hacienda with its two courtyards, fountain, and swimming pool shaded by palms and splashed by bougainvillea. Several one-story, tile-roofed white buildings are scattered about

the grounds, the newer ones with appealing rattan furnishings and papier-mâché wall hangings, the older ones with corner fireplaces. The spacious dining room, warmed on cool nights by several fireplaces, is a crossroads for people from all over—some of whom arrive in their own boats or planes. The owner, Don Johnson, also serves as the American consular agent in Baja California Sur. The hotel is 2 miles south of Mulege on the Mulege River; taxi fare is about $2.50 one way.

WHERE TO EAT

NEVERIA LA PURISIMA "BLANCAS," Zaragoza. Tel. 3-0271.
Specialty: ICE CREAM AND PASTRIES.
$ Prices: Pastry and ice cream $1–$2.
Open: Daily 9am–8pm.
This tiny shop on Zaragoza about a block north of the town square sells delicious bunuelos, fruit-filled empanadas, and homemade ice cream, along with hot coffee to wash them down. For a quick breakfast or afternoon snack, this is the place. A small shrine to the Virgin sits against a wall.

EDUARDO'S BARBECUE, Martínez. Tel. 3-0258.
Specialty: MEXICAN.
$ Prices: Main courses $3.50–$7; hot dogs $1; burgers $3.50; barbecued chicken or pork ribs $5–$7; margaritas $1.25.
Open: Daily 11:30am–10pm.
This thatch-roofed, casual eatery open to the street serves freshly grilled meat at metal checkerboard tables. Piñatas dangling from the ceiling add a festive touch to the simple room. It's on Martínez half a block west of Zaragoza, across from the Pemex gas station.

LOS EQUIPALES, Moctezuma. Tel. 3-0330.
Specialty: MEXICAN/SEAFOOD.
$ Prices: Appetizers $2–$7; main courses $3.50–$13; soup of the day $2; shrimp dishes $6–$8; breakfast courses $3.50; beer $1.
Open: Daily 8am–10pm.
This cheerful new restaurant on the second floor of a recently constructed brick building has graceful arches and an attractive shaded terrace overlooking the street. Plants, piñatas, and blue-and-white tablecloths set with pretty ceramic plates add Mexican charm. It's on Moctezuma half a block west of Zaragoza and the laundry.

HOTEL LAS CASITAS, Madero 50. Tel. 3-0019.
Specialty: MEXICAN/SEAFOOD.
$ Prices: Appetizers $2–$8; main courses $3.50–$15; soup $2; breakfast, burgers, or burritos $3.50–$5; daily specials $3–$9; Sun brunch $6.
Open: Daily 6:30am–10pm.
In a cozy room festively embellished with plants, folk art, and bright plaid tablecloths—or outdoors on a patio lush with tropical greenery—diners enjoy seafood, steak, and Mexican dishes. Take-out lunches for expeditions are also available. It's on Madero a block east of the town plaza.

NEARBY DINING

A visit to either of the next two establishments, both off Highway 1 about 2 miles south of town, should cost around $5 in round-trip taxi fare.

VILLA MARÍA ISABEL RV PARK, south of Mulege.
Specialty: FRENCH/MEXICAN BAKERY.
$ Prices: Baked goods 75¢–$1; whole pizza $8–$10; pizza slice $1.50–$2.
Open: Mon–Sat 9am–5pm.

⭐ The trip out to this RV park is worth the effort, for the bakery here serves excellent French pastries as well as cinnamon rolls, cookies, muffins, onion and cheese rolls, and pizza. It's south of Mulege on Highway 1 about 1½ miles. Turn left at the sign for the RV park; the bakery is to the left of the main office.

LA JUNGLA BAMBU RESTAURANT, south of Mulege. Tel. 2-0300.
    Specialty: ITALIAN/FRENCH/ECLECTIC.
$ Prices: Main courses $6–$13; steak or lobster $14–$16; breakfast dishes, crêpes, blintzes, or cinnamon rolls $3–$5.
    Open: Daily 8am–10pm.

Nestled under a palm grove beside the Mulege River, this American-owned casual restaurant has an impressively eclectic menu that includes mango blintzes, chicken crêpes, shrimp scampi, fish Veracruz, smoked pork chops, and Sonoran steaks. This wide array is suspended only on Monday night during football season, when fans dine on burgers and chili dogs while watching the game on the big-screen TV. The restaurant is south of town on Highway 1 about 1½ miles; turn left at the restaurant sign (between the Oasis Trailer Park and Poncho's Trailer Park).

SHOPPING

It doesn't take long to visit the half dozen or so tourist shops in town. At Madero 47, **Regalos "Nancy"** (tel. 3-0111) has one of the nicest selections of crafts and resort wear; **Bazar La Gaviota,** on Madero adjoining the Hotel Las Casitas (tel. 3-0019), also carries cotton clothing. Try **Casa de Regalos Ann,** Moctezuma 21 (tel. 3-0032), for crafts and dresses; or **Lyta's,** on the west end of Martínez (tel. 3-0040), for huaraches, baskets, and piñatas. There are also some curio stores along Zaragoza.

EVENING ENTERTAINMENT

Mulege is one of those cozy little towns where nightlife means finding out where the party is. The Americans who live here part time or full time keep Margaritaville alive and well in this happy hamlet.

HOTEL SERENIDAD, 2 miles south on Hwy. 1. Tel. 3-0111203.
⭐ On Saturday night from 7 to 10pm the party is definitely at the Hotel Serenidad, where guests gorge themselves at the famous **Pig Roast,** an all-you-can-eat buffet, while mariachis play on the patio. The "guest list" is limited to 200, so make reservations in advance. On Wednesday night from 7 to 10pm the hotel holds a **Mexican Fiesta** with a buffet and mariachis. For the Pig Roast and Mexican Fiesta, make reservations at Regalos Nancy on Madero 47 (tel. 3-0111 or fax 3-0311).
    Admission: $13 Fiesta, $15 Pig Roast, including one margarita.

HOTEL LAS CASITAS, Madero 50. Tel. 3-0019.
    The hotel puts on a Mexican Fiesta on Friday night starting at 7pm. It includes a Mexican buffet (all you can eat), a margarita, and live mariachi music.
    Admission: $11.

LA JUNGLA BAMBU, south of town on Hwy. 1. Tel. 2-0300.
    Sports fans gather here for "Monday Night Football" on TV with burgers, beer, and hot dogs. Drinks run $2 to $4.
    Admission: Free.

5. SANTA ROSALÍA

367 miles N of La Paz, 40 miles N of Mulege, 612 miles S of Tijuana

GETTING THERE   By Bus   North- and southbound buses arrive during the day and evening, starting at 5am (from the south) and 7am (from the north). Several bus lines, including **Tres Estrellas de Oro** (first class) and **Aguila** (second class), serve Santa Rosalía.

By Car   Whether coming from the north or south, the only choice is Mexico Highway 1. The 3- to 4-hour stretch from Guerrero Negro cuts across the peninsula and offers some spectacular desert and mountain scenery. En route you pass Los Tres Virgenes, three extinct volcanoes.

By Ferry   The **SEMATUR ferry** makes the 8-hour crossing from Guaymas to Santa Rosalía on Sunday, Tuesday, Friday, and Saturday, departing Guaymas at 10am. Only Salón-class tickets (bus-type seats in a large room), for $11 one way, are available. In Guaymas, the SEMATUR ticket office is located at Muelle Fiscal, Guaymas, Son. 85400 (tel. 622/2-3392 or 2-3393).

DEPARTING   By Bus   The **main bus station** (tel. 2-0150) is on Highway 1 south of the Pemex gas station; it's open daily from 8am to 2pm and 4 to 10pm. The "station" for the **Aguila** line (tel. 2-0174) is a yellow house with brown trim near the corner of Calle 3a and Constitución, a block west of the town square. It's open daily from 8am to 1pm and 4 to 8pm and sells tickets through the window. The only southbound bus that originates in Santa Rosalía, and on which you can buy a reserved seat the day before, departs from the yellow house daily at 11am, arriving in Loreto around 2pm and in La Paz at 7pm; change buses here for Los Cabos and arrive around 10pm. Northbound buses start arriving at 5am at the main station and take passengers if there's space. To San Ignacio (48 miles north), however, there are two "local" buses (originating in Santa Rosalía) departing from the main station at 2 and 5pm.

By Ferry   The **SEMATUR ferry** to Guaymas departs on Sunday, Tuesday, Friday, and Saturday at 11pm. Only Salón-class tickets (bus-type seats in a large room), for $11 one way, are available for the 8-hour crossing. The Salón section can become crowded; it's not unusual for Salón-class passengers to sleep rolled up in blankets on deck when the Salón seats are full. SEMATUR ferries are usually equipped with a cafeteria, restaurant-bar, and disco. Nevertheless, it's wise to bring some of your own food and bottled water.

Tickets can be purchased on the day of departure at the SEMATUR **ferry terminal building** on the waterfront by the highway, Muelle Fiscal, Santa Rosalía, B.C.S. 23920 (tel. 685/2-0013 or 2-0014).

For more information about ferry service, see "Seeing Baja California" at the beginning of this chapter.

The architecture of this atypical town immediately grabs your attention: Instead of stucco walls topped with red-tile roofs, rows of pastel wooden houses with matching picket fences line the bustling streets of Santa Rosalía (pop. 15,000). A bit of Europe in Baja, Santa Rosalía was founded by the French in 1855 as the "company town" for their Boleo Mine on the slopes just behind the port—the first copper mine in Mexico. Baja is not known for its forests, so the French imported their wood by boat from British Columbia.

Though the French departed in 1953, the Gallic influence remains not only in the architecture—the town boasts the only prefabricated-iron church in the world designed by Gustave Eiffel—but also in the specialty: Santa Rosalía bakes the best bread in Baja.

The town's port and former mine make its rocky waterfront look rather industrial. But the fact that Santa Rosalía is not a tourist town gives this French-built anomaly in Mexico an un-self-conscious charm as well as lower prices. It also makes a good base for whale watching and expeditions to ancient cave paintings. And as the French would say, *Vive la différence!*

ORIENTATION

ARRIVING   By Bus   Most buses arrive at the main station on Highway 1, about half a mile south of town. A taxi from here to most hotels will run $2 to $3. If the bus stops at the yellow house "station," you can walk to one of the two budget hotels in town.

By Ferry   From the ferry dock it's just a short walk to the two budget hotels in town.

INFORMATION   The town has no tourist information office, but sometimes a representative in the mayor's office at the Palacio Municipal (city hall), across from the town square on Carranza (tel. 685/2-0085 or 2-0086), can provide information. Otherwise you must call the state tourist representative in Mulege (tel. 685/3-0019 or 3-0219).

CITY LAYOUT   Santa Rosalía spreads west from the waterfront, its main streets being **Obregón** and **Constitución**. Up the hill to the north of downtown is the **old French neighborhood,** full of beautiful 19th-century wood-frame houses just begging to be restored. The **town square** on Constitución is easy to find—just look for the French-style city hall facing it. If you're driving, pay attention to the one-way signs.

GETTING AROUND

The town is small enough to explore on foot. However, if you're too tired to make the hike up the hill to the French section and the Hotel Francés, wait for the **bus** across the street (Altamirano at Obregón) from the Eiffel iron church; the fare is under $1. Catch **taxis** at the town square or on Obregón near the Conasupo store.

FAST FACTS

Area Code   The telephone area code is 685.
Banks   There are two banks on Obregón, generally open Monday through Friday from 9am to 1pm.
Business Hours   Shops are generally open from 9 or 10am to 7 or 8pm, with a closing for lunch between 1 and 4pm.
Climate   When a norther comes through, Santa Rosalía can get chilly. Take a warm jacket in winter.
Post Office   The Correos is located at Constitución and Calle 2.
Telegraph Office   Telegrams can be sent from the office on Altamirano and Constitución, cater-corner from the town square.
Telephone   Long-distance calls can be made from the **Farmacía California,** at Obregón and Calle 1, which is also a good drugstore.

WHAT TO SEE & DO

Because Santa Rosalía is not a tourist town, there's not much in the way of shopping or special activities for tourists. Nor is there a smooth, sandy beach: The closest swimming beach is rocky **Playa El Morro,** a mile out of town and south of the hotel of the same name. Nevertheless it's a pleasant town to explore on foot, and can be a base for fishing, whale watching, and expeditions to ancient cave paintings.

ARCHITECTURE   A walk around this former French mining town is not without its rewards. Besides the rows of pastel wooden houses with picket fences enclosing flower gardens, you'll find 19th-century public buildings crowned with European-style square clock towers. And a stroll up the hill on the north side of town to what was once the **French residential section** around the Hotel Francés reveals wood-frame colonial mansions and homes that look as if they came straight from a plantation in the French West Indies with their broad, overhanging roofs shading raised front porches. From here there's also a view of the old copper mineworks spilling down the adjacent hillside to the harbor; and across from the Hotel Francés stands an old steam locomotive that probably once carried the copper ore.

The French left their architectural imprint in the downtown area, too: At Obregón and Calle 1 rises the **Iglesia Santa Barbara**—a church of prefabricated iron designed by Gustave Eiffel (designer of the famous tower in Paris) in 1884 and shipped in pieces by boat to Santa Rosalía, where it was installed by 1897.

FISHING Deep-sea fishing trips can be arranged through **Keith Daggett** at Fisherman's Landing at Obregón 48, 2nd Floor (tel. or fax 685/2-0880; or in the U.S. call Rick Cooper at 213/439-9906). Charters on a 30-foot cabin cruiser with captain, mate, and equipment start at $250 a day for up to five people.

SPECIAL EVENT October 19–22 is the **Fiestas de Santa Rosalía.**

WHERE TO STAY

HOTEL OLVERA, Playa 14, Santa Rosalía, B.C.S. 23920. Tel. 685/2-0057. 11 rms (all with bath). A/C
$ **Rates:** $17 single; $22 double.

This two-story, yellow wood-frame building on Calle Playa at Montoya, about a block inland from the waterfront, offers clean, simple rooms (some quite large) with minimal furniture and bare-bulb lighting. The upstairs rooms open onto a shaded communal porch.

HOTEL REAL, Montoya 7, Santa Rosalía, B.C.S. 23920. Tel. 685/2-0068. 13 rms (all with bath). A/C TV
$ **Rates:** $19 single; $23 double; $27 triple.

This small hotel half a block inland from the waterfront offers snug, wood-paneled rooms with plain furniture and an occasional decorative flourish, such as carved trim around a bedroom mirror. A big tree-shaded front porch looks out on the park across the street. Ask for one of the remodeled rooms.

EL MORRO HOTEL, Hwy. 1 km 1.5 Sur (Apdo. Postal 76), Santa Rosalía, B.C.S. 23920. Tel. 685/2-0414. 41 rms (all with bath). A/C TV
$ **Rates:** $25 single; $30 double.

Perched on a bluff overlooking the Sea of Cortez, this hotel offers medium-sized modern rooms with two comfortable double beds and glass doors opening onto a patio in back. Long stone arcades planted with flowers shelter the walkways that edge the one-story wings and lead to the swimming pool. Friendly locals and tourists often gather in the restaurant and bar, which overlook the sea. Ask for a room with an ocean view. The hotel is 1 mile south of town on Highway 1; taxi fare is about $2.50 one way.

WHERE TO EAT

EL BOLEO BAKERY, Obregón and Calle 4. Tel. 2-0310.
Specialty: MEXICAN BAKERY.
$ **Prices:** Bread and pastries 50¢–$2.
Open: Mon–Sat 10am–7:30pm, Sun 10am–1:30pm.

Thanks to the French, Santa Rosalía is known for having the best bread in Baja, and everyone stops here for fresh hot bread, muffins, cookies, or Mexican *pan dulce*. Patrons line up at the cafeteria counter and point to what they want. It's on Obregón about eight blocks inland from the waterfront.

JUGOS CHAPALA, Obregón and Calle 4.
Specialty: FRUIT DRINKS.
$ **Prices:** Juice drinks $1.25–$2.
Open: Daily 6am–8pm.

Order fresh-squeezed orange or pineapple juice or let them whip up a papaya or mango drink for you at this tiny corner juicery, where the fruit is piled up artistically behind the counter. It's on Obregón across from El Boleo Bakery.

SUPER TORTAS ESAR, Calle 4 between Obregón and Constitución. Tel. 2-1206.
Specialty: MEXICAN SANDWICHES.
$ Prices: Tortas $1.25–$2.50; main courses $5–$7; fish $5; shrimp or steak $7; tacos, tamales, burgers, or omelets $1–$4.
Open: Mon–Sat 8am–9pm.

In a small white room with two tables, some of the best tortas—Mexican sandwiches—in town are served. Try the succulent pork carnitas on heavenly bread with a side of fresh french fries.

ASADERO DON DRAGON, Constitución and Guerrero. Tel. 2-1044.
Specialty: MEXICAN GRILL.
$ Prices: Appetizers $2.50; main courses $3–$10; cheese quesadillas or beef tacos $3; roast chicken $7; steak brochette $10.
Open: Daily 1–11:30pm.

Red-checkered tablecloths and rough wood provide the right rustic ambience to go with the grilled steaks, carne asada, and roast chicken. You can also dine at the sidewalk counter on tacos with a tempting assortment of salsas and condiments, while watching the grill at work.

To get there, walk inland on Constitución to the corner of Guerrero.

RESTAURANT SELENE, Playa Sur. Tel. 2-0685.
Specialty: MEXICAN/CHINESE/SEAFOOD.
$ Prices: Appetizers $3–$5; main courses $3.50–$13; soups $3–$6; enchiladas $3.50; seafood platter $13.
Open: June–Oct, daily 7am–midnight; Nov–May, daily 8am–10pm.

For windows looking out on the waves and delightfully tacky, beach-shack decor, take a hike to this restaurant on the waterfront south of town across from the Pemex gas station. Selene makes something for everyone: seafood, Mexican dishes, and Chinese food.

RESTAURANT EL MORRO, in the Hotel El Morro, Hwy. 1 km 1.5 Sur. Tel. 2-0414.
Specialty: INTERNATIONAL.
$ Prices: Appetizers $2–$7; main courses $7–$18; French onion soup $2; jumbo margarita $2; coq au vin, chicken mole, or steamed clams marinara $5–$10; seafood platter $18.
Open: Daily 7am–10pm (sometimes later on weekends).

This cliffside restaurant is the best in town; it's where locals go to celebrate special occasions. Banks of windows on three sides make the most of the fine ocean view, while the massive stone fireplace and cages of parakeets add a comfortable domestic touch. The bar is a pleasant gathering place for meeting residents and visitors, especially over the bartender's potent margaritas. It's on Highway 1 a mile south of town; taxi fare is about $2.50 one way.

EASY EXCURSIONS FROM SANTA ROSALÍA

PREHISTORIC PETROGLYPHS & MODERN WHALES

Santa Rosalía can also serve as a base for visiting the ancient petroglyphs in mountain caves or the whales that migrate to the Pacific coast from January through March.

CAVE PAINTINGS Expeditions to see some of the 100 or so caves painted with ancient petroglyphs can be arranged by guides in Santa Rosalía, San Ignacio, and Guerrero Negro. Although the trips can be made year round, the most pleasant months are October through December; July through September can be uncomfortably hot, especially for one of the longer treks on muleback. No one knows how old the petroglyphs are: estimates range from 300 to 10,000 years.

Note: In arranging any of the trips below, negotiate the fee beforehand and make sure you understand exactly what it covers and what you need to provide (sometimes food, for instance). It is customary to tip the guide 10% to 15% of the tour fee.

From Santa Rosalía: Cave trips can be arranged with local guide **Victor Manuel Fuerte,** who can be reached through the Palacio Municipal (tel. 685/2-0650, 2-0086, or 2-0085; fax 685/2-0545) on the town square. Trips range from 1 hour to all day and start at $20 per person. Fuerte can also set up trips to the mountains to see the wild sheep, and tours to the Pacific coast to see fossils and petrified, prehistoric shark bones.

From San Ignacio (48 miles northwest of Santa Rosalía): **Oscar Fisher** can arrange 1-day visits to cave paintings or longer journeys with mules and camping gear. Rates start at $130 a day for one to six people. Fisher can be reached at the Hotel la Posada, Avenida Carranza 25, San Ignacio, B.C.S. 23930 (tel. 685/13). He recommends making reservations at least 5 days in advance by calling or sending a telegram.

From Guerrero Negro (142 miles northwest of Santa Rosalía): Guides **Enrique Achoy** and **Mario Rueda** are in the process of organizing "Eco Tours Malarrimo" to provide tours to the cave paintings. The 2- to 3-day camping trips will include meals and mules but not sleeping bags and tents—though they say that tents are seldom needed because rain is rare. Reservations must be made in advance by calling Achoy or Rueda at the Malarrimo Restaurant (tel. 685/7-0250), or Achoy at home (tel. 685/7-0020), or by sending them a fax c/o the Guerrero Negro Chamber of Commerce (fax 685/7-0044). Prices and details are still being worked out.

WHALE WATCHING Between January and March (and sometimes as early as December), whales migrate to Laguna San Ignacio (near San Ignacio) and Scammon's Lagoon (near Guerrero Negro) on the Pacific coast.

Both Victor Manuel Fuerte in Santa Rosalía and Oscar Fisher in San Ignacio (see above for telephone numbers) can arrange trips to see the whales in **Laguna San Ignacio,** about a 2-hour trip (17 miles) from San Ignacio over a rough road. Rates start around $40 per person for a minimum party of six.

To see the whales at **Scammon's Lagoon,** contact Enrique Achoy and Mario Rueda in Guerrero Negro. Their whale-watching tours, generally offered from January 20 to March 10, leave between 8am and 9am from the Malarrimo Restaurant on Highway 1 near the east entrance to town, returning around 2pm. The fee of $25 per person includes the round-trip drive to the lagoon, 2 to 3 hours of whale watching from a boat, and a box lunch with soft drinks. Reservations must be made in advance by calling Achoy or Rueda at the Malarrimo Restaurant (tel. 685/7-0250) or Achoy at home (tel. 685/7-0020).

SAN IGNACIO

Another option is to use San Ignacio (48 miles northwest of Santa Rosalía) as a base for whale-watching or cave-paintings tours. It's a little oasis near a palm-fringed river, and boasts one of Baja's loveliest Spanish missions on its main square. Buses to San Ignacio leave Santa Rosalía at 2pm and 5pm, though you could also get on an earlier northbound bus if there's space. From the bus stop on the highway, it's 2 miles into San Ignacio; take a taxi for $1 to $2.

To make the trip from San Ignacio to Laguna San Ignacio on your own, a high-clearance or four-wheel-drive vehicle is necessary.

Note: Although the telephone area code for the region is 685, you must go through the operator to reach San Ignacio.

Where to Stay

HOTEL LA POSADA, Av. Carranza 25, San Ignacio, B.C.S. 23930. Tel. 685/13. 6 rms (all with bath).

$ Rates: $23 double or single.

Owned by local guide Oscar Fisher, this modest hotel about a quarter mile east of the town square (ask locally for directions) offers plain brick rooms with fans arranged around a courtyard and parking area. Though you wouldn't want to spend a week here, it's nice to know about if you need a room.

**HOTEL LA PINTA, Apdo. Postal 37, San Ignacio, B.C.S. 23930. Tel.
685/30,** or toll free 800/336-5454 in the U.S. 28 rms (all with bath). A/C TV
$ Rates: $65 single; $68 double. **Parking:** Free.

★ This white stucco hacienda-style hotel is like San Ignacio: an oasis in the desert. Graceful arches frame courtyards containing a pool and fountains, while wrought iron, Mexican ceramics, folk art, and hand-stenciling decorate the appealing rooms, which come with two double beds. The hotel has a bar and restaurant. It's on the road into San Ignacio, about a mile from town.

Where to Eat

**RESTAURANT TOTA, on the road behind the Hotel La Posada. Tel.
685/42.**
Specialty: MEXICAN/SEAFOOD.
$ Prices: Main courses $4–$13.
Open: Daily 8am–11pm.

You can eat inside or outdoors under a thatched shade while roosters crow next door. This rustic restaurant serves chicken, fresh fish, and huge stuffed clams—two or three can be a meal. To find the restaurant, ask directions at the Hotel La Posada, Avenida Carranza 25.

GUERRERO NEGRO

It may be possible to get from Santa Rosalía to Guerrero Negro (142 miles northwest) in time for the whale-watching tour departure (between 8am and 9am) by catching the 5am northbound bus—*if* there's space on the bus and *if* it arrives on time, for the trip takes about 3 hours. At Guerrero Negro, ask the bus driver to drop you off at the Malarrimo Restaurant (double-check on this and bus schedules when making your tour reservation). The tour usually returns by 2pm, in time to catch a southbound bus back to Santa Rosalía (check locally; buses usually come through every couple of hours or so into the evening). Another option is to spend the night in Guerrero Negro and go on the tour the next day.

To drive to Scammon's Lagoon on your own, near km 209 on Highway 1 (south of Guerrero Negro) take the turnoff heading southwest to the lagoon, marked by the sign LAGUNA OJO DE LIEBRE—if the sign is missing, it's the only road heading toward the coast (away from the mountains) near the km 209 marker. The 18-mile drive over a bumpy but passable dirt road has occasional signs pointing the way to the lagoon.

At the lagoon, local fishermen with small motorboats take tourists to see the whales between 9am and 5pm for $10 to $15 per person, though they usually insist on a minimum party of five. If you don't have enough people, try to join up with other visitors. If all else fails, politely but persistently try negotiating a trip for one or two. Be aware that no rest rooms or public facilities are available here.

Note: Before making the long trip to Guerrero Negro on your own, call the Malarrimo Restaurant (tel. 685/7-0250) to make sure whales are in Scammon's Lagoon (also called "Laguna Ojo de Liebre"). You can also check with the Delegado Municipal in Guerrero Negro (tel. 685/7-0225) or Enrique Achoy at home (tel. 685/7-0020).

Guerrero Negro is a rather bleak strip of a town along the highway in the desert, with little to recommend it besides these tours. On the other hand, the drive itself is spectacular for its majestic desert and mountain scenery with colorful rock formations and extinct volcanic peaks.

Where to Stay

**EL MORRO MOTEL, Blvd. Emiliano Zapata (Hwy. 1), Domicilio Conocido,
Guerrero Negro, B.C.S. Tel. 685/7-0414.** 32 rms (all with bath).
$ Rates: $19 single; $24 double.

For an overnight stay in Guerrero Negro, this plain, two-story motel on the east side of town on Highway 1 offers clean rooms (some of them brand-new) with fans and one or two double beds. TVs are color and receive U.S. channels. There's a restaurant on the premises.

Where to Eat

MALARRIMO RESTAURANT, Hwy. 1. Tel. 7-0250.
Specialty: MEXICAN/SEAFOOD.
$ Prices: Appetizers $1–$3; main courses $4.50–$11.
Open: Daily 7:30am–10pm.

This small restaurant on Highway 1 by the eastern entrance to town serves good Mexican fare and seafood, including such specialties as abalone and giant shrimp. It also has six rooms for rent at $25 a night.

CHAPTER 8
GUADALAJARA

Known as the "City of Roses," Guadalajara is a great metropolis, the second largest in Mexico. It is considered by many the most "Mexican" of cities. Given its charter as *muy leal y muy noble ciudad* ("most loyal and noble city") by none other than Emperor Charles V, it has held a prominent place in Mexican affairs ever since that time. Charles, who ran most of Europe and a lot of the world at the time, certainly knew what he was doing. Today, Guadalajara (pop. 1,700,000) is the capital of the state of Jalisco. Sophisticated and beautiful though it is, the once very visible roses which decorated the city appear only occasionally these days.

As though to emphasize the great things that were expected of it, Guadalajara's Spanish builders gave the city not one but four beautiful plazas in its center. Today the city's leaders have given it a fifth, the enormous Plaza Tapatía, an ambitious stretch of redevelopment extending for about a mile through the urban landscape. Scattered with trees and monuments, sprinkled with fountains, the new super-plaza links the city's major colonial buildings, opens new perspectives for viewing them, and joins the past with the great new buildings of the present. This now-completed, ambitious project is very "Mexican" in its grand scope.

By the way, tapatío (or tapatía) is a word you'll come across often in this city. No one is quite certain where it originated, but *tapatío* means "Guadalajaran"—a thing, a person, even an idea. The way a *charro* (Mexican cowboy) gives his all, or the way a mariachi sings his heart out—that's tapatío!

Guadalajara is as sophisticated and at least as formal as Mexico City. Dress is conservative; resort wear is out of place here.

1. ORIENTATION

ARRIVING

BY PLANE **The Major Airlines** A number of airlines connect Guadalajara with the rest of Mexico and the southern and western parts of the United States: **Aero California** (flights to/from the west coast of Mexico), **Aeromar** (flights to/from Mexico City, San Luis Potosí, Tepic, and Monterrey), **Aeroméxico** (flights to/

WHAT'S SPECIAL ABOUT GUADALAJARA

Historic Center

☐ With its museums, theaters, restaurants, and pedestrian-only streets, it is a magnificent example of urban renewal that preserves the city's history.

Museums

☐ The enormous Instituto Cabanas Cultural, designed by Manuel Tolsa, with fabulous murals by native son Jose Clemente Orozco.

☐ Tlaquepaque's Regional Ceramics Museum and Tonala's National Ceramics Museum, preserving examples of Mexico's master potters.

Villages

☐ Tlaquepaque, a fascinating shopping center in pedestrian-only streets and plazas.

☐ Tonala, famous for its street market and its artists and craftspeople.

Music & Dance

☐ The Ballet Folklorico de la Universidad de Guadalajara, acclaimed as the best folkloric company in all Mexico.

☐ The battle of the mariachis in Tlaquepaque, under the portals of the historic El Parian.

---

from Houston and Los Angeles in the U.S., and Acapulco, Cancún, Culiacan, Monterrey, Puerto Vallarta, and Torreon in Mexico), **Alaska Airlines** (flights to/from San Francisco and Los Angeles), **American Airlines** (flights to/from Dallas/Fort Worth), **Continental Airlines** (flights to/from Houston), and **Delta** (flights to/from Los Angeles). On flights to/from its three Mexican hub cities (Mexico City, Monterrey and Cancún), **Mexicana** offers connections to most major and many minor destinations in the country.

The Airport   Guadalajara's international airport is a 25- to 45-minute ride from the city. On arrival, buy a ticket for the next *colectivo* minivan headed into town; the tickets cost $5.85 and are sold in the arrivals hall (for the return trip, the company picks up at hotels only, charging around the same for the service). Taxis to the heart of Guadalajara cost around $13.

BY TRAIN   The Major Trains   Guadalajara is the country's second-largest train hub. The **National Railways of Mexico** (tel. 50-0826) link Mexico City and Guadalajara with other destinations on Mexico's new first-class train service, *Estrella*. Note that Pacific-coast trains are notoriously unreliable and off schedule. *El Tapatío* runs from Mexico City to Guadalajara, leaving Mexico City at 8:40pm and arriving in Guadalajara at 8:10am. *El Sinaloense* arrives from Mazatlán at 10:05am. From Mexicali, on the California border, *El Tren del Pacífico* departs at 9am Pacific Standard Time, arriving in Guadalajara at 5pm. From Nogales, *Del Pacífico* departs at 2:20pm and arrives in Guadalajara at 5pm. *El Sinaloense* also goes along the Pacific Coast from Los Mochis through Mazatlán and Tepic, but is a less convenient train.

The Train Station   The station, on Calzada Independencia, is within walking distance (with light luggage) of a couple of recommended hotels. Buses marked "Centro" go downtown, and those marked "Estación" go to the station from downtown. Otherwise you're at the mercy of taxis that charge almost $4 to go the short distance anywhere between the station and the city center.

BY BUS   The bus station is 6 miles south of the city center (see "Moving on—Travel Services" for more information).

City buses pick up passengers in front of each terminal building and can become incredibly crowded. Unless you get a seat, there will be no space for even a small suitcase. Any bus marked "Centro" will take you to the downtown area, or you can look specifically for bus no. 301, which travels to Prisciliano Sanchez Street—a good place to look for hotels four blocks from Plaza Tapatía in the center of town.

White **minivans (combis)** also serve the bus terminal and are more comfortable and convenient than city buses. Combi no. 40, with "Centro" or "Nva," or "Nueva Central" on the windshield, travels along Avenida Revolución and begins and ends its route on Calle Ferrocarril between Avenidas 16 de Septiembre and Corona, just a few blocks from Plaza Tapatía and many of our recommended hotels. If your suitcase fits on your lap and isn't higher than about 2 feet, you can be among the 16 or so passengers squeezing into a minivan. Buses and minivans often empty at the beginning of the U where traffic enters in front of the Flecha Amarilla terminal. There, it's easier to get a seat before they get crowded. The cost of both the bus and a minivan is almost pennies.

Buy fixed-price **taxi** tickets from a booth inside each terminal near the exit doors. Rates vary according to destination, but as an example, a taxi from the Central Camionera to the downtown Plaza Tapatía area (a 20-minute ride) costs about $4.

BY CAR   From Nogales on the California border, follow Highway 15. From Barra de Navidad or southeast on the coast, take Highway 80. From Mexico City, Highway 90 leads to Guadalajara, and coming from Colima to the south, take Mexico 110.

CITY LAYOUT

Guadalajara is not a difficult city to negotiate, but it certainly is big. While most of the main attractions are within walking distance of the historic downtown area, others, such as the nearby villages of Tonala, Tlaquepaque, and farther away, Lake Chapala and Ajijic, are accessible by bus. Street names downtown change at the cathedral.

NEIGHBORHOODS IN BRIEF

Historic Center   The heart of the city takes in Plaza de Armas, Plaza de los Laureles, Plaza de los Hombres Ilustres, Plaza Liberación, and Plaza Tapatía. It's the tourist center and includes major museums, theaters, restaurants, hotels, and the largest covered market in Latin America, all linked by wide boulevards and pedestrians-only streets. It's bounded east and west by Avenidas 16 de Septiembre/ Alcalde and Prosperidad (across Calzada Independencia) and north and south by Avenida Hidalgo and Calle Morelos.

Parque Agua Azul   An enormous city park 20 blocks south of the historic center, with a children's area and rubber-wheeled train. Nearby are the state crafts shop, performing arts theaters, and the anthropology museum.

Chapultepec   A fashionable neighborhood with shops and restaurants 25 blocks west of the historic center, reached by Avenida Vallarta. Chapultepec is the main artery through the neighborhood.

Minerva Circle   Almost 40 blocks west of the historic center, Minerva Circle is at the confluence of Avenidas Vallarta and Lopez Mateos and Circunvalción Washington. A fashionable neighborhood, it has several good restaurants and the Hotel Fiesta Americana, all reached by the Par Vial.

Plaza del Sol   The largest shopping center in the city, south of Minerva Circle and southwest of the historic center near the intersection of Avenidas Lopez Mateos and Mariano Otero.

Zapopan   Once a separate village founded in 1542, now a full-fledged suburb 20 minutes northwest of the Plaza Tapatía via Avenida Avilla Camacho. It's noted for its 18th-century basílica and the revered 16th-century image of the Virgin of Zapopan, made of corn paste and honored every October 12. The city's fashionable country club is just south of Zapopan.

Tlaquepaque   Seven miles southeast of the historic center, a village of mansions-turned-shops fronting pedestrians-only streets and plazas.

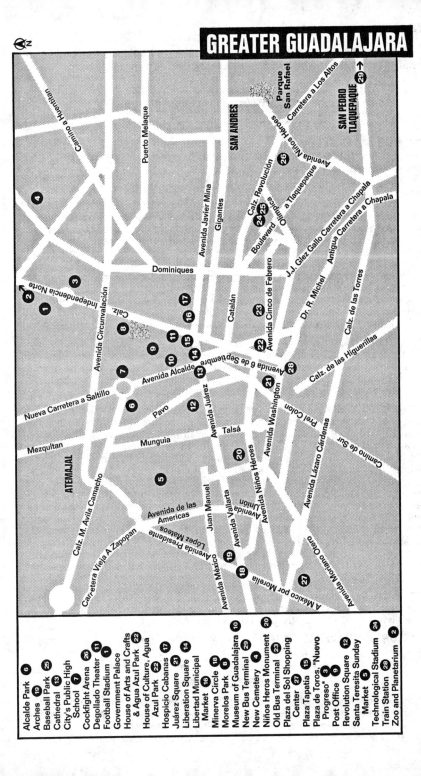

GREATER GUADALAJARA

Alcalde Park **6**
Arches **19**
Baseball Park **25**
Cathedral **13**
City's Public High School **7**
Cockfight Arena **26**
Degollado Theater **11**
Football Stadium **1**
Government Palace
House of Arts and Crafts & Agua Azul Park **22**
House of Culture, Agua Azul Park **22**
Hospicio Cabanas **17**
Juárez Square **21**
Liberation Square **14**
Libertad Municipal Market **16**
Minerva Circle **18**
Morelos Park **8**
Museum of Guadalajara **10**
New Bus Terminal **29**
New Cemetery **4**
Niños Heros Monument **20**
Old Bus Terminal **23**
Plaza del Sol Shopping Center **27**
Plaza Tapatia **15**
Plaza de Toros; "Nuevo Progreso" **3**
Post Office **9**
Revolution Square **12**
Santa Teresita Sunday Market **5**
Technological Stadium **24**
Train Station **28**
Zoo and Planetarium **2**

Tonala   Four miles from Tlaquepaque, a village of over 400 artists working in metal, clay and paper, with a huge street market on Thursday and Sunday.

2. GETTING AROUND

BY BUS & TROLLEY   Two bus routes will satisfy 90% of your intracity transportation needs. Buses marked **"Par Vial"** run a rectangular route east along Avenida Hidalgo to the Mercado Libertad and then west along Avenida Juárez (becoming Avenida Vallarta) to the Glorieta Minerva, near the western edge of the city.

Many buses run north-south along Calzada Independencia (not to be confused with Calle Independencia), but the **"San Juan de Dios–Estación"** bus goes between the points you want: San Juan de Dios church, next to the Mercado Libertad, and the railroad station past Parque Agua Azul. This bus is best because most other buses on Calzada Independencia have longer routes (out to the suburbs, for instance) and thus tend to be more crowded all the time.

When you want to get off a local bus, signal the driver to stop by pushing one of the buzzer buttons on the bus ceiling.

Electric trolleys run the same routes and are quieter, newer, and more pleasant to ride than buses—and cost the same—35¢–50¢.

To get to Tlaquepaque and Tonala by bus, see Section 10, "Easy Excursions."

BY COLECTIVO   Colectivos are minivans running throughout the city day and night picking up and discharging passengers at fixed and unfixed points. They are often a faster and more convenient way to travel than the bus. There are no printed schedules, and the routes and fixed pick up points change frequently. However, locals know the routes by heart and can tell you where and how to use them.

BY RENTAL CAR   All major car-rental agencies are represented at the airport and at various locations in town. The least expensive rates are found by arranging the rental from your home country at least seven days in advance of arrival in Guadalajara. As an example, Avis rates are $38 per day, plus $15 a day insurance and 15% tax. Weekly rates are $159 plus the daily insurance and tax; both are with unlimited mileage. This rate may be higher if you pick up the car on a weekend or major holiday. Keep in mind several main arteries. The Perriferico is a loop around the city that connects to most other highways entering the city. Traffic on the Perriferico is slow because it is heavily potholed, filled with trucks and is only a two lane road. Several important freeway-style thoroughfares crisscross the city. Conzalez Gallo leads south from town center and connects to the road to Tonala and Tlaquepaque or leads straight to Lake Chapala. Hwy 15 from Tepic intersects with both Av. Vallarta and Calz. Lázaro Cárdenas. Vallarta then goes straight to the Plaza Tapatío area. Cárdenas crosses the whole city and intersects the road to Chapala and to Tlaquepaque and Tonala.

BY TAXI   Taxis are an expensive way to get around town. A short 10- to 15-minute ride—for example, from Plaza de Armas to Las Margaritas restaurant—costs an exorbitant $5.25, while a bus there costs only 15¢.

BY HORSE-DRAWN CARRIAGE   Take one of the elegant horse-drawn carriages

IMPRESSIONS

In all Latin-American cities a certain group of older men seem to spend their evenings about the plaza or in the City Club nearby. Perhaps as their wives grow older and the children grow up they lose interest at home.
—LEONIDAS W. RAMSEY, *TIME OUT FOR ADVENTURE: LET'S GO TO MEXICO,* 1934

for a spin around town. The cost is about $13 to $17, depending on route and length of ride—usually about 45 minutes. Drivers congregate near the Mercado Libertad and also behind the Plaza/Rotunda de los Hombres Ilustres and other spots around town.

FAST FACTS GUADALAJARA

American Express   The office is at Avenida Vallarta 2440, Plaza Los Arcos (tel. 30-0200), open Monday through Friday from 9am to 2pm and on Saturday from 9am to noon.

Area Code   The telephone area code is 36.

Baby-sitters   Hotels can usually recommend baby-sitters; ask at the reception desk.

Bookstores   A popular chain of bookstores found throughout the city is Gonvil. There's one across from Plaza de los Hombres Ilustres on Avenida Alcalde and another a few blocks south at Avenida 16 de Septiembre no. 118 (Alcalde becomes 16 de Septiembre south of the cathedral).

Business Hours   In Guadalajara most stores are open Monday through Saturday. Such as travel agencies or other services que and Tona.

Car Rentals   Two to try are: **Auto-Rent de Guadalajara,** Avenida Federalismo Sur 542-A (tel. 25-1515 or 26-2014), and **Aguila,** Avenida Juárez 845-A (tel. 25-9554 or 26-6098). There are many agencies in the airport arrivals area or ask at your hotel.

Climate   Guadalajara has a mild, pleasant, and dry climate year round. Bring a sweater for evenings during November through March. The warmest months— March, April, and May—are hot and dry. From June through September it's rainy and a bit cooler.

Crime   See "Safety," below.

Currency Exchange   Banks will change money and traveler's checks Monday through Friday from 9am to noon.

Many travelers will be delighted/relieved to find a handy **Pocket-Teller.** There's a 24-hour Pocket Teller that takes VISA, Cirrus, and MasterCard at the Banamex bank on the corner of Calle Corona and Avenida Juárez; look for the seven-story gray building cater-corner from the Cafe Madrid.

Dentists   Ask at your hotel, or contact **Ruben E. Moran,** D.D.S., M. S. Angulo 1855 (tel. 52-1001).

Doctors   Contact **Dr. William Fairbank,** Juste Sierra 2515 (tel. 16-4851, or 13-6350 in an emergency).

Drugstores   Ask at your hotel where the closest pharmacy is. **Farmacías Guadalajara** is a chain throughout the city that offers late-night service; there's one near downtown on Avenida Lopez Cotilla (tel. 14-2810 or 14-6657). **Farmacía Varela,** Pedro Moreno 620 (tel. 14-1433), is open from 9am to 11pm. **Farmacía Corona,** S. A. Hidalgo 601 (tel. 14-2201 or 13-2132), has delivery service.

Embassies and Consulates   The world's largest American consular offices are here at 175 Progreso Street (tel. 25-9202 or 25-4445).

Emergencies   For the state **police,** call 17-5838; for the highway police, 21-7194. During the day, call the **Tourist Office** (tel. 14-0606, ext. 114).

For extreme medical emergencies, there's a service from the United States that will fly people to American hospitals, **Air-Evac,** a 24-hour air ambulance; call collect, 24 hours: 713/880-9767 in Houston, 619/278-3822 in San Diego, or 305/772-0003 in Miami.

Eyeglasses   Look for the optic shop right across the plaza from the Tourism Office.

Holidays   See Section 6, "Special Events," below. February and October are the big festival months. At Christmas and Easter, many establishments are closed or have different hours.

? DID YOU KNOW . . . ?

- Guadalajara is Mexico's second-largest city.
- Lake Chapala is the largest lake in Mexico.
- The U.S. Consulate in Guadalajara is the largest American consulate in the world.
- Muralist José Clemente Orozco was born in Guadalajara in 1883.
- The Jarabe Tapatío (Mexican Hat Dance) was developed in Guadalajara.
- The blue agave, from which tequila is made, grows only around Guadalajara near the town of Tequila.
- Mariachi music developed in Cocula, a small town near Guadalajara, where there are now no mariachis.
- A mariachi band can be a group of as few as three musicians to one of a dozen or more.

Hospitals In a medical emergency, go to the **Hospital México-Americano,** Colomos 2110 (tel. 41-0089).

Information The **State of Jalisco Tourist Information Office** is at Calle Morelos 102 (tel. 14-0606, ext. 114), in Plaza Tapatía at the crossroads of Paseo Degollado and Paraje del Rincon del Diablo. It's open Monday through Friday from 9am to 9pm and on Saturday from 9am to 1pm. The English-speaking staff provides good information and an excellent map.

For cultural happenings around town, check with the **Departamento de Bellas Artes,** located at Avenida Jesús Garcia 720, on Parque Alcalde (tel. 14-1614). The office is open Monday through Friday from 9am to 4pm and on Saturday from 9am to 1pm. The **Instituto Cultural Cabañas** (tel. 18-6003, ext. 22) also has information on what's happening around town.

Laundry/Dry Cleaning There are no laundries in the historic downtown area. Hotels generally offer this service (but at a high price).

Lost Property Call the American consulate, the police, or your bus or airline (for property lost in transit).

Luggage Storage/Lockers Luggage storage is available in the main bus station, the Central Camionera, and at the Guadalajara airport.

Newspapers/Magazines The Hotel Fenix, on the corner of Calle Corona and Avenida Lopez Cotilla, has English-language newspapers and magazines and maps. It's also a good place to buy Guadalajara's English newspaper, *The Colony Reporter,* which is published every Saturday, if you don't spot it on a newsstand.

Police See "Emergencies," above.

Post Office The main post office is at the corner of Carranza and Calle Independencia, about four blocks northeast of the cathedral (standing in the plaza behind the cathedral and facing the Degollada Theater, walk to the left and turn left on Carranza; walk past the Hotel Mendoza, cross Calle Independencia, and look for the post office on the left-hand side).

Radio/TV Many English-language U.S. cable TV stations are available in Guadalajara.

Religious Services Check *The Colony Reporter* (see "Newspapers/Magazines," above).

Rest Rooms Use the facilities in a restaurant, museum, or hotel lobby area. Always carry your own toilet paper and soap.

Safety As in any large city, don't be careless with your belongings. Women should avoid walking around alone late at night.

Taxis See Section 2, "Getting Around," above.

Transit Information See Section 2, "Getting Around," above.

3. WHERE TO STAY

DOUBLES FOR LESS THAN $15

HOTEL LISBOA, Huerto 20, Guadalajara, Jal. 44330. Tel. 36/14-2527.

67 rms (all with bath). **Directions:** From Plaza de Armas, walk east on Moreno four blocks to Huerto and turn right.

$ Rates: $7 single; $8 double.

The receptionist is unfriendly and the rooms are minimal in size and decor, but I've included this hotel for its price and prime location. It's on a quiet side street on Plaza Tapatía between Avenida Juárez and the pedestrians-only street of Pedro Moreno. The four-story (no elevator) hotel is also a block from the Libertad Market and the major downtown sights. You'll get a room that's seen many better days, a bed with clean sheets, one very thin towel, enough toilet paper for the night, and a shower.

POSADA ESPANA, Av. Lopez Cotilla 594, Guadalajara, Jal. 44100. Tel. 36/13-5377. 12 rms (all with bath). **Directions:** From the Plaza de Armas, walk two blocks south on Avenida 16 de Septiembre to Avenida Lopez Cotilla, turn right, and walk two more blocks; the hotel is on the right.

$ Rates: $9 single; $12 double.

This establishment, similar to the Posada de la Plata (below), is another aging converted colonial-style home offering large, darkish, basic rooms arranged around a plant-filled central courtyard. The neighborhood is quiet and the hotel is near the former Convento Carmen. Enter this hotel through a locked courtyard with an amiable guard dog, which makes guests feel either secure or paranoid.

POSADA DE LA PLATA, Av. Lopez Cotilla 619, Guadalajara, Jal. 44100. Tel. 36/14-9146. 10 rms (all with bath). **Directions:** From the Plaza de Armas, walk two blocks south on Avenida 16 de Septiembre to Avenida Lopez Cotilla, turn right, and walk two more blocks; the hotel is on the left.

$ Rates: $11 single; $14 double.

A St. Bernard dog greets guests when they knock on the locked gate of this somewhat funky, but pleasant posada. Formerly a private home, this fading beauty has a central, covered courtyard full of potted plants. Rooms tend to be dark, but they're interesting, large, and pleasant enough, although very basically furnished. There's a tiny, purple restaurant/kitchen, where the friendly duena serves meals at two or three tables. It's a 5-minute walk from downtown.

HOTEL ANA-ISABEL, Calle Javier Mina 164, Guadalajara, Jal. 44330. Tel. 36/17-7920 or 17-4859. 42 rms (all with bath). TEL

$ Rates: $11 single; $14 double.

Opposite the Mercado Libertad, this hotel has modest, spotless rooms and a cheerful staff. The lobby is one flight up and overlooks the bustling market across the street. Because the rooms open onto the interior, street noise is not a problem. TVs cost $1.75 per day, and you can make long-distance phone calls here too. There's a parking garage across the street.

HOTEL MEXICO, Calle Javier Mina 230, Guadalajara, Jal. 44330. Tel. 36/17-9978. 80 rms (all with bath).

$ Rates: $10 single; $14 double.

All rooms here have two to four beds, making this a good choice for families or friends traveling together. The bathrooms are clean and extra-large but aging. Rooms facing the street have small balconies, but beware of street noise. The hotel is opposite the Mercado Libertad and one block past the Hotel Ana-Isabel (above).

DOUBLES FOR LESS THAN $25

HOTEL LAS AMERICAS, Av. Hidalgo 76, Guadalajara, Jal. 45120. Tel. 36/13-9622 or 14-1604. 49 rms (all with bath). A/C TV TEL **Directions:** From the cathedral, walk seven blocks east on Avenida Hidalgo and look for the hotel on the left.

$ Rates: $13 single; $16 double.

This four-story budget hotel with a very friendly proprietor, Sr. Valcarcel, is a surprisingly quiet retreat from a very noisy street. New carpeting lines the marble-edged halls and rooms, and there's plenty of purified water available. The clean, carpeted rooms, all with one or two double beds, have windows facing either the street or ample airshafts (these, of course, are quieter).

POSADA REGIS, Av. Corona 171, Guadalajara, Jal. 44100. Tel. 36/13-3026. 22 rms (all with bath). TEL **Directions:** From Plaza de Armas (next to the cathedral) on Avenida 16 de Septiembre, walk three blocks south to Avenida Lopez Cotilla, turn left, and then take the next right.
$ Rates: $18 single; $20 double. **Parking:** $6 in garage.

Opposite the Hotel Fenix, the Posada Regis occupies the second floor of a restored (long ago) old mansion. The carpeted rooms are simply furnished, and arranged around a large, tranquil covered courtyard with sitting areas, a little restaurant, and potted plants. Rooms with balconies facing the street can be quite noisy. Windowless interior rooms are stuffy, so ask for a fan. The beds have plastic covers and "nonbreathing" nylon-type sheets. Bathrooms, which were added to the rooms, are not particularly private, with an open ceiling and no door. I've stayed here and find it particularly serves my budget and my needs for safety and proximity to downtown. A friendly and comfortable atmosphere prevails, with personal attention from the English-speaking manager. Video movies are shown every evening on the TV in the lobby. The restaurant serves a very good and cheap breakfast and lunch. There's personal laundry service too.

HOTEL CONTINENTAL, Av. Corona 450, Guadalajara, Jal. 44100. Tel. 36/14-1117. 129 rms (all with bath). TV TEL.
$ Rates: $15.75 single; $22 double.
The Hotel Continental, on the corner of Libertad, is well worn despite its modernity, and prices reflect the loss of its gleam. The receptionists can be rather incommunicado. All rooms are carpeted, and some have large windows. The cheerful restaurant downstairs is open from 7am to 11pm. To get there, walk eight blocks from the cathedral on Avenida 16 de Septiembre, turn left onto Libertad, and walk one block to Avenida Corona.

HOTEL UNIVERSO, Av. Lopez Cotilla 161, Guadalajara, Jal. 44100. Tel. 36/13-2815. 137 rms (all with bath). A/C TV TEL.
$ Rates: $19 single; $22 double with one bed, $29 double with two beds. **Parking:** Free.
This modern hotel has wall-to-wall carpeting throughout and offers worn but spacious rooms, all with summer-only air conditioning and large windows facing the street or the private parking lot behind the hotel (off-street rooms are quieter). The restaurant downstairs is open daily from 8am to 10:30pm, and there's a travel agency off the lobby. To get there, walk three blocks from Plaza de Armas, turn left on Avenida Lopez Cotilla, and walk three more blocks; the hotel is on the right.

HOTEL NUEVA GALICIA, Av. Corona 610, Guadalajara, Jal. 44100. Tel. 36/14-8780. 95 rms (all with bath). TV TEL **Directions:** Walk or take a local bus about 10 blocks south of the cathedral down Avenida 16 de Septiembre, then turn left onto Nueva Galicia and walk two blocks.
$ Rates: $18 single; $24 double. **Parking:** Free.
Tall and wedge shaped, this modern hotel offers pleasant rooms with lots of windows, and tub/shower combos. The interior rooms are small and dark; the larger rooms face the street and are sunny but noisy. The restaurant downstairs, Cafetera Excelsior, is open from 7am to 11pm. It's clean, bright, and spacious, and serves an excellent comida corrida from noon until 5pm.

DOUBLES FOR LESS THAN $35

HOTEL SAN FRANCISCO PLAZA, Paseo Degollado 267, Guadalajara, Jal. 44100. Tel. 36/13-8954 or 13-8971. 60 rms (all with bath). A/C TV TEL.
$ Rates: $22 single; $26 double. **Parking:** Free.

For a touch of class, try this highly recommended hotel facing a tiny square near Priciliano Sanchez. The management is authorized to charge much more, so you get a lot for the money. Stone arches, brick tile floors, bronze sculptures,

GUADALAJARA ACCOMMODATIONS

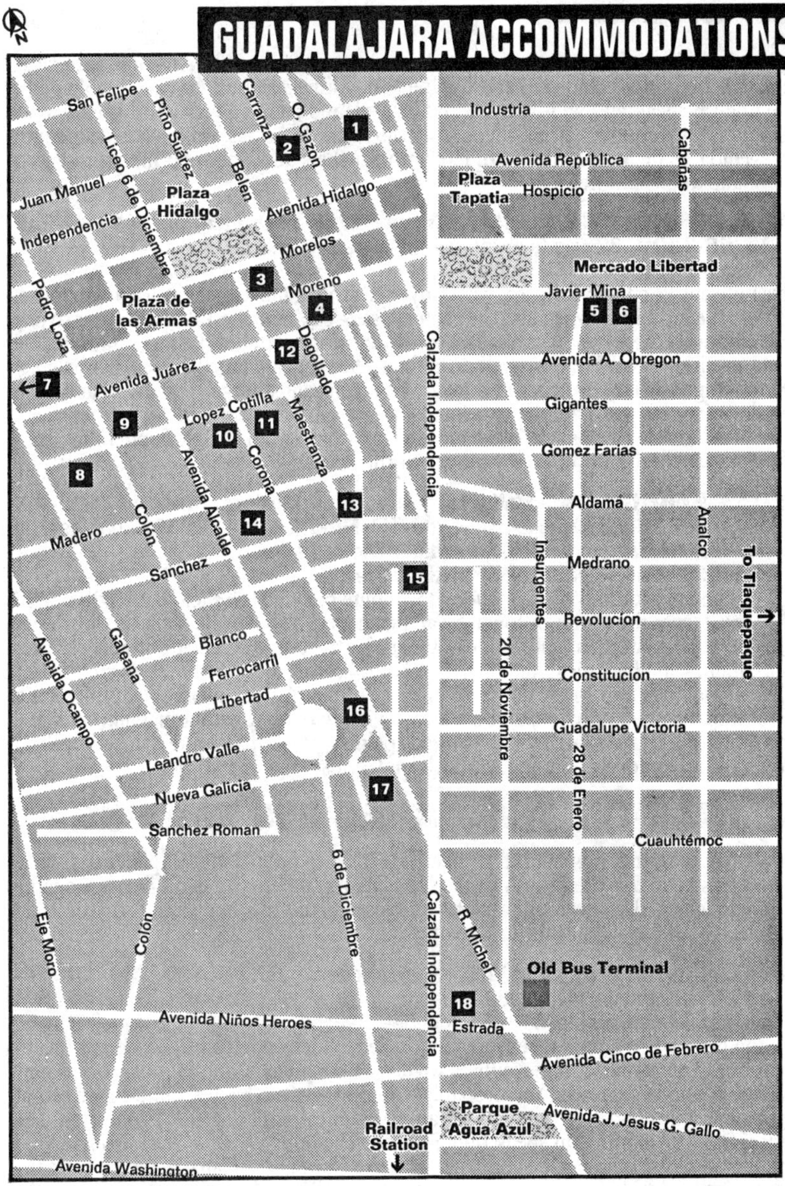

Map labels (streets and landmarks):

San Felipe · Carranza · O. Gazon · Pino Suárez · Belen · Juan Manuel · Liceo 6 de Diciembre · Independencia · Plaza Hidalgo · Avenida Hidalgo · Morelos · Pedro Loza · Moreno · Plaza de las Armas · Degollado · Avenida Juárez · Lopez Cotilla · Maestranza · Avenida Alcalde · Corona · Colón · Madero · Sanchez · Galeana · Blanco · Ferrocarril · Libertad · Avenida Ocampo · Leandro Valle · Nueva Galicia · Sanchez Roman · Eje Moro · Colón · 6 de Diciembre · Avenida Niños Heroes · Railroad Station · Avenida Washington

Industria · Avenida República · Cabañas · Plaza Tapatia · Hospicio · Mercado Libertad · Javier Mina · Avenida A. Obregon · Gigantes · Gomez Farias · Aldama · Analco · Medrano · Insurgentes · To Tlaquepaque · Revolucion · 20 de Noviembre · Constitucion · Guadalupe Victoria · 28 de Enero · Cuauhtémoc · Calzada Independencia · R. Michel · Old Bus Terminal · Estrada · Avenida Cinco de Febrero · Parque Agua Azul · Avenida J. Jesus G. Gallo

Accommodations index:

Las Americas **1**	Don Quijote Plaza **13**	Posada de la Plata **9**
Ana-Isabel **5**	Fenix **10**	Posada España **8**
Aranzazu **15**	Frances **3**	Posada Regis **11**
Canada **18**	Lisboa **4**	San Francisco Plaza **14**
Continental **16**	Mexico 70 **6**	Suites Bernini **7**
De Mendoza **2**	Nueva Galicia **17**	Universo **12**

and potted plants decorate the four spacious central courtyards. All rooms are large and attractive, and include either a double bed, a king-size bed, or two double beds. The English-speaking staff is friendly and helpful, and there's a very good, inexpensive restaurant off the lobby. To get there, from the Plaza de Armas, walk five blocks south on Avenida 16 de Septiembre, turn left onto Sanchez, and walk two blocks to Paseo Degollado and the hotel.

HOTEL DON QUIJOTE PLAZA, Heroes 91, Guadalajara, Jal. 44100. Tel. 36/58-1299. 32 rms (all with bath), 1 suite. TV TEL.
$ Rates: $31 single; $33 double.
This hotel, at Priciliano Sanchez, was converted from a huge, three-story town house. It's near the Hotel Aranzazu and the Hotel Posada San Francisco. You'd expect to pay much more for these rooms, which are softly luxurious with heavy drapes, fashionable pastel furnishings, and wall-to-wall carpeting. The spacious suite has a corner balcony overlooking Priciliano Sanchez and would be an elegant splurge. There's a bar on the first-floor interior patio and an excellent small restaurant off the lobby. To get there, from the Plaza de Armas, walk five blocks south on Avenida 16 de Septiembre, turn left onto Sanchez, and walk two blocks to the hotel.

SUITES BERNINI, Av. Vallarta 1881, Guadalajara, Jal. 44140. Tel. 36/16-6736. 36 suites (all with bath). TEL **Bus:** Take the "Par Vial" bus west on Avenida Juárez from two blocks south of the cathedral.
$ Rates: $34 single or double. **Parking:** Free.
If you don't mind being a 10- or 15-minute bus ride (on the electric "Par Vial" bus) from the center of town, by all means try the Suites Bernini, on the corner of Union (Avenida Juárez, one of the main streets in the center of town), changes names and becomes Avenida Vallarta as it heads west). Marble steps guarded by stone lions lead to the entrance of this elegant 16-story tower. Each suite has a king-size bed, kitchen, and floor-to-ceiling windows, with a magnificent view. The rooms are decorated with potted palms, plush pale-blue carpeting, and artwork—really lovely and spotlessly clean. Choose one or two beds.

NEAR THE TRAIN & OLD BUS STATIONS

Now that the central bus station has been relocated to near Tlaquepaque, there's little reason to stay in this area south of the town center, unless you can't find reasonably priced lodgings elsewhere or want to be close to the old bus station or the train station. It's a 25-minute walk to downtown.

HOTEL CANADA, Estadio 77, Guadalajara, Jal. 44440. Tel. 36/19-4014. 120 rms (all with bath). TEL.
$ Rates: $8–$13 single; $11–$14 double.
My top pick in this area was recently remodeled, which added a bright, cheery feel to the lobby. The rooms got a facelift as well, with fresh paint, and in most rooms new mattresses and bedspreads. You probably wouldn't want to hang around the streets at night here, but it's decent enough for an economical multiday stay in the city. The desk clerks are helpful, but speak only Spanish. The hotel is half a block from the old bus station and should not be confused with the Gran Hotel Canada, which faces the old bus station and is more expensive. To get there from the train station go out the front door and walk straight on Independencia four long blocks and turn right on Estadio; it's on the left.

NEAR THE NEW BUS STATION

HOTEL EL PARADOR, Carretera a Zapotlanejo 1500, Guadalajara, Jal. Tel. 36/59-0142. 630 rms (all with bath). TV TEL
$ Rates: $20 single; $24 double.
With two reception areas, this sprawling hotel is the only lodging near the new Central Camionera (it's just opposite the station, 5½ miles west of the town center). The friendly desk clerks offer efficient computerized check-in, but be sure to get a

receipt. Facilities include a 24-hour restaurant, two swimming pools, and saunas for men. Since rooms serviced by the reception area on the right are slightly farther away from the highway and the busy traffic circle, noise may be less of a problem in this wing. The rooms are clean, simple, and comfortable, with two twin beds. The tile halls carry noise like a megaphone.

WORTH THE EXTRA BUCKS

HOTEL FRANCES, Maestranza 35, Guadalajara, Jal. 44100. Tel. 36/13-1190. 60 rms (all with bath). TV TEL.

$ Rates: $49 single; $58 double.

With caution I mention this 379-year-old hotel, which is practically an institution in downtown Guadalajara. The downstairs disco is so loud that many readers have complained that it keeps them awake until the wee hours of the morning. Desk clerks seem indifferent to complaints. Thus forewarned, it's on a quiet side street off Plaza Libertad and near the Degollado Theater—an excellent location. Though there's an air of elegance about the lobby, with marble floors, central court and fountain, and huge crystal chandelier, the rooms are basic and furnished with old timey furniture. Some are carpeted and some have wood floors, and all have fans. In the lobby bar a piano soloist plays contemporary classics daily from noon to 8pm. There is a restaurant downstairs, and a small "botana" café.

To get there, from the Plaza de Armas, walk one block east on Moreno to Maestranza and turn right; the hotel is on the left.

HOTEL ARANZAZU, Av. Revolución 110, Guadalajara, Jal. 44100. Tel. 36/13-3232. 500 rms (all with bath). A/C TV TEL.

$ Rates: $48 single; $56 double. **Parking:** $5.25 per day.

Located near the intersection of Avenida Corona and Paseo Degollado, this luxury hotel not only has a fine location, but a long list of luxuries as well, including wall-to-wall carpeting, a restaurant and bar, a nightclub with shows, and two terrace swimming pools (one for kids). Check your bed though—some mattresses sag.

To get there, from the Plaza de Armas, walk one block east on Moreno and turn right (south) onto Avenida Corona and walk six blocks.

HOTEL DE MENDOZA, Carranza 16, Guadalajara, Jal. 45120. Tel. 36/13-4646. 104 rms (all with bath). TV TEL.

$ Rates: $53 single; $67 double. **Parking:** $2.25 a day.

This beautifully restored hotel is popular with foreigners for its quiet, colonial atmosphere and modern conveniences. It's at the corner of Avenida Hidalgo, only steps from Liberation Plaza and the Degollado Theater. Almost all the large rooms have wall-to-wall carpeting, and some have a tub and a shower. Rooms face either the street or an interior court with a swimming pool. The hotel's restaurant, La Forga, is very good, and the El Campanario bar offers dance music. Rates may be higher if you call or reserve them from the U.S. Walk-in rates are cheaper—get them quoted in pesos.

To get there, go to the left of the Teatro Degollado and look for Carranza, a block down on the left; turn left at the corner church, adjoining the hotel.

READERS RECOMMEND

Casa Domingo, *Calle Morelos 288, Tlaquepaque, Jal. Tel. 36/57-3846. "On a tree-lined, quiet street, only one block from Tlaquepaque shopping, is a restored mansion that has been turned into one of the most delightful bed-and-breakfast inns it has been our pleasure to find. The rooms are huge and elegantly furnished, and the grounds are gorgeous—lots of flower-filled patio areas and a huge garden in back. The complimentary breakfasts and cocktails and hors d'oeuvres are super, and the Sunday brunch (available to guests at a discount) is superb. For all this, the price is ridiculously affordable, making this one of the best 'buys' in and around Guadalajara."—Ron Wallen and Tom Carillo, Nokomis, Fla. [Author's note: The hotel has five rooms, all with fireplaces. Prices are $60 to $75 single or double, including breakfast and hors d'oeuvres.]*

4. WHERE TO EAT

Although the restaurants below serve food from around the world, I urge you to try a local dish, **birria**. It's a hearty soup of lamb, pork, or goatmeat in a tasty chicken-and-tomato broth, lightly thickened with masa (corn meal) and spiced with oregano, garlic, onions, cumin, chiles, allspice, and cilantro. Restaurants around El Parian in Tlaquepaque have it on the menu daily.

For those on a truly low budget, the second floor of the **Mercado Libertad** will look like heaven. You can get a full, several-course comida corrida here for 50¢ to $2 at any of what seem like hundreds of little restaurant stands. There's a vegetarian section too, and lots of places for tacos, tamales with atole, and enchiladas. But be careful about cleanliness—some people say you should not eat here. Nonetheless, hundreds of people do eat here every day, and seem to be surviving just fine—I've even done it myself. Check it out—it's a fascinating slice of Mexican life. The best time to go is early in the morning, while the food is the freshest.

MEALS FOR $5 OR LESS

TAMALES SINALOENSES, 45B Galvez, at Av. Juárez. No phone.

Specialty: TAMALES/MEXICAN. **Directions:** From Plaza de Armas, walk one block to Avenida Juárez, turn right, and walk three or four blocks to the Templo del Carmen; the café is left of the Templo, facing the plaza.

$ Prices: Tamales 50¢–80¢ (even less to go); pozole $2–$3; atole 50¢; coffee 45¢.

Open: Dinner only, 6:30–10:30pm.

Ⓢ This evening-only restaurant serves pozole, and tamales plus atole, a thick, lightly sweet corn drink that is traditional before bedtime and at breakfast (no alcoholic beverages are served). The tamales are huge (one fills you up), light, and tasty, and they come with beef, pork, and chicken fillings, or in sweet varieties with raisins. The tamales are kept hot in large lidded cans, just the way they're sold in markets. Pozole, a tomato, pork, and chickpea soup, comes in two sizes—large and small. The stainless-steel kitchen is open to view. This is a good place to grab a bite before one of the frequent films, art openings, or concerts at the Carmen Convent just across Avenida Juárez.

EL NUEVO FARO, Av. Lopez Cotilla 24. Tel. 13-1562.

Specialty: MEXICAN. **Directions:** From Plaza de Armas on Avenida Alcalde, walk two blocks south to Avenida Lopez Cotilla, turn left, and walk five short blocks to the restaurant, on the left.

$ Prices: Breakfast $2–$3; antojitos $1.50–$3.25; main courses $3.25–$6; comida corrida $4.

Open: Daily 8am–11pm (comida corrida served 1:30–5pm).

El Nuevo Faro, near Calzada Independencia, offers enchiladas and tacos, many meat and chicken dishes, or an ample, inexpensive breakfast with steaming, hot cafe con leche and warm bread. Leatherette booths, music playing, and a ceiling fan whirring overhead give it a kind of diner atmosphere.

LONCHERIA LA PLAYITA, Av. Juárez 242. Tel. 14-5747.

Specialty: MEXICAN. **Directions:** From Plaza de Armas, walk one block to Avenida Juárez and turn left; it's on the left.

$ Prices: Antojitos $1.25–$2.25; main courses $1.50–$3.25.

Open: Daily 9am–1:30am.

Ⓢ For a snack or light supper, try one of the many loncherias along Avenida Juárez (open for breakfast, "lonch," or supper). La Playita is the best of its kind, serving quesadillas or flautas, hamburgers, hot dogs, toasted sandwiches, and beer, soda, or coffee.

EL AGUACATE LOCO, Enrique Gonzales Martinez 126. No phone.

Specialty: VEGETARIAN. **Directions:** From Plaza de Armas, walk two blocks

GUADALAJARA DINING

San Felipe
Juan Manuel
Independencia
Liceo 6 de Diciembre
Pino Suárez
Belen
Carranza
O. Gazon
Avenida Hidalgo
Plaza Hidalgo
Morelos
Moreno
Plaza de las Armas
Degollado
Maestranza
Pedro Loza
Avenida Juárez
Lopez Cotilla
Corona
Madero
Colón
Avenida Alcalde
Sanchez
Galeana
Blanco
Ferrocarril
Libertad
Avenida Ocampo
Leandro Valle
Nueva Galicia
Sanchez Roman
Eje Moro
Colón
6 de Diciembre
Calzada Independencia
R. Michel
Avenida Niños Heroes
Estrada
Avenida Cinco de Febrero
Avenida J. Jesus G. Gallo
Parque Agua Azul
Railroad Station ↓
Avenida Washington

Industria
Avenida República
Plaza Tapatia
Hospicio
Cabañas
Calzada Independencia
Mercado Libertad
Javier Mina
Avenida A. Obregon
Gigantes
Gomez Farias
Aldama
Insurgentes
Medrano
Revolucion
20 de Noviembre
Constitucion
Guadalupe Victoria
28 de Enero
Cuauhtémoc
Analco
To Tlaquepaque
Old Bus Terminal

El Abajeno Minerva ⑩
Acropolis Cafe and Restaurant/ Pastelería Francesa ⑫
Acuarius ⑭
El Aguacate Loco ⑪
Las Banderillas ①
Cafe Madrid ⑦
Cafe Restaurant Agora ⑫

La Copa de Leche ⑩
Dogos El Meno ⑩
Don Quijote ⑬
El Farol ⑥
Los Itacates Fonda ⑩
Lonchería La Playita ⑧
Las Margaritas ⑪

Mercado Libertad ⑤
Mi Tierra ⑪
El Nuevo Faro ⑨
La Rinconada ③
Rose Cafe/Hotel Frances ④
Sandy's Restaurant ②
Tamales Sinaloenses ⑩

to Avenida Lopez Cotilla, turn right, and walk five blocks to E. G. Martinez; turn right and the restaurant is on the left.
$ Prices: Comida corrida $3.
Open: Mon–Sat 10am–8pm, Sun 10am–4pm.

Translated, this is the "Crazy Avocado Restaurant." Tiny and family operated, this hole-in-the-wall with no menu has the ultimate bargain/delicious vegetarian comida. The menu changes daily, but meals always begin with whole-grain tortillas and a tall glass of fresh jamaica juice (a dark, purple, mildly sweet drink), plus a huge plate of fresh bananas and papayas with lime. Next comes a tasty homemade soup—mine was a rich broth with spinach and whole grains. The main dish included perfectly cooked brown rice and vegetables with a tangy red sauce. Best of all was the moist, homemade banana cake for dessert.

CAFE RESTAURANT AGORA, Av. Juárez 612. Tel. 14-3169.
Specialty: MEXICAN. **Directions:** From Plaza de Armas, walk one block south to Avenida Juárez, turn right, and walk three or four blocks. The Templo del Carmen and its plaza will be on the left; the café is on the right across from the plaza.
$ Prices: Breakfast $1–$2; appetizers $2; sandwiches $1–$2; main courses $2–$5; espresso $1.
Open: Daily 8am–10pm.

Two covered patios next to the former Convento del Carmen (across the street from the church) shelter a casual restaurant and café, which seems to be reorganizing into a coffeehouse: The formerly expansive menu is now tiny, with only a few sandwich and main-dish offerings—including a chicken dish. The $2 huevos rancheros here, however, could be the breakfast deal in town.

DOGOS EL MENO, Golfo Cortez.
Specialty: MEXICAN HOT DOGS. **Bus/Trolley:** Take the "Par Vial" trolley or bus on Avenida Juárez to the Glorieta Minerva circle. Then walk past the tan-arched El Abajeno Minerva restaurant and turn right on Cortez; this upscale "hot-dog stand" is two short blocks on the left (look for a high, green steel fence).
$ Prices: Hot dogs $1–$2; soft drink 50¢; beer $1.
Open: Mon–Sat 9:30am–4pm.

Ordinarily I wouldn't recommend a hot-dog stand, but this one's a step up in hot-dog chic, serving delicious salchicha (Mexican-style hot dogs) on a pleasant shaded patio right outside the Porto Alegre dress shop. A huge, spreading tree on the corner shelters diners at this sit-down "stand."

The three young, enterprising Arias brothers (Roberto, Manuel, and Miguel) started the business with a pushcart on the street corner of Isabel la Católica, and expanded to the patio. The buns, made especially for them, are thick, fresh, and larger and better than ours. The hot dogs come with mustard, heaps of fresh-chopped tomatoes and onions, chile peppers (if you don't want peppers, say "seen *chee*-lay"), and finally a huge dollop of sour cream. The delicious inexpensive and filling concoction keeps customers lined up around the corner.

LAS BANDERILLAS, Av. Alcalde 833. Tel. 13-7926.
Specialty: MEXICAN/BEEF. **Bus:** From the cathedral, hop one of the frequent buses headed north on Avenida Alcalde and get off the bus at Avenida Jesús Garcia (eight blocks); cross Alcalde and look for the restaurant two doors from the corner and Goodyear Tires.
$ Prices: Appetizers 65¢–$6.75; main courses $3.50–$6.75.
Open: Mon–Sat 10am–1am.

For those who like good beef, this long-time local favorite is the place to go. It's a bit away from downtown, but only a few minutes by bus or a 15- or 20-minute walk. Bullfighting posters adorn the blue walls. Cloth-covered wooden tables surround a small stone bridge with a pond and trickling fountain among many plants. Try the cold and delicious, slightly sparkling lemonade, served in a huge terra-cotta mug. The house specialty is a filete relleno, a tender filet stuffed with cheese, ham, and tomato sauce. Freshly made, steaming tortillas accompany the meal, along with two delicious fresh salsas, one heaped with tomatoes, purple onions, and cilantro.

RESTAURANT DON QUIJOTE, in the Hotel San Francisco Plaza, Paseo
Degollado 267. Tel. 13-8954 or 13-8971.
Specialty: MEXICAN. **Directions:** From Plaza de Armas, walk five blocks south on Avenida 16 de Septiembre, turn left onto Sanchez, and walk two more blocks to Paseo Degollado and the hotel.
$ Prices: Breakfast $1–$4; appetizers 90¢–$1.25; main courses $2.25–$5; antojitos $2.25–$5.
Open: Mon–Sat 8am–9:30pm.

This amazingly reasonable and very nice hotel has a restaurant to match. High ceilings, paintings, and wooden tables and chairs make this an agreeable dining room, off a pretty patio filled with plants. The menu includes various Mexican specials, combination plates, and grilled meat and chicken. Those with a craving for mashed potatoes can satisfy it here. The local Guadalajaran beer, Estrella, costs less than a dollar.

MEALS FOR LESS THAN $10

CAFE MADRID, Av. Juárez 264. Tel. 14-9504.
Specialty: MEXICAN. **Directions:** From Plaza de Armas, walk one block to Avenida Juárez and turn left; it's on the left.
$ Prices: Breakfast $3–$5.25; appetizers $1.25–$3; main courses $6–$8; platillo Tapatío $8; comida corrida $6.
Open: Daily 8am–10:30pm (comida corrida served 1–5 or 6pm).

Conveniently located, this popular café serves the best coffee in Guadalajara. The smell of coffee wafts outside the café in the morning—Americano, espresso, cappuccino, and cafe con leche are all excellent eye-openers. Signs above the counter advertise chilaquiles and "ricos wafles," which are just that and served with warm syrup. For a light and inexpensive lunch, try the generous fruit cocktail, chilaquiles rojo or verde (red or green sauce), or a sandwich with french fries or salad. The extra-hearty platillo Tapatío includes fried chicken, a chile relleno, an enchilada, potatoes, and salad.

ACROPOLIS CAFE AND RESTAURANT, Av. Corona 165. Tel. 13-2165.
Specialty: FRENCH PASTRIES/MEXICAN. **Directions:** From Plaza de Armas, walk south on 6 de Diciembre/Avenida Corona three blocks; it's on the left.
$ Prices: Breakfast $3–$9; appetizers $2–$3; main courses $6–$7.50; pastries $1.50–$2; coffee or tea $1–$1.50.
Open: Mon–Sat 8am–9:30pm.
At the front of this restaurant is the **Pastelería Francesa** (French Bakery), with its colorful display of neopolitans, fresh-fruit tarts, creampuffs, tortes, cakes, and pies. The dimly lit, tea room/dining room with pink tablecloths, brass chandeliers, and ceiling fans is a great place to revive. The English-language menu includes salads, sandwiches, and antojitos, plus grilled meats and fish. Fourteen breakfast combinations come with hash browns or beans and salad.

SANDY'S RESTAURANT, Av. 16 de Septiembre and Independencia. Tel.
14-4236.
Specialty: CREPES/MEXICAN. **Directions:** From Plaza de Armas, walk two blocks north along Avenida Alcalde past the cathedral; the restaurant is upstairs on the right on the corner, just past the Rotunda de los Hombres Ilustres.
$ Prices: Breakfast $3.25–$7; sandwiches $4–$5; crêpes $4; appetizers $2–$5; main courses $6–$10.
Open: Daily 8am–10:30pm.

This second-story restaurant, formerly La Chalita, has balconies overlooking the Rotunda de los Hombres Ilustres and the cathedral. Though a bit expensive, it's a nice place for breakfast, when the morning sun and mist play on the flowers and foliage in the park. For lunch, it's a slight escape from the bustle of city life below, and the menu includes niños pobres (poor boys, or subs), and assorted burgers and crêpes. The specialty of the house is crêpes, both dinner and dessert crêpes, and there's an extensive list of fancy drinks, including Irish coffee and cognacs.

EL FAROL, Av. Pedro Moreno 466. Tel. 13-0349.
    Specialty: MEXICAN/TAMALES. **Directions:** From Plaza de Armas, walk two blocks west on Avenida Pedro Moreno; the restaurant is upstairs on the right.
$ Prices: Tamales 90¢–$2.50; tacos $2.25 for four; main courses $3–$6.
    Open: Daily 9am–2am.
For a really authentic Mexican meal, try El Farol, upstairs at the corner of Galeana. Pick a pleasant table by one of the balconies overlooking the pedestrian mall below. House specialties are the soft, rolled, corn-tortilla tacos—18 kinds to choose from. Diners are free to mix and sample the tacos, which come four to an order, or, likewise, the tamales (three to an order). Save some room for the restaurant's famous specialty—cheese pie—or one of the other tasty desserts.

ACUARIUS, Prisciliano Sanchez 416. Tel. 12-6277.
    Specialty: VEGETARIAN. **Directions:** From Plaza de Armas, walk four blocks south on Avenida 16 de Septiembre, turn right onto P. Sanchez, and walk 3½ more blocks; the restaurant is on the right.
$ Prices: Comida corrida $4.50.
    Open: 1:30–8pm.

⭐   This tidy, airy little lunch room has soft music playing, posters of Krishna, ads for yoga groups, and shelves of soy sauce and vitamins. The restaurant serves only a comida corrida daily, but it's a good one. There's a choice of two main dishes, which you can sample first if you can't make up your mind. When I was there the choice was zucchini sautéed with mushrooms in a tangy tomato sauce or a mixed vegetable stew. Whole-grain bread and whole-grain tortillas come with the meal, plus soup, fruit and yogurt or a salad, a tall, cool glass of fruit juice, and dessert.

LOS ITACATES FONDA, Chapultepec Norte 110. Tel. 25-1106.
    Specialty: MEXICAN. **Bus:** Take the "Par Vial" bus line (a 10-minute ride from downtown) west on Avenida Juárez to Chapultepec; turn right and the restaurant is on the right.
$ Prices: Appetizers $1–$5; main courses $3–$6.
    Open: Mon–Sat 8am–11pm, Sun 8am–7pm.
For an excellent meal, try this restaurant, which serves Mexican food "de la vieja cocina Mexicana" (from the old Mexican kitchen). There are three nice dining rooms, one on the patio near the fountain. One fun option here is to order "by the taco," so that you can sample a variety of very tasty dishes for just 45¢ each.

MEALS FOR LESS THAN $15

RESTAURANT LA RINCONADA, Calle Morelos 86. Tel. 13-9914.
    Specialty: MEXICAN. **Directions:** From Plaza de Armas, walk two blocks east on the plaza along Calle Morelos; look for the restaurant behind the theater.
$ Prices: Appetizers $3–$9; main courses $5–$10.
    Open: Mon–Sat 12:30–10:30pm.
Housed in a beautiful old stone mansion on Plaza Tapatía, La Rinconada draws diners in with live music. The dining room is set in the mansion's huge interior patio surrounded by arches and doors leading to smaller rooms with iron-grill-covered windows. The setting is truly lovely, but the slow and inattentive service leaves something to be desired. Though some diners rave about the filets, which are the house special, the cornish hen, pasta, and soup (which tasted like Campbell's) were very disappointing—perhaps the wrong things to order. It's an ideal place to relax after a performance at the Degollado Theater.

RESTAURANT/BAR EL ABAJENO MINERVA, Glorieta Minerva, at the corner of Av. Vallarta and Av. Lopez Mateos. Tel. 30-0307.
    Specialty: MEXICAN. **Bus/Trolley:** Take the "Par Vial" trolley or bus on Avenida Juárez to Glorieta Minerva circle; look for three tan arches to the right of the statue of Minerva's spear (from the rear)—that's the restaurant.
$ Prices: Appetizers $1.25–$4.50; main courses $7.75–$10; antojitos $3–$6.
    Open: Daily 8am–11pm (mariachi music 3–4pm).
Located at the corner of Avenidas Vallarta and Lopez Mateos, El Abajeno Minerva

offers a huge open-air-patio dining area where hearty meat dishes are served and mariachis stroll each afternoon. Though prices are a bit high, I made a delicious and inexpensive meal out of the huge order of guacamole (which contains at least two avocados) and a savory, filling bowl of tlalpeño soup—a spicy hot broth made from chilis with huge chunks of chicken, vegetables, and avocado. All tables receive a plate of garnishes of fresh, chopped cilantro, red onion, mild chile, and lime.

5. ATTRACTIONS

One of the best ways to see Guadalajara's top attractions is to take a walk through the historic downtown area, to acquaint you with the major historical, cultural, and architectural treasures of the city.

WALKING TOUR — Downtown

Start: Plaza de Armas
Finish: Libertad Market
Time: Approximately 3 hours, not including museum and shopping stops.
Best Times: After 10am when museums are open.
Worst Times: Mondays or holidays when the museums are closed.

This walk through downtown Guadalajara will acquaint visitors with the major historical, cultural, and architectural treasures of the city. Begin the tour in the Plaza beside the main cathedral on Avenida Alcalde between Avenida Hidalgo and Calle Morelos in the charming

1. **Plaza de Armas.** This pleasant plaza with wrought iron benches and walkways leading like spokes in a wheel to the ornate, iron French-made, central bandstand, directly in front of:
2. **Palacio del Gobierno.** This eye-catching arched structure that dominates the plaza was built in 1774 and combines the Spanish/Moorish influences prevalent at the time. Be sure to go inside to view the spectacular mural of Hidalgo by Clemente Orozco over the beautiful wooden-railed staircase to the right. The theme in the center, quite obviously, is social struggle. The panel to the right is called "The Contemporary Circus," and the one on the left, "The Ghost of Religion in Alliance with Militarism." Orozco was a native of Guadalajara and is held in high esteem here and nationwide. Wander across the courtyard and you might even catch a rare glimpse of a baby pigeon among the potted citrus trees.
   Going back out the front entrance, turn right and walk to the:
3. **Cathedral.** Begun in 1561, the unusual, multispired facade combines several 17th-century Renaissance styles, including a touch of Gothic. An 1818 earthquake destroyed the original large towers; the present ones were designed by architect Manuel Gomez Ibarra. Inside, look over the sacristy to see the painting believed to be the work of renowned 17th-century artist Bartolome Murillo (1617–82). Leave the cathedral and turn right out the front doors and walk along Avenida Alcalde to the:
4. **Rotunda de los Hombres Ilustres.** Sixteen gleaming-white columns without bases or capitals stand as monuments to Guadalajara's—and the State of Jalisco's—distinguished sons. To learn who they are, visitors need only to stroll around the green, flower-filled park and read the names on the 11 nearly life-size statues of the state's heros. There are 98 burial vaults in the park, only four of which are occupied. East of the plaza, cross Liceo to the:
5. **Regional Museum of Guadalajara.** Built in 1701 in the Churrigueresque style, this museum contains archeological pieces, including a mammoth skeleton

and an 18th-century meteorite, as well as art from the 17th and 18th centuries up to the present—both folk art and crafts and works of art by modern masters such as Orozco, Rivera, Quiroga, Vizcarra and Figueroa. Rooms 6 and 7 are devoted to the history of the state of Jalisco, and others display ethnography and European painting. Another section deals with paleontology, prehistory, and archeology, and features a gigantic reconstructed skeleton of a mammoth and the Meteorite of Zacatecas, found in 1792, weighing 1,715 pounds. The museum also includes the **National Institute of Anthropology and History,** which contains a large, colorful mural by J. G. Nuno showing scenes of the Conquest. Frequent craft shows are held here as well. It's open Tuesday through Sunday from 10am to 4pm. Admission is $3.45 for adults; children enter free. Outside the museum and to the right is the:

6. **Palacio de Justicia.** Built in 1588 as the first convent in Guadalajara, Santa María de Gracia later became a teachers' college and girls' school. In 1952 it was officially designated as the Palace of Justice. Inside, above the stairway, is a huge mural honoring the law profession in Guadalajara; it depicts historic events, including Benito Juárez with the 1857 constitution and laws of reform. Outside the palacio and directly to the right, continuing east on Avenida Hidalgo is the:

7. **Church of Santa María de Gracia,** one of Guadalajara's oldest churches, which was built along with the convent next door. Currently, it's being restored.
   Opposite the church is the:

8. **Teatro Degollado** ("Deh-goh-*yah*-doh"), a beautiful neoclassic 19th-century opera house named for Santos Degollado a local patriot who fought with Juárez against the French and Maximilian. Notice the seven muses in the theater's triangular facade above the columns. The theater hosts various performances during the year, including the Ballet Folklorico on Sunday at noon. **Plaza Liberación** links the cathedral and the Degollado Theater. To the right of the theater, on the opposite side of the plaza from the Santa María de Gracia church, is the:

9. **University of Guadalajara School of Music and the San Agustin Church.** There are continuous services in the church, and sometimes the music school is open to the public. Continuing east on the plaza, be sure to notice the spectacular fountain behind the Degollado Theater depicting Mexican history in low relief. You'll next pass the charming children's fountain, and then the unusual sculpture of a tree with lions with nearby slabs of text by Charles V proclaiming Guadalajara's right to be recognized as a city. The plaza opens up into a huge pedestrian expanse called **Plaza Tapatía,** framed by department stores and offices and dominated by the:

10. **Quetzalcoatl Fountain.** This towering, abstract sculpture/fountain represents the mythical plumed serpent Quetzalcoatl, which figures so broadly in Mexican legend and ancient culture and religion. The smaller pieces represent the serpent/birds; the centerpiece is the serpents' fire.

REFUELING STOP   Take a short break at one of the small ice-cream shops or fast-food restaurants along the plaza, or wait and go to the small cafeteria inside the Hospicio, where they serve hot dogs, sandwiches, cake, soft drinks, coffee, and snacks.

Looking down at the far end of the plaza, you'll spot the:
11. **Hospicio Cabañas.** Formerly called the Cabañas Orphanage, and known today as the **Instituto Cultural Cabañas** (tel. 18-6003), this impressive structure was designed by the famous Mexican architect Manuel Tolsá. It housed homeless children from 1829 until 1980. Today it's a thriving cultural center offering art shows, and classes for children and adults in all the fine arts. The main building has a fine dome and the walls and ceiling are covered by murals painted in 1929 by José Clemente Orozco (1883–1949). The powerful painting in the dome, *Man of Fire,* by Orozco, is a must-see, said to represent the spirit of humanity projecting itself toward the infinite. Several other rooms hold more of

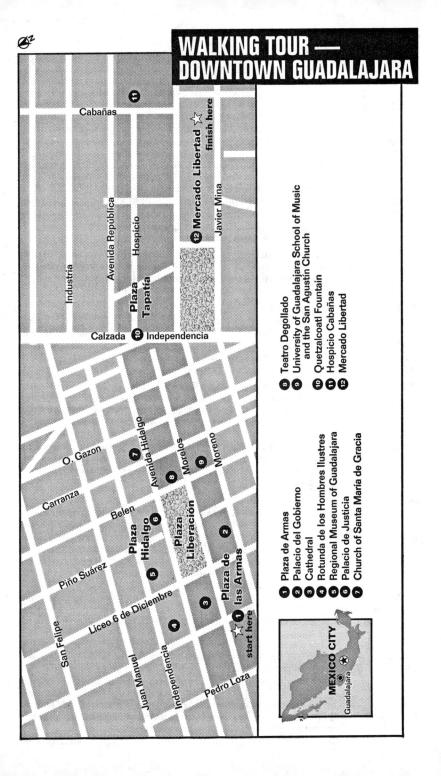

WALKING TOUR —
DOWNTOWN GUADALAJARA

Cabañas

☆ Mercado Libertad
finish here

⓫

⓬ Mercado Libertad

Javier Mina

Avenida República

Hospicio

Plaza
Tapatía

Industria

Calzada ⓾ Independencia

O. Gazon

Carranza

⑦

⑧

Morelos

⑨

Moreno

Avenida Hidalgo

Belen

Plaza
Liberación

Plaza
Hidalgo

⑥

②

Piño Suárez

⑤

Plaza de
las Armas

San Felipe

Liceo 6 de Diciembre

③

①

☆
start here

Juan Manuel

④

Independencia

Pedro Loza

1 Plaza de Armas
2 Palacio del Gobierno
3 Cathedral
4 Rotunda de los Hombres Ilustres
5 Regional Museum of Guadalajara
6 Palacio de Justicia
7 Church of Santa María de Gracia

8 Teatro Degollado
9 University of Guadalajara School of Music
and the San Agustín Church
10 Quetzalcoatl Fountain
11 Hospicio Cabañas
12 Mercado Libertad

MEXICO CITY

Guadalajara

Orozco's work, and there are also excellent temporary exhibits. For a free guided tour, ask for Ruben, who speaks English, at the front desk. Don't miss the contemporary art exhibit in the south wing, with the fascinating and unusual paintings by Javier Arevalo. The institute's own **Ballet Folklorico** performs here every Wednesday at 8:30pm; tickets cost $3.45. The Instituto Cabañas is open Tuesday through Saturday from 10am to 6pm. Call extension 22 about the many cultural events happening around town. For a real change of pace, turn left out the front entrance of the Cabañas and look for a stairway that leads down to the:

12. Mercado Libertad. Guadalajara's gigantic, covered central market, said to be the largest in Latin America. The site has been used for a market plaza since the 1500s and the present buildings were constructed in the early 1950s. This is a great place to buy leather goods, pottery, and just about anything else you can think of.

MORE ATTRACTIONS

PLAZA DE LA UNIVERSIDAD

This formerly charming plaza south of Plaza de Armas is undergoing extensive renovation. There's a huge fountain (a children's favorite) and lots of shoe-shine stands and benches of weary shoppers and people just passing the time.

PLAZA DE LOS MARIACHIS

Half a block from the Libertad Market on Calzada Independencia and Calle Javier Mina, beside the San Juan de Dios Church, is the Plaza de los Mariachis, actually a short street lined with restaurants and cafés. During the day, small bands of mariachis will be loafing around or sipping drinks, but at night the place is packed with them (see Section 9, "Evening Entertainment," below).

PLAZA AND EX-CONVENTO DEL CARMEN

The **Ex-Convento del Carmen,** on Avenida Juárez four blocks west of the historic center, offers a full range of theater, films, and musical events almost nightly. It's open daily from 9am to 10pm. Tickets are usually sold here just a short while before the performance.

Across the street, the **Plaza del Carmen,** with a bubbling fountain, roses, and shade trees, is a nice place to relax. Lovers' embraces may lead to a wedding at the small **Templo del Carmen,** an old church on the plaza. There's usually a mass, wedding, or christening in progress.

PARQUE AGUA AZUL

Located near the former bus station at the south end of Calzada Independencia, this park is a perfect refuge from the bustling city. It contains plants, trees, shrubbery, statues, and fountains. The park is open daily from 10am to 6pm. Admission is 25¢.

For children there's a **Museo Infantil** (children's museum) with displays of traditional toys as well as shows. *El Chuku, Chuku,* a rubber-tired minitrain, circulates through the grounds daily in the summer (on Saturday and Sunday the rest of the year) from 11am to 6pm. A ride costs 45¢.

Near the entrance to the park is the **flower market** where you'll soon discover why Guadalajara is called the City of Roses. Although it's not as big as it once was, people come from all over town to purchase floral arrangements with roses, carnations, birds of paradise, and other flowers.

Half a block farther toward town from the flower market, on the same side of the street, you'll see a sign TEJ for **Teatro Experimental de Jalisco,** marking the entrance to a modern building housing the Experimental Theater of Jalisco. There's also a Children's Theater with performances on Saturday and Sunday at 11am for a small fee.

Across Calzada Independencia from the Experimental Theater is the **Teatro Guadalajara del IMSS,** which offers shows that sound more experimental than the Experimental Theater (see Section 9, "Evening Entertainment," below).

Across the calzada from the flower market in a small, one-story rock building is the

GUADALAJARA ATTRACTIONS

San Felipe
Pino Suárez
Carranza
O. Gazon
Industria
Cabañas

Juan Manuel
Liceo
6 de Diciembre
Belén
Avenida República
Avenida Hidalgo

Independencia
Plaza Hidalgo
Avenida Hidalgo
Hospicio

Pedro Loza
Plaza de las Armas
Morelos
Moreno

Plaza Tapatia

Mercado Libertad
Javier Mina

10 Quetzalcoatl Fountain
11 Hospicio Cabañas
7 Church of Santa Maria de Gracia
6 Palacio de Justicia
5 Regional Museum of Guadalajara
4 Rotunda de los Hombres Ilustres de Jalisco
8 Teatro Degollado
9 Morelos
12 Mercado Libertad

Avenida Juárez

Lopez Cotilla

Maestranza

Avenida A. Obregon

Gigantes

Gomez Farias

Madero

Colón

Avenida Alcalde

Corona

Aldama

Insurgentes

Analco

To Tlaquepaque →

Sanchez

Medrano

Caleana

Blanco

Ferrocarril

Libertad

20 de Noviembre

Revolucion

Constitucion

Avenida Ocampo

Leandro Valle

Nueva Galicia

Sanchez Roman

28 de Enero

Guadalupe Victoria

Cuauhtémoc

6 de Diciembre

Calzada Independencia

R. Michel

Old Bus Terminal

Eje Moro

Colón

Avenida Niños Heroes

Estrada

Avenida Cinco de Febrero

Railroad Station ↓

Parque Agua Azul

Avenida J. Jesus G. Gallo

Avenida Washington

Cathedral **3**
Church of Santa Maria de Gracia **7**
Hospicio Cabañas **11**
Mercado Libertad **12**
Palacio de Justicia **6**
Plaza de Armas **1**
Quetzalcoatl Fountain **10**

Regional Museum of Guadalajara **5**
Rotunda de los Hombres Ilustres de Jalisco **4**
Teatro Degollado **8**
The Palacio del Gobierno **2**
University of Guadalajara School of Music
   and the San Agustín Church **9**

Museo Antropología. It houses a fine collection of pre-Hispanic pottery from the states of Jalisco, Nayarit, and Colima, and is well worth your time. The museum is open daily from 10am to 12:45pm and 3:30 to 7:30pm. There's a small admission charge.

Also across the calzada (opposite Agua Azul Park) is the **Casa de la Cultura,** between Avenida 16 de Septiembre and Calzada Independencia (tel. 19-3611). It offers a variety of classes in local culture by day, as well as a packed evening schedule to which the public is invited (for details, see Section 9, "Evening Entertainment," below).

The state-run **Casa de las Artesanías** is just past the park entrance at the crossroads of Calzada Independencia and Gallo (for details, see Section 8, "Savvy Shopping," below).

JARDIN ZOOLOGICO (ZOO) AND PLANETARIUM

Even those who don't like zoos will like the beautiful and spacious new **Guadalajara Zoo,** which straddles the edge of the breathtaking Huentitlan Ravine at the far northeastern edge of town. It's next to the Technology Center of Guadalajara with its planetarium and Omnimax Theater. A few hours provides a real respite from the hectic downtown pace and affords some great people-, as well as animal, watching. Huge, happy families with toddlers, teens, and patriarchs roam the territory, ogling the animals.

A striking monolithic fountain of bas-relief animals in the turquoise tones of oxidized metal greets visitors at the zoo entrance. Next, a flamboyant flock of flamingos lolls in a large pond. A sightseeing train straight ahead offers a 15-minute tour of the area—a good way to get acquainted. The zoo is nicely integrated into the area's rolling topography, and all the zoo's buildings have an attractive Aztec motif with stout round columns and zigzag painted designs. Modeled after such other great zoos of the world as those in San Diego and Berlin, this roomy zoo gives the larger animals plenty of space to roam and tries to approximate their natural habitats. Huge monkey islands with dead trees strung with vinelike ropes provide hours of entertainment. Most people stand mesmerized around the massive, moon-faced orangutans or the great, placid pumas and panthers. Multiple aviaries house screeching parrots and all types of colorful jungle birds. Informative signs throughout give habitat information and the animals' threatened or endangered status. The zoo (tel. 37-2478) is open daily from 9am to 6pm.

The **planetarium,** right next door (tel. 37-2119 or 37-2050), presents programs every evening, starting at 4, 5, and 6pm, with earlier shows on Saturday. Movies at the **Omnimax Theater** are at 10am and noon, and at 1, 4, 5, and 8pm.

By local bus north on Calzada Independencia, it's about a 30-minute ride; a taxi costs $4 to $5. Those going by bus should look for the large, pale terra-cotta structure on the corner of Independencia Norte and Avenida Flores Magon, on the right-hand side of the street coming from downtown. From Independencia, it's another five- or six-block walk up Avenida Flores Magon to the zoo's entrance, past the huge parking lots.

THE TEQUILA PLANT

You might want to take a tour of the Tequila Sauza bottling plant, at Avenida Vallarta 3273 (tel. 15-6990 or 30-0707), on the left on the way out of town. The tours

---

IMPRESSIONS

Mexico combines the modernity of today with the romance of history. Blending thirteenth-, fifteenth- and twentieth-century civilizations, it presents a stirring picture of Indian, Spanish and western civilizations living side by side. In some cities colonial palaces and cathedrals stand close to steel structures. . . . Pack burros and motor cars, ox carts and airplanes, forked-stick plows and steam tractors—all have their place in this ageless land of mañana.
—Byron Steel, *Let's Visit Mexico,* 1946

begin at 10am Monday through Friday. After the tour there's a "happy hour" where you can enjoy a variety of tequila drinks, prepared by masters of the art. You can skip the tour and come just to drink from 10am to 1pm. Both the tours and the drinks are free.

By the way, this is just a bottling plant. The distillery is in the town of Tequila, off Highway 15 about 25 miles east of Guadalajara. You'll see the spiny blue agave, from which tequila is made, growing everywhere around the little town.

ORGANIZED TOURS

Several times daily, **Panoramex** (tel. 10-5005, 10-5057, or 10-5109) offers bilingual tours of Guadalajara, Lake Chapala, Tequila, and Zapopan, ranging in price from $8 to $17.75. Those without a car might want to consider a tour or two, especially to the outlying regions. The office is open Monday through Friday from 9am to 7pm, or inquire in your hotel.

6. SPECIAL EVENTS

The Jalisco State Band puts on **free concerts** in the Plaza de las Armas, usually every Tuesday, Thursday, and Sunday evening starting about 7pm. Those who want a seat in the park should arrive early.

During September, Mexicans celebrate their **independence** from Spain in a month-long celebration, but Guadalajara really goes all out. Look for poster-size calendars listing attractions that include many performances in theaters all over the city. On September 15, the Governor's Palace fills with well-dressed invited guests as they and the massive crowd in the park below await his reenactment of the traditional *grito* (shout for independence) at 11pm. The grito commemorates Fr. Miguel Hidalgo de Costilla's pronouncement that began the War for Independence in Mexico in 1810. There's live music on a temporary street stage, spontaneous dancing, much shouting of "Viva Mexico!" and fireworks. On September 16 there's a parade that lasts an hour or so. For the next couple of days the park in front of the Degollado Theater resembles a county fair and Mexican market. There are games of chance with stuffed-animal prizes, and a variety of food, including cotton candy and candied apples. Among the many attention-getting gimmicks and games, look for a mechanized, growling, arm-flailing, stuffed gorilla wearing a sombrero. Live entertainment goes on in the park day and night.

October is another month-long celebration, called **Fiestas de Octubre,** that originally began with the procession of Our Lady of Zapopan, but has since added a celebration of all that is notable about Guadalajara and Jalisco. The month kicks off with an enormous parade, usually on the Sunday nearest the first of the month (but it could be Saturday). By the way, those Americans in the parade may be from San Antonio, Texas, Guadalajara's sister city. Festivities continue all month with performing arts, rodeos (*charreadas*), bullfights, art exhibits, regional dancing, a food fair, and a Day of Nations involving all the consulates of Guadalajara. Much of the ongoing displays and events take place in the Benito Juárez Auditorium.

On October 12 around dawn, the small, dark figure of **Our Lady of Zapopan** begins her 5-hour ride from the Cathedral of Guadalajara to the Cathedral of Zapopan, a suburb. The original figure dates from the mid-1500s and the procession tradition began 200 years later. Crowds spend the night all along the route and vie for position as the Virgin passes riding in a new car donated to her for the occasion. In the months before October 12, the figure is carried to churches all over the city. During that time, you may see neighborhoods decorated with paper streamers and banners honoring the passing of the figure to the next church.

The last 2 weeks in February are marked by a series of **cultural events** before the beginning of Lent.

7. SPORTS & RECREATION

BULLFIGHTS Many say that Guadalajara and Mexico City have the best bullfights in the country, so if you want to see one, this is probably an excellent place to do it. Every Sunday at 4:30pm (4pm in summer) there's a bullfight at the Plaza de Toros "Nuevo Progreso," across from the football stadium on Calzada Independencia Norte, north of town. Tickets range from $1.10 for seats in the sun to $62.20 for the best seats in the shade. Buy tickets downtown in the reception area of the Hotel Frances on Thursday from 10am to 2pm or 4 to 7pm. Tickets are also sold in the Restaurant Abajeno Minerva, on the Minerva circle, at the corner of Avenidas Vallarta and Lopez Mateos (tel. 30-0307), or at the Plaza de Toros.

RODEOS To the east of Agua Azul is the **Aceves Galindo Lienzo,** or rodeo ring, at the corner of Dr. R. Michel and Calzada de las Palmas (tel. 19-3232), where there's a Mexican rodeo (*charreada*) on Sunday at noon. Riding, roping, and rope tricks, and a traditional grand promenade are all part of the action at the charreada. Sometimes there are evening shows too.

COCKFIGHTS Also nearby, cockfights are held in the **Palenque/Agua Azul,** at the corner of Washington and Avenida 16 de Septiembre (tel. 19-5993 or 19-5940), but only in the high season, from October to early November. For cockfights the rest of the year, visit the local "pit" at the **Plaza de Gallos, "La Tapatía,"** at Avenida Revolución 2120 (tel. 35-7506), on the way to Tlaquepaque (take a Tlaquepaque bus along Calzada Independencia). Profits from the blood sport go to charity and matches are *usually* held daily. Arrive by 7pm.

8. SAVVY SHOPPING

Besides the mammoth **Mercado Libertad** (see Section 5, "Attractions," above), in which you can find almost anything, Guadalajara boasts the largest modern shopping center in Latin America. The **Plaza del Sol** megacomplex sprawls over 120,000 square yards in an area at the junction of Avenidas Lopez Mateos and Mariano Otero, outside the center of town. Here you can buy anything from a taco to a Volkswagen; you can also cash a check, make a plane reservation, or buy a lottery ticket. There are even hotels and restaurants for weary shoppers! Take bus no. 40 from Calzada Independencia near the Libertad Market.

There's a convenient **pedestrian passageway** that runs under Avenida Juárez where there are many stalls selling candied fruits, leather belts, and other goods. A better place to purchase **leather goods,** however, is down on Avenida Pedro Moreno, a street that runs parallel to Avenida Juárez, and for **shoes,** go to E. Alatorre northeast of the historic center, where 70 shoe stores are located.

One block past the entrance of Agua Azul Park in the direction of the city center (on your right at the crossroads of Calzada Independencia and Gallo), is the **Casa de las Artesanías,** Gallo 20 (tel. 19-4664). It's an enormous two-story, state-run crafts store that sells pottery, silver jewelry, dance masks, and regional clothing from around the state. The best crafts aren't necessarily found here and prices seem somewhat steep, so if you're going to the villages, such as Tonala, you may want to postpone buying. On the right as you enter are museum displays showing crafts and regional costumes from the state of Jalisco. The craft store is open Monday through Friday from 10am to 7pm, on Saturday from 10am to 4pm, and on Sunday from 10am to 2pm.

There's an **outdoor market** every Sunday at Santa Teresita, where you can buy clothes and anything else you have in mind, all at excellent prices; look on the map of Greater Guadalajara for an approximation of where to find it. It stretches out for blocks and blocks.

Some of Mexico's best pottery and crafts are made in the suburbs of **Tlaquepaque** and **Tonala.** These two villages are a must, especially on Thursday or Sunday when Tonala spreads out a huge street market. (See "Tlaquepaque and Tonala" in Section 10, "Easy Excursions," below.)

9. EVENING ENTERTAINMENT

THE PERFORMING ARTS
MUSIC & DANCE

BALLET FOLKLORICO DE LA UNIVERSIDAD DE GUADALAJARA. Tel. 26-5455 or 25-8888, ext. 262, 264, or 266.

This wonderful dance company, acclaimed as the best folklorico company in all of Mexico, provides the light, color, movement, and music that is pure Jalisco. For more than a decade they've been performing at the Degollado Theater. For information, call the university telephone number extension given above. Performances are on Sunday at 10am.

Admission: Tickets, 80¢–$6.

BALLET FOLKLORICO NACIONAL OF THE INSTITUTO CULTURAL CABA-ÑAS. Tel. 18-6003.

Performances are every Wednesday at 8:30pm at the theater of the Instituto Cultural Cabañas.

Admission: Tickets, $2.65.

STATE SYMPHONY ORCHESTRA. Tel. 13-1115.

The orchestra performs regularly at the Degollado Theater. Call for information about the schedule.

Admission: Tickets, 80¢–$6.

CASA DE LA CULTURA, between Av. 16 de Septiembre and Calzada Independencia. Tel. 19-3611.

A variety of performances are offered. The Association of Composers of Jalisco offer new works on Tuesday evenings at 8pm. The state chorus group, the Coral del Estado, also performs here. On Thursday there are literary readings at 8pm, and there are experimental dance performances and Aztec music. Call for information.

EX-CONVENTO DEL CARMEN, Av. Juárez 638. Tel. 14-7184.

At this former convent, just a few blocks from the central plaza, many low-cost concerts are offered. Performances are usually on Monday and Tuesday evenings at 8 or 8:30pm, and tickets are usually sold shortly before the performance.

Admission: Varies; call for information.

THEATER

TEATRO EXPERIMENTAL, Calzada Independencia Sur, near Parque Agua Azul. Tel. 19-3770.

Interesting experimental works are performed at this theater. It's worth going, even if you don't speak Spanish. Performances are every day except Monday from February through November, and begin around 8:30pm Tuesday through Saturday and at 5 and 7pm on Sunday.

Admission: Call for ticket prices.

TEATRO GUADALAJARA DEL IMSS, Av. 16 de Septiembre 868. Tel. 19-4121.

This theater presents modern plays, but is more conventional than the Teatro Experimental. Call for the current schedule.

Admission: Call for ticket prices.

MAJOR PERFORMANCE HALLS

Casa de la Cultura (tel. 19-3611).
Ex-Convento del Carmen (tel. 14-7184).
Degollado Theater (tel. 13-1115).
Teatro Experimental (tel. 19-3770).

THE CLUB & MUSIC SCENE

For rousing music and pure Mexico/Guadalajara ambience, go to **Plaza de los Mariachis,** down by the San Juan de Dios Church and the Libertad Market, at the junction of Calzada Independencia and Avenida Juárez/Calle Javier Mina. Every evening the colorfully dressed mariachis of the city, in various states of inebriation, play for money (if they can get it) or for free. Enjoy a meal, a snack, or a soft drink here, or just stand around spending nothing but time. It's fun and it's free; spend at least one evening here.

Few places in Guadalajara are more enjoyable to me than **El Parian** in Tlaquepaque, where mariachis serenade diners under the portals (see Section 10, "Easy Excursions," below, for more information).

It costs nothing to listen as the mariachis belt away around other diner's tables, but if you ask for a song, ask the price first.

NIGHTCLUBS/CABARET/JAZZ/BLUES

HOTEL FIESTA AMERICANA, Glorieta Minerva. Tel. 25-3434 or 25-4848.
Songs and imitations are presented in the **Caballo Negro Bar** from 7pm until 3am. There is also a continually changing show in the **lobby bar** daily from 7pm until 1am. In another salon, **Estelaris,** there are occasional performances by nationally known artists. Every Thursday at 7:30pm there's a **Mexican Fiesta,** with a dinner buffet, tequila cocktails, mariachis, folk dancing, door prizes, and dance music from Veracruz; reservations are required.
Admission: Fiesta, $20.

RESTAURANT/BAR COPENHAGEN 77, Marcos Castellanos 140-Z. Tel. 25-2803.
This dark, cozy jazz club is by the little Parque de la Revolución, on your left as you walk down Avenida Juárez from downtown. There are linen tablecloths and a red rose on every table. You can come just for a drink, or for the restaurant's specialty, the delicious paella Copenhagen al vino ($9.50). The paella takes a while to prepare, but it's an enjoyable wait, while you sip a drink and listen to the jazz. Open daily from 1pm to 1:30am, a live jazz trio plays Monday through Wednesday from 3 to 4:30pm and 8pm to 12:30am, and Thursday through Saturday from 9pm to 1:30am.
Admission: Free.

DANCE CLUBS/DISCOS

MAXIM'S DISCO CLUB, in the Hotel Frances, Maestranza 35. Tel. 13-1190.
Despite the name, Maxim's is not a disco, but a dance hall with a singer or a live band. There are tables around the dance floor and in the lower bar section.

While you're at the Hotel Frances, check out the **lobby bar,** one of the most enjoyable in Guadalajara, due in large part to the beautiful piano playing of Goyo Flores, who learned to read music by Braille. Flores, who speaks a little English, takes requests and specializes in old, romantic Norteamericano favorites like the theme from *Casablanca* and "Stardust," but he also plays more contemporary classics such as Beatles songs. (Tips are appreciated.) Open daily from 8pm until 3 or 4am; drinks are two-for-one Monday through Wednesday from 8 to 11pm.
Admission: Free.

BAR EL CAMPANARIO, in the Hotel de Mendoza, Carranza 16. Tel. 13-4646.

There is a beautiful view from this penthouse perch in the Hotel de Mendoza. Only couples or mixed-sex groups are allowed in. There is music for dancing Monday through Saturday starting at 9pm. Open Monday through Saturday from 11am to 1am; happy hour is 6 to 7pm. At this writing the bar is temporarily closed, but expected to reopen soon.

MOVIES

Guadalajara is a gold mine for foreign and art films. The best-known *cines de arte* are **Cinematografo Sala Especial,** Avenida Vallarta 1102, at the corner of Argentina (tel. 25-0514), about a 10-minute walk down Avenida Juárez from downtown; and the **Sala Greta Garbo,** at Pino Suárez 183, between Juan Manuel and San Felipe (tel. 14-2275). Also check with the **Instituto Cultural Cabañas** (tel. 17-3097 or 18-6003) for its latest offerings. The **Casa de la Cultura,** near Parque Agua Azul (tel. 19-3611), shows films Saturday and Sunday, usually at 4, 6, and 8pm. The **Ex-Convento del Carmen** (tel. 14-7184) shows foreign and cultural films on Friday and Saturday evenings at 6 and 8pm.

For current film showings in most movie houses around town, consult any of these daily papers: *Informador, Occidental,* and *Ocho Columnas.*

10. EASY EXCURSIONS

There are a number of interesting places to visit near Guadalajara, and Lake Chapala is a popular vacation spot.

TLAQUEPAQUE & TONALA

7–10 miles S of Guadalajara

GETTING THERE By Bus To reach Tlaquepaque (a 25-minute ride), take the A or B no. 275 bus on Avenida 16 de Septiembre/Alcalde in front of the cathedral; wait by the blue bus signs. At Tlaquepaque, get off one or two stops after you see the welcoming arch on the left; then ask for directions to El Parian, Tlaquepaque's central building.

To Tonala, stay on the bus (another 15 minutes) and Tonala is the last stop the bus makes before turning around.

ESSENTIALS The **Tlaquepaque Tourism Office** is in the Presidencia Municipal (opposite El Parian), Calle Guillermo Prieto 80 (tel. 35-1503 or 35-0596), open Monday through Friday from 9am to 3pm and on Saturday from 9am to 1pm.

The **Tonala Tourism Office** is in the Casa de Cultura, at Morelos 180, around the corner from the National Ceramics Museum, upstairs on the right. Hours are Monday through Friday from 9am to 3pm and on Saturday from 9am to 1pm.

Tlaquepaque and Tonala are distant suburbs that are a special treat for shoppers. Market days are Sunday and Thursday in Tonala, but on Sunday many of Tlaquepaque's stores are open only from 10:30am to 2:30pm. To combine a trip to both villages—about 4 or 5 miles apart—Thursday is the best day. Monday through Saturday, stores in Tlaquepaque usually close between 2:30 and 4pm. It makes a nice day to wear yourself out in Tonala then relax at one of Tlaquepaque's nice outdoor restaurants for a sunset meal and wait for the mariachis to warm up at El Parian.

TLAQUEPAQUE

This suburban village is famous for its **fashionable stores** in handsome old stone mansions fronting pedestrians-only streets and its pottery and glass factories. The village is also known for **El Parian,** a circular building dating from the 1800s in the town center, where innumerable mariachis sing songs to diners in sidewalk cafés. The mariachis are especially plentiful, loud, and entertaining on weekend evenings (Sunday is best), but just about any time of day you'll hear them serenading there. The stores, especially on Calle Independencia, offer all the pottery and glass for which the village is famous, plus the best of Mexico's crafts, such as equipales furniture, fine wood sculptures, and papier-mâché.

What to See & Do

Tlaquepaque's **Regional Ceramics Museum,** Independencia 237 (tel. 35-5404), is a good place to see what traditional Jalisco pottery is all about. There are high-quality examples dating back several generations. Note the cross-hatch design known as *petatillo* on some of the pieces; it's one of the region's oldest traditional motifs. There's also a small display of pre-Hispanic pottery, Huichol Indian costumes, and folk art. The museum is open Tuesday through Saturday from 10am to 4pm and on Sunday from 10am to 1pm. (See also the National Museum of Ceramics in Tonala, below.)

Across the street from the museum is a **glass factory.** In a room at the rear of the patio, a dozen scurrying men and boys heat glass bottles and jars on the end of hollow steel poles. Then, blowing furiously, they'll chase across the room, narrowly missing spectators and fellow workers alike as they swing the red-hot glass within an inch of a man who sits placidly rolling an elaborate jug out of another chunk of the cooling glass. Nonchalantly, the old man will leave his own task long enough to clip off the end of the boy's vase at the exact moment at which it comes within reach of his hand. Then he drops the clippers and returns once more to his own task as the youth charges back across the room to reheat the vase in the furnace.

Where to Eat

Read the fine print on menus. The 15% value-added tax, usually included in the written menu price elsewhere in Mexico, may not be included in Tlaquepaque. It may be added on when your bill is presented. Even if the fine print tells you it's included, ask—before ordering.

MARISCOS PROGRESO, Progresso 80. Tel. 57-4995.
   Specialty: SEAFOOD/MEXICAN.
$ Prices: Appetizers $1.25–$6; main courses $6–$8; ceviche $1.25–$3.25.
   Open: Daily 10am–8pm.
Formerly the Restaurant Los Corrales, this renamed restaurant has an all-new, primarily seafood menu. Its cozy tree-shaded patio, filled with leather-covered tables and chairs, makes an inviting place to take a break from your shopping. Mexican food is the specialty here. To get there, cross Avenida Juárez, one of the streets that borders the huge, central El Parian, and look for this corner restaurant.

LOS CAZADORES, Chamizal 606. Tel. 35-1983.
   Specialty: MEXICAN. **Directions:** See below.
$ Prices: Appetizers $4–$6; main courses $6–$18.
   Open: Daily 1–6pm.
Expansive and tranquil, this restaurant resembles a country hacienda and is noted for good service and food in a casual atmosphere. Patrons start drifting in about 1:30pm and the dining rooms and huge shady patio are full by 3pm. The large mariachi group is one of the best I've heard, and plays for free.

Important note: Waiters will bring you extra appetizers (and charge you for them). They all speak English, so make sure they know what you do and don't want. Also, alcoholic drinks can be outrageously expensive, and cocktail prices are not on the menu. Ask the price before you order! As a special treat, folk dancing is presented on Friday from 2 to 3pm and on Saturday and Sunday at 4pm.

To get there, by car or taxi, leave from El Parian (the square in the village) via Independencia (which is one way). At the end of this street, turn left onto Revolución, and drive back toward Guadalajara nine-tenths of a mile. At the traffic circle, go down the street to the right of the Pemex station for two blocks. Los Cazadores is on the right; drive into the parking lot. A taxi will cost around $3.

RESTAURANT WITH NO NAME (Sin Nombre), Madero 80. Tel. 35-4520 or 35-9677.

Specialty: MEXICAN.
$ Prices: Appetizers $6; main courses $11–$13.
Open: Mon–Sat 8:30am–8:30pm, Sun 8:30am–6:30pm.

This all-time favorite offers excellent cuisine in a spectacular garden shaded by banana, peach, palm, and other tropical trees and guarded by strutting peacocks. A trio plays music in midafternoon. The menu is spoken by the bilingual waiter, not written, so ask for prices as you order. I enjoyed the excellent "No Name Chicken," cooked in onions, green peppers, and a buttery sauce, spread around a mound of rice. The quesadillas are outstanding.

Why the unusual name here? When the American-owned restaurant first opened it didn't have a liquor license, so they operated as a speakeasy and early clients gave the place its current appellation. To get there, from the main plaza, follow the narrow street (Independencia) on the right for 1½ blocks; the restaurant is on the corner of Madero and Independencia on the right.

TONALA

Tonala is a pleasant, unpretentious village about 4 miles from Tlaquepaque that many will find more authentic and easier on the wallet. The streets were paved only recently, but there aren't any pedestrians-only thoroughfares yet. The village has been a center for pottery making since pre-Hispanic times; half of the more than 400 artists who reside here produce high- and low-temperature pottery in different colors of clay with a dozen different finishes. Other local artists also work with forged iron, cantera stone, brass and copper, marble, miniatures, papier-mâché, textiles, blown glass, and gesso.

What to See & Do

On Thursday and Sunday **market days** vendors and temporary street stalls under flapping shade cloths fill the streets; "herb-men" sell multicolored, dried medicinal herbs from wheelbarrows; magicians entertain crowds with sleight-of-hand tricks; and craftspeople spread their colorful wares on the plaza's sidewalks. Those who love the hand-blown Mexican glass and folksy ceramics will wish they had a truck to haul the gorgeous and inexpensive handmade items. There is certainly greater variety here than in Tlaquepaque—tacky and chic are often side by side.

Tonala is the home of the **National Museum of Ceramics,** Constitución 104, between Hidalgo and Morelos (tel. 83-0494). The museum occupies a huge two-story mansion with displays of Jalisco work as well as pottery from all over the country. There's a large shop in the front on the right as you enter. The museum is open Tuesday through Friday from 10am to 5pm and on Saturday and Sunday from 10am to 3pm.

Shopping

JOSÉ BERNABE AND SONS, Hidalgo 83. Tel. 83-0040 or 83-0877.

Revered as the best ceramic and stoneware artists in Tonala, José Bernabe and his sons have a workshop and showroom half a block from the Presidencia Municipal. Prices here are high, but the quality is unsurpassable if a bit mass-produced-looking; some pieces are museum quality and all are hand-painted by four generations of Bernabes trained in the art from boyhood. Open Monday through Friday from 10am to 6:30pm and on Saturday and Sunday from 10am to 2pm.

SANTIAGO DE TONALA, Madero 42. Tel. 83-0641 or 39-0543.

Blown glass is made at this factory half a block off the plaza. Enter the factory by the back door to see how the work is done. Open Monday through Friday from 7am to 3pm (the factory is open until 7pm) and on Saturday and Sunday from 7am to 2pm. There's a sales showroom as well where prices are higher than elsewhere because the glasswear is commercial strength, made for heavy use in restaurants, etc.

ARTESANIAS MAYORGA, Madero 43. Tel. 83-0121.

This large shop has a little bit of everything, including all kinds of crafts, from masks to colorful hanging ceramic birds. Open Monday through Saturday from 10am to 6pm, and Sunday from 10am to 5pm.

Where to Eat

LOS GERANIOS, Hidalgo 71. Tel. 83-0010.
   Specialty: MEXICAN.
$ Prices: Appetizers $1.25–$5; main courses $4.50–$8; plate lunches $1.50–$4.
   Open: Sun–Mon 11am–5pm.

This narrow, inviting restaurant next to El Bazar de Sermel offers a cool respite from the blazing sun. Diners can relax in the clean and comfortable white canvas chairs at white-clothed tables or in the small booths. The menu includes Mexican specialties. Start with soup, salad, or nachos or a delicious fruit plate of fresh sliced jicama, oranges, and cucumber (pepita) with lime and sprinkled with chili powder. To get there, with your back toward the plaza, turn right and walk about half a block down Hidalgo; look on the left for a pretty stained-glass sign with red flowers.

LAKE CHAPALA

26 miles S of Guadalajara

GETTING THERE   By Bus   At Guadalajara's Old Central Camionera, look for the **Transportes Guadalajara-Chapala** company (tel. 57-8448). Buses and minibuses run every half hour to Chapala and every hour to Jocotepec, charging 60¢ to 75¢. To get to Ajijic and Jocotepec from Chapala, walk toward the lake from the bus station and you'll spot local buses that travel between Chapala and those villages. In Chapala, the bus from Guadalajara lets you off about three blocks from the lake shore, and in Jocotepec you'll be about five short blocks from the town square.

By Car   Those lucky enough to have a car will be able to enjoy the lake and its towns more fully. Drive to Lake Chapala via Highway 15/80, but be advised that most heavy truck traffic also uses this route to the south. I suggest that you leave Guadalajara via Avenida Gonzalez Gallo, which intersects with Calzada Independencia just before Playa Azul Park. Going south on Independencia, turn left onto Avenida Gallo and follow it all the way out of town past the airport, where it becomes Highway 44, the main road to Chapala. The 25-mile drive is through peaceful farming country. The first view of the lake isn't until just outside of the town of Chapala.

ESSENTIALS   The area's **Tourist Information Office** is at km 6.5 on the road between Chapala and Ajijic, (tel. 376/5-3135). Turn when you see the modernistic cement sculpture on the left; it's next to the Casa Artesanias. Hours are Monday through Friday from 9am to 6pm and Saturday from 9am to 1pm.

Mexico's largest lake has long been popular with foreign vacationers. It boasts a perfect climate, gorgeous scenery, and several charming little shore towns— Chapala, Ajijic, and Jocotepec, each with its own distinct ambience. There's not a lot to see or do here unless you stay long enough to make friends among the Ajijic's large American expatriate community. D. H. Lawrence wrote *The Plumed Serpent* during his stay here.

Lake Chapala is in trouble in part because of upstream use of the Lerma River which feeds the lake. There's much controversy about the lake's health, whether or not it is dying and what the government is doing about it. An observer can see that the water has receded several feet. Local fishermen whose families have lived here for generations say that what's happening has happened before; it's the normal ebb and flow of the lake. Despite the controversy, it's beautiful, ringed by misty mountains, fishing villages, and resorts like Chapala and Ajijic.

CHAPALA

Chapala, Jalisco (pop. 32,000), on the edge of Lake Chapala, is the district's business and administrative center as well as its oldest resort—not that there's much business, or even resort activity. Much of the town's prosperity comes from wealthy retirees who live on the outskirts and come into Chapala to change money, buy groceries, and check the stock ticker. It can be a pretty sleepy place. A newly widened main street (Avenida Madero) leads down to the lakeshore.

Near the Hotel Nido, at Madero 216, is a bookstore, **Libros y Revistas,** that carries English-language newspapers, magazines, and books.

Where to Stay & Eat

HOTEL NIDO, Av. Madero 202, Chapala, Jal. 45900. Tel. 376/5-2116.
31 rms (all with bath).
$ Rates: $16 single; $20 double.
The best budget hotel is in the center of town, half a block from the water. There is a restaurant, bar, swimming pool, and a well-tended garden. The rooms are spacious and those facing the street are the largest. To get there, from the plaza, walk toward the lake about one block and look for the hotel on the right.

The popular restaurant attracts many of the retired people living in Chapala who eat all three meals here and highly recommend the food. The comida corrida costs $5.50.

READERS RECOMMEND

"In Lake Chapala, a good place to catch a snack of soup and bread or a cheap beer is Beto's, just north of the Nido. Also Bings (famous) ice cream is next to the Hotel Nido."—Barbara and Dave Zimmer, Clements, Calif.

AJIJIC

Another town on the lake, Ajijic is a quiet place inhabited by fishermen, artists, and retirees. The cobblestone streets and arts-and-crafts stores give the town a quaint atmosphere, although there aren't as many stores as in past years. The narrow streets lead past a small church and square, and end by the sunny lake.

Buses leave from Chapala for Ajijic every 15 minutes and cost about 40¢. Catch the bus to Ajijic a few blocks down on the main street (to the left, toward the lake) from the small bus station, where the bus from Guadalajara leaves passengers. As you reach Ajijic, the highway becomes a wide, tree-lined boulevard through a wealthy residential district called La Floresta.

What to See & Do

On the left entering Ajijic from Chapala, you'll see a cluster of buildings, one of which is marked **ARTESANÍAS.** The Museum of Anthropology formerly in this same cluster has closed. The shop has a good selection of pottery from all over Mexico as well as locally made crafts of the regions—rugs, etc.

Social life centers around the **Posada Ajijic Cantina,** Calle 16 de Septiembre no. 2, where a band (of sorts) plays for dancing on weekends. In the evening (except Monday), drop in at **El Tapanco Bar and Disco,** on Calle 16 de Septiembre in the same block as the Posada Ajijic, on the other side of the street. They always serve drinks and sometimes have food and music.

Where to Stay

LA NUEVA POSADA, Donato Guerra 9, Ajijic, Jal. Tel. 376/5-3395. 10 bungalows. TV TEL
$ Rates (including full breakfast): $37 single; $50 double. **Parking:** Free.
This beautiful, brand-new posada was built by the former owners of the popular Posada Ajijic, which is now a restaurant under different ownership. Meticulously modeled after a gracious, traditional-style hacienda, La Nueva Posada looks a lot

more expensive than it is. French doors, marble bathrooms, a wine cellar, and a small swimming pool are some of the amenities—not to mention the elegant dining room with a glorious lake view. Pastel rose-and-blue decor with touches of tile and hand-painted flourishes on walls and over doorways create a rich but restful ambience. Original paintings hang in the stylish, color-coordinated rooms and public areas. Some rooms overlook the dazzling lake, others have intimate patios, and all have fans. Owned by the Eager family, the new posada is as popular as (but nothing like) their former hostelry, and the hotel was already booked a year in advance for New Year's. To get there, from the plaza, walk toward the lake on Colón, then turn left onto Calle 16 de Septiembre and look for Donato Guerra; turn right and the hotel is right on the lake.

POSADA LAS CALANDRIAS, main highway poniente no. 8, Ajijic, Jal. Tel. 376/5-2819. 29 rms (all with bath). TEL

$ Rates: $24 single or double.

Outside town, west on the main highway, this two-story brick hotel surrounds a swimming pool with bougainvillea everywhere. Guests come from all over, as the car license plates show: Rhode Island, Montana, and British Columbia. The rooms are comfortable and have kitchens.

HOTEL REAL DE CHAPALA, Paseo del Prado 20, Ajijic, Jal. Tel. 376/5-2416 or 5-2468. 85 suites (80 junior, 5 master). MINIBAR TEL.

$ Rates: $56 single; $69 double.

This five-star hotel with gorgeous grounds and gardens tucked in the La Floresta residential area is a good splurge choice right on the lake. All the rooms are large suites with king-size beds, floor-to-ceiling windows, and sliding glass doors facing the expansive grounds or glimmering lake. The large bathrooms come with huge tiled tubs. A series of dining rooms with white wrought-iron furniture sprawl out on an enormous tree-shaded, flower-filled, lakeside patio with a pool. The glorious nightly sunset silhouettes horseback riders along the beach and sailboats on the lake, while in the background a violinist and pianist serenade guests with soft music—all quite romantic. Those not staying here can soak up the ambience with an evening drink or meal.

The hotel is a little hard to find—it's easiest just to take a taxi from the plaza. But to walk (about 20 minutes from the plaza) go east on 16 Septiembre (a block south of the plaza) to where a median with a stone wall and tall trees divides the street; turn right where the wall ends and look for the sign pointing the way to the hotel.

Where to Eat

DANNY'S, across from Plaza de la Montana on the main highway.

Specialty: MEXICAN/AMERICAN.

$ Prices: Breakfast $2.50–$3; Mexican dishes $2–$4; sandwiches/burgers $3.

Those craving a hamburger or sandwich will enjoy this small, clean, and cheerful café on the main highway across from a small plaza. It has an American-style menu—in fact, it's hard to find the few Mexican items on it—but they're quite good. The Mexican plate with chile relleno, enchiladas, beans, and rice is a tasty choice. There are five breakfast specials that include coffee or tea, beans or home-fries, juice, and toast or tortillas.

RESTAURANT NARANJITOS, Hidalgo 10.

Specialty: MEXICAN/PIZZA.

$ Prices: Appetizers $2–$4.25; main courses $4.45–$10.50; pizzas $3–$9; sandwiches $3–$3.50; desserts $1.30–$2.

Open: Tues–Sun 12:30–9:30pm.

Rustic and trendy, with attractive decor, including yarn "drawings" and unusual fuzzy yarn lights, this restaurant off the central square has a loyal following. Nowhere else can you find spinach-and-watercress salad or quiche on Tuesday and roast beef on Thursday. There's an eclectic, Americanized menu with some Mexican dishes like seafood mojo de ajo. They also specialize in unusual sandwich combinations like the Pancho Villa, with pork, refried beans, cream, and sauce; or the Napolitano, with salami, chutney, cream, lettuce, tomato, and jalapeño. Try the delectable lemon soufflé for dessert. A really nice trio with bass, guitar, and accordion plays at night. To get there, from the plaza facing the church, walk to the right and turn right on the first street; the restaurant is a few doors down on the left.

MANIX RESTAURANT, Ocampo 57. Tel. 5-3449.
  Specialty: INTERNATIONAL.
$ **Prices:** Comida corrida $8.
  Open: Daily 1–9pm.
A favorite of American residents, this small, attractive restaurant with rainbow-colored napkins to brighten up the dark, carved-wood furniture, serves a different international comida daily. Seafood, beef, and sometimes chicken Cordon Bleu are served. To get there, from the plaza with your back to the church, walk straight on Hidalgo and turn right on Ocampo (after Hidalgo and an extension of Constitución); the restaurant is down the street on the right.

LA NUEVA POSADA, Donato Guerra 9. Tel. 5-3395.
  Specialty: INTERNATIONAL.
$ **Prices:** Appetizers $4–$5; lunch $5–$7; main courses $5–$14; brunch specials $8–$11 (includes a drink); daily specials $10–$15.
  Open: Mon–Sat noon–9pm, Sun 10am–8pm; brunch Sun 11am–1pm.
The mouth-watering menu here—especially the brunch specials—includes such offerings as scrambled eggs in a potato nest with sausage, broccoli rarebit, or shrimp-asparagus crêpes Newburg. And for brunch dessert: Danish kringle, granola muffins with strawberry butter, and peaches in caramel sauce. Brunch includes coffee and an alcoholic beverage such as a strawberry daiquiri or the wine of the day. The rest of the varied menu includes seafood, filets, and poultry, with changing daily specials—all too expensive. To get there, from the plaza, walk toward the lake on Colón, turn left onto 16 de Septiembre, and look for Donato Guerra; turn right and the hotel/restaurant is right on the lake.

JOCOTEPEC

West of Ajijic, this small colonial-era village is becoming a center for weavers. Those on a day trip should walk down Hidalgo Street just off the plaza to discover numerous shops selling locally loomed work both large and small—some for the wall and some for the floor. For refreshment, there's a yogurt shop and a couple of outdoor cafés on the central plaza.

Where to Stay

POSADA DEL PESCADOR, Apdo. Postal 67, Jocotepec, Jal. Tel. 376/3-0028. 22 bungalows. TEL
$ **Rates:** $21 bungalow for one; $28 bungalow for two.
This pretty motor inn is on the main highway between Ajijic and Jocotepec on the eastern edge of Jocotopec (on the right if you're coming from Ajijic). Its colonial-style bungalows are scattered around the swimming pool. Each bungalow has a kitchenette, dining area, fireplace, bedroom, and bath.

11. MOVING ON — TRAVEL SERVICES

BY PLANE   International flights require check-in at least 90 minutes before takeoff, at least 60 minutes before departure for domestic flights. **Auto Transportaciones Aeropuerto** (tel. 12-4278, 12-4308, or 12-9337) runs minivans between the airport and city 24 hours a day.
    For reservations or flight information, contact the airlines directly: **Aero California** (tel. 26-1901 or 26-1064, or 89-0924 at the airport), **Aeromar** (tel. 26-4656 or 26-4658), **Aeroméxico** (tel. 25-2559, or 89-0119 at the airport), **Air France** (tel.

30-3721 or 30-3707), **Alaska Airlines** (tel. toll free 95/800-426-0333 in Mexico), **American Airlines** (tel. 89-0304, or 30-0349 at the airport), **Continental Airlines** (tel. 89-0433 or 89-0261), **Delta** (tel. 30-3530 or 30-3226), **Lufthansa** (tel. 16-3175 or 16-3249), and **Mexicana** (tel. 47-2222, or 89-0119 at the airport). Travelers on any Mexicana international flight can receive a 25% discount on domestic flights in Mexico by asking for the VIMEX fare. Tickets for other destinations in Mexico must be purchased within 7 days of arrival in Mexico.

BY TRAIN   Going to **Mexicali,** on the California border, *Del Pacífico* departs Guadalajara at 8:15am and arrives in Tepic at 1:55pm, in Mazatlán at 6:50pm, and in Mexicali at 4:30pm the next day. To **Nogales,** near the Arizona border, *Del Pacífico* departs Guadalajara at 8:15am and arrives in Mazatlán at 6:50pm and in Nogales at 11am; there are no sleeping cars. **To Mexico City,** *El Tapatío,* a train with overnight sleeping compartments, leaves Guadalajara at 8:55pm and arrives in Mexico City at 8:10am; this is a popular train, so reserve a place early.

   Most travel agencies will arrange tickets on the *Del Pacífico,* but there may be a service charge. **MaCulls Travel Agency,** Avenida Lopez Cotilla 361, has up-to-date train information and will make reservations. Located next to the Hotel Universo downtown on the corner of Paseo Degollado, it's open Monday through Friday from 9am to 2pm and 4 to 7pm and on Saturday from 9am to 2pm.

BY BUS   Two bus stations serve Guadalajara—the old one near downtown and the new one 6 miles out on the way to Tonala. A convenient place for bus information is **Servicios Coordinados,** Calzada Independencia 254, a kind of "bus travel agency" located under Plaza Tapatía. There, travelers can make reservations, buy tickets, and receive information on the six main bus lines to all points in Mexico.

The Old Bus Station   For bus trips within a 60-mile radius of Guadalajara, including to **Lake Chapala, Ajijic,** and **Jocotepec,** go to the old bus terminal on Niños Heroes off Calzada Independencia Sur and look for Transportes Guadalajara-Chapala (tel. 19-5675), which has frequent bus and combi service beginning at 6am to Chapala (also see Section 10, "Easy Excursions," above).

The New Bus Station   The **Central Camionera,** about 6 miles and a 20-minute ride east of downtown toward Tonala, provides bus service to or from virtually any point in Mexico. The new terminal resembles an international airport: Seven separate buildings are connected by a covered walkway in a U shape, with one-way traffic entering on the right. Each building houses several first- and second-class bus lines. And that's the only drawback—you must go to each one to find the line or service that suits you best. It's one of the nicest bus stations in Mexico, with amenities like shuttle buses, restaurants, gift shops, luggage storage (*guarda equipaje*), book and magazine shops, liquor stores, Ladatel long-distance telephones, and hotel information. There's also a large, new budget hotel next door (see Section 3, "Where to Stay," above). To get there by bus, take any bus marked **"Diagonal Tonala"** on Avenidas 16 de Septiembre/Alcalde opposite the cathedral in downtown Guadalajara.

   None of the buses from here are of the school-bus variety, but while the price difference between first and second class is small, the difference in speed, comfort, and convenience is often great. To get you started here are a few hints on areas served: To **Aguascalientes** or **Zacatecas,** all lines are on the left and include Camiones de los Altos (tel. 57-6158 or 57-6151), Estrella Blanca (tel. 57-6158 or 57-6151), Transportes Chihuahenses (tel. 57-7431 or 57-8199), Transportes del Norte (tel. 57-8455), and Autobuses al Aguila (tel. 57-8128); to **Tepic** or **San Blas** on the Pacific coast, try Estrella Blanca (tel. 57-6158 or 57-6151); to **Manzanillo,** try Flecha Amarilla (tel. 57-7316), Autobuses del Occidente (tel. 57-6460), or Unidos de la Costa (tel. 57-4933); to **Barra de Navidad** and **San Particio/Melaque,** go to Auto Camiones del Pacífico (tel. 57-4805) or Unidos de la Costa (tel. 57-4933); to **Pátzcuaro, Morelia** or **Uruapan,** go to Flecha Amarilla (tel. 57-7310), Autobuses del Occidente (tel. 57-6460), or Tres Estrellas de Oro (tel. 57-6969 or 57-7225).

CHAPTER 9

INTRODUCING MEXICO CITY

Mexico City glitters with all the fascination and excitement of a world capital. It's a vital, romantic place of monuments, palaces, parks, broad boulevards, tall buildings, and smart boutiques. It's the fountainhead of government, and in every way the center of Mexican life. It's not even "Mexico City" but simply "Mexico" in the lexicon of every Mexican who talks about it.

The region of Mexico City (alt. 7,240 ft.; pop. 20,000,000) has held the most important place in the country's history since the rise of Teotihuacán in 300 B.C. In A.D. 1300 the Aztecs built their great capital of Tenochtitlán on an island in the middle of Lake Texcoco, following a prophecy that they should build where they saw a "sign": an eagle perched on a cactus with a serpent in its beak. Lake Texcoco, now shrunken, once filled the valley to the base of Chapultepec ("Grasshopper Hill" in the Aztec language), and broad causeways connected the island to the shore. Little remains of this magnificent city of 300,000 inhabitants. What we know of Tenochtitlán is from the 16th-century chronicles of the Spanish conquerors, especially of Bernal Díaz del Castillo who saw "the great towers and temples and buildings rising from the water—it was like the enchantments."

After the Aztec defeat, the Spanish made the city their capital, and in the centuries that followed the lake was filled in and the city limits were greatly extended. Maximilian of Hapsburg did much to beautify the city during his short and stormy tenure. He remodeled Chapultepec Palace, built by a Spanish viceroy in 1783, and established the grand boulevard now named the Paseo de la Reforma.

You can see many signs of Mexico City's varied history: The pyramids of Teotihuacán are a short ride from downtown; Xochimilco, a reminder of the Aztec Floating Gardens in Lake Texcoco, is close by; the Zócalo with its cathedral and National Palace is Spain's standard contribution to colonial town planning. And the Mexican Republic has made the city what it is today.

In more ways than these the city is still a creature of its history. In fact, it's literally sinking into it, for the soft lake bottom gives easily under the weight of such formidable structures as the marble palace of the Bellas Artes or the skyscraping Latin American Tower. But it gives only an inch a year, so you needn't worry—take your time in visiting one of the most fascinating capital cities in the world.

You've undoubtedly heard about Mexico City's pollution problem. It is as immense as the city itself. But for the visitor, dealing with the pollution is a matter of luck. On some days you won't notice it; on other days it will make your nose run, your eyes water, and your throat rasp. They say that breathing Mexico City air, when it's bad, is equivalent to smoking two packs of cigarettes a day.

WHAT'S SPECIAL ABOUT MEXICO CITY

Architecture
☐ Pre-Hispanic temple remains, red tezontle stone colonial buildings, magnificent palaces and mansions, and soaring skyscrapers—Mexico City has it all.

Museums
☐ More than 50 sophisticated museums display treasures from the city's and country's abundant cultural and historical wealth.

Performing Arts
☐ Inside theaters and on the streets, from ballet to opera, mariachis to guitar trios, comedy to drama, organ grinders to accordion players, there's something to entertain everyone.

Transportation
☐ This is the country's central transportation hub—you can get to anywhere in Mexico from here.
☐ A quick, efficient Metro, abundant taxis, and inexpensive minivans make getting around relatively easy despite the city's size.

If you have respiratory problems, be very careful; being at an altitude of 7,240 feet makes things even worse. Minimize your exposure to the fumes by refraining from walking busy streets during rush hour. Make Sunday, when many factories are closed and many cars escape the city, your prime sightseeing day. One positive note: The air in the evenings is usually deliciously cool and relatively clean.

1. ORIENTATION

Tackling one of the world's most enormous cities is enough to give the most experienced traveler nightmares, but fortunately Mexico City is quite well organized for the arriving traveler. Try to arrive during daylight hours, but if you can't, don't worry. You won't have to spend the night in some terminal. The following information will help you glide through.

ARRIVING

BY PLANE

Mexico City's **Benito Juárez International Airport** is something of a small city, where you can grab a bite or buy a wardrobe, books, gifts, and insurance, as well as exchange money or arrange a hotel. Near Gate A there's a guarded **baggage-storage area.** The Mexico City Hotel and Motel Association offers a **hotel-reservation service** at their member hotels. Look for their booths before you leave the baggage-claim area and near Gate A on the concourse. They'll make the call according to your specifications for location and price. If they book the hotel, they require one night's advance payment and will give you a voucher showing payment, which you present at the hotel. Ask about hotels with specials, which can substantially reduce the rate. Special low-cost **long-distance telephones** (Ladatel) are strategically placed all along the public concourse (for instructions on how to use them, see the Appendix). For individual airline telephone numbers, see Section 3, "Moving on—Travel Services," below.

GETTING INTO TOWN   The **authorized airport taxis** provide a good, fast service, but are relatively expensive. Here's how to use them: Buy a taxi ticket before exiting the baggage area or outside at either end of the concourse. You must tell the ticket seller your hotel or destination, as price is based on a zone system. Expect to pay around $7 for a ticket to, say, the Plaza de la República, Sullivan Park, or Zona Rosa, or $6 to the Zócalo. Count your change! Present your ticket to a driver at either end of the concourse. Avoid turning your luggage over to a taxi "assistant" who does nothing but take your luggage a few steps to the taxi—naturally, he'll want a tip.

Ignore those who approach you in the arrivals hall offering taxis; these are usually nonlicensed and unauthorized. Take only an authorized cab with all the familiar markings: yellow car, white taxi light on the roof, and TRANSPORTACIÓN TERRESTRE painted on the doors.

The authorized cabbies maintain a monopoly of the airport business. This is not good for travelers. You can try to beat the system by walking to the Terminal Area Metro station (see below), at the intersection of the busy Bulevar Aeropuerto and the airport entrance, and look for a **regular city taxi.** When you see a yellow VW Beetle or little Datsun cab, flag it down. You may save at least 25%, and perhaps 50%, by doing so.

To make sure you get a proper, trustworthy cab, be sure to read the information on taxis in Section 2, "Getting Around," below.

The **Metro,** Mexico City's modern subway system, is cheaper and faster than a taxi. As you come from your plane into the arrivals hall, turn left and walk all the way through the long terminal, out the doors, and along a covered sidewalk. Soon you'll see the distinctive Metro logo that identifies the Terminal Area station, down a flight of stairs. The station is on Metro Line 5. Follow the signs for trains to Pantitlán. At Pantitlán, change for Line 1 ("Observatorio"), which will take you to stations that are just a few blocks south of the Zócalo and the Alameda Central: Pino Suárez, Isabel la Católica, Salto del Agua, Balderas. The fare is astoundingly low—only a few pennies. But wait! You may not be able to go by Metro if you have luggage. Read carefully the Metro information in Section 2, "Getting Around." If you find that you can get on the Metro with luggage, don't plan to take a Metro route that requires you to change

---

IN THEIR FOOTSTEPS

Benito Juárez (1806–1872) A full-blood Zapotec Indian, he was orphaned at the age of 3. He became Governor of Oaxaca in 1847 after which he was exiled to New Orleans by grudge-holding President Santa Anna because Juarez refused to grant him asylum in Oaxaca years before. On becoming President of Mexico first in 1858, his terms were interrupted once during the Reform Wars and again during the French intervention, Juárez cast the deciding vote favoring the execution of Maximilian. He died from a heart attack before completing his fourth term. Devoid of personal excesses, Juárez had a clear vision for Mexico, that included honest leadership, separation of church and state, imposition of civilian rule, reduction of the military, and education reform.

• **Birthplace:** San Pablo Guelatao, Oax. His birthday March 21, is the village's grandest festival day.

• **Residence:** Between 1818 and 1820 he lived at Garcia Vigil 609, Oaxaca, now a Juárez museum. During his presidency he occupied part of the north wing of the National Palace in Mexico City, now The Juárez Museum. During his presidencies in exile, he lived in San Luis Potosi, Chihuahua, and Cd. Juárez all of which commemorate his quarters.

• **Resting Place:** San Fernando Cemetery, Mexico City.

trains at La Raza station. The walk between lines there is 10 to 15 minutes, and you'll be carrying your luggage.

BY TRAIN

The Buenavista railroad station (tel. 547-1097 or 547-1084), three blocks north of the Revolución Metro station along Insurgentes, is officially called the **Terminal de Ferrocarriles Nacionales de México.** You can get away with "Estación Buenavista." Walk out the right-hand set of front doors in the terminal and get your bearings on the front steps. You're facing south. The big boulevard on the right is Avenida Insurgentes, the city's main north-south axis. You can catch a **no. 17 "Indios Verdes–Tlalpan" bus** south along Insurgentes to get to Plaza de la República, Paseo de la Reforma, and the Zona Rosa; catch one north to get to the Terminal Norte (main bus station). Straight ahead of you about 12 blocks away, the dome of the Monument to the Revolution floats on the skyline from its site in Plaza de la República. To the left of it, the spire of the Latin American Tower juts skyward from the intersection of Avenida Juárez and Avenida Lázaro Cárdenas.

Bus no. 22, "Cuatro Caminos–Económica," runs east along Mosqueta (the street in front of the station), and you can catch this bus to the intersection with Avenida Lázaro Cárdenas, then transfer to a trolleybus (no. 27, "Reclusorio Norte–Ciudad Jardin") heading south into the center of town, but these buses are often jam-packed. You may feel better taking a taxi to your chosen hotel.

BY BUS

Mexico City has a bus terminal for each of the four points of the compass: north, east, south, and west. You can't necessarily tell which terminal serves which area of the country by looking at a map, however. See the table in Section 3, "Moving on—Travel Services," for the terminals and destinations they serve (some destinations are served from more than one terminal). All stations have restaurants, book and magazine stands, money exchange booths or banks, post offices, and long distance telephone booths. Each station has a taxi system based on set-price tickets to various zones within the city, operated from a booth or kiosk in or near the entry foyer of the terminal. Locate your destination on a zone map, or tell the seller where you want to go, buy a ticket (boleto) and present it to the driver out front. For bus rider's terms and translations, see the Appendix.

TERMINAL CENTRAL DE AUTOBUSES DEL NORTE Called by shorter names such as "Camiones Norte," "Terminal Norte," or "Central del Norte," or even just "C.N.," this is Mexico's largest bus station, on Avenida de los 100 ("Cien") Metros. It handles most buses coming from the U.S./Mexican border. All buses to/from the Pacific Coast as far south as Puerto Vallarta and Manzanillo, to/from the Gulf Coast as far south as Tampico and Veracruz, and to/from such cities as Guadalajara, San Luis Potosí, Durango, Zacatecas, and Colima arrive and depart from here. You can also get to the pyramids of San Juan Teotihuacán and Tula from here.

The Central del Norte is a mammoth place where you can change money (during normal banking hours), have a meal or a drink, take out insurance, or rent a car. There's even a post office and a long-distance phone installation. A Tourism Information Booth is set up at the center of the terminal's crescent-shaped facade, and nearby there's a hotel-reservations booth. Both can be very helpful.

To get downtown from the Terminal Norte, you have a choice: The Metro has a station (Estación Terminal de Autobuses del Norte, or T.A.N.) right here, so it's easy to hop a train and connect for all points. Walk to the center of the terminal, go out the front door, straight ahead, down the steps, and to the Metro station. This is Línea 5. Follow the signs that say DIRECCIÓN PANTITLÁN. For downtown, you can change trains at either La Raza or Consulado (see the Mexico City Metro map). Be aware that if you change at La Raza, you'll have to walk for 10 to 15 minutes, and you'll encounter stairs. The walk is through a marble-lined underground corridor, but a long way with heavy luggage.

Another way to get downtown is by trolleybus. The stop is on Avenida de los Cien Metros, in front of the terminal. The trolleybus runs right down Avenida Lázaro Cárdenas, the "Eje Central" (Central Artery). Or the no. 17-B bus ("Central Camionera del Norte–Villa Olimpica") goes all the way down Avenida Insurgentes, past the university.

TERMINAL DE AUTOBUSES DE PASAJEROS DE ORIENTE (TAPO) The terminal for eastern routes has a very long name but a conveniently short acronym: TAPO. Take a no. 20 ("Hipodromo-Pantitlán") bus east along Alvarado, Hidalgo, or Donceles to get there. If you take the Metro, go to the San Lázaro station on the eastern portion of Line 1 ("Dirección Pantitlán").

As you emerge from the bus or Metro station, the translucent green dome of TAPO will catch your eye. (If it doesn't, ask anyone: "¿Donde esta el TAPO?") Underneath the dome there are ticket counters, toilets, a post office, a cafeteria, bookstalls, and snack shops. Enter along "Tunel 1" to the Terminal de Salidas under the central dome.

TERMINAL CENTRAL DE AUTOBUSES DEL SUR Mexico City's southern bus terminal is the "Terminal Central de Autobuses del Sur," right next to the Taxqueña Metro stop, last stop on that line. The Central del Sur handles buses to/from Cuernavaca, Taxco, Acapulco, Zihuatanejo, and intermediate points. Easiest way to get to or from the Central del Sur is on the Metro. The station for the terminal is Taxqueña (or Tasqueña, as it's also spelled). Follow the signs that say DIRECCIÓN PANTITLÁN to get downtown. Or take a trolleybus on Avenida Lázaro Cárdenas.

To get downtown by taxi, buy your ticket in the terminal before you exit. The system is the same as at the Central del Norte.

TERMINAL PONIENTE DE AUTOBUSES The western bus terminal is conveniently located right next to the Observatorio Metro station, which you can reach by no. 76 ("Zócalo–km 13") buses.

TOURIST INFORMATION

The Departamento del Distrito Federal (Federal District government) provides several information services for visitors. First of all there are **Infotur** offices, the most convenient of which is in the Zona Rosa at Amberes 54, at the corner of Londres (tel. 525-9380 or 525-9384). Others are at the bus terminals, airport, and railroad station. They're open Monday through Saturday from 8am to 8pm and on Sunday from 8am to 5pm.

The **Secretaría de Turismo (SECTUR)**, Avenida Presidente Masaryk 172 (tel. 250-0151 or 250-0585), north of Chapultepec Park in the district known as Polanco, is a bit out of the way, but any telephone will serve to get you information. They'll speak English and staff the phones 24 hours daily.

The **Mexico City Chamber of Commerce** (tel. 546-5645) maintains an information office with a very friendly, helpful staff who can provide you with a detailed map of the city (or country) and answer some of your questions. It's conveniently located at Reforma 42—look for the Cámara Nacional de Comercio de la Ciudad de México, open Monday through Thursday from 9am to 2pm and 3 to 6pm, and on Friday from 9am to 2pm and 3 to 5:30pm.

CITY LAYOUT

MAIN ARTERIES & STREETS The **Paseo de la Reforma** goes northeast to the Basilica of Our Lady of Guadalupe and west crossing Insurgentes, through Chapultepec Park eventually leading to Toluca. **Avenida Insurgentes Norte** (north), a major north-south artery, goes from Reforma north to the Pyramids of Teotihuacán. To the south it crosses Reforma and becomes **Avenida Insurgentes Sur** (south). This is the artery that leads to San Angel, University City, the Pedregal, and Coyoacan, and farther south it becomes Highway 95 to Taxco and Cuernavaca. Another main north-south artery starts just south of the historic city center at

Servando Teresa de Mier and is called **Calzada San Antonio Abad** until it crosses Miguel Aleman and becomes **Calzada Tlalpan** and continues south terminating in the suburb of Tlalpan.

The **Periferico** (Highway 57) is a loop around the city which is also named Camacho as it heads north. It leads north to Tula, Querétaro, and San Miguel. As it goes south, it crosses Reforma, passes through Chapultepec Park, crosses Constituyentes, and heads south to San Angel before turning east south of University City; eventually it crosses Highway 95 to Taxco, continues past Xochimilco, and finally loops back again to the city center.

In the downtown area the main east-west arteries include **Avenida Juárez,** which runs from Plaza de la República past the south side of the Alameda, and becomes **Avenida Madero,** which ends at the Zócalo. **Cinco de Mayo** runs between the Alameda and the Zócalo. **Hidalgo** runs along the north side of the Alameda, becomes **Calzada Tacuba,** and passes in back of the Metropolitan Cathedral.

Streets change names frequently, as you have probably noted.

FINDING AN ADDRESS   Despite its size, Mexico City is not outrageously hard to understand. The city is divided into 350 *colonias*. But unless you are venturing out of the city center (Colonia Centro), you'll probably have no need for knowing *colonias*. It's helpful to jot them down, however, when trying to find an obscure address, such as a shop or a restaurant that may be unfamiliar to a taxi driver. A few to know are: Colonia Polanco, a fashionable neighborhood, immediately north of Chapultepec Park; and the Lomas (Lomas de Chapultepec, Lomas Tecamachalco, etc.), very exclusive neighborhoods west of Chapultepec Park, the "in" addresses so to speak.

In addresses it's abbreviated "Col." and the full *colonia* name is vital in addressing correspondence.

NEIGHBORHOODS IN BRIEF

Centro   Centro refers to the heart of Mexico City, its business, banking, and historic center, including the areas in and around the Alameda and Zócalo.

Chapultepec   A huge area west of the city center, it mainly includes Chapultepec Park and its immediate environs.

Coyoacán   Farther south from San Angel, 13 miles from the city center, and east of University City, Coyoacán is another colonial-era suburb noted for its beautiful town square, cobblestone streets lined with fine old mansions, and several of the city's most interesting museums.

Polanco   Polanco is a trendy neighborhood of homes, shops, and restaurants north of Chapultepec. President Mazarek is the main artery through it.

San Angel   Once a separate village, 9 miles south of the city center, it's surrounded by the city, yet remains a beautiful suburb of cobblestone streets and beautiful colonial-era homes.

Xochimilco   Xochimilco, 15 miles south of town center, is a village with canals that date from pre-Hispanic times.

Zona Rosa   The "Pink Zone," west of the central city, a trendy multiblock area noted for its pedestrians-only streets, shops, restaurants, and hotels.

STREET MAPS   Should you want more detailed maps of Mexico City than the ones included in this guide, you can obtain them easily. Most bookstores (including Sanborn's), and many newsstands carry a local map-guide entitled *Mexico City Trillas Tourist Guide* ($6.75), a 120-page softbound book of gorgeous block-by-block pictorial maps covering most areas of the city that are of interest to visitors. The text, which includes interesting facts and statistics on Mexico City and its sights, is in English.

Fully detailed street plans of the entire city are published by **Guía Amarilla** and **Guía Roji.** These are probably more detailed than you need or want, unless you have business to conduct in the city. They're available in bookstores and at newsstands.

The **American Automobile Association** publishes a motorist's map of

Mexico and Central America, which includes a very handsome map of downtown Mexico City. The map is available free to AAA members at any AAA office in the United States; it's not available in Mexico.

2. GETTING AROUND

Luckily for budget travelers, Mexico City has a highly developed and remarkably cheap public transportation system. The Metro, first- and second-class buses, minibuses (*colectivos*), and yellow VW taxis will take you anywhere you want to go for very little money.

BY METRO

The subway system in Mexico City offers a smooth ride for one of the lowest fares anywhere in the world. Eight lines are completed in the sprawling system, with plans for nine more in the works.

As you enter the station, buy a boleto (ticket) at the glass caja (ticket booth). Insert your ticket into the slot at the turnstile and pass through; inside you'll see two large signs showing the line's destination (for example, for Line 1, it's Observatorio and Pantitlán). Follow the signs in the direction you want, and *know where you're going,* since there is usually only one map of the routes, at the entrance to the station. There are, however, two signs you'll see everywhere: Salida, which means "exit," and Andenes, which means "platforms." Once inside the train, you'll see above each door a map of the station stops for that line, with symbols and names.

Transfer of lines is indicated by Correspondencias. The ride is smooth, fast, and efficient (although hot and crowded during rush hours). The stations are clean and beautifully designed, and have the added attraction of several archeological ruins unearthed during construction. There is also a subterranean passage that goes between the Pino Suárez and Zócalo stations so you can avoid the crowds and the rain along Pino Suárez. The Zócalo station has dioramas and large photographs of the different periods in the history of the Valley of Mexico, and at Pino Suárez there is the foundation of a pyramid from the Aztec empire.

Important Notes: The Metro system runs Monday through Friday from 6am to 1am and on Saturday and Sunday from 7am to midnight. Also, heavy baggage is not allowed into the system at busy times, especially during rush hours on weekdays. In practice this means that bulky suitcases or backpacks sometimes make you *persona non grata* (but a large shoulder bag such as I use is not classed as luggage, nor is an attaché case, or even a case that's slightly bigger). The reason is that on an average day Mexico City's Metro handles over 5,000,000 riders and that leaves precious little room for bags! But, in effect, if no one stops you as you enter, you're in.

Metro travel is usually very crowded during daylight hours on weekdays, and consequently pretty hot and muggy in summer. In fact, you may find that between 4 and 7pm on weekdays the Metro downtown is virtually unusable because of sardine-can conditions. At some stations there are even separate lanes roped off for women and children because the press of the crowd is so great that someone might get molested. Buses, colectivos, and taxis are all heavily used during these hours. The trick is to leave yourself some time and energy to walk during these hours. On weekends and holidays, the Metro is a joy to ride.

BY BUS

Moving millions of people through this sprawling urban mass is a gargantuan task, but the city officials do a pretty good job of it, though they tend to change bus numbers and routes too frequently. The municipal bus system, operated by the DDF (Departamento del Distrito Federal, or Federal District Department), is run on an enormous grid plan. Odd-numbered buses run roughly north-south, even-numbered buses go east-west, and a special express service runs along the main routes downtown. Maps of the entire system are difficult to find. I'll provide you with most of the routes and numbers you'll need, however.

The buses themselves are modern but they age very rapidly. They tend to be crowded or very crowded. The fare is very low—a few pennies, same as the Metro. Have the exact fare when you board. Downtown bus stops bear signs with full route descriptions.

One of the most important bus routes is the one that runs between the Zócalo and the Auditorio (National Auditorium in Chapultepec Park) or the Observatorio Metro station. The route is via Avenida Madero or Cinco (5) de Mayo, Avenida Juárez, and Paseo de la Reforma; maps of the route are posted at each bus stop. At present, **bus no. 76, "Zócalo–km 13,"** runs along this route.

Another important route is **bus no. 17, "Indios Verdes–Tlalpan,"** which runs along Avenida Insurgentes connecting the northern bus terminal (Terminal Norte), Buenavista railroad station, Reforma, the Zona Rosa, and—far to the south—San Angel and University City. Also, **trolleybuses** run from the Terminal de Autobuses del Norte down Avenida Lázaro Cárdenas to the Tasqueña Metro station.

BY TAXI

Mexico City is pretty easy to negotiate by Metro and bus, and these methods bring you few hassles. Taxis are another matter, but there are times when nothing else will do. Cabs operate under several distinct sets of rules, established in early 1991, and they *may* make using one less of a combat-zone situation than in the past.

Metered Taxis: Yellow-and-white Volkswagen Beetle and coral- and white-colored "sitio" Datsun cabs are your best bet for low cost and good service. Though you will often encounter a gouging driver ("Ah, the meter just broke yesterday; I'll have it fixed tomorrow!"), or one who advances the meter (yes, I've seen it), or drives farther than necessary to run up the tab, most of the service will be quick and adequate. As of early 1991, these taxis began operating strictly by the meter, which starts at 2,000 pesos. If the driver says his meter isn't working, find another taxi.

"Turismo" Taxis: These cabs are unmarked, have special license plates and bags covering their meters, are usually well-kept big cars, and are assigned to specific hotels. The drivers negotiate rates with individual passengers for sightseeing, etc., but rates to and from the airport are established, although higher than the Datsun or VW taxis. Ask the bell captain what the airport rate should be and establish the rate before taking off. These drivers are often English-speaking, licensed guides and can provide exceptional service.

Important Notes: Do *not* use a car that's not an official taxi. Though most of the unauthorized drivers are just guys trying to earn some extra money and make ends meet, others are crooks. Here's how you tell an official, authorized taxi:

All official taxis (except those expensive "Turismo" cabs) are painted yellow or coral. They have white plastic roof signs bearing the word TAXI and they have TAXI or SITIO painted on the doors and they have meters. Look for *all* these indications, not just one or two of them.

There is no need to tip any taxi driver in Mexico unless the driver has performed a special service.

BY COLECTIVO

Also called peseros, these are sedans or minibuses, usually white, that run along major arteries. They pick up and discharge passengers along the route, charge established fares, and provide more comfort and speed than the bus. Routes are displayed on cards in the windshield; often a Metro station will be the destination. One of the most useful routes for tourists is Ruta 2, which runs from the Zócalo along Avenida Juárez, along Reforma to Chapultepec, and back again. Get a colectivo with a sign saying ZÓCALO, not VILLA.

Note that some of the minibuses on this route have automatic sliding doors—you don't have to shut them, a motor does.

As the driver approaches a stop, he may put his hand out the window and hold up

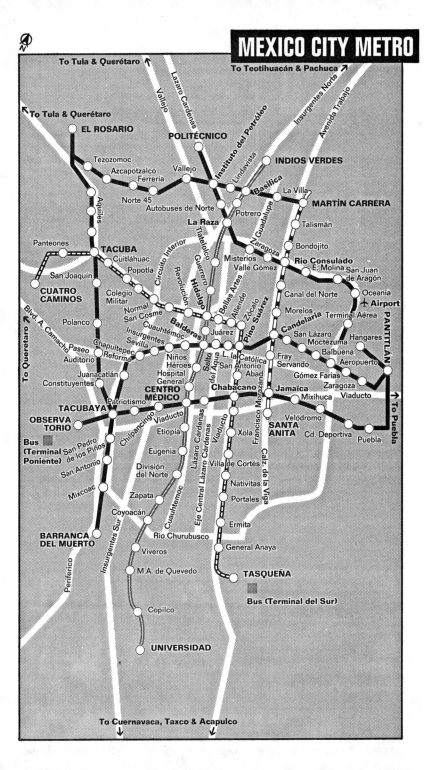

MEXICO CITY METRO

To Tula & Querétaro

To Teotihuacán & Pachuca ↗

To Tula & Querétaro ↖

Lázaro Cárdenas

Vallejo

Instituto del Petróleo

Lindavista

Insurgentes Norte

Avenida Trabajo

EL ROSARIO

POLITÉCNICO

INDIOS VERDES

Tezozomoc

Azcapotzalco

Vallejo

Basílica

La Villa

Ferrería

Norte 45

Autobuses de Norte

Aquiles

La Raza

Potrero

Guadalupe

MARTÍN CARRERA

Talismán

Panteones

TACUBA

Cuitláhuac

Popotla

Circuito Interior

Tlatelolco

Guerrero

Misterios

Valle Gómez

Zaragoza

Bondojito

Río Consulado

E. Molina

San Juan

de Aragón

San Joaquín

**CUATRO
CAMINOS**

Colegio
Militar

Normal

San Cosme

Revolución

Hidalgo

Bellas Artes

Allende

Canal del Norte

Oceanía

✈ Airport

Morelos

Terminal Aérea

PANTITLÁN

Blvd. A. Camacho

Polanco

Cuauhtémoc

Balderas

Juárez

Zócalo

Pino Suárez

Candelaria

San Lázaro

Moctezuma

Hangares

Insurgentes

Sevilla

Chapultepec

Reforma

Niños
Héroes

Salto

del Agua

L. la

San Antonio

Católica

Fray
Servando

Balbuena

Aeropuerto

To Querétaro ↗

Paseo

Auditorio

Juanacatlán

Hospital
General

Abad

Gómez Farías

Constituyentes

**CENTRO
MÉDICO**

Chabacano

Jamaica

Zaragoza

Mixihuca

Viaducto

TACUBAYA

Patriotismo

Chilpancingo

Viaducto

Lázaro Cárdenas

Viaducto

Francisco Morazán

**SANTA
ANITA**

Velódromo

To Puebla ↗

**OBSERVA
TORIO**

Etiopía

Xola

Cd. Deportiva

Bus
**(Terminal
Poniente)**

San Pedro
de los Piños

Eugenia

Villa de Cortés

Calz. de la Viga

Puebla

San Antonio

División
del Norte

Eje Central Lázaro Cárdenas

Nativitas

Mixcoac

Zapata

Cuauhtémoc

Portales

Coyoacán

Río Churubusco

Ermita

**BARRANCA
DEL MUERTO**

Viveros

General Anaya

Periférico

Insurgentes Sur

M.A. de Quevedo

TASQUEÑA

Bus (Terminal del Sur)

Copilco

UNIVERSIDAD

To Cuernavaca, Taxco & Acapulco
↓   ↓

one or more fingers. This is the number of passengers he's willing to take on (vacant seats are difficult to see if you're outside the car).

BY CAR

Generally speaking, renting a car for touring around the world's largest city will be extremely frustrating and I don't recommend it. Besides the usual one-way streets, there are numerous traffic circles, streets change names constantly, and drivers don't heed signs. If you want to spend a few days touring by car outside the capital, don't hesitate to rent one, but time your exit and reentry to the city (to return the car) carefully. The traffic is horrendous and it requires one person to drive and another to navigate. If you arrive late at the airport, ask one of the rental-car employees to drive you and the car to your hotel (pay his taxi fare back to the airport), park the car overnight in protected parking, then leave the city before dawn the next morning when there is almost no traffic. Avoid heavy traffic between 7 and 10am and between 5 and 9pm.

Rental Cars: The least expensive rental car is the manual-shift VW Beetle, which is manufactured in Mexico. The price jump is considerable after the VW Beetle, and you pay more for automatic transmission and air conditioning in any car. Through Avis the basic daily rate for a VW Beetle is $38, plus daily $12 insurance and 15% tax.

Hertz, Budget, National, and Avis car rentals, among others, are represented at the airport, and each has several city offices as well. Daily rates and deductibles vary considerably. Presently Avis has the cheapest rates overall.

Pollution Control: To control pollution in the capital, regulations for car use according to day of the week, tag number, and color are in force as shown in the table below:

PROHIBITED DRIVING DAYS

	Mon.	Tues.	Wed.	Thurs.	Fri.
Tag color	Yellow	Pink	Red	Green	Blue
Tag ends in	5 or 6	7 or 8	3 or 4	1 or 2	9 or 0

This means that if your car tag is yellow and ends in a 5 or 6, you are prohibited from driving in Mexico City on Monday, but you can drive any other day of the week. Note that this applies to rental cars and to tourist cars, but it is not in effect on Saturday or Sunday. There's a $115 fine for violating this regulation.

 MEXICO CITY

In "Fast Facts: Mexico" in Chapter 2, you'll find the answers to all sorts of questions about daily life in Mexico City. But here are a few essentials for getting along in this charming, enormous metropolis:

Altitude   Remember that you are now at an altitude of 7,240 feet—almost a mile and a half in the sky—where there's a lot less oxygen in the air than you're used to. If you run for a bus and feel dizzy when you sit down, that's the altitude; if you think you're in shape, but puff and puff getting up Chapultepec hill, that's the altitude. It takes about 10 days or so to adjust to the scarcity of oxygen. Go easy on food and alcohol the first few days in the city.

American Express   The Mexico City office is at Reforma 234 (tel. 5/533-0380), in the Zona Rosa. It's open for banking, the pickup of American Express clients' mail, and travel advice Monday through Friday from 9am to 6pm and on Saturday from 9am to 1pm.

Area Code   The telephone area code for Mexico City is 5.

Baby-sitters   Hotels can often recommend a baby-sitter.

Banks   Banks are usually open Monday through Friday from 9am to 1:30pm.

Banames is open Monday through Friday from 9am to 5:50pm. Bank branches at the airport are open whenever the airport is busy, including weekends. They usually offer very good rates of exchange.

Bookstores In Mexico City, **Sanborn's** and **Woolworth's** always have books in English, as well as magazines and newspapers. So does the **American Bookstore,** Madero 25 off Bolivar (tel. 512-7284); it's open Monday through Saturday from 9:30am to 7pm. The **American Benevolent Society's Caza Libros,** at Monte Athos 355 (tel. 540-5123), 2½ blocks off Reforma, west of Chapultepec Park in the section called Lomas Barrilaco, has used books in Spanish and English, hardback and paperback, plus magazines. It's open Monday through Saturday from 10am to 5pm. All profits go to charity projects of the society.

French and English books and magazines, especially those dealing with Mexico, its history, archeology, and people, are the specialty of the **Cia. Internacional de Publicaciones, or Librerias (I.P.).** Branches of this firm in Mexico City are located at Serapio Rendon 125 (just off the Jardín del Arte, near the Hotel Sevilla), at Avenida Madero 30 not far from the House of Tiles, and also in Polanco and San Angel.

About the most convenient foreign- and Spanish-language bookstore in Mexico City, with a good selection of guides and books on Mexico, is **Central de Publicaciones—Libreria Mizrachi,** Juárez 4, near Avenida Lázaro Cárdenas (tel. 510-4231), right across from the Bellas Artes. Another shop, nearby, is the **Libreria Britanica,** Madero 30-1, in the Hotel Ritz building (tel. 521-0180). The **Museo Nacional de Antropologia,** in Chapultepec Park (tel. 553-6266), also has an excellent shop with a good selection of books on Mexico, particularly special-interest guides (birds, flowers, geology, mineralogy, archeology, cuisine, folk art, and so forth).

Business Hours Most businesses are open from 10am to 7pm Monday through Friday and until 5pm on Saturday; most are closed Sunday.

Car Rentals See Section 2, "Getting Around," above.

Climate See Section 2, "When to Go," in Chapter 2.

Crime See "Safety," below.

Currency See Section 1, "Information, Entry Requirements, and Money," in Chapter 2.

Currency Exchange The alternative to a bank is a currency-exchange booth, or *casa de cambio.* These are often open Monday through Friday from 8:30am to 5:30pm, and some are open on Saturday from 8:30am to 2:30pm as well; many stay open until 6pm. The exchange rates offered by casas de cambio are sometimes better than—and sometimes worse than—those offered by the banks. Usually, their rates are much better than the rates offered by most hotels.

There are currency-exchange booths in many parts of the city where foreigners circulate, including at Hamburgo 104 (tel. 525-6389), in the Zona Rosa; Londres 118B, at the corner of Genova (tel. 533-2564), in the Zona Rosa; Paseo de la Reforma 80, between Avenida Juárez and Columbus Circle (tel. 535-4352); Paseo de la Reforma 208 (tel. 511-8660); Paseo de la Reforma 320A (tel. 525-6755), facing the U.S. Embassy; and Río Tiber 112B, 1½ blocks from the Independence Monument (tel. 533-0481). The Londres 118B location is open on Saturday from 8:30am to 1pm; the Reforma 208 and Río Tiber 112B offices are open until 2pm on Saturday.

Dentists/Doctors The U.S. and British embassies maintain a reputable list of dentists and doctors.

Drugstores The drug departments at **Sanborn's** stays open late. Check the phone directory for the location nearest you. After hours, check with your hotel staff, who can usually contact the drugstore *de turno* (on call).

Embassies and Consulates A full list of embassies and consulates appears in Chapter 2.

Emergencies The number for the police is 672-0606; tourist assistance is 250-8221. See "Tourist Information" earlier in this chapter, and "Hotlines" below.

Eyeglasses For repairs or prescription services, try **Santosoy,** Hamburgo 99, in the Zona Rosa, open Monday through Saturday from 10am to 8pm.

Hairdressers/Barbers Ask at your hotel. The average cost of a haircut is $10, $12 for a hairdo.

Holidays See Section 2, "When to Go," in Chapter 2.

Hospitals Two hospitals catering to foreigners are in the southern reaches of Mexico City. One is the **American-British Cowdray (A.B.C.) Hospital,** located at Calle Sur 132 no. 136, at the corner of Avenida Observatorio, Colona Las Américas (Sur 132 is the name of the street) (tel. 277-5000 or 277-6211, or for emergencies 515-8359 or 516-8077). Take the Metro (Line 1) to "Observatorio," and the hospital is a short taxi ride from there. Have your insurance up-to-date as the hospital bill is at Stateside prices. The other is the **Hospital Angeles del Pedregal,** Camino de Santa Teresa 1055, Colona Héroes de Padierna (tel. 652-1188 or 652-0422).

Hotlines If you think you've been ripped off in a purchase, call the consumer protection office, the **Procuraduria Nacional del Consumidor** (tel. 761-3811). Another helpful number is that of the **Tourist Assistance Patrols** (tel. 250-8221).

Information See "Tourist Information" in Section 1, "Orientation," above.

Laundry/Dry Cleaning Your hotel can take care of this for you, but you'll save money, and perhaps time, if you take it to a branch of **Lavandería Jiffy** (pronounced "*hee*-fee," not "jiffy"). There are branches at the corner of Río Tiber and Río Lerma, near the Angel Monument; and at the corner of Revillagigedo and Victoria, south of the Alameda Central. Another laundry, north of Plaza de la República, is the **Lavandería Automatica,** Calle Edison 91, between Iglesias and Arriaga. They're open Monday through Friday from 9am to 7pm and on Saturday from 9am to 8pm.

Legal Assistance If you need legal help, call 525-9380, 525-9381, or 525-9382.

Libraries Mexico City has several libraries of English-language books connected with her diplomatic missions. Check out the **Benjamin Franklin (American) Library,** on Niza between Londres and Liverpool. The **Canadian Embassy Library** (Canadian books and periodicals in French and English) is at Schiller 529, in Polanco (tel. 254-3288, ext. 248), open Monday through Friday from 9am to 12:30pm. The **U.S. Embassy** (tel. 211-0042), has a full reference library and numerous U.S. Department of Commerce publications relating to doing business in Mexico. Make arrangements to use it prior to arriving in Mexico. The **American Chamber of Commerce** (tel. 705-0995) has a complete commercial library.

Lost Property See "Insurance" in Chapter 2.

Luggage Storage/Lockers There are *guarda equipaje* rooms at the airport and bus stations. Most hotels have a key-locked storage area for guests who want to leave possessions for a few days.

Newspapers/Magazines The *Mexico City News* is the city's English language daily. See also "Bookstores," above.

Photographic Needs Try **Foto Regis,** Avenida Juárez 80, near the Alameda.

Police Dial 672-0606 for the police.

Post Office The city's main post office, the Correos Mayor, is a block north of the Palacio de Bellas Artes on Avenida Lázaro Cárdenas, at the corner of Tacuba.

Although I don't recommend mailing a package in Mexico, since it may never get to its intended destination, if you must mail one in Mexico City, here's what to do: Take it to the special post office called Correos Internacional no. 2, Calle Dr. Andrade and Río de la Loza (Metro: Balderas or Salto del Agua), open Monday through Friday from 8am to noon. Don't wrap up your package securely until an inspector examines it. (For a glossary of mail terms, see the Appendix.)

Radio Radio VIP (88.9 FM), a CBS affiliate, has all-day English-language broadcasts and news. For jazz and English newscasts, try 90.5 FM. Station XELA (800 AM and 98.5 FM) broadcasts classical music, as do several university stations.

Religious Services Services in English in Mexico City are at the following times and places: **Baptist**—Capital City Baptist Church, Bondojito, at the corner of Calle Sur 138, Colonia Las Americas (tel. 516-1862 or 562-8614), one block from the Observatorio Metro station, across from the American School and the A.B.C. Hospital; Sunday School at 9:45am, services at 11am, evening worship in Spanish at

6pm. **Catholic**—St. Patrick's Church, Bondojito 248, near the A.B.C. Hospital, Colonia Hidalgo (tel. 515-1993); Sunday mass at 10 and 11am and on Saturday at 6pm. **Christian Science**—First Church of Christ Scientist, Calle Dante 21, Colonia Anzures (tel. 514-6603); Sunday service at 11am, bilingual meeting on Wednesday at 7:30pm; Reading Room open Monday, Tuesday, and Thursday through Saturday from 11am to noon and 4 to 7:30pm. **Church of Christ**—Central Church of Christ, Calle 13 de Septiembre no. 26, in Colonia Condesa (on a one-block, one-way street between Tacubaya and Chapultepec); Sunday worship and communion at 9am, Bible classes for all at 10am. **Episcopal**—Christ Church Episcopal, Montes Escandinavos 405, Lomas de Chapultepec, at the corner of Sierra Madre (tel. 520-3763, or 520-1738 for the rectory); Holy Eucharist at 8 and 10am Sunday. **Interdenominational**—Central Church, Balderas 47, at Independencia (tel. 532-7787); special worship service for tourists at 8:30am on Sunday (in the sanctuary of Messiah Methodist Church). **Jewish**—Beth Israel Community Center, Virreyes 1140, Lomas de Chapultepec (tel. 520-8515); services at 8pm on Friday and 9am on Saturday. **Lutheran**—Lutheran Church of the Good Shepherd (La Iglesia Luterana del Buen Pastor), Paseo de las Palmas 1910, Colonia Lomas de Chapultepec (tel. 596-1034); Sunday services at 9:45am, Bible classes at 11am. **Methodist**—Messiah Methodist Church, Balderas 47, between Juárez and Independencia (tel. 512-1608); Sunday service at 8:30am. **Mormon**—Church of Jesus Christ of Latter Day Saints, Sierra Guadarrama 115, Lomas de Chapultepec (tel. 540-2790 or 540-3797); Sunday service from 9am to noon. **Presbyterian**—Gethsemane Presbyterian Church, Allende and Cuauhtémoc, in Coyoacán (tel. 554-8161); Sunday services at 9am. **Quaker**—The Quaker Center, I. Mariscal 132 (tel. 705-0521 or 705-0646); Sunday meetings at 11am. **Union Evangelical Church (Protestant interdenominational)**—Located at Reforma 1870 at Monte Alvernia, in Lomas de Chapultepec (tel. 520-0436 or 520-9931); Sunday School at 9:15am and worship at 10:30am.

Rest Rooms   There are few public rest rooms. Use those in the larger hotels, in cafés and restaurants, and in museums.

Safety   Whenever you're traveling in an unfamiliar city or country, stay alert even in the most heavily touristed areas. Be aware of your immediate surroundings. Wear a moneybelt and don't sling your camera or purse over your shoulder. Note carefully all safety precautions throughout this book and read the section on Safety under "Fast Facts" in Chapter 2.

Watch for pickpockets. Mexico City is unique in many ways, but in one matter it resembles any big city anywhere—pickpockets. Crowded subway cars and buses provide the perfect workplace for petty thieves, as do major museums (inside and out), thronged outdoor markets and bullfights, and indoor theaters. The "touch" can range from light-fingered wallet lifting or purse opening to a fairly rough shoving by two or three petty thieves. Sometimes the ploy is this: Someone drops a coin, and while everyone is looking, pushing, and shoving, your wallet disappears. Watch for them anyplace tourists go in numbers: on the Metro, in Reforma buses, in crowded hotel elevators, at the Ballet Folklorico, at the National Museum of Anthropology. Luckily, violent muggings are pretty infrequent in Mexico City. But if you find yourself up against a handful of these guys in a crowded spot, the best thing to do is to raise a fuss—no matter whether you do it in Spanish or in English. Just a few shouts of "Ladron!" ("Thief!") should put them off.

Shoe Repairs   Ask the bell captain or desk clerk at your hotel.

Spanish Lessons   In Mexico City, there's the **Mexican–North American Institute of Cultural Relations,** Hamburgo 115 (tel. 511-4720). You can sign up for courses in University City as well. Office hours are 9am to 1pm and 3 to 6pm.

Taxes   When you hear or read a price, by law that price should include the 15% tax. It never hurts to ask "¿Más IVA?" (plus tax?) or "¿Con IVA?" (with tax?). There are also airport taxes for domestic and international flights see Section, "Getting Around," in Chapter 2.

Taxis   See Section 2, "Getting Around," above.

Telephones   Public telephones, for local calls, take the 100-peso coin, and many work without coins—free. Even if you must insert a coin, the cost of a call is virtually nil. Long-distance calls within Mexico and to foreign points must be made from special telephones, and are surprisingly expensive. You must read "Telephones and Mail" in the Appendix before placing any sort of long-distance call, even collect. Hotels are beginning to charge for local calls—Mexico City hotels embraced the practice almost immediately, but budget-priced hotels are less likely to charge because they lack the ability to track calls from individual rooms.

Television   "Cablevision" provides CBS, ABC, and NBC, as well as Arts and Entertainment, Movie Channel, and Sports Channel, from 6am to 2am. Many first-class and several budget-category hotels receive these channels.

Transit Information   See Section 2, "Getting Around," above.

Weather and Clothing   Mexico City's altitude means that you'll need a warm jacket and a sweater in winter. In summer it is warm during the day and cool, but not cold, at night. It also rains almost every afternoon or evening between May and October (this is common all over Mexico)—so take a raincoat.

Although most of the restaurant listings in this book are not formal places, you may want to bring along a jacket-and-tie since Mexico City itself is rather formal.

3. MOVING ON — TRAVEL SERVICES

BY PLANE

AIRLINES   For local information on flights, times, and prices, contact the airlines directly. The following numbers may be useful: **Aero California** (tel. 207-1378 or 207-0068 for reservations, 785-1101 or 785-1162 at the airport), **Aeroméxico** (tel. 207-8233 and 207-4900 for reservations, 571-4188 or 762-8060 at the airport), **American** (tel. 399-9222 for reservations, 571-3219 at the airport), **Continental** (tel. 203-1148, 535-7603, or 535-7604 for reservations, 571-3661 at the airport), **Delta** (tel. 202-1608 for reservations, 571-6316 at the airport), **Lufthansa** (tel. 202-8866 for reservations, 571-2713 at the airport), **Mexicana** (tel. 660-4444 for reservations—keep trying, it's always busy—or 571-8888 at the airport), **Pan American** (tel. 395-0077 or 557-8722 for reservations, 571-3219 at the airport), or **United** (tel. 208-8966 for reservations).

For information on reconfirmation of flights, see Chapter 2. *Note:* Telephoning an airline in Mexico City can be frustrating because the city's telephone system is old and in certain sections of the city it's downright nonfunctional. Besides, the airlines often don't have enough telephone lines to handle calls—keep trying. Also check the latest telephone directories for new or additional numbers.

Be sure to allow at least 45 minutes travel time from either the Zona Rosa or the Zócalo area to the airport. Check in at least 90 minutes before international and 60 minutes before domestic flights.

BY TRAIN

From Mexico City's **Buenavista Station,** it's possible to journey by rail to just about any region in the country. It's the hub of a number of Servicio Estrella trains heading for the far corners of the country. (For details on these trains, how to make reservations, and where to get information and timetables, see Chapter 2.) I've included train hours and price information in each of the pertinent sections of this book. *Note:* Significant train reorganization this year may affect the information below, so check these times before planning an itinerary. The following is a glimpse of regions covered by rail from Mexico City:

- The *Constitucionalista* links Mexico City with popular colonial cities a short distance north of the capital. It leaves at 7am, arriving in Querétaro at 10:10am, San Miguel de Allende around noon, and San Luis Potosí at 2pm. The Guanajuato car switches at Querétaro and stops in Irapuato and Silao before reaching Guanajuato around 2pm.
- The *Regiomontaño* leaves Mexico City at 6pm, passes through Monterrey and Saltillo, and arrives the next day in Nuevo Laredo at 12:15am.
- *El Oaxaqueño* takes off from Mexico City at 7pm, arrives in Puebla at midnight, Tehuacán at 2:30am, and Oaxaca at 9:30am the next day.
- *El Jarocho* boards passengers from Mexico City at 9:15pm and drops them off early the next morning in Veracruz at 7am, passing through Puebla, Fortín, Orizaba, and Córdoba en route.
- *El Purepecha*, another overnight train, leaves Mexico City at 10pm, arriving in Morelia at 6:30am, Pátzcuaro at 8am, and Uruapan at 10:10am.
- *El San Marqueño Zacatecano* leaves Mexico City at 8pm, arrives in Irapuato at 2:15am, León at 3:10am, Lagos de Moreno at 4:10am, Aguascalientes at 6:30am, Zacatecas at 8:30am, and in its ultimate destination, Cindad Juárez (opposite El Paso, Texas).
- *El Tapatío* covers the Mexico City to Guadalajara corridor, leaving at 8:40pm for an 8:10am arrival in Guadalajara.

Guadalajara is another hub—see Chapter 8 for details on train travel along the West Coast. Naturally you'll want to reconfirm these times. If you plan to get on and off the train en route, you must tell the agent your exact on/off schedule at the time of your ticket purchase. Make your reservation early because these trains are popular.

BY BUS

Terminal Central de Autobuses del Norte   All of Mexico's major bus companies have desks here where they sell tickets; give information on routes, times, and prices; and check you in for your journey.

Terminal de Autobuses de Pasajeros de Oriente (TAPO) Looking for a bus to Oaxaca, Yucatán, or Guatemala? This is the place to look. Companies that sell tickets here include Autobuses Unidos, Autobuses de Oriente, Fletes y Pasajes, Estrella Roja, and Cristobal Colón. Once in possession of a ticket, a growling mammoth machine will whiz you off to any of those points as well as to Amecameca and Pachuca. To get to TAPO, take a number 20 ("Hipodromo-Pantitlán") bus east along Alvarado, Hidalgo, or Donceles; or take Metro San Lázaro Line 1, ("Dirección Pantitlán").

Terminal de Autobuses del Sur   This terminal is fairly easy to figure out. If you're going to Cuernavaca, head straight for the ticket counters of Autobuses Pullman de Morelos, as their buses depart every 10 or 15 minutes throughout the day for that destination; there's hardly ever a problem getting a seat. If, however, you're headed for Taxco, Acapulco, or Zihuatanejo, go to the first-class line named Estrella de Oro; at their ticket counter, you can choose your bus seat on a computer screen! Other service from the Terminal del Sur is by Lineas Unidas del Sur/Flecha Amarilla, a second-class line which will save you a minuscule sum of money over Estrella de Oro. I recommend going first class.

Terminal Poniente de Autobuses   Smallest of the terminals, the Terminal Poniente's main reason for being is the route between Mexico City and Toluca, but some other cities to the west and northwest are served as well. In general, if your chosen destination is also served from the Terminal Norte, you'd be better off going there. The Terminal Norte simply has more buses and better bus lines.

Buying Bus Tickets Downtown   You'll find a **Greyhound** office at Paseo de la Reforma 27 (tel. 535-2618), where you can buy tickets on their buses and on Mexican connecting lines, into the United States. Office hours are Monday through Friday from 9am to 2pm and 3 to 5pm.

MEXICO CITY BUS TERMINALS & DESTINATIONS

Terminal Norte (North)	T.A.P. Oriente (East)	Terminal Sur (South)	Terminal Poniente (West)
Aguascalientes	Amecameca	Acapulco	Colima
Casas Grandes	Campeche	Cuernavaca	Culiacán
Chapala, Lake	Cancún	Ixtapa	Ensenada
Chihuahua	Chetumal	Taxco	Guadalajara
Ciudad Juárez	Cholula	Zihuatanejo	Hermosillo
Colima	Cozumel		Los Mochis
Durango	Cuautla		Manzanillo
Guadalajara	Ixta-Popo Park		Mazatlán
Guanajuato	Jalapa		Mexicali
Guaymas	Mérida		Morelia
Hermosillo	Oaxaca		Nogales
Los Mochis	Palenque		Pátzcuaro
Manzanillo	Puebla		Playa Azul
Matamoros	Salina Cruz		Puerto Vallarta
Mazatlán	San Cristóbal		Querétaro
Monterrey	de las Casas		San Luis Potosí
Morelia	Tehuacán		Tepic
Nogales	Tehuantepec		Tijuana
Nuevo Laredo	Tuxpan, Ver.		Toluca
Pachuca	Tuxtla Gutierrez		Uruapan
Papantla	Veracruz		
Pátzcuaro	Villahermosa		
Piedras Negras			
Poza Rica			
Puerto Vallarta			
Querétaro			
Reynosa			
Saltillo			
San Luis Potosí			
San Miguel de Allende			
Teotihuacán			
Tepic			
Torreón			
Tula			
Tuxpan, Ver.			
Zacatecas			

BY CAR

Insurgentes Sur becomes Highway 95 to Taxco and Cuernavaca. Insurgentes Norte leads to Teotihuacán and Pachuca. Highway 57, the Pereferico (loop around the city), is called Camacho as it goes north and leads out of the city north to Tula, and Querétaro, etc. Constituyentes leads west out of the city past Chapultepec Park and connects with Highway 15 to Toluca, Morelia, and Pátzcuaro. Zaragoza leads east to Highway 150 to Puebla and Veracruz.

CHAPTER 10

WHERE TO STAY IN MEXICO CITY

It costs less to stay in Mexico City than in most European capitals, or in almost any U.S. city of any size. The city is a bargain when you consider that for $20 to $35 you can find a double room in a fairly central hotel complete with bathroom, and often with such extras as air conditioning, TV, or a balcony. Many hotels have their own garages where guests can park free. Most new construction in the last decade has been luxurious hotels with central air conditioning, elevators, restaurants, and the like; these are usually at the top of our budget. Cheaper hotels tend to be the older ones, well kept but without all the extras that inflate prices.

My recommendations below are grouped around major landmarks in Mexico City, places that are well known by every city dweller and easily identifiable by first-time visitors. To find your chosen hotel area, or to get a bus going in that direction, all you need do is collar any passerby and ask, "¿Donde esta . . . ?" (*Dohn*-deh ess-*tah*) and then the name of the place: "El Monumento a la Revolución," "El Zócalo," "La Zona Rosa," and so on. You'll know your way home in no time at all.

The **Zona Rosa** is Mexico City's Mayfair, Faubourg-St-Honoré, or Central Park West: the status address. The chic boutiques, fancy restaurants and cafés, and expensive hotels are here. My hotel choices, in and near the Zona Rosa, are thus at the top of our daily budget.

Sullivan Park (Jardín del Arte) is a wedge-shaped park extending west from the intersection of Paseo de la Reforma and Avenida Insurgentes. It has a good range of hotels, old and new, colonial and modern, flashy and humble. Many are on quiet streets, some have views of the park, and all are close to the Zona Rosa and to transportation.

The **Revolución Monument** (Monumento a la Revolución) is in the large Plaza de la República, at the very western end of Avenida Juárez. Here you're centrally located, about equidistant from the Zona Rosa and the Zócalo, close to the Alameda, and you're near major transportation routes, but most of the hotel streets are quiet.

The **Alameda Central,** right next to the Palacio de Bellas Artes, is closer to the downtown shopping district, a bit farther from the Zona Rosa. Transportation is still good. Most of the hotels are well-used modern structures on streets to the south of the Alameda.

The **Zócalo** is the heart of historic Mexico City, surrounded by colonial buildings

IMPRESSIONS

Door Knobs in Mexico, for absolutely no reason whatever, are placed so near the frame of the door that it is almost impossible to grasp them without pinching your fingers. . . .
Chiefly from constant contact with tourists, the cab drivers of Mexico City have become notoriously extortionate. . . .
—CHARLES FLANDRAU
VIVA MEXICO, 1908

and Aztec ruins. It's also the heart of the downtown shopping district, with interesting small stores to the west and the gigantic Mercado Merced to the east.

For those arriving tired or late at night, there is a section describing lodging possibilities near the major terminals.

Finally, I've listed some of Mexico City's **apartment hotels,** establishments (mostly in or near the Zona Rosa) where you can rent a fully furnished studio or one-bedroom apartment with kitchen by the week or month, at rates similar to or lower than those in a hotel. If you're traveling with a small group or a family, or if you're staying for a week or more, apartment hotels may be the way to save money.

1. AROUND THE ZONA ROSA

Also see Section 9, "Long-term Stays," for apartment-like hotels in or near the Zona Rosa.

DOUBLES FOR LESS THAN $35

CASA GONZÁLEZ, Río Sena 69, México, D.F. 06500. Tel. 5/514-3302. 22 rms (all with bath). **Metro:** Insurgentes (four blocks away); the hotel is between Río Lerma and Río Panuco.
$ Rates: $18 single; $21–$23 double; $35 suite for four.

Casa González is a two-story hostelry made up of two mansions that have been converted to hold the guest rooms, each of which is different. The houses, with little grassy patios out back and a huge shade tree, make a pleasant and quiet oasis in the middle of the city. Meals (optional) are taken in a dining room bright with stained glass. The owner, Sr. Jorge E. Ortiz González, speaks flawless and effortless English. The price for a single is exceptionally low, but there are only two. Some mattresses sag like a hammock, so check your room first. There's limited parking in the driveway. The Casa González is good, especially for women traveling alone.

HOTEL VIENA, Marsella 28, México, D.F. 06600. Tel. 5/566-0700. 60 rms (all with bath). TV TEL **Metro:** Insurgentes; the hotel is between Berlin and Dinamarca.
$ Rates: $35 double; $36 twin. **Parking:** Small charge.
The Viena is one of several hotels a short walk from the Zona Rosa. The tidy rooms have dated furniture and some rooms have bathrooms with a tub. There's a parking lot beneath the hotel, and a little Swiss-style restaurant at sidewalk level. The rooms at the Viena may be the quietest in the downtown area.

WORTH THE EXTRA BUCKS

HOTEL BRISTOL, Plaza Necaxa 17, México, D.F. 06500. Tel. 5/533-

FROMMER'S SMART TRAVELER: HOTELS

1. Hotel-reservation desks at the airport (both in the baggage-claim area and near Gate A) often know which hotels have discounted promotional rates (*tarifas promocional*) offered only at these airport outlets. This may mean budget prices at nonbudget hotels.
2. Better hotels in the capital often reduce prices on weekends and holidays as much as 50% off normal rates—another way to splurge without paying top dollar.
3. If the hotel isn't full, it never hurts to ask for a better rate than the one quoted.
4. Because of the daily devaluation of the dollar, you'll pay less in the long run if you use a credit card to pay the hotel bill.
5. But be aware that many quality budget hotels don't accept credit cards even if there's a sticker on the window that says they do.
6. Although prices may vary from those quoted here, to avoid being over-charged, if a price seems too high when compared to the price quoted in this book, insist on seeing the official Secretaría de Turismo price sheet (*lista de tarifas*) and compare.

QUESTIONS TO ASK IF YOU'RE ON A BUDGET

1. Are local telephone calls free, or if not, what is the charge per call?
2. Is there a service charge for placing a long-distance call, and if so, is the service charge applied even if the call doesn't go through?
3. Is parking free or is there a charge? Is it on the premises or nearby?

6061 or 208-1717. 134 rms (all with bath). A/C TV TEL **Metro:** Insurgentes (six blocks away); the hotel is between Río Sena and Río Panuco.
$ Rates: $40 single; $48 double.
Across Reforma from the Zona Rosa, the eight-story Hotel Bristol is popular with tour groups and long-term residents, but there are usually rooms to spare. It's modern, shiny, and clean, and in a section of town that's fairly quiet, yet within easy walking distance of major attractions.

HOTEL MARÍA CRISTINA, Río Lerma 31, México, D.F. 06500. Tel. 5/546-9880. Fax 5/566-9194. 150 rms (all with bath). TV TEL
$ Rates: $45 single; $48 double. **Parking:** Free
The colonial-style Hotel María Cristina, at Río Guadiana between Río Amazonas and Río Napoles, in a quiet residential section, is within three blocks of Sullivan Park and five blocks from the heart of the Zona Rosa. It's very popular with out-of-towners because of its comfort, price, and location. The lobby shows rich use of blue-and-white tiles, red velvet, dark wood, and wrought iron. A lounge off the lobby has a nice big fireplace, but you'll probably want to spend your spare minutes on the shady lawn outside.

HOTEL EMPORIO, Reforma 124, México, D.F. 06600. Tel. 5/566-7788. Fax 5/703-1424. 150 rms (all with bath), 11 junior suites, 3 master suites. A/C TV TEL **Metro:** Insurgentes (four blocks away); the hotel is between General Prim and Paris.
$ Rates: $48 single; $55 double; $61 junior suite; $100 master suite.
The recently remodeled Hotel Emporio's lavish use of peach-colored marble in the lobby and the 200-year-old chandelier in the sitting area make a stunning impression usually reserved for more expensive hotels. Throughout there's tasteful bleached-wood furniture and pastel fabrics. Although the Emporio is technically over the edge of our budget, you'd expect to pay more for all this upscale finery. Only one caution:

The air-conditioning in some rooms blows but doesn't cool. There's a bar Thursday through Saturday, and Macho's restaurant features such Stateside dishes as barbecue, blintzes, and fajitas. Like the Hotel Regente a block away, the Emporio's location between the Colón and Cuauhtémoc circles is within walking distance of the Alameda, the Zona Rosa, and Sullivan Park.

2. NEAR SULLIVAN PARK

DOUBLES FOR LESS THAN $35

HOTEL SEVILLA, Serapio Rendon 126, México, D.F. 06470. Tel. 5/566-1866. 125 rms (all with bath). TV TEL **Metro:** San Cosme or Insurgentes; the hotel is near Sullivan.
$ Rates: $22 single; $25 double. **Parking:** Small charge.

The nine-story Hotel Sevilla has clean, carpeted rooms with tiled baths, FM radio stations piped in, and purified water. The hotel's restaurant and bar provides room service.

HOTEL MALLORCA, Serapio Rendon 119, México, D.F. 06470. Tel. 5/566-4833. 118 rms (all with bath). TV TEL **Metro:** Insurgentes; the hotel is between Sullivan and Antonio Caso.
$ Rates: $28 single; $28–$31 double.
Located just off Sullivan Park, the four-story hotel's modern touches include wall-to-wall carpeting almost everywhere, music in each room, a parking garage, and a coffee shop, bar, and restaurant. Every room has its own tiled bath (perhaps with tub) and reading light.

HOTEL REGENTE, Paris 9, México, D.F. 06030. Tel. 5/566-8933. 132 rms (all with bath). TV TEL **Metro:** Revolución or Insurgentes; the hotel is in the triangle formed by Insurgentes Centro, Antonio Caso, and Reforma.
$ Rates: $28 single; $34 double.

One of the older standbys within walking distance of Sullivan Park, the Alameda, and the Zona Rosa, this is a good budget choice. Rooms are comfortable, with carpeting and small bathrooms with showers. The phone system is ancient and phones in some rooms work better than in others. A restaurant and travel-agent desk are in the lobby.

DOUBLES FOR LESS THAN $50

HOTEL DORAL, Sullivan 9, México, D.F. 06470. Tel. 5/592-2866. Fax 5/592-2762. 165 rms (all with bath). TV TEL **Metro:** Insurgentes (eight blocks away); the hotel is between Insurgentes and Carnot.
$ Rates: $38 single; $42 double.
From this high-rise of almost 20 stories, overlooking the Sullivan Park, you can see most of the city from its swimming pool, sundeck, and bar on the roof. Rooms are older and simple, but comfortable, with clean bathrooms. The location couldn't be better.

HOTEL STELLA MARIS, Sullivan 69, México, D.F. 06470. Tel. 5/566-6088. Fax 5/592-5904. 122 rms (all with bath). A/C TV TEL **Metro:** Insurgentes (10 long blocks away); the hotel is at the corner of Sullivan and Rosas Moreno.
$ Rates: $38 single; $48 double.
The rooms in this modern, nine-story hotel are rather small and some are a bit dark, but part of this is due to the agreeable subdued colors. All rooms are equipped with

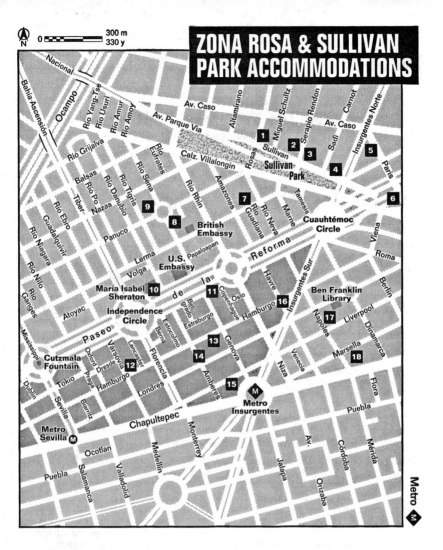

ZONA ROSA & SULLIVAN PARK ACCOMMODATIONS

0 ⌛ 300 m
330 y

MEXICO CITY

Suites Amberes **14**
Aristos Hotel **11**
Bristol Hotel **9**
Century Hotel **15**
Doral Hotel **4**
Emporio Hotel **6**
Galeria Plaza Hotel **12**
Geneve Hotel **13**
Casa Gonzalez **8**
Suites Havre **16**
Mallorca Hotel **2**
María Cristina Hotel **7**

Residencial
 Mision Hotel **17**
Regente Hotel **5**
Sevilla Hotel **3**
María Isabel
 Sheraton Hotel **10**
Viena Hotel **18**

radio and bathrooms with separate washbasin cubicle, and (from front rooms) views of the Jardín and its Sunday art exhibitions are the extras. The hotel's restaurant serves a good fixed-price lunch.

3. NEAR THE REVOLUCIÓN MONUMENT

DOUBLES FOR LESS THAN $25

HOTEL CARLTON, Ignacio Mariscal 32-B, México, D.F. 06030. Tel. 5/566-2911. 41 rms (all with bath). TV TEL **Metro:** Revolución (four blocks away); the hotel is between Arizpe and Ramon Alcazar.
$ Rates: $15 single; $17 double.
The modest, three-story Hotel Carlton has a wonderful location facing the park behind the Museo de San Carlos. The hallways in this hotel are worn, but the guest rooms themselves are quite tidy, with white sheets and cheery draperies and bedspreads. Bathrooms are well worn but clean. There's a bright and convenient little restaurant off the lobby. A bargain!

HOTEL EDISON, Edison 106, México, D.F. 06030. Tel. 5/566-0933. 45 rms (all with bath). TV TEL **Metro:** Revolución (two blocks away); the hotel is between Iglesias and Arriaga.
$ Rates: $17 single; $19 double.
The Hotel Edison, a block from the Revolución Monument, is a real find. In the midst of the city's noise and bustle, its odd two-story construction around a narrow court with grass and trees gives a sense of sanctuary. Some rooms are built in tiers overlooking the court, and even larger ones are hidden away down hallways. These latter rooms tend to be dark, but big and comfortable with huge king-size beds. Blond wood and light colors, piped-in music, and sunlight make this a cheerful place. Services include bathrooms with separate washbasin areas, and some have bidets, plus tub/shower combinations.

GRAN HOTEL TEXAS, Ignacio Mariscal 129, México, D.F. 06030. Tel. 5/546-4626 or 546-4627. 52 rms (all with bath). TV TEL **Metro:** Revolución; the hotel is between Arriaga and Iglesias.
$ Rates: $17 single; $23 double.
At the low end of the price scale, this small, modest, five-story hotel gets high marks for effort. It's consistently clean, friendly, and low priced. Don't look for anything fancy here; rather, notice the smiles that greet you and the tidiness of the premises. The street is relatively quiet, and the location quite convenient.

DOUBLES FOR LESS THAN $35

HOTEL NEW YORK, Edison 45, México, D.F. 06030. Tel. 5/566-9700. 45 rms (all with bath). TV TEL **Metro:** Revolución (five blocks away); the hotel is between Emparan and Baranda.
$ Rates: $24 single; $31 double. **Parking:** Free.
The Hotel New York, two short blocks from the jai-alai fronton, is a large four-story building that's a cubist's dream of mosaic tile, grass-green paneling, and glass. The carpeted rooms have Formica furniture, wood paneling on one wall, and hanging glass lamps. The hotel's small restaurant is open daily from 7am to 10pm.

HOTEL PALACE, Ignacio Remírez 7, México, D.F. 06030. Tel. 5/566-2400. 200 rms (all with bath). A/C TV TEL **Metro:** Revolución (five blocks away); the hotel is between Reforma and Plaza de la República.
$ Rates: $24 single; $31 double.
One of Mexico's outstanding luxury hotels a few decades ago, today the nine-story Hotel Palace retains its comfort, experienced staff, and well-kept rooms. The bustle

of a large hotel surrounds you here, with tobacco kiosk and travel desk in the lobby, bag-bearing bellboys scurrying here and there, and the occasional busload of tourists.

HOTEL CORINTO, Calle Vallarta 24, México, D.F. 06030. Tel. 5/566-6555 or 566-9711. 155 rms (all with bath). TV TEL **Metro:** Revolución (five blocks away); the hotel is near the corner of Gómez Farías opposite the Revolución monument.

$ Rates: $29 single; $34–$36 double.

The modern Hotel Corinto, a nine-story hotel located just a few steps north of Antonio Caso, is a good value within our budget range. It caters to both tourists and Mexican clients, with clean rooms, coordinated furnishings, tiled showers, piped-in music, and special taps for purified water. Just off the lobby is a restaurant, and on the ninth floor is a small swimming pool, sunning area, patch of grass, and a bar. Most rooms have either twin single beds or one double bed.

WORTH THE EXTRA BUCKS

HOTEL JENA, Jesús Teran 12, México, D.F. 06030. Tel. 5/566-0277. Fax 5/566-0455. 161 rms (all with bath). A/C TV TEL **Metro:** Hidalgo (4½ blocks away); the hotel is between Edison and Badillo.

$ Rates: $47 single; $52–$58 double. **Parking:** Free.

Although technically above our budget, considering its appointments the five-story Hotel Jena (pronounced "*Hay*-nah") is a good choice. From the exterior you might think it's more expensive than it is. The rooms are nicely furnished with "hotel Formica," a large mirror, and glistening tile bath. The higher price is for a huge room with a couch, rather like a junior suite. A restaurant is adjacent.

HOTEL CASA BLANCA, Lafragua 7, México, D.F. 06030. Tel. 5/566-3211. Fax 5/705-4197. 272 rms (all with bath). A/C TV TEL **Metro:** Revolución or Hidalgo (five long blocks away); the hotel is between Antonio Caso and Plaza de la República.

$ Rates: $58 single; $66 double.

Just a few steps off Plaza de la República, the Hotel Casa Blanca is located on a quiet street only a block or so from Reforma and Avenida Juárez. The Casa Blanca has been a dependably comfortable and efficient place to stay for many years. Though it's beyond our budget, you certainly get your money's worth here: Marble is used lavishly in the hotel's decor, as is colored glass and brushed stainless steel. There's a modern lounge-bar, and a restaurant. The small kidney-shaped swimming pool and sun deck on the hotel's top floor goes undiscovered by most guests, making it a wonderfully quiet—almost private—getaway. The guest rooms are done in dark tones accented by white stucco and wood. Many rooms open onto interior airshafts, which make them quiet, though without views. There are thoughtful little touches such as individually controlled air conditioning, bottles of purified water, and bedside switches for lights and the TV. There is also underground parking. The Casa Blanca offers a good location, professional staff, and excellent value.

READERS RECOMMEND

Hotel Montemar, Gómez Farías 53. Tel. 5/556-6677. "We've been using the Hotel Montemar near the Revolución Monument. The 86 rooms are well ventilated and newly painted, and all have marble and tile baths, telephones, and color TV. There is a clean little restaurant just off the lobby, with daily specials. An indoor parking lot keeps vehicles safe. The manager, Augusto Sanchez, has good command of English and is very helpful."—Dr. Robert H. MacLeod, Saugerties, N.Y. [*Author's Note*: Rates are $17 to $21.]

Hotel Mayaland, Antonio Caso 23. Tel. 5/566-6066. Fax 5/535-1273. "We would like to suggest one hotel that we were very happy with—the Hotel Mayaland on Antonio Caso. There were two queen-size beds for three of us. It was close to the Paseo de la Reforma as well as a Sanborn's, a Holiday Inn, and a VIPS."—Mr. and Mrs. Herman Birenbaum, Nicoya, Gte., Costa Rica. [*Author's Note*: Rates are $23 single and $32 double.]

4. NEAR THE ALAMEDA CENTRAL

DOUBLES FOR LESS THAN $20

HOTEL CONCORDIA, Uruguay 13, México, D.F. 06000. Tel. 5/510-4100. 56 rms (all with bath). TEL **Metro:** Belles Artes or Salto de Agua (each six blocks away); the hotel is between Bolívar and Cárdenas.
$ Rates: $13 single; $15–$20 double.

⑤ The four-story Hotel Concordia, just off Avenida Lázaro Cárdenas, is opposite the Hotel Capitol, and only two blocks from the Latin American Tower, the Bellas Artes, and the Alameda—a very convenient location. The multipillared lobby is at the end of a corridor. The carpeted rooms are old but decently kept, and some have both a tub and shower. There's an elevator, and a garage for guests with cares.

HOTEL EL SALVADOR, República del Salvador 16, México, D.F. 06000. Tel. 5/521-1247 or 521-2160. 94 rms (all with bath). TV TEL **Metro:** Salto de Agua (six blocks away); the hotel is between Cárdenas and Bolívar.
$ Rates: $17 single; $18 double. **Parking:** Free.
Next choice is a five-story hotel just half a block off Lázaro Cárdenas. Inside, up a few marble steps, the monastically bare lobby is quite unimpressive with red carpeting, low furniture, and wood paneling. The rooms are much better, light, and suffused in a pleasantly soothing monochromatic tan color scheme—Formica furnishings, tan bed throws, drapes, and carpeting. There's a good, though simple, little restaurant on the premises.

DOUBLES FOR LESS THAN $25

HOTEL CONDE, Pescaditos 15, México, D.F. 06070. Tel. 5/521-1084. 80 rms (all with bath). TV TEL **Metro:** Balderas or Juárez; the hotel is at the corner of Revillagigedo.
$ Rates: $16 single; $21 double. **Parking:** Free
The Hotel Conde, just five blocks off Juárez and equally far from Reforma, offers some of the best rooms for the price in this area. The hotel's entrance is at Pescaditos 15, but the building is on the corner of Revillagigedo, and would be numbered about Revillagigedo 56. It's fairly new with a small marbled lobby, and clean bathrooms, wall-to-wall carpet, and FM radio in the rooms, plus free garage parking.

HOTEL MARLOWE, Independencia 17, México, D.F. 06050. Tel. 5/521-9540. 104 rms (all with bath). TV TEL **Metro:** Juárez or Bellas Artes; the hotel is between Lopez and Dolores.
$ Rates: $22 single; $24 double; $26 junior suite.
The Hotel Marlowe, just a block south of Avenida Juárez, is an older, fairly well used structure of nine floors and rooms equipped with double beds, twin beds, or two double beds; and mismatched furnishings. The choicest accommodations here are the junior suites in the corner locations (Room 702, 802, etc.). They're light and airy, with little balconies, some view, and not too much noise, as Independencia is a fairly quiet street.

HOTEL FLEMING, Revillagigedo 35, México, D.F. 06050. Tel. 5/510-4530. 75 rms (all with bath). TV TEL **Metro:** Juárez; the hotel is between Articulo 123 and Victoria.
$ Rates: $23 single; $25 double.
Although well used, with mismatched carpeting, drapes, and spreads, the rooms at the five-story Hotel Fleming are comfortable, and some of the bathrooms are larger and nicer than most. Elevators take you to the upper floors. Doubles have either a double bed or twin beds. A pleasant coffee shop–restaurant located next to the lobby offers a fixed-price lunch daily.

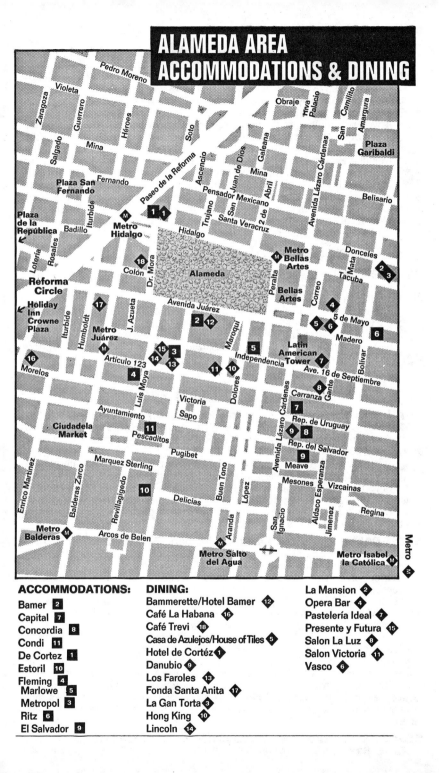

ALAMEDA AREA ACCOMMODATIONS & DINING

ACCOMMODATIONS:

Bamer **2**
Capital **7**
Concordia **8**
Condi **11**
De Cortez **1**
Estoril **10**
Fleming **4**
Marlowe **5**
Metropol **3**
Ritz **6**
El Salvador **9**

DINING:

Bammerette/Hotel Bamer **12**
Café La Habana **16**
Café Trevi **18**
Casa de Azulejos/House of Tiles **5**
Hotel de Cortéz **1**
Danubio **9**
Los Faroles **13**
Fonda Santa Anita **17**
La Gan Torta **3**
Hong King **10**
Lincoln **14**

La Mansion **2**
Opera Bar **4**
Pastelería Ideal **7**
Presente y Futura **15**
Salon La Luz **8**
Salon Victoria **11**
Vasco **6**

DOUBLE FOR LESS THAN $35

HOTEL CAPITOL, Uruguay 12, México, D.F. 06050. Tel. 5/518-1750.
Fax 5/521-1149. 75 rms (all with bath). TV TEL **Metro:** Bellas Artes or Salto de Agua (five blocks away); the hotel is between Cárdenas and Bolívar.
$ Rates: $28 single; $33 double; $40 suite.

A welcome addition to the lineup of Alameda/Zócalo area hotels is the new four-story Hotel Capitol, which opened in late 1989. Rooms open to the lobby atrium and there's a restaurant in back. For a hotel priced on the low end, you wouldn't expect such extras as carpeting, reading lights, or king-size beds, but guests have them here. Double rooms are furnished with either a king-size bed or two doubles. Rooms and bathrooms are large except for the three "suites," which are tiny but have an enormous whirlpool bathtub big enough for two. Rooms along the front have a small balcony opening to Uruguay, while other rooms have interior windows opening to the lobby atrium. This is a good buy within walking distance of the Alameda, Bellas Artes, and historic Zócalo.

DOUBLE FOR LESS THAN $40

HOTEL ESTORIL, Luis Moya 93, México, D.F. 06070. Tel. 5/521-9762.
125 rooms (all with bath). TV TEL **Metro:** Juárez.
$ Rates: $31 single; $36 double.

The recently renovated Estoril, six blocks south of Alameda Park, near Calle Sterling, has an accommodating staff plus clean, quiet rooms, most with one or two double beds; fifth-floor rooms all have king-size beds. The decorator had a field day—walls, carpets, drapes, bedspreads and linens, even bathroom floors and tile are different colors. There's a restaurant off the lobby.

WORTH THE EXTRA BUCKS

HOTEL METROPOL, Luis Moya 39, México, D.F. 06050. Tel. 5/521-4901 or 510-8660. 165 rms (all with bath). A/C TV TEL **Metro:** Juárez (two blocks away); the hotel is between Articulo 123 and Independencia.
$ Rates: $40 single or double.

With a recent total facelift, the Hotel Metropol shed its '60s image and emerged looking more like a small luxury hotel; the prices may go even higher once it reestablishes itself, so take advantage while you can. Each room is beautifully furnished and carpeted, and each one has an in-room safety deposit box, a color TV with U.S. channels, and purified water from a special tap. If it's luxury you want at budget prices, this is the place.

HOTEL BAMER, Avenida Juárez 52, México, D.F. 06050. Tel. 5/521-9060. 111 rms (all with bath) A/C TV TEL **Metro:** Hidalgo or Bellas Artes; the hotel is at the corner of Luis Moya.
$ Rates: $43 single or double; $56 suite for one, $61 suite for two, $70 suite for four.

Facing the Alameda Park and Juárez Hemiciclo monument, the Bamer has been a fixture in Mexico City's downtown for many years. It's well maintained, with spacious rooms, a prime location, and a view of the Alameda Central—pluses hard to top for the price. The 16-story building has two elevators, lustrous wood and huge mirrors in the hallways, and furniture that's more comfy than stylish. Most rooms can accommodate up to four people easily, and come with tub/shower combinations (suites have Jacuzzis as well) and either a king-size bed, two double beds, or two queen-size beds. Suites have separate dining areas. Rooms or suites on the upper floors facing Avenida Juárez and the Alameda have a spectacular view. The hotel's roof restaurant shares the marvelous view. There's a lounge, the Bamerette, with live entertainment, as well.

BEST WESTERN HOTEL RITZ, Avenida Madero 30, México, D.F. 06000. Tel. 5/518-1340, or toll free 800/528-1234 in the U.S. Fax 5/518-3466. 140

rms (all with bath). MINIBAR TV TEL **Metro:** Allende; the hotel is between Bolívar and Motolinía.

$ Rates (including tax): $50 single; $51 double. **Parking:** Valet.

You're well situated here as the Ritz is within walking distance of both the Zócalo and the Alameda, where most of Mexico City's points of interest are found. Popular with Americans, the stylish rooms have a comfy feel and color TV with U.S. channels.

5. NEAR THE ZÓCALO

DOUBLES FOR LESS THAN $25

HOTEL MONTECARLO, Uruguay 69, México, D.F. 06000. Tel. 5/518-1418 or 521-2559. 60 rms (50 with bath). TEL **Metro:** Zócalo or Isabel la Católica; the hotel is between 5 de Febrero and Isabel la Católica, next to the Biblioteca Nacional.

$ Rates: $12 single without bath, $14 single with bath; $14 double without bath, $16 double with bath. **Parking:** Free.

The Hotel Montecarlo has a fascinating history. Built about 1772 as an Augustinian monastery, it later became the residence of D. H. Lawrence for a time. Recently renovated, the large assortment of rooms come in various sizes, with modern baths, new furniture, rugs, and beds. Rooms in the original monastery section, plus the added third story, tend to carry lobby and hallway noise; rooms in the newer section in back are quieter. Note that some rooms have windows looking onto hallways and courtyards, not the outside world. It's a good idea to call ahead to reserve a room, since it's often full. Parking for six or seven cars is reached by driving *through* the lobby.

HOTEL ISABEL, Isabel la Católica 63, México, D.F. 06000. Tel. 5/518-1213. 72 rms (all with bath). TV TEL **Metro:** Isabel la Católica (five blocks away); the hotel is between Uruguay and República del Salvador.

$ Rates: $16 single; $18 double.

The four-story Isabel is an older place with a mix of Mexican and foreign clientele. In the lobby, a somber painting of Queen Isabel gazes out over the vast lobby where a TV provides entertainment. The rooms are old-fashioned and spacious, with dark-wood or painted furniture, carpeting, and bath. Larger rooms have tubs as well as showers, little tiled entrance halls, and frosted-glass doors opening onto wrought-iron balconies. Other comforts include an elevator, a good restaurant and bar, and all-day room service. You can wangle yourself a reduction if they're not full.

HOTEL LAFAYETTE, Motolnía 40, México, D.F. 06000. Tel. 5/521-9640. 61 rms (all with bath). TV TEL **Metro:** Allende; the hotel is between Madero and 16 de Septiembre.

$ Rates: $14 single; $16–$18 double.

The Hotel Lafayette is an older three-story building, kept up-to-date through renovation. It's patronized mostly by Mexican travelers, so there's not much English spoken here, but the staff will figure out your wants. You're right in the center of shopping, on a pedestrians-only street.

HOTEL JUÁREZ, Primer Callejon de Cinco de Mayo no. 17, México, D.F. 06000. Tel. 5/512-6929 or 518-4718. 39 rms (all with bath). TV TEL **Metro:** Zócalo; the hotel is between Motolinía and Isabel la Católica.

$ Rates: $15 single; $20 double.

The five-story Hotel Juárez is on a tiny side street across from the Hotel Canada. Look for the *callejon* (alley) on the north side of Avenida Cinco de Mayo between nos. 48 and 50. Ignore the hotel's grimy facade and look inside, where there's a colonial fountain in the lobby, an elevator, clean guest rooms with marble baths, and blissful quiet. Look at your prospective room before you register; you might want to be sure you're getting one with an outside window, as those with interior windows can be claustrophobic.

HOTEL ANTILLAS, Belisario Dominguez 34, México, D.F. 06010. Tel. 5/526-5674. 70 rms (all with bath). TV TEL **Metro:** Allende (three blocks away); the hotel is between Isabel la Católica and Allende.
$ Rates: $17 single; $18–$25 double. **Parking:** Free.
Another bargain is the Hotel Antillas, a rather old-world, five-story study in burnished red lava block with huge plate-glass windows. Inside, the charming lobby is lit by black wrought-iron chandeliers. The rooms are large and clean, with lots of new paint and new furniture. The Antillas is a top choice of Mexican families.

HOTEL CATEDRAL, Donceles 95, México, D.F. 06010. Tel. 5/518-5232. Fax 5/512-4343. 116 rms (all with bath). TV TEL **Metro:** Zócalo; the hotel is between Brasil and Argentina.
$ Rates: $20–$25 single; $22–$24 double. **Parking:** Available.
One block north of Tacuba is Calle Donceles, a street noted for its bookstores, stationery stores, and gunsmith shops. Here, set back from the street by a shopping arcade, is the six-story Hotel Catedral, half a block from the Templo Mayor, and very popular with Mexico's middle class. In front of the big cool lobby is the hotel's restaurant-bar, bustling with white-jacketed waiters. The hotel is remodeling; rooms are well kept, and some have tub/shower combinations. Bonuses are a bar, parking garage next door, elevator, good housekeeping standards, and rooms on the upper floors with views of Mexico City's mammoth cathedral.

DOUBLES FOR LESS THAN $30

HOTEL CANADA, Avenida Cinco de Mayo no. 47, México, D.F. 06000. Tel. 5/518-2106. 85 rms (all with bath). TV TEL **Metro:** Zócalo (1½ blocks away) the hotel is between Isabel la Católica and Palma.
$ Rates: $22 single; $25 double.
The Hotel Canada, opened in 1984, has up-to-date decor, white Formica furnishings, piped-in music, double beds (one or two of them), and showers. It's comfortable and so different from the rest of the downtown hotels, which tend to be older and somewhat worn.

HOTEL GILLOW, Isabel la Católica 17, México, D.F. 06000. Tel. 5/518-1440. 110 rms (all with bath). TV TEL **Metro:** Allende; the hotel is between Cinco de Mayo and Madero.
$ Rates: $21–$24 single; $26–$28 double.
From the lobby, the six-story Hotel Gillow appears to be among the older, simple-but-dignified downtown Mexico City hotels. But take one of the two elevators up to the guest rooms, and discover behind the old-time facade a modern hotel with rooms grouped in tiers around a long, rectangular, glass-canopied central courtyard at the center of which is a nice colonial fountain. The modern rooms have new tile-and-marble bathrooms, and a feeling of cheery comfort.

WORTH THE EXTRA BUCKS

HOTEL MAJESTIC, Avenida Madero 73, 564 México, D.F. 06000. Tel. 5/521-8600. 85 rms (all with bath). A/C TV TEL **Metro:** Zócalo.
$ Rates: $67 single; $70 double.
If you're feeling flush, the Majestic has rooms that look onto Mexico City's main square, Avenida Madero, or the hotel's own inner court. From the lobby, a place of stone arches, beautiful tiles, and stone fountains, take the elevator to the second floor and its the courtyard, with a floor of glass blocks set with sofas, tables, and chairs great for gazing all the way up to the glass roof six stories above. Each doorway has a border of blue-and-white tiles.

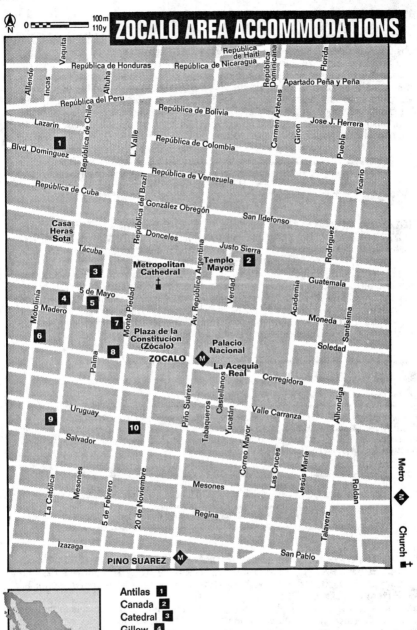

ZOCALO AREA ACCOMMODATIONS

0 — 100m / 110y

N

Vaquita · **República de Honduras** · **República de Nicaragua** · **República de Haiti** · **República Dominicana** · **Florida**

Allende · **Incas** · **Altuña** · **República del Peru** · **Carmen Aztecas** · **Giron** · **Apartado Peña y Peña**

Lazarin · **República de Chile** · **L. Valle** · **República de Bolivia** · **Jose J. Herrera** · **Puebla**

Blvd. Dominguez · **1** · **República de Colombia** · **Vicario**

República de Cuba · **República del Brazil** · **República de Venezuela** · **San Ildefonso** · **Rodriguez**

Casa Heras Sota · **González Obregón**

Tácuba · **Donceles** · **Justo Sierra** · **2** · **Guatemala**

3 · **Metropolitan Cathedral** · **Templo Mayor** · **Av. República Argentina** · **Verdad** · **Academia**

Motolinia · **5 de Mayo** · **4** · **5** · **Monte Piedad** · **Moneda** · **Santisima**

Madero · **7** · **Plaza de la Constitucion (Zócalo)** · **Palacio Nacional** · **Soledad**

6 · **8** · **ZOCALO** · M · **La Acequia Real** · **Corregidora** · **Alhondiga**

Palma · **Piño Suárez** · **Castellanos** · **Valle Carranza**

9 · **Uruguay** · **Tabaqueros** · **Yucatán**

Salvador · **10** · **Correo Mayor** · **Las Cruces** · **Jesús Maria** · **Roldan**

La Católica · **Mesones** · **5 de Febrero** · **20 de Noviembre** · **Mesones** · **Talavera**

Izazaga · **Regina** · **San Pablo**

PINO SUAREZ · M

Metro M · **Church** ✝

MEXICO CITY

Antilas **1**
Canada **2**
Catedral **3**
Gillow **4**
Gran Hotel Ciudad de México (Howard Johnson) **5**
Isabel **6**
Juárez **7**
Lafayette **8**
Majestic **9**
Montecarlo **10**

The comfortably furnished rooms, decorated in pastels, have tile bathrooms with tubs. In rooms on the lower floors facing Avenida Madero noise from the street may be a problem—and you may not go for the quieter rooms that look out onto the interior court (because people look in on you!)—but on the upper floors and in the rooms that front on the Zócalo you needn't worry about voyers. On the other hand, occupants of rooms facing the Zócalo will have the unexpected jolt of the daily 6am flag-raising ceremony on the Zócalo, complete with marching feet, drums, and bugle. The finishing touch to the Majestic is a popular rooftop café-restaurant with umbrella-shaded tables for all three meals.

6. NEAR THE RAILROAD STATION

HOTEL LA RIVIERA, Calle Aldama 9, Col. Cuauhtémoc, México, D.F. 07770. Tel. 5/566-3611. 40 rms (all with bath). TV TEL **Metro:** Revolución; the hotel is at Orozco between Insurgentes and Ejército 1 norte.
$ Rates: $17 single; $26 double. **Parking:** Free.
The Hotel La Riviera, at Orozco y Berra, is half a block from Puente de Alvarado and only five blocks south of Buenavista station; look for the pink tile facade. Although quite worn, it'll do if you're too tired to go farther. It offers heating, carpeting, and piped-in music, and rooms furnished in "motel Formica." The hotel's restaurant—the only hotel that has one for blocks around, incidentally—serves combination breakfasts, a special fixed-price lunch, and is open from 7am to 11pm daily.

READERS RECOMMEND

Hotel Ponte Vedra, Insurgentes Norte 226, México, D.F. 07770. Tel. 5/541-3160 or 541-0684. "I highly recommend the Ponte Vedra, a new hotel directly across the street from the railroad station. The hotel is modern, clean, and friendly, and has free parking. The Buenavista Crafts Market is one block away, a Pemex gas station is at the corner, buses stop in front, and there are several good restaurants nearby." —Bill Anderson, Mill Valley, Calif. [Author's Note: Rates are $19 single and $29 double.]

7. NEAR THE TERMINAL DEL NORTE BUS STATION

HOTEL BRASILIA, Av. de los Cien Metros 4823, México, D.F. 07770. Tel. 5/587-8577. 133 rms (all with bath). TV TEL **Directions:** Exit the terminal, turn left, and walk two blocks; the hotel sign is visible from the terminal.
$ Rates: $23 single; $28 double.
Say you've just arrived in the bus terminal, in almost a liquid state, unable to face the prospect of searching for a hotel. Good news: The V-shaped Hotel Brasilia provides a comfortable refuge for travelers. Rooms have piped-in music and TV with U.S. channels. The hotel has a well-stocked bar and restaurant.

8. NEAR THE AIRPORT

HOTEL RIAZOR, Viaducto Miguel Aleman 297, México, D.F. 08310. Tel.

5/654-3211 or 654-3212. 175 rms (all with bath). TV TEL **Transportation:** Take a taxi from the airport.
$ Rates: $40 single; $44 double.
The six-story Hotel Riazor is only a short cab ride from the airport. You can take shelter in any one of their modern, comfy rooms complete with king-size bed, shower, and perhaps even a view of the city. There's a pool, restaurant, and bar. The hotel fills up by nightfall, but if you arrive early in the day there's a good chance to get a room.

WORTH THE EXTRA BUCKS

If the Riazor is full, the following two hotels, while far out of our range, may be worth a treat, especially if you arrive late and tired and have an early flight. By the time you consider that the cost of a round-trip taxi to a Zócalo-area hotel, for example, would run around $16, then add the cost of the hotel and getting up 45 minutes early to return back to the airport, an airport hotel looks better and better despite the cost.

HOLIDAY INN AEROPUERTO, Bulevar Puerto Aereo 502, México, D.F. **15620. Tel. 5/762-4088,** or toll free 800/465-4329 in the U.S. 324 rms (all with bath). A/C MINIBAR TV TEL **Transportation:** Wait for the courtesy van under the white Holiday Inn shelter in front of the airport.
$ Rates: $115 single or double.
The hotel is close by. To get there, call from the Holiday Inn phone in the airport terminal and the courtesy van will take you on a circuitous block-long ride to the hotel. Recently revamped, the hotel has taken great steps toward improving its sagging image. The staff is attentive and the rooms are fashionably furnished, each with color TV with U.S. channels and purified water from the tap. You'll find several restaurants, a bar, disco, pool, and workout facilities. The hotel also provides a courtesy van to the airport, but those with early flights should leave in plenty of time since the demand for transportation may be greater than the vans can handle.

HOTEL FIESTA AMERICANA AEROPUERTO, Bulevar Puerto Aereo, Méx- **ico, D.F. 15620. Tel. 5/762-0199,** or toll free 800/223-2332 in the U.S. 340 rms (all with bath). A/C MINIBAR TV TEL **Directions:** Find the hotel's elevator in the airport lobby near Gate A, and take it up to the covered walkway connecting the hotel and terminal.
$ Rates: $152 single or double for a standard room.
Built with the super-transient traveler in mind, this hotel has airport flight monitors in the lobby and restaurants. At the hotel elevator in the airport terminal, a bellman will assist you with luggage; you can also make flight reservations and check your baggage in the hotel's lobby. Facilities are resortlike, with a swimming pool and workout room, several restaurants, bar, disco, and shopping arcade. Even if you don't stay overnight, this is a good place to while away some hours between flights.

9. LONG-TERM STAYS

Apartment hotels, often called *suites* ("soo-*wee*-tess"), are found in several city districts, but mostly in or near the Zona Rosa. Who stays here? Families, businesspeople, and consultants on extended stays; people waiting to find houses or permanent apartments; students; tourists staying a week or more. Some apartment hotels rent by the day, but preferential rates really come into play with stops of a week or more.

What if you're planning a truly lengthy stay of several months? The first place to look is in the classified ads section of *The News*. This will give you an idea of the choice neighborhoods and the going rates. To save money, you might then dust off your Spanish and look at the similar sections in the Spanish-language dailies. As landlords advertising in *The News* will obviously be catering to foreigners, their rents may well be higher than the norm.

Another good idea is to make the rounds of the bulletin boards at the various language schools, cultural centers, and other places where foreigners congregate. Sublet and rental notices often find permanent places on such bulletin boards.

SUITES HAVRE, Havre 74, México, D.F. 06010. Tel. 5/533-5670. 56 suites. **Metro:** Insurgentes; the hotel is between Hamburgo and Reforma.
$ Rates: $177 per week ($26 per day), $528 per month ($18 per day).

⑤ On the fringes of the Zona Rosa, the Suites Havre are popular with students of all ages looking for economical lodgings. All suites (really just small apartments) have a two-burner stove, small refrigerator, table and chairs, and two twin beds. Rooms are narrow and some have a window view of an air shaft. The ones overlooking this quiet section of Havre are cheerier and recommended for lengthy stays. The apartments don't rent by the day. An elevator makes all seven floors accessible. Across the street, the Fonda San Diego is a popular gathering place serving economical meals.

HOTEL RESIDENCIAL MISION PALACIO REAL, Napoles 62, México, D.F. 06010. Tel. 5/511-7709. Fax 5/533-1582. 49 rms (all with bath). A/C TV TEL **Metro:** Insurgentes; the hotel is between Liverpool and Marsela on the fringes of the Zona Rosa.
$ Rates (per day for long-term stay; including breakfast): $34 single; $48 double.
Another good choice with cheery modern rooms is the Hotel Residencial Mision Palacio Real. It's especially popular with business types who may want to entertain on a small scale or at the very least have a nice place to unwind at the end of a day. Here numerous amenities are packed into a small space; it's more like a hotel room with extras. Each cozy unit has either a king-size, a double, or two twin beds, shower, love seat that converts to a single bed, side chair, and a hotplate; some have a small refrigerator. A small restaurant in the lobby serves a substantial breakfast which is included in the price of the room. Be sure to check out their inexpensive comida corrida. Rooms without a kitchen rent for a couple of dollars less.

SUITES AMBERES, Amberes 64, México, D.F. 06010. Tel. 5/208-0046. 70 suites (all with bath). TV TEL **Metro:** Insurgentes; the hotel is between Liverpool and Hamburgo.
$ Rates (per day for long-term stay): $54 one-bedroom suite; $63 two-bedroom suite. **Parking:** Free.
The seven-story building is across from Harry's Bar and the Hotel Krystal. High priced but spacious, each one- or two-bedroom apartment (and they are true apartments) has partial carpeting and partial sienna-colored tile, a huge living room, a large balcony with planters and good city views, a nice-size kitchen with bar and stools, and an in-room security box. Furniture is a bit worn and dated, but the overall impression is one of comfort and spaciousness.

CHAPTER 11

WHERE TO EAT IN MEXICO CITY

Everybody eats out in Mexico City, from the wealthy executive to the peasant. Consequently you can find restaurants of every type, size, and price range scattered across the city. Most of them are good, but to cover all of them would be impossible. I get numerous letters each year from readers who have discovered a great restaurant, and indeed they have—and so can you. In this section I have tried to give you a list of some of the tried-and-true establishments; I have sifted through myriad restaurants and have listed those that give the best food for the best price in budget, medium-priced, splurge, and specialty categories.

I have *not* included American-type chains such as Burger Boy, Pizza Hut, Denny's, Woolworth's, and Tastee-Freez. They have standard, familiar fare which, although good to cure a bout of homesickness, tends to be a good deal more expensive for what you get than Mexican food.

A rule of thumb to estimate your restaurant tab would be to select your main course, double its price, and—excluding wine and drinks—you've got a pretty fair estimate of the total bill you'll pay. In the more expensive restaurants, particularly in the Zona Rosa, you'll be able to pay with a major credit card. For tipping suggestions, see "Saving Money on Services" in Section 9, Chapter 2.

The select area known as the Zona Rosa is clearly defined: bounded by Insurgentes, Chapultepec, and Reforma. Within this compound are more charming restaurants than almost anywhere else in the world. You can find any type of food or ambience from the café set to the taco stand.

FROMMER'S SMART TRAVELER: RESTAURANTS

1. Stock up on fruit or bakery goods for an inexpensive breakfast.
2. Stalk the comida corrida at lunch for some good values, with the best deals including dessert and drink.
3. Fine dining is cheaper in Mexico City than a comparable meal in the U.S., so this is the place for an all-out splurge.
4. Drink Mexican-made liquor and wine, which are inexpensive compared to any imported version.
5. For a meal in a bowl, try hearty soups like tlalpeño, tortilla, and pozole.

1. IN & AROUND THE ZONA ROSA

MEALS FOR LESS THAN $5

FONDA SAN DIEGO, Havre 69. Tel. 511-6827.
Specialty: MEXICAN. **Metro:** Insurgentes; it's 1½ blocks south of Reforma, between Insurgentes and Hamburgo.
$ Prices: Comida corrida $3.50.
Open: Mon–Fri 8am–6pm.

On the eastern edge of the Zona Rosa, this is one of those neighborhood eateries I love to discover in any city. Enter through green iron gates, past a narrow courtyard, and go into an old brick town house–turned-restaurant. There's an inviting artsy and bohemian edge to the place, which has red-and-white-checked tablecloths, student art on the walls, and the aroma of good food coming from the kitchen. It's a popular gathering spot for students and office workers. If you come for the comida corrida, there's a choice of two soups, two salads, three meat dishes, soft drink, and dessert, all with a basket of fresh rolls. Portions are not enormous, but the food's delicious and it's hard to beat for the price.

RESTAURANT MARIANNE, Río Rhin 63. Tel. 207-9831.
Specialty: CONTINENTAL. **Metro:** Insurgentes; then walk two blocks north of Reforma, between Río Lerma and Río Panuco.
$ Prices: Lunch $3.50–$4.
Open: Mon–Sat 9am–7pm.

Tucked away one block from the British Embassy is the little Restaurant Marianne, where the atmosphere is European coffeehouse and the specialty is pastries and cappuccino. They also serve an excellent three-course lunch.

RESTAURANT BEATRIZ, Londres 179. Tel. 525-5857.
Specialty: MEXICAN. **Metro:** Sevilla; it's between Florencia and Varsovia.
$ Prices: Tacos $1; soups $2–$3.50; main courses $5.50–$7; mole $4–$6.
Open: Mon–Fri 9am–8pm, Sat–Sun 10:30am–7pm.

You don't have to wander long to find the Restaurant Beatriz—just follow the crowd or your nose. Tortillas are on the grill as you enter a narrow room embellished with brick arches and tables covered in blue-and-white-checked cloths. It's all sparkling clean. Grab a table and choose from 19 different tacos, or 10 kinds of mole, or many soups. Soft drinks and beer are inexpensive for the Zona Rosa.

RESTAURANTE VEGETARIANO YUG, Varsovia 3. Tel. 533-3296.
Specialty: VEGETARIAN. **Metro:** Sevilla (six blocks away); it's between Reforma and Dresden.
$ Prices: Appetizers $3–$5; main courses $2.50–$4; breakfast $2–$5; lunch/dinner $5–$7.
Open: Mon–Fri 7am–10pm, Sat–Sun 1–7pm (buffet served Sun–Fri 1–5pm).

Mexicans are fond of vegetarian and health-food restaurants. The most convenient one in the Zona Rosa is the Restaurante Vegetariano Yug. This upbeat, modern place offers several fixed-price breakfasts, a dozen fantastic salads (the "Africa" features spinach and nuts), plus crêpes, spinach lasagne, and soya "meat" Mexican style. Portions are huge and prices are low.

RESTAURANT Y CAFETERÍA DEL RHIN, Río Rhin 49. Tel. 571-9452.
Specialty: MEXICAN.
$ Prices: Main courses $4.50–$8; comida corrida $3.50–$4; enchiladas suizas $3.
Open: Mon–Sat 8am–8pm.

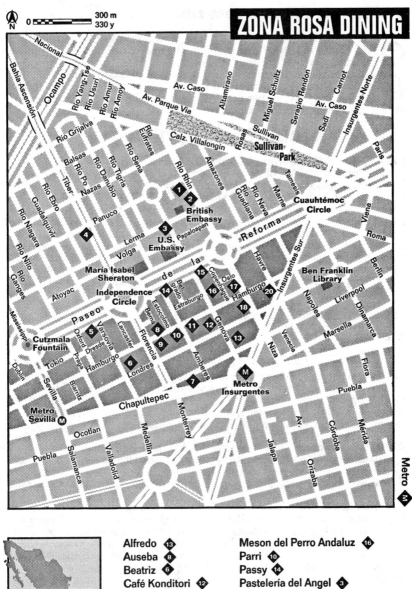

ZONA ROSA DINING

300 m
0
330 y

Nacional

Ocampo

Bahia Ascensión

Rio Yang-Tse
Rio Usuri
Rio Amur
Rio Amoy

Av. Caso

Av. Parque Via

Altamirano
Miguel Schultz
Serapio Rendon
Sadi
Carnot

Av. Caso

Insurgentes Norte

Rio Grijalva

Rio Eufrates

Rio Sena

Calz. Villalongin

Sullivan

Sullivan
Park

Paris

Balsas

Rio Po
Rio Danubio
Rio Tigris

Rio Nilo
Nazas

Rio Rhin

Amazones

Rio Guadiana

Rio Neva

Marne
Tamesis

Tiber

Rio Ebro

Panuco

1
2

Cuauhtémoc
Circle

Vlena

Rio Guadalquivir

Rio Niagara

4

Lerma

Volga

3

British
Embassy

U.S.
Embassy

Papaloapan

Reforma

Roma

Rio Ganges

Maria Isabel
Sheraton

de

la

15

Oslo

Ben Franklin
Library

Berlin

Atoyac

Independence
Circle

14

Belgrado

Estraburgo

16

Copenhague

17

Hamburgo

20

Insurgentes Sur

Napoles

Liverpool

Dinamarca

Paseo

5

Varsovia

Estocolmo

Berna

Londres

8

Florencia

10

11

9

12

Genova

18

13

Venecia

Marsella

Cutzmala
Fountain

Oxford
Dresde
Praga

Lancaster

6

Hamburgo

Amberes

Niza

Flora

Mississippi

Dublin

Tokio

7

M

Metro
Insurgentes

Puebla

Merida

Metro
Sevilla M

Sevilla
Biarritz

Chapultepec

Monterrey

Av.

Córdoba

Orizaba

Ocotlan

Medellin

Jalapa

Metro M

Puebla

Salamanca

Valladolid

MEXICO CITY

Alfredo **13**
Auseba **8**
Beatriz **6**
Café Konditori **12**
La Camela Rosa **16**
Chalet Suiza **18**
Folcolare **17**
Fonda del Refugio **7**
Fonda San Diego **20**
Las Fuentes **4**
Marianne **2**

Meson del Perro Andaluz **16**
Parri **10**
Passy **14**
Pastelería del Angel **3**
Pizza Real **15**
Restaurant y Cafetería
  del Rhin **1**
Salon de The Duca d'Este **9**
Tokyo **11**
Vegetariano Yug **5**

⭐ The Restaurant y Cafetería del Rhin, three blocks north of Reforma between Río Lerma and Río Panuco, is one of those terrific little neighborhood restaurants every travel writer dreams of discovering. The Rhin is a modern

🅢 place: mirrors, tan booths, waiters in natty black-and-white uniforms. The enchiladas suizas are a little triumph of tortillas in a creamy sauce stuffed with Swiss cheese. There are plenty of other Mexican plates—lots of tacos—as well as such comforts as soup, and even filet mignon.

MEALS FOR LESS THAN $10

PARRI, 154-A Hamburgo. Tel. 207-0757.
Specialty: MEXICAN. **Metro:** Insurgentes; it's between Florencia and Amberes.
$ Prices: Appetizers $1.50–$3; main courses $5–$12.
Open: Sun–Thurs 11am–1am; Fri–Sat noon–3am.

For tasty, authentic Mexican food at very reasonable prices in the Zona Rosa, search out the Parri, on Hamburgo near the corner of Florencia. The decor is ranch and big windows look onto the busy sidewalk. Meats are marinated and grilled Sonoran style, and the whole cooking operation is on view from the street or inside tables. You might try a filling tortilla soup, burritos norteñas (which come with refried beans, guacamole, and cheese), enchiladas, or quesadillas, and a dessert of crispy buñuelos or creamy flan. There are also more expensive grilled dishes such as carne asada a la tampiqueña (grilled beef, Tampico style) or chicken brochettes.

LAS FUENTES, Río Panuco 127. Tel. 514-8187.
Specialty: HEALTH FOOD.
$ Prices: Appetizers $3.50–$6; main courses $4–$7; comida corrida $10–$12.
Open: Daily 8am–6pm.

This branch of the "Restaurante Vegetariano y Dietetico," three blocks north of Reforma and the Independence Circle, at the corner of Río Tiber and Río Panuco, is the most modern, expensive, and luxurious of the three. The fresh salad bar is well worth the money. Huge portions are the rule, and you may enjoy lentil soup, carrot-and potato-filled tacos with apple salad, a side order of peas or beans, then coffee or tea and whole-wheat-and-honey cookies. Highly recommended.

ALFREDO, Londres 104 or Genova 74. Tel. 511-3864.
Specialty: ITALIAN. **Metro:** Insurgentes; it's behind the corner of Londres and Genova, with entrances on both streets.
$ Prices: Appetizers $5–$10; pasta courses $6–$7.50; meat or seafood courses $10–$18.
Open: Sun–Fri 1pm–1am.

If you wander around the Zona Rosa long enough, eventually you'll discover the passageway that harbors half a dozen restaurants. Most have sidewalk tables, and all benefit from the lack of street noise. The long-running favorite in the passage is where lowly pasta takes on noble proportions, and other Italian specialties like veal scaloppine crowd the menu. The meal ends with Kahlúa con crema, compliments of the house.

PIZZA REAL, Genova 28. Tel. 511-8834.
Specialty: ITALIAN. **Metro:** Insurgentes; it's between Reforma and Hamburgo.
$ Prices: Pizza $5–$25.
Open: Daily 8am–11:30pm.

⭐ Pizza Real boasts that it serves 50 different varieties of pizza, depending on size and toppings. The "Infante" size is enough for one person. They even serve a selection of four comida corridas featuring soup, fruit salad, pizza, dessert, and coffee, or in the more expensive comidas, an Italian dish such as ravioli. Although it's billed as a pizza joint, Pizza Real is half pizza parlor, half Italian restaurant, with white-brick walls, yellow chairs, a concise menu of pastas and traditional Italian favorites, and a pizza-cutting counter by the front door.

MEALS FOR LESS THAN $20

FOCOLARE, Hamburgo 87. Tel. 525-1487 or 511-2679.

Specialty: REGIONAL MEXICAN. **Metro:** Insurgentes; it's between Niza and Copenhague.

$ Prices: Appetizers $6–$23; main courses $8–$16; Sun breakfast buffet $11; Mexican Fiesta $13.50.

Open: Mon–Fri 7:30am–11:30pm, Sat–Sun 9am–12:30am (Sun breakfast buffet 9am–12:30pm).

Focolare calls itself a restaurant with three souls—Yucatecan, Oaxacan, and Veracruzano. I call it a tribute to three of Mexico's best regional cuisines. As you enter, piano music drifts from both left and right from the bar Pirinola and Cantina Trompo. In the dining area, with its tiled fountain and ceiling of baskets, a trio sings Mexican ballads. By now you are primed to go Mexican all the way. For starters you might try salbutes, a tortilla stuffed with roast suckling pig, from the Yucatán. Soup might be sierra mixteca made with fresh wild Oaxacan mushrooms. For the main course, pok chuk is a sure hit, a flavorful pork specialty from the Yucatán. If you're not too hungry but want to have something tasty, try the sopa Tarasca, a delicious soup honoring the state of Michoacán—yet another state known for its regional specialties. In addition, every day there's a different Oaxacan mole sauce. For drinks, imbibe some of the delicious fruit drinks made from zapote, guanabana, or the spicy-but-smooth horchata blend. Friday and Saturday nights you can reserve space for the lively Mexican Fiesta with music and performing dancers. Dining is à la carte.

MÉSON DEL PERRO ANDALUZ, Copenhague 28. Tel. 533-5306.

Specialty: SPANISH/MEXICAN. **Metro:** Insurgentes; it's between Reforma and Hamburgo.

$ Prices: Appetizers $3–$9; main courses $5.50–$23; lunch specials $5.50–$7.

Open: Daily 1pm–1am.

Very near the Hotel Aristos, Méson del Perro Andaluz has two levels inside, some outdoor tables (always crowded in the evenings), and a very loyal clientele. Prices in the evening are fairly high, but luncheon specials make it especially attractive for a midday meal. Try the tuna-and-avocado salad or a bowl of the hearty minestrone soup. Note that main courses come ungarnished (without vegetables or salad). They have wine, both Mexican and imported. Arrive early in the evening if you want a seat at one of the café tables out front.

LA CAMELLO ROSA, Copenhague 25. Tel. 525-7346.

Specialty: MEXICAN/INTERNATIONAL. **Metro:** Insurgentes; it's between Reforma and Hamburgo.

$ Prices: Appetizers $6–$10; main courses $8–$15.

Open: Daily 1pm–1am.

Of the café-restaurants on the pedestrian street called Copenhague, in the Zona Rosa, the one with the best prices is La Camello Rosa. Sit at one of the Camella Rosa's sidewalk tables. Order filet mignon with mushrooms or jumbo shrimp—these are the most expensive dishes on the menu. Most of the seafood, meats, and Mexican specialties cost a good deal less.

CHALET SUIZO, Niza 37. Tel. 511-7529.

Specialty: INTERNATIONAL. **Metro:** Insurgentes (two blocks away); it's between Hamburgo and Londres.

$ Prices: Appetizers $3–$6; main courses $10–$13.

Open: Daily 12:30pm–midnight.

One of the most dependable restaurants around, the Chalet Suizo has Swiss decor, of course, with checked tablecloths, enormous wooden horns, and alpine landscapes; the service is good. The menu features hearty French onion soup and a wide range of interesting dishes, some of which are changed daily. Among these are sausages with sauerkraut, smoked pork chops, baby veal tongue, sauerbraten, and excellent fondue and pizza.

CAFE KONDITORI, Genova 61. Tel. 511-1589.

Specialty: DANISH. **Metro:** Insurgentes; it's between Hamburgo and Londres.
$ Prices: Appetizers $4–$7; main courses $9–$12; coffee and dessert $4.
Open: Daily 7am–midnight.

Located in the Zona Rosa, the Cafe Konditori advertises itself as a Danish restaurant, bar, and coffee shop. Though it's not what you'd call aggressively Danish, it does have a very pleasant sidewalk-café section. In good weather (which is nearly always), you can sit out in the open air or any time by a window in the restaurant proper. Choose from 11 different coffees. The cappuccino is the perfect accompaniment for one of the Konditori's luscious cakes or tarts. Be sure to inspect the dessert display before you sit down. The café is open for breakfast, lunch, and dinner.

FONDA EL REFUGIO, Liverpool 166. Tel. 207-2732.

Specialty: MEXICAN. **Metro:** Insurgentes; it's between Florencia and Amberes.
$ Prices: Appetizers $4–$5; main courses $10–$12.
Open: Mon–Sat 1pm–midnight.

The Fonda El Refugio is a very special place to dine *a la mexicana*. Although small, it's unusually congenial, with a large fireplace decorated with gleaming copper pots and pans, and rows and rows of culinary awards and citations behind the desk. It manages the almost-impossible task of being elegant and informal at the same time. The menu runs the gamut of Mexican cuisine—a sopa de verduras (vegetable soup), arroz con platanos (rice with fried bananas), tamales de elote con pollo (fresh corn tamales with chicken), chalupas poblanas (tortillas topped with chicken, onions, cheese, lettuce, and green-chile sauce), or perhaps enchiladas con mole poblano, topped with the rich, thick, spicy chocolate sauce of Puebla. If you go all-out and order whatever you like, plus a half bottle of wine, the check shouldn't do too much damage. The Fonda El Refugio is very popular, especially on a Saturday night, so get there early—remember, it's small.

WORTH THE EXTRA BUCKS

RESTAURANT TOKYO, Hamburgo 134. Tel. 525-3775.

Specialty: JAPANESE. **Metro:** Insurgentes; it's between Amberes and Genova.
$ Prices: Appetizers $3–$10; main courses $10–$17.
Open: Mon–Sat 11:30am–midnight, Sun 1pm–midnight.

Mexico's trade with Japan is burgeoning, as is the number of Japanese businessmen who visit the city. This has led to a healthy, and very welcome, growth in the number of restaurants serving Japanese cuisine. Be sure to glance at the "models" of sample meals set out in the glass cabinet by the entryway. Upstairs, the mood is soothing, with quiet Japanese Muzak and a spare but comely decor. The staff is almost unbelieveably friendly. Start with an akadama, a Japanese plum punch. Sukiyaki, shabu-shabu (vegetables in beef broth, cooked at your table), and sashimi (raw fish) are also offered.

LUAU, Niza 38. Tel. 525-7474.

Specialty: CHINESE/POLYNESIAN. **Metro:** Insurgentes; it's between Hamburgo and Londres.
$ Prices: Combination dinner $10–$18.
Open: Mon–Fri 1–11pm, Sat 1pm–midnight, Sun 1–10pm.

Luau is in the heart of the Zona Rosa and its prices reflect it. However, the food is excellent and sometimes nothing else will do because you can't shake your craving for sweet-and-sour something or other. It's an attractive restaurant with a goldfish pond, rock garden with a waterfall, and other typical Polynesian decorative motifs.

RESTAURANT PASSY, Amberes 10. Tel. 511-0257.

Specialty: INTERNATIONAL. **Reservations:** Recommended.
Metro: Insurgentes; it's between Reforma and Hamburgo.
$ Prices: Appetizers $5.50–$8; main courses $10–$20.
Open: Mon–Sat 1–11pm.

An old favorite of locals and visitors alike is the Restaurant Passy, just off Reforma. With low lights, antiques, linen, and candles, the decor is attractive, classic, and restrained. The service is polished and polite, and the menu is traditional in the French way: Oysters Rockefeller, onion soup or shellfish soup "Marseillaise," chicken Cordon Bleu, canard (duck) à l'orange, coq au vin, and beef medallions in chablis sauce are among the continental favorites, but there is also a good selection of fish. The dessert menu is rich in pastries.

RESTAURANT ANGUS, Copenhague 21. Tel. 207-6880.

Specialty: STEAKS. **Metro:** Insurgentes; it's at the corner of Hamburgo.
$ Prices: Appetizers $4–$7; main courses $12–$30; steaks $10–$30.
Open: Daily 1pm–midnight.

The place to go for steak is Restaurant Angus. If you're not lucky enough to grab one of the sidewalk tables on the café street of Copenhague, take a seat in the woody bar behind, or in the attractive dining rooms upstairs. The decor is western but restrained and refined, and steaks range from $10 to $30.

2. NEAR THE REVOLUCIÓN MONUMENT

MEALS FOR LESS THAN $10

RESTAURANT REGIS, Edison 57. Tel. 592-0178.

Specialty: MEXICAN. **Metro:** Hidalgo; it's between Emparan and Alcazar.
$ Prices: Appetizers $2–$4; main courses $3–$6; breakfast $3.75.
Open: Daily 7am–7pm.

Located near Plaza de la República, Restaurant Regis offers friendly service as well as a very good quick meal. Try the enchiladas or tacos, and you can't go wrong with one of the hearty soups or a torta (sandwich).

LA CALESA, Reforma 36.

Specialty: MEXICAN.
$ Prices: Appetizers $4; main courses $5–$7; breakfast $3.50–$5; orange juice $1.50; comida corrida $6.50.
Open: Mon–Sat 7am–10pm.

On your way to a day's sightseeing, you might want to drop in at La Calesa, located near Colón Circle between Donata Guerra and Morelos, for a spot of breakfast. Huevos motulenos consists of two tortillas topped by two eggs covered with ham, cheese, peas, frijoles, and fried bananas. The enormous glass of orange juice is straight from the fruit.

SHIRLEY'S, Reforma 108. Tel. 536-0086.

Specialty: AMERICAN.
$ Prices: Main courses $5.50–$7; breakfast buffet $7 Mon–Fri, $8 Sat–Sun; lunch buffet $9 Mon–Fri.
Open: Daily 7am to 11:30pm.

Right on the east side of Reforma, northeast of the Insurgentes intersection, are two cafeteria-type restaurants, both noted for their good food and comfortable atmosphere. The first of these, Shirley's, is the epitome of efficiency, from the navy-blazer'd maître d' to the light-blue-uniformed waiters and waitresses. Everything runs smoothly, and the atmosphere is one of order and friendliness—a good bet for anyone who's homesick. In fact, from first to last (the check says "Please Pay the Cashier") Shirley's shows its American heritage. The house special is English muffins with cheese and ham, or you can get a hamburger or sandwich with fries for about $7.

MACHOS, Reforma 124. Tel. 703-0781.

Specialty: AMERICAN/MEXICAN.

$ Prices: Appetizers $3–$7; main courses $5–$7; Sun buffet $7.
Open: Daily 7am–2am.

Machos, on Reforma at Paris, between Cuauhtémoc and Colón circles, is one of the latest trendy restaurants along this fashionable boulevard. Technically it's the Hotel Emporio's restaurant, but it has a separate entrance off the street as well as an entrance to the left as you enter the lobby. It's upstairs, and is an entity unto itself. With its green awnings, blond-oak floors and tables, stained glass, ferns, and cactus, you'd swear you'd been transported home. The decor is decidedly American, and so is the menu, with a few Mexican twists to make it interesting. Feel at home here ordering burgers and fries, blintzes, Texas barbecue, fajitas, hot dogs, yogurt, Reuben sandwiches, and assorted familiar foods.

3. NEAR THE ALAMEDA

MEALS FOR LESS THAN $5

RESTAURANT LOS FAROLES, Calle Luis Moya 41. Tel. 521-7634.
Specialty: MEXICAN. **Metro:** Juárez; it's one block south of the Alameda, between Articulo 123 and Independencia, next to the Hotel Metropol.
$ Prices: Appetizers $1.50–$3; main courses $4–$5; comida corrida $4.50–$6.
Open: Daily 8am–7pm.

Through the brick arches you'll see a firepit filled with cazuelas, the big earthenware cooking pots, and a bevy of white-aproned señoras toiling to serve up some of the city's cheapest and most authentic Mexican food. Tacos, enchiladas, caldos (stews), and other truly Mexican dishes are the forte here, and low prices are the rule. Los Faroles is darkish, and not air-conditioned (at those prices?), but good, and it's open every day of the year.

RESTAURANTE PRESENTE Y FUTURO, Independencia 72C. Tel. 521-1913.
Specialty: MEXICAN. **Metro:** Juárez; it's one block south of the Alameda, at the corner of Revillagigedo.
$ Prices: Appetizers $2–$5; main courses $2.50–$5; comida corrida $4–$6.
Open: Daily 7:30am–1am.

South of Avenida Juárez are several good, inexpensive restaurants. The Restaurante Presente y Futuro is open long hours and has an extensive menu filled with inexpensive fare. You'll find lots of soups and sandwiches, including a hamburguesa olmpico con queso ("Olympic cheeseburger"); Mexican traditional favorites such as enchiladas and quesadillas; and substantial restaurant meals based on beef, pork, and chicken. The daily fixed-price meal is three courses. Any night of the week from 5 to 10pm you can have your fortune told in your Turkish coffee cup. If the bright yellow-and-green streetside dining room of booths, tables, and lunch counter is full, make your way upstairs to another one.

MEALS FOR LESS THAN $10

CAFE TREVI, Colón 1. Tel. 512-3020 or 512-5232.
Specialty: ITALIAN/MEXICAN. **Metro:** Hidalgo or Juárez; it's on the western edge of the Alameda, at the corner of Colón and Dr. Mora.
$ Prices: Appetizers $2–$5; main courses $6–$9.50; comida corrida $5–$6.50.
Open: Daily 8am–11:30pm.

Cafe Trevi, facing the Jardín de la Solidaridad (the western extension of the Alameda), is a Mexico City institution. Its white-clothed tables always seem to be busy with enthusiastic diners who've come for the tasty food in decent surroundings at reasonable prices. Right here on the Alameda, facing Avenida Juárez, a meal should cost quite a bit, yet the Trevi serves a five-course comida corrida which might include mozzarella cheese topped with onions, oil, and seasoning; buttered

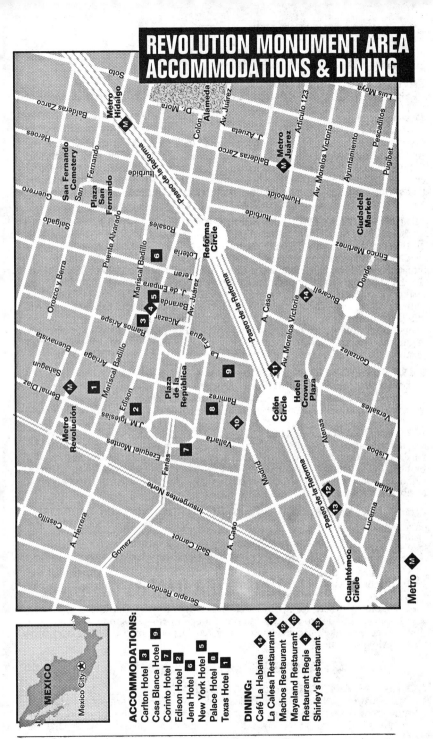

REVOLUTION MONUMENT AREA ACCOMMODATIONS & DINING

ACCOMMODATIONS:

Carlton Hotel **3**
Casa Blanca Hotel **9**
Corinto Hotel **7**
Edison Hotel **2**
Jena Hotel **6**
New York Hotel **5**
Palace Hotel **8**
Texas Hotel **1**

DINING:

Café La Habana **14**
La Calesa Restaurant **11**
Machos Restaurant **12**
Mayaland Restaurant **10**
Restaurant Regis **4**
Shirley's Restaurant **13**

MEXICO

Mexico City ★

Metro **M**

green noodles; scaloppine al marsala; and espresso or cappuccino. The food is simple but good—it's finding a table that's difficult.

CAFE LA HABANA, Morelos 62. Tel. 535-2620.

Specialty: MEXICAN. **Metro:** Juárez (five blocks away); it's at the corner of Morelos and Bucareli.

$ Prices: Appetizers $2.50–$9.50; main courses $5–$10.

Open: Mon–Sat 8am–11pm.

One of the oldest establishments in town, Cafe La Habana is southwest of the Alameda. The cavernous interior reverberates with the sound of clinking glasses and tinkling silver as businessmen and local folk have breakfast, lunch, and dinner, and enjoy the best coffee in town. In the front as you enter is a coffee-roasting machine that's whirring to ensure that the coffee is the freshest. To the delight of my friends, I always bring back bags of their coffee.

FONDA SANTA ANITA, Calle Humboldt 48. Tel. 518-4609.

Specialty: MEXICAN. **Metro:** Juárez; it's between Humboldt and Balderas.

$ Prices: Appetizers $1.50–$3; main courses $3–$9; fixed-price meal $7.

Open: Mon–Sat noon–midnight.

Situated in the little half block south of Avenida Juárez near the Hotel Ambassador, the Fonda Santa Anita doesn't look like much from the outside. But inside it's festooned with colorful banners and it's one of the city's longest-established places with moderate prices and speedy service. There's an English-language menu, and on it you'll find lots of dishes you may not have heard of before. For instance, you can order peppers stuffed with cheese, or bean soup with tortilla strips, or chongos zamoranos (a yogurtlike dessert). You might order the fixed-price *menu turistico,* a four-course meal including a Mexican combination plate.

CASA DE AZULEJOS, Avenida Madero 4. Tel. 512-9820.

Specialty: MEXICAN/AMERICAN. **Metro:** Bellas Artes; it's on the corner of Correo, the alleyway that runs along the main post office.

$ Prices: Appetizers $3–$6; main courses $4–$8; daily specials $5.50–$8; dessert and coffee $3–$4.

Open: Daily 7:30am–10pm.

Located in Sanborn's House of Tiles, this gorgeous antique building was once the palace of the Counts of the Valley of Orizaba. For many years now it has housed a branch of the Sanborn's restaurant and variety-store chain. Dining tables are set in an elaborate courtyard complete with carved pillars, tiles, and peacock frescoes. It's a lovely place for a rest.

LINCOLN RESTAURANT, Revillagigedo 24. Tel. 510-1468 or 510-1102.

Specialty: INTERNATIONAL. **Metro:** Juárez; it's between Articulo 123 and Independencia.

$ Prices: Appetizers $1.50–$7; main courses $6.50–$15.

Open: Mon–Sat 8am–10pm.

Located south of the Alameda Central, across from the Hotel Monte Real, the Lincoln Restaurant is plush in decor but moderate in price. The white tablecloths contrast with the dark paneling, and a portrait of Honest Abe lends dignity. Go here for a full lunch rather than a quick snack, for you'll find yourself wanting to settle in and order soup or perhaps a shrimp cocktail, then something like huachinanguito (baby red snapper), osso buco, or beef brochettes Mexican style.

MEALS FOR LESS THAN $15

RESTAURANTE VASCO, Madero 6. Tel. 512-0613.

Specialty: SPANISH. **Metro:** Bellas Artes; enter the southern end of the arcade at Madero 6 next to Sanborn's, or northern end at Cinco de Mayo no. 7 (also numbered 727); go up the stairs in the center of the passageway, or take the elevator.

$ Prices: Appetizers $3–$6; main courses $9.50–$11; comida corrida $8–9.50.

Open: Lunch only, daily 1–6pm.

Restaurante Vasco, located right next door to Sanborn's House of Tiles, has been serving wonderful, plenteous comidas to generations of satisfied Chilangos (residents of Mexico City) since 1928; it's pure Mexico City tradition, the very best of it. Lunch is the only meal served. Here you'll find a glass-topped atrium with a marble floor and potted palms set with wrought-iron dining tables. Several small rooms opening off it serve as dining rooms as well. Beyond the atrium is a light and spacious front room looking onto the street, with parquet floors, crystal chandeliers, and gilt Corinthian-column trim, all dating from the early part of this century. The waiters are correct and efficient in traditional black-and-white, and the tables are laid with snowy cloths. The fixed-price lunch might include fresh-fruit cocktail, leek-and-potato soup, Spanish omelet, entrecôte of beef sautéed with a hint of garlic and served with french fries, flan for dessert, and coffee to follow. If it's crowded, there are more dining rooms two flights up.

HONG KING, Dolores 25A. Tel. 512-6703.
  Specialty: CHINESE. **Metro:** Bellas Artes; it's between Independencia and Articulo 123.
$ Prices: Appetizers $2.50–$6; main courses $5–$23; fixed-price meals $8.50–$12.
  Open: Daily noon–11:30pm.
One of the better restaurants here, Hong King is a block and a half south of Avenida Juárez. Small and tidy like a luncheonette, the Hong King offers a nice selection. You can get one-person fixed-price Chinese meals and an assortment of à la carte choices. It's not elegant, but it's neat, clean, and conveniently located. Get here early for lunch before the crowds arrive.

RESTAURANT DANUBIO, Uruguay 3. Tel. 512-0912.
  Specialty: INTERNATIONAL. **Metro:** Bellas Artes or Salto de Agua; it's south of the Alameda at the corner of Lázaro Cárdenas.
$ Prices: Appetizers $3–$12; main courses $10–$30; comida corrida $9.50.
  Open: Daily 1pm–midnight (comida corrida served 1–4pm).

Elbow your way past the crowds for a gigantic fixed-price lunch that's practically an institution—it's plenty for two. A typical comida consists of a shrimp or oyster cocktail, maybe Valencia soup or tomato consommé, boiled lentils, a choice of a hot or cold fish dish, a choice of three main courses, custard or fruit, and coffee or tea. The à la carte menu is extensive, but you get better service during the busy time if you stick to the fixed-price meal. They serve cocktails, wine, and beer. There is also a room upstairs to accommodate the lunchtime overflow, although many in the overflow don't know it, so you may find more breathing space aloft. The house specialty is langostinos (baby crayfish) and well worth the splurge!

4. AROUND THE ZÓCALO

MEALS FOR LESS THAN $5

CAFE EL POPULAR, Cinco de Mayo. Tel. 518-6081.
  Specialty: MEXICAN. **Metro:** Zócalo; it's between Isabel La Católica and the Zócalo.
$ Prices: Appetizers $1.50–$2.50; main courses $3–$4; breakfast and tea-time special $2; comida corrida $3; Oaxaca tamal $1.
  Open: Daily 24 hours.

Located on the same side of the street as the Cafe La Blanca, Cafe El Popular not only is popular for its prices but it has the charm La Blanca lacks. It looks like a cozy French café with inviting streetside windows filled with pastries. Go on in—it only looks expensive. You'll find one of the best-priced menus downtown. If the lower level is full, take the narrow stairs up to the loft level. Either way, expect your waitress to greet you with a heaping basket of pastries (they charge you for what you eat). Breakfast or merienda (tea time) specials include a Oaxaca tamal, beans, a cup of atole (a sweet, thick corn drink), or coffee.

CAFETERÍA POPOS, Madero 69. Tel. 512-3438.

Specialty: MEXICAN. **Metro:** Zócalo; it's between Palma and Monte de Piedad alongside the entrance to the Hotel Majestic.

$ Prices: Appetizers $1.50–$2; main courses $3–$5; lunch special $5–$6; Sat pozole special $2.

Open: Mon–Sat 8am–9pm.

Just off the Zócalo is the tiny Cafetería Popos. With fewer than a dozen tables, this clean eatery does a great business because of its inexpensive food and swift service. You can eat and go in no time. The two luncheon specials are often available in the evening and usually include either a soup and sandwich with a prepared fruit drink or coffee, or soup plus a special plate with meat and drink. The Saturday pozole special is reason enough to stop in.

MEALS FOR LESS THAN $10

CAFE CINCO DE MAYO, Cinco de Mayo no. 57. Tel. 510-1995.

Specialty: MEXICAN. **Metro:** Zócalo; it's between Palma and Monte de Piedad.

$ Prices: Appetizers $1.50–$3; main courses $3–$7; comida corrida $7.50.

Open: Daily 7am–11pm.

A real money-saver near the Zócalo, the Cafe Cinco de Mayo is the very picture of a Mexican lunchroom. Less than a block west of the cathedral on the south side of the street, it's bright with fluorescent lights and loud with conversation. The walls bear fake-stone wall covering and mirrors, and its long lunch counter is filled with regulars. Waiters scurry here and there bearing enormous glasses of fresh orange juice, cups of hot coffee, baskets of pan dulce, sandwiches, pork chops—just about anything you can imagine. If you order cafe con leche, a waiter will approach with a big copper coffee pot, pour an inch of thick, bitter coffee into the bottom of your glass, then fill it up with hot milk.

RESTAURANTE VEGETARIANO Y DIETETICO, Madero 56. Tel. 521-6880 or 585-4191.

Specialty: VEGETARIAN. **Metro:** Zócalo; it's upstairs, between Isabel La Católica and Palma.

$ Prices: Main courses and comida corrida $4–$6.

Open: Daily 9am–6pm.

I can't say enough good things about the food at the Restaurante Vegetariano y Dietetico. There's only a small brass plaque with the restaurant's name next to the doorway, so look for a stairway marked PENELLA or the menu posted outside on the entrance; walk one flight up and you'll enter the restaurant. The decor is nothing special—the restaurant was founded in 1942 and probably never redecorated—but the food is fantastic. As the name implies, they serve no meat, but you can easily have your fill, starting with a huge salad, followed by superb soup, a choice of two main courses, and a delicious cake made of whole wheat and honey, served with coffee or tea. The menu is in Spanish only.

There's another Vegetariano at Filomata 13, between Cinco de Mayo and Madero, five blocks west of the Zócalo.

CAFE LA BLANCA, Cinco de Mayo no. 40. Tel. 510-0399.

Specialty: INTERNATIONAL/MEXICAN. **Metro:** Allende; it's between Motolinía and Isabel La Católica.

$ Prices: Appetizers $2–$4; main courses $3–$8.

Open: Daily 7am–11:30pm.

Cafe La Blanca, on the north side of the street, is a large cafeteria-style place with two levels. There's no decor to speak of, but the fare is good, as is indicated by the teeming

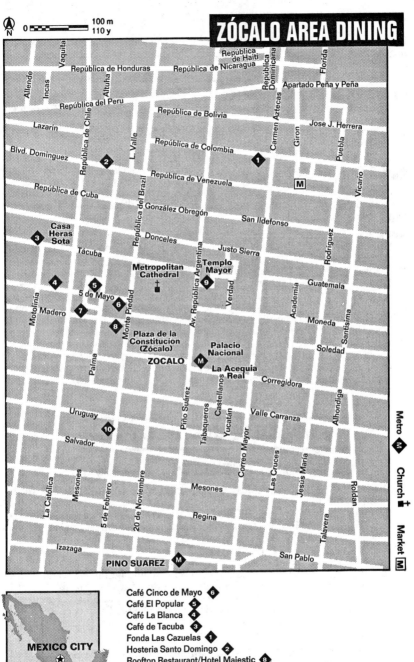

ZÓCALO AREA DINING

0 100 m
   110 y

República de Honduras
Vaquita
Allende
Incas
Altuña
República de Haiti
República de Nicaragua
República Dominicana
Apartado Peña y Peña
Florida
República del Peru
República de Chile
República de Bolivia
Carmen Aztecas
Giron
Jose J. Herrera
Puebla
Lazarin
L. Valle
República de Colombia
República de Venezuela
Vicario
Blvd. Dominguez
República del Brazil
González Obregón
M
República de Cuba
San Ildefonso
Rodriguez
Casa Heras Sota
Donceles
Justo Sierra
Tácuba
Av. República Argentina
Templo Mayor
Academia
Guatemala
Metropolitan Cathedral
Verdad
Motolinia
5 de Mayo
Monte Piedad
Moneda
Santisima
Madero
Soledad
Plaza de la Constitucion (Zócalo)
Palacio Nacional
ZOCALO
M
La Acequia Real
Palma
Corregidora
Pino Suarez
Castellanos
Valle Carranza
Alhondiga
Uruguay
Trabaqueros
Yucatán
Salvador
La Católica
Mesones
5 de Febrero
20 de Noviembre
Mesones
Correo Mayor
Las Cruces
Jesus María
Roldan
Regina
Talavera
Izazaga
Pino Suarez
M
San Pablo

Metro M
Church
Market M

PINO SUAREZ

MEXICO CITY

business they do. They serve only à la carte items but with daily specials like huachinango (red snapper) or jumbo shrimp. You can't go wrong eating here.

MEALS FOR LESS THAN $15

HOSTERIA DE SANTO DOMINGO, Dominguez 72. Tel. 510-1434.
    Specialty: MEXICAN. **Metro:** Allende; it's between República de Brasil and República de Chile.
$ **Prices:** Appetizers $4.50–$8; main courses $7.50–$12; daily specials $5–$9.50.
    Open: Daily 9am–10pm.
    A bit higher in class and price is the Hosteria de Santo Domingo, just east of República de Chile. It is said to be the oldest restaurant in the city still in operation (established 1860). The place has been redecorated in recent times so a lot of the antiquity is gone, but it's still cozy. The food is excellent. Try, for example, the stuffed peppers with cheese, pork loin, or the unusual bread soup. There's live music from 2:30 until 10pm.

CAFE DE TACUBA, Tacuba 28. Tel. 512-8482.
    Specialty: MEXICAN. **Metro:** Allende; it's between República de Chile and Bolívar.
$ **Prices:** Appetizers $3–$6; main courses $7.50–$13; comida corrida $12.50.
    Open: Daily 8am–11:30pm.
    The Cafe de Tacuba looks as though it has been here since the city began—or at least for 100 years or so—but it dates from 1912. The orange, blue, and white wainscoting in the two long dining rooms, the brass lamps, dark and brooding oil paintings, and a large mural of several nuns working in a kitchen create a stately ambience. Soups here are excellent, with the top price going to cream of asparagus with biscuits. The customary fixed-price meal offers a selection of daily lunch plates, served with soup. The best is the last, however, as a tempting selection of what certainly look to be homemade cakes and pastries waits in a glass case near the front of the restaurant.

5. IN CHAPULTEPEC PARK

WORTH THE EXTRA BUCKS

HACIENDA DE LOS MORALES, Calle Vazquez de Mella 525. Tel. 540-3225 or 202-1973.
    Specialty: MEXICAN/AMERICAN/CONTINENTAL. **Reservations:** Necessary. **Transportation:** Take a taxi; the restaurant is northwest of Chapultepec Park at the corner of Avenida Ejercito Nacional.
$ **Prices:** Meal for two $45–$60.
    Open: Mon–Sat 1pm–midnight.
Perhaps your first choice for an extra-special meal should be the Hacienda de los Morales in Chapultepec Morales. Through the doors of a great Spanish colonial house are a cocktail lounge with entertainment, numerous dining rooms of good size and rich decoration, and an inner courtyard with a greenhouse. The service is polished and the food is delicious. In the evening men are required to wear jackets; ties aren't necessary.

RESTAURANT DE CHAPULTEPEC, Segunda Seccion ("2a Seccion") of Chapultepec Park. Tel. 515-9585 or 515-9586.
    Specialty: INTERNATIONAL/CONTINENTAL. **Reservations:** Necessary. **Metro:** Constituyentes or Auditorio to the park; then a taxi from there.
$ **Prices:** Meal for two $50–$75.
    Open: Mon–Sat 1pm–1am.
If your tastes are more modern, the ultra-sophisticated Restaurant de Chapultepec (formerly Del Lago) offers lake-view dining on several levels in a dramatic building

fronted with glass. Tables flicker with faint candlelight, and the romantic atmosphere is great for a special night out. The jacketed waiter will hand you a menu (in English) with such delectables as duck liver pâté, oysters bourguignon, tortilla soup, or lobster bisque for appetizers; grilled brochette of quail, roast beef, or langostinos in garlic for main courses; and wonderfully rich desserts. Prices will vary depending on what you order and what you drink. There's dancing to a combo after dinner, and a cover charge if you haven't come for dinner. Jackets and ties are obligatory for men.

6. SPECIALTY DINING

TEA

AUSEBA, Hamburgo 159B. Tel. 511-3769.
   Specialty: CONTINENTAL. **Metro:** Insurgentes; it's between Florencia and Estocolmo.
$ Prices: Coffee or tea $2–$4; pastries $3–$4; coffee and croissant $2.25.
   Open: Daily 9am–10pm.
The Zona Rosa would be my choice for some fine places for afternoon tea as they serve it on the continent, and one of the finest I've found is Auseba, which serves pastries and candies along with its tea and coffee. The glass cases hold one of the most delicious-looking displays of cookies, meringues, bonbons, cakes, pies, puddings, and tortas I've ever seen in the city. Paintings decorate one wall, and the little cloth-covered circular tables have modern black plastic chairs—eclectic, but comfortable. For a rich pastry and Viennese coffee, you can spend twice as much as coffee and a croissant.

SALON DE THÉ DUCA D'ESTE, Hamburgo 164B. Tel. 525-6374.
   Specialty: CONTINENTAL. **Metro:** Insurgentes; it's at the corner of Florencia and Hamburgo.
$ Prices: Appetizers $4–$5; buffet $4–$6; cake and coffee or breakfast $3–$6.
   Open: Daily 8am–11pm.
This is another favorite of mine, opposite the above-mentioned Auseba. Small tea tables draped in apricot cloths look out onto the bustle of pedestrian traffic on Hamburgo and Florencia. But many of the customers are absorbed in gazing at the Duca d'Este's refrigerated display cases, which shelter many kinds of pastries, and also fresh and candied fruits, ice creams, and other fare. There's a good selection of coffees, teas, and hot chocolates. You can have a light lunch or supper by ordering soup, salad, or salmon.

BAKERIES

PASTELERÍA MADRID, Calle 5 (Cinco) de Febrero no. 25. Tel. 521-3378.
   Specialty: PASTRY. **Metro:** Zócalo; it's 2½ blocks south of the Zócalo between República del Salvador and Uruguay.
$ Prices: 35¢–$10.
   Open: Daily 9am–10pm.
The walls of this enormous, well-lit bakery are lined with deep shelves filled with absolutely fresh, light, puffy pastries, sweet rolls, danish, cookies, biscuits, fresh breads, jam-filled goodies, and custards. Here's how to make these goodies yours: Pick up a circular aluminum tray and a pair of tongs, pile your tray full; then you entrust it to a young lady who deftly transfers the mountain of pastries to a paper bag, totting up the tab at the same time. Come for breakfast (coffee or tea, yogurt, and pastries). Here's a tip: Take your choices from the fullest tray as those are the freshest.

PASTELERÍA IDEAL, Avenida 16 de Septiembre no. 14. Tel. 585-8099.
   Specialty: PASTRY. **Metro:** Bellas Artes; it's 1½ blocks south of the Alameda, between Cárdenas and Gante.

$ Prices: 35¢–$10.
Open: Daily 7am–10pm.

⭐ This classy place has moderate prices and a constant stream of loyal customers. It's sure to charm you with its assortment of confections. Brown-bag your next breakfast from here—if you can resist that long.

PASTELERÍA DEL ANGEL, at the corner of Río Lerma and Río Sena. Tel. 514-4717.
Specialty: BAKERY.
$ Prices: 50¢–$5.
Open: Daily 8:30am–8pm.

⭐ This pastry shop–deli two blocks north of Reforma is just the thing for do-it-yourself breakfasts and snacks with one of the best assortments of rolls, danish, and cookies I've encountered in the capital. And next door (still the same bakery) are ready-made deli sandwiches and meat-filled empanadas. Prices are a bit higher than at pastelerías in less wealthy sections, but you can still make a paper bag heavy with goodies here and pay less than $3. It's only half a block from Casa González.

CANTINAS

SALON LA LUZ, Gante 23. Tel. 512-4246.
Specialty: MEXICAN. **Metro:** Allende; it's 2½ blocks south of the Alameda and House of Tiles, at the corner of Carranza.
$ Prices: Appetizers $4–$15; main courses $10–$12.
Open: Mon–Sat 10am–11pm, Sun 10am–6pm.

Since 1936 the Salon La Luz has been an institution in downtown Mexico City. Not only are women welcome, but the whole family is accommodated. With a recent expansion to include a covered outdoor portion, the salon is putting on airs and music. A trio playing traditional Mexican ballads entertains outdoors from 2 to 6pm and indoors from 7pm to closing. Inside, it's cozy and inviting, with bustling waiters and almost-always-full Formica-topped tables. The specialty here is a delicious carne cruda (steak tartare). If you'd like to try it and something else, order the combination plate. It's enough for two, and includes portions of carne cruda, ham, smoked pork, pâté, and Chihuahua cheese. Come early when the food is freshest.

LA OPERA BAR, Cinco de Mayo no. 14. Tel. 512-8959.
Specialty: INTERNATIONAL. **Reservations:** Recommended at lunch. **Metro:** Bellas Artes; it's between Mata and Correo.
$ Prices: Appetizers $6–$22; main courses $8–$15; mixed drinks $2–$4; beer $1.75; glass of wine $3.
Open: Daily 12:30pm–midnight.

⭐ La Opera Bar, three blocks east of the Alameda, is the most opulent of the city's cantinas. Below gilded baroque ceilings, slide into one of the dark-wood booths with patches of beveled mirror and exquisite small oil paintings of pastoral scenes, or grab a table covered in linen and waiting with a basket of fresh bread. La Opera is the Mexican equivalent of a London club, although it has become so popular for dining that fewer and fewer men play dominoes. In fact, you see more and more people enjoying romantic interludes in one of the cavernous booths, but tables of any kind are hard to find. The best bet is to arrive for lunch when it opens or go after 5pm when the throngs have diminished. The menu is sophisticated and extensive. While you wait for one of the jacketed waiters to bring your meal, look on the ceiling for the bullet hole that legend says Pancho Villa left when he galloped in on a horse.

SALON VICTORIA, Lopez 43. Tel. 512-4340.
Specialty: MEXICAN. **Reservations:** Recommended before 3pm for lunch.
Metro: Bellas Artes; it's at the corner of Marroqui.
$ Prices: Appetizers $3–$11; main courses $8–$18.
Open: Daily 10am–10pm.

The newly remodeled Salon Victoria, at the corner of a pedestrian walkway, is beginning to look like a classy English pub. With brass chandeliers and lamps and brass-framed prints, this is not quite the Salon Victoria of nearly 50 years ago—maybe it's better. Specialties here include paella Valenciana, manchamantales (translated literally "tablecloth stainer"—turkey dish with almost 20 ingredients), and goat-head tacos. The latter are an acquired taste and if you want to try them, you must reserve an order in advance; the supply is limited and the Victoria hoards them for its best customers.

CHAPTER 12

WHAT TO SEE & DO IN MEXICO CITY

- **DID YOU KNOW . . . ?**
1. **THE TOP ATTRACTIONS**
2. **MORE ATTRACTIONS**
3. **WALKING TOURS**
4. **ORGANIZED TOURS**
5. **SPECIAL & FREE EVENTS**
6. **SPORTS & RECREATION**
- **FROMMER'S FAVORITES: MEXICO CITY EXPERIENCES**
7. **SAVVY SHOPPING**
8. **EVENING ENTERTAINMENT**
- **THE MAJOR CONCERT & PERFORMANCE HALLS**

You'll find that in Mexico such routine activities as walking in the park can bring delightful surprises, and even an ordinary stroll in the city's markets presents the opportunity to admire exotic items unavailable at home. The City of Mexico was built on the ruins of the ancient city of Tenochtitlán.

A downtown portion of the city comprising almost 700 blocks and 1,500 buildings has been designated a **Historical Zone.** The area is being reclaimed from years of neglect and restored to its former colonial charm. The center for this transformation is the former home of Don Manuel de Heras y Soto, built in the 18th century at the corner of Donceles and República de Chile, now the **Mexico City Historical Center** (tel. 510-2541). It's open Monday through Friday from 9am to 3pm and 4 to 9pm. On Sunday at 11am the center offers a free guided tour, primarily of the Zócalo area. English-speaking guides may be available if you request one in advance. Don Manuel, by the way, was one of the notables who signed Mexico's Act of National Independence in 1821.

In summer, always be prepared for rain, which comes daily. In winter, carry a jacket or sweater—stone museums are cold inside, and when the sun goes down, the outside air gets chilly.

SUGGESTED ITINERARIES

IF YOU HAVE 1 DAY Arrive at the Museum of Anthropology by 10am and follow the suggested walking tour in this book for the next 2 to 4 hours; it could easily be all-day entertainment, depending on your interest level. Have lunch. Return to your hotel for a rest (remember, this is your first day at 7,240 ft.). In the evening, see a performance of the Ballet Folklorico de México at either the Bellas Artes or Teatro de la Ciudad.

IF YOU HAVE 2 DAYS On the first day, follow the itinerary above.

Start your second day with an early breakfast, then head straight for the Pyramids of Teotihuacán, 30 miles northeast of the city proper. Not counting travel time, seeing the ruins takes between 2 and 5 hours, depending on whether or not you climb the pyramids, stop to read explanatory information, and take photographs. Have a

? DID YOU KNOW . . . ?

- Cortés entered Tenochitlán (today's Mexico City) and first met the Aztec king Moctezuma on November 8, 1519.
- The seige of Tenochitlán began on May 21, 1521, and ended 85 days later.
- The remains of Hernán Cortés, conqueror of Mexico, are in a vault in the chapel of the Hospital of Jesús Nazareno, the oldest functioning hospital in the Americas.
- The first mint in Mexico was established in 1535 in the National Palace in Mexico City, and gold was first coined there in 1679.
- Communist leader Leon Trotsky moved to Mexico City in 1938 and was assassinated here in 1940.
- More than 300,000 students attend the University Atonomia de México (UNAM), in Mexico City, founded in 1551, the oldest university in the New World.
- In 1846 the St. Patrick's Battalion, fighting with Gen. Zachary Taylor during the U.S. invasion of Mexico, deserted the U.S. forces and joined with the Mexicans against the United States.
- One-fourth of Mexico's 80 million inhabitants live in the Mexico City metropolitan area.
- Mexico's two emperors since the Conquest were Augustín Iturbide (1822–23), who lived in the Iturbide Palace on Avenida Madero, and Archduke Maximillian of Hapsburg (1864–67), who lived in Chapultepec Castle. Both were executed by firing squads.
- José Antonio Lopez de Santa Anna, president of Mexico 11 times, died here poor and alone on June 21, 1876. His obituary appeared 2 weeks later.

late lunch there or return to the city. In the early evening, stroll the Zona Rosa and select a restaurant—outdoor or indoors; the choice is immense.

IF YOU HAVE 3 DAYS Spend your first 2 days as suggested above.

Start your third day with a walking tour of the Zócalo, either using the one in this book, or, if it's Sunday, following the free guided tour organized by the Mexico City Historic Center. If you want to combine it with a tour of the adjacent Alameda area, see the Diego Rivera murals in the National Palace, the Templo Mayor Museum, the Museo de la Ciudad de México (Museum of the City), or the Franz Mayer Museum. The Diego Rivera mural *Dream of a Sunday Afternoon in Alameda Park* is in the Parque Solidaridad beside the Alameda.

IF YOU HAVE 5 DAYS For the first 3 days, follow the above itineraries.

On your fourth day, get an early start for touring the southern parts of the city. If it's Saturday, start with the colorful Bazar Sábado (Saturday Bazaar) in San Angel. Otherwise, begin in the suburb of Coyoacán at the museum-home of Frida Kahlo, wife of Diego Rivera. Then walk a few blocks to the house and museum of Leon Trotsky. Have lunch at one of the restaurants around the plaza in Coyoacán, then take a taxi to the Diego Rivera Museum (Museo de Anahuacalli). In the evening, listen to the mariachis around Garibaldi Square.

On your fifth day, if it's Sunday don't miss the Lagunilla Market, especially if you love eclectic flea markets. Mexico City has an enormous variety of stores, quality jewelry, clothing, and good crafts, most of which are in and around the Zona Rosa, Alameda, and the Zócalo. Or take one of the suggested "Easy Excursions from Mexico City" (see Chapter 13). A day trip to Cuernavaca or Toluca would leave plenty of time for looking around either of those cities in time to return in late afternoon.

1. THE TOP ATTRACTIONS

For details on these sights, see the Walking Tours later in this chapter.

NATIONAL MUSEUM OF ANTHROPOLOGY, Chapultepec Park. Tel. 553-6266.

★ Occupying 44,000 square feet, it's regarded as one of the top museums in the world. First-floor rooms are devoted to the pre-Hispanic cultures of Mexico. Second-floor rooms cover contemporary rural cultures through their crafts and everyday life. This museum offers the single best introduction to Mexico.
Admission: $3.50; free Sun.
Open: Tues–Sat 9am–7pm, Sun 10am–6pm. **Metro:** Auditorio.

PYRAMIDS OF TEOTIHUACÁN, 30 miles northeast of the city center.

★ More tourists go to the Pyramids of Teotihuacán than to any other archeologi-cal site in Mexico. Once the city had at least 25,000 inhabitants and covered 95 square miles. Restoration and exploration are ongoing; this city of pyramids is one not to miss. (See Chapter 13 "Easy Excursions from Mexico City.")
Admission: Mon–Sat $4.50, free Sun.
Open: Daily 8am–5pm (visitors are allowed to remain until 6pm).

TEMPLO MAYOR MUSEUM, off the Zócalo. Tel. 542-1717.

★ Opened in 1987 at the site of the newly excavated Aztec Templo Mayor, this quickly became one of the city's top museums. At the time of the Conquest in 1521 the site was the center of religious life for the city of 300,000. No other museum shows the variety and splendor of the Aztec Empire the way this one does. All 6,000 pieces came from the relatively small plot of excavated ruins just in front of the museum. (See "Walking Tour 1—Near the Zócalo," below.)
Admission: $3.50, free Sun.
Open: Tues–Sat 9am–6pm. **Metro:** Zócalo

THE HISTORIC DISTRICT

At least 1,500 buildings and an area of almost 700 acres of historic downtown Mexico City around the Alameda and Zócalo have been earmarked for preservation. Much of the history of Mexico from the 16th to the 20th century is reflected in the grand palaces and buildings in these two areas. (See the walking tours of the Zócalo and the Alameda, below).
Metro: Zócalo or Bellas Artes.

DIEGO RIVERA MURALS

Diego Rivera, one of Mexico's top muralists, left an indelible stamp on Mexico City's walls and, through his painted political themes, affected the way millions view Mexican history. See his stunning and provocative interpretations at the National Palace, the Bellas Artes, the National Preparatory School (his first ones), the Department of Public Education, the National School of Agriculture at Chapingo, the National Institute of Cardiology, and the Museo de la Alameda (formerly in the Hotel Del Prado). (See the walking tours of the Alameda and the Zócalo, below.)

FRANZ MAYER MUSEUM, Hidalgo 45, facing the Alameda. Tel. 518-2265.

★ German immigrant Franz Mayer spent a lifetime collecting rare furniture and other utilitarian decorative pieces dating from the 16th to the 19th century. When he died in 1975, he bequeathed them to the Mexican people with a trust fund for their care and display. (See "Walking Tour 2—Near the Alameda".)
Admission: $1.75 adults, 35¢ students; free for everyone Sun.
Open: Tues–Sun 10am–5pm. **Metro:** Hidalgo or Bellas Artes.

2. MORE ATTRACTIONS

NEAR THE ALAMEDA

North, west, and south of the Alameda proper are other attractions worthy of note. For the major highlights, see "Walking Tour 2—Near the Alameda," later in this chapter.

PLAZA AND CEMETERY OF SAN FERNANDO, Puente de Alvarado and Vicente Guerrero.

At one end of the plaza is the 18th-century San Fernando Church and behind it, 2½ blocks west of the Alameda, is a small cemetery by the same name where a few of Mexico's elite families are buried. It's the only cemetery remaining in the city from the 19th century, and President Benito Juárez was the last person buried here, on July 23, 1872. His tomb is like a Greek temple with a sculpture representing the motherland cradling a beloved son. (Many of Mexico's more infamous are buried in the cemetery behind the original Basilica of Guadalupe.)

Admission: Free.

Open: Daily dawn–dusk.

MUSEO DE SAN CARLOS, Puente de Alvarado 50. Tel. 535-4848 or 592-3721.

The San Carlos Museum shows works from students of the Academy of San Carlos. Most of the country's great painters—Diego Rivera among them—count it as their alma mater. The beautiful converted mansion that houses the museum was built in the early 1800s by architect Manuel Tolsá for the Marqués de Buenavista.

In the mansion's elliptical court are displays of 19th-century Mexican statuary and busts by Manuel Vilar and his pupils, and off to one side is a pretty garden court shaded by rubber trees.

The various rooms on the first and second floors hold some of Mexico's best paintings, by both Mexican and European artists. In Sala IV, for instance, you can view *Christ in Limbo* by Mostaert (ca. 1534–98), and also two paintings by Lucas Cranach the Elder: *Adam and Eve* and *Federico de Sajonia*. Upstairs treats include *La Coquea y el Jovenzuelo* by Fragonard and a portrait of Sir William Stanhope attributed to Sir Joshua Reynolds.

Admission: Free.

Open: Daily 10am–6pm. **Directions:** Walk 5½ blocks west of the Alameda, and 2½ blocks west of San Fernando Plaza, at the corner of Arizpe.

MONUMENTO DE LA REVOLUCIÓN, Plaza de la República, Av. Juárez and La Fragua. Tel. 546-2115 or 566-1902.

The stocky art deco Monument to the Revolution, set in the large Plaza de la República, has a curious and ironic history. The government of Porfirio Díaz, perennially "reelected" as president of Mexico, began construction of what was intended as a new legislative chamber. But only the dome was raised by the time the Mexican Revolution (1910) put an end to his plans—not to mention his dictatorship. In the 1930s, after the turmoil of the Revolution died down, the dome was finished off as a monument; the mortal remains of two revolutionary presidents, Francisco Madero and Venustiano Carranza, were entombed in two of its pillars, and it was dedicated to the Revolution.

Beneath the Monument to the Revolution is the **Museo Nacional de la Revolución.** The tumultuous years from 1867 through the Revolution (which

---

IN THEIR FOOTSTEPS

Pancho Villa (1877–1923) Born Doroteo Arango, he was a noted cattle rustler until effectively leading the northern forces (*Division del Norte*) against the dictatorship of Porfirio Díaz. History remembers him as a bandit, colorful hero, and a notoriously unfaithful husband—he allegedly had at least 23 wives. After the end of the Revolution, he was assasinated and the bullet riddled car he rode in that day is on display in the Museum of the Revolution in Chihuahua.

  • **Birthplace:** A hacienda near La Cuesta, Durango.

  • **Residence:** Quinta Luz, now the Museum of the Revolution, Calle 10, Chihuahua.

  • **Resting Place:** Monument to the Revolution, Mexico City.

started in 1911), to 1917 when the present constitution was signed, are chronicled in exhibits of documents and newspaper stories, photographs and drawings, clothing, costumes, uniforms, weapons, and furnishings from the period.

Admission: Free.

Open: Tues–Sun 9am–5pm. **Directions:** Walk three short blocks south of the Museo de San Carlos along Calle Ramos Arizpe.

PLAZA DE LAS TRES CULTURAS, at the corner of Lázaro Cárdenas and Flores Magón.

Here three cultures converge—Aztec, Spanish, and contemporary. Surrounded by modern office and apartment buildings are large remains of the **Aztec city of Tlatelolco,** site of the last battle of the conquest of Mexico, and off to one side is the **Cathedral of Santiago Tlatelolco.** During the Aztec Empire, Tlatelolco was on the edge of Lake Texcoco, linked to the Aztec capital by a causeway. Bernal Díaz de Castillo, in his *True Story of the Conquest of New Spain,* described the roar from the dazzling market there. Later he described the incredible scene after the last battle of the Conquest in Tlaltelolco on August 13, 1521—the dead bodies were piled so deep that walking there was impossible. That night determined the fate of the country and completed the Spanish Conquest of Mexico.

View the pyramidal remains from raised walkways over the site. The cathedral, off to one side, was built in the 16th century entirely of volcanic stone. The interior has been tastefully restored preserving little patches of fresco in stark-white plaster walls, with a few deep-blue stained-glass windows and an unadorned stone altar. Sunday is a good day to combine a visit here with one to the Sunday Lagunilla street market (see Section 7, "Savvy Shopping," below, for details) which is within walking distance south across Reforma.

Admission: Free.

Open: Daily dawn–dusk. **Directions:** It's about 2 miles north of the Alameda at Flores Magón, just off Reforma, in Colonia Tlatelolco. To walk there from the Alameda, go north on Lázaro Cárdenas straight six long blocks and turn right on Rayón two blocks to the Lagunilla Market. Then turn left and follow the street the short distance to the traffic circle with the Cuitláhuac Monument. The plaza is on the other side of the circle. **Metro:** Line 3 to Tlatelolco; leave the terminal by the exit to Manuel González, and turn right on this street; walk two blocks to Avenida Lázaro Cárdenas and turn right again. The plaza is about half a block south, on the left, just past the Clinico Hospital. The walk takes less than 15 minutes.

SULLIVAN PARK/JARDÍN DEL ARTE, at the intersection of Insurgentes and Reforma.

Though not strictly "near the Alameda," you might want to continue your tour on a 10-minute walk southwest along Reforma to Sullivan Park, which on Sunday becomes Jardín del Arte (Garden of Art). This pretty park begins with the Monumento a la Maternidad (Monument to Motherhood), and continues with trees, shrubs and benches, fountains, and sculpture, into Sullivan Park. On Sunday it's crowded with artists displaying their wares for sale.

Admission: Free.

Open: Daily; artists exhibit on Sun.

IN CHAPULTEPEC PARK

ROTUNDA DE LOS HOMBRES ILUSTRES, Dolores Cemetery, in Section Three of Chapultepec Park, Constituyentes and Av. Civil Dolores.

The din of traffic recedes in the serene environment where Mexico's illustrious military, political, scientific, and artistic elite are buried. It's more like an outdoor museum of monuments than a cemetery. The stone markers are grouped in a double circle around an eternal flame; a stroll here will enliven a conversation about who's who in Mexican history. Among the famous buried here are artists Diego Rivera, Alfredo Siquieros, José Clemente Orozco, and Gerardo Murillo (Dr. Atl); presidents Sebastian Lerdo de Tejada, Valentin Gomez Farías, and Plutarco Calles; musicians

Jaime Nuño (writer of the Mexican National Anthem), Juventino Rosas, and Augustín Lara; and outstanding citizens such as Carlos Pellicer. Stop in the entrance building and the guard will give you a map with a list of those buried here, which includes biographical information.

Admission: Free.
Open: Daily 6am–6pm.

NORTH OF THE CITY CENTER

BASILICA OF GUADALUPE

Within the northern city limits is the famous Basilica of Guadalupe. Tour groups often combine a trip to the basilica with the Plaza of Three Cultures (see above) and the Pyramids of Teotihuacán (see Chapter 13, "Easy Excursions from Mexico City"), which makes a rushed and exhausting day.

The Basilica of Our Lady of Guadalupe is on the site where, on December 9, 1531, a poor Indian named Juan Diego is reputed to have seen a vision of a beautiful lady in a blue mantle. The local bishop was reticent to confirm that Juan had indeed seen the Virgin Mary, and so he asked the peasant for some evidence. Juan saw the vision a second time, on December 12, and it became miraculously emblazoned on the poor peasant's cloak. The bishop immediately ordered the building of a church on the spot, and upon its completion the image was hung in the place of honor, framed in gold. Since that time millions of the devout and the curious have come to view the miraculous image that experts, it is said, are at a loss to explain. The blue-mantled Virgin of Guadalupe is the patron saint of Mexico.

So heavy was the flow of visitors—many of whom approached for hundreds of yards on their knees—that the old church, already fragile, was insufficient to handle it, and an audacious new basilica was built, designed by Pedro Ramírez Vazquez, the same architect who did the breathtaking National Museum of Anthropology.

For a view of the miraculous cloak, which hangs at the altar, go to the lower level of the church. The architect has designed it so that you can look at the image from below through an opening.

At the top of the hill, behind the basilica, is a cemetery for Mexico's more infamous folk (Santa Anna among them) and also several gift shops specializing in trinkets encased in seashells and other folk art. The steps up this hill are lined with flowers, shrubs, and waterfalls, and the climb, although tiring, is worthwhile for the view from the top.

Should you be lucky enough to visit Mexico City on December 12, you can witness the grand festival in honor of the Virgin of Guadalupe. The square in front of the basilica fills up with the pious and the party-minded as prayers, dances, and a carnival atmosphere attract thousands of the devout.

Admission: Free.
Open: Tues–Sun 10am–6pm. **Metro:** Line 3 to the "Básilica" station; take the exit marked SALIDA AV. MONTIEL. A half block or so north of the Metro station, turn right onto Avenida Montiel (the street is crowded with food and trinket vendors);

IN THEIR FOOTSTEPS

Sor Juana Ines de la Cruz (1651–1695) Known as Colonial Mexico's greatest poetess, she distinguished herself as a child intellectual and later was openly critical of the subordinate role of women in society. Rather than marry, she became a nun ("Sor" means "Sister") devoting herself to writing and scholarly studies.

• **Birthplace:** Nepantla, State of Mexico
• **Residence and Resting Place:** Ex-convent of San Jerónimo in Mexico City

after about 15 minutes' walk, you'll see the great church looming ahead. From La Villa station, walk north on Calzada de Guadalupe.

SOUTH OF THE CITY CENTER

POLYFORUM CULTURAL SIQUEIROS, Av. Insurgentes Sur and Filadelfia. Tel. 536-4524.

This gleaming arts center is quite controversial: some say it's bold and imaginative; others say it's a modern monstrosity with overpowering murals, low claustrophobic ceilings, and poor acoustics that echo the slightest sound. Whichever it is, it does contain the world's largest mural (90,655 square feet), *The March of Humanity on Earth* and *Toward the Cosmos,* by the famous Mexican muralist David Alfaro Siqueiros.

Admission: Free.

Open: Daily 10am–3pm and 4–7pm. **Directions:** A colectivo ("San Angel") or bus no. 17 ("Indios Verdes–Tlalpan") or no. 17-B ("Central Norte–Villa Olmpica") south along Insurgentes near the Zona Rosa goes to the Polyforum (the same bus goes to San Angel and the Bazar Sábado, University City, Pedregal, and the Cuicuilco Pyramid).

UNIVERSITY CITY, Av. Insurgentes Sur.

This is the site of the world's most flamboyant college campus and, indeed, of one of the world's most flamboyant architectural groupings, located on Avenida Insurgentes, about 11 miles south of the Alameda Central.

University City (it houses Mexico's National Autonomous University) was planned to be the last and grandest achievement of the regime of former president Miguel Aleman. The original university is said to date back to 1551, which would make it the oldest university in the western hemisphere.

It's an astonishing place and well worth going out to see for its gigantic and brilliantly colored mosaics and murals. The most outstanding of these, by Juan O'Gorman, covers all four sides and 10 complete stories of the library building. Fittingly, the mosaic wall depicts the history of Mexican culture and covers a space in which 2½ million books can be stored. The two lower stories are glass-enclosed and are used as the library's reading rooms.

The administration building, closest to the road, is mostly travertine marble but also has an immense outer mural. This was executed by David Alfaro Siqueiros and depicts Mexican students returning the fruits of their labors to the nation. Diego Rivera contributed the sculpture-painting adorning the world's largest stadium (capacity: 102,000), across the highway.

Wander at random around the campus, which accommodates an enrollment of 300,000. There is a cafeteria on the ground floor of the humanities building which, especially in summer, is well patronized by American students attending classes. All the university cafeterias are open to the public and charge very reasonable prices.

Upstairs in the humanities building, you'll find various notice boards. They merit a few moments' study, as their signs sometimes offer low-priced excursions or rides back to the States on a cost-sharing basis.

South of the university's main campus, but north of the pyramid of Cuicuilco (see below) and east of Avenida Insurgentes Sur, is the **Centro Cultural Universitario,** a large arts-and-performance complex with several important venues.

Metro: The university has its own Metro station ("Universidad"), but it's more than a mile from the library, so you should seek out the "Copilco" or "Viveros" station. **Bus:** 17-A, 17-B, 19, or 19-A along Insurgentes, or catch anything, colectivo or bus, with "Ciudad Universitaria," or simply "C.U.," in the window.

CUICUILCO RUINS

South of the university and its Centro Cultural, across the Periferico, almost where the Periferico and Insurgentes Sur (Highway 95) meet, this circular pyramid represents some of the earliest civilization in the Valley of Mexico. Built in the Preclassic Period, around 1800 B.C., it was completely covered by a volcanic eruption (in A.D. 300), surviving only because it was protected by a strong outer wall.

Admission: $2.75.
Open: Daily 9am–5pm. **Bus:** 17 heading south on Insurgentes; just after it crosses the Anillo Periferico Sur, hop off. From there it's a 15-minute walk east. Or take the Metro as far as Universidad, then a bus on Insurgentes, getting off after crossing the Periferico; then walk east.

THE PEDREGAL

Near University City is Mexico's most luxurious housing development, the **Jardines del Pedregal de San Angel.** The word *pedregal* means lava, and that's precisely what makes up this enormous area. It stretches well beyond the university. In the Jardines del Pedregal, the only restriction placed upon homeowners is that they have enough money to buy at least 2,000 square meters of land and hire an architect to design their home. The result is that all the houses are exceptionally lavish, with swimming pools scooped out of the rock, split levels with indoor gardens, solid glass walls, and in one case, an all-glass sun room on a narrow stilt above the house—like an airport's observation tower.

The lava all came from the now-extinct volcano Xitle, whose eruption covered the Cuicuilco Pyramid. Only in recent times has the pedregal been regarded as anything but a nuisance; at one time many of its caves hid bandits. Today all kinds of odd plants and shrubs grow from its nooks and crevices, and if you're interested in botany, you'll want to take a good look around. The main street is the north-south Avenida Paseo del Pedregal.

THE ANAHUACALLI (Diego Rivera Museum), Calle Museo 150, Col. Tepetlapa. Tel. 677-2984.

Not to be confused with Rivera's Studio Museum near the San Angel Inn, this is probably the most unusual museum in the city. Designed by Rivera before his death in 1957, it's devoted to his works as well as to his extensive collection of pre-Columbian art. Called the Anahuacalli ("House of Mexico") Museum and constructed of pedregal (lava rock with which the area abounds), it resembles Maya and Aztec architecture. The name Anahuac was the old name for the ancient Valley of Mexico.

In front of the museum is a reproduction of a Toltec ball court, and the entrance to the museum itself is via a coffin-shaped door. Light filters in through translucent onyx slabs and is supplemented by lights inside niches and wall cases containing the exhibits. Rivera collected nearly 60,000 pre-Columbian artifacts and the museum showcases thousands of them, in 23 rooms in chronological order, stashed on the shelves, tucked away in corners, and peeking from behind glass cases.

Upstairs, a replica of Rivera's studio has been constructed, and there you'll find the original sketches for some of his murals and two in-progress canvases. His first sketch (of a train) was done at the age of 3, and there's a photo of it, plus a color photograph of him at work later in life in a pair of baggy pants and a blue denim jacket. Rivera (1886–1957) studied in Europe for 15 years, and spent much of his life as a devoted Marxist. Yet he came through political scrapes and personal tragedies with no apparent diminution of creative energy, and a plaque in the museum proclaims him "A man of genius who is among the greatest painters of all time."

Admission: Free.
Open: Tues–Sun 10am–2pm and 3–6pm. **Directions:** It's in the southern outskirts of the city in the suburb of San Pablo Tepetlapán, south of the Frida Kahlo Museum. Take the Metro (Line 2) to the Tasqueña terminal and change to SARO bus no. 136 ("Tasqueña–Peña Pobre") west, which passes the museum. Another way to get there is bus no. 25 ("Zacatenco–Tlalpan") south along Balderas, or no. 59 ("El Rosario–Xochimilco") south along Avenidas Vasconcelos, Nuevo Leon, and Division del Norte; hop off at the Calle del Museo stop.

XOCHIMILCO, about 9 miles south of city center.

As you might guess from its name, Xochimilco (pronounced "so-chee-*meel*-co") is a survival from the civilization of the Aztecs. They built gardens on rafts called *chinampas*, then set them afloat on a series of canals. Now, of course, the gardens are gone, but flower-bedecked boats still run to and fro.

Sad to say, Xochimilco is not in the best of shape today. Aside from the fact that it has become badly commercialized (from the moment you arrive, you'll be pestered by people trying to sell you something or persuading you to take one boat over another), the canals themselves are polluted. On Sunday the place is jammed with foreign tourists and Mexican families with babies and picnic hampers; on weekdays, it's nearly deserted.

When you get to the town of Xochimilco, you'll find a busy market in operation, specializing in brightly decorated pottery. Turn along Madero and follow signs that say LOS EMBARCADEROS. If you can resist the blandishments of the inevitable salesmen and shills, you'll eventually arrive at the docks.

The boats are priced according to their size and the number of people they can hold, plus your skill as a bargainer. The going rate for a medium-sized boat holding five or six people is about $7 per hour. If you have a group of four or five people, a picnic lunch, and drinks, the ride can be a pleasure. Xochimilco is definitely the sort of place that's best enjoyed in a small group.

Admission: Free; charge for boat rides.

Open: Daily, dawn–dusk. **Directions:** Take the Metro to Tasqueña and then a bus. The buses run all the way across the city from north to south to end up at Xochimilco, but they take longer than the Metro. Of the buses coming from the center, the most convenient are nos. 31 and 33 ("La Villa–Xochimilco"), which you catch going south on Correo Mayor and Pino Suárez near the Zócalo; or no. 59, which you catch near Chapultepec on Avenidas Vasconcelos, Nuevo Leon, and Division del Norte.

---

3. WALKING TOURS

The following walking tours cover the top attractions of Mexico City. Some of the tours take only a few hours time, but the major tours can be divided up: Take the first part of the walking tour on one day, and the second half on the following day—depending, of course, on how much time you want to spend at the various attractions. The Museo Nacional de Antropologia, included in the Chapultepec Park walking tour, can, for example, become a tour all on its own.

WALKING TOUR 1 — The Zócalo

Start: The Palacio Nacional on the east end of the Zócalo (Metro: Zócalo).
Finish: Burial vault of Hernán Cortés at the Hospital de Jesús Nazareño.
Time: 1–2 days, depending on the length of time you spend at each stop.
Best Time: Sunday, when the streets are relatively uncrowded, or the week before or after September 15 (Mexican Independence Day), when the Zócalo and surrounding streets are festooned in ribbons and lights.
Worst Time: Monday, when the museums are closed.

1. **The Zócalo.** Every Spanish colonial city in North America was laid out according to a textbook plan, with a plaza at the center surrounded by a church, government buildings, and military headquarters. As capital of New Spain, Mexico City's Zócalo is one of the grandest, and is graced on all sides by stately 17th-century buildings.

   Zócalo actually means "pedestal," or "plinth." A grand monument to Mexico's independence was planned and the pedestal built, but the project was never completed. Nevertheless, the pedestal became a landmark for visitors, and soon everyone was calling the square after the pedestal, even though the pedestal was later removed. Its official name is Plaza de la Constitución. It covers almost 10 acres and is bounded on the north by Cinco de Mayo, on the east by Pino Suárez, on the south by 16 de Septiembre, and on the west by Monte de Piedad. The downtown district, especially to the north of the Templo Mayor site, one of the oldest in the city, has suffered long neglect, but a restoration project is slowly renewing much of its colonial charm. Occupying the entire east side of the Zócalo is the majestic, red tezontle stone:

2. **National Palace,** begun in 1692 on the site of Moctezuma's "new" palace, which became the site of Hernán Cortés's home and the residence of colonial viceroys. It has changed much in 300 years, taking on its present form in the late 1920s when the top floor was added. The complex of countless rooms, wide stone stairways, and numerous courtyards adorned with carved brass balconies is also where the president of Mexico works. But to most visitors it's better known for the fabulous Diego Rivera murals on the second floor depicting the history of Mexico. Just 30 minutes here with an English-speaking guide will provide good background for understanding Mexico's history. The cost of a guide is negotiable, but in general starts around $3.25.

Enter by the central door. Over it hangs the bell from Dolores Hidalgo rung by Padre Miguel Hidalgo when he proclaimed Mexico's independence from Spain in 1810. Each September 15, Independence Day in Mexico, the president of Mexico stands on the balcony above the door to echo Hidalgo's cry to thousands of spectators filling the Zócalo. Take the stairs to the Rivera murals, which were painted during a 25-year period. If you know something of the history of Mexico the content is easy to understand. *The Legend of Quetzalcoatl* depicts the famous legend of the flying serpent bringing a white man with a blond beard to the country. When Cortés arrived, many of the Aztecs remembered this legend, and believed him to be Quetzalcoatl. Another mural tells of the *American Intervention,* during the War of 1847, when American invaders marched into Mexico City. It was on this occasion that the military cadets of Chapultepec Castle (then a military school) fought bravely to the last man. The most notable of Rivera's murals is the *Great City of Tenochtitlán,* a pictorial study of the original settlement in the Valley of Mexico. The city takes up only a small part of the mural, and the remainder is filled with what appears to be four million extras left over from a Hollywood epic. In fact, no matter what their themes, most of the murals incorporate a piece of ancient Mexican history, usually featuring Cortés and a cast of thousands. It's open daily from 8am to 5:30pm. Admission is free.

Inside the corridors of the National Palace, at the northern end, is the comparatively little-known:

3. **Museo Benito Juárez** (tel. 522-5646). Walk north inside the palace, to the statue of Benito Juárez and then up the stairs. To the left is the Juárez Museum and the well-preserved apartments where the former president of Mexico died. It's usually bustling with schoolchildren studying the handwritten letters and papers kept in glass cases around the room. Other cases hold tablecloths, silverware, medals, shirts, watches, a briefcase, and symbolic keys to the city—all personal effects of the much-loved former president. There's a beautiful library here and anyone may study the books.

The last room at the rear is Juárez's bedroom, which gives one the eerie feeling that the former president might walk in at any moment: his dressing gown is laid out on the four-poster bed and a chamber pot peeks from under the bed. The museum is supposedly open Monday through Friday from 9am to 7pm, but hours may be more erratic than that. Admission is free.

Before heading north, you may want to take a look at La Acequia Real (Royal Canal) on the south side of the building at the corner of Corregadora. It was the most important canal in colonial times, carrying commerce from the southern outskirts of the city. A portion of it was recently restored.

From the National Palace, go to the northern edge of the Zócalo and the:

4. **Metropolitan Cathedral** (Metropolitano). An impressive, towering cathedral, begun in 1573 and finished in 1667, it blends Greek and Mexican Churriguresque (baroque) architecture. In your look around the cathedral and the Sagrario next to it, note the sinkage of the building into the soft lake bottom beneath. The base of the facade is far from being level and straight, and when one considers the weight of the immense towers, it's no surprise. Scaffolding may be in place because stabalizing repairs are ongoing. In Mexico, the sacred ground of one religion often becomes the sacred ground of its successor. Cortés and his Spanish

missionaries converted the Aztecs, tore down their temples, and used much of the stone to construct a church on this spot. The church they built was pulled down in 1573 so that the present Metropolitan Cathedral could be built. The immense building of today has five naves and 14 chapels. As you wander past the small chapels, you may hear guides describing some of the cathedral's outstanding features: the tomb of Agustín Iturbide perhaps, placed here in 1838, or the paintings by the Spanish artist Bartolomé Esteban Murillo, or the fact that the stone holy-water fonts ring like metal when tapped with a coin. Like many huge churches, it has catacombs underneath. The much older looking church next to the cathedral is the chapel known as El Sagrario, another tour de force of Mexican baroque architecture built in the mid-1700s.

On the west side of the cathedral is the small Cathedral Museum, with some excellent displays showing the evolution of church building on the Zócalo, with building stones from various epochs (many of which were discovered during restoration) and architectural drawings from the many contributors to the cathedral's design over the centuries. It's open Tuesday through Sunday from 10am to 5pm.

As you walked around to the museum you no doubt noticed a reminder of medieval trade life. The west side of the cathedral is the gathering place of carpenters, plasterers, plumbers, painters, and electricians who have no shops. Each craftsperson displays the tools of his trade, sometimes along with pictures of his work. Go out the front door of the Metropolitano and turn left toward the Palacio Nacional. Continue straight ahead across Seminario to the pedestrians-only street on the left side of the National Palace:

5. Calle de la Moneda (Street of the Treasury or Mint). The street is lined with aged buildings constructed of tezontle, the local volcanic rock. On the left, at the corner of Calle Verdad is the Edificio Arzobispal, the former archbishop's palace. True to Spanish tradition, the chief ecclesiastical official's power base was built smack on top of the Aztecs' Temple of Tezcatlipoca, the multifaceted god who gave life and governed a host of lesser gods. It was on this site that the child Juan Diego revealed the cloak with the figure of the Virgin of Guadalupe for the first time to the archbishop. The building from which the street takes its name is at no. 13, on the right about halfway down, and it houses the:

6. Museum of Cultures (tel. 512-7452). Formerly La Casa de Moneda (the mint), built as a part of the National Palace in the 1500s, it later became the Museum of Anthropology before the new one opened in 1964 in Chapultepec Park. Continuing as a museum, it holds a fascinating assortment of exhibits relating to other world cultures, with especially good pieces from Asia and Africa. It's open Tuesday through Saturday from 9am to 5pm and on Sunday from 9am to 4pm.

REFUELING STOP If you're ready for a break, backtrack on Moneda to the corner of Seminario to the **7. El Nivel Cantina,** founded in 1867 as the first licensed cantina in Mexico City. There's no sign, so look for the wood swinging doors. Once it was covered in gilded mirrors and carved mahogany, but a fire destroyed all that many years ago. A decor of Formica tables and plain wooden booths and chairs is all there is today. Nevertheless, here you can enjoy a limited inexpensive sandwich menu and snacks served free with beer or mixed drinks. It's open daily from 10am to 7pm.

Left around the corner and a half block on the left from the Nivel Cantina, at ground level you'll notice pigeons perched on:

8. The Model of the Lake Region. The model shows the area in what today is the Zócalo and surrounding region as it was when Cortés entered the city for the first time. The two cities of Tenochtitlán (the area where you're standing) and Tlatelolco (roughly, the area around the Plaza of Three Cultures) were surrounded by the waters of Lake Texcoco and linked by raised causeways and canals. The model's fountain fills the canallike "streets" with water just as they did in the heyday of the Aztec capital.

WALKING TOUR — THE ZOCALO

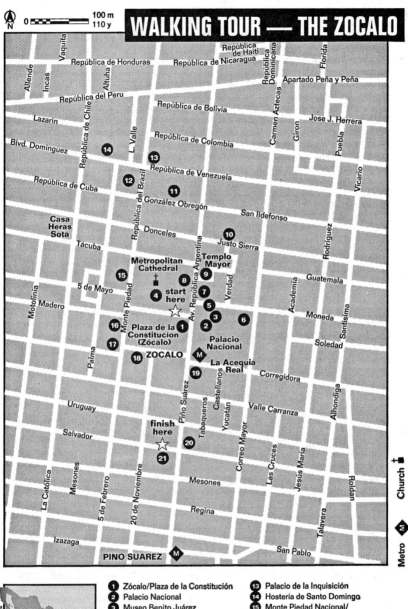

100 m
110 y

República de Haiti
República de Honduras
República de Nicaragua
República Dominicana
Apartado Peña y Peña
Vaquita
Allende
Incas
Altuha
República del Peru
Florida
Carmen Aztecas
República de Bolivia
Jose J. Herrera
Lazarin
República de Chile
L. Valle
República de Colombia
Giron
Puebla
Blvd. Dominguez
Vicario
República de Cuba
República de Brazil
República de Venezuela
Casa Heras Sota
Gonzáles Obregón
San Ildefonso
Donceles
Tácuba
Justo Sierra
Rodriguez
Metropolitan Cathedral
Templo Mayor
Guatemala
5 de Mayo
Academia
Moneda
Motolinia
Madero
Av. República Argentina
Verdad
Santisima
Monte Piedad
start here
Moneda
Plaza de la Constitucion (Zócalo)
Palacio Nacional
Soledad
Palma
ZOCALO
La Acequia Real
Corregidora
Alhondiga
Uruguay
Pino Suárez
Castellanos
Valle Carranza
Salvador
finish here
Tabaqueros
Yucatán
Correo Mayor
Las Cruces
Jesús Maria
Roldan
La Católica
Mesones
5 de Febrero
20 de Noviembre
Mesones
Regina
Izazaga
San Pablo
Talavera
PINO SUAREZ

Metro · Church

MEXICO CITY

1. Zócalo/Plaza de la Constitución
2. Palacio Nacional
3. Museo Benito Juárez
4. Metropolitan Cathedral
5. Calle Moneda
6. Museo de las Culturas
7. El Nivel Cantina
8. Model of the Lake Region
9. Museo Templo Mayor and ruins
10. Escuela Nacional Preparatoria
11. Secretaría de Educación Pública
12. Plaza de Santo Domingo
13. Palacio de la Inquisición
14. Hostería de Santo Domingo
15. Monte Piedad Nacional/ National Pawn Shop
16. Hotel Majestic
17. Gran Hotel Ciudad de México
18. Old and New Federal District Buildings
19. Suprema Corte de Justicia
20. Museo de la Ciudad de México
21. Chapel and Hospital de Jesús Nazareño

Continue on Seminario. Half a block on the right are remnants of pre-Conquest Mexico at the:

9. Templo Mayor Archeological Site and Museum (tel. 542-1717). A small corner of the site had been exposed for years, but it was never excavated. In 1978 a workman, digging on the east side of the Metropolitan Cathedral, next to what is now the National Palace, unearthed an exquisite Aztec stone of the moon goddess Coyolxauhqui. Mexican archeologists followed up the discovery with major excavations, and what they uncovered were interior remains of the Pyramid of Huitzilopochtli, also called the Templo Mayor (Great Temple), the most important religious structure in the Aztec capital. What you see are actually remains of pyramids that were covered by the great pyramid that the Spaniards saw on their arrival in the 16th century.

Strolling along the walkways built over the site, you pass a water-collection conduit constructed during the presidency of Porfirio Díaz (1877–1911), as well as far earlier constructions. Building dates are on explanatory plaques (in Spanish), which give the time frames in which the building took place. Shelters cover the ruins to protect traces of original paintwork and carving. Note especially the Tzompantli, or Altar of Skulls, a common Aztec and Maya design.

To enter the Museo del Templo Mayor (Museum of the Great Temple), which opened in 1987, take the walkway to the large building in the back portion of the site, which contains the fabulous artifacts from on-site excavations.

Inside the door, a model of Tenochtitlán gives a good idea of the scale of the vast city of the Aztecs, which flourished in the century before Cortés arrived (1519). The rooms and exhibits are organized by subject on many levels around a central open space. You'll see some marvelous displays of masks, figurines, tools, jewelry, and other artifacts, including the huge stone wheel of the moon goddess Coyolxauhqui, "she with bells painted upon her face," on the second floor. The goddess ruled the night, so the Aztecs believed, but died at the dawning of every day, slain and dismembered by her brother Xiuhcoatl, the Serpent of Fire.

Look also for the striking jade-and-obsidian mask, and the full-size terra-cotta figures of the *guerreros aguilas,* or "eagle warriors." A cutaway model of the Templo Mayor shows the layers and methods of construction.

Here's a quick guide to the exhibit rooms: Sala 1, "Antecedentes," has exhibits about the early days of Tenochtitlán. Sala 2, "Guerra y Sacrificio," goes into the details of the Aztec religious duties of war and human sacrifice. Sala 3, "Tributo y Comercio," deals with Aztec government, and its alliances and commerce with tributary states. Sala 4, "Huitzilopochtli," treats this most important of Aztec gods, a triumphant warrior, the son of Coatlicue, who bore him without losing her virginity. Huitzilopochtli, the "hummingbird god," was the one who demanded that human sacrifices be made to sustain him. In Sala 5, "Tlaloc," there are exhibits explaining the role of the Aztec rain god in daily and religious life. Sala 6, "Faunas," deals with the wild and domesticated animals common in the Aztec Empire at the time when the capital flourished. Sala 7, "Religion," explains Aztec religious beliefs, which are amazingly complex and sometimes quite confusing because they are so different from the familiar religions of Europe and the Middle East. Sala 8, "Caida de Tenochtitlán," recounts the fall of the great city and its last emperors, Moctezuma and Cuauhtémoc, to Hernan Cortés and his conquistadores. The museum is open Tuesday through Sunday from 9am to 6pm. The entry fee is $3.50 for adults, free for children and free for all on Sunday. Entrance is for both the ruins and the museum.

When you're finished at the museum, exit and return to the entrance on Seminario opposite the cathedral. The street changes to República de Argentina in front of the archeological site. Continuing north a half block, to the corner of Argentina and Donceles, turn right and half a block on the left is the:

10. Escuela Nacional Preparatoria, an 18th-century building of red tezontle stone with murals by three Mexican greats: Rivera, Orozco, and Siqueiros. Today the building is a school.

Continue north on Argentina, cross Calle González Obregón, turn left, and on the right will be the entrance to the:

11. Secretaría de Educación Pública, decorated with a great series of more than 200 Diego Rivera murals, painted in 1923 and 1924. Other artists did a panel here and there, but it's the Rivera murals that are superb. The building dates from 1922 and is open from 9am to 5:30pm.

From the front door of the Secretaría, turn right half a block to the corner of República de Brasil; across the street on the right is:

12. Plaza de Santo Domingo, with a wonderful slice of Mexican life. A fascinating plaza with arcades on one side, a Dominican church on the other, and dominated by a statue of the *corregidora* of Querétaro, Josefa Ortiz de Domínguez, it's best known for the scribes who compose and type letters for clients unable to do so for themselves. Years ago it was full of professional public writers clacking away on ancient typewriters; a few still ply their trade among a proliferation of small print shops. Emperor Cuauhtémoc's palace occupied this land, and later, Dominicans built their monastery here.

Cater-corner across the street at the corner of Venezuela and Brasil is the:

13. Palacio de la Inquisición (Inquisition Palace), built in 1732. For almost 250 years (1571–1820) accused Mexican heretics and other religious criminals were strangled and/or burned at the stake. For close to 100 years this was the building where they were held prisoner and their fates decided. The last accused heretic to be executed was José María Morelos, hero of Mexican Independence. Today it houses several rooms devoted to the Museum of the History of Mexican Medicine, with displays of modern and pre-Hispanic medicine. It's open Monday through Friday from 10am to 6pm.

REFUELING STOP From the front door of the palacio, go straight ahead one block on Dominguez and on the right is the **14. Hostería de Santo Domingo,** (tel. 510-1434), established in 1860 and reportedly the oldest restaurant in Mexico City. Meals and drinks are a little expensive, but it's lively at midday and the service and atmosphere are delightful. It's open Monday through Saturday from 9am to 10pm and on Sunday from 9am to 8:30pm.

From the Hostería de Santo Domingo, double-back to the corner of Dominguez and Brasila and turn right in the direction of the Zócalo, walking 2½ blocks. On the right is the:

15. Monte de Piedad Nacional, or national pawn shop (tel. 597-3455), at the corner of Monte de Piedad and Cinco de Mayo. Whoever heard of touring a pawn shop? In Mexico City it's done all the time in what could be described as the world's largest and most elegant Goodwill/Morgan Memorial thrift store. Electric power tools, jewelry, antique furniture, heavy machine tools, sofa beds, and a bewildering array of other things from trash to treasure are all on display. Buying is not required, but taking a look is recommended. The building is on the site of Moctezuma's "old" Axayácatl palace (his "new" palace occupied the site of the present National Palace, across the street) and the site where the captive Emperor Moctezuma was accidentally killed, and the site later occupied by a viceregal palace constructed by Cortés. The present building was given by Pedro Romero de Terreros, the Count of Regla, an 18th-century silver magnate from Pachuca, so that Mexican people might obtain low-interest loans. It's open Monday through Friday from 8:30am to 5pm and on Saturday from 8:30am to 3pm.

REFUELING STOP For a pause in your walking tour, continue south half a block, crossing Cinco de Mayo, and on the corner is one of the city's most popular hotels and rooftop restaurants, the **16. Hotel Majestic.** From the seventh-floor indoor/outdoor rooftop restaurant, there's a wonderful view of the Zócalo. On a clear day you can even see the Ixta and Popo volcanoes. It's great to begin your Zócalo tour here, stop midday, or pay a late visit to the bar, which adjoins the restaurant where there's a live singer nightly. It's open 7:30am to 10:30pm.

Continue south on Monte de Piedad, with the Majestic Hotel on your right and the Zócalo on your left, to the next corner, 16 de Septiembre, and turn right a few steps to the:

17. **Gran Hotel Ciudad de México.** Originally a department store and later converted to a hotel, it is now operated by the Howard Johnson chain. It has one of the most splendid interiors of any downtown building. Step inside to see the lavish lobby, topped with its breathtaking Tiffany stained-glass canopy, and gilded open elevators on both sides. By the way, the birds are stuffed and their cheery chirps are electronic simulations.

Backtrack half a block east on 16 de Septiembre toward the Zócalo. Across Cinco de Febrero (Monte de Piedad) on the right are the:

18. **Arcades of the 16th-century Old Federal District Building and the New Federal District Building,** which dates from 1935 but looks like the older building. Both are on the south side of the Zócalo.

Continue east across the next street, Pino Suárez, with the National Palace on the left. On your right is the:

19. **Suprema Corte de Justicia** (Supreme Court of Justice), built in the mid-1930s. Inside, on the main staircase and its landings are José Clemente Orozco murals, following a theme of justice which he was given the liberty to interpret.

Some 2½ blocks farther south on Pino Suárez, on the left at the corner of República del Salvador, is the:

20. **Museum of the City of Mexico** (tel. 522-3640 or 542-8356). Before you enter, go to the corner of República del Salvador and look at the enormous stone serpent head, a corner support at the building's base. The stone was once part of an Aztec pyramid. Back at the entrance, a stone doorway opens to the courtyard of this mansion built in 1528 as the House of the Counts of Santiago de Calimaya. This classic old building was converted into the Museum of the City of Mexico in 1964 and should be visited by anyone interested in the country's past. Dealing solely with the Mexico Valley, where the first people arrived in 8000 B.C., there are some fine maps and pictographic presentations of the initial settlements, outlines of the social organization as it developed, and a huge mockup of Tenochtitlán, the city of the Aztecs. The conquest and destruction of Tenochtitlán by the Spaniards is wonderfully portrayed in a mural by Capdevila that appears to have been painted in fire.

After a brief inspection of the elegant old carriage in the courtyard and the little room behind it devoted to the history of transportation in Mexico City, ascend the broad stairs and turn right. The second-floor exhibits begin with a potpourri of beautiful religious paintings, then continue the story of the city's history up to the 1857 revolution. Among the tributes to Juárez and photos of the Villa/Zapata insurrection, there's a marvelously fierce and slightly cross-eyed painting of "the agrarian martyr," Emiliano Zapata, with so much artillery strapped to his chest that he could have won a good-size battle single-handedly.

Calmer, but no less interesting, are the photos and sketches of Mexico City in the present and the future. And on the third floor, you'll find the sun-drenched studio of Mexican impressionist Joaquin Clausell (1866–1935). The walls are completely covered with his fragmentary works, and two easel paintings still stand. It's open Tuesday through Sunday from 9:30am to 7:30pm; admission is free. Cater-corner from the museum, at the corner of Suárez and Salvador, is the:

21. **Chapel and Hospital of Jesús Nazareno,** founded by Hernán Cortés soon after the Conquest. A stone marker outside marks it as the spot where Cortés and Moctezuma reportedly met for the first time. Cortés died in Spain in 1547, but his remains are in a vault inside the chapel (entered by a side door on República del Salvador). Vaults on the opposite wall store the remains of Cortés's relatives. Notice the Orozco mural *The Apocalypse* on the choir ceiling. The chapel is

open Monday through Saturday from 7am to 8pm and on Sunday from 7am to 1pm and 5 to 8pm.

At the end of your tour here, the nearest Metro station is Pino Suárez or Zócalo (equal distance).

WALKING TOUR 2 — Near the Alameda

Start: The Alameda Central (Metro: Bellas Artes).
Finish: Museo de Artes a Industrís Populares.
Time: 1–2 days, depending on the time spent at each location.
Best Time: Saturday, when museums and shops are open, and around Christmas and Independence Day (Sept 15), when the area is festooned in holiday color.
Worst Time: Monday, when the museums are closed.

Today the lovely tree-filled Alameda Central is a magnet for pedestrians, cotton-candy vendors, lovers, organ grinders—everyone enjoying a daily repast in the park. Long ago the site of the Alameda was an Aztec marketplace. When the conquistadores took over in the mid-1500s, heretics were burned at the stake there under the Spanish Inquisition. In 1592 the governor of New Spain, Viceroy Luis de Velasco, converted it to a public park.

As you wander around the Alameda Central, you're bound to notice the:
1. **Juárez Monument,** sometimes called the Hemiciclo (hemicycle, half circle), facing Avenida Juárez. Enthroned as the hero he was, Juárez assumes his proper place here in the pantheon of Mexican patriots. Most of the other statuary in the park was done by European sculptors (mostly French) in the late 19th and early 20th centuries.

On the west side of the Alameda, along Avenida Juárez, where the old Hotel Regis once stood, is the:
2. **Jardín de la Solidaridad,** or Solidarity Garden, built in 1986 in remembrance of those who died during the terrible earthquake of 1985.

Opposite the southeastern edge of the Alameda at the corner of Juárez and Lázaro Cárdenas is:
3. **La Torre Latinoamericana,** or Latin American Tower (tel. 510-2545). See the fabulous views of the whole city and the route of your walking tour from the observation deck on the 42nd floor of this skyscraper soaring above the intersection of Juárez and Cárdenas. Buy a ticket for the deck (open daily from 9am to 11pm) at the booth as you approach the elevators—admission is $2.75 for adults, $2 for children. Tokens for the telescope up top are on sale here too. You then take an elevator to the 37th floor, cross the hall, and take another elevator to the 42nd floor. An employee will ask for your ticket as you get off.

The view is magnificent, with mountains surrounding the capital on all sides, but those to the north are the nearest and Avenida Lázaro Cárdenas seems to head straight for them. To the north just below is the white marble Bellas Artes, and west of it, the green patch of the Alameda. Due west is the Monument to the Revolution, just beyond the intersection of Juárez and Reforma. You can't see Reforma too well because it's hidden by the buildings that line it, but the green swath of Chapultepec Park and its palace on the hilltop are easy to spot. To the east is the Zócalo, dominated by the cathedral. To the south is an area densely packed with homes, factories, and tall apartment buildings.

From the front door of the tower, turn right to the corner and right (west) on Madero (the street name changes from Juárez) a block and a half past the Church of San Francisco to the magnificent:
4. **Palacio de Iturbide,** at Madero 17. This ornate stone palace with huge hand-carved wooden doors and a wildly baroque 40-foot-high carved-stone archway was built in the 1780s for the Marqués de Jaral de Berrio, but by 1821 belonged to Don Agustín de Iturbide, who later became the self-proclaimed Agustín I, Emperor of Mexico (1822–23). His reign lasted only a matter of

months, for although he was a partisan of Mexican independence, his political outlook was basically royalist and conservative. But the future of Mexico lay in the liberal social reforms advocated by the great revolutionaries Hidalgo and Morelos. Iturbide was exiled, and later, upon his unauthorized return, was executed in Padillo, Tamualipas, and buried there. Years later his contribution to Mexican independence was recognized and his body was reburied in the Metropolitan Cathedral (see "Walking Tour 1—The Zócalo"), where it remains today.

Banamex, the present owner of the building, restored the palace in 1972 and the result is beautiful. Enter a courtyard with three tiers of balconies: The ground floor is a banking office and has a temporary art exhibition area; the upper floors have executive offices. Period paintings and statues grace walls and corners, and the second-floor chapel has been beautifully restored. Banamex has a brief (but free) printed guide to the building; ask the guard for one and come in and have a look anytime Monday through Friday from 9am to 5pm.

While you're here you may want to stop in next door at the American Book Store or take a look at the exterior of the Casa Borda that belonged to the silver baron from Taxco, on the same side of the street at the corner of Madero and Allende, across from the bookstore.

Now cross the street to the opposite side of Madero and double-back on Madero toward the Alameda.

REFUELING STOP On the way back from the Iturbide Palace toward the Alameda, whether or not it's time for a break, you must stop in, however briefly, at a downtown institution: **5. The House of Tiles** ("Casa de Azulejos; tel. 510-9613). You can't miss it, all decked out in gorgeous blue-and-white tiles. One of Mexico City's most precious colonial gems and popular meeting places, the building dates from the end of the 1500s, when it was built for the Count of the Valley of Orizaba. The most popular story goes that during the count's defiant youth, his father proclaimed: "You will never build a house of tiles," a tiled house being a sign of success at the time—the father was sure his son would amount to nothing. So when success came, the young count covered his house in tiles, which are a fine example of Puebla craftspeople's work. Today the tile-covered house is a branch of Sanborn's restaurant-newsstand-gift-shop chain. You can stroll through to admire the interior and have a refreshing drink or a full meal. Pause to see the Orozco mural *Omniscience,* on the landing leading to the second floor (where the bathrooms are). It's open daily from 7am to 10pm.

Continuing back toward the Alameda, turn right at the next corner, the busy Avenida Lázaro Cárdenas, and cross it to the beautiful white marble:

6. Palacio de Bellas Artes (pronounced "*Bey*-ahs *Arr*-tess"), at the east end of the Alameda (tel. 512-1282 or 512-5676). The building is a supreme achievement of art deco lyricism. In addition to being the concert hall, it also houses permanent and traveling art shows.

The theater is very turn of the century, built during the Profiriato and covered in Italian Carrara marble on the outside, but completely 1930s art deco inside. It has sunk into the soft belly of Lake Texcoco some 12 feet since construction was begun in 1900 (it was opened in 1934). The palacio is the work of several masters: Italian architect Adam Boari, who made the original plans; Antonio Muñoz and Frederico Mariscal, who modified Boari's plans considerably; and Mexican painter Gerardo Murillo ("Doctor Atl"), who designed the fabulous art nouveau glass curtain which was constructed by Louis Comfort Tiffany in the Tiffany Studios of New York. Made from nearly a million iridescent pieces of colored glass, the glass curtain portrays the Valley of Mexico with its two great volcanoes. You can see the curtain before important performances at the theater, and on Sunday mornings.

On the third level are the famous murals by Rivera, Orozco, and Siqueiros. The controversial Rivera mural *Man in Control of His Universe* was commissioned in 1933 for Rockefeller Center in New York. He completed the work there

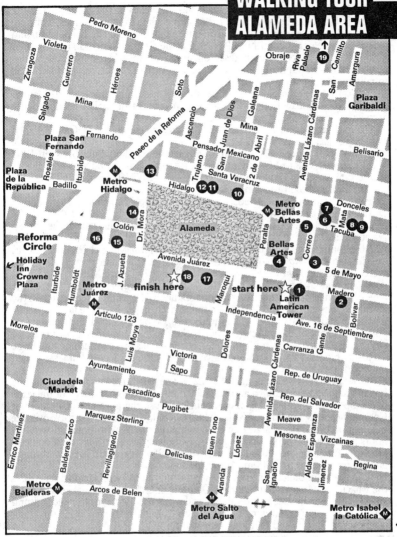

WALKING TOUR — ALAMEDA AREA

Obraje

Plaza Garibaldi

Belisario

Plaza San Fernando

Plaza de la República

Metro Hidalgo

Hidalgo

Metro Bellas Artes

Donceles

Reforma Circle

Alameda

Holiday Inn Crowne Plaza

Metro Juárez

Colón

Bellas Artes

Tacuba

Correo

5 de Mayo

finish here

start here

Latin American Tower

Madero

Avenida Juárez

Independencia

Ave. 16 de Septiembre

Artículo 123

Morelos

Carranza

Victoria

Sapo

Rep. de Uruguay

Ayuntamiento

Ciudadela Market

Pescaditos

Rep. del Salvador

Pugibet

Meave

Marquez Sterling

Mesones

Vizcainas

Delicias

Regina

Metro Balderas

Arcos de Belen

Metro Salto del Agua

Metro Isabel la Católica

Metro

1 Latin American Tower
2 Palacio de Iturbide/Casa Borda
3 House of Tiles
4 Palacio de Bellas Artes
5 Correo/Post Office
6 Plaza Tolsa del Caballito
7 Museo National de Arte and Palacio Minerias
8 La Mansion Restaurant
9 La Gran Torta Restaurant

10 Museo de la Estampa
11 Museo Franz Mayer
12 Cafeteria Franz Mayer
13 Hotel de Cortez
14 Pinoteca Vireynal de San Diego
15 Museo de la Alameda
16 Exposición de Arte Popular
17 Museo de Artes e Industrias Populares
18 Bammerette Restaurant

just as you see it: A giant vacuum sucks up the riches of the earth to feed the factories of callous, card-playing, hard-drinking white capitalist bullies, while the noble workers of the earth, of all races, rally behind the red flag of socialism and its standard-bearer, Lenin. Needless to say, the Rockefellers didn't enjoy their new purchase. Much to their discredit, however, they had it painted over— destroyed. Rivera duplicated the mural here as *Man at the Crossing of the Ways* to preserve it.

You can look around in the building Tuesday through Sunday from 10:30am to 6:30pm. For information on tickets to performances of the Ballet Folklorico, see Section 8, "Evening Entertainment," below.

Go back across Cárdenas. The huge building at the corner of Guardiola and Cárdenas is the:

7. Correos (post office). The beautiful white stone building, built between 1902 and 1907, was designed by Italian architect Adamo Boari, who also contributed to the Bellas Artes. The Museo Filatélico (tel. 521-7760 or 585-3677) on the second floor is closed for remodeling.

From the front of the Correo, go right (north) barely half a block to the corner of Tacuba and turn right again. On the left is the:

8. Plaza Tolsá and El Caballito, a huge equestrian statue in front of the Museo Nacional de Arte. The gallant statue of King Carlos IV of Spain (1788–1808) atop a high-stepping horse was crafted by Mexican sculptor Manuel Tolsá. Mexicans call the statue *El Caballito* ("The Little Horse"), and the name reveals a lot: They prefer not to mention Carlos, who was king shortly before Mexico's Independence movement from Spain began in 1810. The statue is actually one of the largest and most finely crafted equestrian statues in the world. Erected first in the Zócalo, it was later moved (1852) to a traffic circle in the Paseo de la Reforma. A few years ago *El Caballito* was moved to this more dignified and appropriate position in front of the museum opposite the handsome Palacio de Minería (see below), also designed by Tolsá and one of the capital's most handsome buildings.

Just behind the statue is the entrance to one of the city's best, but least-visited museums, the:

9. Museo Nacional de Arte (tel. 512-3224). The palacelike building, designed by Italian architect Silvio Contri and completed in 1911, another legacy of the years of Europe-loving Porfirio Díaz, was built to house the government's offices of Communications and Public Works. The National Museum of Art took over the building in 1982. Wander through the immense rooms with polished wooden floors as you view the wealth of paintings showing Mexico's art development, primarily covering the period from 1810 to 1950. It's open Tuesday through Sunday from 10am to 5:30pm. Admission is $2.75.

The beautiful building across the street from the Museo Nacional de Arte is the Palacio de Minería, built in the 1800s, one of architect Manuel Tolsá's finest works. Formerly the school of mining, today it's used for concerts and cultural events (see Section 8, "Evening Entertainment"). If it's open, step inside for a look at the several patios and fabulous stonework.

REFUELING STOP An indoor outdoor restaurant with colorful umbrellas, **10. La Mansion,** next to the museum (turn left out the front door), is a good place to recharge. It's open Monday through Saturday. Or try **11. La Gran Torta,** next door at Tacuba 10, for great fruit, juices, and inexpensive sandwiches. It's open daily from 7am to 10pm.

Stay on the same side of the block and from here backtrack west on Tacuba, crossing Cárdenas, and walk 1½ blocks. Opposite the north side of the Alameda near the corner of Hidalgo and Trujano is the:

12. Museo de la Estampa, Hidalgo 39 (tel. 521-2244), next door to the Museo Franz Mayer (see below). *Estampa* means engraving or printing, and the museum is devoted to understanding and preserving the graphic arts. Housed in a beautifully restored 16th-century building, the museum has permanent displays on the second floor and changing exhibits on the first floor. Displays include those from pre-Hispanic times when clay seals were used for designs on fabrics, ceramics, and other surfaces. But the most famous works there are probably those of José Guadalupe Posada, Mexico's famous printmaker, who poked fun at death and politicians through his skeleton figure drawings. If your interest in this subject is deep, ask to see the video programs on graphic techniques—woodcuts, lithography, etching, etc. It's open Tuesday through Sunday from 10am to 6pm. Admission is 75¢, free on Sunday.

From here, go right a few steps across the plaza to the entrance of the:

13. Museo Franz Mayer, Hidalgo 45 (tel. 518-2265), one of the capital's foremost museums, which opened in 1986 in a beautifully restored 16th-century building on Plaza de la Santa Veracruz. It's opposite the north side of the Alameda. The extraordinary 10,000-piece collection of antiquities, mostly from Mexico's 16th through 19th centuries, was amassed by one man, Franz Mayer. A German immigrant, he adopted Mexico in 1905 and grew up there. Before his death in 1975 Mayer bequeathed the collection to the country, and arranged for its permanent display through a trust with the Banco Nacional. The pieces, all utilitarian objects (as opposed to pure art objects), include inlaid and richly carved furniture, an enormous collection of Talavera pottery, gold and silver religious pieces, sculptures, tapestries, rare watches and clocks (the oldest is a 1680 lantern clock), wrought iron, old master paintings from Europe and Mexico, and 770 El Quijote volumes, many of which are rare editions or typographically unique. There's so much that it may take two visits to absorb it. Open Tuesday through Sunday from 10am to 5pm. Admission is $1.75 for adults, 35¢ for students, free for all on Sunday. There are guided tours every hour from 10:30am to 1:30pm.

REFUELING STOP If a break is in order at this point, try a light snack at the **14. Cafeteria of the Museo Franz Mayer,** at its marble-topped tables in a pleasant courtyard. It's open the same days and hours as the museum. Or take in another ancient religious structure. Continue one block farther west of the Franz Mayer on Hidalgo to the corner of Reforma and there you'll find the **15. Hotel de Cortés,** converted to a hotel from an 18th-century building that has been both an insane asylum and a hospice for Augustinian monks. Step inside the red tezontle stone edifice to the open courtyard dripping with pink bougainvillea and outfitted in umbrella-clad tables. The restaurant serves rather high-priced Mexican and international dishes. Drinks, however, are inexpensive. It's open daily from 7am to 10:30pm. (See Section 8, "Evening Entertainment," below, for details on the Friday-night Mexican Fiesta.)

From the Hotel de Cortés, cross Hidalgo toward the park and, just at the corner on your right, opposite the Alameda, passing the Centro Cultural José Martí, is the:

16. Pinoteca Virreynal de San Diego, Dr. Mora 7 (tel. 510-2793 or 512-2079). This former church is now a gallery of paintings, mostly from the 16th and 17th centuries, and mostly ecclesiastical in theme. Highlights are apparent immediately as you walk around: In the wing to the right of where the altar would have been is a room with a gorgeous blue-and-gilt ceiling with gleaming rosettes and a striking mural by Federico Cantu (1959), one of the few modern works. Upstairs in a cloister are many small paintings by Hipolito de Rioja (who worked in the second half of the 17th century), Baltazar de Echave Ibia (1610–40), and others. By the way, the tremendous painting on the cloister wall called *Glorificación de la Inmaculada,* by Francisco Antonio Vallejo (1756–83), should be viewed from upstairs—the lighting is better. The Pinoteca is open Tuesday through Sunday from 9am to 5pm; admission is 65¢.

Turn right out the front door, and right again on Colón, a short street facing the Plaza de la Solidaridad, to the entrance to the:

17. Museo de la Alameda (tel. 510-2329), housing Diego Rivera's famous mural *Dream of a Sunday Afternoon in Alameda Park,* which was painted on a wall of the Hotel del Prado in 1947. The hotel was demolished after the 1985 earthquake, but the precious mural, perhaps the best known of Rivera's works, was saved and transferred to its new location in 1986. The huge picture, 50 feet long and 13 feet high, chronicles the history of the park from the time of Cortés onward. Among the historical figures who have made their mark in the history of Mexico are these, portrayed more or less from left to right (but not in chronological order): Cortés; a heretic suffering under the Spanish Inquisition; Sor Juana Inez de la Cruz, a brilliant and progressive woman who became a nun to help those in need; Benito Juárez, putting forth the laws of Mexico's great Reforma; the conservative Gen. Antonio López de Santa Anna, handing the keys to Mexico to the invading American Gen. Winfield Scott; Emperor Maximilian and Empress Carlota; José Martí, the Cuban revolutionary; Death, with the plumed serpent (Quetzalcoatl) entwined about his neck; Gen. Porfirio Díaz, great with age and medals, asleep; a police officer keeping the Alameda free of "riffraff" by ordering a poor family out of the elitist's park; and Francisco Madero, the martyred democratic president who caused the downfall of Díaz, whose betrayal and alleged murder by Gen. Victoriano Huerta (pictured at the right) resulted in years of civil turmoil in Mexico. The museum is open Tuesday through Sunday from 10am to 6pm; admission is $1.75, free for those over age 60, free for all on Sunday.

Folk-art enthusiasts will delight in two excellent government-operated craft shops. For the first one, turn right out the front door of the Museo de la Alameda; at the corner, turn left one block, then right onto Reforma. On the right is the:

18. Exposición Nacional de Arte Popular, Juárez 89 (tel. 518-3058), described in more detail in Section 7, "Savvy Shopping." The ground floor of the 18th-century mansion is loaded with crafts from all over Mexico. It's open Monday through Saturday from 10am to 6pm.

Another, even-larger crafts shop is reached by crossing Reforma and turning left for 2½ blocks. On the right is the:

19. Museo de Artes e Industrías Populares, at Juárez 44 (tel. 521-6679). The building was once the Corpus Christi Convent, built during the 17th century. The upstairs museum portion (closed after the 1985 earthquake) has reopened and you can see it Tuesday through Friday from 9am to 6pm. The downstairs rooms are packed with good-quality regional crafts. The store is open Monday through Friday from 9am to 6pm and on Saturday and Sunday from 10am to 6pm.

A FINAL REFUELING STOP A good place to finish an Alameda tour is **20. Bamerette,** the rooftop restaurant of the Hotel Bamer, opposite the Hipociclo on the south side of the Alameda. There's a fantastic view of the Alameda, and if it's near lunchtime, there's usually a moderately priced comida corrida. It's open daily from 7:30am to 1am. On Friday and Saturday nights there's music beginning at 9pm.

WALKING TOUR 3 — Chapultepec Park

Start: Museum of Anthropology.
Finish: Museum of Natural History.
Time: 2–3 days.
Best Time: Early any weekday.
Worst Time: Monday, when the museums are closed, and Saturday and Sunday, when the park and museums are very crowded. (But the museums are free on Sunday and the zoo is open only Wednesday through Sunday from 9am to 4:45pm.)

Although this is a suggested walking tour, Chapultepec Park has become quite run-down and not the pleasant place it was in years past. So although you can get from place to place on foot, until there is a park renewal, the experience is less than it could be and I recommend that, where possible, you enter and leave the park from outside entrances, rather than walking through it.

CHAPULTEPEC PARK One of the biggest city parks in the world (551 acres), Chapultepec Park is more than a playground: Besides accommodating picnickers upon worn-away grass under centuries-old trees; canoes on the lake (now dirty); vendors of balloons, trinkets, and food; the park contains six museums, a zoo, a garden for senior citizens only, a miniature train, a children's playground, an auditorium, and Los Pinos, home of the president of Mexico. The museums are in great condition and worth the effort to see them.

Covering about 3 square miles, the park is so vast that you'll need some guidance on allotting time. The immensity of the park, plus such barriers as fences and the Periferico Highway, make it more time-consuming to get around on foot than one might suppose from a glance at the map and it's easy to lose your way. Your own interests will dictate how long a visit to Chapultepec Park might take, but here are some general time recommendations: the Museum of Anthropology, at least 4 hours; the Museum of Modern Art, 1½ hours; Chapultepec Castle (National History Museum) and Museo Caracol, 2 hours; the train and zoo, 1 hour; the Technological Museum, 1 hour; the Natural History Museum, 1½ hours. The map isn't to scale and is meant solely as a graphic representation of these areas.

Note: Bring a lunch or a snack; there are street vendors (with questionable food), but the restaurants at the National Anthropology Museum and the Technology Museum, and the expensive Restaurant Del Chapultepec, may be miles from where you are when you want them.

GETTING THERE By Bus Any Ruta 76 "Auditorio" or "Km. 13" bus up Reforma will drop you right outside the Museum of Anthropology, which is situated off the broad boulevard about half a mile past the Diana statue, opposite Chapultepec Park Zoo.

By Metro Line 1 of the Metro will take you to the "Chapultepec" station, outside the park. Line 7 will take you to "Auditorio," which is even closer.

By Car As you come down Reforma, at the foot of Chapultepec hill on the left you'll notice six marble shafts carved as stylized torches placed in a semicircle around a small plaza. This is the Monument to the Boy Heroes (Niños Héroes)—the six cadets who jumped to their death rather than surrender to the U.S. Marines who attacked the castle during the war with Mexico in 1847. Continue on Reforma, crossing Calzada Escobedo, and turn right into the park at the directional sign (second street on the right).

1. **National Museum of Anthropology** (tel. 553-6266), by general consent, is the finest museum of its kind in the world. It was built by architect Pedro Ramírez Vazquez and a team of worthy helpers in 1964—if Sr. Ramírez never did another thing, he'd still deserve the fame of centuries.

The museum, breathtaking in its splendor, with a massive patio half-sheltered by a tremendous stone umbrella designed by José Chávez Morado, will take at least 2 or 3 hours to look around even if you're a dedicated museum rusher. The museum is open Tuesday through Saturday from 9am to 7pm and on Sunday from 10am until 6pm. Admission costs $3.50, free on Sunday. Free tours are available on request (minimum of five people) in English, French, or Spanish Tuesday through Saturday from 10am to 5pm and on Sunday from 10am to 2pm.

There are three sections. First is the entrance hall to the museum proper with a check room and museum bookstore on the left. The bookstore has a superior collection of guidebooks to cultural, culinary, and archeological attractions in Mexico. A good book to buy is *The Mexican National Museum of Anthropology,* written by three museum curators and published by Panorama Books. The room-by-room background provides invaluable information for understanding the thousands of artifacts on display. It's especially useful if you don't read Spanish and don't take a guided tour in English.

Inside the museum proper is an open courtyard with beautifully designed spacious rooms running around three sides on two levels. The ground-floor rooms are theoretically the most significant, and they are the most popular among studious visitors, devoted as they are to history and prehistoric days all the way up to the most recently explored archeological sites. These rooms include dioramas of the way Mexico City looked when the Spaniards first arrived, and reproductions of part of a pyramid at Teotihuacán. The Aztec calendar stone "wheel" takes a proud place here.

Save some of your time and energy, though, for the livelier and more readily understandable ethnographic rooms upstairs. This portion is a "living museum," devoted to the way people throughout Mexico live today, complete with straw-covered huts, tape recordings of songs and dances, crafts, clothing, and lifelike models of village activities. To me, both floors are equally interesting, one dealing with the past and the other dealing with the living past so to speak, because so much Mexican village life retains vestiges of pre-Hispanic customs.

There is a lovely restaurant in the museum with moderate prices, air conditioning, and cheerful patio tables.

After you pass by the ticket taker into the courtyard, here are the museum's highlights, room (sala) by room, beginning on your right:

Sala 1, "Introducción a la Antropología": The entrance mural by Z. González Camarena depicts women of various nations. Exhibits deal with the various races of humanity throughout the world, their progress and development, and how these aspects are studied by anthropologists.

Sala 2, "Mesoamerica": Here you see the cultural interrelation of the Mesoamerican people even though they are dispersed over a large landscape, demonstrated by a large color map showing locations of the great cultures. A timeline puts them in perspective. A mural in the Mesoamerican room, by Raul Anguiano, shows the Maya cosmogony: 13 heavens are held up by a giant ceiba tree; nine hells are beneath. The mural is directly above an exhibit of burial customs.

The next sign you'll see, SALAS DE ETNOGRAFA EN LA PLANTA ALTA, means "Ethnographic Rooms on the Upper Floor." There's a stairway here so you can reach those rooms. But for now, continue around the right side of the courtyard on the main level to:

Sala 3, "Sala Origenes": This "Room of Origins" traces the history of the earliest men and women in the Americas, with specific emphasis on their remains in Mexico. Don't miss the enormous fossilized vertebra believed to be at least 10,000 years old (probably of a type of camel) and carved into the head of an animal.

Sala 4, "Salas Preclasica y Teotihuacana": Exhibits here are of Preclassic times (2000 B.C. to A.D. 300), just before the Mesoamerican cultures reached their zenith. Religion, agriculture, hieroglyphic writing, numbering, and art were in place. Among the early pottery pieces are those of the Olmecs and of Tlatilco (known for its appliqué technique, using clay pieces for figure decoration), many formed in the shape of animals, birds, frogs, and squash. Among the most interesting displays are clay figures that effectively show the appearance of people in those times.

Sala 5, "Teotihuacán": First view the model of this important site, which flourished just outside Mexico City between 100 B.C. and A.D. 700. This room is great preparation before seeing the ruins in person—something you must do. Chronologically displayed pottery gives a clear picture of the development of this utilitarian art at Teotihuacán. Other exhibits show tools for building, sculptures, fresco painting, jewelry making, and weaving. There's a reproduction of the mural *Paradise of the God Tlaloc* and visitors are dwarfed beside the life-size replica of a portion of the temple of Quetzalcoatl.

Sala 6, "Tolteca": Toltec, Chichimec, and Cholulan cultures are preserved

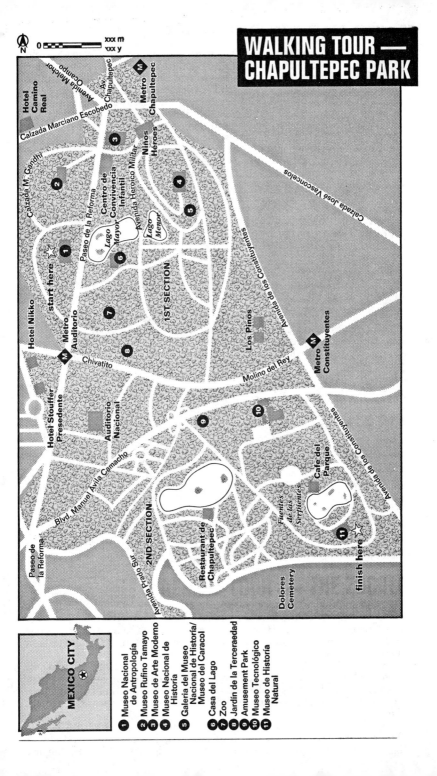

here, but the exhibit begins with Xochicalco, a site between Cuernavaca and Taxco that was both a crossroads of many cultures and perhaps a bridge culture between Teotihuacán and the development of the Toltecs at Tula, north of Mexico City. Xochicalco buildings and pottery show a cross-cultural mix with the Maya, Teotihuacán, and the Toltecs. One of the huge Atlantean-men statues from the Temple of Tlahuizcalpantecutli, at Tula, is in the hall, as well as other great monoliths and pottery. At one end of the room is a model of the pyramid site at Cholula, by volume the largest pyramid in the world, showing its three superimpositions (buildings one on top of another). Cholulan pottery was especially accomplished, so don't miss the displays of it here.

Sala 7, "Mexica": At the far end of the courtyard, lettering on the lintel reads CEM ANAHUAC TENOCHCA TLALPAN, and beneath it is the entrance to one of the most important rooms in the museum. This room is an excellent one to see before visiting the Templo Mayor site and museum near the Zócalo in the historical zone of Mexico City. Among the amazing carved stones are: the Aztec Calendar Stone, which bears symbols for all the ages of humankind (as the Aztecs saw them); the Piedra de Tizoc; Xiuhcoatl, the fire serpent; a Tzompantli, or wall of skulls; the terrifying headless monolith of Coatlicue, goddess of earth and death, with two serpents' heads coming from her neck, a necklace of hands and hearts, and a skirt of serpents; and the stone head of the moon goddess, Coyolxauhqui, with bells on her cheeks, sun disks in her earlobes, and a nose ring.

Amid all this ominous dark volcanic rock, the iridescent feathered headdress of Moctezuma blazes away, as impressive today (a copy) as when the Aztec emperor proceeded regally through the streets of Tenochtitlán. Near the glass case holding the headdress is a large model of Moctezuma's rich capital city; a mural echoes the city's grandeur as well. One of my favorite displays is the enormous diorama of the thriving market at Tlatelolco, which brings to life the description of it by Bernal Díaz de Castillo. (The remains of Tlatelolco are north of the Zócalo in the Plaza of Three Cultures.)

Sala 8, "Oaxaca": After the Mexico room comes that of Oaxaca, with its Zapotec and Mixtec cultures, Olmec influences, and priceless artifacts from the Monte Alban excavations. The huge display of pottery is arranged chronologically to show its evolution, and a deerskin Mixtec codice exemplifies picture writing. The Mixtecs were accomplished metalworkers, gemsmiths, and wood carvers, and you'll see fine examples of their work. Take time to admire the reproduction of Tomb no. 105 from Monte Alban. Go down the stairs to a reproduction of Tomb no. 104, complete with wall frescos and burial figure surrounded by offerings.

Sala 9, "Golfo de Mexico": Divided into four sections, this hall covers the rich cultures of the Huastecas from the northern part of Veracruz and Tamaulipas; the Remojadas and Tononacs, who occupied the middle portion of the region; and the Olmecs of southern Veracruz and northern Tabasco, but whose influence was felt far away. Certainly the most visible highlight here is an enormous multiton, basaltic rock head, but one of the finest is the graceful and beautifully sculpted "wrestler," both by Olmec master stone carvers. The Huastecas were known for their exquisite polychromed pottery with anthropomorphic and zoomorphic forms, and the pottery display does justice to the culture. But the tall, slender stone carved figure of the "Huasteca Adolescent," with a baby on its back, is one of Mesoamerica's most graceful. There are models of the archeological sites at El Tajín, near Papantla, and Zempoala, near the city of Veracruz.

Sala 10, "Maya": Don't miss this room! Not only are the exhibits here wonderful, but Maya art and culture itself has tremendous intrinsic interest. Displays here include a fine collection of well-preserved beautiful Maya carvings, not just from Mexican territory, but from other parts of Mesoamerica (Central America) as well.

Models of ancient cities include Copan (Honduras), Yaxchilan (Chiapas), Tulum (Quintana Roo), and Uaxactun (Guatemala). Downstairs is a model of the fabulous tomb discovered in the Temple of the Inscriptions at Palenque, complete

WALKING TOUR — MUSEO NACIONAL DE ANTROPOLOGIA

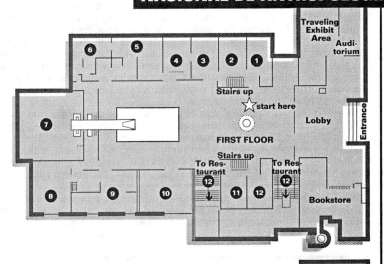

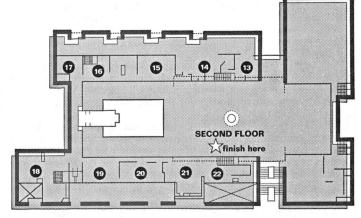

FIRST FLOOR:

1. Introduction to Anthropology
2. Mesoamerica
3. Origins
4. Preclassic and Teotihuacan
5. Teotihuacan
6. Toltec
7. Mexica
8. Oaxaca
9. Gulf of Mexico
10. Maya
11. North and West/Desert Cultures and Valley of Mexico

12. Museum Cafeteria

SECOND FLOOR:

13. Introduction to Ethnography
14. Cora and Huichol Cultures
15. Tarascan Culture
16. Otomi Culture
17. Sierras of Northern Puebla
18. Oaxaca
19. Gulf Coast
20. Maya
21. Northwest Mexico
22. Modern Mexico

with a rich jade mask for the deceased monarch. Outside the exhibit room is a full-scale replica of a temple at Hochob (Campeche), and another of the Temple of Paintings at Bonampak, plus replicas of stele from Quirigua (Guatemala). In all these examples, notice especially the fineness of the carving. In the Tablero de la Cruz Enramada, from Palenque, note the fine work in the glyphs.

Sala 11, "Norte y Occidente": This room deals with the "culture of the desert" from northern Mexico. If you're familiar with the culture of the Native Americans of the southwestern United States, you'll notice many similarities here. Many of the artifacts are from the Casas Grandes pueblo in the state of Chihuahua, where the people lived in adobe pueblos and made pottery very much like that of New Mexico and Arizona.

The occidental (western) exhibits hold echoes of the great civilization of the Valley of Mexico, mostly from sites such as Tzintzuntzan (Michoacán), Ixtlan (Nayarit), Ixtepete (Jalisco), and Chupicuaro (Guanajuato). The Chac-Mool from Ihuatzio, for instance, looks like a bad copy, or a stylized rendering, of the great Chac-Mools of Tula and Chichén-Itzá. There's also a model of a *yacata,* or vast stepped ceremonial platform, as found at many sites in the western zone.

REFUELING STOP   After the Maya room, descend a wide staircase to reach the **2. Cafetería Museo.** No liquor is served, but you can order soft drinks, breakfast, soup and salad, or a sandwich, or more substantial main courses. It's open Tuesday through Saturday from 9am to 7pm and on Sunday from 9am to 6pm.

From here, cross the patio to the stairs leading up to the splendid displays of daily life in the ethnographic section. Begin in the first room on the right:

Sala 13, "Introductoría": Murals, maps, photographs textiles, jewelry, and other objects give perspective on Mexico's daily life from pre-Hispanic times to the present.

Sala 14, "Cora y Huichol": Devoted to inhabitants of the west-coast states of Nayarit and Jalisco, this room displays lifelike figures, clad in traditionally embroidered clothing seated on equipale stools before an authentic indigenous hut. Particularly note the pottery and *morales* (woven bags), all of which are in use in villages today.

Sala 15, "Tarasca": Tarascans live in the state of Michoacán and carry on crafts learned centuries ago under the influence of the first bishop of Pátzcuaro, Vasco de Quiroga. You'll see examples of guitars from Paracho, copper objects from Santa Clara del Cobre, and samples of the fine dinnerware from potters around Lake Pátzcuaro. Note the exquisite black-and-white reversable serape trimmed with stylized designs of quetzal birds and produced by weavers from Angahuan, a village near the Paricutín volcano.

Sala 16, "Otomi": Otomi Indians, who speak several languages within the Otomangue language group, live in the states of Hidalgo, Mexico (which almost surrounds Mexico City), San Luis Potosí, and Querétaro. Here you see figures weaving ixtle fibers of the maguey plant. There are cases of products made for everyday use and trade, such as baskets, belts, jars, blouses, and serapes.

Sala 17, "Sierra Norte de Puebla": The northern part of the state of Puebla is one of the country's most interesting areas, yet it's little visited by tourists. Note the villagers of San Pablito pounding bark into paper, the unfinished pink and black quechquemitl on an unusual loom that rounds corners, and the finely embroidered blouses with flower and animal designs.

Sala 18, "Oaxaca": The southern state of Oaxaca is one of the most interesting in the country, due in part to the numerous varieties of colorful *huipiles* (loose garments) worn by women from different indigenous groups.

Sala 19, "Costa Golfo": This region is comprised of indigeonous groups of Huastecas, Totonacas, and Nahuas. The Huasteca Indians speak a language related to Maya. Inside a hut, women wearing embroidered blouses and ribbons twisted through their braided hair are surrounded by pottery and frozen in the motion of decorating and forming clay by hand.

Sala 20, "Maya": The land of the Maya comprises the states of Tabasco, Chiapas, Yucatán, Campeche, and Quintana Roo. Of these, the most colorful in the country is Chiapas. A market scene from the Chiapas highlands shows men and women in regional attire—heavy wool tunics and colorful loomed and richly brocaded huipiles. In another scene, a woman weaves henequen fiber on a waist loom.

Sala 21, "Noroeste de Mexico": Seri, Tarahumara, and Yaqui Indians live in northwestern Mexico in the states of Sonora, Chihuahua, and Sinaloa, and in Baja California. Among the unusual items, you'll see how the Seri women paint their faces and the fine baskets they weave, which are quite similar to some in the southwestern United States.

Sala 22, "Moderno": In the last room you'll see modern Mexico in motion, blending and molding centuries of culture into a modern one. It ends with a selection of folk art from around the country.

Two tremendous museums in one day would be too much for most people, so you may want to begin a second day at the:

3. Rufino Tamayo Museum (tel. 286-6599 or 286-3572). Turn right off Reforma just after crossing Calzada Escobedo. Oaxaca-born painter Rufino Tamayo not only contributed a great deal to modern Mexican painting, but over the years the artist collected pre-Hispanic, Mexican, and foreign works of art, among them pieces by de Kooning, Warhol, Dalí, and Magritte. The boldly modern museum is the perfect place to display these marvelous and attractive collections. Tamayo's pre-Hispanic collection is in a separate museum in the city of Oaxaca. Here in Mexico City you can see his paintings and his collection of the works of others, unless they are temporarily displaced by a special exhibit. If you see one advertised (in *The News,* for instance), don't miss it, for it's sure to be excellent. The museum is usually open Tuesday through Sunday from 10am to 6pm. Admission is $2.75, free on Sunday.

Doubling back across Reforma, on your left is the:

4. Museum of Modern Art (tel. 553-6233). It's actually in two buildings, set together in a statue-dotted section of grassy park, with two entrances: one on Reforma, the other across from (sort of behind) the Niños Héroes monument. The museum's interior is the perfect vehicle for showing works of art: simple, with handsome parquet floors, marble-and-stone walls, wood-slatted ceiling, and circular windows (always covered by heavy drapes, presumably so the pictures don't get bleached by the sun).

The section at the Reforma entrance has four salons, two on each level, around a central dome of incredible acoustic properties. The salons are attractive in their spaciousness, and give you the nice feeling that you're the only person in the museum. Exhibits in Salons I, II, and III are temporary, and have featured both Mexican and foreign artists including such greats as Magritte, Delvaux, Antonia Guerrero, Bissier, and Nay. Salon IV houses a permanent collection of contemporary art, most of which are by Latin American artists. In the circular rooms across the garden, near the Niños Héroes entrance to the museum, are more temporary exhibits.

The museum is open Tuesday through Sunday from 10am to 5:30pm. Admission costs $3.50, free on Sunday.

Note: The permanent collection of works by Mexican artists that used to be here has been moved to the Museo de Arte Carrillo Gil, in San Angel (see the next walking tour for details). This exceptionally fine collection encompasses works by Rivera, Kahlo, O'Gorman, Siqueiros, Tamayo, Mérida, Orozco, Gerszo, Romero, and others, and deserves a visit by all devotees of modern Mexican painting.

From the Modern Art Museum go left farther into the park and walk straight ahead to the fork and turn right on the Gran Avenida (it goes all around the hill). At the next opportunity, turn left to begin your ascent to:

5. Chapultepec Castle/National Museum of History (tel. 553-6202 or 553-6265). You can walk up the hill from here by following the right fork at the small castlelike gatehouse. The site of Chapultepec Castle had been a fortress since the days of the Aztecs and the present palace was not built until the 1780s.

At the time of the U.S. invasion in 1847 it was in use as a military college, which is how it came about that Mexican army youths, including the unlucky sextet, were defending it.

The castle offers a beautiful view of Mexico City. It's reported that in the days of the French occupation, during the 1860s, Carlotta could sit up in bed and watch her husband Maximilian proceeding down Reforma on his way to work. Carlotta, incidentally, designed the lovely garden surrounding the palace.

Until 1939 this was the official home of Mexico's presidents, and today it houses the National Museum of History, which covers the period between the Conquest in 1521 to the end of the Mexican Revolution in 1917, housing large paintings and statues of Spanish leaders and murals by Orozco, Siqueiros, O'Gorman, and others. On the second floor are rooms displaying jewelry, colonial art objects, and impressive malachite vases. There's even a bust of Cortés, one of the few tangible recognitions of his existence in Mexico. It's an intriguing place through which to stroll, from the elaborate furnishings brought over from Europe by Maximilian and Carlotta, to the patios and fountains and the panorama of the city spread out below. It's open Tuesday through Sunday from 9am to 5pm, but the last ticket is sold at 4pm. Admission is $3.50, free on Sunday. (*Note:* Hold onto the ticket the entire time you're on the hill—you may be asked to show it.)

On your way up the hill, about 200 yards below the castle, you probably noticed the circular glass building that spirals down the hillside. This is the:

6. Galería de la Museo Nacional de Historia, also known as the Museo Caracol (Snail Museum) because of its spiral shape, and as the Museo de la Lucha del Pueblo Mexicano por su Libertad (Museum of the Fight of the Mexican People for Their Liberty) because of its content. It's a condensed chronological history of Mexico for the years 1800 to 1917, complete with portraits, reproductions of documents, and dramatic montages—in three dimensions—of famous scenes from Mexico's past. The more recent years are also represented, with large photographic blowups, and some of the scenes, such as the execution of Maximilian, are staged with a great sense of drama and imagination. The entrance begins with the earliest years and spirals down the hill and through the years showing Mexico's growth toward independence. In many ways it's better presented and more interesting than the National Museum of History on the hill above. It's open Tuesday through Sunday from 10am to 5pm. Admission is free.

From the exit of the Museo Caracol, bear back right to the entrance where you started the ascent to the hill (Gran Avenida), then turn left for some distance, passing the first street (where you see a smelly lake) and taking the next one (past the lake). Turn right, continuing to the:

7. Casa del Lago (you're on the west side of the lake). Originally built as a restaurant, it now houses changing exhibits of local artists from the various art schools in and around Mexico City. Most of the art is for sale. Nearby is the Galería del Bosque, with similar exhibits. It's open Wednesday through Sunday from 11am to 5pm. Admission is free for both galleries.

Continue walking north and on the left you'll come to the:

8. Zoo. It's open Wednesday through Sunday and admission is free. A good way to see the animals without much effort is to join the line of kids waiting to ride the miniature railway, from the train station in the middle of the zoo. For a small fee, you can ride in comfort around the whole zoo, catching tantalizing glimpses of monkeys, hippos, herons, polar bears, zebras, and most of the other creatures. To find the famed Russian pandas, take the main zoo walkway and go right at the main circle. The pandas are behind glass, just past the caged panthers.

To the left of the zoo is the:

9. Jardín de la Tercera Edad (formerly the Jardín Botanico). This section of Chapultepec has been fenced off and is for senior citizens age 55 and older only! The name means Garden of the Third Age, and it's a basic park with benches, but without many vestiges of a botanic garden. On Sunday there's music for dancing around an open-air dance floor between 10am and 2pm. It's open daily from 7am to 5pm—be prepared to prove you're old enough to get in.

To continue from here to the Amusement Park, Museo Tecnologico, and Museo de Historia Natural, exit the main zoo entrance on Reforma and turn left. Walk along Reforma, taking the first possible left (only a few yards from the exit) onto Chivatito. You will actually have made a sort of U-turn and will have crossed over a newly constructed main artery which goes under Reforma from Constituyentes.

Follow Chivatito, bear right and turn left back into the park to the:

10. Amusement Park. This area, complete with roller coaster (named the "Montana Rusa," or Russian Mountain) and ferris wheel, is in New Chapultepec Park—the area at the far western end. Admission costs 10¢ and includes all rides except the roller coaster, which costs 50¢. It's open on Wednesday and Thursday from 11am to 5pm and on Saturday and Sunday from 10:30am to 7pm. You'll have to assess the quality of these rides, some of which seem poorly maintained. There's another amusement park for small children to the left of the Technological Museum; admission and hours are the same. (If you're coming straight from downtown, you can take bus no. 30 along Servando Teresa de Mier, Río de la Loza, and Avenida Chapultepec to Avenida Constituyentes. Get off at the Natural History Museum, and it's a 15-minute walk to the concessions. By Metro, get off at the Constituyentes station.)

The two large buildings to the right of the Amusement Park are the:

11. Technological Museum (tel. 516-0964 or 516-0965). The polyhedral dome outside is the Planetarium, which has scheduled shows at 10am, noon, and 2pm daily. The museum is educational, to say the least. It's always filled with students madly taking notes on scientific developments through the ages. Inside and outside there are trains and planes, mockup factories, experiments of Morse and Edison, and various energy exhibits. When you're thoroughly exhausted, head for the basement, wherein is a cafeteria for food or *refrescos*. The museum is open Tuesday through Saturday from 9am to 4:45pm and on Sunday from 9am to 1:45pm. Entrance is free.

From the Technological Museum, go left toward Avenida Constituyentes, but bear right when the path turns and follow it all the way to a large bend that bears right to the:

12. Museum of Natural History (tel. 516-2848 or 515-6304). It's made up of a series of 10 interconnecting domes which from a distance look like brightly colored inverted bowls surrounded by foliage and flowers. Inside the museum you'll see stuffed and preserved animals and birds, tableaux of such different environments as desert, seashore, tropical forest, and arctic tundra, with the appropriate wildlife (the large display cases of arctic bears and moose have pushbutton lighting on the left). Other domes contain exhibits relating to geology, astronomy, biology, the origin of life, and such displays as a relief map of the world's mountains and an illuminated map of Mexico showing the origin of various minerals.

The museum, fascinating for anyone with the slightest curiosity about nature—and totally absorbing for youngsters—is open Tuesday through Sunday from 10am to 5pm. Admission is 10¢.

Just outside the museum and to the left is the Ferrocarril, a rubber-wheeled train, on which for a few pesos you can ride for 10 minutes around the area.

If you're returning to the downtown area, catch any no. 30 bus outside the museum. Or if you want to get here via Metro, take it to "Chapultepec" and enter the park from Avenida Constituyentes.

WALKING TOUR 4 — San Angel

Start: Museo Colonial del Carmen.
Finish: San Angel Inn.
Time: 3–6 hours.
Best Time: Saturday, to visit the Bazar Sábado.

Worst Time: Monday, when the museums are closed.

San Angel is a fashionable suburb of cobblestone streets, with several worthwhile museums. The nearest Metro station is M. A. Quevedo. From downtown, take a colectivo ("San Angel") or bus no. 17 ("Indios Verdes–Tlalpan") or 17-B ("Central Norte–Villa Olimpica") south along Insurgentes near the Zona Rosa. The colectivo will terminate at the intersection of Insurgentes and Avenida La Paz; as for the bus, ask to get off at La Paz. There's a pretty park here, to the east, and on the west side of Insurgentes is a Sanborn's store and restaurant, good for a quick, moderately priced lunch.

Walk west, up the hill on La Paz, and in a block you'll come to Avenida de la Revolución. To the left (south) is the dark colonial stone bulk of the:

1. **Museo Colonial del Carmen,** Avenida de la Revolución 4 (tel. 548-9849 or 548-2838). This former Carmelite convent, now filled with religious paintings and other ancient artifacts, also keeps a batch of mummified nuns in glass cases in the cellar. The museum, a maze of interlocking halls, corridors, stairways, chapels, and pretty flower-filled patios, is very pleasant to look around. It's open Tuesday through Sunday from 10am to 4:45pm and admission is free.

From the del Carmen follow Revolución to the right (north) three long blocks to the:

2. **Museo de Arte Alvar y Carmen T. Carrillo Gil** Revolución 1608, at the corner of Desierto de los Leones (tel. 548-7467). Sometimes called the Museo de la Esquina (Museum on the Corner) since it's at a major intersection on Avenida de la Revolución, this modern gallery's collection includes rooms dedicated to the works of José Clemente Orozco (1883–1942), Diego Rivera (1886–1957), David Alfaro Siqueiros (1896–1974), and a variety of Mexican painters. It's open Tuesday through Sunday from 9:30am to 6pm. Admission is free.

From the Gil museum, head up the hill through Plaza del Carmen on Calle Dr. Calvez to the:

3. **Plaza San Jacinto.** On Saturday it's filled with artists and their paintings. Many of the old buildings surrounding Plaza San Jacinto have fine courtyards where crafts are sold. While you're there, look for the plaque honoring the St. Patrick's Battalion. When the U.S. invaded Mexico in 1846 this group of Irish Catholic immigrants was persuaded to take the Mexican cause by a Mexican Catholic priest. So they deserted U.S. Gen. Zachary Taylor and joined the Mexicans in the war with Mexico. Some of them were executed on Plaza San Jacinto as traitors—they are considered heros in Mexico.

Up the street and to the right is the:

4. **Bazar Sábado** (Saturday Bazaar). Two stories of shops are jammed into this beautiful colonial building. But this isn't just another curio market—rather, the ordinary is mingled with the extraordinary. Some of Mexico's best designers have shops here, or started out here, so there's ample opportunity to find just the right decorative object, along with crafts and textiles. The crowds inside can be incredible, especially if it's a holiday weekend, but be sure to take a turn through the building, whether or not you intend to buy.

Outside, off to one side, is another area where you're just as likely to see Zapotec Indians from Oaxaca weaving huipiles, or vendors selling masks and wooden fish from the state of Guerrero, as you are to see a contemporary artist with an easel. Prices are fixed inside the bazaar, but out here feel free haggle.

REFUELING STOP   The **5. Sanborn's** on Insurgentes (mentioned above) is a good bet. You can also have the buffet in the courtyard of the **Bazar Sábado** for about $12.

From the front door of the Bazar, turn right and right again at the corner. Cross Amargura, jog left and then right at the next corner, and walk to Avenida Altavista. Turn left and walk four long blocks to the:

6. **Museo Estudio Diego Rivera,** at the corner of Calle Diego Rivera and Avenida

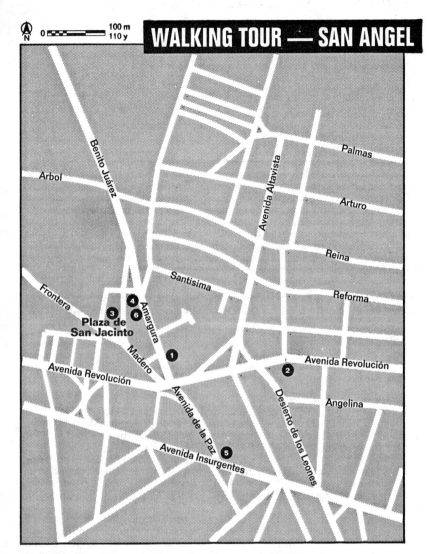

100 m
0
110 y

MEXICO CITY
San Angel
Area

1 Museo Colonial del Carmen
2 Museo de Arte Gil
3 Plaza San Jacinto
4 Bazar Sábado
5 Sanborns
6 Restaurant Bazar Sábado
7 Museo Estudio Diego Rivera
8 Restaurant San Miguel Inn

Altavista (tel. 677-2873). It was here, in the studio designed and built by Juan O'Gorman in 1928, that Rivera drew sketches for his wonderful murals and painted smaller works. He died here in 1957. Now a museum, the Rivera studio holds some of the artist's personal effects and mementos, and there are changing exhibits relating to his life and work. Visiting hours are Tuesday through Sunday from 10am to 6pm; admission is free. (Don't confuse Rivera's studio with his museum, the Anahuacalli, which is in San Pablo Tepetlapan, a different section south of the suburb of Coyoacán.)

Across the street to the right is:

A FINAL REFUELING STOP   Whether or not it's break time, don't leave the area without at least looking around the: **7. San Angel Inn,** at the corner of Palmas and Altavista (tel. 548-6707). This famous colonial hacienda landmark is now one of the city's most fashionable places to dine. It has had many uses, among them a cattle hacienda, later the home of Fanny Calderon de la Barca, and a stint as quarters for Santa Anna's troops. You can order a drink under the portals facing the inn's plant-filled courtyard, or dine inside in the plush dining rooms. The full luncheon will run $15 to $20, but many items are much less.

WALKING TOUR 5 — Coyoacán

Start: National Museum of Popular Cultures.
Finish: National Museum of Interventions.
Time: Half a day.
Best Time: Tuesday through Sunday, when the museums are open.
Worst Time: Monday, when the museums are closed.

Coyoacán is a pretty, and wealthy, suburb with many old houses and cobbled streets dating from the 16th century. At the center are two large, graceful plazas, Plaza Hidalgo and Jardín Centenario, and the Church of San Juan Bautista (1583). Once the capital of the Tepanec kingdom, Coyoacán was later conquered by the Aztecs, then by Cortés. The great conquistador even had a palace here for a while.

From downtown, the Metro, Line 3, can take you to the Coyoacán or Viveros Metro station, within walking distance of Coyoacán's museums. Or bus no. 23 or 23-A ("Iztacala-Coyoacán") will get you from the center to this suburb. Catch the no. 23 going south on Bucareli, or the no. 23-A on Miguel Schultz, Antonio Caso, Río Rhin, or Niza.

Coming from San Angel, catch a no. 56 bus ("Alcantarilla–Col. Agrarista") heading east along the Camino al Desierto de los Leones or Avenida Altavista, near the San Angel Inn. Get off when the bus gets to the corner of Avenida México and Xicotencatl in Coyoacán. Or, simpler, quicker, and easier, take a cab for the 15-minute ride. Sosa, a pretty street, is the main artery into Coyoacán from San Angel.

1. National Museum of Popular Cultures, Hidalgo 289 (tel. 554-3800 or 554-8882), truly a living museum, displays contemporary Mexican rural life within the context of communities throughout the country. Housed in a beautiful old mansion, each exhibition is displayed for about 6 months and is then returned to the community or people whose work was used. Thus each time you go will be a different experience, often with a performance or some other significant activity that complements the display. Call the museum or consult the English-language newspaper *The News* for what's current. Open Tuesday and Thursday from 10am to 4pm, on Wednesday, Friday, and Saturday from 10am to 8pm, and on Sunday from 11am to 5pm. Admission is free.

REFUELING STOP   Coyoacán's beautiful central Plaza Hidalgo, surrounded by sienna-colored colonial buildings, invites lingering. Numerous restaurants are in

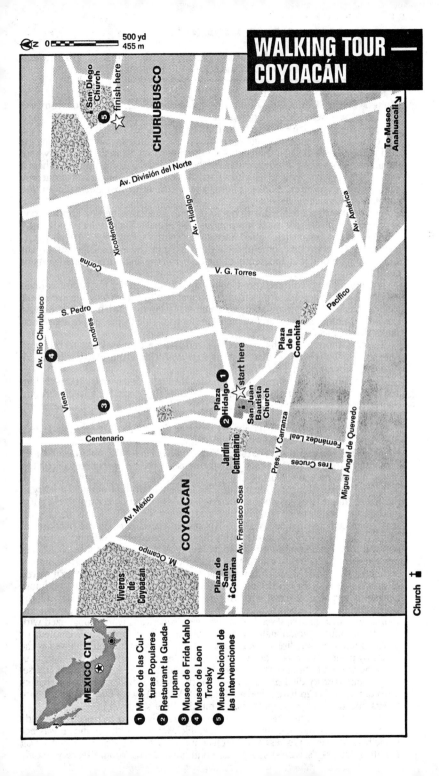

WALKING TOUR —
COYOACÁN

500 yd
0
455 m

† San Diego Church

⑤ finish here

CHURUBUSCO

Av. División del Norte

Av. Hidalgo

Xicoténcatl

Corina

V. G. Torres

Pacífico

S. Pedro

Plaza de la Conchita

Av. Rio Churubusco

Londres

④

① start here

Viena

③

Plaza Hidalgo

San Juan Bautista Church

Pres. V. Carranza

Tres Cruces

Fernández Leal

Miguel Angel de Quevedo

Av. América

To Museo Anahuacalli ↗

Centenario

②

Jardín Centenario

COYOACAN

Av. México

Av. Francisco Sosa

M. Ocampo

Viveros de Coyoacán

Plaza de Santa Catarina †

Church †■

MEXICO CITY

① Museo de las Cul-
turas Populares
② Restaurant la Guada-
lupana
③ Museo de Frida Kahlo
④ Museo de Leon
Trotsky
⑤ Museo Nacional de
las Intervenciones

the area, among them: **2. La Guadalupana,** at the corner of Higuera and Caballocalco, which is good for a snack or a full-length meal.

Six very long blocks north on Allende is the:
3. Museo Frida Kahlo, at Londres 247 (tel. 554-5999), 10 blocks from the Coyoacán or Viveros Metro station. Frida was born here on July 7, 1910, and occupied the house with Rivera from 1929 to 1954. The house is basically as she left it, and as you wander through the rooms you'll get an overwhelming feeling for the life that they led. Their mementos are in every room, from the kitchen, where the names Diego and Frida are written on the walls, to the studio upstairs, where a wheelchair sits next to the easel with a partially completed painting surrounded by paint brushes, palettes, books, photographs, and other paraphernalia of the couple's art-centered lives.

The bookshelves are filled with books in many languages, nestled against a few of Rivera's files bearing such inscriptions as "Protest Rockefeller Vandalism," "Amigos Diego Personales," and "Varios Interesantes y Curiosos." Frida's paintings hang in every room, some of them dominated by the exposed human organs and dripping blood that apparently obsessed her in the final surgery-filled years of her life.

Frida and Diego collected pre-Columbian art, so many of the rooms contain jewelry and terra-cotta figurines from Teotihuacán and Tlatelolco. She even went to the extreme of having a mockup of a temple built in the garden where she could exhibit her numerous pots and statues. On the back side of the temple are several skulls from Chichén-Itzá.

To learn more about the lives of this remarkable couple, I can recommend Bertram D. Wolfe's *Diego Rivera: His Life and Times* and Hayden Herrara's *Frida: A Biography of Frida Kahlo.*

Technically, the museum is open Tuesday through Sunday from 10am to 2pm and 3 to 6pm, but the caretaker has his own idea of the hours. He's usually around even if the door is closed, so keep knocking. Admission is free. No cameras are allowed.

From the Frida Kahlo, turn right out the front door, then right on Allende, two blocks to Viena; turn right and walk 2½ blocks and on the left is the:
4. House and Museum of Trotsky, Viena 45 (tel. 554-4482), between Gómez Farías and Morelos. You will recognize the house by the brick watchtowers on top of the high stone walls. During Lenin's last days, when he was confined to bed, Stalin and Trotsky fought a silent battle for leadership of the Communist Party in the Soviet Union. Trotsky stuck to ideology, while Stalin took control of the party mechanism. Stalin won, and Trotsky was exiled, to continue his ideological struggle elsewhere. Invited by Diego Rivera, he settled here on the outskirts of Mexico City (this area was mostly fields then) to continue his work and writing on political topics and communist ideology. His ideas clashed with those of Stalin in many respects, and Stalin, wanting no opposition or dissension in world Communist ranks, set out to have Trotsky assassinated. A first attempt failed, but it served to give a warning to Trotsky and his household, and from then on the house became a veritable fortress, with riflemen's watchtowers on the corners of the walls, steel doors (Trotsky's bedroom was entered only by thick steel doors), and round-the-clock guards, several of whom were Americans who sympathized with Trotsky's philosophies. Finally a man thought to have been paid, cajoled, or blackmailed by Stalin, directly or indirectly, was able to get himself admitted to the house by posing as a friend of Trotsky's and of his political views. On August 20, 1940, he put a mountaineer's axe into the philosopher's head. He was, of course, caught, but Trotsky died of his wounds shortly afterward. Not long after Trotsky arrived, he and Diego Rivera had a falling out. When Trotsky was murdered, both Rivera and Kahlo were suspects in the murder for a short while.

If you saw the film *The Death of Trotsky* with Richard Burton, you already have a good idea of what the house looks like, for although the movie was not made here, the set was a very good replica of the house and gardens. You can visit Natalia's (Trotsky's wife's) study, the communal dining room, Trotsky's study (with worksheets, newspaper clippings, books, and cylindrical wax dictating records still spread around), and his fortresslike bedroom. Some of the walls still have the bullet holes left during the first attempt on his life. Trotsky's tomb, designed by Juan O'Gorman, is in the garden of the house. There is a thick steel entry door to the house, which more than likely will not be open, but will be opened for you by the caretaker Tuesday through Friday from 10am to 2pm and 3 to 5:30pm, and on Saturday and Sunday from 10:30am to 4pm. Admission is free.

From the Trotsky Museum, turn right and walk to the intersection of Viena and Churubusco; cross the busy Division del Norte and turn at the next available street, jogging right at the first street and left at the next one, to the:

5. **National Museum of Interventions,** 20 de Agosto y General Anaya, Churubusco (tel. 604-0699). Technically, this museum is in Churubusco, the neighbor suburb of Coyoacán. If your country had been invaded as many times as Mexico has, and for some of the most unusual reasons, there would be a museum about it too. Housed in a beautiful old convent, the well-done displays chronicle each intervention, including the French invasions in 1838 and 1862, the war with the United States between 1846 and 1848, and the U.S. invasions of 1914 and 1916. Visitors from France or the States, rather than being in for some American or French bashing, discover just the facts—very well displayed. The building itself was the site of a battle with Mexican General Anaya, his troops, and U.S. deserters on one side, and U.S. Gen. Winfield Scott and his troops on the other. (See "Walking Tour 4—San Angel," for an explanation of the U.S. deserters.) The museum is open Tuesday through Sunday from 9am to 6pm. Admission is $3.50.

Once you've seen Coyoacán, find your way to Avenida México–Coyoacán, and follow it northwest to the Metro station. If you're heading west to San Angel, catch a no. 56 bus on Calle Cuauhtémoc; going east to the Anahuacalli, catch a no. 56 bus on Calle Xicotencatl, then transfer to a no. 25 bus ("Zacatenco-Tlalpan") or no. 59 bus ("El Rosa–Río–Xochimilco") going south on the avenue called Division del Norte.

(The Diego Rivera Museum, Anahuacalli, is a short distance south of Coyoacán. See Section 3, "More Attractions," above, for details.)

4. ORGANIZED TOURS

I've already mentioned that Mexico City is a great place for looking around on your own, and in general this is the cheapest way to see whatever you like. However, if your time is limited, you may wish to acclimate yourself quickly by taking a tour or two.

The most popular tours are the 4-hour city tour that includes such sites as the National Cathedral, the National Palace, and Chapultepec Park and Castle; the 4- to 6-hour tour of the Shrine of Guadalupe and the nearby pyramids in the Teotihuacán archeological zone; and the Sunday tour that begins with the Ballet Folklorico, moves on to the floating gardens of Xochimilco, and may or may not incorporate lunch and the afternoon bullfights. Almost as popular are the 1-day and overnight tours to Cuernavaca and Taxco. There are also several popular nightclub tours.

I feel that I must give some caveats. Many readers have written to say that they were unhappy with the sightseeing tours of this or that company. The reasons are myriad: The tour was too rushed, or the guide knew nothing and made up stories about the sights, or the tour spent most of its time in a handcrafts shop (chosen by the tour company) rather than seeing the sights. Do tour companies get a kickback from souvenir shops? You bet they do! If you meet someone who has recently taken a guided tour and liked it, go with the same company. Otherwise, you might do well to see the sights on your own, following the detailed guidance in this book.

Or I can highly recommend the services of my friend for many years, **Guillermo Arias** (tel. 397-2838), a licensed, English-speaking guide, who can take you anywhere inside or outside the city. Write him at Acacias 82, Viveros de la Loma, 54080 Estado de México—that address is just north of the city center.

5. SPECIAL & FREE EVENTS

Any Monday, Wednesday, or Friday, walk in the front door of the older **National Lottery Building,** where Juárez meets Reforma, go straight up the steps, and take a seat in the small auditorium that faces you. At 8pm sharp a dozen pages clad in maroon uniforms enter to begin the ceremony of picking small wooden balls from two revolving cages. One cage contains 50,000 balls (or more, depending on the number of tickets issued for the lottery), and the other contains balls relating to the number of prizes with the total of each prize on it. As each ball is picked and dropped into cages, the pages keep up a singsong patter of the winning numbers. Winners are posted on a board at the end of the stage. The whole ceremony is broadcast, and the winning numbers are also printed in the newspapers the next morning and listed at all the stands where lottery tickets are sold. Attendance at the lottery takes on a whole different element of suspense if you are clutching a ticket in your hand as the numbers are called.

6. SPORTS & RECREATION

JAI ALAI The strike that closed the **Fronton de Mexico,** Plaza de la República (tel. 546-5369 or 546-3240), is over and jai alai (pronounced "*hi*-lie") is once again being played. It must be the fastest game in the world, and is exciting to watch even without prior knowledge of the sport. It doesn't much matter when you arrive, as there are several games on each night's schedule. As you walk into the fronton, the ticket office is to your left: There you pay and pick up a program, then take a seat.

Jai alai players wear small baskets on their right arms with which they catch and sling a fantastically resilient ball against the wall to the right of where you're sitting. In the best game, four players, two with blue armbands and two with red ones, are competing against each other in a fashion similar to tennis, but even more similar to squash. The member of one team throws the ball against the wall and the other team has to return it. The whole thing is done at an incredible speed—how they manage to see, much less catch, a ball traveling at about 80 miles per hour is marvelous.

The most fun is in the betting; you'd be amazed at how much more exciting a game seems when you have money riding on the result. Wait until the program announces a game of 30 points (*partido a treinta tantos*) and watch the bookies. These colorful gentlemen, wearing burgundy vests, carry little pads of betting slips edged in red (*rojo*) or blue (*azul*), and when the game begins, they'll be offering only a slight edge on one team or another. Bets are placed inside of slashed tennis balls and thrown to bookies during the game. When the scoring starts, however, the odds will change. If you're as good a mathematician as most jai alai aficionados, you'll be able to bet with impunity on both sides at different points of the game—and still finish ahead.

Note: This has become a game for elite spectators, meaning that for men a coat and tie are required. Women must be similarly nicely dressed.

Admission is $7. The box office opens at 6:30pm, and games are held on Tuesday, Wednesday, Thursday, Saturday, and Sunday evenings year round. To get there, head for the northeast corner of Plaza de la República (at the corner of Calle Ramos Arizpe, a few blocks along Juárez west of Reforma). Any bus going west along Juárez will take you to the Juárez-Reforma intersection, and it's a short walk from there. Or you can take the Metro to the Revolución station and walk three blocks down Arriaga (south) to the plaza.

BULLFIGHTS The capital's **Plaza de Toros Monumental México** is among the largest bullrings in the world. It seats 64,000 people and on Sunday during the professional season (usually December through April, but no fixed dates) most seats

FROMMER'S FAVORITES
MEXICO CITY EXPERIENCES

Breakfast or Dinner at the Hotel Majestic Rooftop Restaurant Start or end at least one day under one of the colorful umbrellas overlooking the historic downtown and Zócalo. If you arrive around 6pm, you can watch the military file out of the National Palace and perform the flag-lowering ceremony on the Zócalo.

The Ethnography Section of the Museum of Anthropology Overlooked by many visitors, the Ethnography Section on the second floor is the perfect introduction to Mexican life away from the beaches, resorts, and cities. Fine, unusual weavings, pottery and handcrafts, furniture, huts, plows, and canoes are presented in the context of everyday life. It's a must for those about to visit the interior of the country or who expect their Mexico journeys to be off the well-worn path.

Afternoon Tea at the Salon de Thé Duca d'Este In Mexico, tea and coffee breaks are taken seriously. This cheerful Zona Rosa restaurant and pastry shop is great for sipping a frothy cappuccino and whiling away some time watching passersby through the huge windows facing the street.

The Ballet Folklorico de México Among the best folkloric ballet groups in Mexico are those that perform in Mexico City either at the Teatro Bellas Artes or at the Teatro de la Ciudad. At the Bellas Artes you'll get to see the famed Tiffany glass curtain, which is usually (but not always) shown before each performance.

An Evening in the Zona Rosa The popular Zona Rosa sidewalk cafés and pedestrian streets are ideal for a night of hopping from place to place, without cover charges and taxis, and all to see and be seen. Arrive before dusk to get a good seat for a relaxing drink and to watch the zone come alive for the evening. Copenhague, between Reforma and Hamburgo, is among the best streets for an entire evening or just for drinks. It's a narrow, trafficless artery with awning-covered dining, bustling waiters, and food that's usually good enough to keep the places packed.

The Ruins of Teotihuacán There's nothing to compare with walking down the wide Avenue of the Dead, with the Pyramid of the Moon at one end and pyramidal structures on both sides, imagining what it must have looked like when the walls were embellished with murals on brilliantly colored stucco.

are taken. On other Sundays through the year the arena is given over to the beginners (*novilleros*), most of whom are as bad as the beginners in any other sport. Six fights make up a *corrida,* which begins precisely at 4pm and is one of the few things in Mexico that's always on time.

There are several ways to reach Plaza de Toros, which is situated 2 or 3 miles south along Insurgentes. Any big hotel or tour agency will be happy to book you onto a tour with transportation. In about 25 minutes, the bus will pass the bullring on the right. Most of the people on the bus will alight here, so you'll know you're at the bullring, which is just around the corner ahead.

Dozens of men and women sell nuts, hats, and all kinds of whatnots. Look for a woman or *muchacha* selling chewing gum and waving small "programs." If you buy the chewing gum, she'll give you (free) the one-page sheet that lists the names of the day's *toreros.*

Unless you want to pay more, take your place in the line at one of the windows marked SOL GENERAL. It will be in the sun and it will be high up, but the sun isn't too strong (it sets soon, anyway) and you won't see many other tourists that way. (Try to avoid the seats numbered 1 to 100; for some reason, the roughnecks prefer to gather in this section.) Seats in *la sombra* (shade) are more expensive, of course. Tickets cost $8 to $10 and up. Fights start at 4pm, but get there well in advance for a good seat.

Usually, there are six separate bulls to be killed (two by each matador) in a corrida, but I'd suggest that you leave just before the last bull—to avoid the crowds. Outside, around two sides of the bullring is a scene of frantic activity. Hundreds of tiny stalls have masses of food frying, cold beer stacked high, and radios blaring with a commentary on the action inside the ring.

Or you can take the Metro (to the San Antonio station, on Line 7) or a colectivo; the number of colectivos that normally roam Insurgentes is supplemented by Sunday-afternoon taxis headed for the plaza, and they'll often pick up extra passengers going their way. Or you can catch one of the buses marked PLAZA MÉXICO that travel down Insurgentes on Sunday afternoon, or a no. 17 bus along Insurgentes.

HORSE RACES   Mexico City's racetrack, the **Hipodromo de las Américas,** is as extraordinarily beautiful as many of its other tourist-popular spots. Approached by way of a tree-lined boulevard and containing a small lake on which an occasional swan or heron basks, it has stands built on the hillside for a good view of the track.

You may enter through a special (free) tourist gate, paying only the applicable tax. The normal price of admission is through purchase of a program. If you don't get a program, you won't have much idea what's going on, so you'd better buy one at the gate. Two or more people may enter on one program, but each must pay the program's tax.

Once past the admissions gate, head for the stands and grab a seat. If you're willing to spend the extra loot, you can climb one level higher and sit at a table, where the view is excellent and a minimum amount must be consumed in either food or drink.

You can bet either to win (*primera*), to place (*segunda*), or to show (*tercera*). All windows have signs in both English and Spanish. On certain races, marked SELECCIÓN 1-2 on the program with bold letters, you can win a substantial sum by picking the horses that will come in first and second and placing a bet on your selections. In some races there is an alternative way of betting called the quiniela. This operates on a similar principle, except that your choices for first and second can come in second and first.

Races begin at 2:15pm. The track operates on Tuesday (in winter only), Thursday, Saturday, and Sunday for 11 months of the year; it is closed only for parts of September and October.

To get there, take a colectivo marked HIPODROMO along Reforma, which takes you through Chapultepec to the Anillo Periferico (also called Avenida Manuel Ávila Camacho). The track is just off this main entry, near the intersection with Calzada Legaria. You can also take the Metro to Toreo Quatro Caminos (Line 2); then walk up out of the Metro station, cross over to the bus-marshalling yard (immediately adjacent), go to traffic island 2, the center stall, and look for buses marked HIPODROMO. Get off when you see the ring and a sign. It's a short walk from there.

READERS RECOMMEND

Fiesta de Charros, Constituyentes 500. "We took two colectivos to the Fiesta de Charros and finally arrived 2 hours early as things didn't start until noon. We were the only tourists sitting in the stands and a huge crowd eventually arrived. Promptly at noon there was a grand entry, with riders wearing the traditional dress of the charros. Two bands played, there were speeches, and the flag was brought in very slowly and we stood for all verses of the Mexican National Anthem. A group of charros from Mexico City were competing with some from Celaya, Guanajuato. This is similar to a rodeo in other parts of North America. There was a reining demonstration; I didn't know horses could turn like that. In another event, a rider chased a steer down an alleyway, caught its tail, and turned it over. Two teams of lady riders dressed in long frilly dresses over frilly petticoats rode side-saddle and did a musical ride at full gallop. It was free, although we paid a few pesos for a cushion. The Fiesta de Charros takes place on Sunday from noon to about 2:30pm."—Anne Irwin, Williams Lake, B.C. Canada.

7. SAVVY SHOPPING

Mexico City is a marvelous place to buy crafts of all types. You'll come across numerous places displaying fascinating native products, and you're certain to find something you want as a souvenir. Here's the rundown on the best places to shop, from small, selective crafts shops to vast general markets (for tips on bargaining, see "Saving Money on Shopping" in Chapter 2).

Today it often costs only a little more money to buy these things in the capital than at the source, if one knows a good shop. Several government-run shops and a few excellent privately run shops have exceptionally good collections of Mexico's arts and crafts. As fascinating as a fine-art gallery, these shops deserve a visit whether or not you intend to buy.

The two best districts for browsing are on and off Avenida Juárez facing the Alameda, Avenida Madero and the streets parallel to it, and in the Zona Rosa (for jewelry, Calle Amberes is the place, for instance). A few unique shops deserve particular mention.

SHOPPING A TO Z

CRAFTS

ARTESANÍAS E INDUSTRIAS POPULARES DEL ESTADO DE OAXACA [ARIPO], Londres 117. Tel. 514-2025.

ARIPO, in the Zona Rosa, brings crafts from the state of Oaxaca. It isn't large, and the selection doesn't begin to tap that state's craft possibilities, but it's a good place to see what's just been unpacked. Open Monday through Friday from 10am to 2pm and 3 to 7pm, and on Saturday from 11am to 6pm.

CASA DE LAS ARTESANÍAS DEL ESTADO DE MÉXICO [CASART], Juárez 18-C. Tel. 521-3141.

The state of Mexico operates the Casa de las Artesanías del Estado de México. Look in this small shop for crafts produced in the state of Mexico, which surrounds the Federal District. Open Monday through Saturday from 10am to 7pm.

CASA ROSY, Amberes 69G. Tel. 525-6999.

Casa Rosy is around the corner from the Hotel Krystal and is one of those long-time establishments favored by collectors. It isn't large, so you find yourself studying every corner and shelf. Walls are laden with oodles of masks, and racks and shelves of regional huipiles from Mexico and Guatemala, beaded dresses from San Pablito, wood carvings from Oaxaca, Olinala lacquered gourds, tinware, and more. Open Monday through Saturday from noon to 8pm.

ARTE POPULAR MINIATURA, Hamburgo 130-A, in the Zona Rosa. Tel. 514-1405 or 566-1399.

At the Arte Popular Miniatura, just down from the Restaurant Tokyo in the Zona Rosa, even the shop is miniature. It's about coat-closet size, big enough for a couple of clients, a small display case, and the proprietor. But the walls are jammed with tiny objects like miniature scenes of daily life, tin Christmas ornaments, papier-mâché carnival dolls, tiny skulls, and even miniature figures to make your own miniature display. Open Monday through Saturday from noon to 9:30pm.

EXPOSICIÓN NACIONAL DE ARTE POPULAR, Juárez 89. Tel. 521-6681.

This market has simply everything! There are papier-mâché figurines, woven goods, earthenware, colorfully painted candelabra, hand-carved wooden masks, straw goods, beads, bangles, and glass. It is operated by FONART (Fondo Nacional para el Fomento de las Artes), a government organization that helps village craftspeople. Open daily from 10am to 6pm. Metro: Hidalgo or Juárez.

MULTI EXPORT S.A., Amberes 21. Tel. 533-6130.

Multi Export is another of those stores jammed with crafts—papier-mâché fruit, Olinala chests, Oaxaca animals, Izucar candleholders and masks—some of which are run-of-the-mill and others worth collecting. Open Monday through Friday from 9am to 7:30pm and on Saturday from 10am to 7:30pm.

NATIONAL MUSEUM OF POPULAR INDUSTRIAL ARTS, Juárez 44. Tel. 521-6679.

⭐ The museum, located across the street from the Benito Juárez statue in Alameda Park, has an enormous selection of high-quality Mexican crafts from all over, and because the prices are fixed you can get an idea of quality vs. cost for later use in market bargaining. Open Monday through Saturday from 10am to 6pm.

VICTOR'S ARTES POPULARES MEXICANAS, Madero 10, 2nd Floor, Room 305. Tel. 512-1263.

⭐ Victor's, near the Alameda, is a shop for serious buyers and art collectors owned by the Fosado family who have been in the folk-art business for 60 years. They buy most of their crafts from Indian villages near and far, and supply various exhibits with native craftworks. Theoretically open Tuesday through Friday from 10am to 1pm and 4 to 6pm. Metro: Bellas Artes.

FASHION

GIRASOL, Genova 39A. Tel. 533-3723.

Girasol, with outlets in Acapulco and Cancún, is famous for brightly colored original designs using Mexican motifs and colors. Open Monday through Saturday from 10am to 7pm.

ARTESANÍAS PATRICIA, Londres 139, Col. Juárez. Tel. 525-7192.

Artesanías Patricia, in the Zona Rosa, is another clothing store that specializes in fine-quality embroidered dresses from Oaxaca. The selection is huge and well chosen. Open Monday through Saturday from 10am to 7pm.

FOOD

DULCERÍA DE CELAYA, Motolinía 36. Tel. 518-4548.

⭐ Dulcería de Celaya, between Madero and 16 de Septiembre, is a beautiful old confectioner's shop founded in 1874. In its 19th-century windows you'll see a mouth-watering selection of the sweets for which the city of Celaya is famous: candied fruits of all varieties, jars of sweetened goat milk, sugar-coated almonds, fudge, and pecan candies. Even if your diet doesn't allow you to buy, you should at least take a look at the lovely shop. Open Monday through Saturday from 7am to 8pm.

MARKETS

BAZAR SÁBADO, San Angel.

⭐ The Bazar Sábado in San Angel, a suburb a few miles south of the city, is held on Saturday, as its name indicates. If you like outdoor markets, you'll like this one. Plan to spend all of Saturday touring the attractions on the southern outskirts of the city.

CENTRO ARTESANAL (Mercado de Curiosidades)

This is a rather modern building set back off a plaza on the corner of Ayuntamiento and Dolores. It's composed of a number of stalls on two levels, selling everything from leather to tiles. They have some lovely silver jewelry and, as in most non-fixed-price stores, the asking price is high but the bargained result is often very reasonable. Metro: Salto del Agua.

BUENAVISTA CENTRAL CRAFTS MARKET, Aldama 187 (tel. 529-1254).

Across from Buenavista Railroad Station (Estación Buena Vista) is the Central

Crafts Market, a very tourist-oriented commercial concern with a lot of floor space and an uninspired collection of crafts at rather high prices. They offer customers free soft drinks at a small snack bar in the shop. If you want to take a look, get a no. 17 bus going north on Insurgentes to the railroad station. Get off and walk in front of the station—you'll be heading east. The first real north-south street you come to is Calle Aldama, and the Central Crafts Market is on Aldama just a few steps away. Or you can hop a no. 4 bus going west on Juárez, and it'll drop you right at the market.

Note: The Central Crafts Market employs agents who prowl the length of Avenida Juárez and other tourist-frequented areas to tout the excellence of the market's wares. Offering "free tourist information" or "free guide service," they are friendly and helpful, but their goal is to persuade you to visit the market. Open Monday through Saturday from 9am to 6pm and on Sunday from 9am to 2pm.

LAGUNILLA MARKET, a few blocks north of Plaza de Garibaldi.

This is another market well worth visiting. The best day is Sunday, when the Lagunilla becomes a colorful outdoor market filling the streets for blocks. Vendors sell everything from axes to antiques. Be careful about pickpockets. The two enclosed sections are open all week and are separated by a short street, Calle Juan Alvarez. They have different specialties: the one to the north is noted for clothes, rebozos, and blankets; and the one to the south for tools, pottery, and household goods, such as attractive copper hanging lamps. This is also the area for old and rare books, many at a ridiculously low cost, if you're willing to hunt and bargain. Most, however, are in Spanish. Metro: Allende.

MERCADO DE ARTESANÍAS "LA CIUDADELA," Plaza de la Ciudadela.

An interesting market, large, clean, and with numerous little streets, the Mercado de Artesanías rambles on forever just off Balderas and Ayuntamiento in Plaza de la Ciudadela. The merchandise is of good quality and well displayed, and bartering is a must. I think this is probably the best place for buying—anything you want is here. You might want to come for lunch before shopping; if so, I can highly recommend the restaurant in the market called Fonda Lupita, Local no. 89 (ask someone). It has Spanish decor, and is very simple but clean. A very handsome white-haired lady keeps the place shipshape and also prepares the very tasty food. Open daily from 11am or noon to 8pm. Metro: Juárez.

MERCADO INSURGENTES, on Londres between Florencia and Amberes.

Mercado Insurgentes is a full-fledged crafts market tucked in the Zona Rosa. Because of its Zona Rosa address you might expect exorbitant prices, but vendors in the maze of stalls are eager to bargain and good buys aren't hard to come by.

MERCED MARKET

Try your bargaining skill at the Merced Market, the biggest in the city The Merced Market consists of several modern buildings. The first is mainly for fruits and vegetables; the others contain just about everything you'd find if a department store joined forces with a discount warehouse—a good place to go looking for almost anything. The area to the north of the market is a tangled confusion of trucks and stores, in which cascades of oranges spill gloriously down onto sidewalks.

To get there, take the Metro to the Merced station. To return to the Zócalo or anywhere else in the city, take the Metro (Line 1) from the Merced station, which is just outside the enclosed market. You can change at Pino Suárez (first stop) to take you to the Zócalo.

8. EVENING ENTERTAINMENT

Venture out for an evening's amusement and you can easily end up tens of thousands of pesos poorer. If your entertainments are of the contrived type (say, a supper club at a nice hotel, with drinks and a show, cover charges, minimums, service charges, and tips), you can enjoy them here at a price that compares favorably with any other major city, but that's still a lot of money. On the other hand, if you're willing to let *la vida Mexicana* put on its own fascinating show for you, the bill will be no more than a few dollars, or even nothing at all.

People-watching, café-sitting, music, even a dozen mariachi bands all playing at once, can be yours for next to nothing.

THE ENTERTAINMENT SCENE

For current information on cultural offerings, pick up the Friday edition of *The News,* which has a full listing of cultural events. The *Mexico Daily Bulletin,* a free daily newspaper found in hotel lobbies, is also a good source of current information.

THE ZONA ROSA   Although the Zona Rosa has a well-deserved reputation as Mexico City's high-priced playground, it is also true that by night in summer it's an unending carnival of people and places, lights and sights. You can enjoy yourself here for nothing by window-shopping, people-watching, and generally taking it all in. Or you can spend a few pesos and have dessert and coffee, or perhaps a drink, and watch the ebb and flow. It's worth saving up some extra money to have at least one dinner here (see Chapter 11 for suggestions). Whatever you decide, you'll be glad you came.

Some prime locales for Pink Zone promenades are the streets named **Genova,** Copenhague, and Oslo, which have been turned into pedestrians-only streets (save for the occasional car zipping in to the Aristos Hotel). Sidewalk café-restaurants have sprung up, making **Copenhague** one of Mexico City's most delightful "in" places. Tables are usually packed unless you come early. Some establishments are selected by the cognoscenti as "in," and chairs are then at a premium, while other places do a slower business and have tables more readily available. On **Oslo** the attraction is the several coffeehouses with coffee, pastries, and fortunetellers. Another such crossroads for live entertainment is in the arcade located at **Londres 104,** just off Genova. Half a dozen restaurants here also serve as cafés, and some have live entertainment most evenings.

THE PERFORMING ARTS
THEATER

TEATRO BLANQUITA, Lázaro Cárdenas 14. Tel. 512-8264.
For comedy and vaudeville shows, try the Teatro Blanquita, north of the Latin American Tower. Metro: Bellas Artes.

THE MAJOR CONCERT & PERFORMANCE HALLS

Auditorio Nacional (National Auditorium), on Reforma in Chapultepec Park (tel. 520-3737).
El Granero (The Granary), Chapultepec Park (tel. 520-4331).
Palacio de Bellas Artes, Lázaro Cárdenas (tel. 709-3111, ext. 1041).
Palacio de Minería, Tacuba 5 (tel. 510-1868).
Sala Netzahualcoyotl, Centro Cultural Universitario, Insurgentes Sur 3000 (tel. 655-1344).
Sala Silvestre Revueltos (formerly Sala Ollin Yolixtli), Centro Cultural Universitario, Insurgentes Sur 3000 (tel. 655-3888 or 655-3600).
Teatro Antonio Caso, Reforma Norte 668 (tel. 566-8488).
Teatro Blanquita, Lázaro Cárdenas 14 (tel. 512-8264).
Teatro del Bosque (Theater of the Woods), Chapultepec Park (tel. 520-4332).
Teatro de la Ciudad, Doncelas 36 (tel. 510-2197).
Teatro Fabregas, Donceles 24-A (tel. 566-1644).

TEATRO FABREGAS, Donceles 24-A. Tel. 566-1644.
This theater, in the Alameda area, has plays and musicals all year. Metro: Bellas Artes.

EL GRANERO (The Granary), Chapultepec Park. Tel. 520-4331.
Performances are usually in Spanish, but check local listings. It's behind the National Auditorium, which faces Reforma across from the Hotel Stouffer Presidente. Metro: Auditorio.

TEATRO DEL BOSQUE, Chapultepec Park. Tel. 520-4332.
Theater performances are seasonal. It's behind the National Auditorium. Metro: Auditorio.

TEATRO ANTONIO CASO, Reforma Norte 668. Tel. 566-8488.
North of the town center, in the area near Plaza of Three Cultures, this small theater has occasional plays and readings.

OPERA & BALLET

NATIONAL AUDITORIUM, Chapultepec Park, on Reforma. Tel. 520-3737.
Although currently closed for renovation, the National Auditorium, in Chapultepec Park, is usually the biggest bargain in town. Symphonies, international ballet, opera, and theater companies play here. Prices vary depending on the performance. Metro: Auditorio.

PALACIO DE BELLAS ARTES, Lázaro Cárdenas, on the east side of the Alameda. Tel. 709-3111, ext. 1041.
Besides hosting traveling ballet and opera companies from around the world, performances of Mexico's famed **Ballet Folklorico de México** are held here several times weekly. (See also "Walking Tour 2—Near the Alameda," above.)
The Ballet Folklorico is a celebration of pre- and post-Hispanic dancing in Mexico. A typical program will include Aztec ritual dances, agricultural dances from Jalisco, a fiesta in Veracruz, a Christmas celebration—all welded together with mariachis, marimba players, singers, and dancers.
As many other events are held in the Bellas Artes—visits by foreign opera companies, for instance—there are times when the Ballet Folklorico is moved. Usually, it reappears in the National Auditorium in Chapultepec Park. Check at the Bellas Artes box office. There are two companies—three, if you count the one usually on tour. The show is popular and tickets are bought up rapidly (especially by tour companies), so if you want a seat, go early or book seats through a tour agency (at twice the cost). The box office is on the ground floor of the Bellas Artes, main entrance. Note: The theater tends to be very cold so you may want to bring a sweater.
Prices: Tickets, $8.50–$17 galeria seats, $21 first-floor seats.
Open: Box office, Mon–Sat 11am–3pm and 5–7pm, Sun 8:30am–1pm and 5–7pm; Ballet Folklorico performances, Sun 9:30am–9pm, Wed 9pm.

TEATRO DE LA CUIDAD, Donceles 36. Tel. 510-2197.
An alternative to the Ballet Folklorico de México is the **Ballet Folklorico Nacional Aztlán,** in the beautiful turn-of-the-century Teatro de la Cuidad, a block northeast of the Bellas Artes between Xicotencatl and Allende. Performances here are as good as the better-known ones in the Bellas Artes, but tickets are a lot cheaper and much easier to obtain. Metro: Bellas Artes.
Prices: Tickets, $10.50.
Open: Shows Sun 9:30am and 2:30pm, Tues 8:30pm.

CLASSICAL MUSIC

CENTRO CULTURAL UNIVERSITARIO (University Cultural Center), Insurgentes Sur 3000.

Part of the University of Mexico, it's located south of the university proper but north of the Periferico, in the southern limits of the city (see Section 3, "More Attractions," above). The most popular hall here is the **Netzahualcoyotl Concert Hall** (tel. 655-1344); the other is the **Sala Silvestre Revueltas** (tel. 655-3888). Other theaters there are the **Sala Miguel Covarrubias** movie theater, the **Salas Julio Brecho** and **Carlos Chavez**, and the **Teatro Juan Ruíz de Alarcón** and the **Foro Experimental Sor Juana Ines de la Cruz.**

PALACIO DE MINERÍA, Tacuba 5. Tel. 510-1868.

The handsome 19th-century neoclassical Palacio Minería, near the Alameda, was formerly the school of mining (see "Walking Tour 2—Near the Alameda," above). Today it's used by chamber orchestras and other small cultural events.

THE CLUB & MUSIC SCENE
MARIACHIS

At some time or other, everybody—Mexicans and *turistas* alike—goes to see and hear the mariachi players. The mariachis are strolling musicians who wear distinctive costumes, which make them look like cowboys dressed up for a special occasion. Their costume—tight spangled trousers, fancy jackets, and big floppy bow ties—dates back to the French occupation of Mexico in the mid-19th century, as does their name. *Mariachi* is the Mexican mispronunciation of the French word for marriage, which is where they were often on call for music.

In Mexico City the mariachis make their headquarters around **Plaza de Garibaldi,** a 10-minute stroll north of the Palacio de Bellas Artes up Avenida Lázaro Cárdenas, at Avenida República de Honduras. You'll pass dozens of stores and a couple of burlesque houses.

In Plaza de Garibaldi itself, mariachi players are everywhere. At every corner, guitars are stacked together like rifles in an army training camp. Young musicians strut proudly in their flashy outfits, on the lookout for señoritas to impress. They play when they feel like it, when there's a good chance to gather in some tips, or when someone orders a song—the going rate seems to be around $5 or $10 per song. The best time to hear music in the square itself is after 9 or 10pm, especially on Sunday.

In any of the eating and drinking establishments around the plaza you can enjoy the mariachi music that swirls through the air. **Tlaquepaque,** across the square, is a well-known tourist-oriented restaurant where you can dine to strolling mariachis. But remember—if you give a bandleader the sign, you're the one who pays for the song, just like outside in the square.

Pulquería Hermana Hortensia, Amargura 4 (tel. 529-7828), is perhaps the most adventurous spot for newcomers to Mexico City. It's on Plaza de Garibaldi near the northeast corner at Amargura and República de Honduras. Unlike most pulque bars, La Hermana Hortensia is a *pulquería familiar* (a "family" bar—that is, you can bring your wife, but not your kids). Pulque (that's "*pool*-keh") is a thick and flavorsome drink made by fermenting the juice of a maguey (century) plant. Discovered by the ancient Toltecs and shared with the Aztecs, pulque was a sacred drink forbidden to the common people for centuries. One of the effects of the Spanish Conquest was to liberate pulque for the masses. Was this good or bad? Ask your neighbor in La Hermana Hortensia as you quaff the thick brew. Pulque packs a wallop, although it's not nearly so strong as those other maguey-based drinks, tequila and mezcal. By the way, the pulque here can be ordered with nuts blended in for a different flavor.

Don't get the idea that you'll see only your countryfolk in the Plaza de Garibaldi, for it is indeed a Mexican phenomenon. As evening falls, lots of people from the neighborhood come to stroll or sit.

TRIO MUSIC, JAZZ & FIESTAS
JORONGO BAR, Reforma 325. Tel. 207-3933.

For wonderful Mexican trio music in plush surroundings, make your way to Jorongo Bar at the María Isabel–Sheraton Hotel, facing the Angel Monument. This bar's reputation for good trio music has stood for decades—it's almost an institution. From 7pm to 2am, you can enjoy the smooth and joyous sounds for the price of a drink ($4) and a cover charge (about $10).

HOTEL GALERIA PLAZA, Hamburgo 195, at Varsovia. Tel. 211-0014.
Ever since this luxury hotel opened in the early 1980s it has been known for it's inviting Lobby Bar entertainment. The music is usually jazz, played from 7pm to 1am.

HOTEL DE CORTES, Av. Hidalgo 85. Tel. 518-2182.
Unless it rains, there's a Mexican Fiesta every Saturday at 8pm on the open patio of this colonial-era convent-turned-hotel on the Alameda (see also "Walking Tour 2—Near the Alameda," above). The price of $20 includes drinks, dinner, and the show.

NIGHTCLUBS

MURALTO, on the 41st floor of the Latin American Tower, on Madero at San Juan de Letran. Tel. 521-7751.
For soft piano and violin music to dance by, go to Muralto, high over the city, with a spectacular night view of the city lights. The dress code includes coat and tie for men. It's open daily from 1pm to 1am.

CHEZ'AR, at the Hotel Aristos, Reforma 276, at Copenhague. Tel. 211-0112.
In the French specialty restaurant of the Hotel Aristos there's ballroom and swing dancing nightly for a cover of $6 to $10. You can come for the dancing and not for a meal if you like. Coat and tie preferred.

HOLIDAY INN CROWNE PLAZA, Colón Circle. Tel. 705-1515.
This enormous, fashionable hotel offers one of the best lineups of low-key, late-night entertainment. First there's the **Caballo Negro,** with two shows nightly, usually a musical group of guitarists for one show and a variety act for the other (closed Sunday). One show nightly in **Las Sillas** often features trios singing the best of Mexican ballads; **Barbarela** is classified as a dance hall, but there's also entertainment. Check for current times, prices, and entertainers.

MOVIES

You'll find many current first-run hits playing in Mexico City, usually in the original-language version with Spanish subtitles, and usually under the same title (although the title will be translated into Spanish).

The best place to check for what's currently being shown is in the entertainment section of Mexico City's English-language paper, *The News.* Tickets are inexpensive even at the nice movie houses along Reforma.

CHAPTER 13

EASY EXCURSIONS FROM MEXICO CITY

1. **THE PYRAMIDS OF SAN JUAN TEOTIHUACÁN**
2. **PACHUCA**
3. **IXTA-POPO NATIONAL PARK**
4. **TEPOTZOTLÁN**
5. **TULA**
6. **TOLUCA**
7. **CUERNAVACA**
8. **TAXCO**

Just as Paris has its Versailles and Rome its Villa d'Este, so Mexico City is surrounded by suburban areas that are every bit as fascinating as the city itself—and all of them can be reached by a bus ride that is ridiculously cheap. The places described in this chapter are suitable for 1-day trips that can be followed by an evening back in town (although for Taxco you may want to make an exception and stay overnight).

The first and most exciting stop is at the breath-taking ancient pyramids of Teotihuacán. Later I take you farther afield, southwest over the mountains to Cuernavaca, and thence to the silver city of Taxco, on the road to Acapulco.

If you drive to Teotihuacán and take Highway 132D through the villages, about 15 miles from Mexico City the village of San Cristobal Ecatepec looms off to the left. Note, also on the left, an old wall built centuries ago to keep what was then a lake from flooding the area. When the road forks a mile or so farther north, take the road to the right. About 3 miles farther along this road is the Convent of San Agustín Acolman (1539–60). Not long ago the fortresslike monastery was in ruins: The only sounds were the ticking of a modern clock, the faint bleating of sheep from the fields outside, and the chatter of birds building nests on the roof. At one time it was even flooded with mud. Now, however, the monastery and church are restored and you can wander through the immense halls lined with 16th-century frescoes and colonial-era paintings, and into the cells used by the Augustinian monks. Note the intricately decorated portal, which is considered among the finest examples of plateresque in the country. Over the arched entry note the sculpted lion, angel heads, and horses whose hind portions become leaves and flowers. It's a beautiful place and worth a visit. Admission is $3.50, and the monastery is open daily from 10am to 1pm and 3 to 6pm.

1. THE PYRAMIDS OF SAN JUAN TEOTIHUACÁN

30 miles NE of Mexico City

GETTING THERE By Bus Don't let anyone tell you that it's difficult to get to the pyramids by bus, and that you should take a tour or a cab! It's simple, relatively fast, and inexpensive to go by bus.

Buses leave every half hour (from 5am to 10pm) every day of the week from the **Terminal Central de Autobuses del Norte,** and the trip takes 1 hour. To get to the Terminal del Norte, take bus no. 17 ("Indios Verdes"), or bus no. 17-B ("Central Camionera del Norte") going north on Insurgentes. Or take the Metro (Line 5) to the Terminal de Autobuses Norte station. When you reach the Terminal del Norte, look for the **Autobuses Sahagun** sign located at the far northwest end, all the way down to the sign 8 ESPERA.

Another way to get to the pyramids by bus is to take the Metro (Line 3) to **Indios Verdes,** and catch a bus from there. When you arrive at the Indios Verdes station, head for the exit (*salida*) and you'll see arrows pointing to the various platforms.

By Car Driving to San Juan Teotihuacán on either the toll Highway 85D or free Highway 132D will take about an hour. Head north on Insurgentes to get out of the city. Highway 132D is the scenic route, but is excruciatingly slow because of the surfeit of trucks and buses; Highway 85D, the toll road, is a little duller but faster.

DEPARTING By Bus For the return journey, catch the same bus at the main gate to the museum or take a bus at the traffic circle near the pyramid entrance closest to the Unidad Cultural. The "México-Metro" bus will drop you off at the Indios Verdes Metro station, from which it is a short ride to any other point in the city.

The name Teotihuacán means "Place Where Gods Were Born." The Pyramid of the Sun at Teotihuacán was begun about 100 B.C., the time when the Classical Greeks were building their great monuments on the other side of the world. Teotihuacán was the dominant city during the Classical Period, with its magnificent pyramids, palaces, and houses covering 8 square miles. At its zenith around A.D. 500 there were at least 125,000 inhabitants, more than in contemporary Rome, and its influence was known as far south as Guatemala. But little is known about the city's inhabitants—what language they spoke, where they came from, or why they abandoned the place in A.D. 700, except that a great fire swept the site about that time. Today what remains are the rough stone structures of the three pyramids and sacrificial altars, and some of the grand houses, all of which were once covered in stucco and painted with brilliant frescos, mainly in red. This is one of Mexico's most remarkable ruins, and you shouldn't miss it!

ORIENTATION

INFORMATION A good place to start is the **Unidad Cultural** (Visitor's Center), the only modern building of any size on the grounds of Teotihuacán. It (and an adjacent parking lot) is at the southern end of the site opposite the Ciudadela, and has shops, a restaurant, a book and souvenir shop, and the museum, which provides valuable background before touring the ruins.

First thing you'll notice as you wander into the museum is a statue (a copy, actually) of the goddess Chalchiuhtlicue. She stands in a small pool, which is appropriate as she was the goddess of water. Behind, around, and above her are various exhibits outlining the culture of Teotihuacán, as well as some artifacts found during excavations on the site. A scale model of the city is most useful in planning the rest of your visit.

Do keep in mind these important points: You will be doing a great deal of walking, and perhaps some climbing—it's a full mile from the Visitor's Center to the Pyramid of the Moon and there are 248 steep steps up to the top of the Pyramid of the Sun.

Remember that you're at an altitude of more than 7,000 feet, and you will tire more easily than usual. Take it slowly. Also, the sun and heat can get you. Protect yourself.

In the summer rainy season, it rains almost every afternoon. Plan to be in the museum or a restaurant when the showers come at 2 or 3 o'clock.

SITE LAYOUT Because the site is so vast, I'll describe it in sections. Whichever entrance you use to the site, locate the section nearest you and visit it first—backtracking takes too much time and energy.

The grand buildings of Teotihuacán were laid out on a cosmic plan. The front wall of the **Pyramid of the Sun** is exactly square to (facing) the point on the horizon where the sun sets on the day it reaches its zenith. So if a line were drawn from the pyramid to the sun at noon on the day when the sun reaches its highest point (that is, it seems to be directly overhead), and another line were drawn from the pyramid to the sun when the sun reaches the horizon later that same day, then the pyramid would be exactly square to these lines. The rest of the ceremonial buildings were laid out at right angles to the Pyramid of the Sun.

The main thoroughfare, called by archeologists the **Avenue of the Dead,** runs roughly north-south. The **Pyramid of the Moon** is at the northern end, and the **Unidad Cultural** (Museum/Visitor's Center) and **Ciudadela** are on the southern part of the thoroughfare. Actually, the great street was several miles long in its heyday, but only a mile or so has been uncovered and restored.

WHAT TO SEE & DO

Across the Avenue of the Dead from the Visitor's Center is the **Ciudadela (Citadel),** so named by the Spaniards. Actually, this immense sunken square was not a fortress at all, although the impressive walls make it look like one. It was the grand setting for a temple to Quetzalcoatl, the famed "plumed serpent" who appears so often in Mexican folklore. Once you've admired the great scale of the Ciudadela, go down the steps into the massive court and head for the ruined temple in the middle.

The **Temple of Quetzalcoatl** was covered over by an even-larger structure, a pyramid. As you walk toward the center of the Ciudadela's court, you'll be approaching the pyramid. Walk around to the right of it and soon you'll see the reconstructed temple close behind the pyramid. There's a narrow passage between the two structures, and traffic is supposed to be one way—which is why I directed you to the right.

It was a common practice in Mexico and Central America for early temples to be covered over by later ones. The Pyramid of the Sun may have been built up in this way. As for the Temple of Quetzalcoatl, you'll notice at once the fine big carved serpents' heads jutting out from aureoles of feathers carved in the stone walls. Other feathered serpents are carved in relief low on the walls. The temple provides a vivid example of pre-Columbian public decoration. The decoration at Chichén-Itzá, Uxmal, and Tikal is certainly more elaborate, but these sites are thousands of miles from Mexico City. Luckily, you can still get a good idea of the glory of Mexico's ancient cities from this temple.

The **Avenue of the Dead** got its strange and forbidding name from the Aztecs, who mistook the little temples that line both sides of the avenue for tombs of kings or priests.

As you stroll north along the Avenue of the Dead toward the Pyramid of the Moon, look on the right for a bit of wall sheltered by a modern corrugated roof. Beneath the shelter, the wall still bears a painting of a jaguar. From this fragment you might be able to build a picture of the breathtaking spectacle that must have met the eye when all the paintings along the avenue were intact.

The **Pyramid of the Sun** is located on the east side of the Avenue of the Dead. As pyramids go, this is the third largest in the world. The Great Pyramid of Cholula, near Puebla, is the largest structure ever built. Today it appears as a muddy hill with a church built on top. Second largest is the Pyramid of Cheops on the outskirts of Cairo. In third place is Teotihuacán's Pyramid of the Sun, which is almost—at 730 feet per side—as large as Cheops at the base. But at 210 feet high, this pyramid is only about half as high as its Egyptian rival. No matter, it's still the biggest restored pyramid in the western hemisphere, and an awesome sight. Although the Pyramid of the Sun was not built as a great king's tomb, it does have secret tunnels and chambers beneath it. A natural grotto was enlarged and restructured into a four-room chamber that was used for some occult purpose—no one knows what. The tunnels are not open to the public.

The first structure of the pyramid was probably built a century before Christ, and the temple that used to crown the pyramid was finished about 400 years later (A.D.

300). By the time the pyramid was discovered and restoration was begun (early in our century), the temple had completely disappeared and the pyramid was just a mass of rubble covered with bushes and trees.

If you're game, trudge up the 248 steps to the top. The view is marvelous, if the smog's not too thick.

The **Pyramid of the Moon** faces an interesting plaza at the northern end of the avenue. The plaza is surrounded by little temples, and by the Palace of Quetzal-Mariposa (or Quetzal-Butterfly), on the left (west) side. You get about the same range of view from the top of the Pyramid of the Moon as you do from its larger neighbor, because the moon pyramid is built on higher ground. So if the prospect of dragging yourself up the sun pyramid was just too much, you can go up the 150-foot-high moon pyramid with less effort. The perspective straight down the Avenue of the Dead is magnificent.

The **Palace of Quetzal-Mariposa** lay in ruins until the 1960s, when restoration work began. Today it echoes wonderfully with its former glory, as figures of Quetzal-Mariposa (a mythical exotic bird-butterfly) appear painted on walls or carved in the pillars of the inner court. Behind the Palace of Quetzal-Mariposa is the **Palace of the Jaguars,** complete with murals showing a lively jaguar musical combo, and some frescoes.

Admission: $3.50, free on Sun.

Open: Daily 8am–5pm (visitors are allowed to remain until 6pm).

WHERE TO EAT

You may want to pack a lunch to take to the ruins. Restaurants exist, but a box lunch will save you a long walk. Almost any hotel or restaurant in the city can prepare a box lunch for you, if you like. If you forget your box lunch, don't panic. Drinks and snacks are sold by vendors, so you needn't starve.

There is a restaurant called **Piramid Charlies** upstairs in the Unidad Cultural (Visitor's Center) that's open Monday through Friday from 9am to midnight, on Saturday from 11am to 11pm, and on Sunday from 10am to 6pm. But more economical places exist along the road that rings the archeological site.

LA GRUTA. Tel. 595/6-0127 or 6-0104.
   Specialty: MEXICAN. **Directions:** Walk 10 minutes east of the Pyramid of the Sun (go out the gate behind the pyramid and follow the signs).
$ Prices: Main courses $6–$10; fixed-price lunch $11.
   Open: Daily 11am–7pm.
La Gruta is a huge, delightfully cool natural grotto filled with natty waiters and the sound of clinking glasses. Soft drinks and beer are served until the full bar opens. You have the option of ordering a five-course fixed-price lunch or choosing your own combination—perhaps a hamburger and a soft drink.

HOTEL-RESTAURANT VILLA ARQUEOLOGICA, outside the southern end of the site. Tel. 595/6-0244 or 6-0909.
   Specialty: FRENCH/MEXICAN. **Directions:** Ask directions from wherever you exit; it's just outside the fence around the pyramid grounds.
$ Prices: Main courses $7–$15.

IMPRESSIONS

Even a short stay in Mexico will telescope you through many centuries and, in imagination at least, will transport you to far away countries. Only Egypt has pyramids and prehistoric ruins as monumental as those of Teotihuacán and Chichén-Itzá. Taxco's and Mexico City's cathedrals rival those of Spain and Italy. Even Switzerland can hardly claim grander mountain scenery than Mexico's.
—Byron Steel, *Let's Visit Mexico*, 1946

Open: Daily 7:30am–11pm.

You can enjoy lunch in a fairly elegant dining room, and a postprandial coffee on the patio overlooking the swimming pool. The hotel part of the Villa Arqueologica is the very comfortable Club Méditerranée hotel within view of the ruins, just as at Chichén-Itzá, Cobá, Uxmal, and Cholula. Cactuses line the driveway, and red tiles and white stucco give the place a country ambience. The hotel has a library, tennis court, pool, and souvenir shop, as well as comfortable modern guest rooms, air-conditioned and equipped with private bathrooms, renting for $52 single or $58 double, per night. You can make reservations by calling the hotel, or by contacting Hoteles Villas Arqueologicas, Avenida Presidente Masaryk 183, Colonia Polanco, México, D.F. 11570 (tel. 5/203-3086 or 203-3833, or toll free 800/258-2633 in the U.S.).

DINING CLUSTERS

From the Unidad Cultural, walk out to the traffic circle and turn left. Along the road are several dozen tidy little **cookshops** tended by bright and energetic señoritas. As you walk along examining the premises, each will beckon you to enter, order, dine, and find satisfaction. Pick a place that appeals to you, take a look at what's cooking, and ask prices in advance. Many of them put out little signs advertising mixiotes, a wonderful regional specialty usually of chicken, potatoes, carrots, and a light white sauce (not spicy), all wrapped and cooked in a thin parchment paper made from the maguey leaf. It's delicious and differs from mixiote elsewhere made with beef, pork, or lamb in a red sauce. A full lunch need only cost $2 to $4. Cold soft drinks and beer are served.

---

2. PACHUCA

50 miles NE of Mexico City, 175 W of Tuxpan

GETTING THERE   By Bus   Buses to Pachuca are frequent from the Terminal del Norte in Mexico City and the trip takes about an hour and a half.

By Car   From the Pyramids of Teotihuacán, take the connecting road just north of San Martín de las Pirámides to Highway 85 north to Pachuca. Or you can backtrack south on Highway 132D to Highway 85 north to Pachuca. From the pyramids the trip takes less than an hour. From Tuxpan, the drive on Highway 180, then on Highway 130 at Poza Rica, is a beautiful one though the mountains and picturesque villages of Xicotepec de Juárez and Huauchinango. At Tulancingo, watch for the turnoff onto Highway 180 to Pachuca.

ESSENTIALS   The **telephone area code** is 771. The **State Tourism Office** is upstairs at Allende 406 (tel. 771/2-3253 or 2-3276), about two blocks east of Plaza Independencia.

Pachuca (alt. 8,000 ft.; pop. 180,000) is an attractive old town that's swept by cooling breezes. The women selling socks, handkerchiefs, and scarves in the plaza are constantly having to get up to retrieve items of clothing blown into the street by sudden gusts of wind. In the hills around the town, silver has been mined for at least 5 centuries, and is still produced in large quantities. It's well worth the effort to climb one of the narrow, precipitous streets up the hillside, from which there's an excellent view of the irregular surrounding terrain.

WHAT TO SEE & DO

Pachuca has a small, clean **market** through which it is pleasant to stroll. One section appears to specialize in making funeral wreaths with dozens of different white flowers woven into the greenery. There are many bake shops with appetizing cookies and pastries on show.

The Regional History Museum in the Hidalgo Cultural Center is located in what used to be the **Convent of San Francisco** on Plaza Bartolomé de Medina Plaza, about five blocks south of the main square (ask for directions). The former convent, considered to be the most important and original building in Pachuca, is an architectural gem itself. Built in 1596, it has seen a progression of uses: first as a mission base; then as a mining school, city hospital, and penitentiary; and now home for **National Photographic Archives,** the **Hidalgo State historical memorabilia,** and the **Hidalgo Cultural Center.** Take the time to stop in at this promising first-of-its-kind regional museum and browse through the historical and cultural past of this area. Open daily from 9am to noon and 3 to 5pm. Admission is 50¢.

WHERE TO STAY & EAT

For a place to stay, home in on **Plaza Independencia.** There are several other plazas in town, each unique. You won't miss this one if you look for the massive clock and bell tower. The remainder of the plaza is bare concrete. However, under the bell tower is a subterranean complex housing the cinema El Reloj, where you'll also find a few shops, public bathrooms, and parking. There is no lack of other good restaurants in town; you'll find most either on the plaza or Calle de Matamoros.

HOTEL DE LOS BAÑOS, Calle de Matamoros 205, Pachuca, Hgo. Tel. 771/3-0700. 62 rms (all with bath). TV TEL
$ Rates: $15 single; $17 double.
The old but well-kept Hotel de Los Baños is two blocks south of Plaza Independencia. Here you'll find a vast tile court for a lobby, guarded by sturdy wooden gates. The central court has several tiers of balconies leading to the rooms, some with elaborately carved Spanish furniture, Oriental rugs, and chandeliers; other rooms have modernish, functional hotel furniture. One side of the lobby is a cheery restaurant.

HOTEL EMILY, Plaza Independencia, Pachuca, Hgo. Tel. 771/5-0828 or 5-0868. 30 rms (all with bath). TV TEL
$ Rates: $15 single; $17 double; $28 deluxe suite.
First choice for a room is the Hotel Emily. The entrance faces the clock and bell tower and the marquee for the cinema on the plaza. An upholstered lounge area furnished only with pillows spruces up the lobby. The large rooms, accented with natural pine touches, are very tidy. The deluxe suite features a sitting room and one of the largest king-size beds in Mexico. There's a restaurant as well.

3. IXTA-POPO NATIONAL PARK

135 miles SE of Mexico City

GETTING THERE   By Bus   Take Metro Line 1 east (toward Pantalán) to the San Lazaro stop. As you come to the surface, you'll see the green-domed **TAPO** (Terminal de Autobuses de Pasajeros de Oriente), Mexico City's eastern bus terminal. Walk along Tunel 1, the corridor to the central domed area, and look for **Lineas Unidas–Cristóbal Colón** buses to Amecameca and Popo Park. Buses leave every half hour, every day, on the 1¼-hour trip. The bus will let you off a block and a half from the central square in Amecameca.

To get to Ixta-Popo National Park and the mountain lodge, about 8 miles from Amecameca, you'll have to hire a taxi for about $12 to $16 one way. Check at the Hotel San Carlos, on the square, for other passengers, and perhaps you'll be able to split the cost. Make a deal with the taxi driver to pick you up later since there's no telephone at the lodge; or you can take a chance and try to thumb a ride down the mountain, which is often easily done. Hitchhiking from Amecameca to the lodge isn't recommended because there is little traffic.

By Car   Take the Puebla road (Route 190) out of Mexico City, turning off to the right on Route 115 to the village of Chalco. A few miles farther on is Amecameca. From there, ask directions for the road to the park, 8 miles farther up the mountain on a good paved road that twists through alpine beauty.

Amecameca (pop. 37,000), situated at a height of 7,500 feet, is a fresh, clear town, with a big square and a 200-year-old parish church constructed in the 16th century for priests of the Dominican order. But the reason you are here is to see or perhaps to hike or climb in the Ixta-Popo National Park, whose raison d'être is the volcanoes Popocatépetl and Ixtaccíhihuatl, neither of which has erupted in this century.

WHAT TO SEE & DO

Outside the Albergue is the snow-covered summit of **Popocatépetl**, 18,177 feet at the rim. In the morning, the clouds may drift away for an hour, yielding an incomparable closeup view. Across the valley, Popo's sister volcano, **Ixtaccíhihuatl**, may be exposed as well. When you see them gleaming in the morning sun, surrounded by the chilly morning air, you'll remember the moment for a lifetime.

The Trails: Please take me in dead seriousness when I say that Popocatépetl is no mountain for rookie climbers, or for any expert climber who's not in top shape. At the lodge trailhead the air is so thin that even walking makes a normal, healthy person dizzy—and the air's considerably thinner at 17,887 feet! Besides, it's cold up here, even in the sweltering heat of summer. But if you're an expert climber, check in at the lodge reception or the rescue hut next to the lodge. You may be asked to pass an equipment check and sign your name in the hiker's register before you set out.

Maps of the various trails to the summit, showing the several huts and shelters, are on view in the lodge hut. The trek to the summit takes 9 to 12 hours, depending on what shape you're in and which trail you choose. You must camp at the summit that night and return the next day. Despite the name "rescue hut" on one of the buildings, there is no staff rescue team on hand. *You climb at your own risk,* and rescue—if any—will come from those on hand who pitch in to help.

When you return to the lodge, if all the bunks are taken, no one will mind if you pitch your hiking tent in the pine grove just below the lodge.

WHERE TO STAY & EAT

ALBERGUE VICENTE GUERRERO, Río Elba 20, 10th Floor, Col. Cuauhtémoc 06500 D.F. Tel. 286-9278.
$ Rates: $2 bunk with sheet, pillow case, and blanket.
The Albergue Vicente Guerrero at Tlamacas (alt. 12,800 ft.), in the Parque Nacional Ixta-Popo, was opened in 1978. It's beautiful—a modern mountain lodge done in native stone and natural wood, complete with bunkrooms, showers, a cafeteria, and a restaurant. If you want to stay the night, especially on a weekend, it's best to call or drop by the Mexico City office of the lodge for a reservation at the above address. There are several bunkrooms with six sections of four bunk beds each, which you share with others of mixed gender.

---

4. TEPOTZOTLÁN

27 miles N of Mexico City

GETTING THERE   By Metro and Bus   You can make the trip in a morning or an afternoon by taking the Metro (Line 7) to the Tacuba (not the Tacubaya!) station, walking over Aquiles Serdan on the pedestrian bridge, and then catching a bus (1-hour trip) to Tepotzotlán.

By Car   If you drive, go west on Paseo de la Reforma, and shortly after you pass the Auditorio Municipal (on your left) in Chapultepec Park, turn right (north) onto the Anillo Periferico. This soon becomes Avenida Manuel Ávila Camacho, which in turn becomes Highway 57D, the toll road to Querétaro. About 22½ miles out of the city, look for the turn to Tepotzotlán, which is about 1½ miles west of the highway.

For baroque architecture and a closeup view of small-town Mexican daily life, set aside a morning or afternoon for an excursion to the colonial town of Tepotzotlán.

WHAT TO SEE & DO

Tepotzotlán's **church** (1682) on the Plaza Hidalgo is considered one of the three finest examples of Churrigueresque (Mexican baroque) architecture (the other two are Santa Prisca in Taxco and La Valenciana in Guanajuato).

The grand extravagance of the facade is echoed inside the church, which is richly decorated with carved altarpieces and paintings. The museum attached to the church has a rich collection of paintings (including a Tintoretto), church ceremonial objects, vestments, pottery, and carving. Plan your visit for Tuesday through Sunday; the church and museum are closed on Monday.

When your senses start to reel from the power of it all, stroll outside, turn right, and enjoy the shady park standing in front of the museum.

The **Museo Nacional del Virrienato (National Viceroy's Museum),** Plaza Hidalgo 99 (tel. 987-0332), was once the Novitiate of the Company of Jesus (1585). Besides the dozens of rooms with displays of colonial treasures, be sure to inspect the Domestic Chapel, dating from about the same time as the neighboring church. It's open Tuesday through Sunday from 10am to 6pm and admission is free.

The main church, the **Templo de San Francisco Javier,** has 10 altars in the exaggerated baroque Churrigueresque style, bearing paintings by Miguel Cabrera. There are also 22 canvases by Cristóbal de Villalpando outlining the life of San Ignacio de Loyola, as well as a rich collection of colonial furnishings and artifacts.

After you've seen Tepotzotlán's colonial monuments, you might want to have a look at the **market** across the street, around which are several nice restaurants; or you may prefer simply to wander the cobbled streets for a while.

The bus back to Mexico City passes right through the main square. Those with cars might want to continue on (north) along Highway 57D, the Querétaro toll road, to the ruined Toltec city of Tula (see Section 5, below).

---

5. TULA

50 miles N of Mexico City

GETTING THERE By Bus Buses leave every quarter hour from Mexico City's **Terminal Central de Autobuses del Norte,** reached by a no. 17 city bus ("Indios Verdes") going north along Insurgentes or by Metro to the Terminal de Autobuses Norte station. When you enter the giant bus station, turn left and walk down to the far (western) end to the Tula ticket counter, marked **Autotransportes Valle del Mezquital.** Other companies run buses to Tula, but this one has the most frequent departures, every 15 minutes from 5am to 11pm. If you take the bus, you'll be obliged to walk out to the archeological site from town (about 15 minutes), take a cab, or a minibus "Tlahuelilpan," which runs out to the ruins, about a mile from the center of town.

By Car Driving north on the fast toll road (Highway 57D), there are no fewer than three turnoffs for Tula, at km 58 ("Petrolera-Tula"), km 69 ("Tepeji del Río–Tula"), and km 84 ("Jilotepec-Tula"). Take the first, most southerly, one at km 58 to avoid a toll.

When you reach the town of Tula, ask for directions to the Zona Arqueologica. The road in town that leads to the site is marked by a sign PARQUE NACIONAL TULA. Watch out for a sharp left turn just past a Pemex housing development.

In A.D. 900 or thereabouts, Teotihuacán may have been overrun by a people called the Chichimecs and some of the inhabitants of Teotihuacán may have moved northward to be among the great numbers of Chichimecs who founded the city of Tula, which flourished from 900 to 1150. The inhabitants of Tula, called Toltecs, consisted mainly of people with Chichimec ancestry. But 210 years after the founding of Tula, other Chichimecs ravaged the city, bringing about its demise. Enough of the one-time Toltec capital's impressive remains survived 200 years later to be hauled off to Tenochtitlán; Toltec architectural and design elements were greatly admired by the Aztecs and were incorporated into the building of the Aztec capital beginning in 1325. Modern archeologists have salvaged enough of the remains of Tula's pyramids, giant statues, and curious three-legged pottery to make the site worth a visit.

The city's remains are memorably beautiful, although its history is a sad story. The peace-loving king of the Toltecs, Quetzalcoatl (the "feathered serpent" in later lore) sought to purge his people of such things as human sacrifice and to direct their efforts to peaceful agriculture. The warlike party in Tula disagreed with the king's aims, and forced him and a band of his followers to flee the city in about 987. They wandered as far as the Yucatán and Chichén-Itzá, spreading Toltec culture along the way and giving birth to the legend of Quetzalcoatl (see Chapter 1 for more information).

The Chichimecs seized Tula around 1150, and for the next 200 years or so tribes in the whole region were in a state of flux.

WHAT TO SEE & DO

Most striking of the city's remains are the 15-foot-tall "Atlantean men," gigantic basalt figures mounted atop the **Temple of Tlahuizcalpantecutli** (Toltec for "Morning Star"). Possibly they supported the roof of the temple, but no one knows for sure because they were found at the base of the pyramid during excavations. The city's ball court has been restored beautifully. To the west of the temple is the **Burnt Palace (Quemado)** where you'll be able to see several painted reliefs and a statue of **Chac-Mool,** the reclining figure with head turned to one side. Between the temple and the ball court is a large wall with fantastic reliefs of the feathered serpent, skulls, eagles, and jaguars.

At the parking lot and entrance to the ruins, there's a small **site museum,** which contains a few Toltec artifacts as well as some Aztec pottery. The most interesting items here are the two stone figures once thought to be standard holders.

Both the ruins and the museum are open daily from 9:30am to 4:30pm. Admission is $3.50, free on Sunday.

WHERE TO EAT

CAFE "EL CISNE," on Tula's main street at Leando Valle. Tel. 2-0133.
   Specialty: MEXICAN.
   $ Prices: Fixed-price lunch $4.50.
   Open: Daily 10am–10pm.
You won't find any food at the ruins, so you might want to have a bite in town before you head out. The Cafe "El Cisne," next to Plaza de la Constitución, can fill your lunch wishes admirably and cheaply. Or if you want to eat at the ruins, have the restaurant wrap up some tacos and take them with you.

---

6. TOLUCA
45 miles W of Mexico City

GETTING THERE   By Bus   It's easy to get to Toluca and the market by bus from Mexico City. Take the Metro to the Observatorio station and look for the **Terminal Poniente** bus station. Reserved-seat buses ("Toluca-Directo") of various companies depart every 5 or 10 minutes on the hour-long trip.

By Car From Mexico City, follow Paseo de la Reforma west until it merges with Carretera a Toluca (Highway 15).

ESSENTIALS The **telephone area code** is 721. The **Tourist Office** is in the central city at Lerdo Poniente 101 in the Edificio Plaza Toluca, second floor (tel. 721/3-3014 or 3-2142), open Monday through Friday from 9am to 3pm and 4 to 8pm.

The **American Express** representative is Viajes Corona, Billada No. 445 (tel. 721/2-4189; fax 721/4-2655).

At 8,760 feet, Toluca (pop. 200,000) is the highest city in Mexico, capital of the state of México, and the hour-long trip there from Mexico City offers spectacular scenic views. Pine trees and icy-looking blue lakes dot the landscape, and only an occasional cactus plant or brightly colored painting, drying in the sun, will remind you that you're in Mexico.

Toluca's Friday market was once so popular that a parade of buses loaded up tourists every hour from Chapultepec Park in Mexico City. Toluca declined in popular tourism in the 1970s after its famous Friday market moved from its downtown location to its present one, nearer the outskirts of town by the bus station. Though tourism dropped, business boomed. Today Toluca is a thriving industrial center; you'll see the plants lining the highway as you drive into town. With a healthy business growth came city beautification, as well as new museums and restaurants. In short, with city sights and excellent shopping in Toluca, and easily reached nearby villages, there's good reason to put Toluca back on the tourist itinerary.

ORIENTATION

From Mexico City you'll enter town on the broad **Paseo Tollocan,** a four-lane highway lined with industrial plants like Chrysler and Pfizer. The bus will discharge passengers at the central bus station in front of the famed Friday market. Both are on **Isidro Fabela** near the intersection of Tollocan. If you're going directly to the market, it's behind the bus station. If you're going to a hotel first and have luggage, you'll want to get a taxi. They line up out front and it's a free-for-all. Taxis are inexpensive in Toluca, but bus-station drivers will double or triple the price. Slash the quoted price in half and you may strike a reasonable bargain. If you're traveling light, use the city buses ("Centro") that go to the city center and are also lined up in front.

From the bus station, the center of town is northwest between Lerdo de Tejada and Avenida Hidalgo. It's too far to walk.

WHAT TO SEE & DO

Plan your Toluca foray for a Friday, just so you can say that you saw the market, even if you don't stay long. The crowds and hubub are taxing and an hour or two should do it, even for the die-hard market lover. Follow that by a trip to **CASART,** the state crafts store a long block from the market. Then catch a bus ("Centro") for downtown. The first two should take the better part of the morning. After lunch you'll have time to see the museums and walk around the historic center of town. A trip to nearby archeological sites and the craft villages takes another day.

THE MARKET The gigantic **Mercado Juárez,** at the edge of town on the highway to Mexico City, has both market buildings and open-air grounds. Shops in the buildings are open all week, but it's on Friday that the people from surrounding villages come and crowd the plaza. The bus from Mexico City pulls into a terminal right across the street from the Mercado Juárez. You'll recognize the market by the pair of slender concrete slabs that tower above it to serve as a landmark.

Because of the natives' bargaining powers, a peaceful walk around the market is not an easy matter. Every time you pause to admire such unfamiliar sights as a boxful of chattering chickens, a 2-foot-high pile of assorted shoelaces, or an array of framed saints' pictures, some man or young boy will accost you with cries of "Serapes, rebozos, Señor, very cheap." Some sights will make you pause—a marimba band banging away cheerfully between the stalls or a little open-fronted bakery where chains of tortillas can be seen pouring off a conveyor belt into a basket. But sooner or later the heat and crowdedness of the market will begin to get you down; the man with the pig under his arm or the woman with a turkey sticking its head from the back of her shawl brushing past probably won't even cause you to bat an eye.

THE HISTORIC CENTER   This area in the heart of Toluca is bounded by Avenidas Hidalgo, Juárez, and Sebastian Lerdo de Tejada. Here you'll see the housing for the heart of state government in stately buildings framing the square—the Palace of Justice, Chamber of Deputies, Government Palace, and Municipal Palace, Cosmovitral Botanico, and the cathedral, which was established by the Franciscans in the mid-1800s.

✪ THE COSMOVITRAL BOTANICO (BOTANICAL GARDEN)   Located at the corner of Juárez and Lerdo (tel. 721/14-6785), off Plaza de los Martires between the Chamber of Deputies and the Government Palace, this indoor garden inside the walls of a 19th-century art nouveau building is one of the city's greatest creations. It was the site of the famed Toluca market until 1975. In 1980 it reopened to house the botanical gardens. The upper half of the building is emblazoned with 54 bold stained-glass panels telling the story of humanity in relation to the cosmos. All the elements of a good tale are there—good and evil, happiness and sadness, freedom and imprisonment. From design to completion, it took local artists 3 years. The stained glass, however, is only the frame for the gardens showing plants native to the state of Mexico and other countries. The gardens are open Tuesday through Sunday from 9am to 5pm, and admission is 50¢.

The famous ***portales*** **(arcades)** of Toluca, begun in 1832, are one block east. They are a popular meeting, shopping, and dining place. From the Day of the Dead (November 1–2) through Christmas they're filled with temporary vendors selling the candy for which the state is famous.

✪ CENTRO CULTURAL MEXEQUENSE   Seeing this cultural center is reason enough to stay on in Toluca. In 1987 the Centro Cultural Mexequense (tel. 721/12-4113) opened on the sprawling grounds of the former Hacienda de la Pila, in a southeastern suburb of the city. The ambitious and beautiful museum incorporates four cultural entities and a library that were once scattered throughout Toluca. The various buildings form a one-story U shape around an enormous central yard where orchestras and dancers sometimes entertain.

English-speaking guides are often available for the asking at the library, on your left as you approach the cluster of buildings. Or you are free to wander at your leisure, but all signs are in Spanish.

The center is open Tuesday through Sunday from 9am to 5pm (the restaurant is closed Sunday), and admission is free. To get there, take the "Lineas 2 de Marzo" bus, either from the bus station by the market or as it comes through the central plaza approximately every 15 minutes.

Don't miss the **Popular Arts Museum,** on the right, in the original hacienda

---

IMPRESSIONS

. . . I make solemn affidavit that not even in Russia have I seen such an abnormal proportion of bankrupt plumbing systems, [and] ill-advised electric wiring . . .
—STUART CHASE, *MEXICO: A STUDY OF TWO AMERICANS,* 1931

In the Maison de la Providencia, at Toluca, yesterday, a hungry guest shot Margarito Lopez, a waiter of the establishment, through the hand, because the waiter did not answer his call promptly.
—W. E. CARSON, *MEXICO: THE WONDERLAND OF THE SOUTH,* 1909

building, if you plan to visit any of the state's crafts villages. You'll get a great overview not only of what the state has to offer and where, but also an idea of quality. As you enter, you can't miss the spectacular, building-size, polychrome-clay "trees of life" from the artisans of Metepec. They would have been too huge to bring into the building, so the artists made and fired them inside before the museum opened. As you walk through the salons you'll find exhibits of regional costumes, Persian-like tapestries from Temoaya, leather-covered chests from San Mateo Atenco, and embroidery from Ameyalco among the thousands of objects. In the **Charro Museum** you'll see lariats and swords, a great sombrero display, spurs, bits, and saddles. There's even a 16th-century stirrup and a charro wedding suit. A cozy restaurant (inexpensive), bookstore, and sales shop are in this building.

Opposite the Popular Arts Museum and next to the **library** is the **Museum of Modern Art** (tel. 12-4115) in a building originally intended as an observatory. Here you can study, close up, paintings by Rufino Tamayo, Juan O'Gorman, Jose Chávez Morado, Orozco, and Diego Rivera, all of whom were better known for their murals. The works are quite good and you'll likely discover other lesser-known artists whose efforts rival their better-known contemporaries.

In the middle, straight ahead from the entrance, between the Popular Arts and Modern Art museums, is the **Museum of Anthropology** (tel. 12-4079). The massive number of artifacts are well displayed in a broad and spacious building. Objects from the state's 10 most important archeological sites include beautiful pottery and mural fragments from Teotihuacán and the famous wood drum from Malinalco, showing carved jaguars and eagles. Other excellent displays show the forests and animals by region, insects, butterflies, and a considerable collection of stuffed animals. Memorabilia from colonial days to the present includes a bust of Emperor Maximilian, a fan and lace gloves that belonged to Empress Carlotta, French dresses from the time of Porfirio Díaz, photographs, and the first soft-drink machine in the state of Mexico.

SHOPPING

Besides the famous **Central Market** mentioned above, Toluca and environs offer several good options for shopping, especially for regionally made crafts.

CASART, Paseo Tollocan and Urawa. Tel. 14-0742.

The Centro Cultural Mexequense and the Toluca Market give you two insights into regional crafts; CASART gives the other. You can't miss the showy building on the main road by the central market and bus station. Inside is an enormous showroom and sales outlet for a majority of the state's crafts—blown glass, dinnerware, textiles, wood carving, Persian-style rugs from nearby Temoaya, hand-woven sweaters, rugs and serapes from Guaulapita, baskets of all kinds, silver jewelry from San Felipe el Progreso, and pottery from Metepec. A few crafts from other regions in Mexico are for sale as well, such as lacquer chests from Olinala, Guerrero. Local women sell and demonstrate textile and basket weaving as well. Upstairs are more crafts and excellent photographs of artisans at work, with labels describing the regions and crafts. CASART is open daily from 10am to 8pm.

DULCERÍA EL SOCIO, opposite Woolworth's.

While you're in the vicinity, take a gander at the biggest array of candy in town. Dulcería means sweet shop, and since people in the state of Mexico thrive on candy, this shop feeds the addiction with floor-to-ceiling goodies. You can pick out a gift basket and fill it here. But to save money, buy the sweets here and bargain for a basket from one of the women from neighboring Tlapaltitlan who weave beautiful baskets in many sizes while waiting for their accumulated inventory to sell. You'll find them around the arcades. The shop is open Monday through Saturday from 10am to 9pm.

EASY EXCURSIONS

POTTERY ✪ **Metepec,** approximately 5 miles from the edge of Toluca, is probably the most famous of the crafts villages, known for its pottery and polychrome "trees of life." A trip here is worth the little time it takes: Frequent buses leave the central bus station in Toluca and the trip takes less than 30 minutes. Avoid arriving between 2 and 4pm when many shops are closed. Pottery shops line the main street into town. Potters generally have their workshops away from the city center, so if you want to see them at work, ask around for directions.

ARCHEOLOGICAL SITES   Of the two nearby archeological sites, Teotenango and Calixlahuaca, the latter is the easier to reach by local bus from Toluca's bus station. Frequent buses make the 20-minute trip to the town of **Calixlahuaca**. From there it's a short hike up the hill. The zone is small and dates back more than 3,000 years. The most notable edifice is the circular one devoted to Ehecatl, god of the wind. If your visit coincides with lunch, bring it along and eat while sitting there listening to the sounds of the village drift up. You can see for miles. Locals may try to sell you artifacts they've found, but it's illegal to buy them. There's a small museum at the site.

About 15 miles south of Toluca is the huge, ancient fortified city of **Teotenango**. It was occupied between A.D. 900 and 1200.

The archeological sites are open daily from 9am to 5pm. Admission is $2.75, for each site.

WHERE TO STAY

HOTEL TERMINAL, Felipe Berriozabal 101, Toluca, Edo. de México 50000. Tel. 721/4-4588. 79 rms (all with bath). **Bus:** "Centro" from the city center.
$ Rates: $11–$15 single; $15–$19 double.
The Hotel Terminal has an entrance inside the bus terminal, to the right before you exit the front doors. For a short stay and a slim budget, it's acceptable. However, if you saw it from the trashy street in front, stepping over debris and wedging yourself past elbow-to-elbow street vendors, you might say "No way!" Inside makes a better impression. There are two room categories. Rooms on Floors 1 to 5 have plainish, somewhat dreary, uncarpeted rooms with chenille bedspreads. Rooms on Floors 6 and 7 each come with a carpet and a telephone; a TV is $1.75 extra. The price difference between the categories isn't much, but the quality difference is considerable. The rooms may be packed on weekends (remember that giant Friday market across the street) and thus more noisy too; weekdays you can have your pick.

HOTEL SAN CARLOS, Portal Madero 210, Toluca, Edo. de México 50000. Tel. 721/4-9419. 75 rms (all with bath). TV TEL
$ Rates: $15 single; $20 double.
Across from the Woolworth's is the near-zócalo budget answer. Management is in the process of remodeling the rooms and installing new carpet, so for a while some guests may have "new" rooms and some may have those that are tidy but worn and sparsely furnished. The desk clerks are friendly and helpful, and guests can't go wrong choosing the San Carlos.

HOTEL COLONIAL, Hidalgo Oriente 103, Toluca, Edo. de México 50000. Tel. 721/5-9700 or 4-7066. 40 rms (all with bath).
$ Rates: $16 single; $21 double.
A block and a half farther from the Hotel San Carlos, two blocks east of the *portales*, near the corner of Juárez, the Hotel Colonial is only slightly higher in price for better-quality, although smallish, rooms. As befits its name, the hotel is colonial in feel and built around an interior patio. Its carpeted rooms are cozy, with good beds and nostalgic old armoires and dressers. A small restaurant and bar are attached.

WORTH THE EXTRA BUCKS

HOTEL SAN FRANCISCO, Rayon 104, Toluca, Edo. de México 50000. Tel. 721/3-3114. 74 rms (all with bath). MINIBAR TV TEL
$ Rates: $30 single; $42 double with two beds.
Rayon is a quiet street close to Toluca's center, four blocks east of the *portales*; the

hotel is between Hidalgo and Morelos. The spacious, soaring lobby, with split-level dining, sitting, and bar area, belies its rather small number of rooms (there are only eight floors). Most rooms have double or queen-size beds, but there are a few with king-size beds as well. The beds are excellent and most bathrooms have a tub/shower combination. For its quality and location in a larger Mexican City, it would be twice the price.

HOTEL DEL REY, km 63.5, Toluca, Edo. de México 50000. Tel. 721/2-2122. 150 rms (all with bath). MINIBAR TV TEL
$ Rates: $53 single; $60 double.

The Hotel del Rey is on the industrial parkway leading into Toluca (Highway 15), on the eastern edge of the city—it's on the left after the Chrysler and Nissan assembly plants, but before the Pfizer plant—and is one of several hotels along this strip catering to visiting businesspeople. It's a modern, sprawling hostelry with colonial-style architecture, gift shops, restaurants, a travel agent, and indoor gardens. Rooms are spacious, with king- and queen-size beds. For all its worldly appeal it isn't too far out of our budget range. If you want to save a taxi ride from the bus station to the del Rey to stash luggage before going to the market (which is across from the bus station) tell the driver (you'll notice that he discharges passengers all along the parkway).

WHERE TO EAT

If none of the little **market eateries** appeals to you, there are several alternatives. Search the skyline for the red-and-yellow star sign that identifies the local branch of VIPS (pronounced "beeps"), a clean, bright, and cheery American-style restaurant.

VIPS, Paseo Tollocan. Tel. 17-4974.
   Specialty: MEXICAN/AMERICAN.
$ Prices: Main courses $3.60–$12.
   Open: Daily 8am–11pm.

This light, bright, American-style coffee shop even has a no-smoking section—but, of course, no one pays any attention. It's a casual, modern place much like a slick fast-food place in the U.S. but with Mexican specialties and good old American-style hamburgers. It's one block from the market toward Tollocan around the corner from the state-owned crafts store CASART.

EL PORTON, Paseo Tollocan 1031. Tel. 17-9690.
   Specialty: MEXICAN.
$ Prices: Soups $2–$3; tacos $1.75–$3; plate-lunch special $5–$8.
   Open: Daily 11am–11pm.

This gleaming restaurant, near the market one block south of the state-owned crafts store CASART and half a block to the left of VIPS restaurant, is geared toward tourists who don't speak Spanish. The menu has color photos of all the specialties, making it easy to point and pick from among the soups, tacos, platter meals, and daily special. The service is friendly and swift.

LA VAQUITA NEGRA, Portal Reforma. Tel. 15-6847.
   Specialty: TORTAS/SANDWICHES.
$ Prices: Sandwiches $1.50–$4.
   Open: Mon–Sat 9am–9pm.

La Vaquita Negra is reputed to be the best torta shop in town. It's located just around from the Fonda Rosita on one side of the cathedral. Tortas are sandwiches using the typical bolillo roll. Here you have a choice of fresh ingredients like cheese, sausage, chicken, and avocado. It's a deli too, so choose ingredients in the showcases while rubbing elbows with downtowners doing the same. The prices vary a bit, depending on how you stack your sandwich.

FONDA ROSITA, Portal Madero, Plaza Fray Andrés de Castro. Tel. 5-1394.
   Specialty: MEXICAN.
$ Prices: Appetizers $2–$3; main courses $6.50–$13.

Open: Daily 10am–11pm.

⭐ Inside the *portales* (arcades) of the historic city center on Plaza Fray Andrés Castro, is a bustling place frequented by families. That's usually a sign of quality and value in Mexico. As its sister restaurant Fonda San Felipe in nearby Tlalmimilolpan, the Rosita has enjoyed a well-deserved reputation for high-quality Mexican food. The sopa medula (bone-marrow soup) and baked pork loin are especially good.

7. CUERNAVACA

64 miles S of Mexico City, 50 miles N of Taxco

GETTING THERE   By Plane   The regional airline, **AeroMorelos,** is headquartered in Cuernavaca with a hub in Oaxaca. They use two 40-passenger F-27 planes and a 40-seat Piper Navajo PD 31-350. From Cuernavaca there's a twice-weekly service from Puebla, Acapulco, and Oaxaca. Make reservations through the Cuernavaca office: Paseo del Conquistador 51, Col. Maravillas, Cuernavaca, Mor. 62230 (tel. 73/17-5588 or 17-5582; fax 73/17-2320).

By Bus   The Mexico City **Central de Autobuses del Sur**'s reason for being is the route Mexico City–Cuernavaca–Taxco–Acapulco–Zihuatanejo. Almost 90% of the buses leaving that terminal ply this route, and they do it with great frequency, so you'll have little trouble getting a bus. **Autobuses Pullman de Morelos** is the line with the most frequent departures and the most convenient downtown terminal in Cuernavaca. Buses leave Mexico City's Central del Sur every 10 minutes throughout the day on the 1-hour trip, so reservations are not really necessary. Buy a ticket for the "Centro," not for "Casino de la Selva," which is a bus stop at the northern edge of Cuernavaca. And be careful not to get off at La Selva, as some buses will stop there.

Several other lines serve the city, including **Estrella de Oro** (15 buses daily) and **Lineas Unidas del Sur/Flecha Roja** (8 buses daily).

By Car   From Mexico City, take Paseo de la Reforma to Chapultepec Park and merge with the Periferico that will take you to Highway 95D, the toll road on the far south of town that goes to Cuernavaca. From the Periferico, take the Insurgentes exit and continue until you come to signs for Cuernavaca/Tlalpan. Choose either the Cuernavaca Cuota (toll) or the old Cuernavaca Libre (free) road on the right.

DEPARTING   By Bus   The **Autobuses Pullman de Morelos** bus station, at the corner of Abasolo and Netzahualcoyotl (tel. 73/12-6001), is four blocks south of the center of town. This is the station with the most departures to Mexico City. The **Autobuses Estrella de Oro** terminal in Cuernavaca is at Morelos Sur 900 (tel. 73/12-3055), at the corner of Veracruz, about 15 blocks south of the center of town. This is the terminal with buses to Taxco (6 per day), Zihuatanejo (3 per day), Acapulco, Iguala, and Chilpancingo (10 per day), and Mexico City (13 per day). (For details on how to get to Taxco by bus, see "Easy Excursions from Cuernavaca," below.) The second-class bus line **Autobuses Unidas del Sur/Flecha Roja** has its Cuernavaca terminal at Morelos 255 (tel. 73/12-5797), north of the town center. Any bus going up Morelos will drop you there. Here you'll find the buses to Toluca, Chalma, Ixtapan de la Sal, Taxco, Acapulco, the Cacahuamilpa Caves, and Querétaro. Buses (the school-bus type) load until the aisles are jammed. If you take one of these to the caves or to Taxco your chances of getting a seat are good at the Apulyeca crossroads where many people get off. **Estrella Roja,** at Galeana and Cuauhtemotzin, about eight blocks south of the town center, serves Cuautla, Yautepec, Oaxtepec, and Izucar de Matamoros. But if you're just taking a day trip to Cuautla, there are more buses at the Mercado Central (see "Easy Excursions from Cuernavaca," below, for details).

Cuernavaca (alt. 5,058 ft.; pop. 282,000), capital of the state of Morelos, has been popular as a resort for people from Mexico City ever since the time of Moctezuma.

Emperor Maximilian built a retreat here over a century ago. Mexicans say that the town has a climate of "eternal springs," and on weekends the city is crowded with day-trippers from surrounding cities, especially from the capital, which on weekends results in jammed roads between Mexico City and Cuernavaca, and restaurants and hotels may be full as well. Cuernavaca has a large American colony, plus students attending one of the myriad language and cultural institutes that crowd the city.

The Indian name for this town was Cuauhnahuac, which means "at the edge of the forest." The city's symbol today is an Indian pictogram of a tree speaking. People have lived here, next to the whispering trees, since about A.D. 1200, but only in the early 1400s did it come under the sway of the Aztecs, who established huge hunting parks for themselves—beginning a tradition of Cuauhnahuac as a resort for the wealthy and powerful.

The conquistadores, when they arrived, heard "Cuauhnahuac" but said "Cuernavaca," so the whispering tree became a cow's horn.

Emperor Charles V gave Cuernavaca to Cortés as a fief, and the conquistador built a palace here in 1532 (now the Museo Cuauhnahuac) and lived there on and off for half a dozen years before returning to Spain. Cortés introduced sugarcane cultivation to the area, and Caribbean slaves came to work in the cane fields. His sugar hacienda at the edge of town is now the luxurious Hotel de Cortés. The economics of large sugarcane growers failed to serve the interests of the indigenous farmers and there were numerous uprisings in colonial times.

After independence, mighty landowners from Mexico City gradually dispossessed the remaining small landholders, converting them to virtual serfdom. It was this condition that led to the rise of Emiliano Zapata, the great champion of agrarian reform, who battled the forces of wealth and power, defending the small farmer with the cry of "Tierra y Libertad!" (Land and Liberty!) during the Mexican Revolution following 1910.

In this century, Cuernavaca has seen the influx of wealthy foreigners, and of industrial capital. The giant CIVAC industrial complex on the outskirts has brought wealth to the city, but also the curse of increased traffic, noise, and air pollution.

ORIENTATION

ARRIVING   By Plane   The airport is 15½ miles southwest of Cuernavaca on the highway to Acapulco. There are no colectivo minivans, and taxis to or from the airport cost around $8 one way. Don't tarry in the terminal—there are few flights and taxis disappear quickly.

By Bus   Bus stations are close to town center and most are within walking distance of several of my hotel recommendations. When you arrive in Cuernavaca after the hour-long ride, you'll alight at the last stop, in the **Autobuses Pullman de Morelos** bus station. Walk up the hill (north) on Netzahualcoyotl two blocks to Hidalgo, then turn right onto that street to reach the center of town.

The **Autobuses Estrella de Oro** terminal in Cuernavaca is about a 15- or 20-minute walk south of the center of town. If you arrive at this terminal (say, from Acapulco or Taxco), you should know that the tourist office is less than a block up Morelos (see below). Take any bus going north (uphill) on Morelos to reach the center of town, near the cathedral.

The second-class bus line **Autobuses Unidas del Sur/Flecha Roja** has its Cuernavaca terminal at Morelos 255 (tel. 73/12-5797), north of the town center and too far to walk. Most buses going south on Morelos will drop you near the central plazas, but ask first.

If you arrive in Cuernavaca from Cuautla, more than likely you'll arrive at the **Estrella Roja** station at Galeana and Cuauhtemotzin, about eight blocks south of the center of town. From here, your best bet is a taxi to town.

INFORMATION   Cuernavaca's **State Tourist Office** is at Avenida Morelos Sur 802, between Jalisco and Veracruz (tel. 73/14-3860 or 14-3920), half a block north of the Estrella de Oro bus station, and about a 10- or 15-minute walk south of the cathedral. It's open Monday through Friday from 9am to 8pm and on Saturday and Sunday from 9am to 5pm.

The **Federal Tourism Office,** upstairs at Hidalgo and Comonfort (tel. 73/12-1815 or 12-5414), is open Monday through Friday from 9am to 3pm. Pick up brochures here and maybe a map, but the staff is of little help.

CITY LAYOUT Coming into Cuernavaca from Mexico City, on the east side of town you may pass **La Selva** (The Woods), where there's a fancy hotel and a vast overambitious resort complex called the Casino de la Selva, begun in the 1960s, which was never really completed. Depending on which bus you take, you may pass a dramatic equestrian statue of the popular hero Emiliano Zapata, galloping at full tilt on the northern edge of town.

In the center of the city, are two contiguous plazas. The smaller and more formal of the two is square, with a Victorian gazebo (designed by Monsieur Eiffel of Eiffel Tower fame) at its center. This is the **Jardín Juárez.** The larger, rectangular plaza planted with trees, shrubs, and benches is the **Jardín de los Héroes,** also sometimes called the Plaza de Armas or the Alameda. These two tree-filled plazas are the hub for strolling vendors selling balloons, baskets, bracelets, and other crafts from surrounding villages. It's all easy-going, and one of the best pleasures is grabbing a park bench or table in a nearby restaurant just to watch. On Sunday afternoon orchestras play from the gazebo. At the eastern end of the Alameda is the **Cortés Palace,** the conquistador's residence which now serves as the Museo de Cuauhnahuac.

You should be aware that this city's street-numbering system—or, rather, systems—are extremely confusing. It appears that the city fathers, during the past century or so, became dissatisfied with the street numbers every 10 or 20 years, and imposed a new numbering system each time. Thus you may find an address given as "no. 5" only to find that the building itself bears the number "506." One grand gateway I know bears no fewer than five different and various street numbers, ranging from 2 to 567! In my descriptions of hotels, restaurants, and sights, I'll note the nearest cross street so you can find your way to your chosen destination with a minimum of fuss.

GETTING AROUND

BY BUS Frequent buses go from downtown to all the outlying centers. Just tell a local where you want to go and most will go out of their way to help you.

BY TAXI Taxis are relatively inexpensive in Cuernavaca; $1 should get you from downtown to the outlying Herb Museum, for example. Determine the fare before taking off.

FAST FACTS

American Express The local representative is Viajes Marin, Edificio Las Plazas, Loc. 13 (tel. 73/14-2266; fax 73/12-9297).

Area Code The telephone area code is 73.

Bookstores There's a handy bookstore with English-language books and periodicals just off the main square in the Centro Las Plazas shopping center. It's the Anglo-American Bookstore, also called the **Librería Las Plazas,** at Local 10 in the complex.

Post Office The post office (tel. 73/12-4379) is on the Jardín de los Héroes, right next door to the Cafe Los Arcos.

Spanish Lessons As much as for its springlike weather Cuernavaca is known for its Spanish-language schools, aimed at the foreigner. Generally the schools will help students find lodging with a family, or provide a list of potential places to stay. Rather than make a long-term commitment in a family living situation, try it for a week, then decide. Below are the names of and addresses of some of the schools. The whole experience from classes to lodging can be quite inexpensive and the school may accept credit cards for the class portion. The **Mexican Lyceum of Languages** is located at Isla Mujeres 14, Col. Quintana Roo, Cuernavaca, Mor. 62060, México.

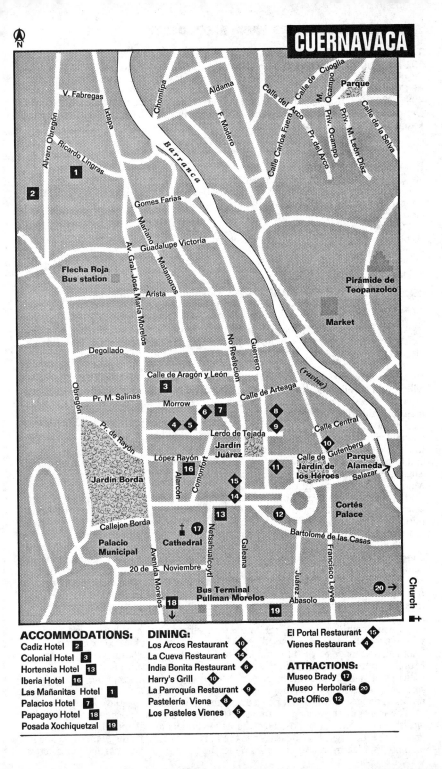

CUERNAVACA

ACCOMMODATIONS:
Cadiz Hotel **2**
Colonial Hotel **3**
Hortensia Hotel **13**
Iberia Hotel **16**
Las Mañanitas Hotel **1**
Palacios Hotel **7**
Papagayo Hotel **18**
Posada Xochiquetzal **19**

DINING:
Los Arcos Restaurant **10**
La Cueva Restaurant **14**
India Bonita Restaurant **6**
Harry's Grill **10**
La Parroquía Restaurant **9**
Pastelería Viena **8**
Los Pasteles Vienes **5**

El Portal Restaurant **15**
Vienes Restaurant **4**

ATTRACTIONS:
Museo Brady **17**
Museo Herbolaria **20**
Post Office **12**

The **Instituto Teopanzolco** is also good and it is located at Calle Teopanzolco 102-bis, Col. Vista Hermosa, Cuernavaca, Mor. 62290, México (or write to Apdo. Postal 103-A, Cuernavaca, Mor. 62280, México). Or you can contact a representative of the school in the U.S., John Díaz, 410 Escobar St., Fremont, CA 94539 (tel. 408/732-0807). Readers have written to recommend **Universal, Centro de Lengua y Comunicación Social A.C.** (the Universal Language School), Apdo. Postal 1-1826, Cuernavaca, Mor. 62000, México.

WHAT TO SEE & DO

If you plan to visit Cuernavaca on a day trip from Mexico City, the best days to do so are Tuesday, Wednesday, or Thursday (and perhaps Friday). On weekends the roads, the city, its hotels and restaurants are filled with people from Mexico City, and prices jump dramatically. On Monday, the museum—which you definitely must see—is closed. So make it Tuesday through Friday.

You can spend 1 or 2 days sightseeing in Cuernavaca pleasantly enough. If you've come on a day trip from Mexico City, you may not have time to make all the excursions listed below, but you'll have enough time to see the sights in town.

First place to visit is the former home of the greatest of the conquistadores, Hernán Cortés:

MUSEO DE CUAUHNAHUAC, in the Cortés Palace.

The museum is housed in the Cortés Palace, the former home of the greatest of the conquistadores, Hernán Cortés. Begun by Cortés in 1530, it was finished by the conquistador's son, Martín, and later served as the legislative headquarters for the state of Morelos. It's in the town center at the eastern end of the Jardín de los Héroes.

Inside the main door, go to the right. If you've recently visited the National Museum of Anthropology in Mexico City, these displays of humanity's early times will be familiar. Passing through these exhibits, you come to a little court in which are the ruins of a Tlahuica temple. In keeping with conquistador policy, Cortés had his mansion built right on top of an older structure.

The northern wing of the palace, on the ground floor, houses exhibits from the colonial era: suits of armor juxtaposed with the arrows, spears, and maces used by the Indians. Upstairs in the northern wing are costumes, domestic furnishings, carriages, and farm implements from Mexico of the 1800s, mostly from *haciendas azucareras* (sugar plantations). There are also mementos of the great revolutionaries Francisco Madero and Emiliano Zapata.

Through the southern door are more exhibits from colonial times, including several fascinating "painted books," or Indian codices, which survived the book burnings of the Spaniards. There's also a clock mechanism (*reloj*) from Cuernavaca's cathedral, thought to be the first public clock on the American continent.

When you get to the east portico on the upper floor, you're in for a treat. A large **Diego Rivera mural** commissioned by Dwight Morrow, U.S. ambassador to Mexico in the 1920s, depicts the history of Cuernavaca from the coming of the Spaniards to the rise of Zapata (1910). It's fascinating to examine the mural in detail. Above the north door, the Spaniards and their Indian allies, armed with firearms, crossbows, and cannon battle the Aztecs, who have clubs, spears, slings, and bows and arrows. Above the door is a scene of Aztec human sacrifice.

Moving southward along the wall, men struggle with a huge tree, perhaps symbolizing the Aztec "universe." Next, the inhabitants of Mexico are enslaved, branded, and made to yield their gold. The figure in a white headscarf is José María Morelos, one of the leaders in Mexico's fight for independence from Spain.

Moving along, malevolent priests, backed by lancers, subjugate the Indians spiritually; dressed in white, they stand peaceably and respectfully, at the orders of the priests. The Spaniards build a new society using the Indians as slave labor.

The scenes on the sugar plantations are from the time after independence when the wealthy and powerful dispossessed the native population of their land in order to create the huge sugar haciendas. While the Indians slave away, the *blancos* recline in hammocks. Nearby, priests and friars direct the building of churches and monasteries by native labor; the churchmen accept gold from the Indians; and only one poor friar sits with the women and children, teaching them the doctrines of the church.

Above the south door is an auto-da-fe, or burning of heretics, from the Spanish Inquisition. The scene is chronologically out of place, but Rivera obviously meant to contrast it to the Aztec sacrifice over the north door, opposite. He's saying, "Aztecs or Catholics, the more it changes, the more it stays the same." Rivera firmly believed that communism would break the cycle of man's inhumanity to man, but the Stalinist purges of the 1930s were yet in the future when Rivera painted this superb mural. It's ironic that his "religion" (Communist ideology) led to the same excesses of ideological fanaticism as did Aztec cosmology and the Catholic Inquisition.

In the upper left corner of the southern door, Indian revolutionaries are hanged by slave-drivers. In the lower left, Zapata leads a group of revolutionary *campesinos* brandishing their farming tools as weapons.

The frieze beneath the mural is interesting as well, done in a chunky 1930s style which is very art deco, but also very Rivera. It looks to me as though he was inspired by the many Aztec friezes.

Admission: Tues–Sat $2.75, Sun free.
Open: Tues–Sun 9:30am–7pm.

CATEDRAL DE LA ASUNCIÓN, at the corner of Hidalgo and Morelos.

As you enter the church precincts and pass down the walk, try to imagine what life in Mexico was like in the old days. Construction on the church was begun in 1533, a mere 12 years after Cortés conquered Tenochtitlán (Mexico City) from the Aztecs. The churchmen could hardly trust their safety to the tenuous allegiance of their new converts, so they built a fortress as a church. The skull-and-crossbones above the main door is not a comment on their feelings about the future, however, but rather a symbol for the Franciscan order, which had its monastery here in the church precincts.

Inside, the church is stark, even severe, having been refurbished in the 1960s. The most curious aspect of the interior is the mystery of the frescoes. Discovered during the refurbishing, they depict Christian missionary activity and persecution in Japan, and are painted in Japanese style. No one is certain who painted them, or why.

Admission: Free.
Open: Daily 8am–11pm. **Directions:** Walk three blocks southwest of the Jardín de los Héroes.

MUSEO CASA ROBERT BRADY, Calle Netzahualcoyotl 4. Tel. 12-1136.

This new museum in the Franciscan cloister of the Cuernavaca cathedral (behind the cathedral between Calles 20 de Noviembre and Hidalgo) contains more than 1,300 works of art. Among them are pre-Hispanic and colonial pieces; oil paintings by Frida Kahlo and Rufino Tamayo; and handcrafts from America, Africa, Asia, and India. Admission includes a guide in Spanish; English and French guides are available if requested at the time of your reservation.

Admission: $3.50.
Open: Thurs–Friday 10am–2pm and 4–6pm, Sat 10am–2pm. *Call ahead for reservations.* Special visits can be arranged during other days at a special price.

PALACIO MUNICIPAL, at the corner of Av. Morelos and Callejon Borda. Tel. 18-5710.

On Cuernavaca's Palacio Municipal (Town Hall) there's a ceramic tile plaque to the right of the door which reads HONORABLE AYUNTAMIENTO DE CUERNAVACA (town council); to the left, CUAUHNAHUAC, with the city's tree symbol. Walk into the brick, stone, and stucco courtyard anytime the building is open. Besides the unusual and attractive building, you should tour the large old oil paintings hung in the arcades on the first and second floors. On the north wall, on the ground floor, paintings explain the making of "feathered mosaics." In the north arcade, on the upper floor, are scenes from Cuernavaca's pre-Hispanic culture: Tlahuicans making pottery, storing corn (maize), being shaken down by an Aztec tax collector, and harvesting cotton. On the east wall, the scenes continue: The Indians gather maguey leaves, pound them to release the fibers, and weave cloth; a priest offers a chicken to the god Tepuztecatl. The Aztec goldsmiths' craft is explained in a canvas with 17 smaller panels. In the

southeastern corner are two murals, done by R. Cueva in 1962, with scenes from the Revolution.
Admission: Free.
Open: Mon–Fri 9am–2pm and 4–6pm (often at other times as well).

JARDÍN BORDA, on Morelos at Hidalgo. Tel. 12-0086.

Half a block from the cathedral is the Jardín Borda, or Borda Gardens. One of the many wealthy builders to choose Cuernavaca was José de la Borda, the Taxco silver magnate, who ordered a sumptuous vacation house built here in the late 1700s. The large enclosed garden next to the house was actually a huge private park, laid out in Andalusian style with little kiosks and an artificial pond. Maximilian found it worthy of an emperor, and took it over as his private preserve in the mid-1800s. But after Max, the Borda Gardens fell on hard times. Decades of neglect followed.

The paintings of the French Intervention enhance a stroll through the gardens. Here are the scenes you'll see: First, Emperor Maximilian and Empress Carlotta arrive in Cuernavaca for the first time; then, Maximilian, while out for a ride, gets his first glimpse of La India Bonita, who was to become his lover. The next scene is of court festivities in the Borda Gardens, with courtiers taking turns rowing little boats. Finally, Maximilian's niece pleads with President Benito Juárez, after the siege of Querétaro, to spare the emperor's life. (At the time, Carlotta was off in Europe, trying to round up support for her husband's cause, without result.) Juárez refused her request, and Maximilian, along with two of his generals, was executed by firing squad on the Hill of Bells in Querétaro a few days thereafter.

On your stroll through the gardens you'll see that same little artificial lake on which Austrian, French, and Mexican nobility rowed in little boats beneath the moonlight. Ducks have taken the place of dukes, however, and there are rowboats for rent. The lake is now artfully adapted as an outdoor theater, with seats for the audience on one side and the stage on the other.

The Borda Gardens have been completely restored, and were reopened in October 1987 as the Jardín Borda Centro de Artes, Avenida Morelos 103. In the gateway building are several galleries for changing exhibits, a café for refreshments and light meals, and several large paintings showing scenes from the life of Maximilian and from the history of the Borda Gardens.
Admission: 50¢.
Open: Tues–Sun 10am–6:30pm.

MUSEO DE LA HERBOLARÍA, Matamoros 200, Acapantzingo.

This museum of traditional herbal medicine, in the southern suburb of Acapantzingo, has been set up in a former resort residence built by Maximilian, the Casa del Olindo, or Casa del Olvido. It was here, during his brief reign, that the Austrian-born emperor would come for trysts with La India Bonita, his Cuernavacan lover. Restored in 1960, the house and gardens now preserve the local wisdom in folk medicine. Take a taxi or, if driving, ask directions.
Admission: Free.
Open: Daily 9am–5pm.

PIRAMIDE DE TEOPANZOLCO, northeast of the center of town.

You'll need a taxi to reach the curious Teopanzolco pyramid, northeast of the center of town. Now set in a park, the pyramid was excavated beginning in 1921. As with most Mesoamerican cultures, the local Tlahuicans reconstructed their principal religious monuments at the end of a major calendar cycle by building a new, larger structure right on top of the older one. Here you can clearly see the two different older and newer structures.
Admission: $2.75.
Open: Daily 9am–5pm.

WHERE TO STAY

Because so many *capitalinos* come down from Mexico City for the day, or for the weekend, the hotel trade here may be heavy on weekends and holidays, light at other times. A few local hoteliers adapt their policies and prices to these weird shifts.

DOUBLES FOR LESS THAN $20

HOTEL COLONIAL, Aragón y León 104, Cuernavaca, Mor. 62000. Tel. 73/12-0099. 14 rms (all with bath).
$ Rates: $12–$13 for one bed (one or two people), $15 for two beds.

The nice, simple little rooms at the Colonial, 4¼ blocks north of Jardín Juárez between Matamoros and Morelos, are the best buys on the street that's full of budget hotels, so get there early before they fill up. The 14 rooms, all with showers, are arranged around a cheery courtyard.

HOTEL PALACIO, Morrow 204, Cuernavaca, Mor. 62000. Tel. 73/12-0553. 16 rms (all with bath).
$ Rates: $14 single; $13–$16 double.

You'll feel at home the moment you enter the patio. The Hotel Palacio, between Matamoros and Comonfort, 1½ blocks north of both plazas, positively shouts 19th-century Mexican town house, which is what it was. Rooms are simply furnished as if carrying on the feel of a genteel city home that's still keeping up appearances although the family money is gone. To the left of the entry is a glass-topped courtyard with a nice restaurant, popular for its not low-priced but bounteous luncheon comida corrida for $10.50; $12 on weekends. If you want to meet some American residents of Cuernavaca, come at lunch; it's a popular hangout at that time.

HOTEL PAPAGAYO, Motolinia 13, Cuernavaca, Mor. 62000. Tel. 73/14-1711 or 14-1924. 74 rms (all with bath).
$ Rates (including breakfast): $17 double Mon–Fri, $33 double Sat–Sun.
Ignore the ugly facade and dinky sign of the rambling Hotel Papagayo—there's a much nicer entryway at the address given above. The Papagayo's scores of rooms must be picked over to find a good, quiet one (it's only a block south of the Autobuses Pullman de Morelos terminal, so there are always buses passing outside), but once you've located a good room, you can enjoy the bonus—a big swimming pool.

HOTEL CADIZ, Alvaro Obregón 329, Cuernavaca, Mor. 62000. Tel. 73/12-2971. 17 rms (all with bath).
$ Rates: $15 single; $17 double; $22 triple.

Every now and then I discover a hotel with the kind of homey charm that makes me want to return. Such is the Hotel Cadiz, near Avenida Ricardo Linares, the ISSTE Hospital, and the Hotel Las Mañanitas, run by the gracious Aguilar family. You may have known it as the Hotel María Cristina, and long before that it was a diet sanitarium. Each of the fresh, simple rooms has a fan and is furnished differently, and there's lots of nostalgic tile and big old sinks. The grounds, set back from the street, make a pleasant respite, plus there's a pool and small inexpensive restaurant open for all three meals.

DOUBLES FOR LESS THAN $30

HOTEL LAS HORTENSIAS, Calle Hidalgo 22, Cuernavaca, Mor. 62000. Tel. 73/12-6152. 23 rms (all with bath).
$ Rates: $21–$23 double Mon–Fri.
The Hotel Las Hortensias, two blocks south of Jardín Juárez, is another convenient downtown hotel converted from an old house on an odd hillside site. Rooms are small, simple, and modernish with colonial accents. Look at your prospective room first—some are dark and some only have windows that look onto the walkways. The nice, quiet little garden with a fountain and green grass provides an oasis in the midst of the city.

HOTEL IBERIA, Rayon 9 (at Alarcón), Cuernavaca, Mor. 62000. Tel. 73/12-6040. 25 rms (all with bath). TEL
$ Rates: $21 single; $26 double.

Rooms in this richly tiled old building are simple but presentable, arranged around a small courtyard where you can park your car (if it's small). The hard-working señoras who run the hotel keep everything in top shape. Note:

There is some street noise in the evenings. It's 2½ long blocks southwest of the central plazas and half a block north of the cathedral.

WORTH THE EXTRA BUCKS

LA POSADA DE XOCHIQUETZAL, Leyva 200 (Apdo. Postal 203), Cuer-navaca, Mor. 62000. Tel. 73/18-5767. 14 rms (all with bath). TV TEL
$ Rates: $60–$70 single or double; $95 suite. **Parking:** Free.

⭐ La Posada de Xochiquetzal (pronounced "so-chee-*ket*-zahl") charges more than the above-mentioned hotels, but you get your money's worth in beauty, for the posada's high walls conceal many delights: a small swimming pool, lush gardens with fountains, tasteful colonial-style furnishings, a good restaurant, patios, and large and small guest rooms. Even if you don't come to stay, come for a meal (see "Where to Eat," below). It's three long blocks to the right of the Cortés Palace, or two blocks east (right) of the Pullman Morelos bus station.

LAS MAÑANITAS, Ricardo Linares 107, Cuernavaca, Mor. 62000. Tel. 73/14-1466 or 12-4646. 22 rms (all with bath). TEL **Bus:** Buses going north on Morelos stop within half a block of the hotel.
$ Rates: $70–$87 double; $124–$240 suite. No credit cards. **Parking:** Valet.
Among Cuernavaca's best-known luxury lodgings is Las Mañanitas, 5½ long blocks north of the Jardín Borda. Antique headboards, heavy brass candlesticks, authentic period furniture and decoration, and large bathrooms make each room a charmer. Many have verdant, vine-encumbered balconies big enough for sitting and sipping while overlooking the emerald lawns where peacocks and other exotic birds strut and preen, and fountains tinkle musically. A few rooms have fireplaces, and the hotel also has a heated swimming pool and valet parking.

Accommodations come in four types, all doubles, but it's the standard rooms that interest us. These simple but charming accommodations allow you to splurge and live the good life when others, staying in the terrace suites, patio suites, and luxurious garden suites, are paying a great deal more than you will.

WHERE TO EAT
MEALS FOR LESS THAN $5

LA CUEVA, Galeana 2, at the corner of Rayon. Tel. 12-1240.
  Specialty: MEXICAN.
$ Prices: Comida corrida $5–$6.
  Open: Daily 9am–11pm.
For simple and cheap dining you might try La Cueva (similar to its next-door neighbor El Portal), pulling up one of the red chairs to a Formica table. The menu is on the mirror and on the blackboard out front, both of which usually feature several daily specials. It's under the portals just off the Alameda, at the corner of Rayon.

EL PORTAL, Galeana 2, at the corner of Rayon. Tel. 12-3449.
  Specialty: MEXICAN.
$ Prices: Comida corrida less than $5.
  Open: Daily 7am–11pm.

ⓢ Like it's neighbor La Cueva, next door, the decor is plain: A crowd of Formica tables and plastic-covered chairs from which you can watch action on the street. Meat roasts on a spit in the front, just to get your taste buds working, and the service is swift even during the busy lunchtime. The tradition of comida corrida is alive here, starting with soup, then rice, followed by the meat course, with a vegetable, a small dessert, and coffee. Nothing fancy, just good plain food.

VIENA PASTELERÍA, Guerrero 104. Tel. 18-1366.
  Specialty: PASTRIES/COFFEE.
$ Prices: Coffee 75¢–$1.75; pastries $1.50–$3.
  Open: Daily 8am–10pm.
This is a great spot for people-watching, which is the specialty here besides pastry eating and coffee drinking. The black coffee (with an emphasis on strong) and the

cappuccino here are reputedly the best in town. It's half a block north of the Alameda, opposite Parque Juárez.

LA PARROQUÍA, Guerrero 102. Tel. 18-5820.
Specialty: MEXICAN/PASTRIES.
$ Prices: Main courses $4–$7; quesadillas con pollo $4.75; beer $1.75.
Open: Daily 7:30am–11:30pm.

This place does a teeming business, partly because of its great location (half a block north of the Alameda, opposite Parque Juárez, and almost next to Viena Pastelería) and partly because it has fairly reasonable prices for Cuernavaca. It's open to the street with a few outdoor café tables and perfect for watching the changing parade of street vendors and park life.

MEALS FOR LESS THAN $10

RESTAURANT VIENES, Lerdo de Tejada 4. Tel. 18-4044.
Specialty: VIENNESE.
$ Prices: Main courses $4–$8.
Open: Wed–Mon 11am–10pm.

Another indication of this city's Viennese immigrant heritage is the Restaurant Vienes, a tidy and somewhat Viennese-looking place a block from the Jardín Juárez between Lerdo de Tejada and Morrow. The menu also has echoes of the Old World, such as grilled trout with vegetables and German potato salad, and apfelstrudel for dessert, followed by Viennese coffee. Salzburger nockerln is another possibility.

LOS PASTELES DEL VIENES, Lerdo de Tejada 120, at the corner of Comonfort. Tel. 14-3404.
Specialty: VIENNESE/PASTRIES.
$ Prices: Appetizers $1–$3; main courses $3–$5.
Open: Daily 8am–10pm.

Los Pasteles del Vienes is the Restaurant Vienes's café and pastry shop (it's next door), but you can get good light meals here as well. In short, it's an authentic European-style café. Brass trim and café curtains make for an elegant atmosphere in which you can enjoy a full selection of soups, salads, and sandwiches, and also more substantial fare such as wienerschnitzel, chicken dishes, and cheese fondue. Pastries and succulent cakes and tarts fill several huge refrigerated cases, so don't fill up before dessert-time.

RESTAURANT LOS ARCOS, Jardín de los Héroes 4. Tel. 12-4486.
Specialty: MEXICAN.
$ Prices: Appetizers $1–$3; main courses $3–$10; fixed-price lunch $5.50.
Open: Daily 7am–11pm.

Cuernavaca's best-located sidewalk café is the Restaurant Los Arcos, right next to the post office on the larger of the city's two plazas. Wrought-iron tables and chairs, shaded by umbrellas, are set out within view of the Cortés Palace, and all three meals are served, every day. The menu runs the gamut from sandwiches and enchiladas to chicken and steaks. There's even a fixed-price lunch, called the *menu del día*. Recommended.

RESTAURANT LA INDIA BONITA, Morrow 6B, near Matamoros. Tel. 12-1266.
Specialty: MEXICAN.
$ Prices: Breakfast $3–$4; desayuno Maximiliano $4.75–$7; main courses $5–$12.
Open: Tues–Sat 8:30am–8pm, Sun 8:30am–6:30pm.

Located right next door to the Hotel Palacio, 1½ blocks north of the Jardín Juárez, between Matamoros and Comonfort, Restaurant La India Bonita boasts that it has been here since 1945. Though it has changed hands several times, it's still a cheery, pleasant restaurant specializing in mole poblano (chicken with a sauce of bitter chocolate and fiery chiles) and a filet a la parrilla (charcoal-grilled steak). An appealing choice is the Mexican plate with seven different foods, unless you want the gigantic desayuno Maximiliano, a huge platter based on enchiladas.

WORTH THE EXTRA BUCKS

LA POSADA DE XOCHIQUETZAL, Leyva 200, at Abasolo. Tel. 18-5767.
Specialty: MEXICAN/ITALIAN.
$ **Prices:** Main courses $7–$15; fixed-price Sun buffet $12.
Open: Mon–Sat 7:30am–11pm, Sun 7:30am–5pm.

⭐ Enter an unimpressive doorway two blocks south of the Cortés Palace, at the corner of Abasolo and Juárez, to find a quiet haven of colonial arches shading inviting sitting areas and open-air or glass-enclosed dining, all with a view of the lush gardens. The popular hostelry is also well known for its good food. Specialties include chicken cacciatore and red snapper veracruzana. Recommended.

RESTAURANT LAS MAÑANITAS, Ricardo Linares 107. Tel. 731/14-1466 or 12-4646.
Specialty: MEXICAN/INTERNATIONAL. **Reservations:** Recommended.
Bus: Buses going north on Morelos stop within half a block of the hotel.
$ **Prices:** Full meal $25–$35. No credit cards.
Open: Lunch daily noon–5pm; dinner daily 7–11pm.
The Restaurant Las Mañanitas, 5½ long blocks north of the Jardín Borda, set the standard for lush and sumptuous in Cuernavaca. Dining tables are set out on an airy, shaded terrace with a view of the gardens. The decor and ambience are lightly colonial and the service is extremely friendly and attentive. When you arrive, you can enjoy cocktails in the cozy sala and when you're ready to dine a waiter will present a large blackboard menu of at least half a dozen daily specials. The specialty is Mexican with an international flare, using whatever fruits and vegetables are in season and offering a full selection of fresh seafood, beef, pork, veal, and fowl. Recommended.

EVENING ENTERTAINMENT

Cuernavaca has a number of cafés right off the Jardín Juárez where people gather to sip coffee or drinks till the wee hours of the morning, the best of which are Los Arcos, La Parroquía, and the Viena Pastelería, (see "Where to Eat," above). There are band concerts in the Jardín Juárez on Thursday and Sunday evenings.

Harry's Grill, Gutenberg 3, at Salazar, just off the main square (tel. 12-7679), is another addition to the Carlos Anderson chain and includes their usual good food and craziness with Mexican revolutionary posters and jaunty waiters. Although they serve full dinners here, I'd recommend that you go for drinks ($2 to $4). Open daily from 1:30 to 11:30pm.

EASY EXCURSIONS FROM CUERNAVACA

If you have enough time, you should try to make some side trips around Cuernavaca. To the north you'll find pine trees and an alpine setting; to the east, lush hills and valleys. On the road north to Mexico City you will climb several thousand feet within a half hour into some gorgeous mountain air. If you have a car you can go for a brisk morning hike (it's cold up there) or a lazy afternoon picnic lunch.

TEPOZTLAN Take one of the frequent buses or minivans by the market. Tourists don't use these much and other passengers generally go out of their way to be helpful and will let you know when to get off. This Tlahuica village pre-dates the Conquest, and still holds the ruins of a temple, plus a **Dominican monastery** (1580) and the thatched huts of the residents. It's a slice of village life only minutes from the big city. There's generally a very good street market around the central square on weekends and holidays, especially during Carnaval (3 days before Ash Wednesday, a moveable date usually in February).

XOCHICALCO RUINS About 16 miles south of Cuernavaca along Highway 95 (the "Libre"—no-toll—road to Taxco) is the town of Alpuyeca, and 9½ miles northeast of Alpuyeca are the ruins of Xochicalco, the "House of Flowers." High on a mountaintop, Xochicalco boasts a magnificent situation, and an interesting complex of buildings dating from about A.D. 600 through 900. Most interesting is the **Temple of the Feathered Serpents**, with beautiful bas-reliefs. There's also a ball court, some underground passages, and other temples. Xochicalco is of interest to archeologists because it seems to have been the point at which the Teotihuacán, Toltec, Zapotec, and Maya cultures met and interacted. You can visit the ruins from 8am to 5pm daily, but you'll need a car to get there. Admission is $3.50.

GRUTAS DE CACAHUAMILPA (CACAHUAMILPA CAVES) These caves lie some 46 miles southwest of Cuernavaca, 5 miles north of the Taxco road, Highway 95. You can join the group tour (every hour on the hour) of these mammoth caverns, said to stretch some 43 miles within the earth (don't worry—you don't get to see the entire 43 miles!). If you have a car and are driving to Taxco, this makes a nice detour. To go by bus, go to the Lineas Unidas/Flecha Roja bus station and take one of the crowded buses which leave frequently. When you get off at the caves, be sure to ask when the buses return.

The caves are truly awesome, worth a visit even if you're not generally a cave fancier. Judging by the graffiti in the caves, everyone important—from Empress Carlotta to Mexican presidents—has come to admire them. The caves are open daily from 10am to 3pm; admission costs less than $2. Tours are in Spanish only, but you'll pick up the salient points, and the geologic grandeur and beauty speak for themselves.

IXTAPAN DE LA SAL The road to Cacahuamilpa, Highway 55, is also the road to Toluca, which is 79 miles north from Highway 95. On the way, 28 miles from Highway 95, is the pretty spa town of Ixtapan de la Sal, with a dozen hotels specializing in the cure: bathing in the natural mineral waters of the area.

A SCENIC TRAIN RIDE The nation's only steam-engine train, **Ferrocarril Escenico** (scenic train), plies the route thrice weekly between **Cuautla** and the 16th-century village of **Yecapixtla.** From Cuautla's 17th-century train station (formerly a Franciscan convent), the engine pulls four turn-of-the-century passenger cars past villages and sugarcane fields. The cars, with wood interior and seats, have been used in numerous movies. The trip takes about an hour. Vans meet the train to transport passengers on the 10-minute trip to Yecapixtla for a 2-hour visit; the passengers are again collected for the return to the Yecapixtla station. The scenic train leaves on Thursday (Yecapixtla's market day), Saturday, and Sunday (another market day). The market is primarily for locals to fill the family pantry, so there are few tourist-oriented curios. Villagers are friendly and enjoy striking up a conversation with visitors. The real attraction here is the 16th-century Augustinian **Convent of San Juan Bautista.** The train ticket includes a guided tour (in Spanish) of the convent. It's the best preserved of all on the convent route in these parts. Most notable are the well-preserved murals with religious themes.

The price for this journey to and from Cuernavaca is an astounding $1, including all bus transportation, the train ticket, and the tour! To take the trip, meet the bus at the **Morelos State Tourism Office,** Avenida Morelos Sur 802, on Thursday at 8:30am, on Saturday at 11:30am, or on Sunday at 9:30am. The state reserves one car for Cuernavaca passengers and supposedly sells only that number of seats. Do verify these times and prices, and it's a good idea to buy tickets a day or two ahead.

TAXCO As popular as Taxco is for a day trip from Cuernavaca, getting there requires knowing the ropes. Here they are. From the **Estrella de Oro** station, there are six *de paso* buses from Cuernavaca to Taxco, at 9 and 10:30am, noon, and 2:30, 4:30, and 8pm daily, all originating in Mexico City. Advance reservations are possible a day ahead only, between 2:45 and 5pm. During those hours the dispatcher calls Mexico City to reserve seats—you pay the same rate as if you were leaving from Mexico City, which saves the seat for you from Mexico City to Taxco, although you get on in Cuernavaca. This procedure is advisable on weekends and holidays, especially Easter week and Christmas. Weekdays seats will probably be available without advance reservation. Go half an hour before the bus is scheduled, wait in line, and buy your ticket when the bus arrives. *De paso* buses return from Taxco to Cuernavaca at 9am and 4, 6, 7, and 9pm.

8. TAXCO
111 miles S of Mexico City, 50 miles S of Cuernavaca, 185 miles N of Acapulco

GETTING THERE   By Bus   From Mexico City, **Estrella de Oro,** Calzada de Tlalpan 2205 (tel. 549-8520), at the **Central de Autobuses del Sur** (Metro: Tasqueña) has five buses a day to Taxco and the trip takes 3 hours. Lineas Unidas del Sur/Flecha Roja also has several buses a day, but is a second choice to Estrella de Oro.

From Cuernavaca, you can catch an Estrella de Oro bus as it passes through, if there are seats available from Mexico City via Cuernavaca (see details above under "Easy Excursions from Cuernavaca" in Section 7, above). It's also possible to stop in Taxco on your way back **from Acapulco or Zihuatanejo;** two buses per day will drop you in Taxco after the 5½-hour ride.

By Car   From Mexico City, take Paseo de la Reforma to Chapultepec Park and merge with the Periferico that will take you to Highway 95D on the south end of town. From the Periferico, take the Insurgentes exit and merge until you come to the sign to Cuernavaca/Tlalpan. Choose either Cuernavaca Cuoto (toll) or Cuernavaca Libre (free). Continue south around Cuernavaca to the Amacuzac interchange and proceed straight ahead for Taxco. The drive from Mexico City takes about 3½ hours. Fill up with gas at Cuernavaca.

ESSENTIALS   The **telephone area code** is 732. The **post office** (Correos) is not far from the Plaza Borda: head down the hills, bearing left at the Los Castillo jewelry shop. The post office is on the lefthand side of the street.

Taxco (pronounced "*Tahs*-ko"; alt. 5,850 ft.; pop. 87,000), famous for its silver, sits on a hill among hills, and almost everywhere you walk in the city there are fantastic views.

Taxco's renowned silver mines, first worked in the time of Cortés, 4 centuries ago, were revived, for all practical purposes, by an American, William Spratling, in the 1930s. Today its fame rests more on the 180 silver shops, most of them little one-man factories, that line the cobbled streets all the way up into the hills. Whether or not you'll find bargains depends on how much you know about the quality and price of silver (some silver prices are actually higher than in Mexico City because of the magnitude of the tourist trade). But there is no doubt that nowhere else in the country will you find the quantity and variety of silver. The artistry and imagination of the local silversmiths are evident in each piece.

You can get the idea of what Taxco's like by spending an afternoon there, but there's much more to this picturesque town than just Plaza Borda and the shops surrounding it. You'll have to stay overnight if you want more time to climb up and down its steep streets, discovering little plazas and fine churches. The main part of town stretches up the hillside from the highway, and although it's a steep walk, it's not a particularly long one. But you don't have to walk: Vehicles make the circuit through the town, up the hill and down, picking up and dropping off passengers along the route. There are *burritos,* white VW minibuses that run the route, and small city buses as well. Both these vehicles run from about 7am until 9pm.

Warning: Self-appointed guides will undoubtedly approach you in the zócalo (Plaza Borda) and offer their services—they get a cut (up to 25%) of all you buy in the shops they take you to. Should you want a **guide,** however, ask to see his Department de Turismo credentials. Call 732/2-1986 or go to the Department of Tourism office on the highway at the north end of town to engage a licensed guide, for about $5 to $8 per hour.

ORIENTATION

ARRIVING By Bus Taxco's bus station is on the southern edge of town. If you have only a small suitcase, white minivans marked SANTA PRISCA stop in front of the station. Otherwise take a taxi; the hills are steep from the station to town.

By Car Arriving from either Cuernavaca or Mexico City, you'll arrive above the town and see it sprawling below in the valley and up the hillsides. Follow the signs into town, but be aware that the streets are extremely narrow and many are one way. You'll probably want to park your car while you're in Taxco and not use it again until you leave.

INFORMATION The State of Guerrero **Dirección de Turismo** (tel. 732/2-2274) has offices at the arches on the main highway at the north end of town, useful if you're driving into town. The office is open Monday through Saturday from 9am to 2pm and 5 to 8pm; and on Sunday from 10am to 3pm. To get there from Plaza Borda, take a combi ("Zócalo Arcos") and get off at the arch over the highway. When you see the arches, you're at the tourism office.

CITY LAYOUT The center of town is the tiny **Plaza Borda,** shaded by perfectly manicured Indian laurel trees. On one side is the imposing, pink-stone, twin-towered **Santa Prisca Church** and the other sides are lined with whitewashed, red-tile buildings housing the famous **silver shops** and a restaurant or two. Beside the church, deep in a crevice of the mountain is the **city market.** Brick-paved streets fill out from here in a helter-skelter fashion up and down the hillsides. Besides the silver-filled shops, the plaza swirls with vendors of everything from hammocks to cotton candy and bark paintings to balloons.

WHAT TO SEE & DO

In a phrase—**shopping for silver!** With almost 200 shops, it's almost impossible to suggest where you might find the piece that will suit your fancy. However, some of the workshops with long-time names in Taxco's silver business are those of Spratling and Castillo (see "Easy Excursions from Taxco," below).

When you've tired of shopping, perhaps you'd like to snoop through local landmarks and museums. You might also consider sneaking in for a look at Juan O'Gorman's mural beside the swimming pool at the **Hotel Posada de la Mision** (on the highway; go via minibus). And don't miss one of Mexico's top three baroque churches, Santa Prisca, on the main square. (Tepotzotlán, north of Mexico City, and the Valenciana Church in Guanajuato are the other two.)

SANTA PRISCA CHURCH, Plaza Borda.

⭐ This is Taxco's centerpiece parish church, around which village life takes place. Located facing the pleasant Plaza Borda, it was built with funds provided by José de la Borda, a French miner who struck it rich in Taxco's silver mines. Completed in 1758 after 8 years of labor, it's one of Mexico's most impressive baroque churches. Outside, the ultra-carved facade is flanked by two elaborately embellished steeples and a colorful tile dome. Inside, the intricacy of the gold-leafed saints and cherubic angels is positively breathtaking. The paintings by Miguel Cabrera, Mexico's most famous colonial-era artist, are the pride of Taxco. A long overdue restoration and cleaning of the interior walls has been going on for several years, thus you'll probably see scaffolding in place.

Guides, both small boys and adults, will approach you outside the church offering to give you a tour. The adults, of course, are more likely to speak English, and it's worth the small price to get a full rendition of what you're seeing. Make sure the guide's English is good, however, and establish whether the price is per person or per tour. It's customary to tip 50¢ or so if the tour is a good one.
   Admission: Free.
   Open: Daily 8am–11pm.

SILVER MUSEUM, Plaza Borda. Tel. 2-0558.

406 · EASY EXCURSIONS FROM MEXICO CITY

The newest addition is the Silver Museum, operated by a local silversmith. After entering the building next to Santa Prisca (it's also the site of the Sr. Costilla's restaurant), look for a sign on the left and the museum is downstairs. It's not a traditional public-sponsored museum. Nevertheless, it does a much-needed job of describing the history of silver in Mexico and Taxco, as well as displaying some historic and contemporary award-winning pieces. Time spent here seeing quality silverwork will make you a more discerning shopper in Taxco's dazzling silver shops.
Admission: Free.
Open: Daily 9am–5pm.

MUSEO DE TAXCO GUILLERMO SPRATLING, Calle Veracruz. Tel. 2-1660.

A plaque (in Spanish) explains that most of the collection of pre-Columbian art displayed here, and the funds for the museum, came from William Spratling, an American born in 1900 who studied architecture in the U.S., later settled in Taxco, and organized the first workshops to turn out high-quality silver jewelry. From this first effort in 1931 the town's reputation as a center of artistic silverwork grew to what it is today. In a real sense, Spratling "put Taxco on the map." He died in 1967 in a car accident. Having said that, you'd expect this to be a silver museum, but it's not—for Spratling silver, go to the Spratling Ranch. The entrance floor of this museum and the one above display a good collection of pre-Columbian statues and implements in clay, stone, and jade. The lower floor has changing exhibits.
To find it, turn left out of the Santa Prisca Church and left again at the corner; the museum is on the left at the end of the street.
Admission: $1.75.
Open: Tues–Sat 10am–5pm.

VON HUMBOLDT HOUSE, Calle Juan Ruíz de Alarcón. Tel. 2-0691.

After the museums, you might like to stroll along Ruíz de Alarcón looking for the richly decorated facade of the Von Humboldt House. The renowned German scientist and explorer Baron Alexander von Humboldt (1769–1859) visited Taxco and stayed in this beautiful house in 1803. Now it's the state-operated **Casa de Artesanías,** where crafts are for sale—but it doesn't begin to represent the fine work for which the state of Guerrero is known. Visitors are allowed to explore the house at leisure, even the rooftop.
To get there, turn left out of the Santa Prisca Church and left again at the corner, following that street to its end; Casa Humbolt is straight ahead.
Admission: Free.
Open: Mon–Sat 10am–3pm and 4–7pm, Sun 10am–2pm.

MERCADO CENTRAL, Plaza Borda.

To the right of the Santa Prisca Church, behind and below Bertas, Taxco's central market meanders deep inside the mountain. Among the curio stores you'll find the food stalls and cook shops, always the best place for a cheap meal.
Open: Daily 7am–8pm.

EVENING ENTERTAINMENT

Taxco's nighttime action is centered in the luxury hotels. The **Hotel Monte Taxco** (tel. 2-1300), **Posada de la Mision** (tel. 2-0063), and **Hotel de la Borda** (tel. 2-0025) all have their clubs or lounges and/or nighttime shows. **Paco's** is just about the most popular place overlooking the square for sipping, nibbling, people-watching, and people-meeting, all of which continues until midnight daily. **La Taberna** (see "Where to Eat," below) stays open until midnight. And finally there's Taxco's dazzling new disco, **Windows,** high up the mountain in the Hotel Monte Taxco. The whole city is on view from there and music runs the gamut from the Hit Parade to hard rock. For a cover of $6 weekends and $4 other days, you can boogie Tuesday through Sunday from 9pm to 3am.
Completely different in tone is **Berta's,** right next to Santa Prisca Church. Opened in the early 1930s by a lady named Berta, who made her fame on a drink of the same name (tequila, soda, lime, and sugar syrup), Berta's is traditionally the

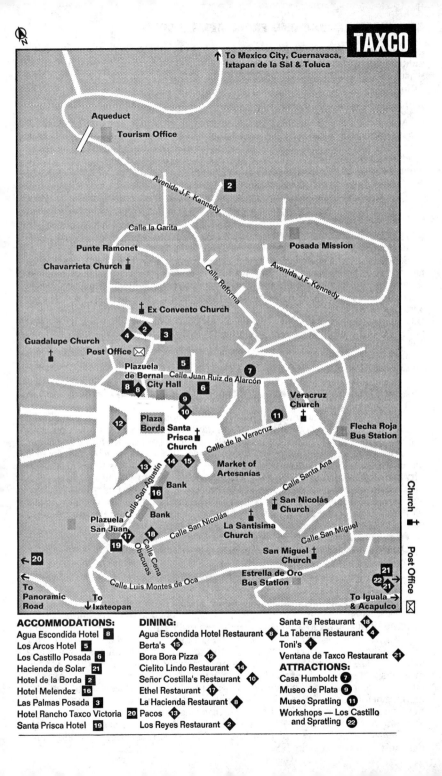

TAXCO

↑ To Mexico City, Cuernavaca, Ixtapan de la Sal & Toluca

Aqueduct

Tourism Office

Avenida J.F. Kennedy

Calle la Garita

Punte Ramonet

Chavarrieta Church ✝

Posada Mission

Calle Reforma

Avenida J.F. Kennedy

✝ Ex Convento Church

Guadalupe Church ✝

◆ 4 ■ 2 ■ 3

Post Office ✉

Plazuela de Bernal

City Hall

■ 5

Calle Juan Ruiz de Alarcón

⑦

Veracruz Church ✝

■ 8 ◆ 8

■ 6

⑨

⑩

⑪

Flecha Roja Bus Station

◆ 12

Plaza Borda

Santa Prisca Church ✝

Calle de la Veracruz

◆ 13 ⑭ ⑮

Market of Artesanías

Calle San Agustín

■ 16

Bank

Calle Santa Ana

✝ San Nicolás Church

Bank

⑱

Plazuela San Juan

■ 17

■ 19

Calle San Nicolás

Calle Cena Obscuras

La Santisima Church ✝

Calle San Miguel

San Miguel Church ✝

◆ 20

Calle Luis Montes de Oca

Estrella de Oro Bus Station

■ 21

㉒

■ 21

← To Panoramic Road

↓ To Ixateopan

To Iguala → & Acapulco

Church ✝

Post Office ✉

ACCOMMODATIONS:
Agua Escondida Hotel ■ 8
Los Arcos Hotel ■ 5
Los Castillo Posada ■ 6
Hacienda de Solar ■ 21
Hotel de la Borda ■ 2
Hotel Melendez ■ 16
Las Palmas Posada ■ 3
Hotel Rancho Taxco Victoria ■ 20
Santa Prisca Hotel ■ 19

DINING:
Agua Escondida Hotel Restaurant ◆ 8
Berta's ⑮
Bora Bora Pizza ◆ 12
Cielito Lindo Restaurant ⑭
Señor Costilla's Restaurant ⑩
Ethel Restaurant ⑰
La Hacienda Restaurant ◆ 8
Pacos ◆ 13
Los Reyes Restaurant ◆ 2

Santa Fe Restaurant ⑱
La Taberna Restaurant ◆ 4
Toni's ①
Ventana de Taxco Restaurant ◆ 21

ATTRACTIONS:
Casa Humboldt ⑦
Museo de Plata ⑨
Museo Spratling ⑪
Workshops — Los Castillo and Spratling ㉒

gathering place of the local gentry. Spurs and old swords decorate the walls, and a saddle is casually slung over the banister of the stairs leading to the second-floor room where tin masks leer from the walls. A Berta costs about $2; rum, the same. Open from 9am to around midnight.

PACO'S BAR, Plaza Borda, upstairs.

After a hard day of shopping and museum hopping, you'll probably be ready for some refreshment. Drinks are anywhere from $1.25 for soft drinks, through beer at about $1.30, with more sophisticated concoctions costing up to $3.75. They've augmented the menu here, hoping to attract diners as well as drinkers. There's a full menu from oysters to lobster, chicken, steak, and Mexican plates, all between $3.75 and $20.

EASY EXCURSIONS FROM TAXCO

SPRATLING RANCH WORKSHOP, 6 miles south of town, on the Acapulco Highway.

Spratling's hacienda-style home/workshop on the outskirts of Taxco once again hums with busy hands reproducing his unique designs. A display case of originals shows the fine skill of design and workmanship that makes Spratling pieces truly distinctive. Those being made today carry the same fine craftsmanship because even Spratling's own workshop foreman is employed again, overseeing the work of a new generation of silversmiths. The only Taxco sales outlet of Spratling work is here and prices are high, but the designs are unusual and considered collectable. To get there, hire a taxi and ask him to wait.

Admission: Free.
Open: Mon–Sat 9am–5pm.

LOS CASTILLOS, 5 miles south of town on the Acapulco Highway, and in Taxco on Plaza Bernal.

Castillo was one of hundreds of young men to whom William Spratling taught the silversmithing trade in the 1930s. And Castillo was one of the first to branch out with his own shops and line of designs, which over the years have earned him a fine name. Now his daughter creates her own noteworthy designs, among which are decorative pieces with silver fused into porcelain. Besides Taxco, Castillo has shops in Mexico City and Cancún, and an outlet at the Madeiras Restaurant in Acapulco. You can visit the Castillo workshop, 5 miles south of town, Monday through Friday between 9am and 5pm, but there's no sales outlet at the workshop. His store, Los Castillos, is just off Plaza Borda, reached by walking down the hill beside City Hall; the store is ahead with a big sign. Customers can watch silversmiths here as well.

Admission: Workshop and store, free.
Open: Workshop, Mon–Fri 9am–5pm; store, daily 9am–7pm.

SPECIAL EVENTS

Taxco's **Silver Fair** takes place from mid-November through mid-December and includes a competition for silver sculptures from among the top silversmiths.

Holy Week in Taxco is one of the most compelling in the country, beginning the Friday a week before Easter with evening processions every night and several during the day. The most riveting procession, on Thursday evening, lasts almost 4 hours and includes villagers from the surrounding area carrying saints, followed by hooded members of a society of self-flagellating penitants chained at the ankles and carrying huge wooden crosses and bundles of penetrating thorny branches. On the Saturday morning before Easter, Plaza Borda fills for the procession of three falls, reinacting the three times Christ stumbled and fell while carrying his cross.

From the middle of May to April 1 are the **Jornadas Alarcones,** featuring plays and literary events in honor of Juan Ruíz de Alarcón (1572–1639), a world-famous dramatist who was born in Taxco.

WHERE TO STAY

Compared to Cuernavaca, Taxco is an overnight-stop visitor's dream: charming and picturesque, not noisy or polluted, with a respectable selection of well-kept and delightful hotels. The prices have gone up so much in recent years that Taxco is no longer the budget traveler's haven it once was. And prices tend to "bulge" even more at holiday times (especially Easter week).

DOUBLE FOR LESS THAN $25

POSADA DE LAS PALMAS, Estacas 1, Taxco, Gro. 40200. Tel. 732/2-3177. 14 rms (all with bath).
$ Rates: $20 single; $22 double; $24 triple; $32 quad.
Find the post office on Calle Juárez and Restaurante Los Reyes. Estacas is the pedestrians-only, stepped-cobblestone street beside the restaurant. Walk down it to the first level and take the high level (left) to the second door. A faded sign announces the hotel, but just in case you have trouble, it's the door on the right. Enter it and go down, down, down. (To enter by the parking lot, ask the manager for directions.) If you follow these directions, you'll discover the office and several of the simple, but pleasant rooms, all with fans. The remainder are across a large, verdant lawn (with a swimming pool). Finding those rooms is like meandering up and down the halls of a rock-walled castle. Here and there are sitting areas with magazines. Rooms A through D are easiest to reach from the front door. There is no elevator, but the hotel rates make it worth the effort.

DOUBLES FOR LESS THAN $30

POSADA DE LOS CASTILLO, Juan Ruíz de Alarcón 3, Taxco, Gro. 40200. Tel. 732/2-1396. Fax 732/2-2935. 15 rms (all with bath).
$ Rates: $20 single; $26 double (one bed or two).
Posada de los Castillo is a beautiful colonial mansion completely restored in 1980. Boasting lots and lots of plants (some even in planters in the bathrooms!), the small rooms surround a courtyard on four levels. Each has a fan and is simply furnished, and bathrooms have either tubs or showers.
To get there, from Plaza Borda, follow the hill down (the Hotel Escondida is on your left), make an immediate right at the bottom of the hill, and the hotel is one block on the right.

HOTEL MELENDEZ, Cuauhtémoc 6, Taxco, Gro. 40200. Tel. 732/2-0006. 33 rms (all with bath).
$ Rates: $22 single; $26 double.
The Hotel Melendez, to the left of Paco's Bar half a block off Plaza Borda, is an old-timey hotel with overpriced, simply furnished rooms. Some of its rooms are airy bedrooms and have blue-tile walls and ornate glass and metalwork doors on the bathrooms. Several have terrific views. However, don't take Room 5, 6, 7, or 8 unless you're desperate—they're oddly located and sort of claustrophobic. And avoid any room next to the stairwell where noise echos through the tile corridors straight into your room. The hotel's restaurant, with windows overlooking Taxco, has fairly reasonable prices.

HOTEL LOS ARCOS, Juan Ruíz de Alarcón 12, Taxco, Gro. 40200. Tel. 732/2-1836. 21 rms (all with bath).
$ Rates: $22 single; $28 double; $28 triple.
This once modestly furnished hotel is undergoing renovation, so guests can expect gradual changes. Los Arcos is, in fact, a converted monastery (1620). Already the handsome inner patio is bedecked with Puebla pottery, equipales tables and chairs in the middle, and a gaily dressed restaurant area to the left, all around a central fountain. Eventually the bar will be in the former living room on the left as you enter. The rooms are being transformed with new beds, spreads, tile, and furniture. You'll be immersed in colonial charm and blissful quiet, yet you're only a 5-minute walk from Plaza Borda (from Plaza Borda, follow the hill

down, with the Hotel Escondida on your left and make an immediate right at the bottom of the hill; the hotel is a block on the left, opposite the Posada de los Castillo).

DOUBLES FOR LESS THAN $45

HOTEL AGUA ESCONDIDA, Plaza Borda 4 (or Calle Spratling 4), Taxco, Gro. 40200. Tel. 732/2-0726 or 2-0736. 70 rms (all with bath).
$ Rates: $30 single; $35 double.
Located at one corner of Plaza Borda, the Hotel Agua Escondida is a simple, modest establishment with tile corridors, but fairly overpriced for the quality of the rooms. It's popular with families, primarily for its swimming pool, and often fills up on weekends. The rooms have such extra touches as vases of fresh flowers and bottles of mineral water at each bedside.

HOTEL SANTA PRISCA, Cena Obscuras 1 (Apdo. Postal 42), Taxco, Gro. 40200. Tel. 732/2-0080 or 2-0980. 34 rms (all with bath).
$ Rates: $35 single; $44 double.
★ The Santa Prisca, one block from Plaza Borda on Plazuela de San Juan, is one of the older and nicer hotels in town. Rooms are small but comfortable, with older bathrooms (showers only), tile floors, wood beams, and a colonial atmosphere. If your stay is a long one, ask for a room in the adjacent "new addition," where the rooms are sunnier, more spacious, and quieter. There's a reading area in an upstairs salon overlooking Taxco, two lush patios with fountains, and a lovely dining room done in mustard and blue.

WORTH THE EXTRA BUCKS

HACIENDA DEL SOLAR, Apdo. Postal 96, Taxco, Gro. 40200. Tel. 732/2-0323. 22 rms (all with bath).
$ Rates: $45–$72 double; $90–$132 junior suite.
Located on a hilltop 2½ miles south of the town center off the highway to Acapulco (look for signs on the left) with magnificent views of the surrounding valleys and the town, several Mexican-style cottages are arranged around the hilltop. The decor is slightly different in each one, but most include bathrooms done in handmade tiles, lots of beautiful handcraft works as accents, colonial-style construction, hand-painted folk murals, and red-tile floors. Beds have bright, cheerful colored spreads to match the warm sunlight that enters each room. Several rooms have Gothic-vaulted tile ceilings and fine private terraces with panoramic views.

Accommodations are rented as doubles only, in three grades. Standard rooms have no terraces and only showers in the baths; deluxe rooms have sunken tubs with showers, and terraces. The largest and most luxurious accommodations are the junior suites. The prices I've quoted here are those given me by the management right at the hotel. If you make a reservation through a travel agent back home, you may be quoted a significantly higher price.

Besides the marvelous hilltop setting, guests at the Hacienda del Solar enjoy a nice big heated swimming pool surrounded by lots of green grass for sunning, beautifully planted grounds with rough-stone walks, flowering shrubs, shade trees, a tennis court, and a cocktail lounge named the Salon Colibri. Meals are served in the hacienda's own restaurant, La Ventana de Taxco (see "Where to Eat," below, for details).

HOTEL RANCHO TAXCO VICTORIA, Apdo. Postal 83, Taxco, Gro. 40200. Tel. 732/2-1014 or 2-0010. 100 rms (all with bath).
$ Rates: $50 single or double.
An older hotel, the Rancho Taxco Victoria clings to the hillside above the town, with breathtaking views from its flower-covered verandas. It's somewhat overpriced, but it has all the charm of old-fashioned Mexico and it's a personal favorite. Furnishings, sometimes a bit worn in a homey sort of way, whisper comfortably of the hotel's heyday in the 1940s. In the guest rooms, nestled into nooks and crannies of the rambling hillside buildings, are vanities constructed with handmade tiles, local tin-craft reading lamps, beamed ceilings, fans, craftwork, bedspreads and throw rugs, a plant or two, bathrooms with tubs, and, in many cases, a small private terrace.

To get there, from Plazuela de San Juan, go up a cobbled, winding street named Carlos J. Nibbi to no. 57, on the hilltop.

WHERE TO EAT

Taxco gets a lot of people down from the capital for the day, or passing through on their way to Acapulco, and there are not enough restaurants to fill the demand so prices are high for what you get. If you have a big breakfast and pack a lunch, you'll save money. Otherwise, listed below are the cheapest meals near the zócalo.

MEALS FOR LESS THAN $10

BORA BORA PIZZA, Callejon de las Delicias 4, in Plaza Borda. Tel. 2-1721.
Specialty: ITALIAN.
$ Prices: Pizza $3.60–$14; spaghetti $3.60–$5; beer $1.25; wine $1.50.
Open: Tues–Sun 5:30pm–midnight.

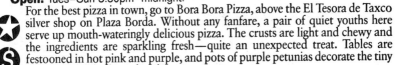

For the best pizza in town, go to Bora Bora Pizza, above the El Tesora de Taxco silver shop on Plaza Borda. Without any fanfare, a pair of quiet youths here serve up mouth-wateringly delicious pizza. The crusts are light and chewy and the ingredients are sparkling fresh—quite an unexpected treat. Tables are festooned in hot pink and purple, and pots of purple petunias decorate the tiny balconies overlooking the plaza.

RESTAURANT ETHEL, Plazuela de San Juan 14. Tel. 2-0788.
Specialty: MEXICAN.
$ Prices: Soup $2; sandwiches $2–$4; main courses $4.50–$8; comida corrida $7.50.
Open: Daily 9am–10pm (comida corrida served 1–5pm).
A family-run place opposite the Hotel Santa Prisca on Plazuela San Juan, one block from Plaza Borda, Restaurant Ethel is kept clean and tidy, with white throws and colorful crumb cloths on the tables and a homey atmosphere. The hearty daily comida corrida consists of soup or pasta, meat (perhaps a small steak), dessert, and coffee.

RESTAURANT SANTA FE, Hidalgo 2. Tel. 2-1170.
Specialty: MEXICAN.
$ Prices: Comida corrida $7.
Open: Daily 7:30am–11pm.
Another family-run eatery that bustles at lunchtime and beckons with good smells from the kitchen, the Restaurant Santa Fe is a second choice to the aforementioned Ethel. Service is friendly, the tables are covered in checked cloths, and the whitewashed walls sport cowboy figures. It's immediately off Plaza San Bernal, around the corner from Restaurant Ethel.

RESTAURANTE LOS REYES, Juárez 9. Tel. 2-1254.
Specialty: MEXICAN.
$ Prices: Soups and sandwiches $3–$4; main courses $4–$7.50; comida corrida $6.50.
Open: Daily 8am–10pm.
For this restaurant, from the Plaza Borda, walk with the Hotel Agua Escondida on your left and bear right to the post office. Across the street and upstairs, look up for a sign and small open vestibule which are visible from the street. There's nothing fancy about the place, but the food is reasonably priced and from here the post office murals are visible on the second floor and Taxco's townsfolk pass below.

HOTEL MELENDEZ, Cuauhtémoc 6. Tel. 2-0006.
Specialty: MEXICAN.

$ Prices: Main courses $3–$5; comida corrida $6.50.
Open: Daily 7:30am–10:30pm.

You will dine in an attractive tiled dining room overlooking the town and the valley (it's to the left of Paco's Bar, half a block from Plaza Borda). The comida corrida includes soup, rice, vegetables, meat course, dessert of fruit or pastry, and coffee or tea. You certainly get your money's worth here.

MEALS FOR LESS THAN $15

RESTAURANT LA HACIENDA, Calle Bailar, off Plaza Borda. Tel. 2-0663.
Specialty: MEXICAN/AMERICAN.
$ Prices: Appetizers $1.50–$3; main courses $4.50–$9.
Open: Daily 7:30am–9pm.

The Restaurant La Hacienda boasts white linen, colorful table settings, a simple colonial decor, and an extensive menu—everything from enchiladas to steak, from pasta to hamburgers. Despite its trappings, it's a small, family-run operation, so the service is friendly if a little slow. Entrance is either through the Hotel Agua Escondida lobby or from a side street off Plaza Borda.

LA TABERNA RESTAURANT/BAR, Juárez 8.
Specialty: ITALIAN.
$ Prices: Appetizers $4–$7; main courses $4–$15.
Open: Daily 1pm–midnight.

La Taberna is the newest eatery in town, and looks as if it ought to fall in the splurge category. It beckons from the porch all decked out in turquoise and white napkins and cloths. Climb the stairs and enter the old stone house with its front sala-turned-bar and pass to the interior plant-filled patio for a welcome respite and al fresco dining. The owners are the same as at Bora Bora Pizza and the food is consistently good. I enjoyed the fettuccine La Taberna, which comes with ham, bacon, tomatoes, and mushrooms. There are six kinds of crêpes, and 14 selections of beef, chicken, and fish. Among them you'll discover chicken Kiev and chicken and beef brochettes.

To get here, from the Plaza Borda, go down the hill beside the Hotel Agua Escondida, bearing leftish, then right to the post office. La Taberna is a few steps farther on your left as you turn the corner.

CIELITO LINDO, Plaza Borda 14. Tel. 2-0603.
Specialty: MEXICAN/INTERNATIONAL.
$ Prices: Appetizers $7.50–$11; main courses $11–$14.
Open: Daily 10am–10pm.

The Cielito Lindo is probably the most popular place on the plaza for lunch, perhaps more for its visibility and colorful decor than for the food—which is fine, not great. The tables, covered in white and laid with blue-and-white local crockery, are usually packed, and plates of food disappear as fast as the waiters can bring them. You can get anything from soup to roast chicken, enchiladas, tacos, steak, and dessert, as well as a frosty margarita.

SR. COSTILLA'S ("Mr. Ribs"), Plaza Borda 1. Tel. 2-3215.
Specialty: INTERNATIONAL.
$ Prices: Appetizers $3.50–$6.50; main courses $10–$16.
Open: Mon–Fri noon–midnight, Sat–Sun noon–1am.

The offbeat decor here includes a marvelous antique jukebox, a fake skeleton, and a ceiling festooned with the usual assortment of cultural flotsam and jetsam. Several tiny balconies hold a few minuscule tables that afford a view of the plaza and church (it's next to the Santa Prisca Church, above Patio de las Artesanías), and these fill up long before the large dining room does. The menu is typical Andersonese (like the other Carlos Anderson restaurants you may have encountered in your Mexican travels), with Spanglish jive and a large selection of everything from soup through steaks, sandwiches, and the eponymous spareribs to desserts and coffee. Wine, beer, and drinks are served.

WORTH THE EXTRA BUCKS

LA VENTANA DE TAXCO, Hwy. 95 south. Tel. 2-0587.

Specialty: ITALIAN/INTERNATIONAL. **Reservations:** Recommended. **Directions:** Drive south of Taxco on the highway to Acapulco; look for signs on the left.

$ Prices: Appetizers $5–$10; main courses $10–$20.

Open: Daily 1–10:30pm.

Dining here is almost synonymous with a visit to Taxco, so if you've been saving for a splurge, this is a good place. Daytime, the floor-to-ceiling windows (*ventanas*) reveal Taxco in all its hillside splendor; at night, flickering candles on each table make it one of the most romantic places in Mexico. Careful and polite service supplements the menu of continental (especially Italian), American, and Mexican specialties.

TONI'S, at the Hotel Monte Taxco. Tel. 2-1300.

Specialty: STEAKS/SEAFOOD. **Reservations:** Recommended. **Transportation:** Take a combi to the convention center/tourist office, then hail a cab from there for around $2.75.

$ Prices: Appetizers $3.50–$6; main courses $18–$30.

Open: Tues–Sat 7pm–1am.

Toni's is the new, intimate, and classy restaurant at the Hotel Monte Taxco, perched high on a mountaintop. The restaurant is enclosed in a huge, cone-shaped thatched palapa with a panoramic view of the city below. The 11 candlelit tables sparkle with crystal and crisp linen. For the best views, try to get a booth by the panoramic windows. The limited menu of shrimp or beef won't keep guests returning night after night, but what they do have is superior. I tried the house salad and the tender, juicy prime roast beef (all the beef is flown in from Chicago), which comes with Yorkshire pudding, creamed spinach, and baked potato. Lobster is also available.

CHAPTER 14

SOUTH OVER THE MOUNTAINS

1. PUEBLA
- WHAT'S SPECIAL
  ABOUT THE
  MOUNTAIN COUNTRY
2. TEHUACÁN
3. OAXACA

Southeast of Mexico City is the mountain country. Puebla and its surrounding villages contain interesting baroque Indian churches, and it is here that the famous Talavera pottery is made. Oaxaca, a center of Indian culture and archeology, is a city of beautiful tiles and colonial buildings. Like the Yucatán, it abounds in ruins of varied Indian cultures: The Zapotec ruins of Monte Alban are a few miles from the city, and the ruins of Yaagul, Lambityeco, and Mitla are easily accessible.

SEEING THE MOUNTAIN REGION

If you have time to explore this area, your best bet is to take the road from Mexico City to Oaxaca, a 12-hour, 325-mile drive over a winding road through the mountains. The road is unusually scenic. Among many distractions, you'll see little shrines built into the sides of the road, churches glistening with brilliantly colored tile domes, produce stands with fruit elaborately piled into pyramids, and, weather permitting, the snow-capped peaks of the volcanos Popocatepetl and Ixtaccihuatl.

Head south from Mexico City to Pueblo (a 2-hour trip) and spend 1 or 2 days seeing the town and its environs. You can stop in Huejotzingo and Cholula on the way to Puebla, or visit these interesting places as excursions from Puebla. Oaxaca can be reached in a day of long driving, but you can break your trip with an overnight stop at Tehuacán. Explore Oaxaca, visit the ruins, and go to some of the outlying markets, which take place on different days of the week.

Oaxaca is an overnight trip by train, and by bus the journey takes at least 12 to 15 hours.

---

1. PUEBLA

80 miles E of Mexico City

GETTING THERE By Plane AeroMorelos has once-a-week flights to and from Puebla, Acapulco, and Cuernavaca. Reservations in Puebla are through Turismo Colonial 3 Oriente, Analco 1003-B (tel. 22/46-6222; fax 22/46-6486).

By Train The first-class *El Oaxaqueño* train from Mexico City to Oaxaca, via Puebla, leaves Buenavista Station in Mexico City at 7pm and arrives in Puebla at 11:50pm.

By Bus The first-class line to Puebla is **Autobuses del Oriente (ADO)** (tel.

WHAT'S SPECIAL ABOUT THE MOUNTAIN COUNTRY

Archeology
- ☐ Monte Alban Zapotec, the mountain-top ceremonial center west of Oaxaca.
- ☐ Yagul, a ceremonial city east of Oaxaca.
- ☐ Mitla, ancient buildings with Greek-like stone mosaics and a church built atop the ruins of an ancient pyramid.

Architectural Highlights
- ☐ The Rosario Chapel in Puebla's Church of Santo Domingo, lavishly embellished with sculpted figures, tile, and gold leaf.
- ☐ The ornate interior of Oaxaca's Santo Domingo Church.
- ☐ Santa María Tonanzintla, an Indian baroque church near Cholula.
- ☐ The fantastic tiled facade of the Church of Acatepec, near Tonanzintla and Cholula.
- ☐ Tiled domes and building facades throughout the state of Puebla.

Shopping
- ☐ Puebla's beautiful and collectable Talavera pottery.
- ☐ Oaxaca's markets and outlying crafts villages

Festivals
- ☐ Oaxaca's Guelaguetza in July, for spectacular regional dancing.
- ☐ December 23, Night of the Radishes in Oaxaca, with huge carved radishes.
- ☐ December 24 in Oaxaca, with religious processions, buñuelos, and hot chocolate.
- ☐ Pre-Lenten Carnaval festivities in Huejotzingo, Puebla.

Museums
- ☐ Regional Museum of Oaxaca, with riches uncovered from archeological sites, plus an ethnographic display of regional clothing and objects.
- ☐ Rufino Tamayo Museum in Oaxaca, showcasing the artist's collection of pre-Hispanic artifacts.
- ☐ Museum of Popular Arts in Puebla, with it's displays of regional costumes, household objects, and a fabulously tiled convent kitchen.
- ☐ Museo Bello in Puebla, a fine collection of European art and Talavera pottery from the 17th to the 19th century.

522-7200 in Mexico City). Buses depart from the capital every 10 minutes from 7am to midnight daily for the 2-hour trip.

Autobuses Unidos (tel. 542-4216 in Mexico City) provides convenient second-class service from Mexico City to Puebla every 15 minutes, from Puebla to Tehuacan (eight buses a day), and to Orizaba, Córdoba, Veracruz, Oaxaca, and Villahermosa, at rates slightly lower than those of the ADO.

By Car There are two roads to Puebla from the capital: Highway 190, an old, winding one that you'll drive with great frustration, following strings of lumbering trucks with no chance to pass; and Highway 150D, a classy, new toll road that's faster. The bus usually follows the new highway.

DEPARTING By Plane Puebla's **airport** is between Huejotzingo and Cholula, at least a 15-minute drive and $10 taxi ride.

By Train Puebla's **railroad station** (tel. 22/46-5158) is at the northern end of Calle 9 Norte. Going to Mexico City, *El Oaxaqueño* leaves at 4:25am and arrives in Mexico City at 9:20am. Going to Oaxaca it leaves at 11:50pm and arrives in Tehuacán at 2:30am and Oaxaca at 9:30am.

By Bus The **ADO** line runs six buses a day from Puebla to Veracruz and back, seven a day to Villahermosa, four a day to Oaxaca, and 20 a day to Tehuacán.

It's also possible to get from Puebla to Cuernavaca, and on to Taxco and Acapulco.

Autobuses Flecha Roja has direct service to Cuernavaca (daily from 5am to 8pm on the hour). The service is second class and takes 3½ hours. Since you cannot reserve seats a day ahead, get there at least half an hour before you intend to leave.

Autobuses Estrella Roja (tel. 41-7671) provides second-class services to Mexico City (every 10 minutes, 24 hours daily).

By Car From Puebla you have a choice of roads **to Oaxaca,** whether you go by bus or car. One route, Highway 190 goes south through Izucár de Matamoros and Acatlan, then to Huajuapan de León, where the road becomes full of curves as it twists through the mountains to Oaxaca. Matamoros is the source of the colorful clay trees of life, but you won't see many here because most of the trees are shipped to the big cities for sale. Acatlan is famous for its red animal pottery.

Another route, which takes about the same time to drive, runs southeast to Tehuacán, the mineral bath town, along Highway 150, which is now paved all the way to Oaxaca (the Tehuacán–Oaxaca portion is called Highway 131). This road is also full of twists and turns, and although it's slow going, you'll be treated to a fine view of the mountains and curious stands of cactus. But before you wind up into the mountains, you might want to stop for lunch, or even overnight, in Tehuacán, a famous spa town from the 1940s.

The highway from Puebla **to Veracruz** is well paved and scenic. You're in for a pleasant drive, whether you take the toll road, Highway 150D, straight to Orizaba, or detour through Tehuacán, before heading through Orizaba, Córdoba, and on to the coast.

Puebla, founded around 1531 as a haven of safety between the capital and the coast, has preserved much of its wealth and architecture from its early years. Many mansions and public buildings were built by and for the "rich and famous" who passed through on their way to and from the capital. The church chose Puebla as a major center, along with San Luis Potosí and Oaxaca. Already known for pottery making before the Conquest, Talavera artisans from Toledo, Spain, blended their talents with those of the native population to create a wonderful pottery and tile tradition. Religion flourished until 1767, when an antireligious movement closed many churches and convents. Some 99 churches survive, along with many grand monasteries, convents, and a magnificent Bishop's Palace next to the cathedral.

Today Puebla (alt. 7,049 ft.; pop 1,250,000) is growing at an amazing rate. The streets teem with people, some of whom sell everything from tacos to kitchen utensils. The streets are jammed with cars and the ever-present buses, which spew fumes, trumpet, and roar.

ORIENTATION

ARRIVING Puebla's **Hermanos Serdan Airport** is located between the towns of Huejotzingo and Cholula, and it's closer to both of those than to Puebla, which is about 15 minutes away by taxi.

The **railroad station** (tel. 22/46-5158) is at the northern end of Calle 9 Norte, a moderate distance from downtown.

All first- and second-class bus services arrive at a modern **bus terminal,** said to be one of the largest in Latin America, which is located on the outskirts of the city. A colectivo taxi to the city center costs $2.25. City buses ("Estación Nueva") travel between the bus station and the downtown area for a fare of 30¢. You can also catch one of the red-and-white buses going downtown, from the corner of Avenida 14 Oriente and Calle 5 de Mayo.

INFORMATION The **Tourist Office** is at Avenida 5 Oriente no. 3 (tel. 46-1285), next to the cathedral and next to the Biblioteca Palafoxiana. The friendly staff can give you a good map of the city, and the office is open Monday through Saturday from 8am to 8pm and on Sunday from 10am to 2pm.

CITY LAYOUT Touristically speaking, the heart of town is the shady zócalo,

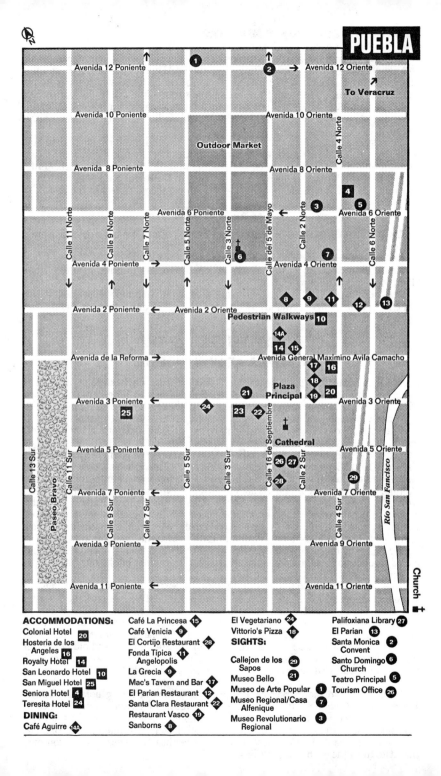

PUEBLA

Avenida 12 Poniente — ① — ② → Avenida 12 Oriente

To Veracruz

Avenida 10 Poniente — Avenida 10 Oriente

Calle 4 Norte

Outdoor Market

Avenida 8 Poniente — Avenida 8 Oriente

④
⑤

Avenida 6 Poniente — ③ — Avenida 6 Oriente

Calle 11 Norte · Calle 9 Norte · Calle 7 Norte · Calle 5 Norte · Calle 3 Norte · Calle del 5 de Mayo · Calle 2 Norte · Calle 6 Norte

⑥

⑦

Avenida 4 Poniente → — Avenida 4 Oriente

⑧ ⑨ ⑪ ⑫ ⑬

Avenida 2 Poniente ← — Avenida 2 Oriente

Pedestrian Walkways ⑩

14A

⑭ ⑮

Avenida de la Reforma → — Avenida General Maximino Avila Camacho

⑰ ⑯
⑱
Plaza Principal ⑳
⑲

㉑

Avenida 3 Poniente ← — Avenida 3 Oriente

㉕

㉔

㉓ ㉒

Calle 16 de Septiembre

† ■
Cathedral

Avenida 5 Poniente → — Avenida 5 Oriente

Calle 13 Sur · Calle 11 Sur · Paseo Bravo · Calle 9 Sur · Calle 7 Sur · Calle 5 Sur · Calle 3 Sur · Calle 2 Sur · Calle 4 Sur

㉖ ㉗

㉘

㉙

Avenida 7 Poniente ← — Avenida 7 Oriente

Avenida 9 Poniente → — Avenida 9 Oriente

Río San Francisco

Avenida 11 Poniente ← — Avenida 11 Oriente

Church †
■ †

ACCOMMODATIONS:
Colonial Hotel ⑳
Hosteria de los Angeles ⑯
Royalty Hotel ⑭
San Leonardo Hotel ⑩
San Miguel Hotel ㉕
Seniora Hotel ④
Teresita Hotel ㉔

DINING:
Café Aguirre 14A
Café La Princesa ⑮
Café Venicia ⑨
El Cortijo Restaurant ㉘
Fonda Típica Angelopolis ⑪
La Grecia ⑨
Mac's Tavern and Bar ⑰
El Parian Restaurant ⑫
Santa Clara Restaurant ㉒
Restaurant Vasco ⑲
Sanborns ⑧

El Vegetariano ㉔
Vittorio's Pizza ⑱

SIGHTS:
Callejon de los Sapos ㉙
Museo Bello ㉑
Museo de Arte Popular ①
Museo Regional/Casa Alfenique ⑦
Museo Revolucionario Regional ③

Palifoxiana Library ㉗
El Parian ⑬
Santa Monica Convent ②
Santo Domingo Church ⑥
Teatro Principal ⑤
Tourism Office ㉖

known as the **Plaza de la Constitución,** a beautiful place with a central bandstand and tile-covered benches. On one side is the cathedral and Calle 3 Oriente, and the other sides are flanked by the portales of colonial-era buildings which today house restaurants, hotels, and shops. These are on the streets Calle del 16 de Septiembre, Calle 2 Sur, and Avenida de la Reforma where it meets Avenida Camacho. Most of the museums, shops, and hotels mentioned here are within walking distance of the zócalo.

Most streets running east and west are *avenidas,* and those running north and south are *calles.* **Avenida de la Reforma** divides the city north and south, with even-numbered avenues to the north and odd-numbered avenues to the south. **Calle del 16 de Septiembre,** which changes its name to **Calle del 5 de Mayo** north of Reforma, is the east-west dividing line, with even-numbered streets to the east.

FAST FACTS

American Express   The American Express office is on Calle del 5 de Mayo, at Plaza Dorada 2 (tel. 37-5558).

Area Code   The telephone area code is 22.

Business Hours   Most shops are open Monday through Saturday from 10am to 1:30pm and 4 to 7pm; closed between 1:30 and 4pm.

Post Office   The Correos (post office) is in the Archbishop's Palace next to the cathedral, at the corner of Avenida 5 Ote. and Calle del 16 de Septiembre, but there is no sign.

WHAT TO SEE & DO
A STROLL AROUND PUEBLA

Puebla is a fascinating place to explore. The immense **cathedral** at Avenida 5 Oriente and Calle del 16 de Septiembre, was ordered built by King Philip of Spain in 1562, and it was completed in 1649. Bells hang in the tower closer to the zócalo (the other tower is empty). According to legend, additional bells were not installed because the Pueblans believed the weight would make the cathedral sink into an underground sea. The cathedral is open daily.

Just across the street from the cathedral, on the corner of Avenida 5 Oriente and Calle del 16 de Septiembre, is the old Archbishop's Palace, which now houses the **Casa de la Cultura** and the **Biblioteca Palafoxiana.** The entrance to the Cultural Center and the Library is about halfway down the block on Avenida 5 Ote. After you enter the courtyard, the marble stairs to the right will take you to the Biblioteca Palafoxiana. This library, the oldest in the Americas (also the most beautiful), was built in 1646 by Juan de Palafoxe y Mendoza, then archbishop and founder of the College of Saints Peter and Paul. It bespeaks the glory of this period with its elegant tile floor, hand-carved wood walls and ceiling, inlaid tables, and gilded wooden statues. Bookcases are filled with 17th-century books and manuscripts in Spanish, Créole, French, and English.

The old **mercado,** one of those Victorian monsters that resembles a railroad station, covers the entire block between Avenidas 4 and 8 Poniente on Calle 3 Norte, and has been renovated into a complex of office buildings and a cultural center. However, the entire area from Avenidas 4 to 10 Pte. and Calle 5 Norte to Calle del 5 de Mayo is still teeming with activity. It's a maze of narrow pathways lined with vendors on mats and knees selling vegetables and plastic trinkets, and old women in brightly colored clothes selling withered fruit. This is the place to buy onyx—most of the onyx mined in Mexico is shipped into Puebla where skilled artisans carve the stone.

While you're in the market area, stop in for a look at the **Iglesia de Santo Domingo** on Calle del 5 de Mayo between Avenidas 5 Ote. and 3 Ote. Finished in 1611, the church was originally part of a monastery. Don't miss the **Capilla del Rosario,** a fantastic symphony of gilt and beautiful stone dedicated to the Virgin of the Rosary and built in 1690. Puebla has many other beautiful churches and convents that date from the 17th and 18th centuries.

Near the **Barrio del Artística** is the **Principal Theater,** said to be the oldest theater in the Americas. The interior has been restored but it's only open for concerts (ask the Tourism Office for schedules).

MUSEUMS

MUSEO BELLO (Museum of Art), Av. 3 Pte. no. 302. Tel. 41-9475.

Located near the corner of Calle Sur 3 and Avenida 3 Pte., this museum is definitely worth a visit. The collection includes some of the finest 17th-, 18th-, and 19th-century art I've seen anywhere. Señor Bello made his fortune in tobacco and began to collect art from all over the world. He never traveled, but he hired art dealers who did. Later, Señor Bello, who was a fine artist and an accomplished organist, founded a museum, which he left to the state when he died. His taste is evident throughout the house: velvet curtains, French porcelain, beautiful hand-carved furniture, several very fine organs, and numerous paintings. The mandatory guided tour (in English or Spanish) is included in the price of admission.
Admission: 50¢.
Open: Tues–Sun 10am–4:30pm.

STATE REGIONAL MUSEUM, Calle 4 Ote. no. 416. Tel. 41-4296.

One of the most interesting parts of this museum is the building itself, called the Casa de Alfenique. The 18th-century house resembles an elaborate wedding cake and, in fact, the name means "sugar-cake house." Inside there is a good collection of pre-Hispanic artifacts and pottery, as well as exhibits of regional crafts and colonial-era furniture. The museum is 3½ blocks northwest of zócalo, between Calle 4 Norte and Calle 6 Norte.
Admission: 65¢.
Open: Tues–Sun 10am–4:30pm.

CONVENT OF SANTA MONICA, Av. 18 Pte. no. 103. Tel. 32-0178.

When the convents in Puebla were closed in 1767, this one and two others operated secretly, using entrances through private homes, which hid the convent from public view. Very few people knew this convent existed before it was rediscovered in 1935. Today it's a museum, kept as it was found. It's at the corner of Avenida 18 Poniente and Calle 3 Sur.
Admission: $1.75.
Open: Tues–Sun 10am–4:30pm.

MUSEUM OF POPULAR ARTS and THE COCINA DE SANTA ROSA, Av. 12 Pte. at Calle 5 Norte. Tel. 46-4526.

The largest convent in Puebla, Santa Rosa belonged to the Dominican order. It has been beautifully restored. The convent is worth a visit just to see the cavernous, beautifully tiled kitchen (*cocina*) where many native Mexican dishes were created. The museum has two floors of elaborate Mexican arts and crafts, including 6-foot earthenware candelabra, regional costumes, minute scenes made of straw and clay, and hand-tooled leather. A small shop sells local crafts, but they aren't as good as the government shops in other cities. Twenty-minute tours of the museum and kitchen are offered, the last one starting at 4:30pm. The museum is eight blocks northwest of the zócalo, between Calle 5 Norte and Calle 3 Norte.
Admission: 50¢.
Open: Tues–Sun 10am–4:30pm.

REGIONAL MEXICAN REVOLUTIONARY MUSEUM, Av. 6 Ote. no. 206. Tel. 42-1076.

This war museum is 3½ blocks north of the zócalo, between Calle 2 Norte and Calle 4 Norte, in the Casa de Aquiles Serdan, an 18th-century structure, complete with bullet holes in the front facade of the house! The collection includes arms and photos of the great turmoil of the mid-19th century: the battle between the Juarists (liberals) and those who followed the imperialists (conservatives). Since Puebla lies between the main seaport of Veracruz and the capital, it was often under bombardment by besieging armies.

Admission: 50¢.
Open: Tues–Sun 10am–4:30pm.

NEARBY ATTRACTIONS

About 2 miles from the zócalo, two forts commemorate the Mexican victory over the French on May 5, 1862. Admission to **Fort Loreto** is $1.75, and **Fort Guadalupe** is free. Some 6,000 Frenchmen led by Maximilian were defeated here by 2,000 Mexicans. You can buy a booklet at Fort Loreto telling the whole story. Streets in every Mexican city and town are named for the date of the battle, "Cinco de Mayo" (May 5).

You can take a cab to the forts or take a "Fuerte" bus from either the corner of 16 de Septiembre and Avenida 9 Ote. or at Calle 2 Sur and Avenida 6 Ote. While you are in the area you can easily visit the Regional Museum and the Planetarium. (The Planetarium however, was out of order on my last visit).

You can also visit the **African Safari game preserve** 10 miles southeast of town at Avenida 11 Oriente no. 2405. If you've seen this kind of park at home, however, you'll probably want to skip this one as there's nothing special about it. It's 15 minutes by car and 30 minutes by bus from downtown. It has a collection of African animals: gazelle, antelope, lions, ostriches, and elephants. Admission and a guided (Spanish) bus tour costs $4 for adults, $3 for children. A bus departs Terminal African at Avenida 12 Ote. and Calle 4 Norte for the round-trip.

SHOPPING

If you're in the market for a set of **Talavera dinnerware,** this is the city. Numerous workshops produce this famous pottery, which is very expensive. Among them is the **Casa Rugerio,** Avenida 18 Poniente no. 111 (tel. 41-3843), a family-owned shop that's been in business for generations. There's a small sales showroom in front and visitors can tour the small production area in back. Orders for complete sets of dinnerware can take 2 to 3 years for delivery, and you must make a down payment. Just for your information, the sales folks are family members who've been at this so long they've forgotten how to smile, so don't expect a flurry of appreciation or joy when you buy or order.

The **Mercado El Parian** is a pedestrians-only open-air shopping area on Calle 8 Norte between Avenidas 2 and 6 Oriente. You'll see rows of neat brick shops selling crafts and souvenirs. Don't judge all Talavera pottery by what you see here, though—artists seem to have gone overboard with design. The shops are open daily from 10am to 8pm. Bargain to get a good price. While you're in this area you can take a look at the Principal Theater.

For some good antiques browsing, go to **Callejon de los Sapos** (Frog Street), about five blocks south of the zócalo near Calle 4 Sur and Avenida 7 Oriente. Wander in and out, there's good stuff large and small. Shops are generally open from 10am to 2pm and 4 to 6pm.

Shoppers should also browse through the old **mercado.**

EVENING ENTERTAINMENT

Mariachis play daily, beginning at 6pm, on **Plaza de Santa Ines,** at Avenida 11 Poniente and Calle 3 Sur. They stroll through the crowds that gather at the sidewalk cafés. Another square that attracts mariachis is **Plaza de los Sapos,** Avenida 7 Oriente near Calle 6 Sur. To get there, walk two blocks south from the zócalo and take a left onto Avenida 7 Oriente, toward the river. To find the plaza, follow the sound of music. A third place to hear mariachis nightly is the **Plaza de Los Trabajos,** at Calle 11 Norte and Avenida 10 Pte.

Teorama, Reforma 540 near Calle 6 Norte (tel. 42-1014), is a wonderful coffeeshop and bookstore which features guitarists and folksingers every evening. This is a good place to meet young local residents.

WHERE TO STAY

Puebla has many hotels, but I haven't found a single well-run budget hotel among them. Perhaps it's Puebla's industrial wealth, such as the gigantic Volkswagen plant on the main highway, cement plants, and faïence works, that keep the hotels full at inflated prices.

DOUBLES FOR LESS THAN $20

HOTEL TERESITA, Av. 3 Pte. no. 309, Puebla, Pla. 72000. Tel. 22/41-7072. 54 rms (37 with bath).
$ Rates: $14.50 single, $16 double, with bath; $11.50 single, $13.50 double without bath.
The small, tidy colonial-style foyer has a staircase leading up to a lot of drab but well-kept rooms. It's location, 1½ blocks west of the zócalo, between Calles 3 Sur and 5 Sur, makes it a good budget choice, but be aware that the clientele is mostly Mexican workers, and I've never seen women here.

DOUBLES FOR LESS THAN $35

HOTEL SAN MIGUEL, Av. 3 Pte. no. 721, Puebla, Pla. 72000. Tel. 22/42-4860. 63 rms (all with bath). TEL
$ Rates: $18 single; $23 double.
The best budget hotel in town is 3½ long blocks west of the cathedral, between Calles 7 Sur and 9 Sur. The hallways are gleaming tile, and the rooms are large and clean. I recommend a quiet interior room. The only drawback here is the limited supply of hot water—it's available from 6 to 11am and 5 to 11pm.

HOTEL SEÑORIAL, Calle 4 Nte. no. 602, Puebla, Pla. 72000. Tel. 22/46-8999. Fax 22/46-8964. 72 rms (all with bath). TEL
$ Rates: $25 single; $30 double.
A modern hotel, it has an aluminum, glass, and shiny black stone facade. The rooms have wall-to-wall carpeting, and facilities include a beauty salon, barbershops, Turkish baths, and a garage. Some rooms have TV. Beware of rooms facing the street where there's plenty of street noise. The hotel is 4½ blocks north of the zócalo, between Avenidas 6 and 8 Oriente.

DOUBLES FOR LESS THAN $45

HOTEL ROYALTY CENTRO, Portal Hidalgo 8, Puebla, Pla. 72000. Tel. 22/42-0202 or 42-4740. 44 rms (all with bath). TV TEL
$ Rates: $33 single; $40 double.
You can't go wrong in this old-fashioned hotel that's as much of an institution as the zócalo across the street. Rooms are comfortably furnished and some have a view of the plaza. Larger rooms or a private refrigerator cost extra.

HOTEL COLONIAL, Calle 4 Sur no. 105, Puebla, Pla. 72000. Tel. 22/46-4199. 70 rms (all with bath). TEL
$ Rates: $32 single; $40 double.
The hotel is charming in an old way, with arches and lots of tiles on the interior public areas. The rooms, too, have tile floors and are neatly furnished in 1940s furniture. It's overpriced, but comfortable and close to all the sights. The restaurant is one of the best in the downtown area. There are also elevators, and garage parking is around the corner. The Colonial is one block east of the zócalo, between Camacho and Avenida 3 Oriente.

HOTEL PALACIO SAN LEONARDO, Av. 2 Ote. no. 211, Puebla, Pla. 72000. Tel. 22/46-0555. 75 rms (all with bath). TV TEL

$ Rates: $33 single; $42 double.

The lobby is entered through massive wooden doors, and there's a crystal chandelier hanging from the ceiling. However, the second you step into the elevator you leave 18th-century style behind: The rooms have carpeting and modern furnishings. Try to get a room on the sixth floor with a great view of the church domes and the surrounding mountains. There's a tiny swimming pool and a terrace on the roof. The hotel is 2½ blocks north of the zócalo, between Calles 2 Norte and 4 Norte.

WHERE TO EAT

The main square, or zócalo, is in the center of town where the two main boulevards cross. There are several restaurants here that offer good food, good value, and a view of the action on the square.

Puebla is known throughout Mexico for the famous **mole poblano,** a sauce with more than 20 ingredients, as well **mixiotes** which is beef, pork, or lamb in a spicy red sauce and baked in maguey paper. **Dulces** (sweets) shops are scattered about, with display windows brim-full of marzipan crafted into various shapes and designs, candied figs, guava paste, and camotes, which are little cylinders of a fruity, sweet-potato paste wrapped in waxed paper.

There are more small, cheap, Puebla-style eateries on **Calle 6 Norte,** all doing their part to uphold the reputation Puebla bears as a culinary fount. Great pots of boiling mole and other mysteriously delectable regional sauces bubble temptingly. Find something you like by peeking into the kitchens right in front. Most restaurants are open daily, but several are closed on Wednesday.

MEALS FOR LESS THAN $5

CAFE VENECIA, Av. 2 Ote. no. 207. Tel. 46-2306.
Specialty: MEXICAN.
$ Prices: Appetizers $1–$2; main courses $2–$5; comida corrida $2.50.
Open: Daily 7am–10pm (comida corrida served 1–5pm).
This is a clean, cheery, but simple place with a good variety of items for lunch or a light dinner at decent prices. For instance, a hamburger, ham sandwich, fruit cocktail, enchiladas, and chicken casserole are all priced between $1.75 and $4. A second-floor dining balcony overlooks the first floor. The café is 4½ blocks north of the zócalo, between Calles 2 Norte and 4 Norte.

MACS TAVERN AND BAR, Camacho and Portal Morelos. Tel. 46-0211.
Specialty: MEXICAN.
$ Prices: Appetizers $2–$3; comida corrida $5–$7.
Open: Daily 7am–midnight.
Here on the northeast corner of the zócalo is one of Puebla's most popular places for lunch. Hungry Poblanos don't come here for the modern setting, but for the three-course, fixed-price lunch and the four-course dinner. One of the lunches will last you the rest of the day. This is also a pleasant place to stop in the evening to enjoy the live organ music.

EL VEGETARIANO, Av. 3 Pte. no. 525. Tel. 46-5462.
Specialty: VEGETARIAN.
$ Prices: Soups and salads $2.50; main courses $4–$5.
Open: Daily 8am–9pm.
Sparsely furnished with plain pine boards reminiscent of an unpretentious Scandinavian kitchen, El Vegetariano is clean and welcoming with good service. Try the refreshing yogurt with fruit, honey, and granola. Besides the extensive menu, a vegetarian comida is served either downstairs or on the mezzanine. If you like french fries, order the delicious papas a la francesa. You'll find the restaurant three blocks west of the zócalo, located between Calles 5 Sur and 7 Sur.

MEALS FOR LESS THAN $10

RESTAURANTE DEL PARIAN, Av. 2 Ote. no. 415. Tel. 46-4798.

Specialty: REGIONAL.
$ Prices: Main courses $3–$5.
Open: Thurs–Tues 10am–10pm.

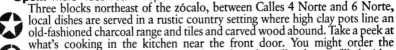

Three blocks northeast of the zócalo, between Calles 4 Norte and 6 Norte, local dishes are served in a rustic country setting where high clay pots line an old-fashioned charcoal range and tiles and carved wood abound. Take a peek at what's cooking in the kitchen near the front door. You might order the Puebla-style enchiladas, or chalupas (boat-shaped tortillas that are filled with a meat mixture), among other tasty delights. No English is spoken here, so ask "Es muy picante?" ("Is it very spicy-hot?") before you order.

FONDA TÍPICA ANGELOPOLIS, Av. 2 Ote. no. 407. Tel. 42-9063.

Specialty: REGIONAL.
$ Prices: Main courses $2–$6.50.
Open: Thurs–Tues 9am–midnight.

This mom-and-pop restaurant is small, spotless, and attractively decorated with ceramic tiles. As you enter, examine the bubbling contents in the clay pots and notice the different colors of Puebla sauces and stews, ranging from green to red and dark brown. The Fonda is two blocks northeast of the zócalo, between Calles 2 Norte and 4 Norte.

LA GRECIA, Av. 2 Ote. no. 207. Tel. 46-2781.

Specialty: MEXICAN.
$ Prices: Appetizers $2.75–$3.75; main courses $4.50–$6.50.
Open: Daily 8am–midnight.

Located in the same building as Cafe Venecia, 1½ blocks north of the zócalo, between Calles 2 Norte and 4 Norte, this restaurant also offers good food for good prices. The roast-meat smell that wafts from this restaurant is enough to draw you in. The featured items are tacos con tortilla arabe, which translates as grilled meat in pita bread, and tortas (sandwiches). And you can get yogurt too.

VITTORIO'S PIZZERIA, Portal Morelos 106. Tel. 32-7900.

Specialty: ITALIAN.
$ Prices: Pastas and salads $3–$5; pizza $5–$17.
Open: Daily 8am–11:30pm.

This upscale restaurant on the east side of the zócalo serves incredibly cheesy pizzas and pastas, as well as regional poblano cuisine. You can dine in the romantic restaurant or outside on the plaza. Pizzas come in three sizes: Small will feed one or two people, medium will satisfy two or three, and the large will feed a party of four to six. This is the place for a good inexpensive cappuccino or espresso.

EL CORTIJO, Calle del 16 de Septiembre no. 506. Tel. 42-0503.

Specialty: MEXICAN. **Directions:** Walk 1½ blocks S of zócalo; it's between Calle 16 de Septiembre and Calle 2 Sur.
$ Prices: Appetizers $2–$4.50; main courses $7.50–$11.
Open: Mon–Sat 10am–7pm, Sun 1–5pm (comida corrida served 1–5pm).

With large wooden doors and a charming patio that's always crowded, El Cortijo has a comfortable atmosphere and tasty food. Dishes range from pork chops to a delicious jumbo shrimp or paella. The cubierto (or comida corrida) consists of a filling five courses with a choice of four different main dishes. This is a good place for that large afternoon meal and a bottle of wine.

CAFE LA PRINCESA, Portal Juárez 101. Tel. 32-1195.

Specialty: MEXICAN.
$ Prices: Breakfast $1.55–$3; appetizers $1.25–$4; main courses $7.50–$9; comida corrida $6.50.
Open: Daily 8am–11:30pm.

Facing the bustle of the downtown and the north side of the shady zócalo, this brightly lit large room is filled with tables draped in red-and-white cloths and with friendly waiters in bow ties. For the comida, you can choose between several appetizers and main dishes.

SANBORN'S, Av. 2 Ote. no. 6. Tel. 42-9436.
   Specialty: MEXICAN.
   $ Prices: Soups, salads, and sandwiches $2–$6; main courses $6–$10.
   Open: Sun–Fri 7:30am–11pm, Sat 7:30am–midnight.
Despite the modern facade, this local restaurant is set up just like those in Mexico City, with sales counters for magazines and cameras. The plush dining room is in a fine colonial courtyard, with tables set out around a stone fountain. The atmosphere is cool and quiet. Stay away from the tenderloin tips and order the chicken with chilaquiles or hamburger and fries instead. Sanborn's is not particularly cheap, but it's very restful. It's 1½ blocks north of the zócalo, between Avenidas 2 Oriente and 4 Oriente.

CAFE AGUIRRE, Calle del 5 de Mayo no. 4. Tel. 41-9270.
   Specialty: MEXICAN.
   $ Prices: Main courses $6.50–$10.
   Open: Mon–Sat 7:30am–10:30pm, Sun 9am–4:30pm.
Located on the northwest corner of the zócalo, at the corner of Camacho, this café is part of a photo shop advertised by a big yellow-and-white Kodak sign. Both young and old enjoy the snacks, sandwiches, and ice cream here. A fixed-price lunch is served daily starting at 1pm.

CAFE EL VASCO, Portal Juárez 105. Tel. 32-8689.
   Specialty: MEXICAN.
   $ Prices: Appetizers $3–$7.50; main courses $5–$10.
   Open: Daily 8am–10:30pm.
Puebla's businessmen prefer this somber and medieval café with sidewalk tables. The decor has a Crusades motif: swords, maces, and paintings of Crusaders off to the Holy Land. The food, anything from soup to enchiladas suizas, red snapper, and chateaubriand, is good and the service is attentive. The café is on the east side of the zócalo under the portals.

FONDA SANTA CLARA, Av. 3 Pte. no. 307. Tel. 42-2659.
   Specialty: REGIONAL.
   $ Prices: Appetizers $2–$5; main courses $4.50–$10.
   Open: Tues–Sat 8am–10:30pm, Sun 8am–9:30pm.
One of the city's most popular and traditional restaurants, serving regional food, it's busy, but cozy and slightly formal. The menu includes local dishes such as pollo mole poblano and mixiotes. The restaurant is opposite the Bello Museum half a block west of the zócalo, between Calles 3 Sur and 5 Sur.

EASY EXCURSIONS FROM PUEBLA

CHOLULA Six miles northwest of Puebla along Highway 190 (not the toll road, 190D), the colonial town of Cholula (pop. 45,000) is one of the holiest places in Mexico. It was here that Quetzalcoatl, the famed feathered serpent, is thought to have lived in exile after he was forced to leave his city of Tula, capital of the Toltecs, in A.D. 900. During pre-Hispanic days pilgrims came here to pay their respects to this great leader. Today it's very easy to get to Cholula from Puebla. From Puebla take one of the red-and-white buses marked "Cholula," at the corner of Av. 8 and Calle 7 Nte. However, schedules and routes were being changed when I checked. Ask at the Puebla Tourist Office for current information, or take a taxi from Puebla.
   The Cholulans strongly resisted Cortés and his men. When the Spaniards discovered that the residents of this town were plotting to overthrow them, at least 3,000 Cholulans were killed.
   Cholula has so many churches it's often said that there's one for every day of the

year. It's also the home of the **University of the Americas**—popular with American students. From Cholula's main plaza, you can see the massive yellow **Los Remedios Church** atop the Great Tepanapa Pyramid, only a 5-minute walk away. To get to the ruins from the plaza at Calle 2 Sur and Avenida Morelos, follow Avenida Morelos and continue over the railroad tracks. Immediately to your right is the entrance to the pyramid. The ruins are open daily from 10:30am to 5pm. Admission is $3.25, free on Sun. and holidays.

What you will see is just the base; the pyramid is actually buried under the "hill." Left from pre-Hispanic times, it is slowly being excavated and restored. I recommend that you hire a guide to show you the hidden tunnels and the fantastic frescoes that are deep inside the mound. The frescoes are some of the most famous in Mexico and date back to the Classic Period.

To reach the little **museum,** containing a scaled-down model of the pyramid, continue straight ahead after crossing the railroad tracks. Admission to the museum is included in the admission to the ruins, so save your ticket.

If you take the stone walkway up the hill you'll reach the lovely chapel of the Virgen de los Remedios. The gilded interior of this little gem is as pretty as its exterior. Some enterprising children sell cold soft drinks in the right portal of the church. While regaining your breath, you'll enjoy the spectacular view of the town's steeples and plaza.

Two Indian Baroque Churches   If you go to Cholula, try to visit the churches of **Santa María Tonantzintla** and **San Francisco Acatepec,** three miles southeast of Cholula. Called Indian baroque because the Indians used pre-Hispanic ideas to present Christian concepts. The churches are elaborately decorated with beautifully colored Puebla tiles and wood carved by local artisans. Saints are swaddled in stylized queztzal bird feathers, once used to depict the god Quetzalcoatl, and clownlike faces protrude from a headdress of corn leaves, in the same way they did in pre-Christian times. The interior of the Tonanzintla church is covered floor to ceiling in fabulous gilded and polychromed faces, cherubs, and foliage—an unforgettable sight. The facade of the Acatepec church is a fantasy of tile though it has a less elaborate interior than the Tonanzintla church.

The churches are only 8 miles outside Cholula and are easy to reach from there by bus. Take one of the red-and-white buses marked "Chupito" which go by the entrance to the ruins. You'll enjoy seeing these Churrigueresque tours de force. Both churches close between 1 and 3pm, and often other hours as well; the caretaker is usually not far away, so ask around for him and chances are he'll appear.

HUEJOTZINGO   Huejotzingo, Puebla (alt. 7,550 ft.; pop. 30,000), is a pleasant town with a large main square 9 miles northwest of Cholula. Fine woolen goods, especially serapes and blankets, are sold at the open-air market on Saturday. Even if you don't come for market day, you can stop and enjoy a glass or two of the sparkling (alcoholic) cider, a local specialty.

While in town, be sure to visit the **Franciscan monastery,** right across the main road from the town plaza. It was built between 1529 and 1570 and is one of the oldest in Mexico. As you walk up the stairs from the main road and enter the monastery compound, stop to admire the little square chapels (*pozos*) topped by pyramidal roofs at each corner of the enclosure. The cross mounted on a pedestal in the courtyard dates from the 1500s as well.

The church, very austere on the outside, has a wonderfully lacy Gothic vault inside, and a dazzling altar in the plateresque style. The monastery building next door, entered through the double-arch doorway, has a few excellent friezes in black and white painted by Fray Antonio de Rola in 1558. There is a lovely chapel, a cloister for the monks, kitchens, and a dining room. The monastery is open Tuesday through Sunday from 10am to 4:30pm; there is a small admission fee.

From Puebla, ask about current transportation; bus schedules were changing at press time. From Cholula, take a taxi from the central plaza for around $6.

Special Event   The colorful story of a bandit, Augustín Lorenzo, and the kidnapping of a beautiful young girl is reenacted in Huejotzingo the Tuesday before

Ash Wednesday with a colorful firecracker-filled **Carnaval** with a cast of thousands wearing brilliantly colored costumes. The story goes that during the colonial era in Huejotzingo, Lorenzo kidnapped the daughter of a rich landowner and spirited her away into the mountains in order to wed her. During the wedding celebration local soldiers came to her rescue. It's one of the most colorful Carnaval celebrations in Mexico; the carnaval market is at least 10 blocks square.

2. TEHUACÁN

65 miles SE of Puebla

GETTING TO & FROM TEHUACÁN   By Train   From Mexico City, the first-class *El Oaxaqueño* arrives in Tehuacán at 2:30am and stops only a few minutes before continuing on to Oaxaca where it arrives at 9:30am the following morning.

By Bus   The **ADO** (tel. 2-0096) first-class bus station is in central Tehuacán at Independencia 119. It serves 25 buses a day each way between Tehuacán and Puebla, 15 to Oaxaca, and 2 per day to and from Veracruz. The bus station has a small cafeteria, but you can easily walk to other restaurants: Just head out the front door of the station, turn right, and in a few minutes you'll be at the center of town, the intersection of Independencia and Reforma.

The route to Oaxaca is also served by several local lines originating in Tehuacán. The new second-class bus station, serving **Autobuses Unidos** lines is at 5 Oriente no. 413 between 3 Sur and 5 Sur. Six buses run to Puebla daily, four to Veracruz, and seven to Mexico City. Downtown is seven blocks from the back of the station.

By Car   The two-lane Highway 150 from Puebla runs through Tehuacán on the way to Oaxaca. The road is rough and poorly maintained, so watch for potholes. The drive from Puebla takes about 90 minutes. From Tehuacán to Oaxaca takes 5 or 6 hours on a twisty mountain road.

ESSENTIALS   The town's two main streets are named **Reforma** (north-south) and **Independencia** (east-west). On Independencia, one block east of the corner of Reforma, is the lovely shady **Parque Juárez,** which functions as the center of town. The **Tourism Office,** on the northeast corner of the Parque, is open Monday through Friday from 9am to 1pm and 4 or 5 to 6pm. The **telephone area code** is 238.

Tehuacán (alt. 5,409 ft.; pop. 90,000) is a clean, attractive town that is popular with the wealthy and ill. The hotels are large and expensive, and the mineral waters are said to be good for hepatitis and for kidney and stomach ailments.

WHAT TO SEE & DO

There's not much to do besides **take the waters** at El Riego, to the west of town, and at San Lorenzo, off the road to Mexico City in the northwest. Both are free. If you don't want to leave town, water is also dispensed at luxurious "cave" next door to the Hotel Hacienda Spa Peñafiel, at the northern end of town. Actually it's a long, downward-sloping hallway with plaster of Paris "rocks" on the ceiling, tile walls, and silvered wrought-iron gates. At the end of the passage is a modern little patio with the waters gushing out of spigots. There's nothing to drink from, so bring an empty bottle. Drink all you want—it's free. The cave is maintained by the Peñafiel bottling company, whose plant adjoins it. It's open to the public daily from 7:30am to 2:30pm.

Once you've tasted the mineral waters and strolled through the **Parque Juárez,** walk up Avenida Reforma Norte to the **Templo del Carmen,** finished in 1783. Its dazzling domes are covered in polychrome faïence. Hidden in the former convent (monastery) connected to the church is the rather worn-out **Museo del Valle de Tehuacán,** open daily from 9am to 1pm; admission is 75¢, and the caretaker seldom has change. Some frescoes remain from the time the monks were in residence, but the exhibits on the lower floor are much older. In the early 1960s Dr. Richard MacNeish discovered that the valley of Tehuacán was the cradle of the earliest maize (corn) cultivation in the world—dating from 5000 B.C. You can also trace the development of sculpture in the valley, from primitive pointy-chin female figurines to beautiful obsidian knives.

There are **public pools** at San Lorenzo. Take one of the red-and-yellow "San Lorenzo" buses from the corner of 1 Norte and 2 Oriente, behind the Templo del Carmen, to the end of the line. Admission to the four large pools is 50¢. You can also swim at the pool at Hotel Spa Penafiel for a small fee. The "San Lorenzo" bus passes the hotel en route.

WHERE TO STAY

HOTEL IBERIA, Av. Independencia 211, Tehuacán, Pla. 75700. Tel. 238/3-1507. 26 rms (all with bath). TEL
$ Rates: $15 single; $18 double.
This mammoth colonial-style hotel, past the park on the left-hand side of Independencia, is my first choice. The Iberia's facelift managed to reverse its sagging image. Even the courtyard has been rejuvenated with a variety of potted plants and rose bushes. The rooms are the same quality as the Monroy, but the location can't be beat. Upstairs rooms are arranged around a nice patio.

HOTEL MONROY, Reforma Norte 217, Tehuacán, Pla. 75700. Tel. 238/2-0491. 28 rms (all with bath).
$ Rates: $12 per person.
Serious budget travelers will like this modern, kelly-green building, trimmed with black and white ceramic stripes. It's across from the Templo del Carmen. The cheerful rooms are plain, but large and scrupulously clean. This is an exceptional value for solo travelers.

HOTEL MÉXICO, Reforma and Independencia, Tehuacán, Pla. 75700. Tel. 238/2-2319. 66 rms (all with bath); 20 suites. TV TEL
$ Rates: $38 single; $44 double; $54–$63 suite. **Parking:** Free.
This is a colonial wonder, without the same full measure of grace as the Penafiel, but nice nonetheless. Rooms are certainly large and comfortable, but prices are a bit high because of the cable color TV. The restaurant serves meals and a daily comida. Parking is adjacent. The hotel is at the corner of Parque Juárez.

WHERE TO EAT

RESTAURANT PENAFIEL, on the east side of Parque Juárez. Tel. 3-2490.
Specialty: MEXICAN.
$ Prices: Appetizers $1.50–$3; meat and fowl courses $5.50–$9.50.
Open: Daily 7am–11pm.
This is the most elegant and expensive place to dine along the Parque Juárez. Waiters wear bow ties and are eager to serve. Big glass windows look onto the park and the passing scene.

There are several less expensive places across the park on the west side, serving meals for 25% to 35% less.

BAGDAD, Reforma Norte. 113.
Specialty: MEXICAN.
$ Prices: Main courses $1–$3.

428 • SOUTH OVER THE MOUNTAINS

Open: Breakfast/lunch daily 8am–3pm; dinner daily 7pm–midnight.

Ideal for a quick snack, this restaurant opposite the Templo del Carmen is one of the many little Mexican grills in Tehuacán. The menu of *ricos antojitos típicos* includes tacos, burritos, grilled meats, and sandwiches. A tall glass of fresh-squeezed orange juice costs $1.

EN ROUTE TO OAXACA

The trip by car takes 4½ hours if you take the new Highway 131. Because the bus stops at Teotitlán, the trip takes slightly longer.

On the road to Oaxaca, you wind through beautiful mountain country, dipping down into valleys filled with mango trees and climbing hillsides crowded with gigantic cacti.

3. OAXACA

325 miles S of Mexico City, 144 miles S of Tehuacán, 168 miles N of Puerto Escondido

GETTING THERE   By Plane   Mexicana flies to Oaxaca from Mexico City, Tuxtla Gutiérrez, Villahermosa, Mérida, Cancún, and several U.S. gateways. **Aeroméxico** flies in from Mexico City, Guadalajara, Monterrey, Ciudad Juárez, and U.S. gateways. **Aerovías Oaxaqueños** flies 28-passenger DC-3s from Puerto Escondido. **AeroMorelos** flies from Acapulco, Huatulco, Puebla, and Puerto Escondido. **Aviacsa** flies in from Tuxtla Gutiérrez. **AeroCaribe** flies from Tuxtla Gutiérrez, Villahermosa, Mérida, and Cancún. **AeroLibertad** flies from Acapulco, Puerto Escondido, and Huatulco.

By Train   The overnight train from Mexico City, *El Oaxaqueño* departs the capital at 7pm, arrives in Puebla at midnight, and at Oaxaca at 9am. Fares are $4 for a first-class seat, $10.50 for a special-class seat (cleaner, better bathrooms), $43.25 for a double sleeper, and $52.45 double for a bedroom with private bath.

By Bus   The first-class bus lines **ADO** serves Oaxaca from the north and west and **Cristóbal Colón** from the south and east.

By Car   It's a 10-hour ride from Mexico City, via Puebla and Tehuacán. Take the toll Highway 190D to Puebla; then Highways 150 and 131 through Tehuacán south to Oaxaca. The road winds through the mountains, cutting your speed considerably. It's unlikely you'll try to do it in one day, so you'll have to plan an overnight stop. Figure that from Mexico City you'll drive 2 hours to get to Puebla, and 3 more hours to get to Tehuacán on a rough, potholed road.

DEPARTING   By Plane   Airline offices are downtown and/or at the airport: **Mexicana,** Fiallo 102, at Avenida Independencia (tel. 6-7352 or 6-2337, or 6-9229 at the airport); **Aeroméxico,** Avenida Hidalgo 513, at 20 de Noviembre (tel. 6-1066 or 6-3765, or at the airport 6-2844). **Aerovías Oaxaqueñas,** Armenta y López 209, between Hidalgo and Guerrero (tel. 6-3833, or 6-1600 at the airport), where tickets should be reserved through the airline ticket office rather than through a travel agency (it's a small company, and there have been mix-ups with telephone reservations); **AeroCaribe** (now belonging to Mexicana), at Murguia 103 (tel. 6-2247); **AeroMorelos,** at the airport (tel. 6-3010); and **AeroLibertad,** at the airport (tel. 6-1687).

By Train   The *Oaxaqueño* night train leaves from Oaxaca's main station (tel. 6-2564 or 6-2253), west of the Cerro del Fortín hill, a moderate distance from the center of town. The first-class train has sleeping cars, and leaves Oaxaca at 7pm, arriving in Puebla at 4am and at Mexico City at 9am. Buy tickets at the station, from El Convento Travel Agency in the Hotel El Presidente, or Travel Agency Centroamerica on the plaza.

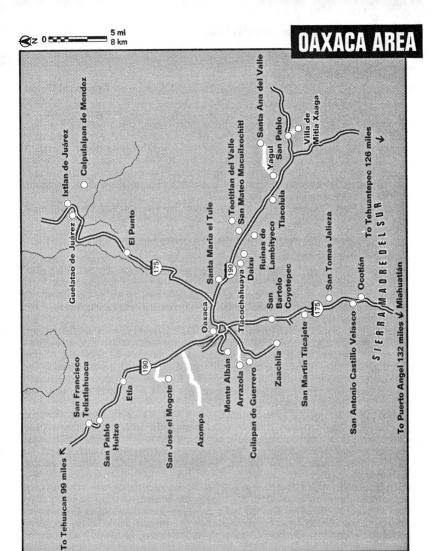

OAXACA AREA

0   5 mi
    8 km

To Tehuacan 99 miles

Calpulpalpan de Mendez

Ixtlan de Juárez

Guelatao de Juárez

El Punto

175

San Francisco Telixtlahuaca

San Pablo Huitzo

Etla

San Jose el Mogote

Azompa

190

Cuilapan de Guerrero

Arrazola

Monte Albán

Oaxaca

Santa Maria el Tule

Teotitlan del Valle

San Mateo Macuilxochitl

Santa Ana del Valle

Yagul

Villa de Mitla Xaaga

San Pablo

Tlacolula

190

Tlacochahuaya

Daizu

Ruinas de Lambityeco

San Bartolo Coyotepec

Zaachila

San Martin Tilcajete

San Tomas Jalieza

175

Ocotlán

San Antonio Castillo Velasco

SIERRA MADRE DEL SUR

To Tehuantepec 126 miles ↓

To Puerto Angel 132 miles ↙ Miahuatlán

MEXICO CITY

Oaxaca

BASKET MAKERS MARKET:
Miahuatlan

CHEESE MARKET:
Etla

GENERAL MARKET:
Tlacolula (Sunday)
Zaachila (Thursday)

POTTERY MARKETS:
Azompa
Ocotlán

WEAVERS MARKET:
Santo Tomas
Santa Ana del Valle
Teotitlán

WOOD CARVERS MARKET:
Arrazola
San Martin Tilcajete

Train travel south of Oaxaca is not recommended—trains are slow, uncomfortable, and plagued by thieves.

By Bus **ADO** (tel. 5-1703) handles most traffic north and west; **Cristóbal Colón** (tel. 5-1214) serves the region south and east of Oaxaca. At least 30 buses a day run to Mexico City's Central del Norte, 12 a day to Puebla, 17 a day between Oaxaca and Tehuacán. There are also buses to Huatulco (two a day); Tehuantepec (11 a day); Tuxtla Gutiérrez (three a day); San Cristóbal de las Casas, a 13-hour trip (one a day); Tapachula (two a day); Veracruz (two a day); and Villahermosa (three a day). A second-class bus for Guelatao (birthplace of Benito Juárez) also leaves from the first-class station. Buy your tickets a day in advance to be sure of space and a good seat.

Autobuses Turisticos has two buses a day to Puerto Escondido, departing from the hotel Mesón del Angel (tel. 6-5327).

Fletes y Pasajes, at the second-class station, has frequent departures for most of the villages surrounding the city.

Oaxaca (pronounced "Wa-*hah*-kah") is a booming commercial and industrial center located in a secluded valley high in the rugged mountains (alt. 5,070 ft.; pop. 800,000). Although prosperity has given the city a cosmopolitan touch, the local residents, called Oaxaqueños (pronounced "Wah-hah-*kehn*-yos"), have carefully preserved the colonial beauty of the central city and most visitors are unaware of the modern industry.

The Zapotec came to this high valley about 800 B.C. and built a beautiful city and a flourishing culture at Monte Albán, 6 miles from the modern city. Evidence shows that there were primitive inhabitants in the valley as early as 8000 B.C. Some authorities who have studied the early inhabitants find a distinct resemblance to the art and calendar system to the Olmecs of the Gulf Coast. In any case, it was certainly the Zapotecs who raised the city's cultural life to a high level and built the monuments visible at the site today.

After this flowering of Zapotec culture (about A.D. 300–700), another tribe, the Mixtecs, built a rival center at Mitla, 36 miles away on the other side of what is today Oaxaca, and the two tribes struggled for control of the valley until the Aztec threat united them against the common enemy. But even the two tribes united were no match for the Aztecs, and in the late 1400s and early 1500s Aztec influence predominated.

The local tribes didn't have to worry about the Aztecs for long, however—an even more formidable enemy appeared in 1521. After the Spanish subdued the valley, they set up a military post called Antequers here; 6 years later the town of Oaxaca was founded. Hernán Cortés was later given the title of Marqués del Valle de Oaxaca by the Habsburg Emperor Charles V, and with the title came grants of land, some of which were controlled by Cortés's descendants until the Mexican Revolution in 1910.

Two of Mexico's presidents, Porfirio Díaz and Benito Juárez, were born near Oaxaca. Nobody does much to remember Díaz these days, but monuments to Juárez are everywhere: statues, murals, streets named for him, even a Benito Juárez University. In fact, the city's official name is Oaxaca de Juárez. A Zapotec, Juárez was born in the nearby village of Guelatao, and "adopted" by a wealthy Oaxacan family who clothed, educated, and taught him Spanish in return for his services as a houseboy. He fell in love with the daughter of the household, and promised that he would become rich and famous and return to marry her. He managed all three, and Oaxaca adores him for it. Juárez attended law school, was the governor of the state of Oaxaca (1847–52), and later a resistance leader and president of the republic. He is a national hero.

Oaxaca has become the destination of choice for travelers seeking colonial surroundings, archeological sites, and indigenous creativity. The city is a beautiful treasure of homes and shops, with blooming jacaranda trees casting a purple haze against the cobalt sky. Museums display classic treasures in gold and jade, galleries exhibit modern masterpieces by local folk artists, and the mountains and valleys of the surrounding countryside are a photographer's dream. Expatriates from the U.S.

and Europe create a bohemian subculture, mingling with the colorful Zapotecs and Mixtecs who live much as their ancestors did long ago.

ORIENTATION

ARRIVING **By Plane** The **airport** is south of town, about a 15-minute cab ride. **Transportaciones Aeropuerto Oaxaca,** Alameda de León 1A (tel. 6-2777), operates an airport minibus service between the hotels in the center of town and the airport. It's at least a 20-minute ride and costs $2.50 each way. It costs more if you have what they consider to be a lot of luggage. Drop by the office next to the Hotel Monte Albán at least a day in advance to reserve your place. The office is open Monday through Saturday from 9am to 2pm and 5 to 8pm. Buy tickets on Saturday if you plan to leave on Monday.

By Bus The **Central Camionera** first-class bus station is north of the center of town on the main highway, a city street called Calle Niños Héroes de Chapultepec. Taxis between here and the zócalo cost about $2.50, and perhaps this is your best bet, as direct city bus transportation must be caught several blocks down the street (turn left as you leave the station) at the intersection of Niños Héroes and Vasconcelos, a long walk with a suitcase. Buses are marked "Col. America" and "Col. Reforma."

The **Central Camionera de Segunda Clase** (second-class bus terminal) is near the railroad station and the new market buildings; head west out Trujano and cross the railroad tracks. Take an "Estación" bus along Hidalgo.

By Train The **railroad station** is about 15 blocks southwest of the plaza. From the train station, taxis to Plaza Principal cost about $2.50, or you can take the "Estación" bus that runs along Avenida Hidalgo between the station and the plaza.

INFORMATION **Amistad International** operates an extremely helpful tourist office in the Palacio Municipal, Independencia at García Vigil (tel. 6-3810).

The **Federal Tourism Office** is at the corner of Matamoros and G. Vigil (tel. 6-0144), open Monday through Saturday from 9am to 3pm and 5 to 7pm.

The state of Oaxaca also maintains a **State and Federal Tourism Office** (Oficina de Turismo) at the corner of Morelos and Cinco de Mayo (tel. 951/6-1955 or 6-4828), open daily from 9am to 8pm. The enthusiastic staff is full of information.

CITY LAYOUT Most of the city's sights are located around **Plaza Principal,** one of the prettiest main plazas in Mexico. The city streets all change names at the plaza, which is bordered by Avenida Hidalgo at the north. Avenida Trujano at the south, García Vigil at the west, and Alcala at the east. Alcala is closed to traffic from Avenida Morelos to Avenida Gurrion, forming a pedestrian mall. Most of the more expensive hotels, restaurants, and galleries are located north of the plaza; the market, red-light district, and inexpensive hotels are south.

GETTING AROUND

BY BUS Colectivo buses to various parts of the city and outlying villages stop at the Central Market and the Abastos market.

BY TAXI Colectivo taxis to the villages depart from the Abastos market. There is a long line-up of taxis along Independencia at the north side of the plaza by the Abastos Market; you can negotiate rides to the ruins based on the number of people in your group.

FAST FACTS

American Express The office is at Valdivieso at Hidalgo, at the northeast corner of the plaza (tel. 951/6-2700 or 6-3010; fax 951/6-7475). Office hours are Monday through Friday from 9am to 2pm and 4 to 6:30pm and on Saturday from 9am to 2pm.

Area Code The telephone area code is 951.

Bookstores There's a good Spanish-English bookstore off the southeast corner of Plaza Principal at Guerrero 108, called **Librería Universitaría.** Most are new books, but there are a few used-book racks. Used books are even cheaper at the **Biblioteca Circulante (Oaxaca Lending Library)** located at Alcala 305.

Consulates Many consulates are located at Grupo Consular, Hidalgo 817 (tel. 951/6-0654). The **United States Consulate** is at Crespo 213 (tel. 6-0654).

Currency Exchange Banks only change dollars Monday through Friday from 9am to 12:30pm. Avoid Banapais, which charges 5%. There are several Casas de Cambio (money-changing storefronts) around the plaza, some of which offer a better exchange rate than at the banks. Most require a tourist card and passport.

Canadian readers have complained that Bancomer, García Vigil 120 (tel. 6-7643), is the only bank in town that will change Canadian currency or checks.

Health For some reason, tourists are more likely to have intestinal problems in Oaxaca. Also, the risk of contracting malaria (*paludismo*) has increased on the Pacific coast, and there have been cases of typhoid fever, a deadly disease. See the section on "Health" in Chapter 2.

Laundry The **Laundry Automatica Clin,** 20 de Noviembre no. 105, is an immaculately clean laundry where helpful women will wash and dry your clothes for a minimum of $3.50 for 3½ kilos (about 7 lb.). The laundry is open Monday through Saturday from 9am to 8pm.

Library The **Biblioteca Circulante,** at Alcala 305, is open Monday through Friday from 10am to 1pm and 4 to 6pm, to members only (fee is $2.25 per year, plus a $10 refundable deposit; teachers and students receive a discount). The library has a good collection of fiction and magazines in English, French, and Spanish, as well as reference materials. It's a quiet, relaxing place for an afternoon stop to read about Benito Juárez. You don't have to be a member to buy the used books displayed in the glass case at the entrance.

Newspapers and Magazines The English newspaper *The News* is sold by enterprising children for 50¢ to $1 at cafés around the plaza, or for 35¢ at newsstands. There is a supply of magazines at the library.

Post Office The Correos (main post office) is at the corner of Independencia and the Alameda Park.

Safety Petty crime is increasing in Oaxaca. Take normal precautions and you should have no trouble. Park your car in a lot overnight, don't leave anything in the car within view, watch your property at all times when you're waiting in the bus station, and be especially careful of very professional pickpockets in the markets and buses—they can take your wallet out of your back pocket, handbag, or knapsack and you won't know it until the time comes to pay for dinner. Luckily, violent crime (including mugging) is still very rare here. In any case, the police are no help at all.

Shipping Oaxaca is a shoppers' delight, and it's hard to keep from accumulating huge quantities of pottery, rugs, and other heavy goods that must be sent home. Many of the better shops can arrange shipping, but if your goods have come from the markets and villages you'll need to ship them yourself. The first rule of shipping is: You must have a receipt. That means carrying a notebook and asking merchants to write out a receipt for you when you shop. Mexicana airlines has a cargo office on Avenida Morelos by the restaurant Catedral, open Monday through Saturday from 9am to 6pm, and can ship your goods to any gateway cities in the U.S. that have U.S. Customs offices. Mexicana requires eight copies of your receipts, and charges a minimum of $38 to send a package to, for example, Los Angeles.

Spanish and Art Classes The **Instituto Cultural Oaxaca A.C.** offers Spanish classes for foreigners, as well as workshops with Mexican artisans such as weavers and potters. There are also lectures emphasizing Oaxaca's history, archeology, anthropology, and botany. The institute can arrange inexpensive housing with families. The address is Avenida Juárez 909 (Apdo. Postal 340), Oaxaca, Oax. 68000, México (tel. 951/5-3404; fax 951/6-1382).

WHAT TO SEE & DO

There are several very good museums, convents, and colonial buildings in Oaxaca, as well as a wonderful zócalo where the band plays every other night and sidewalk cafes

0   275 m
N   250 y

MEXICO CITY

Oaxaca

ACCOMMODATIONS:

Anturios Hotel **1**
Arnel Casa de Hues-
   pedes **4**
Calesa Real Hotel **20**
Francia Hotel **38**
Las Golondrinas
   Hotel **9**
El Méson Hotel **39**
El Méson del Angel
   Hotel **53**
Monte Alban Hotel **33**
Parador Plaza Hotel **26**
Principal Hotel **27**
Reforma Hotel **30**
Las Rosas Hotel **44**
San Carlos Posada **36**
San Pablo Hotel **50**
Santo Tomás Hotel **11**
Senorial Hotel **43**
Stouffer Presidente **31**
Trebol Hotel **52**
Veracruz Hotel **2**
Virreyes Hotel **29**

DINING:

Alex Cafetería **37**
Asador Vasco
   Restaurant **42**
Bamby Cafetería **19**
Bum Bum Refres-
   caría **47**
Catedral Restaurant-
   Bar **18**
Chips Restaurant **45**
Los Danzantes
   Restaurant **40**
Del Jardín
   Restaurant **46**
Flor de Loto
   Restaurant **15**
Los Guajiros
   Restaurant **17**
Guelatao
   Restaurant **48**

El Méson Restaurant **35**
Mi Casita Restaurant **41**
Pisces Restaurant **31**
Pizzeria Alfred da Roma **10**
Quickly Restaurant **23**
Santa Fe Restaurant **24**
El Sol y La Luna Café **12**
El Tio Restaurant **28**
Tipioc de Oaxaca Restaurant **11**

ATTRACTIONS:
Basilica de la Soledad **17**

Cathedral **34**
Instituto de Artes Graficas **6**
Museo Casa Benito Júarez **5**
Museo del Ciudad de Oaxaca **6**
Museo Regional de Oaxaca **7**
Museo Rufino Tamayo **16**
San Juan de Dios Church **51**
Santo Domingo Church **8**
Teatro Macedonio de Alcala **49**
Tito's Cafetería **22**

Pan American Hwy.

Avenida Niños Héroes Chapultepec
To Tule, Mitla → **1**
& Tehuantepec   **Bus Station**
   2

To Mexico City   G. Farías   F.G. Olivera

Juárez Park

Humboldt

Garcia Vigil   Alcalá   Berriozábal

5   **6**   **7**   **Santo Domingo Plaza**
Carranza   **8**
9   Allende   Gurrion   Constitución
  10 **11**   L. Abasolo
Porfirio Díaz   M. Bravo   **12**
  Matamoros   Murguía
19   5 de Mayo
16 **15** **18**   **20** **21** **25** **26** **27** **29**
  23 **24** **28** **30**   Avenida Morelos
17   Avenida Independencia
  32 **33** **34** **35** **36**   Avenida Juárez   Piño Suárez   Libres   Martires de Tacubaya
Mier y Teran   G. Díaz Ordaz   Tinoco y Palacios   Avenida Hidalgo
17   **41**   **48** **49**
31   **38**   **42**   **50**
Trujano   **39**   **47**   Vicente Guerrero
J.P. Garcia   **40**   **43**
  44 **45** **46**   **Plaza Principal**   Xicoténcatl   Doblando   González Ortega
Las Casas Colón   20 de Noviembre   El Magon   **52**
  51 **M**   Aldama Rayón
53   Mina Arteaga
  M. Cabrera   C.M. Bustamente   Armenta y Lopes   Reforma   M. Ocampo
Zaragoza
De Burgoa   M. de Fiallo
Nuño del Mercado Xóchitl
Moctezuma Vega

Atoyac River
Porfirio Díaz Bridge

To Zaachila   To Airport & Coyotepec ↘

provide the perfect place for travelers and locals to watch the action. There are also many interesting excursions to nearby ruins at Monte Albán and Mitla, and visits to the outlying Indian villages for pottery, wood carving, and textiles. You'll want to visit Oaxaca's market and the various popular art shops around town; the craftwork of this state is some of the finest in Mexico. Remember that Oaxaqueños observe the siesta from 2 to 4pm and most shops and museums will be closed.

The life of the city centers around **Plaza Principal**, bordered by Avenidas Hidalgo, Trujano, García Vigil, and Alcala. It's one of the prettiest in Mexico, with a white wrought-iron gazebo in the center and several fountains along the pathways. This is the place from which to orient yourself for seeing the city.

To get a feel for this lovely city, I recommend walking around town to see the churches and monuments, and then (*mañana*) a visit to the Regional Museum and the Rufino Tamayo Museum of pre-Hispanic art.

MUSEUMS

REGIONAL MUSEUM OF OAXACA, Constitución at Cinco de Mayo. Tel. 6-2991.

This former convent next to the Santo Domingo Church six blocks north of Plaza Principal has had a colorful history. It was used as an army barracks during the War of Independence. All the rooms open onto the arched, interior courtyard, where the only sound is that of the fountain. There are faint traces of elaborate frescoes along the walls and ceilings. The building must have been magnificent, judging from what remains. You can still feel the pervasive peacefulness of the place.

On the top floor, the first room to the right contains objects left from the Dominican convent. Counterclockwise, the next three rooms are dedicated to finds from Monte Albán, a nearby Zapotec city, which flourished from 800 B.C. until it was abandoned in A.D. 900. Unfortunately there's no guidebook to the museum, and all the plaques are in Spanish. Here are a few hints: The Zapotecs had a number system of bars and dots, similar to that of the Olmecs and the Maya, and a collection of glyphs which, perhaps, represent a calendar; another thing to note is that most of the ceramic sculpture here has the characteristic Zapotec touches of prominent teeth, proboscises, elaborate headgear (often as an eagle or jaguar mask), and large ear plugs.

IN THEIR FOOTSTEPS

Hernan Cortes (1485–1547) Brash, bold, greedy and a brilliant military leader, 34-year-old Hernán Cortés conquered Mexico in the name of Spain. He sank his ships to prevent desertion and with only 550 men and 16 horses, he overcame a nation of 30,000 and a territory larger than his native country. He became governor and captain general of New Spain immediately after the conquest and later he was given title of Marqués of the Valley of Oaxaca and substantial landholdings. He began silver mining in Taxco and introduced sugar cane cultivation around Cuernavaca. But by 1528 the king sent others to take charge and he was removed from governorship. Cortés died in Spain while seeking proper recognition from the Spanish court which shunned him. Mexicans regard him as the destroyer of a nation and no monuments honor him.

• **Birthplace:** Medellín, Spain.

• **Residences:** The National Palace on the Zócalo in Mexico City and the Cuernavaca Palace facing the Jardín de los Héroes, now the Museum de Cuauhnáhuac were principal residences. During the building of Mexico City he lived in Coyoacan, south of Mexico City proper. According to legend a mansion was under construction for him in Oaxaca, but he died without seeing it; today it's the Museum of the City of Oaxaca.

• **Resting Place:** Church of the Hospital of Jésus Nazareño, Mexico City.

Many of the figures have mouths similar to the ones found in Olmec sculpture—it's thought that the Olmecs influenced the early development of Monte Albán. Be sure to see the incredible treasures found in 1932 in Tomb 7 at Monte Albán. The tomb contained seven bodies (hence its name) and dates from A.D. 500. Whether the tomb was Zapotec or Mixtec is still being debated, but all agree that the jewelry in gold, turquoise, conch shell, amber, obsidian, and the bowls of onyx and glass are very beautiful. Some 500 pieces of jewelry and art were found.

The last rooms on the upper floor are devoted to an ethnographic exhibit of regional crafts and costumes; mannequins dressed in authentic regional dress portray facets of religious, social, and cultural life.

Admission: 50¢, free on Sun and hols.
Open: Tues–Fri 10am–6pm, Sat–Sun 10am–5pm.

RUFINO TAMAYO MUSEUM OF PRE-HISPANIC ART, Av. Morelos 503. Tel. 6-4750.

The artifacts displayed in this unique museum were chosen "solely for the aesthetic rank of the works, their beauty, power, and originality." The result is one of the most beautiful museums in all of Mexico. The collection was amassed over a 20-year period by artist Rufino Tamayo, born in Oaxaca. The artifacts range from the Preclassical Period up to the Aztecs: terra-cotta figurines, scenes of daily life, lots of female fertility figures, Olmecan and Totonac sculpture from the Gulf Coast, and Zapotec long-nosed god figures. Plaques in Spanish give the period, culture, and location of each find, but you find yourself ignoring this information and just admiring the works and the displays. The rooms are beautiful in themselves, and are painted pink, blue, lavender, green, and orange in succession. The museum is four blocks northwest of Plaza Principal at the corner of Tinoco y Palacios.

Admission: $1.75.
Open: Mon–Sat 10am–2pm and 4–7pm, Sun 10am–3pm.

HOUSE OF BENITO JUÁREZ, García Vigil 609.

This house and museum are only moderately interesting. Look for the small plaque over the door which indicates that this was the residence of the local hero from 1818 to 1820. Four rooms around a courtyard show the style in which the great man lived. The school across the street—it looks like a fortress—was once the convent-church of El Carmen, run by the Carmelite order. Next to the convent-church is the nice Plazuela del Carmen Alto, where local craftspeople sell their wares. You might even see some weaving. It's a good place to buy a cool *refresco* and rest. The house is six blocks north of Plaza Principal, and two blocks from the Regional Museum.

Admission: 50¢, free on Sun.
Open: Tues–Sun 9am–7pm.

MUSEUM OF THE CITY OF OAXACA, Alcala 202, at Matamoros. Tel. 6-8499.

Also known as the House of Cortés, this museum 2½ blocks north of Plaza Principal exhibits the work of contemporary artists from around the world. If there's an opening night, join the crowd. There was a reception for a Spanish artist when I was there. Not too long before that 35 artists from Montana took the spotlight. The beautifully restored 16th-century building housing the museum was supposedly built on the order of conqueror Hernán Cortés after receiving the title of Marqués of the Valley of Oaxaca (he died in Spain without seeing it).

Admission: Free.
Open: Daily 9am–9pm.

INSTITUTO DE ARTES GRAFICAS, Alcala 507. Tel. 6-6980.

Franciso Toledo, a Mexican painter, donated his colonial-era home and private graphics collection to found this museum. The collection includes 3,000 works, but not all are on display. Still, what you see are works by world-renowned artists such as Picasso. The museum is between Carranza and Humboldt, opposite the Santo Domingo Church, 8½ blocks north of Plaza Principal.

Admission: Free.
Open: Mon–Sat 10am–2pm and 4–7pm, Sun 11am–5pm.

CHURCHES

CATHEDRAL OF OAXACA, García Vigil, between Independencia and Hidalgo.
Anchoring one end of Plaza Principal is the cathedral, built in 1553, with an elaborate 18th-century baroque facade and a glittering interior with three naves. It contains a bronze altar, a huge pipe organ, and windows with fine, etched-glass representations of the saints.
Admission: Free.
Open: Daily 8am–11pm.

BASILICA DE LA SOLEDAD, Independencia at Galeana.
The basilica, the most important religious center in Oaxaca, is seven blocks west of Plaza Principal. Here is where you'll find an effigy of the town's patron saint carved in black stone. The basilica is actually a huge complex of buildings including a garden, convent, and a smaller theater where spectators can witness the famous Fiesta de la Soledad (see "Special Events," below). Built in 1682–90, the basilica has four levels on the outside, each decorated with carvings of saints. The interior is an overpowering array of chandeliers, lunging angels, gilt ceiling, paintings, and statues. The statue of the Virgin de la Soledad (the patron saint of Oaxaca) is in the museum around the back of the church, to the right as you exit. The statue is draped in black velvet and placed in a chapel filled with white bouquets made of glass, pearl, and plastic. The only other item of interest is a 3-foot-square case of innumerable miniature glass figurines (birds, angels, animals, and flowers) surrounding the Christ Child.
Admission: Free.
Open: Museum, Mon–Sat 10am–2pm.

SANTO DOMINGO CHURCH, Constitución and Cinco de Mayo.
✪ There are 27 churches in Oaxaca, but you should make a special effort to see this one next to the Regional Museum of Oaxaca, six blocks north of Plaza Principal—and don't judge a church by its facade. Started in the 1550s by Dominican friars and finished a century later, it contains the work of all the best artists of that period. The walls and ceiling are covered with ornate plaster statues and flowers, most of them gilded. The sun shines through the yellow stained-glass window, casting a golden glow over the whole interior. There is a large gilded rosary chapel to the right as you enter. Also, be sure to notice the genealogical tree of the Guzman family in the apse (Don Felíz de Guzman founded the church).
Admission: Free.
Open: 8am–11pm.

CHURCH OF SAN FELIPE, Tinoco y Palacio at Independencia.
This church 2½ blocks northeast of Plaza Principal was built in 1636 and displays all the architectural opulence of that period: The altar and nave are covered with ornately carved and gilded wood, and the walls are frescoed—ornate, but not overpowering.
Admission: Free.
Open: Daily 8am–11pm.

SAN JUAN DE DIOS, 20 de Noviembre, between Colón and Arteaga.
The earliest church in Oaxaca, built in 1525–30, the exterior is nothing special but the interior has an ornate altar and paintings on the ceiling by Urbano Olivera. A glass shrine to the Virgin near the entrance and one to Christ (off to the right) are especially revered by Oaxaqueños. Because it's by the market, three blocks south of Plaza Principal, many of the people who visit the church are villagers who've come in to buy and sell.
Admission: Free.
Open: Daily 6am–11pm.

OTHER ATTRACTIONS

TEATRO MACEDONIO DE ALCALA, Independencia at Armenta y López.
This beautiful 1903 Belle Epoque theater, two blocks east of Plaza Principal, holds

1,300 people and is still used for concerts and performances in the evening. Peek through the doors to see the marble stairway and Louis XV vestibule. A list of events is posted by the doors.

Open: Only for events.

CERRO DEL FORTÍN, Díaz Ordaz at Calle Delmonte.

To take all this sightseeing in at a glance, those with cars can drive to this hill at the west of town from which you can get a panoramic view of the city, especially good just before sunset. Recognize the hill by a statue of—who else?—Benito Juárez, and a stadium built to hold 15,000 spectators.

You can walk to the hill as well. Head up Díaz Ordaz/Crespo, and look for the Escaleras del Fortín (Stairway to the Fortress) shortly after you cross Calle Delmonte.

MONTE ALBÁN

⬟ This beautiful ancient city was inhabited for almost 3,000 years, from 1500 B.C. to A.D. 1400. Monte Albán was first inhabited by descendants of the Olmecs who dubbed it a "city of the gods." All that is left from this period are the Danzantes friezes, which, according to Mario Perez Ramírez, illustrate the beginning of pre-Hispanic medicine. According to his book *El Enigma del Arte Hispanica,* Monte Albán was used as a medical research center.

The Zapotecs began to build a ceremonial center here in 500 B.C. It is thought that Monte Albán was an elite center of Zapotec merchants and artists, who were greatly influenced by contemporary cultures outside the valley of Mexico. You can see a resemblance to Maya art in many of the masks and sculptures. When Monte Albán was at its zenith in A.D. 300, Teotihuacán was the most influential city; you can see borrowed ideas from that site in the architecture of the Zapotecs. In the 11th century the site was used by the invading Mixtecs, who came into the valley of Oaxaca from the west. The Mixtecs moved into the abandoned city and did very little building of their own.

Monte Albán covers about 15 square miles and is centered on the Great Plaza, a large grassy area that was once a mountaintop that was flattened by the Zapotecs in 600 B.C. From this plaza, aligned north-south, you can overlook the lush Oaxacan valley, a gorgeous setting for any civilization. The excavations at Monte Albán have revealed 170 tombs, numerous ceremonial altars, stelae, pyramids, and palaces.

SEEING THE RUINS Begin on the eastern side of the **Great Plaza** at the I-shaped ball court. This **ball court** differs slightly from Mayan and Toltec ball courts in that there are no goal rings and the sides of the court are sloped. Also on the east side of the plaza are several altars and pyramids constructed with ocher stone that was once covered with stucco. Note the sloping walls and the wide stairs and ramps, which are typical of Zapotec architecture and resemble the architecture of Teotihuacán. The building slightly out of line with the plaza (not on the north-south axis) is thought to be the **observatory** and was probably aligned with the heavenly bodies rather than with the points of the compass.

The south side of the plaza has a large platform that bore several stelae, most of which are now in the Museum of Anthropology in Mexico City. There is a good view of the surrounding area from the top of this platform.

The west side has more ceremonial platforms and pyramids. On top of the pyramid substructure are four columns that probably held the roof of the temple at one time.

The famous building of the **Dancers (Danzantes)** is on the west side of the plaza. This is the earliest structure at Monte Albán, dating back to 800 B.C. This building is covered with large stone slabs carved into distorted, naked figures. There is speculation as to who carved these figures and what they represent. There is certainly a distinct resemblance to the Olmec "baby faces" seen at La Venta. The distorted bodies and pained expressions of the faces perhaps imply disease. There are clear examples of figures representing childbirth, dwarfism, and infantilism. Because of the fluidity of the figures, they became known as the Danzantes, but this is only a modern label for these ancient and mysterious carvings.

The **Northern Platform** is a maze of temples and palaces interwoven with subterranean tunnels and sanctuaries. Wander around here, for there are numerous reliefs, glyphs, paintings, and friezes along the lintels and jams as well as the walls.

Leaving the Great Plaza, head north to the **cemetery and tombs.** Of the 170 tombs so far excavated the most famous is Tomb 7, to the east of the cemetery. Inside were found some 500 pieces of jewelry made of gold, amber, and turquoise, as well as art objects made of silver, alabaster, and bone. This amazing collection is on display at the Regional Museum of Oaxaca.

If you have more than 1 day to spend at Monte Albán, be sure to visit some of the tombs, for they contain some really magnificent glyphs, paintings, and stone carvings of gods, goddesses, birds, and serpents. Two of the tombs that are especially absorbing, Tombs 104 and 105 are guarded and can be entered via ladders; the guards are usually helpful about pointing out areas of special interest. Ignore the vendors hawking "original" artifacts, supposedly found at the site—if they were real, these guys would hardly need to wander around in the midday sun to sell them!

There is a new museum, a shop selling guidebooks to the ruins, a café, and a crafts shop. I recommend that you purchase one of the guidebooks.

ESSENTIALS Admission to the ruins is $3.50, free on Sunday and holidays. The site is open daily from 8am to 5pm.

To get to Monte Albán, take a bus from the Hotel Mesón del Angel, Mina 518, at Mier y Teran. **Autobuses Turisticos** makes five runs daily, leaving at 8:30, 9:30, and 11:30am, and 1:30 and 3:30pm. Return service leaves the ruins at 11am, noon, and 2, 4, and 5:30pm. The round-trip fare is $1.20. The ride takes a half hour, and your return time is 2 hours after your arrival. It's possible to take a later return for an additional 60¢; inform the driver of your intent (but you won't be guaranteed a seat).

SPECIAL EVENTS

Oaxaca is famous for its festivals, filled with the color and exuberance of traditional life. The three most important ones are during Holy Week at Easter, in July, and in December. Make hotel reservations well in advance if you plan to visit during these times.

During **Holy Week** (which begins the Friday before Easter Sunday) figurines made of palm leaves are made and sold on the streets by village women. On Palm Sunday (the Sunday before Easter) there are colorful parades, and on the Thursday after that, Oaxaca residents follow the Procession of the Seven Churches. Hundreds of the pious move from church to church, taking communion in each one to ensure a prosperous year. Throughout the week each church sponsors concerts, fireworks, fairs, and other entertainments. On Holy Saturday, the day before Easter, the famous *guelaguetza* is danced in Plaza de la Soledad, followed by a candlelight service in the Santo Domingo Church.

In mid-July you can witness the **Fiesta Guelaguetza** (offering) of the Virgin of Carmen. From the second week in July through the following two Mondays there are fairs and exhibits. Regional dances are performed in the stadium on the Cerro del Fortín each Monday. It is a marvelous spectacle of color, costumes, music, and dance. Some 350 different huipils and dresses can be seen during the performance as the

IMPRESSIONS

In Mexico there is always a brooding sense of the past. Turn off the highway, and the rutted road leads you over humpbacked bridges, past the gates of old haciendas, through the villages where the church stands on the plaza as it always has. The high mesa blossoms pink with cosmos in late August, and far away on the edge of the hills shine the tile domes. Farther up the hills are markets where not everyone speaks Spanish, where women are still wearing garments which they weave for themselves.
—ELIZABETH WILDER WEISMANN, *ART AND TIME IN MEXICO,* 1985

villages of the seven regions of Oaxaca present their traditional dances. Admission ranges from $3 to $5 and tickets must be reserved in advance (no later than May). A travel agency could handle this for you, although the Tourism Office will try to help if you do not have reservations. I recommend Sections 5 and 6 in Palco A for the best seating in the Cerro del Fortín Auditorium. The color of your ticket matches the color of your seat. You will be sitting in strong sunlight, so wear a hat and long sleeves. On Sunday night before the Guelaguetza, the university students present an excellent program in Plaza de la Soledad. It is called the Bani Stui Gulal. The programs begin at 8pm, but since the event is free you should get there no later than 5:30 if you want to get a seat.

The **December Festivals** begin on the 18th with the **Fiesta de la Soledad** in honor of the patron saint of Oaxaca. On that night there is a cascade of fire from a "castle" erected for the occasion in Plaza de la Soledad. December 23 is the **Night of the Radishes** when the Oaxaqueños build fantastic sculptures out of radishes (the most prized vegetable cultivated during the colonial period), as well as flowers, leaves, and fruits. They are on display in the garden off the zócalo. On **December 24** each Oaxacan church organizes a procession with music, floats, and crowds bearing candles. **New Year's Eve** is celebrated with the Petition of the Cross where villagers from all over come to a forlorn chapel on the hill beyond Tlacolula (about 22 miles southeast of Oaxaca, near Mitla) to light candles and express their wishes for the coming new year. Mock bargaining, with sticks and stones to represent livestock and produce, is part of the traditional way of expressing hopes for the new year. Tiny symbolic farms and fields are built in the hope for real prosperity.

At festival time in Oaxaca, sidewalk stands are set up in the market area and near the cathedral to sell buñuelos, the Mexican equivalent of a pappadum, only sweet. You'll be served your buñuelo in a cracked or otherwise flawed dish or bowl, and after you're finished you smash the crockery on the sidewalk for good luck. Don't be timid! After a while, you may find yourself buying more and more buñuelos—about 75¢ each—just for the fun of smashing plates.

Note: If you want to come for Christmas or the Guelaguetza, but rooms and transportation are booked, you may want to consider Sanborn's Tours for both festivals. Contact them at 2015 South 10th Street, McAllen, TX 78502 (tel. toll free 800/395-8482).

WHERE TO STAY

Oaxaca is in the midst of a tourism boom (and a room shortage). Most of the available rooms are priced about the same, no matter what they look like. Most of Oaxaca's low-budget hotels are near the market and the red-light district.

IN THEIR FOOTSTEPS

Porfirio Diaz (1830–1915) Born in Oaxaca and schooled in law, at age 32 he distinguished himself at the famous Puebla battle and within 14 years became president of Mexico. He remained as dictator, for the next 34 years, with one four-year interruption. His contributions were enormous: He moved the country from turmoil and bankruptcy into peace and stability through improvements in communication, railroads, agriculture, manufacturing, mining, port enlargement, oil exploration, and foreign investment. He built lavish public buildings, and sent promising art students to Europe on full scholarship. His love for all things French was legendary. He achieved these successes by disregarding the law and at the expense of the poor, Indians, and intellectuals who opposed his methods, all of which brought about his downfall in 1911 and the Mexican Revolution which lasted until 1917. He died in exile in Paris.

- **Birthplace:** Oaxaca, Oax.
- **Residences:** Chapultepec Castle.
- **Resting Place:** Père Lachaise Cemetery, Paris, France.

DOUBLES FOR LESS THAN $20

CASA DE HUÉSPEDES ARNEL, Aldama 404, Colonia Jalatlaco, Oaxaca, Oax. 68080. Tel. 951/5-2856. 39 rms (22 with bath).
$ Rates: $5.50 single without bath, $10.50 single with bath; $9 double without bath; $13 double with bath; $250 single apartment (per month), $300 double apartment (per month). **Parking:** Free.

This good budget choice is slightly removed from the city center, but still within walking distance of most sights. The casa is a U-shaped two-story building built around a cool tropical garden behind the Cruz family home. You'll find a touch of family warmth here; sooner or later you'll meet a member of this large extended family; you'll also be on a first-name basis with the four resident parrots and a dozing cat or two.

The rooms are plain but clean and comfortable; some share a bath among four rooms. If you crave a firm mattress, this is the place—some of them are brick hard. Across the street in the new wing are two rooms with double beds and private baths. There also are two furnished apartments with fully equipped kitchens. In the apartments, stays of 15 days are allowed at half the monthly rate. Breakfast and dinner are served on the family patio.

You'll find the casa six blocks behind the first-class bus station. Turn right out the front door of the station, go two blocks, and turn right onto Aldama. The casa is ahead on your left across from the Iglesia San Matias Jalatlaco.

HOTEL REFORMA, Reforma 102, Oaxaca, Oax. 68000. Tel. 951/6-7144. 14 rms (all with bath).
$ Rates: $8 single; $10 double.
If you're on a tight budget, try this centrally located hotel two blocks northeast of the plaza at the corner of Independencia, between Independencia and Morelos. The clean rooms have tile floors and chenille bedspreads. Four rooms on the rooftop are sunny, cheerful, and distanced from street sounds.

HOTEL VIRREYES, Morelos 1001, Oaxaca, Oax. 68000. Tel. 951/6-5141. 30 rms (all with bath).
$ Rates: $8.50 single; $10.50–$16 double. Discounts of up to 20% are offered during slow times.
The courtyard is covered with painted glass which lets in such a mellow light that the air seems to be colored beige. There is a quiet, relaxed atmosphere, with cool blue walls and tables with white tablecloths. Be sure to look at your room before signing in as the rooms are quite individual. This is not a hotel for the light sleeper because of the street noise and the echo-chamber effect created by the enclosed courtyard. The hotel is two blocks east of the pedestrian zone at Reforma.

HOTEL PRINCIPAL, Calle Cinco de Mayo no. 208, Oaxaca, Oax. 68000. Tel. 951/6-2535. 17 rms (all with bath).
$ Rates: $14.75 single; $18 double; $21.75 triple.
The Principal, 3½ blocks north of Plaza Principal, is a long-time favorite of budget travelers, for good reason. The courtyard is one of the prettiest in town, and the rooms are clean and filled with sunlight. Travelers congregate in the courtyard to share information, and the staff is most helpful. Make reservations in advance if you can.

HOTEL SANTO TOMAS Abasolo 305, Oaxaca, Oax. 68000. Tel. 951/6-3800. 25 rms (all with bath).
$ Rates: $12.50 single; $19 double; $21 triple. **Parking:** Free.
The rooms are all back from the street, making this one of the most peaceful hotels in Oaxaca. They aren't fancy, but the rooms are immaculate and sunny, with windows facing the courtyard. The simple furnishings are coordinated and cheerful, although some of the bathrooms are missing shower curtains. The hotel could use a paint job throughout, and pots of dead plants are detracting. A fully equipped kitchen and common area upstairs is for guest use,

and the friendly management is happy to assist with the lighting of the eccentric gas stove. The hotel is eight blocks northeast of Plaza Principal.

HOTEL FRANCIA, Calle 20 de Noviembre no. 212, Oaxaca, Oax. 68000. Tel. 951/6-4811. 80 rms (all with bath).
$ Rates: $15.75 single; $19.50 double; $22.50 triple.
The Francia, two blocks west of Plaza Principal, is functional and quite pleasant. The rooms are filled with ancient furniture and arranged around a covered courtyard. The hotel has expanded, engulfing several adjoining buildings in the process, so you can choose from a wide selection of rooms. Beware of street noise. The restaurant is open daily from 7:30am to 10pm and has an excellent comida.

POSADA SAN PABLO, De Fiallo 102, Oaxaca, Oax. 68000. Tel. 951/6-4914. 22 rms (all with bath).
$ Rates: $300 single or double per month. **Parking:** Free
This restored hotel once was the Convent of Saint Paul. Today the rooms are simple (as befits a former convent), but very comfortable. All rooms have a two-burner stove and a refrigerator. The drawback is that most have no exterior windows (less cross-breeze, but also less street noise). Since the price is so good, this popular hostelry stays booked, so it's best to make a reservation at least a month or more in advance. You may find a vacancy in February and May if you make a reservation on short notice. They rarely rent by the night. The Posada San Pablo is two blocks east of Plaza Principal.

DOUBLES FOR LESS THAN $30

HOTEL VERACRUZ, Av. Niños Héroes de Chapultepec 1020, Oaxaca, Oax. 68000. Tel. 951/5-0511. 55 rms (all with bath).
$ Rates: $16 single; $21 double.
If you are arriving by bus late at night, the Veracruz is your easiest option—it's on the left as you exit the first-class bus station. The rooms are modern and clean, with plain, motellike decor. As you can imagine, the proximity to the bus station makes this a noisy place to stay; choose your room accordingly.

HOTEL MESÓN DEL REY, Trujano 212, Oaxaca, Oax. 68000. Tel. 951/6-0033. 22 rms (all with bath). TV TEL
$ Rates: $17.50 single; $21.50 double. **Parking:** Free.
There is a *caseta de larga distancia* here, so there are always a few Oaxaqueños waiting in the restaurant for their long-distance phone calls to go through. The hotel is popular with Mexican families, who wander the halls and stairways in their robes. The rooms are plain but comfortable and all have fans; stay at the back away from the street noise. It's 1½ blocks east of Plaza Principal.

HOTEL LAS ROSAS, Trujano 112, Oaxaca, Oax. 68000. Tel. 951/4-2217. 19 rooms (all with bath).
$ Rates: $17 single; $22 double.
The former Plaza Hotel, 1½ blocks west of Plaza Principal, has been renovated and painted bright white. A narrow flight of stairs leads up from the street to the second-story lobby and concrete courtyard painted swimming-pool blue. The rooms open onto the courtyard, and there are no exterior windows, which can give a claustrophobic feeling. The bathrooms have all been remodeled with tiled showers, and though the furnishings are humble and the mattresses thin, you can count on everything being extraordinarily clean.

HOTEL TREBOL, Flores Magon 201, Oaxaca, Oax. 68000. Tel. 951/6-1256. 14 rms (all with bath).
$ Rates: $17 single; $22 double; $27 triple.
This is a peaceful haven, despite its prime location across the street from the bustling market and behind the Government Palace around the corner from the southwest edge of the plaza. The rooms are simple and tasteful, with large windows and double beds. Ask and you may be quoted rates at a 20% discount.

HOTEL MONTE ALBÁN, Alameda de León, Oaxaca, Oax. 68000. Tel. 951/6-2777. 20 rms (all with bath). TV TEL
$ Rates: $24 single; $27 double.

Location and colonial charm are two good reasons to stay at this hotel on the northwest side of the plaza across from the cathedral. The large, airy rooms in the front of the hotel are the most colonial, but the smaller interior rooms are also fine, and a bit lower in price. All rooms have a tile showers and colonial furnishings. The courtyard restaurant is topped by a glass skylight canopy. Here on the Alameda you're in the best of company: the cathedral, the regional headquarters of the PRI, and the post office are right next door.

The hotel hosts a delightful show of folk dances in the courtyard every night from 8:30 to 10pm ($4 admission). Guests who go to bed early might not find the show so delightful night after night.

HOTEL SEÑORIAL, Portal de Flores 6, Oaxaca, Oax. 68000. Tel. 951/6-3933. Fax 951/6-3668. 127 rms (all with bath).
$ Rates: $26 single; $28 double. **Parking:** Free.

Many frequent travelers to Oaxaca wouldn't dream of staying anywhere but the Señorial. The rooms, though comfortably furnished, are not luxurious. Its location on the west side of Plaza Principal is its major plus. If you don't mind constant street noise, choose a room at the front of the hotel for a perfect view of the plaza; otherwise select something farther back. The small swimming pool is another plus, and the rooftop patio is a good spot for people-watching. But reserve in advance—it's frequently full.

DOUBLES FOR LESS THAN $40

MESÓN DEL ANGEL, Mina 518, Oaxaca, Oax. 68000. Tel. 951/6-6666. 34 rms (all with bath).
$ Rates: $27 single; $35.50 double. **Parking:** Free.

The large modern building has louvered windows and screens, a restaurant, a bar, and a swimming pool with slide. You pay a bit extra for the pool, and will sometimes encounter large numbers of screaming children playing on a small set of playground equipment by the pool. But the proximity of the market and the second-class bus station are advantages, and the hotel has the best travel agency in town. Buses leave from here for Monte Albán and Puerto Escondido. It's two blocks west of the market at Mier y Teran.

ANTURIOS, Privada Carranza, Oaxaca, Oax. 68000. 28 rms (all with bath).
$ Rates: $28 single; $36 double. **Parking:** Free.

⭐ By far the nicest hotel near the bus station, the brand-new Anturios is worth the 10-yard walk. Built with the business traveler in mind, the two-story hotel has a pleasant coffee shop, a small sundries store, and a second-story sun deck for peaceful relaxation. The large rooms have fans, firm mattresses with box springs, rocking chairs, huge showers and closets, reading lights over the beds, small desks, and heavy drapes to block the sun.

To get here from the first-class bus station, cross Avenida Niños Héroes de Chapultepec and walk north two blocks. Turn right at the blue fence in front of an elementary school onto Privada Carranza; the hotel is on your right.

CALESA REAL, Vigil 306, Oaxaca, Oax. 68000. Tel. 951/6-5544. 77 rms (all with bath). TV TEL
$ Rates: $29 single; $35.75 double. **Parking:** Free.

⭐ The Calesa Real, in a colonial building 2½ blocks north of Plaza Principal, is a traditional favorite which was closed for quite a while. One of the nicest features here is a small kidney-shaped swimming pool in an overgrown courtyard. Some rooms on the first floor have French doors opening to the pool area, others on the second and third floors have small balconies, and there is a second-story terrace overlooking the pool. The large rooms have fans, blue-tile bathrooms, double beds, and worn furnishings. The elevator seems to run as if by a miracle, and the whole hotel exudes an air of antiquity.

**HOTEL PARADOR PLAZA, Murguía 104, Oaxaca, Oax. 68000. Tel.
951/6-4900.** Fax 951/4-2037. 58 rms (all with bath). TV TEL
$ Rates: $29 single; $36 double.

The former Hotel Isabel, on Murguía between Cinco de Mayo and Alcala, has
undergone extensive remodeling and become an elegant modern hotel unlike any
other in the center city. A mirrored elevator rides up the three stories to large rooms
decorated in blue and peach, with lights over the king-size beds, marble sinks, and
large wall closets. The courtyard lounge is topped by a massive skylight, and the
restaurant glows with candlelight. The only drawback is the lack of outer windows in
many of the rooms; instead, the windows face into the courtyard, where live music
and mingling guests create considerable noise.

WORTH THE EXTRA BUCKS

**HOTEL STOUFFER PRESIDENTE, Av. 5 de Mayo no. 300, Oaxaca, Oax.
68000. Tel. 951/6-061,** or toll free 800/HOTELS-1 in the U.S. Fax. 951/6-
0732. 100 rms (all with bath). TV TEL
$ Rates: $110 single or double. Children under 12 stay free in their parents' room.

Converted from the former four-centuries-old Convent of Santa Catalina, this
hotel is one of the most beautiful of its kind in the country. Through the
centuries it has been used as the city municipal office, government palace, a jail,
movie theater, and twice as a school. Since becoming a hotel, the building has been
designated a "national treasure." It's four blocks northeast of Plaza Principal and one
block east of the pedestrian street at Abasolo.

The hotel's two floors are decorated with frescoes and colonial relics. The rooms
are adorned with Mexican textiles and local pottery, and each has a fan. Facilities
include a swimming pool, laundry, souvenir shops, and all the other amenities of a
first-class hotel. Even if this is way out of our range, you might enjoy walking through
the corridors and public rooms, or dining under one of the porticos. If you decide to
splurge for a night or two here, ask for an interior room—those with windows on the
street echo with passing traffic until the wee hours. Consider splurging on the lavish
Sunday brunch, or just have a cup of coffee in the lounge by the pool for a taste of the
good life.

READERS RECOMMEND

Las Golondrinas, *Tinoco y Palacios 411, Oaxaca, Oax. 68000 (tel. 951/6-8726). "Las
Golondrinas is a charming, clean hotel, eight blocks north of the plaza, newly built, run by an
interesting gentleman, Jorge A. Velasco, who couldn't do enough for us. It's quiet, with banana
trees and other lovely plants filling the courtyard, a place we look forward to returning
to."*—Brenda Lazin, Philadelphia, Pa. [*Author's Note:* A real find, with beautiful rose gardens,
fuschia bougainvillea, and mature palms growing throughout the courtyards of a 100-year-old
hacienda. The 24 rooms are in a complex of one-story buildings and have thick mattresses tiled
baths, small desks and chairs, with windows and doors opening to courtyards. Rates are $17 single,
$21 double. Breakfast is served in a small bamboo-covered café. The name, by the way, means
"the swallows." Velasco hopes his guests will return, much like the swallows in Capistrano.]

WHERE TO EAT

Oaxaca's regional foods are among the best in Mexico. The state is known for its
varieties of mole, cheese, tamales, peppers, tortillas, bread, and chocolate. To see a
magnificent array of these foods, walk through the Abastos Market on Saturday; the
quantity and variety are unforgettable. When you hear women shouting "*tlayuda,
tlayuda,*" take a look at the 12-inch tortillas they're selling. Oaxaca is also known for
pozole Mixteco, a delightfully different version of this hearty soup which includes
chicken and red mole sauce. Restaurants in the city often feature mole, tamales, and
Oaxaca cheese. Fortunately, and at last, good restaurants are becoming easier to find
in Oaxaca and the prices here are better than in almost any other city in Mexico.

To find the city's cheapest **comida corrida,** walk west on Trujano until you
come to the two-block section between 20 de Noviembre and Díaz Ordaz. The little

hole-in-the-wall eateries here are very basic, but very cheap—a four-course meal costs only about $2.

For a snack or light breakfast, pick up your fill of pastries, cookies, sweet rolls, and breads from the large **Panificadora Bamby,** at the corner of Morelos and García Vigil, two blocks north from Plaza Principal. Open daily from 7am to 9pm.

MEALS FOR LESS THAN $5

REFRESCARÍA BUM-BUM, Portal Benito Juárez.
  Specialty: FRUIT DRINKS.
$ Prices: Carrot juice $1.25; tamarind soda 70¢.
  Open: Mon–Sat 11am–10pm, Sun 5–10pm.
In Mexico, do as the Mexicans do—savor the fruits and eat and drink them as you walk around. Sit down here beside Guelatao on the east side of the plaza and drink a tall, fresh-squeezed glass of orange or carrot juice, or carry your juice across the street and rest in the plaza.

CHIPS, Trujano, between Magón and Noviembre.
  Specialty: SANDWICHES.
$ Prices: Sandwiches $1.50; coffee 50¢.
  Open: Daily 10am–9pm.
The three tables by the counter in this tiny café half a block east of the plaza are always filled with regulars who appreciate a fine cup of coffee any time of day. There are a few more tables on a narrow upstairs balcony, and the lone waiter gets a good workout running up and down the stairs. Try a torta oaxaqueña—a soft roll (called a bolillo) stuffed with quesillo cheese and chorizo.

CAFETERÍA TITO'S, García Vigil 116. Tel. 6-7379.
  Specialty: MEXICAN/AMERICAN.
$ Prices: Hot dog $1.75; pozole $1.25; chilaquiles $1.25.
  Open: Mon–Sat 8am–midnight, Sun 9am–3pm.
This lunch counter and café 1½ blocks north of the plaza has a green-and-black-striped awning over the doorway. Inside, local families and young students crowd into orange plastic booths to drink coffee or devour a chicken cooked in the rôtisserie next to the front door. Tito's offers light meals such as sandwiches, hamburgers, and traditional dishes. Try a filling bowl of pozole, the famous rich stew of hominy with meat or chicken, or the burritos with ham, cheese, and a side order of guacamole. But skip the strawberry pie, which is basically red gelatin in a crust.

CAFETERÍA ALEX, Díaz Ordaz and Trujano.
  Specialty: MEXICAN.
$ Prices: Main courses $1.25–$2.
  Open: Mon–Sat 7:30am–9pm, Sun 7:30am–noon.
Here you'll find hours to please the early riser and prices that are hard to beat anywhere else in the city. It's small but clean, and a good bet for breakfast, especially on Sunday when everyplace else seems to be closed. It's three blocks west of the plaza.

RESTAURANT FLOR DE LOTO, Morelos 511.
  Specialty: MEXICAN.
$ Prices: Licuados $1; fruit plate $1.25; chiles rellenos $2.
  Open: Daily 8am–10pm.
The "Lotus Flower" is the best deal in town for vegetarians and carnivores alike. The menu changes daily; you might have fresh-baked whole-wheat bread and butter, fruit plate, soup, chiles rellenos with cheese, vegetables, papaya water, and guayaba dulce (sweet baked guava) for dessert. The decor is simple, the music soft, and the food prepared and presented thoughtfully. Get there early for the best selection. The restaurant is at Morelos and P. Díaz.

LOS GUAJIROS, Alcala 303. Tel. 6-5038.
  Specialty: MEXICAN/AMERICAN.
$ Prices: Salads $2.50; pasta $3.50; rolled tacos $2.25.

Open: Dinner only, Mon–Sat 6pm–1am.
A large courtyard inside an old hacienda with bright-orange walls is the setting for this music club, where salsa bands appear on a small stage. Tables are arranged around the courtyard and on platforms around the edges of the room. Try the rollitos gauchos, spicy rolled tacos with cheese. The crowd amasses after 10pm for mingling and dancing. It's in the pedestrians-only zone, 2½ blocks north of the plaza.

RESTAURANT/BAR LOS DANZANTES, 20 de Noviembre and Trujano. Tel. 6-6880.
Specialty: OAXACAN.
$ Prices: Breakfast $2.75; verde oaxaqueño $4.50; fixed-price lunch $2.50; buffet $4.25.
Open: Mon–Sat 8:30am–10pm.
The setting is gloomy and dark, but the food is savory and filling, especially the dishes featuring delicious regional cuisine, including the savory specialty verde oaxaqueño, a spicy soup of salsa-marinated pork accompanied by green beans and potato. The menu is printed in Spanish, English, German, and French and is a good resource for figuring out the ingredients in local dishes. The restaurant is two blocks southwest of Plaza Principal.

RESTAURANT QUICKLY, Macedonio de Alcala 100. Tel. 6-0313.
Specialty: OAXACAN.
$ Prices: Lunch $3.50; vegetarian lunch $3.25.
Open: Mon–Fri 8am–11pm, Sat–Sun noon–11pm.
Several readers wrote to tell me about this one. If you can get past the bright green, blue, and orange floral decor and the electronic sign that flashes GOOD FOOD . . . BUENA COMIDA over the entrance, you'll sit down to some of the best and cheapest food in Oaxaca. A seven-course vegetarian or meat comida is served throughout the day. There is an extensive à la carte menu as well: good burgers, parrillados (a plate of grilled vegetables, cheese, or meat, served with guacamole and tortillas), and cauliflower crêpes. For breakfast, try the "all-you-can-eat Mexican smörgåsbord." You'll find Restaurant Quickly at the south end of the pedestrians-only zone, 1½ blocks north of the plaza.

DOÑA ELPIDIA, Miguel Cabrera 413. Tel. 6-4292.
Specialty: MEXICAN.
$ Prices: Fixed-price lunch $4.50.
Open: Lunch only, daily 1:30–4pm.
This restaurant is virtually an institution in Oaxaca; Doña Elpidia has been catering to a refined and selective local clientele for more than 40 years. Walking past, you'd hardly think it was a restaurant, but inside the shabby-looking door is a beautiful but run-down courtyard filled with birds and plants. Two large dogs on the roof keep watch. Five tables are set out in the arcade, and there are a dozen more in the indoor dining rooms. Last time I visited, the five-course comida corrida included small portions of an appetizer of chicharron (delicious deep-fried pork rind), vegetable soup, roast chicken with a garnish of warm pickled vegetables, delicately seasoned pork with rice, a dessert of cinnamon rice pudding, and Mexican coffee (with cinnamon). The restaurant only serves the comida corrida, beer, soda, and coffee. It's seven blocks south of the plaza (Cabrera is the southern extension of García Vigil).

GUELATAO, Portal Benito Juárez 102. Tel. 6-2311.
Specialty: MEXICAN.
$ Prices: Fixed-price lunch $2.50; beer $1; main courses $2.25–$4.50.
Open: Daily 7am–10:30pm.
My favorite restaurant on the plaza is one of several located in the arcade on the east side. The fixed-price lunch includes soup, pasta, meat or fish, frijoles or salad, dessert, and coffee. If you don't want that much, just order a portion of lomo de cerdo (roast pork) with potato salad, or perhaps tamales oaxaqueños de mole (corn dough wrapped around bits of chicken, in a dark, rich mole sauce, the whole thing wrapped in banana leaves). The outdoor tables at the Guelatao are distinguished from the tables

of neighboring restaurants by their pastel plaid tablecloths—be sure you're sitting in the right section.

RESTAURANT DEL JARDÍN, Portal de Flores 10. Tel. 6-9719.
Specialty: MEXICAN.
$ Prices: Main courses $1.25–$4.75.
Open: Daily 8am–12:30am.

The beautiful marble tables of this café-restaurant on the west side of the plaza are always occupied by a varied crowd sipping beer or coffee. This is the prime place to wait out one of Oaxaca's brief but intense afternoon thundershowers, provided you get a table when the first drops come down (they fill up fast). They recommend that you dine inside because "the service is faster," but I suspect that they want to keep the sidewalk portion a café rather than a restaurant. The menu includes fixed-price breakfasts available all day, a half dozen Oaxacan specialties, and such dinner choices as tamale oaxaqueño and carne asada Oaxaca style.

RESTAURANT EL MESÓN, Av. Hidalgo. Tel. 6-2729.
Specialty: MEXICAN.
$ Prices: Tacos $1.25; fixed-price lunch $2.50; lunch buffet $4.50.
Open: Daily 8am–1am.

You can watch the señoritas prepare your tacos at what can only be described as the Mexican equivalent of a sushi bar. This restaurant is clean, attractive, and lively. A printed list of dishes serves as menu, order blank, and bill. The prices are printed on it; the taco prices are per taco, so if you want more than one, indicate it when you order. If you don't eat meat, try refried black beans, which come topped with cheese and with a stack of fresh, hot tortillas. If you order the chorizo oaxaqueño, make sure you have a frosty beer for a chaser, and that your "fire insurance" is up-to-date. The restaurant is half a block east of the plaza.

CAFETERÍA BAMBY, Vigil 205. Tel. 6-0333.
Specialty: MEXICAN/BAKERY.
$ Prices: Oaxacan breakfast $4.50; club sandwich $2.50; mole $4.25.
Open: Mon–Sat 8am–10pm.

The owners of the immensely popular Panadificadora Bamby recently opened this coffee shop, which looks as if it belongs in a brand-new hotel. The walls and furnishings are painted in peach and gray tones, and even under the bright lights there isn't a spot of dirt. The food is well prepared and the servings generous, and you can count on good service and food even in the off-hours between lunch and dinner. Those homesick for all-American food will find burgers, filet mignon, and club sandwiches. The small Bamby market next door has a nice selection of Oaxacan cheeses, sliced lunch meats, granolas, and nuts. The cafeteria is 2½ blocks north of the plaza.

EL TÍO, Cinco de Mayo no. 108. Tel. 6-8201.
Specialty: MEXICAN.
$ Prices: Main courses $3–$5.
Open: Daily noon–10pm.

El Tío is the cornerstone of a new dining complex two and a half blocks north of the plaza called La Casa de la Tía, with several small cafés sharing space around a central courtyard. The complex has a clever concept: You can choose from all the menus no matter where you sit down. El Tío specializes in local dishes; try the tasajo, a thin marinated steak served with guacamole, tomatoes, beans, and bolillos. Gino's Pizza serves an incredible seafood pizza with oysters, squid, and anchovies. Las Crepas serves mushroom and chicken crêpes, cakes, and crepas cajetas, covered with caramel sauce. Other cafés include Pollo Brujo and Taco Fans. There are plans for live music at night once the complex is better established.

CAFE EL SOL Y LA LUNA, Murguía 105. Tel. 6-2933.
Specialty: MEXICAN/AMERICAN.
$ Prices: Light meals $2.50–$4.50.
Open: Mon–Sat 7pm–1am.

The local hip crowd gathers here to listen to live jazz and salsa groups playing in a small courtyard with tables set around a wrought-iron staircase. The menu includes melted-cheese plates, yogurt with granola and honey, avocado salads, crêpes, and pastas. Wine and beer are served at competitive prices. A good spot for a late-night snack and for being among the city's artists, the café is four blocks north of the plaza at Reforma.

RESTAURANT PISCES, Av. Hidalgo 119. Tel. 6-2651.
   Specialty: VEGETARIAN.
 $ Prices: Main courses $2.50–$4.
   Open: Lunch only, Mon–Sat 1–4pm.
One of my favorite vegetarian restaurants, the Pisces offers a comida corrida that includes vegetable soup, a plate of lentil stew with carrots and pineapple, frijoles, fruit salad, and tea. The menu changes daily. The true business hours are indicated in this listing despite what the sign says outside the restaurant. It's five blocks west of the plaza.

MEALS FOR LESS THAN $10

RESTAURANT TÍPICO DE OAXACA, Plaza Labastida. Tel. 6-4331.
   Specialty: OAXACAN.
 $ Prices: Main dishes $4–$7.
   Open: Daily 8am–midnight.
Authentic Oaxacan food, some of it not seen elsewhere, is served an a pleasant courtyard with tables arranged around a fountain. The Oaxacan platter features several regional appetizers, and Oaxacan pollo mole is a specialty of the house. Many of the dishes can be ordered without meat for half the price. A band plays here in the evening and the music is often too loud to permit conversation.
   You'll find the restaurant five blocks north of Plaza Principal and one block east of Alcala between Alcala and 5 de Mayo.

MI CASITA, Av. Hidalgo 616. Tel. 6-9256.
   Specialty: OAXACAN.
 $ Prices: Appetizers $3; main courses $5–$15.50.
   Open: Lunch only, daily 1–6pm.
This is one of the best places in town to try authentic Oaxacan cooking. Owner Miguel Najera is always on hand, personally attending to his contented guests. The menu includes plato oaxaqueño (a sampler of nine dishes), chiles relleños, and mole oaxaqueño de pollo. The soups are fantastic. A sideboard is set with dishes prepared from the menu, so you can see what you're about to order. It's a pleasant place for a leisurely lunch without being accosted by vendors between every bite as it's on the second story overlooking the northwest side of the plaza.

RESTAURANT SANTA FE, 5 de Mayo no. 103. Tel. 6-9434.
   Specialty: OAXACAN.
 $ Prices: Fixed-price lunch $4.25; mole $5; filet $7; enchiladas $4.50; crepas cajeta flambé for two $6.50.
   Open: Daily 8am–midnight.
This is another good place to try Oaxacan specialties—15 different ones in all will tempt you. One of them, the excellent and filling chicken and Oaxaca-cheese quesadillas made with fresh flour tortillas, covers a large platter and comes with beans, cheese, lettuce, and tomatoes, and a great guacamole salad alive with the flavor of cilantro. However, pass over the strange-tasting version of Oaxacan tamales. If you're starved for fresh vegetables, the huge mixed salad is almost a meal in itself. Flaming desserts are another specialty. The restaurant is 2½ blocks north of Plaza Principal between Independencia and Morelos.

RESTAURANT BAR CATEDRAL, Morelos 602. Tel. 6-0137.
   Specialty: MEXICAN.
 $ Prices: Main courses $6–$8.
   Open: Daily noon–1am.

Two blocks north of the plaza at Vigil is a cool place to enjoy a leisurely midday meal. A few tables are near the fountain in the small courtyard, while others are in two large rooms to your left and right as you enter. One can sense the elegance here: cloth napkins, more than one fork, and waiters in jackets and ties. The restaurant is known for its excellent cuts of beef. The flan may be the best I've ever had!

PIZZERÍA ALFREDO DA ROMA, Alcala 400. Tel. 6-5058.
  Specialty: ITALIAN.
  $ Prices: Main courses $3–$9.25.
  Open: Daily 1:30–11:30pm.
The small tables covered with red-and-white-checkered tablecloths are full of locals as well as tourists. Many people who stop for take-out pizza spend their time examining the Italian prints that are clustered together on the walls. All prices are posted on a board in the entrance. The lasagne and spaghetti are certainly worth a try, but skip the terrible onion pizza. The pizzeria is at the north end of the pedestrians-only zone, north of plaza.

WORTH THE EXTRA BUCKS

ASADOR VASCO, Plaza Principal. Tel. 6-9719.
  Specialty: MEXICAN.
  $ Prices: Main courses $7.50–$14.
  Open: 1:30–11:30pm.
This restaurant, upstairs on the west side of the plaza, has its strong points: the second-floor location, with balcony tables overlooking the plaza; a menu listing lots of steaks, fish, and chicken, plus some familiar Mexican favorites. The prices are high, but the posted exchange rate for dollars is significantly higher than at the hotels. The hostess may refuse to seat you at a table overlooking the plaza if you are dining alone or are dressed shabbily. A guitarist plays romantic ballads in the bar from 8:30pm until closing.

SHOPPING

It's a toss-up as to what tourists do first in Oaxaca: see the nearby ruins or shop. Oaxaca and the surrounding villages have some of the country's best buys in locally handcrafted pottery, wood carvings, and textiles. It's easy to buy more than you ever imagined, so come prepared with extra suitcases. *Note:* Before you load down with tons of pottery, wood carvings, and weavings, however, keep in mind that your luggage is weighed at flight check-in. You'll be charged a fee for bags over 25 kilos (slightly over 55 lb.). The transport bus to the airport also charges extra for passengers with excess baggage bulk.

CITY MARKETS

BENITO JUÁREZ MARKET, bordered by Señorial, Mina Arteaga, 20 de Noviembre, and Magón.
One block south of the Plaza Principal, this covered market is big and busy every day, but especially on Saturday. The area around it is all open street market, teeming with vendors of chiles, string, parrots, talismans, food, spices, cloth, blankets—one of the most exciting markets in Mexico, because the people who come to sell their wares are so colorful. There's a huge crafts section, but the bulk of the produce trade has been relocated to a new building called the Abastos Market (see below), where the local color is even more profound.

ABASTOS MARKET, across the railroad tracks and near the second-class bus station.
The Abastos Market is open daily but is most active on Saturday, when Indians

from the villages come to town to sell and shop. You'll see huge mounds of dried chiles, herbs, vegetables, crafts, bread, and even burros for sale at this bustling market.

ARTS & CRAFTS

Several of the stores mentioned below are on the **pedestrians-only Alcala,** which has been closed to traffic for three blocks from Morelos to Allende, making it a most pleasant place to browse. The **Benito Juárez Market** (see above) has a huge crafts section. And running alongside it, **20 de Noviembre,** one block west of Plaza Principal, is another good street for browsing although it's not closed to traffic.

MERCADO DE ARTESANÍAS, García at Zaragoza.

This is a good place to get an overview of Oaxaca's folk arts, particularly textiles. Women and men weave rugs, belts, huipils, serapes, and bags on looms, and display their finest work. Ask the artisans where they're from and you'll get an idea of which villages you'd like to visit. Located two blocks south of the Benito Juárez Market and six blocks south of Plaza Principal, it's open daily from 10am to 4pm.

LA MANO MAGICA, Alcala 203. Tel. 6-4275.

⭐ This gallery of contemporary and popular art is across from the City Museum. The name means "magic hand" and it's a true celebration of Oaxacan artistic creativity. Fine exhibits of paintings by local artists occupy the front room. The back room, reached through a courtyard, is full of regional folk art by the area's best artisans. Most of the popular artists are humble folk who carry on an inherited artistic tradition in their village homes. Photographs of the artists at work are often displayed next to their creations. It's located between Morelos and Matamoros opposite the Museum of the City (House of Cortés), and is open Monday through Saturday from 10am to 2pm and 4 to 8pm.

VICTOR'S, Porfirio Díaz 111. Tel. 6-1174.

This art shop in a 17th-century monastery is managed by Sr. Ramon Fosado, who goes to the villages himself in search of the best native art. He speaks English and is very pleasant. If you're shopping for serapes and blankets, be sure to stop at Victor's to do a little research. The quality of these goods varies, and the friendly patrons here are willing to tell you about the differences in materials (wool vs. synthetic), dyes (natural and chemical), and designs. You should also scout around and compare the various products in the open markets. It's open Monday through Saturday from 9am to 2pm and 4 to 8pm.

YALALAG DE OAXACA, Alcala 104. Tel. 6-2108.

This old mansion at the corner of Alcala and Morelos displays a multifarious collection of black pottery, terra-cotta figurines, tin sculpture, jewelry, rugs, beads, necklaces, paper-mâché sculpture, and much more. Owner Enrique de la Lanza speaks English and prices are moderate. Open Monday through Saturday from 9am to 1:30pm and 4 to 8pm.

CASA BRENA, Piño Suarez 700. Tel. 5-3890.

Textiles and some pottery are sold at this 50-year-old shop across the street from the park. Inside is a large courtyard with a *tienda* (store) off to the left and looms in the back. You'll hear the slapping of the wooden paddles as the men tighten the shuttled thread between the warp. Walk back and look around. The boys dye the wool in bright colors from fluorescent pink to canary yellow, the young girls spin the thread, and the men work the looms. All in all, it's an impressive operation, and I can almost guarantee you'll want to buy something. The prices here are about as low as you'll find anywhere, and the quality is the best. The "Colonia Reforma" bus will take you to the corner at Piño Suarez and San Martín. The looms operate Monday through Friday from 8am to 4:30pm and on Saturday from 8am to 2pm. The shop is open Monday through Friday from 9am to 7pm and on Saturday from 9am to 5pm.

ARTESANÍAS Y INDUSTRIAS POPULARES DEL ESTADO DE OAXACA (ARIPO), Vigil 809. Tel. 6-9211.

⭐ The state of Oaxaca runs ARIPO, which includes a shop and is located two blocks farther up the hill beyond the Benito Juárez house. You can hear looms working in the back as you browse through the handcrafts expertly displayed in the many rooms. ARIPO has possibly the widest selection of black pottery in the city. There's also a good supply of masks, clothing, and cutlery. Open Monday through Saturday from 9am to 7:30pm and on Sunday from 9am to 1pm.

MICROINDUSTRIAS, Vigil 601. Tel. 6-5828.

This cooperative of area artisans offers some great bargains at about half the cost of ARIPO. There are only two small rooms and a loft. All the work, including black pottery from Coyotepec, brown, green, and white pottery from Atzompa, and rugs from Teotitlán del Valle are direct from the artists and avoid the middleman's markup. Open Monday through Saturday from 9am to 2pm and 4 to 7pm.

FONART, M. Bravo 116. Tel. 6-5764.

⭐ Oaxaca's branch of this government-supported chain is on M. Bravo at García Vigil. The name stands for Fondo Nacional para el Fomento de las Artesanías. Prices are fixed. Open Monday through Saturday from 9am to 2pm and 4 to 7pm.

GALERÍA ARTE DE OAXACA, Trujano 102. Tel. 6-9719.

Located near the southwest corner of Plaza Principal, this gallery features contemporary Oaxacan painters. Open Monday through Saturday from 11am to 3pm and 5 to 9pm.

VILLAGE SHOPPING

One of the main reasons many people come to Oaxaca is to visit the markets and crafts villages nearby. For market days in outlying villages and directions to the wood carvers and other crafts villages of importance, see "Excursions," below.

EVENING ENTERTAINMENT

The cheapest (and one of the best) evening entertainments is hearing the band concerts in **Plaza Principal.** Music is scheduled on Tuesday, Thursday, and Sunday, and almost daily during the summer. Oaxaca has the jolliest and most active zócalo in all of Mexico, enjoyed by everyone in town, young and old, rich and poor.

The *Guelaguetza,* famous regional dance of Oaxaca, is performed at the **Hotel Stouffer Presidente** on Friday at 7pm for $15 per person. The **Hotel Monte Albán** presents more reasonably priced folk dances daily from 8:30 to 10pm for $3.50. Buy your ticket the day before. When you enter, you'll find your name card placed at your reserved seat.

Concerts and dance programs are offered all year long at the **Teatro Macedonio de Alcala,** at Independencia and Armenta y López. Schedules are posted by the front doors of the theater. The **Casa de la Cultura,** at the corner of Colón and G. Ortega, offers exhibits, lectures, films, and various art and music classes.

The **Cinema Ariel 2000,** at the corner of Juárez and Liceaga (that's the continuation of Berriozabal, six blocks north of Plaza Principal), is new, clean, and modern. Films change every 2 or 3 days.

Cine Oaxaca is on Calle Morelos two blocks south of the zócalo; **Cine Mitla** is east of the plaza on G. Vigil. Movies cost $1.10.

Oaxaca's hottest disco is in the **Hotel Victoria,** on the Cerro del Fortín, northwest of the center of town (tel. 5-2633). You'll need a taxi to get there.

EASY EXCURSIONS FROM OAXACA

Monte Albán and Mitla are the two most important archeological sites near Oaxaca, but there are several smaller ruins that are also interesting. I've also mentioned a few day trips to the more interesting villages outside Oaxaca. (For Puerto Escondido, see

Chapter 6.) The Tourist Office will give you a map showing the nearby villages where beautiful handcrafts are made. It's a fun excursion by car or bus.

MARKET VILLAGES

You could spend nearly a full week in Oaxaca just visiting the various markets held in nearby villages. Each has its specialty—cheese, produce, livestock, weaving, and pottery—and its unique character. **Market days** in the villages are as follows:

Wednesday	**Etla,** known for its cheese; 9½ miles north.
Thursday	**Zaachila,** ruins and agriculture; 11 miles southwest.
	Ejutla, agriculture; 40 miles south.
Friday	**Ocotlán,** pottery, textiles, and food; 18½ miles south.
Saturday	**Oaxaca,** Abastos market.
Sunday	**Tlacolula,** agriculture and crafts (visit the chapel as well); 19½ miles southeast.

GETTING THERE   You can get to any of these crafts villages by taking a bus from the **second-class bus** station. On market days the aisles are crammed with passengers. If you get off the bus between destinations, say, at Dainzu on the way to Mitla or at Culiapan on the way to Zaachila, but want to continue to the next place, return to the highway and hail a passing bus.

It's also possible to take a **colectivo taxi** to the villages that don't have bus service. To find a colectivo, go out the front door of the second-class bus station, face the Abastos Market, and look left. You'll see a large, open plaza to the far left of the market. Cross it and keep going on the left side of the market, where you'll see dozens of parked yellow and white colectivo taxis. The town each one serves is written on the door or trunk. They fill up relatively fast and are an economical way to reach the villages. It's 75¢ per person to Zaachila, for example, and roughly twice that to Mitla. If you're coming from town on the street between the market and the bus station, you'll pass the plaza on your left before you get to the colectivo lot. Be sure to go early; by afternoon the colectivos don't fill up as fast and you'll have to wait.

Viajes Mitla in the Hotel Mesón del Ángel (tel. 6-6175), has tours to all the markets as well as the crafts villages and ruins. The agency has a great map of the area around Oaxaca, with descriptions of the various villages and their market days.

THE ROAD TO MITLA

East of Oaxaca, the Pan American Highway to Mitla includes several important archeological sites, markets, and crafts villages. En route you can visit the famous El Tule tree; the church at Tiacochahuaya; the ruins at Dainzu, Lambityeco, and Yaagul; the weaver's village of Teotitlán del Valle; and Saturday market village of Tlacolula.

Without a car, it's impossible to cover all these destinations in 1 day, and by car the route takes a very long day. On a Sunday you could combine the Tlacolula market with all the archeological sites, which have free admission on Sunday. Save the weaving village of Teotitlán del Valle and the church of Tlacochahua for another day.

The best guided tour of El Tule and Mitla can be arranged through **Viajes Mitla,** at the Hotel Mesón del Angel (tel. 6-6175). The 4-hour tour costs $9 and includes transport and guide, but not the admission fee to the ruins. More expensive tours are offered by the various travel agents in town. However, if you'd like to explore some of the other places along the way (and even if not), the trip can be made easily on your own. (Bring a flashlight in case the tunnels at Mitla are open.)

The **Fletes y Pasajes** bus line (tel. 6-2270) runs buses every 20 minutes from 6am to 8pm to Mitla from the second-class terminal. The terminal is five blocks west of Plaza Principal on Aldama, across the railroad tracks. The trip takes an hour and 15 minutes and costs 60¢ each way. The driver will stop at any point along the way; let him know in advance.

EL TULE TREE   Santa María del Tule is a small town (8 miles outside Oaxaca) that's filled with turkeys, children, and rug vendors. The town is famous for the immense ahuehuete tree (water cypress) in a churchyard just off the main road. The 2,000-year-old tree is so big it takes a person half a minute to walk around it. Unfortunately, now there's a fence around the tree that will keep you from timing it yourself—as if a tree that has survived 2,000 years needs protection! This tree is still growing today, as is evidenced by the foliage, and will likely continue to do so as long as the water level remains high. This whole region around Santa María del Tule was once very marshy; in fact, the word *tule* means reed. Beyond El Tule is agricultural country, and at siesta time you'll see whole families resting in the shade of giant cacti.

CHURCH OF SAN JERONIMO TLACOCHAHUAYA This church is a fine example of how the Spanish borrowed from Zapotec architectural design. Inside you'll see how the church leaders artistically melded the two cultures. Note the elaborately carved altar and the crucified Christ made of dried corn cobs. Because of vandalism, the church is usually closed, except for special holy services. However, you might be able to find the keeper of the keys (inquire at the house across from the church). He'll open the church and show you around (a small tip is suggested). It's on the right side of the road, past the Tule Tree.

The Mitla bus will drop you off at the road leading into town. You can either hitch a ride with locals or walk the distance.

DAINZU Sixteen miles from Oaxaca, this recently excavated site is not very interesting to the layperson because very little restoration has been done on the buildings. A caretaker will show you some of the more interesting points and he has a storeroom of fascinating relics: massive stone carvings that resemble the Danzante carvings seen in Monte Albán. Admission is a few pesos.

The site is located on a dirt road heading southwest from Highway 190 to Mitla. Look for a sign 16 miles from Oaxaca.

LAMBITYECO Visible from the highway, a few miles east of the turnoff to Dainzu, this small site is thought to have been inhabited during the decline of Monte Albán. Admission is free.

✪ TEOTITLÁN DEL VALLE This little town is famous for weaving. The beautiful serapes and heavy blankets can be found in the shops in Oaxaca, but you might enjoy buying from the source. Many of the weavers sell out of their homes, and give demonstrations. The prices are slightly lower than in Oaxaca.

Direct buses make the run between Oaxaca and Teotitlán from the second-class bus station. If you're coming from or going to Mitla, you'll have to hitch or walk from the highway crossroads.

✪ YAAGUL This was a fortress city on a small hill overlooking the valley. It's 20 miles southeast of Oaxaca about half a mile off the road to Mitla. There's a small sign indicating the turnoff to the left. Go down the newly paved road and the last bit is uphill. The setting is absolutely gorgeous, and although the ruins are not nearly as magnificent as Monte Albán, you're likely to have the place to yourself. It's a good place for a picnic lunch.

The city was divided into two sections: the fortress on the hill and the area of palaces lower down the hill. The center of the palace complex is the plaza, surrounded by four temples. In the center is a ceremonial platform, under which is the Triple Tomb. The door of the tomb is a large stone slab decorated on both sides with beautiful hieroglyphs. Unfortunately, the tomb was closed on my last visit.

Look for the beautifully restored ball court, typical of Zapotec ball courts (which are without goal rings). North of the plaza is the incredible palace structure built for the chiefs of the city. It's a maze of huge rooms with six patios, decorated with painted stucco and stone mosaics. Here and there you can see ceremonial mounds and tombs decorated in the same geometric patterns that are found in Mitla. This is one of the most interesting palaces in the area. The panoramic view of the valley from the fortress is worth the rather exhausting climb.

Admission is $3.50, free on Sunday and holidays. The site is open daily from 8am to 5pm.

It's just a few miles farther southeast to Mitla. The turnoff comes at a very obvious fork in the road.

✪ **TLACOLULA**   Located 50 miles from Oaxaca, southeast on the road to Mitla, Tlacolula is famous for its Saturday market and **Dominican chapel,** which is considered by many to be the most beautiful of the Dominican churches in the Americas. The wrought-iron gates, choir loft, and banisters of the pulpit are worth a look, as well as the frescoes and paintings in relief. A few years ago a secret passage was found, leading to a room that contained valuable silver religious pieces. The silver was hidden during the Revolution of 1916 when there was a tide of antireligious sentiment; the articles are now back in the church.

Sunday is market day in Tlacolula.

MITLA

★   Mitla is 2¾ miles from the highway, and the turnoff terminates in the dusty town square. If you've come here by bus, it's about half a mile up the road to the ruins; if you want to hire a cab, there are some available in the square. You'll probably find the drivers anxious to act as guides, and that isn't a bad idea, if you can agree on a reasonable price in advance.

Mitla was settled by the Zapotecs as early as 800 B.C., abandoned in A.D. 900, and resettled by the Mixtecs in the late 10th century. This city of the Mixtecs was still flourishing at the time of the Spanish Conquest, and many of the buildings were used through the 16th century.

The town of Mitla (pop. 10,000) is often bypassed by the tour groups, but is worth a visit. The University of the Americas maintains a small **museum** in town which contains some Zapotec and Mixtec relics. Admission is free after signing in. Be sure to peek through the glass partition at the Leigh collection, which contains some real treasures. (The light switch is next to the outside door.) The museum is housed in the delightful **Posada La Sorpresa,** Avenida Independencia 40, an old hacienda.

There's a pleasant town square where local women sell crafts. A few small shops have opened near the square, including **Mitla Mon Amour,** a gallery with antique religious paintings and statues, jewelry, hand-painted pottery, and antique furniture. The gallery is run by Andrea Ludden, a French archeologist who worked on the excavation of Monte Albán four decades ago. Ludden is now at work restoring a 17th-century hacienda near Mitla which she hopes will someday be a retreat for artists and writers.

Seeing the Ruins   You can easily see the most important buildings in an hour. Mixtec architecture is based on a quadrangle surrounded on three or four sides by patios and chambers, usually rectangular in shape. The chambers have a low roof, which is excellent for defense but which makes the rooms dark and close. The stone buildings are covered with mud and inlaid with small stones cut in geometric patterns.

There are five groups of buildings divided by the Mitla River. The most important buildings are on the east side of the ravine. The **Group of the Columns** consisted of two quadrangles, connected at the corners with palaces. The building to the north has a long chamber with six columns and many rooms decorated with geometric designs. The most common motif is the zigzag pattern, the same one seen repeatedly on the Mitla blankets. Human or animal images are rare in Mixtec art. In fact, only one frieze has been found (in the **Group of the Church,** in the north patio). Here, you'll see a series of figures painted with their name glyphs.

At press time, the tombs were closed for restoration, but may be open when you get there.

Admission to the site is $3.50, free on Sunday and holidays. It's open daily from 9am to 5pm.

Outside the ruins you'll be bombarded by vendors. The moment you step out of a car or taxi, every able-bodied woman and child for 10 miles around comes charging over with shrill cries and a basket full of bargains. Heavily embroidered belts, small pieces of pottery, fake archeological relics, cheap earrings—offer to pay half the price that the vendors ask. There is a modern handcrafts market near the ruins, but prices are lower in town.

Mezcal Outlets   In Mitla and on the highway going south, you'll find *expendios de mezcal,* which are factory outlets for little distilleries that produce the fiery cactus aguardiente. To be authentic, a bottle of mezcal must have a worm floating in it. The liquor is surprisingly cheap, the bottle labels are surprisingly colorful, and the taste is astoundingly horrible. But mix a shot of mezcal with a glass of grapefruit or pomegranate juice and you've got a cocktail that will make you forget the heat, even in Mitla. Watch out for the worm!

ARRAZOLA, CUILAPAN & ZAACHILA

Arrazola is in the foothills of Monte Albán, about 15 miles southwest of Oaxaca. The tiny town's most famous resident is Manuel Jimenez, the septuagenarian grandfather of the resurgence in wood carving as a folk art. Jimenez's polar bears, anteaters, and rabbits carved from copal wood are shown in galleries throughout the world, and his home is a mecca of sorts for folk-art collectors. Now the town is full of other carvers, all making fanciful creatures painted in bright, festive colors. Little boys will greet you at the outskirts of town offering to guide you to individual homes for a small tip. Following them is a good way to know the town and after a bit you can dismiss them.

If you're driving, take the road out of town that goes to Monte Albán, take the left fork after crossing the Atoyac River, and follow the signs for Zaachila. Turn right after the town of Xoxo to reach Arrazola. There are no road signs, but other travelers along the way will direct you. The bus from the second-class station will let you off at the road to Arrazola where it meets the highway. From there it's a pleasant 3½-mile walk to the town, past a few homes, the occupants of which are wood carvers who will invite you in for a look at their work. To return, collectivo taxis make the run to Zaachila and Oaxaca for around $2, which can be shared—it's worth it.

Cuilapan is located about 10 miles southwest of Oaxaca. The Dominican friars built their second monastery here in 1555. However, parts of the convent and church were never completed because funds ran out. The roof of the monastery has fallen, but the cloister and the church remain. The church has been restored and is still used today. There are three naves with lofty arches, large stone columns, and many frescoes. The monastery is visible on the right a short distance from the main road to Zaachila, and there's a sign as well. The bus from the second-class station stops within a few hundred feet of the church.

Farther on from Culiapan, 15 miles southwest of Oaxaca, **Zaachila** is worth a visit only on market day (Thursday). A few baskets and some pottery is sold for local household use. Thousands flock to the produce market and there's an interesting livestock section just as you enter town. The most important attractions, the tombs, are closed to visitors so there's not much to see if you search them out.

At the time of the Spanish Conquest, Zaachila was the last surviving city of the Zapotec rulers. When Cortés marched on the city, the Zapotecs did not resist and instead formed an alliance with him, which outraged the Mixtecs, who invaded Zaachila shortly afterward. Only a few pyramids, mounds, and some very interesting tombs remain—but they aren't open. You'll find the tombs and the pyramids near the church in the main plaza. Most of the artifacts found in the tombs have been moved to the Museum of Anthropology in Mexico City.

To return to Oaxaca, you have a choice of walking several blocks back to the second-class bus station near the animal market, or lining up with the locals for one of the colectivo taxis on the main street across from the market. I prefer the taxi.

SAN BARTOLO COYOTEPEC, SAN MARTIN TILCAJETE & OCOTLÁN

San Bartolo is the home of the black pottery you've seen in all the stores in Oaxaca. It's also one of several little villages named Coyotepec in the area. Buses frequently operate between Oaxaca and this village 23 miles south on Highway 175. More than 50 years ago, a native woman named Doña Rosa invented the technique of smoking the pottery to make it black during firing, and rubbing the with a piece of quartz to produce a sheen, and she opened a factory to produce the distinctive vases, bowls, figurines, and candlesticks. Doña Rosa died in 1979, but villagers carry on the tradition. Rosa's home and factory is a few blocks off the main road; you'll see the sign as you enter town. It's open daily from 9am to 5:30pm.

Black pottery is sold at many shops on the little plaza, or in the artists' homes. Villagers who make pottery often place a piece of their work near their front door, by the gate, or on the street. It's their way of inviting prospective buyers to come in.

San Martín Tilcajete is a recent addition to the tour of folk-art towns. Located about 10 miles south of San Bartolo Coyotepec, San Martín is noted for its wood carvers and their fantastical, brightly painted animals and dragons. The Sosa and Hernández families are especially prolific, and you can easily spend half a day wandering from house to house to see the amazing collections for hot-pink rabbits, bright-blue, 4-foot-long twisting snakes, and two-headed dalmations.

One of the best markets in the area is held on Friday in **Ocotlán de Morelos, 35** miles south of Oaxaca on Highway 175. The variety of goods includes modern dishware and cutlery, hand-molded earthenware jugs, polyester dresses, finely woven cotton or wool rebozos (scarves), hand-dyed and tooled leather, and electronics, as well as produce. You won't find a more varied selection except in Oaxaca. There's not much to see Saturday through Thursday unless you come to visit Ocotlán's most famous potters, the noted Aguilar family. On the right, just at the outskirts of Ocotlán, their row of home-workshops is distinguished by pottery pieces stuck up on the fence. Their work, often figures of daily life, is colorful, sometimes humorous, and highly prized by collectors. Visitors are welcome daily.

GUELATAO

Set high in the mountains north of Oaxaca, this town has become a living monument to its favorite son, Benito Juárez. Although usually peaceful, this lovely town comes to life on Juárez's birthday (Mar 21). The museum, statues, and plaza all attest to the town's obvious devotion to the patriot.

To get here, take the second-class bus from the first-class station at 3:30am, 10am, or 11:30am, or one of several departures from the second-class station. The trip will take at least 2 hours, through gorgeous mountain scenery. Buses return to Oaxaca every 2 hours until 8pm.

EN ROUTE TO SAN CRISTÓBAL DE LAS CASAS

Consider stopping near Tehuantepec if you're making the long haul from Oaxaca to San Cristóbal de las Casas. From Oaxaca to Tehuantepec is a comparatively short trip of 155 miles, but a fairly arduous one if you're driving, since you'll have to negotiate dozens of S-turns and innumerable climbs and descents.

The first thing you'll notice about Tehuantepec (alt. 200 ft.; pop. 102,000) is that it's hot and the women wear long trailing skirts with heavy velvet embroidered huipils. Although beautiful, the full-length skirt seems the last thing one would want to wear in this hot and humid climate. They're sometimes sold in the market. Otherwise, the town has very little to offer, and I wouldn't recommend that you stay or eat here.

If you need a hotel, I recommend those on the highway past the Pemex station on the way to Tuxtla Gutiérrez. If you're headed toward Villahermosa, Palenque, and the Yucatán, you might stop in Acayucan, at the northern end of Highway 185 near the Gulf Coast. See chapters 00 and 00 for details.

CHAPTER 15

THE CENTRAL ROUTE FROM LAREDO & MONTERREY

Most travelers arriving by land from the eastern or midwestern United States use the Laredo, Texas/Nuevo Laredo, Tamaulipas, border crossing. Access to the rest of Mexico is through the two cities of Monterrey and Saltillo. The trip from Laredo to Monterrey on Highway 85, and from Saltillo to San Luis Potosí is a long and boring one of desert, cactus, and joshua trees.

A new border crossing is now under construction a few miles northwest of Laredo at Columbus, Texas.

TRAVELING THE CENTRAL ROUTE

Once across the border, it's a 3-hour trip to Monterrey, or 4 hours to Saltillo. From these two cities, well-maintained highways lead all the way to Mexico City. Highway 85 is two lane to Monterrey, and from Monterrey to San Luis Potosí. A four-lane highway appears between Monterrey and Saltillo, and again before Querétaro into Mexico City. It's a 10- to 12-hour drive from Nuevo Laredo to San Luis Potosí, which can be done in 1 day by leaving the border by 7 or 8am in order to arrive in San Luis before dark. But I recommend a stay along the way, at either Monterrey or Real de Catorce.

ROUTES TO THE INTERIOR

To the Silver Cities: From Monterrey and Saltillo, Hwys. 57 and 54 lead to San Miguel de Allende, San Luis Potosí, Guanajuato, Zacatecas, and Aguascalientes.

To the Capital: Excellent Hwy. 57 south leads from Nuevo Laredo at the Texas border to Mexico City, a 20-hour journey by bus or car.

To Guadalajara: From Saltillo, Hwy. 54 leads straight through Zacatecas to Guadalajara.

To the West Coast: Hwy. 40 goes southwest from Saltillo through Durango to Mazatlán on the Pacific Coast.

To the East Coast: Hwy. 85 from Monterrey offers quick access to Mexico's east-coast gateway city of Ciudad Victoria.

WHAT'S SPECIAL ABOUT THE CENTRAL ROUTE

Architectural Achievement
- [ ] The 40-acre Gran Plaza in Monterrey, which transformed an eyesore into a beautiful cultural hub.

Regional Food
- [ ] Such favorites as flour tortillas, charro beans flavored with beer, small tamales, roast kid, and shredded dried beef (*machacada*).

Natural Spectacles
- [ ] Horsetail Falls recreation area, outside Monterrey.
- [ ] Garcia Caves, between Monterrey and Saltillo, reached by a 2,298-foot cable car.

Shopping
- [ ] Blown glass, a Monterrey specialty.
- [ ] Saltillo, known for the multicolored striped serape/rug by the same name.

Ghost Town
- [ ] Real de Catorce, at an altitude of 9,000 feet, an 18th-century silver-mining town with small rustic hotels and restaurants, hidden in the mountains 140 miles south of Saltillo.

1. MONTERREY

146 miles S of Laredo, Texas; 53 miles NE of Saltillo

GETTING THERE   By Plane   Monterrey has multiple daily air connections with Mexico City, plus nonstop flights to Cancún, Chicago, Chihuahua, Dallas/Fort Worth, Guadalajara, Houston, Los Angeles, Mazatlán, San Antonio, San Luis Potosí, Tampico, and Tijuana. **Domestic flights** are operated by AeroCancún, Aeroméxico, Mexicana, AeroLitoral, AeroMar, Aviación del Noroeste, and AeroSierra. **International flights** are shared by Aeroméxico, Aeromonterrey, American, Continental, and Mexicana.

By Train   The speediest and most comfortable way to get to Monterrey is on **El Regiomontaño,** a first-class Estrella train with chair cars as well as Pullman and diner. It leaves Nuevo Laredo (the border) daily at 3:15pm, arriving in Monterrey at 7pm. From Mexico City it leaves at 6pm and arrives (via San Luis Potosí and Saltillo) in Monterrey at 8:10am the following morning. By March 1992 there may be a new train, the **Royal Eagle,** running between San Antonio, Texas, and Monterrey; for information call toll free 800/666-3232 in the U.S.

Many people drive to the border, leave their cars in a protected lot on the U.S. side, cross over, and take the train to Mexico. For information on secure places to park for extended periods call the Laredo, Texas, Convention and Visitor's Bureau (tel. 512/722-9895).

By Bus   Greyhound buses and their affiliates in the U.S. border towns can usually provide information on bus schedules leaving from the Mexican side to the Mexican interior. In Laredo, Texas, call 512/723-1321.

Transportes del Norte (tel. 72-4965 or 75-5744) runs buses in both directions between Nuevo Laredo and Monterrey every 45 minutes throughout the day for $4.25. In addition, Transportes del Norte has hourly buses between Saltillo and Monterrey, a 1½- or 2-hour trip. **Transportes Monterrey-Saltillo** (tel. 75-5744) has hourly buses to Saltillo from 9am to noon on Saturday and Sunday.

By Car   From Laredo, take Highway 85; the 146 miles takes about 3 hours to drive. From Eagle Pass you can take Mexican Highway 57 south through Sabinas and then go east shortly after Monclova to Monterrey; but it's much faster to take the U.S.

Highway 83 from Eagle Pass to Laredo (about 120 miles) and cross the border there. The route from Laredo (Highway 85) is one of the most popular for visitors from the north because it can be reached conveniently from the northern and eastern United States via Interstate highways.

DEPARTING   By Plane   The office of **Aeroméxico** is located at the corner of Avenida Cuauhtémoc and Padre Mier (tel. 40-8760, or 44-7720 or 44-7730 at the airport). **Mexicana,** which can also book **Aeromonterrey,** an affiliate, has offices on the Gran Plaza, at Zaragoza and Matamoros (tel. 45-3077); in the Gran Hotel Ancira, at Hidalgo and Escobedo (tel. 45-6422); at Hidalgo 922 Poniente (tel. 44-2211); at Cuauhtémoc 716 Norte (tel. 74-1474); and at the airport (tel. 45-0811).

The city office of **Continental** is in the Centro Commercial at Insurgentes 2500, in the Galerías Monterrey, Local 613 (tel. 33-2622, or 44-7505 or 45-7734 at the airport). **American Airlines** has offices downtown on the first floor of the Kalos Building (a couple of blocks from the Jardín Hidalgo), at Zaragoza 1300 Sur (tel. 58-9100, or 45-7946 at the airport). The new regional carrier, **AeroLitoral,** is also in the Kalos building at Zaragoza and Constitución (tel. 58-9977 or 58-9978, or 45-5799 or 45-5809 at the airport); it flies from Monterrey to the Bays of Huatulco, Minatitlán, Tampico, Veracruz, and Villahermosa. **AeroMar,** another regional airline, is at Morelos 177 Poniente in the Motreuvi building (tel. 45-3141 or 45-3201), on one side of the Hotel Ro; AeroMar flies to León, Mexico City, San Luis Potosí, and Tampico from Monterrey. **AeroSierra** (tel. 77-2106 and 59-4768), using Durango as its hub, flies a Monterrey–Torreón–Durango route three times a week.

Reservations on the **AeroCancún** spring/summer direct flight to Cancún from Monterrey are made through Provotel (tel. 44-6416, 44-7711), a Mexican hotel reservation firm, which sells 8-day air-and-hotel packages from Monterrey to Cancún. Provotel makes reservations for several hundred Mexican hotels through its offices in Houston, Texas (tel. 713/449-4900), but only markets air/land packages in Mexico.

By Train   To Saltillo and Mexico City, the *El Regiomontaño* train leaves Monterrey at 7pm and arrives in Saltillo at 10pm, San Luis Potosí at 3:45am, and Mexico City at 10am. The journey between Monterrey and Mexico City, for example, costs around $52.50 (round-trip) for a chair seat, $91 in a Pullman (sleeper). To Nuevo Laredo, *El Regiomontaño* leaves Monterrey at 8:10am and arrives at Nuevo Laredo shortly after noon.

The *Tamaulipeco* leaves Matamoros (across from Brownsville, Texas) at 2pm, stops at Reynosa (across from McAllen, Texas) and leaves there at 3:20pm, arriving in Monterrey at 6:50pm. If you want to park your car in Brownsville and take the train into Mexico, secured parking information is provided by the Brownsville Convention & Visitors Bureau (tel. 512/546-3721). For secured parking in McAllen, call the McAllen Convention and Visitors Bureau (tel. 512/682-2871).

For **general train information** in Monterrey, call 51-1100, extension 215. For the *Regiomontaño,* call 75-4604.

By Bus   Drop by the **Central de Autobuses** (tel. 75-3238) a day before you plan to leave and arrangements to almost anywhere will be a snap to make. **Autobuses Anahuac** (tel. 75-6480) will get you to Mexico City in 10½ hours; they also run to San Luis Potosí, as does **Transportes del Norte** (tel. 72-4965). **Tres Estrellas de Oro** (tel. 74-2410) operates from Monterrey to points all over Mexico. **Autobuses Estrella Blanca** (tel. 75-7216) and **Transportes Frontera** (tel. 75-7557) operate from Monterrey to points south and west. **Camiones de los Altos** (tel. 75-0358) has routes to the Silver Cities and Guadalajara.

By Car   From Monterrey, take Highway 40 to Saltillo. See "En Route To . . ." at the end of this section and the end of the Saltillo section for more details about routes from this region.

Monterrey, capital of the state of Nuevo León, is Mexico's third-largest city (alt. 1,770 ft.; pop. 3.5 million for the metropolitan area) and its main industrial center. Its setting is spectacular: hemmed in by towering, craggy mountains, one of which (Cerro de la Silla, "Saddle Mountain") has become a symbol of the city. This modern city "holds court" in the recently completed Gran Plaza. Its gardens, fountains, monuments, and buildings breathe new life into the city center.

With the industrial sprawl has come serious noise and air pollution, the latter often in the form of a pink pall that hangs in the valley 24 hours a day. But Monterrey, named in 1596 for the Count of Monterrey, Viceroy of New Spain, retains some colonial touches among its shiny new buildings and factories: the town hall, the Government Palace (state capitol of Nuevo León), mansions and hotels, churches and monasteries, and the parks and squares that the colonial planners always laid out in new towns. Hardly the stereotypical laid-back, charming, colonial Mexican town, filled with flowers all year and mariachis each evening, Monterrey is a raw, muscular city, crowded and expensive, that produces a great deal of Mexico's wealth.

ORIENTATION

ARRIVING By Plane   To get from the **airport** into Monterrey, a distance of about 19 miles, take one of the minibuses run by **Aeropuerto Transportaciones** (tel. 45-3330). A seat in a shared minibus (combi) costs $4; a private minibus running as a taxi charges $7. The combis run more frequently in the evenings, when the airport is busier, and there may not be any during nonpeak hours. A shared taxi costs about $8.25 to the area near the bus station.

By Train   The **train station** is near the bus station at Miguel Nieto and Calzada Victoria and quite a distance from town (see "By Bus," below).

By Bus   The bustling **bus station** on Avenida Colón, about 4 miles outside the city center, is a $5.50 taxi ride away. Local buses marked "Centro" (also "Ruta 39") go from the station to the main plaza. For taxis, you'll strike a better deal by skipping those in front of the station and walking to the street just in front; bargaining saves bucks. From the front door of the bus station, town is to the left. The bus depot is a few blocks south of the railroad station. Two blocks south of the bus station, Avenida Madero is a lively, noisy boulevard full of outdoor life and once replete with cheap, fairly good hotels. Most hotel business has moved downtown, however, and so proximity to the bus station and the city's cheapest eateries is about your only advantage here. But since decent and cheap hotel rooms are getting hard to find all over Monterrey, this is still your best bet if you must stick rigidly to your budget.

INFORMATION   The state of Nuevo León maintains an **Infotur** tourist-information office at the corner of Zaragoza and Matamoros, just off the Gran Plaza (down below, at street level; tel. 83/45-0870 or 45-0902), open Monday through Friday from 9am to 1pm and 3 to 7pm, and on Saturday and Sunday from 10am to 5pm.

Should your questions go beyond the Infotur desk, try the main office, a combination of the **State and Federal Tourism Offices,** on the second floor of the Kalos Building, Constitución and Zaragoza (tel. 83/44-4343, 40-1080, or 44-1169), open Monday through Friday from 8am to 4pm. The enthusiastic folks here have plenty of literature and maps, and periodically publish a very helpful *Guía Monterrey* (Monterrey Guide). Tourists with problems can contact this office for assistance Monday through Friday from 8am to 6pm.

CITY LAYOUT   The touristic heart of the city is centered on the modern **Gran Plaza,** which extends north to south from Juan Ignacio Ramón to Avenida de la Constitución and east and west between Ignacio Zaragoza and Juan Zuazua; and on the adjoining **Zona Rosa,** a pedestrians-only shopping-and-restaurant area between Zaragoza and Morelos. **Avenida Colón** is the main market street.

The intersection of Juárez and Aramberri divides Monterrey's street addresses. All numbers north or south of **Aramberri** are *norte* (north) or *sur* (south), respectively. All numbers east or west of **Juárez** are *oriente* (east) or *poniente* (west), respectively;

and the numbers start at this intersection (you might call it the "zero point") and go up.

GETTING AROUND

City bus travel for destinations I describe can be accomplished on the many **"Ruta 1"** buses. The trip from the bus station to the Zona Rosa is easy on Ruta 1. Catch the bus along Pino Suárez; fare is 15¢. You will pass the lovely Alameda Park, then watch the blocks tick off until Hidalgo downtown. The return trip to the bus terminal is also a Ruta 1 bus, only catch it along Juárez. Get off along Colón for a two-block walk to the bus station.

Monterrey's **monorail** became partially operational after I was there. The tourism office should have information on routes and how to use the system.

FAST FACTS

American Express The American Express office is located at Padre Mier Poniente 1424 (tel. 43-8299 or 45-2628).

Area Code The telephone area code is 171.

Consulates The **U.S. Consulate** is at Constitución 411 Poniente (tel. 45-2120). The **Consulate of Great Britain** is at Privada Tamazunchale 104, Colonia Valle, in Garza García in the southwest section of the city.

WHAT TO SEE & DO

Monterrey is a thriving business center, but it's not a major tourist destination although there are lots of Americans in town on business. Still, a day or so here can be spent pleasantly enough.

A STROLL AROUND THE GRAN PLAZA

Monterrey's crown jewel is the **Gran Plaza or Macro Plaza,** dedicated to the new wealth of Monterrey. Covering more than 40 acres of downtown, from the Palacio Municipal (City Hall) to the Palacio de Gobierno (State Capitol), the Gran Plaza has been called the largest in the world, and it may well be. Construction was accomplished in the record time of 3 years, a fact city leaders are proud of.

The enormity of the plaza gives its strollers a kind of anonymity—unlike the communal feeling common to most Mexican plazas. Nevertheless, lovers embrace along the concrete walkways, dwarfed by the spectacular modern architecture, and children play on the verdant lawns among the statuary in the "Hidden Garden" to the tune of bubbling artificial waterfalls and school bands practicing nearby. Gradually, the Gran Plaza is warming into the true "living room" of Monterrey.

Orient yourself at the south end of the plaza, with your back to the steel-and-glass **Palacio Municipal** and the Faro, or Commerce Beacon, ahead and to the right. Padre Mier is the only street that crosses the plaza between you and the Palacio de Gobierno. The following streets pass under the raised plaza: Zaragoza (southbound), Zuazua (northbound), Matamoros, Allende, and Ramón. Parking for 900 vehicles is available under the plaza.

IMPRESSIONS

You cross the border and enter another world, more foreign than Europe. The visitor to Europe, beneath the quality of strangeness, will feel that he is at the source of a culture that belongs to him. He can at least look and see his own roots. The visitor to Mexico will feel no such bond; he will stand perplexed.
—JOHN A. CROW, *MEXICO TODAY,* 1957

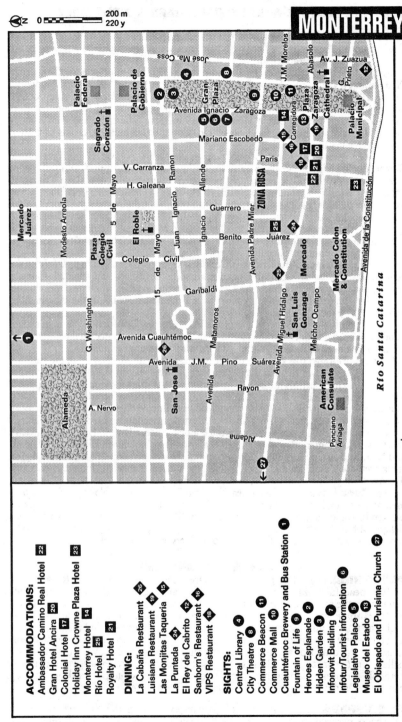

MONTERREY

200 m
220 y

Río Santa Catarina

Church ✝

ACCOMMODATIONS:
Ambassador Camino Real Hotel [22]
Gran Hotel Ancira [20]
Colonial Hotel [17]
Holiday Inn Crowne Plaza Hotel [23]
Monterrey Hotel [14]
Río Hotel [25]
Royalty Hotel [21]

DINING:
La Cabaña Restaurant [26]
Luisiana Restaurant [19]
Las Monjitas Taqueria [15]
La Puntada [24]
El Rey del Cabrito [12]
Sanborn's Restaurant [16]
VIPS Restaurant [18]

SIGHTS:
Central Library [4]
City Theatre [8]
Commerce Beacon [11]
Commerce Mall [10]
Cuauhtémoc Brewery and Bus Station [1]
Fountain of Life [9]
Heroes Esplanade [2]
Hidden Garden [3]
Infonovit Building [7]
Infotur/Tourist information [6]
Legislative Palace [5]
Museo del Estado [13]
El Obispado and Purísima Church [27]

462 · THE CENTRAL ROUTE FROM LAREDO & MONTERREY

On the east side of the plaza is the town's **cathedral,** begun in 1600 but not finished until 150 years later. The lavish paintings, sculpture, and decoration inside are typical of colonial Catholicism.

By far the tallest attraction is the vivid-orange, 230-foot-tall *Faro de Comercio* **(Commerce Beacon).** The well-known architect Luis Barragan designed the monolith for the 100th anniversary of the Monterrey Chamber of Commerce. The bright-orange color signifies the influence of Mexico's folklore. Atop the tower is a green laser that slices the night air every evening except Monday from 7 to 11pm. The fine green beam is barely detectable in the air until it strikes a far-off radio tower or tall building, creating a flash of brilliant green sparks.

Between Padre Mier and Morelos down the stairs on the Gran Plaza is the **Commercial Mall.** The gleaming shops below offer everything from antiques to hot dogs. Back atop the plaza, notice the innovative architecture of the **City Theater,** **Infonavit Building,** and the **Legislative Palace,** all built with a single theme. The *Fountain of Life,* designed by sculptor Luis Sanguino, is the major water-works on the plaza. Neptune with trident, the central figure of the fountain, was designed to symbolically end the water shortage that has plagued Monterrey throughout its history. A great fountain—unfortunately, the water problem persists. The **Central Library,** equally dramatic in its architecture, is next.

The **Bosque Hundido (Hidden Garden)** separates the *Fountain of Life* from the **Heroes Esplanade.** The small fountains, artworks, large trees, and waterfalls-fountain make this green space one of the most comfortable niches in all of Monterrey. Monuments to Hidalgo, Juárez, Escobedo, and Morelos are the largest works in the Esplanade of Heroes.

Farther on is the imposing facade of the **Palacio de Gobierno,** the state capitol building of Nuevo León, interesting for its Spanish-style patio and decorated hallways. The art deco **Federal Building** behind it to the north contains the post office.

The new **Museo del Estado de Nuevo León** (State Museum) is in the graceful, old building that faces the plaza and Zaragoza opposite the cathedral. Its yellow-ocher facade and arched porticos are easy to spot and there's a stone inscription showing that it was the Palacio Municipal from last century. Inside on the right are rooms honoring illustrious locals. Upstairs a series of rooms shows Mexico's origins with fossils and stone bowls, pre-Hispanic pottery from all over Mexico, a section devoted to the country's viceregal era, independence, revolution, the era of President Porfirio Díaz, and Mexico's reform years. An interesting display highlights Monterrey's commercial trio—steel, glass, and beer. And last, a few photographs remind of the U.S. invasion of Mexico (1914–16). It's a well-done museum and is worth the few minutes it takes to look it over. Open Tuesday through Sunday from 10am to 6pm; admission is free.

The **Zona Rosa** (Pink Zone), near the Gran Plaza, is a seven-block pedestrians-only area bounded by Zaragoza, Juárez, Padre Mier, and Morelos. At night and especially on weekends, while families and tourists stroll, the Zona Rosa becomes a street vendor's delight with balloon sellers, pushcarts of hot dogs, corn on the cob, and popcorn, and a few others who spread a small inventory of trinkets and toys on the paving stones.

OTHER ATTRACTIONS

PLAZA HIDALGO This pretty little square is the center of the Zona Rosa. It's the perfect, peaceful plaza for pigeon- and people-watching under the shady trees, while listening to the refreshing burble of the fountain. Be sure to drop into the stately **Gran Hotel Ancira** on the southwest corner of Jardín Hidalgo. The ceiling is about 60 feet high, the floor is alternating squares of black-and-white marble, and the plush chairs and tables give it the air of an elegant living room. A pianist serenades guests with soft music. In the center of all, a magnificent grand staircase coils down from an ornate gallery on the mezzanine. Both food and lodging here are expensive, but this is certainly the prime place to have a coffee or cool drink, write postcards, or pick up bus tour (Osetur) information (see "Organized Tours," below).

EL OBISPADO The best view of Monterrey is from the Bishop's Palace, El Obispado, perched atop a hill at the western end of Avenida Padre Mier. Built in the late 18th century to provide employment for the poor during a famine, it has played an important part in Monterrey's history. During the Mexican-American War U.S. troops slept there. During the yellow fever epidemics of 1898 and 1901 it became a hospital. In 1913 Pancho Villa converted it to a fort. Today it's a museum. Many historical objects, including the first printing press brought to northern Mexico (in 1813), have been moved here. Its chief asset, however, is its view of the city—excellent. It's open from 9am to 5pm and admission is 50¢.

When approaching El Obispado by car, head west on Padre Mier to the end of the street. Turn right, go one block, turn left, and follow the signs to El Obispado. The "Ruta 4" bus (green with a red stripe) on Padre Mier stops within a few blocks of El Obispado—a short but steep climb to the top (get off the bus where it turns left after the straight shot down Padre Mier, then keep walking up the winding streets to the top of the hill). To return to town, take the "Ruta 69" bus on Hidalgo.

A BREWERY TOUR Since Monterrey is synonymous with beer, go on a free tour of the **Cuauhtémoc Brewery,** Avenida Universidad Norte 2202 (tel. 75-2200 or 75-2124), Tuesday through Friday at 11am, noon, and 3pm. An added bonus Tuesday through Sunday from 9am to 5pm is the beer garden where visitors can sit and sip free Carta Blanca. Take a taxi to the brewery or any "Ruta 1" bus from Avenida Juárez.

A CRYSTAL FACTORY Monterrey is famous for its lead crystal, and there is a factory with a showroom specializing in the manufacture and sale of this beautiful product at the **Kristaluxus factory,** José María Vigil 400, Colonia del Norte at Ruíz Cortinez (tel. 83/51-6340 or 51-9393). Prices are only slightly lower than in the stores handling the crystal in town, but the selection is much greater and there's usually a section called "promotional specials," which may or may not be a real deal. Those who know a bit about crystal or prices beforehand can do well. All sales are final. The showroom is open Monday through Friday from 9am to 1pm and 2:30 to 6:30pm, and on Saturday from 9am to 1pm. Tours through the factory are held Monday through Friday at 10:30am, but call ahead to make arrangements.

There is no satisfactory bus service to Kristaluxus, so plan to take a taxi or the city tour, as it's quite a distance from anywhere else.

BULLFIGHTS/CHARREADAS Sunday is the day for bullfights at the **Plaza de Toros,** north of the city off Avenida Cuauhtémoc. Buy tickets at the Tourist Office (see above).

The **Charras Rodeo,** every Sunday at 11am, is held in Villa de Guadalupe, off Highway 85. Buses go to the town plaza; from there it's a bit of a walk to the Charras.

ORGANIZED TOURS

GUIDED TAXI TOURS Walk along Hidalgo near Plaza Hidalgo and every taxi driver and licensed tourist guide you encounter will offer to take you on a tour of Monterrey's sights—for a price. These guides carry identification and an official rate sheet, which you will see as soon as you attempt to bargain for a lower price. It's good to compare prices with several drivers and the official rates before making a commitment. Test the guide's English, then set down exactly what the tour will cover. A good city tour should take you to the Palacio del Gobierno, the Palacio Federal, Pursima Church, El Obispado, University City, and perhaps to the markets, all in about 3 hours. The "official" rate is $35 (regardless of the value of the peso) for the carload. A 4-hour tour in the guide's car to Horsetail Falls for one to five people is $40.

BUS TOURS Osetur (tel. 83/43-6616 or 44-6811) operates out of the San Francisco Building at the corner of San Francisco and Loma Grande, but the major downtown hotels (Ancira, etc.) provide information and sell tickets. If there is enough of a group, the Osetur bus plies Monterrey's hotspots Tuesday through Sunday. The morning tour begins at 9:30am and takes a slightly different, but equally pleasing, route each day—including the Gran Plaza and Kristaluxus, and either the museums or craft shops. The bilingual Osetur brochure includes a daily schedule. The afternoon trips, which are farther afield, begin at 1:30pm. Again, check the brochure as it indicates exactly where each tour goes. For example, on Friday you can visit La Boca

Dam (Bahía Escondido Resort) and Horsetail Falls, whereas on Wednesday it's García Caves. On Sunday there is a special tour that includes the Gran Plaza, Cesar's Curiosidades (arts and crafts), the Obispado (Bishop's Palace), Horsetail Falls, and Villa de Santiago.

Best of all is the price of $5.25 per person for either a morning or an afternoon tour, which includes the tour, entrance tickets at all visits, and the services of a bilingual host. The tour departs from Ocampo and Escobedo, behind the Hotel Ancira.

SHOPPING

The city's four main markets offer good shopping possibilities for Mexican crafts. While there's some overlap in merchandise, the differences are interesting enough so that a visit to all of them won't be repetitious. The **Mercado San Luis** is the first one on your right if you are walking from downtown on Ocampo. Rafters are jammed with funeral wreaths, and huge, colorful piñatas in whimsical shapes of elephants, burros, pigs, etc. At eye level you'll notice piles of hats and pottery and some of the largest casserole dishes with lids that I've seen, plus multitudes of baskets.

Across the street, behind **Más Que Todo** (another market), the **Mercado Colón** has more curios than its neighbor markets in baskets, pottery, hammocks, ceramic horses and cow's heads, copperware, guitars, live ducks, parakeets, parrots, and rabbits.

Cross the street pathway from the Colón to the **Mercado Constitución** and its load of baskets, pottery, miniature piñatas, puppets, lacquered gourds, and handmade toys, including toy airplanes.

An eight-block walk from the city center brings you to the **Mercado Juárez,** an even bigger feast for the senses. Here you'll find a huge section of fresh flowers, more funeral wreaths, baskets big enough to be transformed into clothes hampers, blown-glass animals, sequin portraits of Christ and Mary, stuffed frog bands, huaraches, kitchen utensils (including tortilla presses and hand juicers), wick lanterns, and medicinal soaps and herbs.

CARAPAN, Hidalgo Ote. 305. Tel. 45-4422.

For a truly superb collection of Mexican arts and crafts, stop at Carapan, not far from Plaza Hidalgo. Antiques and modern items, silver and tin, glass and pottery, textiles and toys—the collection is eclectic and obviously done with an expert's eye. Sr. Porfirio Sosa, the owner, has created a work of art (his shop) from works of art—the best of Mexican crafts—but prices are fairly high. Open Tuesday through Saturday from 9am to 1pm and 3 to 7pm.

ANTIGUEDADES "ELIZABETH," Hidalgo Ote. 233. Tel. 40-6151.

For a completely different sort of browsing and shopping, walk the few steps west along Hidalgo to Antiguedades "Elizabeth." The friendly shopkeepers encourage browsing in this cluttered old shop which holds an amazing assortment of stuff from darkened paintings to spurs and chandeliers. Open Tuesday through Saturday from 10am to 1:30pm and 4 to 7pm.

EVENING ENTERTAINMENT

The **Zona Rosa** tends to be the center of Monterrey's social life. On Sunday in summer there are band concerts in **Plaza Hidalgo** and other days of the week there are night concerts at City Hall.

Except for the nicer hotels, most of the bars in town discourage women—it's a real "macho" man's world in there. A good place to start is Los Fundadores, the plush, purple-velvet-trimmed lobby bar at the **Hotel Monterrey** (on Plaza Hidalgo and next to the old Palacio Municipal) or move on to the hotel's El Cid nightclub, which opens at 8pm—both have live music. At the **Holiday Inn Crowne Plaza,** on Constitución, just two blocks west and one block south of the Gran Plaza, there's the Mombasa, a piano bar, open from 8pm to 3am, or the Scaramouche for live entertainment from 10pm to 4am. For the more sedate and sophisticated, there's the elegant Bar 1900 at the **Gran Hotel Ancira,** right on Plaza Hidalgo.

NEARBY ATTRACTIONS

About 25 miles south of Monterrey, on Highway 85, are **La Boca Dam** (near the little village of Santiago) and Horsetail Falls (Cola de Caballo). La Boca has facilities for waterskiing, swimming, and boating, and features boat races almost every Sunday. There are picnic areas and restaurants nearby.

Horsetail Falls (small fee to enter) is located on a private hacienda named Vista Hermosa. Turn right off Highway 85 to the village of El Cercado, and travel about 4 miles up a rough but passable road. The road winds around for about 3 miles from the main road (making the falls accessible only by car or taxi), and leads to a parking area where horses and burros can be hired for the final half mile to the falls. If you walk, it's hard to resist the blandishments of the children who accompany you on burros, making reduced offers all the way until, when you're nearly there, they start bargaining about the return trip. I walked both ways and found it no particular strain.

WHERE TO STAY

The cheaper hotels in Monterrey are a distance from the town center's culture and nightlife. In fact, it's getting harder to find good, clean hotels within our budget range. As this is one of the three largest cities in Mexico and thus relatively high priced (compared to a provincial town), you may want to splurge for a day or two here, and plan to make up the deficit in a smaller, cheaper city later on in your trip. The prime area for accommodations is in and around the Zona Rosa, the modern downtown district near the Gran Plaza and Plaza Hidalgo, a small park nearby. I'll give the low-down on the cheaper hotels near the bus and train stations, 15 long blocks north of downtown, then move up to choices in and around the Zona Rosa.

DOUBLES FOR LESS THAN $25

HOTEL AMADO NERVO, Amado Nervo Nte. 1110, Monterrey, N.L. 64000. Tel. 83/75-4632. 78 rms (all with bath).
$ Rates: $16 single; $18 double with one bed, $21 double with two beds.
Pleasant, tidy, and semi-quiet, the tiled interior has a Mexican feel to it and attracts a sedate and family-oriented clientele. There are 28 air-conditioned rooms, and the rest have fans. Slightly aged blue and ocher bathroom tile (no toilet seats) give a homey feel. The hotel has a clean little corner café with an inexpensive comida corrida.

To get here from the front center door of the Central de Autobuses, cross Avenida Colón (the street in front of the bus station) and turn left. Amado Nervo Norte is the first cross street on the left—it's small and has no sign—almost directly across from the bus station. Turn right and walk two blocks; the hotel is on the right, next door to Hotel Posada (see below).

HOTEL NUEVO LEÓN, Amado Nervo Nte. 1007, Monterrey, N.L. 64000. Tel. 83/74-1900. 72 rms (all with bath).
$ Rates: $16 single; $18 double (with one bed), $24 double (with two beds).
Parking: $1.50 in a garage.
Almost the cheapest option in town, the Hotel Nuevo León is just two blocks from the bus station (follow the directions to the Hotel Amado Nervo, above, but walk only one block from Avenida Colón; it's on the left-hand side). The rooms are all doubles; all have fans (some have phones) and are clean, pleasant, and modern if a bit small. No English is spoken. The emphasis is on "comfort without waste" and cleanliness. Be sure to get a room off the street.

HOTEL POSADA, Amado Nervo Nte. 1138, Monterrey, N.L. 64000. Tel. 83/72-3908. 32 rms (all with bath). TV
$ Rates: $18 single; $20 double.
Your company within the Hotel Posada will be tired families. It's difficult to escape the growling of the buses in this area, but here at least the rooms have no exterior windows and instead face the beginnings of an interior courtyard hosting one potted plant. The rooms are very small but sport decent mattresses and box springs, and either a ceiling or table fan. If you are on the claustrophobic side, be sure to see a

room first. The minuscule restaurant next door can serve your needs until you head for town. The hotel is next door to the Hotel Amado Nervo (see above).

DOUBLES FOR LESS THAN $40

COLONIAL HOTEL, Hidalgo Ote. 475, Monterrey, N.L. 64000. Tel. 83/43-6791 or 42-2040. 85 rms (all with bath). TV
$ Rates: $38 single or double.

The Colonial Hotel is housed in one of the oldest buildings in Monterrey, only two blocks from the Gran Plaza, across the street from the Hotel Ancira and around the corner from Sanborn's and the Zona Rosa's Plaza Hidalgo. Despite its ideal location within walking distance of most of the city's sights, rates for the rooms are surprisingly low. The redecorated rooms feature stenciled walls, tub/shower combinations, and good beds. Some rooms have telephones but the antiquated switchboard causes problems in dialing and receiving calls. Most of the rooms have window air conditioners, but test yours to be sure it's working before you take a room.

WORTH THE EXTRA BUCKS

FASTOS HOTEL, Av. Colón Pte. 956, Monterrey, N.L. 64000. Tel. 83/72-3774 or 72-3721. 150 rms (all with bath). A/C TV TEL
$ Rates: $45–$60 single; $53–$66 double.

Directly across from the bus station, at the corner of Villagran, Fastos is the premier place to stay in this area. It is a seven-story establishment with all the comforts of a four-star hotel, but at prices well below that standing. The carpeted guest rooms are done in natural wood, soft pastel colors, brick, and red tile. Cheerful clerks welcome you at the front desk; the clientele here is mostly Mexican businessmen. A refundable $35 deposit is required at registration. Less luxurious rooms, without TV, air conditioning, or carpeting, cost less and require a $30 refundable key deposit. The Fastos has a bright and spotlessly clean, air-conditioned restaurant, the Fastory, open 24 hours a day.

BEST WESTERN HOTEL MONTERREY, Morelos 574 (Apdo. Postal 349), Monterrey, N.L. 64000. Tel. 83/43-5120 or 43-8820, or toll free 800/528-1234 in the U.S. 197 rms (all with bath). A/C MINIBAR TV TEL
$ Rates: $72 single or double (one to three people).

This is a great place to stay right on the Gran Plaza. Since the recent total refurbishing of its rooms, no single description is sufficient for all rooms since each floor is furnished and colored differently. Rooms offer such touches as bedside control of air conditioning and TV on-and-off switches. Some bathrooms have hairdryers. Each floor has an ice machine—something of a rarity in Mexico. No hotel in the city can top this one for views of the beautiful Plaza Zaragoza and Gran Plaza, so try to get a room on the front.

HOTEL RÍO, Av. Padre Mier 1194, Monterrey, N.L. 64000. Tel. 83/44-9410 or 44-9510. 400 rms (all with bath). A/C MINIBAR TV TEL
$ Rates: $85 single or double; $193 suite. **Parking:** Free, adjacent.
The Hotel Río strives successfully to best its competitors and encroach on its superiors. All rooms in its towers have been refurnished in tones of pale gray and dusty blue, with light-tone furniture and thick carpeting. The rooms come close to the feeling of comfort and luxury you find at the more expensive Ancira. Each guest room has individually controlled heat, two double beds, showers, and some tubs. On the second floor there's a tennis court and large pool, with an even-larger sunning area and a small play area for children. The attractive restaurant is open 24 hours daily. While the $9.50 lunch buffet is a bit steep for our budget, it features a good fresh salad section.

You'll find the Río if you look up for the big red letters on top of this high-rise hotel six short blocks west of the Gran Plaza, at Garibaldi.

HOTEL AMBASSADOR CAMINO REAL, Hidalgo Ote. 310, Monterrey, N.L. 64000. Tel. 83/42-2040 or 40-9390, or toll free 800/228-3000 in the U.S. 240 rms (all with bath). A/C MINIBAR TV TEL
$ Rates: $128–$152 double. There's a 50% weekend discount.
Just two blocks from Gran Plaza, between Melchor Ocampo and Hidalgo, the Hotel Ambassador Camino Real is a luxurious and modern hotel with fine colonial accents such as bevelled and etched glass and polished marble. It's the favorite of those for whom price is no obstacle and luxury living is second nature.

A new health club has been added next to the hotel, connected by a second-story bridge over a newly created park. With this addition guests are offered use of a tennis court, pool, whirlpool, aerobics, sauna, and massage, which are separate for men and women. The Ambassador is a Westin hotel, so reservations can be made in the U.S.

GRAN HOTEL ANCIRA, Hidalgo and Escobedo (Apdo. Postal 697), Monterrey, N.L. 64000. Tel. 83/45-1060 or 45-7575, or toll free 800/327-0200 in the U.S. 246 rms (all with bath). A/C TV TEL
$ Rates: $124–$152 single or double. **Parking:** Free, across the street.
To frequent Monterrey travelers, Monterrey is synonymous with a stay at the Ancira. At the very least, no trip to Monterrey is complete without at least dropping into the magnificent lobby, ordering a drink or coffee, and letting the waiter offer you a selection of the day's newspapers while you soak it all in. Such a handsome respite is reasonable: A cup of cappuccino, for example, costs about $1.30, and you can stay as long as you want. The hotel has as much turn-of-the-century atmosphere and elegance as any in Mexico. All the amenities of a fine five-star hotel are in place: a restaurant, Bar 1900 and a lobby bar, and a small heated swimming pool on the first floor. On the southwest corner of Plaza Hidalgo, one block West of the Gran Plaza, it's part of the Inter-Continental hotel chain.

WHERE TO EAT

Monterrey's best budget-priced downtown eateries look like American chain restaurants, with plastic-laminate counters and booths and illustrated menus. But the food is Mexican and very tasty, so it's easy to ignore the atmosphere.

MEALS FOR LESS THAN $5

LA PUNTADA, Av. Hidalgo Ote. 123. Tel. 40-9985.
Specialty: MEXICAN.
$ Prices: Breakfast 50¢–$1.25; main courses $1.35–$8.
Open: Mon–Sat 7:30am–10pm.

A light, bright Mexican lunch place, La Puntada boasts chrome-and-plastic tables and chairs, a lunch counter, lots of windows, and a loyal local clientele. Though modern, it's also somehow very Mexican. The menu includes breakfast plates, sandwiches, tacos, and other Mexican treats. The most expensive item on the entire menu is T-bone steak. With hotcakes just slightly more than a dollar, this is probably the best breakfast bargain downtown.

To get here from the Gran Plaza, walk three blocks west on Morelos to Galeana and turn left (pass the Taquería Las Monjitas) and turn right at the next street (Hidalgo); the restaurant is about three-quarters of a block on the right.

MEALS FOR LESS THAN $10

TAQUERÍA LAS MONJITAS, Escobedo 936-B. Tel. 45-1319.
Specialty: MEXICAN.
$ Prices: Appetizers $1.60–$5.25; main courses $2.50–$8.
Open: Daily noon–9:30pm.

For good local color, try Taquería Las Monjitas (The Little Nuns), where women dressed as nuns do the cooking and waiting on tables. Service is swift and friendly. The sirloin tacos with fried onions and a spritz of lime juice are quite filling and good. Flautas (filled, rolled tortillas) and quesadillas (tortillas stuffed with cheese) or a small steak might also be an option. The "nun" theme restaurant appears to be popular in Monterrey—there are two other "little nun" eateries in the same vicinity. This one is in the Zona Rosa. From the Gran Plaza walk one block west on Morelos to Escobedo and turn left; the restaurant is about half a block down the street on the left (across from Sanborn's—see below).

SANBORN'S, Escobedo 920.
  Specialty: MEXICAN.
  $ Prices: Breakfast $2–$5; appetizers $1.40–$3; main courses $2.70–$10.70.
  Open: Daily 7:30am–11pm.

Despite its gringo-sounding name, Sanborn's is a Mexican chain of variety stores with restaurants and lunch counters that you'll learn to rely on in your Mexican travels. The stores are bright, modern, spacious, air-conditioned, and stocked with jewelry, gifts, clothing, luggage, stationery, candies and nuts, books (some in English), records, newspapers and magazines—you name it. The restaurants, usually with a section of booths or tables and also a lunch counter, serve Mexican food that is tasty and wholesome, though not extraordinary. At breakfast there's a varied assortments of eggs, hotcakes, toast, refried beans (a breakfast staple in Mexico), and steak. The orange juice is fresh. Later in the day, come for enchiladas, tacos, puntas de filete (sirloin tips), and various sandwiches, including hamburgers. Refreshing, cold beers come in big, blue ceramic Chinese "Willow Ware" mugs.

Sanborn's is in the Zona Rosa. From the Gran Plaza, walk one block down Morelos to Escobedo and turn left; it's about half a block down on the right.

VIPS, Hidalgo Ote. 401, at the corner of Carranza. Tel. 42-5073.
  Specialty: FAST FOOD/REGIONAL/INTERNATIONAL.
  $ Prices: Hamburgers and sandwiches $4–$6; Mexican dishes $4.50–$6; main courses $5.50–$10.
  Open: Daily 24 hours.

Always jammed, this upscale fast-food restaurant, with bright colors and lots of windows, has a varied menu which includes blueberry malts and carrot cake. Because service is good you never have to wait long for a table.

To get here from the Gran Plaza, walk two blocks on Morelos and turn left onto Carranza; VIPS is on the left at the far end of the street.

MEALS FOR LESS THAN $15

LA CABAÑA, Matamoros Pte. 318. Tel. 42-9523.
  Specialty: MEXICAN.
  $ Prices: Appetizers $1.50–$4.50; combination plates $10.50; main courses $6.25–$15.
  Open: Sun–Thurs 11am–1am, Fri–Sat 11am–2am.

For an atmospheric lunch or dinner, go to La Cabaña, about eight blocks from the Gran Plaza on Matamoros between Piño Suárez and Cuauhtémoc. This is an unlikely location, and you'll think that you're lost or that I've given you the wrong address, but persevere and you will indeed come upon a rustic-style ranch house with rough wood and stained glass, air conditioning, and a menu that lists lots of huge and satisfying Mexican combination plates, and such à la carte dishes as steaks, fish, shrimp, and Mexican specialties.

EL REY DEL CABRITO, at the corner of Dr. Coss and Constitución. Tel. 45-3232.
  Specialty: MEXICAN.
  $ Prices: Appetizers $3–$8; cabrito (main courses) $5–$11.
  Open: Daily 10am–10pm.

The best cabrito in Monterrey is at El Rey del Cabrito. You can't miss this large gold-and-brown building. Fifty or more goat kids are usually roasting over the coals in the front window, so there's no mistaking the specialty here. Inside, the decor is Mexican-western-eclectic, with a stuffed pouncing puma in one corner, dozens of other stuffed animals, saddles and tack scattered about, old guns mounted on the walls, and a fountain bubbling in the middle of the downstairs dining room. Not only is this the true "king of cabrito," but with 500 seats it's also one of Monterrey's largest restaurants.

To get here from the east end of the Gran Plaza (by the modern glass-and-steel Palacio Municipal) and facing south, turn left and carefully cross the welter of streets fanning out from the end of the plaza, all leading to Constitución.

MEALS FOR LESS THAN $20

LE PAVILLON, in the Hotel Ambassador, at the corner of Hidalgo and Carranza. Tel. 42-2040, ext. 205.
Specialty: INTERNATIONAL.
$ Prices: Breakfast $2–$5; appetizers $6–$9; main courses $8–$25.
Open: 7am–10pm.
If you come at breakfast there's a selection of fruits, yogurts, pan dulce, eggs, and cereals. The lunch menu includes meat dishes, salads, and soups, as well as tempting desserts. The dinner menu lists numerous soups, red snapper, beef medallions in chipotle sauce, and similar delights, all elegantly served in this demure, pastel-toned dining room. It's two blocks west of the Gran Plaza, between Melchor Ocampo and Hidalgo.

RESTAURANT LUISIANA, Plaza Hidalgo. Tel. 43-1561.
Specialty: CONTINENTAL/MEXICAN. **Reservations:** Recommended.
$ Prices: Appetizers $6–$15; main courses $11–$28.
Open: Daily noon–midnight.
The Restaurant Luisiana has been serving loyal customers for as many years as anyone can remember. The attractive dining rooms are plush and elegant, the food an inviting assortment of cuisines, heavy on seafood and steaks. Adventurous souls can sample such traditional delicacies as maguey worms with guacamole—no doubt the Mexican counterpart of escargots and the most expensive appetizer on the menu.

EN ROUTE TO . . .

CIUDAD VICTORIA If your destination is Mexico's East Coast beginning with Ciudad Victoria (covered in Chapter 18), the distance is 180 miles and takes about 4 hours by bus or car. Those driving should fill up the tank in Monterrey, as unleaded gas may be scarce until Ciudad Victoria. From Monterrey, go southeast on Highway 85, a two-lane road that's mostly straight and fast, with plenty of greenery and the majestic Sierra Madre range towering up on the right (west). There's little else to be seen, however, except an occasional passing car, bus, or cyclist, and lazy cattle grazing by the road. Between Linares and Ciudad Victoria is sugarcane country.

The first town of size is 50 miles southeast, **Montemorelos,** Nuevo León (alt. 1,609 ft.; pop. 18,000), described as Mexico's "Naranjiera Capital" (Orange Capital). Montemorelos is hot in summer and doesn't ever have too much to offer, except the mid-July fiesta, the pecan fair in mid-September, and the sight of the orange and lemon trees in bloom from February to March.

Some 30 miles south of Montemorelos is **Linares,** Nuevo León (alt. 1,272 ft.; pop. 62,000), a clean, pleasant town that is the center of a farming area and some small industry (bricks, furniture). Ciudad Victoria is approximately 100 miles south of Linares.

THE SILVER CITIES From Monterrey to Saltillo, take Highway 40; then bypass Saltillo and connect to Highway 57, which goes all the way, through San Luis Potosí, and Querétaro, to Mexico City. But most people use this route to branch off to the Silver Cities (Chapter 16), beginning with San Luis Potosí and southwest of there on Highway 110 to Dolores Hidalgo and Guanajuato and on Highway 111 to San Miguel de Allende. Between Saltillo and San Luis Potosí is a barren dessert of scrubby grass, cactus, and joshua trees on a road that's nearly straight and is one of the most boring in the country. Once you arrive in San Luis, the scenery improves. There's usually unleaded gas in the main towns along this route, but fill up at every chance anyway.

SAN LUIS POTOSÍ Since the loop around Saltillo was constructed, there's little reason to stop there. Most people barrel on down Highway 57 for the first night at

San Luis Potosí, which is possible by starting early at the border. However, en route from either Monterrey or Saltillo to San Luis Potosí, 140 miles south of Saltillo, is the ghost town of **Real de Catorce,** one of Mexico's most unusual places, like an 18th-century town preserved in a time capsule, and hidden in the mountains west of Matehuala. It's a must if you can spare the time. Be aware, however, that the two hotels in Real de Catorce are comfortable enough but very rustic, and the restaurants are the same. Photographers, historians, lovers of the unusual in Mexico, and people who don't mind a little uncertainty in their travels will count this among the high points of a trip south of the border.

After the discovery of silver in 1773, Real de Catorce became one of Mexico's top three silver-producing towns by the early 1800s, with a population of over 40,000. Streets lined with mansions owned by wealthy mine owners sprouted side by side along with an opera house and a mint. The Mexican Revolution brought the downfall of the town; the mines were flooded and townspeople fled to safety elsewhere and never returned, although many descendants retain ownership and in recent years a few mines have reopened. The latest population census attributes almost 11,000 people to this town, but locals guess that only around 2,000 people live in the immediate area.

What travelers find on arrival is a neat, mountaintop town of closed-up crumbling rock-walled mansions, with cactus and brush growing on the rooflines, a church that attracts 25,000 penitents every October 2, a mint which is sometimes open for "tours," a stone cockpit arena, a fascinating cemetery, a small museum, and a few stores selling food, mining equipment, and Huichol Indian clothing and folk art. Miners and prospectors come to town on horseback and hitch their steeds outside the stores. Sanborn's Auto Insurance/Travel in McAllen, Texas, sells a book about the town, *The Incredible City,* by Lucy H. Wallace. Another book often found in Matehuala is *El Real de Catorce* (in Spanish), by Octaviano Cabrera Ipiña.

On the northern edge of Matehuala there's a sign on Highway 57 which is the Spanish equivalent of "Turn Here for Ghost Town," but it's misleading in the distance it gives, which is just to the turnoff and not to Real de Catorce. Although it's only 30 miles from the turnoff from Highway 57 to Real de Catorce, it takes an hour and a half to drive on a well-maintained cobblestone road that winds up 9,000 feet in the mountains past an onyx quarry and through several tiny, crumbling adobe-walled villages. You'll know you've arrived when you reach the tunnel, which is 2 miles long and the only entrance into the town. Since it's one way, young men at both ends regulate traffic with walkie talkies; there's a small fee for this service. Usually there is little traffic, but in the past deaths from fumes have occurred during the busy October 2 festival season when a stalled car stopped traffic in the tunnel. After passing through the tunnel, take the narrow high street to the right, up into the town. There's one small hotel on the main street and another one on the far side of town on the road to the cemetery. There's only one phone—at the grocery/general store—so it's impossible to make hotel reservations. In winter, bring your heavy clothes, for you're almost 2 miles high and hotels have no heat. Hiking boots are useful, since exploring the area on foot is one of the pleasures here. It's also possible to find horses to rent, done very informally of course, since no one does that exclusively for a living.

Although the town is off the beaten track, hotels sometimes fill up by nightfall. My advice is to arrive and get a room no later than 3pm. If there are no vacant rooms, you'll still have time to look around briefly and return to the highway before dark. If you can't arrive by 3pm, spend the night at one of the several motels on the highway at Matehuala, then get an early start the next day.

Note: Don't plan to go to Real de Catorce the week before or after October 2. Pilgrims honoring the venerated black Christ in the church in Catorce begin arriving and tax the town and its few services beyond capacity.

Matehuala (alt. 5,085 ft.; pop. 55,000) is the second-largest city in the state of San Luis Potosí, although you wouldn't know it as it's so small in appearance. But it's a tidy town with a good central market.

SALTILLO   Taking Highway 40 in the Saltillo direction, you'll find **Chipinque Mesa** about 13 miles from Monterrey. Turn left at Colonia del Valle, pay a small toll, and drive up the pine-covered slopes of the **Sierra Madre.** The road culminates in a breathtaking view of Monterrey from a 4,200-foot plateau.

You can also travel 15 miles along Highway 40 to the village of **Santa Catarina.** Turn left here, go 2 miles more, and you'll find yourselves at **Huasteca Canyon,** a massive rock formation framing dangerously deep ravines. This trip can be hazardous to your car as well as to your nerves.

About 27 miles from Monterrey on Highway 40 are the **Garcia Caves** (Grutas de Garcia), with the usual stalactites and stalagmites, huge chambers, and a subterranean lake.

2. SALTILLO

53 miles SW of Monterrey, 140 miles N of Real de Catorce

GETTING THERE   By Plane   Plane service on Mexicana between San Antonio, Texas, San Luis Potosí and Mexico City was suspended at press time.

By Train   The first-class *El Regiomontaño* departs Nuevo Laredo at 3:15pm and arrives in Saltillo at 10pm. From Mexico City, it leaves at 6pm and arrives in Saltillo at 5:44am.

From Piedras Negras (across from Eagle Pass, Texas), *El Coahuilense* leaves at 1pm and arrives in Saltillo at 8:30pm. Those driving to Eagle Pass to board the train across the border can get information on secured parking lots from the Eagle Pass Chamber of Commerce (tel. 512/773-3224).

By Bus   Buses run to Saltillo from all major towns in Mexico.

By Car   You can drive here on Highway 40 from Monterrey, on Highway 57 from Monclova and Piedras Negras (across the border from Eagle Pass, Texas), or on Highway 40 from Torreón. If your destination is farther into the heartland of Mexico, you can leave the border at Nuevo Laredo around 8am and reach San Luis Potosí before night, so there's no need to stay in Saltillo.

DEPARTING   By Train   *El Regiomontaño* leaves Saltillo at 5:45am and arrives in Nuevo Laredo around noon. Going to Mexico City, it leaves Saltillo at 10pm, arriving in San Luis Potosí at 3:45am and in Mexico City at 10am. If your destination is San Miguel de Allende, see Chapter 16 for details on getting there by train via San Luis Potosí.

El Coahuilense leaves Saltillo at 7am and arrives in Piedras Negras (opposite Eagle Pass, Texas) at 2:30pm.

By Bus   Numerous bus lines operate from Saltillo, including **Transportes del Norte** (tel. 7-0901), **Transportes Monterrey Saltillo** (tel. 7-0195 and 4-2614), **Autobuses Anahuac** (tel. 7-0135), **Tres Estrellas de Oro** (tel. 2-3118), and **Camiones de los Altos** (tel. 7-0195).

Saltillo (alt. 5,280 ft.; pop. 441,000) is the mile-high capital of the state of Coahuila, and holds the State College of Coahuila and the International University, both of which attract American students during the summer. But for most people it's merely an overnight on the journey to a more interesting Mexico farther south. The main tower of the two-century-old cathedral, on the Plaza de Armas, offers a good view of the city, but this, together with the tree- and lake-filled Alameda Park, and shopping present just about the only diversions for the wanderer in this once-colonial, now-industrial city with its noise and air pollution.

ORIENTATION

ARRIVING   The **railroad station** is at the southwest corner of town on Avenida Carranza (Hwy. 57), which parallels Allende. It's rather far to walk; best to flag a taxi.

The **bus station** is inconveniently located on the bypass loop (Calzada L.

Echeverria) on the southern edge of town. If you know when you'll be leaving, it's best to buy your ticket when you arrive to save yourself a trip back. Buses marked "Centro" go to the downtown area and stop in front. A taxi will cost around $5, or it's a 30-minute walk.

INFORMATION The **Tourist Information Office** is in the Convention Center, Boulevard Fundadores km 6.5 (tel. 5-4444 or 5-4504), quite a distance east from downtown.

CITY LAYOUT Saltillo's town center is the zócalo or **Plaza de Armas,** bounded by Zaragoza and Hidalgo running north and south, and Aldama and Victoria running east and west. Here, you'll find the city hall, cathedral and state capital. The main shopping street is **Calle Victoria,** runing west from the zócalo. The **market** is on Allende, two long blocks north of the zócalo.

FAST FACTS

Area Code The telephone area code is 841.

Climate The climate is excellent, with gentle breezes that sweep down from the mountains to dispel lingering heat and humidity in midsummer. Were it not for the dust that comes with the breezes, Saltillo would be ideal. In winter it's chillier than you'd expect—note that most of the budget hotels are not heated.

Currency Exchange The bank across the street from the post office will change money Monday through Friday from 9am to noon.

Post Office The post office at Calle Victoria 453 is open daily, including Sunday.

WHAT TO SEE & DO
A STROLL AROUND DOWNTOWN

Plaza de Armas, or zócalo as it is called locally, between Aldama and Victoria, is centered on a graceful fountain near where Saltillo's more sedate citizens fill wrought-iron benches to take the air in the evenings. Take a close look at the 17th-century **cathedral,** actually two separate naves with a facade that's truly an eyeful. The style is Churrigueresque, a 17th-century Spanish mutation of baroque that carries the style to even more ornate extremes. The nave on the left is quite impressive, but walk all the way to the altar in the nave on the right to see the elaborate side altars of gilded wood. Climb the cathedral's main tower for a good view of the city.

Plaza Acuna, north of the zócalo, is bounded by Allende, Aldama, Padre Flores, and the market, and has action throughout the day: sellers of boiled corn, tacos, candies, and other treats; an army of shoeshine boys; a car being raffled; a public photographer with an antediluvian camera; another man with a more modern camera taking pictures of children astride a plaster horse; a kiddie rocketship ride; old men sunning on benches; pitchmen selling gizmos of every conceivable type. Don't miss this microcosm.

The "formal" park is all that Acuna is not. Saltillo's third park is the **Alameda,** a tree-and-pond oasis at the opposite (west) end of Calle Victoria from Allende, a good place for a late-afternoon stroll.

SHOPPING

The town's main market, **Mercado Juárez,** next to Plaza Acuna, is a three-story enclosed building worthy of a look, especially if you're looking for Mexican crafts. The ground level has rows of souvenirs, from Saltillo serapes to hats and pottery. There are a lot of uninteresting mass-produced items, but among them you'll spot some collectable folk art. Upstairs you'll find food, a restaurant section, piñatas, bird cages, and more pottery and baskets.

After a brief visit to the market, serious shoppers should direct their steps to the main shopping street, **Calle Victoria.** Two doors away from the town's post office is one of the big stores selling the products that give Saltillo its claim to fame, namely the colorful wool or cotton serapes.

EL SALTILLERO, Calle Victoria 469.

Here the famous striped Saltillo serapes come in every shape, size, and color combination, and are reasonably priced. The store also holds a sizable assortment of other handcrafts, including embroidered blouses and shirts, articles in painted papier-mâché (including intricate candelabra), and things made from copper, brass, alabaster, leather, glass, and tin. Some of the helpful staff speak English. It's open Monday through Saturday from 9am to 1pm and 3 to 7pm.

SALTILLO SILVER FACTORY, Calle Victoria 212. Tel. 42-2726.

Even by U.S. standards prices are rather high, but you'll find hand-woven wool sweaters and serapes, wood carvings, sconces, sculptured candles, and of course, a gleaming selection of silver, including some lovely and unusual jewelry. Ask to see the silversmiths at work next door Monday through Friday. Open Monday through Saturday from 9am to 7:30pm.

ZAPATERA VICTORIA, Allende Nte. 642.

Those in the market for a pair of men's boots should try the Zapatera Victoria, half a block from the Restaurant Principal. This long-established bootery offers some handsome footwear in suede and leather. It's open daily from 9am to 1pm and 3 to 8pm.

ESE, Perez Trevino 345, at Padre Flores. Tel. 22-2344.

For fresh Veracruz coffee, either whole or ground, ESE is just down from Allende and beside the market. It's a little cheaper here than at the branch in Monterrey, and there are a couple of grades to choose from—or you can have them mixed. Prices are between $4 and $5 per kilo. Stock up on coffee here. ESE is open Monday through Saturday from 9am to 1pm and 3 to 8pm, and on Sunday from 9am to 1pm.

SPECIAL EVENTS

Those who visit Saltillo in August may be in time for the big fair and exposition, the **Fiesta de Santo Cristo,** an annual event which begins on August 6 displaying local achievements in agriculture and industry art and culture as well as religious ceremonies, traditional dances, and fireworks.

On September 13 the town celebrates the **Fiesta del Ojo de Agua** with commercial and art expositions.

WHERE TO STAY

The hotel situation in Saltillo is bad—and getting worse. The half dozen downtown hostelries that once surrounded guests with at least a modicum of colonial charm—at low prices—have lost business to the new Rodeway Inn and Camino Real hotels on the outskirts of town. As the trade moved out, downtown hotels dwindled. Short of settling into one of the out-of-town hotels at exorbitant prices, you can check out a few places downtown.

To guide you to your hotel and restaurant choices, I'll use the lively Plaza Acuna, next to the market, as a central point, as it's within easy walking distance of all the places listed below.

HOTEL CENTRAL, Echeverría 231, Saltillo, Coah. 25000. Tel. 841/2-8410. 53 rms (all with bath).
$ Rates: $10.50 single; $12 double.
This is a no-frills place, inside and out. The exterior is plain unfinished wood, rivaled only by the starkness of the lobby with its five "waiting room"–style chairs lined up against the wall and a TV pressed against the opposite wall. The rooms, though small, are adequate and clean, with ceiling fans and nice bathrooms too. The Panificadora next door makes delicious sugar doughnuts. The hotel is across from the bus station.

HOTEL PREMIER, Allende Nte. 508, Saltillo, Coah. 25000. Tel. 841/2-1050. 54 rms (all with bath). A/C TV TEL
$ Rates: $17.50 single; $19.50 double. **Parking:** Free, next door.
Considering what you get, the Hotel Premier charges a bit too much. Be sure to look

at a few rooms before you choose one. The downstairs rooms have been remodeled and are a better value than the rooms upstairs, which are scheduled for remodeling.

To get here from Plaza Acuna, go north on Allende; the hotel is on the right side of the street.

HOTEL URDINOLA, Calle Victoria 211, Saltillo, Coah. 25000. Tel. 841/4-0940 or 4-0993. 46 rms (all with bath). TV TEL
$ Rates: $19 single; $21 double. **Parking:** Free, next door.

One of Saltillo's better budget lodging choices for many years, the Urdinola is the place to stay for charm. Originally built in colonial style many years ago, it has undergone periodic renovation to keep it presentable. Some of its nicer features have escaped the ravages of modernization, though: the huge white granite stairway that leads to the second floor and a large stained-glass window, a lovely long sunny patio onto which the rooms open, an elegant ballroom upstairs with a beautiful carved wood fireplace, and a fine tile fountain at the patio's end.

The Urdinola's location on the main shopping street is ideal: From Plaza Acuna, go south on Allende to Guadalupe Victoria (one long block, not counting small side streets); turn right onto Victoria and the hotel is on the left about half a block down.

HOTEL SAADE, Aldama Pte. 397, Saltillo, Coah. 25000. Tel. 841/2-9120 or 2-9121. Fax 841/2-9129. 72 rms (all with bath). A/C
$ Rates: $20–$22 single; $24–$28 double. **Parking:** Free, nearby.

Just down from the San Jorge Hotel (see below) the Hotel Saade is the best-priced downtown hotel by a couple of dollars. It's another of Saltillo's well-kept older hotels, but you might not think so if you judge by the nondescript entrance on a street that sometimes churns with street vendors from the nearby market (it's a block west of Plaza Acuna, where Acuna intersects Aldama). Inside, the clean, quiet lobby and reception area dispel initial misgivings. There are three price categories at the Saade. Those at the low end don't have TV, carpet, or telephone but are quite comfortable. Those at the high end have it all. Be sure to see your room first to choose among those with windows overlooking the street or rooftops and those with windows opening to the parking driveway. The fourth-floor restaurant is closed on Sunday.

SAN JORGE HOTEL, Manuel Acuna 240, Saltillo, Coah. 25000. Tel. 841/2-2222. 120 rms (all with bath). A/C TV TEL
$ Rates: $41 single; $48 double.
The San Jorge is Saltillo's best downtown hotel and is just two blocks from the Plaza Acuna (1½ blocks west on Aldama, then half a block left on Acuna). All the rooms here are modern, heated, clean, and carpeted, with stucco walls and comfortable chairs with leather seats. Quaint pueblo scenes are painted on the headboards and matching bedside stands. The cheerfully decorated El Mirador Restaurant on the sixth floor has a splendid view of the city. Outside the rooftop dining room is a pleasant, breezy patio with a pool and lounge area.

WHERE TO DINE

BOCA DEL RÍO, Acuna Nte. 533. Tel. 2-4105.
Specialty: SEAFOOD.
$ Prices: Appetizers $2.40–$6; main courses $4.50–$9.
Open: Daily 9am–11pm.

Enjoy a delicious meal here from the frosty mug of ice-cold beer, fresh-baked warm bread, and a huge serving of savory guacamole to a variety of excellent seafood dishes. This clean and comfortable restaurant with woven leather chairs sports a huge copper sailfish over the counter. There's a tasty fish cocktail, spicy octopus with shrimp and rice, and the Boca del Río's star performance: the jumbo shrimp en brochette, a tremendous helping of food that's almost heavenly. The excellent fish filet mojo de ajo comes with a generous garnish of garlic. Large portions are the rule here.

To get here from Plaza Acuna, walk west on Aldama one block to Acuna, then turn right onto Acuna and walk 2½ more blocks; the restaurant is on the left-hand side.

RESTAURANT PRINCIPAL, Allende Nte. 702. Tel. 4-3384.
Specialty: MEXICAN.
$ Prices: Appetizers $1–$3; main courses $4.50–$9.
Open: Mon–Sat 8am–midnight.

Bright and modern, with brick arches and a tile kitchen open to view, this is a pleasant place to try the succulent (although a bit greasy) kid cooking over coals in the window. While you can have other things here—chicken or T-bone, for instance— you should come here to have the specialty of the house, cabrito, which comes in all sizes and parts from a leg or kid kidneys to a steamed head of kid "cabecita" (no kidding) or fritada (goat-blood soup). Platters come with a side order of delicious beans. The Principal is four blocks north of Plaza Acuna on Allende, at the corner of Alessio Robles.

EL ZAGUAN and RESTAURANT SAN SEBASTIAN, Ocampo 338. Tel. 47-7667.
Specialty: MEXICAN.
$ Prices: Breakfast $2–$4.50 (San Sebastian only); appetizers $1–2; main courses $3–$6.
Open: El Zaguan, Mon–Sat noon–2am; Restaurant San Sabastian, Mon–Sat 7am–11pm.

For two casual dining/music/bar choices in Saltillo, a couple of blocks from the main square, try El Zaguan downstairs and the Restaurant San Sebastian upstairs. The three-story building, built around an interior courtyard, formerly quartered Franciscan priests assigned to the San Sebastian church across the street. Cushioned sitting areas of El Zaguan are built around numerous arches and rock walls below ground in what was formerly a warehouse for the church. It's cozy and conducive to conversation. Inexpensive drinks and light snacks are staples. From 9pm to 2am a romantic trio plays and there's a cover charge then.

On the second floor, the Restaurant San Sebastian has balcony windows overlooking the street and church, and shares quarters with an art gallery in an adjacent wing. The short, simple, and inexpensive combination breakfast, lunch, and dinner menu has soups, salads, and a small selection of Mexican specialties and breakfasts of fruit, yogurt, eggs, and juice. This is a favorite spot for late-evening desserts and coffee.

To find these places, with your back to the cathedral, cross the plaza and straight ahead is Ocampo, a tiny street between Padre Flores and Allende. Follow it a half a block and the restaurants are on the right.

EN ROUTE TO GUADALAJARA

Highway 54 south of Saltillo is the favored route of those traveling from the border to Guadalajara and the Pacific Coast. From Saltillo, it's 470 miles to Guadalajara, at least 11 hours by car and longer by bus. Zacatecas, almost equidistant between Saltillo and Guadalajara, is 270 miles south of Saltillo and is a wonderful place to stop on the way; but the drive between the two will be at least 6 hours, so start early.

CHAPTER 16

THE COLONIAL SILVER CITIES

Between the mountain ranges of the Sierra Madre lies the heartland of Mexico, a high plateau sculpted by rains and rivers over the eons, now a maze of highlands, lakes, and valleys. This is Anahuac, the center of ancient Mexican civilization, today called the Valley of Mexico.

When the conquistadores had subdued Tenochtitlán (Mexico City) in the early 1500s, they sent their armies and colonists into the other parts of the Valley of Mexico in search of mineral wealth. They found it in abundance—lead, tin, zinc, iron, antimony, and gold. But what made the early Spanish governors (and the cities of the northern valley) rich was silver. So rich were the mines here that the Silver Cities of the northern Valley of Mexico became incredibly wealthy, and stayed that way for centuries. Today these cities are among Mexico's finest colonial showpieces, with outstanding architectural beauty. Guanajuato is almost a fairytale town. San Luis Potosí exudes wealth and civic pride from its grand government buildings, cathedral, and churches. Zacatecas is an architectural gem that lingers in the memory, San Miguel is a city of fine restored mansions and cobblestone streets, and Aguascalientes preserves its charm around its Plaza Principal as Querétaro does around its Plaza de la Independencia. Each city has a lot to offer, and a visitor who has not made the rounds of the Silver Cities hasn't seen Mexico.

SEEING THE REGION

No matter how you're traveling in Mexico, the Silver Cities are easily accessible despite their locations in mountain valleys. Coming overland from El Paso, Zacatecas is the first real colonial city you'll encounter; from Monterrey and Saltillo, Highway 57 goes straight to San Luis Potosí; from Guadalajara, it's only a few hours' drive to Aguascalientes. Mexico City is linked to Querétaro by train and a fast, limited-access toll highway, and from Querétaro you can be in San Miguel de Allende and Guanajuato or any other of the Silver Cities in a few hours' time by train or good two-lane paved road. Bus service is fast, frequent, and comfortable.

As for how to allot your time, much depends on your particular interests. But for the bare minimum, I recommend 2 to 3 days each in San Miguel de Allende, Zacatecas, and Guanajuato, and 1 day each in San Luis Potosí and Aguascalientes.

---

1. ZACATECAS

392 miles NW of Mexico City, 117 miles NW of San Luis Potosí,
197 miles NE of Guadalajara, 186 miles SE of Durango.

GETTING THERE By Plane Mexicana flies nonstop to Zacatecas from Mexico City, Tijuana, and Los Angeles (the flight from Tijuana will be booked months in advance for the Christmas holidays). **AeroSierra** (tel. 50-391 or 50-392), a

WHAT'S SPECIAL ABOUT THE COLONIAL SILVER CITIES

Great Towns/Villages

☐ San Miguel de Allende, with colonial-era mansions, great shopping and dining, and numerous art and language schools

☐ Picturesque Guanajuato, the most Spanish of Mexican villages.

☐ Zacatecas, whose twisting hillside streets are famous for gorgeous pink stone architecture, ornate wrought-iron balconies, and festive late-night *callejoneadas.*

☐ Historic Querétaro, known as the Cradle of Independence, where the Mexican constitution was signed in 1917.

Outstanding Museums

☐ New Museo Rafael Coronel, in Zacatecas, with 4,500 Mexican regional masks and a collection of 350 rare marionettes.

☐ Museo Goitia, in Zacatecas, devoted to the works of Francisco Goita and other 20th century Mexican artists.

☐ Museo Pedro Coronel, in Zacatecas, a fabulous private collection of art from around the world and paintings by Coronel, a highly regarded Mexican artist.

☐ Museum Convent of Guadalupe, in Zacatecas, with a priceless collection of colonial religious art.

☐ National Museum of Masks, in San Luis Potosí, showcasing 700 Mexican masks in an elegant turn-of-the-century mansion.

☐ Museo Regional Alhondiga, in Guanajuato, which occupies a mighty stone granary filled with regional art from pre-Hispanic times to the present.

Gardens

☐ The former Hacienda San Gabriel Barrera, in Guanajuato, with 11 terraced gardens next to a restored 17th-century hacienda and museum.

Architectural Highlights

☐ Convent Church of Santa Rosa de Viterbo, in Querétaro, stunningly adorned with gilded altars and a massive choir screen with 15 saints' portraits framed in gilded wood.

☐ The 18th-century Church of San Cayetano de la Valenciana, in Guanajuato, whose baroque exterior is crowded with carved foliage and saints and whose interior is filled with gilted altars and figures.

Events/Festivals

☐ Cervantino Festival, in Guanajuato, with performing groups from around the world.

☐ Estudiantinas, Guanajuato's roving singing groups in 16th-century garb appearing in the streets and restaurants.

Shopping

☐ San Miguel de Allende, a top shopping town with fine crafts, including the town's specialties—textiles, brass, bronze, and tin.

Junípero Serra Mission Route

☐ Five missions established by Fray Junípero Serra, east of Querétaro, beautifully restored.

---

regional carrier, flies from Durango to Zacatecas and Guadalajara on Monday, Wednesday, and Friday.

By Bus   Almost a dozen bus companies provide service in and out of Zacatecas. For those just passing through Zacatecas who want to take the suggested side trip to Guadalupe, Transportes de Guadalupe goes there every 15 minutes from the Central Camionera (where you'll be if you arrive by bus) for around 30¢.

By Car   Highway 54 comes from Saltillo and Monterrey (5 to 6 hours), Highway 40/49 comes from Torreón, and Highway 45 from Durango.

DEPARTING   By Plane   From Zacatecas, **Mexicana,** Avenida Hidalgo (tel. 406/408 2-7429 or 5-0352 at the airport), flies nonstop to Mexico City, Tijuana, and Los Angeles.

By Bus   Camiones de los Altos has 11 buses leaving the Central Camionero for Guadalajara daily, priced at $4.30. Buses to Aguascalientes go every half hour for around $2.50, and there are hourly buses to Fresnillo.

Zacatecas (alt. 8,200 ft.; pop. 108,000), capital of the state of the same name, was already an old town when the Spaniards arrived in 1546. The name comes from the Nahuatl words *zacatl* (pasture) and *tecatl* (people)—Zacatecas, then, means "people of the pasture." A city made rich by silver mines, it has picturesque brick streets ascending the hillsides, a plaza watched over by a white marble angel atop a column, and a real dearth of tourists.

The facade of the wildly Churrigueresque cathedral is the first sight most visitors want to see. The nearby Convento de Guadalupe and the ruins at La Quemada, are also good for a look. You can see it all from the hilltops that dominate the town, most notably the Cerro de la Bufa.

Remember that it's very hilly here, and you'll be doing a lot of climbing at an altitude of more than 8,000 feet; you'll become winded very quickly going up those hills.

ORIENTATION

ARRIVING   The airport is located about 18 miles north of Zacatecas. **Aero Transportes** (tel. 25-946) provides minibus transportation to and from the airport; allow 30 minutes for the ride. The **Central Camionera** (bus station) is on a hilltop a bit out of town, but a taxi to town costs only $1.30. Ruta 8 buses go to and from here frequently and can be found in front of the station.

CITY LAYOUT   The touristic heart of Zacatecas is centered on **Plaza de Armas,** facing Hidalgo and flanked by government buildings and the cathedral, and opposite the tourism office. The late-night *callejoneadas* wind up here with a last burst of singing, dancing, drinking, and band playing.

INFORMATION   The State of Zacatecas provides two official tourism offices downtown, near the cathedral, both with friendly English-speaking staffs, lots of printed information in English and Spanish, and maps and information on Zacatecas and the entire state. The **Dirección de Turismo** office is located on Avenida Hidalgo (tel. 2-8467 or 2-6683), across the street from the cathedral and the Nevera Acropolis, on the corner of Callejon del Santero. It's open Monday through Friday from 8am to 3pm and 6 to 8pm, but it also has an adjoining information booth open 7 days a week.

Another excellent resource is **Cantera Tours** (tel. 2-9065), with an office located a block south of the cathedral, in the Centro Comercial "El Mercado" on Avenida Hidalgo, open Monday through Saturday from 8:30am to 4pm and 5 to 8pm, and on Sunday from 9am to 1pm and 5 to 8pm. In addition to a pleasant, English-speaking staff loaded with information, they offer free maps and several quality tours with bilingual guides (see "What to See and Do," below, for more information regarding tours).

Turismo Marxal, in the lobby of the Hotel Posada de la Moneda, Avenida Hidalgo 413 (tel. 2-3693), is another good tourism service that also has a helpful English-speaking staff and lots of information. It's open Monday through Friday from 10am to 3pm and 5 to 7pm, and on Saturday from 10am to 3pm.

GETTING AROUND

Zacatecas has excellent inner-city bus service. To reach the Central Camionera (bus station), take a Ruta 8 at Plaza de la Independencia. Ruta 7 goes to the Motel de

Bosque and Teleferico. From the local bus station a block past the Hotel Gallery, buses go to and from Guadalupe every few minutes.

FAST FACTS

American Express   American Express is handled by Viajes Mazzoco, a travel agent at Sierra de Alica 313 (tel. 492/2-5559 or 2-5159; fax 492/2-5559).

Area Code   The telephone area code is 492.

Food Store   The **Casa Jaquez,** Avenida Hidalgo 202 at Callejon de la Bordadora, is a convenient supermarket and wine shop, open Monday through Saturday from 9am to 10pm and on Sunday from 9am to 4pm.

Handcrafts   Zacatecan handcrafts can be found directly across from the Teatro Calderón in the Mercado González Ortega.

Post Office   The Correos is not in the building with the Telegrafos at the corner of Juárez and Hidalgo, but on the side street called Allende, half a block down from Avenida Hidalgo.

WHAT TO SEE & DO

Zacatecas is famous among craftspeople for its serapes, its carvings in stone and wood and its leatherwork. This is a fine place to take a day (or a few days) off for eing, should you be barreling southward from the U.S. border.

A STROLL AROUND TOWN

The **Plaza de Armas,** the town's main square on Avenida Hidalgo, is where you'll find the **cathedral** with its fantastically ornate pink stone facade that has earned it the name of "Parthenon of Mexican Baroque." It took 22 years to build (1730–52). Take a close look at the zigzag carving along the lower surfaces, the huge stone pillars inside, and the quaint corn-motif ceiling. In the **city hall** is a modern mural (1970) by Antonio Rodriguez.

Walking south on Avenida Hidalgo, on the right you'll pass the **Teatro Calderón** (inaugurated in 1891), a stately building with lovely stained-glass windows that's now in use again after a remodeling to regain its former glory. Scenes from the movie *The Old Gringo,* starring Jane Fonda and Gregory Peck, were filmed here. Opera star Placido Domingo sang here in 1990. The theater is named for a poet/political writer from the state of Jalisco.

Continue on Hidalgo, across Juárez, and mount the hill to **Sierra de Alica Park** (the street changes names up the hill and becomes Avenida Gral. Jesús González Ortega). The equestrian statue (1898) is none other than General González Ortega himself, hero of the Battle of Calpulalpan. Behind it is a gazebo with marvelous acoustics and a pleasant, shady park good for a picnic or a romantic stroll. It's also well lit in the evening.

Beginning at Alica Park and extending southward, the famous **Aqueduct of Zacatecas** looms over the street. The wealth of this mining city at the end of the 18th century allowed it to undertake such impressive public works. Water passed along the aqueduct to a large cistern downtown.

IMPRESSIONS

To think of Mexican colonial architecture—whether churches, or houses, hospitals, or haciendas—as a scattering of remarkable buildings is to be astonished at the wrong thing. This was not an architecture of imperial display, marking the high points of the system, but the intimate expression of the life of New Spain.
—ELIZABETH WILDER WEISMANN, *ART AND TIME IN MEXICO,* 1985

There is also the massive **Templo de San Agustín,** west of the cathedral, on the corner of Miguel Auza and Callejon de San Agustín, open Tuesday through Saturday from 8am to 2pm and 4 to 5pm. Behind it is the building of **El Congreso Local del Estado de Zacatecas,** opened in 1985, a replica of the Real Caja (state bank) built in 1763 and destroyed in an explosion during the Revolution.

Down by the **Plaza de la Independencia,** on the south side by Super Pollos Rostizados El Pastor, there's a plaque on the wall announcing it as the birthplace of the first journalist in America, Dr. D. Juan Ignacio Mara de Casterena Ursua y Coyeneche Villareal, "en fecha como hoy" (on a day like today) in 1668.

To take it all in at once, climb slowly (remember the altitude) to the Motel del Bosque on the Cerro Grillo hill, west of the cathedral, and take the **teleferico** (cable car) on a sky ride over Zacatecas to the **Cerro de la Bufa,** a huge knob of a rock on the hilltop (which, by the way, translates as "pig's bladder," named by a local Basque citizen, who was reminded of that part of the animal's anatomy). When the sun is low in the sky, turning the sandstone town to a golden wonder, and the lights begin to twinkle on, it'll all seem magical. Watch the time, though, as the teleferico (tel. 2-5694 or 2-6013) operates only from 12:30 to 7:30pm, and if it's windy it won't be open at all. The cost for a ride is $1.75, one way or round-trip; you can hike up either hill and walk down the other if you wish. Before making that long climb, look to see if the cars are running; they may be in repair, or out of service because of winds. A glance will tell.

Up on Cerro de la Bufa, beside the Museo de la Toma Zacatecas (see below) is the beautiful church **La Capilla de la Virgen del Patrocinio,** patron of Zacatecas, and at the very top of the hill, an observatory used for meteorological purposes. Around the far side of the hill is the Mausoleo de los Hombres Ilustrios de Zacatecas, where many of the city's important revolutionary fighters still keep watch over their town below.

CHURCHES

Of Zacatecas's churches, many are notable: **San Agustín** dates from 1613, when construction was started, although dedication had to wait until 1782. It has been a Catholic church, then a Protestant one (stripped of its architectural ornamentation), a casino, and even ancient condominiums. Today it's an enormous, beautiful shell used for art exhibitions, conferences, and storage and display of pieces of its past glory. Note the mosaics of carved-stone chunks crammed in the archways and other niches. These pieces formerly ornamented the church's ramparts, but now no one knows quite where. It's five blocks south of the cathedral, past the Hotel Posada de la Moneda and right on the next street. Open Tuesday through Saturday from 8am to 2pm and 4 to 5pm.

Four miles from Zacatecas proper is the **Convent of Guadalupe,** the most famous church in the region. See "In Nearby Guadalupe," below, for details.

MUSEUMS

MUSEO F. GOITA, Enrique Estrada 102, Col. Sierra de Alica. Tel. 2-0211.

⭐ Located behind the park, this is a former governor's palace built in 1945. Having been occupied by three governors, each for a 4-year term, it was converted into a high school, and then a very fine museum. Exhibits on the ground floor are the work of Francisco Goita (1882–1960), including *Tata Jesucristo,* one of the artist's most famous, internationally known works. Upstairs are changing exhibits featuring other modern Mexican artists. The graceful marble stairway was supposedly constructed so that one may walk down its steps in perfect rhythm while humming the Triumphal March from *Aïda.*

Admission: 70¢, free Sun.

Open: Tues–Sun 10am–2pm and 5–8pm. **Directions:** Walk seven short blocks south of the cathedral on Hidalgo, crossing Juárez and continuing up the hill. Turn right on Manuel Ponce (look for the aqueduct) and walk two more short blocks. Look for the imposing white "palace" behind the park.

MUSEO PEDRO CORONEL, Plaza de Santo Domingo. Tel. 2-5661 or 2-5085.

This museum is located downtown, next to the ornate Church of Santo Domingo, and contains exhibits from Africa, India, China, Tibet, Thailand, Egypt (even a mummy case!), and ancient Greece and Rome, plus works of such European artists as Dalí, Picasso, Miró, and Chagall, in addition to the works of Coronel. Especially notable is the large collection of native pre-Hispanic art and masks downstairs, matched by a similar display of African masks directly above.

Admission: 70¢, free Sun.

Open: Fri–Wed 10am–2pm and 4–7pm. **Directions:** Facing the cathedral, walk left to the next street, De Veyna, and turn left and walk one block to Plaza de Santo Domingo and the museum.

MUSEO DE LA TOMA DE ZACATECAS, Cerro de la Bufa. Tel. 2-8066.

The Museum of the Taking of Zacatecas, founded in 1984, displays pictures and exhibits explaining the battle between the Federales and the Revolucionarios in the hills surrounding Zacatecas in June 1914. When Pancho Villa arrived from the north to seal the fate of the Federales in this battle, it marked the turning point in the victory of the Revolution.

Admission: 70¢, free Sun.

Open: Tues–Sun 10am–5pm. **Bus:** Ruta 7 from Plaza de la Independencia to the Motel del Bosque and teleferico. Take the teleferico to El Cerro de la Bufa and the museum (or walk, following the directions below to the mine entrance and weave a few more short streets to the hilltop).

LA MINA "EL EDEN," Cerro Grillo. Tel. 2-3002.

Opened in 1586, this mine was carved by hand by the indigenous population, forced into slavery by the Spanish. The Indians began working in the mine at age 10 or 12, and lived to about 30 years of age, dying of accidents, tuberculosis, or silicosis. The mine was one of the richest, yielding gold, copper, zinc, iron, and lead in addition to silver, but was closed after only 60 years when an attempt to use explosives resulted in an inundation of water into the lower shafts. Be sure to take the mine tour, beginning with a short ride on the small train 1,720 feet into the mine. A Spanish-speaking guide takes tourists to interesting points in the mine, which is dramatically lit. Visitors can view the special miners' altar by crossing a shaky (but short) suspension bridge over a deep, dark, water-filled crevasse. The tour is worth the time even for those who don't speak Spanish.

Admission: $2.25 (includes train and tour).

Open: Daily noon–7pm. **Directions:** One entrance is near the teleferico exit and the Motel del Bosque. For the train and tour, take the other entrance, which is a few blocks up Avenida Juárez (which becomes Avenida Torreón). From the cathedral walk down Hidalgo to Juárez (four blocks), turn right on Juárez (which becomes Torreón) and walk about three blocks passing the long, narrow Alameda (park) and the red Seguro Social building, and turn right at the next street, Dovali Jaime, which leads straight to the mine entrance.

RAFAEL CORONEL MUSEUM, Calle Chevano, between Juan de Tolosa and Vergel Nuevo.

This spectacular museum opened in 1990 and may well be Zacatecas's—and Mexico's—most mesmerizing. First, stroll through the gorgeous tranquil gardens and ruins of the former Convento de San Francisco, filled with trailing blossoms and verdant foliage, and framed by ancient arches and blue sky. A small wing contains Coronel's drawings on paper.

Step inside the mask museum and prepare to be dazzled by the sheer number of fantastic masks—4,500 of them—from all over Mexico, but so exotic they look as if they could be from all over the world. There are entire walls of bizarre demons with curling 3-foot-long horns and noses; red devils; animals and unidentifiable creatures spitting snakes, pigs, or rats; conquistadors; anything the amazing Mexican mind can conjure up. Both antique and contemporary, the masks are festooned with all manner of materials, from human hair and animal fur, fabric, plant fibers, and bones to metal screening, steel wool, sequins, plastic, and glitter.

An amazing marionette museum with entire dioramas of a bullfight, battling armies, and even a vision of hell, makes this a great place to bring children.

This superb collection was donated by Rafael Coronel, younger brother of Pedro Coronel, whose work is found in the Museo Pedro Coronel in Zacatecas.

The museum also has a delightful ground-floor café for coffee and pastries and an attractive second-floor cafeteria overlooking the grassy courtyard with its huge, dancing fountain.

Admission: 70¢.

Open: Thurs–Tues 10am–2pm and 4–7pm. **Bus:** Ruta 5, 8, or 10. **Directions:** Facing the cathedral, walk left up Hidalgo to the Founder's Fountain (about two blocks), then take the left fork (Calle Abasolo) two more short blocks; at the large, yellow-ocher building and traffic triangle, take the right fork. You'll spot the large, old temple ahead.

CASCO DE LA HACIENDA BERNARDEO, Pan American Hwy. km 2.5 toward Guadalupe. Tel. 2-1007.

Since Zacatecas is first in Mexico in the production of silver and fourth in gold, it seems only fitting that the art of metalworking is being reborn here. Young silversmiths are learning the trade in an old hacienda, which once belonged to the counts of Laguna, located in the Fraccionamiento Lomas near the golf course. The first class of 11 students (graduated in 1989) were trained not only in the art of jewelry making, but as businesspeople capable of opening their own stores. An association of mining engineers is supporting the school and students. The unusual jewelry designs are taken from the balconies and ironwork in Zacatecas, and after you've seen them, you'll view Zacatecas's architecture with new eyes. The only place to see and buy this jewelry is at the Casco. It might be easier to take a taxi for around $3 than to follow the directions given below; by car it's a 10-minute drive.

Admission: Free.

Open: Mon–Fri 9:30am–5:30pm, Sat 10am–2pm. **Bus:** Ruta 11; tell driver where you're going and he'll let you off, but you'll still have to walk up and down hills for at least a mile. When you see a yellow building, turn right on a dirt path and go under the old remains of the aqueduct; the hacienda is ahead.

IN NEARBY GUADALUPE

The most famous religious edifice, aside from the cathedral in Zacatecas, is the Convento de Guadalupe, in Guadalupe, about 4 miles east of Zacatecas on Highways 45/49. Transportes de Guadalupe buses go from the Central Camionera in Zacatecas or there's a bus to Guadalupe from Callejon del Barro, just up from the Hotel Gallery. The bus stops right in front of the convent. It leaves about every 15 minutes or so, and costs 20¢ for the 20-minute ride. A taxi to Guadalupe will run about $2.25. If you're driving, look for a red-brick church and steeple, and turn right just past it onto Calle Independencia.

CONVENTO DE GUADALUPE, Calle Independencia, Guadalupe

Dating from 1707, the convent now houses the **Museo de Arte Virreinal de Guadalupe** (tel. 2-3322). Enter through a small park or courtyard with stone mosaics—look up at the different domes and doorways of the convent. The museum building is to your right. Inside the convent proper, every wall seems to be covered by paintings, with a series of huge paintings describing the life of St. Francis of Assisi on the ground floor and the life of Christ on the floor above.

Remember, while touring these holy grounds, that they were reserved for men of the cloth; the public was not meant to see them, the paintings, or the sumptuous "cells" where the Franciscan monks spent their spare time. You may catch a glimpse of the brown-robed monks through a slatted wooden door, for the building is still in use today as a college of instruction in the Franciscan order, with only a part of it used for the museum. Here at the third Franciscan monastery established in the New World, missionaries were educated and sent northward into what is now northern Mexico and the southwestern U.S. in the cultural conquest of the Spaniards. (The Dominican order, also important in the Conquest, appears in the artwork of the convent too; but it's the brown-robed Franciscans that are the more familiar figures, the three knots of their sashes signifying their vows of obedience, penitence, and poverty—the occasional fourth knot signifying the additional vow of silence.)

The chapel to the left of the main building (as you face the convent from the front court/park) is called the **Capilla de Napoles.** It must have taken a king's ransom in gold to decorate it, with gold ranging in quality from 6 karat on the lower walls up to 22 karat in the dome above. Guides are available for a tour or to open the chapel, which is visible from either the organ loft or the ground floor—be sure to tip the guide for opening the doors and turning on the lights.

Admission: Museum, 60¢.
Open: Tues–Sun 10am–4:30pm.

MUSEO REGIONAL DE LA HISTORIA, Jardín Juárez, Guadalupe. Tel. 2-6683.

In Guadalupe, to one side of the plaza in a large building that was once a grand hacienda, is this museum with an exhibit of carriages and antique cars collected from all over Mexico, formerly belonging to ex-presidents and famous persons in history.

Admission: Free.
Open: Tues–Sun 10am–5pm.

ORGANIZED TOURS

Cantera Tours (tel. 2-9065) has an excellent 5-hour guided tour that covers Zacatecas, Guadalupe, and the surrounding region (the Convento de Guadalupe, Cerro de la Bufa, the teleferico, etc.); another 5-hour guided tour covers the nearby town of Jerez and the ruins of Chicomostoc (the Zona Arqueologica La Quemada), and is the only way to get directly to Chicomostoc unless you have a car. Prices for these two tours are about $12 per person, which includes all expenses, including the entrance fees to the various sites. Both tours require a minimum of five people and they will pick you up and drop you off at your hotel. The office is located a block south of the cathedral, in the Centro Comercial "El Mercado" on Avenida Hidalgo, open Monday through Saturday from 8:30am to 4pm and 5 to 8pm, and on Sunday from 9am to 1pm and 5 to 8pm.

Another interesting event sponsored by Cantera Tours is the **Callejoneada Zacatecana,** a walk through the city's *callejones* (the little curving alleys and byways and plazas) accompanied by music and dancing, on Saturday evenings beginning at 9pm (8pm in cold weather). This is a traditional activity and pleasure of the region, and a good time is guaranteed for all ages. The price of $17 per person includes dinner, with native wine and mezcal. Again, they will pick you up and drop you off at your hotel, or even give you a ride to your favorite discothèque if you still feel like dancing afterward. However, these fun evenings are held only if there are at least 30 people interested. Be sure to ask if there will be one while you're in town. If you wish to hire a private English-speaking guide, Cantera Tours offers this service too, at a rate of about $1.75 per hour.

Or—for free—just mosey on down to the Alameda García de la Cadena on Torreón (also Juárez) around 9pm and join the group forming there or join a group as it marches through the streets—they're hard to miss with the drums and horns. You'll still get free dancing and mescal in a little ceramic jug with ribbon to wear round your neck—to keep revelers warm in the chilly, mountain-night air.

SPECIAL EVENTS

During Semana Santa or **Holy Week,** before Easter each year, Zacatecas hosts an international cultural festival that the town hopes will soon rival the similar Cervantino festival in Guanajuato. Painters, poets, dancers, musicians, actors, and other artists from around the world converge on the town.

The annual **Feria de Zacatecas,** which celebrates the founding day of the city, begins the Friday before September 8 and lasts for 2 weeks, when cockfights, bullfights, sporting events, band concerts, and general hoopla prevail. Particularly famous toreodores are hired and bullfight tickets go for around $3; buses leave from downtown for the gigantic Plaza de Toros (and also for the nearby cockpit) on days when fights are held. Sports events are held in the Olympic-size sports stadium, and in the equally huge gymnasium; there are even car races at the racetrack outside town.

EVENING ENTERTAINMENT

The **Hotel Aristos** (Loma de la Soledad—see the directions to La Mina El Eden, but follow Torreón all the way to the top of the hill and turn left) and the **Hotel Gallery,** which cater to an upper-class clientele, also have nightclubs with shows, open to guests and visitors alike.

EL MALACATE, Mina El Eden. Tel. 2-3002.
Have you ever been to a discothèque located in a silver mine 1,050 feet underground? Call in advance to reserve yourself a table, since it's a very popular place. The entrance is at the end of Calle Dovale Jaime, which is the street just past the Seguro Social building on Avenida Torreón. Open Thursday through Sunday from 9:30pm to 2am.
Admission: $5.45.

EL ELEFANTE BLANCO, Paseo Díaz Ordaz, next to the teleferico station. Tel. 2-7104.
This unusual dance club, the "White Elephant," is perched on the mountaintop with the Motel del Bosque, right behind the teleferico departure point. It has been remodeled and enlarged, and now has a big video section. The side facing the city is almost round, with windows floor to ceiling, making for a magnificent panoramic view. Here again, you might want to call for a reservation, since this, also, is a very popular spot. It's open Thursday through Saturday from 9pm to 2am and on Sunday from 6 to 11pm.
Admission: $5.45.

EL PARAÍSO, Av. Hidalgo. Tel. 2-6164.
This enjoyable family bar is located in the Centro Comercial "El Mercado," one block south of the cathedral. It's nicely decorated, with potted plants and bar, booths, or tables to choose from. Open Monday through Saturday from 1:30pm to midnight.

WHERE TO STAY

Over on Boulevard Lopez Mateos, near where the bus station used to be, are several hotels: Motel Zacatecas Courts, Hotel Colón, and Hotel Gallery. They tend to be loud, being right on the main highway, and for my money, I'd rather stay downtown. But if you need a room, all three of these are clean and acceptable, and they're not too far a walk from downtown.

ROOMS FOR LESS THAN $20

HOTEL DEL PARQUE, Paseo González Ortega 302, Zacatecas, Zac. 98000. Tel. 492/2-0479. 23 rms (none with bath).
$ Rates: $10 single; $12 double.

This budget hotel is spartan, but clean and quiet—and, I might add, drafty and cold in winter. The hot water is not so hot sometimes; in fact it goes out altogether in the evening once in a while, but the price is definitely a plus. The shared baths are down the hall.

To find the hotel, walk seven short blocks south of the cathedral on Hidalgo, cross Juárez, and continue up the hill; turn right on Manuel Ponce (look for the aqueduct) and walk two more short blocks to Sierra de Alica Park; the hotel is a few doors up the hill from the park.

HOTEL CONDESA, Av. Juárez 5, Zacatecas, Zac. 98000. Tel. 492/2-1160. 60 rms (all with bath). TV TEL
$ Rates: $14 single; $18 double. **Parking:** $1 (nearby).

Right across the street from the Posada de los Condes (near the intersection of Avenidas Juárez and Hidalgo, about three blocks south on Hidalgo from the cathedral and left on Juárez) is this hotel where the prices are lower. The worn but comfortable rooms offer all the basics, with hot water morning and evening, ancient telephones, and purified water. The rooms on all three floors open onto a bright, glass-topped courtyard. The hotel's restaurant is one of the more popular places to dine in Zacatecas (see "Where to Eat," below).

ROOMS FOR LESS THAN $25

HOTEL COLÓN, Lopez Velarde 508, Zacatecas, Zac. 98000. Tel. 492/2-0464. 27 rms (all with bath). TV TEL
$ Rates: $15.75 single; $20 double.
Just a little farther up the hill from the Motel Zacatecas Courts is this hotel, which also sits between busy Boulevard Lopez Mateos and Avenida Lopez Velarde, with signs facing both. (Facing the cathedral, walk/wind to the right around and behind it to Calle Tacuba, which, bearing continuously left, first becomes Guerrero, then Ramón Lopez Velarde, up the hill—a total of about five or six blocks to the hotel.) It's very basic, but clean.

ROOMS FOR LESS THAN $35

POSADA DE LOS CONDES, Juárez 107, Zacatecas, Zac. 98000. Tel. 492/2-1412 or 492/2-1093. 58 rms (all with bath). TV TEL
$ Rates: $24.50 single; $29 double. **Parking:** Small charge.

This is a good hotel choice on the busiest corner in town, the intersection of Avenidas Juárez and Hidalgo (about three blocks south on Hidalgo from the cathedral and left on Juárez; the hotel is on the right side of the street). The building's facade is about 300 years old, but the inside was remodeled in 1968. Rooms facing the street have French doors opening onto small iron-railed balconies; other, quieter rooms have no windows, but do have ceiling ventilation. Be sure to specify which you prefer. Rooms that receive no direct sun are chilly in the winter months. The rooms are in good shape, clean, carpeted, with phone, elevator, TV (with two U.S. channels), and hot water from 7pm to midnight. Parking is nearby.

MOTEL DEL BOSQUE, Paseo Díaz Ordaz, Zacatecas, Zac. 98000. Tel. 492/2-0745. 70 rms (all with bath). TV TEL **Bus:** Ruta 7 from Plaza de la Independencia the Motel del Bosque and teleferico.
$ Rates: $24 single; $30 double. **Parking:** Free.
If you'd prefer to be a bit removed from all the hubbub of downtown, by all means try this hotel perched high above town, with rooms offering views of the city below. Ask to see several rooms, and be specific in your request for a room with a view, for that is the del Bosque's great advantage over downtown places. When you've chosen one, you'll find that your clean, modern room has carpeting and hot water 24 hours a day;

rooms are lined up in rows stretching along the hillside, with parking on the cobblestone driveway between rows. It's quiet and pleasant up here overlooking the city, and you're located near several of Zacatecas's main tourist attractions: the teleferico, the mine, and the hilltop discothèque El Elefante Blanco.

MOTEL ZACATECAS COURTS, Lopez Velarde 602, Zacatecas, Zac. 98000. Tel. 492/2-0328. 64 rms (all with bath). TV TEL
$ Rates: $26 single; $32 double. **Parking:** Free.

S This clean, but somewhat worn, modern-style hotel sits between two main streets, Boulevard Lopez Mateos and Avenida Lopez Velarde, with a sign on both sides. (Facing the cathedral, walk/wind to the right around and behind it to Calle Tacuba, which, bearing continuously left, first becomes Guerrero, then Ramón Lopez Velarde, up the hill—a total of about five or six blocks to the hotel.) It has carpeting, hot water 24 hours a day, enclosed parking, laundry and dry cleaning services, a travel agency, and even a pharmacy and medical services. The restaurant is open daily from 7am to 10:30pm.

POSADA DE LA MONEDA, Av. Hidalgo 413, Zacatecas, Zac. 98000. Tel. 492/2-0881. 36 rms (all with bath). TV TEL
$ Rates: $26 single; $32 double. **Parking:** Small charge.

Right in the heart of town, one block south of the cathedral, the location is ideal, though a bit noisy. Most of the rooms get plenty of light, either with French doors opening onto tiny balconies overlooking the street, or windows facing the sunny interior patio. All rooms have carpets. They also have hot water all day. The bar and restaurant is open daily from 8am to 10pm. The helpful Turismo Marxal travel agency is in the hotel lobby. Enclosed parking is nearby.

WORTH THE EXTRA BUCKS

PARAÍSO RADISSON, Av. Hidalgo 703, Col. Centro, Zacatecas, Zac. 98000. Tel. 492/2-6183, or toll free 800/333-3333 in the U.S. Fax 492/2-6245. 117 rms (all with bath). A/C TV TEL
$ Rates: $64 single; $81 double. **Parking:** Free.

In the heart of historic and beautiful Zacatecas, opposite the cathedral, this hotel opened its doors in 1989 behind the facade of a former colonial-era building that most recently housed the Hotel Reina Cristina. You'll enter a lobby that holds a popular bar and restaurant. The spacious, heated rooms on six floors are fashionably decorated. Rooms facing the plaza have a ringside seat on Zacatecas—the mountains, the central plaza, the cathedral, and those wee-hours *callejoneadas* that end there anywhere between 11pm and 1 or 2am. (I love the pure Zacatecas, late-night exuberance of a *callejoneada*—but if you don't, be forewarned that they sometimes go on loud and long.) Other rooms, facing the interior courtyard, are quieter. All rooms come equipped with TV with U.S. channels, some have king-size beds and others have two double beds.

HOTEL QUINTA REAL, Av. Rayón 434, Zacatecas, Zac. 98000. Tel. 492/2-9104, or toll free 800/445-4565 in the U.S., 800/227-0212 in California. 50 rms. A/C MINIBAR TV TEL
$ Rates: $117 suite without Jacuzzi; $141 suite with Jacuzzi. **Parking:** Free.

If ever there was a place for a splurge in Mexico this is it—it's one of the most beautiful and unusual in the country. Built almost under Zacatecas's ancient aqueduct (walk seven short blocks south of the cathedral on Hidalgo, cross Juárez, and continue to Manuel Ponce) it's handsomely incorporated into one of Mexico's oldest bullfighting rings—more than a century old and built of stone. Each of the 49 exquisite, heated rooms faces the ring's interior, and except for the planters of verbena and bougainvillea, half the stepped edifice remains just as it was when crowds cheered "Ole!" As you register, spirited bullfight music plays softly in the background. But there the bullish theme ends. Rooms are luxuriously formal but cozy, like something in a mansion on "Lifestyles of the Rich and Famous," and each has a private balcony overlooking the verdant Plaza de Toros.

An outdoor restaurant with umbrella-shaded tables uses part of the spectator section. The formal indoor restaurant is plush and sophisticated. A bar on the lower level occupies the former bull chutes and the graffiti remains on the rock walls. Even if you don't stay here, come for a drink or a meal. A variety of international dishes ranges from $6 to $25. Salads and soup are much less. Beer, desserts, and cappuccino are inexpensive.

WHERE TO EAT

Between Plaza de la Independencia and Boulevard Lopez Mateos runs **Calle Ventura Salazar,** lined with taco shops, snack stands, and hole-in-the-wall eateries just fine for a quick bite at ridiculously low prices.

MEALS FOR LESS THAN $5

CAFE NEVERIA ACROPOLIS, Av. Hidalgo and Plazuela Candelario Huzar, Tel. 2-1284.

Specialty: MEXICAN/SNACKS.
$ Prices: Breakfast $4; antojitos $3–$5; malts $2; cakes $1.25–$3; sandwiches $1.25–$3; cappuccino $1.25.
Open: Daily 9am–10pm.

One place I enjoy immensely is one of the most popular places in town for students and university types. It's a soda fountain, sweets, and ice-cream parlor in the daytime, and a hip coffeehouse in the evening. Along the wall are photos and signatures of famous people, including Gregory Peck and Jane Fonda who stayed in Zacatecas for the filming of *The Old Gringo*. This café is a great place for a late-afternoon sightseeing break with tea or coffee and a slab of heavily iced cake. The pastry display case is filled with delectable-looking items. Comfy leatherette booths help make this a popular hangout. It's just across the little street to the right of the cathedral.

HOTEL CONDESA, Av. Juárez 5. Tel. 2-1160.

Specialty: MEXICAN.
$ Prices: Breakfast 90¢–$2; appetizers $1.75; antojitos $1.50–$3.50; main courses $3–$7.50; comida corrida $3.
Open: Tues–Sun 7:30am–11pm.

All the previously mentioned hotels have their own restaurants, and this spot is popular despite its drabness and spartan decoration. You have a choice of 11 types of egg dishes and even the filet mignon. A hearty and tasty comida corrida, about the cheapest in town, is served from 1:30pm until it's gone at around 4 or 4:30pm.

RESTAURANT MESÓN LA MINA, Av. Juárez 15. Tel. 2-2773.

Specialty: MEXICAN.
$ Prices: Breakfast $2–$3.50; appetizers $2; main courses $3–$10; comida corrida $4.
Open: Daily 8am–11pm (comida corrida served 1–4pm).

One of the most popular restaurants in Zacatecas, it's just a few doors up from the Hotel Condesa. Cheery, bright-blue tablecloths over white-and-red-tile floors provide a pleasant, colonial/frontier ambience, especially in the restaurant's rear by the old, dark-wood bar (Pancho Villa could have slung a few down here) with broad, stone arches, carved wooden chairs, and large, round tables. (The front of the restaurant is more cafélike with chrome and Formica.) There's a wide menu selection that includes nine types of soup, four types of chilaquiles, beef filets, chicken, and pork chops with fries. There's also a full bar, and espresso coffee. A popular breakfast on chilly Zacatecas mountain mornings is leche para cafe and a basket of pan dulce. The leche (hot, steamed milk) comes in a tall sundae glass, accompanied by a jar of instant coffee and a long spoon for stirring—sounds tacky, but after watching the happy locals hovering over this steaming, frothy mix and stirring in the dark swirls of Nescafé, I tried one and it's delicious.

ROSTICERÍA EL PASTOR, Independencia 214 and 218. Tel. 2-1635.
   Specialty: CHICKEN.
$ Prices: Chicken $6 whole, $3 half, $1.25 quarter; fries $1; coffee 20¢; beer 60¢–80¢.
   Open: Daily 9am–9pm.
The only thing served at "Super Pollos Rostizados" is "super roast chicken." This cheerful café has white marble floors, bright-orange vegetable-print tablecloths, cute little stools, and the "mono-menu" up on the wall. It's usually packed with people who know good food at a good price. The chicken is excellent and comes with barbecued potato chips, salad, salsa, and tortillas. There's also chicken soup and roast chicken to go. A plaque on the wall out front, by the way, proclaims this house as the birthplace of the first journalist in America (Dr. D. Juan Villareal, born in 1668). It's directly behind the Plaza de la Independencia (south side), a little farther down Juárez from the Fonda El Jacalito.

MEALS FOR LESS THAN $10

FONDA EL JACALITO, in the Posada de los Condes, Av. Juárez 18. Tel. 2-0771.
   Specialty: MEXICAN.
$ Prices: Breakfast 90¢–$2; antojitos $3–$6; main courses $4–$8; comida corrida $7.
   Open: Daily 8am–10pm (comida corrida served 1:30–4pm).
This is another very well-attended restaurant, pleasant and bright in the Mexican neotraditional genre of chrome and Formica. Note the strange walls—are they stone or wood? The fonda serves a no-longer-cheap comida corrida and antojito plates. Those feeling homesick can even order a bowl of Campbell's soup. There's chicken and six kinds of steaks, sandwiches, and various platters. It's across the street from the Restaurant Mesón La Mina (above).

RESTAURANT VILLA DEL MAR, Ventura Salazar 338 and 340. Tel. 2-5004.
   Specialty: SEAFOOD.
$ Prices: Appetizers $2; main courses $3–$10; house special "mosaico" $9; combination specials $6–$11.
   Open: Daily 9am–7pm.
At this clean restaurant there's a wide variety of seafood with several combination specials which include beer, appetizer and dessert. The specialty of the house is the Mosaico Villa del Mar, which includes a breaded fish filet, filet of pike, stuffed crab, frogs' legs, onion rings, and french-fried potatoes. There's a variety of beer and wine, and a bottle of one of Zacatecas's delicious local wines (Los Pioñeros) costs the same as the special.
   To get there, walk past Plaza de la Independencia (just down from the Hotel Condesa on Juárez—see directions above) then turn right on Aldama and take the second left, which is Salazar; the restaurant is on the right.

EL CAMPANARIO, Lopez Velarde 327. Tel. 2-2089.
   Specialty: SEAFOOD/INTERNATIONAL.
$ Prices: Appetizers $3.50–$7; main courses $4.50–$15.
   Open: Daily noon–11pm.
This, modern, tile-floored restaurant has dark wooden tables and chairs, clothed in yellow and white. Paintings of old Zacatecas decorate the walls. Treat yourself to an enjoyable dining experience here with the excellent chicken in white wine sauce, or à l'orange; or try the fish filets prepared in many ways. For more of a splurge, there's a T-bone or sirloin steak, or jumbo shrimp. There is also a full bar.

To find El Campanario, facing the cathedral, walk down the side street to the right (Guerrero, which eventually becomes Lopez Velarde), pass the intersection with the fountain, and continue around to the left to the busy intersection with a green overhead sign. Look for restaurant on the left across the street.

WORTH THE EXTRA BUCKS

HOTEL QUINTA REAL, Av. Rayón 434. Tel. 2-9104.
  Specialty: REGIONAL/INTERNATIONAL.
$ Prices: Breakfast $5–$9; appetizers $4–$13; soups $3; main courses $4.50–$15.
  Open: Daily 7am–11pm.

White linen tablecloths, pastel tapestry-covered chairs, high beamed ceilings, and plants everywhere give an elegant, but comfortable ambience. The wrap-around dining room faces the center of the former bullring and diners gaze out at the twinkling lights in the courtyard's potted trees with the illuminated aqueduct arched gracefully high above. Though it would be easy to spend a fortune here, I had a delicious dinner for less than $13, including a glass of Los Pioñeros Zacatecan wine and two of the house specialties: the tournedo Quinta Real (a perfectly cooked beef filet in a tangy tomato sauce topped with avocado and cheese) and the cream of chile poblano and squash-blossom soup—both excellent. There's an exciting menu featuring all sorts of creative dishes including seafood Pernod, which is shrimp, octopus, and three kinds of oysters "aromatized with Pernod"; a robalo (fish) filet "acueducto," covered with sweet bananas, green peppers, and butter sauce—and much, much more. For desert, try cajeta (goat's milk candy) crêpes, crêpes Suzette, or chocolate mousse.

To get here, walk seven short blocks south of the cathedral on Hidalgo, cross Juárez, and continue to Manuel Ponce; hotel is under the aqueduct on the left.

EASY EXCURSIONS FROM ZACATECAS

CHICOMOSTOC About 34 miles south of Zacatecas, about 1¼ miles off Highway 54 to Guadalajara, is the **Zona Arqueologica La Quemada,** an archeological site of a 12th-century culture developed by the Nahuatlacas tribe. The pyramids here vaguely resemble the ones at Mitla and Monte Alban much farther to the south. The largest pyramid, called the Temple, has been restored and offers you your first glimpse of this fascinating aspect of Mexico's past. The rest of the site is not very well preserved, but the 11 pillars built of granite stones serve to give you an idea of the grandiose palace that once stood here. Stone-paved avenues and terraces crowded with foundations of houses mark the Ciudadela, atop which is an observatory from which the Nahuatlacas studied the movements of stars and planets and—who knows?—tracked the course of early extraterrestrial visitors. You can visit the ruins Tuesday through Sunday from 10am to 5pm. Admission is 60¢, free on Sunday.

If you don't have a car, getting to Chicomostoc may present a challenge, since the public bus only lets you out on the highway, with a walk of a little over a mile to reach the ruins. If you're vigorous, you can make the walk with no trouble. Alternatively, you can take a **guided tour,** either through Cantera Tours (tel. 2-9065) mentioned above, or through Viajes Masoco (tel. 2-5559).

NEARBY HOT SPRINGS Several hot springs are within bus distance of Zacatecas. One of the nicest is **Paraíso Caxcan,** at km 136 (that's 136km—85 miles—from Zacatecas) heading south on Highway 54 toward Guadalajara, before you reach Apozol. It's a well-developed vacation center/thermal-bath facility, with gardens, bar, restaurant, and hotel. Hotel rates are $34 double, or $58 for a cabaña holding up to six people. If you just want to visit for the day, it's 60¢. It's open every day from 11am to 8pm.

Other hot springs in the area are **San Miguel Atotonilco** in Apozol, in the south of the state of Zacatecas; **Balneario Agua Azul,** 40 minutes by bus along the road heading west to Jerez; and **Valparaíso,** 94 miles west of Zacatecas, on the road passing through Fresnillo. You can get more information on these hot springs from any of the tourism offices.

2. AGUASCALIENTES

84 miles S of Zacatecas, 104 miles W of San Luis Potosí,
157 miles NE of Guadalajara

GETTING THERE   By Plane   Aero California flies between Los Angeles and Aguascalientes. **Aeroméxico** has daily flights between Tijuana and Mexico City, and three weekly flights from Los Angeles to Aguascalientes and Mazatlán.

By Bus   Many bus lines operate to and from Aguascalientes. It's about 2 or 3 hours by bus to either Zacatecas or San Luis Potosí. **Chihuahuenses** runs from Zacatecas and costs $2.60.

By Car   Take Highway 49/45 (the Pan American Highway) from Zacatecas, Highway 70 from San Luis Posoti, Mex 54 from Guadalajara.

DEPARTING   By Plane   Aeroméxico has its office at Madero 474 (tel. 7-0252, or 7-2404 at the airport). Allow at least 25 minutes for the trip to the airport. **Aero California** has offices at Montoro 23 (tel. 7-2310 or 7-2153, or toll free 800/237-6225 in the U.S.).

By Bus   There are frequent daily buses to Mexico City, Guadalajara, and most other cities in Mexico. **Flecha Amarilla** serves the León region and Celaya with buses every half hour. **Aguila** and **Anahuac** (tel. 5-8095) go north to Zacatecas, Monterrey, and Saltillo. Besides normal service, **Omnibus de México** (tel. 6-1770) has one first-class *Ejecutivo* (executive) bus that leaves at 11pm and arrives in Mexico City at 5:30am; this bus has a video TV, extra-wide seats (and only half as many as a regular bus), and a card/smoking salon (about $30 one way). There's also a similar daily *Ejecutivo* to Guadalajara for $12.50. **Estrella Blanca** leaves hourly for San Luis Potosí.

Aguascalientes (alt. 6,000 ft.; pop. 514,000), the capital of the state of the same name, means "hot waters," so it isn't hard to figure out that the city has hot springs. Underneath the town is a maze of tunnels believed to have been excavated by some ancient peoples who left no explanation of their feats; the tunnels are not open to the public.

The present town of Aguascalientes was founded by the Spanish in 1575 as La Villa de la Ascunción de las Aguas Calientes, a place of protection and rest along the silver highway between Mexico City, Guanajuato, and Zacatecas, as well as a center of cultivation of food for the mining region. Today Aguascalientes is known for its copper mining, embroidery, and knitwear. In the streets beside and behind the cathedral and Plaza Principal, you'll note several stores selling the products of this industry.

Other major industries have come to Aguascalientes from Japan, France, and the United States, and from Mexico City, augmenting the population considerably. With growth the city has lost some of its colonial charm, although the people here are still friendly and relaxed.

ORIENTATION

ARRIVING   By Plane   Colectivo minivans take passengers to and from the airport, which is 21 miles south of the city. Buy a ticket inside the air terminal; the fare is around $7 one way.

By Bus   The clean bus station has several services for the traveler. Besides plenty of seats in the waiting area and a restaurant, there's a helpful computer-operated

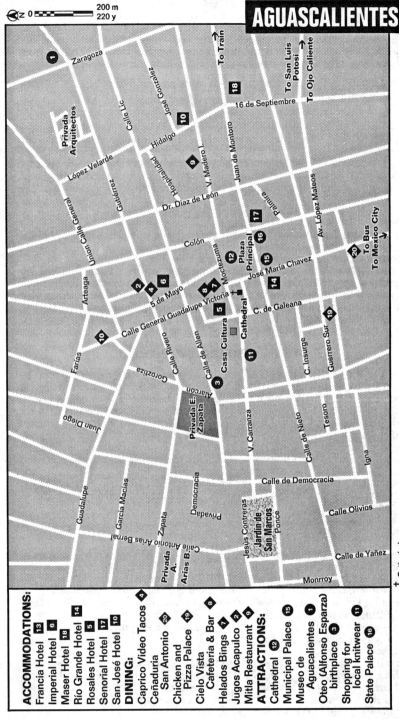

AGUASCALIENTES

0 | 200 m
0 | 220 y

Zaragoza

Privada Arquitectos

José González

Calle Lic

Hidalgo

López Velarde

Gutiérrez

Hospitalidad

V. Madero I.

Dr. Díaz de León

Juan de Montoro

Palmira

16 de Septiembre

To Train

To San Luis Potosí

To Ojo Caliente

Union Calle General

Arteaga

Colón

Plaza Principal

José María Chavez

Av. López Mateos

To Bus

To Mexico City

5 de Mayo

Moctezuma

Farías

Calle Rivero

Corazóza

Calle de Allen

Calle General Guadalupe Victoria

Casa Cultura

Cathedral

C. de Galeana

C. Insurge

Guerrero Sur

Tesoro

Igna

Juan Diego

Privada E. Zapata

Alarcón

V. Carranza

Calle de Nieto

Calle de Democracia

Calle Olivios

Guadalupe

García Macías

Zapata

Democracia

Privadad

Privada A.

Arias B.

Calle Antonio Arias Bernal

Jesús Contreras

Jardín de San Marcos

Ponce

Monrroy

Calle de Yañez

Cathedral

ACCOMMODATIONS:
Francia Hotel 13
Imperial Hotel 6
Maser Hotel 18
Río Grande Hotel 14
Rosales Hotel 5
Senorial Hotel 17
San José Hotel 10

DINING:
Caprico Video Tacos 4
Ceñaduria
San Antonio 20
Chicken and
Pizza Palace 19
Cielo Vista
Cafetería & Bar 8
Helados Bings 7
Jugos Acapulco 2
Mitla Restaurant 9

ATTRACTIONS:
Cathedral 12
Municipal Palace 15
Museo de
Aguacalientes 1
Oteo (Alfonso Esparza)
birthplace 3
Shopping for
local knitwear 11
State Palace 16

telephone service. To use it, just tell the attendant where you want to call. When the call is completed the computer prints out the cost—just for the call—no service charge. It's very efficient and inexpensive. The bus station is around 20 blocks from the city center; taxis and city buses stop out front. Taxi fare is about $2.

CITY LAYOUT   The center of town is also its colonial heart, based on **Plaza Principal** bounded by Madero, Cinco de Mayo/Chávez, Colón, and Montoro. And as usual in towns dating from colonial times, it's flanked by the cathedral and main government offices. The tourism office is there as well.

INFORMATION   The **Tourist Information Office** is on the main plaza, to the left of the cathedral, inside the State Palace or Palacio (tel. 491/5-1155 or 6-0347), with a good map and a guidebook detailing the sights and side trips, as well as plenty of information on hotels and restaurants. It's open Monday through Friday from 8am to 3pm and 5 to 8pm, and on Saturday from 10am to 1pm.

FAST FACTS

American Express   The local representative is Viajes Chavoya, Centro Commercial El Dorado, Local 11 (tel. and fax 491/6-6959).
Area Code   The telephone area code is 491.
Post Office   The Correo is about two blocks from Plaza Principal on Hospitalidad between Hidalgo and Dr. Díaz de León. From the plaza, walk one block east on Madero, turn left on Díaz de León and then right on Hospitalidad; the post office is on the left, halfway down the block.

WHAT TO SEE & DO
A STROLL AROUND DOWNTOWN

The **State Palace** is right on Plaza Principal. As you enter you'll be stopped short by the astonishing perspective of 111 hand-carved pink stone pillars and arches, a sweeping staircase, and the general grandeur of the interior patio. A glorious mural by the Chilean painter Ualdo Ibarra was completed in 1957 and depicts industry mingling with pastoral scenes, long-haired maidens displaying embroidery, miners climbing from the depths, cannons booming, and succulent grapes overflowing their vases. The **Municipal Palace** next door is an 18th-century construction in the same style, with a lovely fountain just inside the entrance; once a soldiers' quarters and police headquarters, it also is arresting in its beauty.

Behind the Municipal Palace is the **Palace Garden,** with two engravings by J. Jesús Contreras, printed in France: Comaxtli, god of hunting, and Centleotl, god of abundance.

The baroque **cathedral,** across the wide plaza, was begun in 1575 as a small chapel. At the rear it contains a small museum with valuable religious paintings dating from the 17th century to the present.

Behind the cathedral about one block, look for the **birthplace of composer Alfonso Esparza Oteo,** at Calle Allende 238, a dark stone house trimmed with white stone and gracefully curving designs. The streets are so narrow, it's easy to miss such treasures, squeezed in between print shops and hairdressers. Every so often a brilliant tile facade on a venerable edifice will take the visitor by surprise. The **Casa de Cultura** is also behind the cathedral, but on Carranza, just a half block down—another lovely old building with arch-lined courtyards with magnificent, two-story-high bougainvillea and strains of beautiful music wafting from various classrooms and studios.

It can be relaxing just to walk along **Avenida Carranza** to the attractive **Jardín de San Marcos,** a lovely enclosed park where the only sounds are those of hundreds of birds in the treetops and the shouts and laughter of children playing around the bandstand. Carranza parallels Nieto and is two blocks north of the tourism office; then left on Carranza to the park.

Bulls, incidentally, are bred in the area, and it's possible to make arrangements to visit two well-known breeding ranches, Hacienda Chichimeco and Hacienda Penuelas. Proprietors can be contacted via the tourism office.

OTHER ATTRACTIONS

MUSEUM OF AGUASCALIENTES, Zaragoza and Vazquez del Mercado. Tel. 5-9043.

This museum is located across from the lovely San Antonio Church, and contains mostly 20th-century Mexican oil paintings, with some from the 17th through 19th centuries as well.

Admission: Free.

Open: Tues–Sat 10am–4pm and 6–8pm, Sun 10am–2pm. **Directions:** From the plaza, walk two blocks north on Colón and turn right on Gutierrez; walk three more blocks, cross Zaragoza, and the museum is straight ahead.

OJO CALIENTE, km 1 on Hwy. 70 to San Luis Potosí. Tel. 5-4721.

This is the principal local spa and it is located on the eastern outskirts of town (a taxi ride here should cost about $1.75 from downtown). The waters here are highly recommended for rheumatism, arthritis, and liver ailments. The water in the hot springs here isn't really hot, as the name implies, but you'll find it pleasantly warm, like a heated swimming pool. All these facilities are located where you see the sign CENTRO DEPORTIVO OJOCALIENTE (Ojocaliente Sports Center) out front.

Admission: Olympic-size swimming pool, $1.30 adults, $1.10 children; "family pools," $6.50–$9 per hour; steambaths and saunas, $1.75–$2.85 per hour; squash and tennis courts, $2.85 per hour.

Open: Daily 7am–7pm. **Bus:** Take the "Emiliano Zapata" bus down Avenida Lopez Mateos or Ruta 12, 15, or 16.

SPECIAL EVENTS

The biggest fair in Mexico is held here annually from April 18 to May 10. It's the **Feria de San Marcos,** held in honor of the town's patron saint. The celebration begins with the crowning of a queen of the festival. Craft and industrial expositions, fireworks, cultural events, rodeos, and bullfights with renowned bullfighters entertain the townspeople. Antojitos (regional food) is sold in the Jardín de San Marcos, where amusement rides are set up for the children. People come from all over to celebrate, so if you want to join in the festivities, make your hotel reservations early and pay in advance.

WHERE TO STAY

DOUBLES FOR LESS THAN $15

HOTEL SAN JOSÉ, Hidalgo 207, Aguascalientes, Ags. 20000. Tel. 491/5-5130 or 5-1431. 31 rms (all with bath).

$ Rates: $9.50 single; $11.50 double. **Parking:** Free.

Just a short block away from the Hotel Maser, this is another good budget hotel. The outside is plain, but it's just fine inside. The spare but clean rooms open onto narrow hallways; all have ample windows for light. It's a popular, friendly place.

To get here from the plaza, walk two blocks east on Madero and turn left on 16 de Septiembre/Hidalgo; the hotel is on the right.

DOUBLES FOR LESS THAN $20

HOTEL ROSALES, Calle Gral. Guadalupe Victoria 104, Aguascalientes, Ags. 20000. Tel. 491/5-2165. 40 rms (all with bath).

$ Rates: $10 single; $12 twin; $18 double.
The lobby is a visual adventure in this clean hotel, with something for everyone, including a TV, a picture of Rin Tin Tin gazing down on a huge potted plant, a statue of the beloved Mexican comedian Cantinflas, and such a variety of staircases that getting to your room may be a bit like being in a life-size version of "Chutes and Ladders." All the rooms have one or two beds and warm water during the day. The rooms are small and slightly stuffy but quiet, and the bathrooms are so minuscule that you could surely perform all functions in two strides. You could also ask for a discount here and probably get it.

From the plaza, turn right on the small street (Guadalupe Victoria) past the Imperial Hotel; the Hotel Rosales is on the left.

HOTEL MASER, Juan de Montoro 303, Aguascalientes, Ags. 20000. Tel. 491/5-3532 or 5-9662. 44 rms (all with bath).
$ Rates: $12 single; $16 double. **Parking:** Free.

Located on the corner of 16 de Septiembre two blocks from the plaza, this is the best budget choice in town. It's spotlessly clean, and with its red mosaic-tile floors, white walls, and ceramic-potted plants all around, it's really very nice, though chilly in winter. Some of its bright, cheerful rooms face the covered courtyard forming the lobby; others, the open courtyard behind.

HOTEL SEÑORIAL, Colón 104, Aguascalientes, Ags. 20000. Tel. 491/5-1630 or 5-1473. 32 rms (all with bath). TEL
$ Rates: $14 single; $18 double.
Right in the heart of things, off the southeast corner of the main plaza, the Hotel Señorial looks as if no speck of dust had ever entered. Try to get one of the sunny rooms facing the street, or especially the corner, with French doors and tiny balconies. Rooms on the interior are, of course, quieter. The cafeteria serves daily between 8am and 11pm. The hotel also offers long-distance phone service. Señora Rosa del Carmen al Dasota DeVega (the dueña) is very friendly and nice, and speaks English.

DOUBLES FOR LESS THAN $25

HOTEL IMPERIAL, Calle 5 de Mayo no. 106, Aguascalientes, Ags. 20000. Tel. 491/5-1664 or 5-1650. 63 rms (all with bath). TEL
$ Rates: $17 single; $23 double.
On Plaza Principal, the Imperial Hotel is housed in a once-imposing stone building. The Imperial's "lobby" is a tiny little entrance at the side of the building—the original lobby was converted into a Bancomer branch. Most of the rooms are big, and the outside ones, with French doors opening onto wrought-iron balconies with views of the magnificent cathedral, are cheerful and especially bright—but beware of the unmerciful street noise. Rooms facing the pleasant, spacious inner courtyard are much quieter.

WORTH THE EXTRA BUCKS

HOTEL FRANCIA, Av. Madero and Plaza Principal, Aguascalientes, Ags. 20000. Tel. 491/5-6080. Fax 491/7-0140. 88 rms (all with bath). A/C TV
$ Rates: $36 single; $45 double. **Parking:** 50¢.

The president of Mexico recently stayed here. The Francia has a synthetic tile floor that looks like marble and a huge blowup print of Aguascaliente's Plaza Principal as it looked a century ago. Its huge, modern rooms are stylish enough, with an overtone of yesteryear. The clientele at the Francia tend to be well-groomed business types, with the occasional wealthy farmer in a sleek cowboy hat. Parking is underground.

The corner restaurant downstairs—one of the best and most popular in town—is open daily from 7:30am to 10:30pm. There's also an elegant restaurant/bar next door, also popular, and a restaurant *típico* open daily from 2pm to midnight.

HOTEL RÍO GRANDE, José María Chávez 101, Aguascalientes, Ags. 20000. Tel. 491/6-1666 or 6-1889. 75 rms (all with bath). A/C TV TEL

$ Rates: $50 single; $52 double. **Parking:** 90¢ underground.

On another corner of the plaza, above the restaurant Las Bugambilias, is this comprehensive hotel which boasts air-conditioned rooms with color TV (with U.S. channels), FM radio, carpeting, and all the other niceties you could ask for. Lobby bar, restaurant, travel agency, and underground parking are also available.

WHERE TO EAT
MEALS FOR LESS THAN $5

JUGOS ACAPULCO, Allende 106.

Specialty: JUICES/SANDWICHES/DESSERTS.
$ Prices: Breakfast $1.25–$2.50; juice $1–$1.50; sandwiches $1.30–$2.25.
Open: Daily 8am–9pm.

As the name implies, this is a good place to go for juice—seven types, fresh-squeezed or made into cool, delicious frothy licuados with milk. Nothing fancy, this clean and cute little brick-arched snack shop also has a sidewalk café with umbrellas and white wrought-iron chairs and tables. Stop here for an inexpensive sandwich, quesadilla, yogurt, cake, or flan.

To find it, from the plaza, turn left on Colón (off the northeast corner), walk one block, and turn left. The café is on the right, halfway down the block.

RESTAURANT MITLA, Madero 220. Tel. 6-3679.

Specialty: MEXICAN.
$ Prices: Breakfast $1.30–$5; appetizers $1.50–$3.50; main courses $3.50–$9.
Open: Daily 8am–midnight.

This nice bar-and-grill restaurant is spotlessly clean, and has such good service that the waiter brings you a plate of rolls, butter, and cheese (cheese at a slight charge) the moment you sit down. The service is excellent and friendly, and at least one waiter will probably speak English—in fact, they like to practice their English. Lots of selection in edibles here. For breakfast, there are several very ample inexpensive combos, and simple egg plates are half that price. Try the Divorciados, a plate of eggs cooked to order and topped with red sauce at one end and green sauce at the other, with chilaquiles in between. Fish filets prepared in any of several ways or antojitos are good lunch and dinner choices. Full bar service too.

CAPRICHO VIDEO TACOS, Calle 5 de Mayo no. 118. Tel. 6-2588.

Specialty: MEXICAN.
$ Prices: Breakfast $2.50–$3; main courses $3–$5; comida corrida $3.
Open: Daily 8am–midnight.

Billed as "the new image in fast foods," this restaurant sports black-and-glass doors and a black-and-white-tile entry on the left as you walk away from Plaza Principal. The black, trendy front room seems designed to focus attention on the TV, suspended above on the wall. But the atmosphere is pleasant and friendly. Great breakfast specials include eggs any style with potatos and unlimited coffee, and each table is set with a basket of fresh sweet rolls. The huge fixed-price lunch is delicious and a bargain. There are nine types of tacos (including Hawaiian style) and various meat dishes, including filet mignon.

CENADURÍA SAN ANTONIO, Chaves 607, at Pimenter. Tel. 6-6525.

Specialty: REGIONAL/MEXICAN.
$ Prices: Main courses 90¢–$5; sampler plate $5.
Open: Dinner only, daily 6pm–midnight.

This is a delightful place, well worth the walk for its inexpensive, tasty regional food and lively atmosphere. An army of white-garbed and turbaned women buzz around a huge counter crammed with tubs of dozens of ingredients and zip from table to table, efficiently taking orders. This former hole-in-the-wall has expanded to two rooms, Renaissance reproductions now bedeck the walls, and well-heeled clients pull up stools at the plastic-covered tables to join the mob of happy diners. I met a lawyer/rancher/industrial park owner who had driven 20 miles to town to pick up enchiladas for his workers. It's easy to see why with a choice of 10 kinds of tamales—sweet ones flavored with rompope or pineapple or nuts, hot ones with green and red chiles; or red mole and meat—seven types of tacos and the platillo hidrocaldo, a sort of sampler plate with a chicken sope, beef tostado, potato taco, beef flauta, cheese enchilada, cream, guacamole, and a sweet tamale. Unlike most Mexican restaurants, here you get a ticket and pay the cashier.

To get here from the plaza, go left from the cathedral, walk about six or seven short blocks down Cháves and across Guerrero Sur/Hornedo; it's on the right.

MEALS FOR LESS THAN $10

CAFETERÍA & BAR CIELO VISTA, Plaza Principal 103. Tel. 5-3000 or 7-0777.
Specialty: MEXICAN.
$ Prices: Main courses $5.50–$11; comida corrida $7.50; sandwiches and antojitos $2–$5.50.
Open: Daily 8am–11pm (comida corrida served 1:30–5pm).
Right off the plaza, this is the place to be in the evening. The café and bar are located in different parts of the same large room; clocks along the wall by the counter show you the time in Mexico City, New York, Madrid, Tokyo, and "Zulu Time." Prices are a little high, but the atmosphere is amiable and pleasant. It's also a good place for dessert and coffee. The bar has live music nightly from 7 to 11pm.

CHICKEN & PIZZA PALACE, Av. Lopez Mateos 207 Pte. Tel. 5-2841.
Specialty: PIZZA/CHICKEN.
$ Prices: Main courses $4–$9; all-you-can-eat lunch buffet $4.
Open: Daily 10am–1am (buffet special served Mon–Sat noon–5pm).
The Chicken & Pizza Palace (which is more humble than palacial) offers the most filling lunch for the lowest price in town—an all-you-can-eat buffet of pizza, spaghetti, various chilled vegetables, fried potatoes, cole slaw, and several potato and pasta salads. You can also order chicken or a pizza—but of course. The food here is not exactly gourmet, but it's not bad either, and it will surely fill you. The decor is nice too, with red tablecloths and dark wooden paneling, revolving ceiling fans, and music playing.

To get here, walk from the plaza on Chávez past the Río Grand Hotel (to the left of the cathedral). Turn right on the second street (Lopez Mateos) and walk 1¾ blocks; the restaurant is on the right.

FOR DESSERTS & ICE CREAM

Just off the main square is **Danny-Yo,** Calle 5 de Mayo 102 (no phone), where you can get frozen yogurt sundaes to go, priced from 75¢ for a small size to $2.50 for a large with a choice of two flavors of frozen yogurt, fresh fruit, and several toppings (which you can select as it's being made). They have popcorn, nacho chips, chocolate-chip cookies, and corn (on or off the cob) here too, or big frozen-yogurt cones for 55¢. Open daily from 9am to 9pm.

For the best ice cream (with the emphasis on cream), go around the corner to a branch of **Helados Bing.** It's 90¢ for a one-scoop cone and $1.70 for two scoops; milkshakes cost $2.70. You can't miss the hot-pink lights facing the plaza. It opens daily at 9:30am and closes at 9:30pm.

EASY EXCURSIONS FROM AGUASCALIENTES

About an hour or less (31 miles) northwest of Aguascalientes is the Sierra Fría, a hilly range containing the **Sierra Fría National Park,** a huge preserve nice for camping and hiking. From Aguascalientes, drive or take the bus to San José de Gracia; ask there, in the Presidencia Municipal (city hall), for permission to camp. They'll give you a map of the forest, and if you like, a guide will take you out there and show you where to go. The town is located right on the Presa Calles, a large reservoir great for fishing.

Fans of colonial architecture might like to visit the small town of **Asientos** (pop.

15,000), about 28 miles northeast of Aguascalientes, easily accessible by bus. It's full of nice old buildings and colonial atmosphere, with many 16th- and 17th-century paintings displayed in its various churches.

Finally, a side trip (or at least a stop) to **Encarnación de Díaz,** a charming little town 26 miles south of Aguascalientes on Highway 45, is worth the trip to see the central plaza, which contains some amazing artwork in the form of living cedar trees. These trees have been pruned into beautiful and unlikely shapes: Columbus with his three ships (the *Nina, Pinta,* and *Santa María*), kings and queens with ermine robes, zebras, and lions, among others, all created by José Cervantes, who has been tending the trees for 40 years.

3. SAN LUIS POTOSÍ

261 miles NW of Mexico City, 216 miles NE of Guadalajara

GETTING THERE   By Plane   A new regional carrier, **AeroMar,** has direct flights daily from Mexico City and Guadalajara, and connections with several cities via Mexico City. **Mexicana** also flies to/from the capital daily, as well as Monterrey, and may resume service with San Antonio, Texas, via Monterrey on a regional carrier called Aero Monterrey.

By Train   The train station (tel. 2-2123 for information, 2-3641 for tickets) is across the street from the Alameda park and within walking distance of most of the recommended hotels. The first-class *El Regiomontaño* departs Mexico City at 6pm and arrives in San Luis at midnight. From Nuevo Laredo, it arrives in San Luis at 3am and leaves quickly, arriving in Mexico City at 9am.

By Bus   It's an easy 8-hour bus ride from Monterrey or Saltillo, and only 3 hours from Zacatecas or Aguascalientes.

By Car   Take Highway 57 from Mexico City or Highway 80 from Guadalajara. There's dramatic scenery on the second half of trip between Aguascalientes and San Luis Potosí—hair-raising hills and scenic "pueblitos."

DEPARTING   By Plane   The **AeroMar** offices are at Carranza 1055-304 (tel. 7-7936 or 3-0559). **Mexicana** is at the corner of Madero and Resti (tel. 4-1119 or 4-1233). For return transportation to the airport, call **Transportes Aeropuerto** (tel. 7-0877 or 4-0054).

By Train   The first-class *El Regiomontaño* departs San Luis Potosí and arrives in Saltillo at 6am, in Monterrey at 8:30am, and in Nuevo Laredo at the Texas border at noon. If you've arrived by train from the Texas border at 3am and you're headed next to San Miguel de Allende, you might want to get a hotel for these wee morning hours; later, tour the town until the *Constitucionalista* leaves San Luis at 2:15pm for a 4:38pm arrival in San Miguel de Allende. It continues to Querétaro, arriving at 6:30pm, and in Mexico City at 10pm.

By Bus   City buses marked "Central" go to the bus station from the Alameda park opposite the train station. There are several daily buses to Guanajuato and San Miguel de Allende, and many to Mexico City via Querétaro. The bus station is in an L-shaped building divided between first- and second-class buses. First-class buses are at the end beyond the restaurant. **Flecha Amarilla** has hourly buses to León, 16 buses a day to Mexico City and Morelia, 17 to Querétaro, 8 to Guanajuato, 4 to Pátzcuaro, and 3 to San Miguel de Allende (at 6, 7:30, and 9:30am). **Estrella Blanca** has direct service to Aguascalientes two times a day (13 *de paso* buses), as do **Chihuahuenses** and **Omnibus de México.**

San Luis Potosí (alt. 6,200 ft.; pop. 526,000) is among the most picturesque and prosperous mining cities of Mexico, and once you visit this bustling city, you'll see why. It has rich colonial architecture accented by the city's long, momentous history. Capital of the state of the same name, San Luis Potosí was named for Louis, saintly king of France and "Potosí," the Quechua word for "richness," borrowed from the incredibly rich Potosí mines of Bolivia, which San Luis's mines were thought to rival. Founded in 1583 by Spaniard Fray Magdalena and Captain Caldera on the site of the Chichimec town of Tanga-Manga, the indigenous people had been living in a town on this spot for 3 centuries before the Spaniards arrived.

The Spaniards came in search of silver and found it, mostly at a small town called San Pedro, 25 miles from San Luis Potosí. But San Luis's mineral springs made it a better place to settle than San Pedro, so this became the mining center. As a state capital, San Luis Potosí exudes prosperity and sophistication, much the way Morelia does. You'll note shady plazas and brick-paved streets.

Along with the prospectors came the friars in search of converts: the Franciscans were the first, followed by the Jesuits and the Carmelites. San Luis owes much of its architectural heritage to the vigor—and lavish expenditure—of these groups.

Later, during the Mexican Revolution, the "Plan of San Luis" was proclaimed here. The city has in fact been twice the capital of Mexico—in 1863 and 1867—when Benito Juárez led the fight against European intervention, governing the country from the Palacio de Gobierno (on Plaza de Armas). From this palace he pronounced the death sentence on Maximilian and his two generals.

Today San Luis Potosí lives on industry rather than silver. Everything from automobiles to mezcal is produced in the factories ringing the city, but fortunately the colonial center has been preserved intact.

ORIENTATION

ARRIVING   The **airport** is about 7 miles from downtown. A taxi or colectivo van will cost a sky-high $10.50 to the city center, but the cost of the taxi can be shared.

The **train station** is within walking distance of town and hotels; go out the front door and turn right—the central plaza is straight ahead.

The city's **Central Camionera** (bus station), on Guadalupe Torres at Diagonal Sur, is a long distance from town. If you arrive there, to get a bus to town go out the front entrance of the station, turn left, and walk two blocks to the corner of Dolores Jimenez y Muro. There you'll find buses to "Alameda Centro" (the Alameda is a huge park and the only one the bus passes). Get off at the second Alameda stop, which will put you across from the train station and a couple of blocks from the central plaza. Cabs from the bus station to town cost $2.25 to $3.50, depending on your bargaining ability.

INFORMATION   The **Tourism Office** is upstairs at Manuel José Othon 130 (tel. 481/2-3143 or 4-2994). Cross the street to the right of the cathedral, turn left, and walk a few doors down; the building is on the right. The staff is knowledgeable and at least one person there will speak English. They also have excellent bilingual color brochures covering San Luis. The office is open Monday through Friday from 9am to 8pm and on Saturday from 10am to 2pm.

CITY LAYOUT   The **Jardín Hidalgo** is the historic city center, bounded on all sides by colonial-era buildings and narrow one-way streets—Carranza, Madero, Allende/5 de Mayo, and Hidalgo/Zaragoza. It's a delightfully walkable city; most of the museums, restaurants, and hotels are all downtown and close to the central jardín. Many of the city's historic structures now house museums and restaurants.

FAST FACTS

American Express   The local representative is Grandes Viajes, Avenida Carranza 1007 (tel. 481/7-6056; fax 481/17-6108).

Area Code   The telephone area code is 481.

Banks   Banamex, one block off the main plaza (Jardín Hidalgo) to the left of the cathedral, will change traveler's checks/money Monday through Friday from 9am to 1pm.

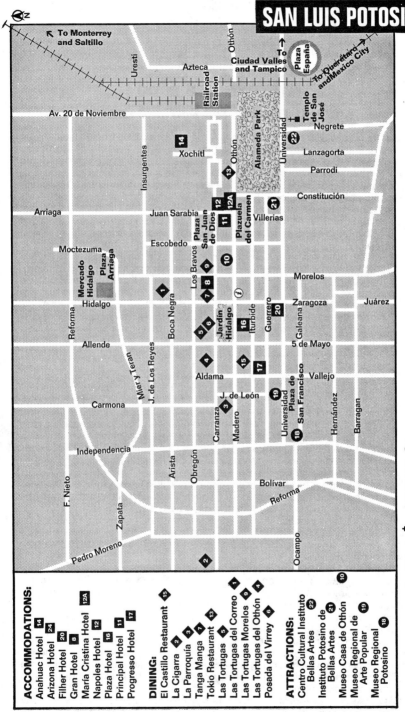

SAN LUIS POTOSÍ

To Monterrey and Saltillo

To Ciudad Valles and Tampico

To Querétaro and Mexico City

Plaza España

Railroad Station

Alameda Park

Templo de San José

Negrete

Lanzagorta

Parrodi

Constitución

Av. 20 de Noviembre

Xochitl

Othón

Universidad

Arriaga

Juan Sarabia

Plaza San Juan de Dios

Plazuela del Carmen

Villerias

Moctezuma

Escobedo

Mercado Hidalgo

Plaza Arriaga

Los Bravos

Morelos

Hidalgo

Boca Negra

Jardin Hidalgo

Iturbide

Zaragoza

Juárez

Allende

5 de Mayo

Aldama

Vallejo

J. de León

Universidad Plaza de San Francisco

Carmona

Independencia

Bolívar

Reforma

Pedro Moreno

Church ✝ Information ⓘ

ACCOMMODATIONS:
Anahuac Hotel 14
Arizona Hotel 24
Filher Hotel 20
Gran Hotel 8
María Cristina Hotel 12A
Napoles Hotel 12
Plaza Hotel 16
Principal Hotel 11
Progresso Hotel 17

DINING:
El Castillo Restaurant 15
La Cigarra 2
La Parroquia 3
Tanga Manga 7
Tokio Restaurant 13
Las Tortugas 5
Las Tortugas del Correo 1
Las Tortugas Morelos 9
Las Tortugas del Othón 4
Posada del Virrey 6

ATTRACTIONS:
Centro Cultural Instituto Bellas Artes 22
Instituto Potosino de Bellas Artes 21
Museo Casa de Othón 10
Museo Regional de Arte Popular 19
Museo Regional Potosino 18

Climate Here it's warm and pleasant year round—the average annual temperature is 67°F. Rain is rare, with an average rainfall of 14 inches; the rainy season is from April through November and the coolest weather is between November and March.

WHAT TO SEE & DO

A STROLL AROUND THE HISTORIC CENTER

The center of town is the **Jardín Hidalgo,** a large plaza dating from the mid-1700s; before that it was a bullring. After the plaza was laid out, the **Palacio de Gobierno** was begun. What you see today of this building has been much repaired, restored, and added to through the centuries—the back and the south facade were redone as recently as 1973. The front of the building retains much of the original 18th-century decoration, at least on the lower floors.

The **bandstand** in the center of the plaza was built in 1947 (although in colonial style), using the pink stone famous to the region. You'll see the stone throughout San Luis. The band plays here on Thursday and Sunday evenings, free, beginning around 7:30 or 8pm.

Across the plaza from the Government Palace is the **cathedral.** The original building had only one bell tower, so the one on the left was built in 1910 to match, although today the newer tower looks to be the older. The **Palacio Municipal,** on the north side of the cathedral, was built in 1850 by the Count of Monterrey and was loaded with great wealth—paintings and sculpture—little of which has survived the plaza's stormy history. When the count died in 1890, the palace was taken over by the bishop, and later in 1921 by the city government. Since that year it has been San Luis's city hall, peaceful for many years until it was firebombed on January 1, 1986, because of political differences. It has all been restored and functions again with business as usual.

The area south of the Jardín Hidalgo is a grid of narrow streets lined with graceful, and for the most part unmodernized, old mansions. These low, elaborate, and ancient homes are built in the Spanish style and each contains a lush central garden courtyard. It's well worth a stroll down here to peek through the delicate iron traceries that cover the windows, and if you're lucky you can catch glimpses of cool, aristocratic rooms lined with gilt and velvet, looking as they have for almost a century.

Heading north out of the Jardín Hidalgo, stroll along Calle Hidalgo. This street is reserved for pedestrians, and it's a treat to walk from the jardín almost all the way to the city's Central Market.

Southeast of the Jardín Hidalgo is one of the city's most famous squares, **Plazuela del Carmen,** named for the Templo del Carmen church. From the jardín, walk east along Madero-Orthon to Escobedo and the plazuela. The entire area you see was once part of the lush grounds of the Carmelite monastery, built in the 17th century. The church survives from that time, and is perhaps the Potosinos' favorite place of worship, but the convent has been destroyed. The beautiful **Teatro de la Paz** now stands on the site, having been built there in 1889.

Attached to the Teatro de la Paz, entered either through the theater's lounge or through the separate entrance on Calle Villerias, the **Sala German Gedovius** (tel. 2-2698) has four galleries for exhibitions of international and local art. Open Tuesday through Sunday from 10am to 2pm and 4 to 6pm.

The square is a fine place to take a rest by the fountain before heading on a few blocks east to get to the **Alameda,** the city's largest downtown park. This is the coolest park, because of the shade trees; walk all the way to the center and you barely notice the traffic on the very busy streets surrounding the Alameda. All around the sides of the park are vendors selling handcrafts, fruits, and all manner of snacks: try a hot fried banana with butter and sugar, or wrapped tortillas filled with cajeta, a wonderful butterscotch made from goat's milk.

Just across Negrete is the magnificent **Templo de San José,** with lots of ornate gold decoration, huge religious paintings, and *El Señor de los Trabajos,* a miracle-working statue with many retablos testifying to the wonders it has performed.

IMPRESSIONS

There are city parks and squares in other countries, but in none do they play the same intimate and important part in the national domestic life that they do in Mexico.
—CHARLES FLANDRAU, *VIVA MEXICO*, 1908

Nearby, on the corner of Avenidas Universidad and Constitución, the **Instituto Potosino de Bellas Artes** is a school of fine arts with classes for both children and adults in painting, dance, music, etc. Here you can find painting exhibits and performances of music and dance on the weekends.

PLAZAS

San Luis Potosí has many more plazas than the two most famous ones mentioned above. **Plaza de San Francisco** (also called **Plaza de Guerrero**) is south of the Palacio de Gobierno along Aldama, between Universidad and Galeana. This shady square, lush with ivy, iris, vine-covered trees, and royal palms, takes its name from the huge monastery of the Franciscan order at the south side of the plaza. The church on the west side, the Church of San Francisco, is dated 1799, and is really worth visiting, with its beautiful stained-glass scenes all around the dome, carved pink-stone altar, its radiant statue of the Virgin surrounded by angels and golden rays, other lovely statues and paintings, and the spectacular crystal chandelier, shaped like a sailing ship, hanging from the center of the dome.

Another square with a church to visit is **Plaza de los Fundadores,** at the intersection of Obregón and Aldama (northwest of the Jardín Hidalgo). Take a peek through the baroque doorway of the Loreto Chapel, dating from the 16th century, and the neighboring headquarters of the Compañia de Jesús—the Jesuit order. In the chapel is a magnificent golden sunburst over the altar, a reminder of past glories.

It's a ways from downtown, but if you have transportation you might be interested in a visit to **Parque Tangamanga** (tel. 481/7-6217), one of the largest parks in Mexico, located on the Boulevard Diagonal Sur at the intersection of Tata Nacho. It covers acres and acres, with three lakes, a Hollywood Bowl–type outdoor theater, a planetarium and observatory, a library, a museum, a children's playground, every kind of sports field you can think of, and many picnic sites set up with barbecue pits, tables, and benches, with slatted shelters for shade. The park is open daily from 6am to 6pm (admission free).

MUSEUMS

MUSEO REGIONAL DE ARTE POPULAR, Jardín Guerrero 6. Tel. 2-7521.

⭐ Next to the Church of San Francisco, on Plaza de San Francisco (three blocks south and one block west of the Jardín Hidalgo), this interesting museum is housed in a turn-of-the-century building, formerly a private home. Notice the unusual, waffle-patterned design of the building's exterior walls. Exhibits displayed in the glassed-in rooms around the open court run the gamut of Potosino crafts: ceramics, inlaid wood, papier-mâché "sculptures," basketry, and local designs in weaving and rebozos.

Admission: Free.

Open: Mon 10am–3pm, Tues–Sat 10am–1:45pm and 4–5:45pm, Sun 10am–2:15pm.

MUSEO REGIONAL POTOSINO, Calle Galeana 450. Tel. 2-5185.

⭐ This museum on Plaza de San Francisco was originally part of the Convent of San Francisco, founded in 1590. Downstairs is a small but excellent museum of pre-Columbian artifacts and stone statues, representing many areas and tribes of ancient Mexico—Maya, Mixteca, Huasteco, Mexica, Totonaca, and Zapoteca—

with a short explanation (in Spanish) about each culture and epoch, and color photographs of the pyramids of the different regions. Upstairs is the beautiful **Capilla de Aranzazu,** constructed in the middle of the 18th century as a private chapel for the Franciscan order and dedicated to the cult of the Virgin of Aranzazu (a Vascuense word for *entre espinas, tu,* roughly translated as "between thorns, you"). The chapel, with its lovely lifelike statue of the Virgin, old-style religious paintings, and fancy gold decoration, is a true blending of baroque and Churrigueresque styles.

   Admission: 25¢, free for students, free for all Sun.
   Open: Tues–Fri 10am–1pm and 3–6pm, Sat 10am–noon, Sun 10am–1pm.

CASA DE LA CULTURA, Av. V. Carranza 1815. Tel. 3-2247.

   Somewhat removed from the city center, this museum is housed in a splendid neoclassical building constructed at the turn of this century, surrounded by large landscaped gardens. There's a collection of archeological items, works of art, historical pieces, and handcrafts. Adjoining is the Center of Historical and Geographical Studies. All kinds of national and international cultural events are held here.

   Admission: Free.
   Open: Tues–Fri 10am–2pm and 4–6pm, Sat 10am–2pm and 6–9pm. **Transportation:** Take a cab or any of the city buses running west on Carranza.

MUSEO NACIONAL DE LA MASCARA, Villerias 2. Tel. 2-3025.

   ✪ Just across from the Teatro de la Paz, the National Mask Museum is the only museum of its kind on the national level in Mexico. It's loaded with regional dance masks from all over the country and is a must-see. In addition to its permanent and temporary exhibits, it offers lectures and workshops on mask making, theater, painting, movies, and history, and a national mask contest at Carnaval (Mardi Gras) time.

   Admission: Free.
   Open: Tues–Fri 10am–2pm and 4–6pm, Sat–Sun 10am–2pm. **Directions:** From the Jardín Hidalgo (Plaza de Armas), walk east along Madero-Orthon to Escobedo to the Plazuela del Carmen. The museum is south, just off the plaza.

MUSEO CASA DE OTHON, Calle Manuel José Othon 225.

   This is the birthplace and home of the poet Othon, who lived from 1858 to 1906. Here are the traditional furnishings of the poet's time, his original poetry manuscripts, and beautiful, tender letters he wrote to his wife. Literary readings and lectures are occasionally held here.

   Admission: Free.
   Open: Tues–Fri 8am–7pm, Sat–Sun 10am–1pm. **Directions:** Walk two blocks east of the Jardín Hidalgo on Othon; the museum is on the left.

CENTRO DE DIFUSION CULTURAL DEL INSTITUTO POTOSINO DE BELLAS ARTES, at the corner of Av. Universidad and Negrete. Tel. 2-4333.

   On one side of the Alameda you'll see this futuristic building. It has four art galleries with rotating art exhibits, as well as space for cultural events, including performances of dance, theater, and music.

   Admission: Free.
   Open: Tues–Sun 10am–2pm and 5–8pm. **Directions:** Walk three blocks east of the Jardín Hidalgo on Othon to the Alameda; the centro is on the opposite side of the Alameda about mid-park.

SHOPPING

It's several blocks along the pedestrian Calle Hidalgo from the Jardín Hidalgo to the city's new **Mercado Hidalgo,** a mammoth building devoted mostly to food but also carrying some baskets, rebozos, and straw furniture. While here, be sure to try some queso de tuna, a specialty of the region. Although called a "cheese," in fact it's a sweet paste—something like dried figs or dates with a molasses or burnt-sugar taste—made from the fruit of the prickly pear cactus. It's delicious, and comes in pieces of various sizes, ranging from a taste to a kilo.

But the walk along **Calle Hidalgo** is itself an introduction to the city's commercial life. Hardware stores, craftspeople's shops, shoe stores, groceries, and taverns all crowd the street. Continuing on past the Mercado Hidalgo, there's another big market, the **Mercado Republica.**

For some real bargains, visit **Plaza de San Francisco** and check the spreads of the colorfully clad ladies from Oaxaca who set up shop on the sidewalk there. On either side of the Oaxacans a local woman and man sell a delightful array of basketry—including tiny bamboo bird cages—all very inexpensive.

WHERE TO STAY

DOUBLES FOR LESS THAN $10

GRAN HOTEL, Los Bravos 235, San Luis Potosí, S.L.P. 78000. Tel. 481/2-2119. 15 rms (7 with bath).
$ Rates: $3.50 single without bath, $4.50 single with bath; or $4.25 double without bath, $5 double with bath.
Speaking of older buildings, if funds are stretched to the limit but you're not quite into park benches, head for this hotel. Although the rooms are washed down each day, no amount of scrubbing is going to put the shine back into the rather dark and desperate Gran Hotel. When all else fails, you can catch a night's sleep here more cheaply than anywhere else in town. The shared bathrooms are separated for men and women.

To get here from the main plaza, walk to the left of the cathedral one block west on Los Bravos.

DOUBLES FOR LESS THAN $20

HOTEL PLAZA, Jardín Hidalgo 22, San Luis Potosí, S.L.P. 78000. Tel. 481/2-4631. 32 rms (all with bath). TEL
$ Rates: $10 single; $12 double. **Parking:** Free.
If you prefer older buildings with the wistful air of better days, try the small Hotel Plaza, conveniently located on the south side of the main plaza. The Plaza's rooms are dark and old-fashioned (except for the few facing the plaza), but are clean and quiet, since most face one of two inner courtyards (one covered, the other open) well back from the street. There's a TV in the lobby and the restaurant downstairs is open daily from 7am to 11pm.

HOTEL PRINCIPAL, Juan Sarabia 145, San Luis Potosí, S.L.P. 78000. Tel. 481/2-0784. 18 rms (all with bath).
$ Rates: $10 single; $14 double; $24 quad.
Although this hotel is directly across from the more expensive María Cristina (from the main plaza, walk three blocks down Othon and turn left on Juan Sarabia; the hotel is on the left), that is where the similarity ends. But a pretty green, white, and gold tiled entryway greets the visitor in this family hotel. The rooms are a bit worn, but clean, pleasant, and freshly painted. Some have carpeting, high windows, and brick trim, and all have fans.

HOTEL PROGRESO, Aldama 415, San Luis Potosí, S.L.P. 78000. Tel. 481/2-0366. 50 rms (all with bath). TEL
$ Rates: $12 single; $13 double.
Many of San Luis Potosi's budget hotels are as much colonial monuments as the grand edifices on the Jardín Hidalgo, although they are much faded, having seen many better days. Such a place is the Hotel Progreso, between Iturbide and Guerrero and opposite Plaza de San Francisco. Like many other hotels in the city, it's an old mansion converted to a hotel. The lofty court (now the lobby) is filled with heavy colonial wood furniture, lovely wood trim carved with boars' and rams' heads over the high

doorways, and two voluptuous but woebegone caryatids supporting the arch at the bottom of the grand staircase leading to the rooms. The rooms are an odd lot, very worn and old-fashioned, but comfortable if you aren't expecting luxury. Inspect your room first, though; housekeeping here is rather lax. The desk clerk can help you with parking.

HOTEL ANAHUAC, Calle Xochitl 140, San Luis Potosí, S.L.P. 78000. **Tel. 481/2-6504** or 2-6505. 42 rms (all with bath). TEL
$ Rates: $12 single; $15 double. **Parking:** 65¢.

A modern and only slightly weather-beaten hotel, the Anahuac has a cavernous, bare lobby. Rooms are equally without frills, but clean and suitable, and the hotel has its own big parking lot. The area around the Anahuac is only a few steps from the railroad station and the Alameda (look for the second, four-story white building on the right side of the street as you walk down Xochitl from Calle de los Bravos). Once it was pretty run-down, but urban renewal has swept away the crumbling buildings and replaced them with parks, public buildings, and a mammoth public parking garage. A dark café in the hotel lobby, brightened by orange and white tablecloths, serves inexpensive breakfasts, antojitos, and a comida.

DOUBLES FOR LESS THAN $35

HOTEL NAPOLES, Juan Sarabia 120, San Luis Potosí, S.L.P. 78000. **Tel. 481/2-8418.** Fax 481/14-2104. 84 rms (all with bath). TV TEL
$ Rates: $29 single; $31 double. **Parking:** $1.35.

⭐ Next door to the María Cristina is its competitor, the Hotel Napoles. (Walk three blocks down Othon from the main plaza and turn left on Juan Sarabia; the hotel is on the right.) Rooms at the Napoles are quite modern and nice. Some of the rooms face the street, others an airshaft, so ask for your preference.

There's a ladies' bar open daily from 3 to 11pm, and a very nice restaurant, La Colomba, with a bilingual menu and gourmet dishes.

HOTEL ARIZONA, Guadalupe Torres 158, San Luis Potosí, S.L.P. 78000. Tel. 481/8-1848. 92 rms (all with bath). A/C TV TEL
$ Rates: $27 single; $30 double; $32 triple.

🅢 The Arizona is the high-rise across the street from the bus station. Its well-kept, carpeted rooms have either a small desk or a table and two chairs. Upper rooms are quieter than those on lower floors, near the bus station bustle.

HOTEL MARÍA CRISTINA, Juan Sarabia 110, San Luis Potosí, S.L.P. 78000. Tel. 481/2-9408. 74 rms (all with bath). TV TEL
$ Rates: $28 single; $32 double; $36 triple. **Parking:** $1.35.

🅢 This is one of San Luis Potosí's most substantial downtown hostelries, with the extra touches some love and others would rather not pay for. If you like the comforts, you'll find them here: a rooftop restaurant and swimming pool, elevators to take you there, carpeting and a color TV with HBO, Cinemax, and sports channels in each of the rooms, and a comfortable lobby that looks just like a European living room, with comfy leather furniture, a crystal chandelier, a gas fireplace, and even an antique French clock on the mantelpiece.

You can get here from the main plaza by walking three blocks on Othon and turning left onto Juan Sarabia; the hotel is on the right.

HOTEL FILHER, Av. Universidad 375, San Luis Potosí, S.L.P. 78000. **Tel. 481/2-1562.** 48 rms (all with bath). TV TEL
$ Rates: $28 single; $32 double.

A good, standard modern place to try is the Hotel Filher, three short blocks from the main square at the corner of Zaragoza and Universidad (look for the white sign). The courtyard has been glassed over, but the hotel still whispers elegance and charm, and prices are reasonable. The rooms are comfortable and some have French doors and balconies. The hotel's restaurant, Los Candiles (open daily from 8am to 9pm), with its cheerful decor of yellow-on-white tablecloths, makes the hotel a nice, comfortable place to dine.

WHERE TO EAT

The hotel restaurants listed above are worth a try in addition to the restaurants listed below.

MEALS FOR LESS THAN $5

TANGA-MANGA, Hidalgo at Los Bravos. Tel. 2-8555.
Specialty: MEXICAN.
$ Prices: Appetizers $2; main courses $3; comida corrida $3.50.
Open: Daily 9am–11pm (comida corrida served noon–5pm).

Scan the menu by the entrance for specials before you walk in and sit down. Modern and shiny-bright, its colorful booths and imitation brick contrast with the weighty solidity of the surrounding architecture. For hanging out at night, there's cappuccino for $1, espresso for even less, and a bar. It's on the main plaza.

POSADA DEL VIRREY, Jardín Hidalgo 3. Tel. 2-7055.
Specialty: MEXICAN.
$ Prices: Main courses $2.50–$5; comida corrida $5.50.
Open: Daily 7am–midnight.

One of the city's most popular restaurants is actually three interconnected mansions. It has great atmosphere—a delightful covered courtyard with a bubbling fountain and singing birds—and is the best place to sample local specialties like enchiladas Potosinas (known elsewhere as empanadas, these come filled with cheese). Obliging waitresses will fix up a sample plate if you'd like to try a variety of empanadas and tacos such as Camila, Aerero, or potosinas—they're different and quite tasty in San Luis. When I dined here a superb cream of tomato soup accompanied the comida corrida, which, though a little high-priced, was huge, delicious, and well worth it.

RESTAURANT/BAR/CAFETERÍA EL CASTILLO, Madero 145. Tel. 2-4221.
Specialty: MEXICAN.
$ Prices: Breakfast $2–$3.50; sandwiches $1–$2.25; main courses $3.50–$5; specialty coffees 70¢–$1.
Open: Daily 8am–11:30pm.

Don't confuse this café with its tiny companion snack/pastry shop of the same name right on the main plaza. This bright and comfy but aging place just off the Jardín Hidalgo is good for a light lunch or snack. The walls are splashed with scenes that would make a Parisian feel right at home—enjoy a view of Montmartre or the Eiffel Tower while checking out the menu. El Castillo is patronized by business-suited types in the morning and late afternoon, and by hip young people in the evening, when there's more of a coffeehouse atmosphere and a variety of specialty coffees in addition to full bar service.

RESTAURANT-CAFE TOKIO, Othon 415. Tel. 2-5899.
Specialty: MEXICAN.
$ Prices: Appetizers $1.25–$3; main courses $3–$6; enchilada plate $3.25; comida corrida $3.25 Mon–Sat, $4.50 Sun.
Open: Daily 7am–midnight (comida corrida served 1–4pm).

Those looking for Japanese food here won't find it. This restaurant is apparently so named because it's owned by a Japanese couple. Facing the Alameda not far from the railroad station, it looks a bit like a station inside—bright and bare and always busy, with waiters and customers scurrying. It serves everything from sandwiches to filet mignon and carne a la tampiqueña (roast beef with salad and guacamole). A good bargain is the enchiladas potosinas plate which comes with five enchiladas topped with chopped onions, cheese, generous dollops of refried beans, guacamole, and salad. The large menu includes inexpensive breakfasts. The Tokio has been dependably good for decades.

LA PARROQUÍA, Carranza 303. Tel. 2-6681.

Specialty: MEXICAN.
$ Prices: Breakfast $2.25–$3.75; appetizers $1.50–$4; main courses $3.75–$7.50; individual pizzas $3.50.
Open: Daily 7am–midnight.

This is one of several spots patronized by the business set. When the cinema next door lets out, the café tables fill up for conversation, seeing and being seen, people-watching—the food is definitely less important than the social life. It's fun, and the menus offer everything from steaks to banana splits. Walk up here for dessert after dinner to take in the nightlife. It's two blocks west of the main plaza.

LA CIGARRA, Carranza 950. Tel. 2-3984.
Specialty: MEXICAN.
$ Prices: Main courses $3–$7.
Open: Daily 8am–4am.

This restaurant is about a 15-minute walk (seven blocks) west of the main plaza. The prices are right and the food is delicious. The house specialty is a fine pozole (a hearty soup of pork and chicken, corn, and other vegetables, served with lime to squirt on top). There's a delicious and inexpensive omelet with ham, potatoes, and beans, or burgers and fries.

LA COLOMBA, in the Hotel Napoles, Juan Sarabia 120. Tel. 2-8418.
Specialty: REGIONAL/INTERNATIONAL.
$ Prices: Appetizers $2.50–$5; main courses $6–$22; chateaubriand for two $20.

The hotel's restaurant, La Colomba, is technically beyond our budget, but its live music and attractive brown-and-white decor make a nice place to dine out for a splurge. The bilingual menu includes seafood, poultry, and meat dishes. Among the gourmet dishes are chateaubriand with béarnaise sauce for two diners and cherries jubilee. To get here from the main plaza, walk three blocks on Othon and turn left on Juan Sarabia.

A CHAIN OF BUDGET RESTAURANTS

Another excellent bargain are the restaurants **Las Tortugas,** all open daily from 7am to 10pm, serving rich, satisfying tortas (sandwiches on a small French roll) for $1 to $1.50—hot or cold—and hamburgers with french fries for $2.60. There are many kinds of tortas from which to choose, put together with all the trimmings: avocado, egg, ham, sausage, and roast beef, to name a few. From its humble beginning as a little sandwich shack, Las Tortugas has become more and more popular, expanding to include several locations, including Las Tortugas Morelos, at the corner of Morelos and Obregon (tel. 4-4713), and Las Tortugas del Correo, on the corner of Morelos and Boca Negra. At all branches, the atmosphere is friendly and informal, the kitchens clean, and the service fast. They also feature free delivery—call 4-6791, the phone number of another Tortugas, this one on the corner of Obregon and Allende, or Los Tortugas del Othon at Carranza 130, at Allende (tel. 2-3682).

EASY EXCURSIONS FROM SAN LUIS POTOSÍ

For a real treat, you can either make a side trip to the **Balneario de Gogorron,** an hour's ride south of San Luis Potosí on the highway heading toward Guanajuato, where you see the sign saying CENTRO VACACIONAL GOGORRON. The attraction here is the thermal water. Unlike many hot springs in the region, which have only lukewarm water, the water here is quite hot, with one small pool of really hot water and a larger, Olympic-size pool, where it's still very warm. There are also private Roman baths. Day rates for the large mineral pools are $3.60 for adults, $2.25 for children; the private Roman baths cost $4.50 per person per hour. A sign in the information house tells the mineral content of the water, known for its health-giving qualities.

The springs area has been made into a complete "vacation center," with a restaurant open from 9am to 8:30pm, a bar, horseback riding on weekends, a wide lawn, and a children's playground in addition to the mineral pools. It's full of happy Mexican families out for a holiday, and all in all it's a relaxing place to be. Open from 8am to 8pm, 365 days a year.

Gogorron has 20 cabañas (cabins) for rent, with 12 more even-larger ones now completed, all spotlessly clean, each with its own private sunken tile tub (large enough for several people to lounge around in the mineral water), two double beds, carpeting, and phone in a spacious, very nice room. Prices, including three meals at the restaurant, are $54 single, $67 double, and $87 triple, for the smaller cabañas; or $80 single, $90 double, and $116 triple for the larger ones. During the week (Monday through Friday only) you can pay for just the cabins (no meals) if you wish, and in that case it's about two-thirds the price.

There's no extra charge to use any of the mineral-water facilities if you're staying overnight. You can make reservations or get additional information by calling Gogorron at 481/4-6655, or by contacting their office in San Luis Potosí, three doors down to the right of the Tourist Office, at Calle Manuel José Othon 100, Suite 52, up on the fourth floor; or write to Apdo. Postal 700, San Luis Potosí, S.L.P. 78000 (tel. 481/2-9435, 2-3636, or 2-1550).

To get to Gogorron from San Luis Potosí, take the highway heading to Mexico City and turn off to the right on the highway heading toward León and Guanajuato; the *balneario* is right on this highway, with lots of trees on your left and a big sign on your right. It's also easy to get there by bus: From the central bus station, take the bus line Flecha Amarilla, which has departures every half hour or so for $1.50, and get off the bus right at the entrance to the *balneario*. Wait at the entrance and flag down a bus when you're ready to go back after a long, relaxing day.

---

4. GUANAJUATO

221 miles NW of Mexico City, 58 miles W of San Miguel de Allende,
130 miles SW of San Luis Potosí, 102 miles N of Morelia

GETTING THERE   By Train   The *Constitucionalista* (one of the first-class Estrella trains) leaves Mexico City at 7am and via Querétaro (departing at 10:20am), Irapuato, and Silao, arrives in Guanajuato at 1:25pm.

By Bus   From Mexico City's Terminal del Norte, the **Flecha Amarilla** line runs buses hourly to Guanajuato. Go to Area 6 ("6 Espera") to find the company's ticket desk and bus platforms. The trip can take as long as 6 hours if you get a local bus that stops in San Juan del Río, Querétaro, Dolores Hidalgo, and San Miguel de Allende. Ask for the express.

Also, **Omnibus de México** serves Guanajuato with one daily bus to/from Guadalajara and two each to/from Querétaro and San Miguel de Allende (at 5pm). From Mexico City **Estrella Blanca** has four daily express buses to Guanajuato, the first at 10am and the last at 6:15pm; the trip takes 5 hours.

By Car   From Mexico City there are two routes. The faster, although it may look the longer, is Highway 57 north to Highway 45D at Querétaro west to Salamanca, where you follow Highway 45 north to Silao and then take Highway 110 east. That route is four-lane road almost all the way. The other route continues north on Highway 57 past Querétaro, then west on Highway 110 through Dolores Hidalgo and continuing on to Guanajuato. From San Luis Potosí, the quickest way is through Dolores Hidalgo.

DEPARTING   By Train   The *Constitucionalista* leaves Guanajuato at 2:30pm and arrives in Querétaro at 5:40pm, where cars are connected with another branch of the *Constitucionalista* to arrive in Mexico City's Buenavista Station at 9pm. Tickets are sold at the Guanajuato train station (tel. 2-1035 or 2-0306) between 8am and 3pm. Weekend travel is heavy, so buy your tickets a day in advance.

By Bus   The bus station is 2 miles northwest of town and frequent buses marked "Central" go between town and the station. **Omnibus de México** has a ticket office in central Guanajuato through a travel agency Viajes Fravsto, Obregón 10, open Monday through Friday from 8:30am to 1pm and 5 to 8pm. from Guanajuato, **Flecha Amarilla** runs 7 buses a day to San Luis Potosí, 7 to Aguascalientes, 13 to Mexico City, 16 to San Miguel de Allende, 10 to Querétaro, and 17 to Guadalajara.

The quickest way to get to San Miguel de Allende is on Flecha Amarilla's "Via Presa" six daily buses; the first is at 6:30am and the last at 6pm, and the trip takes 90 minutes. Eight buses daily go "Via Dolores" and the trip takes 2 hours. Since day trips to San Miguel are popular from Guanajuato, it's a good idea to purchase your ticket a day in advance.

Guanajuato (alt. 6,724 ft.; pop. 113,500) is one of Mexico's hidden gems, discovered by relatively few tourists. Like the other Silver Cities, it harbors architectural treasures, oddities, one of the most charming and beautiful cityscapes in the country, and a wealth of cultural offerings. Clean and beautifully preserved, Guanajuato should be high on anyone's list of Mexico's finest places to visit.

It's an unusually attractive town with an inexplicable air of isolation about it. It was founded in 1559 around the Río Guanajuato, and the narrow, winding streets of today reflect the meanderings of the past. Floods plagued the town though, and finally the river was diverted, leaving an excellent bed for what has now become a subterranean highway with cantilevered houses jutting over the roadway. Most of the stonework and arches you'll see in the tunneled road were already there in the 17th century—all that was needed was stone pavement and street lights. The oldest buildings are those closest to the old riverbed, when the river was used for processing ore, and the town "grew up" from there, covering the hillsides with rock and stucco edifices, some quite colorfully painted.

Rich in history, it was one of the most important colonial cities (along with Querétaro, Zacatecas, San Miguel, and San Luis Potosí) in the 16th, 17th, and 18th centuries. Mines produced a third of all the silver in the world; and like the gold-rush towns in the United States, it bloomed with elaborate churches and mansions, many in the Moorish style. Today, Guanajuato seems like an old Spanish city that has been dumped lock, stock, and barrel into a Mexican river valley.

The name "Guanajuato" is the Spanish adaptation of the Tarascan word *guanaxuato,* meaning "hill of frogs." They called it this because rocks above town appeared to be shaped like frogs. This was especially significant since, to the Tarascan, the frog represented the god of wisdom.

ORIENTATION

ARRIVING By Train The station is in the north part of town close to several hotels.

By Bus The modern station, about 2 miles northwest of town on the road to Celaya, opened in February 1990 and has all the latest conveniences—shops, baggage storage, telephone center with fax and long distance, and a fast-food, cafeteria-style restaurant. If you aren't carting much luggage, take one of the city buses marked "Centro" into town. Otherwise there are taxis.

By Car Try not to lose your sanity before finding a place to park. Such a windy, hilly town as Guanajuato defies good verbal or written directions. Just be alert for one-way streets, and after winding around through the subterranean highway a bit you'll get your bearings enough to park. If in doubt, follow the signs TEATRO JUÁREZ or JARDÍN UNIÓN, which will get you to the center of town, where you can park and collect your wits.

INFORMATION The **Tourist Information Office** is at the intersection of Juárez and Cinco de Mayo (tel. 2-0086 or 2-1574). It's open Monday through Friday from 8:30am to 7:30pm, and on Saturday, Sunday, and holidays from 10am to 2pm, with an English-speaking staff. Here you can get information and a free, detailed map of the city, with a map of the entire state of Guanajuato on the back.

GUANAJUATO

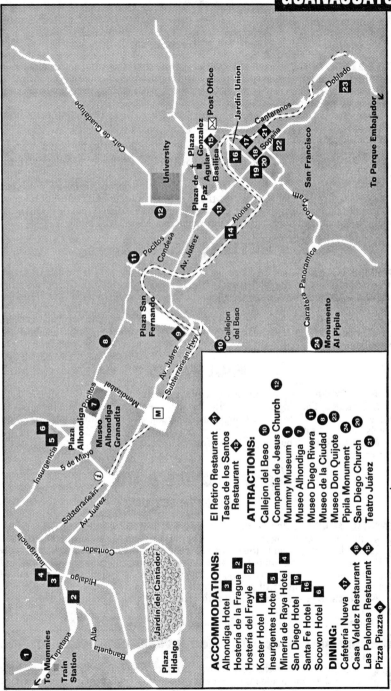

ACCOMMODATIONS:
Alhondiga Hotel **3**
Hosteria de la Fragua **2**
Hosteria del Frayle **22**
Koster Hotel **14**
Insurgentes Hotel **5**
Mineria de Raya Hotel **4**
San Diego Hotel **19**
Santa Fe Hotel **16**
Socovon Hotel **6**

DINING:
Cafeteria Nueva **17**
Casa Valdez Restaurant **18**
Las Palomas Restaurant **15**
Pizza Piazza **9**
El Retiro Restaurant **21**
Tasca de los Santos Restaurant **23**

ATTRACTIONS:
Callejon del Beso **10**
Compania de Jesus Church **12**
Mummy Museum **1**
Museo Alhondiga **7**
Museo Diego Rivera **11**
Museo de la Ciudad **8**
Museo Don Quijote **23**
Pipila Monument **24**
San Diego Church **20**
Teatro Juárez **21**

Post Office ⊠   Information ⓘ   Church ✝

Another resource is **Transportes Tursticos de Guanajuato,** with offices at the bottom of the Basilica Church of San Diego (tel. 2-2838 or 2-2134), open daily from 8am to 8pm. They offer free information in English, as well as an excellent tour of the city (see "Organized Tours" in "What to See and Do," below).

CITY LAYOUT   Guanajuato is a town of narrow streets twisting up the mountains and interspersed by pleasant parks, plazas, and churches. Using our map or any other, you'll soon learn that they aren't to scale, nor is every narrow street or connecting stairstep walkway shown.

Among all Guanajuato's plazas and parks, the **Plaza de la Unión** is the true heart of the city, the place where students, locals, and visitors gather more than any other. On one side are both the Teatro Juárez and Templo de San Diego, and it's within walking distance of almost all the city sights. As another point of orientation, the statue of **Pipila,** high on a mountainside overlooking the town, is in line with the Teatro Juárez and Plaza de la Unión.

If you're driving, an excellent orientation is the **scenic highway** (Carretera Panorámica), from which you can see the city from above. It starts north of town off the road to Irapuato, passes *Pipila,* continues south to the dam (Presa de la Olla), and finally loops around north again to the Valenciana Mine and Church.

GETTING AROUND

Walking is the only way really to get to know this labyrinthine town. For longer stretches, just hop on the main **bus,** marked "Presa-Estación," which operates from one end of town at the railroad station to the other end at Presa de la Olla. Buses use the subterranean highway when going south and subterranean bus stops are along the way; for example, there's one near the Teatro Juárez, off the Jardín da la Unión. **Taxis** are abundant and generally reasonably priced, but as usual you should establish the price before setting out.

FAST FACTS

Area Code   The telephone area code is 473.

Climate   This high-altitude city has mild temperatures in summer, but in winter it can dip to freezing. Bring warm clothing and remember, too, that most hotels have no heat.

Post Office   The post office (Correo) is located on Positos, to the right of the university.

WHAT TO SEE & DO

THE TOP ATTRACTIONS

TEATRO JUÁREZ, Jardín de la Unión. Tel. 2-0183.

Built in 1903 during the opulent era of the Porfiriato when a theater represented all that was elegant, today it's the venue for many productions, especially during the Cervantino festival. Outside are bronze sculptures of lions and lanterns, and inside the five-story U-shaped theater is embellished with carved ornamentation all a flurry of red, gold, and blue.

Admission: 75¢; 50¢ additional with a still camera, $1.75 additional with a video camera.

Open: Tues–Sun 9:15am–1:45pm and 5–7:30pm.

MUSEUM BIRTHPLACE OF DIEGO RIVERA, Calle Positos 47. Tel. 2-1197.

The house where the painter was born on December 8, 1886, has been refurbished and made into a museum; on the wall is a plaque commemorating "el pintor magnifico."

The house, 1½ blocks north of Plaza de la Paz, has been completely redone and now it is more like a museum than a home. Upstairs there's a fine collection of Rivera's early works. He began painting when he was 12 years old, and moved to Paris where he became a Marxist during World War I. You can see the cubist influence in his painting of this period. There are sketches of some of his earlier murals, the ones that made his reputation, but most of his works on display are paintings from 1902 to 1956. On the third floor is a small auditorium where lectures and conferences are held.

Admission: $1.

Open: Tues–Sat 10am–1:30pm and 4–6:30pm, Sun 10am–2:30pm.

MUSEO DEL PUEBLO DE GUANAJUATO, Calle Positos 7. Tel. 2-2990.

Farther down on the same side of the street as the Rivera museum, this special museum is housed in a 17th-century mansion once belonging to the Marquès San Juan de Rayas. It holds a priceless collection of more than 1,000 colonial-era civil and religious pieces gathered by the local distinguished muralist José Chávez Morado. Chávez murals can be seen in this museum as well as the Regional Museum La Alhondiga down the street. Besides the Chávez collection, contemporary displays upstairs show Mexican artists. Every other year the museum hosts the Biennial of Diego Rivera, a showcase for Mexico's up-and-coming artists, which is a truly fine exhibit if you get a chance to see it.

Admission: Free.

Open: Tues–Sat 10am–1:30pm and 4–6:30pm, Sun 10am to 3pm.

REGIONAL MUSEUM LA ALHONDIGA, Mendizábal 6. Tel. 2-1112.

Continuing a long block farther on the same street as the Rivera museum, you'll see the huge Alhondiga on the left. (The entrance is on Positas). The Alhondiga de Granaditas, the doors of which Pipila burned, was built between 1798 and 1809 to be the town granary—such a splendid one that it was called El Palacio del Maiz (the Corn Palace). Although the Spanish had lost the battle when Pipila and company burned down the doors to the Alhondiga where they had taken refuge, they still had not lost the war. A year later the heads of revolutionaries Hidalgo, Allende, Aldama, and Jimenez were brought here and hung in iron cages on the four outside corners of the building—where they remained from 1811 to 1821 to remind the populace of what happens to revolutionaries. On the four corners of the building the name plaques below the cornice commemorate the four heroes of this stormy period. Later on, from 1864 to 1949, the building was a prison.

IN THEIR FOOTSTEPS

Diego Rivera (1886–1957) Considered the most outstanding of Mexico's famous "Big Three" muralists, Rivera's art training began at age 10 at the Academy of San Carlos in Mexico City and continued with scholarships to Europe and foreign travel off and on until 1922. Besides art he adopted a Marxist political philosophy and his grand, and often controversial, murals present Mexico's history through his romanticized Communist eyes. Some of his greatest murals are at the National Palace in Mexico City and the Palacio de Cortés in Cuernavaca. Controversial even in his lifetime, his mural painted for New York City's Rockefeller Center was destroyed because Lenin appeared in it. He later recreated it in the Palacio Belles Artes in Mexico City. At his insistence the Mexican government gave communist leader Leon Trotsky refuge in Mexico City. He married, divorced and remarried artist Frida Kahlo.
Museums of his work and pre-Hispanic art collections are in Mexico City and Guanajuato.

  • **Birthplace:** Guanajuato, Gto.
  • **Residences:** Calle Positos 47, Guanajuato, his birthplace and now the Diego Rivera Museum.
  • **Resting Place:** Dolores Cemetery, Chapultepec Park, Mexico City.

The Alhondiga is now a museum, and one of the best in Mexico. There are two levels to the museum, with rooms off the courtyard. You'll see numerous pre-Columbian relics: pots, decorative seals and stamps, terra-cotta figurines, and stone implements. The lower level (on which you enter) has rooms of regional crafts and several rooms of the pre-Hispanic art collection of José Chávez Morado, the artist responsible for the splendid murals on both stairwells (and whose collection is in the important Museo del Pueblo de Guanajuato). Mexico's most complete collection of pre-Hispanic stamps was donated to the museum by American archeologist Frederick Field. From the southeast part of the state are Chipícuaro ceramics dating from A.D. 350–450, which were saved when the Solis Dam was constructed in 1949, and make up a type of ceramics rarely seen in Mexico. A long corridor contains bronze masks of the revolutionary heroes as well as an eternal flame in their honor.

Upstairs is a Bellas Artes section with shows (both temporary and permanent) of national and international artists. Following are several rooms showing the history of the state of Guanajuato, particularly its revolutionary history, and its dozen mines, the first one begun in 1557 on orders of Charles V. There are some interesting lithographs showing the city as it was in the 18th and 19th centuries, as well as 20th-century photographs.

Admission: $3.50 ($1.50 extra with a camera), free for students with an ID card, free for all on Sun.

Open: Tues–Sat 10am–2pm and 4–5:30pm, Sun 10am–4pm.

EL PIPILA

High above the town, with a great view overlooking the Jardín de la Unión, is the city's monument to José de los Reyes Martínez, nicknamed El Pipila, a brave young miner who, on the orders of Hidalgo, set fire to the strategically situated grain warehouse, the Alhondiga de Granaditas, in which the Royalists were hiding during the War of Independence. Hidalgo, a young priest who had appealed for Mexico's independence from Spain, on September 16, 1810, led an army that captured Guanajuato. In this bloody battle 600 inhabitants and 2,000 Indians were killed, but the revolution was on its way. Guanajuato became the rebel capital, but its history was short—10 months later the revolutionary leader, Hidalgo, was captured, shot in Chihuahua, and his head sent to Guanajuato to be exhibited.

Today, Pipila's statue raises a sword high over the city in everlasting vigilance, and the inscription at his feet proclaims AUN HAY OTRAS ALHONDIGAS POR INCENDIAR— "There are still other alhondigas to burn."

From the statue at the top (you can climb inside the statue too, if you wish), there's a lovely view of the city below. Churches appear everywhere, bronze figures atop the Teatro Juárez, the massive university—all unfold below. It's the best spot in town for photos. There's a little park where kids play ball and families picnic. The atmosphere and view are delightful.

Admission: Free.

Open: Daily 24 hours. **Directions:** Go via automobile or bus ("Pipila"), or on foot on a rugged winding pathway (wear comfortable shoes). Walk up Calle Sopena from the Jardín de la Unión, and turn to the right up Callejon del Calvario. A sign on the wall reads AL PIPILA ("To Pipila").

MUSEO DE LOS MOMIAS (Mummy Museum), Calzada del Panteón. Tel. 2-0639.

✪ At the northwestern end of town is Calzada del Panteón, which leads up to the municipal cemetery. Once there, you'll find a building in which the mummies are displayed in tall showcases and glass caskets. Dryness, plus the earth's gases and minerals, in certain sections of the Panteón cause decomposition to halt. Because of space limitations, people are buried for only 5 years; then, if the relatives can't continue to pay for the grave, the bodies are exhumed to make room for more. Those on display, however, were exhumed between 1865 and 1975. The mummies stand or recline in glass cases, grinning, choking, or staring. It's impossible to resist the temptation to go up and look at them—everybody does—and this is the only graveyard I've seen with souvenir stands next to the main gate, selling sugar effigies of the mummies.

Admission: $1, 75¢ extra with a still camera, $1.75 extra with a movie camera.
Open: Daily 9am–6pm. **Directions:** It's a steep climb on foot, but the bus labeled "Presa-Estación" runs along Juárez and this will take you to the foot of the cobbled hill. Guanajuato's cab drivers, for this trip, will invariably tend to charge what the traffic will bear.

OTHER ATTRACTIONS

The **Church of San Diego,** on the Jardín de la Unión, stands almost as it did in 1633 when it was built under the direction of Franciscan missionaries. After a flood in 1760 that nearly destroyed it, reconstruction was completed in 1786; half the funds were given by the Count of Valenciana. The pink cantera stone facade is a fine example of Mexican baroque (Churrigueresque).

Plazuela del Baratillo, just off the Jardín de la Unión, has a beautiful fountain (a gift from Emperor Maximilian) at its center and you'll always find people sitting around peacefully, some in the shade and others in the sun, for late in the afternoon the plazuela is almost exactly divided between *sol* and *sombra.* **Plazuela San Fernando** is larger and has a stone platform where very often there will be local Mexican dances with the younger generation decked out in bright costumes.

The magnificent **university** was founded in 1732, but its entrance was rebuilt in 1945 in a stately manner so that the building dominates the whole town. The university (Diego Rivera was a graduate) is just behind **Plaza de la Paz,** and open every day and visitors are welcome.

The **Church of the Compañia de Jesús,** next door to the university, was built in 1747 by the Jesuit order and was the biggest of their churches at that time. It is distinctly Churrigueresque on the outside, but the interior, which was restored in the 19th century, is not. This church was built as part of the Jesuit university, founded in 1732 on orders of Philip V, on the site of the present university, the last of 23 universities built by the Jesuit order in Mexico.

READERS RECOMMEND

Museo Iconografico del Quijote, Manuel Doblado 1 (tel. 2-6721). *"The Don Quijote Museum is a gem with all kinds of art centered on the theme of the great adventurer-idealist. Paintings, sculpture in bronze, a stunning mural showing scenes from the life of Cervantes. It's a must to savor and the museum building has all the charm of, say, the Picasso Museum in Barcelona."* —Robert S. Thomson and Josephine Slogget, Vancouver, B.C., Canada. [*Author's note:* It's near Jardín Unión, a few doors south of Hostería del Frayle, and truly a wonderful museum. Don Quijote is represented in many forms by artists including Salvador Dalí, Francisco de Icaza, José Moreno Carbonero, Pedro Coronel, and others from around the world. It's open Tuesday through Saturday from 10am to 1:30pm and 4 to 6:30pm, and on Sunday from 10am to 2:30pm. Admission is free.]

Instituto Falcon, Callejon de la Mora 158, Guanajuato, Gto. Tel. 473/2-3694. *"We studied here last summer for 1 month—our second such experience. The teaching at the instituto was the highest quality. Classes were small, teachers kind, and lessons imaginative. Both the school's director, Jorge Barroso, and our instructors took a personal interest in the students and went out of their way to accommodate varied interests and to ensure rewarding experiences. Our host family was terrific and we are looking forward to returning to the instituto this summer."* —Ann and Greg Oxrieder, Bellevue, Wash.

NEARBY ATTRACTIONS

For a suburban outing, hop any bus that says "Presa" (try at the bus stop in the Subterranean near Jardín de la Unión) to the **Parque de la Acacias** and the **Presa de la Olla,** the artificial lake. There are several parks and lots of trees—it's a good place for a lazy afternoon.

While in the neighborhood, you might note the **Government Palace** on Paseo de la Presa, with its pink stone front and green-tile interior. The neighborhood around here is residential and will give you another glimpse of Guanajuato, away from the bustle of the plazas.

The most famous silver mine is **La Valenciana,** said to have produced a fifth of the silver circulating in the world from 1558 to 1810. It can be reached by taking Route 30, the Dolores Hidalgo road, 3 miles northeast of town (buses are "J. Perones–Marfil" with VALENCIANA written in soap on the windshield). The mine was closed about 40 years ago, but then reopened, and a caretaker is there to show you the eight-sided vertical shaft (1,650 ft. deep) and the once-grandiose courtyard. You can take a look down the long mine shaft (but you can't go down), from which silver is still being extracted today, along with about 50 other minerals and metals. Silver products from this mine are sold in the adjoining silver shop, at not-unreasonable prices.

While you're here in Valenciana, be sure to visit the **Iglesia de San Cayetano,** the magnificent church built in 1765 by the first Count of Valencia. It is one of the most beautiful of the colonial churches in Churrigueresque style—a true masterpiece and one of the finest churches in Mexico, absolutely filled with luxurious floor-to-ceiling carvings of white cedar covered with 18-karat gold, a baroque art form unique to Mexico, what with the Spanish idea of art and the abundant gold of Mexico to manifest the glory. You'll find some beautiful paintings here too. If you're lucky, you may be able to catch a concert of baroque music, performed on the large organ.

All through this mountainous area, more than a dozen mines produced silver. Some are now abandoned, and some, like Valenciana, are still functioning. Also around here there were more than 150 splendid mansion-haciendas of wealthy colonial mine owners. Most are now either in ruins, or restored and privately owned, but there's one you can visit, and I certainly recommend doing so.

Located about 2 miles from town on the ancient road to Marfil, the **Museo Ex-Hacienda San Gabriel de Barrera** is housed in one of the most luxurious of the 18th-century grand haciendas, with magnificent buildings, a gold-adorned chapel, and acres of lovely gardens. You can wander through Italian gardens, English gardens, Chinese gardens, cactus gardens—quite a variety, all decorated with beautiful statues and fountains from the various countries represented. The hacienda, which had remained in the family for 2 centuries, was sold to the Mexican government in 1979 and is now a museum furnished with Mexican and European furniture and open to the public. You can visit it any day from 9am to 6:30pm; admission is $1.25, plus $1 for a still camera or $2.75 for a video camera.

The elegant Hotel San Gabriel de Barrera is also here—see "Worth the Extra Bucks" in "Where to Stay" for information on this, and for directions on how to come out here from town.

IN THEIR FOOTSTEPS

Miguel Hidalgo y Costilla (1753-1811) A small-town priest in the town of Dolores, Guanajuato, before his fame as Father of Mexican Independence, he was better known for his anti-celibacy beliefs, and disbelief in papal supremacy. He taught parishioners how to grow mulberry trees for silkworms (for silkmaking) and grapes (for winemaking prohibited by the crown), and ceramic making; the latter two still thrive in the region. Among several in his area, he secretly conspired to free Mexico from Spanish domination. On the morning of September 16, 1810, a messenger from Josefa Ortiz de Dominguez brought Hidalgo word that the conspiracy was uncovered. He quickly decided to publicly call for independence (known today as the *grito* or "cry") from his parish church after which he galloped from village to village spreading the news, and gathering troops.

• **Birthplace:** Hacienda de San Diego de Corralejo, Gto.
• **Residence:** His small home, today a museum, is on Morelos street, corner of Hidalgo in Dolores Hidalgo, Gto.
• **Resting Place:** Independence Monument, Mexico City.

ORGANIZED TOURS

Perhaps your best bet for seeing Guanajuato is to go to **Transportes Turísticos de Guanajuato,** at the bottom (left side) of the Basílica Church of San Diego (tel. 2-2838 or 2-2134), open daily from 8am to 8pm. They offer free information in English, as well as an excellent bilingual tour of the city that includes the Panteón, the Valenciana mine and church, and *Pípila*, all of which are otherwise hard to reach. The 3½-hour tour costs $4 per person. Passengers are picked up at various hotels, so check to see at what time and where you can catch the minibus.

SPECIAL EVENTS

Every year, from about October 15 to November 4, the state of Guanajuato sponsors the **Festival Cervantino (International Cervantes Festival),** 2 weeks of performing arts from all over the world. In recent years they have had marionettes from Czechoslovakia, the Elliot Feld Dance Company from New York, the Cuban National Ballet, and a host of Mexican artists. The shows are held in open plazas and theaters all over town. These same groups also tour Mexico after the festival, so there's a chance of seeing them elsewhere. Book rooms in well in advance during the festival; if Guanajuato is full, consider staying in nearby San Miguel de Allende.

SHOPPING

The **Mercado Hidalgo,** housed in a building that resembles a Victorian railroad station (built 1909), has a cavernous lower level and an upper balcony that encircles the whole building. It's stacked with lots of little eateries and stalls, and every conceivable kind of pottery and ceramic ware, even including items imported from Japan. From this balcony you can look down onto one of the neatest layouts in Mexico: symmetrical rows of stalls and counters providing splashes of orange, green, red, brown, and black—the tones of the fruits and vegetables they're covered with. Very few people sprawl around on the floor or in the aisles, unlike most markets, but whether this is due to the local ordinance or a sense of orderliness I can't say. The market is open every day, from morning to evening.

The **Gorky González Workshop,** Calle Pastita, by the stadium, is a good place to pick up the Talavera-style pottery for which Sr. González is famous. Hours are irregular, but you may be able to browse through the small showroom Monday through Friday from 9am to 2pm and 4 to 6pm.

EVENING ENTERTAINMENT

The word *entremeses* literally means "intermissions," and it's the term given to short sketches that were written to be presented between performances. In Guanajuato, it means a very special entertainment: an evening under the stars in a medieval-style courtyard, **Plazuela de San Roque,** with about 90 minutes of acting and action by students and faculty of the University of Guanajuato. The *entremeses* are presented several times during the Festival Cervantino and are some of the best theater you'll ever see. Tickets (which must be obtained in advance) can be bought at the Teatro Juárez for $4.45. The Tourism Office (tel. 2-0086) can give you a list of dates for which the performances are scheduled.

Let me emphasize again that these are no ordinary amateur theatricals. If you are in the vicinity, or conceivably can arrange to be in the vicinity of Guanajuato, when a performance is scheduled—drop everything and buy, beg, borrow, or steal a ticket. You'll never regret it! The fact that the show takes place in a real courtyard with galloping horses, water thrown from windows, church bells ringing, gusts of wind blowing out the candles, and people in authentic period costumes looking not too out of place in 20th-century Guanajuato makes it all the more impressive. Don't miss it!

If you don't happen to be there during the Festival Cervantino, you can still catch some worthwhile theater—free—in Plazuela de San Roque at 8pm on any Sunday night when the university is in session, presented by the students as entertainment for all.

Try the bars at the **Hotel San Diego** and the **Hostería del Frayle.** Another more expensive choice is the **Cantarranas Bar** at the Hotel Real de Minas, on the cobblestone road that leads to Mexico City. A piano player entertains on weekends.

WHERE TO STAY

During the International Cervantes Festival held in late October and November, rooms are virtually impossible to find unless you have a reservation, and even then it's good to claim your room early in the day. Some visitors have to stay as far away as Querétaro, León, or San Miguel de Allende, and come to Guanajuato for the day.

If you're not opposed to taking a bus to and from the city center, stay outside town. There are several good choices with reasonable rates, and out here you have the quiet tree-lined streets instead of the city bustle. These hotels are easily reached by taking the "Presa-Estación" bus from the corner of Cinco de Mayo and Juárez, just north of the Mercado. If you're hearty, you can even walk it, once you've gotten there and dropped off your luggage.

DOUBLES FOR LESS THAN $20

CASA KLOSTER, Calle de Alonso 32, Guanajuato, Gto. 36000. Tel. 473/2-0088. 15 rms (none with bath).
$ Rates: $7 single; $9 double.

Those looking for a European-style pension will find it in this hotel located on a quiet side street northwest of the Jardín de la Union, one block west of Juárez, across from Telefonos de México. Run by a warm and friendly old couple, the Kloster has a large central courtyard brilliant with birds and flowers, around which are arranged the very plain but very clean rooms. The common bathrooms, where you light a wood fire under the broiler to make hot water for a shower, are also spotlessly clean. No meals are served, but don't be surprised if Don Jesús, the proprietor, invites you to share a morning coffee in the family kitchen.

HOTEL ALHONDIGA, Insurgencia 49, Guanajuato, Gto. 36000. Tel. 473/2-0525. 30 rms (all with bath).
$ Rates: $12 single; $20 double.
Located just off Plaza Alhondiga, within walking distance of all downtown sights, this hotel has small, basic rooms. Front rooms are the nicest, but also the noisiest, as this is a major corner (if there is such thing in Guanajuato). The hotel has a restaurant and parking.

DOUBLES FOR LESS THAN $30

HOTEL SOCAVON, Alhondiga 41-A, Guanajuato, Gto. 36060. Tel. 473/2-6666. 37 rms (all with bath).
$ Rates: $19 single; $23 double.

All rooms, arranged around a central courtyard, are attractive, clean, and carpeted, with nice touches like copper washbasins in the private baths, and arches all over. The comfortable second-floor restaurant/bar is open daily from 7:30am to 10:30pm. The hotel is at the north end of town along the street that goes to Dolores Hidalgo.

MOTEL EMBAJADORAS, Parque Embajadoras, Guanajuato, Gto. 36000. Tel. 473/2-0081. 25 rms (all with bath). TEL
$ Rates: $23 single or double.

This is the best choice out of downtown on the tree-lined street heading toward Paseo Madero. It's attractive and comfortable, and the very quiet rooms are small but clean. The nicest thing, however, is the quiet surrounding grounds. There's a patio at the rear, with tables, chairs, and a hammock; climbing bougainvilleas complete the tranquil scene. A nice reasonably priced restaurant/bar takes care of meals.

HOSTERÍA DEL FRAYLE, Sopena 3, Guanajuato, Gto. 36000. Tel. 473/2-1179. 37 rms (all with bath). TEL

$ Rates: $20 single; $24 double.

Half a block north of Plaza de la Unión, this is a perfect hotel to sample quarters as they might have been in colonial times. Ore was processed here before it went to the mint during colonial times. Today it has been charmingly converted into a hotel. Each room has tall wooden doors, old hardwood floors, and comfortable furnishings with a cozy hint of yesteryear. It could be plenty drafty and nippy in winter though, so bring your long johns. Management is friendly and there's a nice restaurant serving Italian food to the left off the lobby.

DOUBLES FOR LESS THAN $40

HOTEL EL INSURGENTE, Juárez 226, Guanajuato, Gto. 36000. Tel. 473/2-2294. 83 rms (all with bath). TV TEL
$ Rates: $32 single; $36 double.
During recent remodeling, the nice old stone doorways were left intact and attractive wood and stone were added in the lobby. The rooms, on the other hand, are more modern but not fancy. Although small, each has wall-to-wall carpeting, FM radio, and color TV with U.S. channels. The rooms with windows facing the street aren't claustrophobic as the interior rooms tend to be, but they do have the problem of noise; better to take a small but quiet one on the glassed-in central court, on the third or fourth floor. The hotel is six long blocks north of the Jardín de la Unión.

MESÓN DE LA FRAGUA, Tepetapa 46, Guanajuato, Gto. 36000. Tel. 473/2-2715 or 2-2726. 55 rms (all with bath). TV TEL
$ Rates: $30 single; $36 double; $45 junior suite that sleeps five; $32 master suite that sleeps three.
Enter through elaborately carved doors into a pretty little colonial-style lobby with a restaurant on the right and a tiny swimming pool straight ahead. Stairs and halls meander up and down to the rooms, which are carpeted and furnished with tasteful tile accents, and either double or king-size beds. This hotel is not well known, so it's a good choice if the town is full. It's half a block from the train station.

HOTEL MINERAL DE RAYAS, Alhondiga 7 y Callejon del Apartado 487, Guanajuato, Gto. 36000. Tel. 473/2-1967 or 2-3749. 82 rms (all with bath).
$ Rates: $30 single; $36 double.
Since rooms are overpriced considering their quality and overall maintenance, consider this one only if Guanajuato is full. It's a labyrinthine building with rather dark, carpeted rooms. There's parking, and an indoor tile swimming pool, which may or may not be clean. It's at the north end of town on the street that eventually goes to Dolores Hidalgo.

WORTH THE EXTRA BUCKS

POSADA SANTA FE, Jardín de la Unión 12, Guanajuato, Gto. 36000. Tel. 473/2-0084. 50 rms (all with bath). A/C TV TEL
$ Rates: $50 single; $56 double.
This elegant old-time hotel was converted from a mansion dating from the 18th and 19th centuries. Lobby walls are decorated with paintings of colonial Guanajuato by Fernando Leal. Tile staircases with elaborate ironwork lead up the meandering halls and rooms. The well-kept rooms are carpeted and have furnishings reminiscent of the 1930s. Rooms facing back streets can be noisy. There's a delightful pool and sundeck on the roof. The lobby bar, and both the indoor and outdoor restaurant are among the most popular in town. Student singers stroll in often to serenade diners.

HOTEL SAN GABRIEL DE BARRERA, Camino Antigua a Marfil km 2.5, Guanajuato, Gto. 36050. Tel. 473/2-3980. 139 rms (all with bath). TV TEL
$ Rates: $60 single; $70 double.
Formerly called the Hotel El Presidente Guanajuato, this hotel is 2 miles from the center of town in a pretty valley next to the beautiful and authentic Hacienda San

Gabriel Barrera museum. Flower-covered terraces, a spacious lobby and restaurant, large attractive rooms overlooking a tidy swimming pool, and very friendly staff are what you get. However, transportation presents a problem. Cabs cost $3 between town and the hotel. Take the bus ("Noria Alta" or "Marfil") to Noria Alta, then walk 5 or 10 minutes. Catch the same bus back into town; even though the bus goes right by the hotel, it's not allowed to stop on the twisty road, so you must board or exit at Noria Alta.

HOTEL SAN DIEGO, Jardín de la Unión 1 (Apdo. Postal 8), Guanajuato, Gto. 36000. Tel. 473/2-1300. 43 rms (all with bath). TEL
$ Rates: $52 single; $60 double.
The big open lobby, next to the Iglesia de San Diego, has paintings of Guanajuato in colonial times by artist Fernando Leal. The building was once part of the church complex and the hotel itself features broad arches and interior courtyard where carriages once entered. The recently updated rooms have light-colored furnishings and new beds, but don't expect luxury—the prices here are a reflection of the hotel's prime location. The second-story restaurant-bar overlooking the jardín is a popular spot for people-watching.

WHERE TO EAT

If you find yourself hungry in the **Mercado Hidalgo** area, stop and try one of the many inexpensive eateries inside the huge mercado edifice, or in the building just next door to the south, open all day, every day. Right beside the Mercado Hidalgo is the **Mercado Gavira,** a very different sort of place. Modern, soiled, and bustling with cookshops à la Marrakesh, this is a good place for the fearless to try native cuisine. If your stomach is beyond insult, launch into a serving of birria, barbacoa (barbecue), pozole (stew), or menudo (tripe). Choose kettles that are boiling and you should do all right. Ask for prices—observe the sign that says (in Spanish): "Avoid disappointment, ask to see the price list!"

There are also a number of inexpensive home-style cookshops on both sides of the parking lot in front of the Hotel El Insurgente. From the hotel all the way to the market, you can pick up a comida corrida for about $3, or sandwiches and daily-special plates for even less.

MEALS FOR LESS THAN $5

CASA VALADEZ, Jardín de la Union 3. Tel. 2-1157.
  Specialty: MEXICAN/INTERNATIONAL.
$ Prices: Appetizers $2–$5; main courses $5–$10; comida corrida $4.50.
  Open: Daily 8am–11pm (comida corrida served 2–5pm).
Just across from the Teatro Juárez is this combination restaurant and soda fountain, with reasonable prices. The best deal here is the comida corrida. There's live music every day from 3 to 5pm and again from 7:30 to 9:30pm, helping to make this the popular restaurant, watering hole, and hangout that it is.

CAFETERÍA NUEVA, Jardín de la Unión at Allende 3. Tel. 2-1414.
  Specialty: MEXICAN REGIONAL.
$ Prices: Appetizers $1–$2; main courses $2.25–$3; comida corrida $3.25.
  Open: Daily 8:30am–9:30pm (comida corrida served 1–4pm).
Located on the rear corner of the Jardín de la Unión, this nothing-special eatery is nevertheless popular with students and creative types because of its low prices (perhaps the lowest in town) and informal, friendly atmosphere. Everything on the menu here—from breakfast to sandwiches to steak and potatoes—is low-priced and enjoyably edible. Be sure to notice the graffiti on the ceiling.

CAFE EL RETIRO, Sopena 12. Tel. 2-0622.
  Specialty: MEXICAN.

$ Prices: Appetizers $1.25–$2.25; main courses $3.50–$10; comida corrida $4.75.
Open: Daily 8am–11pm (comida corrida served 1–4:30pm).

Sooner or later everyone—local, student, or visitor—winds up at El Retiro. The best inexpensive lunch in town is served here, consisting of soup, rice with cheese, two or three choices of meat dish, dessert, and coffee. On the à la carte menu you can choose from a variety of antojitos, such as tacos and enchiladas or a quarter chicken. With its vases of flowers on the sideboard, and its cafeteria-modern furniture, El Retiro seems more like somebody's living room than a restaurant, and the service is just as informally friendly. It's half a block south of the Jardín de la Unión, cater-corner to the Teatro Juárez.

RESTAURANT/BAR LAS PALOMAS, Ayuntamiento 19. Tel. 2-4936.
Specialty: MEXICAN.
$ Prices: Appetizers $2.25–$3.75; main courses $5–$10.50; comida corrida $5.
Open: Daily 9am–11pm (comida corrida served 2–5pm).

The decor is something to see at this special restaurant located next door to the post office (Correos) a few blocks north of the Jardín de la Unión. It has high-quality artwork covering every arched adobe wall, colorful tablecloths and flowers on the tables, and classical music playing in the background. A full meal might include filet mignon and mushrooms, with choice of soup, salad, dessert, and coffee.

MEALS FOR LESS THAN $10

PIZZA PIAZZA, San Fernando 24. Tel. 2-3094.
Specialty: ITALIAN.
$ Prices: Pizza $4.50–$10.
Open: Daily 2–11pm.

Young sophisticates and students with a little cash patronize this restaurant which is right on Plazuela San Fernando. Comfortable niche-booths and rough furniture provide an ambience for easy camaraderie: This is one of the best places in town to meet young Mexicans of both sexes. Pizzas come in small, medium, and large—the large can feed five or six people. Beer and sangría are also served, either in the dining room or at the tables under the tree in the plazuela. They serve up lots of spaghetti too, for only $1.50.

There are two more Pizza Piazzas, with the same menu, prices, and hours. One is at Hidalgo 14 (tel. 2-4259), just off the Jardín de la Unión; the other is at Avenida Juárez 69A (tel. 2-5917), up from the Mercado at Plaza los Pastitos.

TASCA DE LOS SANTOS, Plaza de la Paz 28. Tel. 2-2320.
Specialty: MEXICAN REGIONAL.
$ Prices: Appetizers $3–$4.50; main courses $4.25–$15.
Open: Daily 8am–midnight.

This is one of Guanajuato's snazzier restaurants and the menu is completely à la carte. The food, service, and heavy Spanish decor will please you. Paella is a house specialty. They also serve chicken in white wine sauce and beef a la Andaluza. You can order wine by the bottle or glass.

EN ROUTE TO SAN MIGUEL DE ALLENDE

The fastest route from here to Mexico City is south on Highway 45 connecting with Highway 45D to the capital—it's four-lane roadway all the way. The scenic route to Mexico City is Highway 110 north to **Dolores Hidalgo,** then continuing south through San Miguel de Allende. Dolores Hidalgo (pop. 80,000) has little to offer. It's famous because it's where the local priest, Miguel Hidalgo, first made his proclamation of the independence of Mexico, the "Cry of Dolores," on September 16, 1810. The church on the main plaza was the site of the proclamation, and Hidalgo's house, at Morelos 1 (one block from the bus station), is now a museum filled with flags, photos, and documents. Since the drive from Guanajuato to San Miguel takes only about 2 hours, an overnight stop in Dolores isn't really necessary. If you just want refreshments, there are several restaurants on the plaza.

5. SAN MIGUEL DE ALLENDE

180 miles NW of Mexico City, 75 miles W of Guanajuato

GETTING THERE   By Train   First-class direct train service to San Miguel has been suspended, but you can get there most of the way by train and complete the trip by bus. **From Nuevo Laredo:** *El Regiomontaño* leaves Nuevo Laredo at 3:15pm and arrives in San Luis Potosí at 4am. It has both dining and sleeping cars. Continue to San Miguel by bus. **From Mexico City:** Catch the 7am *Constitucionalista* to Querétaro and from there take a bus.

By Bus   From Mexico City: It's a 4- to 5-hour trip. Flecha Amarilla has the most buses daily to and from Mexico City: 17 trips in all, counting all the buses in both directions, and 14 buses a day to Guanajuato, some of which travel via Dolores Hidalgo. Tres Estrellas de Oro has one bus a day to and from Mexico City via Querétaro. Omnibus de México has two buses a day to and from Mexico City, and also one bus a day to and from Guadalajara (via Guanajuato). **From Guanajuato:** Flecha Amarilla has at least 16 buses a day to San Miguel. **From Guadalajara:** Take a bus from the central bus terminal in Guadalajara to the town of Celaya; in Celaya, catch a Flecha Amarilla bus for the last hour of the trip. Flecha Amarilla operates buses between San Miguel and Celaya every 20 minutes from 5:20am to 9pm.

By Car   From Guanajuato: The short route is Highway 110 south; the long route is Highway 110 north through Dolores Hidalgo. **From Mexico City:** The trip takes around 3 hours and you have a choice of two routes—via Querétaro on Highway 57 or via Celaya on Highway 45. Take Highway 57 north, a four-lane freeway, through Querétaro; about 25 miles north of Querétaro, a sign points left to San Miguel. Exit and go west on that two-lane road about 20 miles to San Miguel. For the Celeya route, take Highway 57 north to Querétaro. As you near Querétaro, watch carefully for signs pointing to Celaya and Highway 45. The signs are almost at the point you have to turn. At Celaya, turn right on Highway 51 to San Miguel.

DEPARTING   By Train   The closest train service is in San Luis Potosí or Querétaro. **To Laredo** (from San Luis Potosí): *El Regiomontaño* leaves San Luis at midnight and arrives in Laredo just after noon. **To Mexico City** (from Querétaro): The *Constitucionalista* leaves Querétaro at 5:50pm and arrives in Mexico City at 9pm.

By Bus   There are buses to Dolores Hidalgo every 30 minutes, as well as frequent buses to Atotonilco, Guanajuato, and Querétaro.

San Miguel de Allende (alt. 6,134 ft.; pop. 60,000) founded in 1542, may well be the prettiest town in Mexico and, like Taxco, has been declared a national monument. Virtually all the buildings you see date from the 1600s through the colonial era. Newer buildings must conform to the existing architecture. Because so much of the city remains as it did during the days of silver mining in the region, many of the hotels, restaurants, and shops are housed in beautiful mansions dating from those years. Its cobbled streets are reminiscent of Cornwall or Nantucket, and the best-known view of the town, where the highway enters it from the south, has been featured in innumerable movies and postcards.

You'll awake early in San Miguel with the bells of a score of churches clanging like a score of hammers on a score of different-shaped anvils and soon the booming of the *parroquía* (parish church) will superimpose itself as the others begin to fade away.

The iron benches in the Jardín hold the cast that makes up life in San Miguel. Mornings find people occupied by resident Americans on their way to and from the post office. By midmorning transient tourists arrive and fill the plaza and maze of adjoining streets to shop. (This is one of Mexico's best shopping and dining towns.) Language students come with their tutors, and artists sit sketching a slice of San Miguel life. And throughout the day local residents pass through on their way to the striking Parroquía Church across the street, or to the market several blocks in the other direction. Some sell baskets and balloons, and others, painted pottery. At night it spills over with young folks who still practice the courtship custom of the promenade: the opposite sexes walk in opposite directions until love blossoms and they pair up. Nighttime, too, brings bands of mariachis who wait under surrounding portals to be hired.

A sizable colony of American students and pensioners has established itself here, although the major portion of this group tends to turn over about twice a year. Apart from the financially successful, which includes those who have retired here to live relatively well, the town's American colony is always composed of teachers, painters, writers, and others who have saved up enough to buy themselves 6 months in the sun.

If you can, try to get a look around at least one of the houses in which resident Americans are living (there's a home tour every Sunday). Shabby and almost universally drab from the outside, they open inside onto pretty, cool, flower-filled patios with French doors, lily ponds, and breathtaking views.

ORIENTATION

ARRIVING   By Train   The train station in San Miguel is a couple of miles west of town on Calle Organos. It's a 20-minute walk on a cobblestone street (no sidewalks) or 5 minutes by taxi. Taxis meet each train but are scarce other times.

By Bus   The bus station is about half a mile closer in on the same street, and taxis are generally available at all hours.

INFORMATION   The **Tourist Information Office** is on the southeastern corner of the plaza, left of the church (tel. 2-1747). The English-speaking staff has maps and information about attractions in San Miguel and the surrounding region. It's open Monday through Friday from 10am to 2:45pm and 5 to 7pm, on Saturday from 10am to 1pm, and on Sunday from 10am to noon. Don't get your train or bus information here though; it may not be current.

CITY LAYOUT   San Miguel's beautiful central square, the **Jardín,** shaded by perfectly groomed Indian laurel trees, is the center of city life. It's the point of reference for just about all directions and is bounded by Calles Correo (Post Office Street), San Francisco, Hidalgo, and Reloj.

GETTING AROUND

BY BUS   In San Miguel there are no inner-city buses or minivans as in other cities in Mexico. Buses to outlying villages (Taboada thermal pool, for example) leave from around the market.

IMPRESSIONS

. . . [The traveler] is bound to spend long evenings in the company of compatriots who have gone virtually native, listening as they remove cover after cover from the surface of Mexico until he stares dizzily into a bottomless pit of mysteries, atavisms, sorceries and primitive profundities.
—STUART CHASE, *MEXICO: A STUDY OF TWO AMERICAS*, 1931

BY TAXI In general, taxis are fairly priced, but agree on the price in advance—they don't have meters.

ON FOOT Most of San Miguel's sights are within walking distance of the central Jardín.

FAST FACTS

American Express The local representative is Viajes Vertiz, Hidalgo 1 (tel. 465/2-1856; fax 465/2-0499), open Monday through Friday from 9am to 2pm and 4 to 6pm.

Area Code The telephone area code is 465.

Art Supplies See "Bookstores," below.

Bookstores An English-language bookstore, **El Colibri**, Sollano 30 (tel. 2-0751), located a few blocks off the plaza, offers an excellent selection of current literature, classics, books on Mexico, etc., and even art supplies. Open Monday through Saturday from 10am to 2pm and 4 to 7pm.

Laundry The Lavandería Automatica de San Miguel will do the washing and drying. It's at Potranca 18, Col. Guadiana, located just past the Instituto Allende and facing the Red Cross.

Library The Biblioteca Pública (Public Library), Insurgentes 25 (tel. 2-0293), is the gathering point for the American community. It has a good selection of books in Spanish and English. Here, too, is a courtyard with tables where you can relax and read a book or magazine. Open Monday through Saturday from 10am to 2pm and 4 to 7pm.

Messages San Miguel's unofficial message center is **La Luciernaga**, Aldama 1 (tel. 465/2-1687; fax 465/2-2312), called **Lucy's** for short. They develop film, repair cameras, sell batteries and film, receive or make long-distance calls, and for a small monthly charge they'll receive mail and take messages. There's also a complete computer service in Spanish and English, and courier service for errands to Mexico City. Now that it's the personal business hub of San Miguel, they've opened a small restaurant. It's open Monday through Friday from 8am to 8pm and on Saturday from 8am to 3pm.

Newspaper *Atención*, the English-language paper, has local news as well as a full list of what to see and do. Or if you want to keep up with what's going on in San Miguel, a subscription costs $30. Write Atención, Biblioteca Publica de San Miguel, Insurgentes 25 (Apdo. Postal 119), San Miguel de Allende, Gto. 37700, México.

Photographic Needs See "Messages," above.

Post Office The post office and telegraph office are at Calle Correo 16, open Monday through Friday from 8am to 7pm and on Saturday from 9am to 1pm.

WHAT TO SEE & DO

It's difficult to be bored in San Miguel. The shopping is excellent and you'll run out of time before you can try all the good restaurants. San Miguel is ideally situated for side trips to Dolores Hidalgo, Querétaro, Guanajuato, and San Luis Potosí; and should there be a lull, this is one of Mexico's most popular towns for classes in Spanish and the arts.

THE PARROQUÍA CHURCH, south side of El Jardín.

La Parroquía Church, the parish church, is an imposing Gothic structure of local sandstone built in the late 19th century by a self-made architect, Ceferino Gutierrez. The story goes that he had never seen such a church and used a picture to fashion this one. Neoclassical stone altars have replaced the original ones made of gilded wood, but the bell is original. Step inside on any day and you are likely to find parishioners from surrounding villages carrying on an ancient rite that has both Catholic and pre-Hispanic overtones—quite something in the swirl of modern San Miguel.

Admission: Free.

Open: Daily 8am–2pm and 5–9pm.

MUSEO DE LA CASA DE ALLENDE, southwest corner of El Jardín.

SAN MIGUEL DE ALLENDE

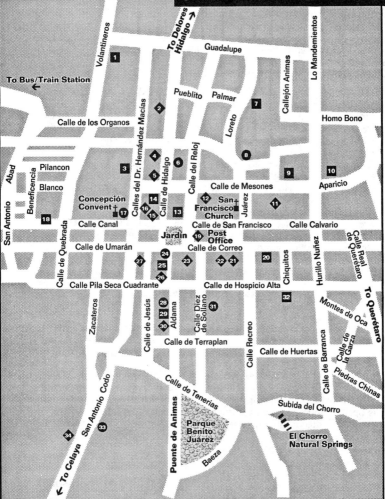

N

To Bus/Train Station ←

To Dolores Hidalgo →

Guadalupe
Volantineros
1
Pueblito
Palmar
2
7
Callejón Animas
Lo Mandemientos
Calle de los Organos
Loreto
Homo Bono
Abad
Pilancon
Blanco
Beneficencia
Calles del Dr. Hernández Macias
4
6
Calle del Reloj
8
Calle de Mesones
9
10
Aparicio
5
San Antonio
Concepción Convent
14
Calle de Hidalgo
13
12
San Francisco Church
Juárez
11
18
17
16
15
Calle Canal
Calle de San Francisco
Calle Calvario
Jardín
19
Post Office
Calle de Quebrada
Calle de Umarán
Calle de Correo
24
23
22
21
20
Chiquitos
Hurillo Nuñez
Calle Real de Querétaro
27
25
26
Calle Pila Seca Cuadrante
Calle de Hospicio Alta
32
To Querétaro
28
29
30
Aldama
31
Calle Diez de Sollano
Montes de Oca
Zacateros
Calle de Jesús
Calle de Terraplan
Calle Recreo
Calle de Huertas
Calle de Barranca
Calle de la Garza
Piedras Chinas
San Antonio Codo
Calle de Tenerias
Puente de Animas
Parque Benito Juárez
Baeza
Subida del Chorro
El Chorro Natural Springs
33
34
To Celaya ←

Church ✝

San Miguel de Allende

MEXICO CITY

ACCOMMODATIONS:
Pensión Casa Carmen 20
Posada Carmina 25
Hacienda de las Flores 32
Quinta Loreto Hotel 7
Posada de las Monjas 18

Mesón de San Antonio 14
Monte Verde Hotel 1
Parador San Sebastian 9
Posada San Francisco 13
Sautto Restaurant 3
Hotel Vianey 10
Vista Hermosa Hotel 29

DINING:
Bugambillia Restaurant 2
El Correo Restaurant 22
La Dolce Vita Restaurant 16
Rincon Español Restaurant 21
La Fragua 26
Hobos Restaurant 34
Mama Mia Restaurant 27
Mesón de San José Fonda 11
Mexas Restaurant 15

Pancho's y Lefty/Pepe's Patio 5
Pepe's Pizza 4
La Terraza Restaurant 23
El Tucán Restaurant 19
Vendimia Café 14
Villa Jacaranda 30
Virginia's Restaurant 12

ATTRACTIONS:
Bellas Artes/Centro Cultural 17
El Colibri Bookstore 31
Instituto Allende 33
Library 8
Lucerniaga (Lucy's) 28
Museo Casa Allende 24
El Ring Disco 6
Tourist Office 23

The birthplace of the famous independence leader Ignacio Allende has been converted into a museum housing colonial-era furnishings and historical documents. In 1810 Allende plotted with Padre Miguel Hidalgo of nearby Dolores and Josefa Domínguez of neighboring Querétaro, among others, to organize for independence from Spain. Allende and Hidalgo were both executed in Chihuahua a year later.

Admission: Free.

Open: Tues–Sun 10am–5pm.

CENTRO CULTURAL IGNACIO RAMÍREZ [BELLAS ARTES/EL NIGRO-MANTE], Hernández Macías 75. Tel. 2-0289.

Housed in the former Convento de la Concepción (1765), between Canal and Insurgentes, two blocks west of the Jardín, this is a branch of the Bellas Artes of Mexico City. It's built on two levels surrounding an enormous courtyard of lush trees, and consists of numerous rooms housing art exhibits and classrooms for drawing, painting, sculpture, lithography, textiles, ceramics, dramatic arts, ballet, regional dance, piano, and guitar. Several murals by David Alfaro Siqueiros, as well as memorabilia of the artist, are worth seeing. A bulletin board lists concerts and lectures given at this institute and elsewhere in the city. The pleasant restaurant serves Italian food daily between 10am and 8pm.

Before you leave, notice the magnificent dome behind the convent. It belongs to the Iglesia de la Concepción and was designed by the same unschooled architect that designed the Parroquia Church.

Admission: Free.

Open: Mon–Fri 9am–9pm, Sat 10am–7pm, Sun 10am–5pm.

MORE ATTRACTIONS

If you're in town on a Sunday, you might be interested in a tour through some of the colonial houses in San Miguel. These **House and Garden Tours** leave from the library every Sunday at 11:30am for a 2-hour tour, with a donation fixed at $8. The tours are a voluntary project sponsored by the library for the benefit of the youth of San Miguel.

The **Travel Institute of San Miguel,** Cuna de Allende 11 (tel. 2-0078), holds walking tours, field trips to colonial and archeological sites, adventure and nature tours, visits to artisans at work, and workshops in marketing, among other things. The office is open Monday through Saturday from 9am to 2pm and 4 to 7pm.

A couple of the most enjoyable walks in town are to the lookout point **El Mirador,** especially at sunset, which colors the whole town and the lake beyond; and to **Parque Juárez,** a lovely and spacious, shady park.

The town's movie theater, the **Aldama,** is on San Francisco, in the block between the Jardín and the San Francisco Church.

One great way to see the mountains around San Miguel is on a **horseback ride.** For $10 an hour or $50 a day you can hire a horse, but at the moment you'll need several days to plan it. Leave a message for Captain Canales at La Luciernaga (tel. 2-1687) (see "Messages" in "Fast Facts," above); he'll get back to you at your hotel to set a time.

The **Taboada hot springs** are located just 5 miles outside San Miguel, about 15 minutes away by car. The Hotel Balneario Taboada is out of the budget range for this book, but next door to it is the most popular hot springs/swimming pool in the area, which you can use for about $2. Buses to Taboada leave from Calle San Francisco by the market supposedly at 9 and 11am, and 1 and 3pm. If you should have trouble getting a bus, you can always take a taxi out to any of the three hot springs; it will cost about $6—not a bad deal if you have several people to split the cost. You can ask the taxi driver to return and pick you up at the end of the day.

NEARBY ATTRACTIONS

One of the most pleasant excursions you can make from San Miguel is to **Atotonilco el Grande,** a rural town that contains a wonderful 16th-century oratorio (the church of an Augustinian monastery). The imaginative and animated frescoes depicting scenes from the Bible were used to teach the Indians. The trip itself is an introduction to super-picturesque Mexican country life. Hop a bus on Calle Llamas ("Oratorio") and you'll trundle out of San Miguel on the road to Taboada. Past Taboada the route goes left at signs reading MANANTIALES DE LA GRUTA and LA FLOR DEL CORTIJO. The road passes two large mansions that are now spas (see above), then an aqueduct and a little narrow bridge. In no time you're in the small town square of Atotonilco with the oratorio in front of you.

Querétaro, Guanajuato, and Dolores Hidalgo are easy day trips from San Miguel. See "Departing," above, for transportation information.

Two companies use San Miguel as a base for trips to see the **monarch butterflies** in the state of Michoacan west of Mexico City. The Travel Institute of San Miguel (mentioned above) offers this trip between November and March. Another company, Columbus Travel, also originates the trip from either San Miguel or Mexico City, returning through San Miguel. Contact them at 6017 Calaghan Rd., San Antonio, TX 78228 (tel. 512/523-1400, or toll free 800/843-1060 in the U.S. and Canada).

SHOPPING

In general, stores in San Miguel open at 9am, close between 2 and 4pm, and reopen from 4 to 7pm. Most are closed Sunday. The town is known for its metalwork—brass, bronze, and tin—and for its textiles and pottery, especially Talavera ware, which is also made in Dolores Hidalgo. But shopping is by no means limited to those. Also, ask to see the charming children's art for sale at the Public Library; the proceeds help support the children's program.

Art Galleries

GALERÍA SAN MIGUEL, Plaza Principal 14. Tel. 2-0454.

This is the best of the art galleries. It is run by a charming and stylish Mexican-American woman, fluent in English, who is a well-known art dealer. She exhibits the work of local residents as well as artists from all over Mexico in all price ranges. Open Monday through Friday from 10am to 2pm and 4 to 7pm, on Saturday from 10am to 2pm and 4 to 8pm, and on Sunday from 10am to 2pm.

Another branch of the gallery, specializing in larger paintings, is located at Umaran 1 (tel. 2-1046), across from the Mama Mía Restaurant, with the same hours, but closed Sunday.

Crafts

CASA MAXWELL, Canal 14. Tel. 2-0247.

It's a beautiful house and garden with every imaginable craft displayed, some high-priced, others fairly reasonable. It's well worth a look around. Open Monday through Saturday from 9am to 2pm and 4 to 7pm.

CERAMICA DE SAN MIGUEL, Canal 45. Tel. 2-0092.

This manufacturer, who also has a ceramics outlet on the road to Querétaro, has a shop here. In addition to Monday through Saturday hours, it's also open on Sunday between 10am and 2pm.

CASA ANGUIANO, corner of Canal and Macías. Tel. 2-0107.

This is one of those places you return to again and again just to see what's new. The inventory of colorful Michoacan foot-loomed fabric by the bolt is extensive, as is the inventory of blown glass, copper, brass, and nativity scenes. It's open daily from 9am to 7pm.

AMADA BOUTIQUE, in the Bazaar Colonial, at the corner of Canal and Hidalgo.

The small shop, tucked in the far right corner of the Bazaar Colonial, is packed literally floor to ceiling with Guatemalan textiles, jewelry, and popular art. It's next to La Dolce Vita Restaurant. Open daily from 10am to 8pm.

CASA COHEN, Reloj 12. Tel. 2-1434.

⭐ Located half a block north of the square, this is the place to find brass and bronze—bowls, plates, house numbers, doorknobs and knockers, and drawer pulls, as well as other utilitarian objects made of iron, aluminum, and carved stone. There's hand-carved wood furniture too. It's open the usual San Miguel hours except on Thursday and Saturday when it closes at 6pm.

MESÓN DE SAN JOSÉ, Mesones 38. Tel. 2-1367.

This lovely old mansion, across from the market between Juárez and Nuñez, houses a dozen shops and a restaurant. One of the shops, Originales Papel Mache, is a manufacturer of papier-mâché and has a good supply of napkin rings and serving trays, as well as a smattering of folk art from around Mexico. Open the usual San Miguel hours plus Sunday from 9:30am to 4pm.

Furniture

CASA MARÍA LUISA, Canal 40, at Zacateros. Tel. 2-0130.

⭐ If your interests are architectural or decorative, you may enjoy browsing here. Among the crowded aisles is its own line of furniture, which might appeal to those with a southwestern decor. Stacked and displayed here and there are decorative ironwork, lamps, masks, pottery, and more. It's loaded. Open daily from 9am to 7pm.

Masks

TONATIU METZTLI, Umaran 24, at Zacateros. Tel. 2-0869.

This shop is a must for the mask collector. Besides the masks hanging all over the shop walls, owner Jorje Guzman has a private collection that he shows by appointment. Open daily (Sunday hours are 10am to 4pm).

Pottery

ZARCO, Sollano 24, at the corner of Hospicio. Tel. 2-0323.

This craft shop doubles as a beauty salon, and has a large selection of pottery seconds. Prices are slightly lower than the "firsts" you'll see elsewhere in town. Select carefully and look for repairs, especially on the clay work from Ocumichu. Your purchases can be delivered to your hotel at no extra charge. This is one store that's also open on Sunday.

SCHOOLS

San Miguel is known for its Spanish-language and art schools. These institutions cater to Americans and often will provide a list of apartments from which to choose for long-term stays. Rates for language classes are usually by the hour and get lower the more hours you take. Some classes are smaller than others, so if you want a chance to practice, it's best to look for smaller classes.

Instituto Allende, Calle Ancha de San Antonio 20, San Miguel de Allende, Gto. 37700 (tel. 465/2-0190; fax 465/2-0190), put San Miguel on the map back in the 1930s when Enrique Fernández Martínez, former governor of the state of Guanajuato, and Stirling Dickinson, an American, opened it. Today it thrives in the 18th-century home of the former counts of Canal, a beautiful place with big grounds, elegant patios and gardens, art exhibits, and murals. You can wander past classrooms where weavers, sculptors, painters, ceramicists, photographers, and struggling language students are at work. The notice board in the entrance lobby carries interesting offers ("Ride offered to L.A.," "Paperbacks for sale, Shayne to Schopenhauer"), and the office maintains a list of local families who rent rooms for stays of a month or more. The institute offers an MFA degree and the school's credits are transferrable to at least 300 colleges and universities in the U.S. and Canada, but noncredit students are welcome too.

Academia Hispano Americana has a reputation for being a tougher-than-most language school with the emphasis on grammar as well as conversation. The registrar writes: "This is a language school, teaching Spanish, history, and the literature of Spain and Mexico. It's small, with classes limited to 12 people; instructors are rotated; grammar is presented and absorbed through example, application, and usage, rather than by rule. It's a serious school, the work is intensive, and we are particularly interested in students who plan to use Spanish in their future careers, people who sincerely feel the need to communicate and understand the other Americas." The school has a continuous program of study of 12 4-week sessions for 35 hours a week. Private lessons cost $9 an hour. A brochure is available from the Registrar, Academia Hispano Americana, Mesones 4 (Apdo. Postal 150), San Miguel de Allende, Gto. 37700 (tel. 465/2-0349; fax 465/2-2333). Office hours are Monday to Friday, 8am to 1pm and 3:30 to 6:30pm. It's a member of the International Association of Language Centers.

Yet another option for studying Spanish is **Inter Idiomas,** Mesones 15, San Miguel de Allende, Gto. 37700 (tel. 465/2-2177), with a maximum of six students per class for 2 hours a day Monday through Friday. The first hour covers grammar and the second conversation. Sign up by the week, but 4 weeks are cheaper. Go between 9 and 11am for a free observation of classes.

Casa de La Luna, Cuadrante 2 (tel. 2-2312), also invites prospective students to sit in on classes before enrolling. Group size is two or three people for 2 hours a day Monday through Friday. It's cheaper the more weeks you are enrolled. Hour-long private classes are in the afternoons only. The office is open Monday through Friday from 9am to 1pm and 4 to 6pm.

Also see the **Centro Cultural Ignacio Ramírez,** above.

SPECIAL EVENTS

Holy Week, a moveable date in the spring, is special in San Miguel, with numerous processions almost daily beginning the Saturday a week before Easter Sunday. On **June 13, Saint Anthony's Day,** children bring decorated animals for a blessing at the Parroquía Church—it's quite an event. San Miguel's main festivity, however, is the **Fiesta de San Miguel** on September 29, honoring the town's patron saint. Events center around the churches and there are processions in the streets.

EVENING ENTERTAINMENT

Clubs and discos here tend to spring up and die quickly. For a pleasant night out enjoying dinner and drinks with live music—be it piano, guitar, South American folkloric, or flamenco—see "Where to Eat," below; where there's live music, I've mentioned it. San Miguel has many such enjoyable restaurants. Finally, be sure to check San Miguel's English-language paper, *Atención,* for other happenings around town while you're here.

LA PRINCESA, Calle Recreo 5. Tel. 2-1043.

This restaurant/bar has a guitar soloist nightly from 8 to 10pm, and flamenco performances from 10pm to 1am. La Princesa is open daily from 1pm to 2am.

PANCHO Y LEFTY'S, Mesones 99. Tel. 2-1958.

Photos of Willie Nelson, Jerry Garcia, Bob Dylan, and many others adorn the entrance to the partially covered courtyard patio, with a raised stage and tables all around. The emphasis is on American music, with a country-music night every Wednesday when there's two-for-one beer and free peanuts all day and night. It has a live band for dancing from 10pm to 1am. You can bring in food from the nice patio restaurant, Pepe's Patio, out back. There's a happy hour daily from 7 to 9pm; regular hours are Tuesday through Sunday from 6pm to 2am.

Admission: $2.50.

MAMA MIA, Umaran 8. Tel. 2-2063.

There's live jazz for dancing or listening in the bar every Thursday, Friday, and Saturday from 9pm to 2am.
    Admission: $2.50.

EL RING, Hidalgo 25-27. Tel. 2-1998.
    Located in a lovely old building on the right side of the street as you come from the main plaza, this disco has a very elaborate layout including strobe lights and other visual hallucinogens (but visual only). Every Wednesday is two-for-one tequila night. Open Tuesday through Sunday from 10pm until 4 or 5am.
    Admission: Fri–Sat $5.50.

DISCO LABYRINTOS, Ancha de San Antonio 7. Tel. 2-0362.
    This is the other disco; but not right downtown. It's a small place, with two postage-stamp-size dance floors, but quite popular, especially with the 18- to 22-year-old set. Its open Thursday through Sunday from 10pm until 4:30am. The cover price changes according to the day.
    Admission: $1–$5.50.

LA FRAGUA, Cuna de Allende 5. Tel. 2-1114.
    San Miguel's artists and writers drift in and out all afternoon and evening at this popular gathering spot of long standing. Housed in an old colonial home, the restaurant has tables around the courtyard where Mexican musicians perform every evening from 8 to 10:30pm. Several other dining rooms and a comfy, living room–like bar are off the courtyard. The emphasis here is on standard Mexican fare. Antojitos range in price from $2.50 for four tacos to $12 for steak tampiqueña. Garlic fans won't want to miss the unusual garlic soup with egg for $2. Bar hours are daily, 2pm to 2am and the restaurant serves from 1pm to midnight.

WHERE TO STAY

There are plenty of accommodations for visitors in San Miguel, but you'll find them hard to get around the Christmas and Easter holidays and around San Miguel's patron saint festival, September 29. October and November are slack months, as are January and February. For a long stay in San Miguel (more than a month), check at the instituto or the academia (see "Schools" in "What to See and Do," above) for their list of apartments or rooms to rent. Most apartments are equipped with kitchens and bedding, some with maid service.

DOUBLES FOR LESS THAN $20

QUINTA LORETO, Callejon Loreto 15, San Miguel de Allende, Gto. 37700. Tel. 465/2-0042. 28 rms (all with bath).
$ Rates: $14 single, $15 double; with two meals daily, $25.50 single, $35 double. Weekly and monthly discounts available.
    This motel is tucked away amid cobblestone lanes and manicured gardens. It has a large pool, tennis court, lovely garden, excellent restaurant, friendly atmosphere, and simple but pleasant rooms. Meals here are a bargain. Make reservations—the Loreto is very popular and is often booked up months in advance.
    To get here from the Jardín, walk two blocks west on Correo past the post office, turn left at the next corner (Juárez) for two blocks, crossing Mesones and continuing three long blocks (the street curves); it's on a small street off Calle Loreto.

PARADOR SAN SEBASTIAN, Calle Mesones 7, San Miguel de Allende, Gto. 37700. Tel. 465/2-0707. 13 rms (all with bath).
$ Rates: $16 single; $18 double.
    The San Sebastian is a colonial-style inn with spacious rooms that include a fireplace and face a lovely courtyard and garden. The rooms are simple and comfortable. They don't take reservations here, so you just have to come and try your luck.
    From the Jardín, walk two blocks west on Correo past the post office, turn left at the next corner (Juárez) for two blocks, turn right on Mesones and then left, and it's one block on the left opposite the market.

DOUBLES FOR LESS THAN $30

MESÓN DE SAN ANTONIO, Mesones 80, San Miguel de Allende, Gto. 37700. Tel. 465/2-0580. 10 rms (all with bath) TV **Directions:** From the Jardín walk 1 block N on Hidalgo and turn left on Mesones and walk 1 block.

$ Rates: $21 standard single or double; $23 triple; $31 junior suite; $486 standard room for 1 month.

In this a converted colonial mansion, rooms are arranged around two nice courtyards with white iron furniture. Rooms are carpeted and standard rooms come with heat (in winter), two beds, TV, desk, and couch. Suites are furnished the same except with king-size beds. Because rooms look onto the courtyards, they're a bit dark. The mesón is one block from Hidalgo on Mesones.

HOTEL SAUTTO, Hernández Macías 59, San Miguel de Allende, Gto. 37700. Tel. 465/2-0052. 25 rms (all with bath).

$ Rates: $18 single; $23 double.

This hotel between Canal and Insurgentes by the Centro Cultural, has a very large, neglected courtyard and grounds—unattended lemon, lime, and orange trees, and sweet-smelling flowers everywhere. The hotel is an old colonial mansion, worn but comfortable, and pleasant in an old style. About half the rooms have both a fireplace and worn carpeting, but it's overpriced for what you get. If you can't do better, stay here.

POSADA DE SAN FRANCISCO, Plaza Principal 2 (Apdo. Postal 40), San Miguel de Allende, Gto. 37700. Tel. 465/2-1466 or 2-2425. 49 rms (all with bath). TEL

$ Rates: $29 single; $23 double.

Right on El Jardín, San Miguel's main square, is this converted colonial mansion with a very pretty courtyard. The San Francisco has large, high-ceilinged rooms and colonial touches. The furniture is a bit worn in some rooms, but still quite serviceable. The large windows have screens to keep out bugs. Bar service is available in the courtyard with its bubbling fountain, and the hotel restaurant serves three meals a day. There's even an elevator.

POSADA CARMINA, Cuna de Allende 7, San Miguel de Allende, Gto. 37700. Tel. 465/2-0458. 10 rms (all with bath).

$ Rates: $23 single; $25 double.

Located on the south side of the plaza next to the Parroquía Church, is this charming and friendly colonial-style place with nicely furnished rooms facing a central courtyard full of orange trees and flowering vines. Around the upstairs terrace are two comfortable living rooms, chairs, and chaise longues. You get more than you pay for here. A restaurant serving good food is open daily from 8am to 9:30pm.

DOUBLES FOR LESS THAN $40

POSADA DE LAS MONJAS, Canal 37, San Miguel de Allende, Gto. 37700. Tel. 465/2-0171. 65 rms (all with bath).

$ Rates: $22 single; $32 double; $38 suite single or double.

This charming little inn and a former convent 3½ long blocks west of the Jardín is of pink-stone construction. Inside, as you'd expect, it's Mexican quaint—lively colors, cavernous wood furniture, lots of beams, arches, and the like. The rooms are tastefully furnished. Double rooms are the best as they have windows and views, but even the tiny singles are good. There are also big rooms with two beds, fireplaces, and suitelike accommodations. The lobby, with fireplace and Persian-style rugs, is especially nice for lounging about with fellow guests.

HOTEL VISTA HERMOSA TABOADA, Allende 11 (Apdo. Postal 100), San Miguel de Allende, Gto. 37700. Tel. 465/2-0078 or 2-0437. 16 rms (all with bath).

$ Rates: $22 room with one bed, $30 room with two beds.

Rooms here have an old-timey feel, with furniture from several eras ago—perhaps several ages—all in one room. Rooms, all facing a small courtyard, are carpeted, dark, and neat, and each has a fireplace. For the location (one block south of El Jardín), it's a good choice although it's a little overpriced.

HOTEL MONTEVERDE, Volanteros 2, San Miguel de Allende, Gto. 37700. Tel. 465/2-1814 or 2-1156. 25 rms, 7 suites (all with bath).
$ Rates: $30 single; $36 double. (Complimentary breakfast included with stays of a week or more.) **Parking:** Free.

Hidden inside this former mansion, which only recently became a hotel, is a large garden with white patio furniture. Rooms are as spacious as the lobby/lounge. Each has brick or tile floors and hand-carved furniture including desks. The restaurant specializes in low-cholesterol food.

To get here from the Jardín, walk three long blocks west on Canal, then turn right onto Quebrada/Volanteros for 2½ long blocks; it's near the corner of Guadalupe.

WORTH THE EXTRA BUCKS

PENSION CASA CARMEN, Correo 31 (Apdo. Postal 152), San Miguel de Allende, Gto. 37700. Tel. 465/2-0844. 11 rms (all with bath).
$ Rates: $33 single; $47 double.

⭐ This small, quiet place with a friendly and relaxed atmosphere is often booked months in advance. The rooms, all with gas heaters, face a lovely colonial courtyard with plants and a fountain; meals are served in a European-style common dining room. You can stay by the day, week, or month.

You can get here from the Jardín by walking east on Correo past the Parroquía Church and post office for 2½ blocks; it's near the corner of Recreo.

READERS RECOMMEND

Hotel Vianey, Aparicio 18, San Miguel de Allende, Gto. 37700 (tel. 465/2-0365). "We stayed in this small hotel, a 5-minute walk from the Quinta Loreto. It was spotlessly clean and had new furniture, plenty of lights, and constant very hot water. We spent a lot of time on the roof sunbathing. The manager, María, doesn't speak English."—Anne Irwin, Williams Lake, B.C., Canada. [Author's Note: The Vianey has 11 rooms, all with private baths. It's one block north and four long blocks east of El Jardín. Prices are around $16 without a kitchen and $23 with one, single or double. Not bad for San Miguel, and it's a good choice for an extended stay.]

Mi Casa B&B, Canal 58 (Apdo. Postal 496), San Miguel de Allende, Gto. (tel. 465/2-2492). "My wife and I discovered Mi Casa B&B, in a charming old colonial dwelling lovingly restored and close to the center of town. It has only two suites, on a flower-filled rooftop courtyard with view, a comfortable covered lanai and a well-stocked honor bar. It's exquisitely decorated with romantic Mexican furnishings. There are lots of books, pictures, pillows, artifacts, decorative mirrors, comfortable chairs, dramatic sunken tiled shower tubs, and plants and flowers to make you feel pampered. One suite even has a beautiful fireplace and sitting room. The owner/host, Carmen McDaniel, a very gracious expatriate from the U.S., is a fountain of information. She'll even pick you up at the train station. The suites are $35 and $45 per night for two, including breakfast and free laundry service. There's an additional $5 charge in high season. A 10% discount is given for stays over 7 nights."—Bill and Posie Anderson, Mill Valley, Calif.

Casa de LuJo, Pila Seca 35 (Apdo. Postal 552), San Miguel de Allende, Gto. 37700. "We would like to recommend the Casa de LuJo following two extended stays in this delightful bed-and-breakfast. Each of the seven rooms has its own flower-bedecked patio, private entrance, and bath. Prices begin at $40 for two, including an outstanding breakfast, "high tea" at 5pm, full maid and laundry service, and substantial discounts for guests at selected restaurants and shops. Weekly and monthly rates are offered by the English-speaking owners and staff."—Bill and Gail Brooks, Laguna Beach, Calif.

WHERE TO EAT

Because of its large foreign colony and its popularity with Mexicans as a tourist destination, San Miguel has the best quality and assortment of restaurants of any small city in Mexico. New places open all the time, while eateries only a few years old close down overnight. As in every Mexican town, the **mercado** offers the least expensive food in town. Rows of fruits and vegetables, and everything else you can think of, and stands with cooked food offer basic meals like chiles rellenos, frijoles, and rice-with-broth, all for about $1 or less.

MEALS FOR LESS THAN $10

EL TUCAN, Calle San Francisco.
Specialty: MEXICAN/TORTAS.
$ Prices: Enchiladas or tacos $1.50–$4; tortas 90¢–$1.95.
Open: Wed–Mon 9am–10pm.

Around the corner from the plaza on Calle San Francisco, you'll see this restaurant on the right which serves some of the richest tortas (sandwiches on a small French roll) I've ever tasted. The tortas are hot and come loaded with lettuce, tomato, mustard, mayonnaise, avocado, chiles, etc. Antojitos (enchiladas, tacos, etc.), hamburgers with french fries, ham or sausage and eggs, and omelets are also served at reasonable prices.

QUINTA LORETO, in the Quinta Loreto Hotel, Callejon Loreto 15. Tel. 2-0042.
Specialty: MEXICAN.
$ Prices: Soups and tacos $1.50–$3.50; main courses $4–$5; comida corrida $5.
Open: Breakfast daily 8–10:30am; lunch and comida corrida daily 1:30–6pm.

Tucked away at the back of the Quinta Loreto (see "Where to Stay," above) is a swimming pool, and adjoining the pool is a café—the best bargain restaurant in town. The comida corrida is excellent, and other menu selections are also well priced. The dining room tends to be a bit noisy; you might want to sit out on the terrace overlooking the garden.

VIRGINIA'S GALLERY AND RESTAURANTE, Mesones 58. Tel. 2-0613.
Specialty: MEXICAN.
$ Prices: Appetizers $2.50–$4; main courses $3–$6.
Open: Mon–Sat 8:30am–10pm, Sun noon–9pm.

Painted sienna and turquoise, it bills itself as a *galería restaurante*. Besides selling handmade rugs, unusual knitted clothing, jewelry, and crystals, the restaurant sells homemade ice cream and gourmet meals to eat in or take out. The weekly special when I was there was Russian food, and there are other equally delicious and unexpected offerings here such as moussaka, tabouleh, and a variety of quiches. There's conversational Spanish on Monday, Wednesday, and Friday between 4 and 6pm, and Thursday poetry readings at 7pm.

To get here from the Jardín, walk north on Reloj for two blocks and turn right onto Mesones for half a block; it's between Juárez and Reloj.

LA DOLCE VITA, Hernández Macías 74.
Specialty: PASTRIES & COFFEE.
$ Prices: Coffee $1–$2.50; pastries $2.25–$3.75
Open: Daily 10am–10pm.

For coffee, my favorite place in town is a European-style café with good, strong coffee, tucked away in the Bazaar Colonial (at the corner of Canal) in the patio of a building full of boutiques and the like. Light meals, including delicious croissant sandwiches, are served as well. Coffee comes with whipped cream and so on. Highly enjoyable.

PEPE PIZZAS, Hidalgo 26. Tel. 2-1832.
Specialty: ITALIAN.
$ Prices: Appetizers $3; pizza $4.75–$15; pasta $4–$5.
Open: Daily 1–11pm.

This Italian restaurant is less extravagant than Mama Mía (see below), but it's simple in an elegant sort of way. You dine in either the carpeted dining rooms or at patio tables out back in a beautiful garden. Some 21 varieties of pizza are served, or choose from pastas like lasagne, spaghetti, and fettuccine.

To get here from the Jardín, walk north on Hidalgo for two long blocks; it's between Hidalgo and Macías.

RESTAURANT/BAR BUGAMBILIA, Hidalgo 42. Tel. 2-1007.
   Specialty: MEXICAN.
   $ Prices: Appetizers $4.50–$5.50; main courses $6–$16.
   Open: Daily noon–11pm.

A good, attractive restaurant 2½ long blocks north of the Jardín, this spot sports tables with *equipales* chairs set in a covered courtyard. Especially delicious is the Aztec soup, a chicken-based stock with tomatoes, cheese, avocados, and toasted mild black chiles. There's a nice menu of both hot and cold dishes—all the basic favorites plus some imaginative concoctions. There's live guitar or piano music from 8:30 to 11pm nightly.

CASA MEXAS, Canal 15 Centro. Tel. 2-2003.
   Specialty: MEXICAN.
   $ Prices: Appetizers $3.25–$5; main courses $6.50–$15; children's plate $2.50–$4; fajita plate $7.50.
   Open: Thurs–Tues 12:30–11pm.

The large dining room is a riot of baskets and colorful piñatas on the ceiling, white tables and chairs decorated with red paper flowers, and white napkins stuffed into whimsical papier-mâché napkin rings. As the name suggests, it's a blend of Mexican food and Tex-Mex, but it's much better than Tex-Mex. Prices are moderate for the large portions of well-seasoned food. A large crunchy chicken or beef fajita plate and the flauta plate are especially filling buys. Put on a bib for the chicken sandwich, piled deep with sliced avocado, lettuce, tomato, and onion, next to which are french fries and either cole slaw or macaroni salad. This is a place kids will like, and they offer plate meals with children in mind. It's across from the Casa Maxwell, one block north of the Jardín on Canal.

EL CORREO, Correo 23. Tel. 2-0151.
   Specialty: AMERICAN.
   $ Prices: Appetizers $1.50–$5.50; main courses $2–$5.50.
   Open: Thurs–Tues 9am–9:30pm.

Housed in a colonial-era building opposite El Correo (the post office) half a block east of the Jardín, it's ideally suited for watching the morning mail ritual among resident Americans. You'll see them lingering over coffee and conversation here—and for that reason the nine tables are often full, especially around breakfast. Persevere—it's worth it! Walls are stenciled for the effect of pale turn-of-the-century wallpaper. A mantel over the fireplace is loaded with cookbooks for patron perusal. Try the platter-size almond-laced "waffles tropical," topped with a heaping pile of fruit—easily enough for two. The migas natural, another good breakfast choice, comes with onion, tomato, and chile, or ranchero sauce. Or you can tank up on apple fritters, orange juice, or fruit with yogurt and granola. For homesick stomachs at lunch there's fried chicken, stuffed baked potato, and soup.

HOBOS, Calle Ancho de San Antonio 31. Tel. 2-1724.
   Specialty: MEXICAN/AMERICAN.
   $ Prices: Appetizers $2–$3; main courses $4.50–$8.
   Open: Daily 9am–8pm.

Despite its down-and-out name, this is an up-and-coming, trendy place that's easy on the wallet. It's half a block south of the Instituto Allende on the road to Celaya. With hardwood floors, and log tables and chairs, it's a cozy place with a hobo motif and a menu to delight a hobo. There's corned beef and cabbage with mashed potatoes, or jambalaya Hobo style, which comes with sautéed shrimp, rice, pork, vegetables, and smoked sausage; and hearty meatloaf with mashed potatoes and vegetables. Or try a filling round of chicken cacciatore with spaghetti. If you drop in for a drink, management is likely to surprise you with a light snack—no charge.

RESTAURANT/BAR LA TERRAZA, on the southeast corner of El Jardín.
Specialty: MEXICAN.
$ Prices: Appetizers $3–$6; main courses $6–$13.
Open: Daily 8am–9pm.
For plaza-watchers, the terrace of this restaurant faces the Jardín and offers lots of sidewalk tables. The ambience is nice and relaxing, and the food on the simple and basic menu is neither too cheap nor too expensive. They've perfected the margarita here, so this is a good place to rest from all that shopping.

MEALS FOR LESS THAN $15

MAMA MÍA, Umaran 8. Tel. 2-2063.
Specialty: ITALIAN.
$ Prices: Appetizers $7–$10; pizzas $7–$11; pastas $5–$10; meat main courses $7–$15; coffees $3–$4.
Open: Daily 9am–11:30pm.
Casual and hip—that sums up the atmosphere at this good-quality Italian restaurant. It's two blocks southwest of El Jardín on Umaran, between Jesús and Macías, set in a tree-shaded brick courtyard where you can dine al fresco and enjoy live folkloric South American and flamenco music nightly. There's also a nice selection of coffee-based drinks, with Kahlúa or brandy.

WORTH THE EXTRA BUCKS

HACIENDA DE LAS FLORES, Hospicio 16. Tel. 2-1808.
Specialty: FRENCH. **Reservations:** Recommended.
$ Prices: Appetizers $5–$6.50; main courses $7.50–$15.
Open: Lunch Tues–Sun 1–4pm; dinner Tues–Sun 7–10pm.
Although beyond our budget range as a hotel, the restaurant has a number of relatively inexpensive selections. It's upstairs in a large room overlooking the garden. Light-apricot walls, lace touches, Talavera pottery filled with huge sprays of flowers, and candles and silk flowers on each of the nine tables set a luxurious mood. One of the nicest qualities about this restaurant is its flexibility: Half orders are priced on the menu. For example, a half order (which was a lot) of savory fettuccine with curry sauce and vegetables can be prepared with or without chicken. There's a whole range of freshly made pasta, and soups are another specialty. I highly recommend the delicately seasoned sopa poblana with corn. The service is not as polished as at other splurge restaurants, but it's definitely worth a visit.

To get here from the Jardín, walk east on Correo one block; turn right on Recreo for one block and then left on Hospicio for half a block.

VILLA JACARANDA, Aldama 53. Tel. 2-1015 or 2-0811.
Specialty: INTERNATIONAL. **Reservations:** Recommended.
$ Prices: Main courses $7–$20; fixed-price lunch or dinner $25–$30.
Open: Tues–Sun 7:30am–10:30pm.
Located in the hotel of the same name (way out of our budget range), back of the Parroquia on Aldama, two long blocks south of the Jardín, this is San Miguel's poshest restaurant. With its decor it could easily be a French dining room, but it's not wildly out of our reach. A steak sandwich for lunch runs $8, for example. The fixed-price meal would include soup and, say, filet mignon, stuffed shrimp, or chicken Cordon Bleu. You'll enjoy it: The soft music, twittering birds, ivy, vines, exotic flowers, and the elegance of the restaurant's decor all make it special.

CAFE VENDIMIA, Hidalgo 12. Tel. 2-2645.
Specialty: FRENCH/CONTINENTAL.
$ Prices: Appetizers $3.25–$5; main courses $15–$20.

Open: Tues–Sat noon–9pm, Sun 11am–4pm.

⭐ Among the newest of San Miguel's many restaurants the Cafe Vendimia, on Hidalgo one long block north of the Jardín, is also one of the best. With its pale-ocher walls, cushioned and painted chairs in forest green, tall blown-glass water goblets, and soft table linens, the effect is elegant country French. The handwritten menu varies daily and with only 12 offerings, each one masterfully presented, is austere to perfection. You'll see appetizers like pâté a la casa or onion soup. The delicious chicken breast tarragon comes in a light sauce served with rice and a delicious vegetable medley. The pescado meunière is lightly breaded and fresh. After you order, the waiter returns with a plate of caraway cheese and a warm loaf of round bread. For all the attention and good food you'd expect to pay much more.

READERS RECOMMEND

Fonda Mesón de San José, *Mesones 38 (tel. 2-3848). "The fonda is a fairly new restaurant in a beautiful courtyard setting and part of a complex of shops across from the market. It's hard to find: Look for the sign* ONO *with red and green circles outside. Then go through a passage which looks like a small handcraft shop to get to the patio. Yogurt and fruit or American or Mexican-style breakfasts cost about $2.50. Dinners are Mexican or vegetarian and cost between $3 and $5. English is spoken."* —William and Hannelore Ring, San Diego, Calif. [*Author's Note: The Fonda is open daily from 8am to 9pm.*]

Mesón de Mesones, *Mesones 103, in front of the Angela Peralta Theater. "We discovered a great, new restaurant. Owner/chef Fernando Ortiz Griffith was born and raised in Lincoln, Nebraska, but his family hailed from San Miguel. The restaurant is small—six tables—and is housed in a flower-decked open courtyard. Diners are offered samples of moles and dishes prior to ordering. Food and service are both outstanding."* —Mary Lee and Norm Seward, Guadalajara, Jal., México. [*Author's Note: The Sewards enclosed a menu showing $2 breakfasts served from 8:30 to 11:30am and a full three-course lunch for $3.50, served from 1:30 to 6:30pm.*]

---

6. QUERÉTARO

138 miles N of Mexico City, 63 miles SE of San Miguel de Allende

GETTING THERE By Train From Mexico City: The first-class *Constitucionalista* leaves at 7am and arrives in Querétaro at 10am. (From here, a car is switched that goes on to Irapuato, Silao, and Guanajuato.) **From Nuevo Laredo:** The train arrives in Querétaro at 6pm.

By Bus In Mexico City's Terminal del Norte at "6 Espera," **Flecha Amarilla,** runs a bus to Querétaro every 10 minutes, 24 hours a day. Return service is just as frequent. Other companies run buses about every 20 minutes. The trip from Mexico City takes around 3 hours. There are also frequent buses from San Miguel and Guanajuato.

By Car From Mexico City, follow Highway 57 all the way north to Querétaro. From San Miguel de Allende, either take Highway 111 which enters Querétaro from the north after connecting with Highway 57, or go south from San Miguel to Celaya and then east on Highway 45D to Querétaro.

DEPARTING By Train To Mexico City: The *Constitucionalista* leaves Querétaro at 6pm and arrives in the capital at 9pm. **To Guanajuato:** The *Constitucionalista* leaves Querétaro at 10:20am and arrives in Guanajuato at 1:25pm.

By Bus From Querétaro to Guanajuato, **Flecha Amarilla** has five buses, the first at 4am and the last at 5:40pm. There are hourly buses to San Miguel beginning at 10:30am.

Historic Querétaro (alt. 5,873 ft.; pop. 455,000) is capital of the state of the same name and also a prosperous city with a fantastic history. It was here that Mexico's fight for independence was instigated by Hidalgo in 1810; here that, with the treaty of Guadalupe, Hidalgo sealed the peace of the Mexican War; here that Emperor Maximilian was executed in 1866; and finally, here that the present Mexican constitution was drafted in 1916.

ORIENTATION

ARRIVING   By Train   Querétaro's handsome, early 20th-century train station (tel. 2-1703) is in the Parque los Alcanfores (eucalyptus forest), a 10-minute drive north of downtown. Plans are to convert it to a museum and move the train terminal farther out, but no date has yet been set on when that will happen. Taxis (the only transportation) can be hard to find if you tarry in the station.

By Bus   From the central bus station near Querétaro's lovely Alameda Park you can walk to several hotels or, in 15 minutes, to the main square (Plaza Obregón). Those in a real hurry or with heavy luggage should take a cab.

INFORMATION   Querétaro's tourism office is the **Dirección de Turismo,** at Calle 5 de Mayo no. 61 (tel. 4-0179 or 4-0428), to the left of the Templo de San Francisco. Right next to this church there is also a kiosk operated by the Dirección de Turismo where you can pick up a map of Querétaro and a limited amount of other information. At the main office you can get much more detailed information and make a reservation for a **free city tour.** The 2-hour tours, held Monday through Saturday at 10:30am, cover the major sights of the city—a great way to see the city in a hurry and the best tour deal I've ever encountered. The tourism office is open Monday through Saturday from 9am to 3pm and 6 to 8pm.

FAST FACTS

American Express   The American Express office is at Turismo Beverly, Avenida Tecnologico 118, Loc. 1 (tel. 421/6-1260; fax 421/6-2524).
Area Code   The telephone area code is 421.

WHAT TO SEE & DO

From Querétaro's central square, **Plaza Obregón,** most of the city's major sights are within walking distance. It's bounded by Juárez and Corregadora running north and south, and by Madero and 16 de Septiembre running east and west. Despite the presence of industry on the outskirts and the fact that it is a state capital, this is a pleasant, slow-paced town, without heavy traffic in the downtown area.

If you arrived by bus, you noticed the **Alameda,** an enormous tree-shaded park just across the street that's a good place for a picnic. The central Plaza Obregón is flanked by the church, the Regional Museum, restaurants, shops, and banks. Across the street is a triangular-looking plaza known as the **Jardín Corregidora,** centered on a graceful statue of the famous Josefa Ortíz de Domínguez.

Walking south of Plaza Obregón and the Jardín Corregidora, you'll find **Plaza de la Constitución,** which once housed the town's market on its raised central square. Nowadays it's a pastel-pink piazza boasting a large statue of Venustiano Carranza, who gazes up the polished stones bordering the square. The pedestrians-only **Plaza de la Independencia** (also called Plaza de Armas), on 5 de Mayo a couple of blocks east of Plaza Obregón, is the most beautiful plaza and the historic heart of the city. Graced by manicured, umbrella-shaped trees, a beautiful fountain, and mansions now housing government offices, it's the most delightful place to stroll. And leading off this plaza are flower-decorated pedestrians-only brick streets leading to other well-tended plazas and a few shops.

THE TOP ATTRACTIONS

REGIONAL MUSEUM, Corregidora 3.
A few steps east of Plaza Obregón, this building was originally the Grand Convent of Saint Francis of Assisi, begun in 1540. In 1861 it was used as a fortress by the Imperialists, who backed Maximilian. The structure is one of

those palatial edifices that the "humble" friars favored, replete with arches and Corinthian columns. The first room as you enter holds fascinating memorabilia. Here, several Mexican paintings are informatively compared with European works of the same time; various classical paintings are presented together with modern ones, accompanied by well-written (in Spanish) texts pointing out similarities in form, theme, color, and so forth. Colonial paintings and furniture are in other rooms, and the Sala de Historia contains numerous items of (perhaps morbid) interest, including Maximilian's coffin and countless period photographs.

The museum bookshop sells mostly Spanish-language books.

Admission: $1.

Open: Tues–Sat 10am–6pm, Sun 10am–3:30pm.

CASA DE LA CORREGIDORA/PALACIO MUNICIPAL, Plaza de la Independencia.

Of all the colonial-era buildings surrounding Plaza de la Independencia, this is the most famous. It's a magnificent building and tourists are welcome to step inside the interior courtyard. On the second floor is the Corregidora's room—where, while under lock and key, she (Dona Josefa Ortíz de Domínguez) managed to send a warning to Father Hidalgo that their conspiracy to declare Mexico's independence from Spain had been discovered. Hidalgo got the message and hurried to publicly shout "Independence" in Dolores Hidalgo. The rest is history. Ask the guard if you can see the room, and take your camera—the view of the square from there is good.

Admission: Free.

Open: Mon–Sat 9am–6pm.

INSTITUTO DE LAS ARTESANÍAS, Pasteur 16, at the corner of Libertad. Tel. 2-9100, ext. 215.

Opposite the Casa de la Corregidora is a state crafts shop in another colonial gem. Walk through the rooms with nicely displayed weavings, regional clothing, pottery, onyx, hand-carved furniture, and opals and jewelry incorporating other semiprecious stones—all from Querétaro and all for sale. There is, as well, a nice quantity of items from other regions of Mexico and Guatemala.

Admission: Free.

Open: Mon–Sat 10am–2pm and 5–8pm.

MUSEO DE ARTE, Allende 14 Sur and the Jardín de Santa Clara. Tel. 2-2357.

Step inside this beautiful restored former convent and you get a double whammy: It's a fine museum in a fabulous baroque building that was originally an 18th-century Augustinian convent. Construction began in 1731 and was finished in 1745. Later it was occupied by soldiers in the 1860s. It was designated a historic monument in 1935, yet it remained neglected, even housing the jail at one time. I saw it years ago when it housed the post office, and seemed destined to crumble away chunk by chunk.

What a rebirth! Now visitors are pulled between an obligatory walk through the museum and gazing at the fabulous interior stonework. (The names of the architects and stonemasons are unknown.) An excellent 15-minute video in Spanish unlocks the mystery of the symbolism in the stone. In case your Spanish is rusty, it tells that elephants, ducks, horses, and pelicans signify Christ, and each hand sign has a different meaning. Inside is a magnificent collection of 16th- and 17th-century Mexican and European paintings, as well as changing exhibits of contemporary Mexican paintings. It's one block north of Plaza Obrégon, between Suárez and Madero.

Admission: Free.

Open: Tues–Sun 11am–7pm.

CERRO DE LAS CAMPANÍA (Hill of Bells), Av. Hidalgo between Tecnológico and Hwy. 57 to San Luis Potosí.

One of the most historic places in Mexico can be easily spotted from Highway 57 as a giant hill topped by a titanic statue of Juárez. Just below the statue is the site of the execution of Maximilian, ruler of the short-lived Empire of Mexico. In 1901 the Austrian government built an Expiatory Chapel on the side of the hill. The caretaker (who is rarely around to let you in) takes pleasure in showing you the three small columns in front of the altar, the stones that mark the exact spot where Maximilian and his generals, Miramón and Mejia, stood before the firing squad. Maximilian was in the middle, but gave that place of honor to Miramón; then he gave each member of the firing squad a gold coin so that they would aim at his chest instead of his head (they complied).

Admission: Free.
Open: Daily dawn–dusk.

MORE ATTRACTIONS

The **Convent of Santa Rosa de Viterbo,** on Arteaga between Ocampo and Ezequiel Montes, was built in the 18th century by Mexico's greatest religious architect, Eduardo Tresguerras. It's known for the unusual inverted flying buttresses on the outside and the baroque retablos on the inside, which are magnificent. It's closed more often than it's open, but try around 4 or 5pm.

EVENING ENTERTAINMENT

On Saturday nights from 6 to 10pm Plaza de la Independencia is given over to live entertainment provided by the city's talented youth, **Sábados Querétenos** (Querétaro Saturdays). Take a chair and enjoy the show along with the townsfolk. The parade of talent may include mimes, guitarists, mariachis, vocalists, and violinists.

WHERE TO STAY

You can choose between three lodging areas in Querétaro. Near the bus station are some nice hotels in the upper reaches of our price range. Downtown near the main square are a few charming old places with very down-to-earth prices, and there's a splurge right on Plaza de la Independencia.

DOUBLES FOR LESS THAN $20

HOTEL HIDALGO, Madero Pte. 11, Querétaro, Qro. 76000. Tel. 421/2-0081. 40 rms (all with bath).
$ Rates: $10–$12 single; $14–$17 double.

IN THEIR FOOTSTEPS

Josefa Ortiz de Dominguez (1768–1829) Known as La Correguidora, wife of the correguidor (mayor) of Quérétaro, she assured her place in history the night she sent a messenger to warn the other conspirators, notably Miguel Hidalgo, that their plot to push for independence from Spain had been discovered by government officials. For her role she was imprisoned several times between 1810 and 1817. She died impoverished and forgotten, but today she is much revered. She was the first woman to appear on a Mexican coin, the 5 centavo piece, minted from 1942 to 1946.

• **Birthplace:** Valladolid (now Morelia), Michoacan.
• **Residence:** The Government Palace on Independence Square, Querétaro, known as the House of the Correguidora.
• **Resting Place:** Cemetery of the Illustrious, Querétaro.

The central patio, paved and arched with heavy stones, doubles as a parking lot. Now under new ownership, the hotel, one block west of Plaza Obregón, is being remodeled down to new beds and mattresses, all due to be finished by the summer of 1991. A TV room with free daily newspaper has been added, and soft drinks and snacks are available 24 hours. The Hidalgo's restaurant, is toward the back of the patio.

HOTEL PLAZA, Juárez Norte 23, Querétaro, Qro. 76000. Tel. 421/2-1138. 29 rms (all with bath).
$ Rates: $14.50 single; $16 double.

This little hotel facing Plaza Obregón offers simple but suitable rooms with carpeting. If you like light you won't like the Plaza, since most of the rooms are quite dark, with windows perhaps to the hall but not to the outside. This used to be a noisy place, but now that the square has been fairly well closed to traffic, it's much quieter.

HOTEL SAN FRANCISCO, Corregidora Sur 144, Querétaro, Qro. 76000. Tel. 421/2-0858. 58 rms (all with bath).
$ Rates: $11.50 single; $16 double.
The rooms here are simple and agreeably priced. Some, with windows facing the hallway, are a bit dark; others have ample windows facing the street or a sunny airshaft. The hotel restaurant downstairs, open daily from 7am to midnight, has piles of its delicious butter cookies arranged in the window.

HOTEL SAN AGUSTÍN, Pino Suárez 12, Querétaro, Qro. 76000. Tel. 421/2-1195. 35 rms (all with bath). TEL
$ Rates: $16 single; $18 double.
More or less back to back with the Hotel Hidalgo, this hotel is also about half a block off the plaza, between Allende and Juárez. Overpriced for the quality, the rooms are spartan but clean and bright, with lots of windows. It's a good choice for the money.

DOUBLES FOR LESS THAN $30

HOTEL IMPALA, Colón 1, Querétaro, Qro. 76000. Tel. 421/2-2570. 108 rms (all with bath). TV TEL
$ Rates: $16 single; $22 double.
Its rooms are worn but clean, with blue-tiled baths. Other services include parking, and tobacco and beauty shops. Watch the noise factor here: The quietest rooms are those that face the Alameda, or one of the spacious airshafts, still offering ample light into every room. It's one block from the Alameda off Zaragoza.

DOUBLES FOR LESS THAN $40

HOTEL AMBERES, Av. Corregidora Sur 188, Querétaro, Qro. 76000. Tel. 421/2-8604. 140 rms (all with bath). TV TEL
$ Rates: $23 single; $33 double.
The hotel has dark halls but is well equipped, with private parking, elevators, two bars, a restaurant, and nondescript rooms with piped-in music. It's quiet here despite its location on a major street opposite the Alameda and near the bus station.

HOTEL MIRABEL, Av. Constituyentes 2 Oriente, Querétaro, Qro. 76000. Tel. 421/4-3535 or 4-3644. 171 rms (all with bath). TV TEL
$ Rates: $32 single; $35–$52 double.
Inside the big, dark building is a bright and shiny lobby, a newsstand, and a restaurant with snowy tablecloths and glittering stemware. The rooms are pleasant, with private bath, large windows with nice views, and wall-to-wall carpeting. And it's equipped

with a nice restaurant and bar. Notice the HOTEL sign on the left as you walk out the front door of the bus station; it's a block away. From here it's an easy walk to most of Querétaro's sights.

WORTH THE EXTRA BUCKS

MESÓN SANTA ROSA, Pasteur 17, Queretero, Qro. 76000. Tel. 421/4-5781. Fax 421/4-0997. 5 junior suites, 14 master suites, 1 presidential suite (all with bath). TV TEL
$ Rates: $85 single or double junior suite; $93 master suite.

The loveliest hotel in Querétaro, the state-owned Mesón Santa Rosa was an 18th-century stable, then quarters for Juárez's troops, and later a tenement house before its splendid rebirth as a hotel in the late 1980s. It's on Plaza de la Independencia, opposite the Casa de Artesanías and cater-corner to the Corregidora's house. Expectations are raised just looking at the hotel from the pedestrians-only street in front: iron-studded doors, sienna-colored walls, two large patios dripping with fuchsia-colored bougainvillea, and white iron tables and chairs on the open patio. The patio is usually filled with patrons sipping cappuccino and eyeing the dessert cart. The suites are spacious, all with king-size beds, heavy hand-loomed bedspreads, and comfortable sitting areas.

The **Restaurant Santa Rosa** is a visual and culinary treat. The color scheme is rose and white, and the deep-rose walls are stenciled to resemble white paper doilies. Tables are covered in white linen and waiters wear black jackets and bow ties. Often there's a pianist or violinist in the adjacent bar. The international menu emphasizes Mexican cuisine. (The enchiladas verdes were featured in Patricia Quintana's *The Taste of Mexico*.) Plan to spend as little as $10 or as much as $35 if you order soup through dessert and wine. Reservations are recommended for lunch and dinner.

HOLIDAY INN QUERÉTARO, Av. 5 de Febrero (Hwy. 57), Querétaro, Qro. 76010. Tel. 421/6-0202. 171 rms (all with bath). A/C MINIBAR TV TEL
$ Rates: $90 single or double.
If you're weary from a day's drive and want to splurge on a night of comfort without the hassle of hunting for the place, this is a good choice—you can't miss it, it's right on the highway leading to Mexico City. The decor is colonial throughout, and the rooms are handsomely furnished and comfortable. There's a pool for a refreshing dip, tennis courts, and miniature golf. The restaurant is open early and late, and there's live music in the lobby bar most evenings.

WHERE TO EAT

In addition to the above-mentioned hotel restaurants, all of which stay open all day every day, several pleasant dining spots are on or near Querétaro's main plaza.

MEALS FOR LESS THAN $5

COMEDOR VEGETARIANO, Vergara 7. Tel. 4-1088.
Specialty: VEGETARIAN.
$ Prices: Main courses $1.50–$2.50; comida corrida $2.75.
Open: Mon–Sat 8am–8pm.

You'll find delicious vegetarian Mexican and international foods here. The restaurant is small and informal, with a counter selling vitamins, herbal teas, natural cosmetics, and everything else you'd expect to find in a natural-food store. The comida corrida here includes a fresh salad, juice, soup, homemade whole-wheat bread, and a main course. Or you could try the soy and mushroom burgers or soy or cheese enchiladas.

This Comedor is on a pedestrians-only street off Plaza de la Independencia. With your back to Mesón Santa Rosa, and with Casa de Artesanías on your left, walk straight ahead on Calle Libertad and turn left at the corner (Vergara); the restaurant is on the left.

There's another branch of the Comedor off Plaza Obregón at Juárez 47.

CAFETERÍA LA MARIPOSA, Angela Peralta 7. Tel. 2-1166.
Specialty: MEXICAN.
$ Prices: Appetizers $2–$3.50; main courses $2.50–$10.
Open: Daily 8am–10pm.

Look for the wrought-iron butterfly sign when you turn left on Peralta (two blocks north of Plaza Obregón) for one of the city's most popular restaurants. It's a good place for light lunches—enchiladas, a fruit salad, or club sandwich—or pastries, ice cream, and coffee.

Right next door is a wickedly tempting sweet shop featuring such irresistibles as candied figs, peaches, bananas, and papaya. You can order these in the restaurant, as the two enterprises are under the same management.

MEALS FOR LESS THAN $10

OSTIONERÍA TAMPICO, Corregidora Norte 3. Tel. 2-3001.
Specialty: SEAFOOD.
$ Prices: Appetizers $2–$5; main courses $3–$6; comida corrida $5.75–$7.
Open: Daily 9am–8pm.

Just off the Obregón, this sparkling-clean restaurant will satisfy your seafood craving. Take a seat at the lunch counter or the Formica tables and chow down on crab ceviche or seafood cocktail, filet of fish, or many other seafood selections.

PIZZAS LA TAVOLA, Av. 16 de Septiembre Ote. 14. Tel. 2-4033.
Specialty: ITALIAN.
$ Prices: Pizza $5–$11.
Open: Daily noon–10:30pm.

At the little garden just off the main square on Corregidora, your nose will lead you to an inviting place to dine on good pizza or pasta. The restaurant sports nice wood-and-wicker decor, and booths with hanging wicker shades. Prices here are excellent, as are the pizzas: plain or with the works. You can even order it to go, if you like.

RESTAURANT/BAR EL CORTIJO DE DON JUAN, Jardín Corregidora 1416. Tel. 4-3037.
Specialty: SPANISH/MEXICAN.
$ Prices: Appetizers $2–$3; main courses $6–$13.
Open: Daily 9am–1am.

For a fancier place, try El Cortido de Don Juan on the Jardín Corregidora. You'll think I should have put it under "Worth the Extra Bucks" until you see the surprisingly low prices. Try one of the main courses, such as charcoal-broiled steak with potatoes, beans, and salad. You can choose to sit outside at the sidewalk tables in the garden, under the striped awning; inside in any of the several small, colonial-style rooms with a traditional Spanish bullfight decor and a mural of a Flamenco dancer on the wall; or in the comfortable, dark-wood bar.

LA FLOR DE QUERÉTARO, Juárez Norte 5. Tel. 2-0199.
Specialty: MEXICAN.
$ Prices: Appetizers $1.50–$2; main courses $4–$10.
Open: Daily 7am–10:30pm.

A few doors down from the Hotel Plaza is one of the best budget choices in town. Its tablecloths are spotless, the wood-paneled walls are adorned with old scenic photos, and all in all, it's a clean, comfortable, and pleasant place, right down to the cushioned red chairs. There's a wide selection of dishes offered for every meal on the bilingual menu, with excellent prices.

READERS RECOMMEND

El Archangel, at the corner of Guerrero and Madero. "This is a nice restaurant three blocks from the Plaza. It looks like an old ice-cream parlor inside, but serves traditional meals and pizza at very reasonable prices. Salads and fruit are washed in purified water. They also serve fruit drinks and cakes."—William and Hannelore Ring, San Diego, Calif.

EASY EXCURSIONS FROM QUERÉTARO
TEQUISQUIAPAN

About 46½ miles from Querétaro, a short distance east off the toll road to Mexico City, is the resort town of Tequisquiapan, Querétaro. From a 16th-century farming town in the rich Bajio ("lowlands") region, Tequisquiapan has grown to become a favorite weekend getaway destination for residents of the great metropolis only 2 hours' drive away.

Besides farming, "Tequis" is famous for its crafts, and for some hot springs that the hotels capitalize on today. The town square with a 16th-century church in its center is surrounded by boutiques, hotels, and restaurants. It's a delightful place to relax, providing you know when to go. Since on weekends hotel prices include meals, plan your visit for between Sunday noon and Friday noon (that's before and after the Capitalinos); most hotels relax the meal requirement between weekends.

Another time to go (but not to stay—it'll be too expensive) is at the end of May and the beginning of June for the **Feria Nacional del Queso y el Vino**—a grand wine-and-cheese festival celebrating these two regional products. Day and night the festivities rage, as sports matches, rodeos, cockfights, even exhibits of children's paintings keep one and all on the go. Wine- and cheese-tasting parties are provided—many of them free of charge—by the big dairies and wineries, and so the gaiety is full blown and long-lived.

Buses run to "Tequis" frequently from Querétaro's Central Camionera, with a lot of extra buses laid on during the wine-and-cheese festival. But be aware that room rates go up dramatically during the fair.

The streets of Tequisquiapan are lined with hotels, large and small, and most have thermal water pools. If these below are full, this side of town is full of other reasonably priced lodging.

Where to Stay & Eat

HOTEL LOS ARCOS, Moctezuma 12, Tequisquiapan, Qro. Tel. 467/3-0566. 9 rms (all with bath).
$ Rates: $25 single or double.

This new hotel about eight blocks west of the central plaza is a good choice, but it doesn't have a pool or hotel grounds. Rooms have fans, and are spacious, well kept, and priced slightly less than the Posada Tequisquiapan (see below). Room rates never include meals, so you can dine around at will. But you'll soon discover that the hotel-owned Restaurant Los Molcajetes, next door, has some of the most reasonably priced meals in town.

POSADA TEQUISQUIAPAN, Moctezuma 6, Tequisquiapan, Qro. Tel. 467/5-0010. 13 rms (all with bath).
$ Rates: Mon–Fri $24 single, $31 double, without meals; Sat–Sun $39 per person, with three meals.

Although this hotel was once better cared for than it is today, it's still a beautiful and relaxing place. The setting of the older section, around gardens and a spring that doubles as the swimming pool, will prove that. There's a small restaurant, too. All rooms have fans. Newer rooms across the street are more modern but lack the charm of the older section. It's about six blocks west of the central plaza.

FRAY JUNÍPERO SERRA MISSIONS

If you're driving, this is a side trip worth making. Five little-known missions established by Fray Junípero Serra, before his journey to California, are in the Sierra Gorda mountain region east of Querétaro. The beautiful buildings have been restored and the state operates three hotels along the route: **Mesón Concá,** near Mision Concá ($22 double in the old section of a hacienda, $52 for the master suite); **Mesón de San Joaquín,** at San Joaquín ($22 double); and **Mesón de Fray Junípero Serra,** at Jalpan ($22 double). Each has a small restaurant. My favorite is the hacienda section of Mesón Concá. The master suite opens to a porch, yard, and steamy thermal water stream—all very relaxing. The largest town is Jalpan; the others are only small farming villages.

From Querétaro the drive (which begins at the Cadereyta turnoff south of Querétaro) is a windy, mountainous one that takes at least 5 hours. En route are two **archeological sites**—Las Ranas, easily accessible, and Toluquilla, reached over a rutted road after which you must climb a mountain to reach the site. Another, less windy route begins far north of Querétaro at the San Luis Potosí turnoff east to Río Verde. From there, go south to Concá and Jalpan.

Whichever route you choose, plan to spend a minimum of 2 nights in the mission zone. The drive is tiring and, although the missions can all be seen in one day, you'd be pushing it to drive out the second afternoon, not to mention rushing through the experience.

Unfortunately there is no local or Querétaro tourism office information on the Franciscan symbolism of the missions' fabulously decorated facades, so bone up on this before you go. The State Tourism Office in Querétaro can make reservations and provide a map to the region, hotels, and missions. Or contact the state promotional office **Prodabitur,** Prospero C. Vega 31, Querétaro, Qro. México 76000 (tel. 463/4-3078; fax 463/4-0997).

TULA

The ancient Toltec capital of Tula is an interesting archeological site, worth a visit. It's 12 miles north from the Querétaro–Mexico City toll road, Highway 57D, on State Highway 126. The bus from Querétaro's Central Camionera will go through Tepeji del Río, where you may have to change to another bus for Tula. (See Chapter 18, Section 1, for more details of this "City of Atlantean Men.")

OTHER SILVER CITIES

Besides the cities founded because of silver that are discussed in this chapter, see also Chapter 13 for Taxco, called the "Silver Capital of Mexico," Pachuca also in Chapter 13, and Real de Catorce in Chapter 15.

TARASCAN COUNTRY

The land of the Tarascans has held a special place in the country's history since before the Spanish conquest of Mexico. Unconquered by the Aztecs, the proud and courageous Tarascan people held themselves and their land apart in majestic forested mountains dotted with misty lakes. Their language and influence were known as far north as the present-day states of Querétaro, Guerrero, Colima, Jalisco, and Guanajuato. Even the name Guanajuato is a Spanish corruption of the Tarascan word *guanaxuato,* meaning "hill of the frogs." Their pyramids, connecting half circles and rectangles, were called *yacatas,* the most visible of which is at Tzintzuntzán, near Pátzcuaro. Good examples of their pottery, stonework, and metalwork are displayed at the Museo del Estado in Morelia.

The true name of the indigenous group and its language is not Tarascan but Purépecha (sometimes spelled Purápecha), a word heard often in the region. When Spaniards married into Indian families, the Indians called them *tarasco,* which means "son in law" in Purépecha, a name the Spaniards heard so often that they named the people Tarascans—and it stuck. The Purépecha language is still spoken by more than 200,000 people; according to the *Cultural Atlas of Mexico,* it's remotely linked to the Mixe and Zoque languages in Mexico, and to the Quecha language of Peru. But even from village to village there are differences in pronunciation within the language.

Two very different leaders stand out in the colonial history of Pátzcuaro. Conquistador Nuño de Guzman's infamous greed led him to terrorize the Tarascan population and burn their chief alive because he wouldn't—or couldn't—disclose the location of gold deposits. After Guzman was arrested, a humane bishop named Vasco de Quiroga was sent to reconstruct the area. De Quiroga taught the Indians several trades, a different one in each village. As a result, today the region is well known for its crafts: handsome hand-loomed fabrics made in Pátzcuaro and Erongaricaro; pottery and straw weavings in Tzintzuntzán; wood carving in Quiroga, Tzintzuntzán, and Pátzcuaro. Santa Clara de Cobre's shops shimmer with copper, and both Pátzcuaro and Uruapan are known for lacquerware. The bishop became so revered that he is still honored today. Streets and hotels are named after him, and his statue stands in the main plaza of Pátzcuaro.

Although most Tarascans have given up truly distinctive regional dress, women still wear their hair braided and interlaced with satin ribbons in the traditional manner, don embroidered blouses and hand-loomed skirts, and wrap themselves in rebozos. In remote villages men (more often boys) wear traditional white cotton homespun pants and shirts.

While the region is completely incorporated into the commerce of mainstream Mexico through agriculture (avocados and coffee) and industry (furniture and lumber), it is still apart, primarily due to the beautiful-but-mountainous terrain.

WHAT'S SPECIAL ABOUT TARASCAN COUNTRY

Phenomena
- ☐ The nesting grounds of the monarch butterfly from Morelia.
- ☐ Paricutín, the volcano, and a lava-covered village near Uruapan.

Great Towns and Villages
- ☐ The stately colonial-era buildings of Morelia.
- ☐ Pátzcuaro's picturesque, red-tile roofs and whitewashed walls.

Museums
- ☐ The Museo del Estado (state museum) in Morelia in the childhood home of Ana Huerta, Empress of Mexico (1862–64), with displays beginning in pre-Hispanic times.

Music
- ☐ The May Organ Festival in Morelia, featuring the cathedral's 4,600 pipe organ.
- ☐ Performances of the Morelia Boys Choir at the Rosas Conservatory of Music.

Shopping
- ☐ House of Eleven Patios in Pátzcuaro, featuring foot-loomed fabrics, copper, embroidery, wood carving, straw weaving, and pottery from Michoacan state.
- ☐ Paracho, the "Guitar Capital of Mexico."
- ☐ Pátzcuaro's handmade traditional furniture.

Special Events
- ☐ Easter Week in Pátzcuaro, combining regional traditions and religious pageantry.
- ☐ Janitzio Island in Lake Pátzcuaro, famous commemoration of the "Days of the Dead," with an all-night candlelight cemetery vigil Nov. 1 and 2.

Architecturally it's almost unchanged from colonial times. Also, it's off the beaten tourist track and therefore relatively low priced. All of this combines to create one of the most enjoyable regions in Mexico to visit.

SEEING THE REGION

Located northwest of Mexico City, the three best-known towns in Tarascan Country—Morelia, Pátzcuaro, and Uruapan—are in the state of Michoacan ("Meech-oh-ah-kahn"), Mexico's sixth-largest state. The distances between the three cities is no more than an hour or two and public transportation is frequent. Plan no less than a day (2 nights) in Morelia and a minimum of 2 days (3 nights) in Pátzcuaro. Uruapan is an easy day trip, but you may want to stay longer for a visit to the Paricutín volcano. Easter week or Day of the Dead (actually 2 days, Nov 1–2), will find the plazas in Pátzcuaro and Uruapan loaded with regional crafts. Processions and other traditional customs make Easter week exceptional in Pátzcuaro. But reserve rooms well in advance for these holidays.

1. MORELIA

195 miles NW of Mexico City, 228 miles SE of Guadalajara

GETTING THERE By Plane The regional airline, **AeroMar,** offers three flights per day between Morelia and Mexico City Sunday through Friday and two flights on Saturday. The fare is $92 one way, $183 round-trip.

By Train   Between Mexico City and Morelia, a 9- to 10-hour overnight trip, a seat on *El Purépecha* costs $8.65 in Primera Especial and $4 in Primera Regular. A sleeping compartment costs $16.50 for one, $27.50 for two. Reserve early for the sleeping compartments—they fill up first. This train can get very cold or very hot, so be prepared.

By Bus   Tres Estrellas de Oro buses to and from Mexico City run every 30 minutes. There are frequent buses from Pátzcuaro.

By Car   Highway 15 runs east and south to Mexico City and west and north to Guadalajara. Both sections are mountainous and have hairpin curves. Although it looks longer on the map, there are fewer curves and therefore it's a shorter drive from Mexico City if you take the turnoff north on Highway 122 just before Hidalgo, then west again at Maravatío through Querendaro to Morelia. Highway 43 north is a fairly direct and noncurvaceous route from San Miguel de Allende and Guanajuato.

DEPARTING   By Plane   Aeropuerto Francisco J. Mugica is a 45-minute drive from the city center on the Carretera Morelia/Cinapecuaro, km. 27 (tel. 3-6074, 3-6177, or 3-6178). The **AeroMar** offices are at Avenida 20 de Noviembre no. 110 (tel. 451/2-8524, or toll free 800/950-0747 in the U.S.; fax 451/3-0555).

By Train   *El Purépecha* train service leaves Morelia for Mexico City at 11pm and arrives in the capital at 7:30am. Or to Pátzcuaro or Uruapan, it leaves at 6:30am and arrives in Pátzcuaro at 7:30am and in Uruapan at 10am. You could use the service for a day trip to either of those villages: The return train from Uruapan leaves at 7pm, stops in Pátzcuaro at 9:40pm, and arrives back in Morelia around 11pm. If you use the train for a day trip, buy a round-trip ticket to be assured a seat on the return train. A taxi to the train station takes about 10 minutes and costs $1.75.

By Bus   The **Central de Autobuses** is at Eduardo Ruíz and Valentin Gomez Farías, seven blocks northwest of the cathedral. **Tres Estrellas de Oro** (tel. 2-1186) runs first-class buses to Mexico City every 30 minutes. **Autotransportes Flecha Amarilla** (tel. 2-5503), and **ADO** (tel. 2-0600) also have frequent service.

By Car   Pátzcuaro is an hour's drive southwest of Morelia by several routes; the shortest route is via Tiripetío. Highway 15 goes via Quiroga and Tzintzuntzán, or you can cut south before Quiroga at El Correro and take Highway 14 to Pátzcuaro. To Uruapan, follow the directions to Pátzcuaro, then take Highway 14 to Uruapan—a beautiful mountainous drive.

For routes to Mexico City, see "Getting There," above.

Morelia (alt. 6,368 ft.; pop. 484,000), the capital of the wildly beautiful state of Michoacan, is a lovely colonial city. Over the years it has earned a reputation as one of Mexico's intellectual and artistic centers. As with much of Mexico, there is layer upon layer of fascinating history here. The area was inhabited first by the indigenous peoples, notably the Tarascans. Founded by the Spanish in 1541, the city was originally named Valladolid, changed later to honor the revolutionary hero José María Morelos, who once lived here.

Morelia's many original colonial buildings add a special touch of ancient Mexican/Spanish elegance. To preserve the architectural harmony, the city government long ago decreed that all new major construction continue the same style and be built no taller than the existing structures. Thus Morelia retains its colonial charm.

ORIENTATION

ARRIVING   A taxi from the airport to downtown takes 45 minutes and costs $11. The bus station is about seven blocks northwest of the cathedral. Taxis line up out front to collect passengers. A ride to hotels around Plaza Principal should cost around $1.25.

INFORMATION The **State Tourism Office** is in a former Jesuit monastery, the Palacio Clavijero, at the corner of Madero and Nigromante (tel. 3-2654). Someone on the helpful staff usually speaks English. They have excellent maps and information on Morelia and Michoacan. It's open daily from 9am to 2pm and 4 to 8pm.

CITY LAYOUT The heart of the city is the pretty central plaza, bounded north and south by Madero and Allende/Valladolid and east and west by Abasolo, Hidalgo, and the cathedral. Streets change directions at the plaza. Most of the major attractions and my recommended hotels are in this historic central zone anchored by the plaza.

GETTING AROUND

Taxis are a fairly good bargain. Although there are no meters, cab drivers are supposed to charge 45¢ per kilometer, or about $1.20 between various points downtown. Here, as anywhere in Mexico, strike your bargain before you enter the cab.

    Combis, at 17¢ a ticket, are cheaper than taxis. The customized vans hold up to 15 passengers and are color-coded according to each route.

    Two types of **buses** will take you anywhere in the city: white buses cost 10¢ and the blue express buses cost 17¢.

FAST FACTS

    American Express The local representative is Lopsa travel agency, in the Centro Comercial, Avenida del Campestre and Artilleros del 47 no. 1520 (tel. 451/4-1950; fax 451/4-7716).

    Area Code The telephone area code is 451.

    Climate At an altitude of more than 6,000 feet, Morelia can be a bit chilly in the evenings, especially from November through February.

    Newspapers: The local paper, *La Voz de Michoacan,* has a "What's New in Morelia This Week" page that appears every Monday and lists all kinds of interesting cultural events around Morelia.

    Post Office and Telegraph Office Both are in the Palacio Federal, on the corner of Madero and Serapio Rendon, five blocks east of the cathedral.

WHAT TO SEE & DO

Morelia is a beautiful city and perfect for walking, since most of the important sights and shopping are all within walking distance of downtown hotels and restaurants.

WALKING TOUR — Morelia's Historic Center

Start: At the Cathedral.
Finish: Casa de la Cultura.
Time: Approximately all day (you can also spread it over 2 days).
Best Times to Go: After 9am when the museums are open.
Worst Times to Go: Monday and holidays, and daily between 2 and 4pm.

IMPRESSIONS

I like Mexico, I like its color, its violence, its raw tumbling mountains, green checkerboard valleys, dizzy trails, purple blue sky and stabbing sun. I like its crumbling monasteries and cathedrals with cactus growing from their roofs, and even more its ancient pyramids rising earth-covered and defiant from jungle plain and mountain top.
    —STUART CHASE, *MEXICO: A STUDY OF TWO AMERICAS,* 1931

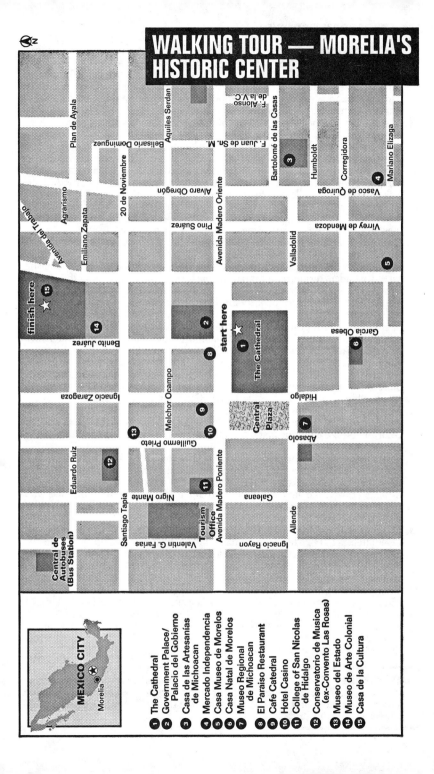

WALKING TOUR — MORELIA'S HISTORIC CENTER

N

Plan de Ayala
Aquiles Serdán
F. Alonso de la V.C.
Belisario Domínguez
F. Juan de Sn. M.
Bartolomé de las Casas
Humboldt
Corregidora
Mariano Elizaga
Agrarismo
20 de Noviembre
Alvaro Obregón
Vasco de Quiroga
Emiliano Zapata
Pino Suárez
Avenida Madero Oriente
Virrey de Mendoza
Avenida del Trabajo
Valladolid

3
4
5

finish here
15
14
2
8
start here
1
6
García Obeso
Benito Juárez
Melchor Ocampo
The Cathedral
Hidalgo

Ignacio Zaragoza
9
13
10
7
Abasolo
Central Plaza
Eduardo Ruiz
12
Guillermo Prieto
11
Galeana
Nigro Mante
Santiago Tapia
Tourism Office
Avenida Madero Poniente
Allende
Valentín G. Farías
Ignacio Rayón

Central de Autobuses (Bus Station)

MEXICO CITY
Morelia

1. The Cathedral
2. Government Palace/ Palacio del Gobierno
3. Casa de las Artesanías de Michoacán
4. Mercado Independencia
5. Casa Museo de Morelos
6. Casa Natal de Morelos
7. Museo Regional de Michoacán
8. El Paraíso Restaurant
9. Cafe Catedral
10. Hotel Casino
11. College of San Nicolás de Hidalgo
12. Conservatorio de Musica (ex-Convento Las Rosas)
13. Museo del Estado
14. Museo de Arte Colonial
15. Casa de la Cultura

548 • TARASCAN COUNTRY

1. The Cathedral. In the heart of Morelia, on Madero between Ignacio Zaragoza and Avenida Morelos Norte, past the plaza, the **cathedral** took 104 years to build (1640–1744) and has two impressive spires over 70 meters (220 ft.) high, which can be climbed (the doors are locked, but the man with the key is usually hanging around at midday). The interior of the church is awesome, particularly if you're fortunate enough to be there when the organist is playing. The organ, with its 4,600 pipes, is one of the best in Latin America. Great organists perform here during the International Organ Festival in May.

Across the street (Madero) from the cathedral,

2. The **Government Palace** was built in 1732 as a seminary, but now contains grand colorful murals depicting the history of the state of Michoacan and of Mexico. Some of them were done by a well-known local artist named Alfredo Zalce. Notice the building's lovely arches.

For one of the best regional museums of art and showrooms of crafts, walk two blocks east on Madero (turn left out the door of the Government Palace) then turn south (right) onto Vasco de Quiroga for one block to the:

3. Casa de las Artesanías de Michoacan (tel. 2-1248), across Plaza de San Francisco in the old colonial building attached to the church of the same name. High-quality traditional-style crafts of all sorts are displayed here: fantastic carved wooden furniture; gigantic, people-size ceramic pots; beautiful, hand-woven clothing; wooden masks—including unpainted ones to decorate yourself. Three large rooms hold lacquerware from Pátzcuaro and Uruapan, including delicately flowered trays inlaid with gold. There are several examples of embutido inlay—the original process involves treating the completed trays with a preparation of colored earth, axle oil, and linseed oil to create a waterproof finish. There's cross-stitch embroidery from Taracuato; pine furniture from Cuanejo, woodwork and guitars from Paracho, and close-woven hats from the Isla de Jaracuaro. Everything on display is for sale at reasonable prices. Upstairs is a crafts museum. The art center is open daily from 9am to 8pm; admission is free.

Four blocks south on Avenida Lázaro Cárdenas is the huge:

4. Mercado Independencia, which is open daily. Browse around and enjoy the wonders of the Mexican marketplace, everything from clothing to cookware to colorful flowers. From the market, walk two blocks west to Avenida Morelos Sur to visit the:

5. Casa Museo de Morelos, Morelos 323 (tel. 3-2651), where the city's namesake lived as an adult. It's a pleasant hacienda with an authentic kitchen from the era, and furniture and personal effects of the hero. It's open Monday through Friday from 9am to 2pm and 4 to 8pm; admission is free. For those who want still more on Morelos, walk another block west to Garcia Obesa, turn right, and on the corner of Corregidora is the:

6. Casa Natal de Morelos (birthplace of Morelos), at Corregidora and Obesa (tel. 2-2703). There's more memorabilia, including historical documents, old posters, and modern murals depicting the Revolution. It's open Monday through Friday from 9am to 2pm and 4 to 8pm.

From here, turn left out the front door half a block to Hidalgo and turn right, and then left again for another block to Allende and the:

7. Museo Regional de Michoacan, Allende and Abasolo (tel. 2-0407). This is a good introduction to the history of the state from prehistoric times to Mexico's Cárdenist period of the 1930s. It's open Tuesday through Saturday from 9am to 7pm and on Sunday from 9am to 2pm. Admission costs 35¢. Head north across the park to Madero, for a:

REFUELING STOP Back on Madero in front of the cathedral is the whole choice of cafés, across from the cathedral beginning with **8. El Paraíso** on the corner of Benito Juárez and running down past the **9. Cafe Catedral** and **10. Hotel Casino** to Prieto.

Continue west on Madero one block to the corner of Nigromante, where, on the right-hand corner, is the:

11. College of San Nicolas de Hidalgo, a beautiful colonial-era university that claims to be "oldest in the western hemisphere." Founded in Pátzcuaro in 1540, it was moved to Valladolid (that is, Morelia) in 1580 and incorporated into the University of Michoacan in 1957. Turn north (right) on Nigromante and walk three short blocks to Santiago Tapia; turn right and on the left-hand side is the:

12. Conservatorio de Musica, in the former *Convento de Las Rosas,* established as a convent for Dominican nuns in 1500. In 1785 it became a school for boys with musical skill, and is now the home of the internationally acclaimed Morelia Boys' Choir. Don't miss them if there's a practice or performance while you're in town; you can listen and observe quietly. Cater-corner across the street is the:

13. Museo del Estado, at the corner of Tapia and Guillermo Prieto (tel. 3-0629), a delightfully well-done, free museum with everything about Michoacan, starting with cavemen, fossils, and fangs to an on-site, intact 19th-century apothecary shop, on up to contemporary art on the second floor. This was the childhood home of Ana Huerta, first empress of Mexico and wife of Emperor Augustín Iturbide. It's open Monday through Friday from 9am to 2pm and 4 to 8pm, and on Saturday, Sunday, and holidays from 9am to 7pm. For another interesting museum, continue east on Santiago Tapia two blocks to Benito Juárez and turn north (left) to the:

14. Museo de Arte colonial, Avenida Benito Juárez 240 (tel. 3-9260). It's filled with religious art from the 16th to the 18th century, housed in another old town house with a central courtyard.

To find out about local cultural events, cross the small street to the north, (around the corner to the right from the museum) and turn left (next street) on Avenida Morelos Norte. Follow the high wrought-iron fence enclosing whimsical, contemporary sculpture made from machine parts to reach the entrance of the:

15. Casa de la Cultura. This cultural complex includes a mask museum, an open-air café, and several art galleries. It's open daily from 10am to 8pm and there's no admission charge. Posters in the entryway announce events happening here and at other locations in town.

A BUS & WALKING TOUR

On Calle Santiago Tapia, just north of Madero, board a "Directo" bus for the trip east, where you'll see the results of the city-hall order to build in colonial style: Banks, office buildings, even Woolworth's, are all in that style.

Leave the bus at the corner of Madero and Avenida Acueducto and walk along the Bosque Cuauhtémoc, which holds the **Museum of Contemporary Art.** Across the street is one of the city's most famous structures, a 3-mile-long **aqueduct,** with 253 arches, built in 1785.

Turn right on Calzada Ventura Puente and you'll pass the **Museum of Natural History** on the right. This museum, run by the University of Michoacan, is open Wednesday through Monday from 1 to 6pm. Admission is free. On your left as you walk along, you'll pass several science buildings belonging to the university.

Continuing on across Avenida Carrillo, board an "Alberca" bus, which will take you south to the Paseo de la Camelina. The city's **planetarium** is at this intersection, with shows Tuesday through Sunday at 6:30pm; admission is 90¢.

From the planetarium, you can board Ruta 2 bus heading west to Parque Juárez, which has a little **zoo,** complete with elephants and tigers, for an admission of 50¢ for adults, 10¢ for children. It's open Wednesday through Monday from 11am until 6pm.

Outside the park, board a "Santa María" bus for the ride north, back to downtown. This last leg of the tour presents an enjoyable view of the narrow streets in the residential quarters of the city's interior.

The bus will take you back to the center of town. Fares are so low that you can ride along this route, hopping off at every interesting prospect, and still end up paying very little for the entire trip.

MORE ATTRACTIONS

The **Templo de los Monjas** is a lovely old church, a few blocks down Madero, east of the cathedral and right beside the massive **Palacio Federal,** which houses, among many other official bureaus, the post and telegraph offices.

SPECIAL EVENTS

The **International Organ Festival** is in May at the cathedral. In June is the **Fiesta de Corpus,** with special cathedral lighting and in September, for the **birthday of Don José María Morelos,** there are independence celebrations.

WHERE TO STAY

HOTEL SAN JORGE, Madero Pte. 719, Morelia, Mich. 58000. Tel. 451/2-4610. 45 rms (all with bath).
$ Rates: $11.50 single; $14 double.
This budget choice offers rooms that are small, clean, nice enough but without frills. Doors and windows open out onto a long common hallway. A simple breakfast is served at several small tables in the lobby. The hotel is at the corner of Guadalupe Victoria and Madero, several blocks west of the cathedral.

HOTEL MINTZICURI, Vasco de Quiroga 227, Morelia, Mich. 58000. Tel. 451/2-0664. 37 rms (all with bath). TEL
$ Rates: $11.50 single; $14.50 double.
This modern, attractive, three-floor budget hotel with an eye-catching blue, orange, and white tile facade has rooms that all face an interior open courtyard, where guests can park their cars. The rooms are pleasant, carpeted, and very clean, with all-new bathrooms. The restaurant was being remodeled and should be open when you travel. The Mintzicuri is three blocks east on Madero from the cathedral, then south (right) on Quiroga three more blocks.

HOTEL PLAZA, Valentín Gomez Farías 278, Morelia, Mich. 58000. Tel. 451/2-3095. 33 rms (all with bath). TEL
$ Rates: $12 single; $16 double.
This hotel, at the corner of Eduardo Ruíz, is near the bus station. It offers rooms that are small and worn, but clean and acceptable. The restaurant downstairs, open

---

IN THEIR FOOTSTEPS

Augustin Iturbide (1783–1824) In an elaborate ceremony that took months to plan, he was crowned Emperor of Mexico and created an elaborate imperial monarchy with titles and right of succession by his children. But he reigned only briefly from 1822 to 1824, when General Santa Anna led a successful rebellion to dethrone him. He returned surreptitiously from exile but was captured and shot by a firing squad in Padilla, Tamaulipas. For years regarded as a usurper and self-interested politican, in a rare move, public sentiment recognized his role in gaining Mexico's independence from Spain and his remains were interred more fittingly in Mexico City.
    • **Birthplace:** Morelia, Michoacan
    • **Residence:** A palace, at Madero 17 in Mexico City, built in the 18th century for the Counts of San Mateo de Valparaiso, became Iturbide's palace residence. It's a Banamex branch today.
    • **Resting Place:** Mexico City Cathedral.

MORELIA ACCOMMODATIONS & DINING

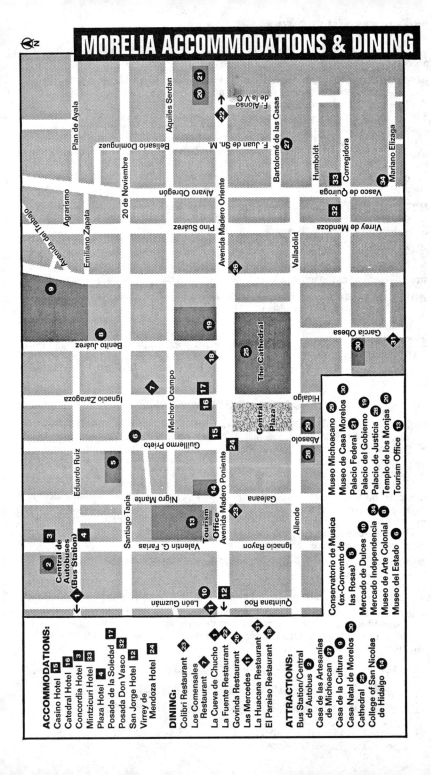

ACCOMMODATIONS:
Casino Hotel **15**
Catedral Hotel **16**
Concordia Hotel **3**
Mintzicuri Hotel **33**
Plaza Hotel **4**
Posada de la Soledad **17**
Posada Don Vasco **32**
San Jorge Hotel **12**
Virrey de
Mendoza Hotel **24**

DINING:
Colibri Restaurant **23**
Los Comensales
Restaurant **7**
La Cueva de Chucho **1**
La Fuente Restaurant **22**
Govinda Restaurant **26**
Las Mercedes **11**
La Huacana Restaurant **31**
El Paraiso Restaurant **18**

ATTRACTIONS:
Bus Station/Central
de Autobus **2**
Casa de las Artesanías
de Michoacan **27**
Casa de la Cultura **9**
Casa Natal de Morelos **30**
Cathedral **25**
College of San Nicolas
de Hidalgo **14**

Conservatorio de Musica
(ex-Convento de
las Rosas) **5**
Mercado de Dulces **10**
Mercado Independencia **34**
Museo de Arte Colonial **8**
Museo del Estado **6**

Museo Michoacano **29**
Museo de Casa Morelos **30**
Palacio Federal **21**
Palacio del Gobierno **19**
Palacio de Justicia **28**
Templo de los Monjas **20**
Tourism Office **13**

Monday through Saturday from 7am to 11pm, has a basic menu and reasonable prices.

POSADA DON VASCO, Vasco de Quiroga 232, Morelia, Mich. 58000.
Tel. 451/2-1484. 36 rms (all with bath). TEL
$ Rates: $13.25 single; $16 double.

This centrally located budget hotel in the bustling neighborhood near the mercado (opposite the Hotel Mintzicuri, above) offers a tranquil and pretty courtyard rampant with cascading flowers. There's a TV in the lobby. The rooms are tidy and pleasant, all with red carpeting and tile baths. La Hostería del Laurel is the hotel's small, extremely popular restaurant—no surprise since it has one of the cheapest comida corridas in town—$2 (served from 2:30 to 5:30pm) and entire breakfasts for slightly more than a dollar.

HOTEL CONCORDIA, Valentín Gomez Farías 328, Morelia, Mich. 58000.
Tel. 451/2-3052. 51 rms (all with bath). TV TEL
$ Rates: $14 single; $18 double.

Many readers recommended this quiet hotel, conveniently located near the bus station and a few blocks from the center of town. The rooms are large and modern, and the staff is friendly. Ask for one of the rooms facing the street—these have the most light and almost a full wall of windows.

HOTEL CASINO, Portal Hidalgo 229, Morelia, Mich. 58000. Tel. 451/3-1003. 50 rms (all with bath). TV TEL
$ Rates: $26 single; $32 double.

This fine old hotel has several nice touches—beams, chandeliers, and columns—along with an excellent location, practically across the street from the cathedral. The immaculate rooms have wall-to-wall carpeting. Downstairs is a large restaurant and bar, upstairs is an enclosed court bordered by classical railings, and outside is a sidewalk café.

WORTH THE EXTRA BUCKS

POSADA DE LA SOLEDAD, Ignacio Zaragoza 90, Morelia, Mich. 58000.
Tel. 451/2-1888. 58 rms, 9 suites (all with bath). TV TEL
$ Rates: $39 single; $47 double. **Parking:** Free.

Enter to a tranquil and beautiful grand hacienda-style manor with stone arches and vines, and surrounding a central courtyard and fountain. Built in 1719, the structure has been a convent, the house of a rich Spaniard, and a carriage house. Some of the rooms have a fireplace, tub as well as shower, and a small balcony. A satellite antenna brings in TV movies. The hotel restaurant and bar, one of the most inviting in Mexico, is open from daily 7am to 10pm, with tables set under the portals.

To get here from the cathedral, walk one block west on Madero to Zaragoza; turn right and hotel is on the right, near Ocampo.

HOTEL CATEDRAL, Zaragoza 37, Morelia, Mich. 58000. Tel. 451/3-0783 or 3-0467. 44 rms (all with bath). TV TEL
$ Rates: $45 single; $59 double. **Parking:** Free.

The Hotel Catedral (one block west of the cathedral, next to the Hotel Casino) is expensive and a splurge—out of our budget range. The rooms are quite comfortable, with wall-to-wall carpeting, and are arranged around an attractive interior courtyard. The elegant restaurant is open daily from 7am to 10:30pm, and you can relax in the bar from 1 to 11pm.

WHERE TO EAT
MEALS FOR LESS THAN $5

LA CUEVA DE CHUCHO, Eduardo Ruíz 620. Tel. 2-3885.
Specialty: MEXICAN.
$ Prices: Breakfast $1.25–$2.50; main courses $3–$4; comida corrida $3.
Open: Daily 7am–11pm (comida corrida served noon–3:30 or 4pm).

Though with its orange-and-red decor, plastic chairs, and tile floors this place has the atmosphere of a bowling alley, it's spotlessly clean, and the food is great and inexpensive. Handmade tortillas are baked fresh daily on a flaming grill. Try the tortitas de carne—delectable, melt-in-your-mouth, lean meat in a spicy tomatillo sauce with a side order of beans. Wash it down with tepache, a delicious fermented pineapple drink that tastes like cider. On Sunday the restaurant's special is paella for $5. The bathrooms here are spotlessly clean as well, and there's even toilet paper—a rarity in Mexico. From the bus terminal, turn right, cross the first street, and the restaurant is on the right.

RESTAURANT EL PARAÍSO, Portal Galeana 103, at the corner of Juárez. Tel. 2-0374.
Specialty: MEXICAN.
$ Prices: Breakfast $3–$4; main courses $2.50–$5; comida corrida $4; buffet $5.
Open: Daily 7:30am–11pm (comida corrida served noon–3:30 or 4pm).

This simple, pleasant restaurant is always crowded with people who enjoy good prices and the casual ambience of a sidewalk café. Inexpensive breakfast combinations come with juice, coffee, and toast; dinner choices come with salad, beans, and french-fried potatoes. The comida corrida is surprisingly ample, with salad, soup, rice, beans, dish of the day, dessert, and coffee.

GOVINDA, Morelos Sur 39. Tel. 3-3886.
Specialty: VEGETARIAN.
$ Prices: Vegetarian hamburgers $2.50; breakfast "integral" $2.50; comida corrida $3.
Open: Daily 9am–5pm (comida corrida served 1:30–5pm).

This vegetarian café looks more like the dining room of an elegant hotel, with its ornate walls and a beautiful stained-glass window. The friendly young owner has visited India three times and cooks up a different kind of Mexi-Hindu combo daily, including vegetables and rice, empanadas, soups, soy dishes, and desserts.

To get here, turn right on the second street east of the cathedral; it's on the left. Enter through an enclosed shopping mall with a branch of Banco Internacional.

MEALS FOR LESS THAN $10

HOTEL CASINO, Portal Hidalgo 229. Tel. 3-1003.
Specialty: MEXICAN.
$ Prices: Breakfast $3–$5.75; appetizers $1.25–$2; main courses $3–$8; comida corrida $6.
Open: Daily 7:30am–9:30pm (comida corrida served noon–6pm).

The Hotel Casino operates one of the many sidewalk cafés that all blend into each other on the lively block across from the cathedral. The Casino also has a quiet, dining room inside with dark-wood tables and chairs, and a bar. It's a slightly more upscale and expensive alternative to the popular El Paraíso on the corner, with a slightly larger and more varied menu.

LA FUENTE, Madero Ote. 493. Tel. 2-6411.
Specialty: VEGETARIAN.
$ Prices: Main courses/comida corrida $4.50–$5.75; *energetica* plates $3.75; soy milkshakes $1.25; yogurt 50¢.
Open: Lunch only, Mon–Sat 1–5:30pm (comida corrida served 1–5:30pm).

The reader who told me about this restaurant called it "the best vegetarian restaurant I encountered in Mexico." It's located six or seven blocks east of the cathedral in an old stone courtyard with lots of arches, now covered and converted into a restaurant. The menu includes typical Mexican selections as well as more unusual items, like Danish apple croquettes. The "energetica" plate consists of fruits, granola, yogurt, and honey.

LA HUACANA, Garcia Obeso and Aldama. Tel. 2-5312.
Specialty: MEXICAN.

$ Prices: Breakfast 50¢–$3; appetizers $1.25–$4.75; main courses $4–$10; comida corrida $5.50.
Open: Daily 8am–9pm.

This local favorite with a clean, expansive two-level dining room is popular with those who enjoy loud live music with their meal. Murals of local scenes decorate the walls and there's a large rendition of the sculpture of the bare-breasted Tarascan maidens holding their basket of fruit—a traditional Morelia trademark taken from the popular sculpture at the Museum of Contemporary Art. The ample, satisfying meals include chicken, lamb, liver and onions, chiles relleños, and the usual Mexican fare. There's also a full bar. It's two blocks south of (behind) the cathedral on Garcia Obesa, between Hidalgo and Morelos Sur.

LOS COMENSALES, Zaragosa 148.
Specialty: MEXICAN/INTERNATIONAL.
$ Prices: Breakfast $1–$3; appetizers $2.50–$4; main courses $4.75–$10; paella $4.50.
Open: Daily 8am–11pm.

This attractive restaurant is in an open courtyard with blooming azaleas and hibiscus, colorful caged birds, and a pretty fountain. Comfortable leather chairs cluster around small tables with terra-cotta–colored cloths. The menu is large and varied, including chicken, beef, and 11 different fish dishes, plus paella and Pátzcuaro white fish. It's a pleasant, sunny place for breakfast, too.

To find Los Comensales from the cathedral, walk one block west to Zaragosa; turn right and look for the restaurant 1½ blocks on the right.

LAS MERCEDES RESTAURANT, León Guzman 47. Tel. 2-6113.
Specialty: MEXICAN/INTERNATIONAL.
$ Prices: Appetizers $2.50–$4; main courses $4.75–$7.
Open: Mon–Sat 1pm–1am.

★ If you eat only one meal in Morelia, eat it here in a stone-arched inner courtyard filled with palms, flowers, and succulents in tubs and pots. One wall is lined with colorful birds in cages and others with exotic murals. At night small spotlights illuminate each table's colorful, fresh flower bouquet. Pastel-clothed tables are set with hand-painted ceramic plates with charming scenes, and wine is presented in a translucent green, hand-blown fluted glass. A plate of small tacos is automatically brought while diners make their choices. Homemade bread also arrives, with three small tubs of different-flavored butter. The menu includes pasta with pinons and pistachios, chicken "a la Michoacana," with a spicy tomato-vegetable sauce, and various seafood and meat offerings.

To get here from the cathedral, walk six short blocks west on Madero. Turn right on León Guzman and look for a small sign on the left over the door.

SPECIALTY DINING

FOR COFFEE & DESSERT Across from the square and cathedral, on the same side of the street as the Hotel Casino and the Restaurant El Paraíso, is an entire block filled with sidewalk cafés. They're all popular and crowded, and prices are competitive. These daytime cafés become Morelia's nightlife after dark. Hot coffee and cold beer are served to a lively college crowd.

For espresso, the best place along here is **Cafe Catedral** (tel. 2-3289 or 3-0467), offering cafe Americano for 85¢, and cappuccino with cookies for $1.30. **Helados Holanda** is here too, always a nice place for an ice-cream sundae. Have a snack—or an entire meal—in Morelia's colonial **Woolworth's Cafe,** Madero 58—you'll never see a Woolworth's like this at home. Wrought-iron chandeliers hang high above from the ancient, vaulted-arch ceilings of stone, but below it's all modern booths. There's a large, varied menu, plus good, inexpensive coffee and cakes.

FOR DRINKS & MUSIC Another nice café and nightspot is **Colibri,** Galeana 36, just across from the Virrey de Mendoza (go two blocks west of the cathedral, then left on Galeana; Colibri is on the right-hand side). Softly strumming his guitar, a singer entertains with a variety of lovely ballads, including Columbian, Mexican, and popular American tunes. On winter evenings around Christmas, the owner personally serves a complimentary cup of the traditional hot fruit punch.

SHOPPING

Besides the **Casa de Artesanías** and **Mercado Independencia** mentioned above, several other places have possibilities.

JARDÍN DEL CONSERVATORIA DE LAS ROSAS, at the corner of Santiago Tapia and Guillermo Prieto.

A couple of blocks north of Madero, this flower market, though named for roses, sells many varieties of flowers.

THE PORTALES, on Madero, between Benito Juárez and Ignacio Zaragoza, across from the cathedral.

The street vendors here have an incredible array of goods, including sunglasses, jewelry, clothing, shoes, and everything else along this one-block stretch. Bargain for the price you want to pay.

MERCADO DE DULCES, behind the Palacio Clavijero, along Valentín Gomez Farías.

This delightful jumble of shops, west on Madero from the cathedral and north on Nigromante, sells cubitos de ate (candied fruit wedges), jelly candies, honey, goat's milk, strawberry jam, and chongos (a combination of milk, sugar, cinnamon, and honey). Upstairs is a shop with all kinds of regional artesanías, and hundreds of picture postcards from all over Michoacan. The mercado is open daily from 7am to 10pm.

AN EASY EXCURSION FROM MORELIA

✪ **THE MONARCH BUTTERFLIES OF MICHOACAN** Visiting the winter nesting grounds of the monarch butterfly in the mountains of Michoacan—a very long day trip from Morelia—is an awesome experience. The monarchs wing down from Canada for the winter, so the best time to see them is from November through February. Take one of the tours offered by a number of travel agents in Morelia, or rough it going by bus on your own. Having done the latter, I recommend the former, since in the long run the tour costs less in time, money, and effort.

On an Organized Tour Tour companies in Morelia offer this trip frequently during peak months for about $33 to $38. The tour takes about 9 hours by van. The travel agent in the lobby of the Hotel Alemeda, on the corner of Madero and G. Prieto (just west of the cathedral), handles this and other tours through Auto Turismo de Michoacan (tel. 2-4987 or 2-6810). Other travel agents to try are Linda Michoacan (4-9943 or 4-0826), Turismo Vallodolid (4-5540 or 4-4621).

On Your Own, By Bus By bus, get up at the crack of dawn (preferably before) and take a bus from the Central Camionera to Zitácuaro (the earliest one is around 7am, costs $3, and takes 3 hours). Once in Zitácuaro, go to the local bus station for the bus to Ocampo. To find this station, get off the bus from Morelia, go left a few blocks to Hidalgo, and look for the other bus station on the corner to the right. Catch one of the frequent buses to Ocampo (50¢ for a 45-minute ride). Once in Ocampo, if you arrive by 12:30pm (hard to do, unless you skip breakfast and lunch), you can catch *the one and only bus* that leaves at that time from the main plaza for the butterfly reserve at El Rosario. Otherwise, a cab will take you the final 45-minute ride to the reserve for $35 (that's right—about the same price as the whole tour from Morelia) or one of the locals will drive you up there for a few dollars less. It's a long, rough road across two streams, so select the driver and vehicle accordingly.

At the tiny, unpaved village of El Rosario, the brilliant butterflies welcome visitors with a blizzard of orange and black. At the nearby El Rosario Sanctuary (admission $2.25; open daily from 10am to 5 or 6pm), a guide (who should be tipped a few dollars) accompanies each group of visitors along the loop trail (about an hour's steep walk at high altitude). But it's worth the time, effort, and expense to be surrounded by the magic of millions of monarchs. Be quiet and listen: This is one of the few places in the world where one can hear the soft sound of butterflies flying—almost a billion wings.

At the high point of the trail, the branches of the tall pine trees bow under their burden of butterflies. For folks unable to tackle the walk, monarchs are visible around the car park. There's also a comprehensive video show at the nearby information center, as well as snacks, soft drinks, and toilets.

By Car   To drive your own car, just follow the main roads to the above towns. Zitácuaro is on Highway 15 between Toluca and Morelia. A Volkswagen Beetle carried us up the final dirt road from Ocampo to El Rosario. To stay overnight, check the **Agua Blanca Spa** at Jungapeo and the **Spa San José Purúa**, both on the same side road off Highway 15. If you're driving from Morelia you'll see the San José Purúa sign after the turnoff to Ocampo and Angangeo. The Zitácuaro turnoff is after them. Both hotels are popular with tour groups during this time, so arrive early and try your luck.

Highly recommended is the **Motel Rancho San Cayatano,** Car. Tuzantla Km. 2.5 (tel. 3-4926), about 4.5 miles south of Zitácuaro near Coatepec on the road to Tuzantla. This 12-room inn (with a pool) run by a French/Vietnamese family is for those who want a special experience and personalized service. A friend who's a long-time Mexico traveler and lives in Pátzcuaro says he had the best meal he ever had in Mexico at San Cayatano's restaurant with its combined French, Mexican, and Vietnamese cuisine.

Tours from Elsewhere   In Mexico City, Turismo Teotihuacán, Río Rhin 64 (tel. 592-4065 or 592-3592), often has 1- or 2-day trips to see the monarchs in January, February, and March, as do travel agencies from San Miguel de Allende. See the section on San Miguel for details. Columbus Travel, 6017 Callaghan Road, San Antonio, TX 78228 (tel. toll free 800/843-1060 in the U.S. and Canada), has frequent trips via Mexico City to the butterflies.

---

2. PÁTZCUARO

231 miles W of Mexico City, 178 miles SE of Guadalajara,
43 miles S of Morelia

GETTING THERE   By Train   *El Purépecha* leaves Mexico City at 10pm and arrives in Pátzcuaro at 7:30am. Seats and sleeping compartments are inexpensive, but reserve early for either one. You can buy tickets shortly before each train leaves.

By Bus   **Autotransportes Galeana** runs between Pátzcuaro and Morelia every half hour, 24 hours a day. The 1-hour trip costs 75¢. The same line has buses to/from Uruapan every 20 minutes and the 1-hour trip costs $1.10. **Flecha Amarilla** and **Autobuses de Occidente** have hourly buses from Mexico City to Pátzcuaro at a cost of $7.65.

By Car   Highway 15 runs between Guadalajara and Mexico City. There are two routes to Pátzcuaro. The first is to turn off Highway 15 onto Highway 120 (west of Morelia) at Quiroga, a scenic drive that follows the eastern edge of Lake Pátzcuaro and passes through Tzintzuntzán, the ancient capital of the Tarascan kingdom. The alternative route is the new highway direct from Morelia, which goes through Tiripetio and is shorter and faster.

DEPARTING   By Train   *El Purépecha* leaves at 9:30pm, gets to Morelia around 11pm, and arrives in Mexico City at 7:30am. Buy your tickets in advance if you want a sleeping compartment. The train from Mexico City goes on to Uruapan after leaving Pátzcuaro. If it isn't late, it leaves just after 7:30am and arrives in Uruapan shortly after 10am. You could use the train for a day trip since the return *Purépecha*

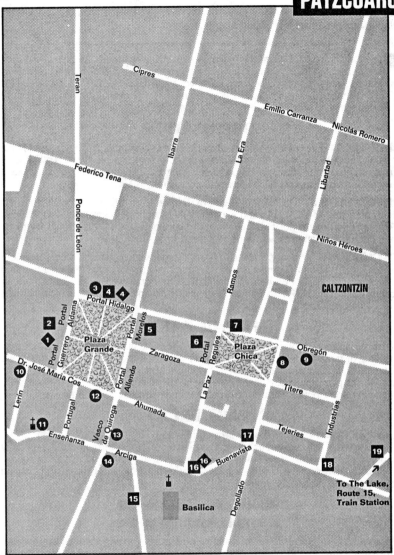

PÁTZCUARO

ACCOMMODATIONS:
Los Escudos Hotel **4**
Gran Hotel **6**
Hosteria de San Felipe **18**
Mansion Iturbe Hotel **5**
Pátzcuaro Motel **19**
Posada de Don Vasco Hotel **19**
Posada de la Basilica **16**
Posada de la Rosa **7**
Posada de la Salud **15**

Posada San Rafael **2**
Valmen Hotel **17**

DINING:
Los Escudos
  Hotel Restaurant **4**
El Patio **1**
Posada de la
  Basilica **16**

ATTRACTIONS:
Casa del Gigante **12**
Casa de Once Patios **10**
Library **8**
Museo Regional del Arte
  Popular **15**
Palacio de Huitzimengari **13**
Post Office **9**
Templo de Companía de Jesus **11**
Tourism Office **3**

leaves Uruapan at 7:15pm and arrives back in Pátzcuaro around 10pm. Check to see if these schedules are still available when you travel.

Pátzcuaro is an old colonial town with low overhanging red-tile roofs, whitewashed buildings, and two plazas. The lakeside vegetation is lush and the climate is pleasant most of the year. The town is known for its lake, one of the world's highest (7,250 ft.), where fishermen catch delicious whitefish with nets of such delicate texture and wide-winged shape that they've been compared to butterflies.

ORIENTATION

ARRIVING   The **train station** is near the lake and far enough from hotels to take a taxi. The **bus station,** on Libramiento Ignacio Zaragoza Highway, is a half mile from the Tourism Office, so if you're spending the day, unencumbered by heavy baggage, it's a pleasant walk. A taxi will cost about $1.60.

INFORMATION   The **State Tourism Office** is on the main square at Portal Hidalgo 9 (tel. 454/2-1214), and is open daily from 9am to 2pm and 4 to 7:30pm. Although you might not find someone who speaks English, the staff will try to be helpful and you can pick up useful maps and brochures.

CITY LAYOUT   In a way, Pátzcuaro has two town centers, both of them plazas and a block apart. **Plaza Grande** is a picturesque tranquil plaza centered on a fountain and statue of Vasco de Quiroga and flanked by hotels, shops, and restaurants in colonial-era edifices. **Plaza Chica** flows into the market plaza and around it swirls the commercial life of Pátzcuaro.

GETTING AROUND

With the exception of Lake Pátzcuaro and the lookout, everything is within easy walking distance from almost any hotel in Pátzcuaro. Although the lake is over a mile from town, buses make the run every 15 minutes from the market plaza, going all the way to the pier (the embarcadero), passing by the train station and all the places I'll name here on Avenida Lázaro Cárdenas (formerly Avenida de las Americas).

FAST FACTS

Area Code   The telephone area code is 454.
Climate   It's cold enough for a heavy sweater October through April, especially mornings and evenings. Few hotels have fireplaces or any source of heat in the rooms.
Post Office   The Correo is located half a block north of the small plaza, on the right-hand side of the street.

WHAT TO SEE & DO
A STROLL AROUND TOWN

Pátzcuaro is a beautiful town, worthy of leisurely strolls through its ancient, unchanged streets and plazas. The **market** has myriad stalls where vendors sell pottery, copper, rebozos, and serapes. Just east of the market is **Plaza de San Agustín,** known as the **Plaza Chica,** with lovely gardens, walkways, and a statue of Gertrudis Bocanegra, heroine of Mexican independence. On the north, facing the small plaza, is the **public library,** also named for Dona Bocanegra, which occupies the former monastery of San Agustín. Inside the library is a huge mural painted by Juan O'Gorman (the artist's first mural), depicting the history of the area from Tarascan legends up to the Revolution. The former living quarters of the monks, next door, was converted into the Teatro Emperador Caltzontzin.

Just a few blocks away is the splendid **Plaza Grande,** a vast tree-shaded expanse of manicured lawns and an elaborate stone fountain. On the north side of the plaza is the **Palacio de Huitzimengari,** built by the Spaniards for the Tarascan emperor—one of the few instances in colonial Mexico of respect and equitable treatment for the indigenous people. Local artisans now occupy the building, which houses workshops and showrooms for traditional Tarascan crafts. The town is much like Colonial Williamsburg from the standpoint of authenticity, and it enjoys a similar monument status. No new buildings interfere with the time-worn harmony of the colonial roofline.

One of the oldest buildings in Pátzcuaro is the **House of the Giant,** on the east side of Plaza Grande at Portal de Matamoros 40. It was named after the 12-foot-high painted statue that supports one of the arches around the patio. This residence was built in 1663 by a Spanish count and certainly represents the colonial taste of that period: carved stone panels, thick columns, and open courtyards.

The **basilica,** east of the small plaza on top of a small hill, was built in the 16th century at the prompting of Bishop Don Vasco and designated a basilica by papal decree in 1907. It opened in 1554, but Don Vasco died before it was completed. Reconstructed now, it has been through many catastrophes, from earthquakes to the civil war of the mid-19th century. Be sure to see the Virgin on the main altar, which is made of "corn-stalk pulp and a mucilage obtained from a prized orchid of the region." She is a very sacred figure to the Indians of this area, and on the eighth day of each month they come from the villages to pay homage to her, particularly for her miraculous healing power.

✪ One block to the south of the basilica is the **Museum of Popular and Regional Arts** (tel. 2-1029). It's yet another beautiful colonial building (1540), originally Don Vasco's College of San Nicolas. The rooms with regional crafts and costumes are located off the central courtyard. The museum is open Tuesday through Saturday from 9am to 7pm and on Sunday from 9am to 3pm. Admission is $3.50 (free on Sunday).

Of the many old churches in Pátzcuaro, one of the most interesting is the **Temple of the Compañía de Jesús,** near the museum. This church was Don Vasco's cathedral before the basilica, and afterward was given to the Jesuits. The buildings to the south of the church were once part of the complex, containing the hospital, soup kitchen, and living quarters for religious scholars.

The **House of the Eleven Patios,** located between José María Cos and Ensenanza, is one of the most outstanding architectural achievements of the colonial period. Formerly a convent of the Catherine nuns, today it houses the **Casa de las Artesanías de Michoacan,** with every type of local artistry on display and for sale: clothing, blankets, and other textile arts, pottery and ceramic dishes, lacquerwork, paintings, wood carvings, jewelry, copperwork, and musical instruments, including the famous Paracho guitars. It's open daily from 9am to 2pm and 4 to 7pm. Don't miss it.

SHOPPING

Pátzcuaro is one of Mexico's best shopping towns because of the textiles, copper, and straw weavings made in the region. There are a couple of shops on the street facing the basilica, several on Plaza Grande, but best of all is the House of the Eleven Patios (mentioned above).

Nearby Tzintzuntzán and Santa Clara de Cobre are must stops for shoppers (see "Easy Excursions from Pátzcuaro," below).

A NEARBY ATTRACTION

No visit to Pátzcuaro is complete without a trip on the lake, preferably across to the isolated island village of ✪ **Janitzio,** dominated by a hilltop statue of José María Morelos. The village church is famous for the annual ceremony on the Day of the Dead, held at midnight on November 1, when villagers climb to the churchyard carrying lighted candles in memory of their dead relatives and then spend the night in graveside vigil. It begins October 30 and lasts through November 2.

The most economical way to get to Janitzio is by colectivo launch, which makes the trip when enough people collect to go—about every 20 to 30 minutes from about 9:30 or 10am until the last trip at 6pm. Round-trip fare is 50¢, for those 5 years of age and older. The ticket office (tel. 2-0681) is open daily from 7am to 5pm.

At the ticket office on the pier (embarcadero), a map of the lake posted on the wall shows all the boat trips possible around the lake, to various islands and lakeshore towns. Launches will take you wherever you want to go, but unless you have a group to split the cost, prices are high. Ask at the ticket office for information.

SPECIAL EVENTS

The island of Janitzio has achieved world fame for the candlelight vigil local residents hold at the cemetery during the nights of November 1 and 2, the **Days of the Dead.**

Easter week is special here too, beginning the Friday before Palm Sunday. Most activity centers around the basilica. There are processions involving the surrounding villages almost nightly and in Tzintzuntzán there's a reenactment of the betrayal of Christ and ceremonial washing of the feet. Although written in 1947, Frances Toor's description of Holy Week in Pátzcuaro, in *A Treasury of Mexican Folkways* (Crown), is still accurate and a good preparation for a visit at that time.

During both events Plaza Principal is loaded with regional crafts. Make hotel reservations months in advance for either event.

WHERE TO STAY
DOUBLES FOR LESS THAN $15

HOTEL VALMEN, Av. Lloreda 34, Pátzcuaro, Mich. 61600. Tel. 454/2-1161. 16 rms (all with bath).
$ Rates: $3.75 single; $5 double.

There's an attractive tiled entryway and small courtyard in this old-fashioned, three-story hotel. On the second floor is a sunny, glassed-in patio, and the entire building is decorated with pretty brown, turquoise, and gold tile. There's a TV in the lobby. Accommodations are modern and comfortable; the clean rooms are arranged around a lovely glass-roofed courtyard. It's an excellent budget choice, though it may be a bit noisy on the busy corner and the front doors are locked tight at 10pm.

To get here from Plaza Principal, walk two blocks north on Ahumada; the hotel is on the left, on the corner of Libertad.

HOTEL POSADA DE LA ROSA, Portal Juárez 29, Pátzcuaro, Mich. 61600. Tel. 454/2-0811. 14 rms (4 with bath).
$ Rates: $5.25 for one to four people, without bath); $10.25 for one to three people, with bath.

This small, clean, and friendly hotel is on the second floor, overlooking the market plaza, which is two blocks north on Zaragoza from the main plaza (look carefully on the left—it's hard to spot, tucked in a small doorway surrounded by vendors). Bright flowers in wooden boxes line the open-air patio onto which all the rooms open. Most rooms do not have private bath, but the common bath and shower facilities (with hot water 24 hours daily) are clean and well maintained. Bring your own toilet paper.

DOUBLES FOR LESS THAN $25

MOTEL PÁTZCUARO, Av. Lázaro Cárdenas 506, Pátzcuaro, Mich. 61600. Tel. 454/2-0767. Fax 454/2-2571. 12 rms (all with bath). **Bus:** Lake buses will stop here; it's north of town on Route 15 on the way to the lake.
$ Rates: $14.50 single; $18 double; camping $9 for two people. **Parking:** Free.
Heading toward town from Route 15, you'll pass this motel, which offers quiet, clean, and rustic rooms, with stone floors, wood-beamed ceilings, wooden furniture, and a fireplace. The friendly owner and his wife speak some English. Facilities include a small swimming pool and two tennis courts (open to the public for $4.50 per hour). Out back are eight spaces for trailers, and several furnished houses. Buses run to town or the lake every 15 minutes.

POSADA DE LA SALUD, Serrato 9, Pátzcuaro, Mich. 61600. Tel. 454/2-0658. 12 rms (all with bath).
$ Rates: $13.50 single; $15.50 double. **Parking:** On street.

This posada offers two tiers of exceptionally quiet rooms built around an attractive courtyard. All rooms have beautiful beds with carved wooden headboards and matching desks. Two rooms have fireplaces.

To get here from the main plaza, walk one block east on P. Allende/V. De Quiroga and turn left on Arciga; walk up the hill and turn right onto Serrato (not marked, but facing the basilica). The hotel is on the right.

GRAN HOTEL, Portal Regules 66, Pátzcuaro, Mich. 61600. Tel. 454/2-0443. 26 rms (all with bath).
$ Rates: $16 single; $20 double.
Popular with Mexican tourists, this hotel on the south side of the small market plaza (Plaza Chica) offers clean but overpriced rooms. The rooms, which don't receive much sun, can be chilly in the winter months. The restaurant serves a comida corrida daily from 1 until 8pm.

POSADA SAN RAFAEL, Plaza Vasco de Quiroga, Pátzcuaro, Mich. 61600. Tel. 454/2-0770 or 2-0779. 104 rms (all with bath). TV
$ Rates: $16 single; $20 double. Children under 12 stay free in parents' room.
Parking: Free in courtyard.
This comfortable, colonial-style inn on the south side of Plaza Principal has stone trim around the dark wooden doors. All the rooms open onto a sunny, central courtyard filled with lush potted plants and a fountain. The rooms have traditional furnishings and are grouped around a handsome wood colonnade. The restaurant is open daily from 7am to 11pm.

HOTEL POSADA DE LA BASILICA, Arciga 6, Pátzcuaro, Mich. 61600. Tel. 454/2-1108. 11 rms (all with bath). TEL
$ Rates: $20 single; $24.50 double. Children under 12 stay free in parents' room.
Parking: Free, enclosed.
A mansion turned hotel, this appealing colonial-style inn across from the basilica offers sunny rooms with wonderful views, red velvet curtains, heavy Spanish-style furniture, and little brick fireplaces. Some mattresses are better than others, so inspect your room before accepting it.

DOUBLES FOR LESS THAN $35

HOSTERÍA DE SAN FELIPE, Av. Lázaro Cárdenas 321 (Apdo. Postal 209), Pátzcuaro, Mich. 61600. Tel. 454/2-1298. 11 rms (all with bath).
$ Rates: $16 single; $26 double. **Parking:** Free.
Located on Route 15 as you come into town, this hotel is very clean, quiet, and comfortable. Rooms are in back, arranged around a green lawn, and each has a fireplace, wall-to-wall carpet, and dark wooden ceilings. The tranquility makes it ideal for a long-term stay.

HOTEL LOS ESCUDOS, Portal Hidalgo 73, Pátzcuaro, Mich. 61600. Tel. 454/2-0138 or 2-1290. 30 rms (all with bath). TV
$ Rates: $22 single; $29 double. Children under 12 stay free in parents' room.
Parking: Free.
This handsome colonial-style hotel on the west side of Plaza Principal decorates rooms with lush red or blue carpeting, red velvet and lace curtains, and scenes of olden-days Pátzcuaro painted on the walls. Some of the rooms have fireplaces, while others have private balconies overlooking the plaza. There's a restaurant off the lobby.

WORTH THE EXTRA BUCKS

HOTEL MANSION ITURBE, Portal Morelos 59, Pátzcuaro, Mich. 61600. Tel. 454/2-0368. 15 rms (all with bath).
$ Rates: $27 single; $49 double. **Parking:** Free.
Located on the south side of Plaza Principal, this hotel has beautiful colonial decor. Heavy, dark wooden Spanish-style furniture, deep-red drapes and bedspreads, along with French doors with lace curtains and cowhide chairs combine to give a feeling of

old-world elegance. The hotel has a cafeteria and restaurant, open daily from 8:30am to 9pm with reasonable prices.

POSADA DE DON VASCO HOTEL AND MOTEL, Av. Lázaro Cárdenas 450, Pátzcuaro, Mich. 61600. Tel. 454/2-0227 or 2-0262, or toll free reservations in the U.S. through Best Western at 800/528-1234. 103 rms (all with bath). A/C TV TEL **Bus:** north of town on Route 15 on the way to the lake.
$ Rates: $58 single; $64 double. **Parking:** Free.

Though this posada is too far away from town center for my taste, some people think staying here is synonymous with a trip to Pátzcuaro. This sprawling colonial-style hotel is about 100 yards up the road from the Motel Pátzcuaro and is made up of a nice motel-style section on one side of the highway opposite the original hotel. It caters to groups, which you'll find lounging around the patios, restaurant, and bar. There's a bowling alley and pool as well. The decor includes crystal chandeliers, antique telephones, and velvet drapes.

CAMPING

Campers with tent or trailer can set up along the lake at **El Pozo Trailer Park,** km 20, Carretera Quiroga (tel. 454/2-0937). With clean facilities, cement pads, lots of grass, and pleasant management, the 20 spaces rent for $10 each. For reservations, write to Apdo. Postal 142, Pátzcuaro, Mich. 61600.

Closer to the center there are eight trailer spaces, renting for $9 each, out behind the **Motel Pátzcuaro** (described above).

WHERE TO EAT

Restaurants open late and close early in Pátzcuaro, so don't plan on hot coffee if you're up to catch the early-morning train, and plan ahead for late-evening hunger pangs. For inexpensive food, try the pushcart taco stands that line up near Plaza Chica and the **market** in the mornings to sell tacos of organ meat (don't ask what, it's just good), or the steamy cups of atole and hot tamales and uchepos sold by housewives. Afternoons, different vendors show up. Evenings, **Plaza Chica** is lined with pushcarts selling another specialty, Pátzcuaro chicken with heaps of fried potatoes and carrots, as well as buñuelos dripping with honey.

EL PATIO, Plaza Vasco de Quiroga 19. Tel. 2-0484.
Specialty: MEXICAN.
$ Prices: Breakfast $2.50–$5; appetizers $1–$5; main courses $4–$6; comida corrida $7.
Open: Daily 8am–9pm (comida corrida served 1:30–4pm).

Wood-beamed ceilings, charming chandeliers woven in basketry, and paintings of local scenes make this a very pleasant restaurant. Be sure to notice the unusual bar made of bottles and a gun imbedded in the stucco. El Patio, on the south side of Plaza Principal, offers delicious, inexpensive meals. Hot bread and butter are served with dishes like carne asada. The five-course comida corrida is delicious and plentiful, and is accompanied by a soloist.

RESTAURANT LOS ESCUDOS, Portal Hidalgo 74. Tel. 2-1290.
Specialty: MEXICAN.
$ Prices: Breakfast $1–$3; appetizers $1–$5; antojitos $1–$4.50; main courses $2–$10.50; soup $1.30; comida corrida $7.
Open: Daily 8am–9:30pm (comida corrida served 2–4pm).

Two very pleasant, wood-paneled dining rooms are decorated with watercolors by local artists. This restaurant, on the west side of Plaza Principal, serves one of the best comidas I've ever tasted—start with the Tarascan soup. There's also a tender and tasty bistek platter for a good price. This is also a good place to watch the morning sun glinting on the lovely plaza fountain at breakfast or to enjoy the free Saturday-night performance at dinner of the traditional "Dance of the Old Men" at 8pm. Service can be a bit slow, however.

RESTAURANT POSADA DE LA BASILICA, Arciga 6. Tel. 2-1108.

Specialty: MEXICAN.
$ **Prices:** Breakfast $2–$5.75; appetizers $1.25–$4; main courses $2.50–$14; comida corrida $7.
Open: Daily 8am–5pm (comida corrida served noon–4pm).

⭐ This hotel restaurant opposite the basilica has a great view of the whole town, down to the lake and up to the hills beyond. The decor includes pink tablecloths and heavy ceramic plates made in the region. The food, while not exactly gourmet, is adequate.

HOSTERÍA DE SAN FELIPE, Av. Lázaro Cárdenas 321. Tel. 2-1298.
Specialty: MEXICAN.
$ **Prices:** Appetizers $3–$6; main courses $4.50–$9.
Open: Daily 9am–9pm.

⭐ A favorite of local residents for banquets and receptions, this place also gets high marks as a restaurant. (It's three blocks north of the main plaza on Ahumada—look for the hotel on the left.) The decor is rustic, with a huge fireplace, hewn-stone wall, linen tablecloths, and plenty of windows from which to see the flowers outside. You can choose among Tarascan, garlic, fish, or chicken soup; the most expensive item on the menu is whitefish. There's a full-service bar.

NEARBY DINING

The traditional place to dine on whitefish is at one of the many restaurants lining the road to the lake. The cheapest way to enjoy the lake's prime product is to wander down to the little open-air restaurants on the wharf (embarcadero), where señoras fry up the delicious fish while you watch. Fish, garnishes, and a soft drink cost $3 or less. The restaurants are open daily from 8am to 6pm.

RESTAURANT LAS REDES, Av. Lázaro Cárdenas 6. Tel. 2-1275.
Specialty: MEXICAN. **Bus:** on the road to the wharf.
$ **Prices:** Appetizers $2–$5; main courses $2.50–$7; comida corrida $5.50–$8.
Open: Daily 9am–8pm (comida corrida served 1–8pm).
Local residents gather at this rustic restaurant on the road to the wharf for the freshest seafood in town. There are two comida corridas: the less expensive one with soup, rice, fish or meat, frijoles, and coffee; and the more expensive one, which comes with whitefish.

CAMINO REAL, Carretera Patz-Tzurumutaro.
Specialty: MEXICAN.
$ **Prices:** Appetizers $1.50–$4; main courses $2–$7.
Open: Daily 7am–midnight.
Locals claim that this hard-to-find restaurant serves the best food in town, and definitely its Tarascan soup has few rivals in the region—a huge, savory bowl at a low price. The chicken and fish dishes are also delicious. It's about a mile outside town on the road to Morelia, behind the Pemex station.

EVENING ENTERTAINMENT

Generally speaking, Pátzcuaro goes to bed before 10pm, so bring a good book or plan to rest up for the remainder of your travels.

The **Danza de los Viejitos** ("Dance of the Old Men") is an ancient mask dance created by the Tarascans to ridicule the Spaniards during the Conquest. It's still performed every Wednesday and Saturday at 9pm in the restaurant of the Hotel Posada de Don Vasco. Dancers in traditional regional costume, wearing comical pink masks with hooked noses and big red smiles, perform a skillful dance, clacking over the floor in wooden sandals, bent over all the while like old men hobbling on wooden canes—but, oh, do their feet fly! There's no charge for admission and the restaurant prices are not expensive; a full dinner will cost $8, but you can dine for much less. After the dancers, an eight-piece mariachi group performs. You can reserve a table, if you wish, on the day of the performance.

Right in town on the main plaza, the Dance of the Old Men is held each Saturday night at 8 at Restaurant Los Escudos in the hotel of the same name (see "Where to Stay," above).

EASY EXCURSIONS FROM PÁTZCUARO

EL ESTRIBO For a good view of the town and the lake, head for the **lookout** at El Estribo, 2 miles from town on the hill to the west. A drive from the main square on Calle Ponce de León, following the signs, will take 10 to 15 minutes. Walking will take you about 45 minutes since it's all up a steep hill. Once you reach the gazebo, you can climb the over-400 steps to the very summit of the hill for a bird's-eye view. The gazebo area is great for a picnic—with barbecue pits and sometimes a couple selling soft drinks and beer.

TZINTZUNTZÁN Take a drive or bus from the Central Camionera to Tzintzuntzán, a village 10 miles on the road from Pátzcuaro to Quiroga. In earlier centuries Tzintzuntzán was the capital of a Tarascan empire that controlled over a hundred other towns and villages. Pyramids upon pyramids—right off the main plaza—still remind visitors of the glorious (and bloody) past. Today the village is known for its straw mobiles, baskets, and figures in every shape and size—skeletons, airplanes, reindeer, turkeys—as well as potters and weavers. The old market is now housed in a new neocolonial building. Across from the **basket market** are several open-air, wood-carving workshops full of photogenic life-size wooden saints, Christs, and other creatures. There is a footpath along the shore of Lake Pátzcuaro.

The week of February 1 the whole village honors **Nuestro Señor del Rescate** (Lord of the Rescue) with religious processions. The village also takes part in Holy Week celebrations.

SANTA CLARA DEL COBRE (VILLA ESCALANTE) Take a bus from the front of the Church of San Francisco or at the far corner of Plaza Chica to this pleasant colonial-era village famous for its copper products. Although the copper mines that existed during pre-Conquest times seem to have been forever lost, local craftsmen still make copper vessels by the age-old methods, each piece pounded out by hand from pieces of scrap pipe, radiators, and bits of electrical wire. The streets are lined with shops and little boys pounce on every visitor to be allowed to direct you to stores (where they get a commission). Buses back to Pátzcuaro run approximately every 45 minutes (or more) from the plaza, but try to join a cab full of people headed back to Pátzcuaro for less than a dollar each. The **National Copper Fair** is held here each August, which coincides on August 15 with the Festival of Our Lady of the Cibary, with folk dancing and parades.

ZIRAHUÉN To see one of Mexico's few remaining pristine lakes, visit Zirahuén, about 7½ miles west of Pátzcuaro on the road to Uruapan. Since there are no regular buses, it's difficult to get to Zirahuén without a car. A taxi costs about $13 one way. But the lake at Zirahuén is what Patzcuaro's overfished and increasingly polluted lake used to be like. And the famous, local whitefish from Zirahuén's pure waters is likewise better.

Right on the lake, the restaurant **La Troje de Ala** (open only on Sunday) offers elegant dining with live music and a great view. Otherwise, choose one of the many pleasant, inexpensive nearby fish stands (inspect carefully for cleanliness and fresh-looking/smelling fish).

---

3. URUAPAN

272 miles W of Mexico City, 77 miles SW of Morelia,
38 miles W of Pátzcuaro

GETTING THERE By Plane The regional carrier, **AeroMar,** flies from Mexico City to Uruapan seven times a week.

By Train *El Purépecha* leaves Mexico City at 10pm, arrives in Pátzcuaro around 7:30am, and in Uruapan shortly after 10am.

By Bus Autotransportes Galeana (tel. 2-0090) operates buses to and from Morelia every 20 minutes for $1.50; the trip takes 2 hours. The **Tres Estrella de Oro** bus line (tel. 2-1083 or 3-4467) has six buses daily to Mexico City (a 7-hour trip) at 1, 3, 5, 10, 11, and 11:30pm for $9; and to Guadalajara (5 hours) at 11am, 2:15pm, and 12:30am for $7.50. The **Flecha Amarilla** bus line (tel. 4-3207 or 3-1870) also serves the region.

By Car Highway 14 goes west to Uruapan from Morelia and Pátzcuaro. From Guadalajara and Lake Chapala, follow Highway 16, then turn right (south) onto Highway 37 at Carapan.

DEPARTING By Plane The **AeroMar** offices are at the airport (tel. 3-5050; fax 3-3455).

By Train Uruapan's train station (tel. 3-1819) is north of town on Highway 15. *El Purépecha* leaves Uruapan at 7pm, reaches Pátzcuaro at 9:30pm, Morelia around 11pm, and Mexico City around 7:30am. Reserve seats early, especially if you want one of the inexpensive sleeping compartments.

Uruapan, Michoacan (alt. 5,500 ft.; pop. 217,000), has long been famous for the lacquered boxes and trays made here. However, in 1943 the city became even better known when Paricutín, a brand-new volcano, suddenly erupted in the middle of a cornfield, pouring lava over two nearby villages and forcing thousands from their homes. The volcano, active for 9 years, is now dormant and can be viewed from a great distance.

Although this town has few tourist attractions of its own, it makes a good base for several interesting side trips. I recommend that you spend the night in Uruapan at one of the inexpensive hotels and take a day trip to the volcano of Paricutín.

ORIENTATION

ARRIVING Uruapan's **train station** is north of town on Highway 15; a taxi from the station costs $2 to $2.50 to our recommended hotels; a local bus, 10¢. Uruapan's main square is 20 blocks from the **bus station.** Local buses come and go constantly between the south side of the plaza and the main bus station; they charge 10¢.

INFORMATION The **Tourist Office** is at 5 de Febrero no. 17, Room 106 (tel. 542/4-0633), just a few doors down from the Nuevo Hotel Alameda, tucked in between various stores. It's open Monday through Friday from 9am to 2pm and 4 to 7pm, and on Saturday from 9am to 2pm.

CITY LAYOUT The main plaza is actually a very long rectangle running east to west, with the churches on the north side and the Hotel Victoria on the south side. Everything you need is within a block or two of the square, including the market, which is behind the churches.

FAST FACTS

Area Code The telephone area code is 542.

Climate Be prepared for cold mornings and evenings from October through April, enough for a heavy sweater and gloves. Few hotels have heat.

WHAT TO SEE & DO
A STROLL AROUND TOWN

Although I wouldn't make a special trip to Uruapan to go to the **market,** it's worth a look when you're in town. Regional goods, including the famous lacquered trays, dishes, and boxes, are sold behind the cathedral on Vasco de Quiroga. The rows of food counters here are particularly clean and appealing. Regional specialties include *uchepos* (tamale with sauce), *atole de grano* or *atole blanco* (a beverage), or *churipo con corundas* (chicken, dried beef, pork, a triangular tamale, and vegetables in a soup).

Uruapan is also proud of its small museum,   ✪ **La Huatapera,** attached to the cathedral—and with good reason. It caters to local residents rather than to tourists, and has authentic charm. It was founded as a hospital in 1533 by Fray Juan de San Miguel, a Franciscan. Residents say that it's the first hospital in Latin America. Visitors duck under the tiny wood-beamed doorways to see the creative and colorful exhibits displayed in a series of thick-walled rooms radiating from a pretty central courtyard, where the locals loll in the sun. The museum collection includes Michoacan ceramic work (with many humorous and fantastic figurines of devils and demons), cloth dolls, and wooden masks—all well labeled and attractively presented. There is also a reasonably priced museum shop. It's open Tuesday through Sunday from 9:30am to 1:30pm and 3:30 to 6pm. Admission is free.

Both **churches** are lovely and also deserve a visit. Be sure to notice the stone angels—each one different—atop the cathedral.

✪ The **Parque Nacional Eduardo Ruíz,** a botanical garden eight blocks west of the main plaza, is worthy of a visit. In front of the telegraph office on the main square buses ("Plaza Toros Quinta" or "Toros Centros Parque") stop at the park. This semitropical paradise includes jungle paths, deep ravines, rushing water, and waterfalls. You may want to "hire" one of the juvenile guides who will offer their services for 85¢ to $2—just to keep the rest at bay. The garden is open daily from 8am to 6pm, and there is a small admission fee.

There's a bus ("Tzaracua") to the impressive **waterfall at Tzararacua,** which is 6 miles from the main plaza. The Río Cupatitzio originates as a bubbling spring in the national park and then forms this cascade on its way toward the Pacific. A trip to Tzararacua and to the national park can be made in a day, even in an afternoon.

SPECIAL EVENTS

Uruapan's main plaza fills with craftsmen from around the state during the week before and after the **Day of the Dead,** November 1 and 2, and before and during **Easter Week.** It's an unbelievable display of wares all neatly displayed. And either one is worth a trip.

WHERE TO STAY

HOTEL MISOLAR, Juan Delgado 10, Uruapan, Mich. 60000. Tel. 452/4-0912. 20 rms (all with bath).
$ Rates: $9 single; $11 double.

S This colonial-style adobe hotel is conveniently located one block north of the plaza, on the west side behind the church. The rooms feel a little ancient and dim, but it's still cheerful and well cared for—an excellent value. Some of the rooms have tubs.

HOTEL MIRADOR, Ocampo 9, Uruapan, Mich. 60000. Tel. 452/4-0473. 49 rms (all with bath).
$ Rates: $9 single; $13 double.
Another colonial-style adobe hotel, the Mirador at the southwestern end of the plaza, shows the wear and tear of time. Ask to see several rooms because all are different; some are big and pleasant, but you'll want to avoid those without windows. There's hot water all day. It's popular with Mexican families.

HOTEL VILLA DE FLORES, Emilio Carranza 15, Uruapan, Mich. 60000. Tel. 452/4-2800. 28 rms (all with bath). TEL
$ Rates: $13 single; $17 double.

S A little more than a block southwest of the plaza, this is one of the nicest hotels in town. It's not fancy—just clean, neat, and highly recommended by those who visit frequently. The colonial-style rooms are nicely furnished and open onto the patio or court full of huge potted plants. The hot water is not always reliable. The restaurant, Fondo de la Villa, serves regional dishes, which usually include corn prepared in some unusual way. The specialties are tamales and buñuelos with atole. The restaurant is open daily from 7am to 10:30pm.

NUEVO HOTEL ALAMEDA, Av. 5 de Febrero no. 11, Uruapan, Mich. 60000. Tel. 452/3-3635 or 3-4100. 72 rms (all with bath). TV TEL
$ Rates: $18 single; $23 double. **Parking:** Free, nearby.
Not as shiny-new as the Hotel Victoria (see below), but cheaper, this five-story hostelry has comfortable, modern rooms. Some of the rooms in the back and on the upper floors have a great view of the city and surrounding mountains. It's half a block south from the east end of the plaza.

WORTH THE EXTRA BUCKS

HOTEL VICTORIA, Cupatitzio 11, Uruapan, Mich. 60000. Tel. 452/3-6700. 83 rms (all with bath). A/C TV TEL
$ Rates: $32 single; $40 double.
The most-advertised hotel in town, the Victoria is very large and offers spotless, well-equipped rooms with wall-to-wall carpeting and extra-large bath towels. The hotel also has an attractive restaurant and bar, which serves good Mexican wines. The hotel is a block southeast of the plaza.

MANSION DEL CUPATITZIO, Uruapan, Mich. 60000. Tel. 452/3-2100, 3-2070, or 3-2090. Fax 452/4-6772. 56 rms (all with bath). TV TEL
$ Rates: $50 single; $48 double.
The city's most charming and restful hotel is next to the Parque Nacional (walk seven blocks west of the main plaza on Emilio Carranza or take one of the frequent local buses to the Parque Nacional from the plaza). Request a room with a view of the park. The landscaped grounds and patios are lovely and blend in well with the park's natural beauty. Rooms surround a central courtyard with a grassy garden and swimming pool. There's also an expensive restaurant and a pretty patio dining area, good for drinks (see "Where to Eat," below).

WHERE TO EAT

RESTAURANT LAS PALMAS, Donato Guerra 2. Tel. 2-0364.
Specialty: MEXICAN.
$ Prices: Breakfast $1–$3; main courses $3; full meal $3.
Open: Daily 8:30am–10pm.
Look for this restaurant next to a craft shop a block north of the western end of the plaza. The decor is giant photomurals, the furniture is bright gold, and the prices are moderate. The menu includes traditional Mexican dishes such as tacos, enchiladas, and quesadillas.

CAFE TRADICIONAL DE URUAPAN, Emilio Carranza 5B.
Specialty: MEXICAN.
$ Prices: Breakfast $3–$4; sandwiches $2–$3; yogurt $2; antojitos 40¢–$2.50; ice cream $2.50.
Open: Daily 8:30am–9pm.
There are actually two such cafés: one a tiny carry-out place right on the plaza and the other a full-blown café/restaurant about a block or so west of the plaza on the left-hand side of the street. This charming café, with carved wooden chairs and tables, serves the renowned local coffee brew and several types of coffee ice cream, including crema, amor, Brasileño, and Romano. There's also a whole case full of delectable-looking pastries. Best of all, they sell the rich Cafe Uruapan by the kilo and will even sew it up in its own little burlap bag with the attractive red Cafe Uruapan logo for only $5.50—great for gifts.

RESTAURANT EMPERADOR, Matamoros 18. Tel. 3-1850 or 8-1130.
Specialty: MEXICAN.
$ Prices: Appetizers $1.50–$3; main courses $3–$7; comida corrida $6.
Open: Daily 8am–11:30pm (comida corrida served from 1pm).
This restaurant on the south side of the main plaza is a popular meeting place for both

young and old. Tacos, chilaquiles, and club sandwiches are reasonable. Coffee drinkers—after dark the place is full of them—can indulge their habit for hours. Sit farther in the back to avoid the street noise.

Stronger drinks are served upstairs at a bar called the **Crystal** (tel. 3-1850), open daily from 7pm to 2am, which has a nice disco and dancing. Although the sign says COUPLES ONLY, women may come unescorted and feel comfortable here.

EL RINCÓN DEL BURRITO, Matamoros 7. Tel. 3-7989.
Specialty: MEXICAN.
$ Prices: Main courses $2–$6; soup $2–$3; ''Clasica Americana'' (hamburger, fries, and malt) $6.
Open: Daily 8am–2am.

It's comfortable here in this semi-fast-food restaurant with white-tile counter and yellow booths. Some 44 combinations of good solid meals with generous portions are listed on the huge menu. The delicious Tarascan soup is thick like barbecue sauce, with shoestrings of crispy fried tortillas sticking out like a bird's nest; it's all topped with sour cream, cheese, and avocado—great filling stuff. Owner Sr. Fernando Cuadra worked 11 years in California in a popular Mexican restaurant chain, and he knows how to please his Norteamericano customers. The restaurant is about mid-plaza, on the south side, across from the churches.

MANSION CUPATITZIO, Parque Nacional. Tel. 3-2100 or 3-2070.
Specialty: MEXICAN. **Bus:** Take one of the frequent local buses at the plaza to the Parque Nacional; or walk seven blocks west of the main plaza on Emilio Carranza to the parque. The hotel is at the northeastern end of the park.
$ Prices: Breakfast $3–$7; appetizers $1.25–$6; soups $2; meat courses $5–$11; Mexican specials $4–$8.
Open: Daily 7am–10:30pm.

Those who can't afford to stay at this hotel might consider dining at the restaurant to enjoy the beauty and tranquility of this establishment. Instead of ordering expensive dishes at lunch or dinner, it's possible to soak up the atmosphere while munching such inexpensive snacks as nachos. After a visit to the parque, the hotel's patio restaurant is a pleasant place to relax with a cool drink or, in general, just a nice place to escape the clamor of the town.

FOR ICE CREAM

Helados Holanda, Cupatitzio 28 (tel. 3-2537), down the same side street as the Hotel Victoria, is an ice-cream parlor boasting 50 flavors. Single-scoop cones are 65¢ and doubles are $1.15. Open daily between 9am and 9pm.

Or try **Cafe Tradicional Uruapan,** Emilio Carranza 5B, with its exotic coffee ice creams.

EASY EXCURSIONS FROM URUAPAN
PARICUTÍN VOLCANO

Get up early, go down to the Central Camionera (city buses from the plaza go there), and take a bus over a newly paved road to Angahuán, a small Tarascan village about 21 miles from Uruapan. Buses leave hourly. The trip costs 90¢ and takes about 1 hour.

If you don't know the story of how Paricutín appeared, stop by the plaza in Angahuán and take a look at the carved wooden door of a house nearby—facing the church, it's around the stone fence to the right, two doors down. The story of the volcano is carved in pictures and words: It shows how a local man was plowing his cornfield in the valley on February 20, 1943, when at 3pm the ground began to boil.

At first he tried to stop it up; when that proved impossible, it seemed better to run. By that evening, rocks, smoke, and fire were flying up out of the ground. Some villagers fled that same night, others days later. The volcano was active for 9 years, growing larger and larger, until finally it breathed its last on March 6, 1952, stopping as suddenly as it had begun.

On arrival in Angahuán, tourists are besieged by guides ready to take them on horseback to see the half-buried **Church of San Juan Parangaricutiro,** looming silently up out of the lava, and to the crater of the volcano. While the horse is not necessary, a guide is advisable.

The road to the volcano—not at all obvious (or marked) in the village—is a few blocks to the left of the plaza, with the church to the right. About half a mile down the road from Angahuán toward the volcano is a state-run lodge and restaurant with bathrooms (the only ones in the area) and a stone patio with a good view of the church and volcanic cone. Unless there's an abundance of hikers or riders headed for the church, orient yourself here, because once you're down in the woods the church is not visible and there are a maze of unmarked trails going every which way. The walk to the church takes about an hour or so.

Those who want to go all the way to the volcano and to climb it should allow at least 8 hours from Angahuán. The round trip is about 14 miles. Take plenty of food and water because there's none along the way. The hike is mostly flat, with some steeper rises toward the end. Climbing the steep crater itself takes only about 40 minutes, for those who exercise regularly, but count on more time to walk around the crater's rim on top (2 to 3km) to enjoy the spectacular view.

By horse, the trip to the church and volcano takes about 6 or 7 hours and costs $20 to $30, plus tip. The asking price for a horse to the volcano is $14 to $17 per horse—and you must also pay that amount for the guide's horse. It's possible to bargain the price down to a total of $20 (for two horses and a guide). However, don't be surprised when, a few kilometers into the ride, the guide asks for a tip to be paid at the end of the trip. My guide requested $7, saying that without it he would make no money and had a family to feed. His services were so good that I chose to give him $10 after the 7-hour trip; he climbed to the top of the crater with me; pointed out various interesting features, including steaming fumeroles; provided riding instructions and a good history of the area. Acting as a guide to the volcano is one of the few opportunities to earn money for the obviously poor Angahuán villagers. Just don't pay until the ride is over and services were as promised.

Plan to spend an entire day for the trip from Uruapan, the ride to the foot of the volcano, the short climb, the return to Angahuán, and the trip back to Uruapan.

Where to Stay & Eat

ALBERGUE PARICUTÍN-ANGAHUÁN, Angahuán. 12 cabañas (all with bath). **$ Rates:** $25 for up to six people. **Parking:** Free.
This state-run lodge with a restaurant and a camping/trailer park is another option for those wishing to visit the volcano and stay nearby. It's about half a mile on the main (dirt) road toward Paricutín Volcano from Angahuán. These rustic stucco cabins are spartan, but tidy and clean. Each has a small fireplace, bathroom with shower, hot water, and bunk beds for six. Firewood costs $2.25 a bundle. There are special larger cabins for groups of up to 12 or 24 people. (There's also a rest room to the left of the restaurant, which can be used by those headed for the buried church or volcano.)

Reservations: Contact the Delegación de Turismo en Uruapan, 5 de Febrero no. 17, Uruapan, Mich. 60000 (tel. 452/4-0633, or 451/2-3658 in Morelia).

PARACHO

Another interesting side trip is to the town of Paracho, the home of fine handmade guitars. They're sold throughout town for prices ranging from $15 to $220. A 30-minute bus ride from the main station on Flecha Amarilla or Servicios Coordinados will get you there for 65¢.

EN ROUTE TO MEXICO CITY OR THE SILVER CITIES

It's a comfortable day's drive (200 miles) from Morelia to **Mexico City.** The route winds through lush mountain country with some breathtaking vistas before leveling off on the plateau. It'll take about 4 hours to get to **Toluca** (see Chapter 13) and another hour to get to the center of Mexico City. The route leads right down the capital's main drag, Paseo de la Reforma, which passes through wealthy residential districts before entering Chapultepec Park and the center of town.

Before going on to the capital, however, I'd advise a detour north to the **Silver Cities** in the central to northern reaches of Mexico (see Chapter 16).

CHAPTER 18
THE GULF COAST

One of Mexico's least-traveled, most interesting parts of the country, the Gulf Coast is also the most economical: Your money will go farther on this coast than anywhere else in the country. In the friendliness and gracious, hospitable pace, it's more like Mexico 20 years ago, and in price it's more like 10 years ago—an immensely appealing discovery when contrasted to Mexico's costly and contrived resorts aimed at well-heeled tourists.

The region is rich in remains of indigenous groups: The **Huastec** occupied the area north of the Cazones River to Soto la Marina, which includes portions of Veracruz, Tamaulipas, and San Luis Potosí; the **Totonac** lived south of the Cazones River to the Papaloapan River, in mid to upper Veracruz; and the **Olmec,** a civilization dating back 3,000 years, from Río Papaloapan to La Venta in southern Veracruz and northern Tabasco. Pyramidal sites dot the coast, some of which, like El Tajín and Zempoala, make for excellent off-the-beaten-track travel. Excellent museums along the way are devoted to explaining these cultures and their impact on Mexico. At least 15% of the people speak Indian languages in seven linguistic groups: Otomi around Puebla spilling into Veracruz, Huasteco, a Maya-linked language in Tamaulipas and San Luis Potosí, and Nauahtl and Totonaco in both Puebla and Veracruz.

SEEING THE GULF COAST

There are a number of ways to see the region: By car or bus you can travel from either Brownsville/Matamoros down coastal Highway 180, or from MacAllen/Reynosa down Highway 97 to Highway 180, through Ciudad Victoria all the way to Lake Catemaco. You won't see much of coastal waters until Tampico, unless you detour off the highway to one of the coastal villages. All along this route maintenance crews burn roadside weeds and the resulting smoke and flames can be dangerous for driving—be very careful.

By ground transportation from the border you could plan your first night in Ciudad Victoria or Tampico. After that, the distances are less than 5 hours from the towns suggested here.

By plane, Monterrey and Ciudad Victoria both have airports and bus travel from either is easy. In Veracruz state, Veracruz has the most flights from the U.S., but if you want to fly from Mexico City to Minatitlán (south of Catemaco), it's very easy to work your way north from there by bus. Veracruz is a natural base for side trips, to Jalapa, capital of Veracruz, and its museums, and the ruins of Zempoala, but allow 3 days. Getting to and seeing Papantla and El Tajín requires around 3 days. Don't plan less than 2 nights in Catemaco and the two Tuxtlas.

1. CIUDAD VICTORIA

420 miles NE of Mexico City, 173 miles SE of Monterrey

GETTING THERE By Plane AeroMar has one daily flight from Mexico City.

By Bus For bus information from the Texas border, call the Greyhond affiliate: at Brownsville/Matamoros, (512/546-7171); at McAllen/Reynosa, 512/682-5513. There's frequent direct service from Monterrey, Tampico, and San Luis Potosí.

By Car Highway 101 from Matamoros (opposite Brownsville, Texas) is probably the best road and the drive takes 4½ hours. Highway 97 from Reynosa (opposite McAllen, Texas) is less well maintained and subject to miles of potholes. From Monterrey, it's a pleasant 4-hour drive, and from Cd. Valles it's about the same; both are on Highway 85, a good, paved two-lane highway.

ESSENTIALS The **telephone area code** is 131.

DEPARTING By Plane Shared minivan transportation (tel. 2-4050) to the airport, 12 miles from downtown, costs $15 one way; make a reservation 24 hours in advance of departure.
   AeroMar has offices at Carrera Torres 14 and Abasolo 742-C (tel. 2-4511; fax 131/2-4435).

By Bus All **Tres Estrellas de Oro** buses (tel. 2-1290) are *de paso* on their frequent trips to Mexico City, Querétaro, San Luis Potosí, León, Morelia, Matamoros, and Reynosa. **Huastecas** (tel. 2-1349), a first-class line, has 12 buses a day to Matamoros and Reynosa, with some originating in Victoria (local) and the remainder *de paso*. **Transportes del Norte** (tel. 2-2122) has seven buses to Mexico City and Tampico, and to Monterrey, three to Reynosa, five to Nuevo Laredo, one to Cd. Valles, and six to San Luis Potosí. **Omnibus de México** (tel. 2-7526 or 2-0060) offers Express service to Guadalajara, and other service to Reynosa, Matamoros, Mexico City, and Querétaro.

Ciudad Victoria (alt. 1,471 ft.; pop. 208,000), capital of the state of Tamaulipas, founded in 1750, was named in 1825 for Mexican revolutionary Guadalupe Victoria, who became the country's first president. Tamaulipas means "between mountains" which it is—distantly. Today, far from being a one-burro town, it has modern architecture, clean wide streets, and two town squares.

ORIENTATION

ARRIVING The **airport** is 12 miles from downtown; shared minivans meet the one flight and cost $15 per person. The **bus station** is 15 blocks northeast of the town center. Taxis cost around $4.

INFORMATION The **State Tourism Office,** eight blocks south of Plaza Juárez at 5 de Mayo and Rosales 272 (tel. 131/2-1057 or 2-7002), is open Monday through Friday from 9am to 7pm.

CITY LAYOUT Touristic interest centers on two downtown plazas—Plaza Hidalgo and Plaza Juárez. **Plaza Hidalgo** is bounded by Morelos and Hidalgo going east and west and Colón and J. Tijerina going north and south. All the hotels I recommend are here. **Plaza Juárez** is eight blocks directly west of Plaza Hidalgo, where you'll find the Centro Cultural, Government Palace (city hall), the state-run artesanías shop, the History and Archeology Museum, theaters, restaurants, and galleries. It's bounded by Hidalgo and Morelos going east and west and Manuel González/Calle 15 and 5 de Mayo/Calle 16 going north and south.

WHAT'S SPECIAL ABOUT THE GULF COAST

Natural History
- [ ] El Cielo, huge cloud-forest reserve south of Ciudad Victoria, with 255 bird species, orchids, black bears, jaguars, and ocelots.
- [ ] Lake Catemaco, haven for 1,000 species of orchids and almost 400 bird species.

Archeological Sites
- [ ] El Tajín, with 20 recently restored buildings and a newly discovered Totonac mural.

Museums
- [ ] Anthropology Museum, in Jalapa, with the country's most complete display of Huastec, Totonac, and Olmec cultures.
- [ ] Huasteca Museum, in Ciudad Valles, devoted to the Huastec culture.
- [ ] Regional Archeology Museum, in Santiago de las Tuxtlas, showcasing Olmec artifacts and a 45-ton Olmec head found nearby.

Cuisine
- [ ] Cafe con leche made with Veracruz-grown coffee.

- [ ] Mollotes, bite-size tamal, and zacahuil (a pig-leg-size tamal), bananas and black-bean combos, smoked pork and pelliscadas (salted lard-fried tortillas).

Music and Dance
- [ ] Marimba bands; the *huapango*, a dance accompanied by harps, violins, guitars, and jaranas (like a ukelele); and *sones*, dances with similar instruments plus singers—in Veracruz.
- [ ] Voladores, who dance and play flutes, then fall suspended by rope from a pole—at Papantla and El Tajín.

Outstanding Plazas
- [ ] Plaza de Armas, in Veracruz, one of the merriest in Mexico, with marimbas and mariachis, restaurants, balloon and hammock vendors.
- [ ] The central plaza in Santiago de las Tuxtlas, one of the most beautiful in Mexico, with a 45-ton stone Olmec head at one end.

There's a confusing street-naming custom in Cd. Victoria. Locals call streets going north and south by their number rather than the name, but street signs have only the name. Ask for both when getting directions.

GETTING AROUND

Plenty of taxis circle the main plazas, but most sites are within walking distance of either central plaza downtown.

WHAT TO SEE & DO

Check local newspapers for what's going on at the **Centro Cultural,** on Plaza Juárez, site of most traveling entertainment. It's almost worth a trip to Plaza Juárez and the **Government Palace** to see the beautiful stone **statue** of the Huasteca goddess Izcuinan Tlazolteotl (representing human base desires), unearthed by a farmer near Altamira, Tam., in 1988. Tall, slender, and exquisitely graceful, with carvings front and back, it's a Postclassic piece dated somewhere between A.D. 1000 and 1521.

Weekend evenings the state band plays in **Plaza Hidalgo.**

The small but good ✪ **Museo Instituto de Investigaciones Historicas,** Calle 9 and Matamoros (tel. 2-6125), is operated by the University of Tamaulipas and dedicated to the state's history from pre-Hispanic to the present time. One large section displays pre-Hispanic artifacts of the Huasteca Indians and is a good introduction to this indigenous group you'll hear a lot about as you journey down the coast.

SHOPPING   Ciudad Victoria's municipal **market,** two blocks east of Plaza

Hidalgo between Morelos and Hidalgo, is one of the cleanest in the country, with a good selection of craft shops around its perimeter.

The government-operated **Tienda Artesanías Voluntariado Tamaulipas** is opposite the Palacio del Gobierno on Plaza Juárez, Calle 16/Hidalgo. Besides a few crafts from other parts of the country, there's regionally made Tula pottery, and woven furniture and palm baskets from Bustamante. It's open Monday through Saturday from 9:30am to 1pm and 4:30 to 8pm.

WHERE TO STAY & EAT

HOTEL SIERRA GORDA, Plaza Hidalgo (Apdo. Postal 107), Cd. Victoria, Tam. 87000. Tel. 131/2-2280. Fax 131/2-9799. 86 rms (all with bath). TV TEL
$ Rates: $22–$42 single or double. **Parking:** 75¢.
The Hotel Sierra Gorda used to be Victoria's prime hostelry, but has competition now from the Everest, cater-corner on the plaza. Rooms have carpeted walls (which cuts down on noise), purified water from a special tap, and tub/shower combinations; there are ice machines on each floor. The less expensive rooms have ceiling fans and black-and-white TV, while the others are air-conditioned and have color TV. One gets the distinct feeling that these prices are only for those who will pay them, however, and that a bit of bargaining will get very dramatic reductions. Ask for the "promotional" rates.

HOTEL EVEREST, Colón 126, Cd. Victoria, Tam. 87000. Tel. 131/2-4050. 100 rms (all with bath). A/C TV TEL
$ Rates: $48 single; $50 double. **Parking:** 75¢.
⭐ Modern and quiet, with a wood-paneled lobby and a popular, reasonably priced restaurant next door, this is a good downtown choice after a day on the road. Rooms are dark but nicely furnished, with carpeting, light-wood furniture, full-length mirrors, and bedside lights. The Everest faces Plaza Hidalgo.

EASY EXCURSIONS FROM CIUDAD VICTORIA

✪ **EL CIELO BIOSPHERE RESERVE** About 50 miles south of Cd. Victoria near the town of Gómez Farías, this unique 357,134-acre cloud-forest reserve was finally set aside in 1985 as an ecologically protected area. Only two other known areas in the world (in China and Germany) resemble the unusual characteristics of this area. Stretching upward from an elevation of 656 feet to 6,235 feet (more than a mile) are visibly different ecosystems—tropical selva, mountainous woods (the cloud-forest area) on the eastern side, oak/pine forest, and scrubby brush and cactus on the western side. The Gulf side of El Cielo gathers cloud moisture (about 103 inches a year) which filters through the limestone rock to rivers providing irrigation waters that convert infertile fields into a breadbasket for hundreds of miles all the way to the coast. The desertlike landward side of the reserve receives only about 12 inches of moisture a year.

The reserve is divided into sectors of use and is rich in orchids and bromeliads, at least 255 species of birds (175 are migratory), almost 200 varieties of butterflies, 40 kinds of bats, 60 different snakes, 21 different frogs, and shelter for endangered black bears, jaguars and ocelots. The most untouched section nearest the top is off-limits to all but authorized scientists.

One part of the reserve was opened to tourism in 1991 with the building of 12 rustic state-operated cabins near the small settlement of San José. Some of the cabins are reserved for research scientists and some are available to tourists interested in natural history. Several of the cabins are similiar to bunkhouses and others are individual units, all with indoor bathrooms for night use and outhouses for day use. Marked paths around the cabin area identify some of the trees, but for the most part visitors are on their own for hiking, birdwatching, etc. A restaurant is available for guests and scholars, but it wouldn't hurt to bring some snack provisions and other essentials.

Though it's only about 25 miles from Gómez Farías, the jolting journey to the cabins, accessible only by four-wheel-drive vehicles, takes 2 hours. The crude, rocky, narrow roads throughout the reserve are left over from logging days and will remain unimproved. (There are no nearby rentals for rugged vehicles, so you must drive your own.)

March through June, August, and September are the best months for seeing flowers. Half the rain falls between July and September. Bring a water canteen for hiking, warm clothing for winter months, and lots of socks and two or three changes of shoes since nothing dries quickly. There's no late-night electricity, so a flashlight is a necessity. Be prepared for rain all year. And there are dangers to be aware of, among them rattlesnakes and fer de lance snakes, and the painful mala mujer (bad woman) plant with fine hairs that penetrate the skin and cause infection.

To enter El Cielo or to reserve a cabin, contact biologist Hector Zamora Treviño, **Dirección de Desarrollo Urbano y Ecologia** (S.A.H.O.S.P.), Gobierno del Estado de Tamaulipas, Apdo. Postal 568, Cd. Victoria, Tam. 87000 (tel. 131/2-9938), or inquire at the **State Tourist Office** in Cd. Victoria (see above for address). Birdwatching trips are also sponsored to another part of the reserve by the **Gorgas Science Foundation,** Southmost College, Brownsville, Texas, which has similar cabin facilities. For details see Chapter 2, "Educational/Adventure Travel."

BALCONES DE MOCTEZUMA ARCHEOLOGICAL SITE   About an hour west of Cd. Victoria, the newly excavated Huasteca Balcones de Moctezuma archeological site is being readied for the public. It is thought to be a Huasteca site for many reasons, among them the Huasteca-style human- and animal-shaped pottery vessels and the characteristic Huasteca circular ceremonial platforms. A terraced slope of 82 semicircular levels leads to a forested mountaintop of stone-walled circles about half of which have been excavated. Portions of more than 100 bodies and 13 full skeletons were unearthed during excavations, most of them children. Among them was a 3-year old girl with chiseled teeth, a practice common among adults, but this is the first discovery in Mexico of the practice on a child. Jade jewelry and metal, pottery, and clay figures found here will be on display in the site museum.

Between August and the end of October **monarch butterflies** alight on the omayel fir trees here on their way south from Canada to Michoacan west of Mexico City.

The rough road from the highway to the site was to have been paved in 1991 and a small site museum opened. Before going, check with the tourist office in Cd. Victoria to be sure it's open, and ask for directions.

TULA   An hour farther on Highway 101 west from the Balcones de Moctezuma, and about a third of the distance to San Luis Potosí, is Tula, founded in 1617 and the oldest town in the state of Tamaulipas. A charming, clean adobe-walled town, set in a desert landscape of cactus and joshua trees so typical of northern Mexico, it's worth a stop. Once its population swelled to 20,000, but today it's almost a ghost town with scarcely 4,000 people. Centered around a central plaza with a frilly iron bandstand and church, there's a bustling, prosperous busy feel about the town despite the fact that behind many doors are empty houses.

Look up Domingo Herrera, a stubble-faced **potter** whose neat courtyard and adjoining lot are crammed with his cream-colored pottery. His home and workshop are at 21 de Noviembre no. 6, about a block behind the church. Emiliano Ledezma Ruíz, **leather craftsman,** and possibly Tula's most famous citizen, is at Guerrero 9. His beautiful fringe-embellished suede charro jackets, with white leather designs, have been commissioned by presidents and even the present pope, who received one in papal purple when he visited Mexico. Hunters like them, too. He makes them individually, so there's no inventory on hand except for a few purses and bags. But if you're interested in a beautiful, one-of-a-kind, collectable jacket, look him up and be fitted.

For a meal or overnight, the inexpensive and charming 13-room **Hotel El Mesón de Mollinedo** opened in 1991 at Calle Morelos 1 (tel. 132/6-0045), near the town plaza. The pretty restaurant off the lobby has a reasonably priced menu. Try the enchiladas Tultecas, a regional specialty more like tacos or chalupas piled high with a variety of delicious ingredients.

LAKE VICENTE GUERRERO   Man-made Lake Guerrero, east of Cd. Victoria, about 45 minutes by car on Highway 101 to Matamoros, has been famous for bass fishing for years. Though diminished in size because of recent droughts, it still attracts fishermen, and numerous lodges around the lake cater to the sports-minded, including hunters. Padilla, a colonial-era town once inundated by the lake, has risen again and you can drive into the ghostly remains, and walk through the remaining buildings and plaza with the marker commemorating the spot where Emperor Augustín Iturbide faced the firing squad.

LA PESCA   About 100 miles east of Cd. Victoria on Highway 70 is La Pesca, a small but growing fishing village facing the Gulf Coast. Several villagers supplement their fishing incomes by taking visitors fishing, so a day of saltwater fishing is what you want, ask around and strike a deal. The village and a huge portion of the coast and inland have been selected for one of the Mexican government's mega-resorts, which could be years in coming.

2. CIUDAD VALLES

140 miles S of Cd. Victoria, 85 miles W of Tampico

GETTING THERE   By Bus   Valles has frequent service from Tampico, mostly on *de paso* buses. Most first-class buses will be full in Tampico, but the second-class station just opposite has frequent buses and more opportunity for a seat.

By Car   Highway 110 from Tampico is well maintained and mostly flat. Highway 85 from Cd. Victoria is well maintained with a few curves.

ESSENTIALS   The **telephone area code** is 138. Hotels can provide most **information.**

Valles (pop. 130,000), in the state of San Luis Potosí, is a good place to take a break in your journey to other places. On your way here you'll pass many stands selling honey and piloncillo (cone-shaped unrefined brown sugar), and you'll see people grinding the raw sugar and cooking it in huge vats. Squash, deep-cooked in brown sugar, hangs temptingly from the rafters of these roadside stands. Stop for a soft drink and look around.

WHAT TO SEE & DO

Relax and do what the local people do in the evening. Go to the **market,** piled high with fresh herbs and spices. Or walk around the **zócalo** and enjoy the fountain and the view over the Río Valles.

Before heading out the next morning, return to the market where Huasteca Indian women wearing beautiful yarn-and-ribbon headdresses sell huge, fresh, steaming Huasteca tamales. Or look for a restaurant in the market area with a SE VENDE ZACAHUIL sign out front that sells a version of the huge tamal wrapped in a banana leaf.

The **Huasteca Anthropology Museum,** south of the market area, is definitely worth a visit. The huge collection of Huasteca artifacts is somewhat dusty, but the mass of material and variety is wonderful. It's open Monday through Friday from 9am to 1pm and 4 to 6pm.

WHERE TO STAY & EAT

HOTEL VALLES, Blvd. 36 Nte. (Hwy. 85), Cd. Valles, S.L.P. 79050. Tel. 138/2-0050. Fax 138/2-0050 ext. 112 (ask for the tone). 100 rms (all with bath).

TV TEL **Directions:** Arriving from Cd. Victoria, it's on the left side before reaching town center.
$ Rates: $38–$62 single; $45–$75 double.
The only good hotel in town, the Hotel Valles is an elaborate hacienda-style motor hotel landscaped with quantities of palm trees and gardens and a splendid 100-foot swimming pool. Rooms are large and comfortably furnished; 96 are air-conditioned and 4 have fans. Prices are a little high for being out in the middle of nowhere.

The Valles also has a thatched cathedral-ceilinged restaurant-bar open daily from 6:30am to 11pm. The fixed-price daily lunch and most main courses cost $6.50. The steak-and-seafood restaurant on the grounds out back is more expensive.

3. TUXPAN

185 miles N of Veracruz, 115 miles S of Tampico

GETTING THERE   By Bus   Buses of the **ADO** line run most frequently from towns along the coast and inland.

By Car   Highway 180 is the fairly well maintained highway that parallels the Gulf Coast. Highway 180/130, also good, is the road to Papantla.

ESSENTIALS   The **ADO bus station** is in the center of the downtown area at Rodríguez and Juárez. Using this centrally located bus station as a starting point, the **market** is across the street, and **Calle Juárez** and my recommended hotels are right out the front door. The **Malecón,** which parallels the Tuxpan River, is to the left.

The **telephone area code** is 783. Ask at your hotel for **tourist information.**
If you're staying in one of the downtown hotels, **parking** is available one block off Juárez at Mina and Morelos for the reasonable rate of $1 per 24-hour period at Parking Iberia. But some hotels have parking, so ask first.

DEPARTING   By Bus   From the **ADO** (tel. 4-0102) station there are 6 buses daily to Papantla, 2 to Huauchinango, and 20 to Tampico and Poza Rica.

Although coming of age now, not long ago Tuxpan, Veracruz (that's "*Toosh*-pahn"; pop. 118,000), was the best example on the Gulf Coast of an unspoiled fishing town. The fishing boats are still moored in town at the mouth of the Río Tuxpan, and a fishing festival is held in early summer, but Tuxpan is growing.

WHAT TO SEE & DO

Why stay in Tuxpan? It's simple: for the unhurried, tropical ambience, the great seafood, and the wide beach, about 6 miles east of town center, facing the Gulf Coast. To get there, take one of the inexpensive colectivo taxis by the market or a bus marked "Playa." They stop a couple of blocks from the beach. The yellow-white sand is fairly packed, and the water is shallow and choppy, so exercise caution and don't wade too far out. Even if you don't want to go to the beach, take the ride anyway; it's an inexpensive way to briefly tour the city since the route skirts the river and goes inland through neighborhoods.

WHERE TO STAY & EAT

Aside from the places listed below, there are good eateries along the beach. All of these are about the same, so see which one is the busiest. Try a fish filet stuffed with seafood or a torta marisco (seafood fried with egg).

HOTEL FLORIDA, Juárez 23, Tuxpan, Ver. 92800. Tel. 783/4-0650 or 4-0602. 76 rms (all with bath). TEL

$ Rates: $15–$27 single; $21–$33 double.

The Florida is three blocks down Juárez from the ADO bus station, on the right at Garizunieta. It's Tuxpan's older and well-used but still sturdy, clean, and serviceable hotel. An elevator serves the several floors, and as some rooms have been remodeled more recently than others it would be good to look before you buy; another reason to look is that the Florida is one of the few hotels with river views—only a few rooms offer this. Lower-priced rooms (38) have fans; interior-facing rooms (38) all have air conditioning and TVs.

The street-level restaurant offers views of downtown's passing scene. There's a full bar as well as a lengthy menu. Main dishes of seafood, beef, or chicken run $5.50 to $8.25; sandwiches and Mexican plates are $2.75 to $5. It's open daily from 7am to 11pm.

HOTEL PLAZA, Juárez 39, Tuxpan, Ver. 92800. Tel. 783/4-0738. Fax 783/4-3535. 57 rms (all with bath). A/C TV TEL
$ Rates: $27 single; $33 double.
At the Hotel Plaza, four blocks on Juárez from the ADO bus station, you can get a modern room. All the conveniences are here: elevator, coordinated wood furniture and headboards, individual room thermostats, tile baths, and marble floors. Interior-facing rooms are quieter.

The Plaza's restaurant is one of the town's more popular places to dine, partly because it's air-conditioned. A couple of photographs of Tuxpan in the 1920s and 1930s spice up the restaurant's otherwise unremarkable modern decor. Breakfast costs $2.50 to $4.25, and main courses for either lunch or dinner run around $3.25 to $8.50. It's open daily from 7am to 11pm.

HOTEL REFORMA, Juárez 25, Tuxpan, Ver. 92800. Tel. 783/4-0210. Fax 783/4-1367. 98 rms (all with bath). TV TEL **Directions:** From the bus station turn right to the corner, then left 3 blocks on Juárez; it's on the right.
$ Rates: $28 single; $35 double.

Although it looks stately and elegant from the outside, the Hotel Reforma is modern, with a lofty inner court preserved from an earlier era. It's furnished with cast-iron tables and chairs, has a little pool with a fountain and bar service. Rooms are comfortably furnished, each with one or two double beds; 84 are air-conditioned and the other 14 have fans.

The Reforma has its own restaurant (open 7am to 11pm), entered from either the court or the street, and it's one of the nicest in the downtown area. Salads and appetizers cost $3.25 to $6.25; sandwiches and Mexican plate specials and most main courses run $7.50 to $9. Friday and Saturday nights an instrumental trio plays from 8pm to midnight.

---

4. PAPANTLA & EL TAJÍN

140 miles NW of Veracruz, 47 miles SE of Tuxpan

GETTING THERE   By Bus   Wherever you are coming from, it's often easier to take one of the frequent buses to Poza Rica and change there to a bus to Papantla. **ADO** has six buses daily to Papantla from Tuxpan.

By Car   From Jalapa it's about a 4-hour drive via Misantla and Martínez de la Torre; then take Highway 180 on the coast. From Veracruz it's about 5 hours using the coastal Highway 180.

ESSENTIALS   The **telephone area code** is 784. The **climate** is sultry, rainy, and hot in summer, cold and rainy in winter—and hotels are unheated.

DEPARTING   By Bus   There are two bus stations in Papantla. The first-class **ADO** station is at the bottom of the hill north of the town center and is preferable to the second-class station on 20 de Noviembre at Calle Olivo, opposite the Hotel

Totonacapan. All ADO buses are *de paso* and there are four daily to Mexico City, three to Tuxpan, and eight to Jalapa and to Poza Rica.

The **second-class buses** are all the school-bus type, with frequent trips to Poza Rica, etc.—but they're famous for pickpockets.

Papantla (pop. 159,000) is the former vanilla capital of the world. The hybrid symbol of the community, displayed at both entrances to the city, is a very large concrete vanilla bean with inscribed hieroglyphs. Vanilla extract can be purchased here for about half the cost in the States. The long, slender, almost-black vanilla beans are also for sale, but more than likely you'll see them fashioned into figures, flowers, or a dozen different designs. Papantla is also noteworthy because of its proximity to the ruins of El Tajín, because of the frequent shows of the flying pole dancers (*voladores*), and also because of the festivities around Corpus Christi Day.

ORIENTATION

ARRIVING   If you arrive by bus you'll be six long blocks from the center of town, which is at the top of the hill. To get to town center, walk out the front door of the bus station, turn left, and go up Juárez five or six blocks to the central park, cathedral, and Hotel Tajín.

CITY LAYOUT   Coming into town, you'll most likely arrive at the bottom of the hill. Fix your eyes on the cathedral and blue facade of the Hotel El Tajín at the top of the hill. That's the center of town, with hotels, markets, plaza, and restaurants.

GETTING AROUND

City buses go to the ruins of El Tajín (see below) and taxis are available around the central plaza. But almost everything worth seeing is within walking distance of the central plaza.

WHAT TO SEE & DO
THE RUINS OF EL TAJÍN

✪   The top attraction is the nearby ruins of El Tajín, which are definitely worth seeing.

Getting There   From Papantla, buses marked "Chote/Tajín" run to El Tajín from beside the Juárez market (at the corner of Reforma and 20 de Noviembre) every hour beginning at 7am—but don't count on it. As an alternative, buses marked "Chote" pass more frequently and will leave you at the Chote crossroads; from there wait for a bus the short distance to El Tajín or take a taxi for around $2.50.

From Veracruz, take Highway 180 to Papantla; from there, take Route 127, which is a back road to Poza Rica, going through Tajín.

Seeing the Ruins   In 1991 the University of Veracruz and the Instituto Nacional e Historia y Antropología completed 2 years of new excavations at the site. Of the 150 buildings, 20 have been excavated and conserved, transforming them from essentially grass-covered mounds to a semblance of their original form. At least 17 ballcourts have been found, though only 3 are visible. Mural fragments led archeologists to discover a Teotihuacan-influenced mural at the top of Building 11, which is being restored.

The ruins at Tajín are divided into the old section (*Tajín viejo*) and the new section (*Tajín chico*). The most impressive structure is in the old section, the **Pyramid of the Niches.** The pyramid is made of stone and adobe, with 365 recesses on all four sides of the building. The pyramid was once covered in painted stucco, and today is one of the most unusual pre-Columbian structures in Mesoamerica. Near this pyramid is a restored **ball court** with beautiful carved reliefs on the vertical playing sides depicting religious scenes and sacrifices.

The **Temple of the Columns** is in the new section. A stairway divides the columns, three on either side, each one decorated with reliefs of priests and warriors plus hieroglyphic dates. Many mounds are still uncovered, but with the reconstruction that has been done so far, it's easier now to see the ruins as a city. The view from on top of one of the pyramids, overlooking the rich, green forests dotted with mounds, is quite impressive. This is definitely worth a stop if you are driving the Gulf Coast highway.

The *Voladores* The *voladores* (fliers) are an additional attraction. These are local Totonac Indians who perform their flying upside-down pole dance. When you hear the sound of a drum and flute, the *voladores* are ready. Five of them, dressed in satin pants, vests, and cone-shaped hats with ribbons and small round mirrors, climb the tall pole (donated by Pemex) to the top where there is a square revolving platform. One stands beating a drum and playing a flute while the four others perch on the four sides of the platform and attach themselves by their waists to a rope. When the time is right, the four lean over backward and fall off, suspended by the rope, revolving 13 times until they reach the ground. The number 13 corresponds to the number of months in the Aztec calendar.

Essentials Admission to the site is $3.50; the *voladores* collect $3.50 from each person in the crowd. The site is open daily from 8am to 5pm; the *voladores* usually perform around 10am, 1pm, and 3pm Monday through Saturday, and on Sunday between noon and 4pm.

SHOPPING

There are at least two markets in Papantla, both near the central plaza. **Mercado Juárez** is opposite the front door of the church. **Mercado Hidalgo** is a block or two down Reforma on the left, away from the plaza. Both have a good selection of locally made baskets and regional clothing. Besides vanilla, a popular local liqueur, **Xanath** makes a good gift and costs around $9.50. Embroidered blouses and dresses, typical attire of the region's Indians, are sold in the market.

SPECIAL EVENTS

The **Feast of Corpus Christi,** the ninth Sunday after Easter, is surrounded by a very special week in Papantla. Well-known Mexican entertainers perform. Also the native *voladores* (see "What to See and Do," above) make special appearances. Lodging is scarce during this week, so be sure to book ahead.

The **zócalo** is lovely in Papantla. Ceramic tile is used throughout and the cathedral wall facing the square is covered with an artist's impression of El Tajín in concrete, and on top of the mountain is an enormous statue of a *volador* ("voh-lah-*dohr*"), famous for the dance that ends in a leap from a tall pole, for which the region is famous.

WHERE TO STAY

EL TAJÍN HOTEL, Nuñez 104, Papantla, Ver. 93400. Tel. 784/2-1012.
Fax 784/2-1062. 60 rms (all with bath). TV TEL
$ Rates: $20 single; $23 double.
Walk along the cathedral wall up the hill to the thriving El Tajín Hotel, the building with the bright-blue facade on top of the hill. The rooms here are small and tidy, and all have fans. The Restaurant Tajín is in the El Tajín Hotel and is clean and inexpensive.

WHERE TO EAT

Mercado Juárez has numerous cookshops that in the morning bring in some outstandingly delicious zacahuil (the huge tamal cooked in a banana leaf). Look around until you see a cook with a line of patrons—that'll be the best zacahuil. Outside the market, rolling cart vendors sell steamy hot atole.

Besides zacahuil, be sure to try mollotes, a small, delicious football-shaped tamal that's served as an appetizer.

CEÑADURÍA M.Y.R., 16 de Septiembre no. 117.

Specialty: REGIONAL.
$ Prices: Mollotes 85¢; tostadas $1.65; main courses $2–$3.50.
Open: Dinner only, daily 6–11pm.

Ceñadurias are dinner places, so don't come for lunch. A "Formica and plastic chair" sort of place, it's short on atmosphere but makes up for it in taste. You get your money's worth here, and the service is good. This is the best place to try mollotes. And you may want to top off any meal with fresh bananas and cream. This ceñaduría is on the street back of the church.

5. JALAPA

188 miles W of Mexico City, 65 miles NW of Veracruz, 111 miles E of Puebla

GETTING THERE   By Plane   Veracruz, 2 hours south, has the closest airport, although some charter flights use the small Jalapa airport.

By Bus   Buses of the **ADO** line arrive every 30 minutes from Veracruz and every hour from Mexico City; there are 7 a day from Orizaba, 11 from Puebla, and 3 from Zempoala, at very odd hours.

By Car   From Veracruz, take Highway 180 to Cardel and then turn left onto Highway 140 past the coffee plantations.
From Mexico City, Puebla, or Tlaxcala, there is danger of dense fog between Perote and Jalapa. Drivers pass even when they can't see on the narrow two-lane highway. On a clear day this drive resembles Switzerland with cows grazing on verdant hillside pastures.

ESSENTIALS   The **telephone area code** is 281. The **climate** is humid and warm in summer, and humid and chilly in winter. All year, be prepared for the *chipi chipi* ("*chee*-pee *chee*-pee") rain that comes and goes.

DEPARTING   By Bus   Both **ADO** and **AU** buses have much the same routes, with frequent service to Mexico City and Veracruz. The trip to Papantla takes 5 to 6 hours over the long route through Perote (with an incredible number of rest stops), so be sure to ask for the short route, and change buses in Poza Rica if necessary. There are buses to the Zempoala ruins at 3am, 4:10am, and 11am.

Capital of the state of Veracruz, Jalapa (or Xalapa; alt. 4,500 ft.; pop. 288,000) is an interesting town to explore for a day. Although modern, the city is riddled with old and narrow streets that wind up and down. Besides being the jalapeño pepper capital of Mexico, this was the hometown of Antonio López de Santa Anna, whose many presidencies of the country spanned 50 years, and whose hacienda is a museum southeast of town. Cortés and his troops passed through nearby Xico on their way from the Gulf Coast to the Aztec capital of Tenochtitlán for the first time. Chroniclers of the Conquest described the hazards of the trip and particularly note the *chipi chipi*, a fine-but-pelting rain that is a frequent part of Jalapa life. Coffee plantations can be seen for miles around, so take time out for a cup of the local brew.

ORIENTATION

ARRIVING   The new **bus station** is less than a mile southeast of the town center on 20 de Noviembre, but the hills make it difficult to walk to town. It resembles a sophisticated airport, with arrivals upstairs and departures downstairs, and an overhanging roof for protection from the weather. Inside it's sleek, with shops, telephone and fax service, car rental and guarded luggage, and a fast-food cafeteria in the center. Taxis are downstairs and charge around $1 to the town center.

INFORMATION   The **State Tourism Office** is far northwest of the town center at Avenida Camacho 91, at Bravo (tel. 8-7186 or 8-7097). Little English is spoken, but they have maps and literature. Hours are Monday through Friday from 9am to 3pm and 6 to 9pm; and on Saturday from 9am to 1pm.

CITY LAYOUT   Jalapa is a hilly town with streets seemingly without much order, which is very confusing to the visitor. The center of town is the beautiful **Plaza Juárez,** where on a clear day the Pico de Orizaba is visible to the southwest. Facing the plaza are the Palacio del Gobierno, the Municipal Palace, and north half a block is the cathedral. A tunnel runs under the park and connects **Avenidas Zaragoza and Ávila Camacho,** the main arteries, which run diagonally across the city southeast to northeast.

GETTING AROUND

Most of my recommended hotels and restaurants are within walking distance of the central Plaza Júarez. Taxis in Jalapa are amazingly inexpensive, around $1 for most places in the city.

WHAT TO SEE & DO
ATTRACTIONS

Take a look at the murals by José Chávez Morado in the **Palacio de Gobierno,** and also a glance in the massive **cathedral.** Walk through the streets and admire the bougainvillea, fruit trees, and flowers. Jalapa is halfway between the mountains and the tropics, so they have coffee plantations and sultry breezes at the same time.

The Agora, a hang-out for artists, students, and other cosmopolitan types, is just off the main park. For books, records, films, conversation, concerts, look here first. Afterward check out the **Teatro del Estado,** at Manuel Ávila Camacho and Ignacio de la Llave. This is Jalapa's official cultural center, and there's always something going on.

In addition, there are two museums worth visiting, as well as the botanical gardens:

MUSEO DE ANTROPOLÓGIA DE JALAPA, Av. Jalapa at Av. Aqueducto. Tel. 7-2551.

Many people come to Jalapa just to visit this suburban museum operated by the University of Veracruz. It's second only to the world-renowned Anthropology Museum in Mexico City, and is a must if you're anywhere nearby. Designed by Edward Durrell Stone (who designed the Kennedy Center in Washington, D.C.), it's divided into sections devoted to the Indian groups on the Gulf Coast—Huastec, Totanac, and Olmec, and specific sites within each one. Good maps show the regions and sites. An ethnographic section shows the daily life of these groups (except the Olmec) as practiced today.

A signature giant Olmec head is the first thing you see upon entering and there are at least two more before you finish. Although the gigantic Olmec pieces are the most visible, and the Olmec culture is the oldest, beginning around 1500 B.C., each culture left powerful artifacts and it's unlikely you'll see any as magnificent as these in other museums. The museum is highly recommended, especially if you plan to visit any of the sites in your travels.

There's a shop and bookstore to the right of the lobby.
Admission: $1.75.
Open: Museum, Tues–Sun 9:30am–5pm; shop, Tues–Sun 10am–2:30pm. and 3:30–5pm. **Bus:** "Museo" from Plaza Juárez, or on Avenida Jalapa or Avenida de las Americas.

HACIENDA LENCERO, km 5 on Hwy. 140 toward Veracruz.

Today known as the Hacienda Lencero, this fabulous country estate 3 miles southeast of the town center was the Hacienda Manga de Clavo, the beloved home of Antonio López de Santa Anna, president of Mexico 11 times from 1842 to 1856. It was his retreat from the world where he sequestered himself as well as received countless notable visitors on occasion. Purchased by the state of Veracruz in 1981, it's one of the best museums of its kind in the country, another must-see for anyone visiting Jalapa.

Rooms in the sprawling mansion are filled with furniture from Mexico, Europe, and Asia, depicting a type of elegance found in Mexico during the 19th century. Included among them is Santa Anna's bed with the national emblem of an eagle holding a snake in its beak. The carefully tended grounds are awash with flowers and shaded by centuries-old trees. Next to the grand house, the spacious servants' quarters, with a gracious, wide covered patio facing a natural spring-fed lake, has been converted to a restaurant serving light snacks, pastries, and soft drinks.

Admission: Free; free Spanish-speaking guides on request.
Open: Tues–Sun 10am–5pm. **Directions:** Drive or take a taxi about 3 miles south of town on Highway 140 toward Veracruz, past the country club; watch for signs on the right.

JARDÍN BOTANICO FRANCISCO CLAVIJERO, Av. Lázaro Cárdenas, km 2.5. Tel. 8-6000, ext. 220.

Though only 1½ miles from Plaza Juárez, it seems much farther, tucked on a hillside just off the busy Cárdenas thoroughfare. Thirteen acres of flat and hillside terrain cradle a dense junglelike park full of palmetto palms, pines, oaks, coffee, and gardens. It's maintained by the Centro Ecológia Veracruz, and visitors wander at leisure.

Admission: Free.
Open: Tues–Sun 8am–5pm. **Directions:** Take a taxi down Cárdenas southwest of Plaza Juárez. It's too far to walk and whizzing traffic on Cárdenas makes it dangerous besides. The narrow, poorly marked entrance off Cárdenas is very difficult to see.

SHOPPING

At **Casa de Artesanías,** Paseo de la Laguna, at Morelos (tel. 7-0804), the quantity and quality of crafts varies from time to time, but you can usually pick up packaged Veracruz coffee, cans of jalapeño peppers, baskets from Papantla, and pottery from San Miguel Aguasuelos, all local products. Open Monday through Friday from 9am to 1pm and 4 to 7pm, and on Saturday from 9am to 1pm. It's off Zaragoza six blocks south of Plaza Juárez.

WHERE TO STAY

HOTEL CONTINENTAL, Zamora 4, Jalapa, Ver. 91000. Tel. 281/7-3530.
18 rms (all with bath).
$ Rates: $10 single; $12–$15 double.
The Hotel Continental is a basic budget hotel with a nice inner courtyard. The large rooms are furnished with old-timey furniture, chenille bedspreads, tile floors, peeling paint, and a bare bulb hanging from the ceiling. The courtyard restaurant serves lunch only, Monday through Saturday from 1 to 6pm.

To get here, with your back to the cathedral, walk two blocks to the left; the hotel is half a block on the right at Calle Carrillo Puerto.

HOTEL CAFETO, Canovas 2, Jalapa, Ver. 91000. Tel. 281/7-0023. 16 rms (all with bath).
$ Rates: $12 single; $15 double; $18 triple.
What a treat to discover this new, colorful, and comfortable town house turned hotel, opened in 1987. It was named for the coffee industry in the region, so there's always a pot of coffee on the burner and guests help themselves anytime. The owners, local architects, gave the rooms colorful Mexican style, with bright bedspreads, royal-blue metal doors and window frames, white walls with painted flower designs, and Mexican tile accents. Windows let in plenty of light and each room is slightly different: Some are small and have two single or two double beds, or a single and a double. TVs can be rented. It's two blocks north of Plaza Juárez.

HOTEL MARÍA VICTORIA, Zaragoza 6, Jalapa, Ver. 91000. Tel. 281/8-6011. 112 rms (all with bath). A/C TV TEL
$ Rates: $34–$41 single; $40–$43 double.
The excellently located Hotel María Victoria—on Zaragoza at Camacho, behind the main plaza—has clean, carpeted, but worn rooms. Some have a view of the pool on the first floor. Interior rooms for two to three people are less noisy. There's a restaurant and bar off the lobby.

WORTH THE EXTRA BUCKS

HOTEL XELAPA, Victoria and Bustamante, Jalapa, Ver. 91000. Tel. 281/8-2222. Fax 281/8-9424. 200 rms (all with bath). A/C MINIBAR TV TEL
$ Rates: $66 single; $70 double.
The gleaming Hotel Xelapa is the capital's best hotel, the place celebrities and politicos stay when they come to town and the venue for balls, receptions, and local coronations. Carpeted and nicely furnished in pastel colors, each heated room has a tub/shower combination. There's a restaurant and bar in the lobby overlooking the enormous pool.

WHERE TO EAT

Walk almost any block in the downtown area and you'll find restaurants of all kinds. **Callejon del Diamante** is a narrow pedestrians-only street a block and a half from Plaza Juárez with half a dozen restaurants—La Fonda and La Sopa El Mayab among them. Prices are reasonable and hours for most are Monday through Saturday from 8am to 10pm. To find it: With your back to the cathedral, walk left on Enríquez across Lucio one block and the callejon is on the left.

HOTEL MÉXICO, Lucio 4. Tel. 8-8000.
Specialty: MEXICAN.
$ Prices: Breakfast $2.65–$4.25; main courses $3.25–$7.50; comida corrida $4.85.
Open: Daily 7am–10pm.

⑤ For years this restaurant, in the far back of the Hotel México parking lot, has been serving the best comida corrida downtown. It begins with fruit, followed by soup, vegetables, meat, rice, dessert, and coffee. You can't go wrong here. It's half a block east of Plaza Juárez, facing the left side of the cathedral.

---

6. VERACRUZ & ZEMPOALA

145 miles E of Mexico City; 68 miles SE of Jalapa

GETTING THERE **By Plane** **Mexicana** flies to Veracruz from Mexico City three times daily. **AeroCaribe** (Mexicana affiliate) flies from Mérida once daily. **AeroLitoral** (Aeroméxico affiliate) flies from Cd. del Carmen, Minatitlán, Monterrey, Tampico, and Villhermosa. **TAESA** (tel. 713/961-1257 in Houston, or toll free 1-800/627-3483 in the U.S.), a government and private-industry charter airline, has twice-weekly flights from Houston and Miami to Veracruz.

By Train The *Jarocho* leaves Mexico City at 9:15pm and arrives in Veracruz at 7am (via Orizaba, Fortin, and Cordoba).

By Bus There are frequent buses to Veracruz from Jalapa, Córdoba, Orizaba, and Mexico City. Buses from Lake Catemaco, Santiago Tuxtla, and San Andres de los Tuxtla are *de paso* and there are fewer of them, so plan travel from there on a weekday when traffic is lighter.
As the bus station is a good distance from downtown, try to make your onward reservations when you arrive in Veracruz.

By Car From Cordoba or Orizaba, take Highway 150 to the coast and then drive north on Highway 180 to Veracruz; it's less than a 2-hour drive. Jalapa also is less than

2 hours away via Highway 140 to the coastal Highway 180 and the toll road into Veracruz, or cut off before the coast at Puente Nacional and go south to Veracruz on toll-free Highway 146.

DEPARTING   By Plane   The **airport** is 2½ miles from the town center. Minibuses of **Transportación Terrestre Aeropuerto** (tel. 34-3520) go out for every departing flight and cost $9.25.

Mexicana offices are at 5 de Mayo and Serdan (tel. 32-2242, or 38-0008 at the airport). **AeroLitoral** has offices in the Hotel de Cortés (tel. 35-0832). **AeroCaribe** offices are at the airport (tel. 37-0260). **TAESA** charter flights to Houston and Miami are handled in Veracruz by Viajes Bojorques, Avenida González Pages 110 (tel. 29/31-0839).

By Train   The **railroad station** (tel. 32-2569) is five long blocks north of Plaza de Armas on Avenida Morelos, just off Plaza de la República. Buy tickets at least a day in advance from the ticket window inside the station to the right of the front entrance. The *reservation window* is open daily from 7 to 11am and 6 to 9:15pm; the *ticket window,* where you pay for and pick up reserved tickets, is at another window inside the station to the left of the front door and open between 7 and 10am and 6 and 9pm—but you may still have to wait. One special night sleeper express, *Jarocho,* leaves Veracruz at 9:30pm and arrives in Mexico City at 7:40am.

By Bus   The **ADO** line (tel. 37-5744) has 14 buses daily to Orizaba, 9 to Córdoba, 29 to San Andres Tuxtla, and buses to Jalapa leave every 30 minutes.

From the **Central Camionera** (tel. 37-6790) buses head from Veracruz to Mexico City (scores of buses every day, a 7-hour trip), Oaxaca, and Mérida (two night buses). Additionally, 10 buses a day make the trip to Villahermosa, 3 a day to Tehuacán, and 6 a day directly to Catemaco. "Díaz Miron" buses go from the town center to the bus station.

Veracruz ("Bay-rah-*croos*"; pop. 328,000) is Mexico's principal port and has been since Hernán Cortés landed there on Good Friday in 1519. His name for the town he founded (which was actually 30 miles north of the present location) was Villa Rica de la Vera Cruz (the Rich Town of the True Cross). The Spaniards once shipped most of their gold and silver out of the port, and looting pirates periodically corraled the townfolk in the parish church, or abandoned them on an island in the bay, while they methodically ransacked the town. The citizens in turn built a high wall around the old town (around Plaza de Armas) and constructed a massive fort, San Juan de Ulua, on what was then an island in the harbor (now connected to the mainland by a curving pier). Despite these formidable precautions the pirates pillaged the port in 1654 and 1712, the French invaded in 1832 and 1861, and the Americans attacked in 1847 and 1914.

Veracruz, a raucous, swinging port town, has an intriguing combination of European and African influences, and a clean and impressive shoreline. Despite its reputation for a good time, especially during Carnaval just before Lent, there's a refreshingly relaxed atmosphere more like the Mexico of 20 years ago.

No trip to Veracruz is complete without indulging in two local customs: drinking coffee at La Paroquía, just off Plaza de Armas, and listening to marimba music beneath the portals on Plaza de Armas.

Note: Telephone numbers throughout the city were being changed at presstime, so numbers given here may have changed by the time you arrive.

IMPRESSIONS

A chronic complaint along the coast of Veracruz is that blast of Boreas called the "Norther." It swoops down upon the sea like a bird of prey, sending ships ashore, and laying low many a forest monarch and many a residence on land.
—FREDERICK A. OBER, *TRAVELS IN MEXICO AND LIFE AMONG THE MEXICANS*, 1884

ORIENTATION

ARRIVING   If you arrive by plane, don't tarry long in the airport in getting to the colectivo minivans that await each flight and cost $3. They fill up and leave rapidly and don't return until the next expected flight.

The **railroad station** is on Plaza de la República, a few blocks north of Plaza de Armas.

The **Central Camionera** is 20 or so blocks south of the town center; taxis cost around $1 to Plaza de Armas. "Díaz Miron" buses go to the town center and leave from across the street on the left corner.

INFORMATION   The **Tourism Office** (tel. 32-9942) with its enthusiastic staff, is right downtown on Plaza de Armas, in the Palacio Municipal (Town Hall), on the south side of the square, and is open daily from 9am to 9pm, although sparsely staffed from 1 to 4pm.

CITY LAYOUT   Parallel to the shoreline, **Paseo del Malecón/Boulevard Camacho** runs north and south, into the town center and out to the beaches and resorts south of town. (Technically the Malecón is named Insurgentes, but that name is seldom used.) City life gravitates around **Plaza de Armas,** one block west of the Malecón. It's bounded by Lerdo and Zamora going east and west, and by Independencia and Morelos going north and south. Most museums, restaurants, and hotels are either here or within a short walk.

GETTING AROUND

City buses are inexpensive and easy to use and I've mentioned the pertinent ones to get you to and from the most important places. **Taxis** are incredibly cheap compared to other cities in Mexico, around $1 almost anywhere in the downtown area, including to the bus station.

FAST FACTS

American Express   Viajes Olymar represents American Express at Boulevard Camacho 2221, Col. Zaragoza (tel. 29/31-4636; fax 29/31-3169).

Area Code   The telephone area code is 29.

Climate   You'll find it hot and sultry in summer, mild in spring, fall, and winter, with windy, sand-blowing *nortes* (northers) from November to March.

Consulate   The **U.S. Consulate** is located on Victimas del 25 de Junio, almost at the corner of Gómez Farías (tel. 31-5821). It's open Monday through Friday from 9am to 1pm.

High Season   June, July and August; December through March.

Post Office   The Correos (post office), located on Avenida de la República, near the Maritime Customs House, is open Monday through Friday from 8am to 8pm.

WHAT TO SEE & DO

More than anything about Veracruz, you'll remember its gaiety. There is a certain carefree spirit about this bustling seaport. From 1 or 2pm until the early morning you'll hear **mariachi** and **marimba** bands playing in Plaza de Armas, and on Thursday and Sunday from 7 to 10pm the state band plays in front of the **Palacio Municipal.** Up and down the **Malecón** and in the square, people gather to socialize, listen to the music, or sell trinkets. It's a lively town, especially on a Sunday, which seems to be the big socializing day.

Sightseeing Trolleys—open-air, rubber-wheeled trolleys, replicas of those that ran on rails in Veracruz until the early 1980s—leave from in front of the train station (by Plaza de la República) every half hour daily (unless the weather is bad) from 9am to 10pm, making an hour-long tour through town. The cost is $1.75 round-trip.

The **Ballet Tradicional de México** (tel. 31-0574 or 32-6693 for reservations) performs at the Teatro J. Clavijero every Saturday at 6pm. Tickets cost $6 to $10 and can be purchased at the tourism office.

SAN JUAN DE ULUA

Built as a limestone rock fortress against pirate invasion, it became more infamous as a prison noted for extreme cruelty and for the famous prisoners who resided there, among them Benito Juárez (from 1858 to 1861), who later became one of the country's most revered presidents. English-speaking guides charge for tours at the entrance or you can go on your own.

Admission: Free.
Open: Tues–Sun 9am–5pm. **Directions:** Drive across the bridge that heads north out of Plaza de Armas between Avenida de la República and Avenida Morelos, and turn right past the piers. **Bus:** "San Juan de Ulua" from the corner of Landero y Coss and Lerdo.

FORT OF SANTIAGO, at the corner of Rayón and Gómez Farías.

The fort was built in 1636 as part of the city fortifications against the pirates, but this bastion is all that's left of the old city walls. It's remarkable to see the type of construction that was used in those days: solid, to say the least. Traveling exhibits are often displayed here.

Admission: Free.
Open: Wed–Mon 10am–7pm. **Directions:** From Plaza de Armas, walk five blocks south on Independencia, then turn left (east) onto Rayón for two more blocks.

CITY MUSEUM, Zaragoza 397.

Recently restored, the 120-year-old City Museum building was converted into a museum years ago. Twelve rooms on two levels off the beautiful interior courtyard house archeological relics from pre-Columbian Gulf Coast sites. The collection is small compared to the museum in Jalapa or Villahermosa, but the displays are attractive and the setting lovely. The Indian cultures represented here are the Olmecs (a civilization of the Preclassic Period from Veracruz and Tabasco), the Totonacs (the Classic civilizations of Tajín and Zempoala, north of Veracruz and south of Tuxpan), and the Huastecas of the upper east coast. Several rooms display regional costumes and crafts.

Admission: 75¢.
Open: Tues–Sat 10am–6pm, Sun 10am–5pm. **Directions:** From the Palacio Municipal, walk 4½ blocks south on Zaragoza; the museum is on the right.

IN THEIR FOOTSTEPS

Antonio Lopez de Santa Anna (1794–1876) One of the most scorned characters in Mexican history, he was President of Mexico 11 times between 1833 and 1855. Audacious, pompous, and self absorbed, his outrageous exploits disgust and infuriate Mexicans even today, but none more than his role in losing half the territory of Mexico to the United States. Defeated and captured at the Battle of San Jacinto outside Houston, Texas, in 1836, among other things he agreed to allow Texas to be a separate republic and to mark the boundary at the Rio Grande. When the U.S. voted to annex Texas, it sparked the Mexican American War which the U.S. won in 1848. In The Treaty of Guadalupe which followed between the two nations, the U.S. paid Mexico 15 million dollars for Texas, New Mexico, California, Arizona, Nevada, Utah, and part of Colorado. Eventually Santa Anna was exiled, but returned two years before he died, poor, alone, and forgotten.

- **Birthplace:** Jalapa, Veracruz.
- **Residences:** Manga de Clavo, now the Museo Lencero, Jalapa, Veracruz.
- **Resting Place:** Guadalupe Cemetery behind the Basilica de Guadalupe, Mexico City.

MORE ATTRACTIONS

GUIDED BOAT TRIPS   Guided boat tours of the harbor (in Spanish only) pass many of the aforementioned sights, as well as many of the international tankers and ships docked in the port. Launches leave sporadically (depending on the weather) from the dock in front of the Hotel Emporio. The cost is $3.50 for adults and $1.75 for children ages 2 to 8, plus a tip for the guide.

BEACHES   Veracruz has beaches, but none of them is very good because the grayish sand is packed and the water tends to be shallow. There are points all along the waterfront downtown where people swim, but the nearest legitimate beach is at the **Villa del Mar,** an open-air terrace and palm-lined promenade at the southern end of town. To get there, take the "Playa V. del Mar" bus, which travels south on Zaragoza. The trip takes about 15 minutes.

About 5 miles south of Veracruz along the Gulf Coast is the beach of **Mocambo,** where boats, snorkeling equipment, and waterskis can be rented. There are large public pools at both Villa del Mar (entrance $1) and Mocambo (entrance $1.50) beaches.

A little farther past Mocambo at the mouth of the Jamapa River is **Boca del Río.** Both of these can easily be reached by taking the buses that leave every 30 minutes (on the hour and half hour) from the corner of Serdan and Zaragoza near the municipal fish market. The bus stop is marked with a sign COSTA VERDE or BOCA DEL RÍO; the trip takes 30 minutes.

✪ A CIGAR FACTORY   The southern part of Veracruz state, around San Andrés de los Tuxtlas, is tobacco-growing country. Leaves grown there are brought to **Puros La Prueba,** Lerdo 500 (tel. 32-2061), in Veracruz and hand-rolled into cigars (*puros*). Visitors are welcome to tour the factory Monday through Friday between 9 and 11:30am. From Plaza de Armas, walk one block north on Independencia and turn left onto Lerdo; walk three more blocks and it's on the left.

SHOPPING

The Veracruz **market** is one of the most interesting in Mexico—it's possible to find just about anything from caged parrots to live iguanas with tethered feet and tied tails. Curio-type shopping is centered in little shops along the **Malecón** opposite the Hotel Oriente and around the corner toward the pier. Here the shopping is more typical beachside junk—full shark's jaws, tacky shell art, ships in a jar, etc.

AN EXCURSION TO THE RUINS OF ZEMPOALA

About 25 miles north of Veracruz, on the way to Jalapa, are the ruins at Zempoala. Surrounded by lush foliage and rich agricultural land, but not quite as large as the site at Tajín, it's still noteworthy. Both Zempoala and Tajín are pre-Columbian ruins of the Totonacs. Both cities flourished during the Classic Period (A.D. 300–900), but Tajín was abandoned in the 13th century when the barbarian Chichimec warriors from the north invaded the city, while Zempoala continued to thrive and was the capital of the Totonacs during the Spanish Conquest. Zempoala means "place of the twenty waters," and was so named for the many rivers that converged at the site. When the conquerors saw Zempoala for the first time, the whitewashed stuccoed walls glimmered like silver in the tropical sun—which naturally drew the Spaniards closer. Though disappointed, the Spaniards still made friends and this city of Totonac Indians became Cortés's first allies. The Spaniards spent considerable time here, learning about the Totonacs' hatred of the Aztecs and about the Aztec Emperor Moctezuma before heading overland to the Aztec capital of Tenochtitlán.

Most buildings at Zempoala date from the 14th and 15th centuries—quite late for pre-Columbian structures. It was, however, inhabited before the time of Christ. The **Great Temple** resembles the Temple of the Sun in Tenochtitlán, probably a result of

Aztec influence during the 15th century. The **Temple of the Little Faces** has stuccoed faces set into the walls, along with hieroglyphs painted on the lower sections. The **Temple of Quetzalcoatl,** the feathered serpent god, is square, and that representing Ehecatl, god of the wind, is, as usual, round.

Admission to the archeological site is $3.50; it's open daily from 9am to 5pm. You can get there on buses of the second-class La Fuega line, which is located just behind the Veracruz first-class A.D.O. terminal; the trip takes 1½ hours, and is truly a beautiful trip through tropical forests. If you're going by car, driving time is 30 minutes north on Highway 180 to Cardel; the ruins of Zempoala are just north of Cardel.

SPECIAL EVENTS

✪ **Carnaval** (Mardi Gras) takes place 3 days before Ash Wednesday, and it's one of the best in Mexico. Visitors from the capital pack the streets and hotels; those without rooms live out of their cars. And the impassive Indians, who've walked a day's journey from their villages, spread their crafts on the sidewalks. Even the townspeople, normally attentive to their own affairs, join the crowds in the music-filled streets.

There are fabulous floats (in Spanish, *carros alegoricos,* "allegorical cars") made with true Mexican flair: bright colors, papier-mâché figures (even the Muppets showed up on one float), large flowers, and live entertainment. Groups from the neighboring villages don their peacock- and pheasant-feathered headdresses in preparation for the dances they will perform during the festivities. There are costumed Draculas and drag queens and girls in sparkling dresses parading down the streets. Most of the nonparade activities center in Plaza de Armas, and begin around noon, lasting well into the night.

If you plan to be in Veracruz for the 3 days of Carnaval, reserve hotel space months in advance, for everything's jammed full at this time. On the Sunday before Ash Wednesday the longest and most lavish of the Carnaval parades takes place on the Malecón. Parades on Monday and Tuesday are scaled-down versions of it (ask at the tourist office about the parade routes on Monday and Tuesday), and by Wednesday it's all over.

WHERE TO STAY

Veracruz has a good assortment of hotels, but be careful of noise in this town—auto and truck noise to be sure, but also marimba and mariachi noise, for this is a festive town that stays up until the early-morning hours.

As a rule of thumb, in the thick of the summer plan to pay for air conditioning if you stay on or very near Plaza de Armas. Hotels six or seven blocks away from the plaza are quieter, and you probably won't have to keep your windows closed as you would have to near the square.

High season is June, July, and August and December through March. *Note:* Veracruz is a favorite weekending spot for tourists from the capital city, who fill every means of transportation on Friday. The flood back up into the mountains is reversed on Sunday. Importers and exporters fill hotel rooms weekdays. Arrive as early in the week, and as early in the day, as possible. You will find a room in any case, but unless you arrive early, it may not be the room you want.

DOUBLES FOR LESS THAN $25

HOTEL VIGO, Av. Molina 56, Veracruz, Ver. 91700. Tel. 29/32-4529. 38 rms (all with bath).

$ Rates: $10 single; $12 double; $17 triple.

The Hotel Vigo has an excellent location facing the Malecón. It's ruled by an eagle-eyed dueña who waters the plants in the lobby with the same seriousness with which she evaluates all guests. This is a last-ditch choice if everything in the city is full.

All rooms in this three-story hotel are "budget green or blue," with decent beds and ceiling fans.

To get here from Plaza de Armas, walk two blocks east to the Malecón, then one long block south; the hotel faces the Malecón.

HOTEL CENTRAL, Av. Díaz Miron 1612, Veracruz, Ver. 91700. Tel. 29/37-2222. 122 rms (all with bath). TEL **Bus:** "Díaz Miron."
$ Rates: $13–$16 single; $14–$22 double.

Though hardly central as its name suggests, the Hotel Central, next to the bus station 20 blocks south of Plaza de Armas, is convenient for those arriving by bus. The marbled halls of the Central lead to rooms with tile showers and well-used furnishings. The 42 rooms on the higher end of the price scale come with air conditioning (the rest have fans). Air conditioning allows you to keep the louvered windows closed and thus the noise out. Because of noise, this place is for emergencies only.

HOTEL CONCHA DORADA, Lerdo de Tejada 77, Veracruz, Ver. 91700. Tel. 29/31-2996. 36 rms (all with bath). TEL
$ Rates: $14 single; $19 double with one bed, $27 double with two beds.

The Hotel Concha Dorada is on Plaza de Armas at the corner of Morelos, almost next door to the Hotel Colonial and Hotel Prendes. Prices are definitely based on the prime location. The clean, smallish rooms are somewhat dark and musty, and have tidy armoires suspended on the walls, tile floors, and overbed lights; 12 are air-conditioned and the rest have fans. The small inner rooms, while a bit claustrophobic, are bound to be quieter than those facing the plaza or street.

HOTEL SANTO DOMINGO, Serdan 451, Veracruz, Ver. 91700. Tel. 29/32-8285. 25 rms (all with bath).
$ Rates: $11 single; $19–$21 double.

The modern stucco building right across from the Hotel Amparo (below) is the recently remodeled Hotel Santo Domingo. The tiny rooms are clean, but barely sufficient for the single or double bed; 15 rooms come with air conditioners (the rest have fans), and 8 have TVs. The staff seems eager to help and even has a map of the city for guests. There's a bakery next door. *Note:* The building is five stories high and has no elevator; the trek to the top, with or without luggage, can be a killer!

To get here from Plaza de Armas, walk two blocks south to Serdan, turn left (east), and the hotel is two short blocks on the left.

HOTEL VILLA RICA, Camacho 165, Veracruz, Ver. 91700. Tel. 29/32-4854. 32 rms (all with bath).
$ Rates: $15 single; $20 double; $24 triple. Ask for lower rates on weekdays.

Right at the northern (beginning) end of Boulevard Manuel Ávila Camacho, the four-story Hotel Villa Rica attracts Mexican families and young people on vacation. Neat and tidy, it's a favorite because it's near the beach and not all that far from downtown. The rooms are small, simple, and clean, with fans and stenciled wall decoration.

To get here from the market, walk 10 blocks east toward the Gulf; the hotel is on corner of Figueroa and Doblado.

HOTEL AMPARO, Serdan 482, Veracruz, Ver. 91700. Tel. 29/32-2738. 64 rms (all with bath).
$ Rates: $10.50 single; $20 double. **Parking:** Free.
The Hotel Amparo has a tile facade, lobby, and corridors, as well as an inner court. All this tilework won't keep you cooler—you'll need the windows open here if it's hot, and the street noise can be fierce, not to mention the very loud band that plays nightly in the restaurant next door. Take a room in the back of the building. Rooms are simple and clean, with fans, old-but-decent furniture, one circular fluorescent light to share between the beds, and a full-length mirror.

You'll find the Amparo two blocks south on Independencia from Plaza de Armas, then left on Serdan one block; it's on the corner, on the right side.

HOTEL BALUARTE, Canal 265, Veracruz, Ver. 91700. Tel. 29/36-0844.
73 rms (all with bath). A/C TV TEL
$ Rates: $19 single; $22 double; $33–$38 suite. **Parking:** Free.

This is an excellent choice for comfort and value. Five stories tall, it's modern and attractive, and the location is quiet. The rooms are clean and some have carpeting. Guests can use the hotel's own parking lot across the street, and a small air-conditioned restaurant off the lobby is good for breakfast or a light meal.

To get here from Plaza de Armas, walk five blocks south on Independencia, then turn left (east) on Canal toward the Gulf for five blocks to 16 de Septiembre; the hotel is on the left, three blocks west of the Malecón.

HOTEL ORIENTE, Miguel Lerdo 20, Veracruz, Ver. 91700. Tel. 29/31-2615. 57 rms (all with bath). A/C TV TEL
$ Rates: $19 single; $25 double.

Near the northeast corner of Plaza de Armas (one block east on Lerdo) with the Malecón on one side, is the four-story Hotel Oriente. The Oriente's huge, bright lobby is rather bare, furnished only with a few plants and low seats. The freshly painted rooms facing Lerdo or the Malecón have balconies and are bright but noisy; interior rooms with windows high up on the wall are dark and quiet. Rooms are well-cared-for and there's a reading light between the beds, which may sag—check yours first.

DOUBLES FOR LESS THAN $40

HOTEL COLONIAL, Plaza de la Constitución, Veracruz, Ver. 91700. Tel. 29/32-0193. Fax 29/32-5393. 182 rms (all with bath). TV TEL
$ Rates: Older section, $24 single; $31 double. Newer section, $31 single; $38 double. **Parking:** $3.25 daily.

The pleasant and ideally located Hotel Colonial has two sections, the older with black-and-white television and centrally controlled air conditioning, and the newer one with color television and individually controlled air conditioning. Rooms are very comfortable and all the expensive hotel services are here, including private covered parking and an indoor swimming pool on the second floor. The Colonial faces Plaza de Armas; there's an entrance on the plaza and another back through the garage.

HOTEL MAR Y TIERRA, Av. Figueroa, Veracruz, Ver. 91700. Tel. 29/31-3866. 160 rms (all with bath). A/C TV TEL **Bus:** "Playa V. de Mar."
$ Rates: Old section, $20–$21 single; $33–$36 double. New section, $29–$31 single; $41–$46 double.

Rooms in the older section have tile floors and black-and-white TV. Those in the newer section are carpeted and have central air conditioning and color television. Many rooms have excellent views, so be sure to look before you lease.

HOTEL PRENDES, Independencia 1064, Veracruz, Ver. 91700. Tel. 29/31-0241. Fax 29/31-0491. 34 rms (all with bath). A/C TV TEL
$ Rates: $34 single or double.

The Hotel Prendes faces the action on Plaza de Armas, but the entrance is on Independencia. An elevator takes you to the three floors of nicely furnished and spacious guest rooms, all with good beds. Exterior rooms have balconies and wood-louvered French doors; interior rooms are much quieter, but, of course, have no windows.

HOTEL VILLA DEL MAR, Blvd. Camacho, Veracruz, Ver. 91700. Tel. 29/31-3366. Fax 29/36-1465. 80 rms, 23 bungalows (all with bath). A/C TV TEL
Bus: "Mocambo" or "Boca del Río" from Plaza de Armas.

$ Rates: $30–$40 single, double, or bungalow. **Parking:** Free.

⭐ ⓢ One of the first hotels on the beach, the pleasant Hotel Villa del Mar is a large, rambling, and completely remodeled place with modernized, air-conditioned rooms. Superior rooms are in the back and are larger and quieter than those in the main building on the Malecón. The 20 bungalows have ceiling fans and kitchens, and rent for the same price as a double. Rooms throughout have overbed reading lights. The hotel has its own private swimming pool, tennis courts, a grassy lawn dotted with palms, and a restaurant and bar. The public beach is just across the busy boulevard. The hotel is 30 blocks south of the plaza at the corner of Bartolomé de las Casas.

WORTH THE EXTRA BUCKS

HOTEL MOCAMBO, Boca del Río (Apdo. Postal 263), Veracruz, Ver. 91700. Tel. 29/37-1531, or 407/367-9306 in the U.S. Fax 29/37-1660. 124 rms, 3 suites (all with bath). A/C TV TEL **Bus:** "Mocambo" from Zaragoza and Serdan by La Prosperidad Restaurant. Buses stopping at the hotel's front gate go into town.

$ Rates: $56 single; $68 double; $80 triple. **Parking:** Free.

The Hotel Macambo, built in 1932, is 9 miles southeast of the town center, right on one of Veracruz's best stretches of beach. Another of the city's first and best hotels, it has hosted presidents, movie stars, and governors. Never out of fashion, it did get a little dated, but it has made a comeback into a comfortable, stylish hotel with the right amount of yesteryear still apparent. A palatial layout with 128 rooms, wide halls, terraces, sauna, Jacuzzi and four pools (two indoor), tennis court, sauna, Ping-Pong, and two restaurants, it's definitely a splurge hotel. All rooms have sea views, but room cost varies depending on view and the size of the room. At least 32 rooms have balconies, and 30 are carpeted. Inquire about the cheaper rooms, as that might not be the first price you are quoted. For its guests, the hotel pays for transportation from the airport in a colectivo van. Even if you don't decide to stay here, you might want to come out for a look, a meal, or a swim. The beach is public—you needn't stay at the hotel.

HOTEL EMPORIO, Malecón, Veracruz, Ver. 91700. Tel. 29/32-7520. Fax 29/31-2261. 202 rms, 17 suites (all with bath). A/C TV TEL

$ Rates: $75–$80 single or double; $104–$135 single or double suite. Ask for a 10%–15% discount (or more) during slow months. **Parking:** $2 daily.

The huge Hotel Emporio, facing the Malecón and harbor, eight blocks east of Plaza de Armas, has been a landmark hotel in Veracruz ever since the 1940s. Remodeled a few years ago, now it's a hotel of the 1990s with fashionably furnished rooms, purified drinking water from special taps in each room, a restaurant, enclosed garage, two huge swimming pools (one of them indoor), and a sun deck. More expensive rooms have whirlpool baths. One caveat: Exterior rooms facing the military academy on the Gulf side will be jolted awake mornings by bugle calls as the naval cadets march in unison and raise the flag.

WHERE TO EAT

On **Plaza de Armas,** the restaurants under the portals that surround it are the focus for eating, drinking, and merrymaking. While they're more expensive than places a few blocks away, the prices are not outrageous.

On Landero y Coss between Arista and Serdan is the **Municipal Fish Market,** its street level chock-a-block with little *ostionerías* (oyster bars) and shrimp stands. Take a stool, ask the price, and order a plate of boiled shrimp, fresh oysters, octopus, or conch. Look upstairs for even more good places.

El Fenix is a *panadería/pastelería* (bakery and pastry shop) which has a very wide selection of Mexican rolls and pastries for prices ranging from 5¢ to 50¢. You can't miss the assortment and the smell at Avenida 5 de Mayo no. 1362, at the corner of Arista. A similar establishment is the **Paris,** at 5 de Mayo and Molina.

MEALS FOR LESS THAN $5

GRAN CAFE DE LA PARROQUÍA, Av. Independencia. Tel. 32-2584.

Specialty: MEXICAN/COFFEE.

$ Prices: Breakfast $1.25–$3; coffee 60¢–80¢; main courses $6–$7; sandwiches $1.50–$4.50; antojitos $3–$4.

Open: Daily 7am–1am.

A trip to Veracruz without partaking of La Parroquía, cater-corner from Plaza de Armas, is like not eating beignets in New Orleans. Bright, bare, always busy, with music at any hour, this restaurant has its coffee ritual and customers who occupy the same tables at the same time every day. Some gather in groups; others nurse coffee and a newspaper for hours. Novice Parroquía patrons can catch onto the ritual quickly. Notice the two waiters scurrying about with big aluminum kettles. One kettle has thick black coffee while the other has hot milk. Order the rich cafe lechera and you'll get a few fingers of coffee in the bottom of your glass. Then pick up your spoon and bang on the glass to call the waiter with the milk—that spoon-banging is a constant chime in La Parroquía. If there's too much coffee in your glass, pour the excess in the waiter's coffee kettle, then he'll pour the milk. Known for coffee and pastries, the café's main courses are quite good too. So popular is La Parroquía, in fact, that there's another branch of the café on Paseo del Malecón just before the Hotel Emporio, open daily from 7pm to 1am. Take your newspaper and try out both.

RESTAURANT EL UNICO, Calle Trigueros 493. Tel. 31-6326.

Specialty: MEXICAN.

$ Prices: Main courses 75¢–$3.50; comida corrida $2; Mexican specialties 85¢–$2.50.

Open: Daily 7am–5:30pm.

Restaurant El Unico may not be the only place where you can get such a good, filling comida corrida, but it's one of the best. The orange decor is nothing much, of course, but the food is very tasty indeed. The señora will bring soup, rice, a choice of meat or fish, dessert, and coffee. The comida corrida is just about all anyone orders during the afternoon, but you can also get plates of fish or other dishes.

To get here from the Palacio Municipal, walk two blocks south, crossing Molina to the slightly diagonal Calle Trigueros; the restaurant is on the left at the corner of Serdan (there's no sign).

RESTAURANT MARTHITA, Calle Trigueros 43. Tel. 32-4428.

Specialty: MEXICAN.

$ Prices: Breakfast $2; main courses $3.50–$7.50; comida corrida $2.50.

Open: Daily 6am–9pm.

What a find! It's hard to beat this restaurant for good, inexpensive food with an inexpensive daily comida that comes with delicious black beans. Choices on the lunch special might include pollo puchero, which is a sort of chicken stew with corn choyote, garbanzos, and carrots. Besides the comida corrida there are several slightly more expensive plate lunches featuring such things as beef with potatoes or with fried bananas, beans, and totopos, or a quarter chicken with the above, plus salad or carne tampiqueño. Service is good even when the place is packed. To get here from the Palacio Municipal, walk two blocks south, crossing Molina to the slightly diagonal Calle Trigueros; the restaurant is on the right before Serdan. The manager told me that may move or open another location. This one is worth tracking down.

MEALS FOR LESS THAN $10

LA PAELLA, Zamora 138. Tel. 32-0322.

Specialty: SPANISH.

$ Prices: Breakfast $1–$3; main courses $3.50–$8; comida corrida $5.

Open: Daily 8:30am–10pm.

Devotees of Spanish food will undoubtedly like La Paella, where the four-course comida corrida is popular, but the portions are small. Three of the courses include such internationally known Spanish specialties as caldo gallego (a fish broth), paella valenciana, and tortilla española (a potato omelet). The walls are festooned with bullfight posters. La Paella is right at the southeast corner of Plaza de Armas near the tourism office—look for its tiled, very colonial facade.

PIZZARÍA PIRO PIRO DA LIUSEPPE, Arista 692. Tel. 31-6144.
Specialty: ITALIAN.
$ Prices: Pizza $8.50; spaghetti $5.75.
Open: Daily 9am–1am.

Piro Piro serves 18 different kinds of medium-size pizza, plus spaghetti eight ways. In a town full of seafood restaurants, it's a nice break. The little place is decorated like a cozy Italian *trattoria,* and is popular with students.

To get here from Plaza de Armas, walk three blocks south on Independencia and then turn left on Arista; the restaurant is on the right.

---

7. CÓRDOBA

187 miles SE of Mexico City; 80 miles SW of Veracruz;
11 miles E of Orizaba

GETTING THERE   By Train   Train no. 49 leaves Mexico City at 6:30 pm and arrives in Córdoba at 1:15 am; take a "Centro" into town.

El Jarocho leaves Mexico City at 9:15pm and arrives in Orizaba at 4:55am the following morning.

By Bus   There are nine buses a day from Veracruz. Local, school-bus-type buses from Orizaba leave from the open market at 9 Oriente and 14 Norte.

By Car   From Veracruz, take Highway 180 south out of town and go west on Highway 170 at the well-marked crossroads.

ESSENTIALS   The **telephone area code** is 271. The **climate** is humid and warm most of the year, with chilly winter mornings and evenings. The **State Tourist Office** is in Orizaba. Hotels have information in Córdoba.

DEPARTING   By Train   The **train station** (tel. 2-0913) is 13 blocks south of the town center on Avenida 11 between Calles 27 and 29. The ticket window is open from 8am to 1pm, 3 to 4:30pm, and 10pm to midnight. The *Jarocho* leaves at 4:55am and arrives at 7am in Veracruz.

By Bus   The small, clean **bus station** is two blocks north of the main plaza on Avenida 3 at Calle 4. Many buses originate here and it's possible to buy tickets a day or so in advance. To Jalapa five buses daily use the short scenic route through Huatusco. Going south to the region of Los Tuxtlas or Lake Catemaco there are four buses. To Villahermosa there are 11; to Cancún, 1; to Campeche and Mérida, 2. And heading west to Mexico City there are 15 daily buses, and to Puebla, 13 *de paso* and 5 *locales.*

This bustling city (alt. 3,000 ft.; pop. 151,000) was founded by Viceroy Diego Fernández de Córdoba in 1618 and a delightful colonial presence makes Córdoba a pleasant stop along the way. With its huge market district, its imposing cathedral (which dates from 1688) with a famous set of bells, and its pretty main square, you can't go wrong. It's a center for Mexico's sugar and coffee industry, several brands of which proudly claim origin in the verdant hills surrounding the town. Sugarcane cutting takes place between December and May when the highways become clogged with cane-laden trucks which scatter cane debris along the roadway. In the distance plumes of smoke billow from tall chimneys on nearby processing haciendas. Prime activity for the traveler in Córdoba is shopping in the huge regional market, people-watching, coffee or cocktail drinking, and dining on the main square.

ORIENTATION

ARRIVING   The train station is 13 blocks south of the town center. Buses marked "centro" go to town from the train station. If you arrive by bus, go out the Ave. 3 door of the station, turn right and the main plaza is two blocks straight ahead.

WHAT TO SEE & DO

General Augustín Iturbide signed Mexico's Act of Independence at the Hotel Zevallos on the main square. Today it's a restaurant with dining under the portals facing the shady plaza, and a prime spot for lolling and people-watching.

Córdoba has one of the most tidy and fascinating **markets** in the country, with baskets, pottery, piles of dried chiles and bread, pumpkins, dried fish, baskets of beans, links of sausage, piñatas, bundles of banana leaves, piloncillo brown sugar cones, medicinal plants, huaraches, hats, bolts of fabric, and banks of fresh flowers for which the region is famous. The market district starts four blocks west of the central plaza and runs four blocks south.

WHERE TO STAY

HOTEL VIRREYNAL, Av. 1 and Calle 5, Córdoba, Ver. 94500. Tel. 271/2-2377. 66 rms (all with bath). TV TEL
$ Rates: $18 single; $22 double. **Parking:** Free, 1½ blocks away.
The facade is baroque, the lobby brilliant with tiles, but the three floors of rooms with fans are modern and comfortable—providing you don't get a room in the front, where the traffic noise and the famous church bells can disturb your sleep. The Virreynal has an excellent restaurant, attractively old-fashioned with wood furniture and white tablecloths. The ample comida corrida will satisfy a hungry appetite. It's served individually from soup tureens and large platters by waiters who bustle back and forth. The hotel is opposite the cathedral and the main square.

WHERE TO EAT

The arcades of the main plaza, from the portal of the Hotel Zevallos to the Hotel Virreynal, are lined with inviting indoor/outdoor café-restaurants, each having a different character and menu.

RESTAURANT & CAFE PARROQUÍA, Av. 1 and Calle 1, Portal Zevallos. Tel. 2-3752.
Specialty: MEXICAN.
$ Prices: Breakfast $1–$2; main courses $3.50–$8.50; antojitos $2–$4; sandwiches $1.50; coffee with milk or cappuccino 65¢.
Open: Daily 8am–midnight.
The restaurant attracts a general mix of people and offers a varied menu. The end of the arcade on the east side of the plaza is a good vantage point for ogling the other cafés and the square while having a meal or drink. It's a good place for an early breakfast.

8. ORIZABA

147 miles SE of Mexico City, 11 miles W of Córdoba,
90 miles SW of Veracruz.

GETTING THERE   By Train   *El Jarocho* leaves Mexico City at 9:15pm and arrives in Orizaba at 4:05am the following morning. Taxis meet each train.

By Bus   From Veracruz, 14 buses daily to go to Orizaba. From Córdoba, take the Autopista bus 1600. This bus discharges passengers at the open market at the corner of 9 Oriente and 14 Norte. Town is 5 blocks ahead on 9 Oriente; turn left at 2 Oriente by the enclosed market.

By Car   From Veracruz, take Highway 180 south out of town, then go west on Highway 170 at the well-marked crossroads.

ESSENTIALS   The **telephone area code** is 272. The **City Tourist Office** (tel. 272/5-1980) was behind the Palacio Municipal when I checked, but they were planning to move, which may have occurred by the time you arrive. The big **market days** are Wednesday and Saturday.

Famous as a manufacturing city, Orizaba, Veracruz (alt. 4,000 ft.; pop. 114,000), sits at the foot of Mexico's highest mountain, Citlaltepetl, or Pico de Orizaba (18,275 ft.), and has a pleasant, cool climate that does little to encourage consumption of its best-known product: various brands of Moctezuma beer. It's a clean, busy city not quite as laid-back as Córdoba, but appealing nonetheless with a colonial town center, well-ordered traffic, and a terrific enclosed market one block west of the central plaza.

WHAT TO SEE & DO

Maximilian and Carlotta had a hacienda on the outskirts of town (now ruined and hardly worth seeing), but the major architectural attraction these days is the fanciful **Palacio Municipal.** The style might be called Victorian gingerbread, but the construction is all steel. Fabricated in Belgium during the 1800s, it was later taken apart, shipped across the Atlantic, and bolted together here in Orizaba. It was scheduled for complete renovation starting in 1991, so it may be in a state of disrepair for some time, but it's a masterpiece no matter what the condition.

Many of the attractions here center on the availability of cold, clear water like **Laguna de Nogales** or **Ojo de Agua** or the hydroelectric plants.

Two other attractions may have more appeal. The **Moctezuma Brewery** is open for tours Monday through Friday from 10am to noon and 4:30 to 5:30pm. Call first for an appointment (tel. 5-3033, ext. 165 or 279).

The second attraction is Mexico's highest mountain, Orizaba, with the Nahuatl name of **Citlaltepetl.** From Orizaba, AU (Autotransportes Unidos) buses go to Tlachichuca. It's possible to hire a Jeep and driver in Tlachichuca for $25 to $40 to drive up to four people to the 14,000-foot-plus point—a rare opportunity for us normally earthbound souls to do some very high climbing. Remember that the summit is covered with snow year round. The best time to climb is from the middle of November through the middle of January.

WHERE TO STAY & EAT

HOTEL ARIES, 6 Oriente no. 265, Orizaba, Ver. 94340. Tel. 272/5-3699. 42 rms (all with bath). TV TEL
$ Rates: $19 single; $21 double.
Should you arrive by ADO bus in Orizaba, the Hotel Aries is a good choice as it's only 2½ blocks from the bus station. There's a good restaurant and bar on the ground floor. The modernized rooms are comfortable, carpeted, and clean. Check your bed for firmness.

---

9. LAKE CATEMACO & LOS TUXTLAS

355 miles SE of Mexico City; 99 miles SE of Veracruz

GETTING THERE   By Bus   From Veracruz, there are approximately 18 daily departures, but most of these will be going only as far as the cigar-making town of San Andrés de los Tuxtlas, 7 miles short of Catemaco. Five first-class buses a day go directly to Catemaco from Veracruz, however, and you should try for one of these. Otherwise, go to San Andrés de los Tuxtlas, and catch a local bus for the last short leg, or hire a taxi (bargain like mad—it shouldn't cost more than $5).

From Orizaba, there are four buses daily to San Andrés.

By Car Highway 180 from either Veracruz or Villhermosa goes to Catemaco.

ESSENTIALS The **telephone area code** is 294. As for the **climate,** Lake Catemaco is a balmy oasis in a region where the rule is muggy heat. Free from extremes of heat and cold, it's more like year-round eternal spring. It's hottest March through May. A jacket is handy December through February. Always be prepared for rain—there are only 150 days of sun.

DEPARTING By Bus The first-class **ADO bus station** in Catemaco is located behind the church, on the corner of Aldama and Bravo. The lake is a block or so behind the station, the cathedral and main plaza are left up the hill, the Hotel Koniapan and the southern end of town facing the lake are to the right. There is service to Puebla, Villhermosa, and Jalapa (one a day), San Andrés de los Tuxtlas and Veracruz (four a day), Mexico City (two), and Alvarado (three). Reserve tickets as far in advance as possible.

There is second-class service from Catemaco as well on **Autotransportes Los Tuxtlas.** Buses make the run to Veracruz throughout the day, for not much less than the more comfortable ADO buses. And they go to San Andrés and Santiago de los Tuxtlas every 10 minutes from midnight to 6pm. The terminal is located on Calle Cuauhtémoc (though this won't help you much, as the streets aren't marked). From the plaza, walking away from the cathedral, take the street that passes the Hotel Brisas on the left and the Hotel Acuario on the right. When the road forks, bear left. You'll be able to see and hear the buses from here.

The beautiful and interesting region around Lake Catemaco (alt, 1,050 ft.; pop. 41,000), includes the two Tuxtlas—San Andrés Tuxtla and Santiago Tuxtla— making an intriguing touristic trio centered on lakeside nature, tobacco, and the Olmec culture. About 6½ miles long and almost 5 miles wide, **Lake Catemaco,** dotted with islands, was formed by the eruption of volcanoes long ago and is one of the most beautiful lakes in Mexico. Ringed by lush forested mountains and two volcanoes, it resembles Lake Atitlan in Guatemala. At least 556 species of birds live or migrate here. Between Catemaco and **San Andrés Tuxtla** is Veracruz tobacco country, with broad green fields awash with the tall leggy plant between July and October and dotted with enormous barns for drying the aromatic leaves, and smaller facilities where the leaves are sorted and sold. Just over the mountain from San Andrés is **Santiago Tuxtla,** a handsome colonial town with one of the most beautiful palm-studded plazas in Mexico. On one side of the plaza is the Museo Regional with Olmec artifacts, and the site Museum of Tres Zapotes is 12 miles away. All are only a few miles from undeveloped beaches on the Gulf of Mexico and within exploring distance of the 500-acre Balzapotes Scientific Station northeast on the coast.

WHAT TO SEE & DO

The lake region is located between the only mountains on the steaming coastal plain that reaches from Tampico to Yucatán. Two volcanic peaks—San Martín and Santa Marta—are in the neighborhood of 7,000 feet. North of Catemaco is Monte Cerro Blanco, where it is rumored that wizards (*brujos*) meet each March. Brujos put out signs in Catemaco the way doctors do in other towns.

Because this was once the site of a pre-Hispanic village, many artifacts have been found in the area. Townsfolk who were children when Catemaco's streets were prepared for paving remember playing with pre-Hispanic artifacts unearthed by bulldozers. Isla Agaltepec, one of four large islands in the lake, was an Olmec ceremonial site. The Catemaco area is richly endowed with bird and animal life. The 556 varieties of migratory and local bird life are apparent upon even a brief walk along the lake. More than 1,000 types of bromeliads have been identified in the region. Many hunters in the area supplement their diets by taking squirrels, armadillos, iguanas, and wild pigs.

If you're sports-minded, boats are available for waterskiing or fishing. If sightseeing is your preference, you can just about choose the trip to fit your budget.

BOAT TRIPS You can take a tour of the lake by boat, passing the black-sand lake beaches, the river, a shrine honoring the local miraculous Virgin, numerous flocks of white herons, a mineral spring called Arroyo Agrio (sour) for its acid content, and another called Coyame—you may have seen its water bottled and on your dinner table. But the most interesting part are the two **monkey islands.** In an experiment to readapt monkeys to the wild, the University of Veracruz brought several families of macaco monkeys from Thailand to two small islands on the lake. One group has learned to swim between the two islands while the other group has not. Because the university sends out food each day, the monkeys line up in hopeful expectation for all approaching boats; have your cameras ready, for as soon as they discover there's no food, they disperse.

In April and May hundreds of **herons** nest on a tiny island called Isla de las Garzas (Heron Island) and the tour boats pass by for a look.

Another stop may be **Nanciyaga,** a rather touristy private nature reserve. Guides lead you across a jungle stream, wind through the woods to a mud-facial house (optional), then back by a pond reserved for nesting crocodiles (it's rather defunct since something was making the crocs sick).

Cost for the 1½-hour lake tour is about $20 per boatload of up to six people. The **Union Permisionaría boat cooperative** is on the Malecón right below the zócalo near La Luna restaurant. Look for posted prices. Ask for "Chovi," who doesn't speak English, but gives a good boat tour.

BEACHES The cheapest way to get to two volcanic sand beaches—**Playa Azul** and **Playa Hermosa**—is by bus. Take the "Montepio" bus (one every 1½ hours) from the second-class bus terminal, or look for the "La Margarita" bus from the town square (though the latter only runs about three times a day). Or you can walk or hitch the 2km (1¼ miles). Be forewarned that these "beaches" are more aptly described as narrow spits of dirt. For real beaches, you have to go to the ocean (reached by the "Montepio" bus in about 45 minutes). The "La Marguarita" bus goes out to the Cuetzalapan River, on the opposite side of the lake, known for its cold transparently clear waters, flowers, bird life, and interesting rock formations.

SPECIAL EVENTS

The El Carmen Church on the zócalo is visited by thousands of pilgrims each year around July 16, the **Feast of El Carmen.** Look for testimonial drawings around the portals. The interior walls are stenciled with a golden-yellow and white floral pattern, while the ceiling is laced with gilded arches. There's also a blessing of the fleet during the festival and decorated boats sail up and down the harbor giving free rides.

WHERE TO STAY

The high season in this area is July, August, Christmas, and Easter week.

POSADA [MOTEL] KONIAPAN, Malecón and Revolución, Catemaco, Ver. 95870. Tel. 294/3-0063. 21 rms (all with bath). TEL
$ Rates: $17 single or double with fan, $21 single or double with air conditioning. **Parking:** Free.

My favorite place to stay in Catemaco is the Posada Koniapan, right on the lakeshore. Bright, and clean, the Koniapan has window screens, small tile bathrooms, and neocolonial furniture. There's a clean swimming pool in the front yard; sometimes an open-air restaurant next to it is open and serving. Rooms have two double beds, and those upstairs have a private balcony and a view of the lake. Good value. Room prices may be a bit higher in July and August when Catemaco is usually busy.

To get here from the ADO bus station, turn right out the front door and go straight for two blocks; the hotel is on the right facing the lake.

HOTEL CATEMACO, Carranza 8, Catemaco, Ver. 95870. Tel. 294/3-0203 or 3-0045. 19 rms (all with bath). A/C TV
$ Rates: $28 single; $33 double. **Parking:** Free.

The clean Hotel Catemaco is located right on the plaza, has a good-sized pool out back and long-distance service, and features Formica furniture, tile floors, two double beds with overbed lights, and air conditioning, which accounts for its rather high prices. It can't fill up at these Mexico City rates, so try offering a lower price and see if they'll go for it.

HOTEL LOS ARCOS, Madero 7, Catemaco, Ver. 95870. Tel. 294/3-0003. 35 rms (all with bath).
$ Rates: $13.50 single; $17 double. **Parking:** Free.

The three-story Hotel Los Arcos has nice, well-kept rooms, with red-tile floors, louvered glass windows, and ceiling fans, but there's good cross-ventilation too; 10 rooms come with TVs. The motel-style walkways to the rooms, which also serve as balconies, have either street or lake views.

To get here from the ADO bus station, walk left out the front door, go around the church, and walk one block past it.

MOTEL PLAYA AZUL, Carretera Sontecomapan km 2, Catemaco, Ver. 95870. Tel. 294/3-0041 or 3-0042. 80 rms (all with bath).
$ Rates: $26–$27 single; $32–$33 double; $37–$43 triple.

The Motel Playa Azul, two miles west along the lake, has two ambiences. Weekdays it's quiet enough to write a novel, but weekends the disco shakes the palm fronds. The setting is beautiful, right on the shores of the lake, with a pool and a restaurant. Rooms have tile floors, ruffled nylon bedspreads, and Formica furniture. The higher prices are for air conditioning (40 rooms); the other rooms have fans.

WHERE TO EAT

Although the lake is famed for its whitefish (mojarra), gastronomy is not always of the highest quality in Catemaco. Besides whitefish, smoked pork is a specialty and is quite good. Pelliscadas are salted tortillas fried in lard, and local clams are made into ceviche.

If the **street market** is in operation around the Hotel Los Arcos, little cookshops will be set up throughout. Here's the cheapest and most colorful place to sample the lake's mojarra, or any of a dozen other sorts of rough-and-ready fare. Prices are not set, and will depend on how the fishing season's going, how much money has been made that day, and how prosperous you seem to be. (Ask the price before you order!)

HOTEL CATEMACO, Carranza 8. Tel. 3-0203 or 3-0045.
Specialty: MEXICAN.
$ Prices: Main courses $3.50–$12.50; sandwiches $3.50; soup $1.65.
Open: Daily 8am–11pm.

Perhaps the best all-around restaurant, good for breakfast, lunch, and dinner, is indoor or outdoor dining at the Hotel Catemaco. A view of the town's busy plaza adds to the pleasant, most refined decor in town. The specialty is steak, and to help you know which cut to order, there's a lighted diagram of a cow with cuts marked in Spanish and English.

LA OLA, Malecón. Tel. 3-0010.
Specialty: MEXICAN.
$ Prices: Breakfast $2–$3.50; seafood $3–$10.50; meat dishes $5–$6.
Open: Daily 7am–9pm.

La Ola, about halfway down on the Malecón, is my favorite lakeside restaurant with its thatched roof and fish-net decorations. A beautiful view adds to the tranquil atmosphere. In the evening concerts of jarocho (Veracruz-style) guitar music are sometimes offered. The fixed-price lunch or dinner at La Ola is offered whenever the custom warrants, which it usually does in summer and on holiday weekends. Otherwise, try barbecued chicken or the famous whitefish (mojarra) of the lake.

LA LUNA, Malecón. Tel. 3-0050.
Specialty: MEXICAN.
$ Prices: Breakfast $2.50–$3.50; main courses $6–$11.

Open: Daily 8am–9pm.

Across the street from La Ola about halfway down on the landward side of the Malécon, facing the lake, La Luna has a more formal atmosphere and a similar menu, though the prices are the same despite the lack of view. A good-sized mojarra cooked one of eight different ways goes for $6.

EASY EXCURSIONS FROM CATEMACO

SAN ANDRÉS TUXTLA

Seven miles northwest of Catemaco, San Andrés Tuxtla (alt. 1,083 ft.; pop. 125,000) is the administrative center of the region. Along the way you'll pass fields of tobacco between July and October, alternated with corn in the off-months. About halfway between Catemaco and San Andrés, at Sihuapan, you'll see signs to **El Salto Eyipantla,** a 150-foot waterfall with 244 steps leading down to it. There's no charge to enter the area and there's a nice restaurant at the top of the stairs.

The town of **Sihuapan** thrives on the tobacco industry. If you pass through, ask for directions to the **"fabrica de tobacco,"** an unmarked tobacco warehouse on your right (if coming from the falls). Depending on the time of year, visitors can usually watch tobacco sorters at work, a fascinating, labor-intensive industry.

San Andrés, a lovely prosperous town with an interesting mix of colonial, Caribbean, and 1960s architecture, is centered around a pretty town square with a frilly white-iron kiosk and church. If you arrive by bus, you'll be by the market packed with locally grown fruits. The town center is up the hill.

What to See & Do

For a fascinating hour, take a tour of the **Te Amo Puro Factory** (*puros* are cigars) and see how the leaves are sorted and graded, then formed by hand into cigars in a gigantic room full of workers, then cured, dried, and packed in wooden boxes. Most of these cigars are exported to the U.S. under brand names of New York, Matacan, Te Amo, and Triunfo. The factory is a couple of blocks from the main plaza. Tours are available Monday through Friday from 9:45am to 2pm and 4 to 6pm. To get there from the main plaza, walk east on Constitución (the church will be on your right) past the PM STEEL sign also on the right, one block to the corner of Pino Suárez. Turn left and the small TE AMO sign is on the left. Tell the guard you'd like a tour.

San Andrés is such a clean, inviting town that you may want to do what the locals do: Pull up a chair, indoors or out, at the Hotel del Parque, cater-corner from the main plaza, order café con leche, and watch the town saunter by.

Where to Stay & Eat

HOTEL DEL PARQUE, Madero 5, San Andrés Tuxtla, Ver. Tel. 294/2-0198. Fax 294/2-3050. 39 rms A/C TV TEL
$ Rates: $26 single; $33 double; $40 triple. **Parking:** Free.

⭐ For being right in the heart of things, there's no better place than the Hotel del Parque, cater-corner from the main plaza, a 1960s-style hotel with comfortable rooms and pleasant management.

The restaurant, which is both indoors and outdoors under the portals facing the street, is the social center of downtown San Andrés. The menu has a wide assortment of inexpensive Mexican dishes including regional specialties of enfrijoladas with chicken, fried bananas with black beans, and dishes from the Yucatán and Oaxaca. Coffee comes six ways, all inexpensive, and there's an extensive cocktail list.

SANTIAGO TUXTLA

Some 13 miles from Lake Catemaco and 8 miles from San Andrés Tuxtla, Santiago Tuxtla (alt. 855 ft.; pop 50,000) is reached by a windy drive over hill and dale, passing herds of grazing cattle and green rolling hills cultivated in sugarcane, corn, oranges, bananas, and mangos, much of it for sale in neatly arranged roadside stands.

The **Regional Museum of Anthropology,** facing the main square, is the reason most tourists seek out this picturesque town. Besides a small, but important, selection of mostly Olmec artifacts, there are examples from the Huasteca and Totonac cultures. It's open Tuesday through Sunday from 9am to 5pm. Admission is $2.75.

On the plaza opposite the museum is a 45-ton **Olmec head** with a scowling face. The **market,** next to the museum, has several good small cookshops and there's a hotel with a nice restaurant and bar across the street.

EN ROUTE TO VILLAHERMOSA

If your destination is the Yucatán or San Cristóbal de las Casas, along the Gulf Coast you'll take Highway 180 past Coatzacoalcos to Villahermosa. This is the route to the Yucatán. From Villahermosa buses cross the mountains on Highway 195 to Tuxtla Gutiérrez and San Cristóbal. There is no reason to travel via Highway 185 which traverses the Isthmus of Tehuantepec, for the isthmus is flat, unscenic, full of traffic, and hot and muggy.

CHAPTER 19

TABASCO & CHIAPAS

1. VILLAHERMOSA
- WHAT'S SPECIAL ABOUT TABASCO & CHIAPAS
2. PALENQUE
3. SAN CRISTÓBAL DE LAS CASAS
4. TUXTLA GUTIÉRREZ

These neighbor states of Tabasco and Chiapas span the distance from the Gulf of Mexico to the Pacific Ocean. Tabasco and it's cities, because of the oil trade along its coast, are more affected by the modern world than is Chiapas, which is hemmed in by majestic mountains and an undeveloped coast. Besides oil, Tabasco is noted for its production of tabacco and cacao. Chiapas produces some of the best coffee in Mexico. Both states boast important indigenous influences. The famous Olmec site of La Venta is in Tabasco state and museums in Villahermosa hold their sculptural remains, while numerous Indian groups in the state still speak Maya-related languages. Villahermosa, Tabasco, is surrounded by indigenous villages each with language, cultural, and craft traditions that are unique in Mexico, and is a main route to the ruins of Palenque and an important gateway to San Cristobal de las Casas, Chiapas.

SEEING TABASCO & CHIAPAS

There are several ways to see the Tabasco-Chiapas region. Some people arrive at Villahermosa and go inland by bus to Palenque and San Cristóbal and out at Tuxtla Gutiérrez. This works well if you're coming from or going to Oaxaca, since commuter planes now connect Tuxtla and Oaxaca, and buses frequently make the long trip. Others arrive from the opposite direction via Tuxtla Gutiérrez, then on to San Cristóbal, Palenque, and Villahermosa. This works well if your ultimate destination is the Yucatán peninsula. Presently airports at both San Cristóbal and Palenque are not operating and both cities use airports nearby.

It's easy to discover that Palenque and San Cristóbal de las Casas are the two stellar attractions here. For apportioning time, spend 1 day in Villahermosa, no less than 1 day (2 nights) at Palenque, and no less than 3 days (4 nights) in San Cristóbal.

1. VILLAHERMOSA

89 miles E of Palenque, 100 miles S of Campeche,
293 miles S of San Cristóbal de las Casas

GETTING THERE   By Plane   Mexicana flies to Villahermosa from Mexico City, Guadalajara, Mérida, Oaxaca, Tuxtla Gutiérrez, and several U.S. gateways. **Aeroméxico** flies from Mexico City, Guadalajara, Mérida, Acapulco, and U.S. gateways. **Aviacsa** flies from Mérida, Mexico City, Tuxtla Gutiérrez, and Oaxaca. **AeroLitoral,** another regional airline, flies from Tampico, Minatitlán, Ciudad

WHAT'S SPECIAL ABOUT TABASCO & CHIAPAS

Outstanding Museums

☐ La Venta Museum of Archeology and Carlos Pellicer Regional Museum of Anthropology, in Villahermosa, two of the country's top museums.

Outstanding Zoo

☐ Miguel Alvarez del Toro Zoo, in Tuxtla Gutiérrez, one of the best zoos in Mexico.

Archeological Sites

☐ Palenque, in a lush tropical setting, with the only pyramid in Mexico built specifically as a tomb.

☐ Bonampak, where magnificent murals depict the greatest battle of pre-Hispanic Mexico.

☐ Comalcalco, near Villahermosa, the only pre-Hispanic center constructed with kilned brick.

☐ Yaxchilán, an important jungle Maya ceremonial site on the Usumacinta River, reached by boat.

Culture

☐ Eight Indian groups, each with distinctive traditions and two different-but-related Maya languages, in Chiapas.

☐ Variations of the rich Maya culture around San Cristóbal de las Casas, Chiapas.

Shopping

☐ San Cristóbal de las Casas, one of the best villages in Mexico for shopping, with its weavers, potters, and leather workers.

Events and Festivals

☐ Carnaval in Chamula, near San Cristóbal, includes the ceremonial custom of running on hot embers.

Carmen, and Monterrey. **AeroCaribe** flies from Villahermosa, Ciudad del Carmen, Tuxtla Gutiérrez, and Mérida.

By Train   The train does connect Mexico City with Villahermosa—or rather with Teapa, an hour by bus from Villahermosa. But everyone says it's a terrible way to travel—dirty, uncomfortable, and dangerous, with only second-class accommodations.

By Bus   The first-class **Omnibus Cristóbal Colón** and **ADO** buses arrive from Tuxtla Gutiérrez, San Cristóbal de las Casas, Tapachula, Oaxaca, and Mexico City; the second-class buses on **Sureste** arrive from Tuxtla, Campeche, and Mérida.

By Car   At the outset, let me warn you not to drive the road between Villahermosa and Chetumal. Besides being isolated, you're in for hundreds of kilometers of potholes, washed-away pavement, and dangerous dips. I've been told that it has been fixed, but I wonder for how long. I'll never drive it again.

Daytime parking in downtown Villahermosa can be difficult, but there are several parking lots near the hotels recommended here; I suggest using one that's guarded around the clock.

ESSENTIALS   The **area code** is 913. **American Express** is represented by Turismo Nieves, Boulevard Simon Sarlat 202 (tel. 913/2-0604 or 2-4390; fax 913/2-5130.

DEPARTING   By Plane   The **Mexicana** ticket office is inconveniently located across from the huge Tabasco 2000 complex and the Palacio Municipal, on Avenida de Los Ríos at Avenida Planeterio (tel. 4-1675 or 3-5487), or at the airport (tel.

2-1164). **Aeroméxico** is at Plaza CICOM between the Teatro Esperanza Iris and the Museo Carlos Pellicer (tel. 2-1164 or 4-1675, or airport 2-0904).

Aviación de Chiapas (Aviacsa) is represented by Viajes Tabasco, Madero 718 (tel. 4-0978 or 2-5318). Aviacsa flies direct to Mérida, Mexico City, Tuxtla Gutiérrez, and Oaxaca. The planes are new, hold 90 passengers, and are far more comfortable than those of the other regional carriers.

AeroLitoral, at the airport (tel. 4-3614), flies to Tampico, Minatitlán, Ciudad del Carmen, and Monterrey. **AeroCaribe,** Mina 1202, near the corner of Paseo Tabasco (tel. 4-3017 or 4-3202), closes the office between 2 and 4:30pm. It's the regional carrier flying between Villahermosa, Ciudad del Carmen, Tuxtla Gutiérrez, and Mérida, with connections to Cancún, Cozumel, Chetumal, and Chichén-Itzá. AeroCaribe tickets are often sold in conjunction with Mexicana tickets.

By Train There's a **Ferrocariles Unidos del Sureste** (tel. 913/2-0165) station in Teapa, an hour by bus from Villahermosa. The one train daily to Mexico City at 7pm is not recommended (see "Getting There," above).

By Bus There are two bus stations in Villahermosa about three blocks apart from each other. The **first-class ADO station** (tel. 2-1226 or 2-8900) is at Mina and Merino, three blocks off Highway 180. The station has a tourist-assistance desk open Monday through Friday from 7am to 9pm and on Saturday from 7am to 1pm (but the main tourist center is much better equipped to assist you).

Buses **to Palenque** leave from the first-class station. Tickets for most destinations (including Palenque) are sold at the first-class ADO station; the bus to Palenque leaves at 4:30, 6, 6:20, and 8am, and 1:30, 4:30, and 6pm.

Omnibus Cristóbal Colón (tel. 2-2937; fax 5/542-3095 in Mexico City) sells tickets to Tuxtla Gutiérrez, San Cristóbal de las Casas, Tapachula, Oaxaca, and Mexico City from a small corner office in the ADO station; you can also order tickets by phone 24 hours in advance and have them delivered. Daily Cristóbal Colón buses ply the route from the tropical savannahs into the rugged Chiapan mountains, and the trip will take around 8 hours.

The **Central Camionera de Segunda Clase** (second-class bus station) is on Highway 180/186, near the traffic circle bearing a statue of a fisherman. It's one of the sleaziest stations in Mexico. From the second-class bus station you can ride **Sureste del Caribe** to Tuxtla and Campeche at 6am, 11am, 3pm, and 7pm; and to Mérida four times daily. **Servicio Somellera** goes to Comalcalco every 30 minutes. **Autobuses Unidos de Tabasco** travels to Veracruz. Be forewarned that the bus station is horrid, and the buses even worse.

By Car Paved Highway 195 connects the Tabascan capital of Villahermosa with Tuxtla Gutiérrez, the capital of the state of Chiapas. Between Villahermosa and San Cristóbal de las Casas, the road, although paved, may be severely potholed in places. Sometimes a portion of the roadway caves in and traffic slows to one lane to avoid it. These conditions occur more frequently during the rainy season between May and October. The trip to San Cristóbal takes a minimum of 10 hours from Villahermosa. The paved, mountainous (and very curvy) road between San Cristóbal and Tuxtla is in good condition and the trip takes about 1½ hours.

The road to Palenque is a good one and the drive should take about 2 hours (3 hours by bus).

Villahermosa (pop. 500,000), the capital of the state of Tabasco, is right at the center of Mexico's oil boom, and seems to grow in size every day. Oil wealth has helped transform this previously dowdy provincial town into an attractive and obviously prosperous modern city.

The boom has brought difficulties as well, and the major one you'll encounter is a shortage of reasonably priced, clean, quiet hotel rooms. Historically, the hotels were able to charge whatever they wanted for rooms without bothering much about maintenance or service—the oilmen had money and were willing to pay high tabs for luxury at the Hyatt and Holiday Inn (both worth a visit if you find your lodgings too humble), and high tabs elsewhere as well since the demand for rooms exceeded the supply. Budget travelers will find themselves in a mid-range of hotels with varying character and clientele.

Prosperity benefited Villahermosa with a beautiful park surrounding the Parque Museo La Venta; a high-class business, residence, and hotel development called Tabasco 2000, with its gleaming office buildings, convention center, golf course, and exclusive residences; the CICOM development, with its theaters and the Museo Regional de Antropología Carlos Pellicer Camara; and the pedestrian mall along Avenida Benito Juárez. You really shouldn't miss the fabulous Parque La Venta, which contains the Olmec remains found at La Venta, west of Villahermosa.

ORIENTATION

ARRIVING   Coming in from Villahermosa's **airport,** which is 6½ miles east of town, you'll cross a bridge over the Río Grijalva and turn left to reach downtown. The airport minibuses charge $2.50; taxis range from $5 to nearly $10, depending on demand and time of day. Don't linger in the terminal and expect a minibus to still be at the curb when you're ready.

Buses marked "Mercado–C. Camionera" or simply "Centro" leave frequently from the **bus station** for the center of town. A taxi from either bus station to downtown hotels will cost about $2.

INFORMATION   The best source of information is the **State Tourism Office** in the Tabasco 2000 complex, Paseo Tabasco 1504, on the second floor in the SEFICOT building, Centro Administrativo del Gobierno (tel. 5-0693 or 5-0694). It's inconveniently located, opposite the Liverpool Department store and enclosed shopping center. It's open Monday through Friday from 9am to 3pm and 6 to 8pm, and on Saturday from 9am to 1pm.

There are three other branches: **at the airport,** staffed Monday through Saturday between 7am and 9pm; **at the ADO bus station,** open the same hours; and **at La Venta Park,** open Monday through Saturday from 8am to 3pm. They can supply rates and telephone numbers for all the city's hotels as well as useful telephone numbers for bus companies and airlines.

CITY LAYOUT   The hotels and restaurants I recommend are located off the three main streets running north and south: **Madero, Piño Suárez, and the Malecón.** Highway 180 skirts the city, so a turn onto Madero or Piño Suárez will take you into the center of town.

Your point of focus in town can be **Plaza Juárez,** the main square, bounded by the streets named Zaragoza, Madero, Sanchez, and Carranza. The plaza is the center of the downtown district, with the Río Grijalva to its east and Highway 186 to its north. Within this area is the **pedestrian zone,** with roads closed to traffic for five blocks (this zone is often called **Centro,** or **Zona Luz**). Villahermosa's main thoroughfare is Av. Madero, running south from Highway 186 past Plaza Juárez to the river, where it intersects with the riverside avenue, the Malecón.

GETTING AROUND

All the **city buses** converge on Avenida Piño Suárez at the market, and are clearly labeled for Tabasco 2000, Parque La Venta, and Centro; most rides cost about 20¢.

A **taxi** from the center of town to Parque La Venta is about $3.

WHAT TO SEE & DO

Major sights in Villahermosa include the Parque La Venta, the Pellicer Anthropology Museum, the History of Tabasco Museum, and the Museum of Popular Culture. You can hit the high points in a day.

If you need to shop for any necessities or luxuries, head to the indoor **shopping mall** at Tabasco 2000, or the shops lining Avenida Madero.

PARQUE MUSEO LA VENTA, Av. Ruíz Cortines (Hwy. 180). Tel. 5-2228.

La Venta was one of three major Olmec cities during the Pre-classic Period (2000

⭐ B.C.–A.D. 300). The mammoth heads you see in the park were found in the tall grass when the ruins of La Venta were discovered in 1938. Today all that remains of the once-impressive city are some grass-covered mounds—once earthen pyramids—84 miles west of Villahermosa. All the gigantic heads and other important sculptures have been moved from the site to this lovely museum/park. Allow at least an hour to wander through the jungle-like sanctuary looking at the 3,000-year-old sculpture and listening to the birds that inhabit the grounds.

On a walk through the park you'll see Olmec relics, sculptures, mosaics, a mockup of the original La Venta, and, of course, three of the colossal Olmec heads. Carved from basalt rock around 1000 B.C., these heads are 6½ feet high and weigh around 40 tons. The faces seem to be half-adult–half-infantile, with the fleshy "jaguar mouth" that's characteristic of Olmecan art. The basalt rock must have been transported from the nearest source, over 70 miles from La Venta, which is all the more impressive when you realize that there were no wheels to move it. The multi-ton rock was brought by raft from the quarry to the site. At least 16 heads have been found: four at La Venta, nine at San Lorenzo, and three at Tres Zapotes—all cities of the Olmecs.

On your stroll through the park, notice the other fine stone sculptures and artistic achievements of the Olmecs, who set forth the first art style in Mesoamerica, chiseling their monumental works without using metal. Their exquisite figurines in jade and serpentine, which can be seen in the Regional Museum of Anthropology, far excelled any other craft of this period.

Admission: $1.75 for nonresidents.
Open: Daily 8am–4:30pm. Sound-and-light show, Fri–Sat at 7pm and 8:15pm; Tues, Thurs, and Sun at 7pm. **Directions:** Take Paseo Tabasco northeast to Highway 180, turn right, and it's less than a mile on your right, next to the Exposition Park.

MUSEO REGIONAL DE ANTROPÓLOGIA CARLOS PELLICER CAMARA, Av. Carlos Pellicer 511. Tel. 2-1803.

⭐ This museum, a mile south of the center of town, along the river's west bank, replaced the Tabasco Museum in 1980. It is architecturally bold and attractive, and very well organized inside. There is more space and therefore the number of pre-Hispanic artifacts on display has greatly increased, to include not only the Tabascan finds (Totonac, Zapotec, and Olmec), but the rest of the Mexican and Central American cultures as well.

The museum itself is beautiful, with parquet floors, wood dividers, and numerous plants. There is a very open and airy feeling about this place. Take the elevator to the top of the museum and walk down past large maps showing the Olmec and Maya lands. Photographs and diagrams make it all easier to comprehend, but the explanatory signs are all in Spanish. Look especially for the figurines that were found in this area and for the colorful Codex (an early book of pictographs).

Admission: $1.75.
Open: Daily 9am–8pm.

MUSEO DE LA HISTORIA DE TABASCO (Casa de los Azulejos), 27 de Febrero and Juárez. Tel. 2-4996.

Take a half hour and see this museum, at the corner of 27 de Febrero and Avenida Juárez, in the pedestrian zone, which presents the history of Tabasco from pre-Columbian times to the present through documents, artifacts, and pictures. Every room is decorated with tiles in the Spanish and Italian baroque style, and the building's blue-and-white-tiled exterior, with wrought-iron balconies, is worth a snapshot. Only some explanations are in English.

Admission: Free.
Open: Daily 9am–8pm.

MUSEO DE CULTURA POPULAR, Calle Zaragoza 810, at Av. Juárez. Tel. 2-1117.

This museum is near the post office, a short three-block walk north of the Museo de la Historia. As you enter, on the right there's a small gift shop with baskets, carved gourds, embroidered regional clothing, and chocolate from Tabasco. Displays in the next room show the state's regional clothing and dance costumes. In the back is a

Chontal hut, complete with typical furnishings and a recorded conversation of two female villagers talking about the high cost of living. Student guides are often on hand for a free explanation. One of them explained that he grew up in a hut like the one on display, but today there are only two huts like it remaining in his village of Tecoluta. Another room shows ceremonial pottery and household utensils.

Admission: Free.
Open: Daily 9am–8pm.

AN EXCURSION TO COMALCALCO

Comalcalco is the only pyramid site in Mexico made of kilned stone. The quiet, shady town also has a beautifully painted church with blue spires and yellow trim. Somellera line buses leave for Comalcalco from the second-class bus station every 30 minutes; ADO has first-class buses at 12:30pm and 8:30pm. Travel agencies in Villahermosa offer a Comalcalco day trip for $45; generally it leaves at 8am and returns around 5pm. The price includes transportation, guide, and entry to the ruins, but not lunch.

WHERE TO STAY

The area around the intersections of Avenidas Juárez and Lerdo, sometimes referred to as the Zona Luz, is now one of the best places to stay; the streets are pedestrian malls closed to traffic. One drawback to this plan is parking, though there are guarded lots on the outskirts of the mall. Room rates in Villahermosa are distressingly high, especially considering what you get.

DOUBLES FOR LESS THAN $25

HOTEL SAN MIGUEL, Av. Lerdo 315, Villahermosa, Tab. 86000. Tel. 913/2-1500. 45 rms (all with bath). TEL
$ Rates: $8–$12 single; $15–$25 double.

The proprietor of this run-down inner-city hotel is a gem, filled with information and plans for the future. The three-story building seems to be undergoing continuous renovation, and the smell of fresh bright-yellow paint overpowers the bug spray. None of the rooms seemed to have been completely remodeled (though all have fans), and you'll have to cope with thin mattresses on narrow metal frames. Still, the location in the center of the pedestrian zone is ideal, and the rates will remain astoundingly low unless the hotel gets a flock of guests or becomes transformed into its owner's vision.

DOUBLES FOR LESS THAN $40

HOTEL RITZ, Av. Madero 1009, Villahermosa, Tab. 86000. Tel. 913/2-1611. 70 rms (all with bath). A/C TV TEL
$ Rates: $30 single; $33 double; $41.50 triple.
Families gravitate to this clean, moderately renovated hotel on the north end of Madero near Boulevard Grijalva, one block off Highway 186 and five blocks from the bus station. The rooms are small, brown, and adequate; the window air conditioners help block the traffic noise. The Ritz tends to fill up quickly, and isn't your best choice late at night. Its access to the highway is a benefit, but the lack of guarded parking is a drawback.

HOTEL MIRAFLORES, Reforma 304, Villahermosa, Tab. 86000. Tel. 913/2-0022. Fax 913/4-0986. 54 rms (all with bath). TV TEL
$ Rates: $30 single; $33.50 double; $36.50 triple.
The elevator in this '50s-style hotel barely makes it to the sixth floor—if you're traveling with lots of luggage, stay closer to the ground. The showers are old and rusty and the paint is chipping on the walls, but the maids do a thorough cleaning job, and the interior rooms are blessedly quiet. The hotel is at the south end of the pedestrian mall, near Madero.

DON CARLOS, Madero 418, Villahermosa, Tab. 86000. Tel. 913/2-2499. Fax 913/2-4622. 94 rms, 8 suites (all with bath). TV TEL

$ Rates: $30 single; $33.50 double; $36.50 triple. **Parking:** Free.
Downtown's largest hotel has been renovated somewhat, and fits the traveling-salesman genre with a business-like lobby, a functioning elevator, and a decent coffee shop. Not all the rooms have been remodeled, and those that have are still an uninspired beige and brown; the eight suites are air-conditioned while 94 rooms all have fans. The drawback here is the incessant traffic noise on Madero; the benefit is guarded parking. The Don Carlos is at the southeast edge of the pedestrian mall.

HOTEL PLAZA INDEPENDENCIA, Independencia 123, Villahermosa, Tab. 86000. Tel. 913/2-7541 or 2-1299. Fax 913/4-4724. 90 rooms (all with bath). A/C TV TEL
$ Rates: $30 single; $33.50 double; $36.50 triple. **Parking:** Free.
Of the many hotels in this price range the Plaza Independencia, by Plaza de Armas, two blocks south of the pedestrian mall, is by far the best. The rooms have avocado drapes and rugs, but the darkness is broken by nice bamboo furnishings, including a small desk. Some rooms have balconies; from the fifth (top) floor you can see the river. It's the only budget hotel with a pool—a blessing in muggy Villahermosa—and enclosed parking. Try to reserve your room in advance.

CHOCO'S HOTEL, Av. Constitución (Lino Merino), Villahermosa, Tab. 86000. Tel. 913/2-9044 or 2-9444. 52 rms (all with bath). A/C TV TEL
$ Rates: $30 single; $34 double.
Creature comforts at budget rates make this a good choice if you don't mind being five blocks from the plaza and a dozen or more from the bus station—it's one block east of the river between Boulevard Grijalva and Avenida Magana, a bit out of the way for those on foot. The bathrooms are bigger and more modern than at other hotels in this bracket—the showers even have doors. The mini-lobby by the elevator on each of the six floors means occasional congregations of partyers—ask for a room down the dark hall.

WHERE TO EAT

MEALS FOR $5 OR LESS

LA BAGUETTE, Av. Juárez 301.
Specialty: BAKERY.
$ Prices: Loaf of bread 75¢; sweet rolls, pastries, and cookies 10¢–$1.
Open: Mon–Sat 9am–9pm.
French bread is the specialty, and on the back wall you'll see fresh loaves lined up like 2-foot-long sentries. The Danish pastries, lavish French tortes, and chocolate-filled croissants should keep your sweet tooth satisfied. Buy some for a late-night snack in your room. La Baguette is in the pedestrian-only zone, opposite the Museo de la Historia.

GALERÍAS MADAN, Madero 408. Tel. 2-1650.
Specialty: MEXICAN.
$ Prices: Breakfast $2–$3; comida corrida $4; hamburger $3.10.
Open: Daily 7am–10pm.
Situated in a lobby of shops on Madero between Lerdo and Reforma, this calm, soft-pink, air-conditioned restaurant serves a comida of soup, rice, pollo mole, vegetables, coffee, and dessert. Large windows look out on the street, and the room has the feel of a hotel coffee shop where downtown shoppers have lunch.

CHILANGO'S SNACK, 27 de Febrero and 5 de Mayo. Tel. 2-3014.
Specialty: MEXICAN.
$ Prices: Fixed-price lunch $3.50; coffee 25¢; beer 75¢.
Open: Daily 7:30am–9pm.

A few white tables border the shady plaza, providing a pretty setting for a bargain lunch of rice, soup, meat, and some sort of vegetable. In the pedestrian zone, half a block east of the Museo de la Historia, it's a good spot to relax, have a meal or cool drink, and review your strategy.

MEALS FOR LESS THAN $10

CHON CUPON, Parque La Choca, Paseo Tabasco and Paseo La Choca, at Tabasco 2000.
   Specialty: MEXICAN/SEAFOOD. **Bus:** "Tabasco 2000" to the end of the line.
$ **Prices:** Appetizers $2; full seafood meals $5.50–$7.50; beer $1.
   Open: Daily 11am–9pm.

If you're craving a decent meal away from the downtown hussle, aim for this giant palapa in an overgrown park, where a miniature train once wove through the jungle's edge. The restaurant appears to have seen better days, but is immensely popular for long, leisurely lunches in the country. The seafood-stuffed quesadillas are a great budget choice; heartier eaters might want grilled fish with rice and vegetables, a chile relleño filled with fish, or the bountiful sopa mariscos. Soft romantic ballads play in the background (when the guitarist can't find any takers for his songs).

The park is at the far east side of Tabasco 2000 by the Río Carrizal; the restaurant is at the entrance.

2. PALENQUE

89 miles W of Villahermosa, 144 miles S of San Cristóbal

GETTING THERE **By Plane** All regularly scheduled flights directly to Palenque have been suspended for some time. Meanwhile the **nearby airport at Comitan** serves all Palenque charter flights. Check with travel agencies in Villahermosa, Tuxtla Guitiérrez, and San Cristóbal de las Casas for information.

   ATC Tours (tel. 924/5-0210 in Palenque) can arrange charter flights to Ocosingo near San Cristóbal de las Casas at $70 per person (four-person minimum).

By Train Plans to add a first-class Mexico City–Mérida Estrella train that would pass through Palenque never seem to materialize, but *this* could be the year. At this writing, the second-class train does stop at Ladron, 6 miles from Palenque, on route from Mexico City to Mérida, but no one favors traveling on it. Horror stories of thefts, breakdowns, and general misery abound.

By Bus From Villahermosa's first-class ADO station there are seven buses to Palenque daily, the trip taking 1½ to 3 hours. From San Cristóbal there's one bus, which leaves at 10am and arrives in Palenque near midnight.

By Car Highway 186 from Villahermosa is in good condition and the trip from there and on the Palenque turnoff should take about an hour and a half. From San Cristóbal Highway 195 is potholed in places, and in some spots the road has washed out, causing traffic to slow to one lane. This is especially true in the rainy season between May and October.

ESSENTIALS The **telephone area code** is 934. **Climate:** Palenque's constant humidity is downright oppressive in the summer months, especially after rain showers. During the winter months the damp air can be chilly, especially in the evenings, so a jacket is a good thing to bring. Raingear is important equipment any time of year.

DEPARTING **By Bus** Three bus stations in Palenque will serve most of your needs for getting in and out of the village. **Auto Transportes Tuxtla** (tel. 5-0369) is on Juárez, on your right about a block from the Pemex station as you enter town.

From here there are five buses daily to Tuxtla Gutiérrez, and five to San Cristóbal beginning at 7:30am (San Cristóbal de las Casas is a 6-hour trip, minimum). The line also has a bus to Agua Azul at 8am; tickets can only be purchased 30 minutes in advance. Luggage storage costs 50¢ per piece.

Two doors down is the **Terminal de Transportes Dag Dug,** known locally as the Mérida station, although only one bus daily goes to Mérida, at 5pm, an 8-hour trip. The bus originates in Palenque so chances of getting a seat are good if you buy a ticket a day in advance. Two buses a day go to Villahermosa, San Cristóbal de las Casas, and Tuxtla Gutiérrez; and one goes to Ocosingo.

By Car The 135-mile trip from Palenque to San Cristóbal on Highway 195 takes 5 to 6 hours and passes through lush jungle and mountain scenery. Take it easy since potholes and other hindrances are common.

The town of Palenque (pop. 63,000) would hardly exist were it not for the ruins. It's a slow-paced, somnolent village accustomed to visitors passing through, but pays them little heed. The ruins of Palenque, on the other hand, are one of the most spectacular Maya archeological sites, with roof-combed temples ensconced in lush vegetation high above the savannahs. The ruins, located on the edge of the jungle in the state of Chiapas, are part of a preserve known as the Parque Nacional Palenque. The surrounding countryside seems to threaten the ruins with extinction once again, and it takes a team of machete wielders to hold the jungle back.

ORIENTATION

ARRIVING Most travelers reach Palenque by bus, arriving near the center of town. Taxis from the bus stations to most hotels cost less than $3; only those hotels surrounding the zócalo are within walking distance if you're carrying heavy luggage.

INFORMATION The **State Tourism Office** is in the Municipal Building on Avenida Hidalgo at the zócalo, but information is scarce and the office is rarely open. Some information is available on the bulletin board outside the office.

CITY LAYOUT The **ruins** are about 5 miles southeast of town. The road from Villahermosa forks just east of town at the impossible-to-miss Maya statue; the ruins are southwest of the statue, and town lies to the east.

Palenque has three separate areas where tourists tend to congregate. The most central area is around the **zócalo,** bordered by Avenidas Hidalgo, 20 de Noviembre, Independencia, and Jiménez. **La Cañada** is a more pleasant area located five blocks east of the zócalo on Merle Green, a partially paved road which runs through a tropical-forest neighborhood. Here you'll find a few small hotels and restaurants and stands of artists who carve and paint. Besides the zócalo area, this is the best location for travelers without cars, since town is within a few blocks and the buses that run to the ruins pass by La Cañada. The third tourist zone is along the **road to the ruins,** where small hotels, RV parks, and campgrounds are tucked into the surrounding jungle. This is an ideal location for those with cars.

GETTING AROUND

The cheapest way to get back and forth from the ruins is on the Chan Balu **colectivo buses,** which depart from the terminal at Avenidas Juárez and Allende every 10 minutes from 7am to 7pm; the fare is 50¢. Chan Balu also has buses five times daily to Misol Ha and Agua Azul; the fare is $5.25. The buses pass by La Cañada and the hotels along the road to the ruins, but they may not stop if they're full.

Taxis from town to the ruins cost $5; drivers may charge more from the ruins back to town.

WHAT TO SEE & DO

The real reason for being here is the ruins, which can be toured in a morning; but many people like to savor Palenque, going both in the morning and afternoon with time out for a siesta during the heat of the day. Although there is much new hotel construction started on the road into town, and despite the fame of the ruins, the town of Palenque remains small and backward. Townsfolk pay little heed to the foreigners who pass through, giving the town an unspoiled, uncommercialized feel; but at the rate of hotel building, that small-town ambience may not last long. There are no sights in the town, so if you have time to spare, sit on the main plaza and observe the goings-on. The La Cañada area east of town is a pleasant spot for a leisurely lunch and browsing through Maya reproductions made by local artists.

PARQUE NACIONAL PALENQUE The ancient Maya city of Palenque was a ceremonial center for the high priests during the Classic Period (A.D. 300–900), with the peak of its civilization around A.D. 600–700. Pottery found during the excavations shows that people lived here as early as 300 B.C. Alberto Ruíz Lhuillier, the archeologist who directed some of the explorations, states that because of "the style of its structures, its hieroglyphic inscriptions, its sculptures, its works in stucco and its pottery, Palenque undoubtedly fell within the great Maya culture. Yet its artistic expressions have a character all their own which is evident in the absolute mastery of craftsmanship, turning the art of Palenque into the most refined of Indian America."

As you enter the ruins, the building to the right is the **Temple of the Inscriptions,** named for the great stone hieroglyphic panels found inside (most of them are now in the Archeological Museum in Mexico City) and famous for the tomb, or Crypt of Pakal, that Lhuiller discovered in its depths in 1949. It took four seasons of digging to clear out the rubble that was put there by the Maya to conceal the crypt. The crypt itself is some 80 feet below the floor of the temple and was covered by a monolithic sepulchral slab 10 feet long and 7 feet wide. Unless you're claustrophobic, you should definitely visit the tomb. The way down is lighted, but the steps can be slippery because of the condensed humidity. This is the only pyramid in Mexico built specifically as a tomb.

Besides the Temple of the Inscriptions, there is the **Palace** with its unique watchtower, the Northern Group (**Temple of the Count** and **Ball Court**), and the group of temples beyond the Palace (**Temple of the Sun, Temple of the Foliated Cross**). The official guidebook has a detailed description of this site and is well worth the money. (For a summary of pre-Columbian history, see Chapter 1.)

The small **museum** has a chronological chart of Maya history, and a modest collection of votive figurines, pieces of statuary, and stones with calendar glyphs. Entrance is free once you have paid for access to the park. Be sure you save your ticket.

Plan to spend a whole day in these wonderful surroundings. A quarter mile back toward town from the parking lot, on the right-hand side (as you approach from town) is a path leading into the **Cascada Motiepa,** a cool, beautiful waterfall good for cooling the feet and resting the soul. Beware of mosquitos. Vendors sell the typical souvenirs along the entranceway to the ruins. Of particular interest are the Lancandon, with long dark hair and simple white tunics. The Lancandon are among the most private and reclusive of Mexico's Indian groups, and it's a bit surprising to see them here, selling bows and arrows.

Admission to the ruins is $5, free on Sunday. Licensed guides charge about $16 for two people for a 2-hour tour. The site is open daily from 8am to 5pm; the museum, from 10am to 5pm; the crypt, 10am to 4pm.

WHERE TO STAY

The three main hotel zones are near the fork in the road at La Cañada, in the village, and on the road to the ruins. Two hotels were under construction by the Maya statue when I was there, and may offer an alternative when you travel.

IN LA CAÑADA

Doubles For Less Than $15

LA POSADA, Av. Cascada Agua Azul, Palenque, Chi. 29960. Tel. 934/5-0437. Fax 934/5-0193. 8 rms (all with bath).

$ Rates: $12.50 single or double. **Parking:** Free.

⭐ 💲 If the rave reviews scribbled all over the lobby walls are any indication, La Posada is the most popular place in town. Owners Sergio and Margarita Valdez are world travelers themselves and understand budget travelers' needs. The rooms, in a long one-story building facing a wide swath of grass, are basic, with fans, concrete platform beds (one per room), thin double mattresses, and tile baths; room numbers are painted in Maya symbols. The main lobby building has a sound system and a great collection of cassettes; Ping-Pong table; refrigerator stocked with juices, yogurt, sandwiches, beer, and mineral water; and plenty of room for guests to mingle. The maids will wash and dry your clothes, and Sergio is always around to answer questions. Tours to Bonampak, Yaxchilán, and San Cristóbal are available.

Few cab drivers will recognize the street address above. The dirt road to it is nameless; the proprietors liked the name and put it in their brochures. It's in La Cañada, left down Merle Green, a dirt road just past the Hotel Maya Tulipanes.

Doubles for Less than $35

HOTEL LA CAÑADA, Av. Hidalgo, Palenque, Chi. 29960. Tel. 934/5-0102. Fax 934/5-0392. 14 rms (all with bath).
$ Rates: $25 single; $31 double; $38 triple.
This secluded group of cottages, on the paved road in La Cañada, about half a mile east of the Maya statue, is surrounded by dense woods. The rooms are a bit musty, which comes with the jungle terrain. Rooms 7, 8, 9, and 10, across the street from the office, are particularly good, and have large bathtubs (a rarity in these climes) and air conditioning; the rest have fans. Señor Carlos Morales Marquez built the hotel 30 years ago, and his 10 sons still help run the place. The palapa restaurant is very good, and the second-story deck is a great place to watch the jungle birds toward sunset.

HOTEL MAYA TULIPANES, Calle Merle Green, Palenque, Chi. 29960. Tel. 934/5-0201. 21 rms (all with bath).
$ Rates: $25.50 single; $31 double; $37.50 triple. **Parking:** Free.
Maya statues, carvings, and paintings fill the hallways and public areas in this rambling, overgrown two-story hotel one long block east of the Maya statue in La Cañada. Some of the windows are even shaped like the Maya corbelled arch. The rooms are dark and musty, showing a decade's use with few repairs; five are air-conditioned and all have fans. You definitely feel like you're in the jungle here, and the dark shade is a cool respite from the sun's glare. Adventure-travel groups sometimes fill the hotel.

IN TOWN

Doubles for Less than $15

HOTEL LACROIX, Hidalgo 18, Palenque, Chi. 29960. Tel. 934/5-0114. 8 rms (all with bath).
$ Rates: $13 single or double.
This dark, dismal hotel has lots of potential but gets little attention, and needs major renovations. Decorated with primitive murals, this hotel offers dark, simple rooms kept cool by ceiling fans, shade, and breezes. Each room opens to a veranda overlooking neglected palm gardens and banana plants. Though dirty, it's often full, since it's the cheapest place by the park; from Avenida Juárez, turn left at the park, then right, and the hotel is down a block on the left, opposite the church.

Doubles for Less than $20

HOTEL MISOL-HA, Av. Juárez 14, Palenque, Chi. 29960. Tel. 934/5-0092. 28 rms (all with bath).
$ Rates: $13 single; $17 double; $21 triple.
Once one of the most popular hotels in town, it has deteriorated badly. Though each

room has a fan, the walls in the rooms are literally falling apart, the shower heads are rusty and corroded, even toilet seats are missing in some rooms. Absolutely see your room before agreeing to a price; you may be able to negotiate. The Misol-Ha is between the bus stations and the zócalo on the north side of Juárez. Hotel parking is three blocks away.

HOTEL VACA VIEJA, Av. Cinco de Mayo no. 42, Palenque, Chi. 29300. Tel. 934/5-0377 or 5-0388. 28 rms (all with bath).

$ Rates: $14.50 single; $18.65 double.

Lack of upkeep is the downfall here. There are fans in all rooms, but the floors are dirty, the plants dead, and the showers curtainless. Hot water is unpredictable, and water of any kind is sometimes unavailable. The owner sold his herd of cattle to build this little inn, which used to be a sure bet. But now Vaca Viejo, the Old Cow, is looking weary, and sadly in need of a spring cleaning. It's about a 10-minute walk east of the bus stations; Cinco de Mayo is one block south of Juárez.

Doubles for Less than $35

HOTEL CASA DE PAKAL, Av. Juárez 18, Palenque, Chi. 29960. 15 rms (all with bath). A/C

$ Rates: $21 single; $29 double; $37.50 triple.

This bright, relatively new hotel one block south of the zócalo far surpasses most others on Juárez, despite the rickety, slatted wooden stairs leading to the rooms. Air conditioning is a big plus here, and the rooms are far brighter and cleaner than at nearby establishments.

CHAN-KAH, Av. Independencía, Palenque, Chi. 29960. Tel. 934/5-0318. Fax 934/5-0489. 17 rms (all with bath). A/C TV

$ Rates: $29 single; $33 double; $37.50 triple.

The only elevator in town is in this impressive wood-and-stone building on the west side of the zócalo, four blocks from the bus stations, overlooking the main plaza and the jungle beyond. Nine rooms have balconies, and the rooms have fans, freshly painted white walls, red-tile floors, large sinks and showers, and soft sheets. When a band is playing in the second-story bar it can be pretty noisy for the rooms in the front of the hotel, but that's not a nightly occurrence.

Camping

There are two camping areas near the ruins, on the left-hand side of the road as you head out from town. The first one is very plain, cheap, and unappealing. You'd do better to continue to the next one, **Camp Mayabell,** within the grounds of the national park. Here you're only 1½ miles from the ruins, which are accessible by colectivo or on foot (about 30 minutes). Mayabell has hookups, showers, and palapas in which to hang your hammock. The price is $1 per person, and you can rent a hammock for 75¢ a night. Mayabell has full hookups for 24 campers for $6 a day. Bring your own hammock and hang it under a thatched palapa for $2.50, which includes use of the showers and bathrooms.

The **Restaurant and Trailer Park María del Mar** is at Carretera Palenque Ruinas km 2.7, Palenque, Chi. 29300 (tel. 934/5-0297). This trailer park has 86 trailer hookups, costing $15 a day. Facilities include showers, toilets, sinks, and a pool. The restaurant is open daily from 7am to 10pm.

Worth the Extra Bucks

HOTEL MISIÓN PALENQUE, Domicilio Conocido, Rancho San Martín de Porres, Palenque, Chi. 29960. Tel. 934/5-0241 or 5-0300. Fax 934/5-0491. 144 rms (all with bath). A/C TEL

$ Rates: $70 single; $80 double; $90 triple.

Palenque's most luxurious hotel is at the far east edge of town, left at the end of Cinco de Mayo, a 20-minute walk from the first-class bus station or a $2 taxi ride. The views of the surrounding, peaceful countryside from the mountains to the jungle are beautiful, and the caged parrots nearby add tropical background noises. The spacious rooms, with high beamed ceilings and cobalt-blue and white walls, are in long, two-story buildings overlooking the gardens; those near the restaurant must bear the music until 10pm. The beds are enormous, the sheets and pillows soft and fragrant, the bathrooms sparkling clean—but the air conditioners are the noisiest I've ever heard. The pool is a blessing after a morning of pyramid climbing or playing tennis on the hotel's courts; there's a hot springs nearby for soaking your weary feet. The restaurant is remarkably good for one that serves busload after busload of European tour groups; it's especially nice on the patio, with candlelight. The hotel's free shuttle goes to and from the ruins six times a day.

ON THE ROAD TO OCOSINGO

MOTEL NUTUTUM VIVA (or Nututun). Tel. 934/5-0100. 40 rms (all with bath).
$ Rates: $35 single; $41 double.
Located on the beautiful Río Usumacinta, this hotel has huge tile rooms with two double beds, large closets, a bathtub, and a shower. Although prices are in the splurge category, swimming in the river after a hot day at the ruins may be worth it. It costs $1 per person to camp on the riverbank using your own equipment.

To get here, go two miles from the Maya statue along the road to the ruins and turn left onto the road toward Ocosingo, Agua Azul, and San Cristóbal.

ON THE ROAD TO THE RUINS

CHAN-KAH, km 31, Carretera Palenque, Palenque, Chi. 29960. 934/5-0318. 18 rms (all with bath).
$ Rates: $58 single; $62.50 double; $66.50 triple.
These comfortable little wood-and-stone bungalows on the left side of the road to the ruins, 2½ miles northwest of the ruins, are spread out in a beautiful jungle setting with fans and sliding glass doors opening to a small patio facing the jungle. Facilities include a large swimming pool—a blessing after the long walk back from the ruins. Taxis are hard to come by here, and there's an extra charge for picking you up at the hotel. A better way to get into town is to walk to the main road and flag down a colectivo or taxi on the road. The hotel has its own restaurant, with adequate but not wonderful food. Christmas holiday prices may be higher than those quoted here, so be sure to ask. And you may be quoted a higher price if you reserve a room in advance from the U.S.

___

READERS RECOMMEND

Kasblan Hotel, 5 de Mayo no. 105, Palenque, Chi. 29960 (tel. 934/5-0297; fax 934/5-0309. "We'd like to recommend the Kasblan Hotel—a new kid on the block, just up the street from the ADO bus station. It's very clean, the staff helpful, and the rooms smallish with ceiling fans, and it costs $16 for a double bed for two people. There's a pleasant dining room—food good, soup wonderful—and a bar with TV showing CNN in English."—Sally Roth, Foster City, Calif.

WHERE TO EAT

Avenida Juárez is lined with many small eateries, none of which is exceptional. A good option are the many markets and *panaderías* (bakeries) along Juárez. **Panificadora La Tehuanito** has fresh cookies firm enough to withstand hours in the bottom of a purse, and **La Bodeguita** has a beautiful display of fresh fruit—just stick with those you can peel.

MEALS FOR LESS THAN $5

RESTAURANTE ECONÓMICO ROSTICERÍA, Av. Juárez.
Specialty: MEXICAN.
$ Prices: Fruit drinks 90¢; tacos $2; breakfast $2; roast chicken with salad and french fries $3.75.
Open: Daily 6am–10pm.

Proximity to the Tuxtla bus station just across Juárez is the best reason to eat here, where the service is desultory at best. Still, the food is basic, relatively satisfying, and cheap, and the setting is clean and cool, with ceiling fans stirring the sluggish air. Count on a fair dose of grease with your fries.

LA OAXAQUEÑA, Av. Juárez at Jorge de la Vega.
Specialty: MEXICAN.
$ Prices: Juices $1; huevos mexicanas $2.60; turkey mole $4.25.
Open: Daily 6am–10pm.

Get a taste of Oaxaca at this bright-orange, barnlike restaurant a block north of the Tuxtla bus station. The walls are bamboo; windows look out to the street. The mole is respectable and the breakfasts basic and filling, but avoid the shrimp omelet.

MEALS FOR LESS THAN $10

LA CAÑADA, Calle Merle Green. Tel. 5-0102.
Specialty: MEXICAN.
$ Prices: Main courses $7–$9; beer $2.50.
Open: Daily 7am–10pm.

This palapa-topped restaurant tucked into the jungle is said to be one of the best restaurants in town, though it never seems crowded. Although the dining room has a dirt floor, the place is spotless, the service attentive, and the food good, if not exceptional. Breakfast is the best bet, or any of the local specialties—tamales, tazajo (thin grilled beef), or corn soup. Near the restaurant, the two-story thatched "club" La Nuit plays disco music and is the most popular dance spot in town. They're in the La Cañada area, on the left, about midway down the road.

RESTAURANT MAYA. Av. Juárez.
Specialty: MEXICAN.
$ Prices: Main courses $4.50–$7; breakfast $2.50.
Open: Daily 7am–10pm.

The most popular place in town among tourists is on the park near the post office, across the street from the west side of the zócalo. It's breezy and open, and although managed by a solicitous family, don't expect anything approaching prompt service. A plus at breakfast is the free coffee refills. Try the tamales.

CHAN-KAH, Av. Independencía. Tel. 5-0318.
Specialty: MEXICAN.
$ Prices: Quesadillas $2; carne asada dinner $5.75.
Open: Daily 7am–11pm.

This attractive restaurant on the west side of the plaza is in the nicest hotel in the center of town, and is the most peaceful place to eat. The waiters are extremely attentive, and the food fairly well prepared. If you're looking to treat yourself to a good meal, try it here. The second-story bar overlooks the plaza, and has live music some weekend nights.

PICCOLINI'S, Av. Juárez.
Specialty: PIZZA.
$ Prices: Pizza $5 small, $6.50 medium, $9.50 large.
Open: Daily 7am–11pm.

This restaurant, one block west of the zócalo near the colectivo station, serves Palenque's best pizza at rickety wood tables with red-checked cloths. Travelers from the U.S. are particularly fond of the place, and wolf down the decent-tasting pizza with relish. Don't count on pepperoni, and the sausage is spicy Mexican chorizo, but it does remind you of home.

EL FOGÓN DE PAKAL, Calle Merle Green. Tel. 5-0210.
Specialty: CHIAPAN. **Directions:** In La Cañada at the end of the road, about ½ mile from the highway.
$ Prices: Main dishes $5–$7; soups $3.
Open: Daily noon–11pm.

This second-story palapa poking above an endless sea of jungle growth is the best place in town to try Chiapan specialties. The tamale sampler has five varieties, including one filled with mashed plantains. The parrillada chiapaneca is a mixed grill feast for two or more; the lomo relleño of chicken wrapped around vegetables and topped with mole, is a culinary treat you won't find anywhere else. All meals begin with a basket of warm tortillas and small bowls of beans, salsas, guacamole, and cheese. The waiters are dressed in the costumes of their home regions, tree limbs wind within the palapa, seeming to bring the jungle within, and soft music blends with the bird calls. In all, an afternoon or nighttime meal here is sheer delight.

WORTH THE EXTRA BUCKS

LA SELVA, Carretera Palenque. Tel. 5-0363.
   Specialty: MEXICAN.
$ Prices: Appetizers $5; full meal $16.
   Open: Daily 11am–10pm.
Palenque's traditional "best" restaurant may get some stiff competition from El Fogón de Pakal, but there's certainly room in town for two classy (in a tropical sense) restaurants serving top-notch local cuisine. Despite its thatched roof, the dining room is large and refined. The pollo Palenque (chicken with potatoes in a tomato-and-onion sauce) is a soothing choice, and save room for the flan. Mexican wines are served by the bottle. La Selva is a 5-minute walk south from the Maya statue toward the ruins.

EASY EXCURSIONS FROM PALENQUE

AGUA AZUL & CASCADA DE MISOL HA   The most popular excursion from Palenque is the day trip to the Agua Azul cascades. For $5, minivans from the Chan Balu Colectivo Service travel to Agua Azul and the Cascada de Misol Ha every day with five round-trips beginning at 10am; the last van departs Agua Azul at 6:30pm. They may wait until six or eight people want to go, so check a day or two in advance of your proposed trip.

✪ **BONAMPAK & YAXCHILÁN**   Adventurers might consider the 2-day excursion to the Maya ruins of Bonampak and Yaxchilán. Several hotels and tour companies offer a 2-day (minimum) tour by four-wheel-drive vehicle to within 4½ miles of Bonampak, known for its painted murals. You must walk the rest of the way to the ruins. After camping overnight, you continue by river to the extensive ruins of the great Maya city, Yaxchilán. Bring rain gear, boots, a flashlight, and bug repellant. All tours include meals, but vary in price ($85 to $100 per person); some take far too many people for comfort (the 7-hour road trip can be unbearable). Among the most reputable tour operators are: **Viajes Shivalva,** Calle Merle Green 1 (Apdo. Postal 237), Palenque, Chi. 29960 (tel. 934/5-0411; fax 934/5-0392); **Transportadora Turisitica de Palenque,** Avenida Cinco de Mayo (and at La Misión Hotel), Palenque, Chi. 29960 (tel. 934/5-0066; fax 934/5-0499); and **ATC Tours and Travel,** Avenida Allende at Juárez, Palenque, Chi. 29960 (tel. 934/5-0201; fax 934/5-0356), whose headquarters is in San Cristóbal at the El Fogón Restaurant. Most of these agencies also have tours to Bonampak and Yaxchilán by plane, and tours to Tikal, San Cristóbal, and other archeological sites in the area. **Sergio Valdez** of the La Posada Hotel also has tours to the ruins.
   An alternative way to reach Bonampak and Yaxchilán is via tours run by the **Chan Balu Colectivo Service,** at Hidalgo and Allende. A minimum of five people are needed to make the trip. The Palenque Bonampak portion is 5 to 7 hours by road and another 2½-hour hike; an overnight stay in rustic huts with wood slat beds and no meals or mosquito netting; and another 2-hour bus ride, a river trip to Yaxchilán, and the long ride back to Palenque. It's a strenuous, no-frills trip that can be absolutely wonderful if you don't expect great service—bring plenty of food and drink, a hammock and net, and plenty of patience. The 2-day trip costs about $50 to $75 per person.
   When negotiating the deal, be sure to ask how many maximum will be in the bus, or you may not have a place to sit for 18 hours of bumpy dirt road.

EN ROUTE TO SAN CRISTÓBAL DE LAS CASAS

After you leave Palenque, you pass the Motel Nututum (see "Where to Stay," above) and then climb into the Chiapan mountains. About 6 miles out of Palenque you'll reach a fork in the road; take the right fork to get to Ocosingo, your intermediate destination. Most of the road is paved these days, but landslides and washouts sometimes slow traffic during the rainy season. After 12½ miles from Palenque (km 47 of the official highway marking system), look for signs to Parque Natural Ejido Misol Ha (a collective farm) on the right (see "Easy Excursions from Palenque," above, for details). About 38½ miles from Palenque is the well-marked turnoff, on the right, to Agua Azul. From the main road, you must go 2¾ miles on a painfully broken road down the hill into the valley to reach the *ejido* (communal property) and the swimming area. After Agua Azul it's about an hour's ride (40 miles) to Ocosingo, which has a few shops and small restaurants right on the highway. From Ocosingo, you have yet to travel 52 miles to reach the junction with the Pan American Highway (Mexican Hwy. 190). From the junction, it's 4½ miles into San Cristóbal.

3. SAN CRISTÓBAL DE LAS CASAS

143 miles S of Palenque, 50 miles W of Tuxtla Gutiérrez, 46 miles SE of Comitan, 104 miles SE of Cuauhtémoc and the Guatemala border

GETTING THERE By Plane There are no commercial flights to San Cristóbal or nearby Ocosingo at this time, though plans are underway to modernize San Cristóbal's airport. Tour agencies in Palenque and San Cristóbal can arrange flights by charter plane between the two cities for a minimum of four people at $70 each.

By Bus From Palenque, four **Auto Transportes Tuxtla** buses make the 6-hour trip daily. The highway between San Cristóbal and Palenque is paved but portions of it are heavily potholed or washed out, or have dangerous dips. Only second-class buses make the trip. If you are prone to motion sickness, be careful not to eat anything before you get on the bus. Buy your ticket the day before your planned departure, if possible.

The best way to get to San Cristóbal from Tuxtla Gutiérrez is to hop on one of the 12 direct buses from the first-class **Cristóbal Colón** bus station for the 1½-hour trip. The road between Tuxtla and San Cristóbal is a curvy one and the buses cover it rapidly, so motion sickness is a consideration. The highway climbs to almost 7,000 feet in a matter of 50 miles and the scenery is spectacular.

By Taxi Strike a deal with a taxi driver, at either the Tuxtla airport or the Cristóbal Colón bus station. For $3.50 per person he'll drive six people or more to San Cristóbal, but you have to wait for five more passengers to assemble; a solo passenger will pay $28 to $35.

By Car The road between Palenque and San Cristóbal de las Casas is an adventure in jungle scenery, with some fascinating hideaways to discover on the way. The trip takes about 5 hours. From Tuxtla it winds through beautiful mountain country and the closer you get to San Cristóbal the more colorfully garbed the Indians you'll see along the roadway.

DEPARTING By Plane Since San Cristóbal's airport is closed, charter flights use the nearby Ocosingo airport. If you need to make flight arrangements on other airlines, **Santa Ana Tours,** 16 de Septiembre no. 6 (tel. 8-0422), just off the zócalo and behind the municipal building, is the representative of Mexicana Airlines as well as several regional carriers including Aviacsa. Their office hours are Monday through Friday from 9am to 1pm and 3 to 6pm, and on Saturday from 9am to 1pm. They can confirm reservations and issue tickets. **Aviacsa** has an office in Plaza Mazariegos (tel. 8-4441). The plans underway for an airport in San Cristóbal include facilities for flights to Guatemala.

By Bus From San Cristóbal to Tuxtla there are only three first-class buses (called *locales*) which originate in San Cristóbal; nine others pass through (*de paso*) and take on passengers if there is space. Seven buses daily will take you to Villahermosa in 7 hours. There's one afternoon bus daily to Oaxaca; be prepared for a 12-hour trip. One bus daily goes to Palenque and the trip takes 6 hours. Or you can sign up for one of the tours to Palenque from San Cristóbal. You have a choice of 17 buses to Tapachula, but they all take at least 9 hours; twelve buses a day go to Comitan.

To ensure a seat on one of the *locales,* purchase your ticket a day in advance at the first-class bus station.

From the second-class **Transportes Tuxtla** bus station, a total of six buses go to Palenque. There are three distinct bus lines here, and you cannot make reservations on three of them as they originate elsewhere. Be sure you get on the bus whose ticket you hold. Twenty buses throughout the day ply the road to Tuxtla, and five go to Comitan.

San Cristóbal (alt. 6,972 ft.; pop. 90,000) is a colonial town set in a lovely valley. The town is the major market center for Indians of various tribes from the surrounding mountains, chiefly the Chamulas, who wear baggy thigh-length trousers and white or black serapes; the Zinacantecans, who dress in light-pink blouses and short pants, with hat ribbons that are tied on married men and dangling loose on bachelors; and the Tenejapa, whose men wear knee-length black tunics and flat straw hats and whose women wear beautiful, heavy wool rust-colored huipils.

San Cristóbal is deep in Mesoamerica where the Maya flourished. In fact, nearly all the Indians in the immediate area speak languages derived from ancient Maya—Tzotzil, Tzeltal. Some don't come into town at all, and one group, the Lacandons (who number only about 450), live so far off in the forests of eastern Chiapas that it takes 6 days on horseback to get to their territory. There are several Indian villages within road access of San Cristóbal—Chamula, with its weavers and non-Christian church; Zinacantan, whose residents practice a unique religion and wear brilliantly colored clothing; Tenejapa, San Andrés, and Magdalena, known for brocaded textiles; Amatenango del Valle, a town of potters; and Aguacatenango, known for embroidery. Most of these "villages" consist of little more than a church and the municipal government, with homes scattered for miles around and a general gathering only for church and market days (usually Sunday).

You'll hear the word *Ladino* here and it means non-Indian Mexicans or people who have taken up modern ways, changed their dress, dropped their traditions and language, and live in town. It is both derogatory and descriptive, depending on who is using it and how it's used.

In recent years San Cristóbal has become more popular with Mexicans, not to mention North Americans and Europeans in search of a charming, cool, "unspoiled," traditional town to visit or settle in. As a result, it's no longer quite as quaint as it once was—but it's by no means ruined.

Although the influx of tourists is increasing and the influence of outsiders (Mexicans as well) is inevitably chipping away at the culture, the Indians aren't really interested in being like the foreigners in their midst; mainly they pay little attention to outsiders. Just in case we think they are envious of our clothing, possessions, or culture, I'll repeat an interesting comment made one night during dinner at Na Balom with a Maya specialist living in San Cristóbal: "They think we are the remains of a leftover civilization and that we eat our babies."

Photography Warning In and around San Cristóbal, taking a photograph of even a chile pepper can be a risky undertaking because of the native belief that a photograph takes away the soul—yes, even of a pepper. Photographers should be very cautious about when, where, and at whom or what they point their cameras. To ensure proper respect by outsiders, villages around San Cristóbal, especially Chamula and Zinacantan, require visitors to go to the municipal building upon arrival and sign an agreement not to take photographs or the punishment will be severe. The penalty for disobeying these regulations is stiff—confiscation of your camera and perhaps a lengthy stay in jail. And they mean it! In San Cristóbal the consequences of pointing

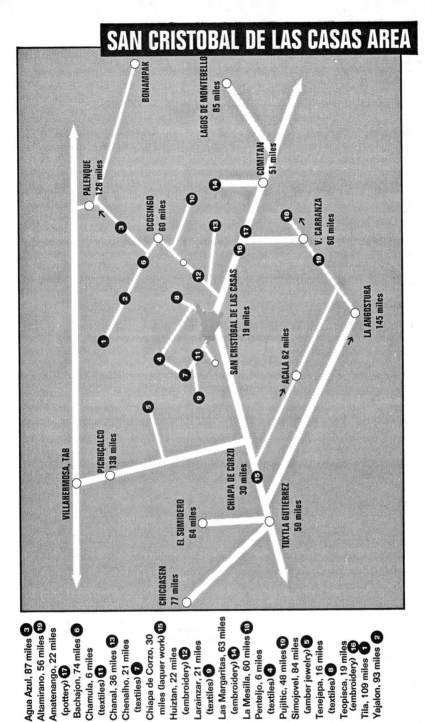

SAN CRISTOBAL DE LAS CASAS AREA

Agua Azul, 87 miles ❸
Altamirano, 56 miles ⓳
Amatenango, 22 miles
(pottery) ⓱
Bachajon, 74 miles ❻
Chamula, 6 miles
(textiles) ⑪
Chanal, 36 miles ⑬
Chenalho, 21 miles
(textiles) ❼
Chiapa de Corzo, 30
miles (laquer work) ⑮
Huiztan, 22 miles
(embroidery) ⑫
Larainzar, 21 miles
(textiles) ❾
Las Margaritas, 63 miles ⑭
(embroidery) ⑭
La Mesilla, 60 miles ⑱
Penteljo, 6 miles
(textiles) ❹
Pujitic, 48 miles ⓳
Simojovel, 84 miles
(amber jewelry) ❺
Tenejapa, 16 miles
(textiles) ❽
Teopisca, 19 miles
(embroidery) ⑯
Tila, 109 miles ❶
Yajalon, 93 miles ❷

your camera are somewhat less—you may only be pelted with fruit, vegetables, and stones. Be respectful and ask first. You might even try offering a small amount of money in exchange for taking a picture. Young handcraft vendors will sometimes offer to be photographed for money.

ORIENTATION

ARRIVING The **first-class Cristóbal Colón bus station** is on Highway 190, which runs on the southern outskirts of San Cristóbal. The street that intersects the highway in front of the bus station is Avenida de los Insurgentes, which is straight up from the central plaza. From the station, the main plaza is nine blocks north along Insurgentes (a 10- or 15-minute walk).

The **second-class Transportes Tuxtla station** is on Calle Pedro Moreno at Allende, three or four blocks away. Walk east along Moreno to get to Insurgentes, then turn left (north) toward the plaza.

INFORMATION The **Municipal Tourism Office,** on the main square in the town hall (tel. 8-0414), next to the cathedral, is well organized with a friendly, helpful staff. The office keeps especially convenient hours: Monday through Friday from 8am to 8pm, on Saturday from 9am to 2pm and 3 to 8pm, and on Sunday from 9am to 2pm. Check the bulletin board here for apartments for rent, shared rides to the States, and cultural events.

CITY LAYOUT The cathedral marks the main plaza, where Avenida de los Insurgentes becomes Utrilla. All streets crossing past the plaza change their names here. The market is nine blocks north along Utrilla, while the bus station is south. From the market, colectivo minibuses trundle to outlying villages.

Take note that this town has at least three streets named "Domínguez." There's Hermanos Domínguez, Belisario Domínguez, and Pantaleón Domínguez.

GETTING AROUND

Most of the sites and shopping in San Cristóbal are within walking distance of the plaza.

Colectivo buses to various parts of the city and the outlying villages depart from the public market at Avenida General Utrilla. Buses late in the day are usually very crowded. Always check to see when the last or next bus returns from wherever you're going, then take the one before that—those last buses sometimes don't materialize and you'll be stranded. Experience is speaking!

As traffic increases in the city it often seems quicker to walk to your destination than grab a **taxi.** Rides from the plaza to most parts of the city are less than $2. There is a taxi stand beside the cathedral at the north side of the plaza.

Rental Cars A car comes in handy for trips to the outlying villages, and may be worth the expense when divided among a group. **Budget Rental,** Avenida Mazar 36 (tel. 8-1871), rents manual-transmission VW Beetles for $35 per day, including insurance.

FAST FACTS

Area Code The telephone area code is 967.

Books *Living Maya* by Walter Morris, with photography by Jeffrey Fox (Abrams), is the best book to read for understanding the culture around San Cristóbal de las Casas.

Bookstore For a good selection of books about local Indians and crafts, go to **Librería Soluna,** Real de Guadelupe 13B.

Climate San Cristóbal can be very cold day or night all year, but especially during the winter months. Most hotels are not heated, although some have fireplaces.

Come prepared to bundle up in layers that can be peeled. I always bring heavy socks, gloves, long johns, and a wool jacket, except in June, July, and August when I leave off the latter three. Then I bring a medium-weight jacket or sweater and always some warm footwear. Some sort of rain gear is handy all year as well, but especially in summer when rains can be torrential.

Parking It's illegal to park your car on most streets of San Cristóbal during the night, so you'll have to find off-street parking. If your hotel doesn't offer it, go to the public parking lot (*Estacionamiento*) in front of the cathedral, just off the main square on 16 de Septiembre. There's a $1 charge per night.

Post Office The post office (Correos) is on Avenida Crecencio Rosas at Cuauhtémoc, half a block south of the main square. It's open Monday through Friday from 8am to 7pm for purchasing stamps and mailing letters (9am to 1pm and 4 to 5pm for mailing packages), and on Saturday and holidays from 9am to 1pm.

Spanish Lessons **Centro Bilingue,** Insurgentes 57 (tel. 8-4157) offers private tutoring in Spanish for $6 an hour.

Telegraph The telegraph office is at Calle Diego de Mazariegos 27 (tel. 8-0661), is just past Avenida 5 de Mayo.

WHAT TO SEE & DO

Although San Cristóbal is a mountain town and somewhat hard to get to, it continues to draw more and more visitors. They come to enjoy the scenery, the air, and hikes in the mountains. But most of all they come to bask in the colorful indigenous culture, carrying on traditional centuries-old daily life wearing beautifully crafted native garb. The life of the Chiapan Maya swirls around you in San Cristóbal, but most travelers take at least one trip to the outlying villages for a clearer vision of the "living Maya."

ATTRACTIONS IN TOWN

NA-BOLOM, Av. Vincente Guerrero 3. Tel. 8-1418.

Those interested in the anthropology of the region will want to visit this museum and library. The home, and headquarters, of anthropologists Franz and Trudy Blom for many years, it is now a focal point for serious study of the region. Na-Bolom offers limited accommodations, with all meals included. The 15 rooms are each decorated with objects and textiles from a particular regional village. Guests are allowed to use the extensive library devoted to Maya literature. Prices (including service and tax) are $40 single, $50 double, and $55 triple (but there's only one triple room). All except two rooms have fireplaces. Meals are optional: Breakfast costs $3; lunch, $6; and dinner, $5. Even if you aren't a guest here, you can come for a meal. Just be sure to make a reservation and arrive on time. The colorful dining room has one large table; you might meet some interesting people.

Admission: $1.

Open: Nonguests can take a tour of the house Tues–Sun at 3:30 and 5:30pm.

Directions: Leave the square on Real de Guadalupe, walk four blocks to Avenida Vicente Guerrero, and turn left; 5½ blocks up Guerrero, just past the intersection with Comitan, is Na-Bolom.

TEMPLO Y CONVENTO SANTO DOMINGO, Av. 20 de Noviembre.

Women from the various villages around San Cristóbal gather here to sell their weavings and tapestries. The carved-stone facade is in a style called plateresque, and there's a beautiful gilded wooden altarpiece inside, built in 1560. Attached to the church is the former Convento Santo Domingo, which now houses a small museum of San Cristóbal and Chiapas. It's five blocks north of the zócalo.

Admission: Church, free; museum, $3.

Open: Museum, Tues–Sun 9am–2pm; Church, 7am–6pm.

CATHEDRAL, Av. 20 de Noviembre at Guadalupe Victoria.

San Cristóbal's main cathedral was built in the 1500s and boasts some fine timberwork and a very fancy pulpit.
Admission: Free.
Open: 7am to 6pm.

PALACIO DE LAS BELLAS ARTES, Av. Hidalgo.

Be sure to check out this building three blocks south of the plaza if you are interested in the arts. I recently saw a fine show of batiks and painting here, and another of folk dancing. There should be a schedule of events and shows posted on the door if the Bellas Artes isn't open. There's a public library right next door.

TEMPLO DE SAN CRISTÓBAL.

For the best overview of San Cristóbal, climb the seemingly endless steps to this church and *mirador* (lookout point). Leave the zócalo on Avenida Hidalgo, turn right onto the third street (Hermanos Domínguez); at the end of the street are the steps you've got to climb. A visit here requires stamina. By the way, there are 22 more churches in town, some of which require a strenuous climb up.

HORSEBACK RIDING

The **Casa de Huespedes Margarita** can arrange horseback rides to San Juan Chamula, or up into the hills for around $20 a day, more if you want to have a guide accompany you. Reserve after 7pm at least a day before you want to ride.

SHOPPING

Many Indian villages near San Cristóbal are noted for their weaving, embroidery, brocaded work, leather, and pottery, making the area one of the best in the country for shopping. The craftspeople make and sell beautiful serapes, colorful native shirts, and rebozos in vivid geometric patterns. In leather they are artisans of the highest rating, making the sandals and men's handbags indigenous to this region. There are numerous shops up and down the streets leading to the **market,** all of them willing to sell you anything from string bags and pottery to colorfully patterned ponchos. **Calle Real de Guadalupe** houses more shops than any other street. There's a proliferation of tie-dyed jaspe from Guatemala in bolts and made into clothing, as well as other textiles from that country.

Crafts

CENTRAL MARKET, Av. Utrilla.

The market buildings, and the streets surrounding them, offer just about anything you need. Market day in San Cristóbal is every morning except Sunday (when each village has its own local market), and you'll probably enjoy looking at the sellers as much as at the things they sell. Remember that photography, even a still-life of a chile pepper, can be a risky undertaking. The mercado is north of the Santo Domingo church, about nine blocks from the zócalo.

PLAZA DE LA CALLE REAL, Calle Real de Guadalupe 5.

A number of boutiques are housed in this beautiful old one-story town house. Shop hours vary, but most are open Monday to Saturday from 10am to 1pm and 4pm to 7pm.

LA GALERÍA, Av. Hidalgo 3. Tel. 8-1547.

This lovely shop beneath a great café has a wonderful selection of paintings and greetings cards by Kiki, a German artist who has found her niche in San Cristóbal. There is also a good selection of Oaxacan rugs and pottery, and unusual silver jewelry. Hours are Monday through Saturday from 10am to 8pm.

Textile Shops

SNA JOLOBIL, Av. 20 de Noviembre.

The "weaver's house" (in the Maya language) is located in the former convent (monastery) of Santo Domingo, next to the Templo de Santo Domingo, between

Navarro and Nicaragua. This cooperative store is operated by groups of Tzotzil and Tzeltal craftspeople, with about 3,000 members who contribute products, help in running the store, and share in the moderate profits. Their works are simply beautiful; prices are set, and high—as is the quality. Be sure to take a look. They're open daily from 9am to 6pm.

PLAZA OF SANTO DOMINGO, Av. Utrilla.

The plazas around this church and the nearby Templo de Caridad are filled with women in native garb selling their wares. Here you'll find women from Chamula weaving belts or embroidering, surrounded by piles of loomed woolen textiles from their village. More and more Guatemalan shawls, belts, and bags are included in their inventory. But there are some excellent buys in Chiapan-made wool vests, jackets, rugs, and shawls similar to those in Sna Jolobil, if you take the time to look and bargain. Vendors arrive daily between 9 and 10am and begin to leave around 3pm.

LA SEGOVIANA, Calle Real de Guadalupe 1. Tel. 8-0346.

For quality and value, this is one of San Cristóbal's premier shops, and it's located just off the zócalo. You'll find beautifully woven sweaters, embroidered native dresses, and other fine crafts. The owner disdains the prevalence of Guatemalan goods in San Cristóbal and specializes only in local wares. He's open Monday through Saturday from 9am to 1pm and 4 to 7pm, and on Sunday from 9am to 1pm.

TZONTEHUITZ, Calle Real de Guadelupe.

About seven blocks from the plaza is one of the best shops on Calle Guadalupe. Owner Janet Giacobone specializes in her own textile designs and weavings. Some of her work is loomed in Guatemala, but you can also watch weavers using foot looms at work in a back room of the shop. Hours are Monday through Saturday from 9am to 2pm and 4 to 7pm.

EXCURSIONS TO NEARBY VILLAGES

I highly recommend that you sign up—a day in advance—for the **tour of local villages** led by a delightful mestiza woman, Mercedes Hernández Gómez. Mercedes, a largely self-trained ethnographer, is immensely informed about the history and folkways of the villages. She explains the religious significance of what you will see in the churches, where shamans try to cure Indian patients of various maladies, and she facilitates firsthand contact with Indians. Mercedes leads her group to the colectivos at the market where they board a bus for the first village on their itinerary; group members then hike with Mercedes from village to village, with a break for lunch, and normally return to the plaza about 4pm. To arrange the tour a day in advance, meet Mercedes at the kiosk in the main plaza at 9am, if possible, although you may be able to join a tour at the last minute. The tour is worth every peso of the $12- to $17-per-person charge, which includes all transportation.

SAN JUAN CHAMULA & ZINACANTAN A side trip to the village of San Juan Chamula really gets one into the spirit of San Cristóbal. Sunday, with the market in full swing, is the best day to go for shopping. But other days are good for seeing the village and church more or less unimpeded by anxious children selling their crafts. Colectivos (minibuses) to San Juan Chamula leave the municipal market in San Cristóbal about every half hour, and charge 50¢. Don't expect anyone in these vans to speak English or Spanish.

The village, 5 miles northeast of San Cristóbal, is the Chamula cultural and ceremonial center. Activity centers on the huge church, the plaza, and the municipal building; each year a new group of citizens is chosen to live in the municipal center as caretakers of the saints, settlers of disputes, and enforcers of village rules.

Carnaval takes place just before Lent and is the big annual festival. The Chamulas are not a very wealthy people as their economy is based on agriculture; but the women are the region's best wool weavers, producing finished pieces for themselves and for other villages. When you arrive, a villager will motion you to a municipal building to pay a small fee and sign a form which in Spanish says that you will take pictures of the exterior of the church and nothing else. During Carnaval, no photographs at all are

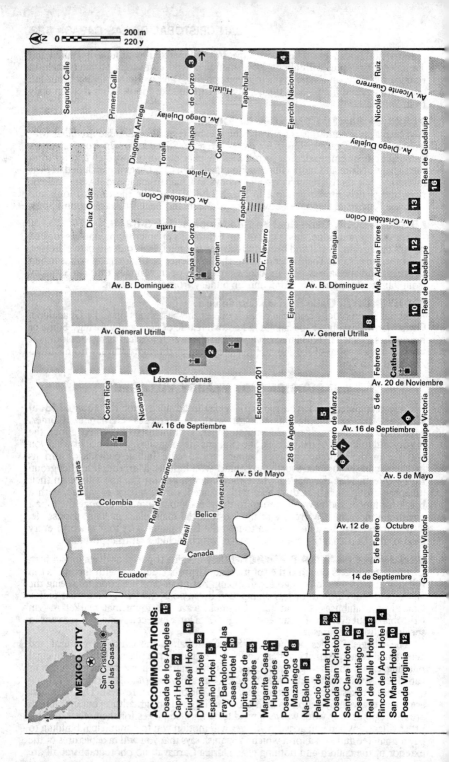

SAN CRISTÓBAL DE LAS CASAS

200 m
0 [scale] 220 y

MEXICO CITY

San Cristóbal
de las Casas

ACCOMMODATIONS:

Posada de los Angeles **15**
Capri Hotel **27**
Ciudad Real Hotel **19**
D'Monica Hotel **32**
Español Hotel **5**
Fray Bartolomé de las Casas Hotel **30**
Lupita Casa de Huespedes **25**
Margarita Casa de Huespedes **11**
Posada Diego de Mazariegos **8**
Na-Balom **3**
Palacio de Moctezuma Hotel **28**
Posada San Cristobal **22**
Santa Clara Hotel **20**
Posada Santiago **16**
Real del Valle Hotel **13**
Rincón del Arco Hotel **4**
San Martin Hotel **10**
Posada Virginia **12**

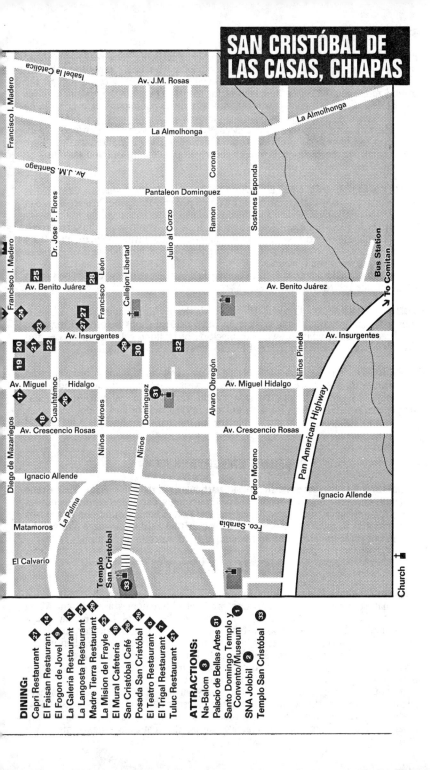

SAN CRISTÓBAL DE LAS CASAS, CHIAPAS

Isabel la Católica
Av. J.M. Rosas
La Almolhonga
La Almolhonga
Francisco I. Madero
Av. J.M. Santiago
Pantaleon Dominguez
Corona
Sostenes Esponda
Dr. Jose F. Flores
Ramon
Julio al Corzo
Bus Station
To Comitan
Francisco Leon
Callejón Libertad
Francisco I. Madero
25
28
Av. Benito Juárez
Av. Benito Juárez
24
27
23
Av. Insurgentes
Av. Insurgentes
20
21
22
29
30
32
Niños Pineda
19
Av. Miguel
Hidalgo
Av. Miguel Hidalgo
17
26
Héroes
Dominguez
31
Alvaro Obregón
18
Cuauhtémoc
Av. Crescencio Rosas
Av. Crescencio Rosas
Diego de Mazariegos
Niños
Niños
Ignacio Allende
Pedro Moreno
Pan American Highway
Ignacio Allende
La Palma
Fco. Sarabia
Matamoros
El Calvario
Templo San Cristóbal
33
Church

DINING:

Capri Restaurant 27
El Faisan Restaurant 4
El Fogon de Jovel 9
La Galeria Restaurant 17
La Langosta Restaurant 24
Madre Tierra Restaurant 29
La Mision del Frayle 23
El Mural Cafetería 18
San Cristóbal Café 25
Posada San Cristóbal 26
El Teatro Restaurant 6
El Trigal Restaurant 7
Tuluc Restaurant 21

ATTRACTIONS:

Na-Balom 3
Palacio de Bellas Artes 31
Santo Domingo Templo y Convento/Museum 1
SNA Jolobil 2
Templo San Cristóbal 33

allowed. Don't dare take pictures inside the church. Folks, they *really* mean this! During Carnaval in 1990 I met a French photographer who took *one* photograph from a hill above town, after which villagers hiding in the bushes wrestled him to the ground and seized the Nikon he was using; he managed to retain the remainder of his camera gear after a struggle. It was the most expensive photograph he ever took, he lamented (see my "Photography Warning" above).

In Zinacantan, before seeing the church, you must also sign a form, which is more rigid than in Chamula—no photos at all. Once permission is granted and you have paid a small fee, an escort will usually show you the church, but you may also be allowed to see it on your own.

AMATENANGO DEL VALLE   About an hour's ride south of San Cristóbal is Amatenango, a town known mostly for women potters. You'll see their work in San Cristóbal—small animals, jars, and large water jugs—but in the village you can visit the potters in their homes. All you have to do is arrive and walk the dirt streets. Villagers will lean over the walls of family compounds and invite you in to select from their inventory. The women wear beautiful red-and-yellow huipils, but if you want to take a photograph, you'll have to pay.

To get there, take a colectivo from the market, but before it lets you off, be sure to ask about the return-trip schedule.

AGUACATENANGO   Located 10 miles south of Amatenango, this village is known for embroidery. If you've been in San Cristóbal shops before arriving here, you'll recognize the white-on-white or black-on-black floral patterns on dresses and blouses for sale. Their own regional blouse, however, is quite different.

TENEJAPA   The weavers of Tenejapa make some of the most beautiful and expensive work you'll see. The best day to visit is on market day (Sunday and Thursday). The weavers of Tenejapa taught the weavers of San Andrés and Magdalena, which accounts for the similarity in their designs and colors.

To get to Tenejapa, try to find a colectivo by the market or hire a taxi for around $20.

EVENING ENTERTAINMENT

Notices around town advertise live music, particularly at the cafés. A favorite pastime is friendly conversation at my recommended restaurants, particularly the coffeehouses with their international clientele. Local residents often hang around one of the two movie theaters in town. There's a slim chance that an English-language film will be shown, but there might be one you wouldn't mind watching in Spanish.

SPECIAL EVENTS

In nearby Chamula, **Carnaval,** the big annual festival, occurs 3 days before Lent. It's a fascinating mingling of the Christian pre-Lenten ceremonies and ancient Maya celebration of the five "lost days" that arise at the end of the 360-day Maya agricultural cycle. Around noon on the Tuesday before Ash Wednesday, groups of village elders run across patches of burning grass as a purification rite, then macho residents run through the streets with a bull. During Carnaval, roads are closed in town and buses drop visitors at the outskirts. *Warning:* No photography of any kind is allowed during the Chamula Carnaval celebrations.

Although perhaps not as dramatic, nearby villages (but not Zinacantan) have celebrations during this time. Visiting them, especially the Sunday before Ash Wednesday, will round out your impression of Carnaval in all its regional varieties. In Tenejapa, the celebrants are still active during the Thursday market after Ash Wednesday.

IMPRESSIONS

*No other race that I can call to mind allowed so wide a disparity between the
simple bread with which they fed their bodies and the arts by which they
nourished their souls. . . . Even today, Mexican Indians have only a rudimentary
development of the so-called instinct of acquisition, and a very sophisticated
development of artistic appreciation as reflected in their craftsmanship.*
—STUART CHASE, *MEXICO: A STUDY OF TWO AMERICAS*, 1931

San Cristóbal explodes with lights, excitement, and hordes of visitors during the
week after Easter, when the annual **Fería de Primavera (Spring Festival)** is held.
Activities include carnival rides, food stalls, handcraft shops, parades, and band
concerts filling an entire week. Hotel rooms are scarce and room prices rise
accordingly.

Another spectacle is staged July 22–25, the date of the annual **Fiesta of San
Cristóbal,** the town's patron saint. The steps up to the San Cristóbal church are lit
with torches at night. Pilgrimages to the church begin several days earlier and on the
night of the 24th there's an all-night vigil.

WHERE TO STAY

San Cristóbal is experiencing a boom, with new hotels and restaurants springing up
overnight. Hot water seems to be temperamental all over town. Many hotels post the
hours for hot water, normally 6am to 10am and 6pm to 10pm. Hotel rates go up 10%
to 20% during peak seasons, including Easter Week.

DOUBLES FOR LESS THAN $15

**CASA DE HUESPEDES MARGARITA, Calle Real de Guadalupe 34, San
Cristóbal de las Casas, Chi. 29200. Tel. 967/8-0957.** 26 rms (12 with
bath).
$ Rates: $6 dorm bed; $8.50 single; $10 double; $12.50 triple.
Part hotel, part youth hostel, this establishment has rooms arranged around a
courtyard where the young backpackers congregate. The rooms have sagging
mattresses and flimsy locks; bathrooms are only fair. There's a general lack of
organization and security here, but an abundance of information and contacts. The
cafeteria is filled with youths in the evening, and there is live music at 8pm. An efficient
laundry service washes clothes for $1.50 per kilo (2.2 lb.). Margarita's also has horse
rentals. It's 1½ blocks east of the plaza between Avenida B Domínguez and Colón.

**CASA DE HUESPEDES LUPITA, Juárez 12, San Cristóbal de la Casas,
Chi. 29200. Tel. 967/8-1421.** 15 rms (none with bath).
$ Rats: $7 single; $12 double.
Forget luxury, privacy, and amenities and concentrate on your budget at this basic
hostelry one block south and one block east of the plaza. Guests share four simple
bathrooms without shower curtains or doors; the rooms have good mattresses, a
wooden chair, and open shelves for your belongings. Guests can use the locked
kitchen, keep perishables in the refrigerator, and wash their clothes in the laundry
tubs. The proprietress does her best to beautify the surroundings, painting every wall
lavender and distributing plants about the hallways.

**HOTEL SAN MARTÍN, Calle Real de Guadalupe 16, San Cristóbal de las
Casas, Chi. 29200. Tel. 967/8-0533.** 26 rms (all with bath).
$ Rates: $8.50 single; $12 double; $14.50 triple.
Long, narrow hallways lead to small, dark rooms in this older three-story, family-run
operation. Peach-colored walls and blue-tile baths add some life to the rooms, and the

chirping caged canaries add a bit of cheer. The location—half a block east of the plaza on Guadalupe, between Utrilla and Domínguez—is a plus since the hotel is within walking distance of almost everything.

DOUBLES FOR LESS THAN $20

POSADA VIRGINIA, Cristóbal Colón 11, San Cristóbal de la Casas, Chi. 29200. Tel. 967/8-1116. 7 rms (all with bath).
$ Rates: $12.50 single; $17 double or triple. **Parking:** Free.

A real find up a quiet street three blocks north of the plaza and one block southeast on Real de Guadalupe, with a view from the second-story rooms of the hillsides surrounding downtown. The rooms and bathrooms are spanking new, with brown patchwork bedspreads and tile floors. The proprietors are extremely helpful and proud of their establishment.

POSADA SANTIAGO, Calle Real de Guadalupe 32, San Cristóbal de las Casas, Chi. 29200. Tel. 967/8-0024. 9 rms (all with bath).
$ Rates: $12.50 single; $17 double.
The rooms are nicer at other establishments in the same price range, though these get plenty of sunlight (especially on the third floor) and the carpeting adds warmth. The beds and rooms are very small, the bathrooms long and narrow. It's 2½ blocks east of the plaza.

REAL DE VALLE, Calle Real de Guadelupe 14, San Cristóbal de las Casas, Chi. 29200. Tel. 967/8-0680. 40 rms (all with bath).
$ Rates: $13.50 single; $16.75 double; $19.50 triple. **Parking:** Free.

You couldn't ask for friendlier or more helpful staff people than here, two blocks east of the plaza, where the manager is quick to change money, seek medical assistance, arrange tours, and help his guests in any way possible. The hotel is under renovation, and the 24 new rooms in the back three-story section have new bathrooms, big closets, and a brown-and-cream decor. There's a rooftop solarium with chaise longues, a small cafeteria, and an upstairs dining room with a big fireplace. Eventually the parking lot will become a courtyard, but for now there is space by the office for five or six small cars.

POSADA SAN CRISTÓBAL, Insurgentes 3, San Cristóbal de las Casas, Chi. 29200. Tel. 967/8-1900. 10 rms (all with bath).
$ Rates: $13.50 single; $16.75 double.
This small hotel is only one block south of the plaza, yet quiet. The small rooms are immaculately clean with simple wooden beds and dressers, and no heat, and the showers tend to flood the bathroom floors. While not fancy, it's convenient, and comfortable.

HOTEL FRAY BARTOLOMÉ DE LAS CASAS, Niños Héroes 2, San Cristó-bal de las Casas, Chi. 29200. Tel. 967/8-0932. 26 rms (all with bath).
$ Rates: $13.50 single; $16.75 double. **Parking:** Free.
This clean, quiet, old colonial inn has plain heated rooms in fair condition: In some the rugs are stained and some showers drip constantly; other rooms are absolutely satisfactory. The courtyard has planters, bentwood furniture, and lots of flowers, and breakfast is served in the small dining room. The hotel is south of the plaza at Insurgentes, next to the Pemex station.

DOUBLES FOR LESS THAN $35

POSADA DE LOS ANGELES, Calle Francisco Madero 17, San Cristóbal de las Casas, Chi. 29200. Tel. 967/8-1173. Fax 967/8-4371. 21 rms (all with bath). TV
$ Rates: $17 single; $21 double; $25.50 triple.
It doesn't look like much from the street, but its vaulted ceilings and skylights make this three-story hotel seem much larger and brighter than many others in the city. The

orange walls may be a bit much, but the bathrooms are large, modern, and immaculately clean, and the windows open to a pretty courtyard with a fountain. The rooftop sun deck is a great siesta spot. The posada is 1½ blocks east of the plaza, on Madero between Juárez and Ortiz de Dominguez.

HOTEL D'MONICA, Insurgentes 33, San Cristóbal de las Casas, Chi. 29200. Tel. 967/8-0732. Fax 967/8-2940. 59 rms (all with bath). TV TEL

$ Rates: $18 single; $22 double; $26 triple. **Parking:** Free.

You can't miss this bright-orange hacienda looming behind a wrought-iron gate, the entrance to one of the best budget buys near the plaza. Tile staircases, stained-glass windows, and an abundance of blooming plants give the feel of a colonial home; the large rooms have blond-wood furnishings, new bathroom fixtures, color TVs with U.S. channels, carpeting, and a blue-and-white decor. There's a restaurant in the hotel and the Madre Tierra restaurant (see "Where to Eat," below) is close. Each room has a fireplace (firewood is $1 extra). The management operates two other hotels, a plain motel at 5 de Febrero no. 18, and a cluster of bungalows on the road to San Juan Chamula. Reservations for all hotels can be arranged at the above phone numbers.

The Hotel d'Monica is four blocks south of the plaza and one block south of the Pemex station, opposite the Fray Bartolomé statue and park.

HOTEL PALACIO DE MOCTEZUMA, Av. Juárez 16, San Cristóbal de las Casas, Chi. 29200. Tel. 967/8-0352 or 8-1142. 36 rms (all with bath). TEL

$ Rates: $20 single; $25 double.

A good choice near the plaza, overgrown with bougainvillea and geraniums, with fresh-cut flowers tucked around tile fountains. The heated rooms have lace curtains, red carpeting, modern tiled showers, and French windows. Overstuffed couches face a large fireplace in the lobby bar, a good spot to warm your toes and catch up on your postcards. On Guadalupe, walk one block east of Insurgentes to Juáres, turn right and walk three blocks south to Francisco León.

HOTEL ESPAÑOL, 1 de Marzo and 16 de Septiembre, San Cristóbal de las Casas, Chi. 29300. Tel. 967/8-0412. 30 rms (all with bath).

$ Rates: $21 single; $27 double; $30 triple.

Blue-and-white-tile fountains and a mass of plants and trees makes this the prettiest courtyard in the city. The old-fashioned rooms arranged around the first courtyard have fireplaces (one bundle of wood is provided free of charge each night), wrought-iron lamps, and modern bathrooms with hand-painted tiles. Those at the back of the courtyard are the quietest. The Español is three blocks northwest of the plaza.

HOTEL RINCÓN DEL ARCO, Ejercito Nacional 66, San Cristóbal de las Casas, Chi. 29200. Tel. 967/8-1313. Fax 967/8-1568. 36 rms (all with bath). TV TEL

$ Rates: $25 single; $30 double. **Parking:** Free.

Those seeking quiet accommodations removed from the center of town, yet still within walking distance of the major sights, should try this cozy colonial mansion nine blocks northeast of the plaza. You will find clean, sizable rooms, each a bit different and furnished in antiques and colonial-style furniture. Some rooms have fireplaces. The management is eager to make your stay a good one. The hotel is six blocks east of the Templo Santo Domingo at the corner of Guerrero.

HOTEL CIUDAD REAL, Plaza 31 de Marzo no. 10, San Cristóbal de las Casas, Chi. 29200. Tel. 967/8-0187. Fax 967/8-0464. 31 rms (all with bath).

$ Rates: $26 single; $30 double.

The decor, the courtyard, and the restaurant with its large fireplace all help make this one of the most inviting hotels in town. Unfortunately, noise from the courtyard can be heard in the rooms, which are small but recently remodeled; all have fireplaces. The rooms on the top floor, with their sloping ceilings, are the most desirable. The main-floor atrium and dining room are good spots to review the day's events. You'll find the hotel on the south side of the plaza, between Hidalgo and Insurgentes.

HOTEL SANTA CLARA, Av. Insurgentes 1, San Cristóbal de las Casas, Chi. 29200. Tel. 967/8-1140. 40 rms (all with bath). TV
$ Rates: $19 single; $32 double; $41.75 triple. **Parking:** Free.
A hacienda-style setting with two-story wings with red-tile roofs framing a central courtyard where scarlet macaws squawk from their cages—there's a certain charm to this old hotel on the south side of the plaza, once called Casa de las Sirenas for the concrete mermaids perched on the outer corners of the building. The rooms have thick carpeting and lots of blankets, but no fireplaces; it can get mighty drafty and cold on wi л ⁚ nights.

WORTH THE EXTRA BUCKS

POSADA DIEGO DE MAZARIEGOS, María Adelina Flores 2 and Cinco de Febrero no. 1, San Cristóbal de las Casas, Chi. 29200. Tel. 967/8-0513 or 8-1825. 54 rms (all with bath). TV TEL
$ Rates: $30 single; $38 double.
⭐ Two separate colonial-style buildings across the street from each other make up this established hotel, one of the best in the city and popular with tour groups. Both buildings are part of former mansions each built around a central courtyard. The colonial decor befits the mountain-town setting. The small rooms in one building have attractive furnishings but little space; those in the other building are very large. Most have fireplaces, but wood costs extra. Facilities include a restaurant, bar, travel agency, and gift shop. The posada is at the corner of Utrilla, 1 block north of the main plaza, where Flores becomes 5 de Febrero.

HOSTELS

For really low-cost lodgings there are basic-but-acceptable *hospedajes* and posadas which charge about $8 for a single and $10 for a double. Usually these places are unadvertised; if you're interested in a very cheap *hospedaje,* ask around in a restaurant or café and you're sure to find one.

To get you started, I suggest looking on Calle Real de Guadalupe, east out of the main square. Some of the best ones are here. Other ones, on Insurgentes near the bus station, tend to be noisy.

WHERE TO EAT

In addition to the dining establishments mentioned below, most hotels have their own restaurants and serve good meals. Be sure to look for regional Chiapan food like large tamales, butifarra (a delicious sausage), and posh (a local firewater similar to aguardiente). But remember that you're about a mile and a half high here and food digests more slowly.

MEALS FOR LESS THAN $10

MADRE TIERRA, Insurgentes 19.
Specialty: MEXICAN/VEGETARIAN.
$ Prices: Granola with yogurt $2.50; quiche $2.50; BLT sandwich $2; comida corrida $5.25.
Open: Restaurant, daily 8am–9:45pm; bakery, Mon–Sat 9am–8pm, Sun 9am–noon.
⭐ This restaurant satisfies the hankerings of both meat lovers and vegetarians, and all those seeking a health fix. The bakery specializes in whole-wheat breads, pastries, pizza by the slice, quiche, grains, granola, and dried fruit (and sells a great postcard collection). The restaurant serves the bakery's goods and other fare in an old mansion with wood-plank floors, long windows looking onto the street, and tables covered in colorful Guatemalan jaspe. Classical music plays softly in the background. It's a good place for a cappuccino and pastry or a meal—the comida

corrida is very filling. The restaurant and back courtyard host appearances by salsa bands, jazz groups, and other artists passing through town. It's opposite the Parque Fray Bartolomé de las Casa, three blocks south of the main plaza.

EL TRIGAL, Calle 1 de Marzo no. 13.

Specialty: MEXICAN.
$ Prices: Tacos $2; main courses $5.
Open: Daily 7am–10pm.

The setting is somewhat tacky and strange, two blocks north of the plaza in the courtyard of an old house painted orange, pink, and red. But the food is excellent, and the service is very friendly—and with only six tables, it's fairly efficient as well. For breakfast, have granola with fruit and homemade yogurt.

RESTAURANT EL FAISAN, Madero 2.

Specialty: MEXICAN.
$ Prices: Main courses $4–$6; comida corrida $5.
Open: Daily 7:30am–11pm.

Low lighting, clay lanterns, glass-top tables, and native embroidery draw a romantic dinner crowd to this small, dark restaurant half a block east of the plaza. If the tables are full downstairs, don't despair; there are more upstairs. The menu includes delicious pollo a la plancha, cochinita guisado, and quesadillas with sliced red peppers. Wine is served.

RESTAURANT TULUC, Insurgentes 5. Tel. 8-2090.

Specialty: MEXICAN.
$ Prices: Main courses $1.50–$6; comida corrida $4.50.
Open: Daily 6am–10pm.

The comida is an exceptional value here—the five-course feast begins with a plentiful fruit plate or a tropical drink, followed by fresh-baked rolls and a generous bowl of soup. You next work your way through a heaping plate of rice and a main dish of your choice (meat, chicken, or fish). Even though that's already five courses, you still get dessert (try pastel tres leches) and a fine cup of coffee. The evening menu is equally popular; the specialty is the filete tuluc, a beef filet wrapped around spinach and cheese, served with fried potatoes and green beans. The Chiapaneco breakfast is a filling quartet of juice, toast, Chiapan tamales, and a choice of tea, coffee, cappuccino, or hot chocolate. The owner speaks seven languages. By the way, there's a portrait of El Tuluc's namesake, the turkey, over the espresso machine. A 15% service charge will be added to your bill. You can change dollars and traveler's checks here. It's a block south of the plaza.

LA GALERÍA, Av. Hidalgo 3. Tel. 8-1547.

Specialty: MEXICAN/AMERICAN.
$ Prices: Yogurt and fruit $2; lemonade and beer $1; spaghetti $3.50; comida corrida $5.
Open: Daily 10am–8pm.

This is a double treat—a shop of folk art, weaving, pottery, and painting, and a café-restaurant upstairs which serves whole-wheat sandwiches, big fruit salads, and desserts. La Galería, half a block southwest of the plaza, is the "in" place for artsy expatriates and tourists; Bonnie Raitt's latest songs play in the background, alternating with the jazzy strands of Sade. There's a stage on the first floor where salsa and jazz bands appear on occasion, and the best tables in the house are along the upstairs balcony overlooking the stage and courtyard fountain. The bulletin board in the stairwell makes for interesting reading. The shop has a separate street entrance.

LA MISIÓN DEL FRAYLE, Insurgentes 10. Tel. 8-1298

Specialty: MEXICAN.
$ Prices: Main courses $4–$7.
Open: Daily 7:30am–11pm.

This sophisticated snack grill is very popular among Mexicans who dine late. Ask to be served "anafre"—individual grills are brought to your table so your food is constantly sizzling. You can also watch the women cook savory beef filets which are served in earthenware crockery. The menu also includes tacos, tostadas, soups, and quesadillas. La Misión is a block south of the plaza.

LA LANGOSTA, Madero 9. Tel. 8-2238.

Specialty: MEXICAN.
$ Prices: Breakfast $2.60; asparagus soup $2; mixed grill brochette $7.
Open: Mon–Sat 10am–1am, Sun 10am–10pm.

This pretty, upscale restaurant a block east of the plaza looks more expensive than it really is, and offers an unusual blend of local dishes with a twist. Try the homemade ginger ale, the chalupas (somewhat like tostadas), and the exceptional spicy mole coleto (chicken). The glass-top tables, blond-wood chairs, and cloth napkins give a sense of class, though the TV does get annoying.

EL FOGÓN DE JOVEL, 16 de Septiembre no. 11. Tel. 7-8257.

Specialty: CHIAPAN.
$ Prices: Corn soup $2; Chiapan tamales $4.25; main courses $5–$8.
Open: Breakfast/lunch daily 9am–5pm; dinner daily 7–10:30pm.

If word-of-mouth doesn't lead you here, the lively sounds of marimba music will. Chiapan food is served at this handsome old town house, built around a central courtyard a block north of the plaza. The waiters wear local costumes. Walls are hung with Guatemalan and Chiapan prints and folk art. Dine outside under the portals around the courtyard or in an interior high-ceilinged room. Each dish and regional drink is explained on the menu in Spanish.

To get you started, I highly recommend an order of Chiapan tamales, which comes with three different and filling tamales. The corn soup is smooth and delicious. The beef-stuffed chile relleño is one of the best buys on the menu. Before your relleño is presented, a basket of steaming warm tortillas arrives, along with six condiments of guacamole, refried beans, cheese, salsa Mexicana, green sauce, and hot pickled vegetables for a make-your-own-taco appetizer. It's really enough for two people. Then comes the huge chile relleño together with a pile of rice. Delicious! On a cold afternoon, a cup of warm fruit punch spiked with a shot of posh, a distilled sugar-and-corn drink popular among the locals, really puts a bloom on the cheeks.

COFFEEHOUSES

Chiapan-grown coffee is highly regarded and so it's natural to find a proliferation of coffeehouses here, most of which are concealed in the nooks and crannies of San Cristóbal's side streets.

CAFETERÍA EL MURAL, Crescencia Rosas 4.

Specialty: MEXICAN.
$ Prices: Cappuccino 80¢; American coffee 50¢; crepas cajetas (caramel crêpes) $2.60; fruit salad $1.75.
Open: Breakfast/lunch Mon–Sat 8:30am–2pm; dinner daily 5–10pm.

After you've eased into one of the comfortable chairs at a small pine table, expect a nice feeling to settle in. Near the door, one clever patron has penned a set of "coffeehouse" cartoons that overcome any language barrier. I like to drop in at this classy place during the evening to sample the local coffee brewed 14 different ways, and blended imaginatively with flavored liqueurs. It's a block southwest of the plaza.

CAFE SAN CRISTÓBAL, Cuauhtémoc 1.

Specialty: COFFEE/CAKE.
$ Prices: Coffee 50¢; cake $1.
Open: Daily 9am–2pm and 4–10pm.

Not only is this a café, but coffee beans are also sold by the kilogram (2.2 lb.) here for $2.75. Chess is the game of choice at the few tables and booths; men hunker over their chessboards for hours, drinking coffee and visiting with friends. A cup of coffee here is a calming respite from the rush outside the door. It's two blocks southwest of the plaza.

READERS RECOMMEND

Capri, on Insurgentes. *"The restaurant Capri, 30 yards from the Hotel Fray Bartolomé walking toward the zócalo, offers good four-course meals at both lunch and dinner. The food was well cooked and served; for each course there was a selection of two to four choices."*—Richard Gucci, Napoli, Italy. [*Author's* Note: The Capri is a very simple storefront-type café with white walls, Formica-type tables, and a full view of the street. It's often completely empty, but gets a crowd during peak dining times. Prices are reasonable—comida corrida is $4; breakfast, $2.75; and enchiladas, $2.75.]

EASY EXCURSIONS FROM SAN CRISTÓBAL

✪ **BONAMPAK & YAXCHILÁN**   The ruins of Bonampak, southeast of Palenque on the Guatemalan border, were uncovered in 1946. The mural discovered on the interior walls of one of the buildings is the greatest battle painting of pre-Hispanic Mexico. Reproductions of the vivid murals found here, deep in the jungle, are on view in the Regional Archeology Museum in Villahermosa. To see the real thing at Bonampak you'll have to hire a small plane to buzz you in, or else hire a sturdy car or Jeep to take you the 5 hours into the jungle. You can visit nearby Yaxchilán on the same trip. Plan to camp overnight, or go and return in a day.

Tours of Bonampak and Yaxchilán can be arranged by several agencies in San Cristóbal. One of them, **ATI,** inside El Fogón restaurant at 16 de Septiembre no. 11 (tel. 967/8-2550; fax 967/8-3145), offers the following program: From the airport in nearby Comitan you fly to Yaxchilán. It's a 5-minute walk from the airstrip to the site. After about 2 hours there, it's a 10-minute flight to Bonampak. A box lunch is included. On the return trip you fly over the Laguna de Miramar and Montebello lakes, and the ruins of Chincultic, before arriving back in Comitan and San Cristóbal. The cost of this all-day excursion is $750 for one to four passengers. A fifth person pays $150. See "Easy Excursions from Palenque" in Section 3, "Palenque," above for details on camping overnight at Yaxchilán.

If you're considering a day trip to the archeological site of Palenque using ATI (mentioned above) or a similar travel agency, here's how it works: Starting at 7 or 8am, within 3 hours you reach the Agua Azul waterfalls where there's a 1½-hour stop to swim. From there it's another 1½-hour drive to Palenque. You'll have about 2 hours to see the site. If your group agrees, you can skip the swim and have more time at Palenque. It'll be a minimum 16-hour day and costs $180 for one or two people, and only slightly more for three or four.

COMITAN & MONTEBELLO NATIONAL PARK   Southeast from San Cristóbal, another 46 miles, lies **Comitan** (alt. 5,018 ft.; pop. 40,000), a pretty town on a hillside, known for a sugarcane-based fire water called *comitecho*. It's also the last big town along the Pan American Highway before the Guatemalan border and it's the location of the nearest airport to San Cristóbal.

What do you do with a free day in Comitan? You take a side trip to the **Montebello National Park** and enjoy the multicolored lakes and exuberant tropical vegetation. Buses run out to the park, but schedules change with the seasons so check for the latest information at the office of Transportes Montebello, on 5a Avenida Sur. Plan to see the park in a day as there are no places to stay overnight.

EN ROUTE TO TUXTLA GUTIÉRREZ

Highway 195 winds from Villahermosa and San Cristóbal to Tuxtla, and shouldn't be taken fast. The road also passes through some of the most gorgeous scenery in all Mexico: Emerald-green mountains, thick banana groves, citrus trees growing wild by the roadside, quaint villages, and breathtaking vistas come one after the other as you wind along. These curves, however, may cause motion sickness even to those not normally prone to it. Consider taking a precautionary pill or bring along some hard candy or gum just in case. It's important to get an early start on this road, especially if you're driving from San Cristóbal, for patches of fog often slow traffic until you climb above the clouds. The trip from San Cristóbal to Tuxtla is about 1½ hours: to Villahermosa it's about 6 to 7 hours by car (7 to 8 by bus).

---

4. TUXTLA GUTIÉRREZ

51 miles E of San Cristóbal, 173 miles E of Villahermosa,
151 miles SE of Ciudad Cuauhtémoc on the Guatemalan border

GETTING THERE **By Plane** **Aviación de Chiapas (Aviacsa)** flies to Tuxtla from Villahermosa, Tapachula, Minatitlán, Huatulco, and Oaxaca. **Mexicana** has daily direct, nonstop flights from Mexico City, and daily flights from Acapulco, Mérida, Oaxaca, and Villahermosa. **AeroCaribe** flies between Tuxtla and several regional destinations.

By Bus First-class **Autobuses Cristóbal Colón** runs 5 daily buses to Tuxtla from Villahermosa, 12 from San Cristóbal, 2 from Oaxaca, and 5 from Comitan.

By Car From Oaxaca or Veracruz, you enter by Highway 190. From Villahermosa or San Cristóbal, you'll enter at the opposite end of town. Eventually, you will end up at the big main square, Plaza Cívica, with its gleaming white church (take a look at the clockwork figures in the tower) and modern buildings.

ESSENTIALS The **American Express** representative is Viajes Marabasco, Plaza Bonampak, Loc. 4, Col. Moctezuma (tel. 961/2-6998; fax 961/2-4053). The **telephone area code** is 961.

DEPARTING **By Plane** **Mexicana,** Avenida Central Poniente 206 (tel. 961/2-0020 or 2-5402, or 3-4921 at the airport), flies from Tuxtla's international Aeropuerto Llano San Juan to Mexico City, Guadalajara, Puerto Escondido, and Acapulco. Check with the local office of Mexicana about van departures to the airport, which leave from in front of the Mexicana offices in time for each flight.
Flights to Oaxaca, Villahermosa, Mérida, and Cancún are handled by **AeroCaribe** (same address and phone as Mexicana), which flies out of a smaller airport, Aeropuerto Francisco Sarabia, only 15 minutes from downtown Tuxtla in the suburb of Teran. This airport is on the edge of a military base, and you must show your ticket and specify the airline. **Aviación de Chiapas (Aviacsa)**, Avenida Norte Poniente 1026 (tel. 3-0978 or 2-8081), also flies from the smaller airport, to Villahermosa, Tapachula, Oaxaca, Chetumal, and Mexico City, but from a different terminal than AeroCaribe.

By Bus First-class **Autobuses Cristóbal Colón** runs 5 daily buses from Tuxtla to Villahermosa, 12 daily buses to San Cristóbal, 2 to Oaxaca, and 5 to Comitan and Ciudad Cuauhtémoc on the Guatemalan border. All 12 buses from Tuxtla to San Cristóbal originate in Tuxtla and are generally easy to book, unless it's a holiday. The first is at 6am and the last is at 9:15pm. The drive by bus or car takes an hour and a half.

By Car From Tuxtla to Villahermosa, take Highway 199, then cut north on Highway 195 to Villahermosa. To San Cristóbal, take Highway 199 all the way. The road winds from Tuxtla and San Cristóbal to Villahermosa, and shouldn't be taken fast. Besides being curvaceous, the road also passes through some of the most gorgeous scenery in all Mexico: Emerald-green mountains, thick banana groves, citrus trees growing wild by the roadside, quaint villages, and breathtaking vistas come one after the other as you wind along. Take precautions against motion sickness. It's important to get an early start on this road, especially if you're driving from San Cristóbal, for patches of fog often slow traffic until you climb above the clouds. The trip from San Cristóbal to Villahermosa takes 5 to 6 hours by car, 6 to 8 hours by bus.

Tuxtla Gutiérrez (alt. 1,838 ft.; pop. 300,000) is the boom-town capital of the state of Chiapas, long Mexico's coffee-growing center, but more recently an oil-prospector's mecca. The mammoth reserves discovered in this wild, mountainous state several years ago have brought people, business, and wealth to Tuxtla. It's not exactly an unpleasant town, but hasn't been able to manage growth with any aesthetic considerations. Tourists are more of a footnote than a necessity. If you have some time to spare, visit the Tuxtla zoo and Sumidero Canyon.

ORIENTATION

ARRIVING From the **international airport** off Highway 190, it's a 40-minute ride to the center of town. The colectivo into town costs $5, and more if there are only a few passengers. Don't tarry at the airport, though—the vans fill up and leave immediately, and taxis charge about five times the price of a collective van for the same trip to downtown Tuxtla.

The **Cristóbal Colón bus terminal,** 2a Avenida Norte and 2a Calle Poniente, is two blocks west of Calle Central.

Taxi drivers solicit riders to San Cristóbal outside the bus station and airports. The going rate of $30 per car can be divided by up to six passengers. You'll have to wait for them to assemble, however, unless fewer than six agree to split the fare.

INFORMATION The **Tourist Office** (tel. 3-3079) is at the western end of town on Avenida Central/Boulevard Domínguez, near the Hotel Bonampak Tuxtla. It's on the second floor in the Plaza de las Instituciones building and is open Monday through Friday from 8am to 8pm.

There's also a helpful **tourist-information booth** at the international airport, staffed when flights are due to arrive.

CITY LAYOUT The city is divided by two "Central" streets: **Calle Central,** running north to south; and **Avenida Central** (also called Avenida 14 de Septiembre), running east to west. The main highway is Avenida Central (also named Boulevard Domínguez west of downtown). Streets are numbered from these central arteries, with the suffix *norte, sur, oriente,* or *poniente* designating the direction of progress from the central arteries.

GETTING AROUND

Buses to all parts of the city converge on Plaza Cívica along Calle Central. **Taxi** fares are higher here than in other regions; for example, a taxi across town from the bus station to the tourist office is $2.50.

WHAT TO SEE & DO

The majority of travelers are simply passing through Tuxtla on their way to San Cristóbal. The excellent zoo, or possibly the Sumidero Canyon, is the best place to spend any hours you have to spare.

PARQUE MADERO, 11A Av. Oriente Norte.

A museum and cultural center are clustered in this park filled with botanical gardens, walking trails, and monuments. The **Regional Museum of Anthropology,** inside the park documents the history of Chiapas and also includes a garden, children's area, and theater. In one short stop, you can learn about Chiapas's past civilizations, its flora, and its present-day accomplishments.

Admission: $3.50.

Open: Museum, Tues–Sun 9am–4pm; botanical gardens, Tues–Sun 9am–6pm; children's area, Tues–Sun 10am–9pm. **Directions:** The park is 11 blocks northeast of the main plaza; catch a colectivo along Avenida Central, or walk about 15 minutes east along 5A Calle Norte Oriente.

MIGUEL ALVAREZ DEL TORO ZOO (ZOOMAT), Blvd. Samuel León Brinois, southeast of downtown.

Located in the forest called El Zapotal, ZOOMAT is one of the best in Mexico, and it's a personal favorite. Its collection of animals and birds indigenous to this area gives the visitor a tangible sense of what Chiapas is like in the wild. Jaguars, howler monkeys, owls, and many more exotic creatures are kept in roomy cages that replicate their home terrain, and the whole zoo is so buried in vegetation that you can almost pretend you're spotting natural habitats. Unlike other zoos I've visited, the animals are almost always on view; many will come to the fence if you make a kissing noise.

Admission: Free; donations solicited.

Open: Tues–Sun 8:30am–5:30pm. **Directions:** The zoo is about 5 miles southeast of downtown; buses for the zoo can be found along Avenida Central and at Parque Madero.

SHOPPING

The government-operated **Casa de las Artesanías,** Boulevard Domínguez 950 (tel. 3-3478), features a fine and extensive collection of crafts from throughout the state of Chiapas. Pottery, weaving, jewelry, and wooden articles are grouped by area and type. The displays are informative as well as for sale. The shop is on the ground floor of Plaza de las Instituciones, the same building housing the tourism office. It's open Monday through Saturday from 9am to 2pm and 5 to 8pm.

WHERE TO STAY

As Tuxtla booms, the center of the hotel industry has moved out of town, west to Highway 190. As you come in from the airport, you'll notice the new motel-style hostelries, all of which charge rates out of our range: the Hotel Flamboyant (it's just that too), the Palace Inn, Hotel Laganja, La Hacienda, and the older Hotel Bonampak Tuxtla. A few less expensive hotels are in the center, but they aren't very good.

HOTEL BONAMPAK TUXTLA, Av. Central/Blvd. Domínguez 180, Tuxtla Gutiérrez, Chi. 29030. Tel. 961/3-2050. Fax 961/2-7737. 112 rms (all with bath). A/C TV TEL

$ Rates: $40 single; $45 double.

This large, sprawling hotel has a swimming pool, barbershop, beauty parlor, tennis court, parking, and restaurant. Rooms are not cheap, but in booming Tuxtla its prices are about the norm. The rooms facing the street are horribly noisy, even with the windows closed and the air conditioning on. But interior rooms are blissfully quiet. Each is comfortable and large, but nothing special. The hotel is on the northwest outskirts of downtown, where Avenida 14 de Septiembre becomes Boulevard Domínguez, across the street from the tourist office.

GRAN HOTEL HUMBERTO, Av. Central 180, Tuxtla Gutiérrez, Chi. 29000. Tel. 961/2-2080 or 2-2504. 105 rms (all with bath). TV TEL

$ Rates: $30 single; $34 double.

This older ten-story inner-city hotel, in the center of downtown, 2½ blocks east of the first-class bus station, is your best bet in booming Tuxtla, which I say with some reservation. It's clean and comfortable enough, but the odor of bug repellant may be a bit much. Hallways are dark and furnishings are circa 1950 in shades of brown. Purified water comes from open jugs in the hallways—I'd suggest bringing your own.

WHERE TO EAT

If you get up before the Flamingo (see below) opens at 7am, you can grab something to eat at the *panadería* (bakery) farther up the same street (1a Calle Poniente, up from Avenida Central). Sweet rolls and danish in hand, walk back down toward the Flamingo, and stop at the Jugos California stand for a huge glass of fresh-squeezed orange juice.

CAFE AVENIDA, Av. Central 230, at 1a Calle Pte.

Specialty: COFFEE.

$ Prices: Coffee 50¢ per cup.

Open: Daily 7am–7pm.

There's not much to do in Tuxtla, but for coffee purists I suggest dropping by the Cafe Avenida (no sign, but it's next to the Hotel Avenida) for a cup or two of the only thing they serve: freshly ground and brewed Chiapan coffee. Huge sacks of beans lean against the counter and the grinder hums away, producing wonderful coffee aromas. The Formica tables have been cleaned so often that the decorative pattern is wearing off. No tea, no sweets, no milk—just coffee, dark roasted (almost burnt), rough flavored, and hearty.

FLAMINGO RESTAURANTE-CAFETERÍA, Zardain Building, 1 Calle Pte. no. 168. Tel. 2-0922.

Specialty: MEXICAN.

$ Prices: Breakfast $2.50; main dishes $2.50–$4; comida corrida $4–$7; coffee 50¢ per cup.

Open: Daily 7am–11pm.

Considered *the* place to eat downtown (not far from Plaza Cívica), it's air-conditioned and busy at all hours. The decor is of the Formica cafeteria genre and reminds me of a Hong Kong dim sum restaurant. The menu features a wide selection of dishes (and prices), served with dispatch. Seafood is flown in frequently, so the oysters, shrimp, and fish specialties are usually fresh, but I wouldn't splurge and expect a great meal.

To get here from the bus station, turn left, then take the first right; walk up and across Avenida Central, and the Zardain Building is on the right side.

CAFETERÍA BONAMPAK, in the Hotel Bonampak, Blvd. Domínguez 180. Tel. 3-2050.

Specialty: MEXICAN.

$ Prices: Hamburger with fries $3; enchiladas $3.25; beer $1.

Open: Daily 7am–11pm.

This hotel dining room is extremely popular with families, businesspeople, and groups of friends throughout the day. The food is basic coffee-shop fare, well prepared. This is the best place for a stomach-settling meal after a long bus ride. It's on the northwestern edge of the city.

LAS PICHANCHAS, Av. Central Ote. 837. Tel. 2-5351.

Specialty: MEXICAN.

$ Prices: Tamales $1 each; main courses $4–$9.

Open: Daily 12:30pm–midnight; live marimba music 2–4pm and 8–11pm, patio dinner show Tues–Sun at 9pm. **Closed:** New Year's Day and 2 days following Easter.

No trip through Tuxtla Gutiérrez is complete without a meal at the restaurant devoted to the regional food and drink of Chiapas. Colorful cut-paper banners stream from the palm-frond roof and inverted *pichanchas* (pots full of holes used to make nixtamal masa dough) are hung on posts as lanterns. The service is good, but the Spanish-only menu requires an interpreter (or bring your dictionary); next to each item is a description of the meal. Avoid the tired bowl of frijoles Zoques and the uninteresting tasajo (dried salted beef strips that are reconstituted for a couple of dishes on the menu). For a sample, try the platon de carnes frías (cold-meat platter) or the platon de botana regional (a variety of hot tidbits). The former is a tasty sampling of different local sausages plus ham, cheese, and tortillas. I especially like the butifarra. Both feed two or three nicely. You can order with confidence the carne asada a la Chamula, which includes grilled steak, an enchilada, and a tostada, along with a small salad and potato chips. Since Chiapan tamales are tastier and larger than any you may have had elsewhere, you must try at least one. Beer and some unusual mixed drinks are offered, along with a nice selection of prepared fruit-water drinks. The refreshing agua de chia (chia-seed water), is a close cousin to lemonade.

From the Hotel Humberto, in the center of downtown, walk six to eight blocks south. When you see the black iron gates on the left, enter a patio surrounded by red-brick walls and tables and chairs under an open porch.

EASY EXCURSIONS FROM TUXTLA GUTIÉRREZ

CHIAPA DE CORZO The small town of Chiapa de Corzo is a 30-minute, 8-mile ride by bus from the main square (buses leave every 15 minutes in the morning, every

30 minutes in the afternoon), or 10 to 15 minutes by taxi. Those going on to San Cristóbal or over the mountains to the Yucatán will pass through this town on their way.

Chiapa has a small **museum** dedicated to lacquered wood, an interesting church, a colonial fountain, and also a small **pyramid,** somewhat restored and visible from the road.

EL SUMIDERO   Another, more spectacular trip is to the canyon of El Sumidero, 10 miles northeast of the center of town along a country road. You can hire a taxi for a road tour of the canyon's rim and five lookout points for about $8.50 an hour. Boat rides through the canyon are offered as tours through hotel agencies or can be done on your own. Take a bus to Chiapa de Corzo and negotiate a ride along the riverbed; the cost should be around $32 for five people for a 2-hour ride. You can also go by bus to Cahuare from the main square and arrange to hire a boat under the Grijalva River Bridge; the rate here may be somewhat less.

CHAPTER 20

INTRODUCING THE YUCATÁN

1. GEOGRAPHY
- WHAT'S SPECIAL ABOUT THE YUCATÁN
2. HISTORY
3. GETTING THERE & GETTING AROUND
4. SEEING THE YUCATÁN

When you travel in Yucatán, you'll be struck by more of Mexico's contrasting layers: Glitzy resorts, and economical beachside hostelries, and snorkeling lagoons are along the coasts as well as jungle and a few archeological sites. Inland there is more jungle, and more ancient sites reached by passing neat, rock-fenced villages, with white stucco or stick and mud-walled cottages usually with palm-thatch roofs and decorated with potted plants and surrounded by fruit trees. Maya village women wear cool cotton embroidered shifts and go about village life oblivious to the peninsula's fame as a premier destination for resort vacationers and archeological wonders. Their day-to-day cultural and belief system holds many elements which can be traced to pre-Hispanic times. Though shy, the Maya are immensely courteous and helpful, and eagerly chat with strangers even when neither can speak the other's language. More than 350,000 Maya living in Yucatan's three states speak Maya and most, especially men, speak Spanish too. Many, especially those serving tourists, slip easily between Maya, Spanish, and English. You'll get along even if English is your only language.

Crumbling henequén haciendas surrounded by fields of maguey, dot the peninsula. Henequén, a yucca like plant from which hemp is made, was the king crop in Yucatán in the 19th century, and the industry is still going strong making rope, packing material, shoes, and purses among other things from the spiney plant. Besides henequén, other crops in the mostly agricultural peninsula are corn, coconuts, oranges, mangoes and bananas.

Four of the world's eight marine turtles nest on Quintana Roo's shores—loggerhead, green, hawksbill, and leatherback—and more than 600 species of birds, reptiles and mammals have been counted.

Sultry, rough-edged, and unfriendly, Quintana Roo's capital, Chetumal, seems far removed at it's far south location, and inappropriate in a state with such natural and touristic riches. Yucatán state, with delightful Mérida as its capital, has, among its crowning attractions, the ruins of Uxmal and Chichén-Itzá. The state's nature reserves include those for flamingos at Celestun and Río Lagartos and a new one, El Palmar, a 1.2 million acre reserve established in 1990 on the upper Yucatán coast.

Campeche has as its capital the beautiful walled city of Campeche, the region is off the beaten path, due to greater touristic interest in the middle and eastern parts of the peninsula. Among it's attractions are the hat and basket weaving towns of Becal and Halacho, and the ruins of Edzná.

1. GEOGRAPHY

Many people think that this peninsula and the state is somewhere in the extreme southeast of Mexico. A look at the map shows that the land of the Maya is actually

WHAT'S SPECIAL ABOUT THE YUCATÁN

Archeology

☐ Uxmal, most beautiful of the Yucatán's pre-Hispanic Maya Cities.

☐ Chichén-Itzá, grand Maya/Toltec site famed for it's architecture, and the yearly appearance of shadow and light serpent.

Crafts

☐ Halacho, known for its beautiful multicolored baskets and Becal, a town of Panama hat weavers, hammock weavers in every village, plus silver and gold filigree work throughout the peninsula.

Nature

☐ Sian Ka'an Reserve, a 1.3 million acre coastal area south of Cancún.

☐ El Palmar Reserve, a 1.2 million acre area on Yucatán's upper coast established in 1990.

☐ Isla Contoy, National Wildlife Refuge island habitat for more than 70 bird species near Isla Mujeres.

☐ Nesting grounds and home to more than 400 species of birds, and 200 reptiles and mammals, including endangered manatee, sea turtles, and flamingos.

Special Cities and Villages

☐ Mérida, with colonial architecture, free nightly cultural events, and the beautiful Museum of Anthropology.

☐ Whitewashed, rock-walled thatched-roofed villages, including Tinum, where visitors stay with villagers, and Ticul, village of tricycle taxis.

☐ Campeche, unique walled city, using baluartes for museums.

Watersports

☐ Reef diving off Cozumel and along the Caribbean Coast, renowned for geologic formations and abundance and diversity of marine life unequaled in Mexico.

☐ Snorkeling in clear Caribbean waters off Yucatán, especially Xcaret and Xel-Ha lagoons, south of Cancún, and Chancanab Park on Cozumel Island.

the far east-central part of the Republic. Mérida is north of the major population centers of Mexico City, Guadalajara, Puebla, and Veracruz. Mérida is also surprisingly close to the tip of Florida: From Mexico City to Mérida it's about 600 miles as the crow flies, and from Mérida to Miami it's a mere 675 miles.

It's edged by the rough and deep-blue aquamarine Gulf of Mexico on the west and north, and the clear cerulean blue Caribbean Sea on the east. The peninsula covers almost 84,000 square miles with nearly 1,000 miles of shoreline. Covered with dense jungle, the porous limestone peninsula is mostly flat, with thin soil supporting a low, scrubby jungle, and almost no surface rivers. Rainwater is filtered by the limestone into underground rivers. Cenotes, or collapsed caves, are natural wells dotting the region. The only sense of height comes from the curvaceous terrain rising from the western shores of Campeche inland to the border of Yucatán state. This rise, called the Puuc hills, is the "Maya Alps," a staggering 980 feet high! Locally they are known as the Sierra de Ticul or Sierra Alta. The highways undulate a little as you go inland, and south of Ticul there's a rise in the highway which provides a marvelous view of the "valley" and misty Puuc hills lining the horizon. Maya towns near the hills favored a style of geometric patterns and masks of Chac giving the style its name—Puuc.

Three states are included in the territory. The Caribbean state of Quintana Roo on the east has the best beaches and the best resort islands—Cancún, Cozumel, and Isla Mujeres—as well as the ruins of Tulum and Coba and the 1.3 million acre Sian Ka'an Biosphere Reserve south of Cancún.

Wedge-shaped Yucatán is in the middle. Campeche, on the peninsula's west coast faces the Gulf of Mexico. The sand on the beaches here is coarser than on the Caribbean, and the water tends to be rough and choppy.

2. HISTORY

Yucatán's history has fascinated the rest of the world since Lord Kingsborough published a study of its ruins in 1831. Just a few years later, New York lawyer John L. Stephens and artist Frederick Catherwood made several trips through Yucatán and Central America. Stephens recorded his adventures in a fascinating series of travel books illustrated by Catherwood's superb drawings, which achieved immediate, and lasting, popularity. The books are still wonderful reading, and are available from Dover Publications, 31 E. 2nd St., Mineola, NY 11501, or through bookstores in North America and Mexico.

Ever since Stephens's adventures, foreigners have been touring Yucatán to view its vast crumbling cities and ponder the fall of the great Maya civilization. The Maya, developed mathematical theories far in advance of European thought, and perfected a calendar even more accurate than the Gregorian one which we use today.

PRE-CLASSIC PERIOD OR FORMATIVE PERIOD

The Olmec civilization took shape between 1500 B.C. to A.D. 300 (the Pre-classic Period), on the Gulf Coast of Mexico. Historians believe the Maya descended from the Olmecs, but a definitive link in the cultures is missing, except for Izapa, a huge site found almost intact on the Pacific Coast of Chiapas. Izapa is considered a transition culture between Olmec and Maya that rose between 400 B.C. and A.D. 400.

Other than conclusions drawn from the stone carvings and historic interpretation of Izapa, the Maya developmental years remain a mystery. Somewhere along the way they perfected the Olmec calendar, refined and developed ornate hieroglyphic writing, developed architecture, and shaped the Maya religion, with its 166 deities. The Maya guided their lives by using a number of interwoven and complex calendars (see the section on Chichén-Itzá in Chapter 21).

THE CLASSIC YEARS

The great years of Maya culture (the so-called **Classic Period**), lasted from A.D. 300 to 900, when Rome was falling to the barbarians and the Dark Ages were spreading over Europe. The finest examples of Maya architecture were conceived and constructed during these years, well before the Gothic style made its appearance in Europe and these supreme achievements of Maya art can be seen at Palenque (near Villahermosa), at Copan in Honduras, and at Quirigua in Guatemala. All these sites flourished during the last part of the 700s.

The Classic Period ended with a century of degradation and collapse, roughly equivalent to the A.D. 800s. By the early 900s, the great ceremonial centers were abandoned and the jungle took them over, but why classic Maya culture collapsed so quickly isn't known.

POST CLASSIC PERIOD

During the years after the Classic Period, the Maya migrated from their historic home in Guatemala and Chiapas into the northern lowlands of Yucatán (roughly the modern states of Yucatán and Campeche) where they spent three centuries from A.D. 900, to 1500 trying to recover their former greatness.

During this period, the cities near Yucatán's low western Puuc (hills) were built. The architecture of the region, called **Puuc style,** is generally characterized by elaborate exterior stonework appearing above doorframes and extending to the roofline. Examples of this architecture can be seen in Kabah, Sayil, Labná, and Xlapak. Even though Maya architecture never regained the heights achieved at Palenque or Tikal, the Puuc buildings, such as the Codz Poop at Kabah and the palaces at Sayil and Labná, are quite beautiful and impressive.

THE PUTÚN MAYA

Yucatán was also profoundly affected by a strong influence from mainland Mexico. Some theories claim that a distantly related branch of the Maya people, called the **Putún Maya,** came from the borders of the Yucatán Peninsula and crowded into Yucatán during the Post Classic Period. The Putún Maya were traders and navigators who had controlled the trade routes along the coast and rivers between mainland Mexico and the classic Maya lands in Petén and Chiapas. They spoke the Maya language poorly and used many Nahuatl (Aztec) words.

THE ITZÁES

When the Putún Maya left their ships and moved inland, they became known as the Itzáes because, after unsuccessfully trying to conquer Yaxuná, they settled 12 miles north in what eventually became known as Chichén-Itzá (well of the Itzá), a perfect place because of it's access to water and it's proximity to centers ripe for conquering. They brought with them years of experience as traders far and wide and thus the influence of the Toltecs that shows up so strongly at Chichén-Itzá. Eventually they were successful in conquering other peninsular kingdoms and creating the vast city of Chichén-Itzá.

THE TOLTEC INVASION THEORY

Though it's long been thought that Chichén-Itzá was invaded by Itzáes joining Toltecs from central Mexico, research detailed in *A Forest of Kings* by Linda Schele and David Freidel (William Morrow and Co., Inc. 1990) shows that the bas relief history at the site does not support a Toltec invasion theory. They believe Chichén-Itzá's adoption of Toltec architecture demonstrates it was a cosmopolitan city that absorbed elements brought by the Itzáes from another place where there were strong ties, but that the continuity of buildings and bas relief figures show it was a continuous Maya site sans Toltecs.

LEGEND OF KUKULKÁN

Legend has it that when the great man-god Quetzalcoatl fled Tula in central Mexico in shame after succumbing to a series of temptations, he took refuge first in the East Coast of Mexico and later in Yucatán. A theory once placed him leading the invasion of Chichén-Itzá, or establishing Mayapan, which came after Chichén-Itzá. Now that theory is out again. That Kukulcán existed isn't in doubt, but precisely how he fit in is being re-examined.

THE XIÚES

According to some authorities, Uxmal was inhabited during this same period (around A.D. 1000), by the tribe known as the Tutul Xiú who came from the region of Oaxaca and Tabasco. Some scholars think that the Xiú took the city from earlier builders because evidence shows that the region around Uxmal was inhabited as early as 800 B.C.

The three great centers of Chichén-Itzá, Mayapán, and Uxmal lived separately. Authorities don't agree on the exact year, but sometime during the 12th Century A.D. the people of Mayapán overthrew the confederation, sacked Chichén-Itzá, conquered Uxmal, and captured the leaders of the Itzá and the Xiú. Held in Mayapán, the Itzá and the Xiú princes reigned over, but did not rule, their former cities and Mayapán remained the seat of the confederation for over 200 years.

The Xiú took their revenge in 1441 when they marched from Uxmal on Mayapán, capturing and destroying the city, and killing the Cocom rulers. They founded a new city at Maní. Battles and skirmishes continued to plague the Maya territory, until it was conquered by the Spanish conquistadores.

SPANISH CONQUEST

The conquest of the Yucatán took 20 years and was achieved by three men all with the same name: Francisco de Montejo, the Elder, (also called El Adelantado, the pioneer), who started the process, his son Francisco Montejo, the Younger (known as El Mozo, the lad), and a cousin. Montejo, the Elder, sailed from Spain in 1527 with 400 soldiers, landed at Cozumel, but was forced to relaunch his campaign from the western coast, where he could more easily receive supplies from New Spain (Mexico).

From Mexico, he conquered what is now the state of Tabasco (1530), pushing onward to the Yucatán. But after four difficult years (1531–1535) he was forced to return to Mexico penniless and exhausted. In 1540, Montejo the Younger and his cousin (another Francisco de Montejo) took over the cause, successfully establishing a town at Campeche, and another at Mérida (1542); by 1546 virtually all of the peninsula was under his control.

A few weeks after the founding of Mérida, the greatest of the several Maya leaders, Ah Kukum Xiú, head of the Xiú people, offered himself as Montejo's vassal, and was baptized giving himself the name Francisco de Montejo Xiú. By allying his people with the Spaniards, Xiú triumphed over the Cocoms, but capitulated the freedom of the Yucatecan Maya. In later centuries warfare, disease, slavery, and emigration all led to the decline of the population of the peninsula. Fray Diego de Landa, second bishop of Yucatán, destroyed much of the history of the Maya culture when he ordered the mass destruction of the priceless Maya codices, or "painted books," at Maní in 1562; only three survived.

INDEPENDENCE

Yucatán struggled along under the heavy yoke of Spanish colonial administration until the **War of Independence** (begun in 1810), liberated Mexico and Yucatán in 1821. In that same year, the Spanish governor of Yucatán resigned and Yucatán, too, became an independent country. Though it decided to join in a union with Mexico two years later, this period of Yucatecan sovereignty is testimony to the Yucatecan spirit of independence. That same spirit arose again in 1846 when Yucatán seceded from Mexico.

After the war, sugarcane and henequen cultivation were introduced on a large scale, organized around vast landed estates, called haciendas, each employing hundreds of Maya virtually as slaves. During the war for secession, weapons were issued to the Maya to defend independent Yucatán against attack from Mexico or the United States, and these were the weapons the Maya used to attack their local oppressors setting off the **War of the Castes** in 1847.

WAR OF THE CASTES

The Maya ruthlessly attacked and sacked Valladolid. They bought more guns and ammunition from British merchants in Belize (British Honduras). By June 1848 they held virtually all of Yucatán except Mérida and Campeche—and Mérida's governor had already decided to abandon the city.

Convinced they had won the war, the Maya fighters then went off to plant the corn. Meanwhile, Mexico sent reinforcements in exchange for Yucatán's resubmission to Mexican authority and government troops took the offensive, driving many of the Maya to the wilds of Quintana Roo, in the southeastern reaches of the peninsula.

Massed in southern Quintana Roo, the Maya seeking inspiration in their war effort, followed the cult of the **Talking Crosses** which was started in 1850 by a Maya ventriloquist and a mestizo "priest," who carried on a tradition of "talking idols" that had flourished for centuries in several places, including Cozumel. The "talking cross" first appeared at Chan Santa Cruz, and soon several crosses were talking and inspiring the Maya.

The Yucatecan authorities seemed content to let the rebels and their talking crosses rule the southern Caribbean coast, which they did with only minor skirmishes until the late 1800s. The rebel government received arms from the British in Belize, and in return allowed the British to cut lumber in rebel territory.

But at the turn of the century, Mexican troops with modern weapons penetrated the rebel territory, soon putting an end to this bizarre, if romantic, episode of Yucatecan history. The town of Chan Santa Cruz was renamed in honor of a Yucatecan governor, Felipe Carrillo Puerto, and Yucatán was finally a full and integral part of Mexico.

RECOMMENDED BOOKS

For some fascinating insights into Yucatecan history and culture, read Fray Diego de Landa's *Yucatán Before and After the Conquest* (Dover Press, 1978); *Incidents of Travel in Central America, Chiapas and Yucatán* by John Stephens, first published in 1841 (Dover Press, 1969); *The Mexican Codices and Their Extraordinary History*, by María Sten (Ediciones Lara, 1980); and *The Living Maya*, a fabulously illustrated account of the life among the present-day Maya of Chiapas by Walter F. Morris, Jr. (Harry N. Abrams, N.Y. 1987).

3. GETTING THERE & GETTING AROUND

BY PLANE Yucatán is linked by major airlines to Cancún, Mérida, and Cozumel and marginally to Campeche and Chetumal. Regional airlines cover shorter and lesser routes to Cozumel, Chetumal, and Chichén-Itzá.

BY TRAIN Trains connect the upper interior of Yucatán from Mérida to Valladolid, with the Gulf Coast from Villahermosa, Palenque, and Campeche. Although I wouldn't recommend it because of long delays, you could even board a train in Mexico City and arrive in the Yucatán. Generally speaking these trains, especially the longer runs, are slow and plagued by thievery. Shorter hauls, say between Mérida and Tinum or Valladolid, can be quite pleasant.

BY BUS The most economical way to see Yucatán is by bus. Service is best between Yucatán's major cities and resorts, but does not measure up in quality or frequency to service found elsewhere in Mexico. You'll spend a lot of time waiting at highway intersections, particularly near Uxmal, Kabah, and along the Caribbean coast. You could easily spend several weeks trying to get to all the major ruins, cities, and beaches in Yucatán by bus. For example, a bus trip from Mérida to Cancún, takes five hours.

BY CAR The best way to see Yucatán is by car. It's one of the most pleasant parts of the country for a driving vacation. The jungle- and beach-lined roads, while narrow and without shoulders, are in generally good condition and have little traffic. Eventually there'll be a four-lane highway between Mérida and Cancún, and between Cancún and Chetumal, so expect construction in those areas for some time. Otherwise the roads are two lane, and straight except in the southern part of Yucatán state and west to Campeche where they undulate through the Yucatán "Alps" (see below).

Be aware of the long distances in the Yucatán. Mérida, for instance, is 400 miles from Villahermosa, 125 miles from Campeche, and 200 miles from Cancún. Leaded gas (Nova) is readily available in the Yucatán; unleaded gas (Magna Sin) is available at most stations.

BY RENTAL CAR The cheapest way to rent a car is to arrange the rental from your home country at least a week in advance of your travel; allow more time if it's a holiday so you can be sure to get the cheapest car. If you rent after arrival the price doubles. Rent the cheapest car, a VW Beetle (made in Mexico), for a week at the unlimited-mileage rate. Total cost for the week, including insurance, rental fee, and 15% IVA tax, would be $257, which comes out to $37 per day (plus gas), using Avis Rental Cars; for the last two years Avis offered the best prices. Several companies offer a weekly unlimited-mileage rate, but watch out for the deductibles. (See the introduction to the book for more information on car rentals.) I prefer dealing with a Stateside company, because I have recourse if the treatment is bad or something goes wrong; but many small local Yucatán agencies rent cars at what appear to be competitive prices. Readers have reported both wonderful and horrible experiences using these agencies. Read the fine print, good luck, and buyer beware.

BY FERRY Frequent ferry service links the island of Cozumel with Playa del Carmen, and Cancún with Isla Mujeres, both on the Caribbean Coast.

4. SEEING THE YUCATÁN

Recently the governments of Mexico, Belize, Guatemala, Honduras, and El Salvador joined together to create the **Ruta Maya** (Maya route). Ideally this will mean diminished red tape for groups traveling to Maya ruins between countries. New inns will be built near ruins. Already, in Mexico there's evidence of long overdue reconstruction and improvement of existing sites in the Yucatán—an effort, it appears, to make Mexico's Maya route exceptional. One hopes, that the new, very high, entrance prices to the ruins are helping pay for the excavations and reconstruction.

You can touch all the high points of Yucatán in a week by rental car, but you'll be traveling fast. Ten days is better, two weeks is excellent, and you can easily spend three weeks or more if you travel off the beaten path by bus. However, it is also possible, using Mérida as your base, to hit the high points in five days to a week.

SUGGESTED ITINERARIES

IF YOU HAVE FIVE DAYS

Since Mérida is an interesting as well as economical city from which to tour Yucatán, here are a few suggestions on planning your visit.

Day 1, Mérida Settle in, get your bearings, change some money, adjust to the heat, and explore the market.

Day 2, Mérida Tour the city, stopping at each of the historic buildings near the Plaza Mayor, and along the Paseo de Montejo. Save time for shopping, and don't miss the free nightly entertainment in local parks.

Day 3, Uxmal If you're driving, stop at Mayapán on your way to Uxmal. These two sites, and perhaps a quick stop in Ticul, will fill your day. Or if you're short on time, skip Mayapán and Ticul and include day four in your itinerary for day three. Return to Mérida for the night, or stay at Uxmal or Ticul.

Day 4, Kabah, Sayil, Labná, Xlapak, and Grutas de Loltún If you stay near Uxmal, spend day four touring these cities and the caves (grutas). If you're absolutely fascinated by ruins, head for Campeche to spend the night, then spend the next day at Edzná, Dzibilnocac, and Hochob. Otherwise return to Mérida.

Day 5, Chichén-Itzá Ride from Mérida through henequen country to

Chichén-Itzá. Find a hotel room, have lunch, perhaps take a nap, then hike out to the ruins and tour until closing time.

IF YOU HAVE TEN DAYS

Day 1, Merida   On the day of arrival, plan to settle in, get your bearings, change money, and adjust to the heat.

Day 2, Merida   Take a self-guided walking tour of this hospitable and colonial city. Save some time for the market.

Day 3, Uxmal   By bus or by car, be sure to see this beautiful site. The stone carvings on the temples are the most elaborate and beautiful in the Yucatán. If you're driving be sure to stop at Mayapán, another site. These two sites, and perhaps a quick stop in Ticul will fill your day. Hotels (except one) in Uxmal far exceed our daily budget, but they are worth the extra money. As an alternative lodging base, the nearby town of Ticul has several budget hotels.

Day 4, Kabah etc. Spend the day touring sites of Kabah, Sayil, Labná, Xlapak, and the Grutas (caves) de Loltún. Have lunch at Oxkutzkab. Continue on to Campeche and more ruins of Edzná, Dzibilnoacac, and Hochob. Or spend the night at or near Uxmal or return to Mérida.

Day 5, Chichén-Itzá   Ride from Mérida through henequén country to Chichén-Itzá. Find a hotel, have lunch, perhaps take a nap, then hike out to the ruins and tour until closing time. If you take a day tour from Mérida or Cancún, you'll arrive and begin to climb pyramids at the very hottest, most crowded time of day, and you'll climb back into your bus for the two-hour return ride just when the light on the ruins is prettiest and the heat is abating. Spend the night at Chichén-Itzá.

Day 6, Cancún   Spend the morning at the ruins of Chichén-Itzá then ride to Cancún in the afternoon. Find a hotel and settle in. You'll want to see this glitzy world-class resort, but don't spend all of your beach time here. Prices are lower on nearby Isla Mujeres; the skindiving and snorkeling are best on Cozumel; the coast south from Cancún to Lago Bacalar is dotted with inexpensive hotels on beautiful beaches.

Day 7, Cancún   Put on your bathing suit, catch a city bus, and head out to the *Zona Hotelera* (Hotel Zone). Spend the day on one of Cancún's fine beaches. In the evening, wander between the restaurants in town.

Day 8, Isla Mujeres   Easily accessible from Cancún, first by city bus and then ferryboat, this small island is great for a day trip, or even better for a stay of several days. Get an early start, and spend the day, especially at Garrafón National Park, with its good snorkeling and diving.

Day 9, Caribbean coast   Using Cancún, Playa del Carmen, the Tulúm junction hotels, or Cozumel as your base, visit Tulúm, Xel-ha, and perhaps other beaches and sites along the coast between Tulúm and Cancún. If you have a car, drive inland to Cobá also. By bus or hitchhiking, Cobá will take at least a full day by itself. Many hotels and resorts along the Caribbean Coast here are much less expensive than either Cancún or Cozumel.

Day 10, Cozumel   Spend a day on Cozumel, taking the passenger ferry from Playa del Carmen, or a flight from Cancún. The largest of Mexico's Caribbean islands, it's a skindiver's paradise. Though more expensive than Isla Mujeres, Cozumel does not offer more variety of activities. It's best beaches are a distance from town, and it's farther from the mainland.

CHAPTER 21

MÉRIDA & THE MAYA CITIES

Beautiful Mérida, Yucatan's cultural center, is the natural launching point for seeing the Yucatán's major archeological sites, with good roads to the ruins branching out like spokes on a wheel. Easy trips to the Gulf Coast and Yucatán's upper coast can be made from Mérida as well. It's especially pleasant for a driving trip, because there are no mountains—roads are fairly well maintained, traffic is light, and stopping in the many rockwalled villages is a delight. In Mérida and throughout Yucatán's central section in and around the ruins, there are numerous choices for economical lodging.

1. MÉRIDA

900 miles E of Mexico City, 200 miles SW of Cancún

GETTING THERE By Plane Mexicana flies between Mexico City, Cancún, Cozumel, and Havana. **Aeroméxico** flies between Mérida and Mexico City, Villahermosa, Cancún, and Miami. **AeroCaribe** and **AeroCozumel,** two regional airlines that were recently purchased by Mexicana Airlines, currently provide service between Mérida and Cozumel, Chetumal, Cancún, Oaxaca, Tuxtla Gutiérrez, Villahermosa, Veracruz, and Minatitlán.

By Bus The ADO line runs from here, as do Union de Camioneros buses, Autotransportes del Sur, Autotransportes Puerto Juárez, Autotransportes del Caribe, and Autotransportes del Sureste.

By Train From Valladolid the train arrives at 8am, from Tizimin at 5pm, and from Campeche at 9:30pm. From Palenque (originating in Mexico City) the arrival time varies anywhere between 1am and 8pm. This is a second-class train without sleeping or dining cars.

By Car Highway 180 from Cancún, Chichén-Itzá, or Valladolid leads into Calle 65, past the market and within one block of Plaza Mayor. Highway 281 from Uxmal (via Muna and Uman) becomes Avenida Itzáes. If you arrive by that route, turn right on Calle 63 to reach Plaza Mayor. From Uxmal (via Ticul and the ruins of Mayapán) the road passes through Kanasin before joining Highway 180 from Valladolid into Mérida.

WHAT'S SPECIAL ABOUT MÉRIDA & THE MAYA CITIES

Architecture
☐ Mérida, with colonial architecture, free nightly cultural events, and the beautiful Museum of Anthropology.

Archeology
☐ Uxmal, most beautiful of the Yucatán's pre-Hispanic Maya Cities.
☐ Chichén-Itzá, grand Maya/Toltec site famed for its architecture and appearance of shadow-and-light serpent each September.

Nature
☐ Flamingo Sanctuary, near Celestún, where thousands of flamingos winter.

Maya Villages
☐ Tinum, a whitewashed, rock-walled village where visitors can stay with villagers.

☐ Ticul, a village of tricycle taxis and seamstresses noted for elaborate embroidered shifts.

Fortified City
☐ Campeche, where unique walled fortifications surround the city and many of the baluartes are museums.

Crafts
☐ Beautiful multicolored baskets woven in damp caves in Halacho.
☐ Panama hat weavers in Becal.
☐ Silver- and gold-filigree work throughout the Yucatán.
☐ Hammock weavers in every village.

A traffic loop encircles Mérida, making it possible to skirt the city and head for a nearby city or site. Directional signs are generally good into the city, but going around it on the loop requires constant vigilance.

DEPARTING   By Plane   **Mexicana** has offices at Calle 58 no. 500, at Calle 61 (tel. 24-6623), at Calle 56-A no. 493, at Paseo de Montejo (tel. 24-7421 or 23-0508), and at the airport (tel. 23-2531). **Aeroméxico** is at Paseo de Montejo 460, between Calles 37 and 35 (tel. 27-9000, or 24-8576 or 24-8554 at the airport). Two regional airlines, **AeroCaribe** and **AeroCozumel,** Paseo de Montejo 460 (tel. 23-0002, or 28-0099 at the airport), have flights to and from Cozumel, Chetumal, Cancún, Oaxaca, Villahermosa, and Ciudad del Carmen. From the city to the airport is by taxi only and costs nearly $7.

By Train   I don't recommend the trains in this part of Mexico; they're uncomfortable (no diners or sleeping cars) and slow, and tourists aboard are easy marks for thieves.
  The train to Mexico City leaves at 8pm from Mérida, arriving in Palenque around 8am, but could take twice as long as the scheduled 24 hours to reach the capital. Trains depart Mérida daily for Valladolid at 4pm, for Tizimin at 6am, for Campeche/Coatzacalcos at 5am, and for Mexico City (via Palenque, Córdoba, and Orizaba) at 8pm. On short runs the trains are usually on time.
  Tickets go on sale 1 hour before departure; the **information booth** (tel. 23-5966 or 23-5212) is open Monday through Saturday from 7am to 10pm and on Sunday from 8 to 11am and 5:30 to 11pm. From downtown, buses to the train station line up on Calle 56 directly behind the Cepeda Peraza Park.

By Bus   The **Central Camionera** is about six blocks northeast of Plaza Mayor on Calle 55 between Calles 48 and 46. ADO buses **to Uxmal** depart at 6, 7, 8, and 9am, noon, and 3, 5:30, and 7pm; return trips are at 6:30, 8:30, and 11:30am, and 2:30, 5:30, and 7:30pm.

For Chichén-Itzá there are first-class ADO buses at 8:45am and 3pm. If you're planning a day trip (something I don't recommend if you enjoy seeing impressive ruins), take the 8:45am bus and reserve a seat on the 3pm return bus.

For Campeche, Autotransportes del Sureste buses (tel. 21-9491) leave from the main bus station about every 30 minutes on the 3- or 4-hour trip, depending on the route: The short way is on Highway 180 via Halacho and Becal, and the longer route is past Uxmal and Kabah via Highway 281.

To Cancún and Puerto Juárez (the dock for boats to Isla Mujeres), a 5-hour trip, there are first-class Autotransportes Puerto Juárez buses (tel. 23-2287) almost hourly on the hour from 6am to just past midnight.

To Valladolid and Playa del Carmen, there are 13 ADO buses, the first leaving at 5am and the last at midnight. About 18 ADO buses per day travel **to Villahermosa** via the Palenque junction, taking 11 or 12 hours. Six buses a day go to **Mexico City.**

Autotransportes del Caribe (tel. 21-9491) first-class buses go via Muna, Ticul, and Oxkutzcab, to Bacalar, Chetumal, Tulum, and Playa del Carmen.

By Car See "Enroute to . . ." at the end of this chapter for suggested routes from Mérida.

Mérida (pop. 558,000), capital of the state of Yucatán, has been the major city in the area ever since the Spanish founded it in the mid-1500s on the site of the defeated Maya city of Tiho. Although the modern city is a major touristic crossroads to the archeological ruins of the peninsula and its glitzy coasts, the city is easygoing and the friendliness of its people remains a trademark.

Downtown Mérida is full of fine examples of colonial-era architecture. Vestiges of the opulent 19th-century era of Mérida's henequen boom remain in the ornate mansions sprinkled throughout the city. In the market and elsewhere, you'll notice items woven from the sisal fiber of the henequen plant. Henequen is still Yucatán's main industry, apart from tourism, and is used to make hammocks, baskets, purses, shoes, tablemats, twine, rope, and packing material, all of which can be seen in the city's throbbing market.

ORIENTATION

ARRIVING By Plane Mérida's **airport** is on the southwestern outskirts of town, where Highway 180 enters the city. The airport has desks for car rental, hotel reservations, and tourist information. **Taxi tickets** to town are sold outside the airport doors under the covered walkway. A colectivo ticket for up to four people costs $2.25 each, but you have to wait for the four to assemble and the taxi lets you off in the center of town, not at individual hotels. Tickets costing around $5 buy taxi service directly to the address of your choice in Mérida, although the ride may still be a shared one.

City bus no. 79 ("Aviación") operates between the town center and the airport. This is the cheapest way to go, with a one-way ticket costing only 30¢, but the buses are not all that frequent. Other city buses run along Avenida de los Itzaes, just out of the airport precincts, heading for downtown.

By Train For buses from the train station, go left out the front door of the train station to the corner where city buses ("Estación") pick up passengers and follow a route along Calle 55.

By Bus From Mérida's main bus station you are only six blocks from Plaza Mayor and within walking distance of several hotels.

Coming from the west (Cancún, Chichén-Itzá, Valladolid), your bus may stop at the old bus station on Calle 50 between Calles 65 and 67. If you're headed for Plaza Mayor, get off here; it's six blocks to the plaza.

INFORMATION The most convenient source of information is the downtown branch of the **State of Yucatán Tourist Information Office,** in the hulking edifice known as the Teatro Peon Contreras, on Calle 60 between Calles 57 and 59 (tel. 24-9290 or 24-9389). It's open daily from 8 to 8pm. Other information booths are staffed at the airport and bus station at roughly the same hours.

CITY LAYOUT   As with most colonial Mexican cities, Mérida's streets were laid out in a grid. **Even-numbered streets** run north-south, **odd-numbered streets** run east-west. In the last few decades, the city has expanded well beyond the grid, and several grand boulevards have been added on the outskirts to ease traffic flow.

When looking for an address, you'll notice that street numbers progress very slowly due to the many unnumbered dwellings and -A, -B, and -C additions. Example: Getting from 504 to 615D on Calle 59 takes 12 blocks.

The center of town is the very pretty **Plaza Mayor** (sometimes called the Plaza Principal), with its shady trees, benches, vendors, and a social life all its own. Around the plaza are the massive cathedral, the Palacio de Gobierno (state government headquarters), the Palacio Municipal, and the Casa de Montejo. Within a few blocks are several smaller plazas, the University of Yucatán, and the sprawling market district.

Mérida's most fashionable address is **Paseo de Montejo,** a wide, tree-lined boulevard seven blocks northwest of Plaza Mayor and home to Yucatán's anthropological museum, several upscale hotels, and the U.S. Consulate.

GETTING AROUND

BY BUS   City buses are the cheapest way to go, charging only 20¢ for a ride. You can take one to the large, shady Parque Centenario on the western outskirts. Look for the bus of the same name ("Centenario") on Calle 64. Most buses on Calle 59 go to the zoo or Museum of Natural History. Those marked "Estación" go to the train station. "Central" buses stop at the bus station, and any bus marked "Mercado" or "Correo" (post office) will take you to the market district.

BY TAXI   Taxi drivers are beginning to overcharge tourists in Mérida as they do in Mexico City. Watch out for the numbers scam. The driver says "*dos*" (2), which you take to mean 2,000 pesos or around 70¢, but on arrival at your destination a few blocks away he announces "*dose*" (12), meaning 12,000 pesos which is closer to $4. A short ride in the downtown area should cost around $2.

BY CAR   Rental cars are handy for your explorations of Mayapán, Uxmal, and Kabah, but you don't need one to get around Mérida, or to Chichén-Itzá or Cancún. Rental cars average $45 to $65 per day for a VW Beetle.

Keep these tips in mind as you scour the city for a rental-car deal: Don't be impressed by a very low daily charge, unless it includes unlimited mileage. Be sure to get the absolutely final figure for a rental before you decide; if you can't get mileage included, estimate the distance you'll travel by adding up the highway mileages, then add 15% for wrong turns and detours. Keep in mind that you can often get lower rates if you arrange the rental before you leave the U.S. and for more than a day or two. If you arrange a rental after arrival, you can often haggle for a lower price, or negotiate lower fees if you promise to pay at the end of the rental in cash dollars (you'll need a credit card at first for the paperwork). Important Note: Deductibles range between $250 and $1,000, so don't fail to get that information before you sign up. For more information, see "Car Rentals" in Chapter 2.

BY HORSE-DRAWN CARRIAGE   Look for a line of them near the cathedral, then haggle for a good price. An hour's tour of the city costs around $11.

ON FOOT   Most tourist attractions are within easy walking distance of the Plaza Mayor.

FAST FACTS

Area Code   The telephone area code is 99.

Bookstore   The **Librería Dante,** Calle 62 at Calle 57 (tel. 24-9522), has a selection of English-language cultural history books on Mexico. It's open Monday through Saturday from 8am to 9:30pm and on Sunday from 10am to 2pm and 4 to 8pm.

Climate   November through February the weather can be chilly, windy, and rainy. You'll need a light jacket or sweater for winter, and thin, cool clothes for summer days. Light raingear is suggested for the brief showers of late May, June, and July, but there's a chance of rain all year in the Yucatán.

Consulates   The **U.S. Consulate** is at Paseo de Montejo 453, at the corner of Avenida Colón (tel. 99/25-5011 or 25-5409), next to the Holiday Inn. It's open Monday through Friday from 7:30am to 4pm. There is a specific schedule for visas and traveler's problems: Visa matters are dealt with only on Monday, Wednesday, and Friday from 7:30 to 11am; other kinds of problems are considered the same days from noon to 3:30pm and on Thursday until 4pm. The telephone number of a duty officer is posted at the entrance. The **British Vice-Consulate** is at Calle 53 no. 489, at the corner of Calle 58 (tel. 99/21-6799). Though in principle it's open Monday through Friday from 9:30am to 1pm, you may find no one there. The vice-consul fields questions about travel to Belize as well as British matters. The **Alliance Française** has a branch at Calle 56 no. 476 (tel. 99/21-6013), between Calle 55 and 57.

Currency Exchange   Banamex, in the Palacio Montejo on Plaza Mayor, has a currency exchange which usually provides a better rate of exchange than other banks, but the lines are often maddeningly long. As an option, there's a money-exchange office just as you enter the bank gates, and more banks are located on and off Calle 65 between Calles 62 and 60.

Doctors   If you're suffering from "Montezuma's Revenge," see Chapter 2 for tips. If it gets serious, ask your hotel to call a doctor—after you've got an estimate of his fee.

Hospitals   The city's **Hospital O'Horan** is on Avenida de los Itzáes at Calle 59A (tel. 99/24-4224 or 24-4111), north of the Parque Centenario.

Post Office   Mérida's main post office (Correo) is in the midst of the market at the corner of Calles 65 and 56. It's open Monday through Friday from 8am to 7pm and on Saturday from 9am to 1pm.

Seasons   There are two high seasons: one in July and August, when the weather is very hot and humid and when Mexicans most commonly take their vacations; and one between December 15 and Easter Sunday, when northerners flock to the Yucatán to escape winter weather and when the weather in the Yucatán is cooler.

Telephones   Long-distance casetas are at the airport, the bus station, at Calles 59 and 62, and Calles 59 and 64, and on Calle 60 between Calles 55 and 53 in "El Calendario Maya." Look also for the blue-and-silver Ladatel phones which are appearing in public places all over Mexico. Remember that international calls, while getting cheaper, are still extremely expensive, but at least from a caseta you won't pay the hotel "service charge." Also see "Telephones" in the Appendix.

WHAT TO SEE & DO

Mérida is pretty and congenial, but summers are also very hot—up to 108°F (42°C), prior to the muggy rainy months (June through September). I recommend you snatch a quick breakfast and begin touring early. When the midday heat is at its worst, have lunch and a siesta, and issue forth in the evening, refreshed and ready for the next round.

If you're lucky enough to be visiting November through January or February, you'll be able to spend most of the day outdoors without discomfort.

SPECIAL EVENTS   Many Mexican cities offer weekend concerts in the park, but Mérida is unique in having almost daily public events, most of which are free.

Sunday   Each Sunday from 9am to 5pm there's a fair called **Mérida Sundays,** the heart of which is in Santa Lucía park. The downtown area is blocked from traffic for the day and alive with children's art classes, antiques vendors, and food stands, as well as concerts of all kinds. At 11am in front of the Palacio del Gobierno, musicians play anything from jazz to semiclassical and folkloric music. Also at 11am, the police orchestra performs Yucatecan tunes at Santa Lucía park. At 11:30am marimba music brightens the Parque Cepeda Peraza (Plaza Hidalgo) on Calle 60 at Calle 59. At 1pm, in front of the Palacio Municipal on Plaza Mayor, folk ballet dancers reenact a typical Yucatecan wedding. All events are free.

Monday   The **City Hall Folkloric Ballet** and the **Police Jaranera Band** perform at 9pm in front of the Palacio Municipal. The music and dancing celebrate the feast after the branding of cattle on Yucatecan haciendas. Free admission.

Tuesday   The theme for Tuesday entertainment is **Musical Memories,** in the Santiago Park at 9pm. The park is on Calle 59 at Calle 72. Tunes range from South American and Mexican to North American. Free Admission. Also at 9pm in the Teatro Peon Contreras, on Calle 60 at Calle 57, the **Yucatán University Folkloric Ballet** presents *Yucatán and Its Roots.* Admission is $3.50.

Wednesday   The **Yucatecan Folkloric Ballet,** guitarists, and poets perform at 8pm at the Mayab Culture House on Calle 63 between Calle 64 and 66. Free Admission.

Thursday   The **Yucalpeten Orchestra** and a variety of soloists present typical Yucatecan music in Santa Lucía park at 9pm. Yucalpeten is a coastal village north of Mérida. Free admission.

Friday   At 9pm in the patio of the Yucatán University, Calle 60 at Calle 57, the **University of Yucatán Folkloric Ballet** performs typical regional dances from the Yucatán. Free admission.

WALKING TOUR—Mérida

Start: Plaza Mayor.
Finish: Iglesia (church) de Santa Lucía.
Time: Allow approximately 2 hours, not counting browsing or time out for refreshment.

Downtown Mérida is a visitor's visual delight, with several tree-shaded parks and most of the finest examples of both colonial and late 19th-century architecture the city has to offer. It's all within an easy stroll of the:

1. **Plaza Mayor,** flanked east and west by Calles 61 and 63, and north and south by Calles 60 and 62, began its history as Plaza de Armas, a training field for Montejo's troops. Later called Plaza Mayor, it was renamed Plaza de la Constitución in 1812, then Plaza de la Independencia in 1821. Other common names for it include Plaza Grande, Plaza Principal, and zócalo. Today this beautiful town square, now shaded by topiary laurel trees, is dressed out in manicured shrubs and lawns with plenty of pleasant iron benches. Numerous public entertainment events take place there throughout the year.
   On the east side of the plaza stands the:
2. **Cathedral,** built between 1561 and 1598. It looks like a fortress, as do many other early churches in Yucatán. (That was actually their function in part for several centuries, as the Maya did not take kindly to European domination.) Much of the stone in the cathedral's walls came from the ruined buildings of Maya Tiho. Inside, decoration is sparse, the most notable feature being a picture over a side door of Ah Kukum Tutul Xiú visiting the Montejo camp.
   To the left of the main altar is a smaller shrine with a curious burnt cross, recovered from the church in the town of Ichmul, which burned down. The figure was carved by a local artist in the 1500s from a miraculous tree which burned but did not char. The figure burned, though, along with the church, and broke out in blisters as it did. The local people named it *Cristo de las Ampollas* (Christ of the Blisters). Also take a look in the side chapel (open from 8 to 11am and 4:30 to 7pm), which has a life-size diorama of the Last Supper. The Mexican Jesus is covered with prayer crosses brought by supplicants asking for intercession.

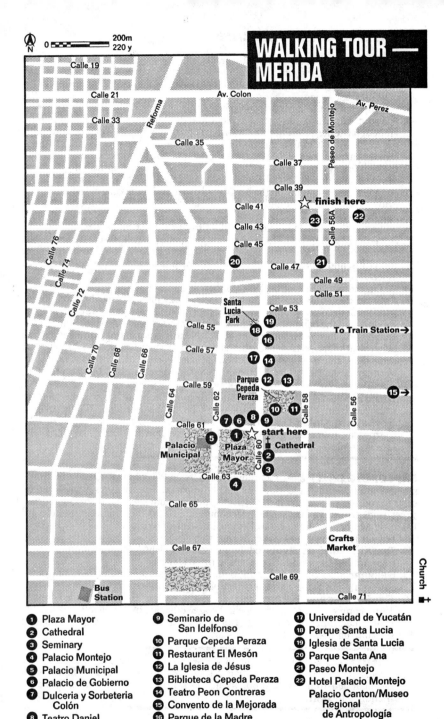

WALKING TOUR — MERIDA

0 ——— 200m
——— 220 y
N

Calle 19
Calle 21
Av. Colon
Av. Perez
Calle 33
Reforma
Paseo de Montejo
Calle 35
Calle 37
Calle 39
Calle 41
☆ finish here
Calle 43
㉓
Calle 56A
㉒
Calle 45
⑳
Calle 47
㉑
Calle 49
Calle 76
Calle 51
Calle 74
Santa
Lucia
Park
Calle 53
⑲
Calle 72
Calle 55
⑱
To Train Station →
⑯
Calle 70
Calle 57
⑰
⑭
Calle 68
Calle 66
Parque
Cepeda
Peraza
⑫
⑬
Calle 59
Calle 64
Calle 62
⑩
⑪
Calle 58
⑦⑥⑧
⑨
Calle 56
⑮ →
Calle 61
☆ start here
⑤
①
Palacio
Municipal
Plaza
Mayor
Calle 60
✝
Cathedral
②
Calle 63
③
④
Calle 65
Calle 67
Crafts
Market
Calle 69
Bus
Station
Church
Calle 71
✝

① Plaza Mayor
② Cathedral
③ Seminary
④ Palacio Montejo
⑤ Palacio Municipal
⑥ Palacio de Gobierno
⑦ Dulceria y Sorbeteria
   Colón
⑧ Teatro Daniel
   de Ayala

⑨ Seminario de
   San Idelfonso
⑩ Parque Cepeda Peraza
⑪ Restaurant El Mesón
⑫ La Iglesia de Jésus
⑬ Biblioteca Cepeda Peraza
⑭ Teatro Peon Contreras
⑮ Convento de la Mejorada
⑯ Parque de la Madre

⑰ Universidad de Yucatán
⑱ Parque Santa Lucia
⑲ Iglesia de Santa Lucia
⑳ Parque Santa Ana
㉑ Paseo Montejo
㉒ Hotel Palacio Montejo
   Palacio Canton/Museo
   Regional
   de Antropología

To the right (south) of the cathedral is a:

3. Seminary and the former sight of the archbishop's palace. The palace was torn down during the Mexican Revolution (1915); part of the seminary remains, but is now used for shops.

On the south side of the square is the:

4. Palacio Montejo, also called the Casa de Montejo. Started in 1549 by Francisco Montejo, "El Mozo," it was occupied by Montejo's descendants until the 1970s. It now houses a bank branch (Banamex), which means you can get a look at parts of the palace just by wandering in during banking hours Monday through Friday from 9am to 1:30pm. Note the arms of the Spanish kings and of the Montejo family on the plateresque facade, along with figures of the conquistadores standing on the heads of "barbarians" overcome by their exploits. Look closely and you'll find the bust of Francisco Montejo the Elder, his wife, and his daughter.

Facing the cathedral, across the plaza from the west side is the:

5. Palacio Municipal (City Hall) with its familiar clock tower. It started out as the *cabildo,* the colonial town hall and lockup, in 1542. It had to be rebuilt in the 1730s, and rebuilt again in the 1850s, when it took on its present romantic aspect.

On the north side of the plaza is the:

6. Palacio de Gobierno, dating from 1892. Large murals painted between 1971 and 1973 decorate interior walls. Scenes from Maya and Mexican history abound, and the painting over the stairway combines the Maya spirit with ears of sacred corn, the "sunbeams of the gods." Nearby is a painting of the mustached benevolent dictator Lázaro Cárdenas, who in 1938 expropriated 17 foreign oil companies and was hailed as a new Mexican liberator. The palace is open Monday through Saturday from 8am to 8pm and on Sunday from 9am to 5pm.

REFUELING STOP Should you decide to take a break before continuing up Calle 60 from Plaza Mayor, you won't be disappointed at: **7. Dulcería y Sorbetería Colón,** on the north side of Plaza Mayor. It's a delightful, inexpensive restaurant spilling onto the covered *portales* facing the plaza. The fare is simple—delicious pastries, soft drinks, and milkshakes.

EXPLORING CALLE 60 Continuing north from Plaza Mayor up Calle 60, you'll see several of Mérida's old churches and little parks. Several stores along Calle 60 cater to tourists selling gold-filigree jewelry, pottery, and folk art. A stroll along this street leads to the Parque Santa Ana, continuing on to the fashionable boulevard Paseo de Montejo and its Museo Regional de Antropológia.

On your left as you leave Plaza Mayor, the:

8. Teatro Daniel de Ayala offers a continuous schedule of performing artists from around the world. Opposite the theater, the:

9. Seminario de San Ildefonso, opposite the Ayala theater, began as one of the city's early hospitals. Three quarters of a block farther is the:

10. Parque Cepeda Peraza (also called the Parque Hidalgo), named for the 19th-century Gen. Manuel Cepeda Peraza, was part of Montejo's original city plan. Small outdoor restaurants front hotels on the park, making it a popular stopping-off place any time of the day.

REFUELING STOP Any one of the several outdoor restaurants on Parque Cepeda Peraza makes an inviting respite. My favorite is: **11. El Mesón,** distinguished from its neighbor by its black iron tables and chairs. Service is friendly and swift.

Bordering Parque Cepeda Peraza,

12. La Iglesia de Jesús, or El Tercer Orden (the Third Order), was built by the Jesuit order in 1618. The entire city block in which the church stands was part of the Jesuit establishment, and the early schools developed into the Universidad de Yucatán. Beside the church is the:

13. Biblioteca (library) Cepeda Peraza, founded by the general in 1867. Next on your right is the:

14. Teatro Peon Contreras, an enormous yellow edifice designed by Italian architect Enrico Deserti in the early years of this century. In one corner you'll see a branch of the State Tourist Information Office facing the park. The main theater entrance, with its Carrara-marble staircase and frescoed dome, is a few steps farther. Domestic and international performers appear here frequently.

East on Calle 59 five blocks past the park and the church is the:

15. former Convento de la Mejorada, a late-1600s work of the Franciscans.

16. Parque de la Madre (also called the Parque Morelos), containing a modern statue of the madonna and child, a copy of the work by Lenoir that stands in the Luxembourg Gardens in Paris.

On the west side of Calle 60, at the corner of Calle 57, the:

17. Universidad de Yucatán, was founded in the 19th century by Felipe Carrillo Puerto with the help of General Cepeda Peraza. The founding is illustrated by the 1961 fresco by Manuel Lizama.

A block farther on your left, past the Hotel Mérida Misión on your left and the Hotel Casa del Balam on your right, is the:

18. Parque Santa Lucía. Surrounded by an arcade on the north and west sides, the parque once was the place at which visitors first alighted in Mérida from their stagecoaches. On Sunday Santa Lucía park is the center of a popular downtown street fair and several evenings a week hosts popular entertainment. And on Thursday nights performers present Yucatecan songs and poems.

Facing the park is the ancient:

19. Iglesia de Santa Lucía (1575).

To reach Paseo de Montejo, continue walking north on Calle 60 to the:

20. Parque Santa Ana, five blocks up Calle 60 from Parque Santa Lucía. Turn right here on Calle 47 for a block and a half, then turn left onto the busy boulevard known as the:

21. Paseo de Montejo, a broad, tree-shaded thoroughfare lined with imposing banks, hotels, and several 19th-century mansions erected by henequen barons, generals, and other Yucatecan potentates. It's Mexico's humble version of the Champs-Elysées.

REFUELING STOP Before or after tackling the Palacio Canton (below), a good place for a break and for watching life on Paseo de Montejo is the lobby restaurant of the: **22. Hotel Palacio Montejo,** which has excellent regional specialties. It's on Paseo de Montejo, a block and a half north of the Palacio Canton.

At the corner of Paseo de Montejo and Calle 43 is the:

23. Palacio Canton, which houses the Museo Regional de Antropológia (anthropology museum) (tel. 23-0055). Designed and built by Enrico Deserti, the architect who designed the Teatro Peon Contreras, it's the most impressive mansion on Paseo de Montejo. It was constructed between 1909 and 1911 during the last years of the Porfiriato as the home of Gen. Francisco Canton Rosado. The general enjoyed his palace for only 6 years before he died in 1917. The house was converted into a school and later became the official residence of Yucatán's governor.

Don't neglect admiring the building itself as you walk around—it's the only paseo mansion that you'll get to visit. Be sure to examine the little art deco elevator—a great luxury at one time. The museum is open Tuesday through Saturday from 8am to 8pm and on Sunday from 8am to 2pm. Admission is $3.50.

On the right as you enter is a room used for changing exhibits. After that are the permanent exhibits, with captions in Spanish only. Starting with fossil mastodon teeth, the exhibits take you down through the ages of Yucatán's history, giving special attention to the daily life of its inhabitants. You'll see how the Maya tied boards to babies' skulls in order to reshape the heads, giving them the slanting forehead that was then a mark of great beauty, and how they filed teeth to sharpen them, or drilled teeth to implant jewels. Enlarged photos show the archeological sites. The one of Mayapán, for instance, clearly shows the city's ancient walls. Even if you know only a little Spanish, the museum provides a good background for Maya explorations.

MORE ATTRACTIONS

West of Plaza Mayor, running along Avenida de los Itzáes between Calle 59 and Calle 85, lies the large **Parque Centenario,** a fine place for an afternoon stroll, especially with children. There's a small train which runs around the park, and a small, but interesting zoo with Yucatecan animals. The cages are close to shady walkways, so it's easy to get a good look at the hairless dogs, numerous monkey and pigeon varieties, alligators, flamingos, parrots, jaguars, pumas, leopards, lions, etc. Throughout the park, sand play areas and swings act as a magnet for children. There's no admission charge, and it's open daily from 8am to 7pm.

The small **Museo de Historia Natural** is just down the block from the Parque Centenario on Calle 59 at Calle 84, housed in an old mansion that was once a military hospital. Among interesting exhibits is a large dried-insect display including the maquech beetle of Maya lore (see "Shopping," below, for more about the maquech). Admission is free; it's open Tuesday through Sunday from 8am to 6pm.

Four blocks east of Plaza Mayor, the **Museo Regional de Arte Popular,** on Calle 59 between Calle 50 and 48, shows regional costumes, pottery, and folk art of the Yucatán. There's a small bookstore and a large sales room with quality crafts from throughout Mexico. Hours are Tuesday through Saturday from 8am to 8pm. Free admission.

WHERE TO STAY

Mérida is a budget traveler's paradise. Most hotels offer at least a few air-conditioned rooms, and a few also have swimming pools. You may find absolutely every room taken in July and August.

Note: Prices could be 10% to 15% less than those quoted below, depending on the season and whether there's much business.

DOUBLES FOR LESS THAN $20

TRINIDAD GALERÍA, Calle 60 no. 456, Mérida, Yuc. 97000. Tel. 99/21-0935 or 23-2463. 31 rms (28 with bath), 1 suite.
$ Rates: $10–$15 single with fan, $20 single with A/C; $12 double with fan, $21–$26 double with A/C; $38 suite for two with A/C. Ask about seasonal discounts. **Parking:** Free, but limited.

Once an enormous home, the rambling structure on Calle 60 at the corner of Calle 49, three blocks north of Santa Lucía park and six blocks north of Plaza Mayor, has been transformed into a hotel with a small, shaded swimming pool, communal refrigerator and shared dining room, original art, and relaxing nooks with comfortable furniture. A lush garden enhances the inner courtyard. Upstairs, a new covered porch runs the length of the hotel. Rooms are darkish and simply furnished, and most don't have windows, but the overall ambience of the hotel is comparable to more expensive inns.

HOTEL MUCUY, Calle 57 no. 481, Mérida, Yuc. 97000. Tel. 99/21-1037. 22 rms (all with bath).
$ Rates: $12–$16 single; $14–$18 double; $15–$20 triple.

Among the most hospitable budget hotels in the country, the Mucuy is named for a small dove said to bring good luck to places where it alights. Owners Alfredo and Ofelia Comin strive to make guests feel welcome, with comfortable outdoor tables and chairs, and such conveniences as a communal refrigerator and laundry and clothesline facilities for guest use. Two floors of freshly painted rooms, with window screens, showers, and ceiling fans, are lined up on one side of the flower-filled garden. The owners live on the premises, and Señora Comin speaks English. The hotel is 3½ blocks northeast of Plaza Mayor and five blocks west of the train station between Calles 56 and 58.

HOTEL MONJAS, Calle 66 no. 509, Mérida, Yuc. 97000. Tel. 99/21-9862. 25 rms (all with bath).
$ Rates: $12 single; $16 double with one bed, $20 double with two beds.
With its inviting modern appearance, the lobby outperforms the rooms at this two-story hotel. But the basically furnished rooms are clean, and include a ceiling fan, and either one or two double beds or a double and a twin. The location is excellent, slightly away from traffic and city hubbub. A small snack bar in the lobby functions on weekends selling sandwiches, breakfast pastries, and soft drinks.

To get here, from Plaza Mayor walk two blocks west on Calle 63; the hotel is on the right corner. From the bus station, turn right out the front door and walk one block; then turn left on Calle 66, walk four blocks, and the hotel is on the left.

HOTEL LATINO, Calle 66 no. 505, Mérida, Yuc. 97000. Tel. 99/21-4831. 27 rms (all with bath).
$ Rates: $12–$15 single; $15–$17 double. **Parking:** Free.
This hotel is overpriced for the quality and cleanliness of the rooms, so consider it a last choice. Rooms have fans (only one is air-conditioned), screened, wood-louvered doors and windows, beds on concrete platforms, fluorescent lighting, old furniture, and no toilet seats. The Latino is between Calles 61 and 63, four blocks north of the bus station and two blocks west of Plaza Mayor.

HOTEL TRINIDAD, Calle 62 no. 464, Mérida, Yuc. 97000. Tel. 99/21-3029 or 23-2033. 13 rms (6 with bath), 1 suite.
$ Rates: $13 single without bath, $26 single with bath; $16 double without bath, $32 double with bath; $40 suite.
This sagging colonial abode is filled with antique furniture. The comfortable lobby doubles as a café, with a TV which receives U.S. channels. Guests can also rent a TV for a small charge. Each room is different, some decorated with paintings or drawings from the owner's interesting art collection, but all have fans.

To get here from Plaza Mayor, walk north on Calle 62 two blocks; the hotel is on Calle 62 near the corner of Calle 57.

CASA BOWEN, Calle 66 no. 521-B, Mérida, Yuc. 97000. Tel. 99/21-6577. 20 rms (all with shower).
$ Rates: $13.50 single; $15.50 double with one bed, $16.50 double with two beds, $16.50 double with one bed and kitchen, $18 double with two beds and kitchen.
Parking: Free, but limited.
Formed from a lovely old mansion plus a modern addition next door, this hospitable, family-run inn is one of the best budget hotels in Mexico. The lobby and courtyard are filled with plants, rattan rockers, and comfortable sitting areas. Among the extras is a paperback book-lending library, rooftop clothesline, well-screened windows, English-speaking management, and several comfortable sitting areas in both sections. Rooms vary in size, with decoration generally around a colonial theme. All are clean, with fans, tile floors, and nice-size windows.

It's on Calle 66 at the corner of Calle 65, three blocks southwest of Plaza Mayor. From the bus station, walk out the front door, turn right, and walk one block; at Calle 66, turn left and walk two more blocks and it's on the left.

CASA BECIL, Calle 67 no. 550-C, Mérida, Yuc. 97000. Tel. 99/21-2957. 14 rms (all with bath).
$ Rates: $16 single; $18 double.
A pleasant family runs this homey *casa de huespedes* between Calles 66 and 68. Most of the plain but serviceable rooms are around a tiny, shady court in back where it's quiet. Toilets may not have seats, but all rooms have fans, windows are well screened, the water in the tap is purified, and there's a small sun deck on the second floor.

There's laundry service, and the English-speaking owner can arrange airline tickets and tours. TVs (optional) rent for a small daily charge. A small coffee shop is scheduled to open just off the lobby.

To get to Casa Becil, from the bus station, turn right out front door, then right again at the first block, Calle 68; walk one block and turn left on Calle 67 and the hotel is on the right.

HOTEL DOLORES ALBA, Calle 63 no. 464, Mérida, Yuc. 97000. Tel. 99/21-3745. 40 rms (all with bath).
$ Rates: $16–$20 single; $19–$25 double; $23–$29 triple.

The Sanchez family converted their family home, between Calles 52 and 54, four blocks west of Plaza Mayor and a block north of the market, into a comfortable hotel with a large open court, and a smaller courtyard with a clean swimming pool. Rooms are decorated with local crafts; four are air-conditioned and the rest have fans. A small dining room opens for breakfast. The Sanchez family also operates the Hotel Janeiro in Mérida, and the Hotel Dolores Alba outside Chichén-Itzá, so you can make reservations at one hotel for another.

DOUBLES FOR LESS THAN $30

HOTEL PENINSULAR, Calle 58 no. 519, Mérida, Yuc. 97000. Tel. 99/23-6996 or 23-6902. 49 rms (all with bath).
$ Rates: $18 single with fan, $21 single with A/C; $21 double with fan, $26 double with A/C.
From the outside this looks like an elegant, pastel-pink and white mansion incongruously set in the midst of the busy market district, three blocks southeast of Plaza Mayor between Calles 65 and 67, and one block west of the market. Located at the end of a long entrance corridor, the rooms are quiet and clean but dark, and vary greatly in size. In back there's a small pool surrounded by a tidy lawn, and in the entry corridor a small restaurant serves inexpensive meals. TVs are available for rent; some rooms have phones.

HOTEL POSADA DEL ANGEL, Calle 67 no. 535, Mérida, Yuc. 97000. Tel. 99/23-2754. 30 rms (all with bath).
$ Rates: $21 single with fan, $25 single with A/C; $22 double with fan, $29 double with A/C. Ask about discounts. **Parking:** Free.
Close to the bus station, but far enough from it to avoid the noise (it's 1½ blocks away), this two-story hotel between Calles 68 and 66 is another "last choice" for late arrivals. It's expensive for what you get. Rooms have red-tile floors and chenille bedspreads, and most have screened, glass-louvered windows, but no toilet seats in the bathrooms. Rooms with air conditioning may not have windows. The few rooms in the front are very noisy because of the buses, but most rooms are in the back. Soft drinks and bottled water are sold in the lobby; there's a small restaurant.

HOTEL JANEIRO, Calle 57 no. 435, Mérida, Yuc. 97000. Tel. 99/23-3602. 22 rms (all with bath).
$ Rates: $18 single or double with fan, $22 single or double with A/C. **Parking:** Free, but limited.

Owned by the same family that runs the Dolores Alba, the Janeiro is between Calles 48 and 50 (from train station, walk out the front door, turn right to the next block, then left one block and right on Calle 57; it's half a block down on the right). A recent refurbishing has improved the rooms. In a quiet courtyard in back there's a little swimming pool and patio tables. You can make reservations here for their hotel near Chichén-Itzá.

HOTEL DEL PARQUE, Calle 60 no. 497, Mérida, Yuc. 97000. Tel. 99/24-7844. Fax 99/28-1429. 20 rms (all with bath). TEL
$ Rates: $20 single with fan, $22 single with A/C; $22 double with fan, $25 double with A/C. **Parking:** Free.

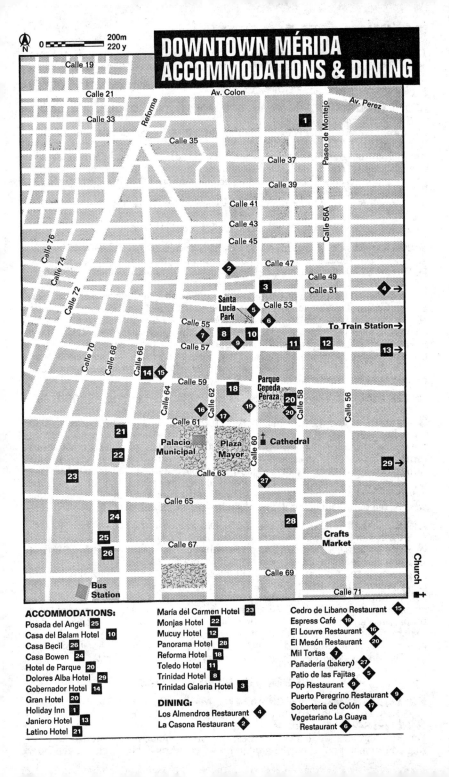

DOWNTOWN MÉRIDA ACCOMMODATIONS & DINING

0 — 200m / 220 y

Calle 19
Calle 21
Av. Colon
Reforma
Calle 33
Calle 35
Paseo de Montejo
Av. Perez
Calle 37
Calle 39
Calle 41
Calle 43
Calle 45
Calle 47
Calle 56A
Calle 76
Calle 74
Calle 72
Calle 49
Calle 51
Calle 53
Santa Lucia Park
Calle 55
To Train Station →
Calle 57
Calle 70
Calle 68
Calle 66
Calle 59
Parque Cepeda Peraza
Calle 58
Calle 56
Calle 64
Calle 62
Calle 61
Palacio Municipal
Plaza Mayor
Calle 60
Cathedral
Calle 63
Church
Calle 65
Crafts Market
Calle 67
Calle 69
Bus Station
Calle 71

ACCOMMODATIONS:
Posada del Angel **25**
Casa del Balam Hotel **10**
Casa Becil **26**
Casa Bowen **24**
Hotel de Parque **20**
Dolores Alba Hotel **29**
Gobernador Hotel **14**
Gran Hotel **20**
Holiday Inn **1**
Janiero Hotel **13**
Latino Hotel **21**

María del Carmen Hotel **23**
Monjas Hotel **22**
Mucuy Hotel **12**
Panorama Hotel **28**
Reforma Hotel **18**
Toledo Hotel **11**
Trinidad Hotel **8**
Trinidad Galeria Hotel **3**

DINING:
Los Almendros Restaurant ◆ **4**
La Casona Restaurant ◆ **2**

Cedro de Libano Restaurant ◆ **15**
Espress Café ◆ **19**
El Louvre Restaurant ◆ **16**
El Mesón Restaurant ◆ **20**
Mil Tortas ◆ **7**
Pañadería (bakery) ◆ **27**
Patio de las Fajitas ◆ **5**
Pop Restaurant ◆ **9**
Puerto Peregrino Restaurant ◆ **9**
Soberteria de Colón ◆ **17**
Vegetariano La Guaya Restaurant ◆ **6**

The small hotel entrance is quite colonial, but the rooms, in the modern structure next door, are carpeted and bright, with floral wallpaper and comfortable furnishings. A favorite of tour groups traveling on a budget, it's opposite Parque Cepeda Peraza, 1½ blocks north of Plaza Mayor at Calle 59.

HOTEL REFORMA, Calle 59 no. 508, Mérida, Yuc. 97000. Tel. 99/24-7922. 45 rms (all with bath).

$ Rates: $22.50 single with fan, $25 single with A/C; $25 double with fan, $31 double with A/C.

Another of the grand old establishments in Mérida is embellished by a twisted wrought-iron staircase, high ceilings, and a central patio with rubber plants in huge pots. Furnishings are old but well kept. The nicest rooms in the hotel are upstairs in the back, around a separate little court and swimming pool. The Reforma is one block north of Plaza Mayor and one block west of Parque Cepeda Peraza.

DOUBLES FOR LESS THAN $40

GRAN HOTEL, Calle 60 no. 496, Mérida, Yuc. 97000. Tel. 99/24-7622. Fax 99/24-7730. 30 rms (all with bath). TEL

$ Rates: $27 single with fan, $31 single with A/C; $31 double with fan, $36 double with A/C.

Perhaps the finest example of old-time hotel architecture in the city, the Gran is on Parque Cepeda Peraza and next to the Hotel Caribe, half a block north of Plaza Mayor between Calles 59 and 61. Here, the ambience is 19th century rather than colonial, and all the more enjoyable for that. The high-ceilinged rooms are on three levels, surrounding a plant-filled central court. Corinthian columns and fancy ironwork vie for your attention with lofty portals and heavy worked wood trim. Despite the hotel's charm, housekeeping is often iffy. El Patio Español, the hotel restaurant, is in a rear courtyard.

HOTEL POSADA TOLEDO, Calle 58 no. 487, Mérida, Yuc. 97000. Tel. 99/23-2256. 19 rms (all with bath).

$ Rates: $25.50 single with fan, $29 single with A/C; $29.50 double with fan, $33 double with A/C.

I'm fond of this colonial inn, which was once a private mansion. It's a cross between a garden dripping with vines and a fading museum with beautifully kept antique furnishings. Most rooms have no windows, but high ceilings and appropriately creaky hardwood floors are standard. The rooftop lounge area is excellent for viewing the city in the cool of the evening. It's on Calle 58 at the corner of Calle 57, seven blocks west of the train station and 2½ blocks northeast of Plaza Mayor.

HOTEL CARIBE, Calle 59 no. 500, Mérida, Yuc. 97000. Tel. 99/24-9022. Fax 99/24-8733. 56 rms (all with bath). TV TEL

$ Rates: $29 single with fan, $33 single with A/C; $34 double with fan, $38 double with A/C; $45 suite double with fan, $56 with A/C. **Parking:** Free.

Step inside the entry of this small, two-story central-city hotel and discover a recently remodeled colonial-style jewel. Nicely coordinated colonial-style furnishings accent new pastel-colored tile floors. Comfortable sitting areas along the three stories of covered open-air walkways become like an extended living room offering a cozy respite any time of day. On the top floor there's a small swimming pool, sun deck, and great views of the cathedral and town. The interior restaurant is arranged around a quiet, central courtyard while the hotel's sidewalk café, El Mesón, is set out in front in the shady Parque Cepeda Peraza.

WORTH THE EXTRA BUCKS

HOTEL COLONIAL, Calle 62 no. 476, Mérida, Yuc. 97000. Tel. 99/23-6444. Fax 99/28-3961. 73 rms (all with bath). A/C TV TEL

$ Rates: $42 single or double.

For price and location, it's hard to beat this bright, modern, multistoried hotel. A small swimming pool is on the ground floor behind the lobby while the top story holds a partially covered plant-filled deck with tables and chairs and great city views. Coordinated pastel furnishings in each of the newly refurbished rooms lend a touch of class usually found in more expensive hotels. It's next to the University of Yucatán, north of Plaza Mayor at the intersection of Calles 62 and 57.

HOTEL DEL GOBERNADOR, Calle 59 no. 535, Mérida, Yuc. 97000. Tel. 99/23-7133. 61 rms (all with bath), 16 junior suites. A/C TV TEL

$ Rates: $43 single or double; $51 junior suite. Extra person $5. Off-season rates may be 30% lower. Suggest a discount and you may get one. **Parking:** Free.

⭐ Modern and sleek, this hotel is one of Mérida's most popular. Built on three levels around an interior swimming pool, all rooms have tile floors and bathrooms with showers. To the left of the lobby is a cozy restaurant and the hotel offers laundry service. It's three blocks west of Parque Cepeda Peraza at the intersection of Calles 59 and 66.

HOTEL MARÍA DEL CARMEN, Calle 63 no. 550 (Apdo. Postal 411), Mérida, Yuc. 97000. Tel. 99/23-9133, or toll-free reservations through Best Western 800/528-1234 in the U.S. Fax 99/23-9290. 89 rms (all with bath). A/C TV TEL

$ Rates: $58 single; $70 double.

⭐ With a good near-town location yet removed from traffic noise found on busier streets, the María del Carmen is an excellent choice. The three-story hotel is built around a pretty swimming pool that's shaded by an enormous rubber tree. The newly remodeled lobby is paved with marble and guest rooms have Asian overtones with maroon-colored furniture. Most have two double beds. To the right of the lobby is a popular restaurant/bar. The hotel is between Calles 68 and 70, 3½ blocks north of the bus station and 4½ blocks west of Plaza Mayor.

CASA DEL BALAM, Calle 60 no. 48, Mérida, Yuc. 97000. Tel. 99/24-8844, or toll free 800/624-8451 in the U.S. 54 rms (all with bath), 2 suites. A/C MINIBAR TV TEL

$ Rates: $65–$80 single or double; $100 suite. **Parking:** Free.

⭐ One of Mérida's most popular and centrally located hotels, it's built around a lush interior courtyard three blocks north of Plaza Mayor. In two sections of three and six stories respectively, each of the colonial-style rooms is accented with Mexican textiles, folk art, dark furniture, iron headboards, and tile floors with area rugs. It's hard to top this place for location and comfort.

WHERE TO EAT

Mérida is a budget diner's delight. American, Mexican, and Yucatecan meals from snacks to banquets are all easy to find, with prices ranging from 50¢ for a sandwich to $10 for a bountiful repast.

LAS MIL TORTAS, Calle 62 no. 479. Tel. 23-7809.
    Specialty: SANDWICHES.
$ Prices: Sandwiches 80¢–$1.90; fruit drinks 55¢–75¢.
    Open: Daily 8am–11pm.

Ⓢ This tiny sandwich shop between Calles 57 and 55, three blocks north of Plaza Mayor and half a block north of the Hotel Colonial, is the mecca for cheap, quick food. The few small tables are often filled with students, but you can get your tortas and *refresco* (soft drink) to go. It's branching out now, so you may see similar shops in other parts of the city.

EL LOUVRE, Calle 62 no. 499. Tel. 24-5073.
    Specialty: MEXICAN.
$ Prices: Main courses $3–$6; fixed-price lunch $3–$4.50.
    Open: Daily 24 hours.
Calle 62 between Plaza Mayor and Calle 57 is a riot of small, rock-bottom food shops offering everything from chalupas to chow mein. This big, open restaurant feeds everybody who comes to Mérida at one time or another—chicle workers, laborers from the henequen fields, planters, and townspeople.

LOS ALMENDROS, Calle 50A no. 493. Tel. 21-2851.
Specialty: YUCATECAN.
$ Prices: Appetizers $3.25–$4.50; main courses $3.50–$8; daily special $5.50–$6.50.
Open: Daily 9am–11pm.

The first Los Almendros is at Ticul, deep in the Maya hinterland, but the branch in Mérida has become the favorite spot to sample local delicacies. Poc-chuc, a delectable concoction of grilled pork, tomatoes, onions, cilantro (fresh coriander leaves), and salt, was created in Mérida at this restaurant, which faces Plaza de Mejorada between Calles 57 and 59, six blocks east of Parque Cepeda Peraza. Ask to see the menu with color photographs of the menu items and descriptions in English.

CEDRO DEL LIBANO, Calle 59 no. 529. Tel. 23-7531.
Specialty: MIDDLE EASTERN.
$ Prices: Appetizers $3.50–$4.50; main courses $3.50–$8.
Open: Daily 11:30am–11pm.

A Middle Eastern restaurant in Yucatán? Why? Because 19th-century Mexico, and particularly Yucatán, had a significant population of Ottoman traders, mostly from the sultan's province of Lebanon. This simple but tidy restaurant has a menu that lists berenjena con tijini (eggplant with tahine), labne (yogurt), labin (like buttermilk), tabouleh, kibi, and alambre de kafta (ground meat grilled on skewers). If you don't know Middle Eastern food, just order and hope; waiters lack the patience to translate. I had the fatta Cedro del Libano, which turned out to be chicken topped with chickpeas, yogurt, and sliced almonds. And just to please everyone, there are sandwiches too, and a wide selection of Mexican specialties. It's on Calle 59 between Calles 64 and 66, down from the Hotel Gobernador and 2½ blocks west of Parque Cepeda Peraza.

EL MESÓN, Parque Cepeda Peraza. Tel. 24-9022.
Specialty: MEXICAN.
$ Prices: Appetizers $2–$5; main courses $4–$10; fixed-price meal $5.50–$6.50; sandwiches $2.50–$3.50.
Open: Daily 7am–11pm.

Soon after your arrival in Mérida you'll discover this tiny restaurant just to the left of the Hotel Caribe's entrance a block north of Plaza Mayor. Wrought-iron tables are set outside in the shady Parque Cepeda Peraza (also called Parque Hidalgo), and they're very often full. I especially enjoy the sopa de verduras (vegetable soup). The fixed-price meal is usually served all evening.

RESTAURANTE VEGETARIANO LA GUAYA, Calle 60 no. 472. Tel. 23-2144.
Specialty: VEGETARIAN.
$ Prices: Appetizers $4–$5; main courses $4–$7.
Open: Dinner only, Mon–Sat 5–11pm.

This little vegetarian restaurant is 4½ blocks north of Plaza Mayor, between Calles 55 and 53, a few steps north of the Parque Santa Lucía. The patio café is combined with a bookstore featuring health-related titles. Lots of different salads are offered here, as well as a Hindu dish of oats, wheat, and fish, named Kama Sutra.

CAFE-RESTAURANT EXPRESS, Calle 59 no. 509. Tel. 28-1691.
Specialty: MEXICAN.
$ Prices: Breakfast $1.80–$3.25; appetizers $1.80; main courses $4.50–$10.50; fixed-price meal $6.50.
Open: Daily 7am–11pm.

The most popular meeting place in town faces Parque Cepeda Peraza near the corner of Calle 60. Hordes of local residents—mainly men—sit and idle the hours away, totally oblivious to the surroundings, with all attention focused on the sidewalk or at least a newspaper. The vast menu includes lengua a la Mexicana (Mexican-style tongue), pollo pibil (the chef wraps and marinates the chicken in banana leaves before cooking), and huachinango milanesa (red snapper). You can also while away some time here with good, strong coffee.

POP, Calle 57 no. 501. Tel. 21-6844.
Specialty: MEXICAN.
$ Prices: Appetizers $1.30–$4; main courses $4.50–$6.50; sandwiches $2–$3.50.
Open: Mon–Fri 7am–midnight, Sun 8am–midnight.

Named after the first month of the 18-month Maya calendar, Pop is perfect for a light lunch. With big windows great for people-watching, it's air-conditioned, clean, bright, and modern. The youth of Mérida seem to frequent this place for snacks in the afternoon. The menu includes the best hamburgers in town, apple pie, and Bavarian fudge cake. Breakfasts are a bit skimpy. Pop is next to the university, two blocks north and one block west of Plaza Mayor between Calles 60 and 62.

A PLAZA CAFE

DULCERÍA Y SORBETERÍA COLÓN, Calle 61 no. 500. Tel. 28-1497.
Specialty: PASTRIES.
$ Prices: Pastries 65¢; ice cream $1–$1.50; soft drinks 40¢; milkshakes $1.25.
Open: Daily 8am–11:30pm.

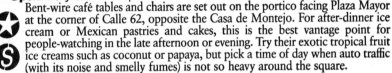

Bent-wire café tables and chairs are set out on the portico facing Plaza Mayor at the corner of Calle 62, opposite the Casa de Montejo. For after-dinner ice cream or Mexican pastries and cakes, this is the best vantage point for people-watching in the late afternoon or evening. Try their exotic tropical fruit ice creams such as coconut or papaya, but pick a time of day when auto traffic (with its noise and smelly fumes) is not so heavy around the square.

BREAKFAST

To make your own breakfast, try the **Panificadora Montejo,** at the corner of Calles 62 and 63, the southwest corner of the main plaza, and choose from a dozen or more delectable breakfast treats. With a hot drink, a light breakfast can be thrown together for about $2.

For those (like me) who can't start a day without fresh orange juice, there's good news. **Juice bars** have sprouted up all over Mérida. Several of these thirst-quenching establishments are on or near the main plaza. A sundae-size glass of orange juice costs $1.30.

WORTH THE EXTRA BUCKS

RESTAURANTE PORTICO DEL PEREGRINO, Calle 57 no. 501. Tel. 21-6844.
Specialty: MEXICAN/INTERNATIONAL. **Reservations:** Advised.
$ Prices: Appetizers $1.80–$4.50; main courses $6.75–$13.50.
Open: Lunch daily noon–3pm; dinner daily 6–11pm.

This romantic restaurant captures the spirit of 19th-century Mexico with its shady little garden court and a cross-topped gateway. If the weather is too warm for outdoor dining, escape to the air-conditioned dining rooms decorated with antique mirrors and elegant sideboards; there's also a modern streetside salon. The extensive menu offers soup, fish filet, a brochette of beef, spaghetti, pollo pibil, and rum-raisin ice cream. The restaurant is between Calles 60 and 62, 2½ blocks north of the main square, next door to Pop and across from the university.

LA CASONA, Calle 60 no. 434. Tel. 23-8348.
Specialty: YUCATECAN/CONTINENTAL. **Reservations:** Suggested.
$ Prices: Appetizers $2.50–$7.75; pasta courses $3.50–$10; meat courses $7.75–$14.
Open: Daily 1pm–midnight.

A gracious old Mérida house and its lush interior garden make a charming and romantic restaurant. The cuisine is Yucatecan and continental, especially Italian, so you can choose among such dishes as pollo pibil, filet mignon with brandy and cream, linguini with mushrooms, or lasagne. It's at the corner of Calle 47, nine blocks north of Plaza Mayor.

EL PATIO DE LAS FAJITAS, Calle 60 no. 467. Tel. 28-3782.
Specialty: MEXICAN.
$ Prices: Appetizers $4.50–$5.50; main courses $9.80–$12; beer $1.50; wine $2.25.
Open: Tues–Sun 1–11pm.

✪ Fajitas are the specialty at this mansion-turned-restaurant where you dine around a central courtyard decorated with plants and colorful tablecloths. The fajitas, grilled before you on the patio, are made of small strips of marinated pork, chicken, or beef, or whole shrimp, all sizzled on an iron griddle with a dash of garlic oil, lime juice, and finally beer for a flaming effect. Each order comes with a delicious guacamole salad, flour tortillas, and fresh Mexican salsa cruda. Although fajitas reign supreme, the menu also offers hamburgers, great quesadillas, beans ranchero style, and other Mexican specialties. You'll find it at the corner of Calle 53, four blocks north of Plaza Mayor.

SHOPPING

Mérida is known for hammocks, guayaberas (typical man's shirt), and Panama hats. But there are good buys in Yucatán-made baskets and pottery, as well as crafts from all over Mexico, especially at the central market. Mérida is also the place to pick up prepared *achiote,* a mixture of ground achiote, oregano, garlic, masa, and other spices used in Yucatecan cuisine, especially on grilled meat and fish—I don't leave the Yucatán without it.

Mérida's bustling **market district,** bounded by Calles 63 to 69 and Calles 62 to 54, is a few blocks southeast of Plaza Mayor. The streets surrounding the market can be as interesting and crowded as the market itself. Heaps of prepared achiote are sold in the food section, or it's sometimes found bottled and already mixed with juice of the sour orange. Buy the prepared achiote only if you are heading home, since it needs refrigeration.

CRAFTS

CRAFTS MARKET, in a separate building of the main market, Calle 67 at Calle 56.
Look for a large pale-green building behind the post office. Climb the steps and wade into the clamor and activity, browsing for leather goods, hammocks, Panama hats, Maya embroidered dresses, men's formal guayabera shirts, and craft items of all kinds.

MUSEO REGIONAL DE ARTESANÍAS, Calle 59 no. 441, between Calles 50 and 48.
It's a branch of the Museo Nacional de Artes e Industrías Populares from Mexico City. Displays of regional costumes and crafts occupy the front rooms. In the back is a large room full of crafts from all over Mexico, including filigree jewelry from Mérida, folk pottery, baskets, and wood carving from the Yucatán. It's open Tuesday through Saturday from 8am to 8pm and on Sunday from 9am to 2pm. Admission is free.

LA CASA DE ARTESANÍAS, Calle 63 no. 513, between Calles 64 and 66. Tel. 24-7776.
This beautiful restored monastery doubles as a regional crafts showplace and salesshop and bookstore. There's a bulletin board listing cultural events, and an inexpensive cafeteria. It's open Monday through Saturday from 8am to 8pm.

HAMMOCKS

The supremely comfortable Yucatecan fine-mesh hammocks (*hamacas*) are made of string from several materials. Silk is wonderful, but extremely expensive, and only for truly serious hammock-sleepers. Nylon is long-lasting. Cotton is attractive, fairly strong, and inexpensive, but it wears out sooner than nylon. There are several grades of cotton string used in hammocks. Here's how to proceed: Look at the string itself. Is it fine and tightly spun? Are the end loops well made and tight? Open the hammock and look at the weave. Are the strings soiled? Are there many mistakes in the pattern of the weave?

To see if the hammock is large enough, grasp the hammock at the point where the wide part and the end strings meet, and hold your hand level with the top of your head. The body should touch the floor; if not, the hammock is too short for you. Keep in mind that any of these hammocks is going to look big when you stretch it open, but many will seem small when you actually lie in them.

Hammocks are sold as *sencillo* (single, 50 pairs of end strings, about $9), *doble* (double, 100 pairs of end strings, $12), *matrimonial* (larger than doble, 150 pairs of end strings, about $16). The biggest hammock of all is called *una hamaca de quatro cajas,* or sometimes *matrimonial especial,* and it's simply enormous, with 175 pairs of end strings; if you can find one, it'll cost you about $25. Buy the biggest hammock you can afford. You'll be glad you did. The bigger ones take up no more room, and are so much more comfortable, even for just one person. (To get long life from your hammock, always remember to remove your shoes and avoid contact between buttons or zippers and the weave.)

Where should you buy your hammock? Street vendors will approach you at every turn: "*Hamacas, señor, señorita?*" Their prices will be low, but so is their quality. If you buy from these vendors, be sure to examine the hammock carefully. Booths in the market will have a larger selection to choose from, at only slightly higher prices.

I've been recommending **La Poblana, S.A.,** Calle 65 no. 492, between Calles 60 and 58 (tel. 21-6503), for years with no complaints. Sr. William Razu C., the owner, is usually on the job and ready to whip out dozens of hammocks for your inspection. Prices are marked so don't try to bargain. If you've spent some time in the market for hammocks and you seem to know what you're talking about, Sr. Razu may usher you upstairs to a room where you can give your prospective purchase a test run. La Poblana sells ropes and mosquito nets for hammocks as well, and also Maya women's dresses and men's guayaberas. Hours are Monday through Saturday from 8am to 7pm.

MAQUECH — THE LEGENDARY MAYA BEETLE

One of the most unusual items for sale in the Yucatán is the live maquech beetle. Storekeepers display bowls of the large dusty-brown insects that have their long black legs and backs sprinkled with multicolored glass "jewels" attached to a small gold chain. The chain hooks to a small safety pin and creates a living brooch to wear. One version of the maquech legend goes that a Maya princess became the forbidden love object of a Maya prince. Without her knowledge, he crept into her garden one night, and just as they met he was captured by the princess's guards. To save the prince, a sorceress turned him into a beetle and put him on a decaying tree near where he was captured. When the princess recovered from her faint, she looked for the prince where she had last seen him, found the bejeweled beetle instead, and in an instant knew it was the prince. Using a few strands of her long hair, she harnessed the beetle and kept it over her heart forever. Another version has it that the prince asked a sorceress to put him close to the heart of his beloved princess. So, because he was very rich, she turned him into a jeweled beetle pin. Either way, putting one close to your heart costs between $7 and $10 and comes with a piece of its favorite wood, a little box with air holes to carry it in, the chain, and a safety pin.

Curios La Carmita, upstairs in the market at Local 18-20, usually has a good supply of the maquech. U.S. Customs, however, doesn't permit the beetle to cross the border, so plan to find it a home before you leave Mexico.

PANAMA HATS

Another very popular item are these soft, pliable hats made from the palm fibers of the jipijapa in several towns along Highway 180, particularly in Becal, in the neighboring state of Campeche. There's no need to journey all the way to Campeche, however, as

Mérida has the hats in abundance. The hats can be rolled up and carried in a suitcase for the trip home since they retain their shape quite well.

Jipi hats come in three grades, judged by the quality (pliability and fineness) of the fibers and closeness of the weave. The coarser, more open weave of fairly large fibers will be sold for a few dollars (or by street vendors in Cancún and Cozumel for up to $10!). The middle grade, a fairly fine, close weave of good fibers, should cost about $10 in a responsible shop. The finest weave, truly a beautiful hat, can cost twice this much.

In **La Casa de los Jipis,** Calle 56 no. 526, near Calle 65, a tried-and-true *sombrerería,* a phlegmatic señora will show you the three grades of hats, grumbling all the while. Find your size, more or less, and the senora will tie a ribbon around the hat for final adjustment. If you'd like to see how the hats are blocked, wander into the depths of the rear of the store.

EVENING ENTERTAINMENT

For a full range of free or low-cost evening entertainment, and Mérida Sunday activities see "Special Events" above.

Teatro Peon Contreras, at Calles 60 and 57, and the **Teatro Ayala,** on Calle 60 at Calle 61, offer a wide range of performing artists from around the world. Stop in and see what's showing.

Action at the hotel bars, lounges, and discos depends on the crowd of customers presently staying at each hotel. Most of Mérida's downtown hotels, however, are filled with tour groups whose members prefer to rest after an exhausting day.

EASY EXCURSIONS FROM MÉRIDA
CELESTÚN

This flamingo sanctuary and offbeat, sand-street fishing village on the Gulf Coast is a 1½-hour drive from Mérida. To get here, take Highway 281 (a single-lane road), past numerous old henequen haciendas. There are also frequent buses from Mérida.

The town is on a narrow strip of land separated from the mainland by a lagoon. Crossing over the lagoon bridge, notice the small boats moored on both sides. They are waiting to take visitors to see the flamingos. A 1½- to 2-hour **flamingo-sighting trip** costs $21, or twice that if you stay a half day. Besides flamingos, you'll see frigatebirds, pelicans, cranes, sandpipers, and other waterfowl feeding on the shallow sandbars. Flamingos are found here all year; some nonbreeding flamingos remain year round even though the larger group takes off around April to nest on the upper Yucatán Peninsula east of Río Lagartos. The best time to go is around 7am and the worst is at midafternoon when sudden storms come up. Be sure not to allow the boatmen to get close enough to frighten the birds; it causes the birds to abandon the habitat.

Essentials The one telephone at the Hotel Gutiérrez (tel. 99/24-6348) serves the entire village. There's a bank, gas station, and grocery store.

Special Events December 8 is the **Feast of the Virgen of Concepción,** the patron saint of the village. On the Sunday nearest **July 15,** a colorful procession takes Celestún's venerated figure of the Virgen of Concepción to meet the sacred figure of the Virgen of Asunción on the highway leading to Celestún. Returning to Celestún, they float away on decorated boats and later return to be ensconced at the church during a mass and celebration.

Where to Stay

To find restaurants and hotels, follow the bridge road a few blocks to the end. On the last street, Calle 12, parallelling the oceanfront, you'll find a few hotels, all with decent rooms but marginal housekeeping standards. Always try to bargain for better rates which could be 30% less in the off season. A hotel under construction next to the Hotel Gutiérrez may be open when you arrive.

HOTEL AGUILAR, Calle 12, Celestún, Yuc. 97367. 12 rooms (all with bath). **$ Rates:** $7–$9 single; $10–$11 double.

Across Calle 12 from the beach, the single-story Aguilar is set back from the street and built around a sandy courtyard. It's the best-kept hotel in town, although you may still find it lacking in that respect. The spacious rooms have fans, hot and cold water, good cross-ventilation, screened windows, tile floors, hammock hooks, one or two double beds, and bathrooms with showers. A small grocery store is in front.

To get here, turn right on Calle 12, go four blocks, and it's on the right (landward side) between Calles 5 and 7.

CASA JULIO, Calle 12 no. 100, Celestún, Yuc. 97367. 9 rms (all with bath).
$ Rates: $7 single; $11.50 double.
Built around a sandy courtyard facing the beach, the rooms (all with fans) are basic and the beds may sag, but the wood louvered windows are well screened and the price is right for a beachfront abode. If there's no one around to rent a room, the manager may be across the street. Casa Julio is two blocks down Calle 12 in the turquoise-colored building at the left on the beach side.

HOTEL GUTIÉRREZ, Calle 14 at Calle 13, Celestún, Yuc. 97367. Tel. 99/24-6348. 18 rms (all with bath).
$ Rates: $13.50 single or double.
Although this hotel appears to be the nicest in town, with its three stories of rooms with fans, all on the beach, housekeeping standards are noticeably lax and promised hot water may never appear. Buy drinking water in the lobby. The hotel also serves as the town's long-distance telephone office. It's on the right about two blocks down from Calle 12.

Where to Eat

RESTAURANT CELESTÚN, Calle 12, on the waterfront.
Specialty: SEAFOOD/MEXICAN.
$ Prices: Main courses $3–$10.
Open: Daily 8am–7pm.
I highly recommend this ocean-view restaurant owned by Elda Cauich and Wenseslao Ojeda, where the service is friendly and swift. The house specialty is a super-delicious shrimp, crab, and squid omelet (called "torta"). To get here, follow the bridge road to the waterfront; the restaurant is immediately left, on Calle 12.

PROGRESO

For another beach escape, go to Progreso, a modern city facing the Gulf less than an hour from Mérida. Here the Malecón, a beautiful oceanfront drive, fronts a vast beach lined with coconut palms that's popular on weekends. A long pier or *muelle* (pronounced "mu-*wey*-yeh") shoots out into the bay to reach water deep enough for ocean-going ships, and a few mediocre seafood restaurants face the Malecón.

From Mérida, buses to Progreso, leave the special bus station at Calle 62 no. 524, between Calles 65 and 67, every 15 minutes during the day, starting at 5am. The trip takes 45 minutes.

In Progreso, the bus station is about four blocks south of Calle 19, which runs along the beach.

DZIBILCHALTÚN

This Maya site, 9 miles north of Mérida along the Progreso road and 4½ miles east off the highway, is worth a stop. Before you go, pick up the detailed official guide written by archeologist E. Wyllys Andrews V, and published by the Instituto Nacional de Antropológia e Historia, complete with descriptions and a handy plan of the central portion of the ruins.

To get there by bus from Mérida, go to the Progreso bus station (see above) where five buses per day (at 7:10 and 10:50am, and 1:20, 5:20, and 7:30pm) go to Chablekal, which is near the entrance to the Dzibilchaltún ruins. I recommend taking the very earliest so as to beat the heat.

There's a small museum at the site with exhibits of stelae, figurines, pottery, and a group of seven strange clay dolls that show a variety of diseases and birth defects.

Though it was founded about 500 B.C. and flourished around A.D. 750, Dzibilchaltún was in decline long before the coming of the conquistadores and wasn't rediscovered until 1941. Today the most interesting buildings are grouped around the **Cenote Xlacah,** the sacred well, and include a complex of buildings around Structure 38, the **Central Group** of temples, the raised **causeways** (or saches), and the **Seven Dolls Group,** centered on the **Temple of the Seven Dolls.** It was beneath the floor of the temple that those seven weird little dolls (now in the museum) were discovered. Admission is $3.50.

MOVING ON TO MAYAPÁN, TICUL & UXMAL

There are two routes to the splendid archeological zone of Uxmal ("Oosh-mahl"), about 50 miles to the south of Mérida. The most direct is on Highway 261 via Uman, the Hacienda Yaxcopoíl, and Muna; the other follows Highway 18 through Kanasin, the ruins of Mayapán, Ticul, and Santa Elena, on a scenic but meandering trip through numerous interesting villages.

It is possible to see Uxmal on a day trip by bus from Mérida. Sunday is a good day to go, since admission is free and means a saving of $14.50 per person, or $20 if Loltún is included. **Autotransportes del Sur** (tel. 24-9055) offers one bus daily on the Mérida–Uxmal–Kabah–Sayil–Labná–Xlapak route. The trip costs $11, departing Mérida at 8am, returning at 2pm. The driver allows passengers to spend around 90 minutes at Uxmal and 30 minutes at each of the other stops before returning. A special bus for the Spanish-language sound-and-light performance at Uxmal costs around $5.50 and departs Mérida at 4:30pm, returning after the show.

The best way to visit the sites, however, is to rent a car, stay 2 nights in a hotel at Uxmal (there's only one budget hotel), or at less expensive hotels in Ticul, and allow 2 full days of sightseeing.

VIA YAXCOPOÍL & MUNA From Mérida via Uman, it's 20 miles to the Hacienda Yaxcopoíl and 40 miles to Muna on Highway 261. Uxmal is 10 miles from Muna.

Ten miles beyond Uman is **Yaxcopoíl,** the tongue-twisting Maya name of a fascinating old hacienda on the right side of the road between Mérida and Uxmal. It's difficult to reach by bus. Take half an hour to tour the house, factory, outbuildings, and museum. You'll see that such haciendas were the administrative, commercial, and social centers of vast private domains, almost little principalities, carved out of the Yucatecan jungle. It's open Monday through Saturday from 8am to dusk and on Sunday from 9am to 1pm.

When you leave Yaxcopoíl, you still have 28 miles to drive to reach Uxmal.

VIA KANASIN, MAYAPÁN & TICUL Taking Calle 67 east, head out of Mérida toward Kanasin and Acanceh ("Ah-*kahn*-keh"), about 12 miles. When Calle 67 ends, bear right, then left at the next big intersection. Follow the wide divided highway complete with speed bumps. At Mérida's *circunvalación* (road that circles the city) you'll see signs to Cancún. You can either cross the circunvalación and go straight into Kanasin or continue to follow the Cancún signs until you see the signs into Kanasin. In Kanasin, watch for signs that say CIRCULACIÓN. As in many Yucatán towns, you're being redirected onto a one-way street through the urban area. Go past the market, church, and main square on your left, and continue straight out of town. The next village you come to, at km 10, is San Antonio Tehuit, an old henequen hacienda. At km 13 is Tepich, another hacienda-centered village, with those funny little henequen-cart tracks criss-crossing the main road. After Tepich comes Petectunich, and finally Acanceh.

A Stop En Route—Acanceh Overlooking Acanceh's main square is a partially restored pyramid to the left of the church, and another, the large **Stucco Palace,** a couple of blocks away. There's little stucco left on the palace, but to find it, follow the street to the right of the market, turn right at the first corner, left at the next one, and right again. The grass-covered pyramid is about halfway down the block. A few animal figures in stucco relief are preserved under a makeshift cover on top. You'll have to find the custodian, Anatolio Narvaez, to unlock the gate to either pyramid; his house is on the street to the right of the main square and about halfway down opposite the market.

From Acanceh's main square, turn right (around the statue of a smiling deer) and head for **Tecoh** with its huge crumbling church (5½ miles) and **Telchaquillo** (7 miles). This route takes you past several old Yucatecan haciendas, each complete with its big house, chapel, factory with smokestack, and workers' houses.

Shortly after the village of Telchaquillo, a sign on the right side of the road will point to the entrance of the ruins of Mayapán.

2. MAYAPÁN & TICUL

MAYAPÁN

Founded by the man-god Quetzalcoatl (Kukulcán in Maya) in about A.D. 1007, Mayapán ranked in importance with Chichén-Itzá and Uxmal and covered at least 2½ square miles. For more than two centuries it was the capital of a Maya confederation of city-states that included Chichén and Uxmal. But before the year 1200 the rulers of Mayapán ended the confederation by attacking and conquering Chichén, and by forcing the rulers of Uxmal to live as vassals in Mayapán. Eventually a successful revolt by the captive Maya rulers brought down Mayapán, which was abandoned during the mid-1400s.

Though ruined, the main pyramid is still impressive. Next to it is a large cenote (natural limestone cavern, used as a well), now full of trees, bushes, and banana plants. Beside it is a small temple with columns and a fine high-relief mask of Chac, the hook-nosed rain god. Jungle paths lead to other small temples, including El Caracol, with its circular tower. These piles of stones give no idea of how the walled city of Mayapán appeared in its heyday. Supplied with water from 20 cenotes, it had over 3,000 buildings in its enclosed boundaries of several square miles. Today, all is covered in dense jungle.

Sr. Fausto Uc Flores, the guard, or his wife, Sra. Magdalena, whom you may meet as you enter the ruins, will sell you the admission ticket for $2.50 (free on Sunday) and provide information. The site is open daily from 8am to 5pm.

FROM MAYAPÁN TO TICUL   The road is a good one, but directional signs through the villages are nonexistent. Stop and ask frequently. From Mayapán, continue along Highway 18 to Tekit (5 miles), turn right, and go to Mama on a road as thrilling as a roller coaster ride (4⅓ miles), and turn right again for Chapab (8 miles).

If you're ready for a break, take time out to visit the **tortilla factory** in Chapab. Turn left when you see a building named Centro Educativo Communitario Chapab; the factory is a couple of blocks farther on the left. As you came into town you probably noticed young Maya girls with masa dough up to their elbows carrying large pans and buckets of it atop their heads. They're returning from the daily ritual of corn grinding, and they'll use the masa to make their own tortillas at home. Other youngsters are carrying out large stacks of finished tortillas. The Matos Sabino family owns the factory and they don't mind if you stop in and watch the action, which goes on daily from 8am to around 3pm. Better yet, buy some tortillas, fill them with avocados, tomatoes, and cheese, and have a picnic on the lawn across the street.

After Capab, you reach Ticul (6¼ miles), the largest town in the region.

TICUL

GETTING THERE   There are frequent buses from Mérida. The Ticul bus station is near the town center on Calle 24 between Calles 25 and 25A. For car information, see the routes above.

ESSENTIALS   The **telephone area code** is 997.

DEPARTING   There are first-class buses to Mérida on Monday at 7am, Sunday through Friday at 2:15pm, on Sunday also at 6:15 and 7pm, and on Saturday at 6pm. Also check with the drivers of the minivans that line up across from the bus station.
   Buses run twice hourly to Muna, where you change to buses to Uxmal.

Many of the 27,000 inhabitants of this sprawling town make their living embroidering huipiles (the Maya women's costume), weaving straw hats, making shoes and gold-filigree jewelry, and shaping pottery. Workshops and stores featuring most of these items are easy to find, especially in the market area.
   The market, most hotels, and Los Almendros, Ticul's best-known restaurant, are on the main street, **Calle 23,** also called Calle Principal.
   Ticul's **annual festival,** complete with bullfights, dancing, and carnival games, is held during the first few days of April.

WHERE TO STAY

HOTEL SAN MIGUEL, Calle 28 no. 195, Ticul, Yuc. 97860. 20 rms (all with bath).
$ Rates: $6.75 single; $9 double with one bed, $11.20 double with two beds.
Some people might call the simply furnished rooms Mexican cell-block style. Though it's not the Ritz, the price is right and each room has a fan and windows on a narrow exterior corridor facing a sunny wall. It's mere steps from the market (from the market, walk half a block north, turn left onto Calle 28, and the narrow doorway to the hotel is on the left).

HOTEL-MOTEL CERRO INN, Calle 23 no. 292, Ticul, Yuc. 97860. Tel. 997/20-260. 9 rms (all with bath). TV
$ Rates: $11 single; $13 double.
Once it was the best motel in town, but now the rooms are only basic, with tile floors and furniture from the 1930s; one is air-conditioned and the rest have fans. The setting, in a cool shady grove, is actually nicer than the rooms. There's a restaurant too, but other places in town have better service and food. It's 1¼ miles from the market on the highway to Muna and Mérida, on the left.

HOTEL BOUGAMBILLIAS FAMILIAR, Calle 23 no. 291A, Ticul, Yuc. 97860. Tel. 997/2-0139. 20 rms (all with bath).
$ Rates: $13 single; $20–$26 double with one or two beds.
Ticul's nicest inn is more like a motel, with parking outside the room section. The half-circle drive into the arched entrance is lined with plants and pottery from the owner's local factory. Ceiling-height windows don't let in much light, but the spotlessly clean rooms have fans, good beds, cool tile floors, and ready hot water. In back is the hotel's pretty restaurant, Xux-Cab (see "Where to Eat," below).
   To get here, follow Calle 23 through Ticul on the road to Muna; it's on the right before you leave town.

WHERE TO EAT

Good restaurants are few in Ticul, but besides those listed here, don't overlook the busy **market** on Calle 23 where you can pick up fresh fruit and grab a bite at one of the little eateries.

XUX-CAB, off Calle 21, in back of the Hotel Bougambillias Familiar. Tel. 2-0139.
   Specialty: YUCATÁN.

$ Prices: Appetizers, free with beer and mixed drinks; main courses $4.
Open: Daily 8am–8pm.

This new, partly open-air and partly sheltered restaurant showed promise on my last visit. Delicious appetizers are served free with alcoholic drinks. Although the menu lists 16 *platillos* (plate meals), only a few may actually be offered; ask what's cooking first. Musicians usually come in the afternoon and evening, making it a pleasant place to relax and eat.

To get here, drive through central Ticul on Calle 23 toward Muna, several blocks past the market; turn into the Hotel Bougambillias Familiar and park in back by the restaurant.

LOS ALMENDROS, Calle 23 no. 207. Tel. 2-0021.

Specialty: YUCATÁN.
$ Prices: Appetizers $3.25; main courses $5.50–$8.
Open: Daily 8am–9pm.

Set in a big old Andalusian-style house, this is the original of the chain with branches now in Mérida and Cancún. The Maya specialties include papadzules (sauce-covered, egg-filled tortillas) poc-chuc, and the spicy pollo ticuleño; as in Mérida, the quality of food varies. Ask for the illustrated menu in English that explains the dishes in detail. The restaurant is two blocks south of the market on the left.

RESTAURANT LOS DELFINES, Calle 27 no. 216.

Specialty: MEXICAN.
$ Prices: To be established.
Open: Daily 8am–6pm.

The owners of my favorite place, Restaurant Delfine, sold out and moved to Querétaro. New owners bought the name, and when I checked recently were preparing to open in a beautiful garden setting near the center of town. The menu and prices were not ready, but it looks promising; see what you think.

From Calle 23 (main street) go past the market and turn left on Calle 28; go two blocks and turn right on Calle 27; it's on the left half a block down.

SHOPPING

Ticul is best known for the manufacture of ladies' dress shoes and it's a center for large-size, commercially produced pottery. Most of the widely sold sienna-colored pottery painted with Maya designs comes from Ticul. If it's a cloudy, humid day the potters may not be working, since part of the process requires sun drying. But they still welcome visitors to purchase finished pieces.

ARTESANÍAS POPULARES, Calle 21 no. 239, between Calles 32 and 34.

The Chan family, owners of the Hotel Bougambillias Familiar, also own a pottery factory which produces much of the Maya-motif pottery you see for sale in the Yucatán, as well as more traditional pottery for gardeners. Drop in between 8am and 5pm Tuesday through Friday, and on Saturday until noon.

UICAB HUCHIN FAMILY, Calle 21 toward Muna, on the right, several blocks past the market.

There's no sign, but look for freshly formed pottery drying on the sidewalk in front of the whitewashed, thatch-roofed family home that doubles as a workshop. It's very informal, with the Uicab sons shaping clay into precisely formed huge pots, Señora Uicab cooking in the kitchen, and children playing. Piles of pots fill every available space, there are no fixed prices, and few small pots for travelers with limited luggage space. Visitors are welcome anytime. If you interrupt the potters for very long, it's considerate to leave a tip.

PLATERÍA SANDY, Calle 21 no. 263, between Calles 36 and 38.

Filigree jewelry is a Yucatán art practiced in this small workshop where a few young men fashion finely worked pieces using crude instruments on a small well-worn table. There's no showroom, so ask to see some finished work. It's open Monday through Saturday from 8am to 1pm and 3 to 6pm.

AN EXCURSION TO YAXNIC CAVES

Just outside the village of Yotolín (also spelled Yohtolín, which is between Ticul and Oxkutcab) are some impressive caves called Yaxnic ("*Yash*-neek"), on the grounds of the old, private Hacienda Yotolín. Virtually undeveloped and full of colored stalactites and stalagmites, the caves are visited by means of a perilous descent in a basket let down on a rope.

Arranging this spelunking challenge takes time, but since the thrill may be worth it, here's the procedure. Several days (or even weeks or months) before your intended cave descent, go to Yotolín and ask for the house of the *commisario*. He will make the proper introductions to the hacienda owners, who in turn will tell you how to prepare for the experience.

EN ROUTE FROM TICUL TO UXMAL

From Ticul to Uxmal, follow the main street through town. At the edge of town, turn left at the sign to Santa Elena. It's 10 miles to Santa Elena; then, at the highway, cut back right for about 2 miles to Uxmal. Or drive straight through Ticul and it's 14 miles to Muna. At Muna, turn left and head south on Highway 261 to Uxmal, 10 miles away.

3. UXMAL

50 miles S of Mérida, 12 miles SW of Ticul, 12 miles S of Muna

GETTING THERE   By Bus   ADO buses to Uxmal depart from Mérida at 6, 7, 8, and 9am, noon, and 3, 5:30, and 7pm; return trips are at 6:30, 8:30, and 11:30am, and 2:30, 5:30, and 7:30pm—wait at the highway in front of the entrance to the ruins.

Autotransportes del Sur (tel. 24-9055) offers one bus daily on the Mérida–Uxmal–Kabah–Sayil–Labná–Xlapak route. The trip, all on the same bus, costs $11, departing Mérida at 8am, returning at 2pm. The driver allows passengers to spend around 90 minutes at Uxmal and 30 minutes at each of the other stops before returning. A special bus for the Spanish-language sound-and-light performance at Uxmal costs around $5.50 and departs Mérida at 4:30pm, returning after the show.

By Car   Two routes are described above, either on Highway 261 from Mérida turning through Muna, or via Highway 18 from Mérida via Kanasin and Mayapán.

Note: There's no gasoline at Uxmal, so top off your tank in Mérida, Muna, or Ticul before continuing.

ESSENTIALS   Uxmal consists of the archeological site, four hotels, and a highway restaurant. There are no phones except at the hotels. Restaurants near Uxmal are expensive, so if you're coming for the day, the smartest thing to do is to bring a lunch. A Sunday visit will save money since admission is free to Uxmal and other recommended sites nearby. Admission to Uxmal is $4.50; Kabah, Sayil, Labná, and Xlapak, $2.75 each; Loltún, $4.50. They are all open daily from 8am to 5pm.

Prepare yourself for one of the highlights of your Yucatán vacation, for the ruins of Uxmal, noted for the rich geometric stone facades, are the most beautiful in the Yucatán. It can give you quite a thrill to ponder what Uxmal must have been like in its heyday: great lords and ladies clad in white embroidered robes and feathered headdresses; and market day, when the commonfolk gathered in a tumultuous scene of barter. Uxmal flourished in the Late Classic Period, about A.D. 600–900, and then fell under the sway of the Xiú princes (who may have come from the Valley of

Mexico) after the year 1000. Some 4½ centuries later the Xiú conquered Mayapán (1440s), and not long afterward the glories of the Maya ended when the Spanish conquistadores arrived.

SEEING THE RUINS

The ruins of Uxmal are open daily from 8am to 5pm. A 45-minute sound-and-light show is staged each evening, in Spanish for $1.50 at 7pm, and in English for $2 at 9pm. The special sound-and-light bus from Mérida only stays for the Spanish show. If you stay for the English, find your own ride back to Mérida. After the impressive show, the chant "Chaaac, Chaaac" will echo in your mind for weeks.

At the main entrance is a modern complex where you'll find toilets, a restaurant, first-aid station, small museum, and shops for publications, photo supplies, and crafts.

The Pyramid of the Magician As you enter the ruins, note the *chultun* (cistern) inside the entrance to the right. Besides the natural underground cisterns (such as cenotes) formed in the porous limestone, chultunes were the principal source of water for the Maya.

Uxmal's dominant building, the Pyramid of the Magician, with its unique rounded sides, looms majestically as you enter. The name comes from a legend about a mystical dwarf who reached adulthood rapidly after being hatched from an egg, and who built this pyramid in 1 night. Beneath it are four temples, since it was common practice for the Maya to build new structures atop old ones, even before the old structures were ruined.

The pyramid is unique because of its oval shape, height, and steepness, and its odd doorway on the opposite (west) side near the top. The doorway's heavy ornamentation, a characteristic of the Chenes style, features 12 stylized masks of the rain god Chac and the doorway itself is a huge open-mouthed Chac mask.

The View from the Top The tiring, and even dangerous, climb is worth it for the view. Next to the Pyramid of the Magician, to the west, is the Nunnery Quadrangle and left of it a conserved ball court, south of which are several large complexes. The biggest building among them is the Governor's Palace, and behind it lies the partially restored Great Pyramid. In the distance is the Dovecote, a palace with a lacy roofcomb (false front) that looks perfect for an apartment complex for pigeons. These are the main structures you'll notice from atop the Pyramid of the Magician.

From this vantage point, note how Uxmal is special among Maya sites for the use of broad terraces or platforms constructed to support the buildings; look closely and you'll see that the Governor's Palace is not on a natural hill or rise, but on a huge square terrace, as is the Nunnery Quadrangle.

The Nunnery The 16th-century Spanish historian Fray Diego López de Cogullado gave the building its name because it resembled Spanish monasteries. Possibly it was a military academy or a training school for princes, who may have lived in the 70-odd rooms. The buildings were constructed at different times: The northern one was first, then the southern one, then the east, then the west, with the western building having the most richly decorated facade, composed of intertwined stone snakes and numerous masks of the hook-nosed rain god Chac.

The corbeled archway on the south was once the main entrance to the Nunnery complex; as you head toward it out of the quadrangle to the south, look above each doorway in that section for the motif of a Maya cottage, or *na*, looking just as they do

IMPRESSIONS

It must be a great experience to be born in Mexico, and to have such a land to come back to and call home.
—STUART CHASE, *MEXICO: A STUDY OF TWO AMERICAS*, 1931

One thing is certain, I should never have gotten on so well had it not been for the friendly and obliging attitude of the Mexicans everywhere.
—CARL LUMHOLTZ, *UNKNOWN MEXICO*, 1902

throughout the Yucatán today. All of this wonderful decoration has been restored, of course—it didn't look this good when the archeologists discovered it.

The Ball Court The unimpressive ball court is conserved to prevent further decay, but keep it in mind to compare with the magnificent restored court at Chichén-Itzá.

The Turtle House Up on the terrace south of the ball court is a little temple decorated with colonnade motif on the facade, and a border of turtles. Though small and simple, its harmony is one of the gems of Uxmal.

The Governor's Palace In size and intricate stonework, this is Uxmal's masterwork, an imposing edifice with a 320-foot-long mosaic facade done in the Puuc style. "Puuc" means "hilly country," the name given to the hills nearby and thus to the predominant style of pre-Hispanic architecture found here. Uxmal has many examples of Puuc decoration, characterized by elaborate stonework from door tops to the roofline. Fray Cogullado, who named the Nunnery, also gave this building its name, and the Governor's Palace may have been just that: the administrative center of the Xiú principality, which included the region around Uxmal. Before you leave the Governor's Palace, note the elaborate stylized headdress patterned in stone over the central doorway.

The Great Pyramid A massive partially restored structure, it has interesting motifs of birds, probably macaws, on its facade, as well as a huge mask. The view from the top is wonderful.

The Dovecote It wasn't built to house doves, but it could well do the job in its lacy roofcomb. The building is remarkable in that roofcombs weren't a common feature of temples in the Puuc hills, although you will see one (of a very different style) on El Mirador at Sayil.

WHERE TO STAY

Uxmal has only one budget hotel; the rest are comfortable, but expensive. This might just be the place to blow your budget. If you've rented a car, more affordable rooms can be found at nearby Ticul.

DOUBLES FOR LESS THAN $25

RANCHO UXMAL, km 70, Carretera Mérida–Uxmal (Calle 26 no. 166, Ticul, Yuc. 97860). 10 rms (all with bath).
$ Rates: $18 single; $23 double. Campsite $3 per person.
This modest little hotel is an exception to the high-priced places near Uxmal. But you'll need strong legs and a sun hat, or a car, to get here—it's a 30-minute walk from the ruins. The rooms are comfortable, and have fans, well-screened windows, showers, and 24-hour electricity. Hot water may not materialize. The restaurant offers main courses for $5 to $6, but don't expect anything great. A primitive campground out back has electrical hookups and use of a shower. The hotel is 2¼ miles north of the ruins on Highway 261.

WORTH THE EXTRA BUCKS

VILLA ARQUEOLÓGICA, Ruinas Uxmal, Uxmal. Yuc. 97844. Tel. toll free 800/258-2633 in the U.S. 46 rms (all with bath). A/C
$ Rates: Low season, $54 single; $56 double. High season, approximately 40% more. Stateside bookings prepay the daily rate and 10% service charge (the 15% tax is collected at the villa). Rates above include all the charges.
A Club Med operation, the beautiful layout around a plant-filled patio and a pool also offers a tennis court, library, and an audiovisual show on the ruins in English, French, and Spanish. The hotel driveway starts at the ruins parking lot. The serene rooms have two oversize single beds. French-inspired meals are à la carte only and cost $15 for breakfast and $25 for lunch or dinner.

To get here, follow the signs to the ruins and turn left to the hotel just before the parking lot at Uxmal.

HOTEL HACIENDA UXMAL, km 78, Carretera Mérida–Uxmal, Uxmal, Yuc. 97844. Tel. 99/4-7142. 78 rms (all with bath).

$ Rates: High season, $67–$80 single or double; low season, 20% less.

One of my favorites, this is also the oldest hotel in Uxmal. Located on the highway across from the ruins, it was built as the headquarters for the archeological staff years ago. Rooms are large and airy, with window screens, ceiling fans (10 are air-conditioned), and heavy furniture. The rooms surround a central garden courtyard with a bar and swimming pool. Other facilities include a dining room and gift shop. Meals are expensive here. A fixed-price breakfast costs $6 to $7.50; lunch, $12.50 to $16; and dinner, $13.50 to $17. A guitar trio usually plays in the evenings.

Reservations: Contact Mayaland Resorts, Hotel Casa del Balam, Calle 60 no. 488, Mérida, Yuc. 97000 (tel. 99/24-8844).

HOTEL MISIÓN UXMAL, km 78, Carretera Mérida–Uxmal, Tel. and fax 99/24-7308, or toll free 91-800/90-038 in Mexico. 49 rms (all with bath).

$ Rates: $64 single; $69 double.

Though it's a distance from the archeological site, the open U form of the hotel, centered around a lovely pool, gives every room a view of the ruins protruding above the distant jungle. Each of the large, comfortable rooms has a fan and a balcony or terrace, but nary a stick of patio furniture for relaxing while enjoying the view. The public areas, however, are comfortably furnished. This hotel restaurant, like the others in Uxmal, is quite expensive: Breakfast is $8; lunch or dinner, $12. The hotel is 1¼ miles north of the ruins on the highway.

WHERE TO EAT

CAFE-BAR NICTE-HA, in the Hotel Hacienda Uxmal, across the highway from the turnoff to the ruins.

Specialty: MEXICAN.

$ Prices: Ham-and-cheese sandwich $4.50; fixed-price lunch $11.

Open: Daily 1–8:30pm.

The small restaurant attached to the Hotel Hacienda Uxmal is visible from the crossroads entrance to the ruins. This is no dining bargain, but the large fixed-price lunch is probably the best deal. Arrive early before tour groups take all the seats.

EASY EXCURSIONS FROM UXMAL
THE OTHER MAYA CITIES

South and west of Uxmal are several other Maya cities worth exploring. Though smaller in scale than either Uxmal or Chichén-Itzá, each has its gems of Maya architecture. The facade of masks on the Palace of Masks at Kabah, the enormous palace at Sayil, and the fantastic caverns of Loltún may be among the high points of your trip. These sites are best photographed in the afternoon light.

Getting There Kabah is 17 miles southeast of Uxmal. From there it's only a few miles to Sayil. Xlapak is almost walking distance (through the jungle) from Sayil, and Labná just a bit farther east. A short drive east from Labná brings you to the caves of Loltún.

If you aren't driving, you can visit all these sites, with the exception of Loltún, by daily bus from Mérida (see "Moving On to Mayapán, Ticul, and Uxmal," above).

To reach Loltún by public transportation, take a bus running every half hour from Mérida to the town of Oxkutzcab, a 1¾-hour trip. From there, a truck (or more expensive, a taxi) will take you the additional 20 minutes to the caves. But there's no reliable return transportation unless your taxi waits.

KABAH If you're off to Kabah, head southwest on Highway 261 to Santa Elena (8½ miles), then south to Kabah (8 miles).

The ancient city of Kabah is on both sides along the highway. From Uxmal, turn right into the parking lot. The site is open daily from 8am to 5pm. Admission is $2.75.

The most outstanding building at Kabah is the huge **Palace of Masks,** or Codz Poop ("rolled-up, mat"), named from a motif in its decoration. You'll notice it first on the right up on a terrace. Its outstanding feature is the facade, completely covered in a repeated pattern of masks of the hook-nosed rain god Chac. There's nothing like this facade in all of Maya architecture.

Once you've seen the Palace of Masks, you've seen the best of Kabah. But you should take a quick look at the other buildings, and follow the paths into the jungle, for a look at the **Tercera Casa** (Third House), or Las Columnas, which has fine colonnaded facades on the front and back. Further restoration is underway at Kabah, so there may be more to see when you arrive.

Across the highway, a conical mound (on your right) was once the **Great Temple,** or Teocalli. Past it is a **great arch** which was much wider at one time, and may have been a monumental gate into the city. Compare this ruined corbeled arch to the one at Labná (below), which is in much better shape.

SAYIL   Just about 3 miles south of Kabah is the turnoff (left, east) to Sayil, Xlapak, Labná, Loltún, and Oxkutzcab. And 2½ miles along this road are the ruins of Sayil, open daily from 8am to 5pm. Admission is $2.75.

Sayil is famous for **El Palacio,** the tremendous 100-room palace that is a masterpiece of Maya architecture. Rows of columns and colonettes give it a Minoan appearance, more impressive for its grandeur and simplicity than for its few decorative details. From the top of El Palacio there's a great view of the Puuc hills. Sometimes it's difficult to tell which are hills and which are unrestored pyramids, as little temples peep out at unlikely places from the jungle. The large circular basin on the ground below the palace is a man-made catch basin for a *chultun* (cistern) since this region has no natural cenotes (wells) to catch rainwater.

Off in the jungle past El Palacio is **El Mirador,** a small temple with an oddly slotted roofcomb. Beyond El Mirador, a crude **stele** has a phallic idol carved on it, with greatly exaggerated proportions.

XLAPAK   Xlapak (pronounced "Shla-pahk") is a small site with one building; it's 3½ miles down the road from Sayil. The **Palace at Xlapak** bears the masks of the rain god, Chac. It's open daily from 8am to 5pm and admission is $2.75.

LABNÁ   Labná is only 1¾ miles past Xlapak and it's open daily from 8am to 5pm. Admission is $2.75.

The first thing you should look at here is the monumental **arch.** Chac can be seen on the corners of one facade, and stylized Maya huts are fashioned in stone above the doorways. **El Mirador,** or El Castillo as it is also called, stands near the arch, with its roofcomb towering above it.

The monumental, yet restrained **Palacio** at Labná is much like the one at Sayil but it's in poorer condition. There is an enormous mask of Chac over a doorway, and a highly stylized serpent's mouth, out of which pops a human head.

LOLTÚN   The caverns of Loltún are 18½ miles past Labná on the way to Oxkutzcab, on the left side of the road. The entrance fee is $4.50 per person and hour-long tours are given at 9:30am, 11am, 12:30pm, and 2:30pm every day. Before going, confirm these times at the information desk at Uxmal.

The fascinating **caves,** homes of ancient Maya, were also used as a refuge and fortress during the War of the Castes (1847–1901). Inside, examine statuary, wall carvings and paintings, *chultunes* (cisterns), and other signs of Maya habitation, but the grandeur and beauty of the caverns alone is impressive.

Note: To return to Mérida from Loltún, drive the few miles to Oxkutzcab and from there head north on Highway 184 to Ticul (12 miles), Muna, and Mérida (62 miles).

OXKUTZCAB

Oxkutzcab (pronounced "Oaks-kootz-kahb", pop. 21,000), 7 miles from Loltún, is the heartland of Yucatán's fruit-growing region, particularly oranges. The tidy village, centered on a beautiful church and the market, is worth a stop if for no other reason than to eat at La Cabaña Suiza before heading back to Mérida, Uxmal, or Ticul, or on to Campeche.

The last week in October and first week in November is the **Orange Festival,** when the village goes all-out with a carnival and orange displays.

Where to Eat

LA CABAÑA SUIZA, Calle 54 no. 101. Tel. 997/5-0057.
  Specialty: CHARCOAL-GRILLED MEAT/MEXICAN.
$ Prices: Meat dishes $3.25; soft drinks and orange juice 50¢.
  Open: Daily 7:30am–6:30pm.
It's worth a trip from Loltún, Ticul, or Uxmal just to feast on the delicious charcoal-grilled meat at this unpretentious eatery in a quiet neighborhood between Calle 49 and Calle 51, three blocks south of the main square. Park in the gravel courtyard, then take a seat at one of the metal tables, either under the palapa roof or outdoors. Señora María Antonia Puerto de Pacho runs the spotless place with an iron hand, and either she or one of her daughters provides swift, friendly service. The menu is limited to filling portions of charcoal-grilled beef, pork, or chicken, all of which are served with salad, rice, tortillas, and a bowl of delicious bean soup.

EN ROUTE TO CAMPECHE

From Oxkutzcab, head back 27 miles to Sayil (if you're coming from Mérida or Uxmal, follow the directions to Sayil in "Easy Excursions from Uxmal," above) then south on Highway 261 to Campeche (78 miles). Along the way are several ruins and caves worth visiting:

XTACUMBILXUNA CAVES   Highway 261 heads south for several miles, passing through a lofty arch marking the boundary between the states of Yucatán and Campeche. Continue on through Bolonchén de Rejon (*bolonchén* means "nine wells").

About 1¾ miles south of Bolonchén, a sign points west to the **Grutas de Xtacumbilxuna** (though the sign spells it XTACUMBINXUNAN). Another sign reads: IT'S WORTH IT TO MAKE A TRIP FROM NEW YORK TO BOLONCHÉN JUST TO SEE XTACUMBILXUNA CAVES (JOHN STEPHENS—EXPLORER). The caves are open whenever the guide is around, which is most of the time. Follow him down for the 30- or 45-minute tour in Spanish, after which a tip is customary.

Legend has it that a Maya girl escaped an unhappy love affair by hiding in these vast limestone caverns, which wouldn't be hard to do, as you'll see. If she hid there, she left no trace. Unlike the fascinating caves at Loltún, filled with traces of Maya occupation, these have only the standard bestiary of limestone shapes: a dog, an eagle, a penguin, madonna and child, snake, and so on—figments of the guide's imagination.

CHENES RUINS   On your route south, you can also take a detour to see several unexcavated, unspoiled ruined cities in the Chenes style. You have to be adventurous for these; pack some food and water. When you get to Hopelchén, take the turnoff for Dzibalchén. When you get to Dzibalchén (25½ miles from Hopelchén), ask for directions to Hochob, San Pedro, Dzehkabtún, El Tabasqueño, and Dzibilnocac.

EDZNÁ   From Hopelchén, Highway 261 heads west. After 26 miles you'll find yourself at the turnoff for the ruined city of Edzná, 12½ miles farther along to the south.

Once a network of Maya canals crisscrossed this entire area, making intensive cultivation possible and no doubt contributing to Edzná's wealth as a ceremonial center. But today it seems more historically important than impressive to see, and perhaps not worth the $3.50 entrance fee and the few minutes it takes to walk it all. What you'll see at this "House of Wry Faces" (that's what Edzná means) is a unique pyramid of five levels with a fine temple, complete with roofcomb, on top. Several other buildings surround an open central yard.

The buildings at Edzná were mostly in the heavily baroque Chenes, or "well country" style, the name given to the region because of its many wells and to the architecture which was ornamented from top to bottom. However, no vestige of the distinctive decorative facades remain at Edzná. (*Note:* The afternoon light is better for photographing the temple.)

Back on Highway 261, it's 8½ miles to the intersection with Highway 180, and then another 19 miles to the very center of Campeche.

---

4. CAMPECHE

1,099 miles E of Mexico City, 157 miles SE of Mérida,
235 miles NE of Villahermosa

GETTING THERE   By Plane   Aeroméxico flies once daily to and from Mexico City.

By Train   Trains arrive from Palenque, Mérida, and Mexico City.

By Bus   Campeche is well connected with Mérida and Villahermosa, and there are four daily buses from Uxmal.

By Car   Highway 180 goes south from Mérida, passing near the basket-making village of Halacho, and Becal, the town of Panama hat weavers. At Tenabo take the shortcut (right) to Campeche rather than going farther to the crossroads near Chencoyí. From Uxmal, Highway 261 passes near some interesting ruins and the Xtacumbilxuna caves.

DEPARTING   By Plane   The **airport** is several miles northeast of town. There's no colectivo transportation from town, and taxis charge around $5 for the trip. **Aeroméxico** has offices at the airport (tel. 6-6656 or 6-5628). Local travel agencies can also make arrangements.

By Train   The **train station** is 2 miles northeast of the downtown waterfront, on Avenida de los Héroes de Nacozari, which intersects Avenida de los Gobernadores. Trains from Campeche depart at 2am for Palenque, arriving at noon; and at 5pm for Mérida, arriving at 10pm. Be careful of thievery on the train between Campeche and Palenque.

By Bus   The **Camioneros de Campeche** line (tel. 6-2802) runs nine second-class buses daily to Mérida, a 2- to 3-hour trip. There are four daily buses to Uxmal, the first of which leaves at 6am and the last at 5pm. These tickets are sold on the Calle Chile side of the bus station. **ADO,** in the front of the station, has one first class *de paso* bus to Palenque at 12:30am.

By Car   For the "Via Corta" (short way) to Celustún or Mérida, go north on Avenida Ruíz Cortínez, bearing left to follow the water (this becomes Avenida Pedro Saliz de Barando, but there's no sign); follow the road as it turns inland, to Highway 180, where you turn left and you're on your way (there's a gas station at the intersection). The route takes you through Becal, a village of Panama hat makers, and Halacho, a village known for beautiful basket making (stores in both villages close between 2 and 4pm).

To Edzná and Uxmal, go north on either Cortínez or Gobernador and turn right onto Madero, which becomes Highway 281.

To Villahermosa, take Cortínez south; it becomes Highway 180.

Campeche (pop. 172,000), capital of the state bearing the same name, is a pleasant coastal town with a leisurely pace. Founded by Francisco de Córdoba in 1517 and claimed for the Spanish Crown by the soldier Francisco de Montejo the Elder in 1531, it was later abandoned and refounded by Montejo the Younger in 1540. To protect against pirates who pillaged the Gulf coastal towns, the townspeople built a wall around the city in the late 1600s. Remnants of these walls, called *baluartes* (bulwarks), are among the city's proudest links with the past.

You'll be able to enjoy this charming city without the crowds, because tourists bypass Campeche on their way to Mérida in favor of the road via Kabah and Uxmal.

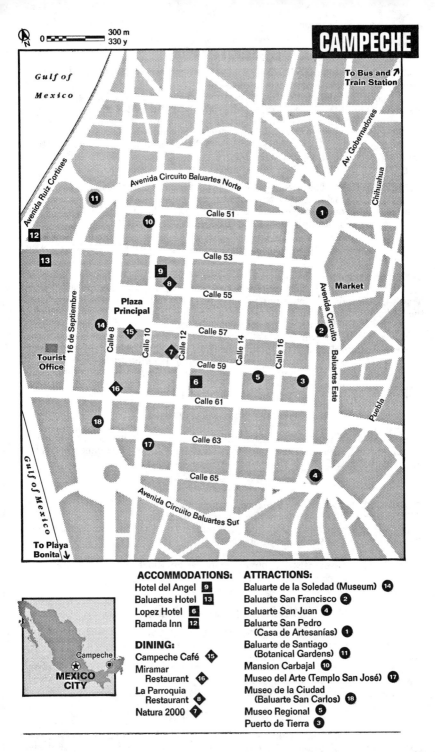

CAMPECHE

0 — 300 m
330 y

Gulf of Mexico

To Bus and ↗
Train Station

Avenida Ruiz Cortines

Av. Gobernadores

Chihuahua

Avenida Circuito Baluartes Norte

Calle 51

Calle 53

Calle 55

Market

Plaza Principal

Calle 57

Calle 59

Calle 61

Calle 63

Calle 65

16 de Septiembre

Calle 8

Calle 10

Calle 12

Calle 14

Calle 16

Avenida Circuito Baluartes Este

Puebla

Tourist Office

Avenida Circuito Baluartes Sur

Gulf of Mexico

To Playa Bonita ↓

Campeche

MEXICO CITY

ACCOMMODATIONS:
Hotel del Angel **9**
Baluartes Hotel **13**
Lopez Hotel **6**
Ramada Inn **12**

DINING:
Campeche Café **15**
Miramar Restaurant **16**
La Parroquia Restaurant **8**
Natura 2000 **7**

ATTRACTIONS:
Baluarte de la Soledad (Museum) **14**
Baluarte San Francisco **2**
Baluarte San Juan **4**
Baluarte San Pedro (Casa de Artesanías) **1**
Baluarte de Santiago (Botanical Gardens) **11**
Mansion Carbajal **10**
Museo del Arte (Templo San José) **17**
Museo de la Ciudad (Baluarte San Carlos) **18**
Museo Regional **5**
Puerto de Tierra **3**

ORIENTATION

ARRIVING If you arrive by plane, you'll have to take a taxi ($5) into town from the **airport,** which is several miles east of town.

Campeche's **train station** is far from town near the airport. Taxis await trains, but don't be too slow getting to them as they are the only means of transportation and you are very far from town. You'll have to pay whatever they charge, around $5; there's no other transportation and they aren't regulated.

The **bus station** is seven long blocks from Plaza Principal. Turn left out the front door, walk one block, turn right at Calle 49, go straight for five blocks, and turn left onto Calle 8; the plaza is three blocks ahead. Taxis cost around $3.

INFORMATION The state of Campeche's convenient **Tourist Office** (tel. 981/6-6068 or 6-6767) is on the waterfront near the Palacio de Gobierno and Parque Principal. Look for the modernistic bulwark with a vertical sign TURISMO on top. The entrance faces the sea (not the ramp in back). It's open Monday through Saturday from 8am to 3pm and 4 to 8:30pm.

An **information booth** at the ADO bus station is open Monday through Saturday.

CITY LAYOUT Most of your time in Campeche will be spent within the confines of the old city walls. The administrative center of town is the modernistic **Plaza Moch-Couoh,** on the waterfront, next to which rises the modern office tower called the Edificio Poderes or Palacio de Gobierno, headquarters for the state of Campeche. Beside it is the futuristic Camara de Diputados, or Casa de Congreso (state legislature's chamber), which looks like an enormous square clam. Just behind it, the **Parque Principal** (central park) will most likely be your reference point for touring.

Campeche boasts a systematic street-numbering plan: Streets running roughly north-south have even numbers, and those running east-west have odd numbers. In addition, the streets are numbered so that numbers ascend toward the south and west. After you walk around for 5 minutes you'll have the system down pat.

GETTING AROUND

Most of the recommended sites, restaurants, and hotels are within walking distance of Parque Principal. Campeche isn't easy to negotiate by bus, so I recommend taxis for the most distant areas.

FAST FACTS

American Express Local offices are at Calle 59 no. 4-5 (tel. 1-1010), in the Edificio Belmar, on the side street opposite the Hotel Balartes. They're open Monday through Friday from 9am to 2pm and 5 to 7pm, and on Saturday from 9am to noon. They don't cash traveler's checks, however.

Area Code The telephone area code is 981.

Mail The **post office** (Correos) is in the Edificio Federal at the corner of Avenida del 16 de Septiembre and Calle 53 (tel. 981/6-2134), near the Baluarte de Santiago. The **telegraph office** is here as well.

WHAT TO SEE & DO

With its city walls, clean brick-paved streets, friendly people, easy pace, and orderly traffic, Campeche is a lovely city, worthy of at least a day in your itinerary. Besides seeing the museums, built within city walls, stroll the streets (especially Calles 55, 57, and 59), and enjoy the typical Mexican colonial-style architecture while looking through large doorways to glimpse the colonial past: high-beamed ceilings, Moorish stone arches, and interior courtyards.

INSIDE THE CITY WALLS

As the busiest port in the region during the 1600s and 1700s, Campeche was a choice target for pirates. The Campechaños began building impressive defenses in 1668 and by 1704 the walls, gates, and bulwarks were in place. Today five of the seven remaining bulwarks are worthy of a visit.

A good place to begin is the pretty little zócalo, or **Plaza Principal,** bounded by Calles 55 and 57 running east and west and Calles 8 and 10 running north and south. Construction of the church on the north side of the square began in 1650, and was finally completed a century and a half later.

For a good introduction to the city, turn south from the park on Calle 8 and walk five blocks to the Museo de la Ciudad (city museum).

BALUARTE DE SAN CARLOS/MUSEO DE LA CIUDAD, Circuito Baluartes and Av. Justo Sierra.

A permanent exhibition of photographs and plans shows the city and its history. The model shows how the city looked in its glory days and gives a good overview for touring within the city walls.

Admission: 35¢.

Open: Tues–Sat 8am–8pm, Sun 8am–1pm.

MUSEO DE ARTE DE CAMPECHE, at Calles 10 and 63. Tel. 6-1424.

For colonial glitter with a touch of modern art, visit this museum, which is actually the restored Templo de San José (1640), where traveling exhibits of Mexican art are displayed. It's just three blocks inland from the Museo de la Ciudad.

Admission: Free.

Open: Mon–Fri 8am–2pm and 5–8pm.

MUSEO REGIONAL DE CAMPECHE, Calle 59 no. 36., between Calle 14 and Calle 16. Tel. 6-9111.

About 2½ blocks farther inland is the city's best museum, which is worthy of a prolonged visit. Housed in the former mansion of the Teniente de Rey (royal governor) it features original Maya artifacts, and pictures, drawings, and models of Campeche's history. The exhibit on the skull-flattening deformation of babies practiced by the Maya includes actual deformed skulls. Another highlight is the Late Classic (A.D. 600–900) Maya stele carved in a metamorphic rock which does not exist in Yucatán, but was transported hundreds of miles from a quarry. Other unusual pre-Hispanic artifacts include clay figures with movable arms and legs, and jade masks and jewelry from the tomb of Calakmul.

A model of the archeological site at Becan shows Maya society in daily life. Other displays demonstrate Maya architecture, techniques of water conservation, aspects of their religion, commerce, art, and their considerable scientific knowledge.

Admission: Free.

Open: Tues–Sat 8am–2pm and 2:30–8pm, Sun 9am–1pm.

PUERTA DE TIERRA (Land Gate), Calle 59 at Circuito Baluartes/Av. de los Gobernadores.

Here is a small museum and light-and-sound show on Friday at 9pm. The 1732 French cannon in the entryway was found in 1990.

Admission: $2.

Open: Mon–Sat 8am–2pm and 4–8pm, Sun 8am–2pm.

BALUARTE DE SAN PEDRO, Circuito Baluartes/Av. de los Gobernadores, at Calle 51.

Traffic skirts this prominent baluarte which houses the **Exposición Permanente de Artesanías.** There's a small selection of crafts, including intricately carved bull horn jewelry (don't mistake it for the prohibited tortoise shell), baskets, pottery, embroidered dresses, hats, and packaged food products all from the state.

Admission: Free.

Open: Mon–Fri 9am–1pm and 5–8pm, Sat 9am–noon.

MANSION CARBAJAL, Calle 10 no. 584. Tel. 6-7560 ext. 17.

Near Calle 51, this beautiful example of Moorish architecture was the home of the Carbajal family and now houses a state-supported crafts shop, carrying crafts similar to those mentioned above, but at higher prices. In case you're ready for a break, there's a nice snack shop in the rear of the casa.

Admission: Free.
Open: Mon–Sat 9am–2pm and 5–8pm.

BALUARTE DE SANTIAGO, at Av. del 16 de Septiembre and Calle 49.

This is the northernmost of the seaside bulwarks, now Campeche's **Jardín Botanico (Botanical Gardens)**, a shady place with both common and exotic plants. Tours in English are given Tuesday through Saturday at noon and 4pm; Spanish tours are offered almost every hour in the morning and evening.
Admission: Free.
Open: Tues–Sat 9am–6pm, Sun 9am–1pm.

BALUARTE DE LA SOLEDAD, at Calle 57 and Calle 8, opposite Plaza Principal.

This bastion houses the Sala de Estelas, or **Chamber of Steles,** a display of Maya votive stones brought from various sites in this ruin-rich state. Many are badly worn, but the excellent line drawings beside the stones allow you to admire their former beauty.
Admission: Free.
Open: Tues–Sat 8am–8pm, Sun 8am–1pm.

MORE ATTRACTIONS

A SCENIC VISTA   For the best view of the city and sea, go south from the tourism office on Avenida Ruíz Cortínez and turn left onto Ruta Escenica, winding up to the **Fuerte San Miguel.** Built in 1771, this fort is the most important of the city's defenses. Santa Anna used this fort when he attacked the city in 1842. Formerly a museum, it's use was undetermined on my last visit. The view is dramatic, whether the building is open or not. To enter the fort, cross the footbridge over the moat.

BEACHES   The **Playa Bonita** is 4 miles west out of town, but it's often dirty.

WHERE TO STAY

Though Campeche's tourist trade is small, there are some good places to stay. If business is slow, these rates may be discounted.

LA POSADA DEL ANGEL, Calle 10 no. 307, Campeche, Camp. 24000. Tel. 981/6-7718. 15 rms (all with bath). A/C

$ Rates: $16 single; $17–$20 double.
Half a block north of Parque Principal, opposite the cathedral, you'll find the three-story La Posada del Angel. Rooms are a little dark, with glass louvered windows opening onto a narrow hall. All are clean and freshly painted, and come with either two double beds or a single and a double. Carpeted halls in the upper two stories should cut down on noise.

HOTEL LÓPEZ, Calle 12 no. 189, Campeche, Camp. 24000. Tel. 981/6-3344. 39 rms (all with bath). TEL

$ Rates: $16–$20 single or double.
Near restaurants and most major sites, this old, three-story hotel 3½ blocks southeast of Parque Principal between Calle 61 and Calle 65 is a good budget choice. The rooms, tiled from floor to ceiling, are semi-clean and well lighted; 25 are air-conditioned and the rest have fans. The hotel's second-floor restaurant is open daily from 7am to 6pm. Before accepting the quoted rate, ask to see the official Secretary of Toursism rate sheet—the desk clerk is not above padding the tab.

READERS RECOMMEND

Hotel America Plaza, Calle 10, Campeche, Camp. 24000. "I spent two nights at the Hotel America Plaza for $12 a night, which I paid with my VISA. I had a nice, clean room, decorated with dark-brown wood and cream walls. The hotel was well run and the management was very attentive."—Donald Korsun, New York, N.Y.

WORTH THE EXTRA BUCKS

HOTEL BALUARTES, Av. Ruíz Cortínez 61, Campeche, Camp. 24000.
Tel. 981/6-3911. Fax 981/6-2410. 100 rms (all with bath). A/C TV TEL
$ Rates: $42 single; $46 double. **Parking:** Free.
Right on the main oceanfront boulevard, two blocks west of Parque Principal, this was the city's original luxury hotel. It's still a nice place, but not quite as modern as the Ramada Inn, next door. Many of the rooms have a sea view, and there is a swimming pool, restaurant, and bar. You're close to all major sites.

RAMADA INN, Av. Ruíz Cortínez 51 (Apdo. Postal 251), Campeche,
Camp. 24000. Tel. 981/6-2233 or 6-4611, or toll free 800/272-6234 in the U.S. 120 rms (all with bath). A/C TV TEL
$ Rates: $55 single or double; $60 junior suite. **Parking:** Free.
Extensively remodeled in 1990, the handsomly furnished rooms all have tile floors and balconies facing the ocean. The restaurant, bar, and coffee shop are popular with local citizens—always a good recommendation. There's a large swimming pool, discothèque, and fenced parking lot behind the hotel. It's on the main oceanfront boulevard, two blocks west of Parque Principal.

WHERE TO EAT

RESTAURANT MIRAMAR, Calle 8 no. 293, at Calle 61. Tel. 6-2883.
Specialty: SEAFOOD/MEXICAN.
$ Prices: Appetizers $2–$3.50; main courses $6.50–$10; sandwiches $2–$3.50.
Open: Mon–Sat 8am–midnight, Sun 8am–7pm.
The best choice in Campeche is very near the town hall building. The decor is airy and pleasant; and the menu offers typical Campeche seafood dishes: lightly fried, breaded shrimp (ask for *camarones empanizados*), arroz con mariscos (shellfish and rice), and for dessert, queso napolitana, a very rich, thick flan. Ask about the changing daily specials.

CAFE Y RESTAURANTE CAMPECHE, Calle 57 no. 4. Tel. 6-2128.
Specialty: MEXICAN/REGIONAL.
$ Prices: Soup 95¢; main courses $2.75–$5.75; plate of the day $2–$2.50; cazon de Campeche $3.50.
Open: Daily 7am–11pm.
When school's out you may have to put up with a blaring TV, but this basic restaurant on Plaza Principal serves good, inexpensive food from an extensive menu. For example, the *comida del día* might have lentil soup, baked chicken, and tortillas. You can try cazon de Campeche, a regional specialty of fresh shark baked in tomato sauce, and traditionally served with pot beans and tortillas.

LA PARROQUÍA, Calle 55 no. 9. Tel. 6-8086.
Specialty: MEXICAN.
$ Prices: Breakfast 75¢–$1.25; main courses $3.50–$4.50; sandwiches $1.50–$2; comida corrida $3.75.
Open: Daily 24 hours.
Despite the sign which has announced for 2 years that this popular but plain restaurant half a block east of Plaza Principal is moving to Calle 8 no. 9, it hasn't yet—but it could. Wherever it is, the same friendly waiters will be on hand, offering the same inexpensive fare, which includes great breakfasts. Selections on the comida corrida might include pot roast, pork or fish, rice or squash, beans, tortillas, and fresh-fruit-flavored water.

NATURA 2000, Calle 12 no. 160.
Specialty: VEGETARIAN.
$ Prices: Comida corrida $2.95; fruit salads $1.75–$2.75.
Open: Mon–Sat 8am–4:30pm.
Though small, with only five tables and a few counter stools, this is a good place for a light meal. "Meat" dishes are made with either oat or soy grain. Fruit salads feature

yogurt, which comes in five flavors, including guanabana and corn. Natura 2000 is on Calle 12 at Calle 59, three blocks north of Plaza Principal.

5. CHICHÉN-ITZÁ

112 miles E of Cancún, 75 miles W of Mérida

GETTING THERE By Plane Day trips on charter flights from Cancún can be arranged by travel agents in the U.S. or Cancún.

By Bus From Mérida first-class ADO buses leave at 8:45am and 3pm. If you go round-trip in a day (a 2½-hour one-way trip) take the 8:45am bus and reserve a seat on the return bus. If you stay in nearby Pisté, only second-class *de paso* buses will stop there, and you may or may not get a seat.

You'll arrive in the village of Pisté, which is only a mile west of Chichén-Itzá, where there's a sidewalk to the archeological zone. The 15-minute walk is comfortable, unless it's the heat of the day. Taxi drivers don't haggle here, so try to find as many people as possible to pile in and split the minimum one-way fare of $3.

By Car Chichén-Itzá is on the main Highway 180 between Mérida and Cancún.

ESSENTIALS The **telephone area code** is 985. **Pisté** is 1½ miles from the ruins.

The fabled pyramids and temples of Chichén-Itzá are Yucatán's best-known ancient monuments. You can't really say you've seen Yucatán until you've gazed at the towering El Castillo, seen the sun from the Maya observatory called El Caracol, or shivered on the brink of the gaping cenote that served as the sacrificial well.

This Maya city was established by Itzáes perhaps sometime during the A.D. 800s. Linda Schele and David Friedel in *A Forest of Kings* (William Morrow, 1990) have cast doubt on the legend that Kukulcán (also called Quetzalcoatl—a name also associated with a legendary god) came here from the Toltec capital of Tula and, along with Putún Maya coastal traders, built a magnificent metropolis combining the Maya Puuc style with Toltec motifs of the feathered serpent, warriors, eagles, and jaguars. Not so, say Schele and Friedel. Reading of Chichén's bas reliefs and hieroglyphs fails to support that legend, but instead shows that Chichén-Itzá was a continuous Maya site influenced by association with Toltecs, but not by an invasion. The truth about Kukulkán's role in Yucatán once again raises questions. (See also Chapter 20, "Introducing the Yucatán.")

Spend the night at Chichén-Itzá (actually, at Pisté) if you can, and take your time seeing the ruins in the cool of the morning and afternoon after 3pm; take a siesta during the midday heat. The next morning, get to the ruins early; when the heat of the day approaches, catch a bus to your next destination. This may involve paying the admission fee more than once (unless you're there on a Sunday when it's free), but the experience is worth it. Day trips generally arrive when it's beginning to get hot, rushing through this marvelous ancient city in order to catch another bus or have lunch. They leave just as the once-fierce sun burnishes the temples a benevolent gold.

WHAT TO SEE & DO

THE MAYA CALENDAR To understand Chichén-Itzá fully, you need to know something about the unique way in which the Maya kept time on several simultaneous calendars.

Although not more accurate than our own calendar, the intricate Maya calendar systems begin (according to many scholars) with 3114 B.C., before Maya culture existed. From that date, the Maya could measure time—and their life cycle—to a point 90 million years in the future! For now, just note that they conceived of world history as a series of cycles moving within cycles.

The Solar Year   The Maya solar year was measured as consisting of 365.24 days. Within that solar year there were 18 "months" of 20 days each, for a total of 360 days, plus a special 5-day period.

The Ceremonial Year   A ceremonial calendar, completely different from the solar calendar, ran its "annual" cycle at the same time. But this was not a crude system like our Gregorian calendar which has saints' days, some fixed feast days, and some movable feasts. It was so intricate that the ordinary Maya depended on the priests to keep track of it. Complex and ingenious, the ceremonial calendar system consisted of 13 "months" of 20 days, but within that cycle of 260 days was another of 20 "weeks" of 13 days. The Maya ceremonial calendar "interlaced" exactly with the solar calendar. Each date of the solar calendar had a name, and each date of the ceremonial calendar also had a name; so every day in Maya history had two names, which were always quoted together.

The Double Cycle   After 52 solar years and 73 ceremonial "years," during which each day had its unique, unduplicated double name, these calendars ended their respective cycles simultaneously on the very same day, and a brand-new, identical double cycle began. Thus, in the longer scheme of things, a day would be identified by the name of the 52-year cycle, the name of the solar day, and the name of the ceremonial day.

Mystic Numbers   As you can see, several numbers were of great significance to the system. The number 20 was perhaps most important, as calendar calculations were done with a number system with base 20. There were 20 "suns" (days) to a "month," 20 years to a *katun*, and 20 *katuns* (20 times 20, or 400 years) to a *baktun*.

The number 52 was of tremendous importance, for it signified, literally, the "end of time"—the end of the double cycle of solar and ceremonial calendars. At the beginning of a new cycle, temples were rebuilt for the "new age," which is why so many Maya temples and pyramids hold within them the structures of earlier, smaller temples and pyramids.

Their Concept of Time   The Maya considered time not as "progress," but the Wheel of Fate, spinning endlessly, determining one's destiny by the combinations of attributes given to days in the solar and ceremonial calendars. The rains came on schedule, the corn was planted on schedule, and the celestial bodies moved in their great dance under the watchful eye of Maya astronomers and astrologers. *The Blood of Kings* (see "Recommended Books" in Chapter 1), has an especially good chapter on the Maya calendar.

As evidence of the Maya obsession with time, Chichén's most impressive structure, El Castillo, is an enormous "time piece."

SEEING THE RUINS   There are actually two parts of Chichén-Itzá: the northern zone, which shows distinct Toltec influence; and the southern zone, which is mostly Puuc architecture. It takes a full day (from 8am to noon and 2 to 5pm) to see all the ruins, which are open daily from 8am to 5pm. Admission is $4.50, free for children under 12, and free for everyone on Sunday and holidays. Parking costs 70¢. Guides are available for around $30 for one to six people; inquire at the entrance.

There's a light-and-sound show in Spanish at 7pm for $1 and one in English at 9pm for $1.50 (its sophisticated computer system frequently breaks down, so before you leave the ruins for dinner, ask if it's working). If you're also going to Uxmal and only want to see one show, many readers think the show at Uxmal is better.

IMPRESSIONS

The architects of pre-Columbian America were more fortunate than most of those of Europe. Their masterpieces were never condemned to invisibility, but stood magnificently isolated, displaying their three dimensions to all beholders. European cathedrals were built within the walls of cities; the temples of the aboriginal American seem, in most cases, to have stood outside.
—ALDOUS HUXLEY, *BEYOND THE MEXIQUE BAY*, 1934

El Castillo As you enter from the tourist center, the beautiful 75-foot El Castillo pyramid is straight ahead. It was built with the calendar in mind: There are a total of 364 stairs plus platform to equal 365 (days of the year), 52 panels on each side which represent the 52-year cycle of the Maya calendars, and nine terraces on each side of the stairways, a total of 18 terraces to represent the 18-month Maya solar calendar. If this isn't proof enough of the mathematical precision of this temple, come for the spring or fall equinox (March 21 or September 22). On those days, during a 34-minute period when the sun goes down, the seven stairs of the northern stairway and the serpent-head carving at the base are touched with the last rays of sunlight and become a "serpent" formed by play of light and shadow. The serpent appears to descend into the earth as the sun leaves each stair from the top. To the Maya this was a fertility symbol: The golden sun has entered the earth; time to plant the corn.

El Castillo, also called the Pyramid of Kukulcán, was built over an earlier structure of Toltec design. A narrow stairway, entered at the western edge of the north staircase, leads inside the structure, where there is a sacrificial altar-throne encrusted with jade, and a Chac-Mool figure. The stairway is open at irregular hours, and is claustrophobic, usually crowded, humid, and uncomfortable; a visit early in the day is best.

Main Ball Court [Juego de Pelota] Northwest of El Castillo is Chichén's main ball court, the largest and best preserved anywhere, and only one of nine ball courts built in this city.

Players on two teams tried to knock a hard rubber ball through one or the other of the two stone rings placed high on either wall, using only their elbows, knees, and hips (no hands). According to legend, the losing players paid for defeat with their lives. However, some experts say that the victors were the only appropriate sacrifices for the gods. Either way, the game must have been exciting, heightened by the marvelous acoustics of the ball court. Have someone walk to the North Temple (at the far end of the ball court), and speak or clap hands. The sound is quite clear at the opposite end, about 450 feet away.

The North Temple This temple has sculptured pillars and more sculptures inside. The bas-reliefs on each wall show two opposing teams facing the center. At the midpoint in the wall, the figure of "Death" accepts the sacrifice of one team's captain, who has been decapitated by the captain of the other team, wielding an obsidian knife.

Temple of Jaguars Near the southeastern corner of the main ball court is a small temple with serpent-columns and carved panels showing jaguars. Up the flight of steps and inside the temple, a mural was found which chronicles a battle between Maya and Toltecs. The Toltecs are the feathered serpents attacking a Maya village.

Tzompantli [Temple of Skulls] To the right of the ball court is the Temple of Skulls, with rows of skulls carved into the stone platform. When a sacrificial victim's head was cut off, it was stuck on a pole and displayed in a tidy row with others. Also carved into the stone are pictures of eagles tearing hearts from human victims. The word *Tzompantli* is not Maya, but came from central Mexico with the Toltecs.

Platform of the Eagles Next to the Tzompantli, this small platform has reliefs showing eagles and jaguars clutching human hearts in their talons and claws.

Platform of Venus East of the Tzompantli and north of El Castillo, near the road to the Sacred Cenote, is the Platform of Venus. In Maya-Toltec lore, Venus is represented by a feathered serpent with a human head in its mouth. It's also called the Tomb of Chac-Mool because a Chac-Mool figure was discovered "buried" within the structure.

Sacred Cenote Follow the dirt road that heads north from the Platform of Venus and after 5 minutes you'll come to the great natural well that may have given Chichén-Itzá (The Well of the Itzáes) its name. It was used for ceremonial purposes, not for drinking water, and according to legend, sacrificial victims were drowned in this pool to honor the rain god Chac. Anatomical research done early in this century by Earnest A. Hooten suggests that children and adults of both sexes were used as sacrificial victims. Judging from Hooten's evidence, the victims may have been outcasts: diseased, feeble-minded, or generally disliked.

Edward Thompson, American consul in Mérida and a Harvard professor, bought the hacienda of Chichén early this century, explored the cenote with dredges and divers, and exposed a fortune in gold and jade. Most of the riches wound up in Harvard's Peabody Museum of Archeology and Ethnology. Later excavations, in the 1960s, brought up more treasure and studies of the recovered objects show offerings from throughout Yucatán, and even farther away.

Temple of the Warriors (Templo de los Guerreros)   Due east of El Castillo is one of the most impressive structures at Chichén, the Temple of the Warriors, named for the carvings of warriors marching along its walls. It's also called the Group of the Thousand Columns, after the many columns flanking it. Climb up the steep stairs at the front to reach a figure of Chac-Mool and several impressive columns carved in relief to look like enormous feathered serpents. South of the temple was a square building called by archeologists the market (*mercado*). Its central court is surrounded by a colonnade. Beyond the temple and the market, in the jungle, are mounds of rubble, parts of which are being reconstructed.

The main Mérida-Cancún highway used to cut straight through the ruins of Chichén, and though it has now been diverted, you can still see the great swath it cut. South and west of the old highway's path are more impressive ruined buildings. On the way to these buildings is a shady stand selling cold drinks.

Tomb of the High Priest (Tumba del Gran Sacerdote)   Past the refreshment stand, to the right of the path, is the Tomb of the High Priest, which stood atop a natural limestone cave in which skeletons and offerings were found, giving the temple its name.

Next building along, on your right, is the **House of Metates (Casa de los Metates)**, named after the concave corn-grinding stones used by the Maya. Past it is the **Temple of the Stag (Templo del Venado)**, fairly tall though ruined. The relief of a stag that gave the temple its name is long gone.

The next temple, **Chichan-chob (Little Holes)**, has a roof comb with little holes, three masks of the rain-god Chac, three rooms, and a good view of the surrounding structures. It's one of the older buildings at Chichén, built in the Puuc style during the Late Classic Period.

Observatory (El Caracol)   Construction of the Observatory, a complex building with a circular tower, was carried out over a long time. No doubt the additions and modifications reflected the Maya's increasing knowledge of celestial movements, and their need for ever more exact measurements. Through slits in the tower's walls, Maya astronomers could observe the cardinal directions and the approach of the all-important spring and autumn equinoxes, and the summer solstice. The temple's name, which means "snail," comes from a spiral staircase inside the structure which is now closed off.

On the east side of El Caracol, a path leads north into the bush to the **Cenote Xtoloc,** a natural limestone well that provided the city's daily water supply. If you see any lizards sunning there, they may well be xtoloc, the lizard for which the cenote is named.

Temple of Panels   Just to the south of El Caracol are the ruins of a **steambath (Temazcalli)**, and the **Templo de los Tableros**, named for the carved panels on top. This was once covered by a much larger structure, only traces of which remain.

Edifice of the Nuns (Edificio de las Monjas)   If you've visited the Puuc sites of Kabah, Sayil, Labná, and Xlapak, the enormous Nunnery here will remind you at once of the "palaces" at the other sites. Built in the Late Classic Period, this new edifice was built over an older one. Suspecting that this was so, Le Plongeon, an archeologist working earlier in this century, put dynamite in between the two and blew part of the newer building to smithereens, thereby revealing part of the old. You can still see the results of Le Plongeon's indelicate exploratory methods.

On the eastern side of the Nunnery is an annex (Anexo Este) in highly ornate Chenes style, with Chac masks and serpents.

The Church   Next to the annex is one of the oldest buildings at Chichén, ridiculously named the Church (La Iglesia). Masks of Chac decorate two upper stories.

Look closely and you'll see among the crowd of Chacs an armadillo, crab, snail, and tortoise. These represent the Maya gods called *bacah,* whose job it was to hold up the sky.

Temple of Obscure Writing [Akab Dzib] The temple is along a path east of the Edifice of the Nuns. Above a door in one of the rooms are some Maya glyphs, which gave the temple its name, since the writings have yet to be deciphered. In other rooms, traces of red handprints are still visible. Reconstructed and expanded over the centuries, at least part of this building is very old, and may well be the oldest at Chichén.

Old Chichén [Chichén Viejo] For a look at more of Chichen's older buildings, constructed well before the Toltecs arrived, follow signs from the Nunnery southwest into the bush to Old Chichén, about half a mile away. Be prepared for this trek with long trousers, insect repellant, and a local guide. The attractions here are the **Temple of the First Inscriptions (Templo de los Inscripciones Iniciales),** with the oldest inscriptions discovered at Chichén, and the restored **Temple of the Lintels (Templo de los Linteles),** a fine Puuc building.

WHERE TO STAY

Many hotels have reservation services in Mérida or Mexico City. Reaching Chichén by phone is difficult.

DOUBLES FOR LESS THAN $25

POSADA CHAC MOOL, Carretera Mérida–Valladolid, Pisté, Yuc. 97751. 5 rms (all with bath).

$ Rates: $18 single; $20 double; $23 triple. Ask for low-season discounts, which may be substantial. **Parking:** Free.

Clean, plain, and new, this no-frills single-story motel opened in 1990 at Calle 15, next to the Central Handcraft Market and almost opposite the Hotel Misión. The basically furnished rooms have fans, new mattresses, red-tile floors, and well-screened windows. Little tables and chairs on the covered walkway outside each room make an inviting place to enjoy a self-made meal.

POSADA NOVELO, Carretera Mérida–Valladolid, Pisté, Yuc. 97751. 8 rms (all with bath).

$ Rates: To be announced.

When I checked, the humble Posada Novelo, in the central village next to the Stardust Inn, was being gutted and completely renewed. It'll still be in the budget price range when completed, but with all new beds, fans, windows, floors, and bathrooms.

DOUBLES FOR LESS THAN $40

HOTEL DOLORES ALBA, km 122, Carretera Valladolid–Chichén-Itzá, Pisté, Yuc. 97751. 18 rms (all with bath).

$ Rates: $21 single; $26 double; $30 triple; $40 for four (in cottage); $2.75 more per room for A/C.

The nice rooms are clean, with matching furniture, tile floors, and showers. There's a swimming pool on the front lawn. The restaurant serves good meals at decent prices, but you should realize that when it comes to dining you have little choice—the nearest alternative is several miles away. Free transportation is provided to the ruins. The Dolores Alba in Mérida, also recommended, is owned by the same family, so either hotel will help you make reservations.

If you go to Chichén-Itzá by bus from Mérida, ask for a ticket on a bus that is going past the ruins—to Valladolid or Puerto Juárez—and then ask the bus driver to stop at the Dolores Alba. Or take a taxi from the ruins to the hotel. It's 1½ miles past the ruins on the road going east to Cancún and Valladolid.

Reservations: Hotel Dolores Alba, Calle 63 no. 464, Mérida, Yuc. 97000 (tel. 97/21-3745; fax 97/28-3163).

PIRAMIDE INN, km 117, Carretera Mérida–Valladolid, Pisté, Yuc. 97751. Tel. Caseta Pisté 985/6-2462 and leave a message. 44 rms (all with bath). A/C

$ Rates: $40 single or double. Ask about low-season discounts.
Less than a mile from the ruins at the edge of Pisté, this hospitable inn has large motellike rooms equipped with firm king-size beds; four rooms come with TVs. There is a pool in the midst of landscaped gardens which include the remains of a pyramid wall. Try to get a room in the back if street noise bothers you. There's also a trailer park next door. If you're coming from Valladolid it's on the left, and from Mérida look for it on the right.

WORTH THE EXTRA BUCKS

HOTEL MISIÓN CHICHÉN-ITZÁ, km 119, Carretera Mérida–Valladolid, Pisté, Yuc. 97751. Tel. Caseta Pisté 985/6-2462. 42 rms (all with bath). A/C

$ Rates: $48 single; $53 double. **Parking:** Free.
The two-story hotel, with comfortable rooms, is built around a pretty pool and grassy inner lawn. The expensive restaurant-bar is popular for tour groups. You can drop in for breakfast ($5), lunch, or dinner ($9.50). It's on the right if you're coming from Valladolid and on the left if you're arriving from Mérida.

Reservations: Hamburgo 227, México, D.F. 06600 (tel. 5/525-0393).

HOTEL VILLA ARQUEOLÓGICA, Zona Archeológica, Chichén-Itzá, Yuc. 97751. Tel. 985/6-2830. 32 rms (all with bath). A/C

$ Rates (including 10% service charge and 15% tax): $75 single; $80 double.
Operated by Club Med, it's almost next to the ruins and built around a swimming pool. The very comfortable rooms are like those at Uxmal and Cobá, each with two oversize single beds. There are tennis courts and a rather expensive restaurant which features French and Yucatecan food (breakfast is $15; lunch or dinner, $25).

Reservations: Liebnitz 34, Mexico City, D.F. (tel. 5/514-4995 or 511-1284, or toll free 800/258-2633 in the U.S.)

HOTEL HACIENDA CHICHÉN, Zona Archeológica, Chichén-Itzá, Yuc. 97751. Tel. 985/6-2513 or 6-2462. 18 rms (all with bath).

$ Rates: $68–$80 single or double. **Closed:** Off-season.
A romantic hotel a short walk from the ruins (follow the signs from the highway), the bungalows were built years ago for those who were excavating the ruins. Each cottage has a fan and is named for an early archeologist working at Chichén. There's a pool which is open to those who drop in for lunch. The dining room is outside under the hacienda portals overlooking the grounds. But any meal is expensive: Breakfast is $5; lunch, around $12; and dinner, $15.

Reservations: Mayaland Resorts, Calle 60 no. 488, Mérida, Yuc. 97000 (tel. 99/25-2122, or toll free 800/624-8451 in the U.S.; fax 99/25-7022).

HOTEL MAYALAND, Zona Archeológica, Chichén-Itzá, Yuc. 97751. Tel. 985/6-2777. 62 rms (all with bath).

$ Rates: $64–$90 single or double; $110 triple; $120 bungalow (Villas Maya).
My choice for a splurge is perhaps the most genteel and sumptuous of Chichén-Itzá hotels. Built hacienda style, it captures the feel of jungle adventure, boasting such subtle touches as a front doorway that frames El

Caracol (the observatory) as you walk outside from the lobby. There are rooms in the main building as well as palapa-roof bungalows, a special treat, with porches facing the grounds, beautifully carved furniture, and mosquito nets; 46 rooms are air-conditioned and the rest have fans. A trio plays evenings by the restaurant-bar. Meals are expensive: breakfast, $7; lunch, $14; and dinner, $20. Fine print on the menu states that prices don't include the 15% tax. There's a lovely swimming pool as well. The hotel is next to the ruins; follow the signs from the highway.

Reservations: Mayaland Resorts, Calle 60 no. 488, Mérida, Yuc. 97000 (tel. 99/25-2122, or toll free 800/451-8891 in the U.S.; fax 25-7022).

WHERE TO EAT

Food is available near the ruins in the expensive hotels, but for the budget traveler I recommend the little restaurants along the highway in the town of Pisté—El Carrousel, La Fiesta, or Nicte-Ha. These days there's little difference in prices or fare between Pisté's restaurants. Meat courses cost $5 to $7. Comida corridas generally are not bargains here. About the cheapest of the town's restaurants is the Parador Maya. Loncherías, like the one next to the Fiesta restaurant and in the arcade across the highway from the church, offer low-priced sandwiches, soup, and similar light lunches.

AN EXCURSION TO GRUTAS [CAVES] DE BALANKANCHE

The Grutas de Balankanche are 3½ miles from Chichén-Itzá on the road to Puerto Juárez. Expect the taxi to cost about $5. I recommend that you tell the taxi to wait while you view the caves. The entire excursion takes about 2 hours. Admission is $4.50. Guided tours in English are at 11am, 1pm, and 3pm; in French at 10am; and Spanish at 9am, noon, 2pm, and 4pm. Double-check these hours at the main entrance to the Chichén ruins.

The natural caves became wartime hideaways after the Toltec invasion of Yucatán. You can still see traces of carving and incense-burning, as well as an underground stream which served as the sanctuary's water supply.

6. VALLADOLID

41 miles E of Mérida, 75 miles W of Cancún, 25 miles E of Chichén-Itzá

GETTING THERE   By Train   From Mérida the train departs at 4pm and arrives in Valladolid at 8pm.

By Bus   Almost hourly buses leave from Mérida, passing through Pisté and Chichén-Itzá on the way to Valladolid and Cancún. There are also regular buses from Cancún and at least six daily buses from Playa del Carmen.

By Car   Highway 180 links Valladolid with both Cancún and Mérida. It's a good, well-marked road, although on my last inspection road repairs slowed traffic considerably just out of Cancún.

ESSENTIALS   The **telephone area code** is 985. All hotels and restaurants are within walking distance of Valladolid's pretty **main square,** Parque Francisco Canton Rosado. The **train station** is eight long blocks straight ahead to the central plaza. The **bus station** is a short two blocks from the main square (going left out the front door of the station). From either Chichén or Cancún, the highway goes right past the main square. Hotels and restaurants here are less crowded than the competition in Chichén.

DEPARTING   By Train   The train station is at the end of Calle 42, eight blocks from the central plaza. Tickets are on sale from 3 to 5am and 7am to noon. The train to Mérida departs at 3:50am and arrives in Mérida at 8am.

By Bus   Because of the frequency of buses to Mérida and Cancún, advance purchase of tickets isn't usually necessary. But the two buses to Cobá, at 4:30am and

1:15pm, may fill early, so buy tickets as soon as possible.

The somewhat sleepy town of Valladolid (pronounced "Bye-*ah*-doh-leet"; pop. 43,000) is an inexpensive alternative to staying in Chichén. You can get an early bus from Mérida, spend the day at the ruins, then travel another hour on to Valladolid.

WHAT TO SEE & DO

Valladolid was founded in 1543 near the site of a Maya religious center called Zací. The Franciscans built an impressive monastery here, called the **Convento de San Bernardino de Siena** (1552), and the town can boast of half a dozen colonial churches and two cenotes. **El Parroquía de San Servasio** (the parish church) is on the south side of the main square, and the **Palacio Municipal** (Town Hall) is on the west.

Embroidered Maya dresses can be found at the **Mercado de Artesanías de Valladolid,** at the corner of Calles 39 and 44, and from women around the main square. The latter also sell—of all things—Barbie doll-size Maya dresses! Just ask "¿*Vestidos para Barbie?*" and out they come.

AN EXCURSION TO TINUM & A MAYAN VILLAGE Adventurous people should consider staying in Tinum, a 30-minute drive from Valladolid, to experience authentic Maya life-style. Some years ago, Ms. Bettina McMakin Erdman left Miami to settle in the tiny village of Tinum. She learned the Maya language, became acquainted with the villagers, and hosted visitors interested in discovering exactly what it's like to live as the Maya do.

The 17-year tradition of hospitality continues, carried on by Jacinto Pool Tuz, whom everyone knows as Don Chivo. He will arrange for you to board with a Maya family in their *na* (house of sticks with a thatched roof), and share their daily life. The cost, paid directly to the family, is about $11 per day. You'll need to bring a hammock to sleep on, or you can write ahead to have one made and waiting for you in Tinum. A double-size hammock is best and will cost around $30. Be sure you realize that this is the real thing: You sleep in your hammock, in a na with a dirt floor, cook on a fire, and use one of the two bathrooms in Dona Bettina's house. You're welcome for 2 or 3 nights.

To get to Tinum, take one of the five daily buses from Valladolid. The trip takes 40 minutes and costs 75¢. By car from Valladolid, head out of town toward Chichén-Itzá; just at the edge of Valladolid you'll see a worn directional sign on your right to Tinum; follow that road straight ahead. The daily train leaves Mérida for Valladolid at 4:30am and stops in Tinum at 7:30am. The bus from Mérida leaves from the Progreso bus station.

When you arrive in town, ask for directions to the home of Don Chivo; everyone knows him. **Advance reservations are necessary,** so to make them, write to Sr. Jacinto Pool "Don Chivo," Calle 24 no. 102A, Tinum, Yuc. 97750.

READERS RECOMMEND

Cenote Dzitnup, *2½ miles west of Valladolid, off Hwy. 180. "A visit to Cenote Dzitnup is well worth the visit. The entrance fee is small; young children lead you down a steep stone stairway into a cave. Stalactites hang from the ceiling and when you enter the main chamber you come across a pool of water in the most amazing color of blue. The water is very clear—catfish can be seen swimming in the water. A tiny hole in the ceiling of the cave allows a few rays of light to further illuminate the water. Quite extraordinary!"—Ellen S. Cristina, Pomfret Center, Conn.*

WHERE TO STAY

HOTEL SAN CLEMENTE, Calle 42 no. 206, Valladolid, Yuc. 97780. Tel. 985/6-2208 or 6-2065. 60 rms (all with bath).
$ Rates: $17 single; $20 double.

This modern, white stucco building is at the southwestern corner of the square, to the right of the cathedral at the corner of Calle 21. The view of the church from the second floor is slightly obstructed. The plain-but-functional rooms are arranged on two floors around a central garden with a swimming pool (which may or may not have water in it). All rooms have fans and 25 come with TVs.

HOTEL ZACÍ, Calle 44 no. 191, Valladolid, Yuc. 97780. Tel. 985/6-2167. 40 rms (all with bath).

$ **Rates:** $14 single; $17 double.

Colonial in architecture, the rooms front a long, quiet courtyard and include a shower; 22 rooms are air-conditioned and the rest have fans. Some of the rooms are newer than others so you'll want to inspect a few before moving in. There are several other small hotels on the same street with the same prices.

To get here from the main square, walk on Calle 39 past the Hotel Marqués on your right; turn right at first block and the Zací is half a block down, between Calle 39 and Calle 37.

HOTEL MARÍA DE LA LUZ, Calle 2 no. 195, Valladolid, Yuc. 97780. Tel. 985/6-2070. 28 rms (all with bath). TV

$ **Rates:** $17–$21 single or double.

The two-stories of rooms are built around an inner pool that isn't kept very clean. Rooms are tidy, if undistinguished, with tile floors and some have king-size beds. A couple of rooms have balconies overlooking the square. The wide, interior covered walkway to the rooms is a nice place to relax in comfortable chairs. Prices vary depending on whether the room is air conditioned (15 rooms) or fan-cooled (13 rooms)—be sure to specify. The hotel is on the west side of the main square, between Calle 39 and Avenida 39.

HOTEL EL MESÓN DEL MARQUÉS, Calle 39 no. 203, Valladolid, Yuc. 97780. Tel. 985/6-2073. Fax 985/6-2208. 34 rms (all with bath). A/C

$ **Rates:** $24–$52 single; $31–$55 double.

This comfortable old colonial-era mansion-turned-hotel, opposite the church on the north side of the square, offers rooms in both the original 200-year-old mansion and in the new addition built around a pool in back. There are several room-price categories, depending on location and amenities, so be sure to ask what rate you are quoted. Though otherwise comfortable, the cheaper rooms (with windows on the side street) will contend with an all-night disco; 13 rooms come with TVs. Hot water may not materialize when you want it, so the best advice is clean up when the water's hot and don't depend on it other times.

WHERE TO EAT

The lowest restaurant prices are in the **Bazar Municipal,** a little arcade of shops beside the Hotel El Mesón del Marqués right on the main square. The cookshops open at mealtimes, with tables and chairs set in the courtyard. You won't find many printed menus, let alone any in English. But a quick look around at nearby tables will tell you what's cooking, and a discreet point of a finger will order it. Ask the price though, so you won't be charged something exorbitant when the bill appears.

HOTEL MARÍA DE LA LUZ, Calle 2 no. 195. Tel. 6-2070.
   Specialty: MEXICAN/YUCATECAN.
$ **Prices:** Breakfast buffet $3.50; main courses $3.50–$5; tamales and sandwiches $1.50–$2.50.
   Open: Daily 7am–10pm.

There's a touch of class here with rattan chairs drawn up to cloth-covered tables. Open to the street on the west side of the main square, this hotel-lobby restaurant is well known for its breezy and inexpensive meals with large portions. Between this and the Mesón del Marqués you'll have the "in" gathering spots covered.

CASA DE LOS ARCOS RESTAURANT, Calle 39 no. 200-A. Tel. 6-2467.
   Specialty: MEXICAN/YUCATECAN.
$ **Prices:** Breakfast $2.50–$3; antojitos $4–$5; main courses $3.50–$9.

Open: Daily 7am–10pm.

A lovely, breezy courtyard with a black-and-white tile floor makes this restaurant especially appealing. Waiters are efficient, and the menu is in English and Spanish. The hearty comida corrida might feature a choice of meat and include red beans, tortillas, and coffee. It's across from the Hotel Don Luis. From the main square, with the Hotel Marqués on your left, take Calle 39 two blocks; the restaurant is on the right.

CAFETERÍA DEL MARQUÉS, Calle 39 no. 203. Tel. 6-2073.
 Specialty: MEXICAN/YUCATECAN.
$ Prices: Breakfast $1.50–$3.50; Mexican plates $2.50–$5; main courses $3.50–$9; sandwiches $2–$3.50; soup $3.
 Open: Daily 7am–9:30pm.

Adjacent to the Hotel del Marqués, it often spills out through the hotel's open portals on an interior courtyard where tables are gaily decorated in hot pink and turquoise and with flowers. It's definitely a popular place on the square, and often crowded at lunch.

EN ROUTE TO CANCÚN & ISLA MUJERES

Having refreshed yourself with a stop in Valladolid, you're ready to head onward to Cancún and Isla Mujeres. These two favorite resort destinations are only a handful of miles apart in distance, but worlds apart in ambience. The 100-mile ride from Valladolid to Cancún or Puerto Juárez will take about 2 hours.

CHAPTER 22
CANCÚN

L ess than two decades ago the name Cancún meant little to anyone. Perhaps a resident of Puerto Juárez or Isla Mujeres linked the name to a hook-shaped island of powdery limestone sand surrounded by coral reefs on the Caribbean side of the Yucatecan coast.

Today Cancún is the magic word in Mexican vacations. After a study to find the best location for a new jet-age resort, Cancún came out on top. The resort that opened with one hotel in 1974, today has 18,000 hotel rooms, and as the luxury hotels sprang up on the deserted sand island, vacationers appeared in search of warm sun and clear waters.

Cancún is the perfect site for a resort because the coast is lush Yucatecan jungle, and the long island with fine sandy beaches is perfect for seaside hotels. The Caribbean waters are incredibly blue and limpid, temperatures (both air and water) are just right, and the coral reefs and tropical climate guarantee brilliant underwater life, snorkeling, and scuba diving. Maya ruins at Tulum, Chichén-Itzá, and Cobá are a short drive away, and for a change of scene the older, less expensive island resorts of Isla Mujeres and Cozumel are close at hand. The coast south of Cancún is exploding with resorts in all price ranges almost all the way to Tulum.

Mexico's second most famous resort (after Acapulco), Cancún (pop. 100,000) was not developed with the cost-conscious independent traveler in mind. Its lavish layout and luxury hotels were meant to attract charter-travel crowds and visitors with bottomless pockets.

But don't let this worry you. It's possible to stay in Cancún, enjoy its fabulous beaches and water sports, take side trips to nearby Maya archeological sites and to the islands of Isla Mujeres and Cozumel, and still remain within our proposed budget. The trick is to spend your nights, and most of your daily budget, in businesslike Ciudad Cancún, and not in the overpriced Zona Turística (also called the Zona Hotelera). Hotels in Ciudad Cancún are comfortable without being flashy, are moderately priced, and convenient to everything. The beaches are a short, cheap bus ride away.

If you're beginning your Yucatecan adventure in Cancún, you should read up on the history of Yucatán in Chapter 20.

1. GETTING THERE

Cancún is 1,114 miles northeast of Mexico City; 125 miles northeast of Chichén-Itzá, 80 miles north of Tulum, 105 miles northeast of Cobá, and 10 miles west of Isla Mujeres.

WHAT'S SPECIAL ABOUT CANCÚN

Beaches
- [ ] All 12 miles of powdery white beaches on Cancún Island are open to the public.

Excursions
- [ ] Use Cancún as a base for day-trips to Sian Ka'an Biosphere Reserve, the ruins of Tulum, and beach resorts north and south.

Restaurants
- [ ] Hundreds of restaurants from world class to Formica class cater to just about every culinary whim and budget.

Nightlife
- [ ] Flashy discos, restaurants, pier dancing, and lobby bars keep Cancún wide awake until the wee hours.

BY PLANE **Mexicana Airlines** has nonstop flights from Chicago, Dallas/Fort Worth, Guadalajara, Los Angeles, Mexico City, Miami, and New York City. **Aeroméxico** offers nonstop service from Mexico City, Houston, Mérida, New York City, and Tijuana.

Regional carriers **AeroCozumel** and **AeroCaribe** (both affiliated with Mexicana) fly from Cozumel, Chetumal, Mérida, Oaxaca, Veracruz, and Ciudad del Carmen. **American** has flights from Dallas/Fort Worth and Raleigh/Durham. **Continental** flies from Houston, New Orleans, and New York. **Northwest** has year-round flights from Tampa and winter flights from Memphis. **United** has numerous connecting flights from the U.S.

BY BUS Buses of the **ADO** line run almost hourly from 6am to midnight from Mérida, stopping at Valladolid and Chichén-Itzá. This company also runs four buses a day on the long (1,100-mile) trip from Mexico City. There are both first- and second-class buses (each has its own ticket window and waiting room).

DEPARTING

BY PLANE As of this writing there is no colectivo service from Cancún City or the Hotel Zone to the airport, so you'll have to hire a taxi from Cancún City for around $10 or $12 or from the Hotel Zone for around $15.

All the airlines have offices in the town and/or at the airport: **Aeroméxico** is at Avenida Cobá 80 (tel. 4-3571, 4-1097, or 4-1186; or 4-2728 or 4-2639 at the airport); it's open Monday through Saturday from 8am to 6:30pm and on Sunday from 9am to 5pm. **AeroCozumel** and **AeroCaribe** are at Avenida Tulum 99, at Uxmal (tel. 4-2000 or 4-2111, or 4-3683 at the airport). **American** is at the airport (tel. 4-2651, or 4-2947 for reservations), as is **Continental** (tel. 4-2540). **Mexicana Airlines** is at Avenida Cobá 39 (tel. 4-1423, 4-1432, 4-1444, or 4-1265; or 4-2427 or 4-2740 at the airport); it's open daily from 9am to 5pm. **United** is at the airport (tel. 4-2528).

BY BUS There is more demand for buses than there is service, so buy your ticket as far in advance of your trip as possible. The **bus station,** though conveniently located near downtown Cancún across the street from the pleasant Hotel Plaza Caribe, is small and crowded with prospective passengers. Both **Autotransportes de Caribe,** the second-class station, and the **ADO** (tel. 4-1378) bus company, next door, are at the intersection of Avenidas Tulum and Uxmal. There are at least 24 Caribe buses daily to Mérida, Valladolid, and Chichén-Itzá; 5 buses to Villhermosa; 3 buses to Coatzcoalcos; 7 buses to Mexico City.

Autotransportes del Caribe recently began 23-seat minibus service direct **to Playa del Carmen** with six daily trips at 5, 8, and 11am and 2, 5, and 6:30pm. It was experimental and you have to know about it to get on; ticket sellers weren't mentioning it in Cancún! Buy a ticket half an hour in advance. ADO has only one reserved-seat bus to Playa del Carmen at 9:30am; all others are *de paso.*

If you have a long wait at the station, escape across the street to the Hotel Plaza Caribe for air conditioning and reasonably priced sandwiches and soft drinks.

BY FERRY   For ferry service to Cozumel or to Isla Mujeres, see Chapter 23.

2. ORIENTATION

ARRIVING   Special minibuses run from Cancún's **international airport** into town for $3 per person. Rates for a cab from the airport to the Zona Hotelera range from $5.80 for one person to $8 for four people.

The **bus station** is in downtown Ciudad Cancún at the intersection of Avenidas Tulum and Uxmal, across the street from the Hotel Plaza Caribe and within walking distance of several of my hotel suggestions. Both the Autotransportes Transportes del Caribe and ADO buses arrive there.

INFORMATION   The **State Tourism Office** (tel. 4-8073) is centrally located downtown on the east side of Avenida Tulum between the Ayuntamiento Benito Juárez building and Comermex Bank, both of which are between Avenidas Cobá and Uxmal. The office is open Monday through Sunday from 9am to 9pm. The addresses and rates of hotels are listed here, as well as ferry schedules.

Many people (the friendliest in town) offer information in exchange for listening to a spiel about the wonders of a Cancún time-sharing or condo purchase.

Pick up a free copy of the monthly *Reader's Digest*–size publication **Cancún Tips** and a tabloid size publication **Cancún Scene.** Both are useful and have fine maps. The publication is owned by the same people who own the Captain's Cove restaurants and a couple of sightseeing boats and time-share hotels, so the information, while good, is not completely unbiased. Don't be surprised if, during your stay, one of their army of employees touts the joys of time-sharing, though more subtly than the others.

CITY LAYOUT   The mainland town, **Ciudad Cancún,** has banks, travel and airline agencies, car-rental firms, restaurants, hotels, and shops, all within an area about nine blocks square.

The main thoroughfare is **Avenida Tulum.** Heading south, Avenida Tulum becomes the highway to the airport, as well as to the ruins of Tulum and to Chetumal; heading north, it joins the Mérida–Puerto Juárez highway, which goes past the Isla Mujeres ferries and on into the Yucatán Peninsula to Mérida.

The **Zona Hotelera,** or **Zona Turística,** stretches out along **Isla Cancún** (Cancún Island), a sandy strip 14 miles long, shaped like a "7." It's now joined by bridges to the mainland at the north and south ends. **Avenida Cobá** from Cancún City becomes **Boulevard Kukulkán,** the island's only main traffic artery—a ferociously busy one. Cancún's international airport is just inland from the base of the "7."

Finding an Address   The street-numbering system is left over from Cancún's beginning days of city lots. Addresses are still given by the number of the building lot and by the *manzana* (block) or *super-manzana* (group of city blocks). Some streets have signs with names, although the establishments along the street may refer to the street only by its number, as Retorno 3, etc. In short, it's very difficult to find a place in Ciudad Cancún just by the numbers. The city is still relatively small and the downtown section can easily be covered on foot. I've tried to be very specific in my directions to recommended establishments. On the island, addresses are given by kilometer number on Kukulkán or by reference to some other well-known location.

3. GETTING AROUND

BY BUS   In town, almost everything is within walking distance. Frequent **Ruta 1** or **Ruta 2** ("Hoteles") city buses operate to the beaches along Avenida Tulum, the main street, all the way to Punta Nizuc at the far end of the Zona Turística on Cancún Island. **Ruta 8** buses go to Puerto Juárez/Punta Sam for ferries to Isla Mujeres. Get them in front of the Tourism Office on Avenida Tulum. Both these city buses operate *between 8am and 10pm daily.*

BY TAXI   Settle on a price in advance. The trip from Ciudad Cancún to the Hotel Camino Real should cost $4 to $5; a short ride between two of the big hotels, $2 to $3; from Ciudad Cancún to the airport, $10 to $12; in Cancún proper, $1 or $2.

BY MOPED   Because of the racetracklike traffic on Boulevard Kukulkán, and congested traffic on the mainland, mopeds are a dangerous way to cruise around. If that's your choice, however, rentals start at $10 an hour or $35 for 6 hours. Ask for a discount if business looks slow. You will have to pay the estimated rental in advance, and perhaps leave a credit-card voucher as security for the moped. You should receive a crash helmet and a lock and chain with the rental. Read the fine print on the back of the rental agreement that states your liability for repair or replacement of the moped in case of accident, theft, or vandalism. There's generally no personal accident insurance, so you rent at considerable risk.

BY RENTAL CAR   There's really no need for a car to get around Cancún since bus service is good, taxis on the mainland are relatively inexpensive, and most things in Cancún City are within walking distance. But if you do rent, the cheapest way is to arrange for the rental before you leave your home country. Otherwise, the daily cost of a rental car will be between $55 and $65 daily if you rent on the spot after arrival.

For seeing the rest of the Yucatán, or taking a couple of days down the coast toward Tulum, I recommend renting a car, since public transportation is sparse. (See "Car Rentals" in Chapter 2.)

 CANCÚN

American Express   The local office is in the Hotel America, Avenida Tulum and Brisas, Loc. A (tel. 4-1999).

Area Code   The telephone area code is 988.

Baby-sitters   Ask at your hotel.

Bookstores   See "Newspapers," below.

Car Rentals   See Section 3, "Getting Around," above.

Climate   Hot! The rainy season is May through October. October, but especially November, can be cloudy, windy, somewhat rainy, and even cool, so a cotton sweater is handy, as is rain protection.

Consulates   The **U.S. Consular Agent** is in the office of Intercaribe Real Estate, Avenida Cobá 30 (tel. 988/4-2411), a block off Avenida Tulum going toward the Zona Hotelera, next to La Dolce Vita Restaurant. The agent is available Monday through Friday from 9am to 2pm and 3 to 4pm; the office is open Monday through Friday from 9am to 2pm and 3 to 6pm. In an emergency, call the U.S. Consulate in Mérida (tel. 99/25-5011 or 99/25-5409).

Crime   Cars break-ins are just about the only crime to speak of, and they happen frequently, especially around the shopping centers in the Zona Hotelera. VW Beetles are frequent targets. Don't leave valuables in plain sight.

Currency   See Section 1, "Information, Entry Requirements, and Money," in Chapter 2.

Currency Exchange   Most banks are downtown along Avenida Tulum, and are usually open Monday through Friday from 9:30am to 1:30pm. There are also

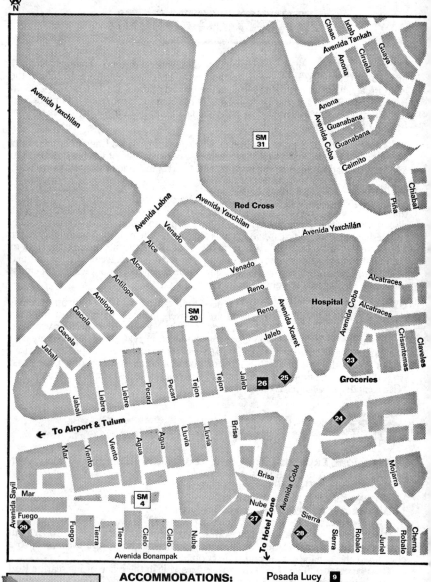

ACCOMMODATIONS:

Antellanos Hotel **18**
Canto Hotel **5**
Caribe Hotel **11**
Coty Hotel **6**
Hacienda Cancún Hotel **2**
Handall Hotel **26**
Helados Bing **12**
Novotel Hotel **13**
Plaza del Sol Hotel **8**

Posada Lucy **9**
Posada Paraíso **14**
Suites Flamboyane **22**
Tankah Hotel **1**

DINING:

Los Alemendros Restaurant **29**
Carrillo Hotel/Restaurant **20**
Ciao Pastelería **28**
Giovanni's Restaurant **27**
Hippocampo Emmy's Restaurant

MEXICO CITY

Cancún

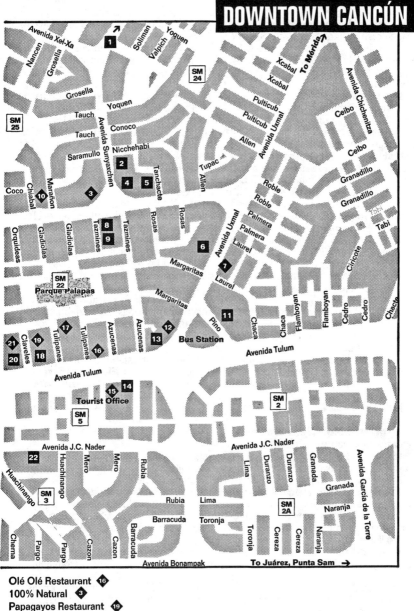

DOWNTOWN CANCÚN

Ole Ole Restaurant ◆16
100% Natural ◆3
Papagayos Restaurant ◆19
Perico's Restaurant ◆10
Pescador Restaurant ◆17
Pop Restaurant ◆15
Rolando's Pizza ◆24
Rosa Mexican Restaurant ◆21
Super Deli ◆25
El Ticolete Restaurant ◆23

a few *casas de cambio* (exchange houses), and downtown merchants are eager to change cash dollars. Island stores don't offer good exchange rates.

Dentists   Ask at your hotel. Or call Dr. Guillermo A. Cabrera Rodriguez, Avenida Xel-Ha 103-5-6, SM 25 (tel. 4-0717 or 49452); he speaks English and French.

Doctors   Ask at your hotel or call one of the hospitals listed under "Emergencies," below.

Drugstores   Next to the Hotel Caribe Internacional, **Pharmacy Escanto,** at Avenida Yaxchilán 36 at Sunyaxchen (tel. 4-4083) is open 24 hours. **Total Assist Hospital** was planning to open a 24-hour pharmacy (tel. 4-8082 or 4-8116).

Emergencies   For first aid, **Cruz Roja** (Red Cross; tel. 4-1616) is on Avenida Yaxchilán between Avenidas Xcaret and Labná, next to the Telemex building. **Total Assist,** a small nine-room emergency hospital with English-speaking doctors, at Claveles 5, SM22, at Avenida Tulum (tel. 4-8082, 4-8116, or 4-8017), is open 24 hours. Desk staff may have limited English. **Clinica Quirurgica del Caribe,** at SM63, Mz Q, Calle 3 inte. no. 36 (tel. 4-2516), is open 24 hours.

Though not tourist-oriented, there's also the **IMSS** (Mexican Social Security Institute) Hospital General de Zona, on Avenida Cobá at Avenida Tulum (tel. 4-1108 or 4-1907). *Urgencias* means "Emergencies."

Eyeglasses   Try **Optica Tolosa Bates,** Avenida Yaxchilán 7, at the corner of Orquídieas, SM 22 (tel. 4-0539), open Monday through Friday from 9am to 2pm and 4 to 9pm; and on Saturday from 9am to 2pm and 4 to 8pm.

Hairdressers/Barbers   Haircuts for men and women cost around $7; style, $11; pedicure or manicure, $7.50.

Holidays   See Section 2, "When to Go," in Chapter 2. Because holidays are when North American visitors come to Cancún, many hotels and restaurants will prepare turkey and dressing on Thanksgiving and Christmas, and organize other familiar traditions to make visitors feel at home.

Hospitals   See "Emergencies," above.

Information   See "Information" in Section 2, "Orientation," above.

Laundry/Dry Cleaning   At Tulum and Crisantemos, **Ela Lavandería** has self-service washers and driers, or they'll do it for you; open Monday through Saturday from 9am to 7pm. Ask about dry cleaning at your hotel.

Lost Property   File a written report with the police (tel. 4-1913). See also "Scams" in Chapter 2.

Luggage Storage/Lockers   Hotels will generally tag and store excess luggage while you travel elsewhere.

Newspapers/Magazines   For English-language newspapers and books, go to **Fama,** on Avenida Tulum between Tulipanes and Claveles (tel. 4-6586), open daily from 8am to 10pm. (Avoid time-share promotions here!)

Photographic Needs   For camera repair, go to **Gerardo Reparaciones,** Tulepanes at Tulum, SM22, Retorno 2, next to Tortas and Pellican, upstairs; it's open Monday through Saturday from 9am to 1pm and 4 to 8pm; and on Sunday until 3pm. For batteries and film, try **Omega** on Avenida Tulum at Tulipanes (tel. 4-3860).

Police   To reach the police, dial 4-1202.

Post Office   The main post office, or Correos, is at the intersection of Avenidas Sunyaxchen and Xel-Ha (tel. 4-1418). It's open Monday through Friday from 8am to 7pm and on Saturday from 9am to 1pm.

Radio/TV   The 24-hour Radio Turquesa (105.1 FM) has broadcasts in English, Spanish, and French, and personal messages in English (tel. 7-0498 or 7-0499).

Religious Services   Check the local phone book.

Rest Rooms   There are few public rest rooms. Use those in restaurants, hotels, and other public establishments.

Safety   There is very little crime in Cancún. People in general are safe late at night in touristed areas; just use ordinary common sense. As in any other beach resort, don't take money or valuables to the beach. See "Crime," above.

Swimming on the Caribbean side presents real dangers from undertow. See "Beaches" in Section 4, "What to See and Do," below for flag warnings.

Shoe Repairs   In Spanish it's *reparación del calzado.* Go to **El Cosario,** in the market, stall 28, SM 28, where Avenidas Tankah and Xpuhil converge.

Taxes See Chapter 2.
Taxis See Section 3, "Getting Around," above.
   Useful Telephone Numbers Police (tel. 4-1913); tourist information (tel. 4-8073).

4. WHAT TO SEE & DO

First thing to do is to explore the sandy, once-deserted island that is this billion-dollar resort's reason for being. Take the Ruta 1 or Ruta 2 bus 12 miles to the end of the island, just to see the fabulous resort and get your bearings. On the return trip, get off the bus at El Parian Centro Comercial, next to the Convention Center, and wander along the beaches from there. The best stretches are dominated by the big hotels.

BEACHES Be especially careful on beaches fronting the open Caribbean—the spine of the island's "7"—the undertow can be deadly. Swim where there's a lifeguard. By contrast, the waters of Mujeres Bay (Bahía Mujeres), at the top of the "7," are usually calm. Get to know Cancún's water-safety pennant system, and make sure to check the **warning flags** at any beach or hotel before entering the water. Here's how it goes:

White	Excellent
Green	Normal conditions (safe)
Yellow	Changeable, uncertain (use caution)
Black or Red	Unsafe—use the swimming pool instead!

Here in the Caribbean, a storm can come up and conditions change from safe to unsafe in a matter of minutes, so be alert: If you see dark clouds heading your way, make your way to shore and wait until the storm passes and the green flag is displayed again.
   All beaches in Mexico are public property, but if you'd rather not esconce yourself on a hotel beach, go to **Playa Tortugas (Turtle Beach)**, the town beach. Activities include swimming and underwater observation. You can also rent a sailboard and take lessons here.

WATER SPORTS Besides snorkeling at **Garrafon National Park**, travel agencies offer an all-day excursion to the natural wildlife habitat of **Isla Contoy**, but it costs more than if you do it on your own from Isla Mujeres. (See Chapter 23 for details.)
   You can go to one of the numerous piers or a travel agency to arrange a day of **deep-sea fishing** for around $70 an hour for up to four people. **Scuba trips** run around $50 and include two tanks; however, Cancún is not the diving mecca that Cozumel is. **Scuba Cancún**, Paseo Kukulkán km 5 (tel. 3-1011 or 4-2336), has the only decompression chamber in Cancún and offers an assortment of diving and certification opportunities. For windsurfing, go to the Playa Tortuga public beach where there's a **Windsurfing School** (tel. 4-2023) with equipment for rent.
   Numerous marinas on the lagoon side have sailboats and waterjets for rent, and offer waterskiing, all of which takes place on the calm Nichupte Lagoon. Prices vary and are negotiable, so check around.

YACHT EXCURSIONS TO ISLA MUJERES Yacht excursions are a favorite pasttime here. Modern motor yachts, trimarans, even old-time sloops take swimmers, sunners, and snorkelers out into the limpid waters, often dropping anchor at **Isla**

Mujeres's Garrafon Beach for lunch and snorkeling around the coral reef, then anchoring for shopping in downtown Isla Mujeres. Most trips depart at 9:30 or 10am, last 5 hours, and include continental breakfast, lunch, and usually an open bar. The cost is $25 to $35 per person.

It's much less expensive to go to Isla Mujeres on your own. From Cancún City, take the Ruta 8 bus to the Puerto Juárez ferry; the ferry docks in downtown Isla Mujeres. From there, take a taxi to Garrafon Park. You can stay as long as you like and return by ferry. (For more details and ferry schedule, see Chapter 23).

The **Corsario** (tel. 3-0200), an "18th-century pirate sloop," leaves from the marina next to the Hotel Stouffer Presidente at 10am and returns at 4pm.

The glass-bottom trimaran **Manta** (tel. 3-1676 or 3-0348; fax 988/3-2529) departs the marina from the pier next to the Plaza Las Glorias. It leaves at 11am and returns at 5pm.

Another motor yacht with an all-day excursion to Isla Mujeres is the **S.S. Stela,** Avenida Bonampak 63, Depto. 103 (tel. 4-2882 or 4-3095; fax 988/4-4426). The yacht leaves at 8:30am from the Playa Tortuga dock near Restaurant Marino in the Zona Hotelera and sails to Isla Mujeres, returning around 4pm.

The new two-decker **Aqua II** (tel. 4-1057 or 4-3194; fax 988/4-1254) is one of several boats going to Isla Mujeres from the Playa Linda dock near the Hotels Calinda and Casa Maya. Departures are Sunday through Friday at 9:30am, returning at 3:30pm. Any of these trips can be booked through a travel agent in Ciudad Cancún—no need to hassle with the telephone or trek out to the Zona Turística. Or you can arrive 30 minutes before departure and buy a ticket—but reconfirm the sailing time first.

RUINAS EL REY   Cancún has its own Maya ruins. They're less impressive than those at Tulum, Cobá, or Chichén-Itzá, but still of interest. The ruins are about 13 miles from town, at the southern reaches of the Zona Hotelera, almost to Punta Nizuc. Look for the Royal Maya Beach Club on the left (east), and then the ruins on the right (west). Admission is free, daily from 8am to 5pm; write your name in the register after you pass through the gate.

The Maya fishermen built this small ceremonial center and settlement very early in the history of Maya culture. It was then abandoned, and later resettled near the end of the Postclassic Period, not long before the arrival of the conquistadores. The platforms of numerous small temples are visible amid the banana plants, papayas, and wildflowers.

BULLFIGHTS   Cancún has a small bullring near the northern (town) end of Paseo Kukulcán. Bullfights are held every Wednesday at 3:30pm during the winter tourist season. There are usually four bulls. Travel agencies in Cancún sell tickets at $26 for adults, $12.50 for children.

5. SAVVY SHOPPING

Although shops in Cancún are more expensive than their equivalent in any other Mexican city, most visitors spend a portion of their time browsing. There are several open-air **crafts markets** easily visible on Avenida Tulum in Cancún City.

Malls on Cancún Island are air-conditioned, and as sleek and sophisticated as any in the States. Most of these come one after another on Paseo Kukulkán between km 7 and km 12: Plaza Lagunas, Costa Brava, La Mansión, Mayfair, Plaza Terramar, Plaza Caracol, and Plaza Flamingo. More are under construction farther out on the island. These malls offer fine shops selling anything from fine crystal and silver to designer clothing and decorative objects. Numerous restaurants are interspersed among the shops and centers, many with prices higher than their branches on the mainland. Store hours are generally daily from 10am to 8 or 10pm. Stores in malls near the convention center generally stay open all day, but some, and especially in malls farther out, close between 2 and 5pm.

6. EVENING ENTERTAINMENT

Ciudad Cancún has a few lively spots that are offshoots of clubs in Mérida or Mexico City. But the real action is in the Zona Turística at the big hotels. Part of the thrill of getting away to the Caribbean is the intrigue of meeting new people, either on the beach or in the cool, dark depths of a disco or nightclub.

THE PERFORMING ARTS   Dinner and a show at the **Convention Center** (tel. 3-0199), on Punta Cancún on the island, includes a table d'hôte dinner at 7pm, followed at 8:30pm by a show with more than 30 dancers and musicians. Though hardly equivalent to the extravaganza staged in Mexico City's Palacio de las Bellas Artes, you may consider it worth the price of $45 for adults (including one drink), $25 for children. Shows are Monday through Saturday at 7:30pm.

The elegant **Hotel Camino Real,** Punta Cancún (tel. 3-1200), is one of several hotels hosting a Mexican Music Night. This exhilarating form of entertainment, which includes dinner, is offered on Friday from 7 to 10pm and costs $30 per person.

THE CLUB & MUSIC SCENE   Many of the big hotels have nightclubs, usually a disco, or at least live music and a lobby bar. Expect to pay a cover charge of between $5 and $16 per person in the discos or show bars. Add drinks at $4 to $7 each and tips to these prices, and you'll see that a night in fabulous Cancún is not all that cheap. Restaurants listed below under "Specialty Dining" offer much of the fun at a fraction of the price of more costly discos.

Flashy **Christine's,** at the Hotel Krystal, Punta Cancún on the island (tel. 3-1133), is one of the most popular discos. Observe the dress code of no shorts and no jeans. Open at 9:30pm nightly.

Dady'O, Paseo Kukulkán km 9.5, on the island, is the newest disco on the island. It opens at 9:30pm nightly.

For one of the least expensive evenings, try the deluxe **Hotel Stouffer Presidente,** km. 8 in the Zona Hotelera (tel. 3-0200). Groups entertain in the lobby bar Thursday through Tuesday nights. There is no cover and no minimum. The music is traditional—mariachis, jarocho—and changes frequently.

There's always something going on in the spacious lobby bar of the **Continental Plaza and Villas,** km. 11 (tel. 3-1400). In the evenings, for the price of drinks, enjoy an assortment of entertainment ranging from light rock and roll to popular Mexican ballads.

Farther out in the hotel zone, the small, off-lobby bar of the new **Paraíso Radisson,** km. 13 (tel. 5-0112), hosts a lively band nightly which you can enjoy for the cost of your drinks.

7. WHERE TO STAY

Now that there are so many hotels competing for the market in Cancún, hoteliers have not raised prices dramatically for a couple of years—a definite boon for vacationers. Ciudad Cancún has many good hotels that are moderately priced or in the budget range. During off-season (from May through November) prices go down 30% to 60%, and it doesn't hurt to bargain for a further price reduction. High season is December 15 through Easter.

If you plan to make hotel reservations from home before leaving for Cancún, be aware that the hotel of your choice may quote you a price as much as two or three times the current local price for a room. If you want to splurge and stay out on the island, never pay the "rack rate," the hotel's published rate to the general public. Package rates through airlines and tour companies can cut the cost considerably.

The hotels below are ranked by low-season double-room prices.

DOUBLES FOR LESS THAN $30

HOTEL TANKAH, Av. Tankah 69, SM 24, Cancún, Q. Roo 77500. Tel. 988/4-4446. 42 rms (all with bath).
$ Rates: $15 single or double with fan, $19 single or double with A/C.

This modest little hotel at the corner of Avenida Xel-Ha, near Plaza Bonita and opposite Restaurant Linus, has a tiled lobby and heavily stuccoed walls. Some rooms have windows only onto the corridor and all come with the bathroom sink conveniently outside the bathroom area. Televisions rent for a small daily charge.

HOTEL COTTY, Uxmal 44, Cancún, Q. Roo 77500. Tel. 988/4-1319. 30 rms (all with bath). A/C
$ Rates: $15–$25 single or double without TV, $27–$31 single or double with TV.
A short walk from the bus station, it's a basic, two-story, rather dreary, no-frills hotel downtown. All the rooms are basically clean, and have windows but no views. It's located two blocks north of bus station near the corner of Margaritas, between Avenidas Tulum and Yaxchilán.

HOTEL CANTO, Av. Yaxchilán at Retorno 5, Cancún, Q. Roo 77500. Tel. 988/4-1267. 24 rms (all with bath). A/C TV TEL
$ Rates: $25 single; $30 double.
With three stories, it's tall enough to stand out, modern enough to satisfy, and cheap enough to please. Though maintenance could be better, rooms are tidy and freshly painted. Each room has a window but no views, and small TVs with U.S. channels. The Canto is behind the Hotel Caribe Internacional; the entrance is on Tanchacte.

HOTEL RIVEMAR, 49-51 Av. Tulum, Cancún, Q. Roo 77500. Tel. 988/4-1199 or 4-1362. 36 rms (all with bath). A/C TV TEL
$ Rates: Off-season, $25 single or double; $31 triple. High season, 50% more.

Right in the heart of downtown Cancún, facing Tulum at Cristantenas, it's hard to be better located. Rooms are clean, with tile floors, two double beds, and small bathrooms. All rooms have windows, some with street views and others the hall view.

PARADOR HOTEL, Av. Tulum 26, Cancún, Q. Roo 77500. Tel. 988/4-1922 or 4-1043. Fax 988/4-9712. 66 rms (all with bath). A/C TV TEL
$ Rates: Off-season, $29 single or double; high season, $50 single or double.

One of the most popular downtown hotels, this three-story hotel is conveniently located on Tulum at Uxmal and the traffic circle, next to Restaurant Pop. Guest rooms are arranged around two long, narrow garden courtyards leading back to a swimming pool (with separate children's pool) and a grassy sunning area. The rooms are modern, with two double beds, showers, and cable TV. Help-yourself bottled drinking water is in the hall. There is a restaurant and bar.

HOTEL HACIENDA CANCÚN, Av. Sunyaxchen 39-40, Cancún, Q. Roo 77500. Tel. 988/4-3672. Fax 988/4-1208. 40 rms (all with bath). A/C TV
$ Rates (including continental breakfast): Off-season, $30 single or double; $33 triple. High season, $43 single or double; $55 triple. **Parking:** Free.
Rooms, some of which hold up to six people, are clean, a little musty, and plainly furnished. All have windows but no views. There's a nice small pool in the back and a restaurant in front. It's also a member of Las Perlas beach club in the hotel zone. The hotel is on Sunyaxchen at Yaxchilán, next to the Hotel Caribe International and opposite 100% Natural.

HOTEL SOBERANIS, Cobá 5 (Apdo. Postal 421), Cancún, Q. Roo 77500. Tel. 988/4-3080 or 4-1858. Fax 988/4-3400. 58 rms (all with bath). A/C TV TEL
$ Rates: Off-season, $32 single or double; $35 triple. High season, $48 single or double; $53 triple.

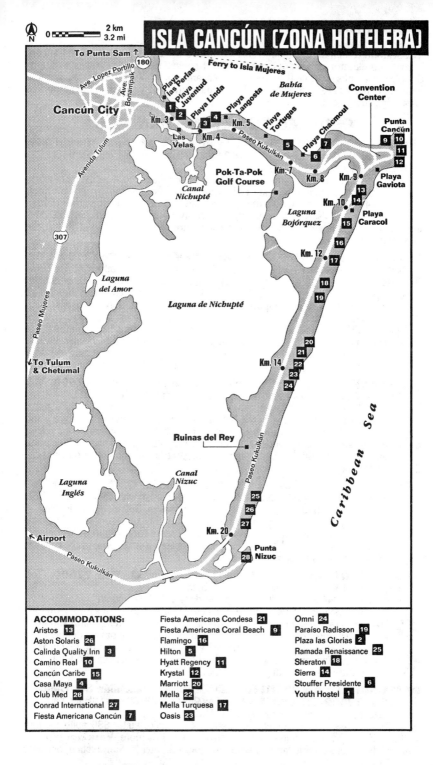

ISLA CANCÚN (ZONA HOTELERA)

0 | 2 km
3.2 mi

N

To Punta Sam ↑

Ferry to Isla Mujeres

Ave. Lopez Portillo
180

Ave. Bonampak

Cancún City

Bahía de Mujeres

Convention Center

Playa las Perlas
Playa Juventud
Playa Linda
Playa Langosta
Playa Tortugas
Playa Chacmool
Punta Cancún

1
2
Km. 3
3 4
Km. 5
Km. 4
Paseo Kukulkán
5
6
7
9 10
11
12

Las Velas

Avenida Tulum

Pok-Ta-Pok Golf Course

Canal Nichupté

Km. 7
Km. 8
Km. 9

Playa Gaviota

307

Laguna Bojórquez

13
14
Km. 10
15

Playa Caracol

16

Km. 12
17

Laguna del Amor

18
19

Laguna de Nichupté

20
21
22
23
24

Paseo Mujeres

↓To Tulum & Chetumal

Km. 14

Ruinas del Rey

Paseo Kukulkán

Canal Nizuc

Laguna Inglés

25
26
27

Caribbean Sea

← Airport

Km. 20

Punta Nizuc

28

Paseo Kukulkán

ACCOMMODATIONS:

Aristos 13
Aston Solaris 26
Calinda Quality Inn 3
Camino Real 10
Cancún Caribe 15
Casa Maya 4
Club Med 28
Conrad International 27
Fiesta Americana Cancún 7

Fiesta Americana Condesa 21
Fiesta Americana Coral Beach 9
Flamingo 16
Hilton 5
Hyatt Regency 11
Krystal 12
Marriott 20
Mella 22
Mella Turquesa 17
Oasis 23

Omni 24
Paraíso Radisson 19
Plaza las Glorias 2
Ramada Renaissance 25
Sheraton 18
Sierra 14
Stouffer Presidente 6
Youth Hostel 1

The seafood restaurant chain Soberanis has both a restaurant and a hotel in Cancún. There's no elevator up to the clean, carpeted rooms. Each room comes with two double beds, sinks separate from the bath area, and small TVs. Bottled water is in the hall. Some rooms are windowless and some have little balconies with unexceptional views. It's south of the town center at Tulum.

DOUBLES FOR LESS THAN $45

NOVOTEL EN CANCÚN, Av. Tulum at Azucenas (Apdo. Postal 70), Cancún, Q. Roo 77500. Tel. 988/4-2999. 40 rms (all with bath).
$ Rates: $35 single or double.
The Novotel is modern, but traditional touches like white stucco walls, metalwork, and colorful craft decorations create a Mexican spirit. The 25 rooms in back overlook a small pool and lawn area with lounge chairs; these have fans only (the other 15 have air conditioning, TVs, and telephone), but are away from the traffic at this busy intersection. This is a popular hotel and rooms are often booked solid. It's at the intersection of Uxmal and Tulum.

HOTEL CANCÚN HANDALL, Av. Tulum 49, Cancún, Q Roo 77500. Tel. 988/4-1122 or 4-1976. Fax 988/4-6352. 50 rms (all with bath). A/C TV TEL
$ Rates: Off-season, $36 single or double; high season, $50–$55 single or double.
Popular with tour groups, rooms in this well-managed two-story hotel, one block west of Cobá, opposite the Hotel America, have recently been refurnished with new tile floors, sinks outside the bath area, and colorful bedspreads. TVs are small but bring in U.S. channels. All rooms have windows, but there's not much of a view. Rooms on the front facing Tulum will be noisier, but the air conditioning drowns most of it out. On the second floor there's a pleasant outdoor lounge area, and on the ground floor in back, a small lap pool and lounge area.

ANTILLANO HOTEL, Calle Claveles 37, Cancún, Q. Roo 77500. Tel. 988/4-1532 or 4-1244. 46 rms, 2 suites (all with bath). A/C TV TEL
$ Rates: Off-season, $33 single; $40 double; $45 triple. High season, 60% more.
This modern wood-and-stucco hotel, half a block west of Tulum by Choco's and Tere's, is one of the nicer downtown establishments. There's a small bar to one side of the reception area. Rooms overlook Tulum, the side streets, and the interior pool. Each has one or two double beds, sink area separate from the bathroom, red-tile floors, and small TVs.

CARRILLO'S, Calle Claveles 1, SM 22, Cancún, Q. Roo 77500. Tel. 988/4-1227 or 4-4833. Fax 988/4-42371. 43 rms (all with bath). A/C TV TEL
$ Rates: Off-season, $35 single or double; high season, $52 single or double.
Walls are highly stuccoed, and standard rooms in this two-story building have plywood vanities and tiled showers. You are paying more for location on Claveles at Tulum, opposite Choco's and Tere's, than decor. There's a small pool in the back, as well as an on-premises restaurant and travel agency.

POSADA LUCY, Gladiolas 25, SM22, Cancún, Q. Roo 77500. Tel. 988/4-4165. 26 rms, 9 suites (all with bath).
$ Rates: $23–$40 single; $35–$40 double daily, $547 per month.
One of Cancún's budget standbys, the Posada Lucy is good for a long-term stay. Six units have a small living room. Two of the units have a refrigerator and small kitchen area. Rooms overall are small, and come with one or two double beds; 25 have air conditioners and 4 have TVs. It's one block east of Yaxchilán at Alcatraces, and one block west of Jardín Palapa, away from the hubbub of Tulum but within walking distance of all the action.

HOTEL-SUITES CARIBE INTERNACIONAL, Av. Yaxchilán 36, Cancún, Q. Roo 77500. Tel. 988/4-3999. Fax 988/4-1993. 82 rms (all with bath), 25 junior suites, 25 master suites. A/C TV TEL
$ Rates: Off-season, $40 single or double; $48 junior suite; $86 suite for four ($21.50 per person). High season, approximately 40% more. **Parking:** Free.
This modern, comfortable, and conveniently located hotel (at Sunyaxchen, opposite

100% Natural) has a number of large rooms, good for several people traveling together. Each room has a balcony overlooking the grassy traffic circle and the town. The junior and master suites are a little expensive for our budget, but they're a good value since they have kitchens and minibars. There's also a snack bar, lobby bar, swimming pool, and guarded parking lot.

SUITES

SUITES RESIDENCIAL "FLAMBOYANES," Av. Carlos J. Nader 101-103, Cancún, Q. Roo 77500. Tel. 988/4-1503. 20 suites. A/C
$ Rates: Off-season, $36 suite for one or two; high season, $48 suite for one or two. Extra person $8. Discounts available for longer stays.

The suites here are arranged in attractive two-story buildings surrounded by tree-shaded lawns with a swimming pool in the center. Suites include a bedroom, living room with couches to sleep two more people, a fully equipped kitchen with a dining area, and a terrace/porch. Remember, you're renting an apartment here, not just a hotel room, and prices are very reasonable for what you get. It's east of Tulum, between Cobá and Uxmal.

For reservations in Mérida, go to Prolongacion 30 no. 78 (tel. 99/7-2498; fax 99/27-5216).

A YOUTH HOSTEL

ALBERGUE DE LA JUVENTUD, Paseo Kukulcán km 3.2 (Apdo. Postal 849), Cancún, Q. Roo 77500. Tel. 988/3-1337. 364 beds.
$ Rates: $3.55 per bed, plus a $7 deposit.
This big, comfortable youth hostel is on the beach on the left at the west end of the hotel zone, near the Hotel Plaza Las Glorias. Look for the hotel sign, VILLA DEPORTIVA JUVENIL, on the left-hand (north) side of Kukulkán. City buses stop in front. There's a swimming pool and a restaurant serving breakfast for $2; lunch or dinner costs $3. Campsites are available for $3 per person. Dorm rooms have fans.

WORTH THE EXTRA BUCKS

HOTEL SAN MARINO, Paseo Kukulkán km 3.5, Cancún, Q. Roo 77500. Tel. 988/3-0815 or 3-1098. Fax 988/3-0522. 40 rms (all with bath). A/C TV TEL
$ Rates: Low season, $40 single or double; high season, $82 single or double.
It's easy to whiz past this hotel without noticing it on the busy Kukulkán boulevard. It's on the lagoon side, sandwiched in with shopping plazas and a boat dock. Thus it's a low-season budget sleeper in the glitz of Cancún. The sparsely furnished lobby with travertine marble floors leads (by elevator) to four stories of rooms with white stucco walls, rustic wood railings, and Moorish overtones. Rooms are large, bright, and cheerful; bathrooms have tub/shower combinations. There's no beach, but a pool and lounge area face the lagoon. There's a good beach across the street.

HOTEL PLAZA DEL SOL, Av. Yaxchilán 31, Cancún, Q. Roo 77500. Tel. 988/4-3888. Fax 988/4-4393. 87 rms (all with bath). A/C TV TEL
$ Rates: Off-season, $46 single or double. High season, $60 single; $70 double.

Don't be put off when I say that this hotel is part of a shopping-and-office complex. Near the intersection of Sunyaxchen, cater-corner from Perico's Restaurant, it's a charming oasis in the midst of a busy resort city, and there are at least a dozen restaurants within a few minutes' walk. The rooms are furnished in Mexican textiles and pale earth tones, and have two double beds, wall-to-wall carpeting, and piped-in music; some have color TVs. Take a dip in the small swimming pool, or the hotel's four-times-a-day (except Monday) shuttle can whisk you out to the hotel's beach club at the Hotel Maya Caribe. Other facilities include a restaurant, coffee shop, lobby bar, pool bar, travel agency, and shopping arcade.

HOTEL PLAZA CARIBE, between Av. Tulum and Uxmal, Cancún, Q. Roo

77500. Tel. 988/4-1377, or toll free 800/528-1234 in the U.S. (through Best Western). Fax 988/4-6352. 200 rms (all with bath). A/C TV TEL

$ Rates: Off-season, $48–$60 single or double; high season, $65 single or double. Ordinarily hotels near bus stations are true budget lodgings, but this one is another oasis in the middle of busy Cancún. Though a bit overpriced because of its location, it's one of the nicer hotels downtown. The modern, comfortable rooms have cool tile floors and two double beds. A cafeteria-restaurant and bar is off the lobby, and there's a nice swimming pool, and gardens in back. It's opposite the bus station on Pino, between Tulum and Uxmal, but the noise from the buses is not really obtrusive.

HOTEL ARISTOS CANCÚN, Paseo Kukulcán km 12 (Apdo. Postal 450), Cancún, Q. Roo 77500. Tel. 988/3-0011, toll free 800/527-4786 in the U.S. 244 rms (all with bath). A/C MINIBAR TV TEL

$ Rates: Off-season, $55 single or double; high season, $80 single or double. One of the island's first hotels, recent remodeling gave it a new adobe-style facade more in keeping with the times than its former 1970s look. Rooms are neat and cool, with red-tile floors, small balconies, and yellow Formica furniture. All rooms face either the Caribbean or the paseo and lagoon; rooms with the best views (and no noise from the paseo) are on the Caribbean side. There's a restaurant, a wide stretch of beach one level below the pool and lobby, a marina with water-sports equipment, two lighted tennis courts, and a baby-sitting service. The large pool is surrounded by plants, lounge chairs, and one of the hotel's several bars.

8. WHERE TO EAT

It's possible to eat well on a budget in Cancún, and here's how: Breakfast and lunch prices are much lower than evening prices along Avenida Tulum, which hosts Ciudad Cancún's evening promenade. If you search the backstreets even just a block or two off Tulum, prices will be lower. I'll describe a few of the long-running budget restaurants as well as the best expensive places, some of which are good for a budget breakfast or lunch.

CANCÚN CITY

MEALS FOR LESS THAN $5

EL TACOLOTE, Cobá 19. Tel. 4-4453.
  Specialty: MEXICAN.
$ Prices: Steaks $3.50–$11; tacos $2–$3.50; beer $1.50; soft drinks 75¢.
  Open: Daily noon–1:30am.

The ranch theme of red brick, wagon wheels, dark-wood tables and chairs, and an open grill is fitting for a place specializing in grilled meats. Steaks are the specialty and northern Mexico–style charro beans are a staple. Tacos come eight ways, plain and really loaded with choices of chile, cheese, bacon, mushrooms, and al pastor. Opposite the IMSS Hospital, half a block west of Tulum, it's usually busy with Mexican families—always a tip-off to good, decently priced food.

RESTAURANT HIPOCAMPO EMMY'S, Uxmal 21-B. Tel. 4-1385.
  Specialty: MEXICAN.
$ Prices: Breakfast $2–$4; sandwiches $2–$3; comida corrida $3–$4.
  Open: Daily 7:30am–9:30pm (breakfast 7:30am–noon; comida corrida served 12:30–2pm).

It's air-conditioned and conveniently located a block north of the bus station (opposite the Hotel Coty), if you're in for a long wait there, and worth a detour if you're farther away. The inexpensive and nice-size meals are the draw, and you'll see more locals than tourists—always an indication of a good deal. The breakfast menu offers eggs seven ways. The large comida corrida comes with soup, meat, rice, dessert, and coffee.

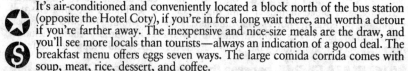

MEALS FOR LESS THAN $10

RESTAURANT POP, Av. Tulum 26. Tel. 4-1991.
Specialty: MEXICAN.
$ Prices: Breakfast $1.50–$6; lunch/dinner, pizza $5–$9.
Open: Mon–Sun 8am–10:30pm.

Look for the green awnings of the popular Restaurant Pop on the east side of Tulum at Uxmal. As at the branch in Mérida, the fare tends to the light, simple, and delicious, with such staples as hamburgers and such specialties as Cuban sandwiches on a long bagguette or chicken breast Louisiana style. It's air-conditioned, and wine and beer are served.

100% NATURAL, Av. Sunyaxchen 6. Tel. 4-1617.
Specialty: SEMI VEGETARIAN.
$ Prices: Breakfast $3–$4; spaghetti $4–$6.50; fruit shakes $1.50–$2; vegetable shakes $2–$3; sandwiches and Mexican plates $2.50–$5.50.
Open: Daily 8am–midnight.

For great mixed-fruit shakes and salads, 100% Natural is *the* place. Quench your thirst with delicious fruit-combination shakes of orange, pineapple, strawberry, and banana, with fruit only or milk added. Full meals include large portions of chicken or fish, spaghetti, or soup and sandwiches. It's between Yaxchilán and Saramuelo, opposite the Hotel Caribe Internacional.

PIZZA ROLANDI, Cobá 12. Tel. 4-4047.
Specialty: ITALIAN.
$ Prices: Appetizers $3–$10; pasta $5–$7; pizza $6–$7.
Open: Mon–Sat 1pm–midnight; Sun noon–11pm.

The outdoor patio of this restaurant is usually very crowded, so elbow your way in. They serve a hearty, wood-oven, cheese-and-tomato pizza, and a full selection of Italian specialties and desserts. Beer and mixed drinks are served.

RESTAURANT LOS ALMENDROS, Av. Bonampak at Sayil. Tel. 4-0807.
Specialty: YUCATECAN.
$ Prices: Appetizers $3–$5; main courses $3.50–$8.
Open: Daily 8am–10:30pm.

The illustrated menu shows color pictures of the typical Yucatecan dishes served here. Some of the regional specialties include lime soup, poc-chuc, and chicken or pork pibil, and appetizers such as panuchos yucatecos. The combinado yucateco is a sampler of four typically Yucatecan main courses—pollos, poc chuc, sausage, and escabeche. Wine and beer are served. The restaurant is six blocks south of Cobá, almost at Sayil.

RESTAURANT EL PESCADOR, Tulipanes 28, off Av. Tulum. Tel. 4-2673.
Specialty: CREOLE/SEAFOOD.
$ Prices: Appetizers $4–$7.50; seafood $10–$25; Mexican plates $7–$10.
Open: Tues–Sun 11am–10:30pm.

There's always a line at this restaurant which serves well-prepared and moderate to high-priced fresh seafood. You can sit on the rustic porch at streetside, in an interior dining room, or upstairs. Feast on cocktails of shrimp, conch, fish, or octopus, Créole-style shrimp (camarones alla criolla), or charcoal-broiled lobster. There's a Mexican specialty menu as well.

OLE, OLE, Av. Tulum 13. Tel. 4-1338.
Specialty: SEAFOOD/MEXICAN.
$ Prices: Appetizers $3–$7; seafood and Mexican plates $6–$12.
Open: Daily 11am–11pm.

At what was formerly the Restaurant El Portal, tables are set inside or out with a perfect view of all the action on Tulum. Neat and friendly, it has some of the best prices and service. Usually there's a special like lobster and steak, which comes with a baked potato, rice, and vegetable. The combination Mexican plate comes with steak, chicken enchilada, quesadilla, chile relleño, rice, beans, and guacamole—and could feed two. The restaurant is on Tulum between Azucenas and Tulipanes.

ON CANCÚN ISLAND

CARLOS 'N' CHARLIE'S, Paseo Kukulkán km 4.5, opposite the Hotel Casa Maya. Tel. 3-0846.
Specialty: MEXICAN.
$ Prices: Main courses $5–$9.
Open: Daily 11:45am–8:30pm; dinner 6pm–midnight.

Another of the popular Carlos Anderson restaurants, here the decor is fish, hats, pigs, and carrots dangling from the T-shirt–draped ceiling, under a casual palapa facing the lagoon. The menu is written on a sack and includes such delicious specialties as black-bean soup, seafood crêpes, fajitas, and barbecue. The lunch menu is less expensive and is a shortened version of the dinner menu. There's open-air pier dancing nightly from 10pm to 3am, for which there's a cover charge if you don't order food.

BOMBAY BICYCLE CLUB RESTAURANT AND VIDEO BAR, Paseo Kukulcán km 6.5.
Specialty: INTERNATIONAL.
$ Prices: Breakfast $5; main courses $6.50–$15; medium pizza $7; lobstertail $10.50.
Open: Daily 7am–11pm.
The Bombay grabs attention with the all-you-can-eat breakfast and such daily specials as ribs and chicken breast or lobstertail. Once inside, you discover other reasons for its popularity. A free salad bar comes with an order of shrimp, fish, or ribeye; the margaritas are enormous; and there's ready iced tea with free refills. Breakfast includes unlimited coffee, multiple trips to the fruit bar, an orange juice, and as much as you want from the regular menu. Pastas are made fresh daily, and they serve pizza, too. If you're coming from Cancún City, the Bombay is after the Hotel Maya Caribe; on the right opposite the Hotel Dos Playas.

CAPTAIN'S COVE II, in the Langosta Shopping Center, Kukulcán. Tel. 3-0669.
Specialty: MEXICAN.
$ Prices: Breakfast buffet $6.25; main courses $4.50–$25 at lunch, $12–$25 at dinner; sandwiches and burgers $5–$7; kids' menu $3–$5.
Open: Daily 8am–11pm.
Though it's open for all three meals, you can enjoy a relatively economical breakfast with a splendid tranquil ocean view, and cool breezes through giant open windows. While seagulls preen and bathe in a small tidal pool and joggers huff past, begin with fresh orange juice, unlimited coffee, a basket of fresh croissants and sweet rolls, and then choose from the menu. Ask about the La Bamba breakfast/Isla Mujeres cruise special which takes off from the dock by the restaurant. The Cove is between the Hotel Casa Maya and Playa Linda beach.

SEÑOR FROGS, Paseo Kukulcán km 4.5. Tel. 3-2931.
Specialty: INTERNATIONAL.
$ Prices: Appetizers $5–$7; main courses $7–$15.
Open: Daily noon–2am.
While lively music entertains, a stuffed bear holds the menu as you enter, a life-size papier-mâché frog stands in the corner, and paper streamers will soon dangle from you as they do from the bear, the frog, the rafters, and the other patrons. Take notice of certain "House Rules"—"no smelling, grinning, chewing with mouth open." Walk across the sawdust-covered floor for a seat near the bandstand, the oyster bar, or the lagoon. The menu offers hamburgers and fries, pastas, oysters, tacos, and quesadillas. There's a cover charge after 8pm for those who don't order dinner, and live music is played from 10:30pm until 2am. It's next to Carlos 'n' Charlie's; opposite the Hotel Casa Maya.

SPECIALTY DINING

The following restaurants in Cancún (as well as Carlos 'n' Charlie's and Señor Frogs, above) provide the customary entertainments of a Mexican seaside resort: sassy waiters, strolling mariachis, perhaps a charro lasso-twirler. The cost for the lively atmosphere is reflected in the dinner prices.

PERICO'S, Av. Yaxchilán 71. Tel. 4-3152.

Specialty: MEXICAN/SEAFOOD.
$ Prices: Appetizers $3–$7; main courses $3–$14.
Open: Daily noon–2am.

Made of sticks to resemble a large Maya house, Perico's has a Guadalupe, Posada, and Emiliano Zapata theme, a ceiling full of baskets, and walls hung with a collection of old musical instruments, photos, and dance masks. It's always booming. The extensive menu offers well-prepared steaks, seafood, and traditional Mexican dishes for moderate rates (except lobster). Witty waiters are part of the fun, and don't be surprised if everybody dons huge Mexican sombreros to bob and snake around the restaurant in a conga dance. You don't have to join in, but it's fun. There's marimba music from 7 to 11:30pm. Perico's is west of Avenida Tulum, between Sunyaxchen and Cobá.

CHOCKO'S & TERE, Calle Claveles 7. Tel. 4-1394.

Specialty: MEXICAN.
$ Prices: Appetizers $4–$8; main courses $4–$15.
Open: Daily 1:30–11pm.

In this semi-open-air collection of dining rooms the noise and fun levels are high. Something's always going on to liven up the already-lively crowd. The food is not the main attraction, although people seem to enjoy it, and the service is casual, witty, and good-natured. Chocko's & Tere is half a block west of Tulum; opposite the Hotel Carrillo.

ICE CREAM

HELADOS BING, Uxmal at Tulum.

Specialty: ICE CREAM.
$ Prices: Single scoop 85¢; milkshake $2.75; sherbet 75¢.
Open: Daily 9am–10pm.

You've seen Helados Bing's hot-pink facade in Acapulco, Puerto Vallarta, and dozens of other Mexican cities. The ice cream is so good and creamy that once you discover the chain, it's hard to pass by without indulging. This branch is next to the Hotel Novotel near the bus station.

PASTRIES

CIAO PASTELERÍA, Cobá 30. Tel. 4-1216.

Specialty: PASTRIES/COFFEE.
$ Prices: Pastries 75¢–$1.75; cup of cappuccino $1.75.
Open: Mon–Sat 8am–10pm; Sun 8–10am.

Like a little French café, with half-curtain windows, a few wood tables and chairs, and a display case of delightful pastries by the slice, it looks more like it belongs in Georgetown or Greenwich Village. Formerly across the street in the Don Giovanni restaurant (it's the Giovanni's bakery), this is a good place to escape from the beach scene for early-morning goodies or after-dinner dessert.

DELICATESSEN

SUPER DELI, Tulum at Xcaret/Cobá. Tel. 4-1122.

Specialty: DELICATESSEN.
$ Prices: Sandwiches $2–$5; bottle of Pedro Domecq Zinfandel $6.
Open: Daily 24 hours.

⭐ You can't miss the trendy awning and outdoor restaurant on the west side of Tulum, half a block south of Xcaret/Cobá next to the Hotel Handall. It's very popular for light meals any time, and inside is a medium-size grocery store with an excellent delicatessen. This is the place to stock up on make-in-your-room sandwiches, snacks for the road, and beer, wine, and cheese, and there are canned goods and coffee, too. There's another branch (smaller) on the island in the Plaza Nautalus.

WORTH THE EXTRA BUCKS

RESTAURANT ROSA MEXICANO, Calle Claveles 4. Tel. 4-6313.
Specialty: MEXICAN HAUTE. **Reservations:** Recommended for parties of six or more.
$ Prices: Appetizers $3–$10; main courses $9–$21.
Open: Dinner only, daily 5–11pm.

⭐ For a nice evening out, try this beautiful little place with candlelit tables and a plant-filled patio. Colorful paper banners and piñatas hang from the ceiling, efficient waiters wear bow ties and cummerbunds color-themed to the Mexican flag, and a trio plays romantic Mexican music nightly. Try the pollo almendro, which is chicken covered in a cream sauce sprinkled with ground almonds, plus rice and vegetables. The steak tampiqueño is a huge platter that comes with guacamole salad, quesadillas, beans, salad, and rice. The restaurant is half a block west of Tulum.

DON GIOVANNI, Cobá 1-12. Tel. 4-5063.
Specialty: ITALIAN.
$ Prices: Appetizers $3.50–$16; pasta $7–$8; seafood $11–$24; chicken $11–$13; fruit plate $3; croissants $6.
Open: Daily 8am–midnight.
From Cancún City, go east on Cobá toward the hotel zone; the restaurant is on the right at Nube (look for the large maroon-and-blue sign). The cozy interior of maroon walls, red-and-white-checked tablecloths, fresh carnations, and green-shaded lights above each table creates a welcoming environment. Pastas are made fresh daily, and all meals come with fresh round loaves of garlic bread. For breakfast, assorted croissants come with several fillings, or there's the traditional fruit plate or spinach crêpes.

9. EASY EXCURSIONS

About 80 miles south of Cancún begins the **Sian Ka'an Biosphere Reserve,** a 1.3-million-acre area set aside in 1986 to preserve a region of tropical forests, savannas, mangroves, canals, lagoons, bays, cenotes, and coral reefs—all of which are home to hundreds of birds, land, and marine animals (see Chapter 23 for details). The Friends of Sian Ka'an, a nonprofit group based in Cancún offers biologist-escorted day trips from Cancún daily (weather permitting) for $80 per person. The price includes lunch, round-trip van transportation to the reserve, guided boat/birding trip through one of the reserve's lagoons, and use of binoculars. For reservations, contact them at Amigos de Sian Ka'an, Plaza America, Avenida Cobá 5, 3rd floor, Suites 48-50 (tel. 4-9583), or make reservations through a Cancún travel agent.

Day-long excursions, or perhaps even an overnight stay, are easy using Cancún as a base. The Maya ruins to the south at **Tulum** or **Cobá** should be your first goal, then perhaps the *caleta* (cove) of **Xel-ha** (see Chapter 23). As long as you're going south, consider a night or two on the island of **Cozumel,** or one of the budget resorts on the **Tulum coast** or **Punta Allen,** south of the Tulum ruins. **Isla Mujeres** is an easy day trip off mainland Cancún (see Chapter 23).

Although I don't recommend it, by driving fast or catching the buses right, one can go inland to **Chichén-Itzá,** explore the ruins, and return in a day, but it's much better to spend several days seeing Chichén-Itzá, Mérida, and Uxmal (see Chapter 21).

CHAPTER 23

ISLA MUJERES, COZUMEL & THE CARIBBEAN COAST

The jungle- and beach-dotted coast from Cancún south to Chetumal has been dubbed the Costa Turquesa (Turquoise Coast), and from Cancún to Tulum it's known as the Tulum Corridor. White powdery beaches stretch from Cancún to Chetumal for 250 miles, and in underwater parks, snorkelers and divers can swim past coral nudged with many-colored fish.

Though expensive resort developments are rising up on this coast in a frenzy, numerous small, inexpensive hideaways dot the coastline a short distance from the highway. Almost 100 miles of this coast, from Tulum to halfway between Felipe Carrillo Puerto and Chetumal, have been saved from developers and set aside as the Sian Ka'an Biosphere Reserve.

SEEING THE CARIBBEAN COAST

The coast is best experienced in a car. It's not impossible to see it by bus, but this requires careful planning, more time, and oodles of patience. Hitching a ride with other travelers is another possibility, but I don't recommend hitchhiking on the highway.

The paved road, Highway 307 south of Cancún, is flanked by jungle on both sides, except where there are beaches and beach settlements. Traffic is scarce so you are seldom slowed by traffic or slow-moving vehicles.

Puerto Morelos, the car-ferry port to Cozumel, is a 45-minute drive from Cancún; to reach the laid-back beachside village of Playa del Carmen takes an hour; Xcaret Lagoon and Pamul, little over an hour; Akumal, an hour and 45 minutes; Xel-Ha and Tulum, around 2 hours. Chetumal is about a 5-hour drive from Cancún.

The most popular agency-led tour is to the ruins of Tulum, followed by a stop at Xel-Ha for a swim and snorkeling in the beautiful clear lagoon. There are frequent buses between Cancún and Chetumal which stop at Playa del Carmen, Tulum, and Felipe Carrillo Puerto. These buses will also let you off on the highway if you want to go to Xel-Ha, Xcaret, or Pamul, but you'll have to walk the mile or so from the highway to your destination. On your return you'll have to walk back and wait to flag a passing bus—you'll be passed by if they're full.

Passenger ferries go to Isla Mujeres from Puerto Juárez, near Cancún, and car-ferries leave from Punta Sam. A car/passenger ferry runs between Puerto Morelos (south of Cancún) and Cozumel. Passenger ferries also run between Playa del Carmen and Cozumel—the preferred way to go.

WHAT'S SPECIAL ABOUT THE CARIBBEAN COAST

Archeology
☐ Pre-Hispanic remains at Tulum and San Gervasio on Cozumel Island

Water Sports
☐ Cozumel, Akumal, Pamul, and Isla Mujeres are Mexico's premier diving playgrounds.

National Parks
☐ Isla Contoy National Wildlife Reserve, on an uninhabited island off Isla Mujeres, sea turtle nesting grounds.
☐ Chancanab Lagoon, in Cozumel and Garrafon on Isla Mujeres, two famed underwater parks.
☐ Sian Ka'an Biosphere Reserve, with hundreds of species of birds and animals.

☐ Underwater National Park, 20 miles of reefs off Cozumel's west coast.
☐ Xel-Ha, a pristine snorkeling lagoon south of Cancún.

Nature
☐ Turtle nesting and hatching on Cozumel, Punta Allen, and Isla Contoy, between June and September.
☐ Birding, especially on Cozumel Island, Punta Allen Peninsula, Chunyaxche and Boca Paila Lagoons, Ruins of Muyil and of Cobá, Ascención and Espiritu Santo Bays, and around Felipe Carrillo Puerto.

Unless you're going to Guatemala or Belize, there's little reason to go to Chetumal. Though it's the capital of Quintana Roo state, it has little to recommend it.

1. ISLA MUJERES

10 miles N of Cancún

GETTING THERE From Mérida First- and second-class buses leave from the bus station several times a day. Your destination is **Puerto Juárez,** from which you take a ferry to the island (see the ferry schedule table). You can also fly from Mérida to Cancún and proceed from there (see Chapter 22).

From Cozumel There are daily flights between Cozumel and Cancún; from the Cancún airport, proceed to the Puerto Juárez ferry terminal, east of downtown Cancún. Or you can take a ferry from Cozumel to Playa del Carmen, then a bus to Puerto Juárez, then another ferry to Isla Mujeres (see below for ferry and bus information from Cozumel).

From Cancún Passenger ferries from mainland Cancún go to Isla Mujeres from **Puerto Juárez** and the passenger/car ferry leaves from **Punta Sam** farther down the same road. To get to either port, take any Ruta 8 city bus from Avenida Tulum.

From Puerto Juárez Puerto Juárez is the dock for the passenger boats to Isla Mujeres. Passenger boats run the 45-minute trip many times daily between Cancún and Isla Mujeres (see the schedule in the accompanying table) at a cost of $1.75. There is no ticket office; pay as you board. The helpful **tourism office** at the dock provides information about hotels, the price of taxis to downtown Cancún (around $2.50), to the Cancún airport ($10 to $13), or to the Hotel Zone ($7), and about ferry schedules in Cancún, Isla Mujeres, Playa del Carmen, and Cozumel. It's open daily from 8am to 6pm.

TRAVELER'S ADVISORY

Except in Cancún, Isla Mujeres, Playa del Carmen, and Cozumel, exchanging money is difficult along this coast. Gas is available at all major towns; most stations have regular and unleaded gas.

From Punta Sam   If you are taking a vehicle to Isla Mujeres, you'll use the Punta Sam port a little farther past Puerto Juárez. The ferry runs the 40-minute trip daily all year except in bad weather (see the schedule in the accompanying table). Cars should arrive an hour in advance of the ferry departure to register for a place in line and pay the posted fee. Passengers without a car pay $1.50 each.

For total, laid-back, inexpensive Caribbean relaxation, it's hard to beat Isla Mujeres. Once called the "poor man's Cancún," Isla's prices have gone up considerably in the last 3 years. While still a bargain compared to Cancún, it's not the deal it once was, though I much prefer it to Cancún. The sand streets have recently been bricked; and painting and refurbishing after Hurricane Gilbert has put a fresh, new face on the island. There's no formal nightlife. Rested and suntanned visitors hang out in open-air cafés, talk, and trade paperback novels until about 10pm when restaurateurs and shop owners start to yawn and the whole island beds down.

There are two versions of how Isla Mujeres got its name. The more popular one claims that pirates parked their women here for safekeeping while they were marauding the Spanish Main. The other account attributes the name to conquistador Francisco Hernández de Córdoba, who was reportedly impressed by the large number of female terra-cotta figurines he found in temples on the island.

ORIENTATION

ARRIVING   Ferries arrive at the dock in the center of town. Taxis are always lined up in front and ask around $2 to $3 to almost any hotel—a true rip-off. The price gets lower if you wait until all passengers have left the area. Unless you're loaded with luggage, you don't need transportation since most hotels are close by.

PUERTO JUÁREZ PASSENGER FERRY SCHEDULE

Cancún to Isla Mujeres	Isla Mujeres to Cancún
6:00am	5:00am
8:30	6:30
9:30	7:30
10:00	8:15
10:30	8:45
11:30	9:30
	10:30
	11:30
12:30pm	12:30pm
1:30	1:30
2:30	2:30
3:30	3:30
4:30	4:15
	5:00
5:30	5:30
6:30	6:30
7:30	
8:30	

PUNTA SAM CAR-FERRY SCHEDULE

Cancún to Isla Mujeres	Isla Mujeres to Cancún
7:15am	6:00am
9:45	8:30
Noon	11:00
2:30pm	1:15pm
5:15	4:00
7:45	6:30
10:00	9:00

INFORMATION The **City Tourist Office** is on Hidalgo in a pink wooden building facing Plaza Principal (tel. 988/2-0316), next to the Palacio Municipal. It's open Monday through Friday from 9am to 2pm and 6 to 8pm.

ISLAND LAYOUT Isla Mujeres is about 5 miles long and 2½ miles wide. The **ferry docks** are right at the center of town, within walking distance of most hotels. The street running along the waterfront is **Rueda Medina,** commonly called the Malecón. The **market** (Mercado Municipal) is by the post office on **Calle Guerrero,** an inland street at the north edge of town, which, like most streets in the town, is unmarked.

FAST FACTS

Area Code   The telephone area code is 988.

Hospital   Half a mile south of the town center, the **Hospital de la Armada,** on Medina at Ojon P. Blanco (tel. 2-0001), has the island's only decompression chamber.

Post Office/Telegraph Office   The Correos is on Calle Guerrero, by the market.

Supermarket   There's a **Super Mercado** facing the main plaza, open daily from 7am to 10pm.

Telephone   There's a long-distance telephone office in the lobby of the Hotel María José, Avenida Madero at Medina, open Monday through Saturday from 9am to 1pm and 4 to 8pm.

GETTING AROUND

The best and most leisurely way to see the island is to rent a **"moto,"** the local sobriquet for motorized bikes and scooters. If you don't want to fool with gears and shifts, rent a fully automatic one for around $22 per day or $6 per hour. They come with seats for one person, but some are large enough for two. Take time to get familiar with the scooter and be careful on the road as you approach blind corners and hills where visibility is poor. There's only one main road with a couple of offshoots—so you won't get lost. The rental price does not include insurance—any injury to yourself or the scooter will come out of your pocket.

WHAT TO SEE & DO

THE BEACHES

There are three beaches, one in town called **Playa Cocoteros** (Coco for short), extending around the northern tip of the island to your left as you get off the boat; another at **Garrafon National Park,** about 3 miles south; and **Playa Langosta,** along the Caribbean edge of the Laguna Makax.

Coco, a beautiful beach, is easily reached on foot from the village. Playa Langosta is a public beach with several rather high-priced palapa-style restaurants (consider bringing your own refreshments). Local buses go to Playa Langosta as far as the El

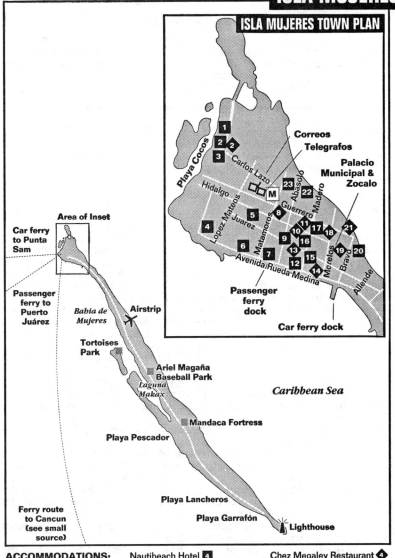

ISLA MUJERES

ISLA MUJERES TOWN PLAN

Playa Cocos

Carlos Lazo

Hidalgo

Lopez Mateos

Juarez

Matamoros

Guerrero

Abasolo

Madero

Morelos

Bravo

Allende

Avenida Rueda Medina

Correos
Telegrafos

Palacio
Municipal &
Zocalo

Passenger
ferry
dock

Car ferry dock

Car ferry
to Punta
Sam

Area of Inset

Passenger
ferry to
Puerto
Juárez

*Bahia de
Mujeres*

Airstrip

Tortoises
Park

Ariel Magaña
Baseball Park

*Laguna
Makax*

Mandaca Fortress

Playa Pescador

Caribbean Sea

Ferry route
to Cancun
(see small
source)

Playa Lancheros

Playa Garrafón

Lighthouse

ACCOMMODATIONS:
Belmar Hotel 11
Berny 9
Buho Hotel/Restaurant 2
Cabañas María del Mar 3
Caribe Maya Hotel 16
Chez Megaley 4
Isleño Hotel 17
María José Hotel 12
Martinez 15
Nabalam Hotel 1

Nautibeach Hotel 4
Perla del Caribe Hotel 22
Pocna Hotel 23
Posada del Mar 6
Posada San Jorge 5
Rocamar Hotel 20
Vistalmar Hotel 7

DINING:
Belmar Restaurant 11
Buho Restaurant 2

Chez Megaley Restaurant 4
Mesón del Bucanero 10
Mirtita's Restaurant 14
Pañadería La Reina 13
La Peña Restaurant 21
Pizza Rolandi 11
Roberts 18
El Sombrero de Gomar 8
Tourist Office 19

IMPRESSIONS

It becomes a virtue, almost a necessity, to do some loafing. The art of leisure is therefore one of Mexico's most stubbornly defended practises [sic] and one of her subtle appeals; a lesson in civilization which we of the hectic north need very badly to learn.
—ANITA BRENNER, *YOUR MEXICAN HOLIDAY*, 1932

Paraíso restaurant on the beach. Most of the beachside restaurants along here have pens with turtles and a nurse shark or two. The marine animals are easily visible in the clear water and it costs nothing to see them, but if you snap a picture of a local holding one up for you, a tip is expected.

WATER SPORTS

Swimming   Wide Playa Coco is the best swimming beach, with Playa Langosta second. There are no lifeguards on duty in Isla Mujeres, and the system of water-safety flags used in Cancún and Cozumel isn't used here either. Be very careful!
✪ Snorkeling   By far the most popular place to snorkel is **Garrafon.** Snorkeling lanes are marked off with ropes so swimmers will neither damage the coral nor be hurt by it. Minibuses to Garrafon start in front of the Muelle Fiscal (commercial pier, a block farther down from the passenger-ferry pier) almost hourly on the half hour beginning at 7:30am; the last one returns from Garrafon at 5:45pm.

Another excellent location is around the lighthouse in the **Bahía de Mujeres** (bay) opposite downtown, where the water is about 6 feet deep. Boatmen will take you around for $10 per person if you have your own snorkeling equipment, or $15 more if you use theirs.

Alex Betancourt, a local snorkeling aficionado, believes that the reef at the end of Avenida Zazil Ha is better than at Garrafon, but cautions that it's not for beginners or weak swimmers because of the strong surf. The jagged reefs on the windward side of the island are good too, he says, but you need to know how to get in and out; otherwise the surf pushes you against the coral. For these two, hire a local guide who knows these waters.

Note: No matter where you snorkel, remember that coral cuts like a knife and causes painful infection.
✪ Diving   The town dive center is **Buzos de México,** on the Malecón at Morelos (tel. 2-0274), next to the Boat Cooperative, with PADI-certified dive masters. Diving sites include the Mancholes and Banderas reefs, both about 35 feet deep; a 400-year-old Spanish galleon at 20 feet, a 200-year-old French sailing ship, and the cave of the sleeping sharks, a 60-foot dive. A 2-hour reef dive costs $45 and includes boat, guide, and gear. The other dives take longer and cost $60 for one dive or $75 for two dives. A 4-day open-water certification course is $350. Make dive arrangements a day in advance. It's open daily from 8am to 6pm.

Fishing   To arrange a day of fishing, which costs around $250, ask at the **Sociedad Cooperativa Turística** (Boatmen's Cooperative; tel. 2-0274) or the travel agency mentioned under Isla Contoy. The cost can be shared with four to six others, and includes lunch and drinks. All year you'll find bonito, mackerel, kingfish, and amberjack. Sailfish and sharks (hammerhead, bull, nurse, lemon, and tiger sharks) are in good supply in April and May. In winter, large grouper and jewelfish are prevalent. The cooperative is open daily from 7:30am to 8pm.

OTHER ATTRACTIONS

Maya Ruin   Just beyond the lighthouse, at the southern end of the island, is a pile of stones that once formed a small Maya pyramid before Hurricane Gilbert. Believed to have been an observatory built to the moon goddess Ix-Chel, now it's reduced to a rocky heap. The location, on a lofty bluff overlooking the sea, is still worth seeing. If you're at Garrafon National Park and want to walk, turn right from Garrafon; when you see the lighthouse, turn toward it down the rocky path. Although there's no need for a guide, the lighthouse keeper's children will gladly give a breathless rendition of the legends of the ruins for a small tip. The keeper has an assortment of cold drinks, snacks, and hammocks for sale.

Pirate's Fortress The Fortress of Mundaca is about 2½ miles in the same direction as Garrafon, about half a mile to the left. The fortress was built by the pirate Mundaca Marecheaga, who in the early 19th century arrived at Isla Mujeres and proceeded to set up a blissful paradise in a pretty, shady spot while making money from selling slaves to Cuba and Belize.

AN EXCURSION TO ISLA CONTOY

If at all possible, plan to visit this pristine, uninhabited island 19 miles by boat from Isla Mujeres, set aside as a national wildlife reserve in 1981. The oddly shaped, 3.8-mile-long island is covered in lush vegetation and harbors 70 species of birds as well as a host of marine and animal life. Bird species that nest on the island include pelicans, brown boobies, frigates, egrets, terns, and cormorants. Flocks of flamingos arrive in April. June, July, and August are good months to plan an overnight trip to witness turtles nesting. Most excursions troll for fish (which will be your lunch), anchor en route for a snorkeling expedition, and leisurely skirt the island for close viewing of the birds without disturbing the habitat. After arrival, there's time to snorkel, laze on the gorgeous beach, or walk in search of birds. A modern visitor's center has excellent displays in Spanish, English, and French explaining the climate, wildlife, and geology of the island.

The trip from Isla Mujeres takes a minimum of an hour and a half one way, more if the waves are choppy. Due to the tight-knit Boatmen's Cooperative, prices for this excursion are the same everywhere—$35. You can buy a ticket at the cooperative, **Sociedad Cooperativa Turística,** on Avenida Rueda Medina, next to Mexico Divers and Las Brisas restaurant, or at one of several travel agencies, such as **La Isleña,** on Morelos at Juárez (tel. 2-0036).

Three types of boats go to Contoy. Small boats have one motor and seat eight or nine people. Medium-size boats have two motors and hold 10 passengers. Large boats have a toilet and hold 16 people. Some boats have a sun cover; others don't. Boat captains should respect the cooperative's regulations regarding capacity and should have enough life jackets to go around. I highly recommend the services of boat owner **Ricardo Gaitan,** who offers the only overnight excursion. Ask for him at the cooperative or write to him directly: Apdo. Postal 42, Isla Mujeres, Q. Roo 77400. He speaks English, and his large boat, the *Estrella Del Norte,* comfortably holds 16 passengers. If you spend the night on the island, be sure to take along mosquito repellent. An inflatable mattress wouldn't be a bad idea, although bedding is provided.

SHOPPING

Shopping is a casual activity here—no glittery, sleek shops or hard sell. Prices are also lower. You'll find silver, Saltillo serapes and Oaxaca rugs, Guerrero masks, Huichol yarn art, Guatemala clothing, pottery, and blown glassware and T-shirts in abundance.

WHERE TO STAY

There are plenty of hotels in all price ranges in Isla Mujeres. High season runs from December through May—a month longer than Cancún—and again in August for some hotels; a few raise rates in mid-November. Rates are at their peak during high season and the headings below reflect double rates during low season from June through mid-November, which is the most economical and least-crowded time to go.

DOUBLES FOR LESS THAN $25

POC-NA, Calle Matamoros 15, Isla Mujeres, Q. Roo 77400. Tel. 988/2-0090. Fax 988/2-0053. 4 bunk rms, 3 hammock rms (none with bath).

$ Rates: Mattress, sheet, and pillow $3; hammock $1; towels 50¢; breakfast 90¢–$1.50.

The Poc-Na claims to be "a basic clean place to stay at the lowest price possible"—and it is. Deposits are necessary for all rentals. The communal sleeping rooms, all with fans, are arranged around a central palapa-shaded dining area with picnic tables. Breakfast is served cafeteria style by a small kitchen. Conveniently located, the hotel is at the end of Calle Matamoros, near the market and only a short walk from Coco beach.

POSADA SAN JORGE, Av. Juárez 29, Isla Mujeres, Q. Roo 77400. Tel. 988/2-0155. 15 rms (all with bath).

$ Rates: High season, $14–$17 single; $15–$20 double. Off-season, $10–$12 single; $13–$15 double.

This modest family-run hotel has decent, clean rooms, a good location, and excellent prices. All rooms come with fans, two lumpy double beds, bedspreads with an African Islamic safari theme, and green-tile floors. Four rooms have refrigerators and rooms on the front have extra windows and more light.

To get here from the pier, turn left one block, then right onto Matamoros, and left half a block on Juárez. It's near Playa Cocoteros.

HOTEL VISTALMAR, Av. Rueda Medina, Isla Mujeres, Q. Roo 77400. Tel. 988/2-0096 or 2-0209. 28 rms (all with bath). TEL

$ Rates: High season, $23 single; $31 double. Low season, $16 single; $18 double. The name means "sea view," which you get if you select a room facing the Malecón; other rooms have interior windows without views. All units have ceiling fans, green-tile floors, and ruffled bedspreads, and are extremely simple, but well kept. The hotel is between Abasolo and Matamoros (from the ferry, turn left onto Medina, the Malecón or main street; it's on the right two blocks down), across from a nice beach, and Coco Beach is almost around the corner. Sixteen more rooms are under construction.

HOTEL MARÍA JOSÉ, Av. Madero and Rueda Medina, Isla Mujeres, Q. Roo 77400. Tel. 988/2-0130. 15 rms (all with bath).

$ Rates: High season, $16–$20 single or double; off-season $11–$15 single or double.

Only a block from the ferry dock, this three-story hotel is a good budget deal. Rooms have fans and are bright, cheery, clean, and comfortable. Some rooms have balconies overlooking the street. The busy long-distance telephone office is in the lobby. From the main pier, turn left onto the Malecón, walk one block to a hot-pink arch, and turn right; the hotel is on the left.

HOTEL MARTÍNEZ, Av. Madero 14, Isla Mujeres, Q. Roo 77400. Tel. 988/2-0154. 14 rms (all with bath).

$ Rates: $17–$20 single or double.

Don't judge the hotel by the cluttered patio as you enter. Guests have been returning to this three-story hotel (no elevator) for years because the basics are dependable: The rooms (all with fans) are clean and freshly painted, the sheets and towels are white (although well used), and each painted bedside table has a seashell lamp. An outdoor sitting area on the second floor catches great cross breezes, as do the rooms.

To get here from the ferry pier, turn left, walk two blocks, and turn right; the hotel is on the right.

HOTEL ISLEÑO, Av. Madero 8, Isla Mujeres, Q. Roo 77400. Tel. 988/2-0302. 20 rms (8 with bath).

$ Rates: Year round, $17 single or double with bath, $13 single or double without bath.

Nothing can beat this hotel for clean, Spartan lodgings at rock-bottom prices. The rooms are bare, but there is good cross-ventilation and fans. Rooms without bath share a clean bathroom on each floor. From the main pier, turn right for one block and left onto Madero, and walk three more blocks; the hotel is on your right at the corner of Guerrero.

HOTEL CARIBE MAYA, Av. Madero 9, Isla Mujeres, Q. Roo 77400. Tel. 988/2-0190. 21 rms (all with bath).

$ Rates: High season, $18–$20 single or double; off-season, $12–$15 single or double.

The rooms in this basic three-story hotel contain furniture that may have seen service in some older and long-gone establishment, green-tile floors, nylon ruffled bedspreads, overbed reading lights, and showers; 12 rooms are air-conditioned and the rest have fans. Upstairs rooms are brighter.

To get here from the main pier, turn left for one block and then right for 1½ blocks.

DOUBLES FOR LESS THAN $35

HOTEL BERNY, Avs. Juárez and Abasolo, Isla Mujeres, Q. Roo 77400. Tel. 988/2-0025. Fax 988/2-0026. 40 rms (all with bath).

$ Rates: High season, $37 single or double; off-season, $25 single or double.

A modern stucco building with handsome red-tile floors, the Hotel Berny offers an interior courtyard with a pretty swimming pool. Each neatly kept room has a single bed, a queen-size bed, and a ceiling fan; some have balconies with sea views. Test the mattress first—some sag. The restaurant serves breakfast and dinner. From the pier, turn left on Medina, walk three blocks, and turn right under the pink arch; the hotel is half a block down on the right.

You can make reservations in Mérida through Amigotel, at Calle 62 no. 515 (tel. 99/28-1351, or toll free 800/458-6888 in the U.S. and Canada).

WORTH THE EXTRA BUCKS

HOTEL POSADA DEL MAR, Av. Rueda Medina 15, Isla Mujeres, Q. Roo 77400. Tel. 988/2-0300. Fax 988/2-0266. 42 rms (all with bath). A/C TEL

$ Rates: High season, $50 single; $64 double. Off-season, $25 bungalow; $25–$35 single or double.

Attractively furnished, this long-established hotel faces the water, and a wide beach three blocks north of the ferry pier. The rooms are in a large garden palm grove in either a three-story hotel building or in one-story bungalow units. For the spacious quality of the rooms and the location, this is among the best buys on the island. A wide, seldom-used but appealing stretch of Playa Coco is across the street. A casual palapa-style restaurant and a pool are set back on the front lawn.

HOTEL BELMAR, Av. Hidalgo, Isla Mujeres, Q. Roo 77400. Tel. 988/2-0430. Fax 988/2-0429. 10 rms (all with bath). A/C TV TEL

$ Rates: High season, $46 single; $58 double. Off-season, $27 single; $45 double.

Situated above Pizza Rolandi, this hotel is run by the same people who serve up those wood-oven pizzas. The simple-but-stylish rooms come with two twin or two double beds and handsome tile accents. Prices are high for no views, but the rooms are nice and a strong TV antenna brings in U.S. channels.

To get here from the pier, walk left half a block and turn right onto Abasolo, then go straight for two blocks and turn left onto Hidalgo; the hotel is half a block down on the right.

HOTEL CABAÑAS MARÍA DEL MAR, Av. Carlos Lazo 11, Isla Mujeres, Q. Roo 77400. Tel. 988/2-0179. Fax 988/2-0213. 25 rms (all with bath). A/C

$ Rates (including continental breakfast at Buho): High season, $75 single or double; $60–$75 bungalow. Off-season, $35–$45 single or double; $30 bungalow.

This three-story hotel, another good choice, is located on Playa Coco, half a block from NaBalam (below). You'll know you're there by the 3-foot-high clay Maya band in the lobby. The 25 nicely outfitted rooms face the beach, all with two single or double beds, refrigerators, and balconies with ocean views. Eleven single-story cabañas are dark but have air conditioning. There's a small but unkempt pool in the garden. Continental breakfast is served across the street at Buho's Restaurant on the patio.

To get here from the pier, walk left one block, turn right onto Matamoros for four blocks, then left onto Lazo, the last street; the hotel is at the end of the block.

HOTEL NABALAM, Zazil Ha 118, Isla Mujeres, Q. Roo 77400. Tel. 988/2-0279. Fax 988/2-0446. 12 suites.

$ Rates: High season, $75 single or double; off-season, $40–$48 single or double.

⭐ This new two-story hotel near the end of (but facing) Coco Beach is a fine addition to the island's lodgings. The lower six units all have terraces, and three of the upper six units have balconies and are higher priced. Each spacious room includes two double beds, a refrigerator, ceiling fan, table, and chairs. A small restaurant serves breakfast and light meals.

From the pier, walk left one block, turn right onto Matamoros for four blocks, then left onto Lazo, the last inland street, for one block, and then turn right; the hotel is half a block down on the left.

HOTEL NAUTIBEACH, Av. Rueda Medina, Isla Mujeres, Q. Roo 77400. Tel. 988/2-0259. Fax 988/2-0487. 13 apartments. A/C

$ Rates: Off-season, $80–$100 double; $100–$130 quad. High season, $20 more.

Located on Coco Beach, 24 units of a 35-unit condominium complex are for rent. All are spacious apartments with two bedrooms and a furnished kitchen/living room with a huge circular glass dining table. There is a terrace or balcony facing the Caribbean, positioned perfectly for sunset watching. The hotel restaurant, Chez Megaley (see "Where to Eat," below) and a pool face the beach. Prices are high for Isla, but this is one of the island's best-planned and most comfortably furnished hotels. It's three long blocks from the pier.

WHERE TO EAT

The **Municipal Market,** next door to the telegraph office and post office on Avenida Guerrero, has several little cookshops operated by obliging and hard-working señoras and enjoyed by numbers of tourists. They set out their steel tables and chairs emblazoned with soft-drink logos early in the morning, and serve up cheap, tasty, filling food all day. Drop by to see what's cooking.

PANADERÍA LA REINA, Av. Madero. Tel. 2-0419.
   Specialty: BAKERY.
$ Prices: Cookies and pan dulce 25¢ each.
   Open: Mon–Sat 7am–9pm.

This bakery near the Hotel Osorio is perhaps your best bet for an inexpensive breakfast. Go in early morning or midafternoon—in the evening the selection is a bit picked-over. There's a refrigerator of juices and yogurt, too. It's one block from Medina at the corner of Avenida Juárez.

ROBERTS, on Morelos between Hidalgo and Guerrero.
   Specialty: MEXICAN.
$ Prices: Main courses $3.50–$4; comida corrida $3.25–$4; tostadas 75¢; sandwiches $1.50; soft drinks 50¢.
   Open: Daily 8am–8pm.

Ⓢ On the central plaza, look for the house (facing the church) with a hot-pink facade and white plastic tables and chairs. Popular with locals and undiscovered by tourists, Roberts has the island's most economical comida corrida. It comes with soup and a meat course, plus salad, rice, or potatoes, depending on the choice of main dish.

RESTAURANT EL SOMBRERO DE GOMAR, Av. Hidalgo at the corner of Matamoros. Tel. 2-0142.
   Specialty: MEXICAN.
$ Prices: Appetizers $3–$5; main courses $4–$8.
   Open: Daily 7am–11pm.

⭐ Among Isla Mujeres's most dependable old stand-bys, the Gomar has an ice-cream parlor on the ground floor; upstairs is the restaurant, overlooking the street and festooned with colorful sombreros and Saltillo serapes. The prices are high, but the service and food are good, and you can see all the action on this busy crossroads.

RESTAURANT LA PENA, Calle Guerrero 5.
  Specialty: SEAFOOD/YUCATÁN.
$ **Prices:** Appetizers $2.50–$3.50; main courses $4.50–$9; pizza $4.50–$15; margarita $2.
  Open: Breakfast daily 7am–noon; lunch daily noon–3pm; dinner daily 3–11pm.
⭐ Under a huge thatched palapa, this popular restaurant behind (east of) the town-square bandstand between Bravo and Morelos has a streetside porch and a seaside terrace. At night candlelight flickers on linen-covered tables. The menu includes a variety of fish and chicken dishes as well as pizza.

PIZZA ROLANDI, Av. Hidalgo, between Madero and Abasolo. Tel. 2-0429.
  Specialty: ITALIAN.
$ **Prices:** Appetizers $3.25–$8; main courses $5.50–$8.
  Open: Daily noon–midnight.
⭐ Pizza Rolandi, the chain that saves the day with dependably good, reasonably priced food in otherwise expensive resorts, comes through in Isla Mujeres as well. The casual dining room is the scene for consumption of plate-size pizza, pasta, and calzones cooked in a wood oven. There's a more expensive specialty menu with fish, beef, and chicken dishes.

MESÓN DEL BUCANERO, Juárez 13 and Hidalgo 11. Tel. 2-0126 or 2-0210.
  Specialty: MEXICAN.
$ **Prices:** Appetizers $1.50–$4; main courses $4–$10.
  Open: Daily 7am–11pm.
The Mesón del Bucanero has a welcoming patio decor of wood, palm trees, and other pirate-friendly design elements. You can come here any day of the year for eggs prepared various ways or for Mexican treats such as enchiladas and tacos. It's opposite Pizza Rolandi between Madero and Abasolo.

RESTAURANT BAR BUHO, Av. Zazil Ha 1. Tel. 2-0213 or 2-0301.
  Specialty: MEXICAN/SEAFOOD.
$ **Prices:** Breakfast $3–$5; main courses $5–$12.
  Open: Daily 7am–11pm.
At the corner of Lazo, facing Coco Beach, this is an inviting place to start the day watching shell hunters, joggers, and walkers on this terrific beach. The fare is the usual fish, tacos, sandwiches, and antojitos—nothing terrific, just a good outdoor place to relax with a view.

MIRTITA'S RESTAURANT AND BAR, Av. Rueda Medina. Tel. 2-0232.
  Specialty: MEXICAN.
$ **Prices:** Breakfast $2.50–$5; main courses $3.50–$10.
  Open: Daily 7am–10pm.
Clean and air-conditioned, this brick restaurant facing the ferry pier resembles a Stateside lunchroom, with a long lunch counter, red booths, and little tables. A sign says CERVEZAS Y PREPARADOS UNICAMENTE DOS POR PERSONA CON ALIMENTOS ("Two drinks or beers per person only with meals"). This rule helps Mirtita's avoid becoming more a tavern than a restaurant. The menu lists fish filet, steak and french fries, seafood salads, shrimp cocktails, onion-and-lemon soup, club sandwiches, and fried chicken.

WORTH THE EXTRA BUCKS
CHEZ MEGALEY, in the Hotel Nautibeach, Av. Rueda Medina. Tel. 2-0436.

Specialty: INTERNATIONAL.
$ Prices: Appetizers $4–$6; main courses $7.50–$24.
Open: Tues–Sun 11am–10pm.

This restaurant at the north end of Medina on Coco Beach has the best view, decor, and food in the central village area. Slip into a matching *equipales* chair and table under a grand palapa inside, or outside on the beachside porch. It's a great location for sunset watching. Tables are festooned in royal blue and blue-tinted blown glasses. Prices are high, but I think you'll enjoy your meal. Try the mixed brochette of shrimp, tender steak, and lobster, which comes with rice and vegetables.

EN ROUTE SOUTH ALONG THE COAST

To enjoy fully the wealth of attractions that Yucatán has to offer, you must wander farther from your Cancún/Isla Mujeres base. Chapter 21 has full information on points west of Cancún such as Chichén-Itzá and Mérida. Let's look now at what lies south of Cancún, on the way to the island of Cozumel and beyond.

If you don't have your own car, transport along the Caribbean coast presents problems. Though there are about a dozen buses a day down the coast (see Chapter 22), you may end up waiting along the sweltering highway for an hour or more only to have a jam-packed bus roar right by you.

---

2. PUERTO MORELOS

21 miles S of Cancún

GETTING THERE **By Bus** Buses from Cancún's bus station going to Tulum and Playa del Carmen usually stop here, but be sure to ask in Cancún if it makes the Puerto Morelos stop.

By Car Drive south from Cancún along Highway 307.

Most people come here to take the car-ferry to Cozumel several hours away. Puerto Morelos has begun to resume the building boom that was beginning when Hurricane Gilbert came through.

WHERE TO STAY & EAT

POSADA AMOR, Apdo. Postal 808, Cancún, Q. Roo 77580. 20 rms (10 with bath).
$ Rates: $13 single without bath, $17 single with bath; $15 double without bath, $22 double with bath.

The simple, cheery little rooms with screens and mosquito netting are quite plain but adequate, and are clustered around a patio in back of the restaurant. The posada's restaurant is rustic and quaint like an English cottage, with whitewashed walls, small shuttered windows, and open rafters, and decorated with primitive paintings and flowers on each table. Prices are reasonable, and an entire meal should cost only $3 to $7 or so. It's open daily from 7:30am to 10pm.

To get here, when you enter town, turn right; with the town square on your left, follow the main street leading to the ferry and the hotel is on the right.

BY CAR-FERRY FROM PUERTO MORELOS TO COZUMEL

The dock is the largest establishment in town and very easy to find. There are no phones in Puerto Morelos, but the car-ferry office can be reached by dialing 987/2-0827 or 2-0938 in Cozumel.

The car-ferry schedule is a complicated one. On Monday there's no ferry service. On Tuesday there are two ferries. For the first one, autos load around 9am if there aren't many cargo trucks. The second ferry leaves at 3pm. On Wednesday and Thursday, autos and campers load at 8am. On Thursday there's a 3pm ferry, but it will be canceled if there's not much cargo. On Friday the main cargo is gasoline trucks. No foot passengers are allowed and only cars with a male driver—no women or children allowed. This ferry is never canceled. On Saturday and Sunday there's one 8am trip. Call in advance to make sure this schedule is still valid.

Cargo takes precedence over cars. Some 25 to 30 cars can fit on each ferry, but there's space for only two to four camper vehicles. Officials suggest that camper drivers stay overnight in the parking lot to be first in line for tickets. In any case, always arrive at least 2 hours in advance of the ferry departure to purchase a ticket and to get in line. The trip to Cozumel takes 3 to 4 hours.

Since passenger-boat service between Playa del Carmen and Cozumel is quite frequent now, I don't recommend that foot passengers bother with this boat.

Check the Cozumel return schedules upon arrival in Cozumel. The return voyage from Cozumel leaves the car-ferry dock, south of town near the Hotel Sol Caribe. Get there early to buy your ticket and get in line. During long bouts of bad weather the boat has been kept at dock for as long as a week.

EN ROUTE TO PLAYA DEL CARMEN

Heading south on Highway 307 from Puerto Morelos, the village of **Muchi** is the next landmark. It's only 20 miles from Puerto Morelos to Playa del Carmen, so you'll be there in a half hour or less.

About 2½ miles before Playa del Carmen, you'll see a sign pointing left to **Punta Bete.** The road is narrow and overgrown, but have faith and keep bearing right to the **Cabañas Xcalacoco.** Soon you'll reach the beach and the compound with seven cabañas facing the ocean. The cabañas are tidy, cinderblock buildings with small porches all on the beach facing the sea. Five have king-size beds and the others have two double beds each. There are camping facilities for those wishing to hang a hammock under a thatch roof. There's a small restaurant, but it's always a good idea to bring along packaged and canned snacks and soft drinks. Singles and doubles rent for $25 to $35 a night. For reservations or information, write to Apdo. Postal 176, Playa del Carmen, Q. Roo 77710.

3. PLAYA DEL CARMEN

20 miles S. of Puerto Morelos, 44 miles S of Cancún

GETTING THERE   By Bus   There are three bus stations in Playa del Carmen, all on Avenida Principal (the main street): **Transportes de Oriente** is 2½ blocks north of the ferry and main square; **Transportes del Caribe** is across the street, near the corner of Avenida Principal and Avenida 5; and the **ADO** station is four blocks north of the ferry dock and two north of the zócalo.

Transportes del Caribe has the best schedule from Cancún, which was experimental when I checked. Minibuses from Cancún leave at 5, 8, and 11am, and 2, 5, and 6:30pm. From Cancún, Transportes de Oriente runs one confirmed-seat bus. Seven *de paso* ADO buses pass through Playa del Carmen on the way to Cancún. The first is at 6:30am. Seven ADO buses go to Valladolid, Chichén-Itzá, and Mérida, and one to Tulum at 10:45am; several second-class buses run the same routes.

By Car   The turnoff to Playa del Carmen from Highway 307 is plainly marked and you'll arrive on the town's widest street, Avenida Principal (not that there's a street sign to that effect).

By Ferry   Of the four ferries mentioned below, the water jet *México I* is the fastest by 10 to 15 minutes (see the schedule in the accompanying table). If the water is choppy, take precautions against seasickness.

DEPARTING   By Bus   Minibuses of **Transportes del Caribe** leave for Cancún at 5:30, 7:30, 9:30, and 11:30am, and 2:15, 5:15, 5:30, 9, and 10pm.

Transportes de Oriente runs seven buses to Cancún, the first at 5am and the last at 9pm, as well as buses to Tulum, Valladolid, Chichén-Itzá, and Mérida. **ADO** also goes to Villahermosa and Mexico City from here.

By Ferry   See the schedule in the accompanying table.

This little Caribbean village came into being because of the passenger-boat service to Cozumel, but recently it has developed quite a tourist trade of its own. Travelers have discovered that Playa del Carmen's long stretches of white beach are far better than those on Cozumel, which are covered with sharp coral or pounded by dangerous surf. Enterprising businesses, many of them foreign owned, are moving in to fill the demand. Rustic cabañas are springing up, but the pace of development has slowed. However, you'll still get much more for your money in Playa than in Cozumel.

Despite the little development, the beach bums and young people aren't about to abandon Playa just yet. The nudist beach has merely been pushed farther and farther north. The once-abundant palm trees were destroyed by Hurricane Gilbert.

Playa del Carmen is even more laid-back than Isla Mujeres. There are few good restaurants and the hotels lean more toward the rustic and plain. Nightlife exists around the few restaurants that stay open until 10pm or so. In short, if you want to relax and do nothing on a budget, with all the beauty of the Caribbean rolled out before you, this is one of those places.

A few vestiges of the preboom days are still visible: Very few streets are paved and there's only one public telephone.

ORIENTATION

ARRIVING   The ferry dock in Playa del Carmen is a block and a half from the main square, and within walking distance of hotels.

FERRY SCHEDULE FROM COZUMEL TO PLAYA DEL CARMEN

México MV	*Xelha* and *Cozumeleño*
4:00am	4:00am
6:30	6:30
8:00	
9:00	9:00
11:00	11:00
1:30pm	1pm
3:30	
4:00	4:00
5:30	
6:30	6:30
	8:00

FERRY SCHEDULE FROM PLAYA DEL CARMEN TO COZUMEL

México MV	*Xelha* and *Cozumeleño*
5:30am	5:30am
7:30	7:30
9:30	
10:15	10:30
12:15pm	Noon
2:30	2:30pm
4:15	
5:30	5:30
6:30	
7:30	7:30
	9:00

CITY LAYOUT   Villagers know and use street names, but few street signs exist. The main street, **Avenida Principal,** leads into town from Highway 307, crossing Avenida 5 one block before it ends at the beach next to the main plaza, or **zócalo.** The other main artery, **Avenida 5,** leads to the ferry dock, two blocks from the zócalo; most restaurants and hotels are either on Avenida 5, or a block or two off of it. The village's beautiful beach parallels Avenida 5 and is only a block from it.

FAST FACTS

Laundry   There's a laundry next to the Hotel Playa del Carmen, two blocks north of the zócalo, open Monday through Saturday from 8am to 8pm and on Sunday and holidays from 7am to noon.

Post Office   The post office (Correos) is on Avenida Principal, three blocks north of the zócalo on the right, past the Hotel Playa del Carmen and laundromat.

Telephone   The Hotel Playa del Carmen, on Avenida Principal, has the village's only telephone, open for long-distance use Monday through Saturday from 7am to 2pm and 3 to 9pm.

WHERE TO STAY

There are motel-style hotels on Avenida Principal, but the more interesting hostelries are the cabaña-style inns along the beach and on Avenida 5.

High season is December through Easter. Low season is all other months, when Playa del Carmen can be quite empty and a bargain vacation. *Price headings below refer to off-season prices.*

DOUBLES FOR LESS THAN $25

CABAÑAS TUCAN, Av. 5 Norte (Apdo. Postal 27), Playa del Carmen, Q. Roo 77710. 8 rms (all with bath).
$ Rates: Low season, $12 single or double; high season, $18 single or double.

The farthest hotel from the ferry (nine blocks away), it's also a block from the beach, on the landward side of Avenida 5 Norte. Each of the austere bungalows has fans, well-screened windows, protective mosquito netting on each bed, tile floors, and white stucco walls. The owners were planning a small outdoor restaurant to serve breakfast.

POSADA CORTO MALTES, Calle 10 and the beach, Playa del Carmen, Q. Roo 77710. 10 bungalows (none with bath).
$ Rates: Low season, $20 single or double; high season, unavailable.

"Rustic but somehow chic" describes these tranquil, French-run quarters. Set among banana trees and flowers, each stick-walled bungalow comes with a peaked thatch roof, fan, screened windows, bed, sink with mirror, and combination shelf and clothes hanger. Each one has a thatched covered "porch" with a hammock and a table and two chairs where a continental breakfast is delivered each morning ($2 extra). Within the compound are four toilets and showers and two sinks.

To get here, walk down Avenida 5 five blocks from Avenida Principal and turn right onto Calle 10; the hotel is on the left.

BANANAS CABAÑAS, Av. 5 at Calle 6, Playa del Carmen, Q. Roo 77710. 19 rms (6 with bath).
$ Rates: High season $17–$28 single or double; off-season, $12–$17 single or double.

The rustically, sophisticated Limones, the best restaurant in Playa del Carmen, is in front of the cabañas and has the same ownership, but the restaurant outshines the cabañas. The cabañas are a rather spartan, well-used assortment of rooms, all clean but very basic. Rooms without bathrooms share a clean bath and toilet facilities (separate for men and women). Across the street, however, the hotel manages another set of rooms, all with private baths, tile floors, and balconies; these are on the high end of the price range. American owned, it's a good place for a long stay on a short budget.

Walk down Avenida 5 six blocks from the ferry pier; the Cabañas are on the left at the fourth cross street.

HOTEL DELFIN, Av. 5 and Calle 6 (Apdo. Postal 38), Playa del Carmen, Q. Roo 77710. 13 rms (all with bath).
$ Rates: High season, $15–$25 single; $30–$35 double. Off-season, $15 single; $20 double.

New in 1990, it's a half a block from the beach, and conveniently located three blocks from the bus station, five blocks down Avenida 5 from the pier, and near restaurants. With two stories, the simple, cheery, and spacious rooms have fans and tile floors. Some rooms have sea views, and on the second floor there's a terrace overlooking the street.

DOUBLES FOR LESS THAN $40

CABAÑAS NUEVO AMANECER, Calle 4 Norte no. 3 (Apdo. Postal 59), Playa de Carmen, Q. Roo 77710. 13 rms (all with bath).
$ Rates: $25–$35 single or double, all year.

American owned, clean, and well kept, the rooms are connected by a thatch-roofed walkway. Each tidy cabaña also has a thatch roof, a fan, well-screened windows, mosquito netting over the bed, tile floors, one double bed, and a hammock. A spare bed can be added. There's a hot tub behind the office for relaxing. It's on the landward side off Avenida 5, a block and a half from the beach, 4½ blocks from the ferry and 2½ blocks from the bus station.

MAYA-BRIC HOTEL, Av. 5 Norte, Playa del Carmen, Q. Roo 77710. Tel./Fax 99/25-1073 in Mérida (at night). 24 rms (all with bath).
$ Rates: $30–$35 single or double, all year

The colorful exterior and flowers of this two-story, beachfront inn will catch your eye. The well-kept rooms have fans, two double beds, and stucco walls. There's a small, clean swimming pool. A restaurant by the office serves breakfast and dinner, and there's another one by the beach open all day. A dive shop on the property rents snorkeling gear and arranges dives. It never hurts to ask for an additional discount here. It's between Calles 8 and 10, 4½ blocks (north) past the zócalo, on the right.

CABAÑAS ALBATROZ, Apdo. Postal 31, Playadel Carmen, Q. Roo 77710. 18 bungalows (all with bath).
$ Rates: High season, $35–$45 cabaña for one or two; off-season $20–$35 cabaña for one or two.

If you want to stay in your own bungalow and swing on a hammock on your doorstep by the beach, you'll pay for it—but this is one of the best places in Carmen to do it. American owned, the colorfully painted huts, each with its own thatch-covered front "porch," are grouped around a flower-filled sandy courtyard. Each comes with a fan and one double bed, but you can ask for an extra single rollaway. Bathrooms are new, tile, and spotless, and have hot water. Room 23, the honeymoon "suite," faces the beach. The restaurant (a good one) serves all three meals, and if you stay a week, the seventh night is free. Someone from the hotel can help with luggage from the street, over the beach, to the hotel.

From Avenida Principal, walk three blocks north on Avenida 5 and then turn right one block to the beach; the hotel is half a block down on the beach.

COSTA DEL MAR, Calle 10 Norte Bis (Apdo. Postal 13), Playa del Carmen, Q. Roo 77710. Tel./Fax 987/2-0231 in Cozumel. 34 rms, 5 bungalows (all with bath).
$ Rates: High season, $42–$52 single or double; $20 bungalow. Low season $24–$40 single or double; $14 bungalows.

More like a traditional hotel found in Isla Mujeres or downtown Cancún, the cheery rooms here have white-tile or travertine marble floors, concrete-platform beds, and good mosquito screens. Most have two double beds. The 19 rooms with air conditioning are larger and are on the high end of the prices. If you choose a palapa-thatched hut or a room with a fan, you'll save a few dollars. A beachside pool and restaurant are farther back on the property.

To get here from Avenida Principal, walk five blocks, turn right onto Calle 10 (at the Maya-Bric Hotel), walk almost to the beach, and turn left; the hotel is on the left.

CAMPING

Playa del Carmen has many little camping areas down along the water. Turn to the left at the beach and head for the **Camping Las Ruinas,** right on the beach and across the street from a tiny Maya ruin. There are small rooms costing $5 to $7, tent space for $2 to $3, trailer and camper spaces for $3.50 to $5, or auto space for 75¢. A shady palapa serves as a restaurant and general gathering area. Coming in from the highway, turn left (north) on the town's main street, go one block, and turn right.

A YOUTH HOSTEL

From the bus station, walk back out in the direction of the highway and follow the signs. A bed in an 18-bunk room with cold water costs $2.75. This includes sheets, pillowcase, and a locker. You can also rent a cabaña for $12 with shared bath. It's a 10- to 15-minute walk from the bus station.

WHERE TO EAT

RESTAURANT MASCARAS, Av. Principal.
   Specialty: ITALIAN.
$ **Prices:** Appetizers $2.50–$6; main courses $5–$21; pizza $4.50–$11.50; pasta $4.75–$6.50.
   Open: Daily 12:30pm–midnight.
If you're in the mood for brick-oven pizza (thin crust and heavy on the tomato), head directly to this place facing the zócalo. The dining room is decorated with Maya and Venetian masks. Besides Italian specialties there are seafood, steak, and chicken dishes. The pride is the bar—ask for anything. Expect an automatic 15% service charge on your bill.

CABAÑAS ALBATROZ, on the beach at the corner of Calle 6.
   Specialty: MEXICAN/ITALIAN.
$ **Prices:** Breakfast $3–$3.50; appetizers $1–$1.75; main courses $3–$7.
   Open: Daily; breakfast 7–11am; lunch 12:30–6pm; dinner 6–10pm.
      On the beach, this is a good place to meet Americans who live here and while away some hours munching and people-watching. The food is dependably good. The lunch menu has sandwiches and tacos, while the evening menu offers pizzas, pastas, and seafood.
      From Avenida Principal, walk three blocks north on Avenida 5 and then turn right for one block on Calle 6 to the beach; the hotel/restaurant is half a block down the beach.

LIMONES, Av. 5 at Calle 6.
   Specialty: MEXICAN/INTERNATIONAL.
$ **Prices:** Breakfast 50¢–$3.50; lunch $2.50–$6; dinner $6.50–$12.
   Open: Daily. High season, breakfast 7am–noon; lunch 2–5pm; dinner 5–11pm. Low season, breakfast 7–11am; dinner 6–10pm.
      This attractive, thatch-roofed restaurant, three blocks from Avenida Principal, is the best in town. The lunch menu offers light meals such as vegetarian pasta, tostadas, flautas, and hamburgers. Dinner is more elegant and the menu

changes daily, but might include jambalaya, or chicken, seafood, or beef brochettes. Most dinner dishes are served with fresh hot garlic bread, vegetables, and either a baked potato or rice and pasta.

4. COZUMEL

12 miles from Playa del Carmen, 44 miles S of Cancún

GETTING THERE   By Plane   AeroCozumel (tel. 2-0928, 2-0503 or 2-0877 or fax 987/2-0500 in Cozumel, 4-2862 in Cancún)—a Mexicana affiliate—has numerous flights to and from Cancún.

American (tel. 2-0988 and 2-0899) flies direct from Dallas/Fort Worth and Raleigh/Durham. **Continental** (tel. 2-0576, 2-0847, or 2-0487) has flights from Houston. **Mexicana,** Melgar Sur 17 at Calle Salas (tel. 2-0157 or 2-0263, or 2-0405 at the airport; fax 987/2-2945), flies from Dallas/Fort Worth, Miami, and Mérida.

By Bus   Buses from Cancún go to Playa del Carmen where there are frequent passenger ferries to Cozumel (see Section 3, above).

By Car   See Section 2, Puerto Morelos, above, for car-ferry information. Or you could drive to Playa del Carmen, find a reliable place to leave your car, and take the ferry from Playa del Carmen (see Section 3, above).

By Ferry   There are several passenger ferries running between Cozumel and Playa del Carmen. **México MV,** the modern water jet, makes the trip in 25 to 30 minutes compared to 40 to 45 minutes on the **Xelha** or the **Cozumeleño.** The MV *México* costs $4.50 one way and is enclosed and air-conditioned, with cushioned seats and video entertainment. The *Cozumeleño* and *Xelha* are open-air vessels with canopies for $2.50. Both companies have ticket booths at the main pier. Be prepared for seasickness on windy days. For the ferry schedules, see Section 3, Playa del Carmen, above, or go to the pier.

DEPARTING   Taxis, no colectivo vans, go to the airport for $2. For the ferry schedule, see Section 3, Playa del Carmen, above. For the car-ferry, check in Cozumel at the car-ferry dock.

Cozumel (pop. 50,000) is Mexico's largest Caribbean island, 28 miles long and 11 miles wide. The only town is San Miguel de Cozumel, usually just called San Miguel. Only 3% of the island is developed, but the construction of 2,000 hotel rooms is planned in 1993 for the area beyond the Stouffer Presidente Hotel and near the Palancar Reef.

If Cancún is the jet-set's port of call and Isla Mujeres is the poor man's Cancún, Cozumel is a little bit of both. More remote than the other two, this island is a place where people come to get away from the day-tripping atmosphere of Isla Mujeres or the megadevelopment of Cancún. Many visitors complain that Cozumel's prices are too high, but if you're diving at Palancar Reef, it all seems worth it; certainly dive packages are a bargain.

All the necessaries for a good vacation are here: excellent snorkeling and scuba places, sailing and water sports, expensive resorts and modest hotels, elegant restaurants and taco shops, even a Maya ruin or two. If, after a while, you do get restless, the ancient Maya city of Tulum, the lagoon of Xel-ha, or the nearby village of Playa del Carmen provide convenient and interesting excursions.

ORIENTATION

ARRIVING   Cozumel's **airport** is near downtown. Aero Transportes colectivo vans at the airport provide transportation into town for $2 and to either the north or south hotel zone for $2 to $4.

INFORMATION   The **Tourism Office** is on the second floor of the Plaza del Sol

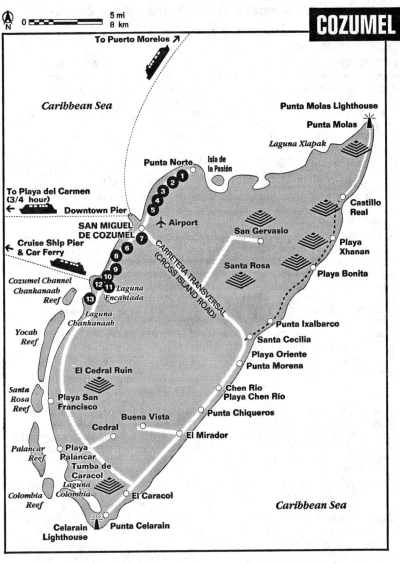

COZUMEL

To Puerto Morelos ↗

0   5 mi / 8 km

Caribbean Sea

Punta Molas Lighthouse
Punta Molas

Laguna Xlapak

Punta Norte
Isla de la Pasión

To Playa del Carmen (3/4 hour) ←
Downtown Pier

Castillo Real

SAN MIGUEL DE COZUMEL

✈ Airport

San Gervasio

Playa Xhanan

Cruise Ship Pier & Car Ferry ←

CARRETERA TRANSVERSAL (CROSS ISLAND ROAD)

Santa Rosa

Playa Bonita

Cozumel Channel
Chankanaab Reef

Laguna Encantada

Laguna Chankanaab

Punta Ixalbarco

Santa Cecilia

Playa Oriente
Punta Morena

Yocab Reef

El Cedral Ruin

Santa Rosa Reef

Playa San Francisco

Chen Rio
Playa Chen Río

Buena Vista

Punta Chiqueros

Cedral

El Mirador

Palancar Reef

Playa Palancar
Tumba de Caracol

Laguna Colombia

Colombia Reef

El Caracol

Caribbean Sea

Celarain Lighthouse
Punta Celarain

MEXICO CITY
★ Cozumel

Cantarell, Hotel ⑤
Casa del Mar ⑩
El Cozumeleño, Hotel ②
Fiesta Americana Sol Caribe Cozumel ⑪
Fiesta Inn Cozumel ⑨
La Ceiba ⑫
Meliá Mayan Cozumel, Hotel ①
Playa Azul, Hotel ④

Plaza Las Glorias Cozumel ⑧
San Miguel, Hotel ⑦
Sol Cabanas del Caribe, Hotel ③
Stouffer President Cozumel ⑬
Villa del Rey, Hotel ⑥

commercial building facing the central plaza (tel. 2-0972). Open Monday through Friday from 9am to 3pm.

CITY LAYOUT San Miguel's main waterfront street is called **Avenida Rafael Melgar,** running along the western shore of the island. Passenger ferries dock right in the center, opposite the main plaza and Melgar. Car-ferries dock south of town near the hotels Sol Caribe, La Ceiba, Fiesta Inn, and Stouffer Presidente.

The town is laid out on a grid, with avenidas running north and south, calles running east and west. The exception is **Avenida Juárez,** which runs right from the passenger-ferry dock through the main square and inland. Juárez divides the town into northern and southern halves.

Heading inland from the dock along Juárez, you'll find that the avenidas you cross are numbered by fives for some reason: "5a Av.," "10a Av.," "15a Av." If you turn left and head north, you'll discover that calles are even-numbered: 2a Norte, 4a Norte, 6a Norte. Turning right from Juárez heads you south, where the streets are odd-numbered: 1a Sur (also called Adolfo Salas), 3a Sur, 5a Sur. The scheme is more systematic than it is practical.

ISLAND LAYOUT The island is cut in half by one road which runs past the airport and the ruins of San Gervasio to the almost-uninhabited southern coast of the island. The northern part of the island has no paved roads. It's scattered with small badly ruined Maya sites, from the age when "Cuzamil" was a land sacred to the moon goddess Ixchel. The sites are best visited by Jeep or boat.

There are many hotels, moderate to expensive, north and south of town. Many cater to divers. Beyond the hotels to the south is **Chancanab National Park,** centered on the beautiful lagoon of the same name. Beyond Chancanab is **Playa Palancar,** and, offshore, the **Palancar Reef** (*arrecife*). At the southern tip of the island is **Punta Celarain** and the lighthouse.

The eastern, seaward shore of the island is mostly surf beach, beautiful for walking but dangerous for swimming.

GETTING AROUND

There is limited **bus** service along Avenida Rafael Melgar from north of town as far south as Palancar, but you can walk to most destinations within town.

The trip from town to Playa San Francisco costs from $5 by **taxi.** For a day at the beach, finding some like-minded fellow travelers and sharing the cost of a cab is the easy, quick way to go. Taxis should charge no more than $4 from the town center to the farthest hotels.

Car rentals are as expensive here as in other parts of Mexico. Open-top Jeeps are popular for rental, but be aware that they are easy to roll, and many tourists have been injured or killed using them.

Moped rentals are all over the village and cost about $25 a day, but terms and prices vary. Carefully inspect the actual moped you'll be renting to see that all the gizmos are in good shape: horn, light, starter, seat, mirror. Be careful of sunburn, there's a tendency to forget that riding in the sun all day is the same as lying on the beach all day. And finally, read the fine print on the back of the moped-rental agreement, which states that you are not insured, you are responsible for paying for any damage to the bike, and you must stay on paved roads.

FAST FACTS

American Express The local representative is **Fiesta Cozumel,** Avenida Melgar 27 (tel. 987/2-0831; fax 987/2-0433).

Area Code The telephone area code is 987.

Bookstore The **Agencia de Publicaciones Gracia,** a small store facing the zócalo at Avenida 5 (tel. 2-0031), has a good selection of English-language novels and magazines. Open daily 9am to 3pm.

Doctors Cozumel has several English-speaking American and Mexican doctors in residence. Your hotel can help you contact one.

Laundry On Salas between Calles 5 Sur and 10 Sur, **Express Laundry** has do-it-yourself washers and dryers, and will do dry cleaning. Open daily from 8am to 9pm.

Post Office   The post office (Correos) is on Avenida Rafael Melgar at Calle 7 Sur, at the southern edge of town.

Recompression Chamber   The new recompression chamber (*camara de recompreción*) is at Discover Cozumel Diving, on Calle 5 Sur between Melgar and Avenida 5 Sur (tel. 2-2387).

Seasons and Climate   High season is December through Easter. November can be very windy, and too dangerous to dive.

Telephone   Long-distance telephones are on Salas between 5th Av. Sur and 10th Av. Sur on the exterior of the telephone building. Use a credit card to get an American operator, or push 01 for the U.S. and Hawaii, wait for an operator, give your area code and number and credit card number; or make it collect; or have a pile of 100 peso coins ready to feed the phone.

WHAT TO SEE & DO
TOURING THE ISLAND

Travel agencies can book you on a group tour of the island for around $12 to $25, depending on if it includes lunch and a stop for snorkeling. A taxi driver charges $40 for a $50 for a 3-hour tour. You can easily rent a motorbike or car for half a day to take you around the southern part of the island (42 miles). If you drive yourself in the downtown area, be aware that north-south traffic has the right of way. Be careful—they don't slow down.

North of town, along Melgar, you'll pass a yacht marina and a string of Cozumel's first hotels as well as some new condominiums. All these hotels have been completely renewed since Hurricane Gilbert and are as up-to-date as those south of town, but are less expensive, though out of our price range. A few of the hotels have nice beaches, which you are welcome to use. This road ends just past the hotels; you can backtrack to the transversal road that cuts across the island from west (the town side) to east and link up with the eastern highway which brings you back to town.

The more interesting route begins by going south of town on Melgar, past the Hotel Barracuda and Hotel La Perla. Remember that no hotel in Mexico "owns" the beach—by law, all beaches are public property—so feel free to use a "hotel" beach. On Cozumel this public ownership is more important than ever, since beaches are relatively few as most of the island is surrounded by coral reefs.

About 5 miles south of town you'll come to the big Sol Caribe and La Ceiba hotels, and also the car-ferry dock for ferries to Puerto Morelos. Go snorkeling out in the water by the Hotel La Ceiba and you might spot a sunken airplane, put there for an underwater movie. Off-shore, from here to the tip of the island at Punta Celarain, 20 miles, is **Underwater National Park,** so designated to protect visitors from damaging the reefs. Dive masters warn not to touch or destroy the underwater growth.

✪ **CHANCANAB NATIONAL PARK**   This lagoon and botanical garden is a mile past the big hotels and 5½ miles south of town. It has long been famous for the color and variety of its sea life. The intrusion of sightseers began to ruin the marine habitat, so now visitors must swim and snorkel in the open sea, not in the lagoon. The beach is wide and beautiful, with plenty of shady thatched umbrellas to sit under, and the snorkeling is good—lots of colorful fish. Arrive early to stake out a chair and palapa before the cruise-ship visitors arrive. There are rest rooms, a gift shop, several snack huts, a restaurant, and a palapa renting snorkeling gear.

Surrounding the lagoon, a botanical garden linked by shady paths has 352 species of tropical and subtropical plants from 22 countries and 451 species from Cozumel. Several Maya structures have been re-created within the gardens to give visitors an idea of Maya life in a jungle setting. There's a small natural-history museum as well.

Admission to the park costs $2.50. It's open daily from 8am to 4:30pm.

BEACHES   After another 10 miles, you'll come to **Playa San Francisco,** and south of it, **Playa Palancar**—on Cozumel they're the best, so plan to spend most of your beach time here. Food (usually overpriced) and equipment rentals are available.

PUNTA CELARAIN   After Playa San Francisco, you plow through the jungle on a straight road for miles until you're 17½ miles from town. (New hotels are being built along this stretch.) Finally, though, you emerge near the southern reaches of the island on the east coast. The **lighthouse** you see in the distance is at Punta Celarain, the island's southernmost tip. The sand track is unsuitable for motorbikes, but in a car you can drive to the lighthouse in about 25 minutes.

THE EASTERN SHORE   The road along the east coast of the island is wonderful. There are views of the sea, the rocky shore, and the pounding surf. On the land side are little farms and forests. Exotic birds take flight as you approach, and monstrous (but harmless) iguanas skitter off into the undergrowth.

Most of the east coast is unsafe for swimming because the surf can create a deadly undertow, which will pull you far out to sea in a matter of minutes. However, there are a few places on this coast where headlands and breakers create safe swimming areas. At **Chen Río** you can swim, and also at **Punta Morena** and **Playa Chiqueros.** Three restaurants catering to tourists are along this part of the coast, complete with sombrero-clad iguanas for a picture companion.

Halfway up the east coast, the paved eastern road meets the paved transversal road (which passes the ruins of San Gervasio) back to town, 9½ miles away. The east-coast road ends when it turns into the transversal, petering out to a narrow track of sandy road by a nice restaurant in front of the Chen Río beach; vehicles, even motorbikes will get stuck on the sand road. If you're a birdwatcher, leave your vehicle on the highway here and walk straight down the sandy road. A lagoon paralleling it on the left is full of waterfowl. Go slowly and quietly and at the least you'll spot many herons and egrets. Farther on are Maya ruins.

MAYA RUINS   One of the most popular trips is to **San Gervasio** (100 B.C.–A.D. 1600). A road leads there from the airport or you can continue on the eastern part of the island following the paved transversal road. The sign to the ruins is worn and easy to miss, but the turnoff to the ruins is about halfway between town and the eastern coast. Stop at the entry gate and pay the 75¢ road-use fee. Go straight ahead over the potholed road to the ruins about 2 miles farther and pay $2.75 to enter.

When it comes to Cozumel's Maya remains, getting there is most of the fun, and you should do it for the trip, not for the ruins. The buildings are conserved, but crudely made and would not be much of a tourist attraction if they were not the island's only cleared and accessible ruins. More significant than beautiful, the site was once an important Maya ceremonial center where they gathered, coming even from the mainland. Tour guides charge $12 for a tour for one to six people, but it's not worth it. Find a copy of the green booklet "San Gervasio," sold at local check-out counters or bookstores, and tour the site on your own. Seeing it takes 30 minutes.

BOAT EXCURSIONS

Boat trips are another popular pastime at Cozumel. Some excursions include snorkeling and scuba diving or a stop at a beach with lunch. Various types of tours can be booked by travel agents, including a glass-bottom-boat tour lasting 1½ hours for $15.

AN EXCURSION TO SIAN KA'AN BIOSPHERE RESERVE

On the mainland south of Cozumel is the Sian Ka'an Biosphere Reserve, 1.3 million acres set aside to protect hundreds of species of birds, animals, and plants (see Section 6, below, for details). **Viajes Internacionales Palancar,** 10a Avenida Sur no. 124, Cozumel, Q. Roo 77600 (tel. 987/2-2259; fax 987/2-2348), offers day-long excursions to the reserve from Cozumel for $88 per person. A minimum of four people is required for the trip, which leaves at 9am, returns at 6pm, and includes a guided boat tour of the reserve with an English-speaking guide, box lunch, and drinks.

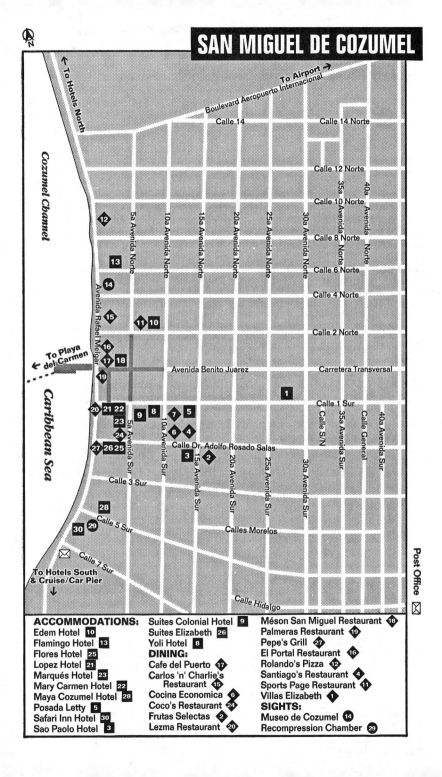

SAN MIGUEL DE COZUMEL

ACCOMMODATIONS:
Edem Hotel 10
Flamingo Hotel 13
Flores Hotel 25
Lopez Hotel 21
Marqués Hotel 23
Mary Carmen Hotel 22
Maya Cozumel Hotel 28
Posada Letty 5
Safari Inn Hotel 30
Sao Paolo Hotel 3

Suites Colonial Hotel 9
Suites Elizabeth 26
Yoli Hotel 8
DINING:
Cafe del Puerto 17
Carlos 'n' Charlie's Restaurant 15
Cocina Economica 6
Coco's Restaurant 24
Frutas Selectas 2
Lezma Restaurant 20

Méson San Miguel Restaurant 18
Palmeras Restaurant 19
Pepe's Grill 27
El Portal Restaurant 16
Rolando's Pizza 12
Santiago's Restaurant 4
Sports Page Restaurant 11
Villas Elizabeth 1
SIGHTS:
Museo de Cozumel 14
Recompression Chamber 29

Post Office ⊠

HISTORY MUSEUM

The new **Museo de la Isla de Cozumel,** on Melgar between Calles 4 and 6 Norte, is a nice place to spend a rainy hour. Exhibits feature the history of the town, as well as the island's ecological systems. It's open Sunday through Friday from 9am to 1pm and 4 to 8pm. Admission is $2; guided tours in English are free. There is a very expensive rooftop restaurant open long hours.

Large sea turtles nest on the beaches south of the town center and from July to part of September the eggs hatch. For $10 the museum takes visitors to the nests and allows them to put the tiny turtles into the ocean after watching them emerge from the nests buried in the sand. Tours leave at 8pm and return around 1am.

WATER SPORTS

✪ **Snorkeling**   Anyone who can swim can go snorkeling. Rental of the snorkel (breathing pipe), goggles, and flippers should only cost about $5 for a half day; a snorkeling trip costs $20. The brilliantly colored tropical fish provide a dazzling show for free.

✪ **Scuba Diving**   Various establishments on the island rent scuba gear—tanks, regulator with pressure gauge, buoyancy compensator, mask, snorkel, and flippers. Many will also arrange a half-day expedition in a boat, complete with lunch, for a set price. Sign up the day before, if you're interested. A day of diving costs between $36 and $45 and includes two tanks. However, if you're a dedicated diver, you'll save many dollars by buying a diving package which includes air, hotel, and usually two dives a day. There's a new recompression chamber on the island (see "Fast Facts," above).

The underwater wonders of the famous **Palancar Reef** are offshore from the beach of the same name. It's the second-largest reef in the world, and in the famous blue depths divers find caves and canyons and huge colorful fish. The **Santa Rosa Reef** is famous for its depth, sea life, coral, and sponges. **San Francisco Reef,** off the beach by the same name south of town, has a drop-off wall, but it's still fairly shallow and the sea life is fascinating. The **Chankanaab Reef,** where divers are joined by game fish, is close to the shore by the national park of the same name. It's shallow and good for novice divers, as is **La Ceiba Reef.** Next going south on the eastern road after Chankanaab, **Yucab Reef** has beautiful coral.

Numerous vessels on the island operate daily diving and snorkeling tours so the best plan is to shop around and sign up for one of those.

Windsurfing   Sailboards are for rent at several hotels south of town.

Fishing   The best months for fishing are April through September, when the catch will be blue and white marlin, sailfish, swordfish, dolfin, wahoo, tuna, and red snapper. A half day of fishing costs $250.

SHOPPING

Shopping has improved beyond the ubiquitous T-shirt shops into expensive resort ware, silver, and better decorative and folk art. Most of the stores are on Melgar.

SPECIAL EVENTS

Carnaval/Mardi Gras is Cozumel's most colorful fiesta, which begins the Thursday before Ash Wednesday with daytime street dancing and nighttime parades on Thursday, Saturday, and Monday, with the latter being the best.

EVENING ENTERTAINMENT

Cozumel is a town frequented by sports-minded visitors, who play hard all day and wind down early at night. People sit in outdoor cafés around the zócalo enjoying the cool night breezes until the restaurants close. **Carlos 'N' Charlies** (see "Where to Eat," below) is always one of the liveliest places in town.

Scaramouche, on Avenida Melgar, two blocks south of the zócalo, is by far the most visible and popular disco. It's open from 9:30pm until. . . . There's usually a cover charge, but it varies.

WHERE TO STAY

Cozumel has a good selection of hotels in all price ranges. You'll have no trouble finding a room from May through November, but during high season—December through Easter—I recommend calling or writing ahead for reservations. Since tourism to Cozumel has been down the last couple of years, many hoteliers have held the same rate all year or raised it only slightly during high season. *Price headings below refer to low-season prices.*

DOUBLES FOR LESS THAN $20

HOTEL YOLI (or Yoly), Calle 1 Sur no. 164, Cozumel, Q. Roo 77600. Tel. 987/2-0024. 10 rms (all with bath).
$ Rates: $9 single; $14 double.

Located between main plaza and 10a Av. Sur, 1½ blocks west of Melgar and half a block west of Avenida 5 Sur, this clean, very simple hotel is one of the most colorful and cheerful in town. Yellow door trim contrasts with aqua doors and aqua tile walls in the hallways. Your room may have a freshly painted fuchsia or pink wall—or maybe both. Furnishings are old-fashioned but comfortable, and lighted with a circular fluorescent light on the wall; all rooms have fans. Towels and soap are laid out on the bed.

HOTEL SAO LIMA, Calle A. Rosado Salas 260, Cozumel, Q. Roo 77600. 20 rms (all with bath).
$ Rates: $10 single; $14 double.
This small, two-story, whitewashed hotel has basic rooms with two double beds or a double and a twin. Rooms on both floors, all with fans face each other separated by a narrow garden running down the middle. It's 2½ blocks west of Melgar between Avs. 10 and 15 Sur.

POSADA EDEM, Calle 2 Norte no. 12, Cozumel, Q. Roo 77600. Tel. 987/2-1166. 15 rms (all with bath).
$ Rates: $12 single; $14 double.
This small, modest hotel is on Calle 2, near the corner of Ave. 5 Norte, near the Sports Page Restaurant and a block and a half from the main square. The rooms—seven with air conditioning, eight with fans—are plain but functional, with tile floors, sheets but no bedspreads, and a single light hanging from the ceiling.

POSADA LETTY, Calle 1 Sur no. 272, Cozumel, Q. Roo 77600. Tel. 987/2-0257. 8 rms (all with bath).
$ Rates: High season, $15 single; $20 double. Low season, $12 single; $14 double.
It's hard to find this hotel because there's no lobby or reception desk, only a tiny sign. But the rooms are available, with ceiling fans, showers, and wooden shutters. The manager works in the little store on the corner past the pension.

To get here, walk west from the zócalo on Calle 1 Sur past Banco del Atlantico until you see a small sign on the right side of street at Av. 15 Sur.

HOTEL FLORES, Calle Adolfo Rosado Salas 72, Cozumel, Q. Roo 77600. Tel. 987/2-1429. Fax 987/2-2475. 32 rms (all with bath).
$ Rates: $12 single; $16 double; $20 triple.

Newly painted throughout and with new mattresses, the three-story Flores (no elevator) is now a good downtown choice. Some rooms have windows facing interior halls and stairs. Corner rooms have two windows to the outside and are bright and cheerful. All rooms have fans. The Flores is one block west of Melgar, a few doors from Suites Elizabeth.

HOTEL FLAMINGO, Calle 6 Norte no. 81, Cozumel, Q. Roo 77600. Tel. 987/2-1264. 22 rms (all with bath).

$ **Rates:** High season, $20 single; $22 double. Low season, $13 single; $17 double.

Built in 1986, the Flamingo offers three floors of quiet rooms, a grassy inner courtyard, and very helpful management. Second- and third-story rooms are spacious. All have fans and white-tile floors. Rooms on the front have balconies overlooking the street. Some doubles have one bed; others have two. Soft drinks and bottled water are available from the refrigerator in the lobby. You get a lot for your money here.

To find it, walk three blocks north on Melgar from the zócalo and turn right on Calle 6; the hotel is on the left.

DOUBLES FOR LESS THAN $30

HOTEL MARY-CARMEN, 5a Av. Sur no. 4, Cozumel, Q. Roo 77600. Tel. 987/2-0581. 27 rms (all with bath). A/C

$ **Rates:** High season, $29 single or double; low season, $23 single or double.

Watched over by eagle-eyed señoras, the two stories of rooms surround an inner courtyard shaded by a large mamey tree. Rooms are clean, with well-screened windows facing the courtyard. Rooms are carpeted and most have two double beds. It's half a block south of the zócalo on the right.

HOTEL EL MARQUÉS, 5a Av. Sur no. 12, Cozumel, Q. Roo 77600. Tel. 987/2-0677. Fax 987/2-0537. 40 rms (all with bath). A/C

$ **Rates:** High season, $26–$30 single or double; low season, $23 single or double.

The three stories of sunny rooms have gold trim and Formica-marble countertops, French provincial overtones, gray and white tile floors, and two double beds. Third-floor rooms have good views. The staff is friendly and attentive. From the zócalo, walk south on Melgar one block to Rosado Salas and turn left; the hotel is on the left.

HOTEL LÓPEZ, Calle 1 Sur no. 7 (Apdo. Postal 44), Cozumel, Q. Roo 77600. Tel. 987/2-0108. 34 rms (all with bath).

$ **Rates:** High season, $21 single; $30 double. Low season, $16 single; $23 double.

Located on the south side of the plaza opposite the passenger ferry pier, this two-story hotel will probably have a vacancy if no one else does. The rooms aren't the cheeriest, but they're large and clean, with blue-tile floors and a single fluorescent light that illuminates the entire room. Most rooms (27) are air-conditioned; the rest have fans.

HOTEL MAYA COZUMEL, Calle 5 Sur no. 4, Cozumel, Q. Roo 77600. Tel. 987/2-0781. Fax 987/2-0011. 38 rms (all with bath). A/C TEL

$ **Rates:** High season, $35 single; $41 double. Low season, $23 single; $29 double.

This bright apricot- and white-colored hotel three blocks down Melgar from the town center has upbeat rooms, with light tile floors and comfortable leather chairs. Through a glass wall in the lobby you can see the grassy rear courtyard surrounding the swimming pool. Ask about dive packages.

HOTEL SUITES BAZAR COLONIAL, Av. 5 Sur no. 9 (Apdo. Postal 286), Cozumel, Q. Roo 77600. Tel. 987/2-0506. Fax 987/2-1387. 28 rms (all with bath). A/C

$ **Rates:** High season, $45 double; low season, $29 double.

Across the street from the El Marqués half a block from the zócalo is a collection of shops, and this nice four-story hotel—with elevator. It's a good deal for the money. The lobby is far back past the shops. You get a quiet, spacious, furnished studio or a one-bedroom apartment with red-tile floors on the first floor. Second- and third-floor rooms have a kitchenette.

DOUBLES FOR LESS THAN $45

HOTEL SAFARI INN, Ave. Melgar at Calle 5 Sur (Apdo. Postal 41), Cozumel, Q. Roo 77600. Tel. 987/2-0101. Fax 987/2-0661. 12 rms (all with bath). A/C

$ **Rates:** $35–$40 single or double.

The nicest budget hotel in town is above and behind the Aqua Dive Shop, 3½ blocks south of the zócalo facing the Caribbean. Natural colors and stucco pervade the interior of this new three-story establishment. The huge rooms come with firm beds, a built-in sofa, and tile floors. The hotel caters to divers and offers some good dive packages.

HOTEL ELIZABETH, Calle Salas 44 (Apdo. Postal 70), Cozumel, Q. Roo 77600. Tel. 987/2-0330. 19 rms (all with bath), 5 suites. A/C
$ Rates: High season, $30–$34 double; $35–$45 suite. Low season, $25 double.
This hotel south of the zócalo, half a block west of Melgar, claims that you'll feel as "comfortable as in your own home." That depends on where you live, but you'll admire its cleanliness, helpful staff, and small, manicured garden. Suites include a living room, bedroom, and kitchen, with refrigerator and utensils.

WHERE TO EAT

There are cheap ways to eat well in Cozumel. On Calle 2 Norte, half a block in from the waterfront, is the **Panificadora Cozumel,** excellent for a do-it-yourself breakfast or for picnic supplies. It's open daily from 6am to 9pm.

MEALS FOR LESS THAN $5

FRUTAS SELECTAS, THE CORNER STORE, Calle 15 Sur at Salas. Tel. 2-1078.
Specialty: FRUIT/PASTRIES.
$ Prices: Fruit salad $2; sandwiches $1.25; fruit shakes $2.50; coffee 75¢.
Open: Daily 8am–9pm.
Just a few steps from the Hotel El Marqués, the sweet smell of fruit greets you as you enter. Juices, liquados, "the best coffee in town," yogurt, sandwiches, salads, fruit shakes, and pastries are served at the counter with space enough for six stools, which are nearly always occupied. It's two blocks south on Melgar to Rosales; turn left and the restaurant is at the next corner.

DELIKATESSEN & DELI'S CAFE, Av. 10 Sur. Tel. 2-0458.
Specialty: INTERNATIONAL.
$ Prices: Cookies 50¢; sandwiches $2.75–$5; salads $1.75–$3.
Open: Mon–Sat 9am–9pm.
Like a cozy neighborhood bakery, here there are a few tables where you can sit and enjoy a sandwich, salad, or dessert. It's a great place for picnic fixings. Whole-wheat bread is baked fresh daily, as are the oatmeal and chocolate-chip cookies, cheesecake, brownies, and, well—everything. It's between Salas and Calle 3 Sur, two blocks south of the zócalo.

COCINA ECONÓMICA MI CHABELITA, Av. 10 Sur. Tel. 2-0896.
Specialty: MEXICAN.
$ Prices: Breakfast $1.75–$3.50; main courses $2.50–$5.
Open: Daily 7am–9pm.
This informal eatery catering to locals is a great place for a filling but economical meal (thus the name—"economical kitchen"). Breakfast features omelets and traditional Yucatecan eggs motuleño style, or enchiladas verdes or mole, and quesadillas. There's fresh orange and carrot juice, but the coffee is instant, unless you ask for *café de olla*, which is brewed and flavored with cinnamon. At lunch and dinner the menu offers tacos, liver and onions, steak and potatoes, fried fish, and soup. It's between Calle 1 Sur and Salas, 1½ blocks south of the zócalo.

MEALS FOR LESS THAN $10

PLAZA LEZA, Calle 1 Sur no. 6. Tel. 2-1041.
Specialty: MEXICAN.
$ Prices: Appetizers $4–$8; main courses $3.50–$16.
Open: Daily 7:30am–11pm.

Conveniently located on the south side of the plaza, this restaurant is great for people-watching. The prices are a bit high, but the breakfasts are excellent. It's most popular in the evening because of its ideal people-watching location.

THE SPORTS PAGE, Av. 5 Norte at Calle 2 Norte. Tel. 2-1199.
  Specialty: AMERICAN.
$ Prices: Breakfast $1.75–$3.50; appetizers $2.50–$6; main courses $4.50–$26; hamburgers $4.50–$6.50.
  Open: Daily 9am–11pm.

Though Mexican owned, it's very American right down to the Stateside-tasting hamburgers and fries, satellite TV antenna to catch U.S. sports action, and U.S. team pennants and T-shirts on the walls. The menu, too, caters to Americans, with luxury nachos, burgers, fajitas, tacos, lobster, steak, and sandwiches. A block north of the zócalo, it's air-conditioned, and prices are in dollars.

SANTIAGO'S GRILL, Calle A. Rosado Salas and Av. 15 Sur. Tel. 2-0175 or 2-2137.
  Specialty: MEXICAN/GRILLED MEAT. **Reservations:** Recommended.
$ Prices: Appetizers $4.50; main courses $4.50–$10.
  Open: Dinner only, daily 5–11pm.

Talk about popular! The crowd willingly waits in line because the word has spread that this patio restaurant serves great food at great prices. Get there early—it's usually packed. Even though they've added tables, the demand exceeds supply. The specialties of grilled seafood and meat, plus Mexican specialties such as fajitas, come with baked potato and vegetables. Santiago himself frequently presides over the grill, and he always bustles about to ensure your satisfaction.

From the zócalo, walk one block south on Avenida 10 Sur to Rosado Salas and turn left; the restaurant is one block down on the left corner.

MEALS FOR LESS THAN $15

LAS PALMERAS, Avs. Juárez and Rafael Melgar. Tel. 2-0532.
  Specialty: MEXICAN/SEAFOOD.
$ Prices: Appetizers $3–$8; main courses $4.50–$15.
  Open: Daily 7am–11pm.

With its prime location—on the zócalo, opposite the passenger-ferry pier—this is easily the busiest restaurant in town. Service and food are good. The tables are shaded from the sun and open to the four winds. It's perfect for breakfast, lunch, dinner, or a late-night snack.

CARLOS 'N' CHARLIE'S, Av. Melgar 1. Tel. 2-0191.
  Specialty: MEXICAN.
$ Prices: Appetizers $6–$7; main courses $8–$17.
  Open: Mon–Sat 9am–midnight, Sun 5pm–midnight.

As always with this popular chain of restaurants, the emphasis is on good clean fun *and* consistently good—but expensive—food. In Cancún the beat is loud and lively; you hear it before you see it on the second floor. There's a moose head over the stairs and the ceiling is full of T-shirts and auto tags. Menu offerings include spaghetti, barbecued ribs, Yucatecan specialties, crêpes, tacos, steak, and fish. The restaurant faces Avenida Melgar 1½ blocks north of the zócalo, between Calles 2 and 4 Norte.

TAVERNA GATTO PARDO, Av. 10 Sur no. 124 Tel. 2-2259.
  Specialty: ITALIAN/MEXICAN.
$ Prices: Appetizers $3–$10; main courses $5.50–$12; pizza $6–$10.
  Open: Dinner only, daily 4–11pm.

The minute you step inside the door, the light aroma of garlic and oregano exudes the aroma of Italian cooking. It's cozy and casual, with low lighting and glossy wood tables and benches. Mugs and doodads hang from the rafters, and there's a stone waterfall on the open patio. The menu includes a range of pastas and pizzas, as well as a combination plate of lasagne, strombolli, and spaghetti; homemade garlic rolls and Mexican specialties, too.

From the zócalo, walk half a block on Avenida 10 Sur, crossing Calle 1 Sur; the restaurant is on the left before Calle Rosado Salas.

PIZZA ROLANDI, Ave. Melgar between Calle 6 and 8 Norte.
   Specialty: ITALIAN.
$ Prices: Appetizers $3.50–$5.50; main courses $7; pizza $7–$8.
   Open: Mon–Sat 11:30am–11:30pm.
Deck chairs and glossy wood tables make the inviting interior garden a restful place in daytime and romantic with candlelight at night. One of seven pizzas on the menu, the Four Seasons pizza, is 8 inches in diameter and serves one person well: It comes topped with black olives, tomatoes, asparagus, cheese, and ham. The Rolandi is four blocks north of the zócalo on Melgar, facing the Caribbean.

WORTH THE EXTRA BUCKS

CAFE DEL PUERTO, Av. Melgar 3. Tel. 2-0316.
   Specialty: INTERNATIONAL.
$ Prices: Appetizers $8–$10; main courses $12–$36.
   Open: Dinner only, daily 5–11pm.
If you want a romantic dinner with a sunset view, try this restaurant, to the left on the corner of the zócalo, opposite the passenger ferry pier. After being greeted at the door, climb the spiral staircase to the main dining room or continue to a higher loft, overlooking the rest of the dining room. Soft piano music entertains in the background. The service is polished and polite, and the menu sophisticated, with choices like mustard steak flambé and shrimp brochette with bacon and pineapple.

READERS RECOMMEND

The Lobster House, Av. Melgar, north of the town center. "*The Lobster House was the most romantic restaurant we have ever been in. No more than six candlelit tables are nestled in a South Pacific–type hut, complete with a thatch roof. Everything about the ambience was intimate, and the service was perfect. You select the lobster tail of your choice, which is then weighed. The side dishes were simple but well prepared. The lobster is expensive: two dinners—medium/small-size lobster tails, no wine, small portions—cost about $40 U.S.*"—Victoria Cotrell, Pittsburgh, Penna.

5. AKUMAL TO TULUM

Of the fledgling resorts south of Playa del Carmen, Akumal is perhaps the most developed, with pricey resort hotels and bungalows scattered among the graceful palms that line the beautiful, soft beach. The beautiful bay here is great for snorkeling. But the beach south of the ancient Maya port city of Tulum is also good. Beach bums flock down the Punta Allen Peninsula south of Tulum, where the generator shuts down at 10pm (if there is one). A few beach cabañas now have reliable power, telephones, and hot showers. If the offbeat beach life is what you're after, grab it now before it disappears. You'll also enjoy a swim in the nearby lagoon of Xel-ha, one of the coast's prettiest spots.

The impressive Maya ruins at Cobá, deep in the jungle, are a worthy detour from your route south. You don't need to stay overnight to see the ruins, but there are a few hotels.

EN ROUTE SOUTH FROM PLAYA DEL CARMEN   Bus transportation from Playa del Carmen south is no longer as chancy, but it's still not great. Buses travel fairly frequently between Playa and Chetumal, stopping at every point of interest along the way. There's even bus service to and from Cobá once a day. There are four bus companies in Playa. Though buses originate here, you may be told that you can't buy tickets ahead of time. Ask the price anyway and make sure the bus driver doesn't overcharge you. (Get into the habit of asking for receipts.) A taxi will demand an unbelievable $70 for a day of driving to Xcaret, Xel-ha, Tulum, and Cobá. If you choose to leave the driving to someone else, be sure to find a driver you like; remember, you'll be with him all day.

XCARET

Xcaret is a magical place with a touch of Maya romance. But the bulldozers are busy carving roads in the woods, so it won't last long. Get there soon.

Xcaret is 5 miles south of Playa del Carmen. At the turnoff there's a nice little **restaurant** on the left. A mile in from the highway brings you to the **Rancho Xcaret,** a turkey farm. Pay the admission of $1 and walk eastward toward the sea along a path. Soon you'll see a clearing of preserved little **Maya temples,** and then get a glimpse of the sea.

At the end of the path is a narrow inlet (*caleta*) bright with sun and flashing with tropical fish. The inlet has already been discovered by snorkelers, who come on foot or in boats, and by one intrepid restaurateur who has built a large palapa hut. The menu is limited, but it's nice to have a beer and quesadillas while looking out over the tropical inlet.

Before the restaurant you'll see a sign to the cenote, only a few dozen yards away. Here in the grotto, you'll find the slightly salty water is as clear as glass, and as warm as a bath. It has been discovered by tourists, but most people prefer the beautiful lagoon.

PAMUL

Some 60 miles south of Cancún, 10 miles south of Xcaret, and half a mile east of the highway is Pamul, a safe cove for swimming and a delightful place for leaving the world behind.

WHAT TO DO

An American PADI-certified dive instructor moved to Pamul a few years ago and opened a fully equipped **dive shop** next to the cabañas. He takes guests on dives 5 miles in either direction. The cost per dive is $18 if you have your own equipment or $28 if you rent.

The **snorkeling** is excellent in this protected bay and the one next to it.

WHERE TO STAY & EAT

CABAÑAS PAMUL, km 85 Cancún–Tulum (Apdo. Postal 83, Playa del Carmen, Q. Roo 77710). Tel. 99/25-9422 in Mérida. 7 bungalows (all with bath), 17 trailer spaces (12 with full hookups).

$ Rates: High season, $35 single; $40 double; trailer $8. Low season $23 single; $26 double.

When you reach this isolated, relaxing hotel you'll see coral and white beachfront bungalows, with covered porches, steps away from the Caribbean. Each cabaña has two double beds, tile floors, rattan furniture, ceiling fans, a hot-water shower, and evening electricity. A small, reasonably priced restaurant by the office serves excellent meals and reasonably priced beer and soft drinks. But bring some nonperishable snacks and bottled drinks—you're miles from stores and other restaurants.

The Pamul turnoff is clearly marked on the highway. By bus, ask the driver to let you off. It's a mile or so on a straight, narrow, paved road to the cabañas.

EN ROUTE TO AKUMAL

About 65 miles south of Cancún and a short distance south of Pamul, you'll come to the new classy development of **Puerto Aventuras,** way out of our budget range.

But the **Museo Cedam** here is worth a stop. Cedam means Center for the Study of Aquatic Sports of Mexico, and the museum houses the history of diving on this coast from pre-Hispanic times to the present. Besides dive-related memorabilia there are displays of pre-Hispanic pottery, figures, and copper bells found in the cenote of Chichén-Itzá, shell fossils, and sunken-ship contents. It's open Wednesday through Monday from 11am to 1pm and 2 to 7pm. If you're hungry, there's a branch of Carlos 'N' Charlies here.

AKUMAL

Continuing on the highway a short distance, you come to Akumal, one of Mexico's stars in Caribbean tourism. Signs point the way in from the highway, and the white arched Akumal gateway is less than half a mile toward the sea. The resort complex here consists of three distinct establishments (all out of our budget range) which share the same wonderful, smooth palm-lined beach that's superb for snorkeling and protected by a breakwater.

WHAT TO DO

You don't have to be a guest here to enjoy the beach, **snorkel** in the beautiful clear bay, and eat at the restaurants. It's an excellent place to spend a day while on a trip down the coast. Besides the excellent snorkeling, ask at the reception desk about **horseback rides** to Chemuyil ($30) and a tour of the Sian Ka'an Biosphere Reserve ($89).

WHERE TO STAY

HOTEL-CLUB AKUMAL CARIBE VILLAS MAYA, km 63 Cancún–Tulum Hwy. 71 rms (all with bath). A/C TV TEL
$ Rates: High season, $92 single or double; $75 bungalow. Low season, $80 single or double; $60 bungalows.
The white arches you drive under (clearly visible from Highway 307) and the entry are not impressive, but the lodging varieties are. The 48 spacious bungalows have beautiful tile floors and comfortable, fashionable furniture, all with fully equipped kitchens. The 21 rooms in the new three-story beachfront hotel are similarly furnished but with small kitchens (no stove), a king-size or two queen-size beds, pale tile floors, and stylish Mexican accents. The hotel has its own pool separate from other facilities on the grounds. The setting is truly relaxing.
Reservations: P.O. Box 13326, El Paso, TX 79950 (tel. 915/584-3552, or toll free 800/351-1622 in the U.S., outside Texas; 800/343-1440 in Canada).

CHEMUYIL & XCACEL

Next down the highway (70 miles south of Cancún) is the beach and trailer park at **Chemuyil,** developed by the government as "the most beautiful beach in the world," or so says the sign on the highway. It is truly beautiful, with deep drifting sand and towering palms. Though sleepy and deserted in summer, it's active in winter, with a snack bar, free medical clinic, and an admission fee of $1.50 per adult (children under 12, free).

Xcacel is 1½ miles south of Chemuyil and a quarter of a mile east of the highway. It's a gorgeous palm-shaded place where you can pitch your tent or park your van for $1.50 per person per night, including use of changing rooms, toilets, and showers. There's a lively restaurant here as well, but you can cook out in a portable grill (yours) as long as you don't do it on the beach.

XEL-HA

The Caribbean coast of the Yucatán is carved by the sea into hundreds of small *caletas* (coves) that form the perfect habitat for tropical marine life, both flora and fauna. Many caletas remain undiscovered and pristine along the coast, but

Xel-Ha, 8 miles south of Akumal, is enjoyed daily by snorkelers and scuba divers who come to luxuriate in its warm waters, palm-lined shore, and brilliant fish. Xel-ha (pronounced "*Shell*-hah") is a bit of paradise for swimming, with no threat of undertow or pollution. Being close to the ruins at Tulum makes Xel-ha the best place for a dip when you've finished clambering around the Maya castles.

The short 8-mile hop north from Tulum to Xel-ha is possible to do by bus. When you get off at the junction for Tulum, ask the restaurant owner when the next buses come by. Otherwise you may have to wait as much as 2 hours on the highway. Most tour companies from Cancún or Cozumel include a trip to Tulum and a swim at Xel-ha in the same journey.

The entrance to Xel-ha is half a mile in from the highway. You'll be asked to pay a $3.50-per-person "contribution" to the upkeep and preservation of the site. Children under 12 are admitted free.

Once in the park, you can rent snorkeling equipment for $7 and an underwater camera for $20. You can also buy an outrageously priced drink or a meal, change clothes, and take showers. When you swim, be careful to observe the SWIM HERE and NO SWIMMING signs. (The greatest variety of fish can be seen right near the ropes marking off the "No Swimming" areas, and near any groups of rocks.) Xel-ha is an exceptionally beautiful place!

Just south of the Xel-ha turnoff on the west side of the highway, don't miss the **Maya ruins** of ancient Xel-ha.

6. TULUM, PUNTA ALLEN & SIAN KA'AN

To get your bearings, think of **Tulum** as four distinct areas: (1) First, there's the junction of Highway 307 and the Tulum access road, where you'll find two small hotels, two restaurants, and a Pemex gas station. (2) Second, on Highway 307, about 1½ miles past the Tulum junction, is the Mexican village of Tulum. (3) Third, a turn at the Tulum junction (before the Tulum village) and by the restaurants (mentioned above) will take you half a mile to the ruins of Tulum and a collection of small restaurants, snack shops, and souvenir stands; enter the ruins here. And (4) fourth, the road past the Tulum ruins parking lot heads south along the narrow **Punta Allen Peninsula,** to Boca de Paila, a portion of the **Sian Ka'an Biosphere Reserve,** and Punta Allen, the lobster-fishing village at the tip end. Though most of this 30-mile-long peninsular stretch of potholed road is uninhabited, there are several rustic inns on a fabulous beach, south of the ruins.

TULUM ARCHEOLOGICAL SITE

At the end of the Classic Period in A.D. 900 the Maya civilization began to decline and most of the large ceremonial centers were deserted. During the Postclassic Period (A.D. 900 to the Spanish Conquest), small rival states developed with a few imported traditions from the Mexicans. Tulum is one such city-state, 8 miles south of Xel-ha. The Maya seaport was built in the 10th century as a fortress overlooking the Caribbean. Aside from the spectacular setting, Tulum is not otherwise an impressive city. There are no magnificent pyramidal structures as are found in the Classic Maya ruins.

The most imposing building in Tulum is the large stone structure on the cliff called the **Castillo (castle),** actually a temple as well as a fortress, once covered with stucco and painted. From on top of the Castillo you get a good view of the limestone city walls. In front of the Castillo are several unrestored palacelike buildings partially covered with stucco. And on the beach below, where the Maya once came ashore, tourists frolic, combining a visit to the ruins with a dip in the Caribbean.

The **Temple of the Frescoes,** directly in front of the Castillo, contains interesting 13th-century wall paintings inside the temple: The lighting is bad, so use a flashlight. Distinctly Maya, they represent the rain god Chac and Ix Chel, the goddess of the moon and medicine. On the cornice of this temple is a relief of the head of a god. If you get a slight distance from the building you will see the eyes, nose, mouth, and chin. Notice the remains of the red-painted stucco on this building—at one time all the buildings at Tulum were painted a bright red.

Much of what we know of Tulum at the time of the Spanish Conquest comes from the writings of Diego de Landa, third bishop of Yucatán. He wrote that Tulum was a small city inhabited by about 600 people, who lived in dwellings situated on platforms along a street and supervised the trade traffic from Honduras to the Yucatán. Tulum survived about 70 years after the Conquest, when it was finally abandoned.

Admission is $3.50, and there's an extra fee to use a video camera. The site is open daily from 8am to 5pm.

WHERE TO STAY & EAT

MOTEL EL CRUCERO, Tulum junction (Apdo. Postal 4), Tulum, Q. Roo. 16 rms (all with bath).

$ Rates: High season, $12 single; $16 double. Low season, $8 single; $12 double. This motel has a very good and festive restaurant, where meals cost $3.50 to $10, and beer runs $1.25. The guest rooms, however, are quite basic; they have fans and may have hot water. There's also a tiny "convenience store." It's at the junction of Highway 307 and the Tulum access road.

HOTEL ACUARIO, km 127 Hwy. 307 (Apdo. Postal 80), Tulum, Q. Roo. Tel. 988/4-4856 in Cancún. 12 rms (all with bath). A/C TV

$ Rates: $30 single or double.

Felipe and Marta Ramírez own this up-and-coming road house that began as a restaurant at the junction of Highway 307 and the Tulum access road. They've added 12 very nice hotel rooms and a pool in back of the restaurant, and there's more abuilding. Plus there's a video bar and laundry service.

The **Restaurant El Faisan y Venado,** which faces the highway in front of the hotel, is similar to that at Crucero (across the street) in price and menu.

SOUTH OF THE RUINS/PUNTA ALLEN PENINSULA

About 3 miles south of the ruins the pavement ends and becomes a narrow, sandy road, with many potholes during the rainy season. Beyond this point is a 30-mile-long peninsula called Punta Allen, split in two at a cut called **Boca Paila,** where a bridge connects the two parts of the peninsula and the Caribbean enters a large lagoon on the right. It is included in the far eastern edge of the 1.3-million-acre Sian Ka'an Biosphere Reserve (see below). Along this road you'll find several cabaña-type inns all on beautiful beaches facing the Caribbean. Taxis from the ruins can take you to most of these, then you can find a ride back to the junction at the end of your stay.

WHAT TO SEE & DO

Besides **lazing** and self-directed **birding** expeditions, between June and August (July is best) **sea turtles nest** on the beaches along here. Alfonso Herrera and wife María Guadalupe Breseño, local residents who live at Rancho Kan Zuul next to the Cabañas Tulum, are state employees hired to protect the nests (*nido* in Spanish) and see that the hatchlings, 45 days later, have a safe journey to the sea. They protect around 1,500 nests of three different turtles a season, with an average of 90 to 170 eggs each. It takes the turtles about 90 exhausting minutes to dig the nest with back flippers, and tourists can watch. But please, no flash pictures or flashlights! Light disorients the turtles, making them switch directions and upset the laborious nesting process. The turtles lumber ashore at night, usually between 10pm and 3am. If you participate, a tip to the family would be courteous.

SIAN KA'AN BIOSPHERE RESERVE Down the peninsula a few miles south of the ruins you'll pass the guard house of the Sian Ka'an Biosphere Reserve, which in 1986 set aside 1.3 million acres to preserve tropical forests, savannas and mangroves, coastal and marine habitats, and 70 miles of the coastal reefs. The area is home to jaguar, puma, ocelot, margay, jaguarundi, spider and howler monkeys, tapir, white-lipped and collared peccary, manatee, brocket and white-tailed deer, crocodiles, and green, loggerhead, hawksbill, and leatherback sea turtles. It also protects 366 species of birds, including ocellated turkey, great cureasow, parrots, toucans and trogons, white ibis, roseate spoonbill, jabiru stork, wood stork, flamingo, and 15 species of herons, egrets, and bitterns. It's separated into three parts: a Core Zone, restricted to research; a Buffer Zone, where visitors and families already living there have restricted use; and a Cooperation Zone, outside the reserve proper but vital to its preservation. If you drive on Highway 307 from Tulum to an imaginary line just below the Bahía (bay) of Espiritu Santo, all you'll see on the Caribbean side is the reserve; but except at the ruins of Muyil (see "En Route to Felipe Carrillo Puerto," below), there's no access. At least 22 archeological sites have been charted within Sian Ka'an.

The best place to sample the reserve is the Punta Allen Peninsula, part of the Buffer Zone. The inns were already in place when the reserve was created. Of these only the Caphe Ha Guest House (mentioned below) offers trips for birding. But anywhere here, bring your own binoculars and birding books and have at it—the birdlife is rich.

At the Boca Paila bridge you can often find fishermen who'll take you into the lagoon on the landward side, where you can fish and see plenty of birdlife; but it's unlikely the boatman will know bird names in English or Spanish. Birding is best just after dawn, especially during the April through July nesting season.

Day trips to the Sian Ka'an are led from Cozumel (see Section 4, above) and by a biologist from the Friends of Sian Ka'an in Cancún. For more information about the reserve or trip reservations, contact them at: Plaza America, Avenida Cobá 5, 3a Piso, Suite 48-50, Cancún, Q. Roo 77500 (telephone 988/4-9583; fax 988/7-3080).

WHERE TO STAY & EAT

Lodgings here vary in quality: Some are quite comfortable, but simple, while others are a lot like camping out. One or two have electricity for a few hours in the evening; most don't have hot water. The first one is a half mile south of the ruins and the farthest one is 15½ miles. Bring plenty of mosquito repellent and mosquito netting, and a flashlight.

CABAÑAS ZAZIL KIN DON ARMANDO, Apdo. Postal 44, Tulum, Q. Roo. Tel. 987/2-1633. 24 bungalows (none with bath).
$ Rates: High season, $12 single or double; low season, $10 single or double. $10 deposit for bedding, key, and flashlight.

A casual place, the stick-walled bungalows are spread over the large beach, mingled with clotheslines flapping with guests' laundry and a restaurant that's notably good. These basic bungalows have a bed on a concrete slab, sheets, a blanket, and occasional mosquito netting, but electricity only in the restaurant. (Bring your own soap, towel, and mosquito netting.) Some of the bungalows have no windows or ventilation, except through the cracks, unless the door is open. There are separate bath facilities for men and women. The friendly, English-speaking owners also run the restaurant. An average meal of chicken, beans, and rice costs $4. It's half a mile south of the Tulum ruins; the sign says ZAZIL KIN.

EL PARAÍSO, Punta Allen Peninsula, km 1 (Apdo. Postal 61), Tulum, Q. Roo. Tel. 987/2-2001 in Cozumel. Fax 987/2-1717. 10 rms (all with bath).
$ Rates: High season, $40 single or double; low season, $23 single or double.

Completely rebuilt after Hurricane Gilbert, it looks a little like a motel. Painted a pleasing pale apricot, the row of cement-walled rooms is closer to the road than to the Caribbean, although the splendid, palm-studded beach and water are close, but farther back on the property. Each room comes with fans, tile floors, two double beds and no bedspreads, hot water, and electricity from 5 to 10:30pm. The rooms are linked by a breezy covered common porch set with comfy chairs. The new, moderately priced restaurant is near the water. The hotel communicates with

Cozumel and Tulum by radio and can call a taxi or receive reservations. It's half a mile south of the Tulum ruins, immediately beyond Cabañas Don Armando.

CABAÑAS SIAN KA'AN OSHO OASIS, Apdo. Postal 99, Tulum, Q. Roo.
20 rms (1 with bath).

$ Rates: Low season, $35 single or double; high season, to be established.
This was formerly the Cabañas Chac Mool, but new owners took over in 1990 and made many improvements. The large, round bungalows are made of stucco and rock, and have thatch roofs and stone floors. All units come with one or two beds suspended from the ceiling and draped with mosquito netting. Screened windows let in cross breezes. Despite its rustic sound, there's an edge of romance to the bungalows and this is one of the most popular places in the area. There are separate shower and bath facilities for men and women, hot water, and electricity between 6:30 and 11pm (bring a flashlight anyway). The restaurant, a huge, round palapa-covered building, serves vegetarian food. Breakfast costs $5; lunch or dinner, $8. The new owners are making many changes, including adding bathrooms to some of the bungalows. Turtles nest on the beach here between June and September. It's 2 miles south of the Tulum ruins.

CABAÑAS LOS ARRECIFES, Punta Allen Peninsula, km 6, Tulum, Q. Roo.
12 huts (8 with bath).

$ Rates: $11 double without bath, $20 double with bath.
This is the most rustic of rustic in the most gorgeous setting of palm-studded drifting sand on the peninsula. The thatch-roofed, stick-walled huts are scattered over the enormous property stretching to the Caribbean. A row of cinderblock rooms is more conventional and these have private baths. There are four shared showers and two toilets. Since there are few guests, it's a lot like being on a private island. Of course there's no electricity or hot water; bring your own drinking water, mosquito netting, candles, and flashlights. There's no restaurant in the off-season, but be prepared for no restaurant in season either—this is a very loose operation. Two restaurants are half a mile away (see below). It's 3½ miles south of the Tulum ruins.

RESTAURANT Y CABAÑAS ANA Y JOSE, Apdo. Postal 80, Tulum, Q. Roo.
Tel. 988/4-9732 or 4-9743 in Cancún. Fax 988/4-7248. 8 rms (all with bath).

$ Rates: $25–$35 single or double.
Four miles south of the Tulum ruins, it started as a restaurant and blossomed into a comfortable inn on the beach. All cabañas have tile floors, two double beds, a cold-water shower, and little patios. The rock-walled cabañas in front are a little larger, some facing the beautiful wide beach just a few yards off. The only drawback is the lack of cross-ventilation in some of the rooms, which can be uncomfortable at night without electricity and fans. Ocean swimming is unsafe since it's on the open sea and subject to dangerous undertows.

The excellent, screened-in restaurant with sand floors under a palapa is open daily from 8am to 10pm. Fish dishes range from $5 to $10, with lobster at $14 in season. Breakfast costs $2 to $4.

CABAÑAS TULUM, Punta Allen Peninsula km 7, Tulum, Q. Roo.
16 rms (all with bath).

$ Rates: High season, $26 single or double; low season, $22 single or double.
Next door to Anna and José's (above), 4 miles south of the Tulum ruins, is a row of bungalows facing a heavenly stretch of ocean and beach; the heavy undertow and pounding surf make swimming unsafe though. Each bungalow includes a cold-water shower, two double beds, screens on the windows (but some have holes), a fan, a table, one electric light, and a veranda where you can hang a hammock. Battered by the hurricane, it's a bit run-down now, but still comfortable. The electricity is on from 6:30 to 10:30pm only, so bring candles or a flashlight. A small restaurant serves beer, soft drinks, and all three meals for reasonable prices. The cabañas are often full between December 15 and Easter, and July and August, so make reservations.

Worth the Extra Bucks

CAPHE HA GUEST HOUSE. 2 rms (1 with bath).

$ Rates (including breakfast and dinner): $75 single; $150–$200 double.

This secluded guesthouse, owned by Sue Brown Baker, is set in a dense coconut-palm grove on a long, fabulous palm-lined beach. There are no restaurants, other inns, or telephones nearby. Lodging is in two mosquito-proof, solar-powered, one-bedroom cottages and a main house; one cottage has a private bath and one is shared with the main house. Rates include as many guided fishing, diving, and birding excursions as guests want. Guests have the run of the main house, and everyone usually pitches in to help with the family-style meals. During the rainy season the potholes are full of water, so allow ample time to arrive before 3pm "mosquito time," as Baker suggests.

To get here from the parking lot of the Tulum ruins, follow the road down the coast. After about 1½ miles the road becomes sand with many potholes. Follow it for about 15 miles (about an hour). When you cross a bridge (Boca Paila), set your odometer. In 3 miles you'll see two posts on the left, the entrance to Caphe Ha.

Reservations: Calle 51 no. 478, Mérida, Yuc. 97000 (tel. 99/21-3404; for information/reservations in the U.S.; Jeff Frankel in New York, (212/219-2198).

EN ROUTE TO COBÁ

About a mile south of the turnoff to Tulum on Highway 307 is the road to Cobá, another fascinating Maya city. Less than a mile past the Cobá road is Tulum village, with little to offer the tourist. If you're driving, turn right when you see the signs to Cobá and continue on that road for 40 miles. When you reach the village, proceed straight until you see the lake and the road curves right; go left. The entrance to the ruins is at the end of that road past some small restaurants.

---

7. COBÁ

105 miles South of Cancún, 40 miles S of the Tulum turnoff.

GETTING THERE & DEPARTING By Bus From Playa del Carmen a bus leaves at 6:30am and noon stopping in Tulum and Cobá and continuing to Valladolid. Two buses leave Valladolid for Cobá at 4:30am and 1:15pm, but they may fill early, so buy tickets as soon as possible. Several buses a day leave Cobá: at 6:30am and 3pm a bus goes to Tulum and Playa del Carmen, and at 6:30pm there's a bus to Valladolid.

The highway into Cobá becomes one main paved street through town, which passes the Bocaditos Restaurant and Hotel on the right (see "Where to Stay and Eat," below), and goes a block to the lake. If you turn right at the lake you reach the Villas Arqueológicas a block farther. Turning left will lead past a couple of informal/primitive restaurants on the left facing the lake, and to the ruins, straight ahead, the equivalent of a block. The village is small and poor, gaining little from visitors passing through to see the ruins. Used clothing (especially for children) would be a welcome gift.

SEEING THE RUINS

The Maya built many breathtaking cities in Yucatán, but few were grander than Cobá—however, much of the site is unexcavated. Linked to important cities many miles distant by excellent, straight roads through the jungle, Cobá covered many square miles on the shores of two Yucatecan lakes.

Once in the site, keep your bearings, as it's very easy to get lost on the maze of dirt roads in the jungle.

The **Grupo Cobá** boasts a large, impressive pyramid near the entry gate to the right. Were you to go straight, you'd pass near the ruined **juego de pelota (ball court).**

Straight in from the entry gate, walk for 10 or 15 minutes to a fork in the road. Left and right you'll notice jungle-covered, unexcavated pyramids. The left fork leads to the **Nohoch Mul** group, which contains **El Castillo**, the tallest pyramid in the Yucatán (taller than the great El Castillo at Chichén-Itzá and the Pyramid of the Magician at Uxmal). Climb to the top and you can see unexcavated, jungle-covered pyramidal structures poking up through the forest all around—ah, if only there were money for research! The right fork (more or less straight on) goes to the **Conjunto Las Pinturas.** Here, the main attraction is the **Pyramid of the Painted Lintel,** a small structure with traces of the original bright colors above the door. You can climb up to get a close look.

Throughout the area, intricately carved stelae stand by pathways, or lie forlornly in the jungle underbrush.

Because of the heat, visit Cobá in the morning, or after the heat of the day has passed. Mosquito repellent and comfortable shoes are imperative. This is a birder's paradise, so bring your binoculars.

Admission is $3.50 (children under 12 and adults over 60, free). The site is open daily from 8am to 5pm.

WHERE TO STAY & EAT

EL BOCADITO, Calle Principal, Cobá, Q. Roo. 9 rms (all with bath).
$ Rates: $8 single; $10 double.

El Bocadito, on the right as you enter the town, could take advantage of being the only game in town besides the much more expensive Villas Arqueológicas—but it doesn't. Next to the hotel's restaurant by the same name, the rooms are arranged in two rows facing an open patio. They're simple, with tile floors, two double beds (no bedspreads), ceiling fan, and wash basin separate from the toilet and cold-water shower cubicle. It's agreeable enough and always full by nightfall, so to secure a room, arrive no later than 3pm. The owner was planning to add rooms in 1991. The clean, open-air restaurant has good meals at reasonable prices, served by a friendly, efficient staff. Bus loads of tour groups stop here at lunch (always a sign of approval). I enjoy Bocadito's casual atmosphere and there's a bookstore with English-language books and a gift shop adjacent to the restaurant.

VILLA ARQUEOLÓGICA COBÁ, Cobá, Q. Roo. Tel. 5/203-3086 in Mexico City, or toll free 800/258-2633 in the U.S. 44 rms (all with bath). A/C
$ Rates: Low season, $54 single; $56 double. High season, approximately 40% more. Stateside bookings prepay the daily rate and 10% service charge; the 15% tax is collected at the Villa. Rates above include all the charges.

Operated by Club Med, but nothing like Club Med villages, this lovely lakeside hotel is a 5-minute walk from the ruins; at the end of the road through the village, turn right and the hotel is straight ahead. The hotel has a French polish and the restaurant is top-notch, though expensive. Breakfast costs $12; lunch or dinner, $25. The rooms, built around a plant-filled courtyard and beautiful swimming pool, are stylish and soothingly comfortable. The hotel also has a library of books on Mesoamerican archeology (with books in French, English, and Spanish). Make reservations; this hotel fills with touring groups.

EN ROUTE TO FELIPE CARRILLO PUERTO

From the Cobá turnoff, the main Highway 307 heads southwest through Tulum village. About 14 miles south of the village are the **ruins of Muyil** (approx. A.D. 1–1540) at the settlement of **Chunyaxche,** on the left-hand side. Tulane University with the Institucion Nacional de Anthrolopólogía de México has done extensive mapping and studies; however, of the 50 or so buildings, caves, and subterranean temples, only a couple of buildings have been excavated. But there's potential. Recent discoveries link this site by canal to the east coast of Yucatán at the **Boca Paila cut** (mentioned above). A French archeologist and nine companions launched boats in a nearby narrow canal and followed it through the dense jungle and mangroves to a sweetwater lagoon and finally on to Boca Paila on the Caribbean. The canal was built by the ancient Maya and there's at least one Maya ruin en route. At the moment, this excursion isn't available to the public, but since the area is in the Sian Ka'an Reserve, the Friends of Sian Ka'an (see above) may organize such trips. Note: The mosquito and dive-bombing fly population is fierce, but this is one of the best places along the coast for birding—go early in the morning.

Admission to the ruins is $1.75, free on Sunday and festival days. The site is open daily from 8am to 5pm.

After Muyil and Chunyaxche, the highway is 45 miles of jungle-bordered road.

---

8. FELIPE CARRILLO PUERTO

95 miles S of Cancún

GETTING THERE By Bus There's frequent bus service south from Cancún and Playa del Carmen.

By Car Coastal Highway 307 from Cancún leads directly here.

Essentials Telephone area code is 983. Banks here don't exchange foreign currency.

Felipe Carrillo Puerto (pop. 47,000) is a busy crossroads in the jungle along the road to Ciudad Chetumal. It has gas stations, a market, a small ice plant, a bus terminal, and a few modest hotels and restaurants.

Since the main road intersects the road back to Mérida, Carrillo Puerto is the turning point for those making a "short circuit" of the Yucatán peninsula. Highway 184 heads west from here to Ticul, Uxmal, Campeche, and Mérida.

As you spend your hour or your overnight in Carrillo Puerto, consider its strange history: This was where the rebels in the War of the Castes took their stand, guided by the "Talking Crosses." Some remnants of that town (named Chan Santa Cruz) are still extant. Look for signs in town pointing the way. For the full story, refer to Chapter 20.

ORIENTATION

The highway goes right through the town, becoming **Avenida Benito Juárez** in town. Driving from the north, you will pass a traffic circle with a bust of the great Juárez. The town **market** is here.

The directions given above assume that you will be driving. If you arrive by bus, the **bus station** is right on the zócalo. From there it's a 10-minute walk east down Calle 67, past the cathedral and banks, to Avenida Juárez. Turn left onto Juárez and you'll find the recommended restaurants, hotels, and the traffic circle I use as a reference point.

WHERE TO STAY

HOTEL-RESTAURANT EL FAISAN Y EL VENADO, Av. Juárez, Felipe Carrillo Puerto, Q. Roo. Tel. 983/4-0043. 21 rms (all with bath).
$ Rates: $8 single; $10 double.
This hotel is adjacent to the popular restaurant of the same name; go one block south from the traffic circle and it's easy to see on the left. The tidy rooms, with hot water, are plain, functional, and comfortable; eight rooms are air-conditioned while the rest have fans, and 13 have TVs. Realistic photographs of the rooms are on display in the restaurant. The restaurant is one of the townfolks' favorites. Modern, with an airy dining room looking onto the street, it's a good place for a stop if you're just passing through. Main courses run $3 to $4; it's open daily from 6am to 10pm.

HOTEL SAN IGNACIO, Av. Juárez, Felipe Carrillo Puerto, Q. Roo. Tel. 983/4-0122. 12 rms (all with bath).

$ Rates: $8 single; $10 double; $12 triple.

This small, simple hotel surrounds a parking lot, a block south of the Hotel/Restaurant El Faisan y Venado, on the left. The rooms are bright and clean, but spare in furnishings. In case the office is closed, the dueña lives next door across the back parking lot and she's thrilled to have guests. Get to bed early—this town wakes up at dawn. The Restaurant 24 Horas is practically next door.

WHERE TO EAT

Besides the popular **Faisan y Venado** (see "Where to Stay," above), there's the **Danesa Ice Cream Parlor** next door to the Restaurant 24 Horas (below).

RESTAURANT 24 HORAS, Av. Juárez. Tel. 4-0020.
Specialty: MEXICAN.
$ Prices: Breakfast $1.75–$3.50; appetizers $2–$3; main courses $2–$4.
Open: Daily 24 hours.

It's comfortable here, and open to breezes, and there's a Maya glyph picture stone on one wall. Come for breakfast—it's the only place in town open early. A full breakfast includes scrambled eggs, ham, instant coffee, and fruit. It's on the left side of Avenida Juárez, opposite the Pemex station.

9. LAGO DE BACALAR

65 miles S of Carrillo Puerto, 23 miles N of Chetumal

GETTING THERE **By Bus** Buses going south from Cancún and Playa del Carmen stop here.

By Car Signs into Bacalar are plainly visible from Highway 307.

The crystal-clear waters of Lake Bacalar are heavenly for swimming. The area is very quiet—the perfect place to relax. If you can arrange it, stopping here sure beats staying in Chetumal or Carrillo Puerto. If you're in your own car, take a detour through the village of Bacalar and down along the lakeshore drive. When you reach town, go five blocks past the *tope* and turn left. Continue to the river and turn right. Drive along marveling at the houses of Quintana Roo which were built by the rich and famous to capture the beautiful view. The hotel will be on the left a distance farther.

WHERE TO STAY

HOTEL LAGUNA, Costera de Bacalar 143, Bacalar, Q. Roo. Tel. 983/2-3517 in Chetumal, 99/27-1304 in Mérida. 22 rms, 4 bungalows (all with bath).
$ Rates: $30 single or double.

The hotel is off the beaten path (turn left off the main street and follow the lakeshore road south to the hotel), so there are almost always rooms available, except in winter when it's full of Canadians. Rooms overlook the pool and have fans and a lovely view of the lake. The water along the shore is very shallow, but you can dive from the hotel's dock into 30-foot water. The hotel's restaurant is fine, with main courses costing about $5 to $12. It's open daily from 8am to 8pm.

WHERE TO EAT

For variety, eat at the **Restaurant Cenote Azul,** a comfortable open-air thatch-roofed restaurant on the edge of the beautiful cenote. Feast on a fresh grilled-fish dinner for $5 to $8. To get there, go left out the hotel's parking lot and follow the road about a mile, bearing right, and you'll see it.

EN ROUTE TO CHETUMAL

As you approach the end of the lake, Highway 307 intersects Highway 186. Turn right and you're headed west to Escacega, Palenque, and Villahermosa; turn left and you'll be going toward Chetumal.

---

10. CHETUMAL

85 miles S of Carrillo Puerto, 23 miles S of Bacalar

GETTING THERE & DEPARTING By Plane AeroCaribe (affiliated with Mexicana) has daily flights from Cancún.

By Bus   The bus station of **Autotransportes del Caribe** (tel. 2-0740) is 20 blocks from the town center. I recommend taking a taxi.

Eight direct first-class buses a day go to **Cancún via Tulum, Playa del Carmen,** and **Puerto Morelos;** eight go to **Mérida.** With changes en route, four first-class buses a day go to **Mexico City,** and one a day goes to **Villahermosa** (a 7- to 8-hour trip).

Second-class bus service includes routes daily to **Tulum** and the coast (two buses), **Mérida** (four buses), **Campeche** (two buses), **Villahermosa** (four buses), and **San Andrés Tuxtla, Veracruz, and Mexico City** (one bus). Sixteen second-class buses run to and from Bacalar daily.

To Belize: Two companies make the run from Chetumal, through Corozal and Orange Walk, to Belize City. **Batty's Bus Service** runs 10 buses per day and **Venus Bus Lines** (tel. 04/2-2132 in Corozal) has seven daily buses, the first at 11am; the 2pm bus is express with fewer stops, and a ticket to Corozal costs 90¢. Seven buses go to Belize City (tel. 02/73354 in Belize) at a cost of $4; the first leaves at 4am and the last at 10am. Though it's a short distance from Chetumal to Corozal, it may take as much as an hour and a half, depending on how long it takes the bus to pass through Customs and Immigration.

By Car   It's a 2½-mile ride from Carrillo Puerto.

ESSENTIALS   The telephone **area code** is 983. Chetumal has many **"no left turn" streets,** with hawk-eyed traffic policemen at each one. Be alert—they love to nail visitors.

Quintana Roo became a state in 1974, and Chetumal (pop. 50,000) is the capital of the new state. While Quintana Roo was still a territory, it was a free-trade zone to encourage trade and immigration between neighboring Guatemala and Belize. The old part of town, down by the river (Río Hondo), has a Caribbean atmosphere and wooden buildings, but the newer parts are modern Mexican. There is lots of noise and heat, so your best plan would be not to stay—it's not a particularly interesting or friendly town.

ORIENTATION

You'll arrive following **Obregón** into town. **Niños Héroes** is the other main cross street. When you reach it, turn left to find the hotels mentioned below.

WHERE TO STAY & EAT

HOTEL JACARANDA, Obregón 201, Chetumal, Q. Roo 77000. Tel. 983/2-1455. 40 rms (all with bath). TEL
$ Rates: $8–$10 single; $11–$13 double.
This semimodern two-story hotel is undistinguished except for its low prices; half the

rooms have air conditioners and half fans. It's located down the hill from the market, on Obregón at Niños Héroes. The restaurant, a brightly lit, Formica-furnished place has efficient service and good food at low prices.

HOTEL PRINCÍPE, Av. Niños Héroes 326, Chetumal, Q. Roo 77000. Tel. 983/2-4799 or 2-5167. Fax 983/2-5191. 51 rms (all with bath). A/C
$ Rates: $30 single; $34 double.

Located six blocks south of the bus station, between the bus station and the center of town, my favorite hotel offers nice rooms arranged around a central courtyard. The dining room has an extensive breakfast menu with dishes ranging from $1.30 to $4.

HOTEL CONTINENTAL CARIBE, Av. Niños Héroes 171, Chetumal, Q. Roo 77000. Tel. 983/2-1100 or 2-1676. 72 rms (all with bath). A/C TV TEL
$ Rates: $44 single; $48 double.

Chetumal is a town where spending more will only get you faded luxury. But if you must, this modern hotel is across from the central market, and has nice rooms and a swimming pool. The restaurant is large, and as cold as a cave. It's on the right side of Niños Héroes, in the market district; the entrance is part of a shopping center.

EN ROUTE TO VILLAHERMOSA & MÉRIDA

From Chetumal, you can cut diagonally across the peninsula to Mérida or retrace your steps to Cancún. You can also go south to Belize and even Guatemala. But if you're thinking of making the long, hot trip to Escarcega and Villahermosa, don't! It's a long, lonely, and badly maintained road. The highway is fine as long as Quintana Roo is maintaining it. But as soon as you cross the state line, ahead of you may lie more than 200km (125 miles) of the worst highway in Mexico. ZONA DE DESLAVE signs are permanent warnings to motorists that parts of the road bed are missing entirely or so badly dipped that they might cause you to lose control of the car. Experience speaks. I've heard that it has improved, but I'll never take it again; annual rains cause constant problems that maintenance can't keep up with.

APPENDIX

A. TELEPHONES & MAIL
B. BUS TERMS
C. VOCABULARY
D. MENU SAVVY

A. TELEPHONES & MAIL

USING THE TELEPHONES

In 1990 Telefonos de Mexico reduced long-distance rates by 40% and at the same time raised local rates. *Long-distance calls are still exorbitantly expensive,* especially out of the country, and now so are local calls.

Public **pay phones** for local use come in two types: In one, the slot at the top holds the 100-peso coin in a gentle grip until your party answers, then it drops; if there's no answer or a busy signal, you can pluck your coin from the slot. With the other type, you insert a coin which disappears into the bowels of the machine, and drops into the cashbox when your call goes through or into the return slot if it doesn't (after you hang up). This type of phone is often jammed, and your coin won't drop, so that when your party answers you will hear them but they won't hear you. Try from another pay phone.

For **long-distance calls** there are several ways to go: The most expensive is through a hotel switchboard, which may add a service charge to your already expensive bill. The least expensive way is to use the Ladatel phones found increasingly in bus stations, airports, and downtown public areas of major cities and tourist zones (see below). Next in cost, and often faster and more convenient, is the *caseta de larga distancia* (long-distance telephone office), found all over Mexico. Most bus stations and airports now have specially staffed rooms exclusively for making long-distance calls and sending faxes. Often they are efficient and inexpensive, providing the client with a computer printout of the time and charges. Long-distance operators are notoriously hard to reach, so no matter what method is used, the process can be time-consuming.

To call the U.S. or Canada collect, dial 09, and tell the *operadora* that you want *una llamada por cobrar* (a collect call), *telefono a telefono* (station-to-station), or *persona a persona* (person-to-person). Collect calls are the least expensive of all, but sometimes caseta offices won't make them, so you'll have to pay on the spot.

To make a long-distance call from Mexico to another country, from a caseta or Ladatel phone first dial 95 for the U.S. and Canada, or 98 for anywhere else in the world. Then, dial the area code and number you are calling. If you need the international (English-speaking) operator after all, dial 09.

To call long distance (abbreviated "lada") within Mexico, dial 91, the area code, then the number. Mexican area codes (*claves*) are listed in the front of the telephone directories, and in the hotel listings for each area in this book. For Mexico City, it's 5; for Acapulco, 74. (But area codes are changing in some places; see above.)

You can save considerably by calling in off-peak periods. The cheapest times to call are daily from 11pm to 8am, and all day Saturday and Sunday. The most expensive times are Monday through Friday from 8am to 5pm.

Long-distance **Ladatel** call stations are at major transportation terminals and other public places of importance. These special pay telephones allow you to dial direct long-distance calls to anywhere in Mexico or the world, at reasonable prices. To use a Ladatel phone, first, have a good supply of 100-peso coins. Next, find out the approximate rate per minute for your call by picking up the handset and punching in the long-distance code (91 for Mexico, 95 for the U.S. and Canada, 98 for the rest of the world), plus the area or country and city codes for the destination of your call. The charge per minute in pesos will appear on the LCD display. For instance, if you press 95-212, you'll get the charge per minute for a call to Manhattan. Once you know the charge per minute, count your coins or tokens, make sure you have as many as you'll need, then dial your number and insert coins. The display will keep you informed of when more coins are needed. Instructions on Ladatel phones are in Spanish, English, and French. Be patient, though; reaching an international telephone operator may take a long time.

To place a **phone call to Mexico** from your home country: dial the international service (011), then Mexico's country code (52), then the Mexican area code (for Mexico City it's 5), then the local number. Thus to call the Secretería de Turismo's information number in Mexico City, you'd dial 011-52-5-250-0123. To dial the SECTUR information office in Acapulco, you'd dial 011-52-74-82-2170.

Keep in mind that calls to Mexico are quite expensive, even if dialed direct from your home phone. As a rule of thumb, it's usually much cheaper to call Europe or the Middle East than it is to call Mexico.

The **telegraph** office may be in a different place from the post office in many cities. Telex works out to be much cheaper than long distance, but you must know the Telex number you want to call. Many businesses, particularly in the travel industry (travel agents and hotels), have Telex numbers.

The effects of reducing long-distance rates while hiking local rates means that hotels have begun to charge for local calls made from hotel room phones. Until now these calls were free. So far, most of the inexpensive hotels listed in this book do not have the equipment to track calls made from individual rooms and therefore telephone use charges are not added to the room bill. But hotels with more sophisticated telephone systems are charging 35¢ to 50¢ per call. To avoid checkout shock, ask at check-in if local calls are extra.

POSTAL GLOSSARY

Airmail Correo Aereo
Customs Aduana
General Delivery Lista de Correos
Insurance (insured mail) Seguros
Mailbox Buzon
Money Order Giro Postale
Parcel Paquete
Post Office Oficina de Correos
Post Office Box (abbreviation) Apdo. Postal
Postal Service Correos
Registered Mail Registrado
Rubber Stamp Sello
Special Delivery, Express Entrega Inmediata
Stamp Estampilla or Timbre

B. BUS TERMS

Bus	**Autobus**
Bus or truck	**Camion**
Lane	**Carril**
Nonstop	**Directo**
Baggage	**Equipajes**
Intercity	**Foraneo**
Luggage storage area	**Guarda equipaje**
Gates	**Llegadas**
Originates at this station	**Local**
Originates elsewhere; stops if seats available	**De paso**
First (class)	**Primera**
Baggage claim area	**Recibo de Equipajes**

Waiting room	**Sala de Espera**
Toilets	**Sanitarios**
Second (class)	**Segunda**
Nonstop	**Sin Escala**
Ticket window	**Taquilla**

C. VOCABULARY

Traveling on or off the beaten track, you will encounter many people in service positions who do not speak English. Many Mexican's who can understand English are embarrassed to speak it. And finally most Mexicans are very patient with foreigners who try to speak their language; it helps a lot to know a few basic phrases.

Berlitz's Latin American Spanish for Travellers, available at most bookstores for $4, cannot be recommended highly enough. But for added convenience, I've included a list of certain simple phrases for expressing basic needs, followed by some menu items presented in the same order in which they'd be found on a Mexican menu.

BASIC VOCABULARY

Good Day	**Buenos días**	bway-nohss dee-ahss
How are you?	**¿Cómo esta usted?**	koh-moh ess-tah oo-sted
Very well	**Muy bien**	mwee byen
Thank you	**Gracias**	grah-see-ahss
You're welcome	**De nada**	day nah-dah
Goodbye	**Adios**	ah-dyohss
Please	**Por favor**	pohr fah-bohr
Yes	**Sí**	see
No	**No**	noh
Excuse me	**Perdóneme**	pehr-doh-ney-may
Give me	**Déme**	day-may
Where is . . . ?	**¿Dónde esta . . . ?**	dchn-day ess-tah
the station	**la estación**	la ess-tah-see-own
a hotel	**un hotel**	oon oh-tel
a gas station	**una gasolinera**	oon-nuh gah-so-lee-nay-rah
a restaurant	**un restaurante**	oon res-tow-rahn-tay
the toilet	**el baño**	el bahn-yoh
a good doctor	**un buen médico**	oon bwayn may-dee-co
the road to	**el camino a . . .**	el cah-mee-noh ah
To the right	**A la derecha**	ah lah day-ray-chuh
To the left	**A la izquierda**	ah lah ees-ky-ehr-dah
Straight ahead	**Derecho**	day-ray-cho
I would like	**Quisiera**	keyh-see-air-ah
I want	**Quiero**	kyehr-oh
to eat	**comer**	ko-mayr
a room	**una habitación**	oon-nuh ha-bee tah-see-own
Do you have?	**¿Tiene usted?**	tyah-nay oos-ted
a book	**un libro**	oon lee-bro
a dictionary	**un diccionario**	oon deek-see-own-ar-eo
How much is it?	**¿Cuanto cuesta?**	kwahn-to kwess-tah
When?	**¿Cuando?**	kwahn-doh
What?	**¿Que?**	kay

English	Spanish	Pronunciation
There is (Is there?)	¿Hay . . .	eye
Yesterday	Ayer	ah-yer
Today	Hoy	oy
Tomorrow	Mañana	mahn-yawn-ah
Good	Bueño	bway-no
Bad	Malo	mah-lo
Better (best)	(Lo) Mejor	(loh) meh-hor
More	Más	mahs
Less	Menos	may-noss
No Smoking	Se prohibe fumar	seh pro-hee-beh foo-mahr
Postcard	Tarjeta postal	tahr-hay-ta pohs-tahl
Insect repellent	Rapellante contra insectos	rah-pey-yahn-te cohn-trah een sehk-tos

1 **uno** (ooh-noh)
2 **dos** (dohs)
3 **tres** (trayss)
4 **cuatro** (kwah-troh)
5 **cinco** (seen-koh)
6 **seis** (sayss)
7 **siete** (syeh-tay)
8 **ocho** (oh-choh)
9 **nueve** (nway-bay)
10 **diez** (dee-ess)
11 **once** (ohn-say)
12 **doce** (doh-say)
13 **trece** (tray-say)
14 **catorce** (kah-tor-say)

15 **quince** (keen-say)
16 **dieciseis** (de-ess-ee-sayss)
17 **diecisiete** (de-ess-ee-see-ay-tay)
18 **dieciocho** (dee-ess-ee-oh-choh)
19 **diecinueve** (dee-ess-ee-nway-bay)
20 **viente** (bayn-tay)
30 **treinta** (trayn-tah)
40 **cuarenta** (kwah-ren-tah)
50 **cincuenta** (seen-kwen-tah)

60 **sesenta** (say-sen-tah)
70 **setenta** (say-ten-tah)
80 **ochenta** (oh-chen-tah)
90 **noventa** (noh-ben-tah)
100 **cien** (see-en)
200 **doscientos** (dos-se-en-tos)
500 **quinientos** (keen-ee-ehn-tos)
1000 **mil** (meal)

USEFUL PHRASES

Do you speak English?	¿Habla usted inglés?
Is there anyone here who speaks English?	¿Hay alguien aquí qué hable inglés?
I speak a little Spanish.	Hablo un poco de español.
I don't understand Spanish very well.	No lo entiendo muy bien el español.
What time is it?	¿Qué hora es?
May I see your menu?	¿Puedo ver su menu?
The check please.	La cuenta por favor.
What do I owe you.	¿Cuanto lo debo?
What did you say?	¿Mande? (colloquial expression for American "Eh?")
I want (to see) a room	Quiero (ver) un cuarto (una habitación)
for two persons	para dos personas
with (without) bath.	con (sin) baño
We are staying here only one night (one week).	Nos quedaremos aqui solamente una noche (una semana).
We are leaving tomorrow.	Partimos mañana.
Do you accept traveler's checks?	¿Acepta usted cheques de viajero?
Please send these clothes to the laundry.	Hágame el favor de mandar esta ropa a la lavandería.

D. MENU SAVVY

GENERAL

almuerzo lunch
cena supper
comida dinner
desayuno breakfast
el menú the menu
la cuenta the check
cocido boiled
empanado breaded

frito fried
poco cocido rare
asado roast
bien cocido well done
milanesa breaded
veracruzana tomato and green olive sauce
entremeses hors d'oeuvres

BREAKFAST (DESAYUNO)

jugo de naranja orange juice
café con crema coffee with cream
pan tostada toast
mermelada jam
leche milk
té tea
huevos eggs
huevos cocidos hard-boiled eggs

huevos poches poached eggs
huevos fritos fried eggs
huevos pasados al agua soft-boiled eggs
huevos revueltos scrambled eggs
tocino bacon
jamón ham

LUNCH AND DINNER

ajo garlic
caldo broth
sopa soup
sopa clara consomme
sopa de lentejas lentil soup
sopa de chicharos pea soup

sopa de arroz dry rice (not soup!)
caldo de pollo chicken broth
salchichas sausages
taco filled tortilla
torta sandwich
tamales russos cabbage rolls

SEAFOOD (MARISCOS)

almejas clams
anchoas anchovies
arenques herring
atun tuna
calamares squid
camarones shrimp
caracoles snails
corvina bass
huachinango red snapper
jaiba crab
langosta lobster
lenguado sole

lobino black bass
mojarra perch
ostiones oysters
pescado fish
pez espada swordfish
robalo sea bass/snook
salmon salmon
salmón ahumado smoked salmon
sardinas sardines
solo pike
trucha arco iris rainbow trout

MEATS (CARNES)

alambre shish kebab
albóndigas meatballs
aves poultry
bistec steak
callos tripe
carne meat
carne fría cold cuts

cerdo pork
chorizo spicy sausage
chuleta chop
chuleta de carnero mutton chop
chuletas de cordero lamb chops
chuletas de puerco pork chops
conejo rabbit

cordero lamb
costillas de cerdo spareribs
faisán pheasant
filete milanesa breaded veal chops
hígado liver
jamón ham
lengua tongue
lomo loin
paloma pigeon
pato duck

pavo turkey
pechuga chicken breast
perdiz partridge
pollo chicken
res beef
riñones kidneys
ternera veal
tocino bacon
venado venison

VEGETABLES [LEGUMBRES]

aceitunas olives
aguacate avocado
arroz rice
betabeles beets
cebolla onions
champinones mushrooms
chicharos peas
col cabbage
coliflor cauliflower
ejotes string beans
elote corn (maize)
esparragos asparagus

espinaca spinach
frijoles beans
hongos mushroom
jicama potato/turnip-like vegetable
lechug lettuce
lentejas lentils
papas potatoes
pepino cucumber
rabanos radishes
tomate tomato
verduras greens, vegetables
zanahoras carrots

SALADS [ENSALADAS]

ensalada de apio celery salad
ensalada de frutas fruit salad
ensalada mixta mixed salad

ensalada de pepinos cucumber
  salad

FRUITS [FRUTAS]

chavacano apricot
ciruela prune
coco coconut
durazno peach
frambuesa raspberry
fresas con crema strawberries with
  cream
fruta cocida stewed fruit
granada pomegranate
guanabana green pear-like fruit
guayaba guava
higos figs

lima lime
limon lemon
mamey sweet orange fruit
mango mango
manzana apple
naranja orange
pera pear
piña pineapple
platano banana
tuna prickly pear fruit
uva grape
zapote sweet brown fruit

DESSERTS [POSTRES]

arroz con leche rice pudding
brunelos de fruta fruit tart
coctel de frutas fruit cocktail
compota stewed fruit
flan custard
galletas crackers or cookies

helado ice cream
nieve sherbet
pastel, torta cake or pastry
queso cheese
yogurt yogurt

BEVERAGES [BEBIDAS]

agua water
brandy brandy
café coffee

café con crema coffee with cream
café de olla coffee with cinnamon
  and sugar

café negro black coffee
cerveza beer
ginebra gin
hielo ice
jerez sherry
jugo de naranja orange juice
jugo de tomate tomato juice
jugo de toronja grapefruit juice
leche milk

manzanita apple juice
refrescos soft drinks
ron rum
sidra cider
sifon soda
té tea
vino blanco white wine
vino tinto red wine

CONDIMENTS & CUTLERY

aceite oil
azucar sugar
bolillo roll
copa goblet
cuchara spoon
cuchillo knife
manteca lard
mantequilla butter
mostaza mustard

pan bread
pimienta pepper
sal salt
sopa soup
taza cup
tenedor fork
vinagre vinegar
vaso glass

PREPARATIONS

asado roasted
cocido cooked
bien cocido well done
poco cocido rare
milanesa Italian breaded
empanado breaded
frito fried

a la parrilla grilled
al horno baked
ahumado smoked
Tampiqueño long strip of thinly
  sliced meat
Veracruzana tomato, garlic and
  onion topped

MENU GLOSSARY

Achiote: small red seed of the annatto tree.

Achiote preparada: a prepared paste found in Yucatán markets made of ground achiote, wheat and corn flour, cumin, cinnamon, salt, onion, garlic, oregano. Use mixed with juice of a sour orange or vinegar and put on broiled or charcoaled fish (tikin-chick) and chicken.

Agua fresca: fruit flavored water, usually watermelon, canteloupe, chia seed with lemon, hibiscus flour, or ground melon seed mixture.

Antojito: a Mexican snack, usually masa based with a variety of toppings such as sausage, cheese, beans, onions; also refers to tostadas, sopes, and garnachas.

Atole: a thick, lightly sweet, warm drink made with finely ground rice or corn and flavored usually with vanilla; often found mornings and evenings at markets.

Birria: lamb or goat meat cooked in a tomato broth spiced with garlic, chiles, cumin, ginger, oregano, cloves, cinnamon, thyme, and garnished with onions and cilantro and fresh lime juice to taste; a specialty of Jalisco state.

Botana: a light snack—an antojito.

Buñelos: round, thin, deep-fried crispy fritters dipped in sugar or dribbled with honey.

Burrito: a large flour tortilla stuffed with beans or sometimes potatoes and onions.

Cabrito: roast kid; a Northern Mexico delicacy.

Cajeta: caramelized cow or goat milk often used in dessert crêpes.

Carnitas: pork that's been deep cooked (not fried) in lard, then steamed and served with corn tortillas for tacos.

Ceviche: fresh raw seafood marinated in fresh lime juice and garnished with chopped tomatoes, onions, chiles and sometimes cilantro and served with crispy, fried whole corn tortillas.

Churro: tube shaped, bread-like fritter, dipped in sugar and sometimes filled with cajeta or chocolate.

Cilantro: an herb grown from the coriander seed chopped and used in salsas and soups.

Chiles rellenos: poblano peppers usually stuffed with cheese, rolled in a batter and baked; but other stuffings may include ground beef spiced with raisins.

Chorizo: a spicy red pork sausage, flavored with different chiles and sometimes with achiote, or cumin and other spices.

Choyote: vegetable pear or merleton, a type of spiney squash boiled and served as an accompaniment to meat dishes.

Cochinita pibil: pig wrapped in banana leaves, flavored with pibil sauce and pit-baked; common in Yucatán.

Corunda: a triangular shaped tamal wrapped in a corn leaf, a Michoacan specialty.

Enchilada: tortilla dipped in a sauce and usually filled with chicken or white cheese and sometimes topped with tomato sauce and sour cream (enchiladas Suizas— Swiss enchiladas) or covered in a green sauce (enchiladas verdes) or topped with onions, sour cream and guacamole (enchiladas Potosiños).

Epazote: leaf of the wormseed plant, used in black beans, and with cheese in quesadillas.

Escabeche: a lightly pickled sauce used in Yucatán chicken stew.

Frijoles charros: beans flavored with beer, a Northern Mexico specialty.

Frijoles refritos: pinto beans mashed and cooked with lard.

Garnachas: a thickish small circle of fried masa with pinched sides, topped with pork or chicken, onions, and avacado or sometimes chopped potatoes, and tomatoes, typical as a botana in Veracruz and Yucatán.

Gorditas: thickish fried corn tortillas, slit and stuffed with choice of cheese, beans, beef, chicken, with or without lettuce, tomato and onion garnish.

Guacamole: mashed avacado, plain or mixed with onions and other spices.

Gusanos de maguey: maguey worms considered a delicacy and delicious when charbroiled to a crisp and served with corn tortillas for tacos.

Horchata: refreshing drink made of ground rice or melon seeds, ground almonds, and lightly sweetened.

Huevos Mexicanos: scrambled eggs with onions, hot peppers, and tomatoes.

Huevos Motulenos: eggs atop a tortilla, garnished with beans, peas, ham, sausage, and grated cheese, a Yucatecan specialty.

Huevos rancheros: fried egg on top of a fried corn tortilla covered in a tomato sauce.

Huitlacoche: sometimes spelled "cuitlacoche," mushroom-flavored black fungus that appears on corn in the rainy season; considered a delicacy.

Machaca: shredded dried beef scrambled with eggs or as salad topping; a specialty of Northern Mexico.

Manchamantel: translated means "tablecloth stainer," a stew of chicken or pork with chiles, tomatoes, pineapple, bananas, and jícama.

Masa: ground corn soaked in lime used as basis for tamales, corn tortillas, and soups.

Mixiote: lamb or chicken baked with carrots, potatoes, and sauce in parchment paper from a maguey leaf.

Mole: pronounced "moh-lay," a sauce made with 20 ingredients including chocolate, peppers, ground tortillas, sesame seeds, cinnamon, tomatoes, onion, garlic, peanuts, pumpkin seeds, cloves, and tomatillos; developed by colonial nuns in Puebla, usually served over chicken or turkey; especially served in Puebla, State of Mexico and Oaxaca with sauces varying from red, to black and brown.

Molletes: a bolillo cut in half and topped with refried beans and cheese, then broiled; popular at breakfast.

Pan de Muerto: sweet or plain bread made around the Days of the Dead (Nov. 1-2), in the form of mummies, dolls, or round with bone designs.

Pan dulce: lightly sweetened bread in many configurations usually served at breakfast or bought at any bakery.

Papadzules: Tortillas are stuffed with hard-boiled eggs and seeds (cucumber or sunflower) in a tomato sauce.

Pavo relleno negro: stuffed turkey, Yucatán style, filled with chopped pork and beef, cooked in a rich, dark sauce.

Pibil: pit baked pork or chicken in a sauce of tomato, onion, mild red pepper, cilantro, and vinegar.

Pipian: sauce made with ground pumpkin seeds, nuts, and mild peppers.

Poc-chuc: slices of pork with onion marinated in a tangy sour orange sauce and charcoal broiled; a Yucatecan specialty.

Pozole: a soup made with hominy and pork or chicken, in either a tomato based broth Jalisco-style, or a white broth Nayarit-style, or green chile sauce Guerrero-style, and topped with choice of chopped white onion, lettuce or cabbage, radishes, oregano, red pepper, and cilantro.

Pulque: drink made of fermented sap of the maguey plant; best in state of Hidalgo and around Mexico City.

Quesadilla: flour tortilla stuffed with melted white cheese and lightly fried or warmed.

Rompope: delicious Mexican eggnog, invented in Puebla, made with eggs, vanilla, sugar, and rum.

Salsa Mexicana: sauce of fresh chopped tomatoes, white onions, and cilantro with a bit of oil; on tables all over Mexico.

Salsa verde: a cooked sauce using the green tomatillo and pureed with mildly hot peppers, onions, garlic, and cilantro; on tables countrywide.

Sopa de calabaza: soup made of chopped squash or pumpkin blossoms.

Sopa de lima: a tangy soup made with chicken broth and accented with fresh lime; popular in Yucatán.

Sopa de medula: bone marrow soup.

Sopa seca: not a soup at all, but a seasoned rice which translated means "dry soup."

Sopa Tarascan: a rib sticking pinto-bean based soup, flavored with onions, garlic, tomatoes, chiles, and chicken broth and garnished with sour cream, white cheese, avocado chunks, and fried tortilla strips; a specialty of Michoacan state.

Sopa Tlalpeña: a hearty soup made with chunks of chicken, chopped carrots, zucchini, corn, onions, garlic, and cilantro.

Sopa tortilla: a traditional chicken broth-based soup, seasoned with chiles, tomatoes, onion, and garlic, bobbing with crisp fried strips of corn tortillas.

Sope: pronounced "soh-pay," a botana similar to a garnacha, except spread with refried beans and topped with crumbled cheese and onions.

Tacos al pastor: thin slices of flavored pork roasted on a revolving cylinder dripping with onion slices and juice of fresh pineapple slice.

Tamal: incorrectly called tamale (tamal singular, tamales plural), meat or sweet filling rolled with fresh masa then wrapped in a corn husk, a corn or banana leaf and steamed; many varieties and sizes throughout the country.

Tepache: drink made of fermented pineapple peelings and brown sugar.

Tikin Xic: also seen on menus as "tikin chick," char-broiled fish brushed with achiote sauce.

Tinga: a stew made with pork tenderloin, sausage, onions, garlic, tomatoes, chiles, and potatoes; popular on menus in Puebla and Hidalgo states.

Torta: sandwich, usually on bolillo bread, usually with sliced avocado, onions, tomatoes, with a choice of meat and often cheese.

Tostadas: crispy fried corn tortillas topped with meat, onions, lettuce, tomatoes, cheese, avocados, and sometimes sour cream.

Venado: Venison (deer) served perhaps as pipian de venado, steamed in banana leaves and served with a sauce of ground squash seeds.

Queso relleno: "Stuffed cheese" is a mild yellow cheese stuffed with minced meat and spices, a Yucatecan specialty.

Xtabentun: (pronounced "Shtah-ben-toon") a Yucatán liquor made of fermented honey, and flavored with anise. It comes seco (dry) or crema (sweet).

Zacahuil: pork leg tamal, packed in thick masa, wrapped in banana leaves and pit baked; sometimes pot-made with tomato and masa; specialty of mid to upper Veracruz.

INDEX

GENERAL INFORMATION

DESTINATIONS

KEY TO ABBREVIATIONS: * = Author's Favorite; $ = Super Value Choice; A = Apartment; W = Worth the extra bucks; YH = Youth Hostel

NOW, SAVE MONEY ON ALL YOUR TRAVELS!
Join Frommer's™ Dollarwise® Travel Club

Saving money while traveling is never easy, which is why the **Dollarwise Travel Club** was formed 32 years ago to provide cost-cutting travel strategies, up-to-date travel information, and a sense of community for value-conscious travelers from all over the world.

In keeping with the money-saving concept, the annual membership fee is low—$20 for U.S. residents and $25 for residents of Canada, Mexico, and other countries—and is immediately exceeded by the value of your benefits, which include:

1. Any TWO books listed on the following pages;
2. Plus any ONE Frommer's City Guide;
3. A subscription to our quarterly newspaper, *The Dollarwise Traveler;*
4. A membership card that entitles you to purchase through the Club all Frommer's publications for 33% to 40% off their retail price.

The eight-page *Dollarwise Traveler* tells you about the latest developments in good-value travel worldwide and includes the following columns: **Hospitality Exchange** (for those offering and seeking hospitality in cities all over the world); and **Share-a-Trip** (for those looking for travel companions to share costs).

Aside from the various Frommer's Guides, the Gault Millau Guides, and the Real Guides you can also choose from our Special Editions, which include such titles as *Caribbean Hideaways* (the 100 most romantic places to stay in the Islands); and *Marilyn Wood's Wonderful Weekends* (a selection of the best mini-vacations within a 200-mile radius of New York City).

To join this Club, send the appropriate membership fee with your name and address to: Frommer's Dollarwise Travel Club, 15 Columbus Circle, New York, NY 10023. Remember to specify which single city guide and which two other guides you wish to receive in your initial package of member's benefits. Or tear out the pages, check off your choices, and send them to us with your membership fee.

FROMMER BOOKS
PRENTICE HALL TRAVEL   Date_____
15 COLUMBUS CIRCLE
NEW YORK, NY 10023

Friends: Please send me the books checked below.

FROMMER'S™ COMPREHENSIVE GUIDES
(Guides listing facilities from budget to deluxe, with emphasis on the medium-priced)

☐ Alaska	$14.95	☐ Italy	$19.00
☐ Australia	$14.95	☐ Japan & Hong Kong	$17.00
☐ Austria & Hungary	$14.95	☐ Morocco	$18.00
☐ Belgium, Holland & Luxembourg	$14.95	☐ Nepal	$18.00
☐ Bermuda & The Bahamas	$17.00	☐ New England	$17.00
☐ Brazil	$14.95	☐ New Mexico	$13.95
☐ California	$18.00	☐ New York State	$19.00
☐ Canada	$16.00	☐ Northwest	$16.95
☐ Caribbean	$17.00	☐ Puerta Vallarta (avail. Feb. '92)	$14.00
☐ Carolinas & Georgia	$17.00	☐ Portugal, Madeira & the Azores	$14.95
☐ Colorado (avail. Jan '92)	$14.00	☐ Scandinavia	$18.95
☐ Cruises (incl. Alaska, Carib, Mex, Hawaii, Panama, Canada & US)	$16.00	☐ Scotland (avail. Feb. '92)	$17.00
		☐ South Pacific	$20.00
☐ Delaware, Maryland, Pennsylvania & the New Jersey Shore (avail. Jan. '92)	$19.00	☐ Southeast Asia	$14.95
		☐ Switzerland & Liechtenstein	$19.00
☐ Egypt	$14.95	☐ Thailand	$20.00
☐ England	$17.00	☐ Virginia (avail. Feb. '92)	$14.00
☐ Florida	$17.00	☐ Virgin Islands	$13.00
☐ France	$15.95	☐ USA	$16.95
☐ Germany	$18.00		

0891492

FROMMER'S CITY GUIDES

(Pocket-size guides to sightseeing and tourist accommodations and facilities in all price ranges)

☐ Amsterdam/Holland $8.95		☐ Minneapolis/St. Paul $8.95	
☐ Athens. $8.95		☐ Montréal/Québec City. $8.95	
☐ Atlanta $8.95		☐ New Orleans. $8.95	
☐ Atlantic City/Cape May $8.95		☐ New York $12.00	
☐ Bangkok. $12.00		☐ Orlando $12.00	
☐ Barcelona $12.00		☐ Paris $8.95	
☐ Belgium $7.95		☐ Philadelphia $11.00	
☐ Berlin. $10.00		☐ Rio $8.95	
☐ Boston. $8.95		☐ Rome. $8.95	
☐ Cancún/Cozumel/Yucatán $8.95		☐ Salt Lake City $8.95	
☐ Chicago $9.95		☐ San Diego. $8.95	
☐ Denver/Boulder/Colorado Springs. . . .$8.95		☐ San Francisco $12.00	
☐ Dublin/Ireland. $10.00		☐ Santa Fe/Taos/Albuquerque. $10.95	
☐ Hawaii $12.00		☐ Seattle/Portland $12.00	
☐ Hong Kong $7.95		☐ St. Louis/Kansas City $9.95	
☐ Las Vegas. $8.95		☐ Sydney. $8.95	
☐ Lisbon/Madrid/Costa del Sol $8.95		☐ Tampa/St. Petersburg $8.95	
☐ London $12.00		☐ Tokyo. $8.95	
☐ Los Angeles $8.95		☐ Toronto $8.95	
☐ Mexico City/Acapulco $8.95		☐ Vancouver/Victoria $7.95	
☐ Miami $8.95		☐ Washington, D.C. $12.00	

FROMMER'S $-A-DAY® GUIDES

(Guides to low-cost tourist accommodations and facilities)

☐ Australia on $40 a Day $13.95		☐ Israel on $40 a Day. $13.95	
☐ Costa Rica, Guatemala & Belize		☐ Mexico on $45 a Day $18.00	
on $35 a Day. $15.95		☐ New York on $65 a Day. $15.00	
☐ Eastern Europe on $25 a Day $16.95		☐ New Zealand on $45 a Day $16.00	
☐ England on $50 a Day. $17.00		☐ Scotland & Wales on $40 a Day $18.00	
☐ Europe on $45 a Day $19.00		☐ South America on $40 a Day $15.95	
☐ Greece on $35 a Day $14.95		☐ Spain on $50 a Day $15.95	
☐ Hawaii on $70 a Day. $18.00		☐ Turkey on $40 a Day. $22.00	
☐ India on $40 a Day $20.00		☐ Washington, D.C., on $45 a Day. $17.00	
☐ Ireland on $40 a Day. $17.00			

FROMMER'S CITY $-A-DAY GUIDES

☐ Berlin on $40 a Day $12.00		☐ Madrid on $50 a Day (avail. Jan '92) . . .$13.00	
☐ Copenhagen on $50 a Day $12.00		☐ Paris on $45 a Day $12.00	
☐ London on $45 a Day $12.00		☐ Stockholm on $50 a Day (avail. Dec. '91)$13.00	

FROMMER'S FAMILY GUIDES

☐ California with Kids $16.95		☐ San Francisco with Kids. $17.00	
☐ Los Angeles with Kids $17.00		☐ Washington, D.C., with Kids (avail. Jan	
☐ New York City with Kids (avail. Jan '92) $18.00		'92) $17.00	

SPECIAL EDITIONS

☐ Beat the High Cost of Travel. $6.95		☐ Marilyn Wood's Wonderful Weekends	
☐ Bed & Breakfast—N. America $14.95		(CT, DE, MA, NH, NJ, NY, PA, RI, VT) . .$11.95	
☐ Caribbean Hideaways. $16.00		☐ Motorist's Phrase Book (Fr/Ger/Sp) $4.95	
☐ Honeymoon Destinations (US, Mex &		☐ The New World of Travel (annual by	
Carib). $14.95		Arthur Frommer for savvy travelers) . . .$16.95	

(TURN PAGE FOR ADDITONAL BOOKS AND ORDER FORM)

0891492

| ☐ Paris Rendez-Vous . . . .$10.95 | ☐ Travel Diary and Record Book. . . . .$5.95 |
| ☐ Swap and Go (Home Exchanging). . . . .$10.95 | ☐ Where to Stay USA (from $3 to $30 a night). . . . .$13.95 |

FROMMER'S TOURING GUIDES

(Color illustrated guides that include walking tours, cultural and historic sites, and practical information)

☐ Amsterdam. $10.95	☐ New York $10.95
☐ Australia $12.95	☐ Paris $8.95
☐ Brazil $10.95	☐ Rome. $10.95
☐ Egypt. $8.95	☐ Scotland. $9.95
☐ Florence. $8.95	☐ Thailand. $12.95
☐ Hong Kong. $10.95	☐ Turkey $10.95
☐ London $12.95	☐ Venice $8.95

GAULT MILLAU

(The only guides that distinguish the truly superlative from the merely overrated)

☐ The Best of Chicago $15.95	☐ The Best of Los Angeles $16.95
☐ The Best of Florida $17.00	☐ The Best of New England $15.95
☐ The Best of France $16.95	☐ The Best of New Orleans. $16.95
☐ The Best of Germany $18.00	☐ The Best of New York $16.95
☐ The Best of Hawaii $16.95	☐ The Best of Paris $16.95
☐ The Best of Hong Kong. $16.95	☐ The Best of San Francisco $16.95
☐ The Best of Italy. $16.95	☐ The Best of Thailand. $17.95
☐ The Best of London $16.95	☐ The Best of Toronto $17.00
	☐ The Best of Washington, D.C. $16.95	

THE REAL GUIDES

(Opinionated, politically aware guides for youthful budget-minded travelers)

☐ Amsterdam $9.95	☐ Mexico. $11.95
☐ Berlin. $11.95	☐ Morocco $12.95
☐ Brazil $13.95	☐ New York $9.95
☐ California & the West Coast $11.95	☐ Paris $9.95
☐ Czechoslovakia $13.95	☐ Peru. $12.95
☐ France $12.95	☐ Poland $13.95
☐ Germany $13.95	☐ Portugal $10.95
☐ Greece. $13.95	☐ San Francisco $11.95
☐ Guatemala $13.95	☐ Scandinavia $14.95
☐ Hong Kong $11.95	☐ Spain. $12.95
☐ Hungary. $12.95	☐ Turkey $12.95
☐ Ireland. $12.95	☐ Venice $11.95
☐ Italy. $13.95	☐ Women Travel. $12.95
☐ Kenya. $12.95	☐ Yugoslavia $12.95

ORDER NOW!

In U.S. include $2 shipping UPS for 1st book; $1 ea. add'l book. Outside U.S. $3 and $1, respectively.

Allow four to six weeks for delivery in U.S., longer outside U.S. We discourage rush order service, but orders arriving with shipping fees plus a $15 surcharge will be handled as rush orders.

Enclosed is my check or money order for $_____

NAME_____

ADDRESS_____

CITY_____ STATE_____ ZIP_____

0891492